Seventh Canadian Edition

ACCOUNTING:
The Basis for Business Decisions

Financial Accounting

Seventh Canadian Edition

ACCOUNTING:

The Basis for Business Decisions

Financial Accounting

ROBERT F. MEIGS, D.B.A.
San Diego State University

WALTER B. MEIGS, Ph.D., C.P.A.
University of Southern California

WAI P. LAM, Ph.D., F.C.A.
University of Windsor

McGraw-Hill Ryerson Limited

Toronto Montreal New York Auckland Bogotá
Caracas Lisbon London Madrid Mexico Milan
New Delhi Paris San Juan Singapore Sydney Tokyo

ACCOUNTING: THE BASIS FOR BUSINESS DECISIONS
Seventh Canadian Edition
Financial Accounting

ISBN: 0-07-552680-8

1 2 3 4 5 6 7 8 9 0 RRD 4 3 2 1 0 9 8 7 6 5

Printed and bound in the United States of America by R. R. Donnelley (Canada) Limited

Sponsoring Editor: Kelly Smyth

Production: Gail Marsden

Cover Design: Dianna Little

Cover Photograph: © G. K. and Vikki Hart/The Image Bank

Printing & Binding: R. R. Donnelley (Canada) Limited

Canadian Cataloguing in Publication Data

Meigs, Robert F.
Accounting : the basis for business decisions : financial accounting

7th Canadian ed.
For use in high schools.
ISBN 0-07-552680-8

1. Accounting. I. Meigs, Walter B., date. II. Lam, Wai P., date. III. Title.

HF5635.M452 1995 657'.044 C95-932063-6

Contents

finished

here

Checklist of Key Figures

1 A-1	Total assets, $507,900
1 A-2	Final cash balance $23,300
1 A-3	(a) Total assets, $368,700
1 A-4	Total assets, Oct. 6, $172,090
1 A-5	(a) Total assets, $43,600
1 B-1	Total assets, $520,000
1 B-2	Final cash balance, $7,600
1 B-3	(a) Total assets, $533,612
1 B-4	Total assets, July 2, $113,700
1 B-5	(a) Total assets, $100,254
2 A-1	No key figure
2 A-2	No key figure
2 A-3	(a) Trial balance totals, $286,450
2 A-4	(b) Trial balance totals, $186,080
2 A-5	(c) Trial balance totals, $105,840
2 A-6	(c) Trial balance totals, $321,300
2 B-1	No key figure
2 B-2	No key figure
2 B-3	(a) Trial balance totals, $792,370
2 B-4	(b) Trial balance totals, $135,080
2 B-5	(c) Trial balance totals, $148,760
2 B-6	(c) Trial balance totals, $662,500
CP-1	(c) Trial balance totals, $1,696,900
3 A-1	No key figure
3 A-2	No key figure
3 A-3	(c) Trial balance totals, $267,280
3 A-4	(b) Total assets, $124,300
3 A-5	(a) Net income, $31,300
3 A-6	(c) Net income, $3,900
3 A-7	(e) Adjusted trial balance, $29,670
3 B-1	No key figure
3 B-2	No key figure
3 B-3	(c) Trial balance totals, $173,452
3 B-4	(a) Net income, $34,500
3 B-5	(a) Total assets, $246,500
3 B-6	(c) Net income, $3,427
3 B-7	(f) Total assets, $1,049,650
4 A-1	No key figure
4 A-2	(b) Total revenue, $9,060
4 A-3	No key figure
4 A-4	Net loss, $340
4 A-5	Adjusted trial balance, $355,900
4 A-6	Adjusted trial balance, $1,424,700
4 A-7	(b) Jan. Expense, $4,000
4 B-1	No key figure
4 B-2	(b) Total revenue, $34,100
4 B-3	Net income, $34,800
4 B-4	Net income, $6,800
4 B-5	Adjusted trial balance, $1,106,625
4 B-6	Adjusted trial balance, $511,125
4 B-7	(b) July revenue, $1,000
CP-2	(c) Adjusted trial balance, $325,720; Net income, $6,500
5-1	(b) Gross profit, $1,738,100
5-2	(c) Units on hand at May 31, 10
5-3	(a) Cost of goods sold, $29,900
5-4	(d) Cost of goods sold, $11,200
5-5	(d) Cost of goods sold, $28,000
5-6	No key figure
5-7	(a) Current liabilities, $227,600
5-8	No key figure
5-9	(a) Net income, $800
5-10	No key figure
5-11	No key figure
5-12	No key figure
5-13	(c) Net income, $45,000
5-14	No key figure
5-15	(c) Net income, $43,400
5-16	(a) Net income, $20,000
5-17	(b) Total assets, $192,800
6-1	No key figure
6-2	(c) Store no. 1, rental revenue, $8.50
6-3	No key figure
6-4	No key figure
6-5	No key figure
6-6	No key figure
6-7	No key figure
6-8	No key figure
6-9	Cash receipts, $46,392
6-10	Cash payments, $113,865
6-11	Cash receipts, $84,228; cash payments, $62,964
6-12	No key figure
6-13	Cash receipts, $43,676; cash payments, $51,193
7 A-1	No key figure
7 A-2	(a) Adjusted cash balance, $41,953
7 A-3	(a) Adjusted cash balance, $21,142.30
7 A-4	(a) Adjusted cash balance, $21,146.50
7 A-5	No key figure
7 A-6	(a) Adjusted cash balance, $18,334
7 A-7	(b) Adjusted cash balance, $8,552
7 B-1	No key figure
7 B-2	Adjusted cash balance, $47,556
7 B-3	(a) Adjusted cash balance, $31,142.30
7 B-4	(a) Adjusted cash balance, $21,007.29
7 B-5	No key figure
7 B-6	(a) Cash shortage, $8,150
7 B-7	(b) Adjusted cash balance, $8,214.50
8 A-1	(a) (1) Accounts receivable turnover. Freshdrink, 13.8 times

8 A-2	(a) Estimated uncollectible accounts, $38,880
8 A-3	(a) Estimated uncollectible accounts, $11,540
8 A-4	(b) Total estimated uncollectible accounts, $52,500
8 A-5	(a) Feb. 2, cash collected from note, $42,653
8 A-6	(c) Total current assets, $373,195
8 A-7	(c) One-year interest charge originally included in face amount, $25,500
8 B-1	(a) (2) Number of days' sales uncollected, Advantec, 81
8 B-2	(a) Estimated uncollectible accounts, $27,180
8 B-3	(b) Net accounts receivable, Jan. 31, $461,280
8 B-4	(a) Estimated uncollectible accounts, $6,740
8 B-5	(a) Feb. 2, cash collected from note, $30,688
8 B-6	(c) Total current assets, $741,232
8 B-7	(c) One-year interest charge originally included in face amount, $13,200
9-1	No key figure
9-2	(a) May 31 inventory, $280
9-3	(a) Sept. 30 inventory balance, $3,450
9-4	(b) (4) Jan. 15 LIFO inventory, $18,500
9-5	(a) (2) FIFO cost of goods sold, $18,100
9-6	(a) (3) LIFO cost of goods sold, $18,700
9-7	(a) (1) Average cost shrinkage loss, $567
9-8	(a) (2) LIFO cost of goods sold, $303,480
9-9	(b) (3) LIFO cost of goods sold, $7,420
9-10	(a) Gross profit rate, 1995, 43%
9-11	(b) (3) Gross profit, $264,144
9-12	(b) (1) Turnover rate, FIFO, 2.4 times
10 A-1	(c) Total cost of equipment, $91,200
10 A-2	Depreciation for 1997, (b) $36,000; (c) $33,750
10 A-3	(a) Depreciation for 1998, (3) $15,000
10 A-4	(c) Depreciation expense for 1996, $134,175
10 A-5	Gain on disposal of moving van, $4,000
10 A-6	No key figure
10 A-7	No key figure
10 A-8	(b) (1) Book value, $17,000
10 B-1	(a) Total cost of equipment, $220,720
10 B-2	Depreciation for 1997, (b) $65,600; (c) $64,800
10 B-3	Depreciation for 1995, (b) $15,000
10 B-4	(a) Accumulated depreciation: Machine C, $36,000
10 B-5	Gain on disposal of truck, $1,000
10 B-6	No key figure
10 B-7	No key figure
10 B-8	(b) (1) Book value, $6,800
CP-3	(a) Total assets: Alpine, $494,400; Nordic, $496,200; (b) revised net income: Alpine, $225,000
11-1	No key figure
11-2	No key figure
11-3	(a) Total current liabilities, $375,403
11-4	(b) Interest expense on Western Bank note, $3,200
11-5	(b) Interest expense on National Bank note, $4,704
11-6	(c) Total current liabilities, $337,186.50
11-7	(c) Unpaid balance, $8,331
11-8	(c) Jan. 1, 1997, unpaid balance, $539,370
11-9	(b) Total payroll cost, $27,538
11-10	(b) (4) Employer's total payroll costs, $251,854
11-11	(c) Total payroll cost, $15,089
12-1	No key figure
12-2	No key figure
12-3	No key figure
12-4	No key figure
12-5	No key figure
12-6	(a) Profit under percentage-of-completion, 1995, $3,000,000
12-7	(a) (1) Gross profit, $184,000
12-8	No key figure
12-9	No key figure
13 A-1	(b) Total assets, $220,800
13 A-2	(a) Net income, $54,000; (c) total assets, $217,720
13 A-3	(a) (4) Pascal's share, $28,000
13 A-4	(c) Stein's share, $26,100
13 A-5	(c) Bonus to Ritter, $30,000
13 A-6	(c) Bonus to Kim, $60,000
13 A-7	(a) Cash to Nix, $11,600
13 B-1	(b) Total assets, $277,800
13 B-2	(a) Net income, $54,500; (c) total assets, $175,500
13 B-3	(a) (2) Martin's share, $58,000
13 B-4	(a) Conrad's share, $102,600
13 B-5	(c) Bonus to Lee, $70,000
13 B-6	(d) Debit to Spence, Capital, $22,500
13 B-7	(b) Cash payment by Merit, $18,000
14 A-1	(b) Dec. 31, 1996, retained earnings, $1,937,000
14 A-2	(a) Total shareholders' equity, $15,370,000
14 A-3	Total shareholders' equity, $2,063,000
14 A-4	(b) Total shareholders' equity, $1,150,960
14 A-5	(b) Total assets, $1,512,100
14 A-6	(e) Total contributed capital, $11,800,000
14 B-1	(b) Dec. 31, 1996, retained earnings, $1,490,000
14 B-2	(a) Total shareholders' equity, $3,405,000
14 B-3	Total shareholders' equity, $2,112,000
14 B-4	(d) Total shareholders' equity, $890,200
14 B-5	(b) Total assets, $1,352,950
14 B-6	(f) Total contributed capital, $9,660,000
15 A-1	(a) Income before extraordinary items, $13,620,000
15 A-2	(a) Cumulative effect, $91,000

15 A-3 (b) Retained earnings, $7,230,000
15 A-4 (a) Net income, $420,000
15 A-5 (1) Total shareholders' equity, $743,600
15 A-6 (b) Total shareholders' equity, $8,792,800
15 A-7 (a) Total contributed capital, $4,990,000; (b) retained earnings, $874,000

15 B-1 (a) Income before extraordinary items, $11,820,000
15 B-2 (a) Retained earnings, $606,800
15 B-3 (b) Retained earnings, $8,220,000
15 B-4 (a) Net income, $190,000
15 B-5 (1) Total shareholders' equity, $4,578,000
15 B-6 (b) Total shareholders' equity, $9,318,000
15 B-7 (b) Retained earnings, $469,800

16-1 (c) Bond interest expense, $1,500,000
16-2 (b) Long-term liabilities, $58,880,000
16-3 (b) Carrying value of bond liability, bonds issued at 101, $60,560,000
16-4 (c) (1) Long-term liabilities, $29,570,000
16-5 (c) (1) Long-term liabilities, $80,800,000
16-6 (b) Gain on retirement of bonds, $8,800
16-7 (b) Loss on early retirement of bonds, $76,480
16-8 (a) (2) Amortization of discount, $5,400
16-9 (c) Long-term liabilities, $9,473,818
16-10 (c) Long-term liabilities, $10,189,225
16-11 (c) Liability, bonds issued at discount, $8,706,000
16-12 No key figure
16-13 (d) Lease payment obligation, $23,870
16-14 (a) Total liabilities, $1,088,620

CP-4 (c) (1) Net income, $383,710; (c) (3) total assets, $32,067,410

Appendix A

1 (d) Present value, $96,120
2 (a) Issuance price, $9,428,500
3 (c) Liability, Dec. 31, $23,197
4 (a) Present value of payments, 10-year lease, $8,032,300
5 (d) Lease payment obligation, Dec. 31, $40,184
6 (b) (2) Discount on Notes Receivable, $259,920

17 A-1 (b) (2) Gain on sale, $3,700
17 A-2 No key figure
17 A-3 (b) Market value, $305,000
17 A-4 (b) (3) Carrying value, Dec. 31, 1996, $4,995,000
17 A-5 (c) Consolidated total assets, $7,525,000
17 A-6 Consolidated total assets, $3,928,000
17 A-7 Consolidated total assets, $1,204,000

17 B-1 (b) (2) Loss on sale, $5,600
17 B-2 No key figure
17 B-3 (b) Market value, $224,000
17 B-4 (b) (3) Carrying value, Dec. 31, 1997, $1,710,000
17 B-5 (c) Consolidated total assets, $10,670,000
17 B-6 Consolidated total assets, $7,760,000
17 B-7 Consolidated total assets, $1,326,000

18 A-1 No key figure
18 A-2 No key figure
18 A-3 Taxable income, $79,920
18 A-4 (a) Capital cost allowance, $225,000
18 A-5 (a) Accounting income, $969,000

18 B-1 No key figure
18 B-2 No key figure
18 B-3 Taxable income, $75,470
18 B-4 (a) Capital cost allowance, $160,000
18 B-5 (a) Accounting income, $150,000

19 A-1 No key figure
19 A-2 Cash provided by operating activities, $514,000
19 A-3 (b) Cash provided by operating activities, $155,000
19 A-4 Cash provided by operating activities, $155,000
19 A-5 (b) Cash provided by operating activities, $204,000
19 A-6 (c) Cash provided by operating activities, $166,000
19 A-7 (c) Cash used in investing activities, $80,000

19 B-1 No key figure
19 B-2 No key figure
19 B-3 (b) Cash provided by operating activities, $144,000
19 B-4 Cash provided by operating activities, $144,000
19 B-5 (b) Cash provided by operating activities, $1,020,000
19 B-6 (c) Cash provided by operating activities, $1,000
19 B-7 (c) Cash provided by operating activities, $580,000

20-1 (a) Net sales, 1995, $2,520,000
20-2 (a) Net income, Sub Zero, 7%
20-3 (c) Operating cycle, 119.8 days
20-4 (a) (6) Return on average assets, 16%
20-5 (a) (3) Operating expenses, $270,000
20-6 (a) (6) Operating cycle, Mondo, 192 days
20-7 (a) (6) Operating cycle, Imports, 168 days
20-8 (b) (3) Working capital, $1,296,000
20-9 No key figure
20-10 Total assets, $1,000; net sales, $1,280
20-11 (c) Price-earnings ratio, Continental, 9.1 times
20-12 (a) (9) Interest coverage ratio, PepsiCo, 2.9 times

CP-5 Part 1: No key figure
Part 2: (a) (6) Accounts receivable turnover rate, 1992, 42 days

Preface

OUR GOALS IN THIS SEVENTH CANADIAN EDITION

We have tried to accomplish many things in this edition. Among our most important goals have been to:

1. Provide students with a better understanding of the environment in which accounting information is developed and used.
2. Shift emphasis from the preparation of accounting information to its interpretation and use.
3. Retain a course structure that meets the specific content requirements of most universities and colleges.

Providing Students with a Better Background

If students are to appreciate the nature of accounting, they first should have a basic understanding of the business environment. We find, however, that many introductory students lack this background.

We give increased attention to explaining business practices before discussing accounting issues. Our focus is upon ***current*** business and accounting practices, not those of the past. For example, virtually every business with external reporting obligations now uses a perpetual inventory system. Yet many accounting textbooks continue to emphasize periodic systems. We emphasize ***perpetual*** inventory systems.

For purposes of illustration, textbooks traditionally assume the use of simple, manually maintained accounting records. Such records do not meet the needs of most modern businesses. We, too, find it convenient to use simple accounting records as the basis for many illustrations. However, we also explain how the information is processed in a computer-based environment.

Attention is given throughout the text to the role of ***professional judgment*** in both the development and interpretation of accounting information. We explain in some depth professional ethics for accountants in the field of public and private accounting. We also discuss audits, reviews, and the independent auditors' potential liability to the users of financial statements. Furthermore, we delineate the development and importance of international accounting standards in today's global business environment.

Shifting to a "User Orientation"

Today, relatively few introductory students will become professional preparers of accounting information. All, however, will become life-long information ***users.*** For this reason, we have shifted our emphasis significantly from the preparation of accounting information to its interpretation and use.

This shift in emphasis affects the text in several ways. For example, we have added new assignment material designed specifically to develop students' analytical, decision-making, and communication skills. Accordingly, a substantial number of stimulating and challenging problems/cases requiring the application of these critical skills have been incorporated in the final section of the assignment material entitled "Analytical and Decision Problems and Cases."

A user-oriented approach also affects topical content and emphasis. Topics relevant to basic business decisions now are addressed, even if these topics traditionally have been deferred to later accounting courses. Examples of such topics include accounting for postretirement costs, audits and reviews, "window dressing," and many of the disclosures that accompany financial statements.

Throughout the text, attention is given to analytical ratios and financial relationships. The chapter on analysis of financial statements now serves primarily as a review.

Increased attention also is given to the use of accounting information ***by management.*** No longer is this topic addressed only in a group of "managerial" chapters; it now is integrated throughout the text.

Some "traditional" accounting topics relate primarily to the preparation of accounting information and are of little significance to the information user. Examples include reversing entries, manual special journals, and alternative methods of recording accruals and deferrals. In our user-oriented approach, such topics are given less emphasis. Often they are presented in Supplemental Topic sections.

ELEMENTS OF THE TEXTBOOK

This seventh Canadian edition introduces many new features and retains all of the time-honoured materials. Such a well-balanced blending makes this text uniquely suitable for today's business environment.

Chapter Introductions and Learning Objectives

Each chapter begins with a brief overview and a set of basic learning objectives. These learning objectives then are integrated with the text discussions.

Cases in Point

A distinctive feature of past editions has been the use of short ***Cases in Point,*** which are based upon actual events. Many new Cases in Point have been created for this edition as part of our increased focus on the contemporary business environment.

Supplemental Topics and Appendixes

A new feature in the structure of this edition is the inclusion of short ***Supplemental Topic*** sections at the end of several chapters. These Supplemental Topics are closely related to the content of the chapters in which they appear.

Students always should read the Supplemental Topic sections, as these discussions will enhance their overall understanding of the chapter. Instructors, however, may decide whether these topics are of sufficient general interest for inclusion in class discussions, homework assignments, and examinations. [Assignment material relating to Supplemental Topics are preceded by an asterisk (*).]

Chapter Reviews

Each chapter is fol1owed by such learning aids as a ***Glossary of Key Terms*** and, in most chapters, a ***Demonstration Problem*** with a complete solution.

Assignment Material

One of the distinctive features of this seventh Canadian edition is the increase in the quantity and variety of the assignment material. Increased emphasis is placed upon the development of students' analytical abilities, decision-making skills, and communication skills. Much of the new assignment material is based upon the operations of well-known companies.

Six categories of assignments accompany the text. These are (1) Discussion Questions, (2) Multiple Choice Questions, (3) Exercises, (4) Problems, (5) Analytical and Decision Problems and Cases, and (6) Comprehensive Problems.

Discussion Questions are short and usually call for expository answers. In addition to developing writing and communication skills, these questions explore students' conceptual understanding of accounting.

Multiple Choice Questions focus on many of the most important concepts in the chapter. These questions are very useful in testing students' understanding of key aspects of the chapter material. They are both stimulating and challenging.

Exercises are short assignments, usually focusing upon a single concept. We have greatly increased the number and the variety of Exercises. By enabling instructors to cover basic concepts quickly, we hope to allow more time for discussing in class such assignments as our Analytical and Decision Problems and Cases.

Problems are longer than the Exercises and address several concepts at one time. Most chapters contain both an *A* and *B* problem series, each providing thorough coverage of the chapter. A few chapters contain a single—but longer—series of problems. The single series accommodates a greater variety of assignments.

Analytical and Decision Problems and Cases emphasize the development of analytical, decision-making, and communication skills. They also provide a wealth of assignment material well suited to in-class discussions.

To encourage the use of these assignments, we have developed a large number of Analytical and Decision Problems and Cases that cover a wide range of time requirements and difficulty levels. Many of our Exercises and Problems also call for analysis and the use of judgment.

We consider our six ***Comprehensive Problems*** to be among the most useful assignments in the text. Each of these problems ties together concepts presented over a span of chapters. Two of the Comprehensive Problems are similar in scope to a "practice set," and another involves the analysis of an actual annual report.

A ***Checklist of Key Figures*** for Problems and Comprehensive Problems appears on the front and back inside covers of the text. The purpose of these check figures is to aid students in verifying their problem solutions and in discovering their own errors.

NEW AND EXTENSIVELY REVISED CHAPTERS

Many chapters in this seventh Canadian edition have been revised significantly. Almost every chapter contains greater emphasis upon the use of accounting information and more assignment material than ever before. Among the changes in topical content that will be noticed most readily are:

Chapter 1, "Accounting: The Language of Business," has been rewritten to provide a more comprehensive introduction to the process of financial reporting. We have added discussions of such topics as reporting requirements of publicly owned companies, auditing, and professional ethics. Also included is a new discussion of the nature and sources of generally accepted accounting principles. Moreover, the importance of a background in accounting as a "stepping stone" to positions in top management is illustrated. Career opportunities in accounting are discussed in a Supplemental Topic section at the end of the chapter.

In ***Chapter 4,*** we have revised the format of the work sheet. Our goal is to focus upon the ***accounting processes*** illustrated within the work sheet, not to present the document itself as a component of the accounting cycle.

Chapter 5, now entitled "Accounting for Merchandising Activities; Classified Financial Statements," exemplifies many of the changes in this edition. The opening pages of this chapter illustrate our concerted effort to explain business practices before discussing the accounting treatments accorded those practices.

In keeping with contemporary business practices, this chapter now emphasizes ***perpetual inventory systems***—the type of system used in every large business organization. Periodic systems still receive thorough coverage; in fact, we have added an explanation of a "shortcut" periodic system that is used by many small businesses. Also, additional coverage on periodic inventory system is presented in a Supplemental Topic section at the end of the chapter.

The final portion of Chapter 5, "Introduction to Classified Financial Statements," typifies our increased emphasis upon the ***use*** of accounting information.

Chapter 6, "Accounting Systems, Internal Control, and Audits," emphasizes the capabilities of computer-based accounting systems, rather than the use of manual special journals. Among the new features of this chapter are examples of how data bases tailor information to meet the needs of different decision makers. New elements of this chapter also include discussions of financial and operational audits, and the related topics of employee fraud and management fraud. However, the coverage of manual special journals is not neglected; it is presented in a Supplemental Topic section at the end of the chapter.

Chapter 8, "Accounts Receivable and Notes Receivable," now includes discussions of the goals of credit management, accounts receivable turnover rates, strategies for quickly converting receivables into cash, and disclosure of concentrations of credit risk. These additions illustrate our increased emphasis on the use of accounting information by management, as well as by persons outside of the business organization.

Our coverage of notes receivable with interest included in the face amount has been moved to a Supplemental Topic section, as such notes are held primarily by financial institutions.

Chapter 9, "Inventories and the Cost of Goods Sold," has been revised extensively in light of our emphasis upon perpetual inventory systems. Also included are discussions of the just-in-time concept, inventory turnover rates, and the objectives of efficient inventory management.

Chapter 10, dealing with capital assets such as plant and equipment, includes extensively revised coverage of trade-ins.

Our coverage of liabilities, contained in ***Chapters 11*** and ***16,*** has been revised extensively. ***Chapter 11*** now focuses upon the types of liabilities ***common to most business entities,*** including long-term instalment debt. ***Chapter 16,*** in contrast, addresses those types of liabilities found primarily in the financial statements of large, publicly owned corporations. This format completes our coverage of accounting for the sole proprietorship type of unincorporated businesses in the first semester. It also heightens students' awareness of the differences in the business environments of small businesses and of large corporations.

Our coverage of liabilities also has been expanded in terms of topical content. Chapter 11 now includes long-term instalment debt, disclosure requirements relating to long-term debts, and increased emphasis on contingent losses and commitments. Extensively revised coverage of payroll liabilities now appears as a Supplemental Topic.

In Chapter 16, new or expanded coverage is given to topics that, because of their materiality, are relevant to the users of corporate financial statements. Examples include deferred income taxes and an employer's obligation for postretirement benefits.

Chapter 12, "Accounting Concepts, Professional Judgment, and Ethical Conduct," is new to this edition. One objective of this chapter is to review at one time many of the generally accepted accounting principles discussed throughout the text. Another objective is to look in some depth at key elements of a code of professional ethics.

Chapter 18, "Income Taxes and Business Decisions," has been substantially updated to include the most recent changes in tax legislation.

Chapter 20, "Analysis and Interpretation of Financial Statements," has been revised to reflect our emphasis of this topic throughout the textbook.

SUPPLEMENTARY MATERIALS

This text is accompanied by a large number of supplementary learning and teaching aids. These supplements are listed below. A complete description of these materials is contained in the ***Instructor's Guide.*** If you would like information and costs on the supplemental materials, please contact your local McGraw-Hill Ryerson representative. We value both your interest and our supplements.

For the Student:

Study Guide to accompany Volume 1 by Meigs, Meigs, Meigs, and Lam
Study Guide to accompany Volume 2 and Volume 3 by Meigs, Meigs, Meigs, and Lam
Accounting Work Sheets, Chapters 1–12 by Meigs, Meigs, and Lam
Accounting Work Sheets, Chapters 13–26 by Meigs, Meigs, and Lam
Blank Forms for Problems and Cases

Accounting Information Manager: A General Ledger Program by John W. Wanlass
Accounting Information Manager: A Spreadsheet Program by John W. Wanlass
MicroGuide Computerized Accounting Tutorial by Jean Gutmann
Manual Simulations and Applications:
- *The Next Dimension: An Accounting Cycle Application* by Mary A. Meigs and Wai P. Lam
- *Remington Restaurant Supply: An Accounting Cycle Application*
- *Valley Building Materials Inc.; A Corporate Accounting Cycle Application*
- *Adders 'n Keyes,* 2/e by Brenda Mallouk
- *Deluxe Spa Products Incorporated: Using Management Accounting for Costing and Decision Making* by Brenda Mallouk and Catherine Seguin
- *Premium Foods Corporation: A Financial Statement Analysis Case* by Christie W. Johnson
- *Facts-by-FAX: An Accounting Cycle Application*
- *Color Copy Co.: An Accounting Cycle Application*
- *Echo Paint Co.: A Small Business Application with Forms* by Richard A. Wright
- *Executive Woodcraft: A Managerial Accounting Application* by Ronald W. Hilton
- *Printer Recharge, Inc.: A Corporate Practice Set* by Phillip Ricci and Wanda G. Spruill

Computer-Based Simulations and Applications:
- *CȲMA General Ledger Package: Shadow Mountain Hotel*
- *CȲMA General Ledger Package: Authenticity and Facts-by-FAX*
- *Echo Paint Co.: A Small Business Application with Forms,* by Richard A. Wright
- *Remington Restaurant Supply: A Computerized Accounting Cycle Application*
- *Electronic Spreadsheet Application to Accompany the Premium Foods Corporation Financial Statement Analysis Case* by Christie W. Johnson

For the Instructor:

Canadian:
Instructor's Manual
Solutions Manual
Overhead Transparencies
Test Bank (Manual and Computerized Versions)
Solutions to accompany The Next Dimension
Solutions to accompany Deluxe Spa Products Incorporated

American:
Lecture Video Series
Case Study Videos for Analysis and Critical Thinking
Instructor's Manual/Critical Thinking Guide to Accompany Case Study Videotapes by Mark S. Bettner
Electronic Classroom Presentations by Glenn Owen

Interactive Solutions Software
Teaching Transparencies
Report Card: Electronic Grading Software
Financial Statement Analysis Problem Set and Software
Solutions to Applications

Acknowledgements

This seventh Canadian edition has benefited from the perceptive inputs of the instructors and students who used the preceding edition. To those instructors and students, I express my sincere appreciation.

I am especially indebted to those reviewers who provided critical and constructive suggestions and to those who bestowed me with valuable advice. The suggestions and advice contributed greatly to the improvement in the text, supplementary, and assignment materials. Accordingly, I wish to thank all of the following individuals:

Mortimer Davis, Vanier College
Bruce W. Densmore, Mount Saint Vincent University
Randy Dickson, Red Deer College
Wendy Doyle, Mount Saint Vincent University
Gary Earle, Loyalist College
Adrian Feigelsohn, Royal Trust
Leo Gallant, St. Francis Xavier University
Peter Henderson, Douglas College
Tilly Jensen, Northern Alberta Institute of Technology
Ross Johnston, University of Windsor
Chris Kellman, Northwest College
Loris Macor, Coopers & Lybrand
Jim Macri, Ernst & Young
John Mitchell, Sault College
R. C. (Bob) Nichols, British Columbia Institute of Technology
Chris O'Neill, Algonquin College
Bill Ralston, Northwest College
Catherine Seguin, University of Toronto
Glen Sikorski, Niagara College
Ralph Sweet, Durham College

I greatly appreciate the expert attention, advice and assistance given to the seventh Canadian edition by the staff of McGraw-Hill Ryerson, especially Kelly Smyth, Susan Calvert, and Betty Tustin. Also, the excellent editing by Gail Marsden is much appreciated. My special thanks go to Sandy Berlasty for her assistance in typing part of the manuscript.

Finally, heartfelt appreciation is due to my family members—Jean, Angela, Lambert, and Gloria. Their patience and understanding have made this important academic endeavour more enjoyable. As well, they have done an outstanding job in typing, editing, and proofreading the manuscript of the text, solutions, and supplements.

Wai P. Lam

PART

1 The Accounting Cycle

In these first four chapters, the continuing example of Roberts Real Estate Company is used to illustrate the concepts of double-entry accrual accounting for a small, service-type business. Accounting for a merchandising concern will be introduced in Part 2.

Also included are two Comprehensive Problems. The first of these focuses upon the nature of double-entry accounting and the interpretation of a balance sheet. The second provides a review of the entire accounting cycle.

CHAPTER

1 Accounting: The Language of Business

The primary purpose of this introductory chapter is to explore the nature of accounting information and the environment in which it is developed and used. We emphasize the financial reporting process, including the roles played by financial statements, generally accepted accounting principles, independent audits, and professional judgment. A basic financial statement—the balance sheet—is illustrated and discussed. We explain the nature of assets, liabilities, and owner's equity, and why a balance sheet always "balances." We also introduce Roberts Real Estate Company, which is used as a continuing example throughout the first four chapters.

This chapter concludes with a discussion of career opportunities in accounting.

Learning Objectives

After studying this chapter you should be able to:

1 *Define accounting, financial reporting, and financial statements.*

2 *Explain the phrase "generally accepted accounting principles."*

3 *Describe and prepare a balance sheet; define assets, liabilities, and owner's equity.*

4 *Describe the accounting principles involved in asset valuation.*

5 *Indicate the effects of various transactions upon the balance sheet and the accounting equation.*

6 *Describe the three forms of business organization.*

7 *Use a balance sheet in evaluating the short-term solvency of a business organization.*

8 *Explain the concept of adequate disclosure.*

9 *Identify factors contributing to the reliability of financial statements.*

10 *Identify several areas in which accountants must exercise professional judgment.*

11 *Describe the relationship between professional accountants and top corporate executives.*

*12 *Describe various career opportunities in accounting.*

* *Supplemental Topic, "Careers in Accounting"*

WHAT IS ACCOUNTING?

*OBJECTIVE 1 **Define accounting, financial reporting, and financial statements.***

Some people think of accounting as a highly technical field that is practised and understood only by professional accountants. Actually, nearly everyone practises "accounting" in one form or another on almost a daily basis. ***Accounting is the art of identifying, measuring, recording, interpreting, and communicating the results of economic activities.*** Whether you are paying your phone bill, balancing your chequebook, preparing your income tax return, or managing an international corporation, you are working with accounting concepts and accounting information.

Accounting has often been called the ***language of business.*** Such terms and concepts as ***assets, liabilities, net income, cash flow, earnings per share, business entity, and going concern*** are but a few examples of technical accounting terms and concepts widely used throughout the business world. Every investor, manager, and business decision maker needs a clear understanding of accounting terms and concepts if he or she is to participate and communicate effectively in the business community.

The use of accounting information is not limited to the business world. We live in an era of accountability. An individual may be required to account for his or her income and file an income tax return. Often an individual must supply personal accounting information in order to qualify for a loan or to obtain a credit card. The federal government, the provinces, the cities, and the school boards all use accounting information as the basis for controlling their resources and measuring their accomplishments. Accounting is just as important to the successful operation of a government, a social program, or a church as it is to a business organization.

The study of accounting should not be limited to students majoring in accounting or finance. Everyone who engages in economic activity—***which means everyone***—will benefit from understanding the nature, significance, and limitations of accounting information.

The Purpose of Accounting

The basic purpose of accounting is to provide decision makers with information ***useful in making economic decisions.*** These decisions concern the allocation and use of scarce economic resources, such as money, land, and labour. The manner in which we allocate and use economic resources shapes the world's economies. Resource allocation decisions determine prices, wages, the goods and services we produce, the adequacy of our food supplies, the quality of our transportation systems, and which countries will enjoy economic growth or suffer economic decline.

Just as there are many different types of economic decisions, there are many types of accounting information. The terms ***financial accounting, management accounting,*** and ***tax accounting*** often are used in describing the types of accounting information most widely used in the business community.

Financial Accounting Financial accounting refers to information describing the financial resources, obligations, equity, and activities of an economic entity (either an organization or an individual). Accountants use the term ***financial position*** to describe an entity's financial resources and obligations at one point in time, and the term ***results of operations*** to describe its financial activities during an accounting period such as a month or a year.

Financial accounting information is designed primarily to assist ***investors*** and ***creditors*** in deciding where to place their scarce investment resources.[1] Such decisions are important to society, as they determine which companies and industries will receive the financial resources necessary for growth, and which will not.

However, many ***other*** decision makers also make use of financial accounting information. A company's managers and employees constantly need such information in order to run and control daily business operations. For example, they need to know the amount of money in the company's bank accounts, the types and quantities of merchandise in the company's warehouse, and the amounts owed to specific creditors. Financial accounting information also is used in income tax returns. In fact, financial accounting information is used for so many ***different purposes*** that it often is called ***general-purpose*** accounting information.

Management Accounting Management (or managerial) accounting involves the development and interpretation of accounting information intended ***specifically to aid management*** in running the business. Managers use this information in setting the company's overall goals, evaluating the performance of departments and individuals, deciding whether to introduce a new line of products—and in making virtually all types of managerial decisions.

Much "management accounting" information is financial in nature but has been organized in a manner relating directly to the decision at hand. However, management accounting information often includes evaluations of "nonfinancial" factors, such as political considerations, the possible effects of various actions upon the environment, the company's public image, and worker productivity.

The enormous storage capacity of computers enables large companies to maintain integrated ***management information systems,*** which provide decision makers with both financial and nonfinancial information. Financial information, however, comprises the largest component of every management information system. The reason is simple: by definition, ***every economic decision involves financial considerations.***

Tax Accounting The preparation of income tax returns is a specialized field within accounting. To a great extent, tax returns are based upon financial accounting information. However, the information often is adjusted or reorganized to conform with income tax reporting requirements.

The most challenging aspect of tax accounting is not the preparation of an income tax return but rather ***tax planning.*** Tax planning means anticipating the "tax effects" of business transactions and structuring these transactions in a manner that will legitimately minimize the income tax burden.

---

[1] CICA, *CICA Handbook* (Toronto), section 1000.11.

Focus of This Text In this textbook, we begin by introducing the basic concepts of financial accounting. These discussions will emphasize both the process of ***financial reporting*** to investors and creditors and the usefulness of financial information to an organization's management and employees. In later chapters, our emphasis will shift toward management accounting and the use of accounting information in specific types of managerial decisions.

Major income tax concepts are discussed at various points throughout the text, and Chapter 18 is devoted entirely to this topic. Comprehensive coverage of income taxes, however, must be deferred to more advanced accounting courses.

Remember that the fields of financial, management, and tax accounting are ***closely related.*** Thus, we often address financial reporting requirements, management's information needs, and income tax considerations within a single chapter. Our emphasis throughout this text will be upon the accounting information developed in ***profit-oriented business organizations.***[2]

Our basic goals in this textbook are to help you develop your abilities to ***understand*** and to ***use*** accounting information effectively in making economic decisions. Throughout this course, you should focus upon the usefulness—and the limitations—of the accounting information available to decision makers.

THE FINANCIAL REPORTING PROCESS

All of the accounting information developed within a business is available to management. However, much of the company's financial accounting information also is used by decision makers ***outside*** the organization. These outsiders include investors, financial analysts, investment advisors, creditors (lenders), labour unions, government agencies, and the public. Each of these groups either supplies money to the business or has some other interest in the financial health of the organization. A labour union, for example, needs information about a company's financial strength and profitability before negotiating a new labour contract.

Supplying general-purpose financial information about a business to people outside the organization is termed ***financial reporting.*** In Canada and most other industrialized countries, large "publicly owned" business organizations make much of their accounting information public, that is, ***available to everyone.***[3] These countries generally have laws to ensure that the ***public information*** provided by these organizations is reasonably ***complete*** and ***reliable.***

Small businesses generally do not provide general-purpose financial information to persons outside the organization. However, banks and other

---

[2] The accounting practices of governmental agencies and other "not-for-profit" organizations differ in a number of ways from those of profit-oriented organizations. "Not-for-profit" accounting is a specialized topic and is addressed in advanced accounting courses.

[3] A company is "publicly owned" whenever ownership "shares" in the company are offered for sale to the general public. Public information about a business can be obtained by writing to the company's corporate secretary.

creditors often ***insist*** upon receiving this information as a condition for making loans to the business.

Financial Statements

The principal means of reporting general-purpose financial information to persons outside a business organization is a set of accounting reports called ***financial statements.*** The persons receiving these reports are termed the ***users*** of the financial statements.

A set of financial statements consists of four related accounting reports that summarize in a few pages the ***financial resources, obligations, equity, profitability,*** and ***cash transactions of a business.*** A complete set of financial statements includes:

1 A ***balance sheet,*** showing at a specific date the ***financial position*** of the company by indicating the resources that it owns, the debts that it owes, and the amount of the owner's ***equity*** (investment) in the business.
2 An ***income statement,*** indicating the ***profitability*** of the business over the preceding year (or other time period).
3 A ***statement of owner's equity,*** explaining certain changes in the amount of the owner's equity (investment) in the business. (In businesses that are organized as corporations, the statement of owner's equity is replaced by a ***statement of retained earnings.***)
4 A ***statement of changes in financial position,*** summarizing the cash receipts and cash payments of the business over the same time period covered by the income statement.

In addition, a complete set of financial statements includes several pages of ***notes,*** containing additional information that accountants believe is ***useful in the interpretation*** of the financial statements.[4]

The basic purpose of financial statements is to assist users in evaluating the ***financial position, profitability,*** and ***future prospects*** of a business. In Canada, the annual (and quarterly) financial statements of all publicly owned corporations are ***public information.***[5]

In deciding where to invest their resources, investors and creditors often compare the financial statements of many different companies. For such comparisons to be valid, the financial statements of these different companies must be reasonably ***comparable***—that is, they must present similar information in a similar format based on some "ground rules." To achieve this goal, financial statements are prepared in conformity with a set of "ground rules" called ***generally accepted accounting principles (GAAP).***

---

[4] A complete set of financial statements, along with the accompanying notes, is illustrated in Comprehensive Problem 5, which follows Chapter 20.

[5] In ***annual*** financial statements, the time period covered by the income statement, statement of retained earnings, and statement of changes in financial position is one year. In ***quarterly*** statements, the period covered in these statements is a quarter of a year (three months). The balance sheet reflects what the business owns and owes at the ***end*** of the time period covered by the other statements.

Financial Statements and Income Tax Returns Revenue Canada requires businesses and individuals with taxable income to file annual income tax returns. ***Taxable income*** is a legal concept defined by income tax laws and regulations. In many instances, income tax laws are similar to generally accepted accounting principles; but in other cases, they are quite different. Therefore, an income tax return is a special accounting report, separate from the company's financial statements. A company's income tax return is sent only to tax authorities such as Revenue Canada; it is ***not*** public information.

The Functions of an Accounting System

Most business organizations have an accounting system for preparing financial statements, income tax returns, reports to managers, bills to customers, and other types of accounting information. An accounting ***system*** consists of the personnel, procedures, devices, forms, and records used by an entity in developing accounting information and in communicating this information to decision makers. Accounting systems often make use of computers and other electronic devices, as well as handwritten forms and records. In fact, the accounting system of any large business organization includes all of these components.

In every accounting system, the economic activities of the organization are ***identified, measured,*** and then ***recorded*** in the accounting records. Next, the recorded data are ***classified*** within the system to accumulate subtotals for various types of economic activities. Finally, the information is ***summarized*** in accounting reports designed to meet the information needs of various decision makers, such as investors, managers, and governmental agencies.

The "Transactions" Approach to Recording Economic Activity Accounting reports summarize information that has been recorded in the accounting system. In recording economic activities, accountants focus upon ***completed transactions***—that is, events that (1) cause an ***immediate change*** in the financial resources or obligations of the business and (2) can be ***measured objectively*** in monetary terms.[6] Examples of transactions include purchasing or selling goods or services, receiving cash, and making cash payments. The recording of transactions in an accounting system may be performed in many ways, such as writing with a pen or pencil, using a cash register, or entering data through a keyboard.

The primary strength of this "transactions approach" lies in the ***reliability*** of the information that is recorded. The recorded information is based upon past events, for which the financial effects upon the business can be measured with a reasonable degree of ***objectivity.***

In another respect, accountants' emphasis upon transactions ***lessens*** the usefulness of accounting reports. Some important events are not recorded in the accounting records, because they do not meet the definition of

[6] Accountants use the term ***objective*** to mean neutral, free from bias, and verifiable in amount. The concept of ***objectivity*** is a generally accepted accounting principle and has a profound effect upon accounting practices and accounting information. This concept is discussed further on page ***16*** and at many points throughout the text.

a transaction. For example, the retirement or death of a key executive, a technological breakthrough by the company's research department, or the introduction of a new product by a competitor are not "transactions," and therefore they are not recorded in the accounting records. These events may cause significant ***future*** changes in the financial resources and obligations of the business, but they do not cause ***immediate*** changes. In addition, the financial effects of these events cannot be measured with much objectivity.

The preceding events are examples of important "nonfinancial" information. Although these events are not recorded in the accounting records, they are recorded elsewhere in the management information system. In addition, these events are disclosed to persons outside of the business organization through press conferences, notes to the financial statements, or the news media.

Internal Control

The decisions made by management are based to a considerable extent upon information developed by the accounting system. Therefore, management needs assurance that all the accounting information it receives is accurate and reliable. This assurance is provided by the company's ***system of internal control.*** A simple example of an internal control procedure is the use of serial numbers on cheques issued. Accounting for an unbroken sequence of serial numbers provides assurance that every cheque issued has been recorded in the accounting records.

A ***system of internal control*** includes all measures used by an organization to guard against errors, waste, and fraud; to assure the reliability of accounting data; to promote compliance with management policies; and to evaluate the level of performance in all divisions of the company. In short, a system of internal control includes all of the measures designed to assure management that the entire organization ***operates according to plan.***

Audits of Financial Statements

What assurance do outsiders have that the financial statements issued by management provide a complete and reliable picture of the company's financial position and operating results? In large part, this assurance is provided by an ***audit*** of the company's financial statements, performed by a firm of ***public accountants.*** These auditors are experts in the field of financial reporting and are ***independent*** of the company issuing the financial statements.

An ***audit*** is an ***investigation*** of a company's financial statements, designed to determine the "fairness" of these statements. Accountants and auditors use the term ***fair*** in describing financial statements that are reliable and complete, conform to generally accepted accounting principles, and are ***not misleading.***

As part of the audit, the auditors investigate the quality of the company's system of internal control, count or observe many of the company's assets, and gather evidence both from within the business and from outside sources. Based upon this careful investigation, the public accounting firm expresses its ***professional opinion*** as to the fairness of the financial statements. This opinion, called the ***auditors' report,*** accompanies the financial statements distributed to persons outside the business organization.

Auditors do not guarantee the accuracy of financial statements; they only express their expert opinion as to the fairness of the statements. However, public accounting firms stake their reputations on the thoroughness of their audits and the dependability of their audit reports. Over many years, audited financial statements have established an impressive track record of reliability.

Annual Reports

As part of the financial reporting process, large business organizations prepare ***annual reports*** for distribution to investors and other users. Included in these annual reports are audited financial statements for each of the last two years. These ***comparative*** financial statements enable users to identify trends in the company's performance and financial position. Annual reports also include the auditor's reports on the comparative statements and discussions by top management of the company's financial position, profitability, and future prospects. In addition, they contain much nonfinancial information about the company's objectives, products, and operations.

CASE IN POINT McDonald's Corporation devoted much of a recent annual report to the company's concern for the environment. Included in the report were discussions of the company's programs for solid waste management, resource conservation, and recycling. (The annual report was printed entirely on recycled paper.)

Financial Reporting: A Multimedia Process

Although financial statements are the ***primary*** means of financial reporting, they are not the ***only*** means. Information about a business is also made available to outside decision makers through news conferences, press releases, annual reports, and filings of public information with governmental agencies. In addition, many financial analysts, investment advisory services, and business magazines continually evaluate the financial position, profitability, and future prospects of publicly owned companies. Many such evaluations are readily available to the public at little or no cost.

CASE IN POINT Financial analysts and financial reporters share their evaluations of the financial position, profitability, and future prospects of many publicly owned companies in such business publications as *The Financial Post, Canadian Business, Financial Times, Financial Post Survey of Industrials, The Investment Reporter,* and *Value Line Investment Survey.*

The Use of Computers in Accounting Systems

Computers are tools widely used by accountants for recording, processing, and storing accounting information. In addition, the use of computers helps make accounting information ***more useful to decision makers.*** First, computers enable accountants to assemble information and deliver it to decision makers far more quickly than is possible in a manual system. Of even greater importance, computers enable accountants to classify and summarize data ***in many different ways.*** For example, the daily sales reports prepared for the manager of a large department store may be most useful if sales are summarized ***by department.*** In sales reports prepared for the store's merchandise buyers, however, it may be more useful to summarize the daily sales ***by product.*** Thus, computers assist accountants in tailoring accounting reports to the needs of specific decision makers.

The Distinction between Accounting and Bookkeeping

Persons with little knowledge of accounting may fail to understand the distinction between accounting and bookkeeping. ***Bookkeeping*** refers to the daily operation of an accounting system—that is, recording and classifying routine transactions. Bookkeeping is a skill that an individual might acquire within a few weeks or months. Most bookkeeping functions can be performed most efficiently through the use of a computer.

Accounting encompasses bookkeeping and it includes identifying and measuring the transactions and events to be recorded as well as interpreting and communicating the recorded information in a meaningful manner to decision makers. Accounting also involves the designing of accounting and internal control systems.

GENERALLY ACCEPTED ACCOUNTING PRINCIPLES (GAAP)

Rules & Regulation

OBJECTIVE 2 Explain the phrase "generally accepted accounting principles."

Generally accepted accounting principles (or ***GAAP***) are the "ground rules" for financial reporting. These principles provide the general framework determining ***what information is included in financial statements and how this information is to be presented.*** The phrase "generally accepted accounting principles" encompasses the basic objectives of financial reporting, as well as numerous broad concepts and many detailed rules. Thus, such terms as ***objectives, standards, concepts, assumptions, methods,*** and ***rules*** often are used in describing specific generally accepted accounting "principles."

We already have discussed two concepts embodied in generally accepted accounting principles: ***comparability*** (among different companies) and ***reliability.*** In this chapter we will discuss six other generally accepted accounting principles: the ***entity principle,*** the ***cost principle,*** the ***going-concern assumption,*** the ***objectivity principle,*** the ***stable-dollar assumption,*** and the ***concept of adequate disclosure.*** These and other accounting principles will be considered further at many points throughout this book.

Let us emphasize, however, that ***there is no comprehensive list of generally accepted accounting principles.*** In fact, new accounting principles emerge continuously as business organizations enter into new forms of business activity.

The Nature of Accounting Principles

Accounting principles are not like physical laws; they do not exist in nature awaiting discovery. Rather, they are ***developed by people,*** in light of what we consider to be the most important objectives of financial reporting. In many ways generally accepted accounting principles are similar to the rules established for an organized sport, such as football or basketball. For example, accounting principles, like sports rules:

- Originate from a combination of tradition, experience, and official decree.
- Require authoritative support and some means of enforcement.
- Are sometimes arbitrary.
- May change over time as shortcomings in the existing rules come to light.
- Must be clearly understood and observed by all participants in the process.

Unfortunately, accounting principles vary somewhat from country to country. The phrase "generally accepted accounting principles" refers to the accounting concepts in use in Canada. However, the principles in use in the United States, Great Britain, and a number of other countries are quite similar. Also, foreign companies that raise capital from Canadian investors usually issue financial statements in conformity with the generally accepted accounting principles in use in Canada.

Several international organizations currently are attempting to establish greater uniformity among the accounting principles in use around the world.

Organizations Influencing Accounting Practice

In Canada, the Canadian Institute of Chartered Accountants (CICA) is the most prominent and influential organization in developing generally accepted accounting principles and in improving the quality of financial reporting. The CICA, through its Accounting Standards Board,[7] has issued a significant number of recommendations on accounting standards. The recommendations are contained in the *CICA Handbook* and are considered as generally accepted accounting principles. Both the Canadian Business Corporations Act and the provincial securities commissions have recog-

[7] The CICA's Accounting Standards Board is composed of a cross section of individuals with various backgrounds and occupations: eight members are appointed by the CICA, and one member is appointed by each of these five organizations—the Canadian Academic Accounting Association, Canadian Council of Financial Analysts, Certified General Accountants' Association of Canada, Financial Executives Institute Canada, and Society of Management Accountants of Canada. However, the Certified General Accountants' Association of Canada has declined to appoint its representative to serve on the Board.

nized the *CICA Handbook* accounting recommendations as generally accepted accounting principles. The CICA is a self-regulated body, not a government agency.

A number of other organizations outside Canada also have an influence on Canadian accounting practices—the Financial Accounting Standards Board (FASB), the American Institute of Certified Public Accountants (AICPA), and the Securities and Exchange Commissions (SEC) in the United States, and the International Accounting Standards Committee located in the United Kingdom.

The FASB is a self-regulated body that issues Statements of Financial Accounting Standards. These statements represent authoritative expression of generally accepted accounting principles in the United States.

"Authoritative Support" for Accounting Principles To qualify as "generally accepted," an accounting principle must have "substantial authoritative support." Accounting recommendations set forth by the CICA's Accounting Standards Board automatically qualify as generally accepted accounting principles. However, many concepts and practices gain substantial authoritative support from ***unofficial*** sources, such as widespread use or recognition in textbooks and other "unofficial" accounting literature. Thus, the phrase "generally accepted accounting principles" includes more concepts and practices than appear in the "official" literature.

FINANCIAL STATEMENTS: THE STARTING POINT IN THE STUDY OF ACCOUNTING

The preparation of financial statements is not the first step in the accounting process, but it is a logical point to begin the ***study*** of accounting. Financial statements convey to management and to interested outsiders a concise picture of the profitability and financial position of a business. These statements summarize, in a few pages, the thousands or even millions of transactions recorded during the year in the company's accounting system. Thus, financial statements are the ***end product*** of the accounting process. The student who acquires a clear understanding of the nature and content of these statements is in a better position to appreciate the objectives of the earlier steps of recording and classifying business transactions.

The three most widely used financial statements are the ***balance sheet,*** the ***income statement,*** and the ***statement of changes in financial position.*** In this introductory chapter and in Chapter 2, we shall explore the nature of the balance sheet, or ***statement of financial position,*** as it is sometimes called. Once we have become familiar with the form and arrangement of the balance sheet and with the meanings of technical terms such as ***assets, liabilities,*** and ***owner's equity,*** it will be as easy to read and understand a report on the financial position of a business as it is for an architect to read a blueprint for a proposed building. (We shall discuss the income statement in Chapter 3, and the statement of changes in financial position later in the course.)

The Balance Sheet

OBJECTIVE 3 Describe and prepare a balance sheet; define assets, liabilities, and owner's equity.

The purpose of a balance sheet is to show the ***financial position*** of a ***given business entity*** at a ***specific date.*** Every business prepares a balance sheet at the end of the year, and most companies prepare one at the end of each month. A balance sheet consists of a listing of the assets, the liabilities, and the owner's equity of a business. The ***balance sheet date*** is important, as the financial position of a business may change quickly. A balance sheet is most useful if it is ***relatively recent.*** The following balance sheet shows the financial position of ***Vagabond Travel Agency*** at ***December 31, 1996.***

A balance sheet shows financial position at a specific date

VAGABOND TRAVEL AGENCY
Balance Sheet
December 31, 1996

Assets		*Liabilities & Owner's Equity*	
Cash	$ 22,500	Liabilities:	
Notes receivable	10,000	Notes payable	$ 41,000
Accounts receivable	60,500	Accounts payable	36,000
Supplies	2,000	Salaries payable	3,000
Land	100,000	Total liabilities	$ 80,000
Building	90,000	Owner's equity:	
Office equipment	15,000	Terry Crane, capital	220,000
Total	$300,000	Total	$300,000

Let us briefly describe several features of this balance sheet. First, the heading sets forth three things: (1) the name of the business entity, (2) the name of the financial statement, and (3) the balance sheet date. The body of the balance sheet also consists of three distinct sections: ***assets, liabilities,*** and ***owner's equity.***

Notice that cash is listed first among the assets, followed by notes receivable, accounts receivable, supplies, and any other assets that will ***soon be converted into cash or consumed in business operations.*** Following these relatively "liquid" assets are the more "permanent" assets, such as land, buildings, and equipment.

Liabilities are shown before owner's equity. Each major type of liability (such as notes payable, accounts payable, and salaries payable) is listed separately, followed by a figure for total liabilities.

Finally, notice that the amount of total assets ($300,000) is ***equal*** to the total amount of liabilities and owner's equity (also $300,000). This relationship ***always exists***—in fact, the ***equality of these totals*** is one reason that this financial statement is called a ***balance*** sheet.

The Concept of the Business Entity Generally accepted accounting principles require that a set of financial statements describe the affairs of a specific business entity. This concept is also called the ***accounting entity concept*** or ***entity principle.***

A ***business entity*** is an economic unit that engages in ***identifiable business activities.*** For accounting purposes, the business entity is regarded as ***separate from the personal affairs of its owner.*** Therefore, the assets and liabilities are related to a specific business, not related to the owner personally. For example, Vagabond is a business organization operating as a travel agency. Its owner, Terry Crane, may have a personal bank account, a home, a car, and even another business, such as a cattle ranch. These items are ***not involved in the operation of the travel agency*** and should not appear in Vagabond's financial statements.

If the owner were to intermingle his or her personal affairs with the transactions of the business, the resulting financial statements would fail to describe clearly the financial position and operating results of the business organization.

Assets

Assets are economic resources that are owned by a business and are expected to benefit future operations. Assets may have definite physical form, as do buildings, machinery, and an inventory of merchandise. On the other hand, some assets exist not in physical or tangible form but in the form of valuable legal claims or rights; examples are accounts receivable (amounts due from customers), investments in government bonds, and patent rights.

One of the most basic and at the same time most controversial problems in accounting is determining dollar values for the various assets of a business. At present, generally accepted accounting principles call for the valuation of assets in a balance sheet at ***cost,*** rather than at current market values. The specific accounting principles supporting cost as the basis for asset valuation are discussed below.

OBJECTIVE 4 Describe the accounting principles involved in asset valuation.

The Cost Principle Assets such as land, buildings, and equipment are typical of the many economic resources that will be used in producing income for the business. The prevailing accounting view is that such assets should be recorded at their acquisition cost. When we say that an asset is shown in the balance sheet at its ***historical cost,*** we mean the dollar amount originally incurred to acquire the asset; this amount may be very different from what we would have to incur today to replace it.

For example, let us assume that a business buys a tract of land for use as a building site, paying $100,000 in cash. The amount to be entered in the accounting records as the value of the asset will be the cost of $100,000. If we assume a booming real estate market, a fair estimate of the sales value of the land 10 years later might be $250,000. Although the market price or economic value of the land has risen greatly, the accounting value as shown in the accounting records and in the balance sheet would continue unchanged at the cost of $100,000. This policy of accounting for assets at their acquisition cost is often referred to as the ***cost principle*** of accounting.

In reading a balance sheet, it is important to bear in mind that the dollar amounts listed do not necessarily indicate the prices at which the assets could be sold nor the prices at which they could be replaced. One useful generalization to be drawn from this discussion is that a balance sheet ***does not*** necessarily show "how much a business is ***worth.***"

The Going-Concern Assumption It is appropriate to ask ***why*** accountants do not change the recorded values of assets to correspond with changing market prices for these properties. One reason is that the land and building being used to house the business were acquired for ***use*** and not for resale; in fact, these assets cannot be sold without disrupting the business. The balance sheet of a business is prepared on the assumption that the business is a continuing enterprise, a "going concern." Consequently, the present estimated prices at which the land and buildings could be sold are of less importance than if these properties were intended for sale.

The Objectivity Principle Another reason for using cost rather than current market values in accounting for assets is the need for a definite, factual basis for valuation. Accountants use the term ***objective*** to describe asset valuations that are factual and can be verified by independent experts. For example, if land is shown on the balance sheet at cost, any public accountant who performed an audit of the business would be able to find objective evidence that the land was actually valued at the cost of acquiring it. Estimated market values, on the other hand, for assets such as buildings and specialized machinery are not factual and objective. Market values are constantly changing, and estimates of the prices at which assets could be sold are largely a matter of personal opinion.

At the date an asset is acquired, the cost and market value usually are the same. The bargaining process that results in the sale of an asset serves to establish both the current market value of the property and the cost to the buyer. With the passage of time, however, the current market value of assets is likely to differ considerably from the cost recorded in the owner's accounting records.

The Stable-Dollar Assumptions Severe inflation in several countries in recent years has raised serious doubts as to the adequacy of the conventional cost basis in accounting for assets. When inflation becomes very severe, historical cost values for assets simply lose their relevance as a basis for making business decisions. Much consideration has been given to the use of balance sheets that would show assets at current appraised values or at replacement costs rather than at historical cost.

Accountants in Canada, by adhering to the cost basis of accounting, are implying that the dollar is a ***stable unit of measurement,*** like the litre, or the kilometre. The cost principle and the stable-dollar assumption work very well in periods of stable prices but are less satisfactory under conditions of rapid inflation. For example, if a company bought land 20 years ago for $100,000 and purchased a second similar tract of land today for $500,000, the total cost of land shown by the accounting records would be $600,000. This treatment ignores the fact that dollars spent 20 years ago had far greater purchasing power than today's dollar. Thus, the $600,000 total for cost of land is a mixture of two kinds of dollars with very different purchasing power.

After much research into this problem, the CICA's Accounting Standards Board required on a trial basis that large corporations report supplementary data showing current replacement costs and price-level adjusted data. However, after a few years, the cost of developing and disclosing such information in financial statements was judged to be greater than the benefits provided. Consequently, the disclosure requirement was eliminated. At the present time, the stable-dollar assumption continues in use in Canada—perhaps until challenged by more severe inflation sometime in the future.

Liabilities

Liabilities are debts. These debts usually require the payment in assets or the rendering of services, or both. All business concerns have liabilities; even the largest and most successful companies find it convenient to purchase merchandise and supplies on credit rather than to pay cash at the time of each purchase. The liability arising from the purchase of goods or services on credit is called an ***account payable,*** and the person or company to whom the account payable is owed is called a ***creditor.*** The liability arising from receiving cash for future services is called unearned fees (such as unearned management fees discussed in Chapter 4).

A business concern frequently finds it desirable to borrow money as a means of supplementing the funds invested by the owner, thus enabling the business to expand more rapidly. The borrowed funds may, for example, be used to buy merchandise that can be sold at a profit to the company's customers. Or the borrowed money might be used to buy new and more efficient machinery, thus enabling the company to turn out a larger volume of products at lower cost. When a business borrows money for any reason, a liability is incurred and the lender becomes a creditor of the business. The form of the liability when money is borrowed is usually a ***note payable,*** a formal written promise to pay a certain amount of money, plus interest, at a definite future time.

An ***account payable,*** as contrasted with a ***note payable,*** does not involve the issuance of a formal written promise to the creditor, and it usually does not call for payment of interest. When a business has both notes payable and accounts payable, the two types of liabilities are shown separately in the balance sheet, with notes payable usually listed first. A figure showing the total of the liabilities should also be inserted, as shown by the illustrated balance sheet on page **14.**

The creditors have claims against the assets of the business, usually not against any particular asset but against the assets in general. The claims of the creditors are liabilities of the business and have priority over the claims of owners. Creditors are entitled to be paid in full even if such payment should exhaust the assets of the business, leaving nothing for the owner.

Owner's Equity

The owner's equity in a business represents the resources invested by the owner (or owners). The equity of the owner is a ***residual claim,*** because the claims of the creditors legally come first. If you are the owner of a business, you are entitled to whatever remains ***after the claims of the creditors are fully satisfied.*** Thus, owner's equity is equal to the ***total***

assets minus the liabilities. For example, using the data from the illustrated balance sheet of Vagabond Travel Agency (page **14**):

Vagabond has total assets of	$300,000
And total liabilities of	80,000
Therefore, the owner's equity must equal	$220,000

Suppose that Vagabond borrows $20,000 from a bank. After recording the additional asset of $20,000 in cash and recording the new liability of $20,000 owed to the bank, we would have the following:

Vagabond now has total assets of	$320,000
And total liabilities are now	100,000
*Therefore, the owner's equity **still** is equal to*	$220,000

It is apparent that the total assets of the business were increased by the act of borrowing money from a bank, but the increase in total assets was exactly offset by an increase in liabilities, and the owner's equity remained unchanged. The owner's equity in a business ***is not increased*** by the incurring of liabilities of any kind.

Increases in Owner's Equity The owner's equity in a business comes from two sources:

1 ***Investment*** by the owner
2 ***Earnings*** from profitable operation of the business

Only the first of these two sources of owner's equity is considered in this chapter. The second source, an increase in owner's equity through earnings of the business, will be discussed in Chapter 3.

Decreases in Owner's Equity If you are the owner of a business, you have the right to withdraw cash or other assets from the business at any time. Because you want to see the business succeed, you will probably not make withdrawals that would handicap the business in operating efficiently. Withdrawals are most often made by writing a cheque drawn on the company's bank account and payable to the owner. Other types of withdrawals also occur, such as taking office equipment out of the business for personal use by the owner or using cash belonging to the business to pay the personal debts of the owner. Every withdrawal by the owner reduces the total assets of the business and also reduces the owner's equity.

In summary, decreases in the owner's equity in a business are caused in two ways:

1 ***Withdrawals*** of cash or other assets by the owner
2 ***Losses*** from unprofitable operation of the business

Accounting for these types of transactions will be explained and illustrated in Chapter 3.

The Accounting Equation

A fundamental characteristic of every balance sheet is that the total dollar amount of assets is ***equal to*** the total of liabilities and owner's equity. As stated earlier, the equality of these two totals is one reason for calling this financial statement a ***balance sheet.*** But ***why*** do total assets always equal the total of liabilities and owner's equity? The answer can be given in one short paragraph.

The dollar totals on the two sides of the balance sheet are always equal because these two sides are merely two views of the same business resources. The listing of assets shows us ***what resources*** the business owns; the listing of liabilities and owner's equity tells us ***who supplied these resources*** to the business and how much each group supplied. Everything that a business owns has been supplied to it by the creditors or by the owner. Therefore, the total claims of the creditors plus the claim of the owner equal the total assets of the business.

The equality of assets on the one hand and of the claims of the creditors and the owner on the other hand is expressed in the equation:

The basic "accounting equation"

Assets = Liabilities + Owner's Equity
\$300,000 = \$80,000 + \$220,000

The amounts listed in the equation were taken from the balance sheet illustrated on page **14.** A balance sheet is simply a detailed statement of this equation. To illustrate this relationship, compare the balance sheet of Vagabond Travel Agency with the above equation.

To emphasize that the equity of the owner is a residual element, secondary to the claims of creditors, it is often helpful to transpose the terms of the equation, as follows:

Alternative form of equation

Assets − Liabilities = Owner's Equity
\$300,000 − \$80,000 = \$220,000

Every business transaction, no matter how simple or how complex, can be expressed in terms of its effect on the accounting equation. A thorough understanding of the equation and some practice in using it are essential to the student of accounting.

Regardless of whether a business grows or contracts, this equality between the assets and the claims against the assets is always maintained. Any increase in the amount of total assets is necessarily accompanied by an equal increase on the other side of the equation, that is, by an increase in either the liabilities or the owner's equity. Any decrease in total assets is necessarily accompanied by a corresponding decrease in liabilities or owner's equity. The continuing equality of the two sides of the balance sheet can best be illustrated by taking a brand-new business as an example and observing the effects of various transactions upon its balance sheet.

Effects of Business Transactions upon the Balance Sheet

Assume that James Roberts, a licensed real estate broker, decided to start a real estate business of his own, to be known as Roberts Real Estate

OBJECTIVE 5 Indicate the effects of various transactions upon the balance sheet and the accounting equation.

Company. The planned operations of the new business call for obtaining "listings" of houses being offered for sale by owners, advertising these houses, and showing them to prospective buyers. The listing agreement signed with each owner provides that Roberts Real Estate Company shall receive at the time of sale a commission equal to 6% of the sales price of the property.

The new business was begun on September 1, when Roberts deposited $180,000 in a bank account in the name of the business, Roberts Real Estate Company. The initial balance sheet of the new business then appeared as follows:

Beginning balance sheet of a new business

ROBERTS REAL ESTATE COMPANY
Balance Sheet
September 1, 19__

Assets		*Owner's Equity*	
Cash	$180,000	James Roberts, capital	$180,000

Observe that the equity of the owner in the assets is designated on the balance sheet by the caption, ***James Roberts, capital.*** The word ***capital*** is the traditional accounting term used in describing the equity of the proprietor in the assets of the business.

Purchase of an Asset for Cash The next transaction entered into by Roberts Real Estate Company was the purchase of land suitable as a site for an office. The price for the land was $141,000 and payment was made in cash on September 3. The effect of this transaction on the balance sheet was twofold: first, cash was decreased by the amount paid out; and second, a new asset, Land, was acquired. After this exchange of cash for land, the balance sheet appeared as follows:

Balance sheet totals unchanged by purchase of land for cash

ROBERTS REAL ESTATE COMPANY
Balance Sheet
September 3, 19__

Assets		*Owner's Equity*	
Cash	$ 39,000	James Roberts, capital	$180,000
Land	141,000		
Total	$180,000	Total	$180,000

Purchase of an Asset for Cash and on Credit On September 5 an opportunity arose to buy from Kent Company a small office building that had to be moved to permit the construction of a freeway. A price of $36,000 was agreed upon, which included the cost of moving the building and installing it upon the Roberts Company's lot. As the building was in excellent condition and would have cost approximately $80,000 to build, Roberts considered this a very fortunate purchase.

The terms provided for an immediate cash payment of $15,000 and payment of the balance of $21,000 within 90 days. Cash was decreased

$15,000, but a new asset, Building, was recorded at cost in the amount of $36,000. Total assets were thus increased by $21,000, but the total of liabilities and owner's equity was also increased as a result of recording the $21,000 account payable as a liability. After this transaction had been recorded, the balance sheet appeared as shown below. (Remember that cash is always the first asset listed in a balance sheet.)

Totals increased equally by purchase on credit

ROBERTS REAL ESTATE COMPANY
Balance Sheet
September 5, 19__

Assets		*Liabilities & Owner's Equity*	
Cash	*$ 24,000*	*Liabilities:*	
Land	*141,000*	*Accounts payable*	*$ 21,000*
Building	*36,000*	*Owner's equity:*	
		James Roberts, capital	*180,000*
Total	*$201,000*	*Total*	*$201,000*

Note that the building appears in the balance sheet at $36,000, its cost to Roberts Real Estate Company. The estimate of $80,000 as the probable cost to construct such a building is irrelevant. Even if someone should offer to buy the building from Roberts Company for $80,000 or more, this offer, if refused, would have no bearing on the balance sheet. In a balance sheet, most assets are valued at their ***cost,*** not at their current market values.

Sale of an Asset on Credit After the office building had been moved to the Roberts Company's lot, Roberts decided that the lot was larger than was needed. The adjoining business, Carter's Drugstore, wanted more room for a parking area, so, on September 10, Roberts Company sold a small, unused corner of the lot to Carter's Drugstore for a price of $11,000. Since the sales price was computed at the same amount per square metre as Roberts Company had paid for the land, there was neither a profit nor a loss on the sale. No down payment was required, but it was agreed that the full price would be paid within three months. In this transaction a new asset, Accounts Receivable, was acquired, but the asset Land was decreased by the same amount. Consequently, there was no change in the amount of total assets. After this transaction, the balance sheet appeared as follows:

No change in totals by sale of land at cost

ROBERTS REAL ESTATE COMPANY
Balance Sheet
September 10, 19__

Assets		*Liabilities & Owner's Equity*	
Cash	*$ 24,000*	*Liabilities:*	
Accounts receivable	*11,000*	*Accounts payable*	*$ 21,000*
Land	*130,000*	*Owner's equity:*	
Building	*36,000*	*James Roberts, capital*	*180,000*
Total	*$201,000*	*Total*	*$201,000*

In the illustration thus far, Roberts Real Estate Company has an account receivable from only one debtor, and an account payable to only one creditor. As the business grows, the number of debtors and creditors will increase, but the Accounts Receivable and Accounts Payable designations will continue to be used. The additional records necessary to show the amount receivable from each individual debtor and the amount owing to each individual creditor will be explained in Chapter 5.

Purchase of an Asset on Credit A complete set of office equipment was purchased on credit from General Equipment, Inc., on September 14 for $5,400. As the result of this transaction the business owned a new asset, Office Equipment, but it had also incurred a new liability in the form of Accounts Payable. The increase in total assets was exactly offset by the increase in liabilities. After this transaction the balance sheet appeared as follows:

Totals increased by acquiring asset on credit

ROBERTS REAL ESTATE COMPANY
Balance Sheet
September 14, 19__

Assets		Liabilities & Owner's Equity	
Cash	$ 24,000	Liabilities:	
Accounts receivable	11,000	Accounts payable	$ 26,400
Land	130,000	Owner's equity:	
Building	36,000	James Roberts, capital	180,000
Office equipment	5,400		
Total	$206,400	Total	$206,400

Collection of an Account Receivable On September 20, cash in the amount of $1,500 was received as partial settlement of the account receivable from Carter's Drugstore. This transaction caused cash to increase and the accounts receivable to decrease by an equal amount. In essence, this transaction was merely the exchange of one asset for another of equal value. Consequently, there was no change in the amount of total assets. After this transaction, the balance sheet appeared as follows:

Totals unchanged by collection of an account receivable

ROBERTS REAL ESTATE COMPANY
Balance Sheet
September 20, 19__

Assets		Liabilities & Owner's Equity	
Cash	$ 25,500	Liabilities:	
Accounts receivable	9,500	Accounts payable	$ 26,400
Land	130,000	Owner's equity:	
Building	36,000	James Roberts, capital	180,000
Office equipment	5,400		
Total	$206,400	Total	$206,400

Payment of a Liability On September 30, Roberts Real Estate Company paid $3,000 in cash to General Equipment, Inc. This payment caused a decrease in cash and an equal decrease in liabilities. Therefore the balance sheet totals were still in balance. After this transaction, the balance sheet appeared as follows:

Totals decreased by paying a liability

ROBERTS REAL ESTATE COMPANY
Balance Sheet
September 30, 19__

Assets		*Liabilities & Owner's Equity*	
Cash	*$ 22,500*	*Liabilities:*	
Accounts receivable	*9,500*	*Accounts payable*	*$ 23,400*
Land	*130,000*	*Owner's equity:*	
Building	*36,000*	*James Roberts, capital*	*180,000*
Office equipment	*5,400*		
Total	*$203,400*	*Total*	*$203,400*

The transactions that have been illustrated for the month of September were merely preliminary to the formal opening for business of Roberts Real Estate Company on October 1. Since we have assumed that the business earned no commissions and incurred no expenses during September, the owner's equity at September 30 is shown in the above balance sheet at $180,000, unchanged from the original investment by Roberts on September 1. September was a month devoted exclusively to organizing the business and not to regular operations. In succeeding chapters we shall continue the example of Roberts Real Estate Company by illustrating operating transactions and considering how the net income of the business can be determined.

Effect of Business Transactions upon the Accounting Equation

A balance sheet is merely a detailed expression of the accounting equation, ***Assets = Liabilities + Owner's Equity.*** To emphasize the relationship between the accounting equation and the balance sheet, let us now repeat the September transactions of Roberts Real Estate Company to show the effect of each transaction upon the accounting equation. Briefly restated, the seven transactions were as follows:

Sept. 1 Began the business by depositing $180,000 in a company bank account.

3 Purchased land for $141,000 cash.

5 Purchased a prefabricated building for $36,000, paying $15,000 cash and incurring a liability of $21,000.

10 Sold part of the land at a price equal to cost of $11,000, collectible within three months.

14 Purchased office equipment on credit for $5,400.

20 Received $1,500 cash as partial collection of the $11,000 account receivable.

30 Paid $3,000 on accounts payable.

The table below shows the effects of each of the September transactions on the accounting equation. The final line in the table corresponds to the amounts in the balance sheet at the end of September. Note that the equality of the two sides of the equation was maintained throughout the recording of the transactions.

	Assets					= Liabilities	+ Owner's Equity
	Cash	+ Accounts Receivable	+ Land	+ Building	+ Office Equipment	= Accounts Payable	+ James Roberts, Capital
Sept. 1	+$180,000	–0–	–0–	–0–	–0–	–0–	+$180,000
Sept. 3	–141,000		+$141,000				
Balances	$39,000	–0–	$141,000	–0–	–0–	–0–	$180,000
Sept. 5	–15,000			+$36,000		+$21,000	
Balances	$24,000	–0–	$141,000	$36,000	–0–	$21,000	$180,000
Sept. 10		+$11,000	–11,000				
Balances	$24,000	$11,000	$130,000	$36,000	–0–	$21,000	$180,000
Sept. 14					+$5,400	+5,400	
Balances	$24,000	$11,000	$130,000	$36,000	$5,400	$26,400	$180,000
Sept. 20	+1,500	–1,500					
Balances	$25,500	$9,500	$130,000	$36,000	$5,400	$26,400	$180,000
Sept. 30	–3,000					–3,000	
Balances	$22,500 +	$9,500 +	$130,000 +	$36,000 +	$5,400 =	$23,400 +	$180,000

FORMS OF BUSINESS ORGANIZATION

OBJECTIVE 6 Describe the three forms of business organization.

In Canada, a business enterprise may be organized as a ***sole proprietorship,*** a ***partnership,*** or a ***corporation.*** Generally accepted accounting principles apply to the financial statements of all three forms of organization.

Sole Proprietorships

A business owned by one person is called a ***sole proprietorship.*** Often the owner also acts as the manager. Roberts Real Estate Company, the company used in our illustration, is a sole proprietorship owned by James Roberts. This form of business organization is common for small retail stores, farms, service businesses, and professional practices in law, medicine, and public accounting. In fact, the sole proprietorship is by far the most common form of business organization in our economy.

From an accounting viewpoint, a sole proprietorship is regarded as a business entity ***separate from the other affairs of its owner.*** From a legal viewpoint, however, the unincorporated business and its owner are not regarded as separate entities. Thus, ***the owner is personally liable*** for the debts of the business. If the business becomes insolvent, creditors can force the owner to sell his or her personal assets to pay the business debts.

Partnerships

An unincorporated business owned by two or more persons voluntarily acting as partners (co-owners) is called a ***partnership.*** Partnerships, like sole proprietorships, are widely used for small businesses. In addition, some very large professional practices, including international public accounting firms, are organized as partnerships. As in the case of the sole proprietorship, the partnership is not legally an entity separate from its owners. Thus, the owners are personally responsible for all debts of the business. From an accounting standpoint, a partnership is viewed as a business entity separate from the personal affairs of its owners.

Corporations

A corporation is the only type of business organization recognized ***under the law*** as an entity separate from its owners. Therefore, the owners of a corporation are ***not*** personally liable for the debts of the business. These owners can lose no more than the amounts they have invested in the business—a concept known as ***limited liability.*** This concept is the principal reason why corporations are the most attractive form of business organization to many investors.

Ownership of a corporation is divided into transferable shares of capital stock, and the owners are called ***shareholders.*** Stock certificates are issued by the corporation to each shareholder showing the number of shares that he or she owns. The shareholders are free to sell some or all of these shares to other investors at any time. This ***transferability of ownership*** adds to the attractiveness of the corporate form of organization, because investors can more easily "get their money out" of the business.

There are more sole proprietorships and partnerships than corporations, but most large businesses are organized as corporations. Thus, corporations are the ***dominant form*** of business organization in terms of the dollar volume of their business activities. In addition, it is primarily corporations that distribute their financial statements to investors and other outsiders.

Reporting Ownership Equity in the Balance Sheet

Assets and liabilities are presented in the same manner in the balance sheets of all three types of business organization. Some differences arise, however, in the presentation of the ownership equity.

Roberts Real Estate Company is a sole proprietorship, owned by one person. Therefore, the owner's equity section of the balance sheet includes only one item: the equity of the proprietor, James Roberts. If the business were a partnership with two or more owners, we would use the term ***Partners' Equity*** instead of Owner's Equity and would list separately the amount of each partner's equity in the business. If the business were organized as a corporation, the caption used in the balance sheet would be ***Shareholders' Equity.*** It is ***not*** customary in a corporation's balance sheet to show separately the equity of each shareholder. In the case of large corporations, this clearly would not be possible, as these businesses often have ***thousands of*** individual shareholders (owners).

In the balance sheet of a corporation, shareholders' equity is subdivided into two general categories: (1) capital stock and (2) retained earnings. ***Capital stock*** represents the amount that the shareholders originally ***invested in the business*** in exchange for shares of the company's stock. ***Retained earnings,*** in contrast, represents the increase in shareholders' equity that has accumulated over the years ***as a result of profitable business operations.***[8]

The three methods of reporting ownership equity in the balance sheet are illustrated below:

Ownership equity as reported in a balance sheet

In a Sole Proprietorship

Owner's equity:		
Dale Nelson, capital		*$ 50,000*

In a Partnership

Partners' equity:		
Pamela Barnes, capital	*$40,000*	
Scott Davis, capital	*35,000*	
Total partners' equity		*$ 75,000*

In a Corporation

Shareholders' equity:		
Capital stock	*$5,000,000*	
Retained earnings	*3,278,000*	
Total shareholders' equity		*$8,278,000*

THE USE OF FINANCIAL STATEMENTS BY OUTSIDERS

Most "outside" decision makers use financial statements in making ***investment decisions***—that is, in selecting those companies in which they will invest resources or to which they will extend credit. For this reason, financial statements are designed primarily to meet the needs of creditors and investors.[9] Two factors of concern to creditors and investors are the ***solvency*** and ***profitability*** of a business organization.

Creditors are interested in solvency—the ability of the business to pay its debts as they come due. Business concerns that are able to pay their debts promptly are said to be ***solvent.*** In contrast, a company that finds itself unable to meet its obligations as they fall due is called ***insolvent.*** Solvency is critical to the very survival of a business organization—a business that becomes insolvent may be forced into ***bankruptcy*** by its creditors. Once bankrupt, a business may be forced by the courts to stop its operations, sell its assets (for the purpose of paying its creditors), and end its existence.

---

[8] If the business operates ***unprofitably,*** retained earnings can become a ***negative*** amount, indicating the extent to which the unprofitable operations have ***decreased*** the shareholders' equity. The implications of negative retained earnings are discussed in Chapter 14.

[9] In this context, ***creditors*** include everyone to whom the business owes money. One may become a creditor of a business either by lending it money or by providing goods and services with payment due at a later date. ***Investors,*** on the other hand, are those persons having or considering an ***ownership*** interest in the organization.

Investors as well as creditors are interested in the solvency of a business organization, but they are even more interested in its ***profitability.***[10] A business is profitable when its revenue exceeds its expenses for an accounting period. Thus, ***profitable operations increase the value of the owners' equity*** in the business. A company that continually operates unprofitably will eventually exhaust its resources and be forced out of existence. Therefore, most users of financial statements study these statements carefully for clues to the company's solvency and future profitability.

The Short Run versus the Long Run In the short run, solvency and profitability may be independent of each other. A business may be operating profitably, but nevertheless run out of cash, and thereby become insolvent. On the other hand, a company may operate unprofitably during a given year, yet have enough cash to pay its bills and remain solvent.

Over a longer term, however, the goals of solvency and profitability go hand in hand. If a business is to survive, it must remain solvent and, in the long run, it must operate profitably.

CASE IN POINT Throughout the 1980s, the business activities of Donald Trump were enormously profitable, increasing Trump's net worth by several billion dollars. Yet in June 1990, the billionaire became insolvent; he did not have enough cash to meet a scheduled interest payment to his creditors. After days of around-the-clock negotiations with numerous banks, Trump was able to borrow enough cash to make his operations solvent again—at least for the moment. Had he not been able to arrange these "eleventh-hour" loans, Trump's creditors might have forced portions of his financial empire into bankruptcy.

However, Olympia & York Developments Ltd. (O & Y), the world's largest developer with properties spanning Canada, the United States, and Britain, was not so fortunate. This multi-billion dollar company became insolvent and collapsed in late 1992. Creditors have been taking over the properties that served as securities for the debts.

OBJECTIVE 7 Use a balance sheet in evaluating the short-term solvency of a business organization.

Evaluating Short-Term Solvency One key indicator of short-term solvency is the relationship between an entity's ***liquid*** assets and the liabilities requiring payment ***in the near future.***[11] By studying the nature of a company's assets and the amounts and due dates of its liabilities, users of financial statements often may anticipate whether the company is likely to have difficulty in meeting its upcoming obligations. This simple type of analysis meets the needs of many ***short-term*** creditors. Evaluating long-term solvency is a more difficult matter and is discussed in later chapters.

In studying financial statements, users should ***always*** read the accompanying notes and the auditors' report.

---

[10] The concept of profitability is discussed further in Chapter 3.

[11] "Liquid" assets are those expected to be converted into cash or consumed in business operations within a short period of time; from a short-term creditor's point of view, by the time payment is due. By definition, cash is the most liquid asset.

The Need for Adequate Disclosure

OBJECTIVE 8 Explain the concept of adequate disclosure.

The concept of adequate disclosure is an important generally accepted accounting principle. Adequate disclosure means that users of financial statements are informed of any facts ***necessary for the proper interpretation*** of the statements. Adequate disclosure may be made either in the body of the financial statements or in ***notes*** accompanying the statements.

Among the events that require disclosure are significant financial events occurring ***after*** the balance sheet date but before the financial statements have been issued to outsiders. For an example, let us refer to the December 31, 1996, balance sheet of Vagabond Travel Agency, illustrated on page 14. Assume that on January 4, ***1997,*** the building owned by Vagabond was completely destroyed by an earthquake. As the building existed at the end of 1996, it properly is included in the balance sheet date of December 31. However, users of this balance sheet need to be informed that the building ***no longer exists.*** The destruction of this building should be disclosed in a note accompanying the financial statements, such as the following:

Note 7: Events occurring subsequent to the balance sheet date

On January 4, 1997, a building shown in the balance sheet at $90,000 was destroyed by an earthquake. The Company does not insure against this type of loss. The financial effects of this loss will be reflected in the Company's 1997 financial statements.

In addition to important "subsequent events," many other situations may require disclosure in notes to the financial statements. Examples include lawsuits against the company, due dates of major liabilities, assets pledged as collateral to secure loans, amounts receivable from officers or other "insiders," and contractual commitments requiring large future cash outlays.

There is no comprehensive list of the items and events that may require disclosure. As a general rule, a company should disclose any financial facts that an intelligent person would consider ***necessary to the proper interpretation*** of the financial statements. Events that clearly are unimportant ***do not*** require disclosure.

The Reliability of Financial Statements

OBJECTIVE 9 Identify factors contributing to the reliability of financial statements.

Why should decision makers outside an organization regard financial statements as being fair and reliable? We already have identified three factors: (1) companies' systems of internal control, (2) the concept of adequate disclosure, and (3) audits performed by independent accounting firms. In Canada, ***corporate and securities laws*** provide additional assurance as to the reliability of financial statements. These laws require that the financial statements of publicly owned companies be prepared in conformity with generally accepted accounting principles, including the concept of adequate disclosure, and that they be audited. Any person who ***knowingly causes such financial statements to be misleading*** may be held financially responsible for the losses incurred by anyone relying upon the statements. These laws apply to the management of the company issuing the statements and also to the independent auditors.

Management's Interest in Financial Statements

The management of a business organization is vitally concerned with the financial position of the business, and also with its profitability. Therefore, management is anxious to receive financial statements as frequently and as quickly as possible, so that it may take action to improve areas of weak performance. Most large organizations provide managers with financial statements on at least a monthly basis.

However, managers have a special interest in the ***annual*** financial statements, as these are the statements most widely used by decision makers outside of the organization. For example, if creditors view the year-end balance sheet as "strong," they will be more willing to extend credit to the business than if they regard the company's financial position as weak. A ***strong*** balance sheet is one that shows relatively little debt and large amounts of liquid assets relative to the liabilities due in the near future. Management can—and does—take steps to make the year-end balance sheet look as strong as possible. For example, cash purchases of assets may be delayed so that substantial amounts of cash will be on hand at the balance sheet date. Liabilities due in the near future may be paid or replaced with longer-term liabilities.

These actions are called ***window dressing***—legitimate measures taken by management to make a business look as strong as possible at the balance sheet date. Users of year-end balance sheets should realize that while these statements are "fair" and "reliable," they may not necessarily describe the "typical" financial position of the business. In its annual financial statements, almost every company tries to "put its best foot forward." Many creditors, therefore, regard monthly balance sheets as providing a more typical picture of a company's financial position.

COMPETENCE, INTEGRITY, AND PROFESSIONAL JUDGMENT

OBJECTIVE 10 Identify several areas in which accountants must exercise professional judgment.

The preparation of accounting reports is not a mechanical task that can be performed by machine or even by well-trained clerical personnel. A characteristic common to all recognized professions—such as medicine, law, engineering, architecture, and accounting—is the need for individual practitioners to resolve many problems with their own ***professional judgment.*** The problems encountered in the practice of a profession are often complex, and the specific circumstances unique. Consequently, no written set of rules exists to provide answers in every situation.

In preparing the financial statements of a large business organization, the company's accountants and its independent auditors must make many "judgment calls." For example:

- What constitutes "adequate" disclosure?
- At what point should a business in financial difficulties cease to be viewed as a going concern?
- What types of investigative procedures are necessary to assure auditors that a company's financial statements represent a "fair" presentation?

- Which efforts by management represent legitimate "window dressing," and which are inappropriate actions that would make the financial statements misleading?
- Which accounting principles are appropriate for the specific business?

Unfortunately, judgmental decisions ***always involve some risk of error.*** Some "errors in judgment" result from carelessness or inexperience on the part of the decision makers. However, others occur simply because future events do not work out as anticipated.

If the public is to have confidence in the judgment of professional accountants, these accountants first must demonstrate that they possess the characteristics of ***competence*** and ***integrity.***

Professional Competence Professional competence means the possession of adequate technical training and proficiency in accountancy. Such training and proficiency is attained in qualifying for a professional designation such as Chartered Accountant (CA), Certified General Accountant (CGA), or Certified Management Accountant (CMA). To ensure continuing competence, professional accountants in public practice are required to take appropriate professional development courses and are subject to practice inspection. Practice inspection involves the review of the public accountant's work on auditing and accounting engagements by an independent external party.

Integrity and Ethics ***Integrity*** means honesty and a strong commitment to ethical conduct—doing the "right thing." For a professional accountant, integrity is just as important as competence. However, it is far more difficult to test or enforce.

Organizations of professional accountants have taken steps to encourage and enforce integrity within the profession. For example, professional organizations have developed ***codes of professional ethics*** for their members.[12] These codes are intended to help professional accountants fulfill their professional obligations with integrity. Violation of these codes may cause a public accountant to lose his or her licence to practise public accounting.

One concept found in all professional codes of ethics for accountants is that accountants must ***never knowingly be associated with misleading accounting information.*** In fact, a professional accountant should ***resign his or her position*** rather than become involved in the preparation or distribution of misleading information.

Of course, the basic concept of ethical conduct—acting with honour and integrity—***applies to management*** as well as to professional accountants.

The users of financial statements should recognize that the reliability of these statements is affected by the ***competence, integrity,*** and ***professional judgment*** of the management, accountants, and auditors involved in the financial reporting process. But as we have previously stated, au-

[12] In accounting, codes of professional ethics have been developed by the institutes of chartered accountants, the certified general accountants' associations, and the societies of certified management accountants.

dited financial statements—and the accounting profession—have established an impressive track record of reliability. More than any other factor, the competence and integrity of professional accountants ensure the fairness and reliability of financial statements.

CASE IN POINT A national survey of a large number of business people on the ethical conducts of sixteen professional and business groups ranks accountants first, followed by dentists and doctors. The others include corporate officers, lawyers, realtors, union leaders, newspaper reporters, and politicians.

Professional Accountants and Top Corporate Executives

OBJECTIVE 11 ***Describe the relationship between professional accountants and top corporate executives.***

While most professional accountants devote their career in public, management, and government accounting, many have become top corporate executives. The chairpersons, presidents, and directors of many large and well-known corporations in Canada have a professional accounting designation. These top executives run the leading corporations in almost all industries—banking, commercial, manufacturing, airline, insurance, publication, brewery, mining, and real estate. Thus, a background in accounting can be a stepping stone to top management.

CASE IN POINT Some of these well-known top corporate executives with a professional accounting background include: Laurant Beaudoin, FCA*, chairman and CEO (chief executive officer) of Bombardier; Paul Beeston, FCA, president of the Toronto Blue Jays; James Black, FCA, chairman of Molson; William Bradford, FCGA, president and CEO of North American Life Assurance; W. Michael Brown, CA, president of Thomson Corp.; Donald G. Campbell, FCA, chairman of McLean Hunter; John Cleghorn, FCA, president of Royal Bank of Canada; Norman T. Currie, FCA, president and CEO of Maple Leaf Mills; Douglas W. Dodds, FCMA, president and CEO of Schneider Corporation; Rhys T. Eyton, FCA, chairman of Canadian Airlines International; Peter Godsoe, CA, president and CEO of Bank of Nova Scotia; John Goudie, CMA, FSMAC, chairman of Alberta and Southern Gas; Gordan Gray, FCA, chairman of Royal LePage; Melvin Hawkrigg, FCA, chairman of Trilon Financial; Paul Ivanier, Ph.D., CA, president and CEO of Ivaco; Lucille Johnstone, CGA, president and COO (chief operating officer) of Rivtow Straits; David W. Kerr, CA, president and CEO of Noranda Inc.; Frank Knowles, CA, president and COO of Power Corp.; Wayne McLeod, FCA, vice-chairman and president, CCL Industries; Adam Zimmerman, FCA, vice-chairman of Noranda.

A number of individuals (other than those listed above) hold multiple directorships of large and well-known corporations. Some examples (since listing all the corporations will be lengthy, only three are mentioned for

---

* The "F" preceding the professional designation CA, CGA, or CMA means "Fellow", which is awarded to the members for their outstanding service and the distinction they brought to the profession.

each): John W. Adams, FCA, LL.D. (C.T. Financial Services, Canada Trust, F.W. Woolworth-U.S.); Marcel Belanger, FCA (BCE Inc., Hudson's Bay, John Labatt); Warren Chippindale, FCA (Alcan Aluminum, BCE Inc., Molson); Robert Despres, FCGA, FSMAC (Domtar, Norcen Energy, Provigo); Geno Francolini, FCA, LL.D. (Bell Canada, Laidlaw Transportation, Schneider Corp.); and Richard Haskayna, FCA (Manufacturers Life, Royal LePage, Canadian Imperial Bank of Commerce).

* Supplemental Topic
Careers in Accounting

THE ACCOUNTING PROFESSION

OBJECTIVE 12 Describe various career opportunities in accounting.

In Canada, there are three major professional accounting organizations: the provincial Institutes (in Quebec, Order) of Chartered Accountants, Societies of Management Accountants (formerly, the Societies of Industrial Accountants), and Certified General Accountants' Association (in Quebec, Professional Corporation). The national organizations of these three accounting bodies are the Canadian Institute of Chartered Accountants, the Society of Management Accountants of Canada, and the Certified General Accountants' Association of Canada. Members of these organizations receive their respective professional designations as chartered accountants (CAs), certified management accountants (CMAs), and certified general accountants (CGAs). The Institutes of Chartered Accountants place more emphasis on public accounting, the Societies of Management Accountants are primarily interested in management accounting, and the Certified General Accountants are interested in management as well as public accounting. In terms of career opportunities, accounting may be divided into four broad areas: (1) public accounting, (2) management accounting, (3) governmental accounting, and (4) accounting education.

PUBLIC ACCOUNTING

Public accounting firms are organizations that offer a variety of accounting services to the public. These firms vary in size from one-person practices to large, international organizations with several thousand professional accountants.

Most of the people in public accounting are ***chartered accountants (CAs).*** Thus, public accounting firms often are called ***CA firms.*** The specific requirements regarding the right to practise public accounting vary among provinces. In some provinces, such as Ontario and Nova Scotia, only chartered accountants have the automatic privilege to practise public accounting. In other provinces, such as Alberta and British Columbia, the practice of public accounting is open only to members of the professional accounting organizations.

The primary services offered by CA firms include auditing, income tax, and management advisory services.

We have already discussed the role of independent audits in the financial reporting process. For many years, auditing has been the principal function of public accountants. Today, however, tax work and management consulting are separate areas of specialization that are rapidly growing in importance.

Providing ***management advisory services*** is, perhaps, the fastest growing area in public accounting. The advisory services extend well beyond tax planning and accounting matters; public accountants advise management on such diverse issues as international mergers, manufacturing processes, and the introduction of new products. The entry of public accountants into the field of management consulting reflects the fact that ***financial considerations enter into every business decision.***

MANAGEMENT ACCOUNTING

In contrast to the public accountant who serves many clients, the management (or managerial) accountant works for one enterprise. Management accountants develop and interpret accounting information designed specifically to meet the various needs of management.

The chief accounting officer of an organization usually is called the ***controller,*** in recognition of the fact that one basic purpose of accounting data is to aid in controlling business operations. The controller is part of the top management team, which is responsible for running the business, setting its objectives, and seeing that these objectives are achieved.

In addition to developing information to assist managers, management accountants are responsible for operating the company's accounting system, including the recording of transactions and the preparation of financial statements, tax returns, and other accounting reports. As the responsibilities of management accountants are so broad, many areas of specialization have developed. Among the more important are the following:

Financial Reporting Management is responsible for a company meeting its financial reporting obligations. Therefore, some management accountants specialize in preparing financial statements and other reports for outsiders. This specialty requires an in-depth knowledge of generally accepted accounting principles.

Design of Management Information Systems Designing an efficient information system is a most challenging task. Management accountants specializing in this area must be knowledgeable about external reporting requirements, the information needs of managers, and the means of achieving adequate internal control. In addition, they must be familiar with the latest computer hardware and software and be able to develop a satisfactory system ***at a reasonable cost.*** Systems design is not a one-time effort; large organizations continuously expand and improve their information systems.

Cost Accounting Knowing the cost of each business operation and of each manufactured product is essential to the efficient management of a business. Determining the per-unit cost of business activities and of manufactured products—and interpreting this cost data—comprise a specialized field called ***cost accounting.***

Financial Forecasting A financial forecast (or budget) is a plan of financial operations for some ***future*** period. Actually, forecasting is much like financial reporting, except that the accountant is estimating future outcomes, rather than measuring past results. A forecast provides each department of a business with financial goals. Comparison of the results actually achieved with these forecast amounts is one widely used means of evaluating departmental performance.

Income Tax Accounting Many companies rely primarily upon public accounting firms for tax planning and the preparation of income tax returns. Large companies, however, usually maintain ***tax departments*** and perform some of these functions "in house."

Internal Auditing Large organizations usually maintain a staff of ***internal auditors.*** Internal auditors are charged with studying the system of internal control and evaluating the efficiency of many different aspects of the company's operations. As employees, internal auditors are not "independent" of the organization. Therefore, they ***do not*** perform independent audits of the company's financial statements.

GOVERNMENTAL ACCOUNTING

Governmental agencies use accounting information in allocating their resources and in controlling their operations. Therefore, the need for management accountants is similar to that in business organizations. However, governmental agencies generally do not have "investors" and, therefore, do less financial reporting.

The accounting standards used in government differ significantly from those in the business world, because earning a profit is not an objective of government. Universities, hospitals, churches, and other ***not-for-profit*** institutions also follow a pattern of accounting similar to that of governmental agencies.

ACCOUNTING EDUCATION: CAREERS AS FACULTY MEMBERS

So many attractive career opportunities exist for accounting majors that most graduates move directly into public accounting, management accounting, or governmental accounting. An interesting alternative, however, is to embark upon the graduate study and research necessary to become an accounting faculty member. The demand for qualified accounting faculty is intense. Individuals with these qualifications are highly mobile; there are positions to be filled in virtually every university.

Accounting faculty positions offer opportunities for research, consulting, and writing and an unusual degree of freedom in developing individual skills. Accounting educators contribute to the accounting profession in many ways: one, of course, lies in effective teaching; another, in publishing significant research findings in professional journals; and a third, in influencing top students to pursue careers in accounting.

CHAPTER REVIEW

KEY TERMS INTRODUCED OR EMPHASIZED IN CHAPTER 1

Note to Students: Each chapter includes a glossary explaining the key accounting terms introduced or emphasized. You should review these glossaries carefully; an understanding of accounting terminology is an essential step in the study of accounting. These terms will appear frequently in later chapters, in problem material, and in examination questions. (Because of the broad and introductory nature of Chapter 1, this glossary is longer than those in later chapters.)

Accounting Accounting is the art of identifying, measuring, recording, interpreting, and communicating the results of economic activity.

Accounting equation Assets are equal to the sum of liabilities plus owner's equity (A = L + OE). This equation is reflected in the format of the balance sheet.

Accounting Standards Board A board of the CICA that is responsible for issuing recommendations with respect to matters of accounting standards. The board's recommendations, which are contained in the *CICA Handbook,* are recognized as an authoritative source of generally accepted accounting principles.

Accounting system The personnel, procedures, records, forms, and devices used by an organization in developing and communicating accounting information.

Annual report A document issued annually by publicly owned corporations to their shareholders. Includes audited financial statements for two years, as well as nonfinancial information about the company and its operations.

Assets Economic resources owned by an entity.

Auditing Performing an investigation enabling the auditors to express an independent opinion (auditors' report) as to the fairness of a set of financial statements.

Balance sheet The financial statement showing the financial position of an entity by summarizing its assets, liabilities, and owner's equity at one specific date.

Business entity An economic unit that controls resources, incurs obligations, and engages in business activities. It is also called accounting entity.

Canadian Institute of Chartered Accountants (CICA) The national organization of chartered accountants (CAs) that carries on extensive research and is influential in developing and improving accounting standards and practices.

Capital stock Transferable units of ownership in a corporation.

Corporation A business organized as a separate legal entity with ownership divided into transferable shares of capital stock.

Cost principle The widely used principle of accounting for assets at their original cost to the current owner.

Creditor A lender; an entity to which money is owed.

Disclosure ("adequate") The accounting principle of providing with financial statements any financial facts necessary for the proper ***interpretation*** of those statements.

Fair A term used by accountants to describe a set of financial statements that are complete, not misleading, and prepared in conformity with generally accepted accounting principles. Auditors express their opinions as to the "fairness" of financial statements.

Financial accounting The development and use of accounting information describing the financial position of an entity and the results of its operations.

Financial position The financial resources and obligations of an organization, as described in a ***balance sheet.***

Financial reporting The process of periodically providing "general-purpose" financial information (such as financial statements) to persons ***outside*** the business organization.

Financial statements Four related accounting reports that concisely summarize the current financial position of an entity and the results of its operations for the preceding year (or other time period).

Generally accepted accounting principles (GAAP) The accounting concepts, measurement techniques, and standards of presentation used in financial statements. Examples include the cost principle and objectivity principle.

Going-concern assumption An assumption by accountants that a business will operate indefinitely unless specific evidence to the contrary exists, such as impending bankruptcy.

Internal control All measures used within an organization to assure management that the organization is operating in accordance with management's policies and plans.

Liabilities Debts or obligations of an entity that have arisen from past transactions. The claims of creditors against the assets of a business.

Objectivity principle Accountants' tendency to base accounting measurements upon dollar amounts that are factual and subject to independent verification.

Owner's equity The excess of assets over liabilities. The amount of an owner's net investment in a business plus profits from successful operations that have been retained in the business.

Partnership An unincorporated business owned by two or more persons voluntarily associated as partners.

Profitability An increase in owner's equity resulting from successful business operations. (This concept is discussed further in Chapter 3.)

Public Accountant An independent professional accountant who offers auditing and other accounting services to clients.

Publicly held corporations Corporations in which members of the general public may buy or sell shares of capital stock.

Retained earnings The portion of the owners' equity in a corporation that has accumulated as a result of profitable business operations.

Sole proprietorship An unincorporated business owned by an individual.

Solvency Having the financial ability to pay debts as they become due.

Stable-dollar assumption An assumption by accountants that the dollar is a stable unit of measure, like the kilometre or the litre. A simplifying assumption that permits adding or subtracting dollar amounts originating in different time periods. Unfortunately, the assumption technically is incorrect and may seriously distort accounting information during periods of severe inflation.

Shareholders Owners of capital stock in a corporation; hence, the owners of the corporation.

Shareholders' equity The ***owners' equity*** in an entity organized as a corporation.

Transaction An event that causes an immediate change in the financial position of an entity and that can be measured objectively in monetary terms. In current practice, transactions serve as the basis for recording financial activity.

Window dressing Legitimate measures taken by management to make a business look as strong as possible at the balance sheet date.

DEMONSTRATION PROBLEM FOR YOUR REVIEW

The accounting data (listed alphabetically) for Crystal Auto Wash at September 30, 19__, are shown below. The figure for Don Johnson, capital is not given, but it can be determined when all the available information is assembled in the form of a balance sheet.

Accounts payable	*$14,000*	*Land*	*$68,000*
Accounts receivable	*800*	*Machinery and equipment*	*65,000*
Building	*52,000*	*Notes payable*	*29,000*
Cash	*9,200*	*Salaries payable*	*3,000*
Don Johnson, capital	*?*	*Supplies*	*400*

INSTRUCTIONS

a Prepare a balance sheet at September 30, 19__.

b Does this balance sheet indicate that the company is in a strong financial position? Explain briefly.

SOLUTION TO DEMONSTRATION PROBLEM

a

CRYSTAL AUTO WASH
Balance Sheet
September 30, 19__

Assets		*Liabilities & Owner's Equity*	
Cash	*$ 9,200*	***Liabilities:***	
Accounts receivable	*800*	*Notes payable*	*$ 29,000*
Supplies	*400*	*Accounts payable*	*14,000*
Land	*68,000*	*Salaries payable*	*3,000*
Building	*52,000*	*Total liabilities*	*$ 46,000*
Machinery & equipment	*65,000*	***Owner's equity:***	
		*Don Johnson, capital**	*149,400*
Total	*$195,400*	*Total*	*$195,400*

* Computed as total assets, $195,400 – total liabilities, $46,000 = Don Johnson, capital, $149,400

b The balance sheet indicates that Crystal Auto Wash is in a ***very weak*** financial position. The highly "liquid" assets—cash and receivables—total only $10,000, but the company has ***$46,000*** in debts due in the near future. Based upon this balance sheet, the company appears to be insolvent.†

ASSIGNMENT MATERIAL

DISCUSSION QUESTIONS

One objective of these questions is to give you an opportunity to demonstrate and develop your ***communication skills.*** Therefore, we ask that you answer each question in your own words.

1 In broad general terms, what is the purpose of accounting?

† Perhaps the company can generate enough cash from its daily operations to pay its debts. A balance sheet does not indicate the ***rate*** at which cash flows into the business. A recent ***statement of changes in financial position*** showing the cash flows would be useful in making a more complete analysis of the company's financial position. Also, as this business is organized as a sole proprietorship, creditors may look to the personal solvency of the owner, Don Johnson. He is personally liable for the debts of the business entity.

2 Why is a knowledge of accounting terms and concepts useful to persons other than professional accountants?

3 What is meant by the term ***financial reporting?*** What impact, if any, does financial reporting have upon our economy?

4 What is ***public information?*** What does this concept have to do with financial reporting?

Mar/97 → 5 In general terms, what does a set of ***financial statements*** describe? Identify the specific statements and other information that comprise a complete ***set*** of financial statements.

6 Are financial statements the ***only means*** by which decision makers outside of management obtain information about the financial position, profitability, and future prospects of a business?

Oct 97 → 7 Define the term ***business transaction.*** Give several examples of business transactions, and several examples of important events in the life of a business that ***do not*** qualify as "transactions." What is the relationship between business transactions and the information contained in financial statements?

8 Explain briefly why each of the following groups is interested in the financial statements of a business.

a Creditors

b Potential investors

c Labour unions

9 What is the purpose of a ***system of internal control?***

10 What is the purpose of an ***audit?*** Would a large corporation or a small sole proprietorship be more likely to retain a public accounting firm to perform an annual audit? Explain.

11 Are computers essential to the operation of an accounting system? Briefly describe several ways in which computers help make accounting information ***more useful*** to decision makers.

12 Distinguish between ***accounting*** and ***bookkeeping.***

13 The following questions relate to the term ***generally accepted accounting principles.***

a What type of accounting reports are prepared in conformity with these principles?

b Why is it important for these principles to be widely recognized?

c Where do these principles come from?

d Give two examples of generally accepted accounting principles relating to the valuation of assets.

14 How do accounting principles become "generally accepted"?

15 With respect to financial reporting, what is the importance of the Accounting Standards Board of the CICA?

Mar/97 16 Explain briefly the concept of the ***business entity.***

→ 17 State briefly the purpose and content of a balance sheet. Does a balance sheet show how much a business is currently "worth"? Explain.

18 Why is owner's equity considered to be a ***residual claim*** to the assets of a business organization? Can the owner's equity in a business be a ***negative*** amount? Explain.

19 The owner's equity in a business arises from what two sources? What two factors can cause decreases in owner's equity?

20 State the accounting equation in two alternative forms.

21 Why are the total assets shown in a balance sheet always equal to the total of the liabilities plus the owner's equity?

22 Can a business transaction cause one asset to increase without affecting any other asset, liability, or the owner's equity?

May/92 → 23 Give examples of business transactions that would:

- a Cause one asset to increase and another asset to decrease, with no effect upon liabilities or owner's equity.
- b Cause both total assets and total liabilities to increase, with no effect upon owner's equity.

24 Assume that a business becomes insolvent. Can the owner (or owners) of the business be held personally liable for the debts of the business? Give separate answers assuming that the business is organized as (a) a sole proprietorship, (b) a partnership, and (c) a corporation.

25 One objective of every business is to operate profitably. What other primary objective must be met for a business to survive? Explain.

26 What is meant by the term ***adequate disclosure?*** Give several examples of items that may require "disclosure" in financial statements.

oct. 97 → 27 Describe three factors that contribute to the ***reliability*** of financial statements.

28 What is meant by the phrase "a ***strong*** balance sheet"?

29 Describe the term ***window dressing.*** Why should users of financial statements be aware of this concept? Explain.

*30 Identify four broad areas of ***career opportunities*** in accounting.

*31 What are the principal types of services rendered by public accountants?

MULTIPLE CHOICE QUESTIONS

(Note: In order to review as many chapter concepts as possible, some questions include more than one correct answer. In these cases, indicate ***all*** of the correct answers.)

oct 97 → 1 A "set" of financial statements: (Indicate all correct answers.)

- a Is intended to assist users in evaluating the financial position, profitability, and future prospects of an entity.
- b Is intended to assist Revenue Canada in determining the amount of income taxes owed by a business organization.
- c Includes "notes" disclosing items necessary for the proper interpretation of the statements.
- d Is intended to assist investors and creditors in making decisions involving the allocation of economic resources.

2 Generally accepted accounting principles: (Indicate all correct answers.)

- a Include only the official pronouncements of the standard-setting organizations, such as the CICA.

---

* *Supplemental Topic, "Careers in Accounting"*

b May include customary accounting practices in widespread use even if not mentioned specifically in official pronouncements.

c Eliminate the need for professional judgment in the preparation of financial statements.

d Change and evolve as business organizations enter into new forms of business activity.

3 Which of the following statements is ***not*** consistent with generally accepted accounting principles relating to asset valuation?

a Assets are originally recorded in accounting records at their cost to the business entity.

b Subtracting total liabilities from total assets indicates what the owner's equity in the business is worth under current market conditions.

c Accountants assume that assets such as office supplies, land, and buildings will be used in business operations, rather than sold at current market prices.

d Accountants prefer to base the valuation of assets upon objective, verifiable evidence rather than upon appraisals or personal opinion.

4 Arrowhead Boat Shop purchased a truck for $12,000, making a down payment of $5,000 cash and signing a $7,000 note payable due in 60 days. (Indicate all correct answers.)

a Total assets increased by $12,000.

b Total liabilities increased by $7,000.

c From the viewpoint of a short-term creditor, this transaction makes the business less solvent.

d This transaction had no immediate effect upon the owner's equity in the business.

5 A transaction caused a $10,000 ***decrease*** in both total assets and total liabilities. This transaction could have been:

a Purchase of a delivery truck for $10,000 cash.

b An asset with a cost of $10,000 was destroyed by fire.

c Repayment of a $10,000 bank loan.

d Collection of a $10,000 account receivable.

6 Which of the following factors contribute to the ***reliability*** of the information contained in financial statements? (Indicate all correct answers.)

a The competence and integrity of professional accountants.

b An audit required by corporate and securities laws.

c Systems of internal control.

d The concept of adequate disclosure.

7 Which of the following statements relating to the role of professional judgment in the financial reporting process are valid? (Indicate all correct answers.)

a Different accountants may evaluate similar situations differently.

b The determination of which items should be "disclosed" in notes to financial statements requires professional judgment.

c Once a complete list of generally accepted accounting principles is prepared, judgment need no longer enter into the financial reporting process.

d The possibility always exists that professional judgment later may prove to have been incorrect.

8 During the current year, the assets of College Sandwich increased by $29,000, and the liabilities decreased by $7,000. If the owner's equity in the business is $79,000 at the end of the year, the owner's equity at the beginning of the year must have been:

a $57,000

b $43,000

c $115,000

d $101,000

EXERCISES

EXERCISE 1-1
Accounting Terminology

Listed below are twelve technical accounting terms emphasized in this chapter.

Financial reporting	*Audit*	*Insolvent*
Financial statements	*Assets*	*Balance sheet*
Corporation	*Liabilities*	*Owner's equity*
Sole proprietorship	*CICA*	*GAAP*

Each of the following statements may (or may not) describe one of these technical terms. For each statement, indicate the term described, or answer "None" if the statement does not correctly describe any of the terms.

a Obligations of an entity arising from past transactions.

b An investigation by independent accountants intended to assure outsiders of the fairness of a company's financial statements.

c The organization primarily responsible for developing new accounting principles by issuing recommendations.

d The process of distributing general-purpose financial information to persons outside a business organization.

e Economic resources owned by an entity.

f Accounting reports describing the financial position, profitability, and cash transactions of a business entity.

g Being able to meet financial obligations as they come due.

h A form of business organization in which the owners are ***personally liable*** for all debts of the business.

i Assets minus liabilities.

j The "ground rules" for presenting information in financial statements.

k The financial statement indicating the profitability of the business for a period of time.

EXERCISE 1-2
The Accounting Equation

A number of business transactions carried out by Green River Farms are shown below:

a Purchased a computer on credit.

b The owner invested cash in the business.

c Purchased office equipment for cash.

d Collected an account receivable.

e Sold land for cash at a price equal to its cost.

f Paid a liability.

g Returned for credit some of the office equipment previously purchased on credit but not yet paid for.

h Borrowed money from a bank.

Indicate the effects of each of these transactions upon the total amounts of the company's assets, liabilities, and owner's equity. Organize your answer in tabular form, using the column headings shown below and the code letters ***I*** for increase, ***D*** for decrease, and ***NE*** for no effect. The answer for transaction **a** is provided as an example:

Transaction	*Assets*	=	*Liabilities*	+	*Owner's Equity*
a	I		I		NE

EXERCISE 1-3
Financial Reporting

A major focus of this course is the process of financial reporting.

a What is meant by the term ***financial reporting?***

b What are the principal accounting reports involved in the financial reporting process? In general terms, what is the purpose of these reports?

c Do all business entities engage in financial reporting? Explain.

d How does society benefit from the financial reporting process?

EXERCISE 1-4
Generally Accepted Accounting Principles

Generally accepted accounting principles play an important role in financial reporting.

a What is meant by the phrase "generally accepted accounting principles"?

b What are the major sources of these principles?

c Is there a comprehensive list of generally accepted accounting principles? Explain.

EXERCISE 1-5
Audits of Financial Statements

The annual financial statements of all large, publicly owned corporations are audited.

a What is an audit of financial statements?

b Who performs these audits?

c What is the basic purpose of an audit?

EXERCISE 1-6
Who? What? When?

At the end of 1995, the accountant for C. Abrams & Sons, a construction company, prepared a year-end balance sheet with the following heading:

ABRAMS CONSTRUCTION
Statement of Financial Position for the Year 1995

INSTRUCTIONS

a Identify any errors in this heading.

b Prepare a corrected heading.

EXERCISE 1-7
The Nature of Assets

Define ***assets.*** Give three examples of assets other than cash that might appear in the balance sheet of (a) **Air Canada** and (b) a professional sports team, such as the **Toronto Blue Jays.**

EXERCISE 1-8
The Nature of Liabilities

Define ***liabilities.*** Give three examples of liabilities that might appear in the balance sheet of (a) **Air Canada** and (b) a professional sports team, such as the **Toronto Blue Jays.**

EXERCISE 1-9
Accounting Principles and Asset Valuation

The following cases relate to the valuation of assets. Consider each case independently:

a World-Wide Travel Agency has office supplies costing $1,700 on hand at the balance sheet date. These supplies were purchased from a supplier that does not give cash refunds. World-Wide's management believes that the company could sell these supplies for no more than $500 if it were to advertise them for sale. However, the company expects to use these supplies and to purchase more when they are gone. In its balance sheet, the supplies are valued at $500.

b Zenith Corporation purchased land in 1955 for $20,000. In 1995, it purchased a similar parcel of land for $300,000. In its 1995 balance sheet, the company valued these two parcels of land at a combined value of $320,000.

c At December 30, 1995, Lenier Company purchased a computer system from a mail-order supplier for $14,000. The retail value of the system—according to the mail-order supplier—was $20,000. On January 7, 1996, the system was stolen during a burglary. In its December 31, 1995, balance sheet, Lenier showed this computer system at $14,000 and made no reference to its retail value or to the burglary.

INSTRUCTIONS In each case, indicate the appropriate balance sheet valuation of the asset under generally accepted accounting principles. If the valuation assigned by the company is incorrect, briefly explain the accounting principles that have been violated. On the other hand, if the valuation is correct, identify the accounting principles that justify this valuation.

EXERCISE 1-10
Using the Accounting Equation

Compute the missing amount in each of the following three lines.

	Assets	=	*Liabilities*	+	*Owner's Equity*
a	$279,000		$171,000		?
b	?		112,500		$ 75,000
c	615,000		?		285,000

EXERCISE 1-11
Preparing a Balance Sheet

The night manager of Majestic Limousine Service, who had no accounting background, prepared the following balance sheet for the company at March 31, 1996. The dollar amounts were taken directly from the company's accounting records and are correct. However, the balance sheet contains a number of errors in its headings, format, and the classification of assets, liabilities, and owner's equity.

MAJESTIC LIMO
Manager's Report
8 PM Thursday

Assets		*Net Worth*	
Cash	*$ 19,000*	*Accounts receivable*	*$ 41,000*
M. Johnson, capital	*48,000*	*Accounts payable*	*24,000*
Automobiles	*96,000*	*Notes payable*	*86,000*
		Interest payable	*5,000*
		Supplies	*7,000*
Total	*$163,000*	*Total*	*$163,000*

INSTRUCTIONS Prepare a corrected balance sheet, including a proper heading.

EXERCISE 1-12
Preparing a Balance Sheet

The items appearing in the balance sheet of Banners by George at December 31, 19__, are listed below in random order. You are to prepare a balance sheet (including a complete heading). Arrange the items in the sequence shown in the balance sheet illustrated on page 14 and include a figure for total liabilities. You must compute the amount for Chris George, capital.

Land	*$135,000*	*Office equipment*	*15,100*
Cash	*18,150*	*Accounts payable*	*21,900*
Accounts receivable	*28,350*	*Building*	*105,000*
Chris George, capital	*?*	*Notes payable*	*97,500*

EXERCISE 1-13
Effects of Business Transactions

For each of the following categories, state concisely a transaction that will have the required effect on the elements of the accounting equation:

a Increase an asset and increase a liability.

b Decrease an asset and decrease a liability.

c Increase one asset and decrease another asset.

d Increase an asset and increase owner's equity.

e Increase one asset, decrease another asset, and increase a liability.

EXERCISE 1-14
Interpreting the Effects of Business Transactions

Five transactions of Lau Architectural are summarized below in equation form, with each of the five transactions identified by a letter. For each of the transactions (a) through (e) you are to write a separate sentence explaining the nature of the transaction. For example, the explanation of transaction **a** could be as follows: Purchased office equipment on credit at a cost of $6,800.

	Assets									=	Liabilities	+	Owner's Equity
	Cash	+	*Accounts Receivable*	+	*Land*	+	*Building*	+	*Office Equipment*	=	*Accounts Payable*	+	*Tom Lau, Capital*
Balances	*$13,000*		*$39,000*		*$65,000*		*$55,000*		*$23,000*		*$42,000*		*$153,000*
a									*+6,800*		*+6,800*		
Balances	*$13,000*		*$39,000*		*$65,000*		*$55,000*		*$29,800*		*$48,800*		*$153,000*
b	*−4,200*										*−4,200*		
Balances	*$ 8,800*		*$39,000*		*$65,000*		*$55,000*		*$29,800*		*$44,600*		*$153,000*
c	*+10,500*		*−10,500*										
Balances	*$19,300*		*$28,500*		*$65,000*		*$55,000*		*$29,800*		*$44,600*		*$153,000*
d	*−300*								*+1,900*		*+1,600*		
Balances	*$19,000*		*$28,500*		*$65,000*		*$55,000*		*$31,700*		*$46,200*		*$153,000*
e	*−5,000*												*−5,000*
Balances	*$14,000*		*$28,500*		*$65,000*		*$55,000*		*$31,700*		*$46,200*		*$148,000*

EXERCISE 1-15
Forms of Business Organization

QWIK Software Company has assets of $850,000 and liabilities of $460,000.

a Prepare the ownership equity section of QWIK's balance sheet under each of the following ***independent*** assumptions:

1 The business is organized as a sole proprietorship, owned by Johanna Schmidt.

2 The business is a partnership, owned by Johanna Schmidt and Mikki Yato. Schmidt's equity amounts to $240,000.

3 The business is a corporation with 25 shareholders, each of whom originally invested $10,000 in exchange for shares of the company's capital stock. The remainder of the shareholders' equity has resulted from profitable operation of the business.

b Assume that you are a loan officer at Security Bank. QWIK has applied to your bank for a large loan to finance the development of new products. Is it likely to matter to a lender whether QWIK is organized as a sole proprietorship, a partnership, or a corporation? Explain.

EXERCISE 1-16
Professional Judgment

Professional judgment plays a major role in the practice of accounting.

a In general terms, explain why judgment enters into the accounting process.

b Identify at least three situations in which accountants must rely upon their professional judgment, rather than upon official rules.

***EXERCISE 1-17**
Careers in Accounting

Four accounting majors, Maria Acosta, Kenzo Nakao, Helen Martin, and Anthony Mandella, recently graduated from Central University and began professional accounting careers. Acosta entered public accounting, Nakao became a management accountant with **IBM,** Martin joined a governmental agency, and Mandella (who had completed a graduate program) became an accounting faculty member.

INSTRUCTIONS

Assume that each of the four graduates was successful in his or her chosen career. Identify the types of accounting ***activities*** in which each of these graduates might find themselves specializing several years after graduation.

PROBLEMS

Group A

PROBLEM 1A-1
Preparing a Balance Sheet; Computing Owner's Equity

Listed below in random order are the items to be included in the balance sheet of Pearl Beach Resort at December 31, 1995:

Sailboats	*$ 15,200*	*Buildings*	*$225,000*
Land	*210,000*	*Cash*	*14,600*
Accounts receivable	*4,800*	*Furnishings*	*29,100*
Accounts payable	*13,500*	*Notes payable*	*320,000*
Equipment	*9,200*	*Nancy Moore, capital*	*?*

INSTRUCTIONS

Prepare a balance sheet at December 31, 1995. Include a proper heading and organize your balance sheet similar to the illustration on page **14.** (After "Buildings," you may list the remaining assets in any order.) You will need to compute the amount of owner's equity.

PROBLEM 1A-2
Recording the Effects of Transactions

Water-Wise Landscaping was organized on September 1 of the current year and had the following account balances at December 31, listed in tabular form.

	Assets				=	*Liabilities*		+	*Owner's Equity*
	Cash +	*Land +*	*Building +*	*Office Equipment*	=	*Notes Payable +*	*Accounts Payable*	+	*J. Green, Capital*
Balances	*$14,800*	*$50,000*	*$45,000*	*$22,500*		*$32,000*	*$25,300*		*$75,000*

Early in January, the company carried out the following transactions:

1. The owner, J. Green, deposited $20,000 in personal funds into the bank account of the business.
2. Purchased land and a small office building for a total price of $80,000, of which $30,000 was the value of the land and $50,000 was the value of the building. Paid $20,000 in cash and signed a note payable for the remaining $60,000.
3. Bought a Xerox copying machine on credit for $9,500 (30-day open account).
4. Obtained a loan from Pacific Coast Bank in the amount of $18,000. Signed a note payable.
5. Paid the $9,500 account payable originating in transaction **3.**

* *Supplemental Topic, "Careers in Accounting"*

INSTRUCTIONS

a List the December 31 balances of assets, liabilities, and owner's equity in tabular form as shown above.

b Record the effects of each of the six transactions in the tabular arrangement illustrated above. Show the totals for all columns after each transaction.

PROBLEM 1A-3
Preparing a Balance Sheet; Effects of a Change in Assets

!HERE COMES TIGER! is the name of a travelling circus owned by Tiger Hayes. The ledger accounts of the business at June 30, 1995, are listed below in alphabetical order.

Accounts payable	$ 17,400	*Notes payable*	$120,000
Accounts receivable	8,900	*Notes receivable*	2,400
Animals	126,040	*Props and equipment*	59,720
Cages	16,400	*Salaries payable*	6,500
Tiger Hayes, capital	?	*Tents*	42,000
Cash	21,680	*Trucks*	42,460
Costumes	21,000	*Wagons*	28,100

INSTRUCTIONS

a Prepare a balance sheet by using these items and computing the amount of the owner's capital. Organize your balance sheet similar to the one illustrated on page 14. (After "Accounts Receivable," you may list the remaining assets in any order.) Include a proper balance sheet heading.

b Assume that late in the evening of June 30, after your balance sheet had been prepared, a fire destroyed one of the tents, which had cost $11,200. The tent was not insured. Explain what changes would be required in your June 30 balance sheet to reflect the loss of this asset.

PROBLEM 1A-4
Preparing a Balance Sheet; Effects of Business Transactions

The balance sheet items of The Original Malt Shop (arranged in alphabetical order) were as follows at the close of business on September 30, 1995:

Accounts payable	$ 8,500	*Furniture & fixtures*	$20,000
Accounts receivable	1,250	*Land*	55,000
Building	45,500	*Notes payable*	?
Kay Martin, capital	54,090	*Supplies*	3,440
Cash	7,400		

Throughout October, the business will be closed for remodeling. The transactions occurring during the first week of October were:

Oct. 3 Martin invested an additional $30,000 cash in the business. The accounts payable were paid in full. (No payment was made on the notes payable.)

Oct. 6 More furniture was purchased on account at a cost of $18,000, to be paid within 30 days. Supplies were purchased for $1,000 cash from a restaurant supply centre that was going out of business. These supplies would have cost $1,875 if purchased under normal circumstances.

INSTRUCTIONS

a Prepare a balance sheet at September 30, 1995. (You are to compute the missing figure for notes payable.)

b Prepare a balance sheet at October 6, 1995.

PROBLEM 1A-5
Preparing a Balance Sheet; Discussion and Application of Accounting Principles

Melonie Austin, owner and manager of Old Town Playhouse, needs to obtain a bank loan to finance the production of the company's next play. As part of the loan application, Austin was asked to prepare a balance sheet for the business. She prepared the following balance sheet, which is arranged correctly but contains several errors with respect to certain accounting principles.

OLD TOWN PLAYHOUSE
Balance Sheet
September 30, 1995

Assets		*Liabilities & Owner's Equity*	
Cash	$ 18,600	Liabilities:	
Accounts receivable	156,200	Accounts payable	$ 4,600
Props and costumes	1,800	Salaries payable	28,200
Theatre building	13,500	Total liabilities	$32,800
Lighting equipment	8,500	Owner's equity:	
Automobile	12,000	Melonie Austin, capital	10,000
Total	$210,600	Total	$42,800

In discussions with Austin and by reviewing the accounting records of Old Town Playhouse, you discover the following facts:

1 The amount of cash, $18,600, includes $12,000 in the company's bank account, $2,100 on hand in the company's safe, and $4,500 in Austin's personal savings account.

2 Accounts receivable include $6,200 owed to the business by Artistic Tours. The remaining $150,000 is Austin's estimate of future ticket sales from September 30 through the end of the year (December 31).

3 Austin explains that the props and costumes were purchased several days ago for $14,800. The business paid $1,800 of this amount in cash and issued a note payable to Actors' Supply Company for the remainder of the purchase price ($13,000). As this note will not be paid until January of next year, it was not included among the company's liabilities. However, the $1,800 was recorded.

4 Old Town Playhouse rents the theatre building from Kievits International at a rate of $1,500 per month. The $13,500 represents the rent paid through September 30 of the current year. Kievits International acquired the building seven years ago at a cost of $126,000.

5 The lighting equipment was purchased on September 26 at a cost of $8,500, but the stage manager says that it isn't worth a dime.

6 The automobile is Austin's classic 1965 Porsche, which she purchased two years ago for $9,600. She recently saw a similar car advertised for sale at $12,000. She does not use the car in the business, but it has a personalized licence plate that reads "PLAHOUS."

7 The accounts payable include business debts of $3,700 and the $900 balance of Austin's personal Visa card.

8 Salaries payable includes $25,000 offered to Mario Dane to play the lead role in a new play opening next December and also $3,200 still owed to stage hands for work done through September 30.

9 When Austin founded Old Town Playhouse four years ago, she invested $10,000 in the business. She has shown this amount as her owner's equity in order to comply with the cost principle. However, Live Theatre, Inc., has offered to buy her business for $30,000, and she believes that perhaps the owner's equity should be changed to this amount.

INSTRUCTIONS

a Prepare a corrected balance sheet for Old Town Playhouse at September 30, 1995.

b For each of the nine numbered items above, explain your reasoning in deciding whether or not to include the items in the balance sheet and in determining the proper dollar valuation.

Group B

PROBLEM 1B-1
Preparing a Balance Sheet; Computing Owner's Equity

Listed below in random order are the items to be included in the balance sheet of Mystery Mountain Lodge at December 31, 1995:

Accounts receivable	*$ 7,800*	*Furniture*	*$ 47,800*
Cash	*19,300*	*Snowmobiles*	*15,700*
Accounts payable	*35,800*	*Equipment*	*18,400*
Daniel Craig, capital	*?*	*Notes payable*	*339,000*
Buildings	*296,000*	*Land*	*115,000*

INSTRUCTIONS Prepare a balance sheet at December 31, 1995. Include a proper heading and organize your balance sheet similar to the illustration on page 14. (After "Buildings," you may list the remaining assets in any order.) You will need to compute the amount of owner's equity.

PROBLEM 1B-2
Recording the Effects of Transactions

The items making up the balance sheet of Travel Connection at December 31 are listed below in tabular form.

	Assets				=	Liabilities		+	Owner's Equity
	Cash +	Accounts Receivable +	Automobiles +	Office Equipment	=	Notes Payable +	Accounts Payable	+	D. Hall Capital
Balances	$9,500	$58,400	$9,000	$3,800		$20,000	$25,200		$35,500

During a short period after December 31, Travel Connection had the following transactions:

1 Bought office equipment at a cost of $5,700. Paid cash.
2 Collected $4,000 of accounts receivable.
3 Paid $7,200 of accounts payable.
4 Borrowed $10,000 from a bank. Signed a note payable for that amount.
5 Purchased an automobile for $15,500. Paid $3,000 cash and signed a note payable for the balance of $12,500.

INSTRUCTIONS

a List the December 31 balances of assets, liabilities, and owner's equity in tabular form as shown above.
b Record the effects of each of the five transactions in the tabular arrangement illustrated above. Show the totals for all columns after each transaction.

PROBLEM 1B-3
Preparing a Balance Sheet; Effect of a Change in Assets

Shown below in random order is a list of balance sheet items for Valencia Farms at September 30, 1996:

Land	*$305,000*	*Fences & gates*	*$ 18,650*
Barns and sheds	*43,500*	*Irrigation system*	*11,180*
Notes payable	*295,000*	*Cash*	*9,285*
Accounts receivable	*12,425*	*Livestock*	*67,100*
Citrus trees	*42,600*	*Farm machinery*	*23,872*
Accounts payable	*42,830*	*Walter Berkeley, capital*	*?*
Property taxes payable	*5,075*	*Wages payable*	*1,010*

INSTRUCTIONS

a Prepare a balance sheet by using these items. Use a sequence of assets similar to that illustrated on page 14. (After "Barns and sheds," you may list the remaining assets in any order.) Include a proper heading for your balance sheet.

b Assume that immediately after this September 30 balance sheet was prepared, a tornado completely destroyed one of the barns. This barn had a cost of $18,400 and was not insured against this type of disaster. Explain what changes would be required in your September 30 balance sheet to reflect the loss of this barn.

PROBLEM 1B-4
Preparing a Balance Sheet; Effects of Business Transactions

The balance sheet items for Gremlin Auto Wash (arranged in alphabetical order) were as follows at June 30, 1996:

Accounts payable	*$ 4,000*	*Equipment*	*$26,000*
Accounts receivable	*300*	*Land*	*40,000*
Building	*20,000*	*Notes payable*	*46,000*
Susan Young, capital	*?*	*Supplies*	*2,800*
Cash	*4,600*		

During the next two days, the following transactions occurred:

July 2 Young invested an additional $15,000 cash in the business. The accounts payable were paid in full. (No payment was made on the notes payable.)

July 3 Equipment was purchased at a cost of $9,000 to be paid within 10 days. Supplies were purchased for $500 cash from another car-washing concern that was going out of business. These supplies would have cost $900 if purchased through normal channels.

INSTRUCTIONS

a Prepare a balance sheet at June 30, 1996.

b Prepare a balance sheet at July 3, 1996.

PROBLEM 1B-5
Preparing a Balance Sheet; Discussion and Application of Accounting Principles

Hollywood Scripts is a service-type enterprise in the entertainment field, and its owner, Bradford Jones, has only a limited knowledge of accounting. Jones prepared the balance sheet below, which, although arranged satisfactorily, contains certain errors with respect to certain accounting principles.

HOLLYWOOD SCRIPTS
Balance Sheet
November 30, 1996

Assets		*Liabilities & Owner's Equity*	
Cash	*$ 940*	*Notes payable*	*$ 67,000*
Notes receivable	*2,900*	*Accounts payable*	*29,800*
Accounts receivable	*2,465*	*Total liabilities*	*$ 96,800*
Land	*70,000*	*Owner's equity:*	
Building	*54,326*	*Bradford Jones, capital*	*63,080*
Office furniture	*6,848*		
Other assets	*22,401*		
Total	*$159,880*	*Total*	*$159,880*

In discussion with Jones and by inspection of the accounting records, you discover the following facts:

1. One of the notes receivable in the amount of $700 is an IOU that Jones received in a poker game about two years ago. The IOU bears only the initials B. K., and Jones does not know the name or address of the maker.
2. The asset land was acquired at a cost of $34,000 but was increased to a valuation of $70,000 when a friend of Jones offered to pay that much for it if Jones would move the building off the lot.

3 Office furniture includes an antique desk purchased November 29 of the current year at a cost of $2,100. Jones explains that no payment is due for the desk until January and therefore this debt is not included among the liabilities.

4 Also included in the amount for office furniture is a typewriter that cost $525 but is not on hand, because Jones gave it to his daughter as a birthday present.

5 The "Other assets" of $22,401 represents the total amount of income taxes Jones has paid over a period of years. Jones believes the income tax law to be unconstitutional, and a friend who attends law school will help Jones recover the taxes paid as soon as he completes his legal education.

INSTRUCTIONS

a Prepare a corrected balance sheet at November 30, 1996.

b For each of the five numbered items above, use a separate numbered paragraph to explain whether the treatment followed by Jones is in accordance with generally accepted accounting principles.

ANALYTICAL AND DECISION PROBLEMS AND CASES (A&D)

A&D 1-1 "Nonfinancial" Information

In 1987, **The Procter & Gamble Company (P&G)** discovered Olestra, a product that greatly reduces the fat content and calories in potato chips and other fried foods. The product is believed to have great market potential, but as of 1990, the government had not yet approved its use and sale.

INSTRUCTIONS

a In 1987, would the discovery of Olestra and its future sales potential have been recorded in P&G's accounting records and reflected in the company's financial statements?

b How did investors, creditors, and other interested people learn of this discovery and its potential benefit to P&G?

A&D 1-2 Reliability of Financial Statements

In the early 1980s, **Chrysler Corporation** was in severe financial difficulty and desperately needed large loans if the company were to survive. What factors prevented Chrysler from simply providing potential lenders with misleading financial statements, making the company look like a risk-free investment?

A&D 1-3 Ethics and "Window Dressing"

The date is November 18, 1995. You are the chief executive officer of Flowerhill Software—a publicly owned company that is currently in financial difficulty. Flowerhill needs large new bank loans if it is to survive.

You have been negotiating with several banks, but each has asked to see your 1995 financial statements, which will be dated December 31. These statements will, of course, be audited. You are now meeting with other corporate officers to discuss the situation, and the following suggestions have been made:

1 "We are planning to buy the WordMaster Software Corporation for $5 million cash in December. The owners of WordMaster are in no hurry; if we delay this acquisition until January, we'll have $5 million more cash at year-end. That should make us look a lot more solvent."

2 "At year-end, we'll owe accounts payable of about $12 million. If we were to show this liability in our balance sheet at half that amount—say, $6 million—no one would know the difference. We could report the other $6 million as shareholders' equity and our financial position would appear much stronger."

3 "We owe Delta Programming $3 million, due in 90 days. I know some people at Delta. If we were to sign a note and agree to pay 9% interest, they'd let us postpone this debt for a year or more."

4 "We own investments that cost us $2 million, but today they are worth at least $6 million. Let's show them at $6 million in our balance sheet, and that will increase our total assets and our shareholders' equity by $4 million."

INSTRUCTIONS Separately evaluate each of these four proposals. Your evaluations should consider ethical and legal issues as well as accounting issues.

A&D 1-4
Using a Balance Sheet in Business Decisions

King Company and Lee Company are in the same line of business and both were recently organized, so it may be assumed that the recorded costs for assets are close to current market values. Balance sheets for the two companies are as follows.

KING COMPANY
Balance Sheet
July 31, 19__

Assets		Liabilities & Owner's Equity	
Cash	$ 4,800	Liabilities:	
Accounts receivable	10,600	Notes payable	
Land	96,000	(due in 60 days)	$ 23,400
Building	60,000	Accounts payable	43,200
Office equipment	12,000	Total liabilities	$ 66,600
		Owner's equity:	
		Susan King, capital	116,800
Total	$183,400	Total	$183,400

LEE COMPANY
Balance Sheet
July 31, 19__

Assets		Liabilities & Owner's Equity	
Cash	$ 18,000	Liabilities:	
Accounts receivable	28,000	Notes payable	
Land	37,200	(due in 60 days)	$ 12,400
Building	38,000	Accounts payable	10,600
Office equipment	1,200	Total liabilities	$ 23,000
		Owner's equity:	
		Ed Lee, capital	99,400
Total	$122,400	Total	$122,400

INSTRUCTIONS

a Assume that you are a banker and that each company has applied to you for a 90-day loan of $16,000. Which is the more favourable prospect? Explain fully.

b Assume that you are an investor considering the purchase of one or both of the companies. Both Susan King and Ed Lee have indicated to you that they would consider selling their respective businesses. In either transaction you would assume the existing liabilities. For which business would you pay the higher price? Explain fully. (It is recognized that for either decision, additional information would be useful, but you are to reach your decisions on the basis of the information available.)

c Assume that Susan King has much greater personal assets than Ed Lee and that, while both King and Lee have other business operations, the total profits from all the other unrelated business operations are far greater for King than Lee. Would such assumptions change your answers to part (**a**) and (**b**)? Explain fully.

A&D 1-5
Application of Accounting Principles and Business Concepts; Preparing a Balance Sheet for a Corporation

Linda Jones and Tom Laing own all the capital stock of Property Management Corporation. Both shareholders also work full time in the business. The company performs management services for apartment house owners, including finding tenants, collecting rents, and doing maintenance and repair work.

When the business was organized early this year, Jones and Laing invested a total of $60,000 to acquire the capital stock. At December 31, a partial list of the corporation's balance sheet items included cash of $16,800, office equipment of $26,100, accounts payable of $36,700, and income taxes payable of $12,900. Additional information on financial position and operations is as follows:

1 Earlier this year the corporation purchased an office building from Jones at a price of $48,000 for the land and $69,000 for the building. Jones had acquired the property several years ago at a cost of $26,000 for the land and $52,000 for the building. At December 31, Jones and Laing estimated that the land was worth $49,000 and the building was worth $78,000. The corporation owes Jones a $54,000 note payable in connection with the purchase of the property.

2 While working, Jones drives her own automobile, which cost $22,600. Laing uses a car owned by the corporation, which cost $20,200.

3 One of the apartment houses managed by the company is owned by Laing. Laing's cost was $100,000 for the land and $190,000 for the building, but the total market value was at least $380,000.

4 Company records show a $1,900 account receivable from Laing's relatives and $23,400 accounts receivable from other clients.

5 Laing has a $20,000 bank account in the same bank used by the corporation. He explains that if the corporation should run out of cash, it may use that $20,000 and repay him later.

6 Company records have not been properly maintained, and the amount of retained earnings is not known.

INSTRUCTIONS

a For each of the above items numbered **1** through **5**, explain your reasoning in deciding whether or not to include the items on the balance sheet and in determining the proper dollar valuation.

b Prepare a balance sheet for the business entity Property Management Corporation at December 31, 19__.

c Even though Laing and Jones invested an equal amount in the business, Laing feels that he is taking a greater risk than Jones should the business fail. Laing's concern is based on the fact that he has more personal assets than Jones. Explain whether Laing's concern is justified.

A&D 1-6
Preparing a Balance Sheet (Instructor Participation)

You are to prepare a ***hypothetical*** balance sheet for an entity (or type of entity) specified by your instructor. Include in your balance sheet the types of assets and liabilities that you think the entity might have, and show these items at what you believe would be realistic dollar amounts. (Note: The purpose of this assignment is to help you visualize the types of assets and liabilities relating to the operations of a specific type of business. You should complete this assignment ***without*** referring to an actual balance sheet for this type of entity.)

A&D 1-7
Using a Balance Sheet (Instructor Participation)

Obtain from the library the ***annual report*** of a well-known company (or a company specified by your instructor).

INSTRUCTIONS

From the balance sheet, notes to the financial statements, and auditors' report, answer the following:

a What public accounting firm audited the company's financial statements, and did the auditors consider the financial statements a "fair" presentation?

b Select three items in the notes accompanying the financial statements and explain briefly the importance of these items to people making decisions about investing in, or extending credit to, this company.

c Assume that you are a lender, and this company has asked to borrow an amount of cash equal to 10% of its total assets, to be repaid in 90 days. Would you consider this company to be a good credit risk? Explain.

CHAPTER

2 Recording Changes in Financial Position

In this chapter we illustrate the accounting cycle—the procedures used by a business to record, classify, and summarize the effects of business transactions in its accounting records. The transactions of Roberts Real Estate Company, as described in Chapter 1, are now recorded in the company's general journal and posted to the general ledger accounts. The preparation of a trial balance is illustrated, and the uses and limitations of the trial balance are discussed. The chapter concludes by comparing the accounting procedures applied in manual accounting systems with those in computer-based systems.

Learning Objectives

After studying this chapter you should be able to:

1. *Describe a ledger account and a ledger.*
2. *State the rules of debit and credit for balance sheet accounts.*
3. *Explain the double-entry system of accounting.*
4. *Explain the purpose of a journal and its relationship to the ledger.*
5. *Prepare journal entries to record common business transactions.*
6. *Prepare a trial balance and explain its uses and limitations.*
7. *Describe the basic steps of the accounting cycle in both manual and computer-based accounting systems.*

The Role of Accounting Records

Many business concerns have several hundred or even several thousand business transactions each day. It would not be practical to prepare a balance sheet after each transaction and it is quite unnecessary to do so. Instead, the many individual transactions are recorded in the accounting records, and, at the end of the month or other accounting period, a balance sheet is prepared from these records. In this chapter, we shall see how business transactions are analyzed, entered in the accounting records, and classified for use in preparing a balance sheet. In later chapters, we shall also see that the accounting records contain the data necessary to prepare an income statement, income tax returns, and other financial reports.

THE LEDGER

OBJECTIVE 1 Describe a ledger account and a ledger.

An accounting system includes a separate record for each item that appears in the balance sheet. For example, a separate record is kept for the asset cash, showing all the increases and decreases in cash that result from the many transactions in which cash is received or paid. A similar record is kept for every other asset, for every liability, and for owner's equity. The form of record used to record increases and decreases in a single balance sheet item is called an ***account,*** or sometimes a ***ledger account.*** All these separate accounts are usually kept in a loose-leaf binder or in a tray containing a separate page for each account, and the entire group of accounts is called a ***ledger.***

Many businesses use computers for maintaining accounting records; they store data on magnetic discs rather than in ledgers. However, an understanding of accounting concepts is most easily acquired by study of a manual accounting system. The knowledge gained by working with manual accounting records is readily transferable to any type of automated accounting system. For these reasons, we shall use standard written accounting records such as ledger accounts in our study of basic accounting concepts. These written records continue to be used by many businesses, but for our purposes they should be viewed as conceptual devices rather than as physical components of an accounting system.

The Use of Ledger Accounts

A ledger account is a means of accumulating in one place all the information about changes in a specific asset, a liability, or owner's equity. For example, a ledger account for the asset cash provides a record of the amount of cash receipts, cash payments, and the current cash balance. By maintaining a Cash account, management can keep track of the amount of cash available for meeting payrolls and for making current purchases of assets or services. This record of cash is also useful in planning future operations and in advance planning of applications for bank loans.

In its simplest form, an account has only three elements: (1) a title, consisting of the name of the particular asset, liability, or owner's equity; (2) a left side, which is called the ***debit*** side; and (3) a right side, which is called the ***credit*** side. This form of account, called a ***T account*** because of its resemblance to the letter **T,** is illustrated below. More complete forms of accounts will be illustrated later.

T account: a ledger account in simplified form

Title of Account	
Left or debit side	*Right or credit side*

Debit and Credit Entries

An amount recorded on the left or debit side of an account is called a ***debit,*** or a ***debit entry;*** an amount entered on the right or credit side is called a ***credit,*** or a ***credit entry.*** Accountants also use the words ***debit*** and ***credit*** as verbs. The act of recording a debit in an account is called ***debiting*** the account; the recording of a credit is called ***crediting*** the account.

Students beginning a course in accounting often have erroneous notions about the meanings of the terms ***debit*** and ***credit.*** For example, to some people unacquainted with accounting, the word ***credit*** may carry a more favourable connotation than does the word ***debit.*** Such connotations have no validity in the field of accounting. Accountants use ***debit*** to mean an entry on the left-hand side of an account and ***credit*** to mean an entry on the right-hand side. Thus, debit and credit simply mean left and right, without any hidden or subtle implications.

To illustrate the recording of debits and credits in an account, let us go back to the cash transactions of Roberts Real Estate Company as described in Chapter 1. When these cash transactions are recorded in an account, the receipts are listed in vertical order on the debit side of the account and the payments are listed on the credit side. The dates of the transactions may also be listed, as shown in the following illustration:

Cash transactions entered in ledger account

Cash					
Sept. 1		180,000	Sept. 3		141,000
Sept. 20		1,500	Sept. 5		15,000
	181,500		Sept. 30	159,000	3,000
Sept. 30 Balance		22,500			

Each debit and credit entry in the Cash account represents a cash receipt or a cash payment. The amount of cash owned by the business at a given date is equal to the ***balance*** of the account on that date.

Determining the Balance of a T Account The balance of a ledger account is the difference in dollars between the total debits and the total credits in the account. If the debit total exceeds the credit total, the account has a ***debit balance;*** if the credit total exceeds the debit total, the account has a ***credit balance.***

In our illustrated Cash account, a rule has been drawn across the account following the last cash transaction recorded in September. The total cash receipts (debits) recorded in September amount to ***$181,500*** and the total cash payments (credits) amount to ***$159,000.*** These totals are entered in small-size figures just above the rule. (Notice that these totals are written well to the left of the regular money columns so that they will not be mistaken for debit or credit entries). By subtracting the credit total from the debit total ($181,500 – $159,000), we determine that the Cash account has a debit balance of ***$22,500*** on September 30.

This debit balance is entered in the debit side of the account just below the rule. In effect, the horizontal rule creates a "fresh start" in our T account, with the month-end balance representing the ***net result*** of all the previous debit and credit entries. The Cash account now shows the amount of cash owned by the business on September 30. In a balance sheet prepared at this date, Cash in the amount of $22,500 would be listed as an asset.

Debit Balances in Asset Accounts In the preceding illustration of a cash account, increases were recorded on the left (debit) side of the account and decreases were recorded on the right (credit) side. The increases were greater than the decreases and the result was a debit balance in the account.

OBJECTIVE 2 State the rules of debit and credit for balance sheet accounts.

All asset accounts ***normally have debit balances;*** in fact, the ownership of cash, land, or any other asset indicates that the increases (debits) to that asset have been greater than the decreases (credits). It is hard to imagine an account for an asset such as land having a credit balance, as this would indicate that the business had disposed of more land than it had acquired and had reached the impossible position of having a negative amount of land.

The fact that assets are located on the ***left*** side of the balance sheet is a convenient means of remembering the rule that an increase in an asset is recorded on the ***left*** (debit) side of the account, and also that an asset account normally has a debit ***(left-hand)*** balance.

Asset accounts normally have debit balances

Any Asset Account

(Debit)	(Credit)
Increase	*Decrease*

Credit Balances in Liability and Owner's Equity Accounts Increases in liability and owner's equity accounts are recorded by credit entries and decreases in these accounts are recorded by debits. The relationship between entries in these accounts and their position on the balance sheet may be summed up as follows: (1) liabilities and owner's equity belong on the ***right*** side of the balance sheet, (2) an increase in a liability or an owner's equity account is recorded on the ***right*** (credit) side of the account, and (3) liability and owner's equity accounts normally have credit ***(right-hand)*** balances.

Liability and owner's equity accounts normally have credit balances

Any Liability Account or Owner's Equity Account

(Debit)	(Credit)
Decrease	*Increase*

Concise Statement of the Rules of Debit and Credit The use of debits and credits to record changes in assets, liabilities, and owner's equity may be summarized as follows:

Rules of debit and credit

Asset Accounts	*Liability & Owner's Equity Accounts*
Increases are recorded by debits	*Increases are recorded by credits*
Decreases are recorded by credits	*Decreases are recorded by debits*

Double-Entry Accounting—The Equality of Debits and Credits

The rules for debits and credits are designed so that ***every transaction is recorded by equal dollar amounts of debits and credits.*** The reason for this equality lies in the relationship of the debit and credit rules to the accounting equation:

Assets = Liabilities + Owner's Equity

If this equation is to remain in balance, any change in the left side of the equation (assets) ***must be accompanied by an equal change*** in the right-hand side (either liabilities or owner's equity). According to the debit and credit rules that we have just described, increases in the left side of the equation (assets) are recorded by ***debits,*** while increases in the right side (liabilities and owner's equity) are recorded by ***credits.***

OBJECTIVE 3 Explain the double-entry system of accounting.

This system is often called ***double-entry accounting.*** The phrase "double-entry" refers to the need for both debit entries and credit entries (equal in dollar amount) to record every transaction. Virtually every business organization uses the double-entry system regardless of whether the company's accounting records are maintained manually or by computer. In addition, the double-entry system allows us to measure net income at the same time we record the effects of transactions upon the balance sheet accounts. (The measurement of net income is discussed in Chapter 3.)

Double-entry accounting is not a new idea. The system has been in use for more than 600 years. The first systematic presentation of the double-entry system appears in a mathematics textbook written by Luca Pacioli, a friend of Leonardo da Vinci. This text was published in 1494—just two years after Columbus discovered America. Although Pacioli wrote the first textbook on this subject, surviving accounting records show that double-entry accounting had already been in use for at least 150 years.

Recording Transactions in Ledger Accounts: Illustration

The use of debits and credits for recording transactions in ledger accounts now will be illustrated using the September transactions of Roberts Real Estate Company. Each transaction will first be analyzed in terms of increases and decreases in assets, liabilities, and owner's equity. Then we shall follow the rules of debit and credit in entering these increases and decreases in T accounts. Asset accounts will be shown on the left side of the page; liability and owner's equity accounts on the right side. For convenience in following the transactions into the ledger accounts, the letter used to identify a given transaction will also appear opposite the debit and credit entries in the ledger. (This use of identifying letters is for illustrative purposes only and is not used in actual accounting practice.)

Transaction (a) Roberts invested $180,000 cash in the business on September 1.

Recording an investment in the business

Analysis	*Rule*	*Entry*
The asset Cash was increased	*Increases in assets are recorded by debits*	*Debit: Cash, $180,000*
The owner's equity was increased	*Increases in owner's equity are recorded by credits*	*Credit: James Roberts, Capital, $180,000*

Cash

Sept. 1	*(a) 180,000*		

James Roberts, Capital

		Sept. 1	*(a) 180,000*

Transaction (b) On September 3, Roberts Real Estate Company purchased land for cash in the amount of $141,000.

Purchase of land for cash

Analysis	*Rule*	*Entry*
The asset Land was increased	*Increases in assets are recorded by debits*	*Debit: Land, $141,000*
The asset Cash was decreased	*Decreases in assets are recorded by credits*	*Credit: Cash, $141,000*

Cash

Sept. 1	*180,000*	*Sept. 3*	*(b) 141,000*

Land

Sept. 3	*(b) 141,000*		

Transaction (c) On September 5, Roberts Real Estate Company purchased a building from Kent Company at a total price of $36,000. The terms of the purchase required a cash payment of $15,000 with the remainder of $21,000 payable within 90 days.

Purchase of an asset, with partial payment

Analysis	Rule	Entry
A new asset, Building, was acquired	*Increases in assets are recorded by debits*	*Debit: Building, $36,000*
The asset Cash was decreased	*Decreases in assets are recorded by credits*	*Credit: Cash, $15,000*
A new liability, Accounts Payable, was incurred	*Increases in liabilities are recorded by credits*	*Credit: Accounts Payable, $21,000*

Cash

Sept. 1	180,000	Sept. 3	141,000
		Sept. 5	(c) 15,000

Accounts Payable

		Sept. 5	(c) 21,000

Building

Sept. 5	(c) 36,000		

Transaction (d) On September 10, Roberts Real Estate Company sold a portion of its land on credit to Carter's Drugstore for a price of $11,000. The land was sold at its cost, so there was no gain or loss on the transaction.

Sale of land on credit (no gain or loss)

Analysis	Rule	Entry
A new asset, Accounts Receivable, was acquired	*Increases in assets are recorded by debits*	*Debit: Accounts Receivable, $11,000*
The asset Land was decreased	*Decreases in assets are recorded by credits*	*Credit: Land, $11,000*

Accounts Receivable

Sept. 10	(d) 11,000		

Land

Sept. 3	141,000	Sept. 10	(d) 11,000

Transaction (e) On September 14, Roberts Real Estate Company purchased office equipment on credit from General Equipment, Inc., in the amount of $5,400.

Purchase of an asset on credit

Analysis	Rule	Entry
A new asset, Office Equipment, was acquired	*Increases in assets are recorded by debits*	*Debit: Office Equipment, $5,400*
A new liability, Accounts Payable, was incurred	*Increases in liabilities are recorded by credits*	*Credit: Accounts Payable, $5,400*

Office Equipment

Sept. 14 (e) 5,400	

Accounts Payable

	Sept. 5 21,000
	Sept. 14 (e) 5,400

Transaction (f) On September 20, cash of $1,500 was received as partial collection of the account receivable from Carter's Drugstore.

Collection of an account receivable

Analysis	Rule	Entry
The asset Cash was increased	*Increases in assets are recorded by debits*	*Debit: Cash, $1,500*
The asset Accounts Receivable was decreased	*Decreases in assets are recorded by credits*	*Credit: Accounts Receivable, $1,500*

Cash

Sept. 1 180,000	Sept. 3 141,000
Sept. 20 (f) 1,500	Sept. 5 15,000

Accounts Receivable

Sept. 10 11,000	Sept. 20 (f) 1,500

Transaction (g) A cash payment of $3,000 was made on September 30 in partial settlement of the amount owing to General Equipment, Inc.

Payment of a liability

Analysis	Rule	Entry
The liability Accounts Payable was decreased	*Decreases in liabilities are recorded by debits*	*Debit: Accounts Payable, $3,000*
The asset Cash was decreased	*Decreases in assets are recorded by credits*	*Credit: Cash, $3,000*

Cash

Sept. 1	180,000	Sept. 3	141,000
Sept. 20	1,500	Sept. 5	15,000
		Sept. 30 (g)	3,000

Accounts Payable

Sept. 30	(g) 3,000	Sept. 5	21,000
		Sept. 14	5,400

Running Balance Form of Accounts

T accounts are widely used in the classroom and in accounting textbooks, because they provide a concise conceptual picture of the financial effects of a business transaction. In actual practice, however, most businesses prefer to use the ***running balance*** form of ledger account. This form of account has special columns for recording additional information, as illustrated below with the Cash account of Roberts Real Estate Company:

Cash — Account No. 1

Date		Explanation	Ref	Debit	Credit	Balance
19 —						
Sept	1			180000		180000
	3				141000	39000
	5				15000	24000
	20			1500		25500
	30				3000	22500

The ***Date*** column shows the date of the transaction—which is not necessarily the same as the date the entry is recorded in the account. The ***Explanation*** column is needed only for unusual items, and in many companies it is seldom used. The ***Ref*** (Reference) column is used to list the page number of the journal in which the transaction is recorded, thus making it possible to trace ledger entries back to their source. (The use of a ***journal*** is explained later in this chapter.) In the ***Balance*** column of the account, the new balance is entered each time the account is debited or credited. Thus the current balance of the account can always be observed at a glance.

The "Normal" Balance of an Account The running balance form of ledger account does not indicate specifically whether the balance of the account is a debit or credit balance. However, this causes no difficulty because we know that asset accounts normally have debit balances and that accounts for liabilities and owner's equity normally have credit balances.

Occasionally an asset account may temporarily acquire a credit balance, either as the result of an accounting error or because of an unusual transaction. For example, an account receivable may acquire a credit balance because of overpayment by a customer. However, a credit balance in the Building account could be created only by an accounting error.

Sequence and Numbering of Ledger Accounts Accounts are usually arranged in the ledger in ***financial statement order,*** that is, assets first, followed by liabilities, owner's equity, revenue, and expenses. The number of accounts needed by a business will depend upon its size, the nature of its operations, and the extent to which management and regulatory agencies want detailed classification of information. An identification number is assigned to each account. A ***chart of accounts*** is a listing of the account titles and account numbers being used by a given business.

In the following list of accounts, certain numbers have not been assigned; these numbers are held in reserve so that additional accounts can be inserted in the ledger in proper sequence whenever such accounts become necessary. In this illustration, the numbers from 1 to 29 are used exclusively for asset accounts; numbers from 30 to 49 are reserved for liabilities; and numbers in the 50s signify owner's equity accounts. Numbers in the 60s represent revenue accounts and numbers from 70 to 99 designate expense accounts. Revenue and expense will be discussed in Chapter 3. The balance sheet accounts used thus far in our Roberts Real Estate illustration are numbered as shown in the following ***chart of accounts:***

System for numbering ledger accounts

Account Title	Account No.
Assets:	
Cash	1
Accounts receivable	4
Land	20
Building	22
Office equipment	25
Liabilities:	
Accounts payable	32
Owner's equity:	
James Roberts, capital	50

In large businesses with hundreds or thousands of accounts, a more elaborate numbering system is used. Some companies use an eight- or ten-digit number for each ledger account; each of the digits carries special significance as to the classification of the account.

Sequence of Asset Accounts As shown in all the balance sheets we have illustrated, cash is listed first among the assets. It is followed by such assets as marketable securities, short-term notes receivable, accounts receivable, inventories of merchandise, and supplies. These are the most common examples of current assets. The term ***current assets*** includes cash and those assets that will quickly be converted into cash or used up in operations. Next on the balance sheet come the relatively permanent assets used in the business (often called ***plant assets***). Of this group, land is listed first and is followed by buildings. After these two items, any order is acceptable for other assets used in the business, such as automobiles, furniture and fixtures, computers, office equipment, store equipment, etc.

THE JOURNAL

OBJECTIVE 4 Explain the purpose of a journal and its relationship to the ledger.

In our preceding discussion, we recorded business transactions directly in the company's ledger accounts. We did this in order to stress the effects of business transactions upon the individual asset, liability, and owner's equity accounts appearing in the company's balance sheet. In an actual accounting system, however, the information about each business transaction is initially recorded in an accounting record called the ***journal.*** After the transaction has been recorded in the journal, the debit and credit changes in the individual accounts are entered in the ledger. Since the journal is the accounting record in which transactions are ***first recorded,*** it is sometimes called the ***book of original entry.***

The journal is a chronological (day-by-day) record of business transactions. The information recorded about each transaction includes the date of the transaction, the debit and credit changes in specific ledger accounts, and a brief explanation of the transaction. At convenient intervals, the debit and credit amounts recorded in the journal are transferred ***(posted)*** to the accounts in the ledger. The updated ledger accounts, in turn, serve as the basis for preparing the balance sheet and other financial statements.

Why Use a Journal?

Since it is technically possible to record transactions directly in the ledger, why bother to maintain a journal? The answer is that the unit of organization for the journal is the ***transaction,*** whereas the unit of organization for the ledger is the ***account.*** By having both a journal and a ledger, we achieve several advantages that would not be possible if transactions were recorded directly in ledger accounts:

1 **The journal shows all information about a transaction in one place and also provides an explanation of the transaction.** In a journal entry, the debits and credits for a given transaction are recorded together, but when the transaction is recorded in the ledger, the debits and credits are entered in different accounts. Since a ledger may contain hundreds of accounts, it would be very difficult to locate all the facts about a particular transaction by looking in the ledger. The journal is the record that shows the complete story of a transaction in one entry.

2 **The journal provides a chronological record of all the events in the life of a business.** If we want to look up the facts about a transaction of some months or years back, all we need is the date of the transaction in order to locate it in the journal.

3 **The use of a journal helps to prevent errors.** If transactions were recorded directly in the ledger, it would be very easy to make errors such as omitting the debit or the credit, or entering the debit twice or the credit twice. Such errors are not likely to be made in the journal, since the offsetting debits and credits appear together for each transaction.

The General Journal: Illustration of Entries

OBJECTIVE 5 Prepare journal entries to record common business transactions.

Many businesses maintain several types of journals. The nature of operations and the volume of transactions in the particular business determine the number and type of journals needed. The simplest type of journal is called a ***general journal*** and is shown on the next page. A general journal has only two money columns, one for debits and the other for credits; it may be used for all types of transactions.

The process of recording a transaction in a journal is called ***journalizing*** the transaction. To illustrate the use of the general journal, we shall now journalize the September transactions of Roberts Real Estate Company which have been discussed previously.

Efficient use of a general journal requires two things: (1) ability to analyze the effect of a transaction upon assets, liabilities, and owner's equity and (2) familiarity with the standard form and arrangement of journal entries. Our primary interest is in the analytical phase of journalizing; the procedural steps can be learned quickly by observing the following points in the illustration of journal entries:

1 The year, month, and day of the first entry on the page are written in the date column. The year and month need not be repeated for subsequent entries until a new page or a new month is begun.

2 The name of the account to be debited is written for the first line of the entry and is customarily placed at the extreme left next to the date column. The amount of the debit is entered on the same line in the ***left-hand*** money column.

3 The name of the account to be credited is entered on the line below the debit entry and is ***indented,*** that is, placed about 1 centimetre to the right of the date column. The amount credited is entered on the same line in the ***right-hand*** money column.

4 A brief explanation of the transaction begins on the line immediately below the last account credited. This explanation includes any data needed to identify the transaction, such as the name of the customer or supplier. The explanation is not indented.

5 A blank line should be left after each entry. This spacing causes each journal entry to stand out clearly as a separate unit and makes the journal easier to read.

6 An entry that includes more than one debit or more than one credit (such as the entry on September 5) is called a ***compound journal entry.*** Regardless of how many debits or credits are contained in a compound journal entry, ***all the debits*** are entered ***before any credits*** are listed.

7 The LP (ledger page) column just to the left of the debit money column is left blank at the time of making the journal entry. When the debits and credits are later transferred to ledger accounts, the numbers of the ledger accounts will be listed in this column to provide a convenient cross-reference with the ledger.

In journalizing transactions, remember that the ***exact title*** of the ledger accounts to be debited and credited should be used. For example, in recording the purchase of office equipment for cash, ***do not*** make a journal

September journal entries for Roberts Real Estate Company

General Journal — Page 1

Date		Account Titles and Explanation	LP	Debit	Credit
19—					
Sept	1	Cash		180000	
		James Roberts, Capital			180000
		Invested cash in the business.			
	3	Land		141000	
		Cash			141000
		Purchased land for office site.			
	5	Building		36000	
		Cash			15000
		Accounts Payable			21000
		Purchased building to be moved to our lot. Paid part cash; balance payable within 90 days to Kent Company			
	10	Accounts Receivable		11000	
		Land			11000
		Sold the unused part of our lot at cost to Carter's Drugstore. Due within 3 months.			
	14	Office Equipment		5400	
		Accounts Payable			5400
		Purchased equipment on credit from General Equipment, Inc.			
	20	Cash		1500	
		Accounts Receivable			1500
		Collected part of receivable from Carter's Drugstore.			
	30	Accounts Payable		3000	
		Cash			3000
		Made partial payment of the liability to General Equipment, Inc.			

entry debiting "Office Equipment Purchased" and crediting "Cash Paid Out." There are no ledger accounts with such titles. The proper journal entry would consist of a debit to ***Office Equipment*** and a credit to ***Cash.***

A familiarity with the general journal form of describing transactions is just as essential to the study of accounting as a familiarity with plus and minus signs is to the study of mathematics. The journal entry is a ***tool*** for ***analyzing*** and ***describing*** the impact of various transactions upon a business entity. The ability to describe a transaction in journal entry form requires an understanding of the nature of the transaction and its effects upon the financial position of the business.

Posting

The process of transferring the debits and credits from the general journal to the proper ledger accounts is called ***posting.*** Each amount listed in the debit column of the journal is posted by entering it on the debit side of an account in the ledger, and each amount listed in the credit column of the journal is posted to the credit side of a ledger account.

The mechanics of posting may vary somewhat with the preferences of the individual. The following sequence is commonly used:

1 Locate in the ledger the first account named in the journal entry.
2 Enter in the debit column of the ledger account the amount of the debit as shown in the journal.
3 Enter the date of the transaction in the ledger account.
4 Enter in the reference column of the ledger account the number of the journal page from which the entry is being posted.
5 The recording of the debit in the ledger account is now complete; as evidence of this fact, return to the journal and enter in the LP (ledger page) column the number of the ledger account to which the debit was posted.
6 Repeat the posting process described in the preceding five steps for the credit side of the journal entry.

Illustration of Posting To illustrate the posting process, the journal entry for the first transaction of Roberts Real Estate Company is repeated at this point along with the two ledger accounts affected by this entry.

Note that the ***Ref*** (Reference) column of each of the two ledger accounts contains the number 1, indicating that the posting was made from ***page 1*** of the journal. Entering the journal page number in the ledger account and listing the ledger account number in the journal provide a ***cross-reference*** between these two records. It is often necessary to refer to the journal entry in order to obtain more information about an amount listed in a ledger account. A cross-reference between the ledger and journal is therefore essential to efficient use of the records. Another advantage gained from entering in the journal the number of the ledger account to which a posting has been made is to provide evidence throughout the posting work as to which items have been posted. Otherwise, any interruption in the posting might leave some doubt as to which entries had been posted.

Journalizing and posting by hand is a useful method for the study of accounting, both for problem assignments and for examinations. The manual approach is also followed in many small businesses. One shortcoming is the opportunity for error that exists whenever information is being cop-

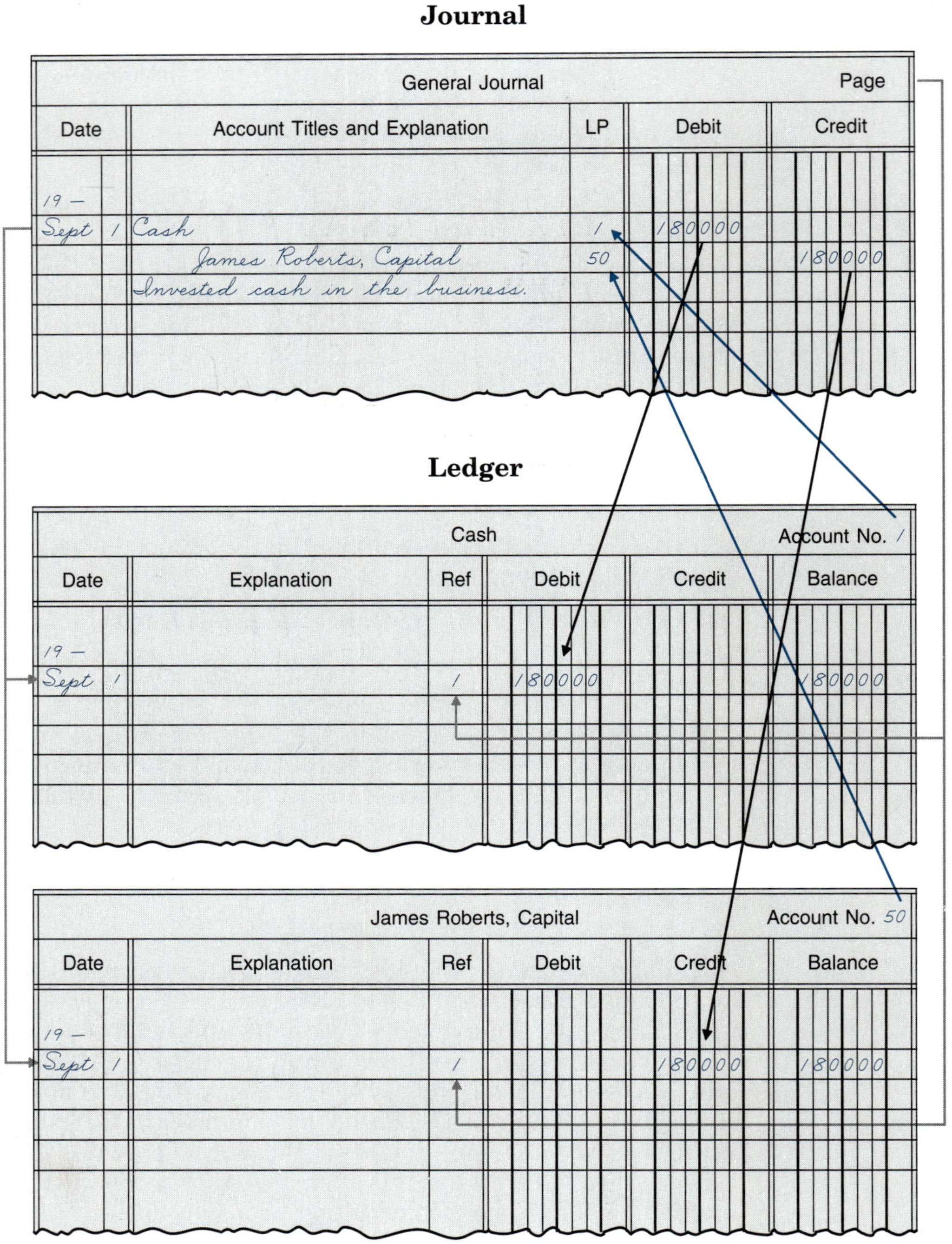

ied from one record to another. In businesses having a large volume of transactions, the posting of ledger accounts is performed automatically by computer, which speeds up the work and reduces errors.

Ledger Accounts after Posting After all the September transactions have been posted, the ledger of Roberts Real Estate Company appears as shown on pages 69 and 70. The accounts are arranged in the ledger in the same order as in the balance sheet, that is, assets first, followed by liabilities and owner's equity.

To conserve space in this illustration, several ledger accounts appear on a single page. In actual practice, however, each account occupies a separate page in the ledger.

Ledger showing September transactions

Cash						Account No. 1
Date		Explanation	Ref	Debit	Credit	Balance
19—						
Sept	1		1	180000		180000
	3		1		141000	39000
	5		1		15000	24000
	20		1	1500		25500
	30		1		3000	22500

Accounts Receivable						Account No. 4
Date		Explanation	Ref	Debit	Credit	Balance
19—						
Sept	10		1	11000		11000
	20		1		1500	9500

Land						Account No. 20
Date		Explanation	Ref	Debit	Credit	Balance
19—						
Sept	3		1	141000		141000
	10		1		11000	130000

Building						Account No. 22
Date		Explanation	Ref	Debit	Credit	Balance
19—						
Sept	5		1	36000		36000

Office Equipment — Account No. 25

Date		Explanation	Ref	Debit	Credit	Balance
19—						
Sept	14		1	5400		5400

Accounts Payable — Account No. 32

Date		Explanation	Ref	Debit	Credit	Balance
19—						
Sept	5		1		21000	21000
	14		1		5400	26400
	30		1	3000		23400

James Roberts, Capital — Account No. 50

Date		Explanation	Ref	Debit	Credit	Balance
19—						
Sept	1		1		180000	180000

THE TRIAL BALANCE

OBJECTIVE 6 ***Prepare a trial balance and explain its uses and limitations.***

Since equal dollar amounts of debits and credits are entered in the accounts for every transaction recorded, the sum of all the debits in the ledger must be equal to the sum of all the credits. If the computation of account balances has been accurate, it follows that the total of the accounts with debit balances must be equal to the total of the accounts with credit balances.

Before using the account balances to prepare a balance sheet, it is desirable to ***prove*** that the total of accounts with debit balances is in fact equal to the total of accounts with credit balances. This proof of the equality of debit and credit balances is called a ***trial balance.*** A trial balance is a two-column schedule listing the names and balances of all the accounts ***in the order in which they appear in the ledger;*** the debit balances are listed in the left-hand column and the credit balances in the right-hand column. The totals of the two columns should agree. A trial balance taken from the ledger of Roberts Real Estate Company follows.

Trial balance at month-end proves ledger is in balance

ROBERTS REAL ESTATE COMPANY
Trial Balance
September 30, 19__

Cash	$ 22,500	
Accounts receivable	9,500	
Land	130,000	
Building	36,000	
Office equipment	5,400	
Accounts payable		$ 23,400
James Roberts, capital		180,000
	$203,400	$203,400

Uses and Limitations of the Trial Balance

The trial balance provides proof that the ledger is in balance. The agreement of the debit and credit totals of the trial balance gives assurance that:

1 Equal debits and credits have been recorded for all transactions.
2 The debit or credit balance of each account has been correctly computed.
3 The addition of the account balances in the trial balance has been correctly performed.

Suppose that the debit and credit totals of the trial balance do not agree. This situation indicates that one or more errors have been made. Typical of such errors are (1) the posting of a debit as a credit, or vice versa; (2) arithmetic mistakes in computing the account balance; (3) clerical errors in copying account balances into the trial balance; (4) listing a debit balance in the credit column of the trial balance, or vice versa; and (5) errors in addition of the trial balance.

The preparation of a trial balance does not prove that transactions have been correctly analyzed and recorded in the proper accounts. If, for example, a receipt of cash were erroneously recorded by debiting the Land account instead of the Cash account, the trial balance would still balance. Also, if a transaction were completely omitted from the ledger, the error would not be disclosed by the trial balance. In brief, ***the trial balance proves only one aspect of the ledger, and that is the equality of debits and credits.***

Despite these limitations, the trial balance is a useful device. It not only provides assurance that the ledger is in balance, but it also serves as a convenient stepping-stone for the preparation of financial statements. As explained in Chapter 1, the balance sheet is a formal statement showing the financial position of the business, intended for distribution to managers, owners, bankers, and various outsiders. The trial balance, on the other hand, is merely a working paper, useful to the accountant but not intended for distribution to others. The balance sheet and other financial statements can be prepared more conveniently from the trial balance than directly from the ledger, especially if there are a great many ledger accounts.

Locating Errors

In the illustration given, the trial balance was in balance. Every accounting student soon discovers in working problems, however, that errors are easily made which prevent trial balances from balancing. The lack of balance may be the result of a single error or a combination of several errors. An error may have been made in adding the trial balance columns or in copying the balances from the ledger accounts. If the preparation of the trial balance has been accurate, then the error may lie in the accounting records, either in the journal or in the ledger accounts. What is the most efficient approach to locating the error or errors? There is no single technique that will give the best results every time, but the following procedures, done in sequence, will often save considerable time and effort in locating errors.

1 Prove the addition of the trial balance columns by adding these columns in the opposite direction from that previously followed.

2 If the error does not lie in addition, next determine the exact amount by which the schedule is out of balance. The amount of the discrepancy is often a clue to the source of the error. If the discrepancy is ***divisible by 9,*** this suggests either a ***transposition*** error or a ***slide.*** For example, assume that the Cash account has a balance of $2,175, but in copying the balance into the trial balance the figures are ***transposed*** and written as $2,157. The resulting error is $18, and like all transposition errors is ***divisible by 9.*** Another common error is the ***slide,*** or incorrect placement of the decimal point, as when $2,175.00 is copied as $21.75. The resulting discrepancy in the trial balance will also be an amount ***divisible by 9.***

   To illustrate another method of using the amount of a discrepancy as a clue to locating the error, assume that the Office Equipment account has a ***debit*** balance of $420, but that it is erroneously listed in the ***credit*** column of the trial balance. This will cause a discrepancy of two times $420, or $840, in the trial balance totals. Since such errors as recording a debit in a credit column are not uncommon, it is advisable, after determining the discrepancy in the trial balance totals, to scan the columns for an amount equal to exactly ***one-half*** of the discrepancy. It is also advisable to look over the transactions for an item of the exact amount of the discrepancy. An error may have been made by recording the debit side of the transaction and forgetting to enter the credit side.

3 Compare the amounts in the trial balance with the balances in the ledger. Make sure that each ledger account balance has been included in the correct column of the trial balance.

4 Recompute the balance of each ledger account.

5 Trace all postings from the journal to the ledger accounts. As this is done, place a check mark in the journal and in the ledger after each

figure verified. When the operation is completed, look through the journal and the ledger for unchecked amounts. In tracing postings, be alert not only for errors in amount but also for debits entered as credits, or vice versa.

Some Tips on Record-Keeping Procedures

Dollar signs are not used in journals or ledgers. Some accountants use dollar signs in trial balances; some do not. In this book, dollar signs are used in trial balances. Dollar signs should always be used in the balance sheet, the income statement, and other formal financial reports. In the balance sheet, for example, a dollar sign is placed by the first amount in each column and also by the final amount or total. Many accountants also place a dollar sign by each subtotal or other amount listed below an underlining. In the published financial statements of large corporations, the use of dollar signs is often limited to the first and last figures in a column.

When dollar amounts are being entered in the columnar paper used in journals and ledgers, commas and decimal points are not needed. On unruled paper, commas and decimal points should be used. Most of the problems and illustrations in this book are in even dollar amounts. In such cases the cents column can be left blank or, if desired, zeros or dashes may be used. A dollar amount that represents a final total within a schedule is underlined by a double rule.

THE ACCOUNTING CYCLE: AN INTRODUCTION

OBJECTIVE 7 ***Describe the basic steps of the accounting cycle in both manual and computer-based accounting systems.***

The sequence of accounting procedures used to record, classify, and summarize accounting information is often termed the ***accounting cycle.*** The accounting cycle begins with the initial recording of business transactions and concludes with the preparation of formal financial statements summarizing the effects of these transactions upon the assets, liabilities, and owner's equity of the business. The term ***cycle*** indicates that these procedures must be repeated continuously to enable the business to prepare new, up-to-date financial statements at reasonable intervals.

At this point, we have illustrated a complete accounting cycle as it relates to the preparation of a balance sheet for a service-type business with a manual accounting system. The accounting procedures discussed to this point may be summarized as follows:

1 **Record transaction in the journal.** As each business transaction occurs, it is entered in the journal, thus creating a chronological record of events. This procedure completes the recording step in the accounting cycle.

2 **Post to ledger accounts.** The debit and credit changes in account balances are posted from the journal to the ledger. This procedure classifies the effects of the business transactions in terms of specific asset, liability, and owner's equity accounts.

3 **Prepare a trial balance.** A trial balance proves the equality of the debit and credit entries in the ledger. The purpose of this procedure is to verify the accuracy of the posting process and the computation of ledger account balances.

4 **Prepare financial statements.** At this point, we have discussed only one financial statement—the balance sheet. This statement shows the financial position of the business at a specific date. The preparation of financial statements summarizes the effects of business transactions occurring through the date of the statements and completes the accounting cycle.

In the next section of this chapter, and throughout this textbook, we will extend our discussion to include computer-based accounting systems. In Chapters 3 and 4, we will expand the accounting cycle to include the measurement of business income and the preparation of an income statement.

Manual and Computer-Based Systems: A Comparison

In our preceding discussion, we have assumed the use of a manual accounting system, in which all the accounting procedures are performed manually by the company's accounting personnel. You may wonder about the relevance of such a discussion in an era when even many small businesses use computer-based accounting systems. However, the concepts and procedures involved in the operation of manual and computer-based accounting systems are ***essentially the same.*** The differences are largely a question of whether specific procedures require human attention, or whether they can be performed automatically by machine, based on programs stored in the computer.

Computers can be programmed to perform mechanical tasks with great speed and accuracy. For example, they can be programmed to read data, to perform mathematical computations, and to rearrange data into any desired format. However, computers cannot think. Therefore, they are not able to ***analyze*** business transactions. Without human guidance, computers cannot determine which events should be recorded in the accounting records, or which accounts should be debited and credited to record an event. With these abilities and limitations in mind, we will explore the effects of computer-based systems upon the basic accounting cycle.

Recording Business Transactions The recording of transactions requires two steps. First, the transaction must be ***analyzed*** to determine whether it should be recorded in the accounting records and, if so, which accounts should be debited and credited and for what dollar amounts. Second, the transaction must be ***physically entered*** (recorded) in the accounting system. As computers do not know which transactions should be recorded or how to record them properly, these two functions must be performed by accounting personnel in both manual and computerized systems.

Differences do exist, however, in the manner in which data are physically entered into manual and computer-based systems. In manual systems, the data are entered in the form of handwritten journal entries. In a computer-based system, the data will be entered through a keyboard, an optical scanner, or other input device. Also, data entered into a computer-based system need ***not*** be arranged in the format of a journal entry. The data usually are entered into a ***data base,*** instead of a journal.

What Is a Data Base? A data base is a warehouse of information stored within a computer system. The purpose of the data base is to allow information that will be used for several different purposes to be entered into the computer system ***only once.*** Data are originally entered into the data base. Then, as data are needed, the computer refers to the data base, selects the appropriate data, and arranges them in the desired format.

The information that must be entered into the data base is the same as that contained in a journal entry—the date, the accounts to be debited and credited, the dollar amounts, and an explanation of the transaction. However, this information need not be arranged in the format of a journal entry. For example, in a data base, accounts usually are identified by number, rather than by title. Also, abbreviations such as "D" or "C" are used to indicate whether an account should be debited or credited. Once information has been entered in the data base, the computer, based on the instructions in the computer programs prepared by someone with accounting knowledge, can arrange this information into any desired format, such as journal entries, ledger accounts, and financial statements.

Posting to Ledger Accounts Posting merely transfers existing information from one accounting record to another—a function that can be easily performed by a computer. In a computer-based system, data posted to the ledger accounts come directly from the data base, rather than from the journal.

Preparation of a Trial Balance Preparation of a trial balance involves three steps: (1) determining the balances of ledger accounts, (2) arranging the account balances in the format of a trial balance, and (3) adding up the trial balance columns and comparing the column totals. All these functions involve information already contained in the data base and can be performed by the computer.

Preparation of Financial Statements and Related Disclosures The preparation of a balance sheet and of the related disclosures are two very different tasks. The balance sheet—like the trial balance—consists of account titles and dollar amounts taken directly from the ledger. Hence, a balance sheet may be prepared automatically in a computer-based system.

Making the appropriate ***disclosures*** to accompany a set of financial statements, however, is a very different matter. Determining the items to be disclosed and wording the appropriate notes to the financial statements are tasks requiring ***professional judgment.*** Therefore, appropriate disclosures ***cannot be prepared automatically by a computer;*** they must be prepared carefully by people with ***sound judgment,*** as well as extensive knowledge of generally accepted accounting principles and financial reporting requirements.

At this point, our discussion of financial statements is limited to the preparation of a balance sheet. The preparation of an income statement involves additional procedures that will be discussed in the following chapter.

In Summary . . . Computers can eliminate the need for copying and rearranging information that already has been entered into the system. They also can perform mathematical computations. In short, computers eliminate most of the "paper work" involved in the operation of an accounting system. However, they ***do not*** eliminate the need for accounting personnel who can analyze business transactions and explain these events in conformity with generally accepted accounting principles.

The differences in manual and computer-based systems with respect to the accounting procedures discussed in this chapter are summarized graphically in the flowcharts below. Functions that are performed by accounting personnel are printed on a white background, and tasks that can be performed automatically by the computer are printed on a gray shaded background.

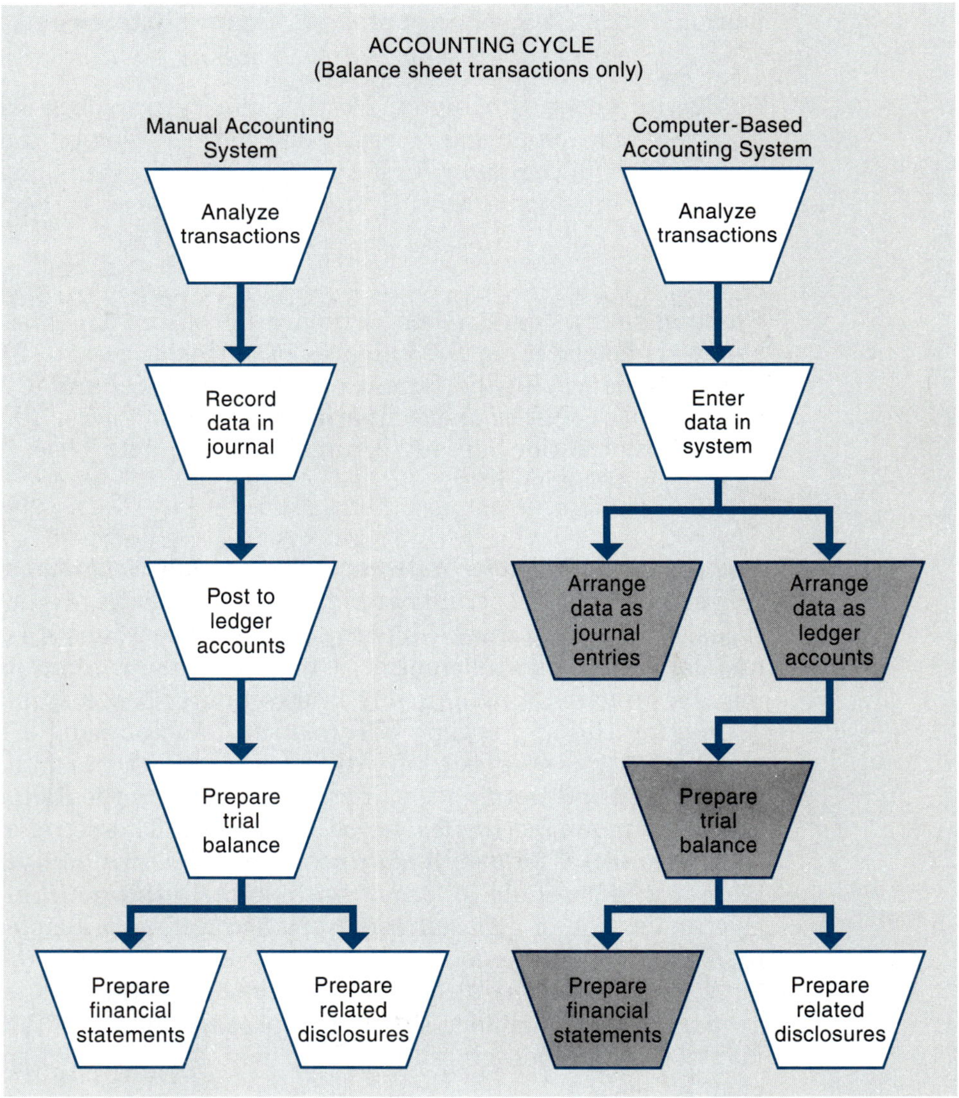

JOURNALS, LEDGERS, AND ACCOUNTING EDUCATION

In this chapter, our discussion of journals and ledgers has focused upon the simplest forms of these accounting records—a manually maintained "general" journal and T accounts. While these records might be sufficient for a very small business, most organizations use more complicated and more efficient types of journals and ledgers. An increasing number of organizations use computer-based accounting systems. Even when a manual system is in use, the recording of transactions can be done much more quickly in "special journals" than in the two-column general journal.[1] The formats of accounting software differ somewhat from one package to the next; also, the formats of special journals vary from one company to the next.

However, general journal entries and T accounts ***illustrate the effects of transactions upon the financial position of a business*** more clearly than do accounting software displays or entries in special journals. Despite their limited use in accounting practice, general journal entries and T accounts remain the preferred method of illustrating the effects of business transactions in accounting classrooms and accounting textbooks.

As a student, you should view general journal entries and T accounts as ***tools for analyzing transactions and illustrating their financial effects,*** not elements of actual accounting systems. Remember, our primary goal in this course is to develop your ability to ***understand and use*** accounting information, not to train you in record-keeping procedures.[2]

The Usefulness of Journals and Ledgers to Managers

Managers continually make use of the information contained in the accounting records. For example, to obtain information about a specific business transaction, managers may refer to the journal entry in which the transaction was recorded. To learn the current balance in such critical accounts as Cash, Accounts Receivable, and Accounts Payable, managers look to the ledger. Managers need not wait until financial statements are issued to obtain financial information about the business. They may obtain this information whenever they need it—often through desktop computers with "read only" access to the company's accounting system.[3]

In contrast, investors, creditors, and other outsiders ***do not*** have direct access to a company's accounting records. They obtain financial information about the business only ***periodically***—when financial statements are issued.[4]

---

1 Special journals are journals designed to record ***one*** particular type of transaction quickly and efficiently. By having several different kinds of special journals, a business may be able to record efficiently ***all*** types of transactions that ***occur frequently.*** Special journals will be discussed further in Chapter 6.

2 Although the format of accounting records varies from one business to the next, a student who understands the basic concepts of double-entry accounting should have little trouble in learning to understand and use the accounting records of any specific organization.

3 "Read only" is an internal control that allows users of a specific computer terminal to read data, but not to alter the data or input new data into the system.

4 Certain financial events may be disclosed to outsiders between financial statement dates, through such media as press conferences. Still, managers have far more timely access to most accounting information than do outside decision makers.

CHAPTER REVIEW

KEY TERMS INTRODUCED OR EMPHASIZED IN CHAPTER 2

Account A record used to summarize all increases and decreases in a particular asset, such as Cash, or any other type of asset, liability, owner's equity, revenue, or expense.

Accounting cycle The sequence of accounting procedures applied in recording, classifying, and summarizing accounting information. The cycle begins with the occurrence of business transactions and concludes with the preparation of financial statements. This concept will be expanded in later chapters.

Chart of accounts A listing of the ledger account titles and numbers being used by a given business.

Credit An amount entered on the right-hand side of an account. A credit is used to record a decrease in an asset and an increase in a liability or in owner's equity.

Data base A storage centre of information within a computer-based accounting system. The idea behind a data base is that data intended for a variety of uses may be entered into the computer system only once, at which time the information is stored in the data base. Then, as the information is needed, the computer can retrieve it from the data base and arrange it in the desired format.

Debit An amount entered on the left-hand side of an account. A debit is used to record an increase in an asset and a decrease in a liability or in owner's equity.

Double-entry accounting A system of recording every business transaction with equal dollar amounts of both debit and credit entries. As a result of this system, the accounting equation always remains in balance; in addition, the system makes possible the measurement of net income and also the use of error-detecting devices such as a trial balance.

Journal A chronological record of transactions, showing for each transaction the debits and credits to be entered in specific ledger accounts. The simplest type of journal is called a general journal.

Ledger A loose-leaf book, tray, or other record containing all the separate accounts of a business.

Posting The process of transferring information from the journal to individual accounts in the ledger.

Trial balance A two-column schedule listing the names and the debit or credit balances of all accounts in the ledger.

DEMONSTRATION PROBLEM FOR YOUR REVIEW

Stadium Parking was organized on July 2 to operate a parking lot near a new sports arena. The following transactions occurred during July prior to the company beginning its regular business operations.

July 2 Sylvia Snyder opened a bank account in the name of the business with a deposit of $49,000 cash.

July 3 Purchased land to be used as the parking lot for a total price of $140,000. A cash down payment of $28,000 was made and a note payable was issued for the balance of the purchase price.

July 5 Purchased a small portable building for $8,000 cash. The purchase price included installation of the building on the parking lot.

July 12 Purchased office equipment on credit from Suzuki & Company for $3,000.

July 28 Paid $2,000 of the amount owed to Suzuki & Company.

The account titles and account numbers used by Stadium Parking to record these transactions are as follows:

Cash	*1*	*Notes payable*	*30*
Land	*20*	*Accounts payable*	*32*
Building	*22*	*Sylvia Snyder, capital*	*50*
Office equipment	*25*		

INSTRUCTIONS

a Prepare journal entries for the month of July.

b Post to ledger accounts of the three-column running balance form.

c Prepare a trial balance at July 31.

SOLUTION TO DEMONSTRATION PROBLEM

a

General Journal — *Page 1*

Date		Account Titles and Explanations	LP	Debit	Credit
19__					
July	2	Cash	1	49,000	
		Sylvia Snyder, Capital	50		49,000
		Owner invested cash to begin business.			
	3	Land	20	140,000	
		Cash	1		28,000
		Notes Payable	30		112,000
		Purchased land. Paid part cash and issued a note payable for the balance.			
	5	Building	22	8,000	
		Cash	1		8,000
		Purchased a small portable building for cash.			
	12	Office Equipment	25	3,000	
		Accounts Payable	32		3,000
		Purchased office equipment on credit from Suzuki & Co.			
	28	Accounts Payable	32	2,000	
		Cash	1		2,000
		Paid part of account payable to Suzuki & Co.			

b

Cash — Account No. 1

Date		Explanation	Ref	Debit	Credit	Balance
19—						
July	2		1	49000		49000
	3		1		28000	21000
	5		1		8000	13000
	28		1		2000	11000

Land					Account No. 20
Date	Explanation	Ref	Debit	Credit	Balance
19—					
July 3		1	140000		140000

Building					Account No. 22
Date	Explanation	Ref	Debit	Credit	Balance
19—					
July 5		1	8000		8000

Office Equipment					Account No. 25
Date	Explanation	Ref	Debit	Credit	Balance
19—					
July 12		1	3000		3000

Notes Payable					Account No. 30
Date	Explanation	Ref	Debit	Credit	Balance
19—					
July 3		1		112000	112000

Accounts Payable					Account No. 32
Date	Explanation	Ref	Debit	Credit	Balance
19—					
July 12		1		3000	3000
28		1	2000		1000

Sylvia Snyder, Capital					Account No. 50
Date	Explanation	Ref	Debit	Credit	Balance
19—					
July 2		1		49000	49000

c

STADIUM PARKING
Trial Balance
July 31, 19__

	Debit	Credit
Cash	$ 11,000	
Land	140,000	
Building	8,000	
Office equipment	3,000	
Notes payable		$112,000
Accounts payable		1,000
Sylvia Snyder, capital		49,000
	$162,000	$162,000

ASSIGNMENT MATERIAL

DISCUSSION QUESTIONS

1 In its simplest form, an account has only three elements or basic parts. What are these three elements?

2 At the beginning of the year, the Office Equipment account of Atlantic Coast Airlines had a debit balance of **$126,900.** During the year, debit entries of **$23,400** and credit entries of **$38,200** were posted to the account. What was the balance of this account at the end of the year? (Indicate debit or credit balance.)

3 What relationship exists between the position of an account on the balance sheet and the rules for recording increases in that account?

4 State briefly the rules of debit and credit as applied to asset accounts and as applied to liability and owner's equity accounts.

5 Does the term ***debit*** mean increase and the term ***credit*** mean decrease? Explain.

6 What requirement is imposed by the double-entry system in the recording of any business transaction?

7 Explain precisely what is meant by each of the phrases listed below. Whenever appropriate, indicate whether the left or right side of an account is affected and whether an increase or a decrease is indicated.

a A debit to the Land account

b Credit balance

c Credit side of an account

d A debit of $200 to the Cash account

e A debit of $600 to Accounts Payable

f A credit of $50 to Accounts Receivable

8 For each of the following transactions, indicate whether the account in parentheses should be debited or credited, and give the reason for your answer.

a Purchased a copying machine on credit, promising to make payment in full within 30 days. (Accounts Payable)

b Purchased land for cash. (Cash)

c Sold an old, unneeded typewriter on 30-day credit. (Office Equipment)

d Obtained a loan of $30,000 from a bank. (Cash)

e James Brown began the business of Brown Sporting Goods Shop by depositing $20,000 cash in a bank account in the name of the business. (James Brown, Capital)

9 For each of the following accounts, state whether it is an asset, a liability, or owner's equity, and whether it would normally have a debit or a credit balance: (a) Office Equipment, (b) John Williams, Capital, (c) Accounts Receivable, (d) Accounts Payable, (e) Cash, (f) Notes Payable, (g) Land.

10 Why is a journal sometimes called the ***book of original entry?***

11 Compare and contrast a ***journal*** and a ***ledger.***

12 What is a ***compound journal entry?***

13 Since it is possible to record the effects of business transactions directly in ledger accounts, why is it desirable for a business to maintain a journal?

14 What purposes are served by a trial balance?

15 In preparing a trial balance, an accounting student listed the balance of the Office Equipment account in the credit column. This account had a balance of $2,450. What would be the amount of the discrepancy in the trial balance totals? Explain.

16 Are dollar signs used in journal entries? In ledger accounts? In trial balances? In financial statements?

17 List the following five items in a logical sequence to illustrate the flow of accounting information through a manual accounting system:

a Information entered in the journal

b Preparation of financial statements

c Occurrence of a business transaction

d Debits and credits posted from journal to ledger

e Preparation of a trial balance

18 Which step in the recording of transactions requires greater understanding of accounting principles: (a) the entering of transactions in the journal or (b) the posting of entries to ledger accounts?

19 List the procedures in the ***accounting cycle*** as described in this chapter.

20 What is a ***data base?*** How does a data base relate to the preparation of journal entries and ledger accounts in a computer-based system?

MULTIPLE-CHOICE QUESTIONS

1 According to the rules of debit and credit for balance sheet accounts:

a Increases in asset, liability, and owner's equity accounts are recorded by debits.

b Decreases in asset and liability accounts are recorded by credits.

c Increases in asset and owner's equity accounts are recorded by debits.

d Decreases in liability and owner's equity accounts are recorded by debits.

2 Which of the following statements about accounting procedures is ***not*** correct?

a The journal shows in one place all the information about specific transactions, arranged in chronological order.

b A ledger account shows in one place all the information about changes in a specific asset or liability, or in owner's equity.

c Posting is the process of transferring debit and credit changes in account balances from the ledger to the journal.

d The end product of the accounting cycle consists of formal financial statements, such as the balance sheet and the income statement.

3 On March 31, the ledger for Odette Office Cleaning consists of the following:

Cleaning equipment	*$27,800*	*Accounts receivable*	*$21,000*
Accounts payable	*15,700*	*Cash*	*6,900*
M. Poppins, capital	*20,000*	*Salaries payable*	*9,600*
Office equipment	*2,000*	*Cleaning supplies*	*2,600*
Automobile	*7,500*	*Notes payable*	*22,500*

In a trial balance prepared on March 31, the total of the credit column is:

a $67,800 b $93,100 c $25,300 d $65,300

4 Sunset Tours has a $3,500 account receivable from the Del Mar Rotary. On January 20, the Rotary makes a partial payment of $2,100 to Sunset Tours. The journal entry made on January 20 by Sunset Tours to record this transaction includes:

a A debit to the Cash Received account of $2,100.

b A credit to the Accounts Receivable account of $2,100.

c A debit to the Cash account of $1,400.

d A debit to the Accounts Receivable account of $1,400.

5 The following journal entry was made in Russel Stores' accounting records:

Cash	*12,000*	
Notes Receivable	*48,000*	
Land		*60,000*

This transaction:

a Involves the purchase of land for $60,000.

b Involves a $12,000 cash payment.

c Involves the sale of land for $60,000.

d Causes an increase in total assets of $12,000.

EXERCISES

EXERCISE 2-1
Accounting Terminology

Listed below are nine technical accounting terms introduced in this chapter:

Ledger	*Account*	*Data base*
Posting	*Credit*	*Double-entry*
Trial balance	*Debit*	*Journal*

Each of the following statements may (or may not) describe one of these technical terms. For each statement, indicate the accounting term described, or answer "None" if the statement does not correctly describe any of the terms.

a The system of accounting in which all transactions are recorded both in the journal and in the ledger

b An entry on the left-hand side of a ledger account

c The process of transferring information from a journal to the ledger

d The accounting record in which transactions are initially recorded in a manual accounting system

e Information stored in a computer-based accounting system that can be arranged into any desired format

f A device that proves the equality of debits and credits posted to the ledger

g The accounting record from which a trial balance is prepared

EXERCISE 2-2
Double-Entry and the Accounting Equation

A number of transactions are described below in terms of the balance sheet accounts debited and credited:

1 Debit Cash, credit Accounts Receivable.

2 Debit Accounts Payable, credit Cash.

3 Debit Cash, credit Tom Hill, Capital.

4 Debit Equipment, credit Accounts Payable.

5 Debit Land, credit Cash and Notes Payable.

6 Debit Accounts Payable, credit Equipment.

INSTRUCTIONS

a Indicate the effects of each transaction upon the elements of the accounting equation, using the code letters ***I*** for increase, ***D*** for decrease, and ***NE*** for no effect. Organize your answer in tabular form using the column headings shown below. The answer for transaction **1** is provided as an example.

Transaction	*Assets*	=	*Liabilities*	+	*Owner's Equity*
1	NE		NE		NE

b Write a one-sentence description of each transaction.

EXERCISE 2-3
Double-Entry Accounting: Debit and Credit Rules

Analyze separately each of the following transactions, using the format illustrated at the end of the exercise. In each situation, explain the debit portion of the transaction before the credit portion.

a On April 2, Ginger Denton organized Metro Insurance Agency by opening a bank account in the company name with a deposit of $80,000 cash.

b On April 11, the new business purchased an office building in an industrial park for a total price of $128,000, of which $72,000 was applicable to the land and $56,000 to the building. A cash down payment of $34,500 was made and a note payable was issued for the balance of the purchase price.

c On April 21, office equipment was purchased on credit from ADR Company at a price of $6,400. The account payable was to be paid on May 21.

d On April 29, a portion of the office equipment purchased on April 21 was found to be defective and was returned to ADR Company. ADR Company agreed that Metro would not be charged for the defective equipment, which had cost $950.

e On May 21, the remaining liability to ADR Company was paid in full.

Note: The type of analysis to be made is shown by the following illustration, using transaction **a** as an example:

a **(1)** The asset Cash was increased. Increases in assets are recorded by debits. Debit Cash, $80,000.

(2) The owner's equity was increased. Increases in owner's equity are recorded by credits. Credit Ginger Denton, Capital, $80,000.

EXERCISE 2-4
T Accounts

Enter the following transactions in T accounts drawn on ordinary notebook paper. Label each debit and credit with the letter identifying the transaction. Prepare a trial balance at June 30.

a On June 8, Lynne Jones opened a bank account in the name of her new business, Bluegrass Company, by making a bank deposit of $82,000 cash.

b On June 12, land was acquired for $36,000 cash.

c On June 14, a prefabricated building was purchased from E-Z Built Corporation at a cost of $40,800. A cash payment of $10,200 was made and a note payable was issued for the balance.

d On June 20, office equipment was purchased at a cost of $7,100. A cash down payment of $1,100 was made, and it was agreed that the balance should be paid within 30 days.

e On June 26, $3,400 of the amount due E-Z Built Corporation was paid.

EXERCISE 2-5
Effects of Debits and Credits on Ledger Account Balances

The first six transactions of Broadway Travel Agency appear in the following T accounts.

Cash

(1)	60,000	(2)	20,000
(6)	2,300	(5)	15,000

Office Equipment

(3)	20,000	(4)	5,000

Accounts Receivable

(4)	5,000	(6)	2,300

Notes Payable

		(2)	100,000

Land

(2)	72,000		

Accounts Payable

(5)	15,000	(3)	20,000

Building

(2)	48,000		

Michael Chan, Capital

		(1)	60,000

For each of the six transactions in turn, indicate the type of accounts affected (asset, liability, or owner's equity) and whether the account was increased or decreased. Arrange your answers in the form illustrated for transaction ***(1),*** shown here as an example.

	Account(s) Debited		Account(s) Credited	
Transaction	***Type of Account(s)***	***Increase or Decrease***	***Type of Account(s)***	***Increase or Decrease***
(1)	*Asset*	*Increase*	*Owner's equity*	*Increase*

EXERCISE 2-6
Recording Transactions in a Journal

Enter the following transactions in the two-column journal of Jenkins Sporting Goods. Include a brief explanation of the transaction as part of each journal entry.

Nov. 1 The owner, Dan Jenkins, invested an additional $40,000 cash in the business.

Nov. 3 Purchased an adjacent vacant lot for use as parking space. The price was $98,500, of which $28,500 was paid in cash; a note payable was issued for the balance.

Nov. 12 Collected an account receivable of $4,500 from a customer, Jean Krieger.

Nov. 17 Acquired office equipment from Tower Company for $7,600 cash.

Nov. 21 Issued a cheque for $764 in full payment of an account payable to Hampton Supply Co.

Nov. 28 Borrowed $25,000 cash from the bank by signing a 90-day note payable.

EXERCISE 2-7
Journal Entries to Illustrate Effects of Transactions

Prepare general journal entries to illustrate the effects of each of the following transactions upon the financial statements of Seacoast Airline. You are to determine appropriate account titles.

Jan. 4 Purchased two seaplanes from Scout Aircraft at a total cost of $790,000. Paid $390,000 in cash and signed a note payable to Island Bank for the remainder.

Jan. 8 Purchased spare parts for the new planes from Breckwoldt Aviation. The parts cost $17,600, and were purchased on credit.

Jan. 12 Issued to Earl Scoggins, the owner of Scoggins' Flight School, a $500,000 note payable in exchange for a parcel of waterfront land and a floating aircraft hangar in La Salle Bay. The current value of the land is appraised at $300,000, and of the floating hangar, $200,000.

Jan. 15 Returned to Breckwoldt Aviation $4,300 of the aircraft parts purchased on January 8. The return of these parts reduced by $4,300 the amount owed to Breckwoldt.

Feb. 2 Paid the remaining balance owed to Breckwoldt Aviation from the purchase on January 8.

EXERCISE 2-8
Relationship between Journal and Ledger Accounts

Transactions are recorded ***first*** in a journal and ***then*** posted to ledger accounts. In this exercise, however, your understanding of the relationship between journal and ledger is tested by asking you to study some ledger accounts and determine the journal entries that probably were made by the company's accountant to produce these ledger entries. The following accounts show the first six transactions of Gutierrez Construction Company. Prepare a journal entry (including written explanation) for each transaction.

Cash

Nov. 1	60,000	Nov. 8	33,600
Nov. 30	35,000	Nov. 25	10,000

Notes Payable

Nov. 25	10,000	Nov. 8	100,000

Land

Nov. 8	70,000		

Accounts Payable

Nov. 21	480	Nov. 15	3,200

Building

Nov. 8	63,600		

Joe Gutierrez, Capital

		Nov. 1	60,000
		Nov. 30	35,000

Office Equipment

Nov. 15	3,200	Nov. 21	480

EXERCISE 2-9
Preparing a Trial Balance

Using the information in the ledger accounts presented in Exercise 2-8, prepare a trial balance for Gutierrez Construction Company at November 30, 19__.

EXERCISE 2-10
Uses and Limitations of a Trial Balance

Some of the following errors would cause the debit and credit columns of the trial balance to have unequal totals. For each of the four paragraphs, write a statement explaining whether the error would cause unequal totals in the trial balance. Each paragraph is to be considered independently of the others.

a A payment of $400 to a creditor was recorded by a debit to Accounts Payable of $400 and a credit to Cash of $40.

b A $540 payment for a new typewriter was recorded by a debit to Office Equipment of $54 and a credit to Cash of $54.

c An account receivable in the amount of $800 was collected in full. The collection was recorded by a debit to Cash for $800 and a debit to Accounts Payable for $800.

d An account payable was paid by issuing a cheque for $350. The payment was recorded by debiting Accounts Payable $350 and crediting Accounts Receivable $350.

EXERCISE 2-11
Uses and Limitations of a Trial Balance

The trial balance prepared by Discount Plumbing Service at June 30 was not in balance. In searching for the error, an employee discovered that a transaction for the purchase of a calculator on credit for $380 had been recorded by a ***debit*** of $380 to the Office Equipment account and a ***debit*** of $380 to Accounts Payable. The credit column of the incorrect trial balance has a total of $129,640.

In answering each of the following five questions, explain fully the reasons underlying your answer and state the dollar amount of the error if any.

a Was the Office Equipment account overstated, understated, or correctly stated in the trial balance?

b Was the total of the debit column of the trial balance overstated, understated, or correctly stated?

c Was the Accounts Payable account overstated, understated, or correctly stated in the trial balance?

d Was the total of the credit column of the trial balance overstated, understated, or correctly stated?

e How much was the total of the debit column of the trial balance before correction of the error?

EXERCISE 2-12
Steps in the Accounting Cycle; Computerized Accounting Systems

Various steps and decisions involved in the accounting cycle are described in the seven lettered statements below. Indicate which of these procedures are mechanical functions that can be performed by machine in a computerized accounting system and which require the judgment of people familiar with accounting principles and concepts.

a Decide whether or not events should be recorded in the accounting records.

b Determine which ledger accounts should be debited and credited to describe specific business transactions.

c Arrange recorded data in the format of journal entries.

d Arrange recorded data in the format of ledger accounts.

e Prepare a trial balance.

f Prepare financial statements (a balance sheet).

g Evaluate the debt-paying ability of one company relative to another.

EXERCISE 2-13
Manual vs. Computer-based Systems

For each of the following steps in the accounting cycle, explain whether the step requires human judgment or whether it can be performed automatically by a computer in a computer-based accounting system.

a Record transactions as they occur.

b Post recorded data to ledger accounts.

c Prepare a trial balance.

d Prepare a balance sheet and related disclosures.

EXERCISE 2-14
Different Uses for Journals and Ledgers

Briefly explain the usefulness of journal entries and of ledger accounts:

a In the operation of an accounting system.

b From the viewpoint of business managers who are ***not*** personally responsible for maintaining accounting records or preparing their company's financial statements.

c From the viewpoint of an accounting student or an accounting instructor (assuming ***general*** journal entries and T accounts).

PROBLEMS

Group A

PROBLEM 2A-1
Recording Transactions in a Journal

Elizabeth Carver, a chartered accountant, resigned from her position with a large CA firm in order to begin her own public accounting practice. The business transactions during September while the new venture was being organized are listed below.

Sept. 1 Carver opened a bank account in the name of her firm, Elizabeth Carver, Chartered Accountant, by depositing $52,000 that she had saved over a period of years.

Sept. 10 Purchased a small office building located on a large lot for a total price of $116,200, of which $48,000 was applicable to the land and $68,200 to the building. A cash payment of $28,200 was made and a note payable was issued for the balance of the purchase price.

Sept. 15 Purchased a microcomputer system from Computer Stores, Inc., for $6,680 cash.

Sept. 19 Purchased office furniture, filing cabinets, and a typewriter from Davidson Office Supply Company at a cost of $3,960. A cash down payment of $720 was made, the balance to be paid in three equal instalments due September 28, October 28, and November 28. The purchase was on open account and did not require signing of a promissory note.

Sept. 26 A $360 monitor in the microcomputer system purchased on September 15 stopped working. The monitor was returned to Computer Stores, Inc., which promised to refund the $360 within five days.

Sept. 28 Paid Davidson Office Supply Company $1,080 cash as the first instalment due on the account payable for office equipment.

Sept. 30 Received $360 cash from Computer Stores, Inc., in full settlement of the account receivable created on September 26.

INSTRUCTIONS Prepare journal entries to record the above transactions. Select the appropriate account titles from the following chart of accounts:

Cash	*Office equipment*
Accounts receivable	*Notes payable*
Land	*Accounts payable*
Building	*Elizabeth Carver, capital*

PROBLEM 2A-2
Analyzing Transactions and Preparing Journal Entries

The Tool Shed was organized to rent trailers, tools, and other equipment to its customers. The organization of the business began on May 1, and the following transactions occurred in May before the company began regular operations on June 1.

1 On May 1, Mark O'Brien opened a bank account in the name of his new company with a deposit of $100,000 cash.

2 On May 3, The Tool Shed bought land for use in its operations at a total cost of $75,000. A cash down payment of $15,000 was made, and a note payable (payable within 90 days without interest) was issued for the balance.

3 On May 5, a movable building was purchased for $62,000 cash and installed on the lot.

4 On May 10, equipment was purchased on credit from Ace Tool Company at a cost of $14,100. The account payable was to be paid within 30 days. (The asset account is entitled Rental Equipment.)

5 On May 31, a cash payment of $20,000 was made in partial settlement of the note payable issued on May 3.

INSTRUCTIONS **a** Prepare an analysis of each of the above transactions. The form of analysis to be used is as follows, using transaction **1** above as an example:

1 (a) The asset Cash was increased. Increases in assets are recorded by debits. Debit Cash, $100,000.

(b) The owner's equity was increased. Increases in owner's equity are recorded by credits. Credit Mark O'Brien, Capital, $100,000.

b Prepare journal entries for the above five transactions. Include an explanation as a part of each journal entry.

PROBLEM 2A-3
Preparing a Trial Balance and a Balance Sheet

Environmental Services is a weather forecasting service that provides information to growers and dealers in perishable commodities. Its ledger account balances at November 30 were as shown in the following alphabetical list.

Accounts payable	$ 7,000	Land	$ 85,200
Accounts receivable	16,700	Notes payable	145,000
Automobiles	14,600	Notes receivable	2,400
Building	110,000	Office furniture	12,900
Carl Ford, capital	129,650	Office supplies	850
Cash	17,650	Property taxes payable	1,060
Computer	18,800	Salaries payable	3,740
Computer software	5,450	Technical library	1,900

INSTRUCTIONS

a Prepare a trial balance with the accounts arranged in financial statement order. Include a proper heading for your trial balance.

b Prepare a balance sheet. Include a subtotal for total liabilities.

PROBLEM 2A-4
Posting to Ledger Accounts; Preparing a Trial Balance and a Balance Sheet

Mei Yi is a veterinarian. In January, she began organizing her own animal hospital, to be known as Animal Care Centre. Mei Yi has prepared the following journal entries to record all January business transactions. She has not posted these entries to ledger accounts. The ledger account numbers to be used are: Cash, 1; Office Supplies, 10; Land, 20; Building, 25; Medical Equipment, 27; Notes Payable, 30; Accounts Payable, 31; and Mei Yi, Capital, 50.

General Journal — **Page 1**

Jan	2	Cash		60,000	
		Mei Yi, Capital			60,000
		Investment in business by owner.			
	4	Land		45,000	
		Building		115,000	
		Cash			40,000
		Notes Payable			120,000
		Purchased land and building.			
	7	Medical Equipment		7,480	
		Accounts Payable			7,480
		Bought equipment on credit from Medco, Inc.			
	8	Office Supplies		590	
		Accounts Payable			590
		Bought supplies from Miller Supply.			
	13	Accounts Payable		1,400	
		Medical Equipment			1,400
		Returned defective medical equipment to Medco, Inc., for credit on account.			
	18	Accounts Payable		590	
		Cash			590
		Made payment of liability to Miller Supply.			

INSTRUCTIONS

a Post the journal entries to ledger accounts of the three-column running balance form.

b Prepare a trial balance at January 31 from the ledger accounts completed in part **a.**

c Prepare a balance sheet at January 31, 19__.

PROBLEM 2A-5
Preparing Journal Entries, Posting, and Preparing a Trial Balance

Ann Ryan, a licensed real estate broker, on October 1 began the organization of her own business, to be known as Ryan Land Company. The following events occurred during October:

Oct. 2 Ann Ryan opened a bank account in the name of the business by depositing personal savings of $35,000.

Oct. 6 Purchased land and a small office building at a total price of $98,500, of which $64,000 was applicable to land and $34,500 to the building. The terms of the purchase required a cash payment of $29,500 and the issuance of a note payable for $69,000.

Oct. 15 Sold one-quarter of the land at its cost of $16,000 to a neighbouring business, Village Medical Clinic, which wanted to expand its parking lot. No down payment was required; Village Medical Clinic issued a note promising payment of the $16,000 in a series of five monthly instalments of $3,200 each, beginning October 30 (ignore interest). As the land was sold at cost, there was no gain or loss on this transaction.

Oct. 20 Purchased office equipment on credit from Buffington Company in the amount of $5,280.

Oct. 30 Paid $3,440 as partial settlement of the liability to Buffington Company.

Oct. 31 Received the first $3,200 monthly instalment on the note receivable from Village Medical Clinic.

The account titles and account numbers to be used are:

Cash	1	*Office equipment*	26
Notes receivable	5	*Notes payable*	30
Land	21	*Accounts payable*	32
Building	23	*Ann Ryan, capital*	50

INSTRUCTIONS

a Prepare journal entries for the month of October.

b Post to ledger accounts of the three-column running balance form.

c Prepare a trial balance at October 31, 19__.

PROBLEM 2A-6
Preparing Journal Entries, Posting, and Preparing a Trial Balance

After playing several seasons of professional football, George Harris had saved enough money to start a business, to be called Number One Auto Rental. The transactions during March while the new business was being organized are listed below:

Mar. 1 George Harris invested $140,000 cash in the business by making a deposit in a bank account in the name of the new company.

Mar. 3 The new company purchased land and a building at a cost of $140,000, of which $72,000 was regarded as applicable to the land and $68,000 to the building. The transaction involved a cash payment of $41,500 and the issuance of a note payable for $98,500.

Mar. 5 Purchased 10 new automobiles at $17,200 each from Fleet Sales Limited. Paid $40,000 cash, and agreed to pay $32,000 by March 31 and the remaining balance by April 15. The liability is viewed as an account payable.

Mar. 7 Sold an automobile at cost to Harris's father-in-law, Howard Facey, who paid $2,400 in cash and agreed to pay the balance within 30 days.

Mar. 8 One of the automobiles was found to be defective and was returned to Fleet Sales Limited. The amount payable to this creditor was thereby reduced by $17,200.

Mar. 20 Purchased office equipment at a cost of $4,000 cash.

Mar. 31 Issued a cheque for $32,000 in partial payment of the liability to Fleet Sales Limited.

The account titles and the account numbers used by the company are as follows:

Cash	*10*	*Automobiles*	*22*
Accounts receivable	*11*	*Notes payable*	*31*
Land	*16*	*Accounts payable*	*32*
Building	*17*	*George Harris, capital*	*50*
Office equipment	*20*		

INSTRUCTIONS

a Journalize the March transactions.

b Post to ledger accounts. Use the running balance form of ledger account.

c Prepare a trial balance at March 31, 19__.

Group B

PROBLEM 2B-1
Recording Transactions in a Journal

In May, James Colby, a physician, decided to open his own medical practice. During May, the new business engaged in the following transactions:

May 4 Colby opened a bank account in the name of his medical practice, James Colby, M.D., by depositing $36,000 cash.

May 16 Purchased a small medical office. The purchase price was $115,400, which included land valued at $50,000 and a building valued at $65,400. A cash down payment was made for $21,000, and a note payable was issued for the balance of the purchase price.

May 19 Purchased office furniture on credit from Modern Office Company, $6,820.

May 22 Purchased medical supplies for cash from Denton Labs, $1,630.

May 23 Returned to Denton Labs $225 of the medical supplies purchased yesterday as these items were not exactly what Colby had ordered. Denton Labs agreed to refund the $225 within 10 days.

May 30 Made an $1,170 partial payment on the account payable to Modern Office Company.

May 31 Received the $225 refund from Denton Labs for the supplies on May 23.

INSTRUCTIONS Prepare journal entries to record the above transactions. Select the appropriate account titles from the following chart of accounts:

Cash	*Land*	*Notes payable*
Accounts receivable	*Building*	*Accounts payable*
Medical supplies	*Office furniture*	*James Colby, capital*

PROBLEM 2B-2
Analyzing Transactions and Preparing Journal Entries

Iris McGill is the founder and owner of Perfect Portraits, a photographic studio. A few of the company's business transactions occurring during July are described below.

1 On July 2, purchased photographic equipment for $2,525, paying $750 in cash and charging the remainder on the company's 30-day account at Camera Supply Company.

2 On July 7, Iris McGill made an additional investment in Perfect Portraits by depositing $5,000 cash in the company bank account.

3 On July 9, returned to Camera Supply Company $400 of photographic equipment that did not work properly. The return of this equipment reduced by $400 the amount owed to Camera Supply Company.

4 On July 25, collected cash of $900 from customers in settlement of accounts receivable.

5 On July 31, paid the remaining $1,375 owed to Camera Supply Company.

INSTRUCTIONS

a Prepare an analysis of each of the above transactions. The form to be used is as follows, using transaction **1** as an example:

1 (a) The asset Photographic Equipment was increased. Increases in assets are recorded by debits. Debit Photographic Equipment, $2,525.

(b) The asset Cash was decreased. Decreases in assets are recorded by credits. Credit Cash, $750. A liability was incurred. Increases in liabilities are recorded by credits. Credit Accounts Payable, $1,775.

b Prepare journal entries, including explanations, for the above transactions.

PROBLEM 2B-3
Preparing a Trial Balance and a Balance Sheet

The ledger accounts of Black Mountain Golf Club at September 30 are shown below in alphabetical order.

Accounts payable	*$ 15,340*	*Lighting equipment*	*$ 52,900*
Accounts receivable	*1,300*	*Maintenance equipment*	*36,500*
Building	*184,200*	*Notes payable*	*390,000*
Robert Jones, capital	*384,060*	*Notes receivable*	*24,000*
Cash	*14,960*	*Office equipment*	*1,420*
Fences	*23,600*	*Office supplies*	*490*
Golf carts	*28,000*	*Sprinkler system*	*50,000*
Land	*375,000*	*Property taxes payable*	*2,970*

INSTRUCTIONS

a Prepare a trial balance with the ledger accounts arranged in the usual financial statement order. Include a proper heading.

b Prepare a balance sheet at September 30, 19__. Include a subtotal showing total liabilities.

PROBLEM 2B-4
Posting to Ledger Accounts; Preparing a Trial Balance and a Balance Sheet

After several seasons of professional tennis competition, Jim Hand had saved enough money to start his own tennis school, to be known as Winners' Tennis College. During July, while organizing the business, Hand prepared the following journal entries to record all July transactions. He has not posted these entries to ledger accounts. The ledger account numbers to be used are: Cash 1, Office Supplies 9, Land 20, Tennis Courts 22, Tennis Equipment 25, Notes Payable 30, Accounts Payable 31, and Jim Hand, Capital 50.

General Journal **Page 1**

July	2	Cash		30,000	
		Jim Hand, Capital			30,000
		Investment in business by owner.			
	3	Land		48,400	
		Tennis Courts		75,000	
		Cash			20,000
		Notes Payable			103,400
		Purchased land and tennis courts.			
	6	Tennis Equipment		1,680	
		Accounts Payable			1,680
		Bought equipment on credit from Rackets, Inc.			
	7	Office Supplies		315	
		Accounts Payable			315
		Bought supplies from Miller Supply.			
	12	Tennis Equipment		725	
		Accounts Payable			725
		Bought equipment on credit from Rackets, Inc.			
	17	Accounts Payable		315	
		Cash			315
		Made payment of liability to Miller Supply.			
	22	Accounts Payable		725	
		Cash			725
		Made payment of liability to Rackets, Inc., for purchase of July 12.			

INSTRUCTIONS

a Post the journal entries to ledger accounts of the three-column running balance form.

b Prepare a trial balance at July 31 from the ledger accounts completed in part **a.**

c Prepare a balance sheet at July 31, 19__.

PROBLEM 2B-5
Preparing Journal Entries, Posting, and Preparing a Trial Balance

Beach Property Management was started on November 1 by Rosa Garcia to provide management services for the owners of apartment buildings. The organizational period extended throughout November and included the transactions listed below.

Nov. 1 Garcia opened a bank account in the name of the business with a deposit of $25,000 cash.

Nov. 4 Purchased land and an office building for a price of $140,000, of which $75,000 was considered applicable to the land and $65,000 attributable to the building. A cash down payment of $20,000 was made and a note payable for $120,000 was issued for the balance of the purchase price.

Nov. 7 Purchased office equipment on credit from Harvard Office Equipment, $5,850.

Nov. 9 A typewriter (cost $490), which was part of the November 7 purchase of office equipment, proved defective and was returned for credit to Harvard Office Equipment.

Nov. 17 Sold one-third of the land acquired on November 4 to Ace Parking Lots at a price of $25,000. This price is equal to Beach Property's cost for this portion of the land, so there is no gain or loss on this transaction.

Beach received a $5,000 cash down payment from Ace Parking Lots and a note receivable in the amount of $20,000, due in four monthly instalments of $5,000 each, beginning on November 30 (ignore interest).

Nov. 28 Paid $1,600 in partial settlement of the liability to Harvard Office Equipment.

Nov. 30 Received cash of $5,000 as partial collection of the note receivable from Ace Parking Lots.

The account titles and account numbers to be used are

Cash	1	*Office equipment*	25
Notes receivable	5	*Notes payable*	31
Land	21	*Accounts payable*	32
Building	23	*Rosa Garcia, capital*	51

INSTRUCTIONS

- **a** Prepare journal entries for the month of November.
- **b** Post to ledger accounts of the three-column running balance form.
- **c** Prepare a trial balance at November 30, 19__.

PROBLEM 2B-6
The Accounting Cycle: a Comprehensive Problem

Community TV was organized in February 1996 to operate as a local television station. The account titles and numbers used by the business are listed below:

Cash	11	*Telecasting equipment*	24
Accounts receivable	15	*Film library*	25
Supplies	19	*Notes payable*	31
Land	21	*Accounts payable*	32
Building	22	*James Ward, capital*	51
Transmitter	23		

The transactions for February were as follows:

Feb. 1 James Ward deposited $400,000 cash in a bank account in the name of the business, Community TV.

Feb. 3 Community TV purchased the land, building, and telecasting equipment previously used by a local television station that had gone bankrupt. The total purchase price was $300,000, of which $100,000 was attributable to the land, $90,000 to the building, and the remainder to the telecasting equipment. The terms of the purchase required a cash payment of $200,000 and the issuance of a note payable for the balance.

Feb. 5 Purchased a transmitter at a cost of $225,000 from AC Manufacturing, making a cash down payment of $75,000. The balance, in the form of a note payable, was to be paid in monthly instalments of $12,500, beginning February 15. (Interest expense is to be ignored.)

Feb. 9 Purchased a film library at a cost of $40,000 from Modern Film Productions, making a down payment of $15,000 cash, with the balance on account payable in 30 days.

Feb. 12 Bought supplies costing $3500, paying cash.

Feb. 15 Paid $12,500 to AC Manufacturing as the first monthly payment on the note payable created on February 5. (Interest expense to be ignored.)

Feb. 25 Sold part of the film library to City College; cost was $9,000 and the selling price also was $9,000. City College agreed to pay the full amount in 30 days.

INSTRUCTIONS

a Prepare journal entries for the month of February.

b Post to ledger accounts of the three-column running balance form.

c Prepare a trial balance at February 29, 1996.

d Prepare a balance sheet at February 29, 1996.

ANALYTICAL AND DECISION PROBLEMS AND CASES

A&D 2-1 Computer-Based Accounting Systems

Bill Gates is planning to create a computer-based accounting system for small businesses. His system will be developed from a data base program and will be suitable for use on personal computers.

The idea underlying data base software is that data needed for a variety of uses is entered into the data base only once. The computer is programmed to arrange this data into any number of desired formats. In the case of Gates's accounting system, the company's accounting personnel must enter the relevant information about each business transaction into the data base. The program that Gates plans to write will then enable the computer operator to have the information arranged by the computer into the formats of (1) journal entries (with written explanations), (2) three-column running balance form ledger accounts, (3) a trial balance, and (4) a balance sheet.

INSTRUCTIONS

a Identify the relevant information about each business transaction that the company's accounting personnel must enter into the data base to enable Gates's program to prepare the four types of accounting records and statements described above.

b As described in this chapter, the accounting cycle includes the steps of (1) analyzing and recording business transactions, (2) posting the debit and credit amounts to ledger accounts, (3) preparing a trial balance, and (4) preparing financial statements (at this stage, only a balance sheet). Indicate which of these functions can be performed automatically by Gates's computer program and which must still be performed by the company's accounting personnel.

A&D 2-2 Preparing Balance Sheets and an Introduction to Measuring Income

Susan Lee, a college student with several summers' experience as a guide on canoe camping trips and with savings of $2,800 from her last summer's earnings of $4,600, decided to go into business for herself. On June 1, Lee organized Birchbark Canoe Trails by depositing $1,600 of personal savings in a bank account in the name of the business. Also on June 1, the business borrowed an additional $3,200 cash from John Lee (Susan's father) by issuing a three-year note payable. To help the business get started, John Lee agreed that no interest would be charged on the loan. The following transactions were also carried out by the business on June 1:

1 Bought a number of canoes at a total cost of $6,200; paid $2,000 cash and agreed to pay the balance within 60 days.

2 Bought camping equipment at a cost of $3,400, payable in 60 days.

3 Bought supplies for cash, $700.

After the close of the season on September 1, Lee asked another student, David Ray, who had taken a course in accounting, to help determine the financial position of the business.

The only record Lee had maintained was a chequebook with memorandum notes written on the cheque stubs. From this source Ray discovered that Lee had invested an additional $1,200 of savings in the business on July 2, and also that the accounts payable arising from the purchase of the canoes and camping equipment had been paid in full. A bank statement received from the bank on September 1 showed a balance on deposit of $2,790.

Lee informed Ray that all cash received by the business had been deposited in the bank and all bills had been paid by cheque immediately upon receipt; consequently, as of September 1 all bills for the season had been paid. However, nothing had been paid on the note payable.

The canoes and camping equipment were all in excellent condition at the end of the season and Lee planned to resume operations the following summer. In fact, she had already accepted reservations from many customers who wished to return.

Ray felt that some consideration should be given to the wear and tear on the canoes and equipment, but he agreed with Lee that for the present purpose the canoes and equipment should be listed in the balance sheet at the original cost. The supplies remaining on hand had cost $50, and Lee felt that these supplies could be used next summer.

Ray suggested that two balance sheets be prepared, one to show the condition of the business on June 1 and the other showing the condition on September 1. He also recommended to Lee that a complete set of accounting records be established.

INSTRUCTIONS

a Use the information in the first paragraph (including the three numbered transactions) as a basis for preparing a balance sheet dated June 1.

b Prepare a balance sheet at September 1. (Because of the incomplete information available, it is not possible to determine the amount of cash at September 1 by adding cash receipts and deducting cash payments throughout the season. The amount on deposit as reported by the bank at September 1 is to be regarded as the total cash belonging to the business at that date.)

c Determine the change in owner's equity and the sources of this change. Explain whether you consider the business to be successful. Also comment on the cash position at the beginning and end of the season.

COMPREHENSIVE PROBLEM 1

LITTLE BEAR RAILROAD, INC.

A REVIEW OF CHAPTERS 1 AND 2

Note to students: This problem includes several issues that will be discussed later in the textbook. A basic purpose of the problem is to have you ***think about situations that you have not seen illustrated and explained.*** Use your best judgment in resolving any questionable issues, and be prepared to ask questions and to voice your opinion if the problem is discussed in class.

For many years Kim-Chung (K-C) Jones has owned and operated Little Bear Railroad, a narrow gauge railroad operating inside a national park. The Little Bear operates for only eight months each year—April 1 through November 30—offering park visitors a 22-kilometre scenic tour of the redwood forest. The train consists of a woodburning locomotive and three passenger cars. Until March 1995, the business had been organized as a sole proprietorship.

In March, prior to opening for the 1995 season, Jones decided to reorganize the business as Little Bear Railroad, Inc., a corporation. The following events occurred as the new corporation was being organized:

Mar. 1 Jones transferred into the new corporation all of the assets and liabilities of Little Bear Railroad, in exchange for which the corporation issued 50,000 shares of capital stock. The business assets and liabilities and their value at March 1 were as follows:

Cash	*$ 48,000*
Accounts receivable	*8,600*
Supplies	*4,900*
Spare parts	*10,400*
Buildings	*170,000*
Equipment & rolling stock	*415,000*
Roadbed, track, & ties	*250,000*
Notes payable (due in 2001)	*300,000*
Accounts payable	*6,900*

In addition to the assets and liabilities listed above, Jones also transferred into the corporation a permanent "right-of-way" allowing the railroad to operate on specific portions of the national park's land. (Notice that the railroad owns no land; the land upon which it operates is part of the national park.) Jones acquired the right-of-way from Parks Canada many years ago at a cost of $100,000. However, this asset was considered to be worth $400,000 at the date that Jones transferred it into the new corporation.

Mar. 4 Jones sold 10% of her capital stock in the corporation to Adrian Wong-Boren, a relative, for $115,000 cash. Jones deposited this money in her personal bank account.

Mar. 10 The corporation borrowed $100,000 cash from Pine City Bank to provide capital for expanding its operations. A note payable was issued, due in 90 days. (Ignore interest charges.)

Mar. 12 Signed an agreement with Jay Gould Construction to build a three-kilometre extension of roadbed and track within company's right-of-way through the park. Work will begin on April 1 and is to be completed by August 15, 1995. The total cost will be $240,000, payable in thirds as each kilometre of track is completed.

Mar. 15 The corporation purchased a replica of an 1865 steam-driven locomotive and an original 1898 dining car from The Spud, a narrow-gauge railroad in Regina that had gone bankrupt. The purchase price was $380,000; Little Bear, Inc., paid $90,000 in cash and issued a note payable for the balance. The note, payable to Yees Trust, is due in one year.

INSTRUCTIONS

a Prepare all general journal entries necessary through March 15 to record these events in the accounting records of the new corporation. (Not all of these events require journal entries.) In your entry on March 1, enter in the accounts of the new corporation the assets invested by Jones, and ***also the liabilities*** (notes payable and accounts payable) that the corporation is assuming. Credit an account entitled ***Capital Stock*** for Jones's ownership equity in the new company.

b Post to ledger accounts of the three-column form. (You are to create the company's ledger by assigning names and numbers to an appropriate number of ledger accounts.)

c Prepare a trial balance at March 15, 1995.

d Prepare a balance sheet at March 15, 1995. Also, draft a note accompanying this balance sheet to disclose the company's contractual commitment to Jay Gould Construction. (Presentation of the shareholders' equity in the balance sheet of a corporation was illustrated in Chapter 1. As this corporation has not yet begun operations, it has no retained earnings; the shareholders' equity consists only of the amount shown as capital stock.)

e Assume that you are a loan officer at Union Bank. Little Bear Railroad, Inc., wants to borrow from your bank the $240,000 to pay for the three-kilometre extension of its track. The corporation intends to repay this loan in one year. Based solely upon the available information, does the corporation appear to be a reasonably good credit risk? Explain the reasons for your conclusion.

CHAPTER

3 Measuring Business Income

In Chapter 3 our coverage of the accounting cycle is expanded to include the measurement of business income. Attention is focused upon the nature of revenue, expenses, net income, and owner's equity. Several important accounting principles are introduced, including the time period principle, the realization (recognition) principle, and the matching principle. The continuing example of Roberts Real Estate Company is used to illustrate the recording of revenue and expense transactions and the preparation of an income statement and a statement of owner's equity. End-of-period ***adjusting entries*** and ***closing procedures*** also are explained and illustrated. Finally the cash and accrual bases of accounting are discussed.

Learning Objectives

After studying this chapter you should be able to:

1. *Explain the nature of net income, revenue, expenses, and the time period principle.*
2. *Apply the realization (recognition) and matching principles in recording revenue and expenses.*
3. *Apply the rules of debit and credit in recording revenue and expenses.*
4. *Define and record depreciation* expense.*
5. *Describe and prepare an income statement and a statement of owner's equity. Explain how these statements relate to the balance sheet.*
6. *Explain the purposes served by closing entries; prepare these entries.*
7. *Describe the sequence of procedures in the accounting cycle.*
8. *Distinguish between the accrual basis and the cash basis of accounting.*

---

* While section 3060 of the *CICA Handbook* uses the term "amortization" to encompass the commonly used terms "depreciation" and "depletion," it indicates that the latter two terms may also be used. In practice, the terms "depreciation" and "depletion" are still most widely used. Also, these two terms are used in the most recent CICA's *Financial Reporting in Canada* (Twentieth Edition, 1993). Accordingly, the terms "depreciation" and "depletion" are used in this text.

WHAT IS NET INCOME?

Jan./99

OBJECTIVE 1 Explain the nature of net income, revenue, expenses, and the time period principle.

In Chapter 1, we stated that a basic objective of every business is to earn a profit, or net income. Why? The answer lies in the very definition of ***net income: an increase in owner's equity resulting from the profitable operation of the business.*** The opposite of net income, a ***decrease*** in owner's equity resulting from unprofitable operation of the business, is termed a ***net loss.***

If you were to organize a business of your own, you would do so with the hope and expectation that the business would produce a net income, thereby increasing your ownership equity. Individuals who invest in the capital stock of a large corporation also expect the business to earn a net income that will increase the value of their investment.

Notice that net income does not consist of cash or any other specific asset. Rather, net income is a ***computation*** of the overall effects of many business transactions upon ***owner's equity.*** The increase in owner's equity resulting from profitable operations usually is accompanied by an increase in total assets, though not necessarily an increase in cash. In some cases, however, an increase in owner's equity is accompanied by a decrease in total liabilities.

Our point is that net income represents an ***increase in owner's equity*** and has no direct relationship to the types or amounts of assets on hand. Consequently even a business earning a net income may run short of cash and become insolvent.

In the balance sheet, the changes in owner's equity resulting from profitable or unprofitable operations are reflected in the balance of the ***owner's capital account.*** The assets of the business organization appear in the ***assets*** section of the balance sheet.

Some of the largest corporations have become large by consistently retaining in the business most of the resources generated by profitable operations.

CASE IN POINT A recent annual report of George Weston Limited shows total owner's equity amounting to nearly $1.2 billion. The owners originally invested only about $141 million—less than 12% of the current equity—in exchange for capital stock. By operating profitably and retaining earnings, George Weston has added more than $1 billion to its ownership equity.

The Income Statement: A Preview

An income statement is a one-page financial statement that summarizes the profitability of the business entity over a specified period of time. In this statement, net income is determined by comparing for the time period: (1) the ***sales price*** of the goods sold and services rendered by the business with (2) the ***cost*** to the business of the goods and services used up in business operations. The technical accounting terms for these components of net income are ***revenue*** and ***expenses.*** Therefore, accountants say that ***net income*** is equal to ***revenue minus expenses,*** as shown in the following income statement.

Income statement for October

ROBERTS REAL ESTATE COMPANY
Income Statement
For the Month Ended October 31, 19__

Revenue:		
Sales commissions earned		*$12,290*
Expenses:		
Advertising expense	*$ 1,680*	
Salaries expense	*7,700*	
Telephone expense	*144*	
Depreciation expense: building	*150*	
Depreciation expense: office equipment	*45*	*9,719*
Net income		*$ 2,571*

When we measure the net income earned by a business we are measuring its economic performance—its success or failure as a business enterprise. The owner, managers, and major creditors are anxious to see the latest available income statement and thereby judge how well the company is doing. If the business is organized as a corporation, the shareholders and prospective investors also will be keenly interested in each successive income statement.

Later in this chapter we will show how this income statement is developed from the accounting records of Roberts Real Estate Company. For the moment, however, this illustration will assist us in discussing some of the basic concepts involved in measuring business income.

Income Must Be Related to a Specified Period of Time Notice that our sample income statement covers a ***period*** of time—namely, the month of October. A balance sheet shows the financial position of a business at a ***particular date.*** An income statement, on the other hand, shows the results of business operations over a span of time. We cannot evaluate net income unless it is associated with a specific time period. For example, if an executive says, "My business earns a net income of $10,000," the profitability of the business is unclear. Does it earn $10,000 per week, per month, or per year?

CASE IN POINT The late J. Paul Getty, one of the world's first billionaires, was once interviewed by a group of business students. One of the students asked Getty to estimate the amount of his income. As the student had not specified a time period, Getty decided to have some fun with his audience and responded, "About $11,000 . . . " He paused long enough to allow the group to express surprise over this seemingly low amount and then completed his sentence, " . . . an hour." Incidentally, $11,000 per hour (24 hours per day) amounts to about $100 million per year.

Accounting Periods The period of time covered by an income statement is termed the company's ***accounting period.*** To provide the users of financial statements with timely information, net income is measured for relatively short accounting periods of equal length. This concept, called the

time period principle, is one of the generally accepted accounting principles that guide the interpretation of financial events and the preparation of financial statements.

The length of a company's accounting period depends upon how frequently managers, investors, and other interested people require information about the company's performance. Every business prepares annual income statements, and most businesses prepare quarterly and monthly income statements as well. (Quarterly statements cover a three-month period and are prepared by all large corporations for distribution to their shareholders.)

The 12-month accounting period used by an entity is called its ***fiscal year.*** The fiscal year used by most companies coincides with the calendar year and ends on December 31. Some businesses, however, elect to use a fiscal year that ends on some other date. It may be convenient for a business to end its fiscal year during a slack season rather than during a time of peak activity.

CASE IN POINT Walt Disney Company ends its fiscal year on September 30. Why? One reason is that September and October are relatively slow months at Disney's theme parks; another is that September financial statements provide timely information about the preceding summer, which is the company's busiest season.

As another example, many department stores, including The Bay, K mart, F. W. Woolworth, and Zellers end their fiscal years on January 31—after the rush of the holiday season.

Let us now explore the meaning of the accounting terms ***revenue*** and ***expenses.***

Revenue

Revenue is the price of goods sold and services rendered during a given accounting period. Earning revenue causes owner's equity to increase. When a business renders services or sells merchandise to its customers, it usually receives cash or acquires an account receivable from the customer. The inflow of cash and receivables from customers increases the total assets of the company. On the other side of the accounting equation, the liabilities do not change, but owner's equity increases to match the increase in total assets. Thus revenue is the ***gross increase in owner's equity*** resulting from operation of the business.

Various terms are used to describe different types of revenue; for example, the revenue earned by a real estate broker might be called ***Sales Commissions Earned,*** or alternatively, ***Commissions Revenue.*** In the professional practice of lawyers, physicians, dentists, and public accountants, the revenue is called ***Fees Earned.*** A business that sells merchandise rather than services will use the term ***Sales*** to describe the revenue earned. Another type of revenue is ***Interest Earned,*** which means the amount received as interest on notes receivable, bank deposits, government bonds, or other securities.

When to Record Revenue: The Realization (Recognition) Principle When is revenue recorded in the accounting records? For example, assume that on May 24, a real estate company signs a contract to represent a client in selling the client's personal residence. The contract entitles the real estate company to a commission equal to 6% of the selling price, due 30 days after the date of sale. On June 10, the real estate company sells the house at a price of $100,000, thereby earning a $6,000 commission ($100,000 × 6%), to be received on July 10. When should the company recognize this $6,000 commission revenue—in May, June, or July?

OBJECTIVE 2 ***Apply the realization (recognition) and matching principles in recording revenue and expenses.***

The company should recognize this revenue on June 10—the day it ***rendered the service*** of selling the client's house. As the company will not collect this commission until July, it must also record an account receivable on June 10. In July, when this receivable is collected, the company must not record revenue a second time. Collecting an account receivable increases one asset, Cash, and decreases another asset, Accounts Receivable. Thus, collecting an account receivable ***does not increase owner's equity*** and does not represent revenue.

Our answer illustrates a generally accepted accounting principle called the ***realization (recognition) principle.*** This principle states that a business should recognize revenue at the time ***services are rendered to customers*** or ***goods sold are delivered to customers.***[1] In short, revenue is recorded when it is ***earned,*** without regard as to when the cash is received.

Expenses

Expenses are the costs of the goods and services used up in the process of earning revenue. Incurring an expense causes a ***decrease in owner's equity.*** The related changes in the accounting equation can be either (1) a decrease in assets or (2) an increase in liabilities. An expense reduces assets if payment occurs at the time that the expense is incurred (or if payment has been made in advance). If the expense will not be paid until later, as, for example, the purchase of advertising services on account, the recording of the expense will be accompanied by an increase in liabilities.

Examples include the cost of employees' salaries, advertising, rent, utilities, and the gradual wearing-out (depreciation) of such assets as buildings, automobiles, and office equipment. All these costs are necessary to attract and serve customers and thereby earn revenue. Expenses are often called the "costs of doing business," that is, the cost of the various activities necessary to carry on a business.

When to Record Expenses: The Matching Principle A significant relationship exists between revenue and expenses. Expenses are incurred for the ***purpose of producing revenue.*** In measuring net income for a period, revenue should be offset by ***all the expenses incurred in producing that revenue.*** This concept of offsetting expenses against revenue on a basis of "cause and effect" is called the ***matching principle.***

---

[1] CICA, *CICA Handbook* (Toronto), Section 3400.06–.08, 3400.11.

Timing is an important factor in matching (offsetting) revenue with the related expenses. For example, in preparing monthly income statements, it is important to offset this month's expenses against this month's revenue. We should not offset this month's expenses against last month's revenue, because there is no cause and effect relationship between the two.

To illustrate the matching principle, assume that the salaries earned by sales personnel serving customers during July are not paid until early August. In which month should these salaries be regarded as an expense? The answer is ***July,*** because this is the month in which the sales personnel's services ***helped to produce revenue.***

We previously explained that revenue and cash receipts are not one and the same thing. Similarly, expenses and cash payments are not identical. The cash payment for an expense may occur before, after, or in the same period that an expense helps to produce revenue. In deciding when to record an expense, the critical question is ***"In what period will this expenditure help to produce revenue?"*** not "When will the cash payment occur?"

Expenditures Benefiting More Than One Accounting Period Many expenditures made by a business benefit two or more accounting periods. Fire insurance policies, for example, usually cover a period of 12 months. If a company prepares monthly income statements, a portion of the cost of such a policy should be allocated to insurance expense each month that the policy is in force. In this case, apportionment of the cost of the policy by months is an easy matter. If the 12-month policy costs $2,400 for example, the insurance expense for each month amounts to $200 ($2,400 ÷ 12 months).

Not all transactions can be so precisely divided by accounting periods. The purchase of a building, furniture and fixtures, machinery, a typewriter, or an automobile provides benefits to the business over all the years in which such an asset is used. No one can determine in advance exactly how many years of service will be received from such long-lived assets. Nevertheless, in measuring the net income of a business for a period of one year or less, the accountant must ***estimate*** what portion of the cost of the building and other long-lived assets is applicable to the current year. Since the allocations of these costs are estimates rather than precise measurements, it follows that income statements should be regarded as useful ***approximations*** of net income rather than as absolutely exact measurements.

For some expenditures, such as those for advertising or employee training programs, it is not possible to estimate objectively the number of accounting periods over which revenue is likely to be produced. In such cases, generally accepted accounting principles require that the expenditure be charged ***immediately to expense.*** This treatment is based upon the accounting principle of ***objectivity*** and the concept of ***conservatism.*** Accountants require ***objective evidence*** that an expenditure will produce revenue in future periods before they will view the expenditure as creating an asset. When this objective evidence does not exist, they follow the conservative practice of recording the expenditure as an expense. ***Conservatism,*** in this context, means applying the accounting treatment that results in the ***lowest*** (most conservative) estimate of net income for the current period.

Debit and Credit Rules for Revenue and Expense

OBJECTIVE 3 Apply the rules of debit and credit in recording revenue and expenses.

We have stressed that revenue increases owner's equity and that expenses decrease owner's equity. The debit and credit rules for recording revenue and expenses in the ledger accounts are a natural extension of the rules for recording changes in owner's equity. The rules previously stated for recording increases and decreases in owner's equity were as follows:

- ***Increases*** in owner's equity are recorded by ***credits.***
- ***Decreases*** in owner's equity are recorded by ***debits.***

This rule is now extended to cover revenue and expense accounts:

- Revenue ***increases*** owner's equity; therefore revenue is recorded by a ***credit.***
- Expenses ***decrease*** owner's equity; therefore expenses are recorded by ***debits.***

Ledger Accounts for Revenue and Expenses

During the course of an accounting period, a great many revenue and expense transactions occur in the average business. To classify and summarize these numerous transactions, a separate ledger account is maintained for each major type of revenue and expense. For example, almost every business maintains accounts for advertising expense, telephone expense, and salaries expense. At the end of the period, all the advertising expenses appear as debits in the Advertising Expense account. The debit balance of this account represents the total advertising expense of the period and is listed as one of the expense items in the income statement.

Revenue accounts are usually much less numerous than expense accounts. A small business such as Roberts Real Estate Company in our continuing illustration may have only one or two types of revenue, such as commissions earned from arranging sales of real estate, and fees earned from managing properties on behalf of clients. In a business of this type, the revenue accounts might be called Sales Commissions Earned and Management Fees Earned.

Investments and Withdrawals by the Owner

The owner of an unincorporated business may at any time invest assets or withdraw assets from the business. These "investment transactions" cause changes in the amount of owner's equity, but they are ***not*** considered revenue or expenses of the business.

Investments of assets by the owner are recorded by debiting the asset accounts and crediting the owner's capital account. This transaction is not viewed as revenue, because the business has not sold any merchandise or rendered any service in exchange for the assets received.

The income statement of a sole proprietorship does not include any salary expense representing the managerial services rendered by the owner. One reason for not including a salary to the owner-manager is that individuals in such positions are able to set their salaries at any amount they choose. The use of an unrealistic salary to the proprietor would tend to destroy the usefulness of the income statement for measuring the profitability of the business. Thus, accountants regard the owner-manager as working to earn the ***entire net income*** of the business, rather than as working for a salary.

Even though the owner does not technically receive a salary, he or she usually makes withdrawals of cash from time to time for personal use. These withdrawals reduce the assets and owner's equity of the business, but they are ***not*** expenses. Expenses are incurred for the purpose of ***generating revenue,*** and withdrawals by the owner do not have this purpose.

Withdrawals could be recorded by debiting the owner's capital account. However, a clearer record is created if a separate Drawing account is debited. (In our Roberts Real Estate Company example, we will use an account entitled ***James Roberts, Drawing*** to record withdrawals by the owner.)

Debits to the owner's drawing account result from such transactions as:

1 Withdrawals of cash.
2 Withdrawals of other assets. The owner of a clothing store, for example, may withdraw merchandise for his or her personal use. The amount of the debit to the drawing account would be for the cost of the goods that were withdrawn.
3 Payment of the owner's personal bills out of company funds.

As investments and withdrawals by the owner are not classified as revenue and expenses, they are not included in the income statement. Instead, they are summarized in the statement of owner's equity, which will be discussed later in this chapter.

Recording Revenue and Expense Transactions: An Illustration

The organization of Roberts Real Estate Company during September has already been described. The illustration is now continued for October, during which the company earned commissions by selling several residences for its clients. Bear in mind that the company does not own any residential property; it merely acts as a broker or an agent for clients wishing to sell their houses. A commission of 6% of the sales price of the house is charged for this service. During October the company not only earned commissions but also incurred a number of expenses.

Note that each illustrated transaction that affects an income statement account also affects a balance sheet account. This pattern is consistent with our previous discussion of revenue and expenses. In recording revenue transactions, we debit the assets received and credit a revenue account. In recording expense transactions, we debit an expense account and credit the asset Cash, or a liability account if payment is to be made later. The transactions for October were as follows:

Oct. 1 Paid $360 for publication of newspaper advertising describing various houses offered for sale.

Advertising expense incurred and paid

Analysis	Rule	Entry
The cost of advertising is an expense	*Expenses decrease the owner's equity and are recorded by debits*	*Debit: Advertising Expense, $360*
The asset Cash was decreased	*Decreases in assets are recorded by credits*	*Credit: Cash, $360*

Oct. 6 Earned and collected a commission of $3,900 by selling a residence previously listed by a client.

Revenue earned and collected

Analysis	Rule	Entry
The asset Cash was increased	*Increases in assets are recorded by debits*	*Debit: Cash, $3,900*
Revenue was earned	*Revenue increases the owner's equity and is recorded by a credit*	*Credit: Sales Commissions Earned, $3,900*

Oct. 16 Television advertising was purchased at a price of $1,320, payment to be made within 30 days.

Advertising expense incurred; to be paid later

Analysis	Rule	Entry
The cost of advertising is an expense	*Expenses decrease the owner's equity and are recorded by debits*	*Debit: Advertising Expense, $1,320*
An account payable, a liability, was incurred	*Increases in liabilities are recorded by credits*	*Credit: Accounts Payable, $1,320*

Oct. 20 A commission of $8,390 was earned by selling a client's residence. The sales agreement provided that the commission would be received in 60 days.

Revenue earned; to be collected later

Analysis	Rule	Entry
An asset in the form of an account receivable was acquired	*Increases in assets are recorded by debits*	*Debit: Accounts Receivable, $8,390*
Revenue was earned	*Revenue increases the owner's equity and is recorded by a credit*	*Credit: Sales Commissions Earned, $8,390*

Oct. 25 Roberts withdrew $2,800 for personal use.

Withdrawal of cash by the owner

Analysis	Rule	Entry
Withdrawal of assets by the owner decreases the owner's equity	*Decreases in owner's equity are recorded by debits*	*Debit: James Roberts, Drawing, $2,800*
The asset Cash was decreased	*Decreases in assets are recorded by credits*	*Credit: Cash, $2,800*

Oct. 30 Roberts found that he did not need all of the $2,800 withdrawn on October 25, and he redeposited $1,000 of this amount in the company's bank account.

Additional investment by the owner

Analysis	Rule	Entry
The asset Cash was increased	*Increases in assets are recorded by debits*	*Debit: Cash, $1,000*
The owner's equity was increased	*Increases in owner's equity are recorded by credits*	*Credit: James Roberts, Capital, $1,000*

Oct. 31 Paid salaries of $7,700 to employees for services rendered during October.

Salaries expense incurred and paid

Analysis	Rule	Entry
Salaries of employees are an expense	*Expenses decrease the owner's equity and are recorded by debits*	*Debit: Salaries Expense, $7,700*
The asset Cash was decreased	*Decreases in assets are recorded by credits*	*Credit: Cash, $7,700*

Oct. 31 A telephone bill for October amounting to $144 was received. Payment was required by November 10.

Telephone expense incurred; to be paid later

Analysis	Rule	Entry
The cost of telephone service is an expense	*Expenses decrease the owner's equity and are recorded by debits*	*Debit: Telephone Expense, $144*
An account payable, a liability, was incurred	*Increases in liabilities are recorded by credits*	*Credit: Accounts Payable, $144*

The journal entries to record the October transactions are as follows:

October journal entries for Roberts Real Estate Company

General Journal — **Page 2**

Date		Account Titles and Explanation	LP	Debit	Credit
19__					
Oct	1	Advertising Expense	70	360	
		Cash	1		360
		Paid for newspaper advertising.			
	6	Cash	1	3,900	
		Sales Commissions Earned	60		3,900
		Earned and collected commission by selling residence for client.			
	16	Advertising Expense	70	1,320	
		Accounts Payable	32		1,320
		Purchased television advertising; payable in 30 days.			
	20	Accounts Receivable	4	8,390	
		Sales Commissions Earned	60		8,390
		Earned commission by selling residence for client; commission to be received in 60 days.			
	25	James Roberts, Drawing	51	2,800	
		Cash	1		2,800
		Withdrawal of cash by owner.			
	30	Cash	1	1,000	
		James Roberts, Capital	50		1,000
		Additional investment by owner.			
	31	Salaries Expense	72	7,700	
		Cash	1		7,700
		Paid salaries for October.			
	31	Telephone Expense	74	144	
		Accounts Payable	32		144
		To record liability for October telephone service.			

The column headings at the top of the illustrated journal page (***Date, Account Titles and Explanation, LP, Debit,*** and ***Credit***) are seldom used in practice. They are included here as an instructional guide but will be omitted from some of the later illustrations of journal entries.

The Ledger

The ledger of Roberts Real Estate Company after the October transactions have been posted is now illustrated. To conserve space in this illustration, several ledger accounts appear on a single page; in actual practice, however, each account occupies a separate page in the ledger.

Cash						Account No. 1
Date		Explanation	Ref	Debit	Credit	Balance
19—						
Sept	1		1	180000		180000
	3		1		141000	39000
	5		1		15000	24000
	20		1	1500		25500
	30		1		3000	22500
Oct	1		2		360	22140
	6		2	3900		26040
	25		2		2800	23240
	30		2	1000		24240
	31		2		7700	16540

Accounts Receivable						Account No. 4
Date		Explanation	Ref	Debit	Credit	Balance
19—						
Sept	10		1	11000		11000
	20		1		1500	9500
Oct	20		2	8390		17890

Land						Account No. 20
Date		Explanation	Ref	Debit	Credit	Balance
19—						
Sept	3		1	141000		141000
	10		1		11000	130000

Building						Account No. 22
Date		Explanation	Ref	Debit	Credit	Balance
19—						
Sept	5		1	36000		36000

Office Equipment — Account No. 25

Date		Explanation	Ref	Debit	Credit	Balance
19 —						
Sept.	14		1	5400		5400

Accounts Payable — Account No. 32

Date		Explanation	Ref	Debit	Credit	Balance
19 —						
Sept.	5		1		21000	21000
	14		1		5400	26400
	30		1	3000		23400
Oct.	16		2		1320	24720
	31		2		144	24864

James Roberts, Capital — Account No. 50

Date		Explanation	Ref	Debit	Credit	Balance
19 —						
Sept.	1		1		180000	180000
Oct	30		2		1000	181000

James Roberts, Drawing — Account No. 51

Date		Explanation	Ref	Debit	Credit	Balance
19 —						
Oct	25		2	2800		2800

Sales Commissions Earned						Account No. 60
Date		Explanation	Ref	Debit	Credit	Balance
19—						
Oct	6		2		3900	3900
	20		2		8390	12290

Advertising Expense						Account No. 70
Date		Explanation	Ref	Debit	Credit	Balance
19—						
Oct	1		2	360		360
	16		2	1320		1680

Salaries Expense						Account No. 72
Date		Explanation	Ref	Debit	Credit	Balance
19—						
Oct	31		2	7700		7700

Telephone Expense						Account No. 74
Date		Explanation	Ref	Debit	Credit	Balance
19—						
Oct	31		2	144		144

The accounts in this illustration are listed in ***financial statement order***—that is, balance sheet accounts first (assets, liabilities, and owner's equity), followed by income statement accounts. The sequence of accounts within the balance sheet categories was discussed in Chapter 2. Within the categories of revenue and expense, accounts may be listed in any order.

The Trial Balance

A trial balance prepared from the ledger accounts of Roberts Real Estate Company is shown below:

Proving the equality of debits and credits

ROBERTS REAL ESTATE COMPANY
Trial Balance
October 31, 19__

Cash	$ 16,540	
Accounts receivable	17,890	
Land	130,000	
Building	36,000	
Office equipment	5,400	
Accounts payable		$ 24,864
James Roberts, capital		181,000
James Roberts, drawing	2,800	
Sales commissions earned		12,290
Advertising expense	1,680	
Salaries expense	7,700	
Telephone expense	144	
	$218,154	$218,154

This trial balance proves the equality of the debit and credit entries in the company's ledger. Notice that the trial balance contains income statement accounts as well as balance sheet accounts.

ADJUSTING ENTRIES: THE NEXT STEP IN THE ACCOUNTING CYCLE

Many transactions affect the revenue or expenses of two or more accounting periods. For example, a business may purchase equipment that will last for many years, insurance policies that cover 12 months, or enough office supplies to last for several months. Each of these assets is gradually used up—that is, becomes expense. How do accountants allocate the cost of these assets to expense over a span of several accounting periods? The answer is ***adjusting entries.***

Adjusting entries are made at the end of each accounting period so that the information in the financial statements will be accurate and complete. There are several different types of adjusting entries; in fact, many businesses make a dozen or more adjusting entries at the end of every accounting period. In this chapter, we introduce the concept of end-of-period adjustments with the entry to record ***depreciation expense.*** This is the most common of all adjusting entries; every business that owns a building or equipment must record depreciation expense at the end of each accounting period. In the next chapter, adjusting entries will be shown for some other items in addition to depreciation.

OBJECTIVE 4 Define and record depreciation expense.

Depreciation Expense Our definition of expense is the cost of goods and services used up in the process of earning revenue. Buildings and equipment are examples of goods that are purchased in advance but that are used up gradually over many accounting periods. Each year a portion of the usefulness of these assets expires, and a portion of their total cost should be recognized as ***depreciation expense.*** The term ***depreciation*** means the ***systematic allocation of the cost of an asset to expense*** over the accounting periods making up the asset's useful life.

Although depreciation expense occurs each month, it does not involve monthly transactions. Thus, adjusting entries are needed at the end of each accounting period to record the appropriate amount of depreciation expense. Failure to make these adjusting entries would result in understating the expenses of the period and consequently overstating net income.

Building The office building purchased by Roberts Real Estate Company at a cost of $36,000 is estimated to have a useful life of 20 years. The purpose of the $36,000 expenditure was to provide a place in which to carry on the business and thereby to obtain revenue. After 20 years of use the building is expected to be worthless and the original cost of $36,000 will have been entirely consumed. In effect, the company has purchased 20 years of "housing services" at a total cost of $36,000. A portion of this cost expires during each year of use of the building. If we assume that each year's operations should bear an equal share of the total cost (straight-line depreciation), the annual depreciation expense will amount to $\frac{1}{20}$ of $36,000, or $1,800. On a monthly basis, depreciation expense is $150 ($36,000 cost ÷ 240 months). There are alternative methods of spreading the cost of a depreciable asset over its useful life, some of which will be considered in Chapter 10.

The journal entry to record depreciation of the building during October follows:

Recording depreciation of the building

General Journal *Page 2*

Date		Account Titles and Explanation	LP	Debit	Credit
19__					
Oct	31	Depreciation Expense: Building	76	150	
		Accumulated Depreciation: Building	23		150
		To record depreciation for October. Cost of $36,000 ÷ 240 months = $150 a month.			

The depreciation expense account will appear in the income statement for October along with the other expenses of salaries, advertising, and telephone. The Accumulated Depreciation: Building account will appear in the balance sheet as a deduction from the Building account, as shown by the following illustration of a partial balance sheet:

ROBERTS REAL ESTATE COMPANY
Partial Balance Sheet
October 31, 19__

Showing accumulated depreciation in the balance sheet

Building (at cost)	*$36,000*	
Less: Accumulated depreciation	*150*	*$35,850*

The end result of crediting the Accumulated Depreciation: Building account is much the same as if the credit had been made to the Building account; that is, the net amount shown on the balance sheet for the building is reduced from $36,000 to $35,850. Although the credit side of a depreciation entry ***could*** be made directly to the asset account, it is customary and more efficient to record such credits in a separate account entitled Accumulated Depreciation. The original cost of the asset and the total amount of depreciation recorded over the years can more easily be determined from the ledger when separate accounts are maintained for the asset and for the accumulated depreciation.

Accumulated Depreciation: Building is an example of a ***contra-asset account,*** because it has a credit balance and is offset against an asset account (Building) to produce the proper balance sheet amount for the asset.

Office Equipment Depreciation on the office equipment of Roberts Real Estate Company must also be recorded at the end of October. This equipment cost $5,400 and is assumed to have a useful life of 10 years. Monthly depreciation expense on the straight-line basis is, therefore, $45, computed by dividing the cost of $5,400 by the useful life of 120 months. The journal entry is as follows:

Recording depreciation of office equipment

General Journal — *Page 2*

Date		Account Titles and Explanation	LP	Debit	Credit
19__					
Oct	31	Depreciation Expense: Office Equipment	78	45	
		Accumulated Depreciation: Office Equipment	26		45
		To record depreciation for October. Cost of $5,400 ÷ 120 months = $45 a month.			

No depreciation was recorded on the building and office equipment for September, the month in which these assets were acquired, because regular operations did not begin until October. Generally, depreciation is not recognized until the business begins active operation and the assets are ***placed in use.***

The Adjusted Trial Balance

After all the necessary adjusting entries have been journalized and posted, an ***adjusted trial balance*** is prepared to prove that the ledger is still in balance. It also provides a complete listing of the account balances to be used in preparing the financial statements. The following adjusted trial balance differs from the trial balance shown on page 114 because it includes accounts for depreciation expense and accumulated depreciation.

Adjusted trial balance

ROBERTS REAL ESTATE COMPANY
Adjusted Trial Balance
October 31, 19__

Cash	$ 16,540	
Accounts receivable	17,890	
Land	130,000	
Building	36,000	
Accumulated depreciation: building		$ 150
Office equipment	5,400	
Accumulated depreciation: office equipment		45
Accounts payable		24,864
James Roberts, capital		181,000
James Roberts, drawing	2,800	
Sales commissions earned		12,290
Advertising expense	1,680	
Salaries expense	7,700	
Telephone expense	144	
Depreciation expense: building	150	
Depreciation expense: office equipment	45	
	$218,349	$218,349

PREPARING A "SET" OF FINANCIAL STATEMENTS

Now that Roberts Real Estate Company has been operating for a month, managers and outside parties will want to know more about the company than just its financial position. They will want to know the results of operations—whether the month's activities have been profitable or unprofitable. To provide this additional information, we will prepare a more complete set of financial statements, consisting of an income statement, a statement of owner's equity, and a balance sheet.[2] These statements are illustrated on page 118.

The Income Statement

OBJECTIVE 5 Describe and prepare an income statement and a statement of owner's equity. Explain how these statements relate to the balance sheet.

The revenue and expenses shown in the income statement are taken directly from the company's adjusted trial balance. The income statement of Roberts Real Estate Company shows that revenue earned in October exceeded the expenses of the month, thus producing a net income of $2,571. Bear in mind, however, that our measurement of net income is not absolutely accurate or precise, because of the assumptions and estimates in the accounting process.

An income statement has certain limitations. Remember that the amounts shown for depreciation expense are based upon ***estimates*** of the useful lives of the company's building and office equipment. Also, the income statement includes only those events that have been ***evidenced by business transactions.*** Perhaps during October, Roberts Real Estate Company has made contact with many people who are right on the verge of buying or selling homes. Good business contacts are an important step

[2] A complete set of financial statements also includes a ***statement of changes in financial position,*** which will be discussed in Chapter 19.

ROBERTS REAL ESTATE COMPANY
Income Statement
For the Month Ended October 31, 19__

Revenue:		
Sales commissions earned		$12,290
Expenses:		
Advertising expense	$1,680	
Salaries expense	7,700	
Telephone expense	144	
Depreciation expense: building	150	
Depreciation expense: office equipment	45	9,719
Net income		$ 2,571

Net income is an increase in owner's equity

ROBERTS REAL ESTATE COMPANY
Statement of Owner's Equity
For the Month Ended October 31, 19__

James Roberts, capital, Sept. 30, 19__	$180,000
Add: Net income for October	2,571
Additional investment by owner	1,000
Subtotal	$183,571
Less: Withdrawals by owner	2,800
James Roberts, capital, Oct. 31, 19__	$180,771

The ending balance of owner's equity appears in the balance sheet

ROBERTS REAL ESTATE COMPANY
Balance Sheet
October 31, 19__

Assets

Cash		$ 16,540
Accounts receivable		17,890
Land		130,000
Building	$36,000	
Less: Accumulated depreciation	150	35,850
Office equipment	$ 5,400	
Less: Accumulated depreciation	45	5,355
Total assets		$205,635

Liabilities & Owner's Equity

Liabilities	
Accounts payable	$ 24,864
Owner's equity:	
James Roberts, capital, Oct. 31, 19__	180,771
Total liabilities & owner's equity	$205,635

toward profitable operations. However, such contacts are not reflected in the income statement because their value cannot be measured ***objectively*** until actual transactions take place. Despite these limitations, the income statement is of vital importance and indicates that the new business has been profitable during its first month of operation.

Alternative titles for the income statement include ***statement of earnings, statement of operations,*** and ***profit and loss statement.*** However, ***income statement*** is one of the two most popular terms for this important financial statement.[3] In summary, we can say that an income statement is used to summarize the ***operating results*** of a business by matching the revenue earned during a given time period with the expenses incurred in obtaining that revenue.

The Statement of Owner's Equity

This financial statement summarizes the increases and decreases during the accounting period in the amount of owner's equity. Increases result from earning net income and from additional investments by the owner; decreases result from net losses and from withdrawals of assets by the owner.

The owner's equity at the beginning of the period ($180,000) may be obtained from the ledger or from the balance sheet of the preceding period. As we have just illustrated, the amount of net income or net loss for the period is determined in the company's ***income statement.*** Additional investments by the owner may be determined by reviewing the credit column of the owner's capital account in the ledger. Withdrawals during the period are indicated by the balance in the owner's drawing account. By adjusting the beginning amount of owner's equity for the increases and decreases occurring during the period, we are able to determine the owner's equity at the end of the period. This amount, ***$180,771*** in our example, will also appear in the company's October 31 balance sheet.

The Balance Sheet

The balance sheet lists the amounts of the company's assets, liabilities, and owner's equity at the ***end*** of the accounting period. The balances of the asset and liability accounts are taken directly from the adjusted trial balance on page 117. The amount of owner's equity at the end of the period, $180,771, was determined in the ***statement of owner's equity.***

Previous illustrations of balance sheets have been arranged in ***account form***—that is, with assets on the left and liabilities and owner's equity on the right. The illustration on page 118 is arranged in ***report form,*** with the liabilities and owner's equity sections listed below rather than to the right of the asset section. Both the account form and the report form of balance sheet are widely used, with the latter being far more popular.[4]

Relationship among the Financial Statements

A set of financial statements becomes easier to understand if we recognize that the income statement, statement of owner's equity, and balance sheet

---

[3] CICA, *Financial Reporting in Canada,* Twentieth Edition (Toronto, 1993), p. 150.

[4] Ibid., p. 85.

all are related to one another. These relationships are emphasized by the arrows in the right-hand margin of our illustration on page 118.

The balance sheet prepared at the end of the preceding period and the one prepared at the end of the current period each show the amount of owner's equity at the respective balance sheet dates. The statement of owner's equity summarizes the changes in owner's equity occurring between these two balance sheet dates. The income statement provides a detailed explanation of the most important change in owner's equity—the amount of net income or net loss for the accounting period. Thus, the income statement and the statement of owner's equity explain the change in the amount of owner's equity shown in successive balance sheets.

CLOSING THE TEMPORARY ACCOUNTS

OBJECTIVE 6 Explain the purposes served by closing entries; prepare these entries.

As previously stated, revenue increases owner's equity, and expenses and withdrawals by the owner decrease owner's equity. If the only financial statement that we needed was a balance sheet, these changes in owner's equity could be recorded directly in the owner's capital account. However, owners, managers, investors, and others need to know amounts of specific revenues and expenses, and the amount of net income earned in the period. Therefore, we maintain separate ledger accounts to measure each type of revenue and expense, and the owner's drawings.

These revenue, expense, and drawing accounts are called ***temporary*** accounts, or ***nominal*** accounts, because they accumulate the transactions of ***only one accounting period.*** At the end of this accounting period, the changes in owner's equity accumulated in these temporary accounts are transferred into the owner's capital account, through a temporary clearing account called ***Income Summary.*** This process serves two purposes. First, it ***updates the balance of the owner's capital account*** for changes in owner's equity occurring during the accounting period. Second, it ***returns the balances of the temporary accounts to zero,*** so that they are ready for measuring the revenue, expenses, and drawings of the next accounting period.

The owner's capital account and other balance sheet accounts are called ***permanent*** or ***real*** accounts, because their balances continue to exist beyond the current accounting period. The process of transferring the balances of the temporary accounts into the owner's permanent capital account is called ***closing*** the accounts. The journal entries made for the purpose of closing the temporary accounts are called ***closing entries.***

It is common practice to close the accounts only once a year, but for illustration, we will now demonstrate the closing of the accounts of Roberts Real Estate Company at October 31 after one month's operation.

Closing Entries for Revenue Accounts

Revenue accounts have credit balances. Closing a revenue account, therefore, means transferring its credit balance to the Income Summary account. This transfer is accomplished by a journal entry debiting the revenue account in an amount equal to its credit balance, with an offsetting credit to the Income Summary account. The debit portion of this closing entry returns the balance of the revenue account to zero; the credit portion transfers the former balance of the revenue account into the Income Summary account. The only revenue account of Roberts Real Estate Company is Sales Commissions Earned, which had a credit balance of $12,290 at October 31. The closing entry is as follows:

Closing a revenue account

General Journal					Page 3
Date		**Account Titles and Explanation**	**LP**	**Debit**	**Credit**
19__					
Oct	31	Sales Commissions Earned.............	60	12,290	
		Income Summary.................	53		12,290
		To close the Sales Commissions Earned account.			

After this closing entry has been posted, the two accounts affected will appear as follows. A few details of account structure have been omitted to simplify the illustration; a directional arrow has been added to show the transfer of the $12,290 balance of the revenue account into the Income Summary account.

Sales Commissions Earned 60

Date		Exp.	Ref	Debit	Credit	Balance
Oct	6		2		3,900	3,900
	20		2		8,390	12,290
	31	To close	3	12,290		-0-

Income Summary 53

Date		Exp.	Ref	Debit	Credit	Balance
Oct	31		3		12,290	12,290

Closing Entries for Expense Accounts

Expense accounts have debit balances. Closing an expense account means transferring its debit balance to the Income Summary account. The journal entry to close an expense account, therefore, consists of a credit to the expense account in an amount equal to its debit balance, with an offsetting debit to the Income Summary account.

There are five expense accounts in the ledger of Roberts Real Estate Company. Five separate journal entries could be made to close these five expense accounts, but the use of one ***compound journal entry*** is an easier, time-saving method of closing all five expense accounts. A compound journal entry is an entry that includes debits to more than one account or credits to more than one account.

Closing the various expense accounts by use of a compound journal entry

General Journal					Page 3
Date		**Account Titles and Explanation**	**LP**	**Debit**	**Credit**
19__					
Oct	31	Income Summary......................	53	9,719	
		Advertising Expense...............	70		1,680
		Salaries Expense..................	72		7,700
		Telephone Expense.................	74		144
		Depreciation Expense: Building.....	76		150
		Depreciation Expense: Office Equipment.........................	78		45
		To close the expense accounts.			

After this closing entry has been posted, the Income Summary account has a credit balance of $2,571, and the five expense accounts have zero balances, as shown on the following page.

Closing the Income Summary Account

The five expense accounts have now been closed and the total amount of $9,719 formerly contained in these accounts appears in the debit column of the Income Summary account. The commissions of $12,290 earned during October appear in the credit column of the Income Summary account. Since the credit entry of $12,290 representing October revenue is larger than the debit of $9,719 representing October expenses, the account has a credit balance of $2,571—the net income for October.

The net income of $2,571 earned during October causes the owner's equity to increase. The ***credit*** balance of the Income Summary account is, therefore, transferred to the owner's capital account by the following closing entry.

Net income increases the owner's equity

General Journal — **Page 3**

Date		Account Titles and Explanation	LP	Debit	Credit
19__					
Oct	31	Income Summary	53	2,571	
		James Roberts, Capital............	50		2,571
		To close the Income Summary account for October by transferring the net income to the owner's capital account.			

After this closing entry has been posted, the Income Summary account has a zero balance, and the net income for October will appear as an increase (or credit entry) in the owner's capital account as shown below.

Income Summary account is closed into the owner's capital account

Income Summary — **Account No. 53**

Date		Explanation	Ref	Debit	Credit	Balance
19__						
Oct	31	Revenue	3		12,290	12,290
	31	Expenses	3	9,719		2,571
	31	To close	3	2,571		-0-

James Roberts, Capital — **Account No. 50**

Date		Explanation	Ref	Debit	Credit	Balance
19__						
Sept	1	Investment by owner	1		180,000	180,000
Oct	30	Additional investment	2		1,000	181,000
	31	Net income for October	3		2,571	183,571

In our illustration the business has operated profitably with revenue in excess of expenses. Not every business is so fortunate: if the expenses of a business are larger than its revenue, the Income Summary account will

Advertising Expense — Account No. 70

Date		Explanation	Ref	Debit	Credit	Balance
19__						
Oct	2		2	360		360
	16		2	1,320		1,680
	31	To close	3		1,680	-0-

Salaries Expense — Account No. 72

Date		Explanation	Ref	Debit	Credit	Balance
19__						
Oct	31		2	7,700		7,700
	31	To close	3		7,700	-0-

Telephone Expense — Account No. 74

Date		Explanation	Ref	Debit	Credit	Balance
19__						
Oct	31		2	144		144
	31	To close	3		144	-0-

Depreciation Expense: Building — Account No. 76

Date		Explanation	Ref	Debit	Credit	Balance
19__						
Oct	31		2	150		150
	31	To close	3		150	-0-

Depreciation Expense: Office Equipment — Account No. 78

Date		Explanation	Ref	Debit	Credit	Balance
19__						
Oct	31		2	45		45
	31	To close	3		45	-0-

Income Summary — Account No. 53

Date		Explanation	Ref	Debit	Credit	Balance
19__						
Oct	31		3		12,290	12,290
	31		3	9,719		2,571

have a ***debit*** balance, representing a ***net loss*** for the accounting period. In that case, the closing of the Income Summary account requires a debit to the owner's capital account and an offsetting credit to the Income Summary account. The owner's equity will, of course, be reduced by the amount of the loss debited to the capital account.

Note that the Income Summary account is used only at the end of the period when the accounts are being closed. The Income Summary account has no entries and no balance except during the process of closing the accounts at the end of the accounting period.

Closing the Owner's Drawing Account

As explained earlier in this chapter, withdrawals of cash or other assets by the owner are not considered as an expense of the business and, therefore, are not a factor in determining the net income for the period. Since drawings by the owner do not constitute an expense, the owner's drawing account is closed not into the Income Summary account but directly to the owner's capital account. The following journal entry serves to close the drawing account in the ledger of Roberts Real Estate Company at October 31.

Drawing account is closed into the owner's capital account

General Journal — **Page 3**

Date		Account Titles and Explanation	LP	Debit	Credit
19__					
Oct	31	James Roberts, Capital	50	2,800	
		James Roberts, Drawing	51		2,800
		To close the owner's drawing account.			

After this closing entry has been posted, the drawing account will have a zero balance, and the amount withdrawn by Roberts during October will appear as a deduction or debit entry in the capital account.

James Roberts, Drawing — **Account No. 51**

Date		Explanation	Ref	Debit	Credit	Balance
19__						
Oct	31	Withdrawal	2	2,800		2,800
	31	To close	3		2,800	–0–

One account now shows the total equity of the owner

James Roberts, Capital — **Account No. 50**

Date		Explanation	Ref	Debit	Credit	Balance
19__						
Sept	1	Investment by owner	1		180,000	180,000
Oct	30	Additional investment	2		1,000	181,000
	31	Net income for October	3		2,571	183,571
	31	From owner's drawing account	3	2,800		180,771

Summary of the Closing Process

Let us now summarize the process of closing the accounts.

1 Close the various ***revenue*** accounts by transferring their balances into the Income Summary account.

2 Close the various ***expense*** accounts by transferring their balances into the Income Summary account.

3 Close the ***Income Summary account*** by transferring its balance into the owner's capital account.

4 Close the owner's ***drawing*** account into the owner's capital account. (The balance of the owner's capital account in the ledger will now be the same as the amount of owner's equity appearing in the balance sheet.)

The closing of the accounts may be illustrated graphically by use of T accounts as follows:

Flowchart of the closing process

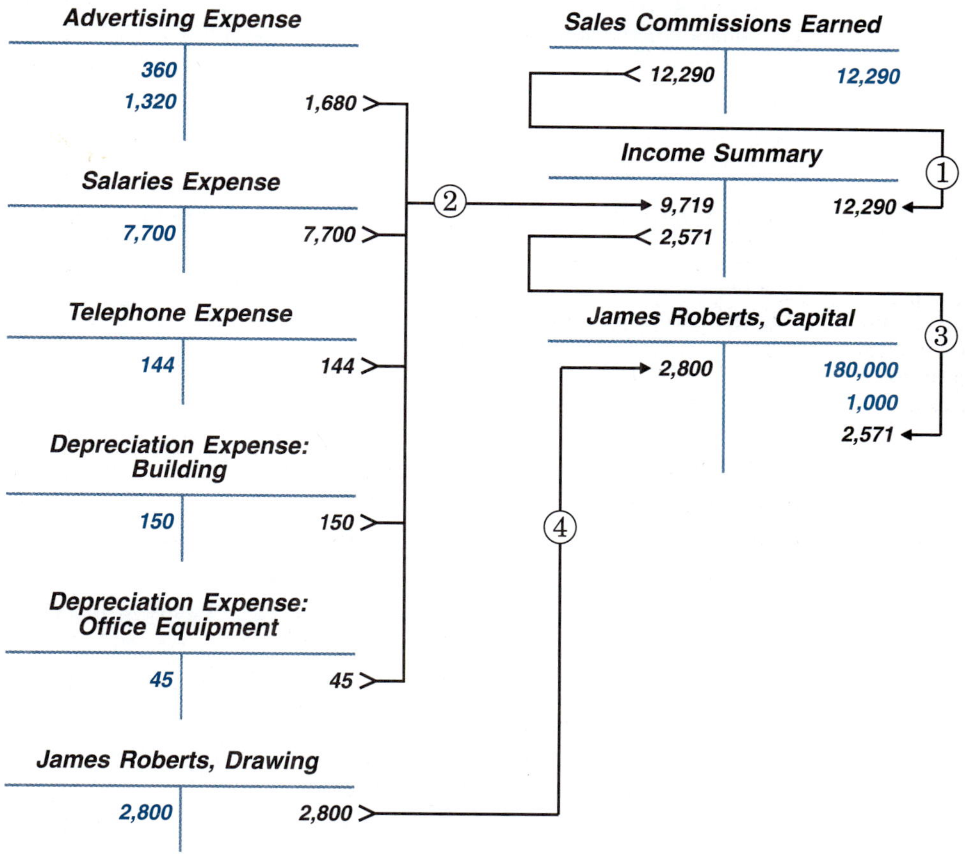

After-Closing Trial Balance

After the revenue and expense accounts have been closed, it is desirable to prepare an ***after-closing trial balance,*** which will consist of balance sheet accounts ***only.*** There is always the possibility that an error in posting the closing entries may have upset the equality of debits and credits in the ledger. The after-closing trial balance is prepared from the ledger. It gives assurance that the accounts are in balance and ready for the recording of the transactions of the new accounting period. The after-closing trial balance of Roberts Real Estate Company follows:

Only the balance sheet accounts remain open

ROBERTS REAL ESTATE COMPANY
After-Closing Trial Balance
October 31, 19__

Cash	*$ 16,540*	
Accounts receivable	*17,890*	
Land	*130,000*	
Building	*36,000*	
Accumulated depreciation: building		*$ 150*
Office equipment	*5,400*	
Accumulated depreciation: office equipment		*45*
Accounts payable		*24,864*
James Roberts, capital		*180,771*
	$205,830	*$205,830*

SEQUENCE OF PROCEDURES IN THE ACCOUNTING CYCLE

Jan./99

OBJECTIVE 7 Describe the sequence of procedures in the accounting cycle.

The accounting procedures described to this point may be summarized in eight steps, as follows:

1 **Journalize transactions.** Enter all transactions in the general journal, thus creating a chronological record of events.

2 **Post to ledger accounts.** Post debits and credits from the general journal to the proper ledger accounts, thus creating a record classified by accounts.

3 **Prepare a trial balance.** Prove the equality of debits and credits in the ledger.

4 **Make end-of-period adjustments.** Draft adjusting entries in the general journal, and post to ledger accounts. Thus far we have illustrated only one type of adjustment: the recording of depreciation at the end of the period.

5 **Prepare an adjusted trial balance.** Prove again the equality of debits and credits in the ledger.

6 **Prepare financial statements and appropriate disclosures.** An income statement shows the results of operations for the period. A statement of owner's equity shows the changes in owner's equity during the period and the ending balance. A balance sheet shows the financial position of the business at the end of the period. Financial statements should be accompanied by ***notes*** disclosing any facts necessary for the ***proper interpretation*** of those statements.

7 **Journalize and post closing entries.** The closing entries clear the revenue, expense, and drawing accounts, making them ready for record-

ing the events of the next accounting period. The closing entries also transfer the net income or loss of the completed period to the owner's capital account.

8 **Prepare an after-closing trial balance.** This step ensures that the ledger remains in balance after posting of the closing entries.

These eight procedures represent a complete accounting cycle. In Chapter 4, however, we shall see that the preparation of a ***work sheet*** will enable us to consolidate several of these procedures.

Accounting Procedures in a Computer-Based System

The sequence of procedures performed in computer-based systems is essentially the same as in manual systems. Of course, the computer is ***programmed*** to perform a number of these steps automatically. In the preceding list, procedures **1** and **4** both involve the analysis of business transactions and judgmental decisions as to accounts to be debited and credited and the dollar amounts. These two steps in the accounting cycle require human judgment, regardless of whether the data is processed manually or by computer. As mentioned in Chapter 2, a computer-based system may call for recording transactions first in a data base, rather than in a journal. The computer then arranges the data, based on the program designed by someone with accounting knowledge, into the format of journal entries, ledger accounts, trial balances, and financial statements.

Procedures such as posting and the preparation of trial balances and financial statements merely involve the ***rearrangement*** of recorded data and may easily be performed by computer. Of course, drafting the appropriate ***disclosures*** that accompany financial statements requires human judgment.

The preparation and posting of closing entries are mechanical tasks, involving the transfer of recorded data from one ledger account to another. Thus, closing entries ***may be performed automatically*** in a computer-based system.

The Accrual Basis of Accounting

OBJECTIVE 8 ***Distinguish between the accrual basis and the cash basis of accounting.***

The policy of recognizing revenue in the accounting records when it is ***earned*** and recognizing expenses when the related goods or services are ***used*** is called the ***accrual basis*** of accounting. The purpose of accrual accounting is to measure the profitability of the ***economic activities conducted*** during the accounting period.

The most important concept involved in accrual accounting is the ***matching principle.*** Revenue is offset with all of the expenses incurred in generating that revenue, thus providing a measure of the overall profitability of the economic activity.

An alternative to the accrual basis is something called ***cash basis*** accounting. Under cash basis accounting, revenue is recognized when cash is collected from the customer, rather than when the company sells goods or renders services. Expenses are recognized when payment is made, rather than when the related goods or services are used in business operations.

The cash basis of accounting measures the amounts of cash received and paid out during the period, but it does ***not*** provide a good measure of the ***profitability of activities*** undertaken during the period.

CASE IN POINT Airlines sell many tickets weeks or even months ***in advance*** of scheduled flights. Yet many expenses relating to a flight—such as salaries of the flight crew and the cost of fuel used—may not be paid until ***after*** the flight has occurred. Thus, the cash basis often would fail to "match" in one accounting period both the revenue and all expenses relating to specific flights.

Generally accepted accounting principles usually ***require*** use of the accrual basis in measuring revenue, expenses, and net income. However, the cash basis is generally acceptable for use in individuals' income tax returns.

In this textbook, we will emphasize the ***accrual basis*** of accounting. Accrual basis accounting is used by virtually all businesses that distribute their financial statements to investors, shareholders, creditors, and other decision makers outside the business.

The Usefulness of Revenue and Expense Data to Managers

The revenue and expense data used by managers in planning and controlling business operations differ significantly from the income statements used by outsiders. Outsiders usually receive income statements on either a quarterly or an annual basis. Managers, on the other hand, need information about daily, weekly, and monthly performance. Also, the income statements distributed to investors and creditors describe the profitability of the business ***viewed as a whole.*** Managers need to know the revenue and expenses relating to ***specific departments*** within the organization.

In summary, the revenue and expense information used by managers generally covers much shorter time periods and is more detailed than the information contained in a formal income statement. For example, the manager of a large department store might receive a sales report every morning, showing separately the revenue earned by each sales department in the store on the preceding day.

The revenue and expense reports prepared daily or weekly for use by managers show only ***selected*** revenue and expenses—usually those items that are under the ***direct control*** of individual managers. Thus, revenue and expense reports usually do not contain all of the information necessary to determine net income.

Managers may compare the revenue and expenses of individual departments with such standards as past performance, budgeted performance for the current and future periods, and the performance of other departments. Their basic goal is to see that resources are being ***used efficiently*** throughout the organization.

CHAPTER REVIEW

KEY TERMS INTRODUCED OR EMPHASIZED IN CHAPTER 3

Accounting period The span of time covered by an income statement. One year is a standard accounting period, but many companies also prepare monthly and quarterly financial statements.

Accrual basis of accounting Calls for recording revenue in the period in which it is earned and recording expenses in the period in which they are incurred. The effect of events on the business is recognized as services are rendered or consumed rather than when cash is received or paid.

Accumulated depreciation account A contra-asset account shown as a deduction from the related asset account in the balance sheet. Depreciation taken throughout the useful life of an asset is accumulated in this account.

Adjusted trial balance A listing of all ledger account balances after the amounts have been changed to include the adjusting entries made at the end of the period.

Adjusting entries Entries required at the end of the period to update the accounts before financial statements are prepared. Adjusting entries serve to apportion transactions properly between the accounting periods affected and to record any revenue earned or expenses incurred that have not been recorded prior to the end of the period.

After-closing trial balance A trial balance prepared after all closing entries have been made and posted. Consists only of accounts for assets, liabilities, and owner's equity.

Cash basis of accounting Revenue is recorded when received in cash and expenses are recorded in the period in which cash payment is made. Does not lead to a logical measurement of net income.

Closing entries Journal entries made at the end of the period for the purpose of closing temporary accounts (revenue, expense, and drawing accounts) and transferring balances to the owner's equity account.

Conservatism The traditional accounting practice of resolving uncertainty by choosing the solution that leads to the lower (more conservative) amount of income being recognized in the current accounting period. This concept is designed to avoid overstatement of financial strength or earnings.

Contra-asset account An account with a credit balance that is offset against or deducted from an asset account to produce the proper balance sheet amount for the asset.

Depreciation The systematic allocation of the cost of an asset to expense during the periods of its useful life.

Drawing account The account used to record the withdrawals of cash or other assets by the owner. Closed at the end of the period by transferring its balance to the owner's capital account.

Expenses The costs of the goods and services used up in the process of obtaining revenue.

Fiscal year Any 12-month accounting period adopted by a business.

Income statement A financial statement summarizing the results of operations of a business by matching its revenue and related expenses for a particular accounting period. Shows the net income or net loss.

Income Summary account The temporary clearing account in the ledger to which revenue and expense accounts are closed at the end of the period. The balance (credit balance for a net income, debit balance for a net loss) is transferred to the owner's capital account.

Matching principle The revenue earned during an accounting period is matched (offset) with the expenses incurred in generating this revenue.

Net income An increase in owner's equity resulting from profitable operations. Also, the excess of revenue earned over the related expenses for a given period.

Realization (Recognition) principle The generally accepted accounting principle that determines when revenue should be recognized in the accounting records. Revenue is realized when services are rendered to customers or when goods sold are delivered to customers.

Revenue The price of goods sold and services rendered by a business.

Statement of owner's equity A financial statement summarizing the increases and decreases in owner's equity during an accounting period.

Time period principle To provide the users of financial statements with timely information, net income is measured for relatively short accounting periods of equal length. The period of time covered by an income statement is termed the company's accounting period.

DEMONSTRATION PROBLEM FOR YOUR REVIEW

Key Insurance Agency was organized on September 1, 19__. Assume that the accounts are closed and financial statements prepared each month. The company occupies rented office space but owns office equipment estimated to have a useful life of 10 years from date of acquisition, September 1. The unadjusted trial balance for Key Insurance Agency at November 30 is shown below.

Cash	$ 3,750	
Accounts receivable	1,210	
Office equipment	4,800	
Accumulated depreciation: office equipment		$ 80
Accounts payable		1,640
Jane Carl, capital		7,490
Jane Carl, drawing	500	
Commissions earned		6,220
Advertising expense	800	
Salaries expense	3,600	
Rent expense	770	
	$15,430	$15,430

INSTRUCTIONS

a Prepare the adjusting journal entry to record depreciation of the office equipment for the month of November.

b Prepare an adjusted trial balance at November 30, 19__.

c Prepare an income statement and a statement of owner's equity for the month ended November 30, 19__, and a balance sheet in report form at November 30, 19__.

SOLUTION TO DEMONSTRATION PROBLEM

a Adjusting journal entry:

Depreciation Expense: Office Equipment	40	
Accumulated Depreciation: Office Equipment		40
To record depreciation for November ($4,800 ÷ 120 months).		

b

KEY INSURANCE AGENCY
Adjusted Trial Balance
November 30, 19__

Cash	$ 3,750	
Accounts receivable	1,210	
Office equipment	4,800	
Accumulated depreciation: office equipment		$ 120
Accounts payable		1,640
Jane Carl, capital		7,490
Jane Carl, drawing	500	
Commissions earned		6,220
Advertising expense	800	
Salaries expense	3,600	
Rent expense	770	
Depreciation expense: office equipment	40	
	$15,470	$15,470

c

KEY INSURANCE AGENCY
Income Statement
For the Month Ended November 30, 19__

Commissions earned		$6,220
Expenses:		
Advertising expense	$ 800	
Salaries expense	3,600	
Rent expense	770	
Depreciation expense: office equipment	40	5,210
Net income		$1,010

KEY INSURANCE AGENCY
Statement of Owner's Equity
For the Month Ended November 30, 19__

Jane Carl, capital, Oct. 31, 19__	$7,490
Add: Net income for the month	1,010
Subtotal	$8,500
Less: Withdrawals by owner	500
Jane Carl, capital, Nov. 31, 19__	$8,000

KEY INSURANCE AGENCY
Balance Sheet
November 30, 19__

Assets

Cash		*$3,750*
Accounts receivable		*1,210*
Office equipment	*$4,800*	
Less: Accumulated depreciation	*120*	*4,680*
Total assets		*$9,640*

Liabilities & Owner's Equity

Liabilities:	
Accounts payable	*$1,640*
Owner's equity:	
Jane Carl, capital	*8,000*
Total liabilities & owner's equity	*$9,640*

ASSIGNMENT MATERIAL

DISCUSSION QUESTIONS

1 Explain the effect of operating profitably upon the balance sheet of a business entity.

2 Does net income represent a supply of cash that can be withdrawn by the owner of a business? Explain.

3 What is the meaning of the term ***revenue?*** Does the receipt of cash by a business indicate that revenue has been earned? Explain.

4 What is the meaning of the term ***expenses?*** Does the payment of cash by a business indicate that an expense has been incurred? Explain.

5 A service enterprise performs services in the amount of $500 for a customer in May and receives payment in June. In which month is the $500 of revenue recognized? What is the journal entry to be made in May and the entry to be made in June?

6 When do accountants consider revenue to be realized? What basic question about recording revenue in accounting records is answered by the ***realization (recognition) principle?***

7 Late in March, Classic Auto Painters purchased paint on account, with payment due in 60 days. The company used the paint to paint customers' cars during the first three weeks of April. Late in May, the company paid the paint store from which the paint had been purchased. In which month should Classic Auto Painters recognize the cost of this paint as expense? What generally accepted accounting principle determines the answer to this question?

8 In what accounting period does the ***matching principle*** indicate that an expense should be recognized?

9 Explain the rules of debit and credit with respect to transactions recorded in revenue and expense accounts.

10 Supply the appropriate term (debit or credit) to complete the following statements.

a The owner's equity account and revenue accounts are increased by ____________ entries.

b Asset accounts and expense accounts are increased by ____________ entries.

c Liability accounts and owner's equity accounts are decreased by ____________ entries.

11 Why does any company that owns equipment or buildings need to make adjusting entries at the end of every accounting period?

12 Does a well-prepared income statement provide an exact measurement of net income for the period, or does it represent merely an approximation of net income? Explain.

13 How does depreciation expense differ from other operating expenses?

14 All ledger accounts belong in one of the following five groups: asset, liability, owner's equity, revenue, and expense. For each of the following accounts, state the group in which it belongs. Also indicate whether the normal balance would be a debit or a credit.

a Fees Earned

b Notes Payable

c Telephone Expense

d John Jones, Capital

e Building

f Depreciation Expense

g Accumulated Depreciation: Building

15 For each of the following financial statements, indicate whether the statement relates to a particular date or to a period of time:

a Balance sheet

b Income statement

c Statement of owner's equity

16 Briefly describe the content and format of an income statement and of a statement of owner's equity.

17 Explain the relationships among the three financial statements discussed in this chapter—that is, the income statement, the statement of owner's equity, and the balance sheet.

18 Which of the following accounts are closed at the end of the accounting period?

Cash	*Donna Jackson, drawing*
Fees earned	*Donna Jackson, capital*
Income summary	*Accumulated depreciation*
Accounts payable	*Accounts receivable*
Telephone expense	*Depreciation expense*

19 Supply the appropriate term (debit or credit) to complete the following statements.

a When a business is operating ***profitably,*** the journal entry to close the Income Summary account will consist of a ____________ to that account and a ____________ to the owner's capital account.

b When a business is operating at a ***loss,*** the journal entry to close the Income Summary account will consist of a ____________ to that account and a ____________ to the owner's capital account.

c The journal entry to close the owner's drawing account consists of a ____________ to that account and a ____________ to the owner's capital account.

20 How does the accrual basis of accounting differ from the cash basis of accounting? Which gives a more accurate picture of the profitability of a business? Explain.

MULTIPLE CHOICE QUESTIONS

1 Identify any of the following statements that correctly describe net income. (Indicate all correct answers.) Net income:

a Is computed in the income statement, appears in the statement of owner's equity, and increases owner's equity in the balance sheet.

b Is equal to revenue minus expenses.

c Is computed in the income statement, appears in the statement of owner's equity, and increases the amount of cash shown in the balance sheet.

d Can be determined using the account balances appearing in an adjusted trial balance.

2 Which of the following are based upon the realization (recognition) principle and the matching principle? (Indicate all correct answers.)

a Adjusting entries.

b Closing entries.

c The accrual basis of accounting.

d The measurement of net income under generally accepted accounting principles.

3 Which of the following explains the debit and credit rules relating to the recording of revenue and expenses?

a Expenses appear on the left side of the balance sheet and are recorded by debits; revenue appears on the right side of the balance sheet and is recorded by credits.

b Expenses appear on the left side of the income statement and are recorded by debits; revenue appears on the right side of the income statement and is recorded by credits.

c The effects of revenue and expenses upon owner's equity.

d The realization principle and the matching principle.

4 The entry to recognize ***depreciation expense:*** (Indicate all correct answers.)

a Is an application of the matching principle.

b Is a closing entry.

c Usually includes an offsetting credit either to Cash or to Accounts Payable.

d Is an adjusting entry.

5 In the accounting cycle: (Indicate all correct answers.)

a Closing entries are made before adjusting entries.

b Financial statements may be prepared as soon as an adjusted trial balance is complete.

c The owner's equity account is not up-to-date until closing entries have been posted.

d Adjusting entries are made before financial statements are prepared.

6 The balance in the owner's capital account of Dayton Company at the beginning of the year was $65,000. During the year, the company earned revenue of $430,000 and incurred expenses of $360,000, the owner withdrew $50,000 in assets, and the balance of the Cash account increased by $10,000. At year-end, the company's net income and the year-end balance in the owner's capital account were, respectively:

a $20,000 and $95,000 c $60,000 and $75,000

b $70,000 and $95,000 d $70,000 and $85,000

Use the following information in questions **7** and **8**.

Accounts appearing in the trial balance of Westside Plumbing at May 31 are listed below in alphabetical order:

Accounts payable	*$2,450*	*Equipment*	*$16,200*
Accounts receivable	*3,100*	*J. T. Golden, capital*	*11,000*
Accumulated depreciation: equipment	*8,100*	*J. T. Golden, drawing*	*2,100*
		Other expenses	*900*
Advertising expense	*150*	*Service revenue*	*4,800*
Cash	*2,900*	*Supplies expense*	*1,000*

No adjusting entry has yet been made to record depreciation expense of $270 for the month of May.

7 The balance of J. T. Golden's capital account appearing in the May 31 balance sheet should be:
a $11,650 b $8,630 c $11,380 d Some other amount

8 In an ***after-closing*** trial balance prepared at May 31, the total of the credit column will be:
a $26,620 b $22,200 c $13,830 d Some other amount

EXERCISES

EXERCISE 3-1 Accounting Terminology

Listed below are 12 technical accounting terms introduced in this chapter:

Accounting period	*Depreciation*	*Net income*
Accrual basis of accounting	*Expenses*	*Realization*
Cash basis of accounting	*Income statement*	*Revenue*
Closing entries	*Matching*	*Conservatism*

Each of the following statements may (or may not) describe one of these technical terms. For each statement, indicate the accounting term described, or answer "None" if the statement does not correctly describe any of the terms.

a The span of time covered by an income statement.

b An increase in owner's equity as a result of earning revenue and incurring expenses.

c An accounting concept intended to avoid overstatement of financial strength or earnings.

d The generally accepted accounting principle used in determining when expenses should be offset against revenue.

- **e** The generally accepted accounting principle used in determining when to recognize revenue.
- **f** Recognizing revenue when it is earned and expenses when the related goods or services are used in the effort to obtain revenue.
- **g** The systematic allocation of the cost of a long-lived asset, such as a building or equipment, to expense over the useful life of the asset.
- **h** The procedures for transferring the balances of the revenue, expense, Income Summary, and owner's drawing accounts into the owner's capital account.
- **i** The cost of goods and services used up in the process of earning revenue.

EXERCISE 3-2
Effects of Transactions; the Accounting Equation

E. E. Ford Trucking Company closes its accounts at the end of each month. Among the events occurring in ***November*** were the following:

- **a** Hauled freight for a credit customer; payment due December 10.
- **b** Paid Truck Service Centre for repairs to trucks performed in October.
- **c** Collected in full the amount due from a credit customer for hauling done in October.
- **d** Received a bill from Apex Truck Stops for fuel used in November. Payment due December 15.
- **e** Prepared an adjusting entry to record depreciation on trucks in November.
- **f** Purchased two new trucks on November 30, paying part cash and issuing a note payable for the balance. The trucks are first scheduled for use on December 3.

INSTRUCTIONS

Indicate the effects that each of these transactions will have upon the following six ***total amounts*** in the company's financial statements for the month of ***November.*** Organize your answer in tabular form, using the column headings shown below, and use the code letters ***I*** for increase, ***D*** for decrease, and ***NE*** for no effect. The answer to transaction **a** is provided as an example.

	Income Statement			*Balance Sheet*		
Transaction	*Revenue* –	*Expenses* =	*Net Income*	*Assets* =	*Liabilities* +	*Owner's Equity*
a	I	NE	I	I	NE	I

EXERCISE 3-3
Effects of Transactions

A number of transactions of PanAm Steamship Lines, Inc., are described below in terms of the accounts debited and credited:

1. Debit Wages Expense, credit Cash.
2. Debit Accounts Receivable, credit Freight Revenue.
3. Debit Depreciation Expense: Ships; credit Accumulated Depreciation: Ships.
4. Debit Repairs Expense, credit Accounts Payable.
5. Debit Cash, credit Accounts Receivable.
6. Debit Accounts Payable, credit Cash.

INSTRUCTIONS

- **a** Indicate the effects of each transaction upon the elements of the income statement and the balance sheet. Use the code letters ***I*** for increase, ***D*** for decrease, and ***NE*** for no effect. Organize your answer in tabular form using the following column headings. The answer for transaction **1** is provided as an example.

	Income Statement			Balance Sheet		
Transaction	Revenue –	Expenses =	Net Income	Assets =	Liabilities +	Owners' Equity
1	NE	I	D	D	NE	D

b Write a one-sentence description of each transaction.

EXERCISE 3-4
Relationship between Net Income and Owner's Equity

Total assets and total liabilities of Yato Talent Agency as shown by the balance sheets at the beginning and end of the year were as follows:

	Beginning of Year	End of Year
Assets	$230,000	$290,000
Liabilities	110,000	140,000

INSTRUCTIONS

Compute the net income or net loss from operations for the year in each of the following independent cases:

a Yato made no withdrawals during the year and no additional investments.

b Yato made no withdrawals during the year but made an additional capital investment of $50,000.

c Yato made withdrawals of $20,000 during the year but made no additional investments.

d Yato made withdrawals of $80,000 during the year and made an additional capital investment of $25,000.

EXERCISE 3-5
Relationship between Net Income and Owner's Equity

Supply the missing figure in the following independent cases:

a	Owner's equity at beginning of year	$130,000
	Net income for the year	–?–
	Owner's drawings during the year	32,000
	Owner's equity at end of year	145,500
b	Owner's equity at beginning of year	91,200
	Net income for the year	28,500
	Owner's drawings during the year	–?–
	Owner's equity at end of year	99,700
c	Owner's equity at beginning of year	–?–
	Net income for the year	189,400
	Owner's drawings during the year	106,000
	Owner's equity at end of year	532,900
d	Owner's equity at beginning of year	74,000
	Additional investment by owner during the year	10,000
	Net income for the year	17,500
	Owner's drawings during the year	12,000
	Owner's equity at end of year	–?–
e	Owner's equity at beginning of year	362,500
	Additional investment by owner during the year	85,000
	Net income for the year	–?–
	Owner's drawings during the year	30,000
	Owner's equity at end of year	469,100

EXERCISE 3-6
Financial Statement Relationships

Shown below is a list of abbreviated terms, each representing an element of financial statements.

Term	*Explanation*
REV	*Revenue of the period*
EXP	*Expenses of the period*
NI	*Net Income for the period*
DRW	*Drawings by the owner during the period*
OE_{BEG}	*Owner's equity, beginning of the period*
OE_{END}	*Owner's equity, end of the period*

INSTRUCTIONS

Shown below are five incomplete formulas describing interrelationships among the elements of financial statements. You are to complete the right-hand side of each formula by adding or subtracting the appropriate terms from the list provided above. (The number of question marks indicates the number of terms needed to complete each formula.)

a ***NI = REV*** (+ or − ?)

b ***EXP = REV*** (+ or − ?)

c ***REV = EXP*** (+ or − ?)

d $OE_{END} = OE_{BEG}$ (+ or − ? and ?)

e $OE_{BEG} = OE_{END}$ (+ or − ? and ?)

EXERCISE 3-7
Heading of an Income Statement

On January 14, 1995, the accountant for Sunray Appliance Company prepared an income statement for the year ended December 31, 1994. The accountant used the following heading on this financial statement:

SUNRAY CO.
Income Statement
January 14, 1995

INSTRUCTIONS

a Identify any errors in this heading.

b Prepare a corrected heading.

EXERCISE 3-8
When Is Revenue Realized?

The following transactions were carried out during the month of June by K. Lansing and Company, a firm of real estate brokers. For each of the five transactions, you are to state whether the transaction represented revenue to the firm during the month of June. Give reasons for your decision in each case.

a Lansing invested an additional $6,400 cash in the business.

b Borrowed $12,800 from Century Bank to be repaid in three months.

c Earned $63 interest on a company bank account during the month of June. No withdrawals were made from this account in June.

d Collected cash of $2,400 from an account receivable. The receivable originated in May from services rendered to a client.

e Arranged a sale of an apartment building owned by a client. The commission for making the sale was $14,400, but this amount will not be received until August 20.

EXERCISE 3-9
When Are Expenses Incurred?

Evergreen Landscaping carried out the following transactions during May. Which of these transactions represented expenses in May? Explain.

a Paid a lawyer $560 for legal services rendered in April.

b The owner withdrew $1,600 from the business for personal use.

c Purchased a copying machine for $2,750 cash.

d Paid $192 for gasoline purchases for a delivery truck during May.

e Paid $1,280 salary to an employee for time worked during May.

EXERCISE 3-10
Preparing Journal Entries to Record Revenue, Expense, and Drawings Transactions

Shown below are selected transactions of the law firm of Emmons & Associates. You are to prepare journal entries to record the transactions in the firm's accounting records. The firm closes its accounts at the end of each calendar year.

Mar. 19 Drafted a prenuptial agreement for C. J. McCall. Sent McCall an invoice for $750, requesting payment within 30 days. (The appropriate revenue account is entitled Legal Fees Earned.)

May 31 Received a bill from Lawyers' Delivery Service for process service during the month of May, $1,150. Payment due by June 10. (The appropriate expense account is entitled Process Service Expense.)

Aug. 7 Ralph Emmons, owner of the law firm, withdrew $15,000 cash for personal purposes.

Dec. 31 Made a year-end adjusting entry to record depreciation expense on the firm's law library, $2,700.

EXERCISE 3-11
Adjusting Entry for Depreciation

Ahmed Pharmacy acquired a delivery truck at a cost of $9,600. Estimated life of the truck is four years. State the amount of depreciation expense per year and per month. Give the adjusting entry to record depreciation on the truck at the end of the first month, and explain where the accounts involved would appear in the financial statements.

EXERCISE 3-12
Preparing an Income Statement and Statement of Owner's Equity

From the following account balances, prepare first an income statement and then a statement of owner's equity for Ross Painting Contractors for the year ended December 31, 1995. Include the proper headings on both financial statements.

T. Ross, capital, Dec. 31, 1994	*$ 27,200*	*Rent expense*	*$9,600*
T. Ross, drawing	*18,000*	*Advertising expense*	*3,200*
Painting fees earned	*140,000*	*Depreciation expense: painting equipment*	*1,200*
Paint & supplies expense	*27,500*		
Salaries expense	*66,800*		

EXERCISE 3-13
Preparing Closing Entries

Prepare the year-end closing entries for Ross Painting Contractors, using the data given in Exercise 3-12. Use four separate entries, as illustrated in this chapter. Indicate the balance in the owner's capital account that should appear in the balance sheet dated December 31, 1995.

EXERCISE 3-14
Closing Entries

During the absence of the regular accountant of Liuku Lawn Care Company, a new employee, Ralph Jones, prepared the following closing entries for the year ended December 31, 19__.

Entry 1

Lawn Service Revenue	*78,000*	
Accumulated Depreciation	*8,000*	
Accounts Payable	*27,000*	
Income Summary		*113,000*
To close the revenue accounts.		

Entry 2

Income Summary	*73,000*	
Salaries Expense		*56,000*
J. Mallory, Drawing		*11,000*
Advertising Expense		*4,000*
Depreciation Expense		*2,000*
To close the expense accounts.		

Entry 3

J. Mallory, Capital	*28,000*	
Income Summary		*28,000*
To close the owner's capital account.		

INSTRUCTIONS

a Identify any errors that Jones made.

b Prepare four correct closing entries.

EXERCISE 3-15
The Accounting cycle

Listed below in random order are the eight steps comprising a complete accounting cycle.

a Prepare a trial balance.

b Journalize and post the closing entries.

c Prepare financial statements and appropriate disclosures.

d Post transaction data to the ledger.

e Prepare an adjusted trial balance.

f Make end-of-period adjusting entries.

g Journalize transactions.

h Prepare an after-closing trial balance.

INSTRUCTIONS

a List these eight steps in the logical sequence in which they would be performed.

b Indicate which of these steps are mechanical functions that can be performed by machine in a computerized accounting system and which require the judgment of people familiar with accounting principles and concepts.

PROBLEMS

Group A

PROBLEM 3A-1
Preparing Journal Entries

Bay Plumbers performs repair work on both a cash and credit basis. Credit customers are required to pay within 30 days from date of billing. The ledger accounts used by the company include:

Cash	*David Cohen, drawing*
Accounts receivable	*Repair service revenue*
Tools	*Advertising expense*
Notes payable	*Rent expense*
Accounts payable	*Salaries expense*

Among the September transactions were the following:

Sept. 1 Performed repair work for Arden Hardware, a credit customer. Sent bill for $1,322.

Sept. 2 Paid rent for September, $750.

Sept. 3 Purchased tools with estimated life of 10 years for $1,275 cash.

Sept. 10 Performed repairs for Harris Drugs and collected in full the charge of $565.

Sept. 15 Newspaper advertising to appear today was arranged at a cost of $275. Received bill from *Tribune* requiring payment within 30 days.

Sept. 18 Received payment in full of the $1,322 account receivable from Arden Hardware for our services on September 1.

Sept. 20 David Cohen, owner of Bay Plumbers, withdrew $1,100 cash from the business for personal use.

Sept. 30 Paid salaries of $3,425 to employees for services rendered during September.

INSTRUCTIONS Prepare a journal entry (including explanation) for each of the above transactions.

PROBLEM 3A-2 Analyzing Transactions and Preparing Journal Entries

The July transactions of Auto Haus, an automobile repair shop, included the following:

1. On July 1, paid rent for the month of July, $2,400.
2. On July 3, at request of National Insurance, Inc., made repairs on car of Stanley West. Sent bill for $610 for services rendered to National Insurance, Inc.
3. On July 9, made repairs to car of H. F. Smith and collected in full the charge of $430.
4. On July 14, placed advertisement in *Daily Star* to be published in issue on July 16 at cost of $150, payment to be made within 30 days.
5. On July 25, received a cheque for $610 from National Insurance, Inc., representing collection of the receivable of July 3.
6. On July 31, the owner, Hans Klauder, withdrew $3,600 cash for personal use.
7. On July 31, paid salaries of $1,800 for July.

INSTRUCTIONS

a. Write an analysis of each transaction. An example of the type of analysis desired is as follows for transaction **1** above:
   1 (a) Rent is an operating expense. Expenses are recorded by debits. Debit Rent Expense, $2,400.
   (b) The asset Cash was decreased. Decreases in assets are recorded by credits. Credit Cash, $2,400.
b. Prepare a journal entry (including explanation) for each of the above transactions.

PROBLEM 3A-3 Preparing Journal Entries, Posting, and Preparing a Trial Balance

In June 1995, Chris Scott organized a crop-dusting business. The company, a sole proprietorship, called Scott Crop Dusting, began operations immediately. Transactions during the month of June were as follows:

June 1 Scott deposited $60,000 cash in a bank account in the name of the business.

June 2 Purchased a crop-dusting aircraft from Utility Aircraft for $225,000. Made a $45,000 cash down payment and issued a note payable for $180,000.

June 4 Paid Woodrow Airport $2,500 to rent office and hangar space for the month.

June 15 Billed customers $8,320 for crop-dusting services rendered during the first half of June.

June 15 Paid $5,880 salaries to employees for services rendered during the first half of June.

June 18 Paid Hannigan's Hangar $1,890 for maintenance and repair services.

June 25 Collected $4,910 of the amounts billed to customers on June 15.

June 30 Billed customers $16,450 for crop-dusting services rendered during the second half of the month.

June 30 Paid $6,000 salaries to employees for services rendered during the second half of June.

June 30 Received a fuel bill from Henry's Feed & Fuel for $2,510 of aircraft fuel purchased during June. This amount is due by July 10.

June 30 Scott withdrew $2,000 cash from the business for personal use.

The account titles and numbers used by Scott Crop Dusting were:

Cash	1	*Chris Scott, drawing*	43
Accounts receivable	5	*Crop-dusting revenue*	51
Aircraft	15	*Maintenance expense*	61
Notes payable	31	*Fuel expense*	62
Accounts payable	32	*Salaries expense*	63
Chris Scott, capital	41	*Rent expenses*	64

INSTRUCTIONS Based on the foregoing transactions:

a Prepare journal entries. (Number journal pages to permit cross-reference to ledger.)

b Post to ledger accounts. (Number ledger accounts to permit cross-reference to journal.) Enter ledger account numbers in the LP column of the journal as the posting work is done.

c Prepare a trial balance at June 30, 1995.

PROBLEM 3A-4
Assembling Financial Statements from an Adjusted Trial Balance

Playland operates a miniature golf course on rented land within a city park. Following is the company's adjusted trial balance at December 31, 1995. The company closes its accounts at the end of each calendar year.

PLAYLAND
Adjusted Trial Balance
December 31, 1995

Cash	$ 13,500	
Accounts receivable	2,800	
Building	60,000	
Accumulated depreciation: building		$ 12,000
Golf course structures	90,000	
Accumulated depreciation: golf course structures		30,000
Accounts payable		7,700
Salaries payable		2,300
Lynn George, capital		108,000
Lynn George, drawing	25,000	
Admissions revenue		192,000
Advertising expense	15,000	
Rent expense	36,000	
Repairs expense	5,200	
Salaries expense	79,000	
Light & power expense	4,500	
Depreciation expense: building	6,000	
Depreciation expense: golf course structures	15,000	
	$352,000	$352,000

INSTRUCTIONS

a Prepare an income statement and a statement of owner's equity for the year ended December 31, 1995.

b Prepare a balance sheet (in report form) as of December 31, 1995.

PROBLEM 3A-5
Preparing Closing Entries

Using the adjusted trial balance presented in Problem 3A-4:

a Prepare journal entries to close the accounts. Use four entries: (1) to close the revenue account, (2) to close the expense accounts, (3) to close the Income Summary account, and (4) to close the owner's drawing account.

b Assume that in the following year Playland again had $192,000 of admissions revenue but expenses increased to ***$200,000.*** Assuming that the revenue account and all the expense accounts had been closed into the Income Summary account at December 31, prepare a journal entry to close the Income Summary account.

PROBLEM 3A-6
End-of-Period Adjusting and Closing Procedures; Preparing Financial Statements

The operations of Sunset Realty consist of obtaining listings of houses being offered for sale by owners, advertising these houses, and showing them to prospective buyers. The company earns revenue in the form of commissions. The building and office equipment used in the business were acquired on January 1 of the current year and were immediately placed in use. Useful life of the building was estimated to be 30 years and that of the office equipment 5 years. The company closes its accounts monthly; on March 31 of the current year, the trial balance is as follows:

SUNSET REALTY
Trial Balance
March 31, 19__

Cash	$ 6,500	
Accounts receivable	5,000	
Land	25,000	
Building	72,000	
Accumulated depreciation: building		$ 400
Office equipment	24,000	
Accumulated depreciation: office equipment		800
Notes payable		81,000
Accounts payable		10,000
Ellen Norton, capital		37,800
Ellen Norton, drawing	2,000	
Commissions earned		20,000
Advertising expense	900	
Automobile rental expense	700	
Salaries expense	13,300	
Telephone expense	600	
	$150,000	$150,000

INSTRUCTIONS From the trial balance and supplementary data given, prepare the following as of March 31, 19__.

a Adjusting entries for depreciation during March of building and of office equipment

b Adjusted trial balance

c Income statement and a statement of owner's equity for the month of March, and a balance sheet at March 31 in report form

d Closing entries

e After-closing trial balance

PROBLEM 3A-7
Complete Accounting Cycle

April Stein, M.D., after completing her medical education, established her own practice on May 1. The following transactions occurred during the first month.

May 1 Stein opened a bank account in the name of the practice, April Stein, M.D., by making a deposit of $12,000.

May 1 Paid office rent for May, $1,700.

May 2 Purchased office equipment for cash, $7,200.

May 3 Purchased medical equipment from Niles Medeq, Inc., at a cost of $9,000. A cash down payment of $1,000 was made and a note payable was issued for the remaining $8,000.

May 4 Retained by Mercer Hospital to be on call for emergency service at a monthly fee of $1,000. The fee for May was collected in cash.

May 15 Excluding the retainer of May 4, fees earned during the first 15 days of the month amounted to $2,800, of which $600 was in cash and $2,200 was in accounts receivable.

May 15 Paid office salary for the first half of May, $1,200.

May 16 Dr. Stein withdrew $975 for personal use.

May 19 Treated Michael Tracy at Mercer Hospital's emergency department for minor injuries received in an accident.

May 27 Treated Cynthia Knight (a foreign student without medical insurance), who paid $25 cash for an office visit and who agreed to pay $35 on June 1 for laboratory medical tests completed May 27.

May 31 Excluding the treatment of Cynthia Knight on May 27, fees earned during the last half of month amounted to $4,800, of which $200 was in cash and $4,600 was in accounts receivable.

May 31 Paid office salary for the second half of month, $1,200.

May 31 Received a bill from McGraw Medical Supplies in the amount of $640 representing the amount of medical supplies used during May.

May 31 Paid utilities for the month, $300.

OTHER INFORMATION

Dr. Stein estimated the useful life of medical equipment at three years and of office equipment at five years. The account titles to be used and the account numbers are as follows:

Cash	*10*	*April Stein, drawing*	*41*
Accounts receivable	*13*	*Income summary*	*45*
Medical equipment	*20*	*Fees earned*	*49*
Accumulated depreciation: medical equipment	*21*	*Medical supplies expense*	*50*
Office equipment	*22*	*Rent expense*	*51*
Accumulated depreciation: office equipment	*23*	*Salaries expense*	*52*
Notes payable	*30*	*Utilities expense*	*53*
Accounts payable	*31*	*Depreciation expense: medical equipment*	*54*
April Stein, capital	*40*	*Depreciation expense: office equipment*	*55*

INSTRUCTIONS

a Journalize the above transactions. (Number journal pages to permit cross-reference to ledger.)

b Post to ledger accounts. (Use running balance form of ledger account. Number ledger accounts to permit cross-reference to journal.)

c Prepare a trial balance at May 31, 19__.

d Prepare adjusting entries to record depreciation for the month of May and post to ledger accounts.

e Prepare an adjusted trial balance.

f Prepare an income statement and a statement of owner's equity for the month of May, and a balance sheet in report form at May 31. (As this is a new business, the first line in the statement of owner's equity should be: "Initial investment by owner, May 1, 19__, $12,000.")

g Prepare closing entries and post to ledger accounts.

h Prepare an after-closing trial balance.

Group B

PROBLEM 3B-1 Preparing Journal Entries

Air Wolfe provides transportation by helicopter for skiers, backpackers, and others to remote mountainous areas. Among the ledger accounts used by the company are the following:

Cash	*Advertising expense*
Accounts payable	*Fuel expense*
Amy Wolfe, capital	*Rent expense*
Amy Wolfe, drawing	*Repair & maintenance expense*
Passenger fare revenue	*Salaries expense*

Some of the January transactions of Air Wolfe are listed below:

Jan. 3 Paid $1,600 rent for the building for January.

Jan. 4 Placed advertising in local newspapers for publication during January. The agreed price of $520 was payable within 10 days after the end of the month.

Jan. 15 Cash receipts from passengers for the first half of January amounted to $9,470.

Jan. 16 Amy Wolfe, the owner, withdrew $3,000 cash for personal use.

Jan. 16 Paid salaries to employees for services rendered in first half of January, $5,265.

Jan. 29 Received a bill for fuel used from Western Oil Limited, amounting to $1,930, and payable by February 10.

Jan. 31 Paid $1,642 to Stevens Aircraft for repair and maintenance work during January.

INSTRUCTIONS Prepare a journal entry (including an explanation) for each of the above transactions.

PROBLEM 3B-2 Analyzing Transactions and Preparing Journal Entries

Garwood Marine is a boat repair yard. During August its transactions included the following:

1 On August 1, paid rent for the month of August, $4,000.

2 On August 3, at request of Kiwi Insurance, Inc., made repairs on boat of Michael Fay. Sent bill for $4,680 for services rendered to Kiwi Insurance, Inc.

3 On August 9, made repairs to boat of Dennis Conner and collected in full the charge of $1,575.

4 On August 14, purchased some special parts for repairing a boat today at cost of $95, payment to be made within 30 days.

5 On August 25, received a cheque for $4,680 from Kiwi Insurance, Inc., representing collection of the receivable of August 3.

6 On August 30, paid the liability incurred on August 14.

7 On August 31, Barbara Garwood, owner of Garwood Marine, withdrew $3,500 from the business for personal use.

INSTRUCTIONS

a Write an analysis of each transaction. An example of the type of analysis desired is as follows for transaction **1** above:

1 (a) Rent is an operating expense. Expenses are recorded by debits. Debit Rent Expense, $4,000.

(b) The asset Cash was decreased. Decreases in assets are recorded by credits. Credit Cash, $4,000.

b Prepare a journal entry (including explanation) for each of the above transactions.

PROBLEM 3B-3
Preparing Journal Entries, Posting, and Preparing a Trial Balance

Metro Park was organized on March 1 for the purpose of operating an automobile parking lot. Included in the company's ledger are the following ledger accounts and their identification numbers.

Cash	*11*	*Tony Poletti, drawing*	*42*
Land	*21*	*Parking fees earned*	*51*
Notes payable	*31*	*Advertising expense*	*61*
Accounts payable	*32*	*Utilities expense*	*63*
Tony Poletti, capital	*41*	*Salaries expense*	*65*

The business was organized and operations were begun during the month of March. Transactions during March were as follows:

Mar. 1 Tony Poletti deposited $50,000 cash in a bank account in the name of the business.

Mar. 5 Purchased land for $160,000, of which $40,000 was paid in cash. A short-term note payable was issued for the balance of $120,000.

Mar. 6 An arrangement was made with the Century Club to provide parking privileges for its customers. Century Club agreed to pay $1,200 monthly, payable in advance. Cash was collected for the month of March.

Mar. 7 Arranged with Times Printing Company for a regular advertisement in the *Times* at a monthly cost of $390. Paid for advertising during March by cheque, $390.

Mar. 15 Parking receipts for the first half of the month were $1,836, exclusive of the monthly fee from Century Club.

Mar. 31 Received bill for light and power from Pacific Power in the amount of $78, to be paid by April 10.

Mar. 31 Paid $2,720 to employees for services rendered during the month. (Payroll taxes are to be ignored.)

Mar. 31 Parking receipts for the second half of the month amounted to $5,338.

Mar. 31 Poletti withdrew $2,000 for personal use.

Mar. 31 Paid $5,000 cash on the note payable incurred with the purchase of land. (You are to ignore any interest on the note.)

INSTRUCTIONS

a Journalize the March transactions.

b Post to ledger accounts. Enter ledger account numbers in the LP column of the journal as the posting work is done.

c Prepare a trial balance at March 31.

PROBLEM 3B-4
Preparing Closing Entries

An adjusted trial balance for Okoye Insurance Agency at December 31 appears as follows.

OKOYE INSURANCE AGENCY
Adjusted Trial Balance
December 31, 1995

Cash	*$ 10,200*	
Accounts receivable	*20,000*	
Office equipment	*15,000*	
Accumulated depreciation: office equipment		*$ 3,000*
Accounts payable		*6,000*
Christian Okoye, capital		*19,700*
Christian Okoye, drawing	*18,000*	
Commissions earned		*185,000*
Advertising expense	*36,500*	
Rent expense	*32,000*	
Salaries expense	*64,500*	
Utilities expense	*16,000*	
Depreciation expense: office equipment	*1,500*	
	$213,700	*$213,700*

INSTRUCTIONS

a Prepare journal entries to close the accounts. Use four entries: (1) to close the revenue account, (2) to close the expense accounts, (3) to close the Income Summary account, and (4) to close the owner's drawing account.

b Does the amount of net income or net loss appear in the closing entries? Explain fully.

PROBLEM 3B-5
Preparing Financial Statements and Closing Entries

Celebrity Agency closes its accounts and prepares financial statements at the end of each calendar year. The following adjusted trial balance was prepared at December 31 of the most recent year.

CELEBRITY AGENCY
Adjusted Trial Balance
December 31, 1995

Cash	*$ 7,300*	
Notes receivable	*6,000*	
Accounts receivable	*12,800*	
Land	*140,000*	
Building	*90,000*	
Accumulated depreciation: building		*$ 12,000*
Office equipment	*4,000*	
Accumulated depreciation: office equipment		*1,600*
Notes payable		*100,000*
Accounts payable		*16,200*
Halley St. James, capital		*132,300*
Halley St. James, drawing	*24,000*	
Consulting fees earned		*89,500*
Advertising expense	*12,500*	
Insurance expense	*2,800*	
Utilities expense	*2,600*	
Salaries expense	*46,200*	
Depreciation expense: building	*3,000*	
Depreciation expense: office equipment	*400*	
	$351,600	*$351,600*

INSTRUCTIONS

a Prepare an income statement and a statement of owner's equity for the year ended December 31, and a balance sheet in report form as of December 31, 1995.

b Prepare closing entries at December 31, 1995. Use four entries as illustrated in this chapter.

PROBLEM 3B-6
End-of-Period Adjusting and Closing Procedures; Preparing Financial Statements

Home Repair Club is a new business that began operations on July 2. The company follows a policy of closing its accounts and preparing financial statements at the end of each month. A trial balance at September 30 appears below.

HOME REPAIR CLUB
Trial Balance
September 30, 19__

Cash	$ 2,500	
Accounts receivable	1,500	
Land	29,400	
Building	50,400	
Accumulated depreciation: building		$ 336
Repair equipment	7,500	
Accumulated depreciation: repair equipment		250
Notes payable		28,000
Accounts payable		1,594
Paul Morgan, capital		58,800
Paul Morgan, drawing	1,400	
Repair service revenue		8,520
Advertising expense	150	
Repair parts expense	700	
Utilities expense	170	
Wages expense	3,780	
	$97,500	$97,500

INSTRUCTIONS

a Prepare adjusting entries at September 30 to record depreciation. Use one entry to record depreciation on the building and a second entry to record depreciation on the repair equipment. The amounts of depreciation for September are $168 on the building and $125 on the repair equipment.

b Prepare an ***adjusted*** trial balance at September 30.

c Prepare an income statement and a statement of owner's equity for the month ended September 30, and a balance sheet in report form.

d Prepare journal entries to close the accounts. Use four entries.

e Prepare an after-closing trial balance.

PROBLEM 3B-7
The Accounting Cycle; a Comprehensive Problem

On November 1, 19__, Ken Ryan organized Continental Moving Company. The transactions occurring during the first month of operations were as follows:

Nov. 1 Ryan deposited $400,000 cash in a bank account in the name of the business.

Nov. 2 Purchased land for $170,000 and building for $360,000, paying $130,000 cash and signing a $400,000 note payable to Secure Mortgage Company bearing interest at 9%.

Nov. 3 Purchased six trucks from Willis Motors at a total cost of $432,000. A cash down payment of $200,000 was made, and a note payable was issued for the balance of the purchase price. (This note is due in 60 days and does not call for the payment of interest.)

Nov. 6 Purchased office equipment for cash, $24,000.

Nov. 6 Moved furniture for Mr. and Mrs. Don Fitch from London to Montreal for $8,650. Collected $4,850 in cash, balance to be paid within 30 days.

Nov. 9 Moved furniture for various clients for $32,350. Collected $18,350 in cash, balance to be paid within 30 days.

Nov. 15 Paid salaries to employees for the first half of the month, $17,400.

Nov. 25 Moved furniture for various clients for a total of $27,000. Cash collected in full.

Nov. 30 Salaries paid for the second half of November amounted to $13,250.

Nov. 30 Received a gasoline bill for the month of November from Lucier Oil Company in the amount of $17,500, to be paid by December 10.

Nov. 30 Received bill of $1,250 for repair work on trucks during November by Newport Repair Company. Payment is due within 30 days.

Nov. 30 Paid $5,000 to Secure Mortgage Company. This $5,000 payment included $3,000 interest expense for November and a $2,000 reduction in the balance of the note payable issued on November 2.

Nov. 30 Ryan withdrew $4,000 cash from the business for his personal use.

Estimated useful life of the building is 20 years, trucks 4 years, and office equipment 10 years. The account titles to be used and the account numbers are as follows:

Cash	*1*	*Ken Ryan, capital*	*40*
Accounts receivable	*3*	*Ken Ryan, drawing*	*41*
Land	*11*	*Income summary*	*50*
Building	*12*	*Moving service revenue*	*60*
Accumulated depreciation: building	*13*	*Salaries expense*	*70*
Trucks	*15*	*Gasoline expense*	*71*
Accumulated depreciation: trucks	*16*	*Repairs & maintenance expense*	*72*
Office equipment	*18*	*Interest expense*	*73*
Accumulated depreciation: office equipment	*19*	*Depreciation expense: building*	*74*
Notes payable	*30*	*Depreciation expense: trucks*	*75*
Accounts payable	*31*	*Depreciation expense: office equipment*	*76*

INSTRUCTIONS

a Prepare journal entries. (Number journal pages to permit cross-reference to ledger.)

b Post to ledger accounts. (Number ledger accounts to permit cross-reference to journal.)

c Prepare a trial balance at November 30, 19__.

d Prepare adjusting entries and post to ledger accounts.

e Prepare an adjusted trial balance at November 30.

f Prepare an income statement and a statement of owner's equity for the month of November, and a balance sheet in report form at November 30. (As this is a new business, the first line in the statement of owner's equity should be: "Initial investment by owner, November 1, 19__, $400,000.")

g Prepare closing entries at November 30 and post to ledger accounts.

h Prepare an after-closing trial balance at November 30, 19__.

ANALYTICAL AND DECISION PROBLEMS AND CASES

A&D 3-1 Revenue Recognition

The realization principle determines when a business should recognize revenue. Listed below are three common business situations involving revenue. After each situation, we give two alternatives as to the accounting period (or periods) in which the business might recognize this revenue. Select the appropriate alternative by applying the realization principle, and explain your reasoning.

a Airline ticket revenue: Most airlines sell tickets well before the scheduled date of the flight. (Period ticket sold, period of flight)

b Sales on account: In June 1994, a Toronto based furniture store had a big sale featuring "no payments until 1995." (Period furniture sold; periods that payments are received from customers)

c Magazine subscriptions revenue: Most magazine publishers sell subscriptions for future delivery of the magazine. (Period subscription sold; periods that magazines are mailed to customers)

A&D 3-2 Expense Recognition

As a basis for deciding when to recognize expense, we have discussed the ***matching principle,*** the need for ***objective evidence*** to recognize the existence of an asset, and the concept of ***conservatism.*** Shown below are three costs that ultimately become expenses. Each situation is followed by two alternatives as to when the business might record this expense. Select the appropriate alternative based upon the principles described above, and explain your answer.

a Computers: Most businesses own them, and they are expensive. Due to the rapid advances in technology, it is very difficult to estimate in advance how long the business will keep them. (Period computers purchased; periods of an estimated useful life)

b Advertising: **Apple Computer** launched the Macintosh with an expensive television advertising campaign. The Macintosh line has been a major source of revenue for Apple ever since. (Period in which advertising was done; periods in estimated production life of the original model Macintosh)

c Interest expense: On some loans, the borrower does not pay any interest until the end of the loan. This practice is very common on short-term loans, such as 60 or 90 days, but may also occur in some special types of long-term borrowing. (Periods comprising the life of the loan; period in which interest is paid)

A&D 3-3 Accrual Accounting; Relationship of Depreciation Expense to Cash Outlays

The Dark Room is a business that develops film within one hour, using a large and expensive developing machine. The business is organized as a sole proprietorship and operates in rented quarters in a large shopping centre. Christine Douglas, owner of The Dark Room, plans to retire and has offered the business for sale. A typical monthly income statement for The Dark Room appears below:

Revenue:		
Fees earned		*$8,900*
Operating expenses:		
Wages	*$1,600*	
Rent	*1,850*	
Supplies	*920*	
Depreciation: developing machine	*1,510*	
Miscellaneous	*460*	*6,340*
Net income		*$2,560*

Revenue is received in cash at the time that film is developed. The wages, rent, supplies, and miscellaneous expenses are all paid in cash on a monthly basis.

Douglas explains that the developing machine, which is 12 months old and is fully paid for, is being depreciated over a period of 5 years. She is using this estimated useful life because she believes that faster and more efficient machines will probably be available at that time. However, if the business does not purchase a new machine, the existing machine should last for 10 years or more.

Dave Berg, a friend of yours, is negotiating with Douglas to buy The Dark Room. Berg does not have enough money to pay the entire purchase price in cash. However, Douglas has offered to accept a note payable from Berg for a substantial portion of the purchase price. The note would call for 18 monthly payments in the amount of $2,500, which would pay off the remainder of the purchase price as well as the interest charges on the note. Douglas points out that these monthly payments can be made "out of the monthly earnings of the business."

Berg comes to you for advice. He feels that the sales price asked by Douglas is very reasonable and that the owner-financing makes this an excellent opportunity. However, he is worried about turning over $2,500 of the business's earnings to Douglas each month. Berg states, "This arrangement will only leave me with about $60 each month. I figure that my family and I need to take about $1,200 out of this business each month just to meet our living expenses." Also, Berg is concerned about the depreciation expense. He does not understand when or to whom the depreciation expense must be paid, or how long this expense will continue.

INSTRUCTIONS

a Explain to Berg the nature of depreciation expense, including when this expense is paid and what effect, if any, it has upon monthly cash expenditures.

b Advise Berg as to how much cash the business will generate each month. Will this amount enable Berg to pay $2,500 per month to the former owner and still withdraw $1,200 per month to meet his personal living expenses?

c Caution Berg about the need to replace the developing machine. Briefly discuss when this expenditure might occur and how much control, if any, Berg has over the timing and dollar amount of this expenditure.

A&D 3-4
A Good Buy?

Lisome King, owner of a small business called Imports from China, has accepted a salaried position overseas and is trying to interest Jane McKay in buying the business. King describes the operating results of the business as follows: "The business has been in existence for only 18 months, but the growth trend is very impressive. Just look at these figures."

	Cash collections from customers
First six-month period	$120,000
Second six-month period	160,000
Third six-month period	180,000

"I think you'll agree those figures show real growth," King concluded.

McKay then asked King whether sales were made only for cash or on both a cash and credit basis. King replied as follows:

"At first we sold both for cash and on open account. In the first six months we made total sales of $200,000 and 70% of those sales were made on credit. We had $80,000 of accounts receivable at the end of the first six-month period."

"During the second six-month period, we tried to discourage selling on credit because of the extra paper work involved and the time required to follow up on slow-paying customers. Our sales on credit in that second six-month period amounted to $70,000, and our total accounts receivable were down to $60,000 at the end of that period."

"During the third six-month period we made sales only for cash. Although we prefer to operate on a cash basis only, we did very well at collecting receivables. We collected in full from every customer to whom we ever sold on credit and we don't have a dollar of accounts receivable at this time."

INSTRUCTIONS

a Jane McKay has come to you for advice. She is unsure whether the use of cash collections from customers is the best basis for evaluating the "growth trend" of the business and wants your comment on it. She also asks you to provide her with an alternative analysis to determine whether King's business is a good buy and whether the "cash sales only" policy has been beneficial.

b Based upon your analysis in **a**, advise Jane McKay on whether she should buy King's business and whether the "cash sales only" policy has been beneficial.

CHAPTER

4 Completion of the Accounting Cycle

In Chapter 4 we complete our coverage of the accounting cycle for a service-type business. The chapter consists of two major sections. In the first, we take a closer look at the various types of ***adjusting entries*** needed to measure the net income of a specific time period. An important new accounting principle—materiality—is introduced and explained. In the second section of the chapter, we introduce the ***work sheet,*** an informal accounting schedule illustrating the "flow" of financial information from a trial balance into financial statements.

Reversing entries—an optional step in the accounting cycle—are discussed in a Supplemental Topic section.

Learning Objectives

After studying this chapter you should be able to:

1. *State the purpose of adjusting entries and explain how these entries relate to the concepts of accrual accounting.*
2. *Describe the four basic types of adjusting entries; prepare these entries.*
3. *Explain the concept of materiality.*
4. *Prepare a work sheet and explain its usefulness.*
5. *Describe the sequence of steps in the accounting cycle when a work sheet is prepared.*

*6 *Explain when and why reversing entries may be used.*

* *Supplemental Topic, "Reversing Entries"*

Accounting Periods and Financial Statements

For the purpose of measuring net income and preparing financial statements, the life of a business is divided into accounting periods of equal length. Because accounting periods are equal in length, we can compare the income of the current period with that of prior periods to see if operating results are improving or declining.

As explained in Chapter 3, the ***accounting period*** means the span of time covered by an income statement. The usual accounting period for which complete financial statements are prepared and distributed to investors, bankers, and governmental agencies is one year. However, most businesses also prepare quarterly and monthly financial statements so that management will be informed on the profitability of the business from month to month.

Transactions Affecting More Than One Accounting Period

Dividing the life of a business into relatively short accounting periods requires the use of ***adjusting entries*** at the end of each period. Adjusting entries are required for those transactions that affect the revenue or the expenses of ***more than one accounting period***. For example, assume that a company that prepares monthly financial statements purchases a one-year insurance policy at a cost of $1,200. Clearly, the entire $1,200 does not represent the insurance expense of the current month. Rather, it is the insurance expense for ***12*** months; only $\frac{1}{12}$ of this cost, or $100, should be recognized as expense in each month covered by the policy. The allocation of this cost to expense in 12 separate accounting periods is accomplished by making an ***adjusting entry*** at the end of each period.

Some transactions affect the revenue or expense of only one accounting period. An example is the payment of a monthly salary to an employee on the last day of each month. Adjusting entries are not required for transactions of this type.

ADJUSTING ENTRIES: A CLOSER LOOK

OBJECTIVE 1 ***State the purpose of adjusting entries and explain how these entries relate to the concepts of accrual accounting.***

The ***realization principle,*** as explained in Chapter 3, requires that revenue be recognized and recorded in the period it is earned. The ***matching principle*** stresses that expenses are incurred in order to produce revenue. To measure net income for an accounting period, we must "match" or compare the revenue earned during the period with the expenses incurred to produce that revenue. At the end of an accounting period, adjusting entries are needed so that all revenue ***earned*** is reflected in the accounts regardless of whether it has been collected. Adjusting entries are also needed for expenses to assure that all expenses ***incurred*** are matched against the revenue of the current period, regardless of when cash payment of the expense occurs.

Thus, adjusting entries help in achieving the goals of accrual accounting—recording revenue when it is ***earned*** and recording expenses when the related goods and services are ***used.*** The realization principle and the matching principle are key elements of accrual accounting. Adjusting entries are a technique of applying these principles to transactions that affect two or more accounting periods.

In Chapter 3, the concept of adjusting entries was introduced when Roberts Real Estate Company recorded depreciation for the month of October. Adjusting entries are necessary to record depreciation expense, because buildings and equipment are purchased in a single accounting period but are used over many periods. Some portion of the cost of these assets should be allocated to expense in each period of the asset's estimated life. In this chapter, we will see that the use of adjusting entries is not limited to recording depreciation expense. Adjusting entries are needed ***whenever transactions affect the revenue or expense of more than one accounting period.***

Types of Adjusting Entries

OBJECTIVE 2 Describe the four basic types of adjusting entries; prepare these entries.

A business may need to make a dozen or more adjusting entries at the end of each accounting period. The exact number of adjustments will depend upon the nature of the company's business activities. All adjusting entries fall into one of five general categories. However, we will focus on the following ***four*** in this chapter.[1]

1. **Entries to apportion recorded costs.** A cost that will benefit more than one accounting period usually is recorded by debiting an asset account. In each period that benefits from the use of this asset, an adjusting entry is made to allocate a portion of the asset's cost to expense.
2. **Entries to apportion unearned revenue.** A business may collect in advance for services to be rendered to customers in future accounting periods. In the period in which services are rendered, an adjusting entry is made to record the portion of the revenue earned during the period.
3. **Entries to record unrecorded expenses.** An expense may be incurred in the current accounting period even though no bill has yet been received and payment will not occur until a future period. Such unrecorded expenses are recorded by an adjusting entry made at the end of the accounting period.
4. **Entries to record unrecorded revenue.** Revenue may be earned during the current period, but not yet billed to customers or recorded in the accounting records. Such unrecorded revenue is recorded by making an adjusting entry at the end of the period.

Characteristics of Adjusting Entries

It will be helpful to keep in mind two important characteristics of all adjusting entries. First, every adjusting entry ***involves the recognition of either revenue or expense.*** Revenue and expenses represent changes in owner's equity. However, owner's equity cannot change by itself; there also must be a corresponding change in either assets or liabilities. ***Thus, every***

[1] A fifth category of adjusting entries consists of adjustments to the balance sheet valuation of certain assets, such as marketable securities and accounts receivable. Valuation adjustments will be explained and illustrated in later chapters.

adjusting entry affects both an income statement account (revenue or expense) ***and a balance sheet account*** (asset or liability).

Second, adjusting entries are based upon the concepts of accrual accounting, ***not upon monthly bills or month-end transactions.*** No one sends us a bill saying, "Depreciation expense on your building amounts to $500 this month." Yet, we must be aware of the need to estimate and record depreciation expense if we are to measure net income properly for the period. Making adjusting entries requires a greater understanding of accrual accounting concepts than does the recording of routine business transactions. In many businesses, the adjusting entries are made by the company's controller or by a professional accountant, rather than by the regular accounting staff.

To demonstrate the various types of adjusting entries, the illustration of Roberts Real Estate Company will be continued for November. We shall consider in detail only those November transactions that require adjusting entries at the end of the month.

In the next few pages we illustrate several ***transactions*** as well as the related ***adjusting entries.*** To help highlight the distinction between transactions and adjusting entries, journal entries recording regular transactions are shown in ***black,*** and adjusting entries are printed in ***blue.***

Apportioning Recorded Costs

When a business makes an expenditure that will benefit more than one accounting period, the amount usually is debited to an asset account. At the end of each period benefiting from this expenditure, an adjusting entry is made to transfer an appropriate portion of the cost from the asset account to an expense account. This adjusting entry reflects the fact that part of the asset has been used up—that is, become expense—during the current accounting period.

An adjusting entry to apportion a recorded cost consists of a debit to an expense account and a credit to an asset account (or a contra-asset account). Examples of these adjustments include the entries to record depreciation expense and to apportion the costs of ***prepaid expenses.***

Prepaid Expenses Payments in advance are often made for such items as insurance, rent, and office supplies. If the advance payment (or prepayment) will benefit more than just the current accounting period, the cost ***represents an asset*** rather than an expense. The cost of this asset will be allocated to expense in the accounting periods in which the services or the supplies are used. In summary, ***prepaid expenses are assets;*** they become expenses only as the goods or services are used up.

Insurance To illustrate these concepts, assume that on November 1, Roberts Real Estate Company paid $600 for a one-year fire insurance policy covering the building. This expenditure was debited to an asset account by the following journal entry:

Expenditure for insurance policy recorded as asset

Unexpired Insurance	*600*	
Cash		*600*
Purchased a one-year fire insurance policy.		

Since this expenditure of $600 will protect the company against fire loss for one year, the insurance expense applicable to each month's operations is $\frac{1}{12}$ of the annual expense, or $50. In order that the accounting records for November show insurance expense of $50, the following ***adjusting entry*** is required at November 30:

Adjusting entry. Portion of asset expires (becomes expense)

Insurance Expense	*50*	
Unexpired Insurance		*50*
To record insurance expense for November.		

This adjusting entry serves two purposes: (1) it apportions the proper amount of insurance expense to November operations, and (2) it reduces the asset account to $550 so that the correct amount of unexpired insurance will appear in the balance sheet at November 30.

What would be the effect on the income statement for November if the above adjustment were not made? The expenses would be understated by $50 and consequently the net income would be overstated by $50. The balance sheet also would be affected by failure to make the adjustment: the assets would be overstated by $50 and so would the owner's equity. The overstatement of the owner's equity would result from the overstated amount of net income transferred to the owner's equity account when the accounts were closed at November 30.

Office Supplies On November 2, Roberts Real Estate Company purchased enough stationery and other office supplies to last for several months. The cost of the supplies was $720, and this amount was debited to an asset account by the following journal entry:

Expenditure for office supplies recorded as asset

Office Supplies	*720*	
Cash		*720*
Purchased office supplies.		

No entries were made during November to record the day-to-day usage of office supplies, but on November 30 the office manager estimated that supplies costing about $500 were still on hand. Thus, supplies costing about $220 were used during November. On the basis of this month-end estimate, an adjusting entry is made debiting an expense account $220 (the cost of supplies consumed during November) and reducing the asset account by $220. The ***adjusting entry*** follows:

Adjusting entry. Portion of supplies used represents expense

Office Supplies Expense	*220*	
Office Supplies		*220*
To record consumption of office supplies in November.		

After this entry is posted, the asset account Office Supplies will have a balance of $500, representing the estimated cost of office supplies on hand at November 30. The Office Supplies account will appear in the balance sheet as an asset; the Office Supplies Expense account will be shown in the income statement.

How would failure to make this adjustment affect the financial statements? In the income statement for November, the expenses would be understated by $220 and the net income overstated by the same amount. Since the overstated amount for net income in November would be transferred into the owner's equity account in the process of closing the accounts, the owner's equity section of the balance sheet would be overstated by $220. Assets also would be overstated because Office Supplies would be listed at $220 too much.

Recording Prepayments Directly in the Expense Accounts In our illustration, payments for insurance and office supplies that are expected to provide benefits for more than one accounting period are recorded by debiting an asset account, such as Unexpired Insurance or Office Supplies. However, some companies follow an alternative practice of debiting these prepayments directly to an expense account such as Insurance Expense. At the end of the period, the adjusting entry would then consist of a debit to Unexpired Insurance and a credit to Insurance Expense for the portion of the insurance cost ***that has not yet expired.***

This alternative method leads to the same results in the balance sheet and income statement as does the method used in our illustration. Under both procedures, the cost of benefits consumed in the current period is treated as an expense, and the cost of benefits applicable to future periods is carried forward in the balance sheet as an asset.

In this text and in the end-of-chapter problem material, we will follow the practice of recording prepayments in ***asset accounts*** and then making adjusting entries to transfer these costs to expense accounts as the assets expire. This approach correctly describes the ***conceptual flow of costs*** through the elements of financial statements. That is, a prepayment ***is*** an asset that later becomes an expense. The alternative approach is used widely in practice only because it is an efficient short-cut, which standardizes the recording of transactions and may reduce the number of adjusting entries needed at the end of the period. Remember, our goal in this course is to develop your ability to ***understand and use*** accounting information, not to train you in the most efficient bookkeeping procedures.

Depreciation of Building The recording of depreciation expense at the end of an accounting period provides another example of an adjusting entry that ***apportions a recorded cost.*** The November 30 adjusting entry to record depreciation of the building used by Roberts Real Estate Company is exactly the same as the October 31 ***adjusting entry*** explained in Chapter 3.

Adjusting entry. Cost of building is gradually converted to expense

Depreciation Expense: Building	*150*	
Accumulated Depreciation: Building		*150*
To record depreciation for November.		

This allocation of depreciation expense to November operations is based on the following facts: the building cost $36,000 and is estimated to have a useful life of 20 years (240 months). Using the straight-line method of depreciation, the portion of the original cost that expires each month is $\frac{1}{240}$ of $36,000, or $150.

The Accumulated Depreciation: Building account now has a credit balance of $300 as a result of the October and November credits of $150 each. The book value of the building is $35,700; that is, the original cost of

$36,000 minus the accumulated depreciation of $300. The term ***book value*** means the net amount at which an asset is shown in the accounting records, as distinguished from its market value. ***Carrying value*** is an alternative term, with the same meaning as book value.

Depreciation of Office Equipment The November 30 adjusting entry to record depreciation of the office equipment is the same as the ***adjusting entry*** for depreciation a month earlier, as shown in Chapter 3.

Adjusting entry. Cost of office equipment gradually converted to expense

Depreciation Expense: Office Equipment	45	
Accumulated Depreciation: Office Equipment		45
To record depreciation for November.		

The original cost of the office equipment was $5,400, and the estimated useful life was 10 years (120 months). Depreciation each month under the straight-line method is therefore $\frac{1}{120}$ of $5,400, or $45.

What is the book value of the office equipment at this point? The original cost of $5,400 minus accumulated depreciation of $90 for two months leaves a book value of $5,310.

Apportioning Unearned Revenue

In some instances, a business may ***collect in advance*** for services to be rendered to customers in later accounting periods. For example, a football team collects much of its revenue in advance through the sale of season tickets. Health clubs collect in advance by selling long-term membership contracts. Airlines sell many of their tickets well in advance of a scheduled flight.

For accounting purposes, amounts collected in advance ***do not represent revenue,*** because these amounts have ***not yet been earned.*** Amounts collected from customers in advance are recorded by debiting the Cash account and crediting an ***unearned revenue*** account. Unearned revenue also may be called ***deferred revenue.***

When a company collects money in advance from its customers, it has an ***obligation*** to render services in the future. Therefore, the balance of an unearned revenue account is considered to be a liability; ***it appears in the liability section of the balance sheet, not in the income statement.*** Unearned revenue differs from other liabilities because it usually will be settled by rendering services, rather than by making payment in cash. In short, it will be ***worked off*** rather than ***paid off.*** Of course if the business is unable to render the service, it must discharge this liability by refunding money to its customers.

CASE IN POINT One of the largest liabilities in the balance sheet of Air Canada is "Advance ticket sales." This account, with a balance of approximately $192 million, represents unearned revenue resulting from the sale of tickets for future flights. Most of this unearned revenue will be earned as the future flights occur. Some customers, however, will change their plans and will return their tickets to Air Canada for a cash refund.

When the company renders the services for which customers have paid in advance, it is working off its liability to these customers and is earning the revenue. At the end of the accounting period in which the revenue is earned, an ***adjusting entry*** is made to transfer an appropriate amount from the unearned revenue account to a revenue account. This adjusting entry consists of a debit to a liability account (unearned revenue) and a credit to a revenue account.

To illustrate these concepts, assume that on November 1, Roberts Real Estate Company agreed to act as manager of some rental properties for a monthly fee of $300. The owner of the properties, Frank Day, was leaving the country on an extended trip and therefore paid the company for six months' service in advance. The journal entry by Roberts Real Estate Company to record the transaction on November 1 was:

Management fee collected but not yet earned

Cash	*1,800*	
Unearned Management Fees		*1,800*
Collected in advance six months' fees for management of properties owned by Frank Day.		

Remember that Unearned Management Fees is a ***liability*** account, not a revenue account. This management fee will be earned gradually over a period of six months as Roberts Real Estate Company performs the required services. At the end of each monthly accounting period, the company will make an adjusting entry transferring $\frac{1}{6}$ of this management fee, or $300, from the unearned revenue account to a revenue account. The first in this series of monthly transfers will be made on November 30 by the following ***adjusting entry:***

Adjusting entry to recognize earning of a part of management fee

Unearned Management Fees	*300*	
Management Fees Earned		*300*
Fee earned by managing Frank Day property during November.		

After this entry has been posted, the Unearned Management Fees account will have a $1,500 credit balance. This balance represents the company's obligation to render $1,500 worth of services over the next five months and will appear in the liability section of the company's balance sheet. The Management Fees Earned account will be shown as revenue in the November income statement.

Recording Advance Collections Directly in the Revenue Accounts We have stressed that amounts collected from customers in advance represent liabilities, not revenue. However, some companies prefer to follow an accounting practice of crediting these advance collections directly to revenue accounts. Under this practice, the adjusting entry required at the end of the period would consist of a debit to the revenue account and a credit to the unearned revenue account for the portion of the advance payment ***not yet earned.*** This alternative accounting practice leads to the same results in the financial statements as does the method used in our Roberts Real Estate Company illustration.

Throughout this book, we will follow the originally described practice of crediting advance payments from customers to an unearned revenue account.

Recording Unrecorded Expenses

This type of adjusting entry recognizes expenses that will be paid in ***future*** transactions; thus, no cost has yet been recorded in the accounting records. Salaries of employees and interest on borrowed money are common examples of expenses that accumulate from day to day but that usually are not recorded until they are paid. These expenses are said to ***accrue*** over time, that is, to grow or to accumulate. At the end of the accounting period, an adjusting entry should be made to record any expenses that have accrued but that have not yet been recorded. Since these expenses will be paid at a future date, the adjusting entry consists of a debit to an expense account and a credit to a liability account. We shall now use the example of Roberts Real Estate Company to illustrate this type of adjusting entry.

Accrual of Interest On November 1, Roberts Real Estate Company borrowed the sum of $3,000 from a bank for a period of three months. Banks require every borrower to sign a ***promissory note,*** that is, a formal, written promise to repay the amount borrowed plus interest at an agreed future date. (Various forms of notes in common use and the accounting problems involved will be discussed more fully in Chapter 11.) The note signed by Roberts, with certain details omitted, is shown below:

Note payable issued to bank

$3,000 Leamington, Ontario November 1, 19__

Three months after date I promise to pay

to the order of National Bank

---Three thousand and no/100--- dollars

for value received, with interest at 12 percent per year

Roberts Real Estate Company

By James Roberts

The note payable is a liability of Roberts Real Estate Company, similar to an account payable but different in that a formal written promise to pay is required and interest is charged on the amount borrowed. A Notes Payable account is credited when the note is issued; the Notes Payable account will be debited three months later when the note is paid. Interest accrues throughout the life of the note payable, but it is not payable until the note matures on February 1. To the bank making the loan, the note signed by Roberts is an asset, a note receivable.

The journal entry made on November 1 by Roberts Real Estate Company to record the borrowing of $3,000 from the bank was as follows:

Entry when bank loan is obtained

Cash	*3,000*	
Notes Payable		*3,000*
Obtained from bank three-month loan with interest at 12% a year.		

Three months later, Roberts Real Estate Company must pay the bank $3,090, representing repayment of the $3,000 note payable plus $90 interest ($3,000 × .12 × $\frac{3}{12}$).[2] The $90 is the total interest expense for the three months. Although no payment will be made for three months, one-third of the interest expense ($30) is ***incurred*** each month, as shown in the chart below.

Accrual of interest

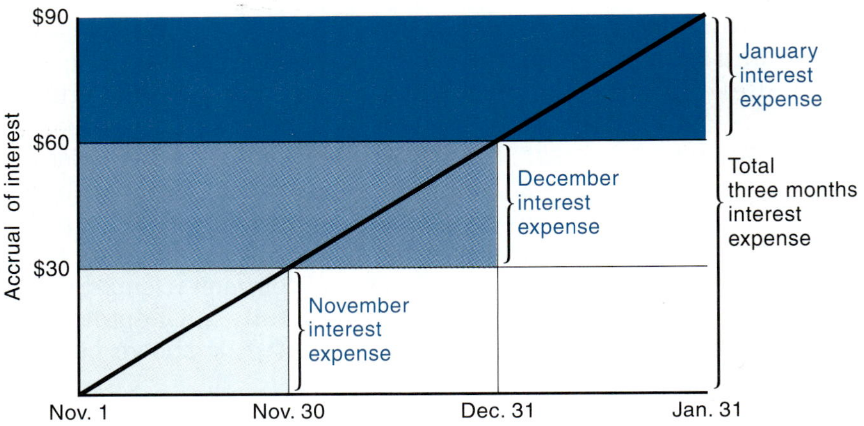

The following ***adjusting entry*** is made at November 30 to charge November operations with one month's interest expense and also to record the amount of interest owed to the bank at the end of November.

Adjusting entry for interest expense incurred in November

Interest Expense	*30*	
Interest Payable		*30*
To record interest expense accrued during November on note payable ($3,000 × 12% × $\frac{1}{12}$).		

The debit balance in the Interest Expense account will appear in the November income statement; the credit balances in the Interest Payable and Notes Payable accounts will be shown in the balance sheet as liabilities. These two liability accounts will remain in the records until the maturity date of the loan, at which time a cash payment to the bank will wipe out both the Notes Payable account and the Interest Payable account.

Accrual of Salary On November 20, Roberts hired Carl Nelson as a part-time salesperson whose job was to work evenings calling on property own-

---

[2] To simplify the interest calculation for demonstration purposes, the months rather than the days are used and thus the three days of grace for a note payable are not included.

ers to secure listings of property for sale or rent. The agreed salary was $225 for a five-evening week, payable each Friday; payment for the first week was made on Friday, November 24. Personal income taxes and other taxes relating to payroll are ignored in this illustration.

Assume that the last day of the accounting period, November 30, fell on Thursday. Nelson had worked four evenings since being paid the preceding Friday and therefore had earned $180 ($\frac{4}{5} \times \$225$). In order that this $180 of November salary expense be reflected in the accounts before the financial statements are prepared, an ***adjusting entry*** is necessary at November 30.

Adjusting entry for salaries expense incurred but unpaid at November 30

Salaries Expense	*180*	
Salaries Payable		*180*
To record salary expense and related liability to salesperson for last four evenings' work in November.		

The debit balance in the Salaries Expense account will appear as an expense in the November income statement; the credit balance of $180 in the Salaries Payable account is the amount owing to the salesperson for work performed during the last four days of November and will appear among the liabilities in the balance sheet at November 30.

The next regular payday for Nelson will be Friday, December 1, which is the first day of the new accounting period. Since the accounts were adjusted and closed on November 30, all the revenue and expense accounts have zero balances at the beginning of business on December 1. The payment of a week's salary to Nelson will be recorded by the following entry on December 1:

Payment of salary overlapping two accounting periods

Salaries Payable	***180***	
Salaries Expense	***45***	
Cash		***225***
Paid weekly salary to salesperson.		

Note that the net result of the November 30 accrual entry has been to split the salesperson's weekly salary expense between November and December. Four days of the work week fell in November, so four days' pay, or $180, was recognized as November expense. One day of the work week fell in December, so $45 was recorded as December expense.

No accrual entry is necessary for other salaries in Roberts Real Estate Company because everyone except Nelson is paid regularly on the last working day of the month.

Recording Unrecorded Revenue

A business may earn revenue during the current accounting period but might not bill the customer until a future accounting period. This situation is likely to occur if additional services will be performed for the same customer, in which case the bill might not be prepared until all services are completed. Any revenue that has been ***earned but not recorded*** during the current accounting period should be recorded at the end of the period by means of an adjusting entry. This adjusting entry consists of a debit to an account receivable and a credit to the appropriate revenue account. The term ***accrued revenue*** often is used to describe revenue that has been earned during the period but that has ***not been recorded*** prior to the making of adjusting entries.

To illustrate this type of adjusting entry, assume that on November 16, Roberts Real Estate Company entered into a management agreement with Angela Clayton, the owner of a small office building. The company agreed to manage the Clayton property for a fee of $240 a month, payable on the fifteenth of each month. No entry is made in the accounting records at the time of signing a contract, because no services have yet been rendered and no change has occurred in assets or liabilities. The managerial duties are to begin immediately, but the first monthly fee will not be received until December 15. The following ***adjusting entry*** is therefore necessary at November 30:

Adjusting entry for fees earned but not yet billed

Management Fees Receivable	*120*	
Management Fees Earned		*120*
To record accrued revenue from services rendered to Angela Clayton during November.		

The debit balance in the Management Fees Receivable account will be shown in the balance sheet as an asset. The credit balance of the Management Fees Earned account, including earnings from both the Frank Day and the Angela Clayton contracts, will appear in the November income statement.

The collection of the first monthly fee from Clayton will occur in the next accounting period (December 15, to be exact). Of this $240 cash receipt, half represents collection of the asset account, Management Fees Receivable, created at November 30 by the adjusting entry. The other half of the $240 cash receipt represents revenue earned during December; this should be credited to the December revenue account for Management Fees Earned. The entry on December 15 is as follows:

Management fee applicable to two accounting periods

Cash	*240*	
Management Fees Receivable		*120*
Management Fees Earned		*120*
Collected management fee from Angela Clayton for month ended December 15.		

The net result of the November 30 accrual entry has been to divide the revenue from managing the Clayton properties between November and December in accordance with the timing of the services rendered.

Adjusting Entries and the Accrual Basis of Accounting

Adjusting entries help make accrual basis accounting work successfully. By preparing adjusting entries, we can recognize revenue in the accounting period in which it is ***earned*** and also recognize any unrecorded expenses that helped to ***produce that revenue.*** For example, the adjusting entry to record revenue that has been earned but not yet recorded helps achieve our goal of including in the income statement all the revenue ***realized*** during the accounting period. The adjusting entries that recognize expenses help to achieve the ***matching principle***—that is, offsetting revenues with all the expenses incurred in generating that revenue.

The Concept of Materiality

Jan./99

OBJECTIVE 3 Explain the concept of materiality.

The term ***materiality*** refers to the ***relative importance*** of an item or an event. An item is "material" if knowledge of the item might reasonably ***influence the decisions*** of users of financial statements. Accountants must be sure that all material items are properly reported in financial statements.

However, the financial reporting process should be ***cost effective***—that is, the value of the information should exceed the cost of its preparation. By definition, the accounting treatment accorded to ***immaterial*** items is of ***little or no consequence to decision makers.*** Therefore, accountants do not waste time accounting for immaterial items; these items may be handled in the ***easiest and most convenient manner.***

In summary, the concept of materiality allows accountants to use estimated amounts and even to ignore other accounting principles if the results of these actions ***do not have a "material effect"*** upon the financial statements. Materiality is one of the most important generally accepted accounting principles; we will encounter applications of this concept throughout the study of accounting.

Materiality and Adjusting Entries The concept of materiality enables accountants to shorten and simplify the process of making adjusting entries in several ways. For example:

1 Businesses purchase many "assets" that have a very low cost, or that will be consumed quickly in business operations. Examples include wastebaskets, lightbulbs, and janitorial supplies. The materiality concept permits charging such purchases ***directly to expense accounts,*** rather than to asset accounts. This treatment conveniently eliminates the need for an adjusting entry at the end of the period to transfer a portion of these costs from an asset account to expense. This accounting short-cut is acceptable as long as the cost of the ***unused*** items on hand at the end of the period is "immaterial."

2 Some expenses, such as telephone bills and utility bills, may be charged to expense as the bills are ***paid,*** rather than as the services are used. Technically this treatment violates the ***matching principle.*** However, accounting for utility bills on a cash basis is very convenient, as the monthly cost of utility service is not even known until the utility bill is received. Under this "cash basis" approach, one month's utility bill is charged to expense each month. Although the bill charged to expense is actually the ***prior*** month's bill, the resulting "error" in the financial statements is not likely to be material.

3 Adjusting entries to accrue unrecorded expenses or unrecorded revenue may be ignored if the dollar amounts are immaterial.

4 If the amount of error is not likely to be material, adjusting entries may be based on ***estimates.*** For example, on page 157 we illustrate an adjusting entry allocating part of the $720 balance in the Office Supplies account to expense. The amount of supplies used during the period ($220) was based upon an ***estimate*** of the supplies still on hand ($500). This $500 estimate is an educated guess; no one actually counted every pen, pencil, and pad of paper on hand at month-end.

Materiality Is a Matter of Professional Judgment Whether or not a specific item or event is "material" is a matter of ***professional judgment.*** In making these judgments, accountants consider several factors.

First, what constitutes a "material amount" varies with the size of the organization. For example, a $1,000 expenditure may be material in relation to the financial statements of a small business but not to the statements of a large corporation such as General Motors.[3] There are no official rules as to what constitutes a "material amount," but most accountants would consider amounts of less than 2 or 3% of net income to be ***immaterial.***

Next, accountants must consider the ***cumulative effect*** of numerous "immaterial" events. Each of a dozen items may be immaterial when considered by itself. When viewed together, however, the ***combined effect*** of all twelve items may be material.

Finally, materiality depends upon the ***nature*** of the item, as well as its dollar amount. Assume, for example, that several managers systematically have been stealing money from the company that they manage. Shareholders probably would consider this fact important even if the dollar amounts were but a small percentage of the company's total resources.

Note to students: In the assignment material accompanying this textbook, you are to consider all dollar amounts to be material, unless the problem specifically states otherwise.

THE WORK SHEET

OBJECTIVE 4 Prepare a work sheet and explain its usefulness.

The work necessary at the end of an accounting period includes construction of a trial balance, journalizing and posting of adjusting entries, preparation of financial statements, and journalizing and posting of closing entries. So many details are involved in these end-of-period procedures that it is easy to make errors. If these errors are recorded in the journal and in the ledger accounts, considerable time and effort can be wasted in correcting them. Both the journal and the ledger are formal, permanent records. One way of avoiding errors in the permanent accounting records and also of simplifying the work to be done at the end of the period is to use a ***work sheet.***

In a manual accounting system, a work sheet is a large columnar sheet of paper, specially designed to arrange in a convenient systematic form all the accounting data required at the end of the period. The work sheet is not a part of the permanent accounting records; it is prepared in pencil by accountants for their own convenience. (The use of a computer to prepare a work sheet is discussed later in this chapter.) If an error is made on the work sheet, it may be erased and corrected much more easily than an error in the formal accounting records. Furthermore, the work sheet is designed to reduce errors by automatically bringing to light many types of discrepancies that otherwise might be entered in the journal and posted to the ledger accounts. Dollar signs, decimal points, and commas are not used

---

[3] This point is emphasized by the fact that GM rounds the dollar amounts shown in its financial statements to the nearest million dollars. This rounding of financial statement amounts is, in itself, an application of the materiality concept.

with the amounts entered on work sheets, although commas are shown in this example. A work sheet for Roberts Real Estate Company appears on page 168.

The work sheet may be thought of as a testing ground on which the ledger accounts are adjusted, balanced, and arranged in the general form of financial statements. The satisfactory completion of a work sheet provides considerable assurance that all the details of the end-of-period accounting procedures have been properly brought together. After this point has been established, the work sheet then serves as the source from which the formal financial statements are prepared and the adjusting and closing entries are made in the journal.

Preparing the Work Sheet

Notice that the heading of the work sheet illustrated for Roberts Real Estate Company consists of three parts: (1) the name of the business, (2) the title ***Work Sheet,*** and (3) the period of time covered. The body of the work sheet contains five pairs of money columns, each pair consisting of a debit and a credit column. The procedures to be followed in preparing a work sheet will now be illustrated in five simple steps.

1 **Enter the ledger account balances in the Trial Balance columns.** The titles and balances of the ledger accounts at November 30 are copied directly from the ledger into the Trial Balance columns of the work sheet, as illustrated on page 168.[4] It would be a duplication of work to prepare a trial balance as a separate schedule and then to copy this information into the work sheet. As soon as the account balances have been listed on the work sheet, these two columns should be added and the totals entered.

Notice that in our work sheet we have inserted captions indicating which ledger accounts relate to the ***balance sheet*** and which relate to the ***income statement.***[5] The sequence of accounts in the ledger lends itself to these captions, because ledger accounts are arranged in financial statement order—that is, the balance sheet accounts appear first.

Including these "Balance sheet" and "Income statement" captions in a trial balance is an optional procedure, but the technique is widely used in practice. We strongly favour the use of these captions for ***educational purposes.*** They help emphasize, for example, that every adjusting entry affects ***both the balance sheet and the income statement.*** Also these captions help to clarify one of the final steps in completing a work sheet—extending the amounts shown in the adjusted trial balance to the appropriate financial statement columns.

If the work sheet is prepared manually, the accountant should leave a few ***blank lines*** after the last "balance sheet" account.[6] If additional balance sheet accounts are needed during the preparation of adjusting

---

[4] The November balances of the ledger accounts reflect all transactions that occurred in the month, even though only those transactions that require adjusting entries have been presented so that we can concentrate on the demonstration of adjustments and work sheet.

[5] The Drawing account is included among the balance sheet accounts because withdrawals affect the amount of owner's equity, but they do ***not*** appear in the income statement.

[6] In a computer-based system, it is not necessary to leave any blank lines; additional lines may be inserted at any point.

Step 1: Prepare a trial balance

ROBERTS REAL ESTATE COMPANY
Work Sheet
For the Month Ended November 30, 19__

	Trial Balance		Adjustments		Adjusted Trial Balance		Income Statement		Balance Sheet	
	Dr	Cr	Dr	Cr	Dr	Cr	Dr	Cr	Dr	Cr
Balance sheet accounts:										
Cash	21,740									
Accounts receivable	16,990									
Unexpired insurance	600									
Office supplies	720									
Land	130,000									
Building	36,000									
Accumulated depreciation: building		150								
Office equipment	5,400									
Accumulated depreciation: office equipment		45								
Notes payable		3,000								
Accounts payable		23,595								
Unearned management fees		1,800								
James Roberts, capital		180,771								
James Roberts, drawing	1,500									
Income statement accounts:										
Sales commissions earned		15,484								
Advertising expense	1,275									
Salaries expense	9,425									
Telephone expense	1,195									
	224,845	224,845								

entries, they can be added on these lines. Additional income statement accounts needed during the adjustment process may be added below the trial balance totals.

2 **Enter the adjustments in the Adjustments columns.** The required adjustments for Roberts Real Estate Company were explained earlier in this chapter; these same adjustments are now entered in the Adjustments columns of the work sheet. (See the following page.)

As a cross-reference, the debit and credit parts of each adjustment are keyed together by placing a key letter to the left of each amount. For example, the adjustment debiting Insurance Expense and crediting Unexpired Insurance is identified by the key letter (a). The use of the key letters makes it easy to match a debit entry in the Adjustments columns with its related credit. The identifying letters also key the debit and credit entries in the Adjustments columns to the brief explanations that appear at the bottom of the work sheet.

In some cases, adjusting entries may require the use of accounts that were not included in the original trial balance. These accounts must be added to the work sheet. Balance sheet accounts—assets and liabilities—are added in the lines that had been left blank following the last balance sheet account in the trial balance. Income statement accounts—revenue and expenses—can be added on lines below the totals for the trial balance columns. After all the adjustment debits and credits have been entered in the Adjustments columns, this pair of columns must be totalled. Proving the equality of debit and credit totals helps to detect any arithmetical errors and to prevent them from being carried over into other columns of the work sheet.

3 **Enter the account balances as adjusted in the Adjusted Trial Balance columns.** The work sheet as it appears after completion of the Adjusted Trial Balance columns is illustrated on page 171. Each account balance in the first pair of columns is combined with the adjustment, if any, in the second pair of columns, and the combined amount is entered in the Adjusted Trial Balance columns. This process of combining the items on each line throughout the first four columns of the work sheet requires horizontal addition or subtraction.

For example, the Office Supplies account has a debit balance of $720 in the Trial Balance columns. This $720 debit amount is combined with the $220 credit appearing on the same line in the Adjustments column; the combination of a $720 ***debit*** with a $220 ***credit*** produces an adjusted debit amount of ***$500*** in the Adjusted Trial Balance debit column. As another example, consider the Office Supplies Expense account. This account had no balance in the Trial Balance columns but shows a $220 debit in the Adjustments debit column. The combination of a zero starting balance and $220 debit adjustment produces a $220 debit amount in the Adjusted Trial Balance.

Many of the accounts in the trial balance are not affected by the adjustments made at the end of the month; the balances of these accounts (such as Cash, Land, Building, or Notes Payable in the illustrated work sheet) are entered in the Adjusted Trial Balance columns in exactly the ***same amounts*** as shown in the Trial Balance columns. After all the accounts have been extended into the Adjusted Trial Bal-

Step 2: Prepare adjusting entries in "columnar form"

ROBERTS REAL ESTATE COMPANY
Work Sheet
For the Month Ended November 30, 19__

	Trial Balance		Adjustments*		Adjusted Trial Balance		Income Statement		Balance Sheet	
	Dr	Cr	Dr	Cr	Dr	Cr	Dr	Cr	Dr	Cr
Balance sheet accounts:										
Cash	21,740									
Accounts receivable	16,990									
Unexpired insurance	600			(a) 50						
Office supplies	720			(b) 220						
Land	130,000									
Building	36,000									
Accumulated depreciation: building		150		(c) 150						
Office equipment	5,400									
Accumulated depreciation: office equipment		45		(d) 45						
Notes payable		3,000								
Accounts payable		23,595								
Unearned management fees		1,800	(e) 300							
James Roberts, capital		180,771								
James Roberts, drawing	1,500									
Interest payable				(f) 30						
Salaries payable				(g) 180						
Management fees receivable			(h) 120							
Income statement accounts:										
Sales commissions earned		15,484								
Advertising expense	1,275									
Salaries expense	9,425		(g) 180							
Telephone expense	1,195									
	224,845	224,845								
Insurance expense			(a) 50							
Office supplies expense			(b) 220							
Depreciation expense: building			(c) 150							
Depreciation expense: office equipment			(d) 45							
Management fees earned				(e) 300						
				(h) 120						
Interest expense			(f) 30							
			1,095	1,095						

Explanatory footnotes keyed to adjustments

* Adjustments:

(a) Portion of insurance cost that expired during November.
(b) Office supplies used during November.
(c) Depreciation of building during November.
(d) Depreciation of office equipment during November.
(e) Earned one-sixth of the fee collected in advance on the Day properties.
(f) Interest expense accrued during November on note payable ($3,000 × 12% × 1/12).
(g) Salesperson's salary for last four days of November.
(h) Management fee accrued on Clayton contract in November.

Step 3: Determine the adjusted balances and enter them in Adjusted Trial Balance columns

ROBERTS REAL ESTATE COMPANY
Work Sheet
For the Month Ended November 30, 19__

	Trial Balance		Adjustments*		Adjusted Trial Balance		Income Statement		Balance Sheet	
	Dr	Cr	Dr	Cr	Dr	Cr	Dr	Cr	Dr	Cr
Balance sheet accounts:										
Cash	21,740				21,740					
Accounts receivable	16,990				16,990					
Unexpired insurance	600			(a) 50	550					
Office supplies	720			(b) 220	500					
Land	130,000				130,000					
Building	36,000				36,000					
Accumulated depreciation: building		150		(c) 150		300				
Office equipment	5,400				5,400					
Accumulated depreciation: office equipment		45		(d) 45		90				
Notes payable		3,000				3,000				
Accounts payable		23,595				23,595				
Unearned management fees		1,800	(e) 300			1,500				
James Roberts, capital		180,771				180,771				
James Roberts, drawing	1,500				1,500					
Interest payable				(f) 30		30				
Salaries payable				(g) 180		180				
Management fees receivable			(h) 120		120					
Income statement accounts:										
Sales commissions earned		15,484				15,484				
Advertising expense	1,275				1,275					
Salaries expense	9,425		(g) 180		9,605					
Telephone expense	1,195				1,195					
	224,845	224,845								
Insurance expense			(a) 50		50					
Office supplies expense			(b) 220		220					
Depreciation expense: building			(c) 150		150					
Depreciation expense: office equipment			(d) 45		45					
Management fees earned				(e) 300		420				
				(h) 120						
Interest expense			(f) 30		30					
			1,095	1,095	225,370	225,370				

* Explanatory notes relating to adjustments are the same as on page 170.

ance columns, this pair of columns is totalled to prove that no arithmetical errors have been made up to this point.

4 **Extend each amount in the Adjusted Trial Balance columns into the Income Statement columns or into the Balance Sheet columns.** Assets, liabilities, and the owner's capital and drawing accounts are extended to the Balance Sheet columns; revenue and expense accounts are extended to the Income Statement columns.

The process of extending amounts horizontally across the work sheet should begin with the account at the top of the work sheet, which is usually Cash. The cash figure is extended to the Balance Sheet debit column. Then the accountant goes down the work sheet line by line, extending each account balance to the appropriate Balance Sheet or Income Statement column. The likelihood of error is much less when each account is extended in the order of its appearance on the work sheet, than if accounts are extended in random order. The work sheet as it appears after completion of this sorting process is illustrated on page 173. Note that each amount in the Adjusted Trial Balance columns is extended to one ***and only one*** of the four remaining columns.

5 **Total the Income Statement columns and the Balance Sheet columns. Enter the net income or net loss as a balancing figure in both pairs of columns, and again compute column totals.** The work sheet as it appears after this final step is shown on page 174.

The net income or net loss for the period is determined by computing the difference between the totals of the two Income Statement columns. In the illustrated work sheet, the credit column total is the larger and the excess represents net income:

Income Statement credit column total (revenue)	*$15,904*
Income Statement debit column total (expenses)	*12,570*
Difference: net income for period	*$ 3,334*

Note on the work sheet that the net income of $3,334 is entered in the Income Statement ***debit*** column as a balancing figure and also on the same line as a balancing figure in the Balance Sheet ***credit*** column. The caption ***Net Income*** is written in the space for account titles to identify and explain this item. New totals are then computed for both the Income Statement columns and the Balance Sheet columns. Each pair of columns is now in balance.

The reason for entering the net income of $3,334 in the Balance Sheet credit column is that the net income accumulated during the period in the revenue and expense accounts causes an increase in the owner's equity. If the balance sheet columns did not have equal totals after the net income had been recorded in the credit column, the lack of agreement would indicate that an error had been made in the work sheet.

Let us assume for a moment that the month's operations had produced a ***net loss*** rather than a net income. In that case the Income Statement debit column would exceed the credit column. The excess of the debits (expenses) over the credits (revenue) would have to be entered in the ***credit column*** in order to bring the two Income Statement

Step 4: Extend each adjusted amount to the appropriate financial statement columns

ROBERTS REAL ESTATE COMPANY
Work Sheet
For the Month Ended November 30, 19__

	Trial Balance		Adjustments*		Adjusted Trial Balance		Income Statement		Balance Sheet	
	Dr	Cr	Dr	Cr	Dr	Cr	Dr	Cr	Dr	Cr
Balance sheet accounts:										
Cash	21,740				21,740				21,740	
Accounts receivable	16,990				16,990				16,990	
Unexpired insurance	600			(a) 50	550				550	
Office supplies	720			(b) 220	500				500	
Land	130,000				130,000				130,000	
Building	36,000				36,000				36,000	
Accumulated depreciation: building		150		(c) 150		300				300
Office equipment	5,400				5,400				5,400	
Accumulated depreciation: office equipment		45		(d) 45		90				90
Notes payable		3,000				3,000				3,000
Accounts payable		23,595				23,595				23,595
Unearned management fees		1,800	(e) 300			1,500				1,500
James Roberts, capital		180,771				180,771				180,771
James Roberts, drawing	1,500				1,500				1,500	
Interest payable				(f) 30		30				30
Salaries payable				(g) 180		180				180
Management fees receivable			(h) 120		120				120	
Income statement accounts:										
Sales commissions earned		15,484				15,484		15,484		
Advertising expense	1,275				1,275		1,275			
Salaries expense	9,425		(g) 180		9,605		9,605			
Telephone expense	1,195				1,195		1,195			
	224,845	224,845								
Insurance expense			(a) 50		50		50			
Office supplies expense			(b) 220		220		220			
Depreciation expense: building			(c) 150		150		150			
Depreciation expense: office equipment			(d) 45		45		45			
Management fees earned				(e) 300		420		420		
				(h) 120						
Interest expense			(f) 30		30		30			
			1,095	1,095	225,370	225,370				

* Explanatory notes relating to adjustments are the same as on page 170.

Step 5: Total both sets of financial statement columns; then enter net income as the "balancing figure"

ROBERTS REAL ESTATE COMPANY
Work Sheet
For the Month Ended November 30, 19__

	Trial Balance		Adjustments*		Adjusted Trial Balance		Income Statement		Balance Sheet	
	Dr	Cr	Dr	Cr	Dr	Cr	Dr	Cr	Dr	Cr
Balance sheet accounts:										
Cash	21,740				21,740				21,740	
Accounts receivable	16,990				16,990				16,990	
Unexpired insurance	600			(a) 50	550				550	
Office supplies	720			(b) 220	500				500	
Land	130,000				130,000				130,000	
Building	36,000				36,000				36,000	
Accumulated depreciation: building		150		(c) 150		300				300
Office equipment	5,400				5,400				5,400	
Accumulated depreciation: office equipment		45		(d) 45		90				90
Notes payable		3,000				3,000				3,000
Accounts payable		23,595				23,595				23,595
Unearned management fees		1,800	(e) 300			1,500				1,500
James Roberts, capital		180,771				180,771				180,771
James Roberts, drawing	1,500				1,500				1,500	
Interest payable				(f) 30		30				30
Salaries payable				(g) 180		180				180
Management fees receivable			(h) 120		120				120	
Income statement accounts:										
Sales commissions earned		15,484				15,484		15,484		
Advertising expense	1,275				1,275		1,275			
Salaries expense	9,425		(g) 180		9,605		9,605			
Telephone expense	1,195				1,195		1,195			
	224,845	224,845								
Insurance expense			(a) 50		50		50			
Office supplies expense			(b) 220		220		220			
Depreciation expense: building			(c) 150		150		150			
Depreciation expense: office equipment			(d) 45		45		45			
Management fees earned				(e) 300		420		420		
				(h) 120						
Interest expense			(f) 30		30		30			
			1,095	1,095	225,370	225,370	12,570	15,904	212,800	209,466
Net income							3,334			3,334
							15,904	15,904	212,800	212,800

* Explanatory notes relating to adjustments are the same as on page 170.

Enter net income to balance the Income Statement columns

Extend net income to bring Balance Sheet columns into balance

columns into balance. The incurring of a net loss would decrease the owner's equity; therefore, the net loss would be entered as a balancing figure in the Balance Sheet ***debit column.*** The Balance Sheet columns would then have equal totals.

Self-Balancing Nature of the Work Sheet Why does the entering of the net income or net loss in one of the Balance Sheet columns bring this pair of columns into balance? The answer is short and simple. All the accounts in the Balance Sheet columns have November 30 balances with the exception of the owner's capital account, which still shows the October 31 balance (because there was no additional investment by the owner, otherwise it would be the beginning balance plus additional investments). By bringing in the current month's net income as an addition to the October 31 capital, the capital account is brought up to date as of November 30 (except for the drawing account which is later closed to the capital account). The Balance Sheet columns now prove the familiar proposition that assets are equal to the total of liabilities and owner's equity.

Uses for the Work Sheet

Preparing Financial Statements Preparing the formal financial statements from the work sheet is an easy step. All the information needed for both the income statement and the balance sheet has already been sorted and arranged in convenient form in the work sheet. For example, compare the amounts in the following income statement with the amounts listed in the Income Statement columns of the completed work sheet.[7]

Data taken from income statement columns of work sheet

ROBERTS REAL ESTATE COMPANY
Income Statement
For the Month Ended November 30, 19__

Revenue:		
Sales commissions earned		$15,484
Management fees earned		420
Total revenue		$15,904
Expenses:		
Advertising	$1,275	
Salaries	9,605	
Telephone	1,195	
Insurance	50	
Office supplies	220	
Depreciation: building	150	
Depreciation: office equipment	45	
Interest	30	
Total expenses		12,570
Net income		$ 3,334

[7] Since there are two revenue accounts and a large number of expense accounts, a subheading is used for total revenue and total expenses, which was not used in Chapter 3.

Notice that in our November 30 work sheet, the owner's capital account still contains its November 1 balance of $180,771. This is because all the changes in owner's equity occurring in the month were recorded in the ***temporary*** accounts (the revenue, expense, and drawing accounts), rather than in the owner's capital account. In the ledger, the owner's capital account will be brought up-to-date when the November closing entries are recorded and posted.

The work sheet provides us with all the information we need to compute the amount of owner's equity at November 30. During November, owner's equity was increased by the earning of net income ($3,334) and decreased by the withdrawal of assets by the owner ($1,500).

The November statement of owner's equity for Roberts Real Estate Company is shown below:

Net income exceeded withdrawals by owner

ROBERTS REAL ESTATE COMPANY
Statement of Owner's Equity
For the Month Ended November 30, 19__

James Roberts, capital, Nov. 1, 19__	*$180,771*
Add: Net income	*3,334*
Subtotal	*$184,105*
Less: Withdrawals	*1,500*
James Roberts, capital, Nov. 30, 19__	*$182,605*

Finally, the November 30 balance sheet for Roberts Real Estate Company contains the amounts for assets and liabilities listed in the Balance Sheet columns of the work sheet, along with the ***new balance*** of owner's equity.

Compare these amounts with figures in balance sheet columns of work sheet

ROBERTS REAL ESTATE COMPANY
Balance Sheet
November 30, 19__

Assets

Cash		*$ 21,740*
Accounts receivable		*16,990*
Management fees receivable		*120*
Unexpired insurance		*550*
Office supplies		*500*
Land		*130,000*
Building	*$36,000*	
Less: Accumulated depreciation	*300*	*35,700*
Office equipment	*$ 5,400*	
Less: Accumulated depreciation	*90*	*5,310*
Total assets		*$210,910*

Liabilities & Owner's Equity

Liabilities:	
Notes payable	*$ 3,000*
Accounts payable	*23,595*
Interest payable	*30*
Salaries payable	*180*
Unearned management fees	*1,500*
Total liabilities	*$ 28,305*
Owner's equity:	
James Roberts, capital	*182,605*
Total liabilities & owner's equity	*$210,910*

Recording Adjusting Entries in the Accounting Records After the financial statements have been prepared from the work sheet at the end of the period, adjusting journal entries are prepared to bring the ledger accounts into agreement with the financial statements. This is an easy step because the adjustments have already been computed on the work sheet. The amounts appearing in the Adjustments columns of the work sheet and the related explanations at the bottom of the work sheet provide all the necessary information for the adjusting entries, as shown below. These adjusting entries are first entered in the journal and then posted to the ledger accounts.

Adjustments on work sheet are entered in general journal

General Journal — **Page 5**

Date		Account Titles and Explanation	LP	Debit	Credit
19__					
Nov	30	Insurance Expense		50	
		Unexpired Insurance			50
		Insurance expense for November.			
	30	Office Supplies Expense		220	
		Office Supplies			220
		Office supplies used during November.			
	30	Depreciation Expense: Building		150	
		Accumulated Depreciation: Building			150
		Depreciation for November ($36,000 ÷ 240 = $150).			
	30	Depreciation Expense: Office Equipment		45	
		Accumulated Depreciation: Office Equipment			45
		Depreciation for November ($5,400 ÷ 120 = $45).			
	30	Unearned Management Fees		300	
		Management Fees Earned			300
		Earned one-sixth of fee collected in advance for management of the properties owned by Frank Day.			

General Journal **Page 5**

Date		Account Titles and Explanation	LP	Debit	Credit
19__					
Nov	30	Interest Expense		30	
		Interest Payable			30
		Interest expense accrued during November on note payable ($3,000 × 12% × $\frac{1}{12}$).			
	30	Salaries Expense		180	
		Salaries Payable..................			180
		To record expense and related liability to salesperson for last four evenings' work in November.			
	30	Management Fees Receivable		120	
		Management Fees Earned..........			120
		To record the receivable and related revenue earned for managing properties owned by Angela Clayton.			

Recording Closing Entries When the financial statements have been prepared, the revenue and expense accounts have served their purpose for the current period and should be closed. These accounts then will have ***zero balances*** and will be ready for the recording of revenue and expenses during the next fiscal period. The completed work sheet provides in convenient form all the information needed to make the closing entries. The preparation of closing entries from the work sheet may be summarized as follows:

1 To close the accounts listed in the Income Statement credit column, debit the revenue accounts and credit Income Summary.

2 To close the accounts listed in the Income Statement debit column, debit Income Summary and credit the expense accounts.

3 To close the Income Summary account, transfer the balancing figure in the Income Statement columns of the work sheet ($3,334 in the illustration) to the owner's capital account. A net income is transferred by debiting Income Summary and crediting the capital account; a net loss is transferred by debiting the capital account and crediting Income Summary.

4 To close the owner's drawing account, debit the capital account and credit the drawing account. Notice on the work sheet that the account, James Roberts, Drawing, is extended from the Adjusted Trial Balance debit column to the Balance Sheet debit column. It does not appear in the Income Statement columns because a withdrawal of cash by the owner is not regarded as an expense of the business.

The closing entries at November 30 are shown as follows:

Closing entries derived from work sheet

General Journal — **Page 6**

Date		Account Titles and Explanation	LP	Debit	Credit
19__					
Nov	30	Sales Commissions Earned		15,484	
		Management Fees Earned		420	
		Income Summary			15,904
		To close the revenue accounts.			
	30	Income Summary		12,570	
		Advertising Expense			1,275
		Salaries Expense			9,605
		Telephone Expense			1,195
		Insurance Expense			50
		Office Supplies Expense			220
		Depreciation Expense: Building			150
		Depreciation Expense: Office Equipment			45
		Interest Expense			30
		To close the expense accounts.			
	30	Income Summary		3,334	
		James Roberts, Capital			3,334
		To close the Income Summary account.			
	30	James Roberts, Capital		1,500	
		James Roberts, Drawing			1,500
		To close the owner's drawing account.			

Work Sheets in Computer-Based Systems The "work sheet" in a computer-based accounting system usually consists of one or more displays on the monitor screen rather than a sheet of columnar paper. Spreadsheet programs, such as Lotus 1-2-3 and VP Planner, are ideally suited to preparing a work sheet in a computerized accounting system.

Most of the steps involved in preparing a work sheet are mechanical and can be performed automatically in a computer-based system. Thus, the work sheet can be prepared faster and more easily than in a manual system. A trial balance, for example, is merely a listing of the ledger account balances and can be prepared instantly by computer. Entering the adjustments, on the other hand, requires human judgment and analysis. Someone familiar with generally accepted accounting principles and with the unrecorded business activities of the company must decide what adjustments are necessary and must enter the adjustment data. Once the adjustments have been entered, the computer can instantly complete the work sheet. When the accountant is satisfied that the adjustments shown in the work sheet are correct, the adjusting and closing entries can be entered in the formal accounting records with the touch of a button.

The Accounting Cycle

As stated at the beginning of this chapter, the life of a business is divided into accounting periods of equal length. In each period we repeat a stan-

OBJECTIVE 5 Describe the sequence of steps in the accounting cycle when a work sheet is prepared.

dard sequence of accounting procedures beginning with the journalizing of transactions and concluding with an after-closing trial balance.

Because the work sheet includes the trial balance, the adjusting entries in preliminary form, and an adjusted trial balance, the use of a work sheet will modify the sequence of procedures given in Chapter 3, as follows:

1 **Journalize transactions.** Analyze business transactions as they occur and record them promptly in a journal.

2 **Post to ledger accounts.** Transfer debits and credits from journal entries to ledger accounts.

3 **Prepare a work sheet.** Begin with a trial balance of the ledger, enter all necessary adjustments, extend the adjusted account balances of the income statement accounts and balance sheet accounts, and determine the net income or net loss.

4 **Prepare financial statements and appropriate notes.** Utilize the information in the work sheet to prepare an income statement, a statement of owner's equity, and a balance sheet. (The appropriate notes come from a variety of other sources.)

5 **Journalize and post the adjusting and closing entries.** Using the information in the work sheet as a guide, enter the adjusting entries in the journal. Post these entries to ledger accounts. Prepare and post journal entries to close the revenue and expense accounts into the Income Summary account and to transfer the net income or net loss to the owner's capital account. Also prepare and post a journal entry to close the owner's drawing account into the owner's capital account.

6 **Prepare an after-closing trial balance.** Prove that equality of debit and credit balances in the ledger has not been upset by the adjusting and closing procedures.

The above sequence of accounting procedures constitutes a complete accounting process. The regular repetition of this standardized set of procedures in each accounting period is often referred to as the ***accounting cycle.*** The procedures of a complete accounting cycle are illustrated in the flowchart on the following page. The numbered white symbols indicate the accounting procedures; the shaded symbols represent accounting records, schedules, and statements.

Note that the preparing of financial statements (Step 4) comes before entering adjusting and closing entries in the journal and posting these entries to the ledger (Step 5). This sequence reflects the fact that ***management wants the financial statements as soon as possible.*** Once the work sheet is complete, all information required for the financial statements is available. Top priority then goes to preparation of the financial statements.

In most business concerns the accounts are closed only once a year; for these companies the accounting cycle is one year in length. For purposes of illustration in a textbook, however, it is often convenient to assume that the entire accounting cycle is performed within the time period of one month. The completion of the accounting cycle is the occasion for preparing financial statements and closing the revenue and expense accounts.

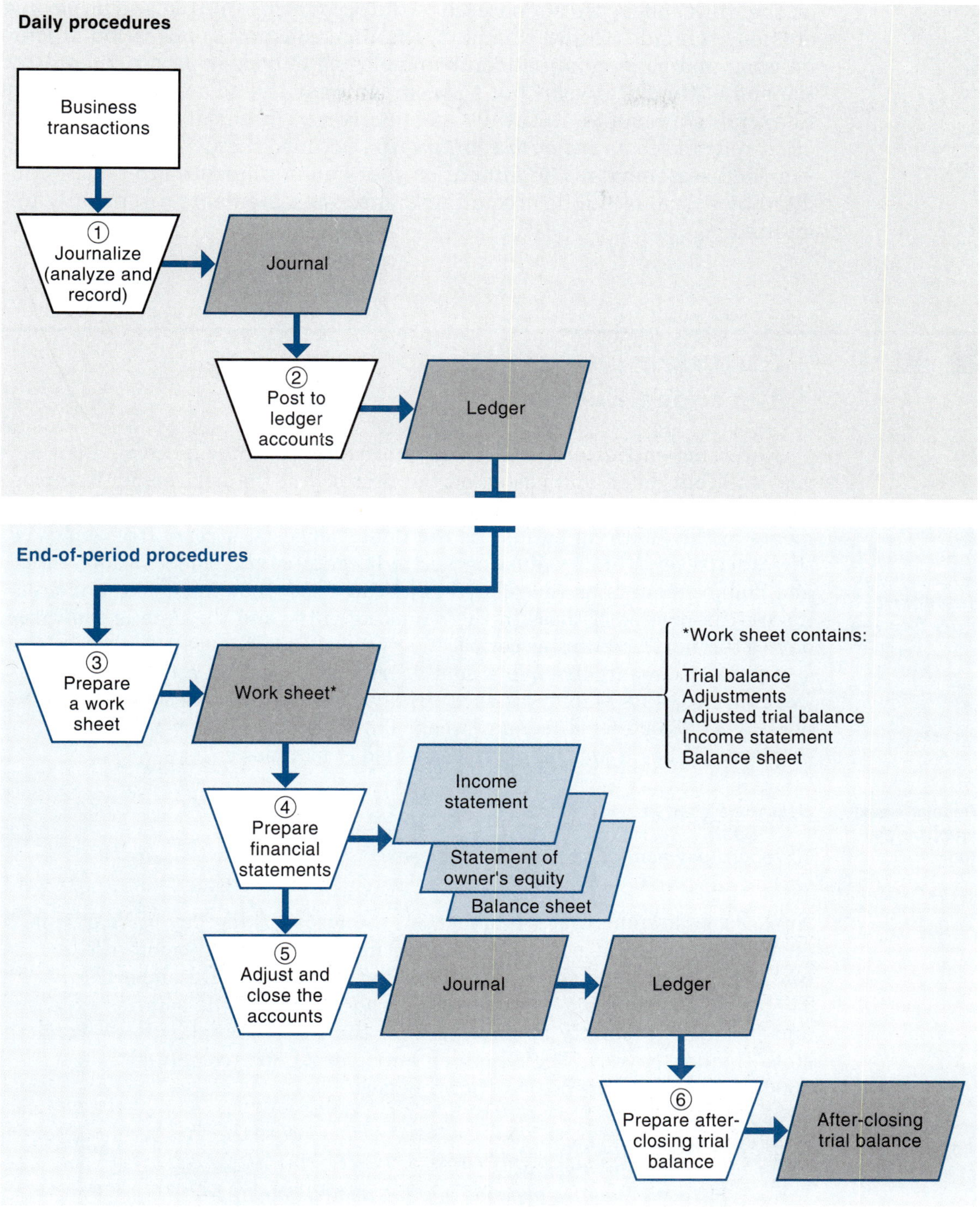

Preparing Monthly Financial Statements without Closing the Accounts

Many companies that close their accounts only once a year nevertheless prepare ***monthly*** financial statements for managerial use. These monthly statements are prepared from work sheets, but the adjustments indicated on the work sheets are not entered in the accounting records and no closing entries are made. Under this plan, the time-consuming operation of journalizing and posting adjustments and closing entries is performed only at the end of the fiscal year, but the company has the advantage of monthly financial statements. Monthly and quarterly financial statements are often referred to as ***interim statements,*** because they are in between the year-end statements. The annual or year-end statements are usually audited by a firm of public accountants; interim statements are usually unaudited.

* *Supplemental Topic*
Reversing Entries

OBJECTIVE 6 Explain when and why reversing entries may be used.

Reversing entries are an optional procedure that may be carried out at year-end (but dated and posted on the first day of the next accounting period) to simplify the recording of certain routine cash receipts and payments in the following period. As the name suggests, a ***reversing entry*** is the exact reverse of an adjusting entry. It contains the same account titles and dollar amounts as the related adjusting entry, but the debits and credits are the reverse of those in the adjusting entry and the date is the first day of the next accounting period.

Let us use as an example a small company that is on a five-day work week and pays its employees each Friday. Assume that the payroll is $600 per day or $3,000 for a five-day week. Throughout the year, a company employee makes a journal entry each Friday as follows:

Regular weekly entry for payroll

Salaries Expense	*3,000*	
Cash		*3,000*
To record payment of salaries for the week.		

Next, let us assume that December 31, the last working day of Year 1, falls on Wednesday. All expenses of the year must be recorded before the accounts are closed and financial statements prepared at December 31. Therefore, an adjusting entry must be made to record the salaries expense and the related liability to employees for the three days they have worked since the last payday. The adjusting entry for $1,800 (computed as 3 × $600 daily salary expense) is shown below:

Adjusting entry at end of year

Dec. 31	*Salaries Expense*	*1,800*	
	Salaries Payable		*1,800*
	To record salaries expense and the related liability to employees for last three days worked in December.		

The closing of the accounts on December 31 will reduce the Salaries Expense account to zero, but the liability account, Salaries Payable, will remain open with its $1,800 credit balance at the beginning of the new year. On the next regular payday, Friday, January 2, an employee can record the $3,000 payroll by a debit of $1,800 to Salaries Payable, a debit of $1,200 to Salaries Expense, and a credit of $3,000 to Cash. However, splitting the debit side of the entry in this manner ($1,800 to the liability account and $1,200 to expense) requires more understanding and alertness from company accounting personnel than if the entry were identical with the other 51 payroll entries made during the year.

By making a ***reversing entry*** as of the first day of the new accounting period, we can simplify the recording of routine transactions and avoid the need for the company's accounting staff to refer to prior adjusting entries for guidance. The reversing entry for the $1,800 year-end accrual of salaries would be dated January 1, Year 2, and would probably be made under the direction of the accountant responsible for the year-end closing of the accounts and preparation of financial statements. The entry would be as follows:

Reversing entry makes possible . . .

Jan. 1	*Salaries Payable*	*1,800*	
	Salaries Expense		*1,800*
	To reverse the accrual of salaries made on Dec. 31, Year 1.		

This reversing entry closes the Salaries Payable account by transferring the $1,800 liability to the credit side of the Salaries Expense account. Thus, the Salaries Expense account begins the new year with an abnormal credit balance of $1,800. On Friday, January 2, the normal payroll entry for $3,000 will be made to the same accounts as on every other Friday during the year.

. . . regular payroll entry for first payday of new year

Jan. 2	*Salaries Expense*	*3,000*	
	Cash		*3,000*
	Paid salaries for week ended Jan. 2, Year 2.		

After this January 2 entry has been posted, the ledger account for Salaries Expense will show a debit balance of $1,200, the result of this $3,000 debit and the $1,800 credit from the reversing entry on January 1. The amount of $1,200 is the correct expense for the two workdays of the new year at $600 a day. The results, of course, are ***exactly the same*** as if no reversing entry had been used and the company's accounting personnel had split the debit side of the January 2 payroll entry between Salaries Payable and Salaries Expense.

The ledger accounts for Salaries Expense and for Salaries Payable illustrate the effects of posting the adjusting entry and the reversing entry.

Salaries Expense

Date		Explanation	Ref	Debit	Credit	Balance
Year 1						
Various		(51 weekly entries of $3,000)				153000
Dec.	31	Adjusting entry (3 days @$600)		1800		154800
	31	To close at year-end			154800	-0-
Year 2						
Jan.	1	Reversing entry			1800	1800 cr
	2	Weekly payroll		3000		1200

Salaries Payable						
				Debit	Credit	Balance
Year 1						
Dec.	31	Adjusting entry (3 days @$600)			1800	1800
Year 2						
Jan.	1	Reversing entry		1800		-0-

Which Adjusting Entries Should Be Reversed? Even when a company follows a policy of making reversing entries, ***not all adjusting entries should be reversed.*** Only those adjustments that ***create an account receivable or a short-term liability*** should be reversed. These adjustments will be followed by cash receipts or cash payments within the near future. Reversing these adjusting entries will enable the company's personnel to record the upcoming cash transactions in a routine manner.

An adjusting entry that apportions an amount recorded in the past ***should not be reversed.*** Thus we do ***not*** reverse the adjusting entries that apportion recorded costs (such as depreciation) or that record the earning of revenue collected in advance.

In summary, reversing entries may be made for those adjusting entries that record ***unrecorded expenses*** or ***unrecorded revenue.*** Reversing entries are ***not*** made for adjustments that apportion recorded costs or recorded revenue.

Reversing Entries in a Computer-Based System Reversing entries do not require any analysis of transactions. Rather, they merely involve reversing the debit and credit amounts of specific adjusting entries. The adjusting entries to be reversed can be identified by a simple rule—namely, reverse those adjustments that increase accounts receivable or short-term liabilities. Thus, a computer may be programmed to prepare reversing entries automatically.

Finally, remember that reversing entries are ***optional.*** They are intended to simplify the accounting process, but they are ***not essential*** in the application of generally accepted accounting principles or in the preparation of financial statements.

CHAPTER REVIEW

KEY TERMS INTRODUCED OR EMPHASIZED IN CHAPTER 4

Accounting cycle The sequence of accounting procedures performed during an accounting period. The procedures include journalizing transactions, posting, preparation of a work sheet and financial statements, adjusting and closing the accounts, and preparation of an after-closing trial balance.

Accrued expenses Expenses such as salaries of employees and interest on notes payable that have been accumulating day-by-day but are unrecorded and unpaid at the end of the period. Also called ***unrecorded expenses.***

Accrued revenue Revenue that has been earned during the accounting period but has not been recorded or collected prior to the closing date. Also called ***unrecorded revenue.***

Adjusting entries Entries required at the end of the period to update the accounts before financial statements are prepared. Adjusting entries serve to apportion transactions properly between the accounting periods affected and to record any revenue earned or expenses incurred that have not been recorded prior to the end of the period.

Book value The net amount at which an asset is shown in accounting records. For depreciable assets, book value equals cost minus accumulated depreciation. Also called ***carrying value.***

Carrying value See book value.

Deferred revenue See unearned revenue.

Interim statements Financial statements prepared at intervals of less than one year. Usually quarterly and monthly statements.

Materiality The relative importance of an amount or item. An item that is not significant enough to influence the decisions of users of financial statements is considered ***immaterial.*** The accounting treatment of immaterial items may be guided by convenience rather than by theoretical principles.

Prepaid expenses Advance payments for such expenses as rent and insurance. The portion that has not been used up at the end of the accounting period is included in the balance sheet as an asset.

Promissory note A formal written promise to repay an amount borrowed plus interest at a future date.

*__Reversing entries__ An optional year-end procedure consisting of the reversal on the first day of the new accounting period of those year-end adjusting entries that accrue expenses or revenue and thus will be followed by later cash payments or receipts. Purpose is to permit company accounting personnel to record routine transactions in a standard manner without referring to prior adjusting entries.

Unearned revenue An obligation to render services or deliver goods in the future because of receipt of advance payment. Also called ***deferred revenue.***

Unrecorded expenses See accrued expenses.

Unrecorded revenue See accrued revenue.

Work sheet A large columnar sheet designed to arrange in convenient form all the accounting data required at the end of the period. Facilitates preparation of financial statements and the work of adjusting and closing the accounts.

---

* *Supplemental topic, "Reversing Entries."*

DEMONSTRATION PROBLEM FOR YOUR REVIEW

Reed Geophysical Company adjusts and closes its accounts at the end of the calendar year. At December 31, 19__, the balances in the ledger accounts ***prior to making adjusting entries*** were as follows:

REED GEOPHYSICAL COMPANY
Trial Balance
December 31, 19__

Cash	$ 12,540	
Prepaid rent	3,300	
Prepaid dues and subscriptions	960	
Supplies	1,300	
Equipment	20,000	
Accumulated depreciation: equipment		$ 1,200
Notes payable		5,000
Unearned consulting fees		35,650
Glen Reed, capital		17,040
Glen Reed, drawing	27,000	
Consulting fees earned		90,860
Salaries expense	66,900	
Telephone expense	2,550	
Rent expense	11,000	
Miscellaneous expenses	4,200	
	$149,750	$149,750

OTHER DATA

a For the first 11 months of the year, office rent had been charged to the Rent Expense account at a rate of $1,000 per month. On December 1, however, the company signed a new rental agreement and paid three months' rent in advance at a rate of $1,100 per month. This advance payment was debited to the Prepaid Rent account.

b Dues and subscriptions expired during the year in the total amount of $710.

c An estimate of supplies on hand was made at December 31; the estimated cost of the unused supplies was $450.

d The useful life of the equipment has been estimated at 10 years from date of acquisition. No depreciation expense has been recorded for the current year.

e Accrued interest on notes payable amounted to $100 at year-end.

f Consulting services valued at $32,550 were rendered during the year for clients who had made payment in advance.

g It is the custom of the firm to bill clients only when consulting work is completed or, in the case of prolonged engagements, at six-month intervals. At December 31, engineering services valued at $3,000 had been rendered to clients but not yet billed. No advance payments had been received from these clients.

h Salaries earned by employees but not yet paid amounted to $2,200 at December 31.

INSTRUCTIONS Prepare a work sheet for the year ended December 31, 19__.

SOLUTION TO DEMONSTRATION PROBLEM

REED GEOPHYSICAL COMPANY
Work Sheet
For the Year Ended December 31, 19__

	Trial Balance		Adjustments*		Adjusted Trial Balance		Income Statement		Balance Sheet	
	Dr	Cr	Dr	Cr	Dr	Cr	Dr	Cr	Dr	Cr
Balance sheet accounts:										
Cash	12,540				12,540				12,540	
Prepaid rent	3,300			(a) 1,100	2,200				2,200	
Prepaid dues and subscriptions	960			(b) 710	250				250	
Supplies	1,300			(c) 850	450				450	
Equipment	20,000				20,000				20,000	
Accumulated depreciation: equipment		1,200		(d) 2,000		3,200				3,200
Notes payable		5,000				5,000				5,000
Unearned consulting fees		35,650	(f) 32,550			3,100				3,100
Glen Reed, capital		17,040				17,040				17,040
Glen Reed, drawing	27,000				27,000				27,000	
Interest payable				(e) 100		100				100
Consulting fees receivable			(g) 3,000		3,000				3,000	
Salaries payable				(h) 2,200		2,200				2,200
Income statement accounts:										
Consulting fees earned		90,860		(f) 32,550		126,410		126,410		
				(g) 3,000						
Salaries expense	66,900		(h) 2,200		69,100		69,100			
Telephone expense	2,550				2,550		2,550			
Rent expense	11,000		(a) 1,100		12,100		12,100			
Miscellaneous expense	4,200				4,200		4,200			
	149,750	149,750								
Dues and subscriptions expense			(b) 710		710		710			
Supplies expense			(c) 850		850		850			
Depreciation expense: equipment			(d) 2,000		2,000		2,000			
Interest expense			(e) 100		100		100			
			42,510	42,510	157,050	157,050	91,610	126,410	65,440	30,640
Net income							34,800			34,800
							126,410	126,410	65,440	65,440

* Adjustments:
(a) Rent expense for December.
(b) Dues and subscriptions expense for year.
(c) Supplies used for year ($1,300 − $450 = $850).
(d) Depreciation expense for year ($20,000 ÷ 10 = $2,000).
(e) Accrued interest on notes payable.
(f) Consulting services performed for clients who paid in advance.
(g) Services rendered but not billed.
(h) Salaries earned but not paid.

ASSIGNMENT MATERIAL

DISCUSSION QUESTIONS

1 What is the purpose of making adjusting entries? Your answer should relate adjusting entries to the goals of accrual accounting.

2 Do all transactions involving revenue or expenses require adjusting entries at the end of the accounting period? If not, what is the distinguishing characteristic of those transactions that do require adjusting entries?

3 Do adjusting entries affect income statement accounts, balance sheet accounts, or both? Explain.

4 Why does the recording of adjusting entries require a better understanding of the concepts of accrual accounting than does the recording of routine revenue and expense transactions occurring throughout the period?

5 Why does the purchase of a one-year insurance policy four months ago give rise to insurance expense in the current month?

6 If services have been rendered to customers during the current accounting period but no revenue has been recorded and no bill has been sent to the customers, why is an adjusting entry needed? What types of accounts should be debited and credited by this entry?

7 What is meant by the term ***unearned revenue?*** Where should an unearned revenue account appear in the financial statements? As the work is done, what happens to the balance of an unearned revenue account?

8 The weekly payroll for employees of Ryan Company, who work a five-day week, amounts to $20,000. All employees are paid up-to-date at the close of business each Friday. If December 31 falls on Thursday, what year-end adjusting entry is needed?

9 The Marvin Company purchased a one-year fire insurance policy on August 1 and debited the entire cost of $3,600 to Unexpired Insurance. The accounts were not adjusted or closed until the end of the year. Give the adjusting entry at December 31.

10 At year-end the adjusting entry to reduce the Unexpired Insurance account by the amount of insurance premium applicable to the current period was accidentally omitted. Which items in the income statement will be in error? Will these items be overstated or understated? Which items in the balance sheet will be in error? Will they be overstated or understated?

11 Briefly explain the concept of ***materiality.*** If an item is not material, how is the item treated for financial reporting purposes?

12 In Chapter 1, assets were defined as economic resources owned by a business and expected to benefit future business operations. By this definition, the gasoline in the tank of a business automobile, unused typewriter ribbons, and even ballpoint pens are actually "assets." Why, then, are purchases of such items routinely charged directly to expense?

13 What is the purpose of a work sheet?

14 In performing the regular end-of-period accounting procedures, does the preparation of the work sheet precede or follow the posting of adjusting entries to ledger accounts? Why?

15 Assume that when the Income Statement columns of a work sheet are first totalled, the total of the debit column exceeds the total of the credit column by $60,000. Explain how the amount of net income (or net loss) should be entered in the work sheet columns.

16 Does the ending balance of the owner's capital account appear in the work sheet? Explain.

17 Can each step in the preparation of a work sheet be performed automatically in a computer-based accounting system? Explain.

18 List in order the procedures comprising the accounting cycle when a work sheet is used.

19 Is a work sheet ever prepared when there is no intention of closing the accounts?

*20 The weekly payroll of Stevens Company, which has a five-day work week, amounts to $15,000 and employees are paid up to date every Friday. On January 1 of the current year, the Salaries Expense account showed a credit balance of $9,000. Explain the nature of the accounting entry or entries that probably led to this balance.

*21 Four general types of adjusting entries were discussed in this chapter. If reversing entries are made, which of these types of adjusting entries should be reversed? Why?

MULTIPLE CHOICE QUESTIONS

1 The purpose of adjusting entries is to:

a Adjust the owner's capital account for the revenue, expense, and withdrawal transactions that occurred during the year.

b Adjust daily the balances in asset, liability, revenue, and expense accounts for the effects of business transactions.

c Apply the realization principle and the matching principle to transactions affecting two or more accounting periods.

d Prepare revenue and expense accounts for recording the transactions of the next accounting period.

2 Before month-end adjustments are made, the January 31 trial balance of Rover Excursions contains revenue of $9,300 and expenses of $5,780. Adjustments are necessary for the following items:
—portion of prepaid rent applicable to January, $900
—depreciation for January, $480
—portion of fees collected in advance earned in January, $1,100
—fees earned in January not yet billed to customers, $650

Net income in Rover Excursions' January income statement is:

a $3,520 b $5,690 c $2,590 d Some other amount

3 The public accounting firm auditing Tucker's Studio found that owner's equity was understated and liabilities were overstated. Which of the following errors could have been the cause?

a Making the adjustment entry for depreciation expense twice.

b Failure to record interest accrued on a note payable.

* Supplemental Topic, "Reversing Entries"

c Failure to make the adjusting entry to record revenue that had been earned but not yet billed to customers.

d Failure to record the earned portion of fees received in advance.

4 The concept of ***materiality:*** (Indicate all correct answers)

a Requires that financial statements are accurate to the nearest dollar but need not show cents.

b Is based upon what users of financial statements are thought to consider important.

c Permits accountants to ignore other generally accepted accounting principles in certain situations.

d Permits accountants to use the easiest and most convenient means of accounting for events that are ***immaterial.***

5 When a work sheet is prepared at year-end:

a Revenue and expense accounts do not have to be closed to the Income Summary account because the income statement is prepared from the work sheet and net income is already computed.

b Adjusting entries must be journalized and posted, even though the Adjustments column is properly completed.

c The amount of net income appears as a credit in the Income Statement column of the worksheet when revenue exceeds total expenses.

d The Income Statement columns and Balance Sheet columns of the work sheet eliminate the need to prepare formal financial statements.

*6 On December 31, Elite Property Management made an adjusting entry to record $300 management fees earned but not yet billed to Marge Carson, a client. This entry was reversed on January 1. On January 15, Carson paid Elite $1,200, of which $900 was applicable to the period January 1 through January 15. The journal entry made by Elite to record receipt of the $1,200 on January 15 includes:

a A credit to Management Fees Earned of $1,200.

b A credit to Accounts Receivable of $300.

c A debit to Management Fees Earned of $300.

d A credit to Management Fees Earned of $900.

EXERCISES

EXERCISE 4-1 Accounting Terminology

Listed below are nine technical accounting terms used in this chapter:

Unrecorded revenue	*Adjusting entries*	*Accrued expenses*
Work sheet	**Reversing entries*	*Book value*
Unearned revenue	*Materiality*	*Prepaid expenses*

Each of the following statements may (or may not) describe one of these technical terms. For each statement, indicate the accounting term described, or answer "None" if the statement does not correctly describe any of the terms.

a The net amount at which an asset is carried in the accounting records as distinguished from its market value.

---

* *Supplemental Topic, "Reversing Entries"*

b An accounting concept that may justify departure from other accounting principles for purposes of convenience and economy.

c A device for organizing all the data needed at the end of the period to prepare financial statements and to make entries to adjust and close the accounts.

d Revenue earned during the current accounting period but not yet recorded or billed, which requires an adjusting entry at the end of the period.

e Entries made at the end of the period to achieve the goals of accrual accounting by recording revenue when it is earned and by recording expenses when the related goods and services are used.

f A type of account credited when customers pay in advance for services to be rendered in the future.

g A balance sheet category used for reporting advance payments of such items as insurance, rent, and office supplies.

h Entries made during the accounting period to correct errors in the original recording of complex transactions.

EXERCISE 4-2
Effects of Adjusting Entries

Security Service Company adjusts and closes its accounts at the end of the month. On November 30, adjusting entries are prepared to record:

a Depreciation expense for November.

b Interest expense that has accrued during November.

c Revenue earned during November that has not yet been billed to customers.

d Salaries payable to company employees that have accrued since the last payday in November.

e The portion of the company's prepaid insurance that has expired during November.

f Earning a portion of the amount collected in advance from a customer, Harbour Restaurant.

INSTRUCTIONS Indicate the effect of each of these adjusting entries upon the major elements of the company's financial statements—that is, upon revenue, expenses, net income, assets, liabilities, and owner's equity. Organize your answer in tabular form, using the column headings shown below and the symbols ***I*** for increase, ***D*** for decrease, and ***NE*** for no effect. The answer for adjusting entry **a** is provided as an example.

Adjusting Entry	*Income Statement*			*Balance Sheet*		
	Revenue –	*Expenses =*	*Net Income*	*Assets =*	*Liabilities +*	*Owner's Equity*
a	NE	I	D	D	NE	D

EXERCISE 4-3
Preparing Adjusting Entries for Recorded Costs and Recorded Revenue

The Outlaws, a professional football team, prepare financial statements on a monthly basis. Football season begins in August, but in July the team engaged in the following transactions:

a Paid $1,500,000 to Skydome as advance rent for use of its facilities for the five-month period from August 1 through December 31. This payment was debited to the asset account, Prepaid Rent.

b Collected $2,560,000 cash from sales of season tickets for the team's eight home games. This amount was credited to Unearned Ticket Revenue.

During the month of August, The Outlaws played one home game and two games on the road. Their record was two wins, one loss.

INSTRUCTIONS Prepare the two adjusting entries required at August 31 to apportion this recorded cost and recorded revenue.

EXERCISE 4-4
Preparing Adjusting Entries for Unrecorded Revenue and Expenses

The law firm of Davis & Askins prepares its financial statements on an annual basis at December 31. Among the situations requiring year-end adjusting entries were the following:

a Salaries to staff lawyers are paid on the fifteenth day of each month. Salaries accrued since December 15 amount to $17,800 and have not yet been recorded.

b The firm is defending J. R. Stone in a civil lawsuit. The agreed-upon legal fees are $2,100 per day while the trial is in progress. The trial has been in progress for nine days during December and is not expected to end until late January. No legal fees have yet been billed to Stone. (Legal fees are recorded in an account entitled Legal Fees Earned.)

INSTRUCTIONS Prepare the two adjusting entries required at December 31 to record the accrued salaries expense and the accrued legal fees revenue.

EXERCISE 4-5
Get Your Tickets Early

When **Air Canada** sells tickets for future flights, it debits cash and credits an account entitled Advance Ticket Sales. With respect to this Advance Ticket Sales account:

a What does the balance of the account represent? Where should the account appear in Air Canada's financial statements?

b Explain the activity that normally ***reduces*** the balance of this account. Can you think of any ***other*** transaction that would reduce this account?

EXERCISE 4-6
Preparing Various Adjusting Entries

Hill Corporation adjusts and closes its accounts at the end of the calendar year. Prepare the necessary adjusting entries required at December 31 based on the following information.

a A bank loan had been obtained on September 1. Accrued interest on the loan at December 31 amounts to $4,800. No interest expense has yet been recorded.

b Depreciation of office equipment is based on an estimated life of five years. The balance in the Office Equipment account is $25,000; no change has occurred in the account during the year.

c Interest receivable on government bonds owned at December 31 amounts to $2,300. This accrued interest revenue has not been recorded.

d On December 31, an agreement was signed to lease a truck for 12 months beginning January 1 at a rate of 35 cents a kilometre. Usage is expected to be 2,000 kilometres per month and the contract specifies a minimum payment equivalent to 18,000 kilometres a year.

e The company's policy is to pay all employees up-to-date each Friday. Since December 31 fell on Monday, there was a liability to employees at December 31 for one day's pay amounting to $2,800.

EXERCISE 4-7
Adjusting Entry and Subsequent Business Transaction

On Friday of each week, Regis Products, Inc., pays its sales personnel weekly salaries amounting to $60,000 for a five-day work week.

a Draft the necessary adjusting entry at year-end, assuming that December 31 falls on Wednesday.

b Also draft the journal entry for the payment by Regis of a week's salaries to its sales personnel on Friday, January 2, the first payday of the new year. (Assume that the company does not use reversing entries.)

EXERCISE 4-8
Notes Payable and Interest

Venture Company adjusts and closes its accounts on December 31. On November 30, 1995, Venture Company signed a note payable and borrowed $12,000 from a bank for a period of six months at an annual interest rate of 10%.

a How much is the total interest expense over the life of the note? How much is the monthly interest expense? (Assume equal amounts of interest expense each month.)

b In the company's annual balance sheet at December 31, 1995, what is the amount of the liability to the bank?

c Prepare the journal entry to record issuance of the note payable on November 30, 1995.

d Prepare the adjusting entry to accrue interest on the note at December 31, 1995.

e Assume the company prepared a balance sheet at March 31, 1996. State the amount of the liability to the bank at this date.

EXERCISE 4-9
Relationship of Adjusting Entries to Business Transactions

Among the ledger accounts used by Windsor Raceway are the following: Prepaid Rent, Rent Expense, Unearned Admissions Revenue, Admissions Revenue, Prepaid Printing, Printing Expense, Concessions Receivable, and Concessions Revenue. For each of the following items, write first the journal entry (if one is needed) to record the external transaction and second the adjusting entry, if any, required on May 31, the end of the fiscal year.

a On May 1, borrowed $300,000 cash from National Bank by issuing a 12% note payable due in three months.

b On May 1, paid rent for six months beginning May 1 at $30,000 per month.

c On May 2, sold season tickets for a total of $910,000 cash. The season includes 70 racing days: 20 in May, 25 in June, and 25 in July.

d On May 4, an agreement was reached with Snack-Bars, Inc., allowing that company to sell refreshments at the track in return for 10% of the gross receipts from refreshment sales.

e On May 6, schedules for the 20 racing days in May and the first 10 racing days in June were printed and paid for at a cost of $12,000.

f On May 31, Snack-Bars, Inc., reported that the gross receipts from refreshment sales in May had been $165,000 and that the 10% owed to Windsor Raceway would be remitted on June 10.

EXERCISE 4-10
Concept of Materiality

The concept of materiality is a generally accepted accounting principle.

a Briefly explain the concept of materiality.

b Is $2,500 a "material" dollar amount? Explain.

c Describe two ways in which the concept of materiality may save accountants' time and effort in making adjusting entries.

EXERCISE 4-11
Materiality: a Specific Application at Year-End

The income statement of **Southwest Airlines Company** for a recent year is reproduced below. Assume you learn that $100,000 of the fuel and oil charged to expense in 1994 actually had been on hand in the company's storage tanks at year-end. Would you consider this to be a "material" error in the company's financial statements? Explain fully.

SOUTHWEST AIRLINES COMPANY
Consolidated Statement of Income
For the Year Ended December 31, 1994
(In thousands)

Operating revenues:	
Passenger	*$ 973,568*
Freight	*18,771*
Other	*22,713*
Total operating revenues	*$1,015,052*
Operating expenses:	
Salaries, wages, and benefits	*$ 301,066*
Fuel and oil	*168,579*
Maintenance and repairs	*75,842*
Agency commissions	*61,362*
Aircraft rentals	*21,636*
Landing fees and other rentals	*51,902*
Depreciation	*72,343*
Other operating expenses	*164,696*
Total operating expenses	*$ 917,426*
Operating income	*$ 97,626*
Other expenses (income):	
Interest expense (net of amounts capitalized)	*$ 23,269*
Interest income	*(16,637)*
Nonoperating gains, net	*(19,988)*
Total other expenses (income)	*$ (13,356)*
Income before income taxes	*$ 110,982*
Provision for income taxes	*39,424*
Net income	*$ 71,558*

$100,000 to Exp → Asset (Inventory) understated & Exp overstated → n/Income understated → but this error is minor. 100,000 ÷ 71 million = .0014

EXERCISE 4-12
Adjusting Entries—A Working Backwards Exercise

Shown below are the Trial Balance and Adjusted Trial Balance columns of the work sheet prepared for Fisher Insurance Agency for the month ended November 30, 1995.

	Trial Balance		Adjusted Trial Balance	
	Dr	Cr	Dr	Cr
Balance sheet accounts:				
Cash	4,980		4,980	
Commissions receivable	3,000		3,850	
Office supplies	600		240	
Office equipment	6,600		6,600	
Accumulated depreciation: office equipment		2,420		2,530
Accounts payable		1,660		1,660
Salaries payable				550
Unearned commissions		400		190
Pat Fisher, capital		12,300		12,300
Pat Fisher, drawing	1,000		1,000	
Income statement accounts:				
Commissions earned		6,900		7,960
Salaries expense	6,000		6,550	
Rent expense	1,500		1,500	
Office supplies expense			360	
Depreciation expense: office equipment			110	
	23,680	23,680	25,190	25,190

INSTRUCTIONS By comparing the two trial balances shown above, it is possible to determine which accounts have been adjusted. You are to prepare the adjusting journal entries that must have been made to cause these changes in account balances. Include an explanation as part of each adjusting entry.

EXERCISE 4-13
Preparing Financial Statements from a Work Sheet

From the adjusted trial balance columns of the work sheet shown in Exercise 4-12, prepare an income statement and a statement of owner's equity for Fisher Insurance Agency for the month ended November 30, 1995, and also a balance sheet (in report form) at November 30.

EXERCISE 4-14
The Accounting Cycle with a Work Sheet

Listed below in random order are the steps comprising the accounting cycle when a work sheet is prepared:

a Prepare the work sheet.
b Prepare an after-closing trial balance.
c Journalize and post the adjusting and closing entries.
d Prepare financial statements and appropriate disclosures.
e Post transaction data to the ledger.
f Journalize transactions.

INSTRUCTIONS a List these six steps in the logical sequence in which they would be performed.

b Indicate which of these steps are mechanical functions that can be performed by machine in a computerized accounting system and which require the judgment of people familiar with accounting principles and concepts. (In some cases, human judgment may be required to complete only a ***portion*** of the step. If so, explain.)

***EXERCISE 4-15**
Preparing Reversing Entries

Blue Company closes its accounts at the end of each calendar year. The company operates on a five-day work week and pays its employees up to date each Friday. The weekly payroll is regularly $10,000. On Thursday, December 31, 1994, an adjusting entry was made to accrue $8,000 salaries expense for the four days worked since the last payday. The company ***did not*** make a reversing entry. On Friday, January 1, 1995, the regular weekly payroll of $10,000 was paid and recorded by the usual entry debiting Salaries Expense $10,000 and crediting Cash $10,000.

Were Blue Company's accounting records correct for the year 1994? For 1995? Explain two alternatives the company might have followed with respect to payroll at year-end. One of the alternatives should include a reversing entry.

EXERCISE 4-16
Accounting Principles

For each of the situations described below, indicate the generally accepted accounting principle that is being ***violated.*** Choose from the following principles:

Matching	*Materiality*
Cost	*Realization*
Objectivity	*Adequate disclosure*

If you do not believe that the practice violates any of these principles, answer "None," and explain.

a The financial statements include no mention of a large lawsuit filed against the company, because the suit has not been settled as of year-end.

b The bookkeeper of a large metropolitan auto dealership depreciates the $7.20 cost of metal wastebaskets over a period of 10 years.

c A small commuter airline recognizes no depreciation expense on its aircraft because the planes are maintained in "as good as new" condition.

d Palm Beach Hotel recognizes room rental revenue on the date that a reservation is received. For the winter season, many guests make reservations as much as a year in advance.

PROBLEMS

Group A

PROBLEM 4A-1
Preparing Adjusting Entries

Alta Sequoia Resort adjusts and closes its accounts ***once a year*** on December 31. Most guests of the resort pay at the time they check out, and the amounts collected are credited to Rental Revenue. A few guests pay in advance for rooms, and these amounts are credited to Unearned Rental Revenue at the time of receipt. The following information is available as a source for preparing adjusting entries at December 31.

a Salaries earned by employees but not yet recorded or paid amount to $7,900.

b As of December 31, Alta Sequoia has earned $11,075 rental revenue from current guests who will not be billed until they are ready to check out.

c On November 1, a suite of rooms was rented to a corporation for six months at a monthly rental of $3,200. The entire six months' rent of $19,200 was collected in advance and credited to Unearned Rental Revenue. At December 31, two

* *Supplemental Topic, "Reversing Entries"*

months' rent is considered to be earned; the remainder is for the first four months of the following year.

d A limousine to carry guests to and from the airport had been rented beginning December 19 from Transport Rentals, Inc., at a daily rate of $120. No rental payment has yet been made. (The limousine has been rented for 13 days in December.)

e A six-month loan in the amount of $30,000 had been obtained on December 1. Interest is to be computed at a rate of 15% per year and is payable when the loan is due. No interest has been paid and no interest expense has been recorded.

f Depreciation on the resort's buildings is based upon an estimated useful life of 30 years. The original cost of the buildings was $1,755,000.

g In December, Alta Sequoia Resort entered into an agreement to host the annual symposium of ACE (Academics for a Clean Environment) in April of next year. The resort expects to earn rental revenue of at least $45,000.

h A one-year fire insurance policy had been purchased on September 1. The premium of $7,200 for the entire life of the policy had been paid on September 1 and recorded as Unexpired Insurance.

INSTRUCTIONS For each of the above lettered paragraphs, draft a separate adjusting journal entry (including explanation) if the information indicates that an adjusting entry is needed.

PROBLEM 4A-2
Preparing Adjusting Entries from a Trial Balance

On April 1, 1995, Pat Hamilton, a lawyer, opened her own legal practice, to be known as the Law Office of Pat Hamilton. The business adjusts and closes its accounts at the end of each month. The following trial balance was prepared at April 30, 1995, ***after one month*** of operations:

LAW OFFICE OF PAT HAMILTON
Trial Balance
April 30, 1995

Cash	*$10,060*	
Legal fees receivable	*—0—*	
Unexpired insurance	*3,000*	
Prepaid office rent	*4,800*	
Office supplies	*1,460*	
Office equipment	*26,400*	
Accumulated depreciation: office equipment		*$—0—*
Notes payable		*16,000*
Interest payable		*—0—*
Salaries payable		*—0—*
Unearned retainer fees		*15,020*
Pat Hamilton, capital		*20,000*
Pat Hamilton, drawing	*3,000*	
Legal fees earned		*1,580*
Salaries expense	*2,680*	
Miscellaneous expense	*1,200*	
Office rent expense	*—0—*	
Office supplies expense	*—0—*	
Depreciation expense: office equipment	*—0—*	
Interest expense	*—0—*	
Insurance expense	*—0—*	
	$52,600	*$52,600*

OTHER DATA

a No interest has yet been paid on the note payable. Accrued interest at April 30 amounts to $200.

b Salaries earned by the office staff but not yet recorded or paid amounted to $970 at April 30.

c Many clients are asked to make an advance payment for the legal services to be rendered in future months. These advance payments are credited to the Unearned Retainer Fees account. During April, $4,700 of these advances were earned by the business.

d Some clients are not billed until all services relating to their matter have been rendered. As of April 30, services priced at $2,780 had been rendered to these clients but had not yet been recorded in the accounting records.

e A professional liability insurance policy was purchased on April 1. The premium of $3,000 for the first six months was paid and recorded as Unexpired Insurance.

f The business rents an office at a monthly rate of $1,600. On April 1, three months' rent was paid in advance and charged to the Prepaid Rent account.

g Office supplies on hand at April 30 amounted to $800.

h The office equipment was purchased on April 1 and is being depreciated over an estimated useful life of 10 years.

INSTRUCTIONS

a Prepare the adjusting entries required at April 30.

b Determine the amount of ***revenue*** that should appear in the company's income statement for the month ended April 30.

PROBLEM 4A-3
Analysis of Adjusted Data; Preparing Adjusting Entries

Sea Cat, Inc., operates a large catamaran that takes tourists at several island resorts on diving and sailing excursions. The company adjusts and closes its accounts at the end of each month. Selected account balances appearing on the June 30 ***adjusted*** trial balance are as follows:

Prepaid rent	*$ 6,000*	
Unexpired insurance	*1,400*	
Catamaran	*46,200*	
Accumulated depreciation: catamaran		*$9,240*
Unearned passenger revenue		*825*

OTHER DATA

a Six months' rent had been prepaid on June 1.

b The unexpired insurance is a 12-month fire insurance policy purchased on March 1.

c The catamaran is being depreciated over a 10-year estimated useful life, with no residual value.

d The unearned passenger revenue represents tickets good for future rides sold to a resort hotel for $15 per ticket on June 1. During June, 145 of the tickets were used.

INSTRUCTIONS

a Determine

1 The monthly rent expense

2 The original cost of the 12-month fire insurance policy

3 The age of the catamaran in months

4 How many $15 tickets for future rides were sold to the resort hotel on June 1

b Prepare the adjusting entries that were made on June 30.

PROBLEM 4A-4
Format of a Work Sheet

Shown below are the first 4 columns of the 10-column work sheet to be prepared for Geotechnical Testing Services for the month ended April 30, 1995.

GEOTECHNICAL TESTING SERVICES
Work Sheet
For the Month Ended April 30, 1995

	Trial Balance		Adjustments*	
	Dr	Cr	Dr	Cr
Balance sheet accounts:				
Cash	3,700			
Accounts receivable	2,900			
Unexpired insurance	490			(a) 70
Supplies	1,460			(b) 560
Equipment	18,600			
Accumulated depreciation: equipment		2,480		(c) 310
Notes payable		10,000		
Unearned revenue		1,200	(e) 400	
Max Benton, capital		14,190		
Max Benton, drawing	1,500			
Interest payable				(d) 80
Salaries payable				(f) 500
Income statement accounts:				
Revenue from services		5,130		(e) 400
Rent expense	2,450			
Salaries expense	1,900		(f) 500	
	33,000	33,000		
Insurance expense			(a) 70	
Supplies expense			(b) 560	
Depreciation expense: equipment			(c) 310	
Interest expense			(d) 80	
			1,920	1,920

* Adjustments
(a) Insurance expired for the month.
(b) Cost of supplies used, based on estimate of supplies at April 30.
(c) Depreciation expense on equipment.
(d) Interest accrued on notes payable at April 30.
(e) Advance payments by customers earned during April.
(f) Salaries earned by employees but not yet recorded or paid.

INSTRUCTIONS Prepare a 10-column work sheet utilizing the trial balance and adjustments shown above in the first 4 columns.

PROBLEM 4A-5
Preparing a Work Sheet

Village Theatre closes its accounts ***each month.*** At July 31, the trial balance and other information given below were available for adjusting and closing the accounts.

VILLAGE THEATRE
Trial Balance
July 31, 19__

Cash	$ 20,000	
Prepaid film rental	31,200	
Land	80,000	
Building	168,000	
Accumulated depreciation: building		$ 10,500
Projection equipment	36,000	
Accumulated depreciation: projection equipment		3,000
Notes payable		190,000
Accounts payable		4,400
Unearned admissions revenue (YMCA)		1,000
Li Trong, capital		103,400
Li Trong, drawing	3,500	
Admissions revenue		36,900
Salaries expense	8,700	
Light and power expense	1,800	
	$349,200	$349,200

OTHER DATA

a Film rental expense for July amounts to $21,050. However, the film rental expense for several months had been paid in advance.

b The building is being depreciated over a period of 20 years.

c The projection equipment is being depreciated over 5 years.

d At July 31, accrued interest payable on the note payable amounts to $1,650. No entry has yet been made to record interest expense for the month of July.

e Village Theatre allows the local YMCA to bring children attending summer camp to the movies on any weekday afternoon for a fixed fee of $500 per month. On May 28, the YMCA made a $1,500 advance payment covering the months of June, July, and August.

f Village Theatre receives a percentage of the revenue earned by Tastie Corporation, the concessionaire operating the snack bar. For snack bar sales in July, Tastie owes Village Theatre $2,250, payable on August 10. No entry has yet been made to record this concessions revenue.

g Salaries owed to employees but not recorded or paid as of July 31 amount to $1,500.

INSTRUCTIONS Prepare a 10-column work sheet utilizing the trial balance and adjusting data provided. Include at the bottom of the work sheet a brief explanation keyed to each adjusting entry.

PROBLEM 4A-6
Preparing a Work Sheet, Financial Statements, and Adjusting and Closing Entries

Island Hopper is an airline providing passenger and freight service among some Pacific islands. The accounts are adjusted and closed each month. At June 30 the following trial balance was prepared from the ledger.

ISLAND HOPPER
Trial Balance
June 30, 1995

Cash	$ 23,600	
Accounts receivable	7,200	
Prepaid rent	9,600	
Unexpired insurance	21,000	
Aircraft	1,200,000	
Accumulated depreciation: aircraft		$ 380,000
Notes payable		600,000
Advance ticket sales		60,000
Mary Earhart, capital		230,850
Mary Earhart, drawing	7,000	
Freight revenue		130,950
Fuel expense	53,800	
Salaries expense	66,700	
Maintenance expense	12,900	
	$1,401,800	$1,401,800

OTHER DATA

a The aircraft has an estimated useful life of 10 years.

b During June, $38,650 of the advance ticket sales was earned by the airline.

c Salaries earned by employees but not yet recorded or paid amount to $3,300 at June 30.

d Accrued interest on notes payable amounts to $5,000 at June 30 and has not yet been recorded.

e One of Island Hopper's regular customers is Pacific Trading Corporation. The airline keeps track of the weight of shipments carried for the trading company during the month and sends a bill shortly after month-end. No entry has yet been made to record $4,600 earned in June carrying freight for Pacific Trading.

f Three months' rent had been prepaid on May 1.

g On April 1, a 12-month insurance policy had been purchased for $25,200.

INSTRUCTIONS

a Prepare a work sheet for the month ended June 30, 1995.

b Prepare an income statement, a statement of owner's equity, and a balance sheet.

c Prepare adjusting and closing journal entries.

***PROBLEM 4A-7**
Reversing Entries

Investor's Journal adjusts and closes its accounts at the end of each calendar year. The company works a five-day week and pays its employees up-to-date each Friday. The weekly salaries are $10,000 ($2,000 per day). Near year-end, the following events occurred relating to salaries:

---

* *Supplemental Topic, "Reversing Entries"*

Dec. 26 (Friday) Recorded payment of regular weekly salaries of $10,000.

Dec. 31 (Wednesday) Prepared an adjusting entry for accrued salaries of $6,000.

Jan. 1 (Thursday) Made a reversing entry for accrued salaries.

Jan. 2 (Friday) Recorded payment of regular weekly salaries of $10,000.

INSTRUCTIONS

a Prepare journal entries (with explanations) for the four events relating to salaries.

b How much of the $10,000 in salaries paid on January 2 represents a January expense? Explain.

c Assume that no reversing entry was made by the company; prepare the journal entry required to record the payment of salaries on January 2.

Group B

PROBLEM 4B-1
Preparing Adjusting Entries

Silver Spur Ranch operates a dude ranch and resort. Most of its guests pay at the time they check out, and the amounts collected are credited to Rental Revenue. The following information is available as a source for preparing adjusting entries at December 31, the year-end date.

a Among the assets owned by Silver Spur is an investment in government bonds in the face amount of $75,000. Accrued interest receivable on the bonds at December 31 was computed to be $2,250. None of the interest has yet been received.

b A 12-month bank loan in the amount of $90,000 had been obtained on November 1. Interest is to be computed at an annual rate of 12% and is payable when the loan becomes due. No interest has been paid and no interest expense has yet been recorded.

c Depreciation on a station wagon owned by the ranch was based on a four-year life. The vehicle had been purchased new on September 1 of the current year at a cost of $25,200.

d Management of the ranch signed an agreement on December 28 to lease a truck from Ace Motors for a period of 6 months beginning January 1 at a rate of 20 cents per kilometre, with a clause providing for a minimum monthly charge of $400.

e Salaries earned by employees but not yet paid amounted to $9,900 at the end of the year.

f As of December 31, Silver Spur has earned $12,500 rental revenue from current guests who will not be billed until they are ready to check out.

g A portion of land owned by Silver Spur had been leased on August 1 of the current year to a service station operator at a yearly rental rate of $18,000. Six months' rent was collected in advance at the date of the lease and credited to Unearned Rental Revenue.

h A bus to carry guests to and from town and the airport had been rented early on December 10 at a daily rate of $50. No rental payment has been made, although Silver Spur has had use of the bus for 22 days in December.

INSTRUCTIONS

For each of the above lettered paragraphs, draft a separate adjusting journal entry (including explanation) if the information indicates that an adjusting entry is needed.

PROBLEM 4B-2
Preparing Adjusting Entries from a Trial Balance

Nick Charles operates a private investigating business called Nick Charles Investigations. Some clients are required to pay in advance for the company's services, while others are billed after the services have been rendered. Advance payments are credited to an account entitled Unearned Retainer Fees. The business adjusts and closes its accounts each month. At May 31, the trial balance appeared as follows:

NICK CHARLES INVESTIGATIONS
Trial Balance
May 31, 19__

Cash	*$ 17,150*	
Fees receivable	*37,800*	
Unexpired insurance	*2,000*	
Prepaid rent	*5,400*	
Office supplies	*1,050*	
Office equipment	*17,100*	
Accumulated depreciation: office equipment		*$ 5,700*
Accounts payable		*3,900*
Unearned retainer fees		*24,000*
Nick Charles, capital		*48,600*
Nick Charles, drawing	*2,400*	
Fees earned		*24,800*
Telephone expense	*1,200*	
Travel expense	*3,400*	
Salaries expense	*19,500*	
	$107,000	*$107,000*

OTHER DATA

a The useful life of the office equipment was estimated at five years.

b Fees of $6,400 were earned during the month by performing services for clients who had paid in advance.

c Salaries earned by employees during the month but not yet recorded or paid amounted to $1,700.

d On May 1, the business moved into a new office and paid the first three months' rent in advance.

e Investigative services rendered during the month but not yet collected or billed to clients amounted to $2,900.

f Office supplies on hand May 31 amounted to $600.

g On April 1, $2,400 was paid as the premium for six months' liability insurance.

INSTRUCTIONS

a Prepare the adjusting entries required at May 31.

b Determine the amount of revenue that should appear in the company's income statement for the month ended May 31.

PROBLEM 4B-3
Making Use of a Completed Work Sheet

A 10-column work sheet for Reed Geophysical Company is illustrated on page 187.

INSTRUCTIONS

Using the information contained in that work sheet, prepare in journal entry form the adjusting and closing entries for Reed Geophysical Company at December 31, 19__.

PROBLEM 4B-4
Format of a Work Sheet

Shown below are the first 4 columns of a 10-column work sheet to be prepared for Lakeside Executive Golf Course for the month ended October 31, 1995. The golf course operates on land rented from the city.

LAKESIDE EXECUTIVE GOLF COURSE
Work Sheet
For the Month Ended October 31, 1995

	Trial Balance		Adjustments*	
	Dr	Cr	Dr	Cr
Balance sheet accounts:				
Cash	20,900			
Unexpired insurance	7,200			(a) 800
Prepaid rent	18,000			(b) 6,000
Equipment	24,000			
Accumulated depreciation: equipment		7,600		(c) 400
Notes payable		10,000		
Unearned greens' fees revenue		6,400	(d) 2,200	
Walter Nelson, capital		38,200		
Walter Nelson, drawing	5,900			
Salaries payable				(e) 1,900
Interest payable				(f) 100
Income statement accounts:				
Greens' fees revenue		26,400		(d) 2,200
Salaries expense	8,600		(e) 1,900	
Water expense	1,200			
Advertising expense	600			
Repairs and maintenance expense	1,500			
Miscellaneous expense	700			
	88,600	88,600		
Insurance expense			(a) 800	
Rent expense			(b) 6,000	
Depreciation expense: equipment			(c) 400	
Interest expense			(f) 100	
			11,400	11,400

* Adjustments
(a) Insurance expiring in October.
(b) Prepaid rent applicable to October.
(c) Depreciation for the month.
(d) Portion of revenue collected in advance but earned during October.
(e) Salaries owed to employees but unpaid as of month-end.
(f) Accrued interest on notes payable at October 31.

INSTRUCTIONS Prepare a 10-column work sheet utilizing the trial balance and adjustments shown above in the first 4 columns.

PROBLEM 4B-5
Preparing a Work Sheet

O'Connell's Air Service operates several small airplanes providing passenger and freight service to small towns, oil fields, fishing lodges, and other remote locations in the Yukon. The company adjusts and closes its accounts at the end of ***each month.*** At April 30, the following trial balance was prepared from the ledger:

O'CONNELL'S AIR SERVICE
Trial Balance
April 30, 19__

Cash	$ 22,750	
Accounts receivable	28,300	
Prepaid rent	8,100	
Unexpired insurance	36,900	
Airplanes	855,000	
Accumulated depreciation: airplanes		$ 232,750
Notes payable		450,000
Advance ticket sales		175,250
Maggie O'Connell, capital		171,750
Maggie O'Connell, drawing	7,750	
Freight revenue		54,250
Fuel expense	47,600	
Salaries expense	70,900	
Maintenance expense	6,700	
	$1,084,000	$1,084,000

OTHER DATA

- **a** One of O'Connell's regular customers is Yukon Oil Limited. The airline keeps track of the number of trips carrying freight for the oil company and sends a bill shortly after month-end. No entry has yet been made in the airline's accounting records to record $11,750 freight revenue earned in April from Yukon Oil.
- **b** Three months' rent ($8,100) had been prepaid on April 1.
- **c** On January 1, a 12-month insurance policy had been purchased for $49,200.
- **d** O'Connell's depreciates its airplanes over a period of 15 years.
- **e** Accrued interest on notes payable amounts to $4,500 at April 30 and has not yet been recorded.
- **f** During April, $94,750 of the advance ticket sales was earned by the airline.
- **g** Salaries owed to airline employees but not yet recorded or paid amount to $1,625 at April 30.

INSTRUCTIONS

Prepare a 10-column work sheet using the trial balance and adjusting data provided. Include at the bottom of the work sheet a brief explanation keyed to each adjusting entry.

PROBLEM 4B-6
A Comprehensive Work Sheet Problem

A trial balance and supplementary information needed for adjustments at September 30 are shown on the following page for Cinemax Stage & Theatre. The company follows a policy of adjusting and closing its accounts at the ***end of each month.***

CINEMAX STAGE & THEATRE
Trial Balance
September 30, 1995

Cash	$ 17,500	
Prepaid film rental	65,000	
Land	75,000	
Building	210,000	
Accumulated depreciation: building		$ 6,125
Projection equipment	90,000	
Accumulated depreciation: projection equipment		7,500
Notes payable		200,000
Accounts payable		8,500
Unearned admissions revenue		5,200
Helen James, capital		200,925
Helen James, drawing	10,500	
Admissions revenue		68,750
Salaries expenses	21,250	
Utilities expense	7,750	
	$497,000	$497,000

OTHER DATA

a Film rental expense for the month is $42,275, all of which had been paid in advance.

b The building has an estimated useful life of 20 years.

c The projection equipment has an estimated useful life of 5 years.

d No entry has yet been made to record interest payable accrued during September. At September 30, accrued interest totals $1,800.

e When tickets are sold to future performances, Cinemax credits its Unearned Admissions Revenue account. No entry has yet been made recording that $3,650 of these advance ticket sales were for performances given during September.

f Cinemax receives a percentage of the revenue earned by Variety Corp., the concessionaire operating the snack bar. For snack bar sales in September, Variety Corp. owes Cinemax $6,200, payable on October 10. No entry has yet been made to record this concession revenue.

g Salaries earned by employees, but unrecorded and unpaid as of September 30, amount to $3,750.

INSTRUCTIONS Prepare

a A work sheet for the month ended September 30, 1995.

b An income statement for the month.

c A statement of owner's equity for the month.

d A balance sheet as of September 30.

e The adjusting and closing entries required at month's end.

***PROBLEM 4B-7 Reversing Entries**

Lawton Industries holds a note receivable in the amount of $300,000, dated March 10, 1995, due in 24 months. Interest of $3,000 is received monthly on the tenth of each month, computed at an annual rate of 12%. Lawton maintains its accounts on

* *Supplemental Topic, "Reversing Entries"*

the basis of a fiscal year ending June 30. During June and July, the following events occurred relating to this note receivable.

June 10 Received regular monthly interest cheque of $3,000 for the preceding month ending June 10.

June 30 Prepared an adjusting entry to record interest revenue for the last 20 days of June.

July 1 Prepared a reversing entry for accrued interest revenue.

July 10 Received regular monthly interest cheque of $3,000 for the month ending July 10.

INSTRUCTIONS

a Prepare journal entries (with explanations) for the four above items relating to interest.

b How much of the $3,000 in interest received on July 10 represents July revenue?

c Assume that no reversing entry had been made by Lawton. Prepare the journal entry for receipt of interest on July 10.

ANALYTICAL AND DECISION PROBLEMS AND CASES

A&D 4-1
Canadian Air Group

Canadian Air Group, Inc. credits the proceeds from advance ticket sales to an account entitled Air Traffic Liability. The company's recent annual report shows the following trend in the balance of this account over a three-year period:

	Year 4	*Year 5*	*Year 6*
Air traffic liability (in millions)	*$41.6*	*$46.8*	*$58.3*

INSTRUCTIONS

a What does the balance in the Air Traffic Liability account represent?

b How does the airline normally discharge this liability?

c Explain the most probable reason for the increases in the amount of this liability from year-to-year.

d Based solely upon the trend in the amount of this liability, would you expect the annual amounts of passenger revenue earned by the airlines to be increasing or decreasing over this three-year period? Explain.

A&D 4-2
Adjusting Entries?

The purpose of this problem is to help you understand the need for adjusting entries in a specific business situation. You are to prepare examples of "typical" adjusting entries that might be made at the end of an accounting period by a company that owns and operates a ***large hotel.*** You are to decide upon the types of assets, liabilities, revenue, and expenses that might be involved in these entries. Prepare two examples of ***each of the four basic types of adjusting entries.*** Thus, you will prepare a total of eight adjusting entries.

You need not include dollar amounts—simply enter ***"xxx"*** in the debit and credit columns. However, your written explanations of each entry should describe specific facts that make the adjustment necessary. For example, one adjusting entry that a hotel might make to apportion unearned revenue is shown below.

a Examples of adjusting entries to apportion recorded revenue:

(1) Unearned Banquet Revenue	*xxx*	
Banquet Revenue		*xxx*
To recognize revenue earned this period from catering the Canadian Football League awards banquet in the hotel. The League had paid for this banquet in an earlier accounting period.		

A&D 4-3 Adjusting Entries? An Alternative Case

This problem is an alternative to A&D 4-2. You are to follow the same instructions as in A&D 4-2, but use a large ***law firm*** as the business entity. However, you are to prepare only ***one*** example of each of the four basic types of adjusting entries.

A&D 4-4 Should This Be Adjusted?

Property Management Professionals provides building management services to owners of office buildings and shopping centres. The company closes its accounts at the ***end of the calendar year.*** The manner in which the company has recorded several transactions occurring during 1995 is described below:

- a On September 1, received advance payment from a shopping centre for property management services to be performed over the three-month period beginning September 1. The entire amount received was credited directly to a ***revenue*** account.
- b On December 1, received advance payment from the same customer described in part **a** for services to be rendered over the three-month period beginning December 1. This time, the entire amount received was credited to an ***unearned revenue*** account.
- c Rendered management services for many customers in December. Normal procedure is to record revenue on the date the customer is billed, which is early in the month after the services have been rendered.
- d On December 15, made full payment for a one-year insurance policy that goes into effect on January 1, 1996. The cost of the policy was debited to Unexpired Insurance.
- e Numerous purchases of equipment were debited to asset accounts, rather than to expense accounts.
- f Payroll expense is recorded when employees are paid. Payday for the last two weeks of December falls on January 2, 1996.

INSTRUCTIONS

For each transaction, explain whether an adjusting entry is needed at ***December 31, 1995,*** and state the reasons for your answer. If you recommend an adjusting entry, explain the effects this entry would have upon assets, liabilities, owner's equity, revenue, and expense in the 1995 financial statements.

A&D 4-5 Adjusting Entries

Selected accounts with their normal balances from the December 31 (year-end) trial balance and adjusted trial balance of Adanac Company are as follows:

	Trial Balance	Adjusted Trial Balance
Cash	$ 6,200	$ 6,200
Prepaid rent	2,100	-0-
Office supplies	780	180
Equipment	30,000	30,000
Notes payable	10,000	10,000
Salaries payable	-0-	970
Unearned consulting fees	4,800	2,300
Iris McGill, Drawing	26,500	26,500
Consulting fees earned	76,500	79,600
Salaries expense	15,700	16,670
Telephone expense	3,200	3,200
Rent expense	-0-	2,100
Office supplies expense	-0-	600
Depreciaton expense: equipment	-0-	3,000
Interest Expense	-0-	1,080

INSTRUCTIONS Prepare all the adjusting entries (with explanations) that you can derive from the two trial balances.

A&D 4-6
What To Adjust?

Gisele Moore, a recent graduate with a degree in sociology and anthropology, decided to start a formal wear and costume rental business rather than to continue her futile efforts in seeking employment in her field. Thus, on August 1, Gisele withdrew $2,000 from her savings account and deposited it in a bank account in the name of her business, Moore's Place. To obtain more capital to finance the acquisition of the needed tuxedos, gowns, and costumes, as well as furniture and fixtures, Gisele borrowed $8,000 from her mother and deposited the cash in the bank account of the business.

August 1 was a very busy day for Gisele. She rented a store from Houston Property Management. Houston would give Gisele a better deal if she paid rent in advance every three months. Gisele accepted the offer and paid $2,700 to Houston. On the same day, she purchased furniture and fixtures for $6,000, paying $1,000 cash and signing a one-year note payable for the balance at an annual interest rate of 6%, payable at maturity. The furniture and fixtures were estimated to have a useful life of five years. To obtain a volume discount, Gisele purchased two months of office supplies on account for $300. Also, Gisele purchased tuxedos, gowns, and costumes from Designer Fashions Limited for $8,400, paying $3,000 cash and agreeing to pay the balance in 60 days. The management of Designer Fashions told Gisele that these items would have a useful life of seven years.

To attract business, Gisele advertised extensively in local newspapers and weekly magazines. On August 3, she paid $1,800 for the advertisements to ensure there would be adequate and equal promotion for two months.

Apparently, the advertisements paid off. Revenue for the first two weeks of operation was $2,600, all paid in cash. In addition, on August 16, the Theatre Players Group paid $2,500 to rent some costumes for a month for the performances in a local casino. The costumes will be returned on September 16.

On Monday, August 28, Gisele hired a part-time employee to help with the increasing volume of business for $250 for a five-day work week. The first week's salary is payable on Friday, September 1.

The business continued to grow. The last two weeks' revenue was $5,200, of which $1,200 was in cash, $3,000 on account, and $1,000 yet to be billed. Feeling that the first month had been a success, Gisele withdrew $1,500 cash from the business. To ensure that she would have sufficient cash to make payments in September, Gisele called the utilities company to find out when she would be paying utilities for August. Gisele was happy to find out that she owed only $230 and it would not be due until early September.

INSTRUCTIONS Prepare the necessary adjusting entries at August 31.

A&D 4-7
Closing Entries

Carlita Shannon, owner of Luu Enterprise, wants you to help her close the books because the part-time bookkeeper has suddenly left the company. She manages to obtain the following information from the bookkeeper's drawers (the accounts are in alphabetical order).

	December 31 (Year-end)	
	Trial Balance	*Adjusted Trial Balance*
Accounts payable	$ 2,300	$ 2,600
Accounts receivable	7,800	8,800
Accumulated depreciation: equipment	3,000	5,000
Cash	1,900	1,900
Depreciation expense: equipment	–0–	2,000
Equipment	20,000	20,000
Interest expense	–0–	720
Interest payable	–0–	720
Management fees earned	108,000	112,900
Office supplies expense	300	900
Prepaid rent	3,200	1,600
Rent expense	8,000	9,600
Salaries expense	26,200	29,500
Carlita Shannon, drawing	49,800	49,800
Telephone expense	2,800	3,180
Unearned management fees	6,900	3,000

INSTRUCTIONS Prepare the closing entries (with explanations) based on the information provided by Carlita.

A&D 4-8
Completing a Worksheet

An unexpected virus attacked the microcomputer system of Gaffar Management Services. As a result, Alice Gaffar, the owner, is left with the partially completed work sheet on page 211 and asks for your assistance.

INSTRUCTIONS Complete the worksheet for Alice Gaffer.

GAFFAR MANAGEMENT SERVICES
Work Sheet
For the Month Ended June 30, 19__

	Trial Balance		Adjustments		Income Statement		Balance Sheet	
	Debit	Credit	Debit	Credit	Debit	Credit	Debit	Credit
Balance sheet accounts:								
Cash							*12,610*	
Management fees receivable	*15,485*						*15,785*	
Prepaid rent				*800*			*800*	
Unexpired insurance							*450*	
Office supplies	*1,080*							
Office equipment	*9,600*							
Accumulated depreciation: office equipment								*300*
Notes payable								*8,000*
Accounts payable		*890*						
Unearned management fees		*3,700*						*1,700*
Alice Gaffar, capital		*23,715*						
Alice Gaffar, drawing							*2,250*	
Salaries payable				*290*				*290*
Interest payable								*60*
Income statement accounts:								
Management fees earned				*300* }		*25,580*		
Rent expense					*1,600*			
Salaries expense								
Telephone expense	*1,260*				*1,260*			
Insurance expense			*450*					
Office supplies expense			*380*		*380*			
Depreciation expense: office equipment			*100*					
Interest expense			*60*					
Net income								*7,240*
						25,580		

A&D 4-9
The Concept of Materiality

The concept of materiality is one of the most basic generally accepted accounting principles.

a Answer the following questions:

1 Why is the materiality of a transaction or an event a matter of professional judgment?

2 What criteria should accountants consider in determining whether a transaction or an event is "material"?

3 Does the concept of materiality mean that financial statements are not precise, down to the last dollar? Does this concept make financial statements less useful to most users?

b **Avis Rent-a-Car** purchases a large number of cars each year for its rental fleet. The cost of any individual automobile is immaterial to Avis, which is a very large corporation. Would it be acceptable for Avis to charge the purchase of automobiles for its rental fleet directly to expense, rather than to an asset account? Explain.

A&D 4-10
Materiality in Practice

During the current year, East-West Airlines earned net income of $50 million from total revenue of $350 million. The company services primarily cities in Canada but also has service to several foreign countries. Three events are described below, along with the treatment accorded to these events in the company's financial statements.

a During the year, the company purchased $5 million in spare parts to be used in aircraft maintenance. All of these purchases were charged immediately to Maintenance Expense. No adjusting entry was made at year-end to reflect approximately $50,000 in spare parts remaining on hand, because the amount was considered immaterial.

b The company's internal auditors discovered that the vice president of in-flight services had embezzled $100,000 from the airlines by authorizing payments to a fictitious supplier of in-flight meals. The vice president was fired, and criminal charges currently are pending against her, as is a civil lawsuit to recover the embezzled funds. In the income statement, this $100,000 loss was deducted from revenue as part of the Flight Operations Expenses, which totalled more than $200 million. No special disclosures were made, because the amount of the embezzlement was considered immaterial.

c Shortly after year-end, the company suspended all flight operations to a particular foreign country as a result of political unrest. These flights provided approximately 2% of the company's revenue and net income during the current year. Cancellation of service to this country was not disclosed in notes to the current year's financial statements, because operations of the current year were not affected.

INSTRUCTIONS

Explain whether in your own judgment you concur or disagree with the treatment accorded to these events by East-West in its current financial statements. If you recommend a different financial statement presentation, explain why you do so. In each case, indicate whether or not you consider the item "material," and explain your reasons. Consider each of these three situations ***independently*** of the others.

A&D 4-11
Computer-Based Accounting System

In A&D 2-1, Bill Gates used data base software to design a simple accounting system for use on personal computers. Gates's first system prepared only a balance sheet; he is now ready to design an enhanced system that will perform all of the steps in the accounting cycle and will produce a complete set of financial statements. This enhanced system also will utilize data base software.

The idea underlying data base software is that data intended for a variety of different uses must be entered into the data base only once. The computer can then arrange these data into any number of desired formats. It can also combine data and perform mathematical computations using data in the data base.

In Gates's new accounting system, the computer will arrange the data into the following formats: (1) journal entries (with explanations) for all transactions, (2) three-column running balance ledger accounts, (3) a 10-column work sheet, (4) a complete set of financial statements and appropriate disclosures, (5) journal entries for all adjusting and closing entries, (6) an after-closing trial balance, and (7) reversing entries.* As each of these records and statements is prepared, any totals or subtotals in the record are included automatically in the data base. For example, when ledger accounts are updated, the new account balances become part of the data base.

INSTRUCTIONS

In Chapter 4, the steps of the accounting cycle were described as follows: (a) journalize transactions, (b) post to ledger accounts, (c) prepare a work sheet, (d) prepare financial statements and appropriate disclosures, (e) adjust and close the accounts, (f) prepare an after-closing trial balance, and (g) prepare reversing entries.* For each step in this cycle, briefly describe the types of data used in performing the step. Indicate whether the data are already contained in the data base, or whether the computer operator must enter data to enable the computer to perform the step.

A&D 4-12
A Sure Thing?

Adam Peitou is interested in buying Foxie's, an aerobic dance studio. He has come to you for help in interpreting the company's financial statements and to seek your advice about purchasing the business.

Foxie's has been in operation for one year. The business is a sole proprietorship owned by Sandy Beech. Foxie's rents the building in which it operates, as well as all of its exercise equipment. As the business is small, Beech has maintained the accounting records on a cash basis. She has prepared the following income statement and balance sheet from these cash basis records at December 31, the year-end date:

Income Statement

Revenue:		
Membership fees	*$150,000*	
Membership dues	*30,000*	*$180,000*
Expenses:		
Rent	*$ 18,000*	
Wages	*52,000*	
Advertising	*20,000*	
Miscellaneous	*15,000*	*105,000*
Net income		*$ 75,000*

Balance Sheet

Assets

Cash	*$ 25,000*

Liabilities & Owner's Equity

Sandy Beech, capital	*$ 25,000*

Beech is offering to sell Foxie's for the balance of her capital account − $25,000. Peitou is very enthusiastic and states, "How can I go wrong? I'll be paying $25,000 to buy $25,000 cash, and I'll be getting a very profitable business that generates large amounts of cash in the deal."

In a meeting with you and Peitou, Beech makes the following statement: "This business has been very good to me. In the first year of operations, I've been able to

* *Supplemental Topic, "Reversing Entries"*

withdraw $50,000 in cash. Yet the business is still quite solvent—it has lots of cash and no debts."

You ask Beech to explain the difference between membership fees and membership dues. She responds, "Foxie's is an exclusive club. We cater only to members. This year, we sold 500 five-year memberships. Each membership requires the customer to pay $300 cash in advance and to pay dues of $10 per month for five years. I credited the advance payments to the Membership Fees account and credited the $10 monthly payments to Membership Dues. Thus, all the revenue is hard cash—no 'paper profits' like you see in so many businesses."

You then enquire as to when these five-year memberships were sold. Beech responds, "On the average, these memberships are only six months old. No members have dropped out, so Foxie's should continue receiving dues from these people for another four and one-half years, thus assuring future profitability. Another beneficial factor is that the company hasn't sold any new memberships in the last several months. Therefore, I think that the company could discontinue its advertising and further increase future profitability. Since further advertising may not produce any new members, the $3,000 television commercial for early next year, for which I have paid, is really worthless and I have included it in the $20,000 advertising expense of this year."

INSTRUCTIONS

a Prepare a revised income statement and balance sheet based on generally accepted accounting principles.

b Assume that none of the 500 members drop out of Foxie's during the next year, and that the business sells no new memberships. What would be the amount of the company's expected cash receipts? Assuming that advertising expense is discontinued but that other expenses remain the same, what would be the expected amount of cash payments for the coming year?

c Use the information in your analysis in parts **a** and **b** to draft a letter to Peitou advising him on the wisdom of purchasing Foxie's for $25,000.

COMPREHENSIVE PROBLEM 2

FRIEND WITH A TRUCK

A SHORT PRACTICE SET, BASED UPON A SERVICE BUSINESS

On June 1, 19__, Anthony Ferrara organized a business called Friend With A Truck for the purpose of operating an equipment rental yard. The new business was able to begin operations immediately by purchasing the assets and taking over the location of Rent-All, an equipment rental company that was going out of business.

Friend With A Truck uses the following chart of accounts:

Cash	1	Anthony Ferrara, Capital	30
Accounts Receivable	4	Anthony Ferrara, Drawing	35
Prepaid Rent	6	Income Summary	40
Office Supplies	8	Rental Fees Earned	50
Rental Equipment	10	Salaries Expense	60
Accumulated Depreciation:		Maintenance Expense	61
Rental Equipment	12	Utilities Expense	62
Notes Payable	20	Rent Expense	63
Accounts Payable	22	Office Supplies Expense	64
Interest Payable	25	Depreciation Expense	65
Salaries Payable	26	Interest Expense	66
Unearned Rental Fees	29		

The company closes its accounts and prepares financial statements at the end of each month. During June, the company entered into the following transactions:

June 1 Anthony Ferrara deposited $150,000 cash in a bank account in the name of the business, Friend With A Truck.

June 1 Purchased for $240,000 all the equipment formerly owned by Rent-All. Paid $100,000 cash and issued a one-year note payable for $140,000, plus interest at the annual rate of 9%. The equipment is estimated to have a useful life of 10 years.

June 1 Paid $10,000 to Morrison Realty as four months' advance rent on the rental yard and office formerly occupied by Rent-All.

June 3 Received $12,000 cash as advance payment on equipment rental from McBryan Construction Company.

June 5 Purchased office supplies on account from Newport Office Company, $1,850. Payment due in 30 days. (These supplies are expected to last for several months.)

June 9 Purchased on account from Foley Parts Distributor $290 in parts needed immediately to repair a rental tractor. Payment is due in 10 days.

June 12 Paid salaries for the first two weeks in June, $3,200.

June 15 Excluding the advance payment from the McBryan Construction Company, equipment rental fees earned during the first 15 days of June amounted to $8,900, of which $7,200 was received in cash.

June 18 Paid the account payable to Foley Parts Distributor, $290.

June 19 Collected $800 of the accounts receivable recorded on June 15.

June 24 Rented a backhoe to Mission Landscaping at a price of $110 per day, to be paid when the backhoe is returned. Mission Landscaping expects to keep the backhoe for about two or three weeks.

June 26 Paid biweekly salaries, $3,200.

June 29 Anthony Ferrara withdrew $3,000 cash from the business to make a mortgage payment for his personal residence.

June 30 Equipment rental fees earned during the second half of June and received in cash amounted to $7,850.

June 30 Received a bill from Western Utilities for the month of June, $340. Payment is due in 30 days.

The information available on June 30 is as follows: the office supplies on hand are estimated at $1,160; $3,210 of the advance payment from McBryan Construction has been earned; salaries earned by employees since the last payroll are $960.

INSTRUCTIONS

a Journalize the above transactions.

b Post to ledger accounts. (Use running balance form of ledger accounts. Enter numbers of journal pages and ledger accounts to complete the cross-referencing between the journal and ledger.)

c Prepare a 10-column work sheet for the month ended June 30, 19__.

d Prepare an income statement and a statement of owner's equity for the month of June, and a balance sheet (in report form) as of June 30.

e Prepare adjusting and closing entries and post to ledger accounts.

f Prepare an after-closing trial balance as of June 30.

***g** Prepare appropriate reversing entries (dated July 1) and post to ledger accounts.

* *Supplemental Topic, "Reversing Entries"*

PART

2 Merchandising Concerns and the Design of Accounting Systems

This part contains two chapters. In the first, we explain the accounting concepts relating to merchandising activities—that is, to the sale of products rather than services. In the second chapter, we explore several characteristics of the accounting systems used in large organizations. These characteristics include the ability to process a large volume of transactions, the need for internal control, and financial and operational audits.

CHAPTER

5 Accounting for Merchandising Activities; Classified Financial Statements

Here the accounting cycle is expanded to include companies that are selling goods rather than services. First, basic merchandising transactions are discussed. More specialized merchandising transactions and comprehensive coverage on periodic inventory system are presented as supplemental topics.

Our second topic is the preparation and use of classified financial statements. We show how creditors and investors use key financial statement relationships in evaluating the solvency, profitability, and future prospects of a business.

Learning Objectives

After studying this chapter you should be able to:

1 *Describe the operating cycle of a merchandising company.*

2 *Explain the need for various subsidiary ledgers in accounting for merchandising transactions.*

3 *Account for purchases and sales of merchandise using a perpetual inventory system.*

4 *Distinguish between perpetual and periodic inventory systems.*

5 *Prepare a classified balance sheet. Compute the current ratio and amount of working capital.*

6 *Identify two standards for comparison widely used in evaluating financial ratios.*

7 *Analyze an income statement; evaluate the adequacy of net income.*

*8 *Account for cash discounts, merchandise returns, transportation costs, and sales taxes.*

**9 *Explain the characteristics, advantages, and disadvantages of a periodic inventory system.*

**10 *Account for transactions using a periodic inventory system.*

**11 *Prepare closing entries in a periodic inventory system, including the entry to "reopen" the inventory account.*

---

* *Supplemental Topic A, "Additional Merchandising Transactions"*
** *Supplemental Topic B," More about Periodic Inventory System"*

ACCOUNTING FOR MERCHANDISING ACTIVITIES

Merchandising Companies

In the preceding four chapters we have illustrated the accounting cycle for businesses that render ***services*** to their customers. Merchandising companies, in contrast to service-type businesses, earn revenue by selling ***goods*** rather than services.

The goods that a merchandising company sells to its customers are called ***inventory*** (or merchandise), regardless of the type of products that the company sells. Thus, the inventory of an automobile dealership consists of automobiles offered for sale, whereas the inventory of a grocery store consists of a wide variety of food items.

Merchandising companies often have large amounts of money invested in their inventories. In fact, inventory is one of the most costly assets appearing in the balance sheets of most merchandising companies. Fortunately, inventory is a relatively "liquid" asset—that is, it usually will be sold within a few weeks or months, thereby generating accounts receivable and cash receipts. For this reason, the asset inventory appears near the top of the balance sheet, immediately below accounts receivable.

The "Operating Cycle" of a Merchandising Company The series of transactions through which a business generates its revenue and its cash receipts from customers is called the ***operating cycle.*** The operating cycle of a merchandising company consists of the following basic transactions: (1) purchases of merchandise; (2) sales of the merchandise, often on account (on credit); and (3) collection of the accounts receivable from customers. As the word ***cycle*** suggests, this sequence of transactions is repeated continuously. Some of the cash collected from the customer is used to purchase more merchandise, and the cycle begins anew.

OBJECTIVE 1 Describe the operating cycle of a merchandising company.

This continuous sequence of merchandising transactions is illustrated in the following diagram:

The operating cycle repeats continuously

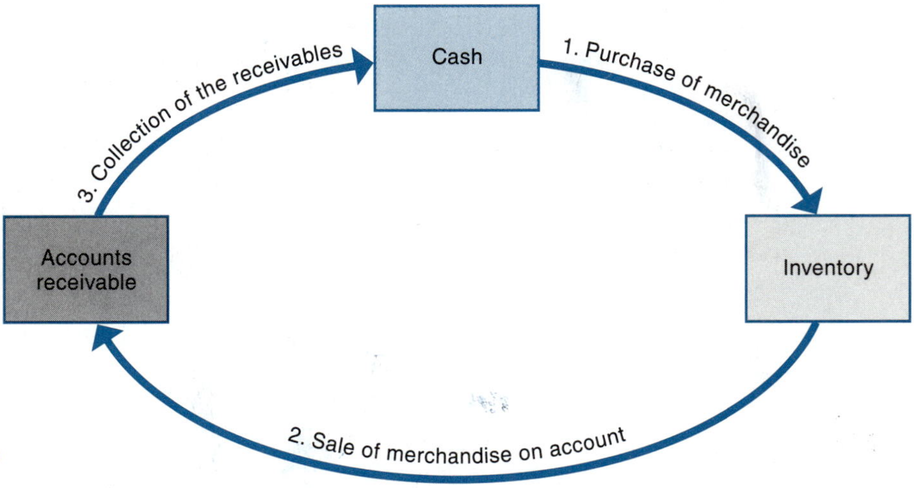

Merchandising Activities Compared with Manufacturing Most merchandising companies purchase their inventories from other business organizations in a ***ready-to-sell*** condition. Companies that ***manufacture*** their inventories, such as General Motors, Alcan Aluminium, and Bombardier, are called ***manufacturers,*** rather than merchandisers. The operating cycle of a manufacturing company is longer and more complex than that of a merchandising company, because the first transaction—purchasing merchandise—is replaced by the many transactions involved in manufacturing the merchandise.

The concepts discussed in this chapter apply equally to merchandising businesses and to manufacturers. However, accounting for manufacturing activities also involves many additional concepts that are addressed in later chapters. For this reason, our examples and illustrations in this chapter are limited to companies that purchase their inventory in a ready-to-sell condition.

Retailers and Wholesalers Merchandising companies include both retailers and wholesalers. A ***retailer*** is a business that sells merchandise directly to the public. Retailers may be large or small; they vary in size from giant department store chains, such as The Bay and Sears, to small neighbourhood businesses, such as gas stations and gift shops. In fact, more businesses engage in retail sales than in any other type of business activity.

The other major type of merchandising company is the ***wholesaler.*** Wholesalers buy large quantities of merchandise from several different manufacturers and then resell this merchandise to many different retailers. As wholesalers do not sell directly to the public, even the largest wholesalers are not well known to most consumers. Nonetheless, wholesaling is a major type of merchandising activity.

The concepts discussed in the remainder of this chapter apply equally to retailers and to wholesalers.

Income Statement of a Merchandising Company

Selling merchandise introduces a new and major cost of doing business: the ***cost*** to the merchandising company of the goods that it resells to its customers. This cost is termed the ***cost of goods sold.*** In essence, the cost of goods sold ***is an expense;*** however, this item is of such importance to a merchandising company that it is shown separate from other expenses in the income statement.

A ***highly condensed*** income statement for a merchandising business is shown below. In comparison with the income statement of a service-type business, the new features of this statement are the inclusion of the ***cost of goods sold*** and a subtotal called ***gross profit.***

Condensed income statement for a merchandising company

COMPUTER BARN
Income Statement
For the Year Ended December 31, 1995

Revenue from sales	$900,000
Less: Cost of goods sold	540,000
Gross profit	$360,000
Less: Expenses	270,000
Net income	$ 90,000

Revenue from sales represents the ***sales price*** of merchandise sold to customers during the period. The cost of goods sold, on the other hand, represents the ***cost*** incurred by the merchandising company in purchasing these goods from the company's suppliers. The difference between revenue from sales and the cost of goods sold is called ***gross profit*** (or gross margin).

Gross profit is a useful means of measuring the profitability of sales transactions, but it does ***not*** represent the overall profitability of the business. A merchandising company has many expenses ***other than*** the cost of goods sold. Examples include salaries, rent, advertising, and depreciation. The company only earns a net income if its gross profit exceeds the sum of these other expenses.

What Accounting Information Does a Merchandising Company Need?

Before we illustrate how a merchandising company accounts for the transactions in its operating cycle, let us consider the basic ***types of information*** that the company's accounting system should develop. The company needs accounting information that will (1) meet its financial reporting requirements, (2) serve the needs of company personnel in conducting daily business operations, and (3) meet any special reporting requirements, such as information required by income tax authorities.

To meet its financial reporting requirements, a merchandising company must measure and record its revenue from sales transactions, and also the cost of goods sold. (Other types of revenue and expenses must also be recorded, but this is done in the same manner as in a service-type business.) In addition, the accounting system must provide a complete record of the company's assets and liabilities.

The information appearing in financial statements is highly summarized. For example, the amount shown as accounts receivable in a balance sheet represents the ***total*** accounts receivable at the balance sheet date. Managers and other company employees need ***much more detailed*** accounting information than that provided in financial statements. In billing customers, for example, the company's billing clerks need to know the amount receivable from ***each credit customer.*** In addition, the accounting system must provide the billing clerks with the dates and amounts of all charges and payments affecting each customer's account.

Businesses that are organized as corporations must file corporate income tax returns.[1] In many respects, the information needed for income tax purposes parallels that used in the financial statements. Differences between income tax rules and financial reporting requirements will be discussed in later chapters.

Let us now see how the accounting system of a merchandising company meets the company's needs for financial information.

---

[1] The taxable income of a ***sole proprietorship*** is included in the personal income tax return of the ***business owner,*** rather than in a tax return filed by the business entity.

General Ledger Accounts

Up to now, we have been recording transactions only in ***general ledger*** accounts. These general ledger accounts are used in preparing financial statements and other accounting reports that ***summarize*** the financial position of a business and the results of its operations.

Although general ledger accounts provide a useful ***overview*** of a company's financial activities, they do not provide much of the detailed information needed by managers and other company employees in daily business operations. This detailed information is found in accounting records called ***subsidiary ledgers.***

Subsidiary Ledgers: A Source of More Detail

OBJECTIVE 2 Explain the need for various subsidiary ledgers in accounting for merchandising transactions.

A subsidiary ledger shows separately the individual items that comprise the balance of a general ledger account. For example, an ***accounts receivable subsidiary ledger*** (or customers ledger) contains a ***separate account for each credit customer.*** If the company has 500 credit customers, there will be 500 separate accounts in the accounts receivable subsidiary ledger. The balances of these 500 subsidiary ledger accounts add up to the balance in the Accounts Receivable account in the general ledger.

An accounts receivable subsidiary ledger contains all the information about a specific customer, including the amounts due, the dates and amounts of credit sales and past payments, the dates that payments are due, the credit limit, and the customer's billing address. In fact, each subsidiary account provides a complete history of the credit transactions between the company and a particular credit customer.

Most businesses maintain several different subsidiary ledgers, each providing details about the composition of a different general ledger account. A general ledger account that summarizes the content of a subsidiary ledger is called a ***controlling account*** (or control account).

For convenience, the word ***subsidiary*** often is omitted in describing a specific subsidiary ledger. Thus, an accounts receivable subsidiary ledger might simply be called the accounts receivable ledger (or customers ledger).

Subsidiary Ledgers Needed for Merchandising Transactions In addition to a subsidiary ledger for accounts receivable, every merchandising company also maintains an ***accounts payable subsidiary ledger,*** showing the amount owed to each creditor. Most merchandising companies also maintain an ***inventory subsidiary ledger,*** with a separate account for each type of merchandise that the company sells. Thus, the inventory ledger of a large department store contains thousands of accounts. Each of these accounts shows for ***one type of product*** the quantities, per-unit costs, and total costs of all units purchased, sold, and currently "in inventory."

The following diagram shows the relationship between several subsidiary ledgers and the related controlling accounts in the general ledger:

Relationship of subsidiary ledgers and controlling accounts

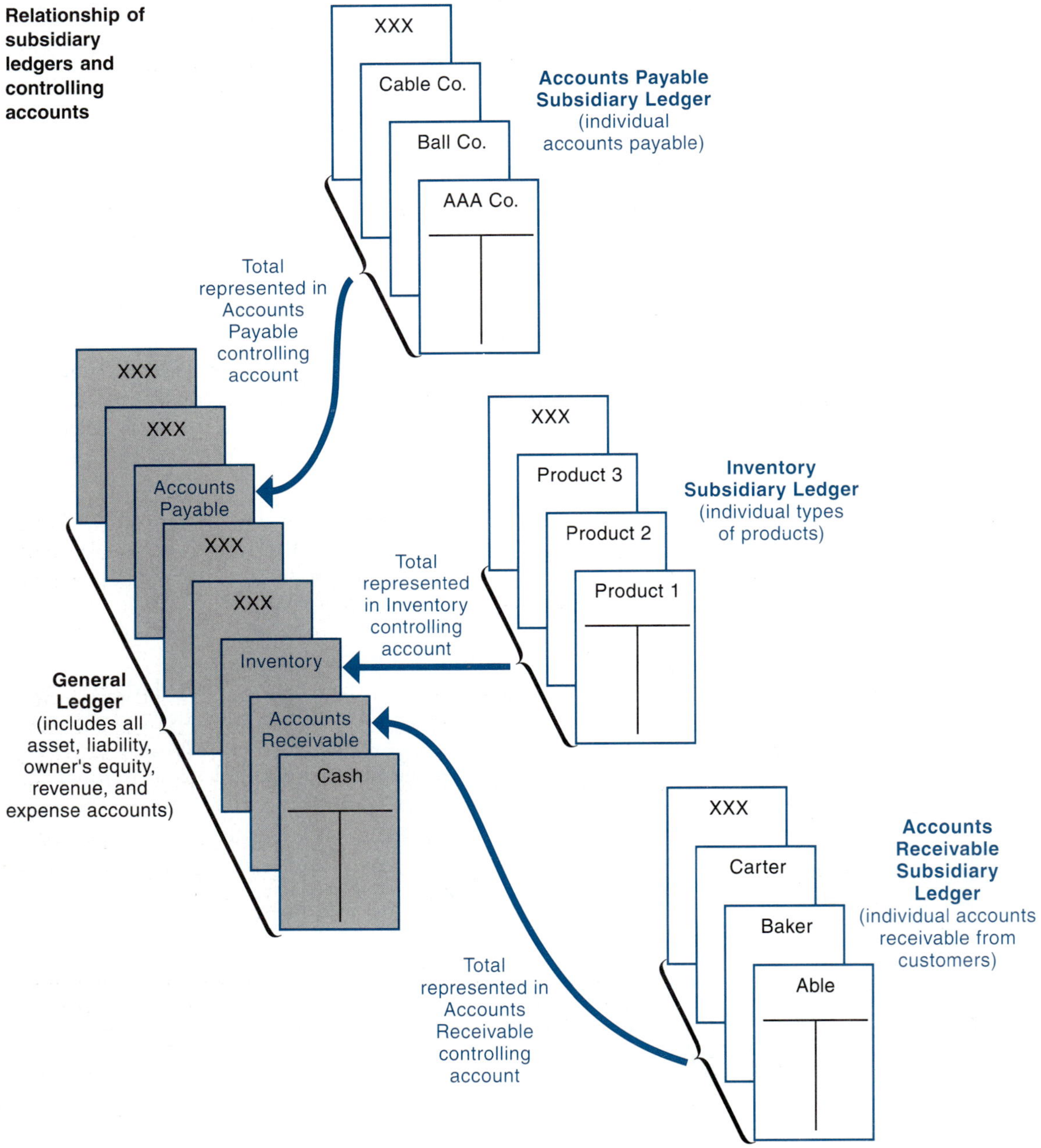

Other Types of Subsidiary Ledgers In this chapter, we discuss the subsidiary ledgers for inventory, accounts payable, and accounts receivable. However, subsidiary ledgers also are maintained for many other general ledger accounts. The following schedule lists some of the general ledger accounts usually supported by a subsidiary ledger:

Controlling Account in the General Ledger	Unit of Organization within the Subsidiary Ledger
Cash	*Each bank account*
Notes receivable	*Each note receivable*
Accounts receivable	*Individual credit customers*
Inventory	*Each type of product offered for sale*
Plant assets	*Each asset (group of similar assets)*
Notes payable	*Each note payable*
Accounts payable	*Each creditor*
Capital stock (only in a business organized as a corporation)	*Each shareholder (this ledger shows each shareholder's name, address, and the number of shares owned)*
Sales (or any revenue account)	*Each department, branch location, or product line*
Cost of goods sold	*Same organization as the sales ledger*
Any expense account	*Each department incurring this type of expense*

Subsidiary ledgers are intended to meet the information needs of the company's ***managers and employees.*** These accounting records are ***not*** used in the preparation of financial statements, nor are they usually made available to persons outside of the business organization.

Posting to Subsidiary Ledger Accounts Any entry that affects the balance of a subsidiary ledger account ***also*** affects the balance of the related controlling account. Thus, entries affecting subsidiary ledger accounts must be ***posted twice***—once to the subsidiary ledger account and once to the controlling account in the general ledger.

To illustrate, assume that on July 12 Hillside Company collects a $1,000 account receivable from L. Brown, a credit customer. This transaction is illustrated below in the form of a general journal entry:

Date		Account Titles and Explanation	LP	Debit	Credit
July	*12*	*Cash*		*1,000*	
		Accounts Receivable (L. Brown)			*1,000*
		Collected an account receivable.			

Assume that in the general ledger the account number for the Cash account is ***101*** and the account number of the Accounts Receivable controlling account is ***120.*** Hillside also maintains an accounts receivable subsidiary ledger, in which customers' accounts are arranged alphabetically. We will assume that the company has only one bank account and, therefore, does not maintain a subsidiary ledger for cash.

Our original journal entry is repeated below, along with the appropriate posting references included in the LP (Ledger Page) column:

Notice the "double posting" of the credit entry

Date		Account Titles and Explanation	LP	Debit	Credit
July	12	Cash	101	1,000	
		Accounts Receivable (L. Brown) ...	✓/120		1,000
		Collected an account receivable.			

The account numbers ***101*** and ***120*** entered in this column indicate that the entry has been posted to both the Cash account and the Accounts Receivable controlling account in the general ledger. The check mark (✓) indicates that the credit portion of the entry also has been posted to the account for L. Brown in the accounts receivable subsidiary ledger.

(In working homework assignments in this text, you often are asked to describe the effects of business transactions in the form of general journal entries. You should ***not*** include posting references in these entries ***unless you actually have posted the data*** to ledger accounts.)

Reconciling Subsidiary Ledgers with the Controlling Account As previously mentioned, the balance in a general ledger controlling account should be equal to the ***sum*** of the balances of all of the accounts in the related subsidiary ledger. Periodically, accountants ***reconcile*** a subsidiary ledger with the controlling account—that is, they determine that the sum of the subsidiary ledger account balances ***does,*** in fact, equal that of the controlling account.

Reconciling a subsidiary ledger is an ***internal control procedure*** that may bring to light certain types of errors. For example, this procedure should detect a failure to post a transaction to the subsidiary ledger or a mechanical error in computing an account balance. Unfortunately, it does ***not*** provide assurance that all transactions were posted to the ***correct account*** within the subsidiary ledger. If a debit or credit entry is posted to the ***wrong account*** in the subsidiary ledger, the subsidiary ledger and controlling account will ***remain "in balance."*** These types of posting errors are difficult to detect and are one reason why individuals and businesses that purchase merchandise on account should review carefully the monthly billings that they receive from their suppliers.

Subsidiary Ledgers in Computer-Based Systems At first, it may seem that maintaining subsidiary ledgers with hundreds or thousands of separate accounts would involve a great deal of work. However, business organizations that are large enough to require large subsidiary ledgers use computer-based accounting systems. In a computer-based accounting system, subsidiary ledger accounts and general ledger accounts all are posted ***automatically*** as transactions are recorded. In addition, the computer automatically reconciles the subsidiary ledgers with the controlling accounts. Thus, no significant effort is required of accounting personnel to maintain subsidiary ledgers in a computer-based system.[2]

[2] The maintenance of subsidiary ledgers was one of the earliest applications of computers in the business world. For a large organization, the time savings in this area alone may justify the cost of a computer-based accounting system. Prior to the use of computers, large business organizations employed many clerical workers for the sole purpose of posting transactions to subsidiary ledger accounts.

Two Approaches Widely Used in Accounting for Merchandising Transactions

Either of two approaches may be used in accounting for merchandising transactions: (1) a ***perpetual inventory system*** or (2) a ***periodic inventory system.*** In past decades, both systems were in widespread use. Today, however, virtually all large businesses (and many smaller ones) use perpetual systems. Periodic systems are used primarily in very small businesses that do not have significant financial reporting requirements.

Perpetual Inventory System

OBJECTIVE 3 Account for purchases and sales of merchandise using a perpetual inventory system.

In a perpetual inventory system, merchandising transactions are recorded ***as they occur.*** The system draws its name from the fact that the accounting records are kept perpetually up-to-date. Purchases of merchandise are recorded by debiting an asset account entitled Inventory. When merchandise is sold, two entries are necessary: one to recognize the ***revenue earned*** and the second to recognize the related ***cost of goods sold.*** This second entry also reduces the balance of the Inventory account to reflect the sale of some of the company's inventory.

A perpetual inventory system usually includes an ***inventory subsidiary ledger.*** This ledger provides company personnel with up-to-date information about every type of product that the company sells, including the cost and the number of units purchased, sold, and currently on hand.

To illustrate the perpetual inventory system, we will follow specific items of merchandise through the operating cycle of Computer Barn, a retail store. The transactions comprising this illustration are as follows:

Sept. 1 Purchased 10 Regent CX-21 computer monitors on account from Okawa Wholesale Company. The monitors cost $600 each, for a total of $6,000; payment is due in 30 days.

Sept. 7 Sold 2 monitors on account to RJ Travel Agency at a retail sales price of $1,000 each, for a total of $2,000. Payment is due in 30 days.

Oct. 1 Paid the $6,000 account payable to Okawa Wholesale Company.

Oct. 7 Collected the $2,000 account receivable from RJ Travel Agency.

In addition to a general ledger, Computer Barn maintains separate subsidiary ledgers for accounts receivable, inventory, and accounts payable.

Purchases of Merchandise Purchases of inventory are recorded at cost. Thus, Computer Barn records its purchase of the 10 computer monitors on September 1 as follows:

Entry to record a purchase

Inventory	*6,000*	
Accounts Payable (Okawa Wholesale Co.)		*6,000*
Purchased 10 Regent CX-21 computer monitors for $600 each; payment due in 30 days.		

The data contained in this entry is posted to the general ledger and also to the subsidiary ledgers. First, the entry is posted to the Inventory and Accounts Payable controlling accounts in the general ledger. The debit to Inventory also is posted to the Regent CX-21 Monitors account in the inventory subsidiary ledger.[3] The quantity of monitors purchased (10) and the per-unit cost ($600) also are recorded in this subsidiary ledger account. (This subsidiary ledger account is illustrated on page 229.)

The credit to Accounts Payable also is posted to the account for Okawa Wholesale Company in Computer Barn's accounts payable subsidiary ledger.

Sales of Merchandise The revenue earned in a sales transaction is equal to the ***sales price*** of the merchandise and is credited to a revenue account entitled ***Sales.*** Except in rare circumstances, sales revenue is considered "realized" when the merchandise is ***delivered to the customer,*** even if the sale is made on account. Therefore, Computer Barn will recognize the revenue from the sale to RJ Travel Agency on September 7, as shown below:

Entries to record a sale . . .

Accounts Receivable (RJ Travel Agency)	*2,000*	
Sales		*2,000*
Sold 2 Regent CX-21 monitors for $1,000 each; payment due in 30 days.		

The ***matching principle*** requires that revenue be matched (offset) with all of the costs and expenses incurred in producing that revenue. Therefore, a ***second journal entry*** is required at the date of sale to record the cost of goods sold.

. . . and the related cost of goods sold

Cost of Goods Sold	*1,200*	
Inventory		*1,200*
To transfer the cost of 2 Regent CX-21 monitors ($600 apiece) from Inventory to the Cost of Goods Sold account.		

Notice that this second entry is based upon the ***cost*** of the merchandise to Computer Barn, not upon its retail sales price. The per-unit cost of the Regent monitors ($600) was determined from the inventory subsidiary ledger (see page 229).

Both of the journal entries relating to this sales transaction are posted to Computer Barn's general ledger. In addition, the $2,000 debit to Accounts Receivable (first entry) is posted to the account for RJ Travel Agency in the accounts receivable subsidiary ledger. The credit to Inventory (second entry) also is posted to the Regent CX-21 Monitors account in the inventory subsidiary ledger (see page 229).

Payment of Accounts Payable to Suppliers The payment to Okawa Wholesale Company on October 1 is recorded as follows:

Accounts Payable (Okawa Wholesale Co.)	*6,000*	
Cash		*6,000*
Paid account payable.		

[3] In journal entries, it is common practice to indicate specific suppliers and customers using a parenthetic note following the account title "Accounts Payable" or "Accounts Receivable." Similar notations usually are ***not*** used with the Inventory account, because ***many different types of products*** may be purchased in a single transaction. The detailed product information used in posting to the inventory ledger is found in the ***invoice*** (bill) that the seller sends to the buyer.

Both portions of this entry are posted to the general ledger. In addition, payment of the account payable is entered in the Okawa Wholesale Company account in the Computer Barn's accounts payable subsidiary ledger.

Collection of Accounts Receivable from Customers On October 7, collection of the account receivable from RJ Travel Agency is recorded as follows:

Cash	*2,000*	
Accounts Receivable (RJ Travel Agency)		*2,000*
Collected an account receivable from a credit customer.		

Both portions of this entry are posted to the general ledger; the credit to Accounts Receivable also is posted to the RJ Travel Agency account in the accounts receivable subsidiary ledger.

Collection of the cash from RJ Travel Agency completes Computer Barn's operating cycle with respect to these two units of merchandise.

The Inventory Subsidiary Ledger An inventory subsidiary ledger includes a separate account (or "inventory card") for each type of product in the company's inventory. Computer Barn's subsidiary inventory record for Regent monitors is illustrated below:

Inventory subsidiary ledger account

Item Regent CX-21 — Primary supplier Okawa Wholesale Company
Description 21 Gray scale monitor — Second supplier Forbes Importers, Inc.
Location Storeroom 2 — Inventory level: Min: 2 Max: 10

	PURCHASED			SOLD			BALANCE		
Date	Units	Unit Cost	Total	Units	Unit Cost	Cost of Goods Sold	Units	Unit Cost	Total
Sept. 1	10	$600	$6,000				10	$600	$6,000
7				2	$600	$1,200	8	$600	$4,800

When Regent CX-21 monitors are purchased, the quantity, unit cost, and total cost are entered in this subsidiary ledger account. When any of these monitors are sold, the number of units, unit cost, and total cost of the units sold also are recorded in this subsidiary ledger account. After each purchase or sales transaction, the "Balance" columns are updated to show the quantity, unit cost, and total cost of the monitors still on hand.[4]

[4] In our illustration, all of the Regent monitors were purchased on the same date and have the same unit cost. Often a company's inventory of a given product includes units acquired at several ***different*** per-unit costs. This situation is addressed in Chapter 9.

An inventory ledger provides useful information to a variety of company personnel. A few examples of the company personnel who utilize this information on a daily basis are listed below:

- ***Sales managers*** use the inventory ledger to see at a glance which products are selling quickly and which are not.
- ***Accounting personnel*** use these records to determine the unit costs of merchandise sold.
- ***Sales personnel*** use this subsidiary ledger to determine the quantities of specific products currently on hand and the physical location of this merchandise.
- ***Employees responsible for ordering merchandise*** refer to the inventory ledger to determine when specific products should be reordered, the quantities to order, and the names of major suppliers.

When a ***physical inventory*** is taken, management uses the inventory ledger to determine on a product-by-product basis whether ***inventory shrinkage*** has been reasonable or excessive.

Taking a Physical Inventory

The basic characteristic of the perpetual inventory system is that the Inventory account is ***continuously updated*** for all purchases and sales of merchandise. Over time, however, normal inventory shrinkage usually causes some discrepancies between the quantities of merchandise shown in the inventory records and the quantities actually on hand. ***Inventory shrinkage*** refers to unrecorded decreases in inventory resulting from such factors as breakage, spoilage, employee theft, and shoplifting.

In order to ensure the accuracy of their perpetual inventory records, most businesses take a ***complete physical count*** of the merchandise on hand at least once a year. This procedure is called ***taking a physical inventory,*** and it usually is performed near year-end.

Once the quantity of merchandise on hand has been determined by a physical count, the per-unit costs in the inventory ledger accounts are used to determine the total cost of the inventory. The Inventory controlling account and also the accounts in the inventory subsidiary ledger then are ***adjusted*** to the quantities and dollar amounts indicated by the physical inventory.

To illustrate, assume that at year-end the Inventory controlling account and inventory subsidiary ledger of Computer Barn both show an inventory with a cost of ***$72,200.*** A physical count, however, reveals that some of the merchandise listed in the accounting records is missing; the items actually on hand have a total cost of ***$70,000.*** Computer Barn would make the following adjusting entry to correct its Inventory controlling account:

Adjusting for inventory shrinkage

Cost of Goods Sold	*2,200*	
Inventory		*2,200*
To adjust the perpetual inventory records to reflect the results of the year-end physical count.		

Computer Barn also will adjust the appropriate accounts in its inventory subsidiary ledger to reflect the quantities indicated by the physical count.

Reasonable amounts of inventory shrinkage are viewed as a normal cost of doing business and simply are debited to the Cost of Goods Sold account, as illustrated on the preceding page.[5]

Closing Entries in a Perpetual Inventory System

As explained and illustrated in Chapter 3, revenue and expense accounts are ***closed*** at the end of each accounting period. A merchandising business with a perpetual inventory system makes closing entries that parallel those of a service-type business. The Sales account is a revenue account and is closed into the Income Summary along with other revenue accounts. The Cost of Goods Sold account is closed into the Income Summary in the same manner as the other expense accounts.

Periodic Inventory System

OBJECTIVE 4 ***Distinguish between perpetual and periodic inventory systems.***

The alternative to the perpetual inventory system is called the ***periodic inventory system.*** In a periodic inventory system, no effort is made either to update the Inventory account or to record the cost of goods sold as transactions occur throughout the year. Rather, the accounting records are updated only "periodically"—usually at year-end.

The fact that the accounting records are not updated until year-end explains why this system is ***not satisfactory*** for a business that makes use of accounting information throughout the year. However, a periodic system is easy and inexpensive to operate and may meet the needs of a very small business.

A traditional periodic system operates as follows. When merchandise is purchased, its cost is debited to an account entitled ***Purchases,*** rather than to the Inventory account. When merchandise is sold, an entry is made to recognize the sales revenue earned, but ***no entry is made to record the cost of goods sold.***

The foundation of the periodic inventory system is the taking of a ***complete physical inventory*** at year-end. This year-end count determines the amount of inventory to appear in the balance sheet and also is used as the basis for computing the cost of goods sold.

Under the periodic inventory system, the cost of goods sold for the entire year is determined at year-end by a short computation, as follows:

Computing the cost of goods sold in a periodic system

Inventory, beginning of the year	$ 12,000
Add: Purchases	130,000
Cost of goods available for sale	$142,000
Less: Inventory, end of the year	8,000
Cost of goods sold	$134,000

In this example, the business had merchandise costing ***$12,000*** on hand at the beginning of the year. During the year, it purchased additional mer-

[5] If a large inventory shortage is caused by an event such as a fire or theft, the cost of the missing or damaged merchandise may be debited to a special loss account, such as Fire Loss. In the income statement, a loss is deducted from revenue in the same manner as an expense.

chandise at a cost of ***$130,000.*** Therefore, merchandise with a total cost of ***$142,000*** was available for sale during the year.

At year-end, merchandise with a cost of ***$8,000*** remains on hand. Thus, merchandise that had cost ***$134,000*** is no longer on hand, and is presumed to have been sold.[6]

Three amounts are used in computing the cost of goods sold: (1) the inventory at the beginning of the year, (2) purchases made during the year, and (3) the inventory at the end of the year. The amounts of inventory on hand at the beginning and end of each year are determined by taking a complete physical inventory at year-end. (Only one physical inventory is taken each year; the ending inventory of one year represents the beginning inventory of the following year.) The cost of all merchandise purchased during the year is indicated by the year-end balance in the Purchases account.

In a periodic inventory system, the closing entries are somewhat more complex than in a perpetual inventory system. A more comprehensive coverage of the periodic inventory system is presented in the Supplemental Topic section at the end of this chapter.

Comparison of Perpetual and Periodic Inventory Systems

Both the perpetual and periodic inventory systems produce the ***same results*** in ***annual*** financial statements. Throughout the year, however, the perpetual inventory system provides a company with a great deal of useful information that simply is ***not available*** in a periodic system.

A perpetual inventory system provides up-to-date information about the quantity and cost of the inventory on hand and also about the cost of goods sold. This enables the company to prepare monthly or quarterly financial statements directly from the accounting records. In a periodic system, however, the amounts of inventory on hand and the cost of goods sold are ***not known*** until a physical inventory is taken at year-end. If interim financial statements are prepared, the amounts of inventory on hand and the cost of goods sold can only be estimated.

Also, a perpetual inventory system usually includes an inventory subsidiary ledger, showing for each type of product the cost and quantities of units purchased, sold, and currently on hand. A periodic system does ***not*** provide management with an inventory subsidiary ledger.

If a perpetual inventory system provides so much more useful information, why would any company use a periodic system? The periodic system has only one advantage: it is not necessary to record the cost of goods sold as sales transactions occur. Prior to the invention of electronic ***point-of-sale terminals,*** businesses that sold many different products had ***no choice*** but to use a periodic inventory system. A supermarket, for example, may sell between 5,000 and 10,000 different items ***per hour.*** Imagine the difficulty of determining and recording the cost of each item sold if the accounting records were maintained by hand.

With modern point-of-sale terminals, however, even supermarkets are now able to use a perpetual inventory system.

---

6 In a periodic inventory system, inventory shrinkage losses are included in the amount identified as "cost of goods sold."

CASE IN POINT Supermarkets, department stores, and many other retailers use electronic cash registers called "point-of-sale terminals." Through an optical scanner, these devices are able to read "product codes" (a pattern of thick and thin vertical bars) that are printed on each item of merchandise. These product codes identify the product to the computer, which then looks up both the cost and the retail sales price of the product in a computer-based inventory ledger. The computer then automatically records the sale and the cost of goods sold and also updates the inventory ledger.

Notice that no accounting personnel are involved in recording or posting these sales transactions. Transactions are recorded automatically as the cashier passes the magnetically coded merchandise over an optical scanner.

In summary, technology has made the periodic inventory system all but obsolete. All large merchandising companies and manufacturing firms use perpetual inventory systems for every significant component of their inventory. Throughout this textbook, you may assume that a perpetual inventory system is in use unless we specifically state otherwise.

Periodic systems are used only by some small businesses with manual accounting systems and by some larger companies to account for relatively minor components of their total inventory. When a periodic system is in use, it usually is modified along the lines described below.

A Short-Cut System for Small Inventories

Some businesses maintain very little inventory, yet still sell substantial amounts of merchandise. This situation is especially likely to arise if the inventory is highly perishable. For example, restaurants, flower shops, and fish markets maintain very little inventory. In any given month, these businesses usually purchase about the same quantity of merchandise as they sell.

Such businesses often follow a policy of immediately debiting the Cost of Goods Sold account for the cost of all merchandise purchased. This approach enables a company to prepare monthly income statements without taking a physical inventory ***or*** recording separately the cost of each sales transaction. If the amount of inventory on hand at year-end is ***material in dollar amount,*** a physical inventory is taken. The Inventory account then is adjusted to reflect the amount indicated by the physical count, with the offsetting debit or credit posted to the Cost of Goods Sold account. If the inventory on hand is ***immaterial,*** it may be omitted from the balance sheet altogether or shown at a small, estimated dollar amount.

This "short-cut" approach appeals to small businesses with manual accounting systems because very little record keeping is required. However, this approach does ***not*** produce satisfactory results if the size of the company's inventory ***fluctuates*** significantly from month to month. Also, this short-cut system does not provide management with the benefits of an inventory subsidiary ledger.

Despite these limitations, this system works well in some small businesses. Also, some large businesses use this system in accounting for insignificant components of their inventory. A department store, for example, may use this system in its candy department, in its cafeteria, and in accounting for low-cost products such as shoelaces and novelty items.

Our objective in describing this modified periodic system is not to illustrate the accounting practices of fish markets and flower shops. Rather, it is intended to make an important point. Accounting systems are designed to meet the company's needs for accounting information ***as efficiently as possible.*** It is neither necessary, nor desirable, to develop more accounting information than is needed or wanted.

Specialized Types of Merchandising Transactions

In addition to the basic transactions comprising the operating cycle, merchandising companies must account for a number of more specialized merchandising transactions. Examples include discounts offered to credit customers for prompt payment, returns of merchandise by dissatisfied customers, and the handling of sales taxes.

In most merchandising companies, these types of transactions do not have a ***material*** effect upon the financial position of the business. Nonetheless, these transactions must be recorded properly if the business is to keep track of the amounts owed to each creditor and the amount due from each customer. We discuss many of these transactions in the Supplemental Topic section at the end of this chapter.

CLASSIFIED FINANCIAL STATEMENTS

Most business organizations prepare ***classified*** financial statements, meaning that items with certain characteristics are placed together in a group, or "classification." The purpose of these classifications is to ***develop useful subtotals*** that will assist users of the statements in evaluating the company's solvency, profitability, and future prospects. These classifications and subtotals are standardized throughout most businesses, thus assisting decision makers in comparing the financial statements of different companies.

A Classified Balance Sheet

OBJECTIVE 5 ***Prepare a classified balance sheet . . .***

In a classified balance sheet, assets usually are presented in three groups: (1) current assets, (2) plant and equipment,[7] and (3) other assets. Liabilities are classified into two categories: (1) current liabilities and (2) long-term liabilities. A classified balance sheet for Computer Barn is illustrated on page 235:

[7] Section 3060 of the *CICA Handbook* uses the general term "capital assets" to encompass three groups of long-term assets: property, plant, and equipment; intangible assets; and natural resources. Since each of these three groups of assets is usually presented separately in the financial statements, it is more descriptive to use the specific terms "property, plant, and equipment," "intangible assets," and "natural resources." Also, these three specific terms are most widely used in published financial statements. In fact, the 1993 edition of *Financial Reporting in Canada,* published by the CICA, uses the terms "property, plant, and equipment" and "intangible assets."

A classified balance sheet

COMPUTER BARN
Balance Sheet
December 31, 1995

Assets			
Current assets:			
Cash			$ 30,000
Marketable securities			11,000
Notes receivable			5,000
Accounts receivable			60,000
Inventory			70,000
Prepaid expenses			4,000
Total current assets			$180,000
Plant and equipment:			
Land		$151,000	
Building	$120,000		
Less: Accumulated depreciation	9,000	111,000	
Fixtures & equipment	$ 45,000		
Less: Accumulated depreciation	27,000	18,000	
Total plant and equipment			280,000
Other assets:			
Land held as a future building site			170,000
Total assets			$630,000
Liabilities & Owner's Equity			
Current liabilities:			
Notes payable (due in 6 months)			$ 20,000
Accounts payable			65,000
Sales taxes payable			3,000
Salaries payable			8,000
Unearned revenue and customer deposits			4,000
Total current liabilities			$100,000
Long-term liabilities:			
Mortgage payable (due in 15 years)			210,000
Total liabilities			$310,000
Owner's equity:			
Pat O'Brien, capital			320,000
Total liabilities & owner's equity			$630,000

Using a Classified Balance Sheet in Evaluating Solvency

The classifications ***current assets*** and ***current liabilities*** are especially useful to short-term creditors in evaluating the immediate debt-paying ability, or ***solvency,*** of the business entity.

Current Assets Current assets are relatively "liquid" resources; this category includes cash, investments in marketable securities, receivables, inventories, and prepaid expenses. To qualify as a current asset, an asset must be capable of ***being converted into cash*** within a relatively short period of time without interfering with normal business operations.[8]

The time period in which current assets are expected to be converted into cash is usually one year. If a company requires more than a year to complete its normal operating cycle, however, the ***length of the operating cycle*** is used as the time period defining current assets. Thus, ***inventory*** and ***accounts receivable from customers*** normally are classified as current assets, even if the conversion of these assets into cash will not be completed within one year.[9]

In a balance sheet, current assets are listed in order of liquidity (the closer an asset is to becoming cash, the greater its liquidity). Thus, cash always is listed first among the current assets, followed by marketable securities, receivables, inventory, and prepaid expenses.

Current Liabilities Current liabilities are ***existing debts*** that must be paid within the ***same time period*** used in defining current assets. Among the most common current liabilities are notes payable (due within one year), accounts payable, unearned revenue, and accrued expenses, such as salaries payable and interest payable. In the balance sheet, notes payable usually are listed first, followed by accounts payable; other types of current liabilities may be listed in any sequence.

The ***relationship*** between current assets and current liabilities is more important than the total dollar amount in either category. Current liabilities must be paid in the near future, and the money to pay these liabilities usually comes—in large part—from the conversion of current assets into cash. Thus, decision makers evaluating the solvency of a business often compare the amounts of current assets and current liabilities.

The Current Ratio

OBJECTIVE 5 . . . Compute the current ratio and amount of working capital.

The most widely used measure of short-term debt-paying ability is the current ratio. The reader of a balance sheet may compute this ratio by ***dividing*** total current assets by total current liabilities.

In the balance sheet of Computer Barn illustrated previously, current assets amount to $180,000 and current liabilities total $100,000, indicating a current ratio of ***1.8 to 1*** ($180,000 ÷ $100,000 = 1.8). A current ratio of 1.8 to 1 means that the company's current assets are 1.8 times as large as its current liabilities.

The higher the current ratio, the more solvent the company appears to be. Many bankers and other short-term creditors traditionally have believed that a retailer should have a current ratio of at least 2 to 1 to qualify as a good credit risk. By this standard, Computer Barn comes up

---

[8] Prepaid expenses are not actually "converted" into cash, but they ***substitute*** for cash by eliminating the need to make certain future cash payments.

[9] The time period used in defining current assets is one year or the length of the operating cycle, whichever is ***longer.*** Most businesses have operating cycles far shorter than one year. However, companies that sell merchandise on long-term instalment contracts or that manufacture products such as ships may have operating cycles requiring several years to complete. The user of financial statements should recognize that the current assets of such companies are converted into cash ***much more slowly*** than are the current assets of most businesses.

a little short; the company probably would ***not*** receive a top credit rating from a bank or other short-term creditor that applied this criteria.

Working Capital

Working capital is another measurement often used to express the relationship between current assets and current liabilities. Working capital is the ***excess*** of current assets over current liabilities.[10] Our illustrated balance sheet indicates that at the end of 1995, Computer Barn has working capital of ***$80,000*** ($180,000 – $100,000).

The amount of working capital that a company needs to remain solvent varies with the size of the organization and the nature of its business activities. An analyst familiar with the nature of a company's operations usually can determine from the amount of working capital whether the company is in a sound financial position or is soon likely to encounter financial difficulties.

Evaluating Financial Ratios

We caution users of financial statements ***against*** placing much confidence in general rules, such as "a current ratio should be at least 2 to 1." To interpret any financial ratio properly, the decision maker must first understand the unique characteristics of the company and of the industry in which it operates.

Retailers and wholesalers, for example, tend to have lower current ratios than do manufacturing companies. Service-type businesses—which have no inventory—generally have lower current ratios than do merchandising or manufacturing companies. Large businesses with highly reliable sources of revenue and cash receipts are able to operate with lower current ratios than are smaller companies with less stable earnings.

CASE IN POINT Large telephone companies are regarded within the business community as "pillars of financial strength." Yet these companies usually do not have high current ratios. Such financially sound companies as Bell Canada, British Columbia Telephone, New Brunswick Telephone, and Maritime Telephone and Telegraph often maintain current ratios of much less than 1 to 1.

Although a high current ratio is one indication of strong debt-paying ability, an extremely high ratio—say, 4 or 5 to 1—may indicate that ***too much*** of the company's resources are "tied up" in current assets. In maintaining such a highly liquid position, the company may be passing up opportunities for growth.

[10] A company with current liabilities in excess of its current assets has a ***negative*** amount of working capital. Negative working capital does ***not*** necessarily mean that a company is insolvent. Any company with a current ratio of less than 1 to 1 has a negative amount of working capital.

Standards for Comparison We have seen that Computer Barn has a current ratio of 1.8 to 1. What standards for comparison are commonly used in evaluating such a statistic?

OBJECTIVE 6 Identify two standards for comparison widely used in evaluating financial ratios.

Users of financial information generally use two criteria in evaluating the reasonableness of a financial ratio. One criterion is the ***trend*** in the ratio over a period of years. By reviewing this trend, the analyst is able to determine whether a company's performance or financial strength is improving or deteriorating. Second, an analyst compares a company's financial ratios with the ratios of ***similar companies*** and also with ***industry-wide averages.*** These comparisons assist the analyst in evaluating a particular ratio in light of the company's current business environment.

In summary, ratios are useful tools; but they can be interpreted properly only by individuals who understand the characteristics of the company and its environment.

Publicly owned corporations issue ***annual reports*** providing a great deal of information about the company, including comparative financial data for several years, and a discussion and analysis by management of the company's financial condition and the results of its recent operations. Financial information about ***entire industries*** is available through a number of financial publications and on-line computer data bases.

CASE IN POINT Dun & Bradstreet Canada Limited annually publishes *Key Business Ratios Canada-Corporation* for many industries. Recent editions of this publication cover more than 800 different lines of business.

As an example of this "industry data," the average current ratios of several industry groups are shown below for a recent year:

Industry Group	Average Current Ratio
Air transport	1 to 1
Retail—general merchandise	1.3 to 1
Wholesale—hardware, plumbing & heating	1.5 to 1
Manufacturing—small appliances	2.2 to 1
Telephone (Bell Canada and three regional companies)	0.6 to 1*
Mining—gold	3.1 to 1
Services—hotel	0.7 to 1

* Telephone company data were accumulated directly from annual reports.

Usefulness and Limitations of Ratios Analysis A financial ratio expresses the relationship of one quantity or amount relative to another. Most users of financial statements find that certain ratios assist them in quickly evaluating the financial position, profitability, and future prospects of a business. A comparison of key ratios for several successive years may indicate whether the business is becoming stronger or weaker. Ratios also provide a means of comparing quickly the financial strength and profitability of different companies.

Users of financial statements should recognize, however, that ratios have several limitations. For example, management may enter into year-end transactions that temporarily improve key ratios. To illustrate, the balance sheet of Computer Barn includes current assets of $180,000 and current liabilities of $100,000, resulting in a current ratio of ***1.8 to 1.*** What would happen if shortly before year-end, management were to use $20,000 of the company's cash to pay off accounts payable? This transaction would reduce current assets to $160,000 and current liabilities to $80,000. However, it would also increase the company's year-end current ratio to a more impressive ***2 to 1*** ($160,000 ÷ $80,000 = 2).

Financial statement ratios contain the same limitations as do the dollar amounts used in financial statements. For example, assets usually are valued at historical cost rather than at current market value. Also, financial statement ratios express only ***financial*** relationships. They give no indication of a company's progress in achieving nonfinancial goals, such as creating new jobs or protecting the environment. A thorough analysis of the future prospects of any business involves more than merely computing and comparing financial ratios.

The Owner's Responsibility for Debts of the Business

Accountants view a business entity as separate from the other economic activities of the business owner (or owners). The law, however, draws an important distinction between corporations and unincorporated business organizations.

Under the law, the owners of ***unincorporated*** businesses (sole proprietorships and partnerships) are ***personally liable*** for any and all debts of the business organization. Therefore, creditors of unincorporated businesses often base their lending decisions upon the solvency of the business ***owners*** rather than upon the financial position of the business itself.

If a business is organized as a ***corporation,*** however, the owners (shareholders) are ***not*** personally responsible for the debts of the business. Creditors may look ***only to the business entity*** in seeking payment of their claims. Thus, the solvency of the business entity becomes much more important if the business is organized as a corporation.

Small Corporations and Loan "Guarantees" Often small corporations do not have sufficient financial resources to qualify for credit. In such cases, creditors may require that one or more of the company's shareholders personally guarantee (or "co-sign") specific debts of the business entity. By co-signing debts of the corporation, individual shareholders become personally liable for the debt if the corporation fails to make payment.

CASE IN POINT A small, family-owned wholesale business was organized as a corporation. To operate efficiently, the business needed to purchase merchandise on account. However, the corporation had so few liquid assets that suppliers were unwilling to extend credit. To obtain credit for the business, a major shareholder pledged his vacation home—a condominium on the Hawaiian island of Maui—to secure the company's debt to a particular supplier. With this additional security, the supplier allowed the business to purchase large quantities of merchandise on account.

Unfortunately, however, the small wholesale business became insolvent and was forced into bankruptcy. Not only did the owners' equity in this business become worthless, but one shareholder also lost his vacation home to the company's creditors.

Classifications in an Income Statement

An income statement may be prepared in either the ***multiple-step*** or the ***single-step*** format. The multiple-step income statement is more useful in illustrating accounting concepts and has been used in all of our illustrations thus far. A multiple-step income statement for Computer Barn is illustrated below:

A multiple-step income statement

COMPUTER BARN
Income Statement
For the Year Ended December 31, 1995

Net sales			$900,000
Less: Cost of goods sold (including transportation-in)			540,000
Gross profit			$360,000
Less: Operating expenses:			
Selling expenses:			
Sales salaries and commissions	$78,800		
Advertising	42,000		
Delivery service	14,200		
Depreciation: store equipment	9,000		
Other selling expenses	6,000		
Total selling expenses		$150,000	
General & administrative expenses:			
Administrative & office salaries	$73,000		
Utilities	6,500		
Depreciation: building	8,500		
Other general & administrative expenses	11,000		
Total general & administrative expenses		99,000	
Total operating expense			249,000
Operating income			$111,000
Less (add): Nonoperating items:			
Interest expense		$23,000	
Purchase discounts lost		1,200	
Interest revenue		(3,200)	21,000
Net income			$ 90,000

This income statement also is ***classified,*** meaning that revenue and expenses have been classified into several categories. (For comparative purposes, this income statement is illustrated in single-step format on page 243.)

Multiple-Step Income Statements

The multiple-step income statement is so named because of a ***series of steps*** in which costs and expenses are deducted from revenue. As a first step, the cost of goods sold is deducted from sales revenue to determine the subtotal ***gross profit.*** As a second step, operating expenses are deducted to obtain a subtotal called ***operating income*** (or income from operations). As a final step, "nonoperating" items are taken into consideration to arrive at ***net income.***

Notice that the income statement is divided into four major sections: (1) revenue, (2) cost of goods sold, (3) operating expenses, and (4) nonoperating items. Multiple-step income statements are noted for their numerous sections and the development of significant subtotals.

The Revenue Section The revenue section of an income statement usually contains only one line, entitled ***Net sales.*** Net sales represents the balance in the sales revenue account, less some minor adjustments for transactions such as refunds made to customers. These adjustments to sales revenue usually are not material in dollar amount and seldom are shown as separate items in the body of the income statement. (We illustrate and explain these transactions in the Supplemental Topic section at the end of this chapter.)

The ***trend*** in net sales from period to period is considered by many users of financial statements to be a key indicator of a company's future prospects. Increasing sales suggest the probability of larger profits in future periods. Declining sales, on the other hand, may provide advance warning of financial difficulties.

In our economy, most prices increase over time. The ***average*** increase in prices during the year is called the ***rate of inflation.*** Because of inflation, a company's total dollar sales may increase somewhat from year-to-year without any increase in the quantity of merchandise sold. If a company is selling more merchandise each year, its net sales usually increase ***faster*** than the rate of inflation.

The Cost of Goods Sold Section The ***matching principle*** requires that revenue be offset by the costs and expenses incurred in generating that revenue. Therefore, revenue from sales must be offset by the cost to the merchandising business of acquiring the goods that it sells. The cost of goods sold usually is shown as a single amount in the income statement.

Gross Profit: A Key Subtotal Gross profit is the ***difference*** between the sales revenue earned during the period and the ***cost*** to the business of the merchandise it has sold. In evaluating the performance of a merchandising company, many analysts find it useful to express the gross profit as a ***percentage*** of net sales. This percentage is called the ***gross profit rate.*** In 1995, Computer Barn has an average gross profit rate of ***40%*** (gross profit, \$360,000, divided by net sales, \$900,000, equals 40%).

By computing the gross profit rate earned in successive accounting periods, users of financial statements may gain insight into the strength of the company's products in the marketplace. A rising gross profit rate usually means that demand for the company's products is strong enough that the company has been able to increase its sales prices.[11] A declining gross profit rate, on the other hand, generally indicates a weakness in demand for the company's products.

In evaluating the rate of gross profit earned by a particular company, the users of the financial statements should consider the rate earned by the company in prior periods and also the gross profit rates earned by other companies in the same industry. In most merchandising companies, the gross profit rate remains reasonably consistent from one period to the next.

Gross profit rates usually lie between 30% and 50% of net sales, depending upon the type of merchandise sold. The gross profit rate usually is lowest on fast-moving merchandise, such as groceries, and highest on low-volume goods, such as fine jewellery.

The Operating Expense Section Operating expenses are incurred for the purpose of ***producing revenue.*** These expenses often are subdivided into functional classifications, such as ***selling expenses*** and ***general and administrative expenses.*** Subdividing operating expenses into functional classifications aids management and other users of the statements in evaluating different aspects of the company's operations separately.

The classification of operating expenses into subcategories is a common practice, but it is ***not required*** under generally accepted accounting principles. Also, the categories into which operating expenses are classified often vary from one company to the next.

Operating Income: Another Key Subtotal Operating income (or income from operations) shows the relationship between revenue ***earned from customers*** and expenses incurred in ***producing this revenue.*** In effect, operating income measures the profitability of a company's ***basic business operations*** and "leaves out" other types of revenue and expenses.

Nonoperating Items Revenue and expenses that are not directly related to the company's primary business activities are listed in a final section of the income statement following the determination of operating income.

Two significant "nonoperating items" are interest expense and corporate income taxes expense. Interest expense stems from the manner in which assets are ***financed,*** not the manner in which these assets are ***used*** in business operations. Corporate income taxes are not viewed as operating expenses because paying income taxes does not help produce revenue.[12]

Any nonoperating revenue, such as interest revenue earned on investments, also is listed in this section of the income statement.

Net Income Most equity investors—that is, the owners—consider net income (or net loss) to be the most important figure in the income statement.

---

[11] An alternative explanation could be that the company is reducing its cost of goods sold relative to its selling prices. Reductions in the cost of goods sold are more likely to occur in companies that ***manufacture*** their inventories than in merchandising companies.

[12] Only those businesses organized as corporations are subject to corporate income taxes. Because Computer Barn (the company used in our example) is organized as a sole proprietorship, no income taxes expense appears in the company's income statement.

This amount represents the overall increase (or decrease) in owners' equity resulting from business operations during the period.

Single-Step Income Statements

With its several classifications and subtotals, a multiple-step income statement highlights significant relationships. For this reason, it is widely used in accounting textbooks and in classroom illustrations. However, many large corporations use a ***single-step*** format in the income statements appearing in their annual reports.

The single-step format income statement takes its name from the fact that all costs and expenses are deducted from total revenue in a single step. No subtotals are shown for gross profit or for operating income, although the statement provides investors with enough information to compute these subtotals on their own. The 1995 income statement of Computer Barn, previously illustrated in the multiple-step format, is rearranged below in the single-step format:

A single-step income statement

COMPUTER BARN
Income Statement
For the Year Ended December 31, 1995

Revenue:		
Net sales		$900,000
Interest earned		3,200
Total revenue		$903,200
Costs and expenses:		
Cost of goods sold	$540,000	
Selling expenses	150,000	
General & administrative expenses	99,000	
Interest expense	23,000	
Purchase discounts lost	1,200	
Total costs and expenses		813,200
Net income		$ 90,000

Evaluating the Adequacy of Net Income

OBJECTIVE 7 Analyze an income statement; evaluate the adequacy of net income.

Should the $90,000 net income of Computer Barn be viewed as excellent, fair, or poor performance for a business of this size? First, notice that Computer Barn is organized as a ***sole proprietorship.*** In an unincorporated business, no "salary expense" is deducted for the value of the personal services rendered to the business by the owner.[13] Any amounts paid to the owner are recorded as "withdrawals." Thus, the net income of a sole proprietorship represents, in part, compensation to the owner for any time and effort devoted to running the business.

[13] The reason for omitting the owner's "salary" from the expenses is that the owner could set this salary at any desired level. An unrealistic salary to the owner, whether too high or too low, would lessen the usefulness of the income statement as a measure of the earning power of the business.

The owner of a business also may have a substantial amount of money invested in the business in the form of owner's equity. Thus, the net income of the business also represents the owner's "return" on this financial investment.

Finally, the net income of a business should be adequate to compensate the owner for taking significant ***risks.*** Some studies show that more than half of all new businesses fail in their first year. Remember, in an unincorporated business, the owners are ***personally liable*** for the debts of the business. Therefore, if an unincorporated business sustains large losses, the owners can lose more than the amount of their equity investment. In fact, they can lose almost everything they own.

In summary, the net income of an unincorporated business should be sufficient to compensate the owner for three factors: (1) personal services rendered to the business, (2) a return on capital invested, and (3) the degree of financial risk that the owner is taking. Using these criteria, let us now appraise the adequacy of the $90,000 net income of Computer Barn.

Assume that Pat O'Brien, the owner of Computer Barn, works full time in the business. Also assume that if he were not running his own business, he could earn a salary of $50,000 per year managing a similar store.

Also notice that O'Brien has $320,000 invested in Computer Barn as of the end of the year. Let us assume that this also was the average amount of his ownership equity throughout the year. If this money had been invested in savings bonds, or in an interest-bearing bank account, O'Brien might have earned investment income of, say, $25,000.

Thus, the two factors of the owner's personal services and financial investment indicate a need for the company to earn at least $75,000 per year to be considered successful. As the business actually earned $90,000, it has provided a $15,000 "cushion" to compensate O'Brien for the risk involved in owning this type of business.

Whether or not $15,000 is adequate compensation for these risks depends upon the degree of risk involved in this type of business activity and upon O'Brien's personal attitude toward risk taking.

Remember, Computer Barn's profitability in the current year is no guarantee that the business will remain profitable in future years. By looking at the ***trend*** in net income over a period of several years, a user of the financial statements can see whether the business is becoming more or less profitable.

Evaluating the Net Income of a Corporation If Computer Barn were organized as a corporation, both the amount of net income for the year and our evaluation of this net income would have been somewhat different. First, profitable corporations incur the expense of corporate income taxes, whereas unincorporated businesses do not. Also, corporations record as expenses all salaries paid to employees, even if these employees are owners (shareholders) of the business. Thus, if Computer Barn were organized as a corporation, its net income would have been lower by the amount of O'Brien's salary and the income taxes expense for the period. On the other hand, we then could ignore the value of O'Brien's personal services in evaluating the adequacy of the company's net income.

Shareholders tend to evaluate the net income of a corporation only in terms of (1) the amount of their financial investment and (2) the degree of risk that they are taking. Remember, however, that shareholders usually are exposed to ***less*** financial risk than are the owners of an unincorporated business, as they are ***not personally liable*** for the debts of the business entity.

We will discuss specific techniques for evaluating the adequacy of a corporation's earnings in later chapters.

* Supplemental Topic A
Additional Merchandising Transactions

OBJECTIVE 8 Account for cash discounts, merchandise returns, transportation costs, and sales taxes.

In addition to the basic transactions illustrated and explained in this chapter, merchandising companies must account for a variety of additional transactions relating to purchases and sales of merchandise. Examples include discounts offered to credit customers for prompt payment, merchandise returns and refunds, transportation costs, and collecting and remitting sales taxes.

TRANSACTIONS RELATING TO PURCHASES

Purchases of merchandise are recorded at cost. However, this cost may be affected by such factors as cash discounts and transportation charges.

Credit Terms and Cash Discounts

Manufacturers and wholesalers normally sell merchandise ***on account (on credit).*** The credit terms are stated in the seller's bill, or ***invoice.*** One common example of credit terms is "net 30 days," or "n/30," meaning full payment is due in 30 days. Another common form of credit terms is "10 eom," meaning payment is due 10 days after the end of the month in which the purchase occurred.

Manufacturers and wholesalers usually allow their customers 30 or 60 days in which to pay for credit purchases. Frequently, however, sellers offer their customers a small discount to encourage earlier payment.

Perhaps the most common credit terms offered by manufacturers and wholesalers are ***"2/10, n/30."*** This expression is read "2, 10, net 30," and it means that full payment is due in 30 days, but that the buyer may take a ***2% discount*** if payment is made within 10 days. The period during which the discount is available is termed the ***discount period.*** Because the discount provides an incentive for the customer to make an early cash payment, it is called a ***cash discount.*** Buyers, however, often refer to these discounts as ***purchase discounts,*** while sellers frequently call them ***sales discounts.***

Most well-managed companies have a policy of taking advantage of all cash discounts available on purchases of merchandise.[14] These companies

[14] The terms 2/10, n/30 offer the buyer a 2% discount for sending payment 20 days before it is otherwise due. Saving 2% over only 20 days is equivalent to earning an annual rate of return of more than 36% (2% × 365/20 = 36.5%). Thus, taking cash discounts represents an excellent investment opportunity. Most companies take advantage of all cash discounts, even if they must borrow from a bank the cash necessary to make payment within the discount period.

initially record purchases of merchandise at the ***net cost***—that is, the invoice price ***minus*** any available discount. After all, this is the amount that the company expects to pay.

To illustrate, assume that on November 3 Computer Barn purchases 100 spreadsheet programs from PC Products. The cost of these programs is $100 each, for a total of $10,000. However, PC Products offers credit terms of 2/10, n/30. If Computer Barn pays for this purchase within the discount period, it will have to pay only ***$9,800,*** or 98% of the full invoice price. Therefore, Computer Barn will record this purchase as follows:

Purchase recorded at net cost

Inventory	*9,800*	
Accounts Payable (PC Products)		*9,800*
To record purchase of 100 spreadsheet programs at net cost ($100 × 98% × 100 units).		

If the invoice is paid within the discount period, Computer Barn simply records payment of a $9,800 account payable.

Through oversight or carelessness, Computer Barn might fail to make payment within the discount period. In this event, Computer Barn must pay PC Products the entire invoice price of ***$10,000,*** rather than the recorded liability of $9,800. The journal entry to record payment ***after the discount period***—on, say, December 3—is:

Recording the loss of a cash discount

Accounts Payable (PC Products)	*9,800*	
Purchase Discounts Lost	*200*	
Cash		*10,000*
To record payment of invoice after expiration of discount period.		

Notice that the additional $200 paid because the discount period has expired is debited to an account entitled Purchase Discounts Lost. Purchase Discounts Lost is an ***expense account.*** The only benefit to Computer Barn from this $200 expenditure was a ***20-day delay*** in paying an account payable. Thus, the lost purchase discount is basically a ***finance charge,*** similar to interest expense. In an income statement, finance charges usually are classified as nonoperating expenses.

The fact that purchase discounts ***not taken*** are recorded in a separate expense account is the primary reason why a company should record purchases of merchandise at ***net cost.*** The use of a Purchase Discounts Lost account immediately brings to management's attention any failure to take advantage of the cash discounts offered by suppliers.

Returns of Unsatisfactory Merchandise

On occasion, a purchaser may find the purchased merchandise unsatisfactory and want to return it to the seller for a refund. Most sellers permit such returns.

To illustrate, assume that on November 9 Computer Barn returns to PC Products five of the spreadsheet programs purchased on November 3, because these programs were not properly labeled. As Computer Barn has not yet paid for this merchandise, the return will reduce the amount that Computer Barn owes PC Products. The gross invoice price of the returned merchandise was $500 ($100 per program). Remember, however, that Computer Barn records purchases at ***net cost.*** Therefore, these spreadsheet programs are carried in Computer Barn's inventory subsidiary ledger at a per-unit cost of ***$98,*** or $490 for the five programs being returned. The entry to record this purchase return is:

Return is based upon recorded acquisition cost

Accounts Payable (PC Products)	*490*	
Inventory		*490*
Returned 5 defective spreadsheet programs to supplier. Net cost of the returned items, $490 ($100 × 98% × 5 units).		

The reduction in inventory must also be recorded in the subsidiary ledger accounts.

Transportation Costs on Purchases

The purchaser sometimes may pay the costs of having the purchased merchandise delivered to its premises. Transportation costs relating to the ***acquisition*** of inventory or any other asset are ***not expenses*** of the current period; rather, these charges are ***part of the cost of the asset*** being acquired.[15] If the purchaser is able to associate transportation costs with specific products, these costs should be debited directly to the Inventory account as part of the "cost" of the merchandise.

Often, many different products arrive in a single shipment. In such cases, it may be impractical for the purchaser to determine the amount of the total transportation cost that is applicable to each product. For this reason, many companies follow the convenient policy of debiting all transportation costs on inbound shipments of merchandise to an account entitled ***Transportation-in.*** The dollar amount of transportation-in usually is too small to show separately in the financial statements. Therefore, this amount is merely included in the amount reported in the income statement as cost of goods sold. At the end of the period, the Transportation-in account is closed into the Income Summary in the same manner as the Cost of Goods Sold account.

This treatment of transportation costs is not entirely consistent with the matching principle. Some of the transportation costs may apply to merchandise still in inventory rather than to goods sold during the current period. We have mentioned, however, that transportation costs are relatively small in dollar amount. The accounting principle of ***materiality,*** therefore, usually justifies accounting for these costs in the most convenient manner.

TRANSACTIONS RELATING TO SALES

Credit terms and merchandise returns also affect the amount of sales revenue earned by the seller. To the extent that credit customers take advantage of cash discounts or return merchandise for a refund, the seller's revenue is reduced. Thus, revenue shown in the income statement of a merchandising concern is often called ***net sales.***

---

15 The "cost" of an asset includes all reasonable and necessary costs of getting the asset to an appropriate location and putting it into usable condition.

The term ***net sales*** means total sales revenue ***minus*** sales returns and allowances and ***minus*** sales discounts. The following partial income statement illustrates this relationship:

COMPUTER BARN
Partial Income Statement
For the Year Ended December 31, 1995

What is "net sales"?

Revenue:		
Sales		*$912,000*
Less: Sales returns and allowances	*$8,000*	
Sales discounts	*4,000*	*12,000*
Net sales		*$900,000*

As we stated earlier in the chapter, the details of this computation seldom are shown in an actual income statement. The normal practice is to begin the income statement with the amount of net sales.

Sales Returns and Allowances

Most merchandising companies allow customers to obtain a refund by returning any merchandise considered to be unsatisfactory. If the merchandise has only minor defects, customers sometimes agree to keep the merchandise if an ***allowance*** (reduction) is made in the sales price.

Under the perpetual inventory system, two entries are needed to record the sale of merchandise: one to recognize the revenue earned and the other to transfer the cost of the merchandise from the Inventory account to Cost of Goods Sold. If some of the merchandise is returned, both of these entries are partially reversed.

First, let us consider the effects upon revenue of granting either a refund or an allowance. Both refunds and allowances have the effect of nullifying previously recorded sales and reducing the amount of revenue earned by the business. The journal entry to reduce sales revenue as the result of a sales return (or allowance) is shown below:

Sales Returns and Allowances	*200*	
Accounts Receivable (or Cash)		*200*
Customer returned merchandise purchased on account for $200. Allowed customer full credit for returned merchandise.		

Sales Returns and Allowances is a ***contra-revenue*** account—that is, it is deducted from gross sales as a step in determining net sales.

Why use a separate Sales Returns and Allowances account rather than merely debiting the Sales account? The answer is that using a separate contra-revenue account enables management to see both the total amount of sales ***and also*** the amount of sales returns and allowances. The relationship between these amounts gives management an indication of customer satisfaction with the merchandise.

If merchandise is returned by the customer, a second entry is made to remove the cost of this merchandise from the Cost of Goods Sold account and restore it to the inventory records. This entry is:

Inventory	*160*	
Cost of Goods Sold		*160*
To restore in the Inventory account the cost of merchandise returned by a customer.		

Notice that this entry is based upon the ***cost*** of the returned merchandise to the seller, ***not upon its sales price.*** (This entry is not necessary when a sales ***allowance*** is granted to a customer who keeps the merchandise.)

Special accounts are maintained in the inventory subsidiary ledger for returned merchandise. Often this merchandise will be returned to the supplier or sold to a damaged-goods "liquidator" rather than again being offered for sale to the company's regular customers.[16]

Sales Discounts

We have explained that sellers frequently offer cash discounts, such as 2/10, n/30, to encourage their customers to make early payments for purchases on account.

Sellers and buyers account for cash discounts quite differently. To the seller, the "cost" associated with cash discounts is not the discounts ***lost*** when payments are delayed, but rather the discounts ***taken*** by customers that do pay within the discount period. Therefore, sellers design their accounting systems to measure the sales discounts ***taken*** by their customers. To achieve this goal, the seller records the sale and the related account receivable at the ***gross*** (full) invoice price.

To illustrate, assume that Computer Barn sells merchandise to Susan Hall for $1,000, offering terms of 2/10, n/30. The sales revenue is recorded at the full invoice price, as shown below:

Sales are recorded at the gross sales price

Accounts Receivable (Susan Hall)	*1,000*	
Sales		*1,000*
Sold merchandise on account. Invoice price, $1,000; terms, 2/10, n/30.		

If Hall makes payment after the discount period has expired, Computer Barn merely records the receipt of $1,000 cash in full payment of this account receivable. If Hall pays ***within*** the discount period, however, she will pay only ***$980*** to settle her account. In this case, Computer Barn will record the receipt of Hall's payment as follows:

Cash	*980*	
Sales Discounts	*20*	
Accounts Receivable (Susan Hall)		*1,000*
Collected a $1,000 account receivable from a customer who took a 2% discount for early payment.		

---

[16] An inventory of returned merchandise should not be valued in the accounting records at a cost that exceeds its ***net realizable value.*** The possible need to write down the carrying value of inventory is discussed in Chapter 9.

Sales Discounts is a ***contra-revenue*** account. In computing net sales, sales discounts are deducted from gross sales along with any sales returns and allowances. (If the customer has returned part of the merchandise, a discount may be taken only on the gross amount owed ***after*** the return.)

Contra-revenue accounts have much in common with expense accounts; both are deducted from gross revenue in determining net, and both have debit balances. Thus, contra-revenue accounts (Sales Returns and Allowances and Sales Discounts) are closed into the Income Summary account in the same manner as expense accounts.

Delivery Expenses

If the seller incurs any costs in delivering merchandise to the customer, these costs are debited to an expense account entitled Delivery Expense. In an income statement, delivery expense is classified as a ***selling expense,*** not as part of the cost of goods sold.

Accounting for Sales Taxes

Sales taxes are levied by the federal and provincial governments on retail sales. Sales taxes actually are imposed upon the consumer, not upon the seller. For example, the recent goods and services tax (known as GST) of 7% is levied by the federal government on the final consumer. However, businesses have to first pay the GST on their purchases and later receive full credit for the GST on their sales to consumers. The GST applies to almost all the goods sold and services rendered. Thus, the seller must collect the tax, file tax returns at times specified by law, and remit the taxes owed on all reported sales.

For cash sales, sales tax is collected from the customer at the time of the sales transaction. For credit sales, the sales tax is included in the amount charged to the customer's account. The liability to the governmental unit for sales taxes may be recorded at the time the sale is made as shown in the following journal entry:

Sales tax recorded at time of sale

Cash (or Accounts Receivable)	*1,150*	
Sales Tax Payable		*150*
Sales		*1,000*
To record sales of $1,000 subject to 7% goods and services tax and 8% provincial tax.		

This approach requires a separate credit entry to the Sales Tax Payable account for each sale. At first glance, this may seem to require an excessive amount of bookkeeping. However, today's electronic cash registers can be programmed to record automatically the sales tax liability at the time of each sale.

An Alternative Approach to Sales Taxes Instead of recording the sales tax liability at the time of sale, some businesses prefer to credit the Sales account with the entire amount collected, including the sales tax, and to make an adjustment at the end of each period to reflect sales tax payable. For example, suppose that the total recorded sales for the period under this method were $345,000. Since the Sales account includes both the sales price and the sales tax (of 15%), it is apparent that $345,000 is ***115%*** of the actual sales figure. Actual sales are $300,000 (computed $345,000 ÷ 1.15) and the amount of sales tax due is $45,000. (Proof: 15% of $300,000 = $45,000.) The entry to record the liability for sales taxes would be

Sales tax recorded as adjustment of sales

Sales	*45,000*	
Sales Tax Payable		*45,000*
To remove sales taxes of 15% on $300,000 of sales from the Sales account, and record as a liability.		

This second approach is widely used in businesses that do not use electronic devices for recording each sales transaction.

If some of the products being sold are not subject to sales tax, the business must keep separate records of taxable and nontaxable sales.

**Supplemental Topic B
More about Periodic Inventory System

Characteristics of a Periodic Inventory System

A periodic inventory system is an ***alternative*** to a perpetual inventory system. The basic characteristics of a periodic system are:

OBJECTIVE 9 ***Explain the characteristics, advantages, and disadvantages of a periodic inventory system.***

1 During an accounting period no entries are made in the Inventory account to record the cost of merchandise purchased or sold. Purchases are recorded by debiting an account called ***Purchases.*** When merchandise is sold, the revenue is recorded, but no effort is made to record the cost of goods sold. Thus, the balance in the Inventory account remains ***unchanged*** throughout the year, and the accounting records do not indicate the cost of goods sold.

2 At the end of each year, a complete ***physical inventory*** is taken. The merchandise on hand is counted, and its cost is determined. (The procedures for assigning per-unit costs to the items in inventory are discussed in Chapter 9.)

3 As stated above, the cost of goods sold is ***not recorded*** as individual sales transactions occur. Rather, the cost of goods sold for the entire year is determined at year-end by a computation such as the one that follows:

Inventory, beginning of the year (per last year's physical count)	*$ 10,000*
Add: Purchases	*140,000*
Cost of goods available for sale during the year	*$150,000*
Less: Ending inventory (per this year's physical count)	*12,000*
Cost of goods sold	*$138,000*

Advantages and Disadvantages of a Periodic System As compared with a perpetual inventory system, a periodic inventory system has one advantage: no entries are required to record the cost of goods sold relating to individual sales transactions. As a direct result, however, the accounting records do not indicate the amount of inventory on hand, or the cost of goods sold, until a complete physical inventory is taken.

Taking a complete physical inventory is both inconvenient and costly. Therefore, a physical inventory usually is taken only at year-end. Thus, a periodic inventory system is well suited to the preparation of annual financial statements, but not to preparing financial statements for shorter periods, such as quarters or months.

Another shortcoming of the periodic system is the lack of an inventory subsidiary ledger. An inventory subsidiary ledger indicates by type of product the costs and quantities of merchandise sold during the period and currently in inventory. This information—absent in a periodic inventory system—is useful to management in developing marketing strategies and in deciding what products to purchase, when to reorder merchandise, and the quantities of merchandise to be purchased.

In order to manage inventories in an efficient manner, and also to meet their quarterly reporting obligations, ***all large companies use perpetual inventory systems.*** Also, all businesses with point-of-sale terminals or computerized inventory accounting systems use the perpetual approach. For a small business with a manual accounting system, however, the fact that a periodic system requires less record keeping than does a perpetual system may outweigh all other considerations.

In businesses in which accounting records are maintained manually by the owner, or by a professional accountant who visits the business on a weekly or monthly basis, a periodic inventory system may be the ***only*** practical means of accounting for inventory.

CASE IN POINT Dale's Market is a small grocery store, in which sales are recorded on mechanical cash registers. The daily register tapes list the retail prices of the items sold but do not identify the products in any other way. Even if Dale were willing to spend all night recording the costs of merchandise sold, he would have no place to start. His accounting system does not identify the types of products that have been sold.

A business with a manual accounting system may be able to use a perpetual inventory system if it sells a relatively small quantity of high-cost items. Examples of such businesses are antique stores, art galleries, and jewellery stores. On the other hand, a business that sells a high volume of low-cost items, such as Dale's Market, can maintain a perpetual inventory system only by installing electronic point-of-sale terminals. (The capabilities of these terminals are discussed in this chapter and Chapter 6.)

Operation of a Periodic Inventory System

In a periodic inventory system, the amount of inventory on hand at the end of each accounting period is determined by physical count. The inventory at the end of one accounting period also represents the ***beginning inventory*** of the following period.

OBJECTIVE 10 Account for transactions using a periodic inventory system.

In summary, a periodic inventory system requires that a complete physical inventory be taken at the end of each accounting period. Annual financial statements may be prepared by taking inventory at the end of the fiscal year. The preparation of monthly financial statements, however, would require monthly inventories.[17]

Purchases of Merchandise Under a periodic inventory system, the cost of merchandise purchased for resale is recorded by debiting an account entitled ***Purchases,*** as shown below:

Purchases	1,960	
Accounts Payable (Beta Wholesale Co.)		1,960
Purchased merchandise on account; gross price, $2,000; terms 2/10, n/30. ($2,000, less 2% = $1,960.)		

Purchases may be recorded either at the gross invoice price, or at net price—that is, net of available cash discounts. In this chapter, we will record purchases at the ***net*** cost.

Other Accounts Included in the Cost of Goods Sold In our earlier illustration, we used only three items in computing the cost of goods sold: beginning inventory, purchases, and ending inventory. In most cases, however, two additional accounts are involved in this computation: Purchase Returns and Allowances, and Transportation-in.

Purchase Returns and Allowances When merchandise purchased from suppliers is found to be unsatisfactory, the goods may be returned or a request may be made for an allowance on the price. A return of goods to the supplier is recorded as follows:

Journal entry for return of goods to supplier

Accounts Payable (Beta Wholesale Co.)	180	
Purchase Returns and Allowances		180
To reduce liability to Beta Wholesale Co. by the cost of goods returned for credit.		

Assuming that the purchase had been recorded at net cost, the purchase return also should be recorded at the net cost of the merchandise.

The Purchase Returns and Allowances account may be viewed as a reduction in the cost of purchases made during the period. It is preferable to credit this "contra-purchases" account when merchandise is returned to a supplier rather than crediting the Purchases account directly. Together, these two accounts show both the total amount of purchases and the amount of cost adjustments and returns. Management is interested in the percentage relationship between goods purchased and the portion of these goods that must be returned. Returning merchandise is time-consuming and expensive and also may result in a loss of sales opportunities. Excessive returns may suggest a need to find more reliable suppliers.

[17] In Chapter 9, we discuss several estimating techniques that may be used in preparing monthly or quarterly financial statements. If inventory (and the cost of goods sold) are based upon such estimating techniques, this fact should be disclosed in the financial statements.

Transportation-in Transportation charges relating to merchandise are accounted for in the same manner in periodic and perpetual inventory systems. The freight charges paid on ***inbound*** shipments are debited to an account entitled ***Transportation-in,*** which is added to the cost of goods sold. Delivery costs on ***outbound*** shipments are debited to Delivery Expense, which is classified as a selling expense.

Purchase Discounts We follow the policy of recording purchases at their net cost. Under this net method, the amount paid to the supplier will be equal to the recorded liability, assuming that payment will be made within the discount period. If payment is not made until after the discount period has expired, the purchaser must pay the gross invoice price. The additional amount paid is debited to an account entitled ***Purchase Discounts Lost,*** an expense account representing a form of interest expense. We strongly recommend this net method, as it focuses management's attention upon any failures to take advantage of available cash discounts.[18]

Accounting for Sales Transactions

Accounting for sales transactions is the same under periodic and perpetual inventory systems, with one notable exception. In a periodic system, no entries are made transferring costs from the Inventory account to the Cost of Goods Sold account.

To illustrate, assume that Farrow's Bait & Tackle Shop sells merchandise on account to South Shore Marina for $1,200; terms, 2/10, net/30. South Shore finds $200 worth of this merchandise defective and returns it to Farrow's immediately. South Shore then pays for the remainder of these goods within the discount period. Farrow's should record the original sales transaction as shown below:

Accounts Receivable (South Shore Marina)	1,200	
Sales		1,200
To record credit sale, terms 2/10, n/30.		

Notice that ***only one entry*** is needed to record a sale. The primary advantage of a periodic inventory system is that it is not necessary to record the cost of goods sold relating to individual sales transactions. (As in a perpetual inventory system, sales usually are recorded at the ***gross*** invoice price, not at the net amount.)

[18] An alternative approach is to record purchases at the gross invoice price. If payment is made within the discount period, the buyer will then pay the supplier less than the recorded amount of the liability. This "cost savings" is credited to an account called Purchase Discounts Taken. Purchase Discounts Taken is a contra-purchases account, similar to Purchase Returns and Allowances. In terms of net income, the "gross method" and "net method" produce essentially the same results.

Farrow's would record the sales return by South Shore as follows:

Sales Returns and Allowances	*200*	
Accounts Receivable (South Shore Marina)		*200*
Credit customer returned defective merchandise.		

Again, only one entry is necessary. Under a periodic inventory system, no entry is made to update the Inventory account or to adjust the cost of goods sold for goods returned by customers.

Following this sales return, South Shore owes Farrow's $1,000. If South Shore pays within the discount period, however, it may take a 2% cash discount. The entry to record the collection of this account receivable within the discount period is:

Cash	*980*	
Sales Discounts	*20*	
Accounts Receivable (South Shore Marina)		*1,000*
To record collection of account receivable within the discount period.		

Both Sales Returns & Allowances and Sales Discounts are ***contra-revenue*** accounts, which are deducted from gross sales revenue as a step in determining net sales. These debit balance accounts reduce the revenue of a specific time period. At the end of the period, they are closed into the Income Summary along with the company's expense accounts.

Income Statement for a Company Using a Periodic Inventory System

To pull together the concepts discussed so far, let us look at a detailed income statement of a business using a periodic inventory system.

Olympic Sporting Goods is a small retail store organized as a sole proprietorship and operated by Robert Riley. The business has no external reporting responsibilities, other than determining its annual income for inclusion in Riley's personal income tax return. Also, Riley works in the store on a daily basis and is intimately familiar with the inventory on hand. Thus, Olympic Sporting Goods is able to meet Riley's needs for accounting information with a periodic inventory system. The company's 1996 income statement is illustrated on the next page.

OLYMPIC SPORTING GOODS
Income Statement
For the Year Ending December 31, 1996

Revenue:			
Sales			$627,000
Less: Sales returns and allowances		$ 12,000	
Sales discounts		5,000	17,000
Net sales			$610,000
Cost of goods sold:			
Inventory, Jan. 1		$ 60,000	
Purchases	$375,000		
Less: Purchase returns and allowances	10,000		
Net purchases	$365,000		
Add: Transportation-in	11,000		
Delivered cost of purchases		376,000	
Cost of goods available for sale		$436,000	
Less: Inventory, Dec. 31		70,000	
Cost of goods sold			366,000
Gross profit			$244,000
Operating expenses:			
Selling expenses:			
Sales salaries	$ 74,000		
Advertising	29,000		
Delivery service	7,000		
Depreciation	6,000		
Total selling expenses		$116,000	
General and administrative expenses:			
Office salaries	$ 55,000		
Utilities	2,100		
Depreciation	2,000		
Total general and administrative expenses		59,100	
Total operating expenses			175,100
Income from operations			$ 68,900
Nonoperating expenses:			
Purchase discounts lost		$ 1,000	
Interest expense		8,200	9,200
Net income			$ 59,700

Notice the computation of the cost of goods sold

Work Sheet for a Merchandising Business

In Chapter 4, we illustrated the preparation of a work sheet as a means of organizing the data used in making adjusting and closing entries and in preparing financial statements. A merchandising business using a periodic inventory system also may elect to prepare a work sheet. In fact, it is small businesses with periodic inventory systems and manual accounting records that are most likely to actually prepare such a schedule.[19]

[19] Remember that a work sheet is ***not*** an essential step in the accounting cycle. In essence, it is "scratch paper," upon which an accountant may work out certain entries before making entries in the accounting records. You should regard the work sheets in this text as illustrations of accounting ***processes,*** not of account documents. In practice, accountants often perform the illustrated processes ***without*** first preparing a work sheet.

In most respects, a work sheet prepared by a merchandising company with a periodic inventory system parallels the work sheet explained and illustrated in Chapter 4. There are, however, a few new features—namely, the Inventory account and other accounts used in recording merchandising transactions. As an illustration, a year-end work sheet for Olympic Sporting Goods is illustrated on the following page. For emphasis, the new types of accounts included in this work sheet are shown in black.

Trial Balance Columns The trial balance columns are prepared by listing the account balances in the ledger at December 31, ***prior*** to making adjusting and closing entries. The Inventory account, however, is ***not*** up-to-date; its $60,000 balance represents the inventory at the ***beginning of the year.*** (A distinctive feature of the periodic inventory system is that the Inventory account is ***not*** updated throughout the year for purchases and sales of merchandise.)

Adjustment Columns and Adjusted Trial Balance The adjustments required in a merchandising company at the end of the period are similar to those of a service business. In our illustration, we assume that the only adjustment needed at December 31 is an entry to record depreciation expense for the year.

The merchandising accounts (shown in black) usually do not require adjustment. Therefore, their balances are extended directly from the Trial Balance columns to the Adjusted Trial Balance columns.

Income Statement Columns The accounts used in the determination of net income are extended from the Adjusted Trial Balance columns into the Income Statement columns. These are the revenue accounts, expense accounts, and ***all accounts used in the computation of the cost of goods sold.***

Notice that the $60,000 balance in the Inventory account is extended into the ***Income Statement*** debit column, instead of the Balance Sheet debit column. This is because the $60,000 balance in this account represents the inventory at the ***beginning*** of the year. At year-end, the beginning inventory is ***no longer an asset;*** rather, it has become ***part of the cost of goods sold.*** The cost of goods sold, of course, is offset against revenue in the income statement.

Treatment of the Inventory Account The most unique element of this work sheet is the treatment accorded to the Inventory account. As we have explained, the $60,000 beginning balance is extended into the Income Statement debit column, not into the Balance Sheet columns. Now, however, it is time to ***update*** the Inventory account to show the $70,000 ***ending inventory,*** as determined by a physical inventory taken at year-end.

Updating the Inventory account requires ***two entries*** in the work sheet. Notice that the cost of the ending inventory appears both in the ***Income Statement credit column*** and in the ***Balance Sheet debit column.*** (For emphasis, these two entries are shown in black.)

Let us briefly explain the reasoning behind these entries. The cost of the ending inventory is entered into the Balance Sheet debit column because this amount will appear in the December 31 balance sheet. The amount also is entered into the Income Statement credit column because,

Note the treatment of the beginning and the ending inventories

OLYMPIC SPORTING GOODS
Work Sheet
For the Year Ended December 31, 1996

	Trial Balance		Adjustments*		Adjusted Trial Balance		Income Statement		Balance Sheet	
	Dr	Cr	Dr	Cr	Dr	Cr	Dr	Cr	Dr	Cr
Balance sheet accounts:										
Cash	19,400				19,400				19,400	
Accounts receivable	48,300				48,300				48,300	
Inventory	60,000				60,000		60,000	70,000	70,000	
Land	52,000				52,000				52,000	
Building	160,000				160,000				160,000	
Accumulated depreciation: building		56,000		(a) 8,000		64,000				64,000
Notes payable		82,000				82,000				82,000
Accounts payable		55,000				55,000				55,000
Robert Riley, capital		115,000				115,000				115,000
Robert Riley, drawing	26,000				26,000				26,000	
Income statement accounts:										
Sales		627,000				627,000		627,000		
Sales returns and allowances	12,000				12,000		12,000			
Sales discounts	5,000				5,000		5,000			
Purchases	375,000				375,000		375,000			
Purchase returns and allowances		10,000				10,000		10,000		
Transportation-in	11,000				11,000		11,000			
Sales salaries	74,000				74,000		74,000			
Advertising expense	29,000				29,000		29,000			
Delivery service	7,000				7,000		7,000			
Office salaries	55,000				55,000		55,000			
Utilities expense	2,100				2,100		2,100			
Purchase discounts lost	1,000				1,000		1,000			
Interest expense	8,200				8,200		8,200			
	945,000	945,000								
Depreciation expense: building			(a) 8,000		8,000		8,000			
			8,000	8,000	953,000	953,000				
							647,300	707,000	375,700	316,000
Net income							59,700			59,700
Totals							707,000	707,000	375,700	375,700

Explanatory footnotes keyed to adjustments
* Adjustment
(a) Depreciation of building for the year.

in a periodic inventory system, the amount of ending inventory ***enters into the determination of net income.***

In a periodic inventory system, the cost of goods sold is determined by ***subtracting ending inventory*** from the total of beginning inventory, purchases, and transportation-in. By entering the ending inventory in the Income Statement ***credit*** column, we in effect are ***deducting*** it from the sum of the beginning inventory, purchases, and transportation-in, all of which were extended into the Income Statement ***debit*** column.

One of the functions of the Income Statement columns is to bring together all of the accounts involved in determining the cost of goods sold. The accounts with debit balances are the beginning Inventory, Purchases, and Transportation-in; these accounts total $446,000. Against this total the two credit items of Purchase Returns & Allowances, $10,000, and ending Inventory, $70,000, are offset. The three accounts with debit balances exceed the total of the two credit balances by ***$366,000;*** this amount is the ***cost of goods sold,*** as shown in the income statement for Olympic Sporting Goods, which appeared earlier in this supplemental section.

Completing the Work Sheet When all the accounts on the work sheet have been extended into the Income Statement or Balance Sheet columns, the final four columns are totalled. The net income is computed, and the work sheet completed in the same manner as illustrated in Chapter 4 for a service business.

Financial Statements

The work to be done at the end of the period is much the same for a merchandising business as for a service-type firm. First, the work sheet is completed; then, financial statements are prepared from the data in the work sheet; next, the adjusting and closing entries are entered in the journal and posted to the ledger accounts; and finally, an after-closing trial balance is prepared. This completes the accounting cycle.

The income statement presented earlier was prepared from the Olympic Sporting Goods work sheet. Note particularly the arrangement of items in the cost of goods sold section of the income statement; this portion of the income statement illustrates many of the essential accounting concepts covered in this supplemental section.

Closing Entries

OBJECTIVE 11 Prepare closing entries in a periodic inventory system, including the entry to "re-open" the inventory account.

In a ***perpetual*** inventory system, the Cost of Goods Sold account simply is closed along with the company's expense accounts. In a ***periodic*** inventory system, a single Cost of Goods Sold account is not used throughout the accounting period. Instead, separate ledger accounts are maintained for the various components of the cost of goods sold, each of which is closed at year-end. The major new elements in the closing process for a merchandising business using a periodic inventory system are the entries showing the ***elimination*** of the beginning inventory and the ***recording*** of the ending inventory.

The beginning inventory is cleared out of the Inventory account by a debit to Income Summary and a credit to Inventory. A separate entry could be made for this purpose, but we can save time by making one compound entry that will debit the Income Summary account with the balance of the beginning inventory and with the balances of all temporary accounts having debit balances.

The ***temporary*** accounts are those that appear in the income statement, including those that enter into the computation of the cost of goods sold. As the name suggests, the temporary accounts are used to accumulate temporarily the increases and decreases in owner's equity resulting from operation of the business. The entry to close the beginning inventory and income statement accounts with debit balances is illustrated below. (For emphasis, the accounts relating specifically to merchandising transactions are shown in black.)

Closing beginning inventory and income statement accounts with debit balances

Dec. 31	Income Summary	647,300	
	Inventory (Jan. 1)		60,000
	Sales Returns and Allowances		12,000
	Sales Discounts		5,000
	Purchases		375,000
	Transportation-in		11,000
	Sales Salaries		74,000
	Advertising Expense		29,000
	Delivery Service		7,000
	Office Salaries		55,000
	Utilities Expense		2,100
	Purchase Discounts Lost		1,000
	Interest Expense		8,200
	Depreciation Expense: Building		8,000
	To close out the beginning inventory and the income statement accounts with debit balances.		

The preceding closing entry closes all the operating expense accounts, as well as the accounts used to accumulate the cost of goods sold. It also closes the accounts for Sales Returns and Allowances and for Sales Discounts, as well as Purchase Discounts Lost. After this first closing entry, the Inventory account has a zero balance. Therefore, it is time to record in this account the new inventory of $70,000 determined by a physical count at December 31.

To bring the ending inventory into the accounting records after the physical inventory on December 31, we could make a separate entry debiting Inventory and crediting the Income Summary account. It is more convenient, however, to combine this step with the closing of the Sales account and any other income statement accounts having credit balances, as illustrated in the following closing entry:

Closing income statement accounts with credit balances and recording ending inventory

Dec. 31	Inventory (Dec. 31)	70,000	
	Sales	627,000	
	Purchase Returns and Allowances	10,000	
	Income Summary		707,000
	To record the ending inventory and to close all income statement accounts with credit balances.		

In this entry, we "close" the Sales account and the Purchase Returns and Allowances account, as each of these accounts will have a ***zero balance*** after the closing entry is posted. On the other hand, the Inventory account had been "closed" in the ***preceding*** entry, which transferred its entire balance into the Income Summary account. Therefore, debiting the Inventory account for the amount of the ending inventory should be viewed as ***"reopening"*** the Inventory account.

The remaining closing entries serve to transfer the balance of the Income Summary account to the owner's capital account and to close the drawing account, as follows:

Closing the Income Summary account and Owner's Drawing account

Dec. 31	Income Summary	59,700	
	Robert Riley, Capital		59,700
	To close the Income Summary account.		
Dec. 31	Robert Riley, Capital	26,000	
	Robert Riley, Drawing		26,000
	To close the drawing account.		

After the preceding four closing entries have been posted to the ledger, the only ledger accounts left with dollar balances will be balance sheet accounts. An after-closing trial balance should be prepared to prove that the ledger is in balance after the year-end entries to adjust and close the accounts have been recorded.

Record-Keeping Requirements in a Periodic System

At first glance, the more complex closing procedures may seem to negate the basic advantage of a periodic inventory system—that is, a reduction in the amount of required record keeping. However, recording the cost of goods sold relating to each sales transaction may require dozens, scores, or hundreds of entries ***each day.*** In contrast, the end-of-the-year closing procedures for a periodic inventory system involve only two additional elements: "closing out" the beginning inventory and "reopening" the Inventory account at the proper ending inventory amount. As closing procedures are usually handled by experienced accountants, use of a periodic system adds only a couple of minutes to the closing process.

CHAPTER REVIEW

KEY TERMS INTRODUCED OR EMPHASIZED IN CHAPTER 5

Classified financial statements Financial statements in which similar items are arranged in groups; subtotals are shown to assist users in analyzing the statements.

Controlling account A general ledger account that summarizes the content of a specific subsidiary ledger.

Cost of goods sold The cost to a merchandising company of the goods that it has sold to its customers during the period.

Current assets Cash and other assets that can be converted into cash within one year or the operating cycle (whichever is longer) without interfering with normal business operations.

Current liabilities Existing liabilities that must be paid within one year or the operating cycle (whichever is longer).

Current ratio Current assets divided by current liabilities. A measure of short-term debt-paying ability.

Gross profit Net sales minus the cost of goods sold.

Gross profit rate Gross profit expressed as a percentage of net sales. Provides a useful measure over time of the strength of a company's products in the marketplace.

Inventory The goods that a merchandising company sells to its customers.

Inventory shrinkage The loss of merchandise through such causes as shoplifting, breakage, and spoilage.

Multiple-step income statement An income statement in which the cost of goods sold and expenses are subtracted from revenue in a series of steps, thus producing a number of useful subtotals.

Net sales Gross sales revenue less sales returns and allowances and minus sales discounts. Usually the first figure shown in an income statement.

Operating cycle The repeating sequence of transactions by which a business generates its revenue and cash receipts from customers.

Operating income A subtotal in an income statement representing the revenue earned from customers less only those expenses incurred for the purpose of generating that revenue.

Periodic inventory system An alternative to the perpetual inventory system that eliminates the need for recording the cost of goods sold as sales occur. However, the amounts of inventory and the cost of goods sold are not known until a complete physical inventory is taken at year-end.

Perpetual inventory system A system of accounting for merchandising transactions in which the Inventory and Cost of Goods Sold accounts are kept perpetually up-to-date.

Point-of-sale terminals Electronic cash registers used for computer-based processing of sales transactions. Capable of recording sales and the cost of goods sold and also of updating accounts receivable and inventory subsidiary records. Permit the use of a perpetual inventory system even in a business selling a high volume of merchandise.

Single-step income statement An income statement in which the cost of goods sold and all expenses are combined and deducted from total revenue in a single step.

Subsidiary ledger A ledger containing separate accounts for each of the items comprising the balance of a controlling account in the general ledger. The total of the account balances in a subsidiary ledger is equal to the balance in the general ledger controlling account.

Working capital Current assets minus current liabilities. A measure of short-run debt-paying ability.

DEMONSTRATION PROBLEM FOR YOUR REVIEW

Whitby Wholesale Corporation sold 100 pairs of boots to Boot Hill, a chain of retail stores. The sales price was $5,000 ($50 per pair), with terms of 2/10, n/30. United Express charged $162 to deliver this merchandise to Boot Hill's stores; these charges were split evenly between the buyer and seller and were paid in cash.

Boot Hill returned 10 pairs of these boots to Whitby Wholesale because they were the wrong style. Whitby Wholesale agreed to accept this return and credit Boot Hill's account for the full invoice price. Boot Hill then paid the remaining balance within the discount period.

Both companies use perpetual inventory systems.

INSTRUCTIONS

a Record this sequence of transactions in the general journal of Whitby Wholesale Corporation. The company records sales at the full invoice price; these boots had cost Whitby Wholesale $32 per pair.

b Record this sequence of transactions in the general journal of Boot Hill. The company records purchases of merchandise at ***net cost*** and uses a Transportation-in account in recording transportation charges on inbound shipments.

SOLUTION TO DEMONSTRATION PROBLEM

General Journal

a Journal entries by Whitby Wholesale Corporation:

Accounts Receivable (Boot Hill)	5,000	
Sales		5,000
Sold merchandise on account; terms, 2/10, n/30.		
Cost of Goods Sold	3,200	
Inventory		3,200
To record cost of merchandise sold ($32/pr. × 100 pr.).		
Delivery Expense	81	
Cash		81
Paid delivery charges on outbound shipment.		
Sales Returns and Allowances	500	
Accounts Receivable (Boot Hill)		500
Customer returned merchandise with a sales price of $500.		
Inventory	320	
Cost of Goods Sold		320
Reduce cost of goods sold for cost of returned merchandise ($32/pr. × 10 pr.).		
Cash	4,410	
Sales Discounts	90	
Accounts Receivable (Boot Hill)		4,500
Collected amount due from credit sale to Boot Hill, less $500 return and less 2% cash discount on remaining $4,500 balance ($4,500 × 2% = $90).		

b Journal entries by Boot Hill:

Inventory	4,900	
Accounts Payable (Whitby Wholesale Corp.)		4,900
Purchased 100 pairs of boots on account; terms, 2/10, n/30. Net cost, $49 cost, $49 per pair ($50, less 2%).		
Transportation-in	81	
Cash		81
Paid transportation charges in inbound shipment.		
Accounts Payable (Whitby Wholesale Corp.)	490	
Inventory		490
Returned 10 pairs of boots to supplier. (Net cost, $49 per pair × 10 pairs = $490.)		
Accounts Payable (Whitby Wholesale Corp.)	4,410	
Cash		4,410
Paid within discount period balance owed to Whitby Wholesale Corp. ($4,900 − $490 = $4,410).		

ASSIGNMENT MATERIAL

DISCUSSION QUESTIONS

1 Describe the operating cycle of a merchandising company.

2 Compare and contrast the merchandising activities of a wholesaler and a retailer.

3 The income statement of a merchandising company includes a major type of cost that does not appear in the income statement of a service-type business. Identify this cost and explain what it represents.

4 During the current year, Green Bay Company earned a gross profit of $350,000, whereas New England Company earned a gross profit of only $280,000. Does this mean that Green Bay is more profitable than New England? Explain.

5 Thornhill Company's income statement shows gross profit of $432,000, cost of goods sold of $638,000, and other expenses totalling $390,000. Compute the amounts of (a) revenue from sales (net sales) and (b) net income.

6 Explain the need for subsidiary ledgers in accounting for merchandising activities.

7 All Night Auto Parts, Inc., maintains subsidiary ledgers for accounts receivable, inventory, and accounts payable. Explain in detail what information from the following journal entry should be posted, and to which subsidiary and general ledger accounts.

Inventory	*420*	
Accounts Payable (Boss Automotive)		*420*
Purchased 12 Boss LoadMaster II shock absorbers. Cost, $35 per unit.		

8 What is meant by the phrase "reconciling a subsidiary ledger"? In general terms, what is the purpose of this procedure?

9 Define the term ***inventory shrinkage.*** How is the amount of inventory shrinkage determined in a business using a perpetual inventory system, and how is this shrinkage recorded in the accounting records?

10 Briefly contrast the accounting procedures in ***perpetual*** and ***periodic*** inventory systems.

11 Miracle Home Cleanser uses a ***periodic*** inventory system. During the current year the company purchased merchandise with a cost of $55,000. State the cost of goods sold for the year under each of the following alternative assumptions:

a No beginning inventory; ending inventory $3,500.

b Beginning inventory $10,000; no ending inventory.

c Beginning inventory $2,000; ending inventory $7,200.

d Beginning inventory $8,000; ending inventory $1,400.

12 Evaluate the following statement: "Without electronic point-of-sale terminals, it simply would not be possible to use perpetual inventory systems in businesses that sell large quantities of many different products."

13 Some companies use a modified version of the periodic inventory system in which purchases are charged directly to the Cost of Goods Sold account. Under what circumstances will such a system produce satisfactory results?

14 How does interest expense differ from normal operating expenses such as advertising and salaries? How is interest expense presented in a multiple-step income statement?

Nov./97 15 What is the basic purpose of ***classifications*** in financial statements?

16 What is the basic characteristic of ***current assets?*** Many retail stores regularly sell merchandise on "instalment plans," calling for payments over a period of 24 or 36 months. Do such receivables qualify as current assets? Explain.

17 Madison Corporation has current assets of $570,000 and current liabilities of $300,000. Compute the current ratio and the amount of working capital.

18 Identify two criteria that users of financial statements often use in evaluating the reasonableness of the financial ratios of a particular company.

19 Briefly describe the extent of a business owner's personal liability for the debts of (a) an unincorporated business and (b) a corporation.

20 Describe the format of a multiple-step income statement and that of a single-step income statement.

Nov. 97 21 Define the term ***gross profit rate.*** Explain two factors that may cause a company's gross profit rate to increase.

22 Distinguish between ***operating income*** and ***net income.***

23 Identify the three basic factors for which the net income of a sole proprietorship compensates the owner.

*24 How does a balance arise in the Purchase Discounts Lost account? Why does management pay careful attention to the balance (if any) in this account?

*25 European Imports pay substantial freight charges to obtain inbound shipments of purchased merchandise. Should these freight charges be debited to the company's Delivery Expense account? Explain.

*26 Outback Sporting Goods purchases merchandise on terms of 4/10, n/60. The company has a "line of credit" that enables it to borrow money as needed from Northern Bank at an annual interest rate of 11%. Should Outback pay its suppliers within the 10 day discount period if it must draw on its line of credit (borrow from Northern Bank) to make these early payments? Explain.

*27 TireCo is a retail store in a province that has a combined goods and service tax and sales tax of 15%. Would you expect to find sales tax expense and sales tax payable in TireCo's financial statements? Explain.

*28 A seller generally records sales at the full invoice price, but the buyer usually records purchases at ***net cost.*** Explain the logic of the buyer and seller recording the transaction at different amounts.

**29 Berlasty Company uses the periodic inventory system and maintains its accounting records on a calendar-year basis. Does the beginning or the ending inventory figure appear in the trial balance prepared from the ledger on December 31?

**30 Compute the amount of cost of goods sold, given the following account balances: beginning inventory $48,000, purchases $100,800, purchase returns and allowances $5,400, transportation-in $1,200, and ending inventory $43,200.

* *Supplemental Topic A, "Additional Merchandising Transactions"*

** *Supplemental Topic B, "More about Periodic Inventory System"*

**31 Under the periodic inventory system, what is the purpose of a closing entry consisting of a debit to the Income Summary account and a credit to the Inventory account?

MULTIPLE CHOICE QUESTIONS

1 Mark and Amanda Carter own an appliance store and a restaurant. The appliance store sells merchandise on a 12-month instalment plan; the restaurant sells only for cash. (More than one answer may be correct.)

- a The appliance store has a longer operating cycle than the restaurant.
- b The appliance store probably uses a perpetual inventory system, whereas the restaurant probably uses a periodic system.
- c Both businesses require subsidiary ledgers for accounts receivable and inventory.
- d Both businesses probably have subsidiary ledgers for accounts payable.

2 Which of the following types of information are found in subsidiary ledgers, but ***not*** in the general ledger? (More than one answer may be correct.)

- a Total cost of goods sold for the period.
- b The quantity of a particular product sold during the period.
- c The dollar amount owed to a particular creditor.
- d The portion of total current assets that consists of cash.

3 The two basic approaches to accounting for inventory and the cost of goods sold are the ***perpetual*** inventory system and the ***periodic*** inventory system. Indicate which of the following statements are correct. (More than one answer may be correct.)

- a Most large merchandising companies and manufacturing businesses use periodic inventory systems.
- b As a practical matter, a grocery store or a large department store could not maintain a perpetual inventory system without the use of point-of-sale terminals.
- c In a periodic inventory system the cost of goods sold is not determined until a complete physical inventory is taken.
- d In a perpetual inventory system, the Cost of Goods Sold account is debited promptly for the cost of merchandise sold.

4 Pisces Market presently has current assets totalling $300,000 and a current ratio of 2.5 to 1. Compute the current ratio immediately ***after*** Pisces pays $30,000 of its accounts payable.

a 3 to 1 b 3.33 to 1 c 2.2 to 1 d 2.25 to 1

5 Which of the following items are deducted as expense in the income statement of a merchandising business organized as a corporation, but ***not*** in the income statement of an unincorporated business? (More than one answer may be correct.)

- a Cost of goods sold.
- b Income taxes expense.
- c Sales taxes expense.
- d Amounts paid to the owner for services rendered to the business.

** *Supplemental Topic B, "More about Periodic Inventory System"*

*6 Big Brother, a retail store, purchased 100 television sets from Krueger Electronics on account at a cost of $200 each. Krueger offers credit terms of 2/10, n/30. Big Brother uses a perpetual inventory system and records purchases at ***net cost.*** Big Brother determines that 10 of these television sets are defective and returns them to Krueger for full credit. In recording this return, Big Brother will:

- a Debit Sales Returns and Allowances.
- b Debit Accounts Payable, $1,960.
- c Debit Cost of Goods Sold, $1,960.
- d Credit Inventory, $2,000.

**7 Chungsun Fabric Outlet uses a periodic inventory system. Its accounting records include the following for January:

Sales	*$163,000*	*Transportation-in*	*$1,000*
Purchases	*130,000*	*Purchase Returns & Allowances*	*4,500*
Sales Discounts	*3,000*		

A physical count determined the cost of inventory on hand at January 31 to be $17,000. If gross profit amounts to 25% of net sales, compute the beginning inventory at January 1.

a $12,750 b $9,750 c $23,500 d $10,500

**8 The closing entries for a merchandising company using a periodic inventory system would not include:

- a A debit to Inventory (ending).
- b A debit to Transportation-in.
- c A credit to Purchases.
- d A credit to Inventory (beginning).

EXERCISES

EXERCISE 5-1
Accounting Terminology

Listed below are nine technical accounting terms introduced in this chapter.

Perpetual inventory system	*Periodic inventory system*	*Classified financial statements*
Gross profit	*Current ratio*	*Subsidiary ledger*
Cost of goods sold	*Working capital*	*Operating income*

Each of the following statements may (or may not) describe one of these technical terms. For each statement, indicate the term described, or answer "None" if the statement does not correctly describe any of the terms.

- a Current assets plus current liabilities.
- b An item deducted from revenue in the income statement of a merchandising company that ***does not appear*** in the income statement of a service-type business.
- c Revenue earned from customers, less expenses relating directly to the production of this revenue.

---

* *Supplemental Topic A, "Additional Merchandising Transactions"*

** *Supplemental Topic B, "More about Periodic Inventory System"*

d An approach to accounting for inventory and determining the cost of goods sold that is based upon complete annual physical counts of the inventory.

e An accounting record providing detail about the individual items comprising the balance of a controlling account.

f The difference between the sales price and the cost of all merchandise sold during the period.

g An approach to accounting for inventory and the cost of goods sold that produces up-to-date accounting records, including an inventory subsidiary ledger.

EXERCISE 5-2
Effects of Basic Merchandising Transactions

Shown below are selected transactions of Marston's, a retail store that uses a perpetual inventory system:

a Purchased merchandise on account.

b Recognized the revenue from a sale of merchandise on account. (Ignore the related cost of goods sold.)

c Recognized the cost of goods sold relating to the sale in transaction **b.**

d Collected in cash the account receivable from the customer in transaction **b.**

e Following the taking of a physical inventory at year-end, made an adjusting entry to record a normal amount of inventory shrinkage.

Indicate the effects of each of these transactions upon the elements of the company's financial statements shown below. Organize your answer in tabular form, using the column headings shown below. (Notice that the cost of goods sold is shown separately from all other expenses.) Use the code letters ***I*** for increase, ***D*** for decrease, and ***NE*** for no effect.

	Income Statement				*Balance Sheet*		
Transaction	*Net Sales –*	*Cost of Goods Sold –*	*All Other Expenses =*	*Net Income*	*Assets =*	*Liabilities +*	*Owner's Equity*
a							

EXERCISE 5-3
Subsidiary Ledgers

Listed below are eight typical merchandising transactions of Everyday Auto Parts, a retail auto supply store.

a Purchased merchandise from Acme Wholesale on account.

b Paid an account payable to a supplier.

c Sold merchandise for cash.

d Sold merchandise on account.

e Collected an account receivable from a customer.

***f** Returned merchandise to a supplier, receiving credit against the amount owed.

***g** Gave a cash refund to a customer who returned merchandise.

***h** Reduced the account receivable from a credit customer who returned merchandise.

Among the account records of Everyday Auto Parts are subsidiary ledgers for inventory, accounts receivable, and accounts payable. For each of the eight transactions, you are to indicate any subsidiary ledger (or ledgers) to which the transaction would be posted. Use the codes below:

Inv = Inventory subsidiary ledger

AR = Accounts receivable subsidiary ledger

AP = Accounts payable subsidiary ledger

---

* *Supplemental Topic A, "Additional Merchandising Transactions"*

Also indicate whether each posting causes the balance in the subsidiary ledger account to ***increase*** or ***decrease.*** Organize your answer in tabular form as illustrated below. The answer for transaction **a** is provided as an example.

Transaction	Subsidiary Ledger	Effect upon Subsidiary Account Balance
a	Inv	Increase
	AP	Increase

EXERCISE 5-4
Posting to Subsidiary Ledgers

In addition to a general ledger, LeatherWorks maintains subsidiary ledgers for accounts receivable, inventory, and accounts payable (the company does not maintain a subsidiary ledger for cash). Two entries appearing in the company's journal are illustrated below, along with the posting references that have been entered in the LP column:

General Journal

Accounts Titles and Explanation	LP	Debit	Credit
Inventory	✓/130	2,500	
Accounts Payable (Pucci, Inc.)	✓		2,500
Purchased 50 shoulder bags from Pucci, Inc., @ $50; payment due in 30 days.			
Cash	101	6,000	
Accounts Receivable (The Bag Man)	105		6,000
Collected an account receivable.			

INSTRUCTIONS

a Based upon the posting references shown, explain in detail the accounts to which the debit and credit portions of each journal entry apparently have been posted.

b Does it appear that the posting of each entry has been completed properly? Explain. (Assume that illustrated account numbers are correct.)

EXERCISE 5-5
Perpetual Inventory System

Caliente Products uses a perpetual inventory system. On January 1 the Inventory account had a balance of $93,500. During the first few days of January the following transactions occurred:

Jan. 2 Purchased merchandise on credit from Bell Company for $12,500.

Jan. 3 Sold merchandise for cash, $9,000. The cost of this merchandise was $6,300.

INSTRUCTIONS

a Prepare entries in general journal form to record the above transactions.

b What was the balance of the Inventory account at the close of business January 3?

EXERCISE 5-6
Taking a Physical Inventory

Electronics Warehouse uses a perpetual inventory system. At year-end, the Inventory account has a balance of $314,000, but a physical count shows that the merchandise on hand has a cost of only $307,500.

INSTRUCTIONS

a Explain the probable reason(s) for this discrepancy.

b Prepare the journal entry required in this situation.

c Indicate all the accounting records to which your journal entry in part **b** should be posted.

EXERCISE 5-7
Periodic Inventory System

Hanson's Gift Shop uses a periodic inventory system. At the end of 1995, the accounting records include the following information:

Inventory, December 31, 1994	*$ 6,700*
Inventory, December 31, 1995	*4,400*
Net sales	*160,400*
Purchases	*81,500*

INSTRUCTIONS

a How were the amounts of beginning and ending inventory determined?

b Compute the amount of the cost of goods sold in 1995.

c Prepare a partial income statement showing the shop's gross profit in the year.

EXERCISE 5-8
A Quick Look at IBM's Current Position

A balance sheet of **IBM** contained the following items among others. (Dollar amounts are stated in millions.)

Cash	*$ 770*
Investment in marketable securities (current asset)	*6,197*
Notes & accounts receivable (net)	*12,757*
Other current receivables	*1,092*
Inventories	*8,645*
Prepaid expenses and other current assets	*1,559*
Plant & other property (net of depreciation)	*20,082*
Accounts payable	*2,627*
Loans payable (short term)	*1,629*
Taxes payable	*2,534*
Other current liabilities	*6,587*
Long-term debt	*3,858*
Shareholders' equity	*38,263*

INSTRUCTIONS

a From the above information, compute the amount of IBM's current assets and the amount of its current liabilities.

b How much working capital does IBM have?

c Compute the current ratio to the nearest tenth of a percent.

EXERCISE 5-9
Recognition of Industry Characteristics

Reebok is a manufacturer of popular athletic footware. **Maritime Telephone & Telegraph** is one of the largest telephone companies in the Maritimes. Both companies are solvent and profitable. Which company would you expect to have the higher current ratio? Which company do you believe has the greater debt-paying ability? Explain fully the reasons for your answers.

EXERCISE 5-10
Logical Gross Profit Relationships

Several factors must be considered in interpreting a company's gross profit rate.

a Companies such as **Lotus Development** and **Microsoft** usually enjoy a higher gross profit rate on sales of a particular software product when it is first introduced than they do in later years. Why?

b For each of the following pairs of businesses, indicate which you would expect to have the highest gross profit rate. Briefly explain the reasons for your answer.

1 A grocery store, or a retail furniture store.

2 **The Bay** (a chain of department stores), or **Zellers** (a chain of discount stores).

EXERCISE 5-11
Classifications Within an Income Statement

Coast Hardware and Fashion Centre are sole proprietorships of similar size. Also, both businesses earn similar amounts of revenue, incur similar amounts of operating expenses, and earn similar net incomes. However, Coast has a higher cost of goods sold, while Fashion Centre has higher interest expense.

Indicate which of these companies has the higher (a) gross profit rate and (b) operating income. In each case, explain the reasons for your answer.

***EXERCISE 5-12**
Cash Discounts

Key Imports sold merchandise to Marine Systems for $7,500, offering terms of 2/10, n/30. Marine Systems paid for the merchandise within the discount period. Both companies use perpetual inventory systems.

INSTRUCTIONS

a Prepare journal entries in the accounting records of Key Imports to account for this sale and the subsequent collection. Assume the original cost of the merchandise to Key Imports had been $4,100.

b Prepare journal entries in the accounting records of Marine Systems to account for the purchase and subsequent payment. Marine Systems records purchases of merchandise at ***net cost.***

c Assume that because of a change in personnel, Marine Systems failed to pay for this merchandise within the discount period. Prepare the journal entry in the accounting records of Marine Systems to record payment ***after*** the discount period.

***EXERCISE 5-13**
Net Sales and Gross Profit

Glamour, Inc., is a retail store. In 1995, the company had gross sales revenue of $2,490,000, cost of goods sold of $1,248,000, sales returns and allowances of $59,000, and allowed sales discounts of $31,000.

Compute for the year (a) net sales, (b) gross profit, and (c) gross profit rate. Show supporting computations.

***EXERCISE 5-14**
Returned Merchandise

College Bookstore returned certain merchandise that it had purchased from McGraw-Hill Ryerson. McGraw-Hill Ryerson allowed the bookstore full credit for this return against the account receivable from the bookstore.

The returned merchandise had been purchased by College Bookstore for $5,000, terms 2/10, n/30. College Bookstore records purchases of merchandise ***net*** of any available cash discounts.

INSTRUCTIONS

Prepare journal entries to record the return of this merchandise in the accounting records of (a) College Bookstore and (b) McGraw-Hill Ryerson. (Assume that the cost of the merchandise to McGraw-Hill Ryerson had been $3,900.)

***EXERCISE 5-15**
Accounting for Sales Taxes

Trophy Shop operates in an area in which a sales tax of 15% (goods and service tax plus provincial tax) is levied on all products handled by the store. On cash sales, the salesclerks include the sales tax in the amount collected from the customer and ring up the entire amount on the cash register without recording separately the tax liability. On credit sales, the customer is charged for the list price of the merchandise plus 15%, and the entire amount is debited to Accounts Receivable and credited to the Sales account. On sales of less than one dollar, the tax collected is rounded to the nearest cent.

Sales tax must be remitted to the government authorities periodically. At March 31 the Sales account showed a balance of $326,025 for the period ended March 31.

INSTRUCTIONS

a What amount of sales tax is owed at March 31?

b Give the journal entry to record the sales tax liability in the accounting records.

* *Supplemental Topic A, "Additional Merchandising Transactions"*

****EXERCISE 5-16**
Relationships among Merchandising Accounts

The income statement of Three-Hole Miniature Golf Shop included the following items:

Net Sales	*900,000*
Gross profit	*360,000*
Beginning inventory	*67,500*
Purchase returns & allowances	*9,000*
Transportation-in	*13,500*
Operating expenses	*180,000*
Purchases	*562,500*

Using the appropriate items from this list as a basis for computing (a) the cost of goods sold, (b) the cost of goods available for sale, and (c) the ending inventory.

PROBLEMS

Note: This chapter contains an unusually wide variety of problem assignments. In order to make all of these problems readily available to all users of the text, we present them in ***one consecutive series,*** rather than splitting them into A and B groups. This series is supported in ***both*** the Group A and Group B packages of accounting work sheets.

PROBLEM 5-1
Perpetual Inventory System and Performance Evaluation

Indian Lake Lumber Company is the only lumberyard in Beaumont, a remote mountain town and popular ski resort. Some of Indian Lake's transactions during 1995 are as follows:

Nov. 5 Sold lumber on account to Dally Construction Company, $38,400. The inventory subsidiary ledger shows the cost of this merchandise to Indian Lake was $22,950.

Nov. 9 Purchased lumber on account from Pine Valley Mill, $104,000.

Dec. 5 Collected in cash the $38,400 account receivable from Dally Construction Company.

Dec. 9 Paid the $104,000 owed to Pine Valley Mill.

Dec. 31 Company personnel counted the inventory on hand and determined its cost to be $964,360. The accounting records, however, indicate inventory of $975,130 and a cost of goods sold of $3,217,130. The physical count of the inventory was observed by the company's auditors and is considered correct.

INSTRUCTIONS

a Prepare journal entries to record these transactions and events in the accounting records of Indian Lake Lumber Company. (The company uses a perpetual inventory system.)

b Prepare a partial income statement showing the company's gross profit for the year. (Net sales for the year amount to $4,966,000.)

c Indian Lake purchases lumber at the same wholesale prices as other lumber companies. Due to its remote mountain location, however, the company must pay between $90,000 and $100,000 per year in extra transportation charges to receive delivery of its purchased lumber. (These additional charges are included in the amount shown as cost of goods sold.)

Assume that an index of key business ratios in your library shows retail lumberyards of Indian Lake's approximate size (in total assets) average net sales of $5,000,000 per year and a gross profit rate of **27%.**

** *Supplemental Topic B, "More about Periodic Inventory System"*

Is Indian Lake Lumber Company able to pass its extra transportation costs on to its customers? Does the company appear to suffer or benefit financially from its remote location? Explain your reasoning and support your conclusions with specific accounting data comparing the operations of Indian Lake Lumber Company with the industry averages.

PROBLEM 5-2
Perpetual Inventory System and an Inventory Subsidiary Ledger

Facts-by-FAX sells facsimile machines, copiers, and other types of office equipment. On May 10, the company purchased for the first time a new "plain-paper" fax manufactured by Mitsui Corporation. Transactions relating to this product during May and June were as follows:

May 10 Purchased five P-500 facsimile machines on account from Mitsui Corporation, at a cost of $540 each. Payment due in 30 days.

May 23 Sold four P-500 facsimile machines on account to Foster & Cole, stockbrokers; sales price, $900 per machine. Payment due in 30 days.

May 24 Purchased an additional nine P-500 facsimile machines on account from Mitsui. Cost, $540 per machine; payment due in 30 days.

June 9 Paid $2,700 cash to Mitsui Corporation for the facsimile machines purchased on May 10.

June 19 Sold two P-500 facsimile machines to Tri-County Realty for cash. Sales price, $950 per machine.

June 22 Collected $3,600 from Foster & Cole in full settlement of the credit sale on May 23.

INSTRUCTIONS

a Prepare journal entries to record these transactions in the accounting records of Facts-by-FAX. (The company uses a perpetual inventory system.)

b Post the appropriate information from these journal entries to an inventory subsidiary ledger account like the one illustrated in this chapter.

c How many Mitsui P-500 facsimile machines were in inventory on May 31? From what accounting record did you obtain the answer to this question?

d Describe the types of information contained in any inventory subsidiary ledger account and explain how this information may be useful to various company personnel in conducting daily business operations.

PROBLEM 5-3
The Periodic Inventory System

Mountain Mabel's is a small general store located just outside of Point Pelee National Park. The store uses a periodic inventory system. Every January 1, Mabel and her husband close the store and take a complete physical inventory. Last year, the inventory amounted to $1,700; this year it totalled $2,800. During the current year, the business recorded sales of $105,000 and purchases of $31,000.

INSTRUCTIONS

a Compute the cost of goods sold for the current year.

b Explain why a small business such as this might use the periodic inventory system.

c Explain some of the ***disadvantages*** of the periodic system to a larger business, such as a Sears store.

PROBLEM 5-4
Comparison of Inventory Systems

Satellite Trackers sells satellite tracking systems for receiving television broadcasts from satellites in outer space. At December 31 last year, the company's inventory amounted to $22,000. During the first week of January this year, the company made only one purchase and one sale. These transactions were as follows:

Jan. 3 Sold one tracking system costing $11,200 to Mystery Mountain Resort for cash, $18,900.

Jan. 6 Purchased merchandise on account from Yamaha, $9,600. Terms, net 30 days.

INSTRUCTIONS

a Prepare journal entries to record these transactions assuming that Satellite Trackers uses the perpetual inventory system.

b Compute the balance of the Inventory account on January 7.

c Prepare journal entries to record the two transactions assuming that Satellite Trackers uses the periodic inventory system.

d Compute the cost of goods sold for the first week of January assuming use of a periodic inventory system. Use your answer to part **b** as the ending inventory.

e Which inventory system do you believe that a company such as Satellite Trackers would probably use? Explain your reasoning.

PROBLEM 5-5
Alternate to Problem 5-4

Halley's Space Scope sells state-of-the-art telescopes to individuals and organizations interested in studying the solar system. At December 31 last year, the company's inventory amounted to $90,000. During the first week of January this year, the company made only one purchase and one sale. These transactions were as follows:

Jan. 2 Sold one telescope costing $28,000 to Eastern University for cash, $40,000.

Jan. 5 Purchased merchandise on account from Solar Optics, $18,500. Terms, net 30 days.

INSTRUCTIONS

a Prepare journal entries to record these transactions assuming that Halley's Space Scope uses the perpetual inventory system.

b Compute the balance of the Inventory account on January 7.

c Prepare journal entries to record the two transactions assuming that Halley's Space Scope uses the periodic inventory system.

d Compute the cost of goods sold for the first week of January assuming use of a periodic inventory system. Use your answer to part **b** as the ending inventory.

e Which inventory system do you believe that a company such as Halley's Space Scope would probably use? Explain your reasoning.

PROBLEM 5-6
Closing entries

Henry Cheng owns a wholesale business called Beacon Hill Enterprise. The following statements provide a partial picture of its operations.

Income Statement
For the Year Ended August 31, 1996

Sales			$986,200
Less: Cost of goods sold			443,790
Gross profit			$542,410
Less: Operating expense:			
Selling expense:			
Advertising	$ 55,100		
Rent	60,000		
Sales commissions	138,000		
Insurance	8,900		
Total selling expense		$262,000	
General expense			
Office salaries	$110,000		
Depreciation—building	36,000		
Telephone expense	9,300		
Miscellaneous	2,200		
Total general expense		157,500	
Total operating expense			419,500
Operating income			$122,910
Less (add): Nonoperating items:			
Interest expense		$ 18,000	
Purchase discount lost		2,900	
Investment income		(6,800)	14,100
Net income			$108,810

Statement of Owner's Equity
For the Year Ended August 31, 1996

Henry Cheng, capital, August 31, 1995	$628,000
Add: Net income	108,810
Investment by owner	80,000
	$816,810
Less: Withdrawals by owner	98,610
Henry Cheng, capital, August 31, 1996	$718,200

INSTRUCTIONS Prepare the closing entries.

PROBLEM 5-7
Computing Current Ratio and Working Capital; Evaluating Solvency

Some of the accounts appearing in the year-end financial statements of Diet Frozen Dinners (a corporation) appear below. This list includes all of the company's current assets and current liabilities.

Sales	*$1,980,000*
Accumulated depreciation: equipment	*370,000*
Notes payable (due in 90 days)	*80,000*
Cash	*47,600*
Capital stock	*150,000*
Marketable securities	*175,040*
Accounts payable	*125,430*
Mortgage payable (due in 15 years)	*320,000*
Salaries payable	*7,570*
Interest payable	*4,600*
Accounts receivable	*230,540*
Inventory	*179,600*
Unearned revenue	*10,000*
Unexpired insurance	*4,500*

INSTRUCTIONS

a Prepare a partial balance sheet for Diet Frozen Dinners consisting of the current asset section and the current liability section ***only.*** Select the appropriate items from the above list.

b Compute the current ratio and the amount of working capital. Explain how each of these measurements is computed. State with reasons whether you consider the company to be in a strong or weak current position.

PROBLEM 5-8
Classified Income Statement

Sharon Carpio is very happy about her new business, S. Carpio Company. The operations for the first year have been fantastic and she is going to show the financial statements to her banker to get some money to finance another store. However, she cannot locate the income statement for the year ended December 31, 1996. Fortunately, she remembers from her accounting courses that the following information may help.

Sales	*689,200*	
Interest revenue	*2,800*	
Income summary		*692,000*
To close the revenue accounts		
Income summary	*572,280*	
Cost of goods sold		*329,520*
Transportation-in		*14,700*
Advertising expense		*20,800*
Delivery expense		*19,500*
Depreciation: Store equipment		*8,000*
Sales salaries expense		*72,080*
Miscellaneous selling expense		*1,690*
General office salaries expense		*63,900*
Depreciation expense: office building		*18,000*
Utilities expense		*9,210*
Insurance expense		*2,300*
Office supplies expense		*1,900*
Interest expense		*9,780*
Purchase discount lost		*900*
To close the Cost of Goods Sold account and other expense accounts		
Income summary	*119,720*	
Sharon Carpio, capital		*119,720*
To close the Income Summary account		
Sharon Carpio, capital	*78,000*	
Sharon Carpio, drawing		*78,000*
To close the owner's drawing account		

INSTRUCTIONS Prepare a classified income statement.

PROBLEM 5-9
Classified Financial Statements and Financial Ratios

Westport Department Store has advertised for an accounting student to work in its accounting department during the summer, and you have applied for the job. To determine whether you are familiar with the content of classified financial statements, the controller of Westport has developed the following problem based upon the store's operations in the year ended December 31, 1995:

Available information (dollar amounts in thousands):

Net sales	*$10,000*
Net income	*?*
Current liabilities	*2,000*
Selling expenses	*1,000*
Long-term liabilities	*1,600*
Total assets (and Total liabilities & shareholder's equity)	*6,800*
Shareholders' equity	*?*
Gross profit	*?*
Cost of goods sold	*7,000*
Current assets	*4,000*
Income taxes expense and other nonoperating items	*220*
Operating income	*?*
General and administrative expenses	*980*
Plant and equipment	*2,600*
Other assets	*?*

INSTRUCTIONS

a Using the captions given above, prepare for Westport Department Store a condensed:

1 Classified balance sheet at December 31, 1995.

2 Multiple-step income statement for the year ended December 31, 1995. Show supporting computations used in determining any missing amounts. (***Note:*** Your financial statements should include only as much detail as these captions permit. For example, the first asset listed in your balance sheet will be "Current assets . . . $4,000." Notice also that this company is a corporation and that "shareholders' equity" is to be summarized in the balance sheet as a single dollar amount.)

b Using the classified financial statements developed in part **a,** compute the following:

1 Current ratio

2 Working capital

3 Gross profit rate for 1995

***PROBLEM 5-10**
Effects of Merchandising Transactions

Southeast Medical Supply sells medical supplies to other businesses, such as drugstores and hospitals. Selected merchandising transactions are listed below:

a Paid air freight charges in order to receive overnight delivery of purchased merchandise needed immediately.

b Paid transportation charges to deliver merchandise to a customer.

c Returned defective merchandise to a supplier, receiving full credit against amounts currently owed.

d Paid an account payable to a merchandise supplier within the discount period.

e Paid an account payable to a merchandise supplier after the discount period had expired.

f A credit customer returned merchandise because its customer had cancelled the order. Gave the customer full credit on its account receivable. [Show the effects of this transaction on two lines: (1) to record crediting the account receivable and (2) to record replacement of the returned merchandise into inventory.]

g Collected an account receivable from a customer making payment within the discount period.

h Collected an account receivable from a customer making payment after the discount period had expired.

To interpret properly the effects of these transactions upon Southeast's financial statements, you first must be familiar with some of the company's accounting policies:

- Southeast uses a perpetual inventory system.
- All purchases are recorded ***net*** of available cash discounts.
- Transportation costs on inbound shipments of merchandise are debited to a Transportation-in account, which in the income statement is combined with the cost of goods sold.
- All credit sales are made on terms 2/10, n/30 and are recorded at the full invoice price.
- The liability for sales taxes payable is recorded at the time of sale.

INSTRUCTIONS

Indicate the effects of each of these transactions upon the following elements of the company's financial statements. Organize your answer in tabular form, using the following column headings. (Notice that the cost of goods sold is shown separately

* *Supplemental Topic A, "Additional Merchandising Transactions"*

from all other expenses.) Use the code letters ***I*** for increase, ***D*** for decrease, and ***NE*** for no effect.

	Income Statement				Balance Sheet		
Transaction	*Net Sales –*	*Cost of Goods Sold –*	*All Other Expenses =*	*Net Income*	*Assets =*	*Liabilities +*	*Owner's Equity*
a							

***PROBLEM 5-11**
Cash Discounts and Merchandise Returns

21st Century Sound purchased 50 compact disc players from Advance Technology at a price of $200 apiece. The terms of the sale were 2/10, n/30. 21st Century found two of the disc players to be defective and returned them immediately to the seller. 21st then paid for the remaining 48 disc players within the discount period.

INSTRUCTIONS

a Record this sequence of transactions in the general journal of 21st Century. The company uses a perpetual inventory system and records purchases of merchandise at net cost.

b Record this sequence of transactions in the general journal of Advance Technology. Advance uses a perpetual inventory system and records sales transactions at the full invoice price. (Assume the cost of the disc players to Advance was $105 each.)

***PROBLEM 5-12**
Merchandising Transactions— A Short Comprehensive Problem

Riviera Fashions, a wholesaler, regularly sells merchandise on account to Caroline's, a chain of retail stores. Among the transactions between these companies are the following:

Mar. 3 Sold 1,000 cashmere sweaters to Caroline's on account, terms, 2/10, n/30. These sweaters had cost Riviera Fashions $32 each; the sales price to Caroline's was $50 per sweater.

Mar. 5 Caroline's returned 100 of the sweaters because they were the wrong colour. Riviera Fashions always allows such returns.

Mar. 13 Caroline's paid within the discount period the remaining amount owed to Riviera Fashions, after allowing for the purchase return on Mar. 5.

Both companies use perpetual inventory systems. Caroline's records purchases of merchandise at ***net cost.***

INSTRUCTIONS

a Prepare journal entries to record these transactions in the accounting records of Riviera Fashions.

b Prepare journal entries to record these transactions in the accounting records of Caroline's.

c Assume that Caroline's had not paid the remaining balance of its account payable to Riviera Fashions until April 2. Record this payment after the discount period in:

1 The accounting records of Riviera Fashions.

2 The accounting records of Caroline's.

****PROBLEM 5-13**
Income Statement Relationships with a Periodic Inventory System

This exercise stresses the sequence and relationship of items in a multiple-step income statement for a merchandising business using a periodic inventory system. Each of the five horizontal lines in the table represents a separate set of income statement items. You are to copy the table and fill in the missing amounts. A net loss in the right-hand column is to be indicated by placing brackets before and after the amount, as for example, in line **e** (25,000).

* *Supplemental Topic A, "Additional Merchandising Transactions"*

** *Supplemental Topic B, "More about Periodic Inventory System"*

	Net Sales	Beginning Inventory	Net Purchases	Ending Inventory	Cost of Goods Sold	Gross Profit	Expenses	Net Income or (Loss)
a	300,000	95,000	130,000	44,000	?	119,000	90,000	?
b	600,000	90,000	340,000	?	330,000	?	?	25,000
c	700,000	230,000	?	185,000	490,000	210,000	165,000	?
d	900,000	?	500,000	150,000	?	260,000	300,000	?
e	?	260,000	?	255,000	660,000	225,000	?	(25,000)

****PROBLEM 5-14**
Journal Entries for Merchandising Transactions

Runners' World deals in a wide variety of low-priced merchandise and uses a periodic inventory system. The company's accounting policies call for recording credit sales at the gross invoice price, but recording purchases at net cost. The following is a partial list of the transactions occurring during May:

May 2 Purchased merchandise (running shoes) on credit from MinuteMan Shoes, $9,500. Terms, 2/10, n/30.

May 3 Paid freight charges of $45 on the shipment of merchandise purchased from MinuteMan Shoes.

May 4 Upon unpacking the shipment from MinuteMan, discovered that some of the shoes were the wrong style. Returned these shoes, which had a gross invoice price of $400 ($392 net cost) to MinuteMan and received full credit.

May 9 Sold merchandise on account to Fun Spa Hotel, $4,100. Terms, 2/10, n/30.

May 11 Paid $22 freight charges on the outbound shipment to Fun Spa Hotel.

May 12 Paid MinuteMan Shoes within the discount period the remaining amount owed for the May 2 purchase, after allowing for the purchase return on May 4.

May 16 Sold merchandise on account to Holiday Sportswear, $2,755. Terms, 2/10, n/30.

May 19 Received cheque from Fun Spa Hotel within the discount period in full settlement of the May 9 sale.

May 21 Holiday Sportswear returned $650 of the merchandise it had purchased on May 16. Runners' World has a policy of accepting all merchandise returns within 30 days of the date of sale without question. Full credit was given to Holiday for the returned merchandise.

INSTRUCTIONS Prepare journal entries to record each of these transactions in the accounting records of Runners' World. Include a written explanation for each journal entry.

****PROBLEM 5-15**
Preparing an Income Statement and Closing Entries

Listed below are the accounts relating to income of Leather Bandit for the three-month period ended March 31, 1996:

Sales	*$500,000*	*Inventory, Jan. 1, 1996*	*$170,100*
Sales returns & allowances	*15,000*	*Inventory, Mar. 31, 1996 (estimated)*	*165,000*
Sales discounts	*7,800*	*Operating expenses*	*121,400*
Purchases	*302,000*	*Purchase discounts lost*	*400*
Purchase returns & allowances	*4,500*	*Interest expense*	*7,500*
Transportation-in	*1,900*		

** *Supplemental Topic B, "More about Periodic Inventory System"*

INSTRUCTIONS

a Compute the amount of net sales for the three-month period.

b Compute the cost of goods sold.

c Prepare a ***condensed*** multiple-step income statement. Show both net sales and the cost of goods sold as "one-line items," without showing the accounts used to compute these amounts. Interest expense and purchase discounts lost should be shown after determining income from operations.

d Prepare closing entries for the period ended March 31, 1996. Only three closing entries are required as the owner, John Brown, made no withdrawals during the year.

****PROBLEM 5-16**
Completing a Work Sheet and Adjusting and Closing Entries

Westport Landing is a small company maintaining its accounts on a calendar-year basis and using a periodic inventory system. A four-column schedule consisting of the first four columns of a 10-column work sheet appears below.

WESTPORT LANDING
Work Sheet
For the Year Ended December 31, 19__

	Trial Balance		Adjustments	
	Debit	*Credit*	*Debit*	*Credit*
Balance sheet accounts:				
Cash	6,400			
Accounts receivable	16,000			
Inventory (Jan. 1)	60,000			
Unexpired insurance	4,400			(b) 2,800
Equipment	22,000			
Accumulated depreciation: equipment		6,600		(a) 2,200
Accounts payable		20,400		
Jane Hill, capital		83,800		
Jane Hill, drawing	21,000			
Income statement accounts:				
Sales		529,000		
Sales returns & allowances	21,000			
Sales discounts	8,000			
Purchases	361,000			
Purchase returns & allowances		18,000		
Transportation-in	12,000			
Advertising expense	32,000			
Rent expense	25,000			
Salaries expense	68,000			
Purchase discounts lost	1,000			
	657,800	657,800		
Depreciation expense			(a) 2,200	
Insurance expense			(b) 2,800	
			5,000	5,000

** *Supplemental Topic B, "More about Periodic Inventory System"*

The completed Adjustments columns have been included in the work sheet to minimize the detail work involved. These adjustments were derived from the following information available at December 31.

a Depreciation expense for the year on equipment, $2,200.

b Insurance premiums expired during the year, $2,800.

A physical inventory taken at December 31 showed the ending inventory to be $66,000.

INSTRUCTIONS

a Prepare a 10-column work sheet following the format illustrated in Supplemental Topic B. Include at the bottom of the work sheet a legend consisting of a brief explanation keyed to each adjusting entry.

b Prepare the two journal entries needed to adjust the accounts at December 31.

c Prepare the necessary journal entries to close the accounts on December 31.

****PROBLEM 5-17**
Preparing a Work Sheet, Financial Statements, Adjusting Entries, and Closing Entries

Shown below is a trial balance prepared from the ledger of Western Supply at December 31, 19__. The accounts are maintained on a calendar-year basis and are adjusted and closed annually.

WESTERN SUPPLY
Trial Balance
December 31, 19__

Cash	$ 16,300	
Accounts receivable	49,200	
Inventory (Jan. 1, 19__)	62,000	
Unexpired insurance	1,800	
Office supplies	800	
Land	17,000	
Building	60,000	
Accumulated depreciation: building		$ 2,400
Equipment	16,000	
Accumulated depreciation: equipment		4,800
Accounts payable		47,900
Mary Lane, capital		99,500
Mary Lane, drawing	18,000	
Sales		326,000
Sales returns & allowances	4,100	
Sales discounts	1,100	
Purchases	190,000	
Purchase returns & allowances		2,000
Purchase discounts lost	400	
Transportation-in	4,800	
Salaries and wages expense	40,000	
Property taxes expense	1,100	
	$482,600	$482,600

OTHER DATA

a Examination of policies showed $600 ***unexpired*** insurance on December 31.

b Office supplies on hand at December 31 were estimated to amount to $300.

** *Supplemental Topic B, "More about Periodic Inventory System"*

c The building is being depreciated over a 25-year useful life. The equipment is being depreciated over a 10-year useful life.

d Accrued salaries payable as of December 31 were $5,000.

e Inventory of merchandise on December 31 was $44,600.

INSTRUCTIONS

a Prepare a 10-column work sheet at December 31, 19__.

b Prepare an income statement, a statement of owner's equity, and a classified balance sheet.

c Prepare adjusting entries.

d Prepare closing entries.

ANALYTICAL AND DECISION PROBLEMS AND CASES

A&D 5-1
What Information Is Really Needed?

Always Fresh is a fish market operating on the pier near the Halifax harbour. It sells fresh fish by the kilogram, and also fish sandwiches. All sales are made for cash. Every day, the market buys for cash a few hundred kilograms of "whatever looks best" directly from incoming fishing boats. At closing time, it sells any left-over inventory to Best Friend, a cannery that makes pet food.

a Would Always Fresh benefit from using a perpetual inventory system? Explain.

b Briefly discuss the company's needs (if any) for subsidiary ledgers for inventory, accounts receivable, and accounts payable.

c Describe accounting procedures for recording purchases and sales that you believe will efficiently meet this company's needs.

A&D 5-2
Evaluating Debt-Paying Ability

You are a loan officer with Martindale Bank. Dan Scott owns two successful restaurants, each of which has applied to your bank for a $250,000 one-year loan for the purpose of opening a second location. Condensed balance sheets for the two business entities are shown below:

RIVERSIDE STEAK RANCH
Balance Sheet
December 31, 1995

Assets		Liabilities & Shareholders' Equity	
Current assets	$ 75,000	Current liabilities	$ 30,000
Plant and equipment	300,000	Long-term liabilities	200,000
		Capital stock	100,000
		Retained earnings	45,000
Total assets	$375,000	Total liabilities & shareholders' equity	$375,000

THE STOCKYARDS
Balance Sheet
December 31, 1995

Assets		Liabilities & Owner's Equity	
Current assets	$ 24,000	Current liabilities	$ 30,000
Plant and equipment	301,000	Long-term liabilities	200,000
		Dan Scott, Capital	95,000
Total assets	$325,000	Total liabilities & owner's equity	$325,000

Both restaurants are popular and have been successful over the last several years. Riverside Steak Ranch has been slightly more profitable, but the operating results for the two businesses have been quite similar. You think that either restaurant's second location should be successful. On the other hand, you know that restaurants are a very "faddish" type of business, and that their popularity and profitability can change very quickly.

Dan Scott is one of the wealthiest people in Alberta. He made a fortune—estimated at more than $60 million—as the founder of Micro Time, a highly successful manufacturer of computer software. Scott now is retired and spends most of his time at Second Life, his huge cattle ranch. Both of his restaurants are run by experienced professional managers.

INSTRUCTIONS

a Compute the current ratio and working capital of each business entity.

b Based upon the information provided in this case, which of these businesses do you consider to be the better credit risk? Explain fully.

c What simple measure might you insist upon that would make the other business as good a credit risk as the one you identified in part **b**? Explain.

A&D 5-3
Hey, You! Put That Back!

Village Hardware is a retail store selling hardware, small appliances, and sporting goods. The business follows a policy of selling all merchandise at exactly twice the amount of its cost to the store and uses a ***periodic*** inventory system.

At year-end, the following information is taken from the accounting records:

Net sales	*$400,000*
Inventory, January 1	*40,000*
Purchases	*205,000*

A physical count indicates merchandise costing $34,000 is on hand at December 31. Ending Inv.

INSTRUCTIONS

a Prepare a partial income statement showing computation of the gross profit for the year. 189,000

b Upon seeing your income statement, the owner of the store makes the following comment: "Inventory shrinkage losses are really costing me. If it weren't for shrinkage losses, the store's gross profit would be 50% of net sales. I'm going to hire a security guard and put an end to shoplifting once and for all."

Determine the amount of loss from inventory "shrinkage" stated (1) at cost, and (2) at retail sales value.

c Assume that Village Hardware could virtually eliminate shoplifting by hiring a security guard at a cost of $1,500 per month. Would this strategy be profitable? Explain your reasoning. The cost is the result of In. shrinkage not resale value
guard salary is $18,000, saving $11,000

A&D 5-4
Strategies to Improve the Current Ratio

Home Improvement Centres owns a chain of nine retail stores that sell building materials, hardware, and garden supplies. In early October, the company's current ratio is 1.7 to 1. This is about normal for the company but is lower than the current ratios of several large competitors. Management feels that to qualify for the best credit terms from its suppliers, the company's year-end balance sheet should indicate a current ratio of at least 2 to 1.

INSTRUCTIONS

a Indicate whether taking each of the following actions would increase or decrease the company's current ratio. Explain your reasoning.

1 Pay some of the company's current liabilities.

2 Purchase large amounts of inventory on account.

3 Offer credit customers a special discount if they pay their account balance prior to year-end.

b Propose several other ***legitimate*** steps that management might take to increase the company's current ratio prior to year-end.

A&D 5-5
What Am I Getting Myself Into?

Megan DeLong, an experienced engineer, is considering buying Taichung Engineering Company at year-end from its current owner, Jack Peterson. Taichung Engineering Company, a sole proprietorship, has been a profitable business, earning about \$70,000 to \$75,000 each year. DeLong is certain she could operate the business just as profitably. The principal activity of the business has been the performance of engineering studies for government agencies interested in the development of air and water pollution control programs.

Peterson has agreed to sell the business for "what he has in it"—namely, \$200,000. DeLong comes to you with the balance sheet of Taichung Engineering Company, which follows, and asks your advice about buying the business.

TAICHUNG ENGINEERING COMPANY
Balance Sheet
December 31, 19__

Assets		*Liabilities & Owner's Equity*	
Cash	\$ 40,500	Notes Payable	\$ 60,000
Government contract receivable	110,000	Accounts payable	20,600
Other contracts receivable	21,500	Wages payable	5,400
Equipment (net of depreciation)	76,000	J. Peterson, capital	200,000
Patents	38,000		
Total assets	\$286,000	Total liabilities & owner's equity	\$286,000

DeLong immediately points out, as evidence of the firm's solvency, that the current ratio for Taichung Engineering is 2 to 1. In discussing the specific items on the balance sheet, you find that the patents were recently purchased by Taichung, and DeLong believes them to be worth their \$38,000 cost. The notes payable liability consists of one note to the manufacturer of the equipment owned by Taichung, which Peterson had incurred five years ago to finance the purchase of the equipment. The note becomes payable, however, in February of the coming year. The accounts payable all will become due within 30 to 60 days.

Since DeLong does not have enough cash to buy Peterson's equity in the business, she is considering the following terms of purchase: (1) Peterson will withdraw all the cash from the business, thus reducing his equity to \$159,500, (2) Peterson will also keep the \$110,000 receivable from the government, leaving his equity in the business at \$49,500, and (3) by borrowing heavily, DeLong thinks she can raise \$49,500 in cash, which she will pay to Peterson for his remaining equity. DeLong will assume the existing liabilities of the business.

INSTRUCTIONS DeLong wants you to write her a memorandum explaining what problems she may encounter if she purchases the business as planned. (Support your answer with proper analyses.)

***A&D 5-6**
Journal Entries for Additional Merchandising Transactions

Diana Carpio, owner of Major Cosmos, is quite upset that her bookkeeper has misplaced all the accounting records for July, the first month of operation. Fortunately, the following account balances at July 31 are available from one of Carpio's files:

* *Supplemental Topic A, "Additional Merchandising Transactions"*

Cash	*$ 600*
Accounts receivable	*1,500*
Accounts payable	*490*
Sales	*9,800*
Sales returns & allowances	*800*
Sales discounts	*60*
Purchases	*4,508*
Purchase returns & allowances	*588*
Transportation-in	*182*
Selling and general expenses	*930*

Even though Major Cosmos prefers cash sales, the July sales, after returns and allowances, were equally divided between cash and credit. Of the credit sales, two-thirds were collected during the month and the customers were given a 2% discount of $60. Sales returns and allowances for July amounted to $800, all of which were related to credit sales. All purchases were for credit; $588 of which were returned to suppliers because of defects. Major Cosmos used the net cost to record its purchase and paid its accounts payable promptly to take advantage of the 2% discount from its suppliers. The transportation-in and selling and general expenses were all paid in cash.

Diana Carpio wonders whether you, an accounting student, would be able to reconstruct the journal entries in summary form, for the month of July, based on the above information.

INSTRUCTIONS Prepare all the journal entries (including explanations) in a general journal format, to summarize the business transactions for July.

****A&D 5-7 What Would You Expect?**

In each of the following situations, indicate whether you would expect the business to use a periodic inventory system or a perpetual inventory system. Explain the reasons for your answer.

- **a** The Frontier Shop is a small retail store that sells boots and western clothing. The store is operated by the owner, who works full time in the business, and by one part-time salesclerk. Sales transactions are recorded on an antique cash register. The business uses a manual accounting system, which is maintained by ACE Bookkeeping Service. At the end of each month, an employee of ACE visits The Frontier Shop to update its account records, prepare sales tax returns, and perform other necessary accounting services.
- **b** Allister's Corner is an art gallery in Yorkville Village in downtown Toronto. All accounting records are maintained manually by the owner, who works in the store on a full-time basis. The store sells three or four paintings each week, at sales prices ranging from about $5,000 to $50,000 per painting.
- **c** A large publicly owned corporation publishes about 200 titles of college-level textbooks. The books are sold to college bookstores throughout the country. Books are distributed to these bookstores from four central warehouses, located in Vancouver, Toronto, Montreal, and Halifax.
- **d** Toys-4-You operates a national chain of 86 retail toy stores. The company has a "state-of-the-art" computerized accounting system. All sales transactions are recorded on electronic point-of-sale terminals. These terminals are tied into a central computer system that provides the national headquarters with information about the profitability of each store on a weekly basis.
- **e** Mr. Jingles is an independently owned and operated ice cream truck.

** *Supplemental Topic B, "More about Periodic Inventory System"*

f TransComm is a small company that sells very large quantities of a single product. The product is a low-cost, 3.5 inch, double-sided, double-density computer floppy disk, manufactured by a large Japanese company. Sales are made only in large quantities, primarily to chains of computer stores and large discount stores. This year, the average sales transaction has amounted to $14,206 worth of merchandise. All accounting records are maintained by a full-time employee using commercial accounting software and a personal computer.

****A&D 5-8**
Closing Entries

Larry Moon operates Modern Boutique, a merchandising business, which has not been doing well. To relieve his depression brought on by the business, Moon took a couple of trips to Barbados. As a result, he had withdrawn $16,000 from the business during April. He was very disturbed by the following income statement for the month of April:

Revenue:			
Sales			*$200,000*
Less: Sales returns and allowances			*10,000*
Net sales			*$190,000*
Cost of goods sold			
Inventory, April 1		*$ 35,000*	
Purchases	*$166,000*		
Less: Purchase returns and allowances	*6,000*		
Net Purchases	*$160,000*		
Add: Transportation-in	*8,000*	*168,000*	
Cost of goods available for sale		*$203,000*	
Less: Inventory, April 30		*43,000*	*160,000*
Gross profit			*$ 30,000*
Operating expense			
Selling expense		*$ 15,000*	
General expense		*28,000*	*43,000*
Loss from operations			*$ 13,000*
Interest income			*1,000*
Net loss			*$ 12,000*

INSTRUCTIONS Prepare the necessary closing entries (including explanations).

** *Supplemental Topic B, "More about Periodic Inventory System"*

CHAPTER

6 Accounting Systems, Internal Control, and Audits

In the first part of this chapter we discuss various techniques for speeding up the operation of an accounting system to meet the needs of a sizable business organization. Emphasis is placed upon such concepts as special journals, data bases, and on-line systems. Manual special journals are presented in the Supplemental Topic section. In the second section of the chapter, we explore the topic of internal control. After explaining the relationship between internal control and accounting, we discuss several methods of achieving strong internal control. The chapter concludes with a discussion of the nature and purposes of financial audits, reviews, and operational audits.

Learning Objectives

After studying this chapter you should be able to:

1 *Explain why the structure of the accounting system varies from one organization to the next.*

2 *Define special journals and explain the reasons for their use.*

3 *Describe a data base and explain its usefulness.*

4 *Code transaction data so that they may be classified using alternative criteria.*

5 *Describe the objectives of internal controls.*

6 *Identify several specific policies and procedures (measures) useful in achieving strong internal control.*

7 *Explain the role of purchase orders and receiving reports in verifying a purchase invoice.*

8 *Distinguish between employee fraud and management fraud.*

9 *Explain the nature and purposes of financial audits, reviews, and operational audits.*

*10 *Explain why the types and formats of manual special journals vary from one business to the next.*

*11 *Record transactions in an appropriate manual special journal.*

*12 *Design a manual special journal for efficiently recording a particular type of business transaction.*

* *Supplemental Topic, "Manual Special Journals"*

ACCOUNTING SYSTEMS

OBJECTIVE 1 Explain why the structure of the accounting system varies from one organization to the next.

As defined in Chapter 1, an accounting system consists of the personnel, procedures, devices, forms, and records used by an entity to develop accounting information and to communicate this information to decision makers. The structure and capabilities of these systems vary greatly from one organization to the next. Accounting systems in common use range from simple manual systems that are operated entirely by the business owner, to highly sophisticated systems that make use of computers, communication satellites, and a large staff of professional accountants. In every case, however, the basic purpose of the accounting system remains the same: ***to meet the organization's needs for accounting information as efficiently as possible.***

Many factors affect the structure of the accounting system within a particular organization. Among the most important are (1) the company's needs for accounting information and (2) the resources available for operation of the system.

Determining a Company's Information Needs

The types of accounting information that a company must generate vary with such factors as the size of the organization, whether it is publicly owned, and the philosophy of management. The need for some types of accounting information may be prescribed by law. For example, income tax regulations require every corporation to have an accounting system that can measure the company's taxable income and explain the nature and source of every item in the company's income tax return. Corporate and securities laws require publicly owned companies to prepare financial statements in conformity with generally accepted accounting principles. These statements must be filed with the regulatory authorities and distributed to shareholders.

Other types of accounting information are required as matters of practical necessity. For example, every business needs to know the amounts receivable from each customer and the amounts owed to each creditor.

Although much accounting information clearly is essential to business operations, management still has many choices as to the types and amount of accounting information to be developed. For example, should the accounting system of a department store measure separately the sales of each department and of each line of merchandise? The answer to such questions depends upon the ***usefulness*** of this information and the ***cost*** of developing it.

The Cost of Producing Accounting Information

Accounting systems should be ***cost-effective***—that is, the value of the information produced should ***exceed the cost*** of producing it. Management has little choice but to produce the types of accounting reports required by law. In other cases, however, management may use cost-effectiveness as the criterion for deciding whether or not to produce the information.[1]

[1] The FASB in the United States considers cost-effectiveness as one criterion in the formulation of new accounting standards. The Board also has eliminated some reporting requirements for which it considered the cost of compliance to exceed the benefits.

In recent years, the development and installation of computer-based accounting systems have increased greatly the types and amounts of accounting information that can be produced in a cost-effective manner. In many cases, the installation of a computer-based system increases the amount of accounting information available to management and also ***reduces*** the cost of operating the accounting system.

Basic Functions of an Accounting System

In developing information about the financial position of a business and the results of its operations, every accounting system performs the following basic functions:

1 ***Record*** the effects of business transactions.

2 ***Classify*** the effects of similar transactions in a manner that permits development of the various totals and subtotals needed in business operations and for external reporting purposes.

3 ***Summarize and communicate*** the data contained in the system in a manner useful to decision makers.

The differences in accounting systems arise primarily in the manner, speed, and extent of detail with which these functions are performed.

In most of our textbook illustrations, we assume the use of a manual accounting system. In this system, transactions are recorded in a general journal, classified in both general and subsidiary ledger accounts, and summarized in the financial statements and various other schedules and reports. While such a system is useful in illustrating basic accounting concepts, it is too slow and cumbersome to meet the needs of a large business organization.

In a large business, transactions may occur at a rate of several hundred or several thousand per hour. To keep pace with such a rapid flow of accounting information, these companies must use computer-based accounting systems. Many small businesses continue to use manual accounting systems. However, these companies usually modify their accounting systems to process accounting information as quickly and efficiently as possible.

Design of Accounting Systems

The design of accounting systems is an area of specialization within the field of accounting. Large businesses have a staff of systems analysts, internal auditors, and other professionals who work full time in designing and improving the accounting system. Medium-size companies often hire a public accounting firm to design or update their systems. Small businesses with limited resources usually purchase one of the many "packaged" accounting systems specially designed for small companies in a particular line of business. These packaged systems are available through many office supply stores, computer stores, and bookkeeping services.

We will now address the challenge of speeding up an accounting system to process information quickly and efficiently. We also will discuss how the system may be expanded to provide management with useful and detailed information about business operations.

Recording Business Transactions: The Need for Special Journals

*OBJECTIVE 2 **Define special journals and explain the reasons for their use.***

A journal is sometimes called a "book of original entry," because the journal is the accounting record in which the effects of transactions are first recorded within the accounting system. In our preceding chapters, we have been using a general journal to illustrate the recording of transactions. Journals, however, come in many different forms. In fact, many journals are ***machines*** rather than paper accounting records.

Characteristics of a General Journal The general journal is unique among journals, because it may be used to record ***any type*** of business transaction. The flexibility of a general journal makes it ideal for use in textbook illustrations. However, this flexibility also makes a general journal a relatively inefficient device for recording large numbers of routine transactions.

Recording all transactions in a general journal simply is not cost-effective. First, every entry in a general journal involves quite a bit of writing—at least two account titles, two dollar amounts, and a written explanation. Also, if all types of business transactions are recorded in a single journal, the person maintaining this journal must be a highly skilled accountant. For an accounting system to be cost-effective, routine transactions must be recorded by clerical personnel or by machines—not by professional accountants.

Special Journals Most businesses are able to speed up and simplify the recording process by designing various ***special journals.*** Each special journal is an accounting record or device designed for recording ***a particular type of transaction*** quickly and efficiently. As only one type of transaction is recorded in each special journal, the person maintaining this journal need not be an expert in accounting.

Two concepts enter into the design of an efficient special journal. First, the person recording the transaction should have to enter ***as little data as possible.*** Second, the recording of transactions should be ***combined with other essential business activities*** in a manner that minimizes the time and effort involved in accounting functions.

"RRRrrrring!" It's a Special Journal The old-fashioned mechanical cash register provides a familiar example of a special journal. As the salesclerk or cashier "rings up" each cash sale, the dollar amount is printed on a tape within the cash register. This tape provides a record of each cash sale.

Let us now identify some of the ways in which a cash register reduces the time and cost of recording transactions. First, notice that ***no accounting personnel*** are involved in recording the numerous cash sales—these transactions are recorded by the company's salesclerks as they accept payment and make change. Also notice how quickly the transactions are recorded. The only data that the salesclerk records on the cash register is the dollar amount of the sale. Ledger account titles and written explanations are not necessary, because ***every*** transaction recorded on the register is a cash sale.

The use of a cash register also saves time in posting the effects of transactions to the ledger. At the end of each day, only the ***total*** appearing at the end of the register tape is posted to the ledger (as a debit to Cash and a credit to Sales). This total amount may represent the overall effects of hundreds—perhaps thousands—of individual transactions.[2]

Point-of-Sale Terminals: A More Efficient Special Journal Modern ***point-of-sale*** terminals (cash registers tied into computer systems) are even more efficient special journals than the old-fashioned cash registers. With a point-of-sale terminal, data entry is reduced to a minimum and the need for manual posting is eliminated entirely. The salesclerk passes the merchandise over an optical scanner; this scanner reads a "product code" attached to the merchandise and enters the code into the computer system. Using this product code, the computer determines the cost and sales price of the merchandise from computer-based files, records the sale and the cost of goods sold, and updates the related general ledger accounts and also the inventory subsidiary ledger.

When sales are made on account, the salesclerk records the credit card number by either "reading" the credit card with the scanner or by entering the customer's credit card number into the terminal. This number identifies the customer to the computer, and the computer automatically updates the accounts receivable subsidiary ledger.

On-Line, Real-Time Systems In an on-line, real-time ***(OLRT)*** computer system, the accounting records are updated instantly for certain business transactions. The OLRT concept requires that transactions be recorded through an ***on-line*** input device ***as the transactions occur.*** An input device is "on-line" when it has direct and immediate access to the computer-based accounting records.

Point-of-sale terminals are on-line. When sales are recorded on these terminals, the general ledger and subsidiary ledger accounts are updated immediately.

An OLRT system allows managers and other company personnel to view through computer terminals accounting information that is ***absolutely current.*** For example, a salesperson may determine at any time how many units of a particular product are currently on hand. Department managers can review the daily sales of their departments at the end of each working day—or, for that matter, as of any point within the day.

Notice that point-of-sale terminals are located on the sales floor, not in the accounting department. As these input devices are used only in recording sales transactions, they may be located ***where the transactions occur.*** Placing on-line recording devices where transactions occur is essential to the concept of an OLRT system. In addition, this practice may facilitate recording transactions in conjunction with performing related business functions.

Even in a sophisticated accounting system, not all of the accounting records can be kept continuously up-to-date. Depreciation expense, for ex-

[2] Most cash registers also permit the recording of sales on account. Credit sales are accumulated separately on the register tape, and the daily total is posted as a debit to Accounts Receivable and a credit to Sales. In recording a credit sale, the salesclerk must record the customer's account number as well as the dollar amount of the sale. The customer's account number is needed for updating the accounts receivable subsidiary ledger.

ample, is recorded only at the end of each accounting period. Among the accounts that ***can*** be kept continuously up-to-date are the general and subsidiary ledger accounts for cash, accounts receivable, inventory, accounts payable, sales revenue, and the cost of goods sold.

Other Types of Automated Special Journals Many special journals are machines. We have emphasized the point-of-sale terminals often used in retail stores; however, many other businesses also record their routine transactions in a highly automated manner. On-line terminals are widely used by banks (for recording deposits and withdrawals) and by airlines (for recording ticket sales). The gas meters, electric meters, and water meters located on most buildings also are types of special journals. These meters automatically record the utility companies' credit sales to individual customers.

Manual Special Journals Not all special journals are automated devices. There are many ***manual*** special journals, in which transactions can be recorded far faster and more efficiently than in a general journal. Perhaps the most common manual special journal is the ***cheque register*** found in every chequebook. A cheque register can be used for efficiently recording every cash disbursement as the cheque is being issued. If the cheque register is maintained properly, it should contain all of the data necessary to post these cash transactions to the company's general and subsidiary ledger accounts. Other common examples of manual special journals include sales journals, cash receipts journals, purchases journals, voucher registers, and payroll registers.

In the Supplemental Topic section at the end of this chapter we illustrate a "typical" set of manual special journals for a merchandising business. These journals illustrate many of the basic concepts widely used to increase the efficiency of manual accounting systems. Bear in mind, however, that the number and format of special journals vary significantly from one business to the next.

This textbook is accompanied by a number of supplemental ***Accounting Applications*** demonstrating the operation of either manual or computer-based accounting systems. Several of these applications make use of special journals similar to those illustrated in the Supplemental Topic section at the end of this chapter. Therefore, if you intend to use these applications, you should first study the Supplemental Topic at the end of this chapter.

Recording Budgeted Amounts

Up to this point, we have discussed recording in the accounting system only the results of ***actual*** business transactions. Many businesses also enter into their accounting system ***forecasts*** (or ***budgets***) of the levels of activity ***expected in future periods.*** As the actual results are recorded in the system, reports are generated showing the ***differences*** between the forecasts and the actual results. These reports aid managers in identifying those areas of the business that are performing above or below expectation.

Classifying and Storing Data in an Accounting System

Two methods of classifying and storing data within an accounting system are in widespread use: ledger accounts and computerized data bases.

Ledger Accounts

In both manual and computer-based accounting systems, the effects of business transactions are classified in terms of the company's chart of ledger accounts. The phrase ***chart of accounts*** refers to the number and titles of the ledger accounts used by the business.

In designing the ledger of any given business, questions always arise as to the ***extent of detail*** needed in the chart of accounts. For example, should one ledger account be used for advertising expense, or should separate accounts be maintained for newspaper advertising, direct mail advertising, and television advertising?

The extent of detail included in the chart of accounts depends primarily upon the types of information that management considers useful. The information appearing in financial statements and income tax returns is classified into broad general categories. Therefore, the preparation of these types of reports ***does not*** require a highly detailed chart of accounts. Management, however, usually finds more detailed accounting information useful in planning and controlling business operations. For example, management may want information about departmental revenue and expenses.

The chart of revenue and expense accounts often is designed along lines of ***managerial responsibility.*** Separate accounts are used for recording the revenue and expenses attributable to each department (or other area of managerial responsibility) within the organization. This ***responsibility accounting system*** provides top management with information useful in evaluating the performance of individual departments and department managers. (Responsibility accounting systems are discussed further in Chapter 24.)

A general ledger with a great many accounts would be unwieldy and difficult to use. Therefore, the accounts showing the detailed composition of specific assets, liabilities, revenue, and expenses usually are placed in ***subsidiary ledgers.*** Only the related ***controlling accounts*** appear in the general ledger.

Data Base Systems

OBJECTIVE 3 Describe a data base and explain its usefulness.

A data base provides greater flexibility in the classification of data than does even a highly detailed chart of ledger accounts. When transaction data are stored in a data base, they may be sorted into many ***different*** categories, according to a variety of classification criteria. A data base consists of ***unclassified*** data, which have not yet been grouped into categories. However, the data are accompanied by various classification ***codes.*** Each of these codes enables the computer to classify (or ***sort***) the data according to different criteria.

An Illustration of a Data Base We will use the sales transactions of a department store to illustrate the concepts of a data base and of "coded" transaction data. Assume that our store has several different sales departments, such as appliances, furniture, men's clothing, shoes, women's clothing, etc. Sales transactions are recorded at on-line point-of-sale terminals located in each sales department.

OBJECTIVE 4 Code transaction data so that they may be classified using alternative criteria.

The first step in designing a data base is to determine the alternative ways in which the transaction data will be used. Assume that the management of our department store intends to use the data about sales transactions in the following ways:

1 General ledger accounts for Cash, Accounts Receivable, Inventory, Sales, and Cost of Goods Sold will be kept continuously up-to-date.

2 Subsidiary ledgers will be maintained for inventory and accounts receivable.

3 Daily sales reports will be developed for the store manager showing the total dollar sales within each of the store's sales departments.

4 Weekly sales reports will be developed for the store's merchandise buyers showing the ***number of units*** of each product that have been sold during the week.

To provide these types of information, the accounting system must be able to classify sales transaction data by (1) general ledger accounts, (2) customer account number, (3) sales department, and (4) product sold.

In recording each transaction, the salesperson enters into the computer terminal a ***product code*** identifying each item sold. If the merchandise is sold on account, the salesperson also must enter the number designating the customer's account in the accounts receivable subsidiary ledger.

Very little time is required for the salesperson to enter these codes. The computer automatically reads the product codes as the salesperson passes the merchandise over an optical scanner. To record customers' account numbers, the salesperson may either pass the customer's credit card over the scanner or enter the customer's account number on a keyboard. (If no customer number is entered, the computer accounts for the transaction as a cash sale.) Thus, each sales transaction can be recorded in a few seconds.

"Fields" of Information The computer places each of the codes entered through the terminal in a separate space called a ***data field.*** All of the data fields relating to a given sales transaction are linked together in the data base. The data entered through the terminal enables the computer to complete the three data fields shown below. These fields may appear in any sequence.

1 Product Code	2* Customer Account No.	3 Quantity Sold
— — —	— — —	— —

* For cash sales, zeros automatically are entered in the second field.

In addition, the date of the transaction is entered in a fourth data field. We have omitted the date field in order to conserve space later in our illustration.

The size of each data field depends upon the length of the required code. For example, a one-digit field can accept any of ten numeric code symbols (***0*** through ***9***). A three-digit field can accept one thousand combinations of numeric codes (***000*** through ***999***).[3]

Recording the Classification Codes To illustrate this coding system, assume that a salesperson in the appliance department sells two Zenith television sets on account to Dave Stewart. This particular model of television set has a product code of ***218,*** and Stewart's account number in the customer ledger is ***830.*** As the salesperson passes the scanner over the merchandise and the customer's credit card, the following information is entered in the data base:

Product Code	Customer Account No.	Quantity Sold
2 1 8	8 3 0	0 2

The computer then uses the product code to determine the unit sales price and unit cost of the television sets from computer-based files. In addition, the computer records the number identifying the ***department*** in which the sale is made. (Assume that the appliance department is dept. no. 1.) Thus, the computer automatically fills in three more data fields, as shown below:

Data Fields for One Sales Transaction

Data Entered at Terminal			Fields Completed by the Computer		
1 Product Code	2 Customer Account No.	3 Quantity Sold	4 Unit Sales Price	5 Unit Cost	6 Sales Dept.
2 1 8	8 3 0	0 2	$ 3 0 0 . 0 0	$ 1 8 0 . 0 0	1

These six data fields are stored together in the data base. (The dollar signs and decimal points in fields 4 and 5 are shown only for illustrative purposes and would not occupy space in the data base.)

Using Coded Data To continue our illustration, assume that the following ten coded transactions have been entered in the data base during a given day. (The transactions are lettered **a** through **j** merely for reference. These identification letters are not entered in the data base.)

Data Fields

	1	2	3	4	5	6
a	218 -	830 -	02 -	$300.00 -	$180.00 -	1
b	130 -	000 -	01 -	$110.00 -	$065.50 -	6
c	301 -	830 -	05 -	$025.00 -	$015.00 -	2
d	206 -	110 -	04 -	$120.00 -	$085.00 -	1
e	420 -	000 -	01 -	$035.90 -	$023.10 -	3

Data Fields

	1	2	3	4	5	6
f	218 -	000 -	01 -	$300.00 -	$180.00 -	1
g	080 -	716 -	02 -	$124.00 -	$072.50 -	3
h	067 -	000 -	03 -	$012.00 -	$008.00 -	4
i	201 -	425 -	01 -	$600.00 -	$460.00 -	1
j	075 -	122 -	01 -	$099.00 -	$056.50 -	5

Note: Field 2 represents the account number of credit customers. Three zeros in this field indicate a cash sale.

---

[3] In terms of the number of required digits, alphabetic codes are more efficient than numeric codes, as any of 26 letters may be placed in each space. Thus, a three-digit field can accept 17,576 possible combinations (26^3). Despite the apparent space savings of alphabetic coding, most computer systems process numerically coded data more efficiently. We will use numeric coding in our illustrations and problem material.

Let us now see how this coded data can be classified in different ways to meet the four objectives specified by management:

1 **Updating the general ledger accounts.** Using the data in fields 3 and 4 (quantity sold and unit sales price), the computer is able to compute the total sales price. This amount immediately is debited to the Accounts Receivable controlling account (or Cash account) and credited to the Sales account in the general ledger. The cost of goods sold (field 3 × field 5) is debited to the Cost of Goods Sold account and credited to the Inventory controlling account.

2 **Updating the subsidiary ledgers.** Field 1 informs the computer of the products sold and field 2 identifies credit customers' account numbers. This information enables the computer to update the inventory and accounts receivable subsidiary ledgers for each sales transaction.

3 **Daily reports of departmental sales.** The special reports for various managers are prepared by computer routines that sort the transaction data according to a particular data field. For example, the store manager is to receive a daily report in which sales are classified by sales department. This report is prepared by sorting the transaction data by department (field 6) and then computing the total sales of each department.

4 **Weekly reports of unit sales, sorted by product.** These reports are prepared by first sorting the transaction data according to product code (field 1) and then totalling the unit sales for each product (field 3).

Comparison of Ledgers and Data Bases In a ledger-based system, the effects of transactions are classified in terms of specific ledger accounts ***at the time transactions are recorded.*** Thus, transaction data are classified in terms of the company's chart of accounts. In a data base, the effects of transactions are stored in an ***unclassified format.*** The computer has the capability of arranging the data in different ways at different times, depending upon the needs of decision makers.

A data base is not a substitute for a ledger; rather, it is intended to provide additional information about certain types of transactions. In order for the accounting system to supply financial statements quickly and efficiently, the effects of all business transactions must be classified within the company's ledger accounts. Only those transactions that management wants to see classified according to several different criteria are entered into the data base. Transactions entered into a data base often include departmental revenue, departmental expense, cash receipts, and cash payments.

Summarizing and Communicating Information

In general terms, the usefulness of accounting information to decision makers depends upon (1) the ***relevance*** of the information to the decisions at hand, (2) the ***timeliness*** of the information, and (3) its ***reliability.*** At this point, we will discuss only the first two factors—the relevance and timeliness of accounting information. The third factor—reliability—is closely related to the topics of internal control and audits of financial statements. These topics are discussed in the following sections of this chapter.

Both the relevance and timeliness of accounting information have been enhanced greatly by recent advancements in the technologies of computers and communications. Computer-based charts of ledger accounts and data base systems permit the preparation of accounting reports ***tailored to the needs*** of specific decision makers. Computers can arrange the data in the accounting system into the formats of accounting reports almost instantly. Through computer networks, electronic mail, facsimile machines, and communications satellites these reports can be transmitted quickly anywhere in the world. In OLRT systems, decision makers may use computer terminals to access information that is ***completely current.*** Thus, advances in technology are rapidly increasing the usefulness of accounting information.

Differences between Manual and Computer-Based Accounting Systems: A Summary

In the following table, we summarize the differences between a simple manual accounting system (such as the one used in our textbook illustrations) and the computer-based systems in use in most large organizations. Notice that both types of systems perform the same basic functions. The differences between these systems lie in the methods and devices used in performing these functions.

Basic Functions of an Accounting System	Means of Performing These Functions		
	The manual system in our illustrations	A computer-based system in a modern business	Comments on the computer-based systems
Recording effects of transactions	General journal (all transactions)	Special journals (routine transactions) General journal (unusual transactions) Some transactions recorded using on-line input devices	Special journals may be on-line and located at transaction sites Budgeted data may be entered for comparative purposes
Classifying and storing effects of transactions	Simple chart of ledger accounts Some use of subsidiary ledgers	Detailed chart of ledger accounts and a data base Extensive use of subsidiary ledger	Data base allows classification in many different ways Revenue and expenses often classified along lines of managerial responsibility
Summarizing and communicating accounting information	Periodic printed reports	Printed reports and computer displays Some information up-to-date and accessible on-line	On-line data may be completely current

In years ahead, readers may expect accounting systems to continue performing the functions shown in the left-hand column. The means of performing these functions are likely to change, however, as technological innovations occur in the fields of computers and communications.

INTERNAL CONTROL

OBJECTIVE 5 Describe the objectives of internal controls.

Internal controls are all policies and procedures (measures) taken by an organization for the purposes of (1) protecting its resources against waste, fraud, or inefficient use; (2) ensuring the reliability of accounting data; (3) securing compliance with management's policies; and (4) evaluating the performance of all employees, managers, and departments within the organization. Thus, all policies and procedures intended to assure management that the entire business is operating according to management's objectives and plans may be described as internal controls. Collectively, the internal controls in force throughout the organization are also called the internal control structure or the system of internal control.

Relationship between Accounting System and Internal Control

The primary objective of an accounting system is to provide useful financial information to decision makers. The objective of internal control is to keep the business "on track," operating in accordance with the objectives and plans of management. These two systems are closely related; in fact, each depends greatly upon the other.

The accounting system depends upon internal control to ensure the ***reliability*** of accounting data. Internal control, on the other hand, makes use of accounting data in keeping track of assets and monitoring the performance of departments. The need for adequate internal control explains the nature and the very existence of many accounting records, reports, documents, and procedures. Thus, the topic of internal control and the study of accounting go hand-in-hand.

Accounting Controls and Administrative Controls

Internal controls fall into two broad categories: accounting controls and administrative controls. ***Accounting controls*** are policies and procedures (measures) that relate directly to the protection of assets or to the reliability of accounting information. An example is the use of cash registers to create an immediate record of cash receipts. Another example is the policy of making an annual physical count of inventory even when a perpetual inventory system is in use.

Administrative controls are policies and procedures (measures) designed to increase operational efficiency; they have ***no direct bearing*** upon the reliability of the accounting records. An example of an administrative control is a requirement that travelling salespeople submit reports showing the names of customers called upon each day. Another example is the requirement that airline pilots have annual medical examinations.

In this textbook, we will emphasize ***internal accounting controls***—those controls that have a ***direct bearing*** upon the reliability of accounting records, financial statements, and other accounting reports. Bear in mind, however, that sound administrative controls also play a vital role in the successful operation of a business.

Guidelines to Achieving Strong Internal Control

OBJECTIVE 6 Identify several specific policies and procedures (measures) useful in achieving strong internal control.

Establish Clear Lines of Responsibility Every organization should indicate clearly the persons or departments responsible for such functions as sales, purchasing, receiving incoming shipments, paying bills, and maintaining accounting records. The lines of authority and responsibility can be shown in an organization chart. (A partial organization chart is illustrated on the next page.) The organization chart should be supported by written job descriptions and by procedures manuals that explain in detail the authority and responsibilities of each person or department appearing in the chart.

Establish Routine Procedures for Processing Each Type of Transaction If management is to direct the activities of a business according to plan, every transaction should go through four separate steps; it should be authorized, approved, executed, and recorded. For example, consider the sale of merchandise on credit. Top management has the authority and responsibility to authorize credit sales to categories of customers who meet certain standards. The credit department is responsible for approving a credit sale of a given dollar amount to a particular customer. The transaction is executed by the shipping department, which ships or delivers the merchandise to the customer. Finally, the transaction is recorded in the accounting department by an entry debiting Accounts Receivable and crediting Sales.

If not one Person can be in charge of every thing in Accts. Cash can't → receive it & Deposit it or spend it

Subdivision of Duties Perhaps the most important concept in achieving internal control is an appropriate subdivision—or separation—of duties. Responsibilities should be assigned so that ***no one person or department handles a transaction completely from beginning to end.*** When duties are divided in this manner, the work of one employee serves to verify that of another and any errors that occur tend to be detected promptly.

To illustrate this concept, let us review the typical procedures followed by a wholesaler in processing a credit sale. The sales department of the company is responsible for securing the order from the customer; the credit department must approve the customer's credit before the order is filled; the stock room assembles the goods ordered; the shipping department packs and ships the goods; the billing department prepares the sales invoice; and the accounting department records the transaction.

Each department receives written evidence of the action by the other departments and reviews the documents describing the transaction to see that the actions taken correspond in all details. The shipping department, for instance, does not release the merchandise until after the credit department has approved the customer as a credit risk. The accounting department does not record the sale until it has received documentary evidence that (1) an order was received from a customer, (2) the extension of credit was approved, (3) the merchandise was shipped to the customer, and (4) a sales invoice was prepared and mailed to the customer.

PORTION OF AN ORGANIZATION CHART

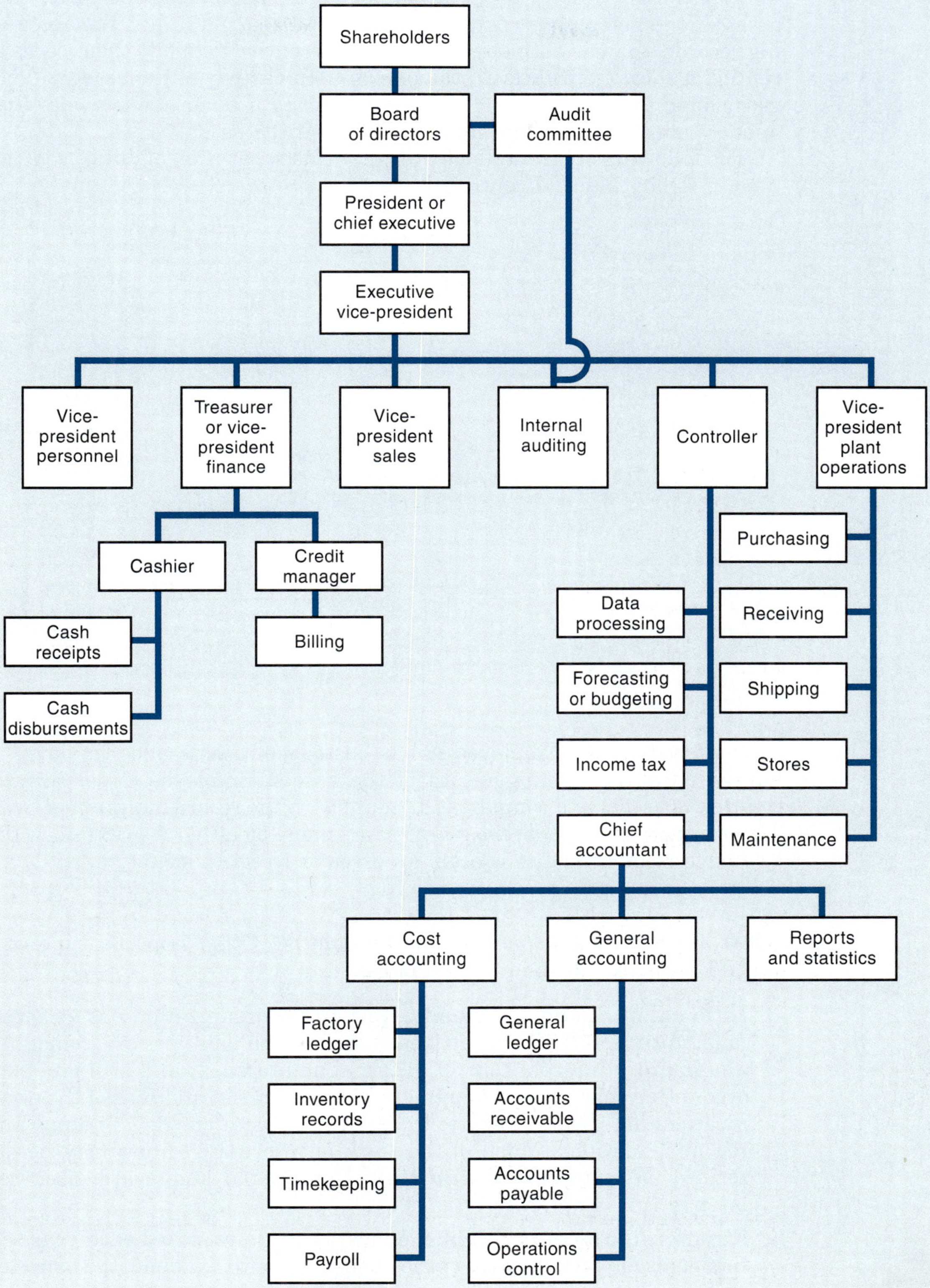

Accounting Function Separate from Custody of Assets Basic to the separation of duties is the concept that an employee who has custody of an asset (or access to an asset) should not maintain the accounting record for that asset. If one person has custody of assets and also maintains the accounting records, there is both opportunity and incentive to falsify the records to conceal a shortage. However, the person with custody of the asset will not be inclined to waste it, steal it, or give it away if he or she is aware that another employee is maintaining a record of the asset.

The following diagram illustrates how this separation of duties contributes to strong internal control.

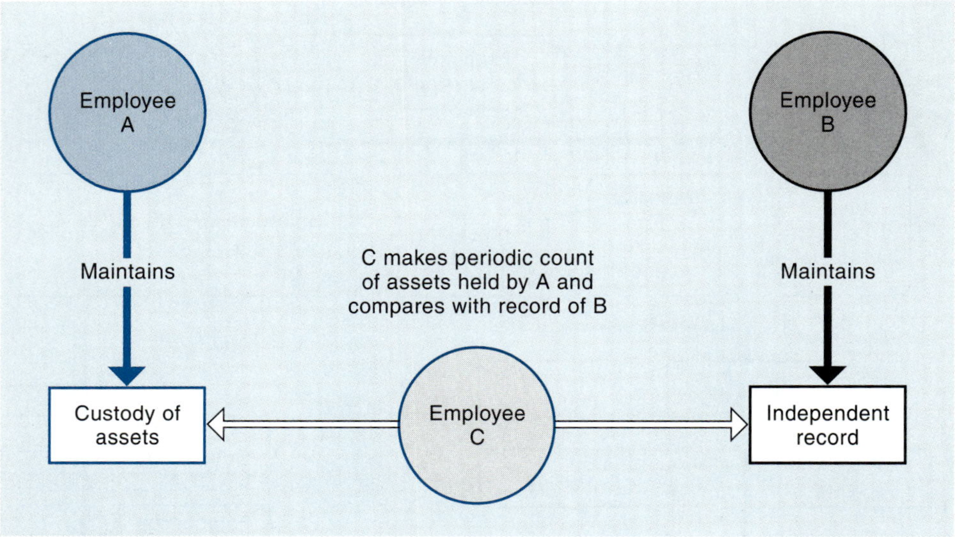

In this diagram Employee A has custody of assets and Employee B maintains an accounting record of the assets. Employee C periodically counts the assets and compares the count with the record maintained by B. This comparison should reveal any errors made by either A or B unless the two have collaborated to conceal an error or irregularity.

Other Steps Toward Achieving Internal Control Other important internal control measures include the following:

1 **Internal auditing.** Virtually every ***large*** organization has an internal auditing staff. The objectives of the internal auditors are to monitor and improve internal control. Internal auditors test and evaluate both accounting controls and administrative controls in all areas of the organization and prepare reports to top management on their findings and recommendations. Much of the work of internal auditors may be described as ***operational auditing.*** Operational audits are discussed later in this chapter.

2 **Financial forecasts.** A plan of operations is prepared each year setting goals for each division of the business, as, for example, the expected

volume of sales, amounts of expenses, and future cash balances. ***Actual*** results are compared with ***forecast*** amounts month by month. This comparison strengthens control because variations from planned results are investigated promptly.

3 **Competent personnel.** Even the best-designed internal control will not work well unless the people using it are competent. Competence of employees is in part developed through training programs, but it is also related to the policies for selection of personnel and to the adequacy of supervision.

4 **Rotation of employees.** The rotation of employees from one job assignment to another may strengthen internal control. When employees know that another person will soon be taking over their duties, they are more likely to maintain records with care and to follow established procedures. The rotation of employees also may bring to light errors or irregularities caused by the employee formerly performing a given task.

5 **Serially numbered documents.** Documents such as cheques, purchase orders, and sales invoices should be serially numbered. If a document is misplaced or concealed, the break in the sequence of numbers will call attention to the missing item.

The Role of Business Documents

OBJECTIVE 7 Explain the role of purchase orders and receiving reports in verifying a purchase invoice.

We have made the point that strong internal control requires subdivision of duties among the departments of the business. How does each department know that the other departments have fulfilled their responsibilities? The answer lies in the use of carefully designed ***business documents.*** Some of the more important business documents used in controlling purchases of merchandise are summarized below:

Business Document	Initiated by	Sent to
Purchase requisition		
Issued when quantity of goods on hand falls below established reorder point	*Departmental sales managers or stores department*	*Original to purchasing department, copy to accounting department*
Purchase order		
Issued when order is placed; indicates type, quantities, and prices of merchandise ordered	*Purchasing department*	*Original to selling company (vendor, supplier), copies to department requisitioning goods and the accounting department*
Invoice		
Confirms that goods have been shipped and requests payment	*Seller (supplier)*	*Accounting department of buying company*

Business Document	Initiated by	Sent to
Receiving report		
Based on count and inspection of goods received	*Receiving department of buying company*	*Original to accounting department, copies to purchasing department and to department requisitioning goods*
Invoice approval form		
Based upon the documents listed above; authorizes payment of the purchase invoice	*Accounting department of buying company*	*Finance department, to support issuance of cheque Returned to accounting department with a copy of the cheque*

Purchase Requisition A purchase requisition is a request from the sales department or stores department (warehousing) for the purchasing department to order merchandise. Thus, the purchasing department is not authorized to order goods ***unless it has first received a purchase requisition.*** A copy of the purchase requisition is sent to the accounting department.

Purchase Orders Once a purchase requisition has been received, the purchasing department determines the lowest-cost supplier of the merchandise and places an order. This order is documented in a ***purchase order.*** A purchase order issued by Fairway Pro Shop to Adams Manufacturing Company is illustrated below:

A serially numbered purchase order

PURCHASE ORDER — **Order no. *999***

FAIRWAY PRO SHOP
10 Fairway Avenue, Toronto, Ontario

To: Adams Manufacturing Company
169 Union Street, S.W.
Calgary, Alberta

Date: November 10, 19—
Ship via: Jones Truck Co.
Terms: 2/10, n/30

Please enter our order for the following:

Quantity	Description	Price	Total
15 sets	Model S irons	$ 120.00	$ 1,800.00
50 dozen	X3Y Shur-Par golf balls	14.00	700.00
			$2,500.00

Fairway Pro Shop

By *DD McCarthy*

Several copies of a purchase order are usually prepared. The original is sent to the supplier; it constitutes an authorization to deliver the merchandise and to submit a bill based on the prices listed. A second copy is sent to the department that initiated the purchase requisition to show that the requisition has been acted upon. Another copy is sent to the accounting department of the buying company.

The issuance of a purchase order does not call for any entries in the accounting records of either the prospective buyer or seller. The company that receives an order does not consider that a sale has been made ***until the merchandise is delivered.*** At that point ownership of the goods changes, and both buyer and seller should make accounting entries to record the transaction.

Invoices When a manufacturer or wholesaler receives an order for its products, it takes two actions. One is to ship the goods to the customer and the other is to send the customer an invoice. By the act of shipping the merchandise, the seller is giving up ownership of one type of asset, inventory; by issuing the invoice, the seller is recording ownership of another form of asset, an account receivable.

An invoice contains a description of the goods being sold, the quantities, prices, credit terms, and method of shipment. The illustration below shows an invoice issued by Adams Manufacturing Company in response to the previously illustrated purchase order from Fairway Pro Shop.

Invoice is basis for accounting entry

INVOICE
ADAMS MANUFACTURING COMPANY
169 Union Street, S.W.
Calgary, Alberta

Invoice no. *782*

Sold to: Fairway Pro Shop
10 Fairway Avenue
Toronto, Ontario

Invoice date: November 15, 19—
Your purchase order no. 999
Date shipped: November 15, 19—

Shipped to: Same
Shipped via: Jones Truck Co.

Terms: 2/10, n/30

Quantity	Description	Price	Total
15 sets	Model S irons	$ 120.00	$ 1,800.00
50 dozen	X3Y Shur-Par golf balls	14.00	700.00
			$2,500.00

From the viewpoint of the seller, an invoice is a ***sales invoice;*** from the buyer's viewpoint it is a ***purchase invoice.*** The invoice is the basis for an entry in the accounting records of ***both*** the seller and the buyer because it evidences the ***transfer of ownership of goods.*** At the time of issuing the invoice, the selling company makes an entry debiting Accounts Receivable and crediting Sales. The buying company, however, does not record the invoice as a liability until the invoice has been approved for payment.

Receiving Report Evidence that the merchandise has been received in good condition is obtained from the receiving department. The receiving department receives all incoming goods, inspects them as to quality and condition, and determines the quantities received by counting, measuring, or weighing. The receiving department then prepares a serially numbered report for each shipment received; one copy of this ***receiving report*** is sent to the accounting department for use in approving the invoice for payment.

Invoice Approval Form The approval of the invoice in the accounting department is accomplished by comparing the purchase requisition, the purchase order, the invoice, and the receiving report. Comparison of these documents establishes that the merchandise described in the invoice was actually ordered, has been received in good condition, and was billed at the prices specified in the purchase order.

The person who performs these comparisons then records the liability (debit Inventory, credit Accounts Payable) and signs an ***invoice approval form*** authorizing payment of the invoice by the finance department. (One type of invoice approval form, called a ***voucher,*** is discussed further in Chapter 7.)

As explained in Chapter 5, most well-managed companies follow a policy of recording purchases at ***net cost***—that is, the invoice price less any available cash discount. This internal control policy requires the use of a Purchase Discounts Lost account that will call management's attention to any failures to take advantage of available cash discount.

Debit and Credit Memoranda (Debit Memos, Credit Memos) If merchandise purchased on account is unsatisfactory and is to be returned to the supplier (or if a price reduction is agreed upon), a ***debit memorandum*** may be prepared by the purchasing company and sent to the supplier. The debit memorandum informs the supplier that the buyer has debited (reduced) its liability to the supplier and explains the circumstances.

Upon being informed of the return of damaged merchandise (or having agreed to a reduction in price), the seller will send the buyer a ***credit memorandum*** indicating that the account receivable from the buyer has been credited (reduced).

Notice that issuing a credit memorandum has the same effect upon a customer's account as does receiving payment from the customer—that is, the account receivable is credited (reduced). Thus, an employee with authority to issue credit memoranda ***should not be allowed to handle cash receipts from customers.*** If both of these duties were assigned to the same employee, that person could abstract some of the cash collected from customers and conceal this theft by issuing fictitious credit memoranda.

Internal Control in Computer-Based Systems

Computers do not eliminate the need for internal control. In fact, most recent cases of large-scale fraud have occurred in companies with computer-based accounting systems.

CASE IN POINT An outside computer consultant for a major bank once used the bank's computer system to transfer $10 million of the bank's money into his personal account at another bank. The consultant's knowledge of the bank's computer system enabled him to commit this fraud. He had observed how bank employees used the computer to make legitimate transfers of funds. In addition, he had noticed that the "secret" computer codes used in these transfers were posted on the wall next to the computer terminal.

Despite the preceding case in point, computer-based accounting systems lend themselves well to the implementation of internal control procedures. One such procedure is the use of ***access codes*** or passwords, which limit access to the system to authorized users and also identify the user responsible for each entry. (Obviously these access codes should not be posted on the wall.)

In fact, computer-based accounting systems create many opportunities for implementing internal control procedures that might not be practicable in a manual accounting system.

CASE IN POINT When on-line terminals are used in recording credit sales, the salesperson enters the customer's credit card number into the system. The computer then determines whether the proposed sales transaction will cause the customer's account balance to exceed any predetermined credit limit. Also, the computer compares the customer's card number with a list of credit cards reported lost or stolen. If either of these procedures indicates that credit should not be extended to this customer, the computer immediately notifies the salesperson not to make the sale.

We have mentioned that in computer-based accounting systems, company personnel may be able to view accounting information on a computer monitor. For internal control purposes, these monitors should have ***read-only access*** to the accounting system. Read-only means that the computer user may view the information but ***may not change it*** in any way.

Limitations and Cost of Internal Control

Although internal control is highly effective in increasing the reliability of accounting data and in safeguarding assets, no system of internal control provides complete protection against fraud, theft, or errors. For example, controls based upon a subdivision of duties may be defeated—at least temporarily—by ***collusion*** among two or more employees. Carelessness on the part of employees also may cause a breakdown in internal control.

In designing internal control, the question of cost cannot be ignored. The internal control ***should be cost-effective.*** Too elaborate an internal control may entail greater expense than is justified by the protection gained.

Internal control is more difficult to achieve in a small business than in a large one because, with only a few employees, it is not possible to arrange an extensive subdivision of duties. Also, such internal controls as an internal audit staff usually are not cost-effective in a small business. An essential element of maintaining a reasonable degree of internal control in a small business is active participation by the owner-manager in strategic control procedures. In summary, internal control must be tailored to meet the needs of the individual business.

Prevention of Fraud

Perhaps the most highly publicized objective of internal control is the prevention of fraud. ***Fraud*** may be defined as the deliberate misrepresentation of facts with the intent of deceiving someone. If the purpose of this deception is personal gain or causing harm to another, fraud may be a criminal act. In discussing the role of internal control in preventing acts of fraud, it is useful to distinguish between ***errors*** in the accounting records and ***irregularities.***

Accountants use the term ***errors*** in reference to unintentional mistakes. ***Irregularities,*** on the other hand, refer to ***intentional*** mistakes, entered into accounting records or accounting reports for some fraudulent purpose. Irregularities may be further subdivided into the classifications of ***employee fraud*** and ***management fraud.***

Employee Fraud

OBJECTIVE 8 Distinguish between employee fraud and management fraud.

Employee fraud refers to dishonest acts performed by the employees of a company ***in spite of management's efforts to prevent these actions.*** Examples of employee fraud include theft of assets, charging lower sales prices to favoured customers, receiving kickbacks from suppliers, overstating hours worked, padding expense accounts, and embezzlement. (***Embezzlement*** is a theft of assets that is concealed by falsification of the accounting records.)

If one employee handles all aspects of a transaction, the danger of irregularities increases. Studies of fraud cases suggest that individuals may be tempted into dishonest acts if given complete control of company property. Most of these persons, however, would not engage in fraud if doing so required collaboration with other employees. Thus, subdivision of duties is believed to substantially reduce the risk of employee fraud.

In addition to subdivision of duties, the risk of employee fraud is reduced by such control procedures as investigating the backgrounds of job applicants, periodic rotation of employees to different job assignments, and frequent comparisons of assets actually on hand with the quantities shown in the accounting records.

Fidelity Bonds No internal control can provide absolute protection against losses from dishonest employees. Therefore, many companies require that employees who handle cash or other negotiable assets be ***bonded.*** A ***fidelity bond*** is a type of insurance contract in which the bonding company agrees to reimburse an employer up to agreed dollar limits for losses caused by fraud or embezzlement by bonded employees.

Management Fraud

Management fraud refers to deliberate misrepresentation made by the ***top management*** of a business to persons ***outside*** the business organization. This type of fraud often involves the issuance of fraudulent financial statements intended to mislead investors and creditors.

CASE IN POINT The bankruptcy of Atlantic Acceptance Corporation Limited in 1965, then the sixth largest sales finance company in Canada, with assets of over $150,000,000, was caused mainly by management fraud. Both its assets and net income were greatly overstated over a twelve-year period. In addition, its president engaged in fraudulent actions against the company. The total loss to the shareholders and noteholders exceeded $60 million. It had a detrimental impact on the Canadian-owned finance companies because, after the Atlantic failure, they had more difficulty raising funds in the money market than the American-owned companies.

CASE IN POINT Some years ago, the bankruptcy of Allied Crude Vegetable Oil Corporation stunned the financial world. Allied had borrowed money from 51 different companies and banks, using as collateral its inventory of nearly 2 billion gallons of salad oil. After the company's bankruptcy, investigators learned that much of Allied's "inventory" consisted of nothing more than forged warehouse receipts. Inventory listed at $175 million in Allied's balance sheet simply did not exist.

Misuse of Company Assets Another form of management fraud involves the misuse of company assets for the personal benefit of top management. The misuse of company assets may take many forms. Examples include excessive salaries to top managers and/or their relatives, and allowing managers to make extensive personal use of such company-owned assets as homes, yachts, and aircraft. Another area of possible abuse is fraudulently structured business transactions between the company and its top management.

The Impact of Management Fraud In cases of management fraud, top management is a ***willing participant*** in the fraudulent acts. One characteristic of such fraud is that management uses its position of trust and authority to ***override internal control*** and to enrich itself at the expense of the company and/or outsiders. The persons most often injured by management fraud are investors and creditors. However, the company's employees and customers and the general public also may be harmed severely.

The basic purpose of accounting is to ***aid decision makers in allocating and using economic resources efficiently.*** Cases of management fraud are far more destructive to this basic purpose than are most cases of employee fraud. The damage caused by employee fraud usually is limited to relatively small losses incurred by a specific company. Seldom, however, does employee fraud force a business into bankruptcy or affect the efficient allocation of resources throughout the economy.

When the financial statements of large companies are altered to mislead investors and creditors, however, the resulting losses may be substantial. In addition, the misallocation of economic resources may even affect the national economy.

CASE IN POINT Management fraud played a major role in the savings and loan crisis in the United States. Some savings and loan companies falsified their accounting records and financial statements to conceal from investors and government regulators their deteriorating financial positions and managements' misuse of company assets.

Ultimately, the savings and loan crisis may cost the American taxpayer—who insures deposits in these institutions—more than $500 billion. In addition, this crisis has contributed to an economic recession, federal income tax increases, and the loss of many jobs.

Management fraud is ***not*** commonplace in our society. The managers and directors of most large business organizations are people of integrity. However, even a few isolated instances of management fraud can adversely affect the economy. Whenever the management of a large publicly owned company engages in fraud, investors, creditors, and the public tend to lose confidence in the business community and the financial reporting process. This loss of confidence may create doubts and reservations that impede the efficient allocation of investment capital for many years.

Protecting Society from Management Fraud To a limited extent, internal control protects outside decision makers against the possibility of a large-scale management fraud. Internal accounting controls are designed primarily to assure ***management*** that the company's accounting information is reliable. However, top management may be able to override these controls when it comes to reporting to people outside the organization.

The limited protection that internal control does provide against management fraud arises from the subdivision of duties within the organization. Many people in management and in the company's accounting department would be aware of a large-scale management fraud. Presumably, some of these people would refuse to participate in the fraud and would "blow the whistle" on a dishonest management.

Financial audits are more oriented toward providing outside decision makers with assurance as to the reliability of financial statements than is internal control.

AUDITS

Audits of Financial Statements

OBJECTIVE 9
Explain the nature and purposes of financial audits, reviews, and operational audits.

A financial audit is an examination of a company's financial statements performed by a firm of public accountants. The basic purpose of this audit is to provide decision makers outside the business organization with an independent expert's ***opinion*** as to the ***fairness*** of the financial statements. Auditors use the term "fair" in describing financial statements that are presented in conformity with generally accepted accounting principles, that is, complete, unbiased, and reliable.

The Nature of a Financial Audit The financial statements of a business are prepared by the company's management. An audit of these financial statements is intended to bridge the "credibility gap" that otherwise might exist between the company's management and the users of these statements. For the auditors' opinion to have credibility, however, the auditors must (1) be ***independent*** of the company issuing the statements and of its management and (2) have a sound basis for their opinion. The term ***audit*** describes the ***investigation*** that the auditors undertake to provide the basis for their opinion.

As part of a financial audit, public accountants obtain an understanding of and test the internal control within the company issuing the financial statements. Such work gives them a "feel" for the accuracy and reliability of the information in the company's accounting system.

Next, the auditors gather evidence to substantiate every material item shown in the company's financial statements. For example, the auditors count portions of the company's inventory and compare these test counts with the company's inventory records. They ***confirm*** some of the accounts receivable by contacting the debtor. In those areas in which internal control is weak, the auditors must gather more evidence from outside the organization, as they have less reason to rely upon the information contained in the company's accounting system.

In addition to substantiating the items shown in a company's financial statements, auditors perform procedures to determine that these statements and the accompanying notes are complete. For example, auditors apply procedures that are designed to bring to light any unrecorded liabilities.

Auditors' Reports Upon concluding their investigation, the auditors issue an auditors' report, expressing their opinion as to the fairness of the financial statements. This report accompanies the financial statements whenever they are issued to persons outside the business organization.

Auditors also issue a report to the company's management—often called the ***internal control letter***—detailing the auditors' recommendations for improving the company's internal control. Auditors have considerable expertise in the area of internal control, as they are continually considering the internal control of many different organizations.

Audits and the Detection of Fraud The primary purpose of financial audits is to determine the overall fairness of a set of financial statements, ***not*** to detect any and all acts of fraud. Users of financial statements should recognize that auditors cannot guarantee that financial statements are completely free of errors and irregularities. Most audit procedures are based upon samples; it simply is not possible for the auditors to verify all of the transactions of a large organization. Therefore, there is always the possibility that errors or irregularities may exist among the transactions that were not examined by the auditors.

Auditors design their examination to detect those errors and irregularities that are ***material*** in relation to the financial statements.[4] We have explained the concept of materiality in earlier chapters. With respect to financial statements, an item is "material" if knowledge of the item might reasonably be expected to ***influence the decisions of users of the statements.***

Some cases of employee fraud, such as the theft of a few items from inventory, involve such small dollar amounts that they do not affect the overall fairness of the financial statements. An audit should not be expected to detect every such irregularity.

Any fraud of a scale that causes the financial statements to become misleading, however, ***is*** material. Such situations ***should*** be brought to light in the normal course of an audit. The principal purpose of an audit is to provide outsiders with assurance that the financial statements are a fair presentation. If these audited statements are misleading, the audit has failed to serve its purpose.

As explained in Chapter 1, audits are not the only factor contributing to the reliability of financial statements. Other factors include the company's internal control and corporate and securities laws. A most important element of reliable financial reporting is the personal commitment of professional accountants to ***ethical conduct.*** If these individuals do not conduct themselves with integrity, the financial reporting process may be rendered ineffective.

The importance of ethical conduct—that is, honourable behaviour—has long been understood by members of the accounting profession. The major associations of professional accountants have developed codes of ethics to provide their members with guidelines for conducting themselves in a manner consistent with their responsibilities to society.

Auditors' Liability to the Users of Financial Statements If auditors perform an audit with ***due professional care,*** they are ***not responsible*** for damages stemming from errors or irregularities that go undetected. On the other hand, if the audit is performed in a ***negligent*** manner, the auditors may be held financially liable for losses sustained by users of these statements.[5]

Although audits do not provide an absolute guarantee of reliability, audited financial statements have established an impressive track record of reliability in comparison with unaudited accounting information. The financial statements of Allied Crude Vegetable Oil, for example, were ***un-***

---

[4] CICA, *CICA Handbook* (Toronto), section 5135.

[5] In the context of auditing, ***negligence*** is a legal term that means failure to exercise due professional care.

audited. Had creditors insisted upon receiving financial statements that had been audited prior to extending credit, the inventory shortages would have been discovered long before reaching such large amounts.

Corporate and securities laws require all publicly owned companies to have their annual financial statements audited. In dealing with nonpublic companies, creditors and investors often insist upon receiving financial statements that have been either audited or reviewed before making substantial investments.

Reviews of Financial Statements An audit is both time-consuming and expensive. (The cost of the audit normally is paid by the company issuing the financial statements.) All accounting information, including audited financial statements, should be cost-effective. For this reason, many nonpublic companies have their financial statements ***reviewed*** by a firm of public accountants, rather than having these statements audited.

Reviews are different from financial audits because the scope of the former is much less than that of the latter and the level of assurance is accordingly much lower. A review consists primarily of enquiry, analytical procedures, and discussion related to the financial statements. The objective of a review is to assess whether the financial statements are plausible, that is, worthy of belief. After the completion of a review, the public accountants provide a ***negative assurance*** on whether the financial statements are in accordance with generally accepted accounting principles. A negative assurance is the public accountants' assertion that nothing has come to their attention to cause them to believe that the financial statements are not in accordance with generally accepted accounting principles. Since a review can be performed much more quickly and is much less time consuming than an audit, its cost is a small fraction of an audit.

Special-Purpose Audits

When public accountants perform a financial audit, their findings usually are made available to all users of the company's financial statements. Tax authorities and some regulatory agencies, however, frequently perform special-purpose audits to determine whether a company is in compliance with the rules and regulations. For example, each year Revenue Canada audits the income tax returns of selected taxpayers. The results of special-purpose audits generally are ***not*** made available to the public or to other outside decision makers.

Operational Auditing

Financial audits focus primarily upon the verification of financial measurements. An operational audit, in contrast, focuses upon the ***efficiency*** and ***effectiveness*** of an operating unit within an organization.

An operational audit involves studying, testing, and evaluating the operating procedures and internal controls relating to a specific unit within an organization. The subject of the operational audit might be the accounting department, the purchasing department, a branch office, or any other subunit within the company. The purpose of the audit is to make recommendations to management for ***improving the operational effectiveness and efficiency*** of the department under study. The results normally are not communicated to decision makers outside the business organization.

Operational auditing is a rapidly growing field of specialization within accounting. Current economic pressures are forcing private companies, not-for-profit organizations, and all levels of government to reduce costs and to increase the effectiveness and efficiency of their operations. Within large organizations, operational auditing is a function of the internal audit staff. Smaller organizations may engage public accounting firms to perform operational audits.

* Supplemental Topic
Manual Special Journals

Why Study Manual Special Journals?

Prior to the use of computers, all accounting records were maintained manually, with the assistance of some mechanical devices such as cash registers. Today more and more businesses use computers in developing accounting information. Why, then, study the "old style" manual accounting records?

We offer several answers to this question. First, manual special journals ***remain in widespread use—and probably always will.*** Many individuals and small businesses rely almost entirely upon manual records for developing their accounting information. Many large businesses use manual special journals on a temporary basis—whenever their computerized systems "go down." And in some situations, it simply is more convenient to record transactions in handwriting than to use a machine. Also, you will find that the study of manual special journals will ***enhance your understanding*** of the operation of every accounting system—large and small.

CHEQUE REGISTER: THE MOST COMMON SPECIAL JOURNAL OF THEM ALL

Cheque registers probably outnumber all other special journals combined. A cheque register, found inside every chequebook, is a special journal for recording all of the transactions in a particular bank chequing account. Almost everyone with a chequing account maintains this type of special journal.

If a business has more than one chequing account, ***a separate cheque register is maintained for each account.*** When cheques are printed by computer, the computer automatically maintains a cheque register. When cheques are written "in the field," however, it often is convenient for the person issuing the cheque to record the transaction in the manual cheque register contained in the chequebook. A manual cheque register is illustrated on the following page.

A special journal found in every chequebook

Cheque Register					
Date	**Cheque No.**	**Name of Payee and Transaction Description**	**Amounts Deposits**	**Cheques**	**Cash Balance**
Mar. 31		Balance			$9,875
Apr. 1	364	Mall Mgmt. Corp. (Store rent for April)		$2,250	(2,250) $7,625
Apr. 1	365	ADP Wholesale Co. (Invoice dated Mar. 22)		3,205	(3,205) $4,420
Apr. 1		Day's cash receipts (All cash sales)	$1,950		1,950 $6,370
Apr. 2	366	. . .			

The transactions recorded in a cheque register may be posted periodically to the company's general ledger accounts, just as are transactions recorded in a general journal. For example, the first transactions in the illustrated cheque register would be posted as a debit to Rent Expense and as a credit to Cash. Some entries—such as payment of an account payable—also are posted to subsidiary ledger accounts.

Large businesses generally post these entries promptly. Small businesses sometimes leave this task for a professional accountant who visits the business only on a monthly or quarterly basis. A special feature of a manual cheque register, however, is a column indicating the ***current balance*** in the chequing account. Thus, even if entries in the cheque register have not yet been posted to the general ledger, the business has an up-to-date record of the amount of cash in its chequing account.

OTHER TYPES OF SPECIAL JOURNALS

OBJECTIVE 10 Explain why the types and formats of manual special journals vary from one business to the next.

Special journals are not all alike; each is designed for recording a ***specific type*** of business transaction. The number and format of the special journals in use at a particular business will vary with the nature and the volume of the company's transactions.

To illustrate the design and use of special journals, let us use the common example of a small merchandising operation. Ski Chalet is a ski shop with a manual accounting system. Like many small businesses with manual accounting systems, Ski Chalet uses a ***periodic inventory system.***[6]

The savings of time and effort are greatest when a separate special journal is designed to record each type of transaction that ***occurs frequently.*** In most merchandising businesses, the vast majority of transactions (perhaps 90% to 95%) fall into four major categories: (1) sales on account, (2) purchases of merchandise on account, (3) cash receipts, and

[6] Characteristics of periodic inventory systems are discussed in Chapter 5. Characteristics central to this illustration are (1) purchases of merchandise are debited to a ***Purchases*** account, rather than to the Inventory account; and (2) no entries are made recording the cost of goods sold as sales transactions occur.

(4) cash payments. Ski Chalet uses four separate special journals for recording these types of transactions, as shown below:

Types of Transactions That Occur Frequently	Corresponding Special Journal
Sales of merchandise on account	Sales journal
Purchases of merchandise on account	Purchases journal
Cash receipts	Cash receipts journal
Cash payments	Cash payments journal

In addition to these four special journals, Ski Chalet uses a ***general journal*** to record any transactions that ***do not fit*** into one of the special journals. Examples of transactions recorded in the general journal include sales returns, end-of-period adjusting entries, and closing entries.

We will now explain and illustrate the use of each of Ski Chalet's four special journals.

Sales Journal

OBJECTIVE 11 Record transactions in an appropriate manual special journal.

Ski Chalet uses its sales journal for recording only one type of transaction—***sales of merchandise on account.*** If a sales transaction involves even a partial cash down payment, it is recorded in the cash receipts journal (discussed in the Supplemental Topic) rather than in the sales journal.

Ski Chalet's sales journal for the month of November is illustrated below:

Sales Journal — Page 8

Date		Account Receivable Debited	Invoice No.	Terms	✓	Amount
19__						
Nov	1	Jill Adams	301	2/10, n/30	✓	3,000
	3	Harold Black	302	2/10, n/30	✓	1,400
	10	C. D. Early	303	net 30	✓	900
	18	Terry Frost	304	10 e.o.m.	✓	1,280
	26	Nordic Ski Rentals	305	2/10, n/30	✓	8,600
	28	Nordic Ski Rentals	306	2/10, n/30	✓	430
	30	Total for the month				15,610

Notice that ***special columns*** are provided for recording each aspect of the sale. The data entered in each column can be quickly copied from the ***sales invoice*** prepared for each credit sale.

Advantages of the Sales Journal Note that each of the six sales transactions is recorded on a single line. Each entry consists of a debit to a customer's account; the offsetting credit to the Sales account is understood without being written, because every transaction recorded in this special journal is a sale.

An entry in a sales journal ***need not include an explanation;*** if more information about the transaction is desired it can be obtained by referring to the file copy of the sales invoice. The invoice number is listed in the sales journal as part of each entry. The one-line entry in the sales journal requires much less writing than would be necessary to record a sales transaction in the general journal. Since there may be several hundred or several thousand sales transactions each month, the time saved in recording transactions in this streamlined manner becomes quite important.

Another advantage of recording transactions in special journals is that much time may be saved in posting the effects of transactions to the company's general ledger accounts.

Posting Entries from the Sales Journal The posting of transaction data from Ski Chalet's sales journal is illustrated below.

Posting a Sales Journal

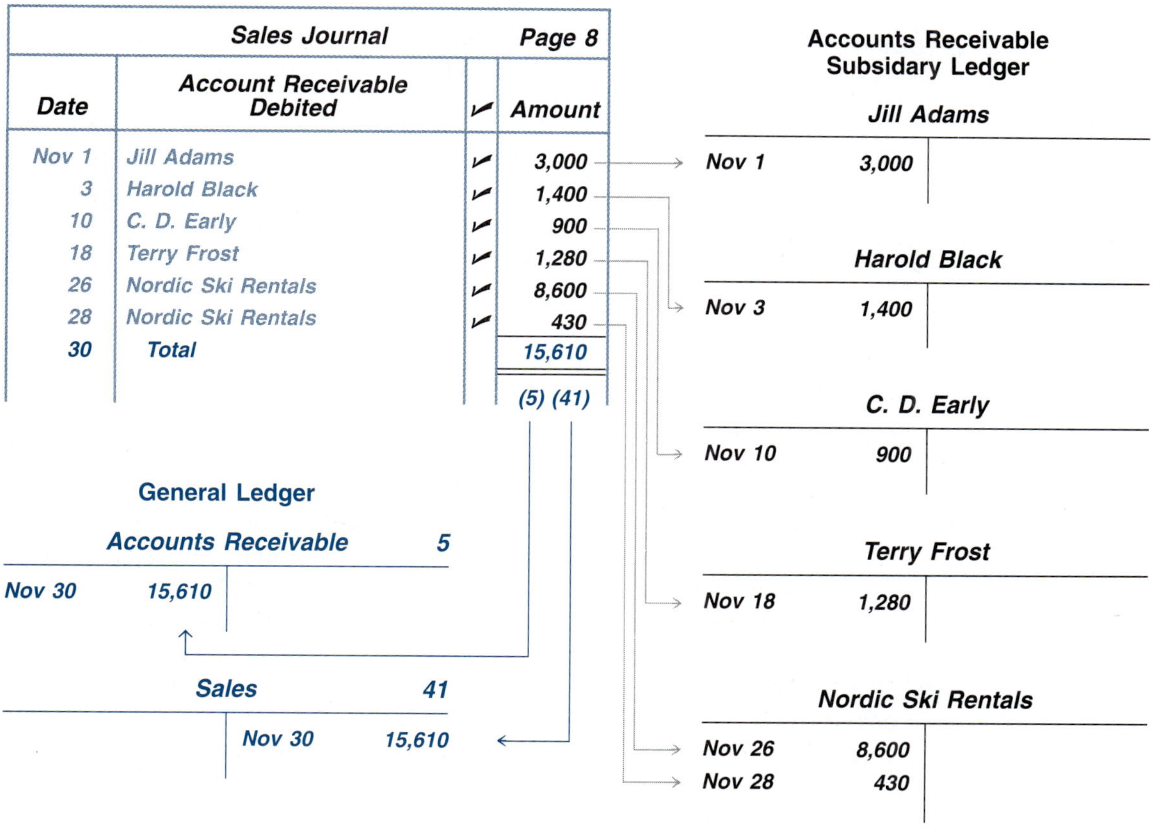

Each credit sales transaction is posted promptly as a ***debit*** to the customer's account in the accounts receivable ***subsidiary ledger.*** (These postings are illustrated in black.) Whenever a posting is made to a subsidiary ledger account, a check mark (✓) is placed in the sales journal posting reference column.

Use of a special journal does not save time in posting transaction data to subsidiary ledger accounts. It does, however, save great amounts of time in posting to ***general ledger*** accounts. As we have seen in Chapter 2, all entries in a general journal are posted separately to the general ledger accounts.

In the illustrated sales journal, however, every transaction is a credit sale, to be recorded as a debit to Accounts Receivable and a credit to Sales. Instead of posting each of these transactions to the general ledger separately, we wait until month-end and then post ***one amount representing all of these credit sales.***

At month-end, the Amount column in the sales journal is ***totalled.*** This total, ***$15,610,*** is posted as a debit to the Accounts Receivable controlling account in the general ledger, and also as a credit to the Sales account. (These postings are shown in dark blue.) The account numbers for these two general ledger accounts (5 and 41) then are placed in parentheses below the column total to show that this amount has been posted.

Notice that the amount debited to the Accounts Receivable controlling account, $15,610, is equal to the ***sum*** of the six separate amounts debited during the month to the accounts receivable subsidiary ledger.

In effect, the six credit sales transactions occurring during November were posted to the general ledger ***as one dollar amount.*** In actual practice, this one posting might represent 600, or even 6,000, separate credit sales transactions.

Purchases Journal

Ski Chalet records all of its ***purchases of merchandise on account*** in a special ***purchases journal.*** This journal is illustrated on the next page, along with arrows indicating how the transaction data are posted to accounts in the accounts payable ledger and the general ledger.

Because Ski Chalet uses a ***periodic*** inventory system, the costs of merchandise purchased are debited to a general ledger account entitled ***Purchases*** rather than to the Inventory account.

Ski Chalet has a policy of taking advantage of all cash discounts offerred by its suppliers. Therefore, purchases are recorded at ***net cost***—that is, at invoice price ***less any available cash discount.*** The two columns in the purchases journal showing the credit terms and invoice date of each purchase assist the company's accounting personnel in determining when each invoice must be paid.

This purchases journal is used in recording only one type of transaction—***purchases of merchandise on account.*** Cash purchases are recorded in the cash payments journal, not the purchases journal. When assets ***other than*** merchandise are purchased, the journal used in recording the transaction depends upon whether a cash payment is made. If assets of this type are purchased for cash, the transaction is recorded in the cash payments journal; if the acquisition is made on account, the general journal is used.

Posting the Purchases Journal Each credit purchase is posted immediately as a credit to the appropriate account in the accounts payable subsidiary ledger. As these postings are made, a check mark (✓) is placed in the purchases journal.

At the end of the month, the Amount column is totalled. This total—representing all credit purchases for the month—is posted to the general ledger as a debit to the Purchases account and as a credit to the Accounts

Purchases journal and . . .

Purchases Journal — ***Page 6***

Date		Account Payable Credited	Invoice Date	Terms	✓	Net Cost
19__						
Nov	*2*	*Alpine Ski Equip.*	*Nov 2*	*net 30*	✓	*5,210*
	4	*Backcountry Sports*	*4*	*2/10, n/30*	✓	*3,920*
	10	*Downhill Specialists*	*9*	*net 30*	✓	*1,860*
	17	*Heads & Tails*	*16*	*2/10, n/30*	✓	*2,450*
	27	*Quick Release Bindings Co.*	*25*	*net 30*	✓	*790*
	30	*Total for the month*				*14,230*
						(50)(21)

. . . posting procedures

General Ledger

Purchases — ***50***

Nov 30	*14,230*		

Accounts Payable — ***21***

		Nov 30	*14,230*

Accounts Payable Subsidiary Ledger

Alpine Ski Equip.

		Nov 2	*5,210*

Backcountry Sports

		Nov 4	*3,920*

Downhill Specialists

		Nov 10	*1,860*

Heads & Tails

		Nov 17	*2,450*

Quick Release Bindings Co.

		Nov 27	*790*

Payable controlling account. The account numbers of these two general ledger accounts then are entered in parentheses just below the column total to show that these postings have been made.

Special Journals for Cash Transactions

A great many transactions involve either the receipt or the payment of cash. As shown earlier in this Supplemental Topic section, the cash receipts and cash payments of a very small business may be summarized in a cheque register. Most businesses, however, also maintain a separate ***cash receipts journal*** and ***cash payments journal.***

When these special cash journals are in use, a cheque register is still maintained for each chequing account. However, the purpose of each cheque register is primarily to indicate the current balance in a particular chequing account. The cash receipts and cash payments journals provide more detailed information about cash transactions and are used as the basis for posting transactions to the ledger accounts.

Cash Receipts Journal

Ski Chalet's cash receipts journal is used for recording ***every transaction that involves the receipt of cash.*** Cash receipts arise from a variety of sources. Therefore, the cash receipts journal is more complicated than the "single-column" special journals that the company uses for recording credit sales and purchases on account.

Ski Chalet's most common source of cash receipts is the sale of merchandise for cash. As each cash sale is made, it is rung up on a cash register. At the end of the day, the total of the cash sales is computed by striking a total key on the register. This total is entered as cash sales in the cash receipts journal, which therefore contains one entry for each day's total cash sales.[7] For other types of cash receipts, such as the collection of an account receivable, a separate entry is made for each transaction.

The cash receipts journal illustrated on the following page contains entries for all of the November transactions of Ski Chalet ***involving the receipt of cash.*** These transactions are described below:

Nov. 1 The owner, G. G. Nuccio, made an additional investment in the business of $30,000 cash.

Nov. 1 Cash sales for the day totalled $1,200.

Nov. 2 Cash sales for the day totalled $910.

Nov. 8 Collected $2,940 from Jill Adams in full settlement of sales invoice no. 301. Payment received within the discount period.

Nov. 10 Sold a small portion of land not needed in the business for a total price of $27,000, receiving $7,000 cash and a note receivable for $20,000. The cost of the land was $25,000; thus, a $2,000 gain was realized on the sale.

Nov. 12 Collected $1,372 from Harold Black in full settlement of sales invoice no. 302. Payment received within the discount period.

Nov. 28 Collected $500 from C. D. Early as a partial payment on sales invoice no. 303.

Nov. 30 Cash sales (since Nov. 2) totalled $18,300.

Nov. 30 Obtained a $15,000 bank loan by issuing a note payable.

Columns in a Cash Receipts Journal Notice that the illustrated cash receipts journal has several columns for recording debits and several for recording credits. Providing a separate column for debit or credit entries to a specific account ***speeds up*** both the recording and posting of these entries.

An entry is recorded in a special column merely by entering the dollar amount; it is not necessary to write the account title, as all entries in the column affect the same account. Also, all of the entries in a specific column

---

[7] To conserve space, our illustration includes daily entries for cash sales only on the first two days of the month. The remaining cash sales for the month are summarized in a single entry dated November 30.

Includes all transactions involving receipt of cash

Cash Receipts Journal

Page 7

Date		Explanation	Debits: Cash	Debits: Sales Discounts	Debits: Other Accounts: Name	Debits: Other Accounts: LP	Debits: Other Accounts: Amount	Account Credited	Credits: Accounts Receivable: ✓	Credits: Accounts Receivable: Amount	Credits: Sales	Credits: Other Accounts: LP	Credits: Other Accounts: Amount
19__													
Nov	1	Investment by owner	30,000					G. G. Nuccio, Capital				30	30,000
	1	Cash sales	1,200								1,200		
	2	Cash sales	910								910		
	8	Invoice 301, less 2%	2,940	60				Jill Adams	✓	3,000			
	10	Sale of land	7,000		Notes Receivable	3	20,000	Land				11	25,000
								Gain on Sale of Land				40	2,000
	12	Invoice 302, less 2%	1,372	28				Harold Black	✓	1,400			
	28	Invoice 303, partial											
		payment received	500					C. D. Early	✓	500			
	30	Cash sales	18,300								18,300		
	30	Obtained bank loan	15,000					Notes Payable				20	15,000
	30	Totals for the month	77,222	88			20,000			4,900	20,410		72,000
			(1)	(43)			(X)			(5)	(41)		(X)

have a similar effect upon the account—that is, they are either all debits or all credits. Therefore, it is not necessary to separately post each transaction to the general ledger account. Instead, all of the entries may be posted simply by posting the column total at the end of each month.

In designing a cash receipts journal, a separate column should be provided for any type of debit or credit entry that ***occurs frequently.*** For example, every cash receipt transaction includes a debit to the Cash account. Therefore, a column is provided for recording these debits. As Ski Chalet often collects its accounts receivable within the discount period, it includes a debit column for recording sales discounts taken by customers. When cash is received, the offsetting credit most often is to either Accounts Receivable or to Sales. Therefore, separate columns are provided for recording these credit entries.

In a manual journal, it usually is not practical to have more than eight or ten columns. Thus, "Other Accounts" columns must be included to accommodate entries to accounts for which there is no special column. A computerized system may (in effect) include separate columns for ***every*** ledger account. In this section, however, we are focusing upon manual systems.

Using the Other Accounts Columns Notice that "Other Accounts" columns are provided on both the debit and credit sides of the journal. These columns can accommodate debit or credit entries to ***any*** ledger account.

Space is provided in the Other Accounts columns for writing both the name of the account and the dollar amount of the debit or credit entry. For example, the entry of November 10 in the illustrated journal shows that cash and a note receivable were received when land was sold. The amount of cash received, $7,000, simply is entered in the Cash debit column; the title Notes Receivable is written in the Other Accounts debit column along with the amount of the debit to this account ($20,000). These two debits are offset by credit entries to Land, $25,000, and Gain on Sale of Land, $2,000, in the Other Accounts credit column. (Notice that a transaction that involves several "other accounts" occupies more than one line in the cash receipts journal.)

Posting the Cash Receipts Journal Three distinct posting processes are involved for the cash receipts journal:

1 As with other special journals, amounts affecting ***subsidiary ledger*** accounts are posted immediately. In the cash receipts journal, these entries are the credits to the accounts receivable from specific customers. A check mark (✔) is entered in the cash receipts journal as evidence that each of these entries has been posted. (For purposes of illustration, the amounts to be posted daily to subsidiary ledgers are shown in black type.)

2 The entries to ***general ledger accounts recorded in the Other Accounts column*** also should be posted daily. As these postings are made, the number of the ledger account is entered in the LP (ledger page) column of the cash receipts journal opposite the item posted. (In our illustration, amounts that should be posted immediately to general ledger accounts appear in gray.)

3 At month-end, each of the debit and credit amount columns is totalled. Before any column totals are posted, it is first important to determine that the sum of the debit column totals is ***equal*** to the sum of the credit column totals. This ***crossfooting*** of the journal is an error-catching procedure, similar to the preparation of a trial balance.

After the column totals have been crossfooted, any debit or credit total ***relating to a specific general ledger account*** is posted to that account. This posting updates the accounts for all of the individual entries recorded in the column during the month. As evidence of this month-end posting, the number of the general ledger account is entered in parentheses just below the column total. (Column totals to be posted at month-end are illustrated in dark blue.)

The totals of the Other Accounts columns are ***not posted*** at month-end for two reasons. First, these column totals often include entries affecting several different ledger accounts. Next, the individual amounts comprising these column totals have ***already been posted,*** as described in step ***2,*** on page 322. The symbol ***(X)*** is placed below the totals of the Other Accounts columns to indicate that these amounts should not be posted.

Cash Payments Journal

Another widely used special journal is the cash payments journal, sometimes called the cash disbursements journal, in which ***all payments of cash*** are recorded. Among the more common of these transactions are payments of accounts payable to creditors, payment of operating expenses, and cash purchases of merchandise.

The cash payments journal illustrated on the following page contains entries for all November transactions of Ski Chalet that required the ***payment of cash.*** These transactions are:

Nov. 1 Paid Powder Bowl Mall rent on store building for November, $2,400.

Nov. 2 Purchased merchandise from Uller Products for cash, $250.

Nov. 5 Bought land, $60,000, and building, $100,000, for use as a future business site. Paid cash of $35,000 to Western Co., and signed a note payable for the $125,000 balance of the purchase price.

Nov. 17 Paid salaries of $3,600 by issuing one cheque for the entire payroll amount to Commerce Bank.

Nov. 27 Paid $2,450 to Heads & Tails in full settlement of $2,500 purchase on Nov. 17, less 2% discount.

Nov. 27 Purchased merchandise from Mountain High for $800 cash.

Nov. 28 Purchased office supplies from Office World for $325, cash.

Nov. 29 Paid for newspaper advertising in Snow Report, $450.

Nov. 30 Paid Backcountry Sports the full $4,000 invoice amount for the purchase on Nov. 4. This invoice was inadvertently overlooked and was not paid within the discount period. (Remember, the purchase originally had been recorded at a ***net cost*** of $3,920.)

Notice in the illustrated cash payments journal that the two credit columns (Cash and Other Accounts) are located ***to the left*** of the three debit

Includes all transactions involving payment of cash

Cash Payments Journal — Page 12

Date		Cheque No.	Payee	Credits				Account Debited	Debits				
				Cash	Other Accounts				Accounts Payable		Purchases	Other Accounts	
					Name	LP	Amount		✓	Amount		LP	Amount
19__													
Nov	1	420	Powder Bowl Mall	2,400				Store Rent Expense				54	2,400
	2	421	Uller Products	250							250		
	5	423	Western Co.	35,000	Notes Payable	20	125,000	Land				11	60,000
								Building				12	100,000
	17	424	Commerce Bank	3,600				Salaries Expense				53	3,600
	27	425	Heads & Tails	2,450				Heads & Tails	✓	2,450			
	27	426	Mountain High	800							800		
	28	427	Office World	325				Office Supplies				5	325
	29	428	Snow Report	450				Advertising Expense				55	450
	30	429	Backcountry Sports	4,000				Backcountry Sports	✓	3,920			
								Purchase Discounts Lost				70	80
	30		**Totals for the month**	**49,275**			125,000			**6,370**	**1,050**		166,855
				(1)			(X)			**(21)**	**(50)**		(X)

columns. Any sequence of columns is satisfactory as long as the column headings clearly indicate whether the account is being debited or credited. The Cash column often is placed first in both the cash receipts journal and the cash payments journal simply because this column is used in recording every transaction.

Good internal control over cash disbursements requires that all payments be made by cheque. The cheques are serially numbered and as each transaction is entered in the cash payments journal, the cheque number is listed in a special column provided just to the right of the date column. An unbroken sequence of cheque numbers in this column gives assurance that every cheque issued has been recorded in the accounting records.

Posting the Cash Payments Journal The posting of the cash payments journal falls into the same phases already described for the cash receipts journal. The first phase consists of the daily posting of entries in the Accounts Payable debit column to the individual accounts of creditors in the accounts payable subsidiary ledger. Check marks (✓) are entered opposite those items to show that the posting has been made. (Amounts to be posted to the subsidiary ledger accounts are shown in black.)

The individual debit and credit entries in the Other Accounts columns of the cash payment journal may be posted daily or at convenient intervals during the month. As the posting of these individual items are made, the number of the ledger account debited or credited is entered in the LP (ledger page) column of the cash payments journal opposite the item posted. (Amounts to be posted to general ledger accounts on a daily basis are shown in gray.)

The third phase of posting the cash payments journal is performed at the end of the month. When all the transactions of the month have been journalized, the cash payments journal is ruled as shown in our illustration, and the five money columns are totalled. The equality of debits and credits is then proved before posting.

After the totals of the cash payments journal have been proved to be in balance, the totals of the columns for Cash, Accounts Payable, and Purchases are posted to the corresponding accounts in the general ledger. (The column totals to be posted are shown in dark blue.) The numbers of the accounts to which these postings are made are listed in parentheses just below the respective column totals in the cash payments journal. The totals of the Other Accounts columns in both the debit and credit section of this special journal are not to be posted, and the symbol ***(X)*** is placed below the totals of these two columns to indicate that no posting is required.

The General Journal

When all transactions involving cash or the purchase and sale of merchandise on credit are recorded in special journals, only a few types of transactions remain to be entered in the general journal. Examples include the purchase or sale of plant and equipment on credit, the return of merchandise for credit to a supplier, and the return of merchandise by customers for credit to their accounts. The general journal is also used for adjusting and closing entries at the end of the accounting period.

The following transactions of Ski Chalet during November could not conveniently be handled in any of the four special journals and were therefore entered in the general journal.

Nov. 22 A customer, Terry Frost, returned for credit $210 worth of merchandise that had been sold to her on Nov. 18.

Nov. 28 Ski Chalet returned to a supplier, Quick Release Bindings, for credit $158 worth of the merchandise purchased on Nov. 27.

Nov. 29 Purchased for use in the business office equipment costing $3,600. Agreed to make payment within 30 days to Wolfe Computer.

Each of the following three entries includes a debit or credit to a controlling account (Accounts Receivable or Accounts Payable) and also identifies by name a particular creditor or customer. When a ***controlling account*** is debited or credited by a general journal entry, the debit or credit must be posted ***twice:*** one posting to the controlling account in the ***general ledger*** and another posting to a customer's account or a creditor's account in a ***subsidiary ledger.*** This double posting is necessary to keep the controlling account in agreement with the subsidiary ledger.

Transactions that do not "fit" in any of the special journals

General Journal **Page 4**

Date		Account Titles and Explanation	LP	Dr	Cr
19__ Nov	22	Sales Returns and Allowances	42	210	
		Accounts Receivable (Terry Frost)....	5/✓		210
		Allowed credit to customer for return of merchandise from sale of Nov. 18.			
	28	Accounts Payable (Quick Release Bindings)	21/✓	158	
		Purchase Returns and Allowances ...	51		158
		Returned to supplier for credit a portion of merchandise purchased on Nov. 27.			
	29	Office Equipment	14	3,600	
		Accounts Payable (Wolfe Computer)	21/✓		3,600
		Purchased office equipment on 30-day credit.			

For example, in the illustrated entry of November 22 for the return of merchandise by a customer, the credit part of the entry is posted twice:

1. To the Accounts Receivable controlling account in the general ledger; this posting is evidenced by listing the account number (5) in the LP column of the general ledger.
2. To the account of Terry Frost in the subsidiary ledger for accounts receivable; this posting is indicated by the check mark (✓) placed in the LP column of the general journal.

Showing the Source of Postings in Ledger Accounts

When a general journal and several special journals are in use, the ledger accounts should indicate the book of original entry from which each debit and credit was posted. An identifying symbol is placed opposite each entry in the reference column of the account. The symbols used in this text are as follows:

- ***S8*** meaning page 8 of the sales journal
- ***P6*** meaning page 6 of the purchases journal
- ***CR7*** meaning page 7 of the cash receipts journal
- ***CP12*** meaning page 12 of the cash payments journal
- ***J4*** meaning page 4 of the general journal

The following illustration shows a typical customer's account in a subsidiary ledger for accounts receivable:

Customer: C. D. Early					Credit terms net 30 Credit limit $2,000
Date		**Ref**	**Debit**	**Credit**	**Balance**
19__					
Nov	10	S8	900		900
	28	CR7		500	400

Notice that the Reference column shows the source of each debit and credit entry. Similar references are entered in general ledger accounts.

Reconciling Subsidiary Ledgers with Controlling Accounts

We have made the point that the balance in a controlling account should be equal to the sum of the balances of the subsidiary ledger accounts. Proving the equality is termed ***reconciling*** the subsidiary ledger with its controlling account. This process may bring to light errors in either the subsidiary ledger or in the controlling account.

The first step in reconciling a subsidiary ledger is to prepare a schedule of the balances of the subsidiary ledger accounts. For example, the balances in Ski Chalet's accounts receivable subsidiary ledger at November 30 are shown below. The total of this schedule should agree with the balance in the controlling account in the general ledger.

Schedule of Accounts Receivable
November 30, 19__

C. D. Early	$ 400
Terry Frost	1,070
Nordic Ski Rentals	9,030
Total (per Accounts Receivable controlling account)	$10,500

Reconciling subsidiary ledgers with their controlling accounts is an important internal control procedure and should be performed at least once a month. This procedure may disclose such errors in the subsidiary ledger as failure to post transactions, transposition or slide errors, or mathematical errors in determining the balances of specific accounts receivable or accounts payable. However, this procedure will ***not*** disclose an entry that was posted to the wrong account within the subsidiary ledger.

If the subsidiary ledger and controlling account are ***not*** in agreement, the error may be difficult to find. The disagreement may be caused by an incorrect posting or by an error in the computation of an account balance. Thus, we may need to verify postings and recompute account balances until the error is found. Fortunately, most businesses use computer programs to maintain accounts receivable records. These programs have built-in internal control procedures that effectively prevent differences between amounts posted to the subsidiary ledger and to the related controlling account.

Variations in Special Journals

OBJECTIVE 12 ***Design a special manual journal for efficiently recording a particular type of business transaction.***

The number of special journals used in a business, and the number of columns in those journals, depends upon the nature of the business and the volume of the various kinds of transactions. For example, a business with a large volume of merchandise returns might establish a special ***sales returns and allowances journal.***

Special Journals in Perpetual Inventory Systems The company in our illustration in this Supplemental Topic section used a periodic inventory system. Periodic inventory systems are used primarily in small businesses that sell a wide variety of low cost merchandise and that have manual accounting systems. Most large businesses today use ***perpetual*** inventory systems, in which the Inventory and Cost of Goods Sold accounts are kept up-to-date. Of course, these large companies also have computer-based accounting systems that enable them to efficiently record the cost of goods sold relating to each sales transaction.

A small business with manual accounting records can maintain a perpetual inventory system only if the company sells a ***low volume*** of high-cost merchandise. Examples of such businesses include art galleries, furniture stores, and used car dealerships.

To modify the illustrated special journals for a perpetual inventory system, two basic changes are necessary:

1 The name of the Purchases columns in the purchases journal and in the cash payments journal is changed to ***Inventory.*** Entries in these Inventory columns should be posted daily as debits to the appropriate accounts in the inventory subsidiary ledger. At month-end, the column totals are posted to the general ledger as debits to the Inventory controlling account and as credits to the Accounts Payable controlling account.

2 A ***Cost of Goods Sold column*** is added to the sales journal. As sales transactions are recorded in this journal, the cost of the items sold is entered in this Cost of Goods Sold column. The individual entries in this column are posted daily as credits to the inventory subsidiary ledger. At month-end, the column total is posted to the general ledgers as a debit to the Cost of Goods Sold account and a credit to the Inventory controlling account.

In Conclusion . . . Special journals should be regarded as laboursaving devices designed to meet the needs of a particular business. Every business can benefit by using some form of special journal for recording any type of transaction that ***occurs frequently.***

CHAPTER REVIEW

KEY TERMS INTRODUCED OR EMPHASIZED IN CHAPTER 6

Accounting system The personnel, procedures, devices, forms, and records used by an entity to develop accounting information and to communicate this information to decision makers.

Auditors' report The expert opinion expressed by auditors as to the fairness of financial statements.

Cost-effective Having economic value in excess of its cost.

Credit memorandum A document issued by a seller to a buyer indicating that the seller is reducing (crediting) its account receivable from the buyer as the result of a sales return or allowance.

Data base A "warehouse" within a computer system in which unclassified coded data are stored. Data in the data base may be sorted and classified in any manner permitted by the classification codes attached to the data.

Debit memorandum A document issued by the buyer to the seller indicating that the buyer is reducing (debiting) its account payable to the seller in connection with a purchase return or allowance.

Embezzlement A theft of assets that is concealed by falsification of the accounting records.

Employee fraud Fraud perpetrated against a company by one or more of its employees.

Errors Unintentional mistakes; one source of erroneous accounting information. A distinction is drawn between errors and ***irregularities.***

Fair presentation A term used by auditors and accountants in describing financial statements that are in conformity with generally accepted accounting principles, that is, complete, unbiased, and reliable.

Fidelity bond A type of insurance that reimburses an employer for losses caused by fraud or embezzlement by bonded employees.

Financial audit A thorough examination of a company's financial statements by an independent public accounting firm, conducted for the purpose of expressing an expert opinion as to the reliability and completeness (or "fairness") of the financial statements.

Fraud Misrepresentation with the intent to deceive. An illegal act if the purpose is financial gain or to cause loss to another.

Internal auditors Professional accountants employed by an organization to continually test and evaluate internal control and to report their findings and recommendations to top management.

Internal control All policies and procedures used by a business to guard against errors, waste, or fraud and to assure the reliability of accounting data. Designed to aid in the efficient operation of a business and to encourage compliance with company policies.

Invoice An itemized statement of goods being bought or sold. Shows quantities, prices, and credit terms. Serves as the basis for an entry in the accounting records of both seller and buyer because it evidences the transfer of ownership of goods.

Invoice approval form A business document prepared by a purchasing company's accounting department prior to recording or approving payment of a purchase invoice. Preliminary steps include comparing the purchase order and receiving report with the purchase invoice.

Irregularities Intentional "mistakes" introduced into accounting information for some fraudulent purpose.

Management fraud Fraud perpetrated by a company's management against outsiders. Usually involves the issuance of misleading financial statements.

On-line, real-time A computer system in which certain accounting records are kept completely up-to-date by recording transactions as they occur.

Operational auditing Studying, testing, and evaluating the efficiency and effectiveness of an operating unit within a larger organization. The purpose of an operational audit is to make recommendations to management for improving the operational efficiency and effectiveness of the unit.

Purchase order A serially numbered document sent by the purchasing department of a business to a supplier or vendor for the purpose of ordering materials or services.

Receiving report An internal form prepared by the receiving department for each incoming shipment showing the quantity and condition of goods received.

Review (of financial statements) Enquiry, analytical procedures, and discussion related to the financial statements for the purpose of providing a ***negative assurance*** that the statements do not seem to deviate from generally accepted accounting principles. A review is substantially less in scope than an audit but also is much less costly.

Special journal An accounting record or device designed for recording a particular type of transaction quickly and efficiently. A business may use many different types of special journals.

ASSIGNMENT MATERIAL

DISCUSSION QUESTIONS

1 What are the basic factors affecting the design and structure of a company's accounting system?

2 Identify the sources from which an organization's accounting system may come. In other words, who designs it?

3 An accounting system should meet the specific needs of a business organization. Identify several examples of (a) information needs that are common to all publicly owned corporations and (b) accounting information that management may want developed for its own use in managing the business.

4 With respect to accounting information, define the term ***cost-effective.*** How does this concept affect the design and output of an accounting system?

5 Explain the unique characteristics of (a) a general journal and (b) a special journal.

6 How is it possible for cashiers using point-of-sale terminals to record cash sales by entering only a "product code" into the terminal? Why is it not necessary to enter the dollar amount of the sale and to instruct the computer to debit the Cash account and credit the Sales account?

7 Define an ***on-line, real-time*** accounting system. Identify several business situations in which on-line, real-time information would be useful to company personnel.

8 What is meant by the term ***responsibility accounting system?*** What are the implications of a responsibility accounting system with respect to a company's chart of ledger accounts?

9 Briefly explain the usefulness of a data base.

10 Identify two general criteria (other than reliability) that affect the usefulness of an accounting report to a decision maker. How has technology affected these criteria in recent years?

11 List four specific objectives of internal control.

12 Internal control includes ***accounting controls*** and ***administrative controls.*** Describe each group and give an example of each.

13 Briefly explain the concept of ***subdivision of duties.*** How does this concept reduce the risk of errors and irregularities?

14 Suggest a control device to protect against the loss of nondelivery of invoices or other business documents that are routed from one department to another.

15 Name three business documents that are needed by the accounting department to verify that a purchase of merchandise has occurred and that payment of the invoice should be made.

16 Radio House received a shipment of 30 cellular car phones from Yamaha Corporation. The receiving report showed that 3 of these phones were defective and are being returned to Yamaha. Should Radio House issue Yamaha a debit memorandum or a credit memorandum when it returns this merchandise?

17 Briefly explain why a person who handles cash receipts from customers should not also have authority to issue credit memoranda for sales returns and allowances.

18 Is internal control necessary in a company with a highly reliable computer system? Explain.

19 Explain several reasons why internal control may ***fail*** to prevent certain errors or irregularities.

20 Is it usually easier to achieve strong internal control in a large business or in a very small one? Explain the reasons for your answer.

21 Distinguish between ***employee fraud*** and ***management fraud.*** Provide an example of each.

22 Describe the nature and purpose of a financial audit. Who performs these audits?

23 Do auditors guarantee the reliability of audited financial statements? If the statements should turn out to be highly misleading, can the auditors be held financially liable for the losses sustained by decision makers relying upon the statements? Explain.

24 Distinguish between a ***financial audit*** and a ***review*** of financial statements. Who performs these services? Who pays for them?

25 Describe the nature and purpose of an operational audit. Who performs these audits?

*26 Bridge Company uses a general journal and four special journals. Which journal should the company use to record (a) cash sales, (b) depreciation, and (c) credit sales? Explain.

*27 The column total of one of the four special journals is posted at month-end to two general ledger accounts. One of these two accounts is Accounts Payable. What is the name of the special journal? What account is debited and what account is credited with this total?

*28 FOB Variety Store makes about 600 sales on account each month, using only a two-column general journal to record these transactions. What would be the extent of the work saved by using a sales journal?

MULTIPLE CHOICE QUESTIONS

1 Which of the following factors is ***not*** a significant consideration in designing an accounting system for a business?

- a The types of accounting information that the business is required by law to report to agencies or persons outside the organization.
- b The cost of developing various types of accounting information.
- c The need for subsidiary ledgers and other detailed information in conducting daily business operations.
- d None of the above answers is correct.

2 Identify all answers that describe characteristics of special journals.

- a Less familiarity with accounting principles is required of an employee maintaining a special journal than of an employee maintaining a general journal.
- b The transactions best suited to special journals are routine transactions that occur frequently.
- c For purposes of strong internal control, all special journals are located in the accounting department.
- d Special journals are essential in an on-line, real-time accounting system.

3 In comparison with a manual accounting system, a computer-based system with point-of-sale terminals and a data base should reduce greatly which of the following? (More than one answer may be correct.)

- a The time and effort spent in recording transactions.
- b The need for internal control.
- c The time and effort involved in maintaining subsidiary ledger accounts.
- d The number of ways in which transaction data may be classified in special reports to management.

4 One means of achieving internal control is an appropriate subdivision of duties. Identify all answers consistent with this concept.

- a No one employee should handle all aspects of a transaction.

* *Supplemental Topic, "Manual Special Journals"*

b Each employee's area of responsibility should be carefully defined.

c To the extent practicable, employees should be rotated periodically to different job assignments.

d Employees with custody of assets should not maintain the accounting records relating to those assets.

5 Which of the following statements concerning internal control is ***not*** correct?

a One purpose of operational audits is to improve internal control.

b It is easier to achieve strong internal control in a small business than in a large one.

c Internal control is more effective in preventing large-scale employee fraud than large-scale management fraud.

d No internal control provides complete protection against errors and irregularities.

6 Parker Corporation has recently issued capital stock to the public and now must be audited annually by an independent firm of public accountants. These annual audits should eliminate the need for:

a Internal control.

b Operational audits by the company's internal auditors.

c Fidelity bonds on employees who handle negotiable assets.

d None of the above.

7 Assume that audited financial statements turn out to be misleading and investors relying upon these statements sustain losses. Which of the following best describes the auditors' potential liability for these losses?

a The auditors may be liable, because they have guaranteed the reliability of the statements.

b The auditors are not liable, as they have only issued an opinion as to the reliability of the statements.

c The auditors may be liable if they performed their audit in a negligent manner.

d The auditors may be liable, but only if the statements were misleading because of management fraud.

*8 Bockus Company is a small business that uses only a general journal. The company makes approximately 90 credit sales each month. If the company were to use a one-column sales journal in recording these transactions:

a The number of transactions to be journalized each month would be significantly reduced.

b The number of credit sales transactions posted to the general ledger each month would be reduced by almost two-thirds.

c Only one amount would be posted each month to the accounts receivable subsidiary ledger.

d Monthly credit sales could be entered in the general ledger by posting a single amount to two different accounts.

* *Supplemental Topic, "Manual Special Journals"*

EXERCISES

EXERCISE 6-1
Accounting Terminology

Listed below are nine technical terms related to accounting systems and/or internal control:

Internal control	*Responsibility accounting system*	*On-line, real-time system*
Special journal	*Data base*	*Purchase order*
General journal	*Debit memorandum*	*Receiving report*

Each of the following statements may (or may not) describe one of these technical terms. For each statement, indicate the term described, or answer "None" if the statement does not correctly describe any of the terms.

- **a** A chart of accounts that permits separate measurement of departmental revenue and expense.
- **b** A document used in verifying the unit prices in a purchase invoice.
- **c** A journal used in recording unusual types of transactions.
- **d** An element of a computer-based accounting system that enables information to be classified according to various criteria.
- **e** Policies and procedures intended to make all aspects of a business operate according to management's plans and policies.
- **f** A system in which certain accounting records are kept continuously up-to-date.
- **g** A business document that might be issued to conceal the theft of cash collected from a credit customer.

EXERCISE 6-2
Accounting Terminology—Fraud and Auditing

Listed below are nine technical terms relating to fraud and/or auditing:

Management fraud	*Financial audit*	*Embezzlement*
Employee fraud	*Operational audit*	*Errors*
Fidelity bond	*Review*	*Irregularities*

Each of the following statements may (or may not) describe one of these technical terms. For each statement, indicate the term described, or answer "None" if the statement does not correctly describe any of the terms.

- **a** An examination conducted by a company's internal auditors for the purpose of providing outsiders with an independent opinion upon the fairness of the company's financial statements.
- **b** A theft of assets that is concealed by falsification of the accounting records.
- **c** An investigation intended to provide negative assurance that the financial statements do not seem to deviate from generally accepted accounting principles.
- **d** Intentional misstatements within financial statements that may result from employee fraud or may represent management fraud.
- **e** A form of insurance policy that compensates users of financial statements for losses sustained as a result of management fraud.
- **f** An investigation conducted for the purpose of evaluating the efficiency and effectiveness of a department or other subunit within an organization.
- **g** An effort to deceive outsiders through the issuance of misleading financial statements.

EXERCISE 6-3
Special Journals

In every accounting system, transactions initially are recorded in some type of journal.

- **a** Compare and contrast basic characteristics of a ***general journal*** and a ***special journal.***

b Is more knowledge of accounting required to maintain a general journal or a special journal? Explain.

c Provide several examples of special journals that you have observed in operation. Explain the nature of the transactions recorded in these journals.

d Does a business with highly efficient special journals also need a general journal? Explain.

EXERCISE 6-4
Ledgers and Data Bases

In computer-based accounting systems, data relating to certain types of transactions may be stored in a data base as well as in ledger accounts.

a Briefly distinguish between ***ledger accounts*** and a ***data base*** as a means of storing and classifying data.

b Is a data base more useful in preparing financial statements or reports to management? Explain.

EXERCISE 6-5
Coding Transaction Data

The Home Improvement Centre program stores data relating to sales transactions in a data base. Department no. 7 has just sold 3 units of product no. 310 to a credit customer. The sales price of this product is $79.50 per unit, and its cost to Home Improvement Centre was $40.00 per unit. The customer's account number in the accounts receivable ledger is 1004. In the data base, this transaction is coded as follows:

1004 - 310 - 3 - 79.50 - 40.00 - 7

a Show how the following transaction would be coded in the data base: Department no. 2 sells on account 5 units of product no. 132. The customer's account number is 4699; product no. 132 has a per-unit cost of $10.40 and a per-unit sales price of $19.95.

b Prepare a brief written description of the following coded transaction. (Your description should be similar to that appearing in part **a.**)

2102 - 218 - 2 - 46.50 - 29.80 - 4

EXERCISE 6-6
Internal Control and Business Documents

In each of the following independent cases, indicate the internal control that appears to be missing in the purchaser's invoice approval procedures.

a Baxter Construction Company, a builder of tract homes, ordered 100 mahogany front doors from Anderson Door Company at the agreed-upon price of $79 each. In the sales invoice, Anderson erroneously listed the price of these doors at $97 each. Baxter paid the invoice total of $9,700 without detecting the error.

b Jet Auto Parts ordered 50 Sure-Start auto batteries from Allied Battery at a price of $20 each. Allied sent Jet a sales invoice for 50 batteries at $20 but delivered only 20 batteries. Jet's accounting personnel recorded the transaction directly from the invoice, debiting Inventory and crediting Accounts Payable for $1,000.

EXERCISE 6-7
Internal Control and Fidelity Bonds

Strong internal control protects a company's assets against waste, fraud, and inefficient use. Fidelity bonds provide a means by which a company may recover losses caused by dishonest acts of employees. Would it be reasonable for a company to maintain strong internal control and also pay for a fidelity bond? Explain. Would you regard fidelity bonds as a satisfactory substitute for internal control? Explain.

EXERCISE 6-8
Internal Control and Fraud Prevention

Golden Valley Farm Supply retained a firm of public accountants to design internal controls especially for its operations. Assuming that the accounting firm has finished its work and the newly designed internal control is in use, answer fully the following:

a Will it be possible for any type of fraud to occur without immediate detection once the new internal control is in full operation?

b Describe two limitations inherent in internal control that prevent it from providing absolute assurance against inefficiency and fraud.

EXERCISE 6-9
Types of Audits

Briefly distinguish among the following types of audits: (a) a financial audit, (b) a Revenue Canada audit of a taxpayer's income tax return, and (c) the ongoing operational audits in a large business organization. You should address such issues as the basic purpose of each audit, who performs the audit, and who makes use of the auditors' findings.

***EXERCISE 6-10**
Recording Transactions in Special Journals

Tustin Company uses a cash receipts journal, a cash payments journal, a sales journal, a purchases journal, and a general journal. Indicate which journal should be used to record each of the following transactions.

a Payment of property taxes
b Purchase of office equipment on credit
c Sale of merchandise on credit
d Sale of merchandise for cash
e Cash refund to a customer who returned merchandise
f Return of merchandise to a supplier for credit
g Adjusting entry to record depreciation
h Purchase of delivery truck for cash
i Purchase of merchandise on credit
j Return of merchandise by a customer company for credit to its account

***EXERCISE 6-11**
Using Subsidiary Ledgers

Holiday Products uses a sales journal to record all sales of merchandise on credit. During June the transactions in this journal were as follows:

Sales Journal

Date		Account Debited	Invoice No.	Amount
June	3	Jim Cando	637	3,600
	15	Hollister Company	638	8,610
	17	Pell & Warden	639	1,029
	26	Stonewall Corporation	640	17,500
	27	Jim Cando	641	3,000
				33,739

Entries in the general journal during June include one for the return of merchandise by a customer, as follows:

June	18	Sales Returns & Allowance	500	
		Accounts Receivable, Hollister Company		500
		Allowed credit to customer for return of merchandise from sale of June 15		

a Prepare a subsidiary ledger for accounts receivable by opening a T account for each of the four customers listed above. Post the entries in the sales journal to these individual customers' accounts. From the general journal, post the credit to the account of Hollister Company.

b Prepare a general ledger account in T form as follows: a controlling account for Accounts Receivable, a Sales account, and a Sales Returns and Allowances ac-

* *Supplemental Topic, "Manual Special Journals"*

count. Post to these accounts the appropriate entries from the sales journal and general journal.

c Prepare a schedule of accounts receivable at June 30 to prove that this subsidiary ledger is in agreement with its controlling account.

PROBLEMS

Note: Due to the nature of the problem material in this chapter, two sets of problems would result in substantial repetition. For this reason, we present the problems in one series, rather than our usual A and B groups. Both the A and B sets of accounting work sheets contain working papers for all of these problems. However, many of these problems also can be answered either on ordinary notebook paper or by using a word processor.

PROBLEM 6-1
Accounting Systems

Evaluate each of the following statements, indicating any areas of agreement and disagreement.

a Transactions can be recorded more efficiently in special journals than in a general journal. Therefore, a well-designed accounting system should use only special journals.

b The transaction data stored in a data base can be arranged in the format of ledger accounts. Therefore, a business with a computer-based accounting system does not need a ledger. Whenever the balance of any ledger account is needed for any purpose, the computer can sort through the data base and determine this amount.

c In an on-line, real-time accounting system, a manager may view the up-to-the-moment balance of any ledger account from a computer terminal.

d Advances in the technologies of computers and communications have increased the usefulness of accounting information to decision makers.

e In recording cash sales, a cashier using a point-of-sale terminal may record a cash sale by entering only a product code that identifies the merchandise sold. This is single-entry accounting, not double-entry accounting.

PROBLEM 6-2
Operation of a Data Base

Video Outlet operates two stores that rent and sell video tapes. (Tapes offered for sale are all new and are stored separately from the rental tapes.) The company sells annual memberships to most of its customers. Members are entitled to lower prices on tape rentals than are nonmembers.

Rental and sales transactions are recorded using point-of-sale terminals located in each store. Each tape has a label that can be read by an optical scanner. This label indicates the title of the tape and whether the tape is a rental or a product offered for sale. The data from these revenue transactions are stored in a data base and are coded as follows:

Field 1 Nature of the revenue; ***0*** indicates a rental, ***1*** indicates a sale.

Field 2 Store in which the transaction originates. Stores are coded ***1*** and ***2.***

Field 3 Member number; three zeros in this field indicates a transaction with a nonmember. (Member numbers are recorded because members who have rented 20 tapes during the year receive an additional discount on future rentals.)

Field 4 Title of tape rented or sold. Each title is identified by a three-digit code number.

Field 5 Revenue earned. For rental transactions, this is the rental price; for sales transactions, the sales price is stored in this field. No sales price exceeds $99.99.

Field 6 Cost of goods sold. This field is completed only for sales transactions; zeros are entered whenever a ***0*** appears in Field 1.

INSTRUCTIONS

a Identify the various ways in which this system enables Video Outlet to classify its revenue.

b In recording both rental and sales transactions, the salesperson passes the tape over the optical scanner, enabling the computer to read the label on the tape. Indicate for each of the six data fields whether this action provides the computer with enough information to complete the field, or whether additional action is required of the terminal operator. In each case, explain the source of the data entered into each field.

c To test your understanding of this data base, 10 coded transactions are shown below. [The numbers (1) through (10) are provided for reference only and are not part of the transaction coding.]

(1) 1 - 2 - 122 - 096 - 29.95 - 10.20
(2) 0 - 1 - 318 - 110 - 02.50 - 00.00
(3) 0 - 2 - 000 - 096 - 03.50 - 00.00
(4) 1 - 2 - 449 - 110 - 49.95 - 35.00
(5) 1 - 1 - 000 - 096 - 29.95 - 10.20
(6) 1 - 1 - 147 - 110 - 49.95 - 35.00
(7) 1 - 2 - 000 - 157 - 79.95 - 32.48
(8) 0 - 1 - 000 - 123 - 03.50 - 00.00
(9) 1 - 1 - 303 - 110 - 49.95 - 35.00
(10) 0 - 1 - 012 - 062 - 02.50 - 00.00

Although this function normally is performed automatically by the computer, you are to sort this transaction data to determine:

1 Total rental revenue earned from store no. 1.

2 Total revenue from sales of tape no. 110 (combine both stores).

3 Total gross profit earned from sales transactions at store no. 2.

4 Total rental revenue earned from nonmembers (combine both stores).

d Show how the following transactions would be coded in this data base:

1 Store no. 1 sells tape no. 143 to member no. 702 for $39.95. The cost of this tape to Video Outlet was $19.30.

2 Store no. 2 rents tape no. 110 for $3.50 to a nonmember.

PROBLEM 6-3
Purpose of Internal Control

Three executives of Jetlab, a small electronics firm, disagree as to their company's need for internal control. Jones argues as follows: "If we are going to spend money on fidelity bonds, it is a complete waste to duplicate that kind of protection by maintaining our own internal control." Smith disagrees and expresses the following view: "The benefits we would receive from strong internal control would go way beyond protection against fraud." Adams says: "The best internal control in my opinion is to maintain two complete but separate sets of accounting records. If all our transactions are recorded twice by different employees, the two independent sets of records and financial statements can be compared and any discrepancies investigated."

Evaluate the views expressed by each of the three executives.

PROBLEM 6-4
Internal Control Measures

The lettered paragraphs that follow describe seven errors or problems that might occur in a merchandising business. Also listed are five internal control measures. List the letter (**a** through **g**) designating each of these errors or problems. Beside each letter, place the number indicating the internal control measure that would prevent this type of error or problem from occurring. If none of the specified control measures would effectively prevent the error or problem, place "0" after the letter.

Possible Errors or Problems

a Paid an invoice in which the supplier had accidentally doubled the price of the merchandise.

b Paid a supplier for goods that were delivered but that were never ordered.

c Purchased merchandise that turned out not to be popular with customers.

d Several sales invoices were misplaced and the accounts receivable department is therefore unaware of the unrecorded credit sales.

e Paid a supplier for goods that were never received.

f The purchasing department ordered goods from one supplier when a better price could have been obtained by ordering from another supplier.

g The cashier conceals the embezzlement of cash by reducing the balance of the Cash account.

Internal Control Measures

1 Comparison of purchase invoice with the receiving report

2 Comparison of purchase invoice with the purchase order

3 Separation of the accounting function from custody of assets

4 Separation of the responsibilities for approving and recording transactions

5 Use of serially numbered documents

0 None of the above control procedures can effectively prevent this error or problem from occurring.

PROBLEM 6-5 Internal Control Measures—Emphasis upon Computer-Based Systems

The lettered paragraphs below describe seven possible errors or problems that might occur in a retail business. Also listed are five internal control measures. List the letters (**a** through **g**) designating the errors or problems. Beside each letter, place the number indicating the internal control measure that should prevent this type of error or problem from occurring. If none of the specified internal control measures would effectively prevent the error or problem, place a "0" opposite the letter. Assume that a computer-based accounting system is in use.

Possible Errors or Problems

a A salesclerk unknowingly makes a credit sale to a customer whose account has already reached the customer's prearranged credit limit.

b The cashier of a business conceals a theft of cash by adjusting the balance of the Cash account in the company's computer-based accounting records.

c Certain merchandise proves to be so unpopular with customers that it cannot be sold except at a price well below its original cost.

d A salesclerk rings up a sale at an incorrect price.

e A salesclerk uses a point-of-sale terminal to improperly reduce the balance of a friend's account in the company's accounts receivable records.

f One of the salesclerks is quite lazy and leaves most of the work of serving customers to the other salesclerks in the department.

g A shoplifter steals merchandise while the salesclerk is busy with another customer.

Internal Control Measures

1 Limiting the types of transactions that can be processed from point-of-sale terminals to cash sales and credit sales.

2 All merchandise has a magnetically coded label that can be read automatically by an optical scanner on a point-of-sale terminal. This code identifies to the computer the merchandise being sold.

3 Credit cards issued by the store have magnetic codes that can be read automatically by a device attached to the electronic cash register. Credit approval and posting to customers' accounts are handled by the computer.

4 The computer prepares a report with separate daily sales totals for each salesperson.

5 Employees with custody of assets do not have access to accounting records.

0 None of the above control measures effectively prevents this type of error or problem from occurring.

PROBLEM 6-6
Types of Fraud

Cases of fraud often are described either as ***employee fraud*** or ***management fraud.***

a Briefly distinguish between employee fraud and management fraud.

b Identify three types of actions that constitute employee fraud.

c Identify three types of actions that constitute management fraud.

d Which type of fraud is likely to have the greatest impact upon the national economy? Explain the reasons for your answer.

PROBLEM 6-7
An Overview of Financial Audits

Answer each of the following questions concerning an audit of the financial statements of a publicly owned company.

a What is the basic purpose of this type of audit?

b Who performs the audit?

c Why is the concept of independence important in a financial audit?

d What consideration do these auditors give to the company's internal control?

e To whom are the auditors' findings made available?

f Do the auditors guarantee the reliability of the audited financial statements? If the audited statements are misleading, are the auditors held financially liable for losses incurred by people relying upon these statements? Explain.

g Who pays for the audit?

h Briefly distinguish between a financial audit and a review of financial statements by a public accounting firm.

PROBLEM 6-8
Characteristics of Financial Audits and of Operational Audits

Listed below are nine statements about auditing. Indicate whether each statement applies to ***financial audits, operational audits, both,*** or ***neither.*** Explain your reasons for each answer.

a As part of their examination, the auditors obtain an understanding of the internal control maintained by the company.

b The auditors guarantee the reliability of the financial statements to outside decision makers.

c The auditors' findings are communicated only to management and to Revenue Canada.

d One major purpose of the audit is to determine compliance with generally accepted accounting principles.

e The audit usually focuses upon a department or subunit within the organization.

f In a large organization, these audits may be conducted continuously as part of the professional responsibilities of certain company employees.

g If the auditors are negligent, they may be held financially liable for losses incurred by decision makers outside the organization.

h The auditors are independent of the company and its management.

i The basic purpose of the audit is the detection of fraud.

***PROBLEM 6-9**
Using a Sales Journal and Cash Receipts Journal

The accounting records of Video Games, a wholesale distributor of packaged software, include a general journal and four special journals similar to those illustrated in the Supplemental Topic section. The company maintains a general ledger and subsidiary ledgers for accounts receivable and accounts payable, and uses a periodic inventory system.

Among the general ledger accounts used by Video Games are:

Cash	*10*	*Sales*	*50*
Notes receivable	*15*	*Sales returns & allowances*	*52*
Accounts receivable	*17*	*Sales discounts*	*54*
Notes payable	*30*	*Purchase returns & allowances*	*62*
Accounts payable	*32*		

Transactions in June involving the sale of merchandise and the receipt of cash are shown below.

June 1 Sold merchandise to The Game Store for cash, $472.

June 4 Sold merchandise to Bravo Company, $8,500. Invoice no. 618; terms 2/10, n/30.

June 5 Received cash refund of $1,088 for merchandise returned to a supplier.

June 8 Sold merchandise to Micro Stores for $4,320. Invoice no. 619; terms e.o.m.

June 11 Received $2,310 cash as partial collection of a $6,310 account receivable from Olympus Corporation. Also received a note receivable for the $4,000 remaining balance due.

June 13 Received cheque from Bravo Company in settlement of invoice dated June 4, less discount.

June 16 Sold merchandise to Books, Etc. for $4,040. Invoice no. 620; terms 2/10, n/30.

June 16 Returned merchandise costing $960 to supplier, Software Co., for reduction of account payable.

June 20 Sold merchandise to Graphics, Inc., for $7,000. Invoice no. 621; terms 2/10, n/30.

June 21 Books, Etc. returned for credit $640 of merchandise purchased on June 16.

June 23 Borrowed $24,000 cash from a bank, signing a six-month note payable.

June 25 Received $3,332 from Books, Etc., in full settlement of invoice dated June 16, less return on June 21 and 2% discount.

June 30 Collected from Graphics, Inc., amount of invoice dated June 20, less 2% discount.

June 30 Received a 60-day note receivable for $4,320 from Micro Stores in settlement of invoice dated June 8.

INSTRUCTIONS Record the above transactions in the appropriate journals. Use a single-column sales journal, a six-column cash receipts journal, and a two-column general journal. Foot and rule the special journals. Indicate how postings would be made by placing ledger account numbers and check marks in the appropriate columns of the journals. (You are not required to post to ledger accounts.)

* *Supplemental Topic, "Manual Special Journals"*

***PROBLEM 6-10**
Special Journals; Purchases and Cash Payments

Poison Creek Drug Store uses a periodic inventory system and the types of manual special journals illustrated in the Supplemental Topic section. Among the ledger accounts used by the company are the following:

Cash	*10*	*Accounts payable*	*30*
Office supplies	*18*	*Purchases*	*50*
Land	*20*	*Purchase returns & allowances*	*52*
Building	*22*	*Salaries expense*	*60*
Notes payable	*28*	*Purchase discounts lost*	*80*

The August transactions relating to the purchase of merchandise for resale and to accounts payable are listed below along with selected other transactions. It is Poison Creek Drug's policy to record purchases of merchandise at ***net cost.***

Aug. 1 Purchased merchandise from Medco Labs at a gross invoice price of $8,450. Invoice dated today; terms 2/10, n/30.

Aug. 4 Purchased merchandise from Alishan Products at a gross invoice price of $19,300. Invoice dated August 3; terms 2/10, n/30.

Aug. 5 Returned for credit to Medco Labs defective merchandise having an invoice price of $1,200 (net cost, $1,176).

Aug. 6 Received shipment of merchandise from Tricor Corporation and their invoice dated August 5 in amount of $14,560. Terms net 30 days.

Aug. 8 Purchased merchandise from Vita-Life, Inc., $24,480. Invoice dated today; terms net 30.

Aug. 10 Purchased merchandise from King Corporation at an invoice price of $30,000. Invoice dated August 9; terms 2/10, n/30.

Aug. 10 Issued cheque no. 631 for $7,105 to Medco Labs in settlement of balance resulting from purchase of August 1 and purchase return of August 5.

Aug. 18 Issued cheque no. 632 to Alishan Products for $19,300, in payment of the August 3 invoice. This invoice temporarily had been misplaced, and Poison Creek failed to make payment in time to take advantage of the 2% cash discount.

Aug. 18 Issued cheque no. 633 for $29,400 to King Corporation in settlement of invoice dated August 9, less 2% discount.

Aug. 20 Purchased merchandise for cash, $1,080. Issued cheque no. 634 to Candy Corp.

Aug. 21 Bought land and building for $208,800. Land was worth $64,800, and building, $144,000. Paid cash of $36,000 and signed a promissory note for the balance of $172,800. Cheque no. 635, in the amount of $36,000, was issued to Security Co.

Aug. 23 Purchased merchandise from Novelty Products for cash, $900. Issued cheque no. 636.

Aug. 26 Purchased merchandise from Ralston Company for a gross invoice price of $32,400. Invoice dated August 26, terms 2/10, n/30.

Aug. 28 Paid cash for office supplies, $270. Issued cheque no. 637 to Super Office, Inc.

Aug. 29 Purchased merchandise from Candy Corp. for cash, $1,890. Cheque no. 638.

---

* *Supplemental Topic, "Manual Special Journals"*

Aug. 31 Paid salaries for August, $17,920. Issued cheque no. 639 to National Bank, which handles the distribution of the payroll to employees. (Ignore payroll taxes.)

INSTRUCTIONS

a Record the transactions in the appropriate journals. Use a single-column purchases journal, a five-column cash payments journal, and a two-column general journal. Foot and rule the special journals. Make all postings to the proper general ledger accounts and to the accounts payable subsidiary ledger.

b Prepare a schedule of accounts payable at August 31 to prove that the subsidiary ledger is in balance with the controlling account for accounts payable.

***PROBLEM 6-11**
Using Special Journals to Record Cash Transactions

J. D. Thomas Co. wholesales furniture to interior designers and retail furniture stores. The company uses a periodic inventory system and special journals similar to those illustrated in the Supplemental Topic section. Purchases of merchandise are recorded at ***net cost*** in a purchases journal.

In this problem, you are to record only the ***cash transactions*** of J. D. Thomas Co. during October. These transactions are listed below:

Oct. 1 Issued cheque no. 734 to Furniture Trade Centre in payment of store rent for October, $2,200.

Oct. 3 Purchased office equipment for $8,400 from MicroDesk, issuing cheque no. 735 as a $1,400 cash down payment and issuing a 90-day, 10% note payable for the $7,000 balance.

Oct. 4 The owner, J. D. Thomas, invested an additional $20,000 cash in the business.

Oct. 8 Paid an account payable to Colonial House, taking the allowable 2% cash discount. Issued cheque no. 736 in the amount of $14,700.

Oct. 9 Sold merchandise for cash to Southwest Design Studios, $16,300.

Oct. 10 Received $3,600 as a partial collection of an $18,000 account receivable from Myra's Interiors. Also received a $14,400 note receivable for the uncollected balance.

Oct. 12 Received $7,742 from Furniture Gallery in settlement of our $7,900 sales invoice dated Oct. 2, less 2%.

Oct. 15 Cash sales of merchandise, $18,750.

Oct. 22 Purchased merchandise from Quebec Furniture Co. for cash, $11,200. Issued cheque no. 737.

Oct. 25 Issued cheque no. 738 in payment of account payable to Fabrics Unlimited, $6,664.

Oct. 27 Purchased merchandise from Oak World, $16,700. Issued cheque no. 739.

Oct. 29 Received cheque for $17,836 from Lambert's in settlement of our $18,200 sales invoice dated Oct. 19, less 2%.

Oct. 31 Paid monthly salaries, $8,470. Issued one cheque, no. 740, to Merchants' Bank in the full amount of these salaries. (The bank handles the distribution of the payroll to individual employees.)

Oct. 31 Paid Merchants' Bank instalment due today on a note payable. Issued cheque no. 741 in the amount of $1,630, representing $480 interest expense and a reduction in the balance of the note payable of the remaining $1,150.

* *Supplemental Topic, "Manual Special Journals"*

INSTRUCTIONS Enter the above transactions in either a six-column cash receipts journal or a five-column cash payments journal. Total the money columns in each journal and determine the equality of the debit and credit column totals.

***PROBLEM 6-12 Relationship between Subsidiary Ledgers and Controlling Accounts**

First Sports Products sells skis and ski clothing. The company uses manual general and special journals and ledgers. At November 30, the subsidiary ledger for accounts receivable included accounts with individual customers as shown below. Note that these accounts include postings from three different journals.

Peektou Sportswear

Date		Explanation	Ref	Debit	Credit	Balance
19 —						
Oct.	31	Balance				12400
Nov.	10		J1		630	11770
	11		S4	8000		19770
	30		CR2		11770	8000

Laurentian Ski Shop

Date		Explanation	Ref	Debit	Credit	Balance
19 —						
Nov.	4		S4	28160		28160
	29		S4	7680		35840
	29		CR2		28160	7680

Whistler Sports Centre

Date		Explanation	Ref	Debit	Credit	Balance
19 —						
Nov.	3		S4	2240		2240
	9		S4	4160		6400
	27		CR2		2240	4160

* *Supplemental Topic, "Manual Special Journals"*

Banff Stores, Inc.						
Date		Explanation	Ref	Debit	Credit	Balance
19—						
Oct.	31	Balance				20736
Nov.	8		CR2		12800	7936
	8		J1		2560	5376
	28		CR2		5376	-0-

INSTRUCTIONS Based on the information in the subsidiary accounts, recreate the Accounts Receivable controlling account in the general ledger (use a three-column, running balance form), including the beginning balance and all the entries in November.

***PROBLEM 6-13**
Using Special Journals: A Comprehensive Problem

The transactions of Mody Store during June, 1996 were as follows (purchases to be recorded at ***net cost***):

June 1 Sold merchandise for cash $6,000.

June 1 Purchased merchandise on account from Dunlop Co. at a gross invoice price of $12,000. Invoice was dated today with terms of 2/10, n/30.

June 2 Purchased supplies for $350 from Waterloo Wholesale. Issued cheque no. 603.

June 3 Sold merchandise to Filmore Company, $9,200. Invoice No. 428; terms 2/10, n/30.

June 7 Issued cheque no. 604 to pay the Dunlop invoice dated June 1.

June 10 Purchased merchandise from Burton Company at a gross invoice price of $11,700. Invoice dated June 9 with terms of 1/10, n/30.

June 11 Collected from Filmore Company for Invoice No. 428, dated June 3.

June 12 Sold merchandise to Payless Inc. $7,360, Invoice No. 429; terms 2/10, n/30.

June 13 Issued cheque no. 605 to pay freight charges of $740 to Dominion Transport on goods purchased from Burton Company.

June 15 Sold land for $90,000, receiving cash of $20,000 and a note receivable for the balance. The land had been acquired at a cost of $75,000 for use in the business, but due to a change of plans it was no longer needed.

June 16 Issued credit memorandum No. 68 in favour of Payless Inc., upon their return of $360 of merchandise.

June 17 Issued cheque no. 606 to General Insurance Limited for $1,400 for one-year fire insurance policy.

June 18 Purchased merchandise for $2,700. Issued cheque no. 607 to London Ltd.

June 19 Paid the Burton Company invoice dated June 9. Issued cheque no. 608.

---

* *Supplemental Topic, "Manual Special Journals"*

June 20 Sold merchandise on account to Peat Brothers, $7,000. Invoice No. 430. Required customer to sign a 30-day non-interest-bearing note. (Record this sale in the Sales Journal by a charge to Accounts Receivable, then transfer from Accounts Receivable to Notes Receivable by means of any entry in the general journal.)

June 20 Purchased merchandise for $1,500. Issued cheque no. 609 to Totten Ltd.

June 21 Sold merchandise for cash, $1,800.

June 21 Received payment from Payless Inc., for Invoice No. 429. Customer made deduction for credit memorandum No. 68 issued June 16 and took 2% discount.

June 25 Purchased merchandise from Amber Company $9,500. Invoice dated June 24, with terms 2/10, n/30.

June 26 Issued debit memorandum No. 42 to Amber Company in connection with merchandise returned today to Amber amounting to $300.

June 29 Purchased equipment having a list price of $21,600 from Lichee Ltd. Paid $3,600 down by issuing cheque no. 610 and signed a promissory note for the balance of $18,000.

June 30 Paid monthly salaries of $15,300 for services rendered by employees during June. Issued cheque no. 611 to Hong Kong Bank, which handles the distribution of payroll. (Ignore payroll taxes.)

June 30 Issued cheque no. 612 to New Trust Co. for monthly instalment on mortgage, $2,260 of which $1,370 was interest.

The following ledger accounts are used by Mody Store.

Cash	10	*L. Liukoo, drawing*	52
Notes receivable	14	*Sales*	60
Accounts receivable	16	*Sales returns & allowances*	62
Supplies	17	*Sales discounts*	64
Unexpired insurance	18	*Purchases*	70
Land	20	*Purchase returns & allowances*	72
Equipment	26	*Transportation-in*	76
Accumulated depreciation:		*Salaries expense*	80
Equipment	28	*Depreciation expense:*	
Notes payable	30	*Equipment*	88
Accounts payable	32	*Gain on sale of land*	90
Mortgage payable	40	*Interest expense*	92
L. Liukoo, capital	50		

INSTRUCTIONS

a Record the June transactions in the following journals:
General journal—two columns
Sales journal—one column
Purchases journal—one column
Cash receipts journal—six columns
Cash payments journal—five columns

b Foot and rule all special journals.

c Show how postings would be made by placing ledger account numbers and check marks in the appropriate columns of the journals.

ANALYTICAL AND DECISION PROBLEMS AND CASES

A&D 6-1
The Baker Street Diversion

Printing Made Easy sells a variety of printers for use with personal computers. Last April, Arthur Doyle, the company's purchasing agent, discovered a weakness in internal control and engaged in a scheme to steal printers. Doyle issued a purchase order for 20 printers to one of the company's regular suppliers, but he included a typewritten note on company letterhead stationery requesting that the printers be delivered to 221B Baker Street, a warehouse in which Doyle had rented space.

The supplier shipped the printers to Baker Street and sent a sales invoice to Printing Made Easy. When the invoice arrived, an accounting clerk carefully complied with company policy and compared the invoice with a copy of the purchase order. After noting agreement between these documents as to quantities, prices, and model numbers, the clerk recorded the transaction in the accounting records and authorized payment of the invoice.

INSTRUCTIONS

What is the weakness in internal control discovered by the purchasing agent to enable him to commit this theft? What changes would you recommend in the company's internal documentation and invoice approval procedures to prevent such problems in the future?

A&D 6-2
Internal Control in a Computer-Based System

Mission Stores uses point-of-sale terminals to record its sales transactions. All merchandise bears a magnetic code number that can be read by an optical scanner. When merchandise is sold, the salesclerk passes each item over the scanner. The computer reads the code number, determines the price of the item from a master price list, and displays the price on a screen for the customer to see. After each item has been passed over the scanner, the computer displays the total amount of the sale and records the transaction in the company's accounting records.

If the transaction is a credit sale, the salesclerk enters the customer's credit card number into the register. The computer checks the customer's credit status and updates the accounts receivable subsidiary ledger.

INSTRUCTIONS

Statements **a** through **d** describe problems that may arise in a retailing business that uses manual cash registers and accounting records. Explain how the point-of-sale terminals used by Mission Stores will help reduce or eliminate these problems. If the point-of-sale terminals will not help to eliminate the problems, explain why not.

a A salesclerk is unaware of a recent change in the price of a particular item.

b Merchandise is stolen by a shoplifter.

c A salesclerk fails to record a cash sale and keeps the cash received from the customer.

d A customer buys merchandise on account using a stolen Mission Stores credit card.

A&D 6-3
Internal Control in a Typical Restaurant

Alice's Restaurant has internal controls that are similar to most restaurants. A waiter or waitress (food server) writes each customer's order on a serially numbered sales ticket. The servers give these sales tickets to the kitchen staff, which prepares the meals. While the customer is eating, the server fills in the prices on the sales ticket and leaves it at the customer's table.

When the customers are ready to leave, they present the completed sales ticket, along with the payment due, to the cashier. The cashier verifies the prices listed on the sales ticket, rings up the sale on a cash register, and gives the customer an appropriate amount of change.

A manager is always on hand observing operations throughout the restaurant. At the end of each shift, the manager determines that all of the sales tickets issued by the food servers have been collected by the cashier and computes the total dollar amount of these tickets. Next, the manager counts the cash receipts and compares this amount with the total shown on the register tape and the total developed from the serially numbered sales tickets.

INSTRUCTIONS

Identify the control procedures (if any) that prevent:

a Food servers from providing free meals to family and friends simply by not preparing a sales ticket.

b Food servers from undercharging favoured customers.

c Food servers from collecting the amount due from the customer and keeping the cash for themselves.

d The cashier from pocketing some of the customers' payment and concealing this theft by ringing up lower amounts on the cash register.

A&D 6-4
Internal Control: Another Short Case

At the Uptown Theatre, the cashier is located in a box office at the front of the building. The cashier receives cash from customers and operates a ticket machine that ejects serially numbered tickets. The serial number appears on each end of the ticket. The tickets come from the printer in large rolls that fit into the ticket machine and are removed at the end of each cashier's working period.

After purchasing a ticket from the cashier, in order to be admitted to the theatre a customer must hand the ticket to a ticket taker stationed some 10 metres from the box office at the entrance to the theatre lobby. The ticket taker tears the ticket in half and returns the ticket stub to the customer. The other half of the ticket is dropped by the ticket taker into a locked box.

INSTRUCTIONS

a Describe the internal controls present in Uptown Theatre's method of handling cash receipts.

b What steps should be taken regularly by the theatre manager or other supervisor to make these and other internal controls work most effectively?

c Assume that the cashier and the ticket taker decided to collaborate in an effort to abstract cash receipts. What action might they take?

d On the assumption made in part **c** of collaboration between the cashier and the ticket taker, what features of the control procedures would be most likely to disclose this employee fraud?

***A&D 6-5**
Designing a Special Journal and Explaining Its Use

Leisure Clothing is a mail-order company that sells clothes to the public at discount prices. Recently Leisure Clothing initiated a new policy allowing a 10-day free trial on all clothes bought from the company. At the end of the 10-day period, the customer may either pay cash for the purchase or return the goods to Leisure Clothing. The new policy caused such a large boost in sales that, even after considering the many sales returns, the policy appeared quite profitable.

The accounting system of Leisure Clothing includes a sales journal, purchases journal, cash receipts journal, cash payments journal, and general journal. As an internal control procedure, an officer of the company reviews and initials every entry in the general journal before the amounts are posted to the ledger accounts. Since the 10-day free trial policy has been in effect, hundreds of entries recording sales returns have been entered in the general journal each week. Each of these entries has been reviewed and initialled by an officer of the company, and the amounts have been posted to Sales Returns & Allowances and to the Accounts

---

* *Supplemental Topic, "Manual Special Journals"*

Receivable controlling account in the general ledger, and also to the customer's account in the accounts receivable subsidiary ledger.

Since these sales return entries are so numerous, it has been suggested that a special journal be designed to handle them. This could not only save time in journalizing and posting the entries, but also eliminate the time-consuming individual review of each of these repetitious entries by an officer of the company.

INSTRUCTIONS

a How many amounts are entered in the general journal to describe a single sales return transaction? Are these amounts the same?

b Explain why these sales return transactions are suited to the use of a special journal. Explain in detail how many money columns the special journal should have, and what postings would have to be done either at the time of the transaction or at the end of the period.

c Assume that there were 3,000 sales returns during the month. How many postings would have to be made during the month if these transactions were entered in the general journal? How many postings would have to be made if the special journal you designed in **b** were used? (Assume a one-month accounting period.)

***A&D 6-6**
Posting from Special Journals

Kaiser Company's manual accounting system includes a general journal and four special journals for cash receipts, cash payments, sales, and purchases of merchandise. On May 31, after all May posting had been completed, the Accounts Receivable controlling account in the general ledger had a debit balance of $320,000 and the Accounts Payable controlling account had a credit balance of $96,000.

The June transactions recorded in the four special journals can be summarized as follows:

Sales journal	*Column total, $192,000*
Purchases journal	*Column total, $112,000*
Cash receipts journal	*Accounts Receivable column total, $153,600*
Cash payments journal	*Accounts Payable column total, $134,400*

INSTRUCTIONS

a Indicate what posting would be made of each of these column totals on June 30?

b Indicate what posting would be made of the individual amounts in each of these column totals.

c State the balances of the Accounts Receivable controlling account and the Accounts Payable controlling account in the general ledger after completion of posting at June 30.

***A&D 6-7**
Locating Errors in Special Journals and Subsidiary Ledgers

Mody Variety Store maintains a manual accounting system with four special journals and a general journal. During August the following errors were made.

a A purchase of merchandise on credit from Lisome Limited in the amount of $3,000 was erroneously entered in the purchases journal as a $300 purchase.

b Incorrectly added the entries in a customer's account in the accounts receivable subsidiary ledger as $1,900 when it should have been $1,100.

c Recorded correctly in the sales journal a $900 sale of merchandise on credit but posted the transaction to the customer's account in the subsidiary ledger as a $90 sale.

INSTRUCTIONS For each of the errors you are to explain how and when the error will be brought to light.

* *Supplemental Topic, "Manual Special Journals"*

PART

3 Accounting for Assets

The manner in which a business records and values its assets affects both the balance sheet and the income statement. By studying the accounting principles involved in asset valuation, we will learn much about the content and limitations of financial statements.

This part concludes with a Comprehensive Problem in which we review various methods of asset valuation and the resulting effects upon net income.

CHAPTER

7 The Control of Cash Transactions

As our chapter title suggests, this chapter focuses in large part upon internal control. The need for internal control over cash transactions should be apparent, as cash is the asset most susceptible to theft and embezzlement. Also, cash transactions affect every element of the financial statements—assets, liabilities, owner's equity, revenue, and expenses. If cash transactions are not recorded properly, none of a company's accounting data should be considered reliable.

Learning Objectives

After studying this chapter you should be able to:

1. *Describe the balance sheet presentation of cash and state the basic objectives of "cash management."*
2. *Explain the major steps in achieving internal control over cash transactions.*
3. *Describe how a voucher system contributes to internal control over cash disbursements.*
4. *Prepare a bank reconciliation and explain its purpose.*
5. *Describe the operation of a petty cash fund.*

What Do Accountants Mean by "Cash"?

Accountants define ***cash*** as money on deposit in banks and any items that a bank will accept for deposit. These items include not only coins and paper money but also cheques, money orders, travellers' cheques, and the charge slips signed by customers using bank credit cards, such as Visa and MasterCard.

Most companies maintain several bank accounts and also may keep small amounts of cash on hand. Therefore, the Cash account in the general ledger is a ***controlling account.*** A cash subsidiary ledger includes a separate account corresponding to each of the company's bank accounts and also to each petty cash fund or change fund within the organization.

Reporting Cash in the Balance Sheet

OBJECTIVE 1 Describe the balance sheet presentation of cash and state the basic objectives of "cash management."

Cash is listed first in the balance sheet because it represents a resource that can be used immediately to pay any type of obligation. The term ***liquid assets*** is used to describe assets that can be converted quickly into cash. In the current asset section of the balance sheet, assets are listed in the order of their liquidity. Thus cash—being the ultimate in liquidity—is listed first.

For purposes of balance sheet presentation, however, the balance in the Cash controlling account generally is combined with the controlling account for cash equivalents.

Cash Equivalents Some short-term or temporary investments are so liquid that they are termed ***cash equivalents.*** (Cash equivalents will be discussed fully in Chapter 19.) Examples include money market funds, treasury bills, certificates of deposit (CDs), and high-grade commercial paper. These items are considered so similar to cash that they often are combined with the amount of cash in the balance sheet. Therefore, many businesses call the first asset shown in the balance sheet ***"Cash and short-term investments."***

Evaluating Solvency Bankers, credit managers, and other creditors who study a balance sheet always are interested in the amount of cash and short-term investments as compared to other balance sheet items, such as accounts payable. These users of a company's financial statements are interested in evaluating the company's ***solvency***—that is, its ability to pay its debts as they come due. Creditors need to know the amount of liquid resources available to the business, but not such details as the balance in each of the bank accounts or the amount of cash on hand as compared to cash in banks.

Lines of Credit Many businesses have arranged lines of credit with their banks. A line of credit means that the bank has agreed in advance to lend the company any amount of money up to a specified limit. The company can borrow this money at any time, by drawing cheques upon a special bank account. A liability to the bank arises as soon as any of the money is borrowed—that is, as soon as a portion of the line of credit is used.

The ***unused*** portion of a line of credit is neither an asset nor a liability; it represents only the ***ability*** to borrow money quickly and easily. Although an unused line of credit does not appear as an asset or a liability in the balance sheet, it does affect the company's solvency. For this reason, unused lines of credit are ***disclosed*** in notes accompanying the financial statements.

CASE IN POINT A recent annual report of Canadian Pacific Limited, a giant conglomerate, included the following note to the financial statements:

> Unused lines of credit for short term financing, subject to periodic review, repayable on demand and at various maturities up to 365 days, amounted to $1,140.4 million on which interest rates vary with bank prime or money market rates.

"Restricted" Cash Some bank accounts are restricted as to their use, so that they are not available to meet normal operating needs of the business. For example, a bank account may contain cash specifically earmarked for the acquisition of plant assets. Bank accounts in some foreign countries are restricted by laws that prohibit transferring the money to another country. Restricted bank accounts are not regarded as current assets if their balances are not available for use in paying current liabilities. Therefore, "restricted cash balances" may be listed just below the current asset section of the balance sheet in the section entitled ***long-term investments.***

The Statement of Changes in Financial Position

The balance sheet indicates the amount of cash owned by the business at a particular date. A separate financial statement, called the statement of changes in financial position, summarizes all of the cash ***activity*** (receipts and disbursements) during the accounting period. Interpreting this statement requires an understanding of many types of business transactions, including the operating, investing, and financing activities of large corporations. Therefore, we will defer discussion of this financial statement to Chapter 19.

Management Responsibilities Relating to Cash

The term ***cash management*** refers to planning, controlling, and accounting for cash transactions and cash balances. Efficient cash management is essential to the success—even to the survival—of every business organization. The basic objectives of cash management are:

- ***Provide accurate accounting for cash receipts, cash disbursements, and cash balances.*** A large portion of the total transactions of a business involve the receipt or disbursement of cash. Also, cash transactions affect every classification within the financial statements—assets, liabilities, owner's equity, revenue, and expenses. If financial statements are to be reliable, it is ***absolutely essential*** that cash transactions be recorded correctly.

- ***Prevent or minimize losses from theft or fraud.*** Cash is more susceptible to theft than any other asset and, therefore, requires physical protection.
- ***Anticipate the need for borrowing and assure the availability of adequate amounts of cash for conducting business operations.*** Every business organization must have sufficient cash to meet its financial obligations as they come due. Otherwise, its creditors may force the business into bankruptcy.
- ***Prevent unnecessarily large amounts of cash from sitting idle in bank accounts that produce little or no revenue.*** Well-managed corporations should frequently review their bank balances for the purpose of transferring any excess cash into short-term investments that generate more revenue.

How Much Cash Is "Enough?" Every business needs sufficient cash, cash equivalents, or lines of credit to meet the company's obligations on a timely basis. However, maintaining larger amounts of cash than necessary is ***not*** an efficient use of resources.

A large cash balance is a relatively nonproductive asset. Corporate accounts do not usually earn interest. Because cash equivalents are such safe and highly liquid investments, they earn very modest rates of return. Such investments are an efficient way of investing ***temporary*** surpluses of cash that soon will be needed for other purposes. However, if a business has large amounts of cash that can be invested on a long-term basis, it should try to earn a substantially ***higher*** rate of return than is available from cash equivalents.

Efficient uses of cash balances that are available on a long-term basis often include financing the growth and expansion of the business, taking advantage of unusual investment opportunities, and repaying interest-bearing liabilities. Simply holding large amounts of cash and cash equivalents increases a company's solvency but adds little to its profitability.

The amount of cash needed to keep a company operating smoothly varies greatly from one business to the next. Most businesses, however, have no more than 5 or 10% of their total assets in the form of cash and cash equivalents, unless they are accumulating the money for some specific purpose. Cash that cannot be utilized efficiently within a particular business should be distributed to the company's owners, so that they may invest it elsewhere.

Cash Balances and Corporate Dividends

In the early chapters of this textbook, most of our illustrations have involved businesses organized as sole proprietorships. In these organizations, the owner may withdraw excess cash balances from the business at will. In a corporation, however, the decision of whether to distribute company-owned cash to the owners (shareholders) rests with the company's ***board of directors.***[1]

---

1 The board of directors is the highest level of corporate management.

A distribution of cash by a corporation to its shareholders is called a ***dividend.***[2] The timing and dollar amounts of dividend payments are determined by the corporation's directors and top management. (Limits upon dividend payments also may be imposed by corporate laws and by contractual agreements with creditors.) Among the factors that most influence the amount of dividends that a corporation pays are the:

- Company's profitability in recent periods.
- Amount of cash on hand that is not needed in business operations.
- Goals and philosophy of the company's top management.

By studying financial statements, investors easily can determine for recent periods a company's net income, the amount of cash on hand, and the amounts of dividends paid to the shareholders. The relationships among these factors can shed much light upon management's attitude toward the payment of dividends and can assist investors in evaluating the prospects of receiving future dividend distributions.

Internal Control over Cash

Internal control over cash is sometimes regarded merely as a means of preventing fraud and theft. A good system of internal control, however, will also aid in achieving the other objectives of efficient cash management, including accurate accounting for cash transactions, anticipating the need for borrowing, and the maintenance of adequate but not excessive cash balances.

*OBJECTIVE 2 **Explain the major steps in achieving internal control over cash transactions.***

1. Separate the function of handling cash from the maintenance of accounting records. Employees who handle cash ***should not have access to the accounting records,*** and accounting personnel should not have access to cash.
2. Prepare for each department within the organization a ***cash budget*** (or forecast) of planned cash receipts, cash payments, and cash balances, scheduled month-by-month for the coming year. (Departmental budgets assume the use of a ***responsibility accounting system.***[3])
3. Prepare a ***control listing*** of cash receipts at the time and place the money is received. For cash sales, this listing may be a cash register tape, created by ringing up each sale on a cash register. For cheques received through the mail, a control listing of incoming cheques should be prepared by the employee assigned to open the mail.
4. Require that all cash receipts be ***deposited daily*** in the bank.
5. Make all payments ***by cheque.*** The only exception should be for small payments to be made in cash from a ***petty cash fund.*** (Petty cash funds are discussed later in this chapter.)

---

[2] Accounting for dividends is explained and illustrated in later chapters.

[3] A ***responsibility accounting system*** includes a chart of accounts sufficiently detailed to measure separately the activities of each department (or area of managerial responsibility) within the organization. These systems were described in Chapter 6.

6 Require that the validity and amount of every expenditure be verified ***before*** a cheque is issued in payment. Separate the function of approving expenditures from the function of signing cheques.

7 Promptly reconcile bank statements with the accounting records.

The application of these principles in building an adequate system of internal control over cash can best be illustrated by considering separately the topics of cash receipts and cash disbursements. A company may supplement its system of internal control by obtaining a fidelity bond from an insurance company. Under a fidelity bond, the insurance company agrees to reimburse an employer for ***proven*** losses resulting from fraud or embezzlement by bonded employees.

Cash Receipts

Cash receipts consist primarily of two types: cash received through the mail as collections of accounts receivable, and cash received over the counter from cash sales.

Cash Received Through the Mail Cash received through the mail should be in the form of cheques made payable to the company. When the mail is first opened, an employee should stamp the back of each cheque with a restrictive endorsement stamp, indicating that the cheque is ***"For Deposit Only"*** into the company's bank account. This ***restrictive endorsement*** prevents anyone else from being able to cash the cheque or deposit it into another bank account.

Next, the employee should prepare a ***control listing*** of the cheques received each day. This list shows each customer's name (or account number) and the amount received. One copy of this list is sent with the customers' cheques to the cashier, who deposits the money in the bank. Another copy is sent to the accounting department, to be recorded in the accounting records. Daily comparisons of this control listing with the amounts deposited by the cashier and with the receipts recorded by the accounting department should bring to light any cash shortages or recording errors.

Cash Received over the Counter Cash sales should be rung up on a cash register so located that the customer can see the amount recorded. The register has a locked-in tape, which serves as a control listing for cash sales. When the salesperson ends a workday, he or she will count the cash in the register and turn it over to the cashier. A representative of the accounting department will remove the tape from the cash register, compare the total shown on the tape with the amount turned in to the cashier, and record the cash sales in the accounting records.

As explained in earlier chapters, most larger stores now use on-line ***point-of-sale terminals.*** When these terminals are in use, sales transactions are recorded instantly in the accounting records as the salesclerk passes the merchandise over an optical scanner. At first glance, it may appear that the salesclerk both handles cash and has access to the accounting records. Actually, the salesclerks do ***not*** have direct access to the accounting records; all entries in the accounting records are made automatically by the point-of-sale terminal.

Use of Prenumbered Sales Tickets Another means of establishing internal control over cash sales is by writing out a prenumbered sales ticket in duplicate at the time of each sale. The original is given to the customer and the carbon copy is retained. Prenumbered sales tickets are often used in businesses such as restaurants in which one central cashier rings up the sales made by all salespeople.

At the end of the day, an employee computes the total sales figure from these sales tickets and also makes sure that no tickets are missing from the series. This total sales figure is then compared with the cash register tape and the total cash receipts.

Cash Over and Short In handling over-the-counter cash receipts, a few errors in making change inevitably will occur. These errors will cause a cash shortage or overage at the end of the day, when the cash is counted and compared with the reading on the cash register.

For example, assume that total cash sales recorded on the point-of-sale terminals during the day amount to $4,500.00. However, the cash receipts in the register drawers total only $4,487.30. The following entry would be made to adjust the accounting records for this $12.70 shortage in the cash receipts:

Cash Over and Short	12.70	
Cash		12.70
To record a $12.70 shortage in cash receipts for the day ($4,500.00 – $4,487.30).		

The account entitled Cash Over and Short is debited with shortages and credited with overages. If the cash shortages during an entire accounting period are in excess of the cash overages, the Cash Over and Short account will have a debit balance and will be shown as miscellaneous ***expense*** in the income statement. On the other hand, if the overages exceed the shortages, the Cash Over and Short account will show a credit balance at the end of the period and should be treated as an item of miscellaneous ***revenue.*** Management should review the daily entries to this account so as to be aware of any material cash shortages or consistent pattern of small shortages.

Subdivision of Duties Employees who handle cash receipts should ***not have access to the accounting records.*** This combination of duties might enable the employee to alter the accounting records and thereby conceal a cash shortage.

Employees who handle cash receipts also should ***not have authority to issue credit memoranda for sales returns.*** This combination of duties might enable the employee to conceal cash shortages by issuing fictitious credit memoranda. Assume, for example, that an employee with these responsibilities collects $500 cash from a customer as payment of the customer's account. The employee might remove this cash and issue a $500 credit memorandum, indicating that the customer had returned the merchandise instead of paying the account. The credit memoranda would cause the account receivable from this customer to be credited. However, the offsetting debit would be to the Sales Returns & Allowances account, not to the Cash account. Thus, the books would remain in balance, the customer would receive credit for the abstracted payment, and there would be no record of cash having been received.

Using Departmental Cash Budgets Departmental cash budgets provide estimates of the cash receipts ***expected*** within each department during the accounting period. Management should investigate to determine ***why*** a department falls significantly short of the budgeted amounts. Perhaps this investigation will show that the budgeted amounts were overly optimistic; in this case, management will change the budget estimates for future months. On the other hand, the investigation may reveal weak departmental performance or fraud on the part of certain personnel. In either of these situations, management will want to initiate corrective action.

Cash Disbursements

To achieve adequate internal control over cash payments, all disbursements of significant dollar amount should be ***made by cheque.*** Cheques should be prenumbered. Any spoiled cheques should be marked "Void" and filed in sequence so that all numbers in the series can be accounted for.

Every transaction requiring a cash disbursement should be verified and approved before payment is made. The official designated to ***sign*** cheques should not be given authority to ***approve*** invoices for payment or to make entries in the accounting records. When a cheque is presented to a company official for signature, it should be accompanied by the approved invoice and voucher showing that the transaction has been fully verified and that payment is justified. When the cheque is signed, the supporting invoices and vouchers should be perforated or stamped "Paid" to eliminate any possibility of their being presented later in support of another cheque. If these rules are followed, it is almost impossible for a fraudulent cash disbursement to be concealed without the collusion of two or more persons.

The Voucher System

OBJECTIVE 3 ***Describe how a voucher system contributes to internal control over cash disbursements.***

One widely used method of establishing control over cash disbursements is the voucher system. The basic idea of this system is that every transaction that will result in a cash disbursement must be verified, approved in writing, and recorded before a cheque is issued. A written authorization called a ***voucher*** is prepared for every transaction that will require a cash payment, regardless of whether the transaction is for payment of an expense, purchase of inventory or a plant asset, or for payment of a liability.[4] Notice that ***every purchase is treated as an independent transaction*** even though many purchases may be made from the same supplier. Vouchers are serially numbered so that the loss or misplacement of a voucher would be immediately apparent.

To demonstrate the internal control inherent in a voucher system, consider the way a voucher is used in verifying an invoice received from a supplier. A serially numbered voucher is attached to each incoming in-

---

[4] Other names for a ***"voucher"*** include ***"invoice approval form"*** and ***"cheque authorization."***

Use of voucher ensures verification of invoice

BROADHILL CORPORATION
Montreal, Quebec

Voucher No. 241 ← Serial number

Pay to	Black Company	Date	May 1, 19—
	3160 Main Street	Date due	May 10, 19—
	Toronto, Ontario		

Date of Invoice	April 30, 19—	Gross amount	$ 1,000.00
Invoice number	847	Less: Cash discount	20.00
Credit terms	2/10, n30	Net amount	$ 980.00

Approval

	Dates	Approved by
Extensions and footings verified	May 1, 19—	RG
Prices in agreement with purchase order	May 1, 19—	RG
Quantities in agreement with receiving report	May 1, 19—	RG
Credit terms in agreement with purchase order	May 1, 19—	RG
Account distribution & recording approved	William Cross	
Approved for payment	Judith Davis	

Accounting Supervisor

← Verification procedures
← Approved for payment

Reverse side of voucher

Voucher No. 241

Account distribution

	Amount		
		Date	May 1, 19—
Inventory	$ 980.00		
Transportation-in		Date due	May 10, 19—
Repairs			
Heat, light, and power		Payee	Black Company
Advertising			3160 Main Street
Delivery expense			Toronto, Ontario
Misc. general expense		Amount of invoice	$ 1,000.00
Telephone and telegraph		Less: Cash discount	20.00
Sales salaries		Net amount	$ 980.00
Office salaries			
		Paid by cheque no.	632
		Date of cheque	May 10, 19—
Credit vouchers payable (total)	980.00	Amount of cheque	$ 980.00
Account distribution by	K.R.D.	Entered in voucher register by	A.S.

Accounts debited →
Accounts credited →

voice. The voucher has spaces for listing the data from the invoice and for showing the ledger accounts to be debited and credited in recording the transaction. Space is also provided for approval signatures for each step in the verification and approval process. A completed voucher provides a description of the transaction and also of the work performed in verifying the liability and approving the cash disbursement.

Preparing a Voucher To illustrate the functioning of a voucher system, let us begin with the receipt of an invoice from a supplier. A voucher is prepared by filling in the appropriate blanks with information taken from the invoice, such as the invoice date, invoice number, amount, and the creditor's name and address. The voucher with the supplier's invoice attached is then sent to the employees responsible for verifying the extensions and footings on the invoice and for comparing prices, quantities, and terms with those specified in the purchase order and receiving report. When completion of the verification process has been evidenced by approval signatures of the persons performing these steps, the voucher and supporting documents are sent to an employee of the accounting department, who indicates on the voucher the accounts to be debited and credited. The voucher is then reviewed by an accounting official to provide assurance that the verification procedures have been satisfactorily completed and that the liability is a proper one.

Recording Approved Vouchers

After receiving the supervisory approval explained above, the voucher is entered in a special journal called a ***voucher register.*** Entries in the voucher register indicate the nature of the expenditure by debiting the appropriate asset, expense, or liability accounts. The credit portion of each entry is always to a short-term liability account entitled Vouchers Payable. Note that the entry in the voucher register is not made ***until the liability has been verified and approved.***

In a company using the voucher system, the ledger account, Vouchers Payable, replaces Accounts Payable. For purposes of balance sheet presentation, however, most companies continue to use the more widely understood term Accounts Payable.

Voucher systems are used principally by larger companies that process transactions by computer. Because our interest in voucher systems is in their internal control features and because manual voucher systems are rare, our discussion does not include illustration of a hand-operated voucher register.

Paying the Voucher within the Discount Period After the voucher has been entered in the voucher register, it is placed (with the supporting documents attached) in a tickler file according to the date of required payment. Cash discount periods generally run from the date of the invoice. Since a voucher is prepared for each invoice, the required date of payment is the last day on which a cheque can be prepared and mailed to the creditor in time to qualify for the discount.

When the payment date arrives, an employee in the accounting department removes the voucher from the unpaid file, draws a cheque for signature by the treasurer, and records payment of the voucher in a special journal called a ***cheque register.*** Since cheques are issued only in payment of approved vouchers, every entry in the cheque register represents a debit to Vouchers Payable and a credit to Cash.

An important factor in achieving internal control is that the employee in the accounting department who prepares the cheque ***is not authorized to sign it.*** The unsigned cheque and the supporting voucher are now sent to the treasurer or other designated official in the finance department. The treasurer reviews the voucher, especially the approval signatures, and signs the cheque. Thus, the invoice is ***approved for payment*** in the accounting department, but the actual cash disbursement is made by the finance department. ***No one person or department is in a position both to approve invoices for payment and to issue signed cheques.***

Once the cheque has been signed, the treasurer should mail it directly to the creditor. The voucher and all supporting documents are then perforated with a PAID stamp and are forwarded to the accounting department, which will note payment of the voucher in the voucher register and will file the paid voucher. The operation of a voucher system is illustrated in the flowchart on the following page. Notes have been made on the illustration identifying the most important internal control features in the system.

Establishing Control over the Issuance of Cheques In a small business, the officer authorized to sign cheques is held responsible for signing only those cheques that have been properly authorized. In a large company that issues hundreds or thousands of cheques daily, it is not practicable for a company official to sign each cheque manually. Instead, cheque-signing machines with various built-in control devices are used. This automation of the cheque-signing function does not weaken the system of internal control if attention is given to proper use of the machine and to control of the cheques both before and after they pass through the cheque-signing machine.

CASE IN POINT A large construction company issued a great many cheques every day but paid little attention to internal controls over its cash payments. Stacks of unissued cheques were kept in an unlocked supply closet along with Styrofoam coffee cups. Because the number of cheques issued was too great for the treasurer to sign them manually, a cheque-signing machine was used. This machine, after signing the cheques, ejected them into a box equipped with a lock. In spite of warnings from the company's auditors, company officials found that it was "too inconvenient" to keep the box locked. The company also failed to make any use of the cheque-counting device built into the cheque-signing machine. Although the company maintained very large amounts on deposit in its bank accounts, it did not bother to reconcile bank statements for weeks or months at a time.

These weaknesses in internal control led to a crisis when an employee was given a three-week-old bank statement and a bundle of paid cheques and told to prepare a bank reconciliation. The employee found that the bundle of paid cheques accompanying the bank statement was incomplete. No paid cheques were on hand to support over $700,000 of charges deducted on the bank statement. Further investigation revealed that over $1 million in unauthorized and unrecorded cheques had been paid from the

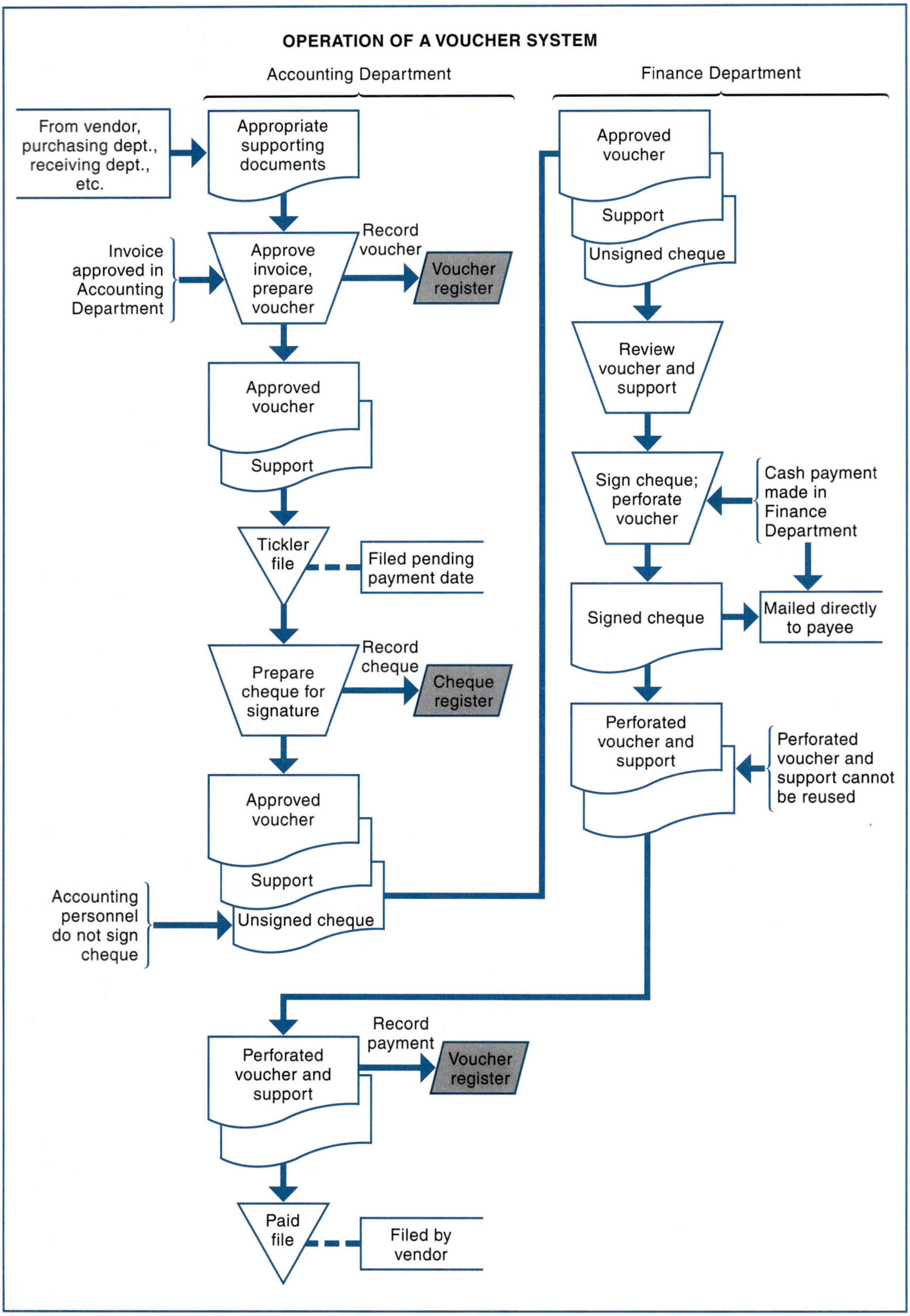
OPERATION OF A VOUCHER SYSTEM
Accounting Department
Finance Department
From vendor, purchasing dept., receiving dept., etc.
Appropriate supporting documents
Invoice approved in Accounting Department
Approve invoice, prepare voucher
Record voucher
Voucher register
Approved voucher
Support
Tickler file
Filed pending payment date
Prepare cheque for signature
Record cheque
Cheque register
Approved voucher
Support
Unsigned cheque
Accounting personnel do not sign cheque
Approved voucher
Support
Unsigned cheque
Review voucher and support
Sign cheque; perforate voucher
Cash payment made in Finance Department
Signed cheque
Mailed directly to payee
Perforated voucher and support
Perforated voucher and support cannot be reused
Perforated voucher and support
Record payment
Voucher register
Paid file
Filed by vendor

corporation's bank accounts. These cheques had been issued out of serial number sequence and had been run through the company cheque-signing machine. It was never determined who had carried out the theft and the money was not recovered.

Chequing Accounts

Virtually every business organization maintains one or more chequing accounts, which are opened and maintained in much the same way as a personal chequing account. The use of chequing accounts contributes to strong internal control in many ways. For example:

1 Chequing accounts eliminate the need for keeping large amounts of currency on hand.
2 The owner of the business must notify the bank of the names of all persons authorized to sign cheques. Thus, access to cash is limited to those company officers and employees designated by the business owner (or, for a corporation, by the board of directors).
3 The person responsible for each cash disbursement is readily identified by the signature on the cheque.
4 The bank returns to the depositor all cheques that it has paid from the account. Thus, the depositor has documentary evidence showing the date and amount of each cash payment, and the identity of the person receiving the money.
5 Comparison of the monthly ***bank statement*** with the depositor's accounting records can bring to light many types of errors made either by the bank or by the depositor in accounting for cash transactions.

Bank Statements

Every month, banks provide each depositor with a bank statement summarizing the activity in the depositor's account.[5] The bank statement is accompanied by all of the cheques that the bank has paid from the account and also by documents indicating the nature and amount of any other changes in the account balance. As illustrated on the next page, a bank statement shows the balance on deposit at the beginning of the month, the deposits, the cheques paid, any other debits and credits during the month, and the new balance at the end of the month. (To keep the illustration short, we have shown only the beginning and ending portion of the statement.)

Reconciling the Bank Statement

OBJECTIVE 4 Prepare a bank reconciliation and explain its purpose.

A ***bank reconciliation*** is a schedule ***explaining any differences*** between the balance shown in the bank statement and the balance shown in the depositor's accounting records. Remember that both the bank and the depositor are maintaining independent records of the deposits, the cheques, and the current balance of the bank account. Each month, the

[5] Large businesses usually receive bank statements on a weekly basis.

A bank statement provides an independent record of cash transactions.

NATIONAL BANK
260 Bland Street
Toronto, Ontario M4W 1G5

Account No. 238484

In account with
Parkview Company
109 Parkview Road
Toronto, Ontario M5K 1B9

Under your agreement with the bank, this statement will be considered correct except as to errors or omissions of which you notify the bank within 30 days after it is delivered or mailed to you
Please notify the bank of any change of address

	Date			Amount	
Balance Forward	30	6	96	5,029	30

Code	Description	Debits	Credits	Date D	M	Yr	Balance
CD			300.00	2	7	96	5,329.30
CD			1,250.00	3	7	96	6,579.30
Ch	Cheque No. 830	1,100.00		3	7	96	5,479.30
Ch	Cheque No. 836	415.20		4	7	96	5,064.10
DM	Cheque returned	50.25		28	7	96	2,798.82
CD			1,083.25	29	7	96	3,882.07
CM	Proceeds of note		500.00	30	7	96	4,382.07
DM	Collection fee	5.00		30	7	96	4,377.07
SC		12.00		31	7	96	4,365.07
CD			610.36	31	7	96	4,975.43
IN			24.74	31	7	96	5,000.17

NO. OF DEBITS	*TOTAL AMOUNT–DEBITS*	NO. OF CREDITS	TOTAL AMOUNT–CREDITS
16	8,367.54	11	8,338.41

EXPLANATION OF CHARACTERS

CC Certified Cheque · *CD Customer Deposit* · *CH Cheque* · *CM Credit Memo*
DD Direct Deposit · *DM Debit Memo* · *EC Error Corrected*
EX Foreign Exchange · *IN Interest* · *LT Total Several Cheques*
OD Balance Overdrawn · *RI Returned Item* · *SC Service Charge*

depositor should prepare a bank reconciliation to verify that these independent sets of records are in agreement. This reconciliation may disclose internal control failures, such as unauthorized cash disbursements or failures to deposit cash receipts, as well as errors in either the bank statement or the depositor's accounting records. In addition, the reconciliation identifies certain transactions that must be recorded in the depositor's accounting records, and helps to determine the "actual" amount of cash on deposit.

For strong internal control, the employee who reconciles the bank statement should not have any other responsibilities for cash.

Normal Differences between Bank Statements and Accounting Records The balance shown in a monthly bank statement seldom equals the balance appearing in the depositor's accounting records. Certain transactions recorded by the depositor may not have been recorded by the bank. The most common examples are:

1 **Outstanding cheques.** Cheques issued and recorded by the company but not yet presented to the bank for payment.

2 **Deposits in transit.** Cash receipts recorded by the depositor but that reached the bank too late to be included in the bank statement for the current month.

In addition, certain transactions appearing in the bank statement may not have been recorded by the depositor. For example:

1 **Service charges.** Banks often charge a fee for handling small accounts. The amount of this charge usually depends upon both the average balance of the account and the number of cheques paid during the month.

2 **Charges for depositing NSF cheques.** NSF stands for "Not Sufficient Funds." When cheques are deposited, the bank increases (credits) the depositor's account. On occasion, one of these cheques may prove to be uncollectible, because the maker of the cheque does not have sufficient funds in his or her account. In such cases, the bank will reduce the depositor's account by a debit memorandum for the amount of this uncollectible item and return the cheque to the depositor marked "NSF."

   The depositor should view an NSF cheque as an account receivable from the maker of the cheque, not as cash. The accounting entry required consists of a debit to the account receivable from the customer and credit to cash.

3 **Credits for interest earned.** Most banks offer some chequing accounts that earn interest. At month-end, this interest is credited to the depositor's account and reported on the bank statement.

4 **Miscellaneous bank charges and credits.** Banks charge for services—such as printing cheques, handling collections of notes receivable, and processing NSF cheques. The bank deducts these charges from the depositor's account and notifies the depositor by including a debit memorandum in the monthly bank statement.[6] If the bank collects a note receivable on behalf of the depositor, it adds the money to the depositor's account and issues a credit memorandum describing the collection.

In a bank reconciliation, the balances shown in the bank statement and in the accounting records both are adjusted for any unrecorded transactions. Additional adjustment may be required to correct any errors discovered in the bank statement or in the accounting records.

Steps in Preparing a Bank Reconciliation To prepare a bank reconciliation, we determine those items that make up the difference between the

---

6 Banks view each depositor's account as a liability. Debit memoranda are issued for transactions that ***reduce*** this liability, such as bank service charges. Credit memoranda are issued to recognize an ***increase*** in this liability, as results, for example, from interest earned by the depositor.

ending ***balance shown on the bank statement and the balance of cash according to the depositor's records.*** By listing and studying these reconciling items we can determine the correct figure for cash owned. This is the amount that should appear in the balance sheet. The specific steps to be taken in preparing a bank reconciliation are:

1 Compare the deposits listed on the bank statement with the deposits shown in the company's records. Any deposits not yet recorded by the bank are deposits in transit and should be added to the balance shown in the bank statement. If there were any deposits in transit listed in the prior month's bank reconciliation, these amounts should appear as deposits in the current month's bank statement. If they do not appear, immediate investigation is necessary.

2 Arrange the paid cheques returned by the bank in sequence by serial numbers and compare each cheque with the corresponding entry in the cheque register. Any cheques issued but not yet paid by the bank should be listed as outstanding cheques to be deducted from the balance reported in the bank statement. Determine whether the cheques listed as ***outstanding*** (i.e., issued but not cashed) in the bank reconciliation for the ***preceding month*** have cleared the bank this month. If not, such cheques should still be listed as outstanding in the current reconciliation.

3 Add to the balance per the depositor's accounting records any credit memoranda issued by the bank that have not been recorded by the depositor. Examples in the illustrated bank statement on page 366 are the $500 credit from collection of a note receivable and the $24.74 credit for interest earned.

4 Deduct from the balance per the depositor's records any debit memoranda issued by the bank that have not been recorded by the depositor. Examples in the illustrated bank statement on page 366 are the $5 collection fee, the $50.25 NSF cheque, and the $12 service charge.

5 Make appropriate additions or deductions to correct any errors in the balance per bank statement or the balance per depositor's records. An example in the illustrated bank reconciliation on page 369 is the $27 error by the company in recording cheque no. 875.

6 Determine that the adjusted balance of the bank statement is equal to the adjusted balance in the depositor's records.

7 Prepare journal entries to record any items in the bank reconciliation listed as adjustments to the balance per the depositor's records.

Illustration of a Bank Reconciliation The July bank statement sent by the bank to Parkview Company was illustrated earlier. This statement shows a balance of cash on deposit at July 31 of $5,000.17. Assume that on July 31, Parkview's ledger shows a bank balance of $4,262.83. The employee preparing the bank reconciliation has identified the following reconciling items:

Bank
Cash Journal
(book)

1 A deposit of $410.90 made after banking hours on July 31 does not appear in the bank statement.

2 Four cheques, one issued in June and three issued in July, have not yet been paid by the bank. These cheques are:

Cheque No.	Date	Amount
801	June 15	$100.00
888	July 24	10.25
890	July 27	402.50
891	July 30	205.00

3 Two credit memoranda were included in the bank statement:

Date	Amount	Explanation
July 30	$500.00	Proceeds from collection of a non-interest-bearing note receivable from J. David. Parkview Company had left this note with the bank's collection department.
July 31	24.74	Interest earned on average account balance during July.

4 Three debit memoranda accompanied the bank statement:

Date	Amount	Explanation
July 28	$50.25	Cheque from customer J. B. Ball deposited by Parkview Company charged back as NSF.
July 30	5.00	Fee charged by bank for handling collection of note receivable.
July 31	12.00	Service charge by bank for the month of July.

5 Cheque no. 875 was issued July 20 in the amount of $85 but was erroneously recorded in the cash payments journal as $58. The cheque, in payment of telephone expense, was paid by the bank and correctly listed at $85 in the bank statement. In Parkview's ledger, the Cash account is ***overstated*** by $27 because of this error ($85 − $58 = $27).

The July 31 bank reconciliation for Parkview Company is shown below. (The numbered arrows coincide both with the steps in preparing a bank reconciliation listed on page 368 and with the reconciling items listed above.)

PARKVIEW COMPANY
Bank Reconciliation
July 31, 1996

	Balance per bank statement, July 31		$5,000.17
1	Add: Deposit of July 31 not recorded by bank		410.90
			$5,411.07
2	Deduct: Outstanding cheques:		
	No. 801	$100.00	
	No. 888	10.25	
	No. 890	402.50	
	No. 891	205.00	717.75
	Adjusted cash balance		**$4,693.32**
	Balance per depositor's records, July 31		$4,262.83
3	Add: Note receivable collected for us by bank	$500.00	
	Interest earned during July	24.74	524.74
			$4,787.57
4	Deduct: NSF cheque of J. B. Ball	$ 50.25	
	Collection fee	5.00	
	Service charge	12.00	
5	Error on cheque stub no. 875	27.00	94.25
	Adjusted cash balance (as above)		**$4,693.32**

6 (the two adjusted cash balances agree)

Updating the Accounting Records The last step in a bank reconciliation is to update the depositor's accounting records for any unrecorded cash transactions brought to light. In the bank reconciliation, every adjustment to the ***balance per depositor's records*** is a cash receipt or a cash payment that has not been recorded in the depositor's accounts. Therefore, ***each of these items should be recorded.***

In this illustration and in our assignment material, we will follow a policy of making one journal entry to record the unrecorded cash receipts and another to record the unrecorded cash reductions. (Acceptable alternatives would be to make separate journal entries for each item or to make one compound entry for all items.) Based on our recording policy, the entries to update the accounting records of Parkview Company are:

Per bank credit memoranda . . .	*Cash*	*524.74*	
	Notes Receivable		*500.00*
	Interest Revenue		*24.74*
	To record collection of note receivable from J. David collected by bank and interest earned on bank account in July.		
. . . per bank debit memoranda (and correction of an error)	*Miscellaneous Expense (or Bank Service Charges)*	*17.00*	
	Accounts Receivable, J. B. Ball	*50.25*	
	Telephone Expense	*27.00*	
	Cash		*94.25*
	To record bank charges (service charge, $12; collection fee, $5), to reclassify NSF cheque from customer J. B. Ball as an account receivable, and to correct understatement of cash payment for telephone expense.		

Electronic Funds Transfer Systems

Banks today allow depositors to use a wide variety of electronic funds transfer systems. These systems enable depositors to transfer money in and out of their bank accounts without actually bringing deposits to the bank or writing cheques. Common examples of these systems include automatic teller machines, automatic bill payment plans, transfers authorized by telephone, and the use of "debit cards."

Many businesses now use electronic funds transfers in meeting their payrolls. Every "payday," the business provides the bank with data indicating the amounts owed to specific employees. The bank electronically transfers these amounts from the company's bank account to the employees' personal bank accounts. Thus, employees receive their money immediately, and the employer is spared the nuisance of issuing and distributing paycheques.

Banks take many precautions to ensure that all electronic funds transfers are properly authorized by the depositor. Also, these transactions are fully documented in the monthly bank statements.

Petty Cash Funds

We have emphasized the importance of making all significant cash disbursements by cheque. However, every business finds it convenient to have a small amount of cash on hand with which to make some minor expendi-

OBJECTIVE 5 Describe the operation of a petty cash fund.

tures. Examples of these expenditures include such things as small purchases of office supplies, taxi fares, and doughnuts for an office meeting.

Establishing a Petty Cash Fund To create a petty cash fund, a cheque is written payable to Petty Cash for a round amount such as $100 or $200, which will cover the small expenditures to be paid in cash for a period of two or three weeks. This cheque is cashed and the money kept on hand in a locked petty cash box or drawer in the office. One employee is designated as the ***custodian*** of the fund.

The entry for the issuance of the cheque creating a petty cash fund is:

Creating the petty cash fund

Petty Cash	200	
Cash		200
To establish a petty cash fund.		

Making Disbursements from a Petty Cash Fund As cash payments are made from the petty cash box, the custodian of the fund is required to fill out a ***petty cash voucher*** for each expenditure. A petty cash voucher shows the date, the amount paid, the purpose of the expenditure, and the signature of the person receiving the money. A petty cash voucher should be prepared for every payment made from the fund. The petty cash box should, therefore, always contain cash and/or vouchers ***totalling the exact amount of the fund.***

The petty cash custodian should be informed that occasional surprise counts of the fund will be made and that he or she is personally responsible for the fund being intact at all times.

Replenishing a Petty Cash Fund Assume that a petty cash fund of $200 was established on June 1. On June 18, the custodian of the fund reports that the cash remaining in the fund is down to $20. Since the $200 originally placed in the fund is nearly exhausted, the fund should be replenished. To replenish a petty cash fund means to restore the fund to its original balance. Thus, a cheque is drawn for $180. This cheque is cashed and the money placed in the petty cash box.

The journal entry to record the issuance of the cheque includes debits to the expense accounts indicated by inspection of the vouchers, as follows:

Replenishing a petty cash fund

Office Supplies Expense	80.60	
Postage Expense	29.00	
Travel & Entertainment Expense	70.40	
Cash		180.00
To replenish the petty cash fund.		

The petty cash vouchers are perforated to prevent their being resubmitted and are filed in support of the replenishment cheque.

Note that ***expense accounts*** are debited each time the fund is replenished. The Petty Cash account is debited only when the fund is first established. There ordinarily will be no further entries in the Petty Cash account after the fund is established, unless the fund is discontinued or a decision is made to change its size from the original $200 amount.

The petty cash fund is usually replenished at the end of an accounting period, even though the fund is not running low, so that all vouchers in the fund are charged to expense accounts before these accounts are closed and financial statements prepared. It is not uncommon for small errors to be made in petty cash transactions. Therefore, small discrepancies may arise between the amount of cash needed to replenish a petty cash fund and the sum of the vouchers documenting disbursements. Any discrepancies should be recorded in a Cash Over and Short account.

Employee Fraud Involving Petty Cash There is a tendency to believe that internal control over petty cash funds is not important because the size of these funds is relatively small. However, these funds may be replenished frequently. Hence, a pattern of recurring irregularities may accumulate to significant dollar amounts.

To ensure the propriety of petty cash expenditures, ***one person*** (the custodian) should be responsible for approving and documenting all disbursements from the fund. When the fund is replenished, the accounting department should review the vouchers prepared by the fund custodian to determine the reasonableness of the expenditures and the adequacy of the documentation.

The use of a Cash Over and Short account helps bring to management's attention a pattern of recurring shortages.

The Cash Budget as a Control over Departmental Expenditures

Many businesses prepare detailed cash budgets that include forecasts of the monthly cash expenditures of each department within the organization. Management (or the internal auditors) will investigate any expenditures that are substantially in excess of the budgeted amounts. Thus, each department manager is held accountable for the monthly cash outlays occurring within his or her department.

Frequent comparisons of actual results with budgeted levels of performance greatly reduce the risks of fraud and waste. Of course, such comparisons require the use of a ***responsibility accounting system,*** that is, a chart of accounts that is sufficiently detailed to measure separately the activities of each department.

CHAPTER REVIEW

KEY TERMS INTRODUCED OR EMPHASIZED IN CHAPTER 7

Bank reconciliation An analysis that explains the difference between the balance of cash shown on the bank statement and the balance of cash shown in the depositor's records.

Board of directors The highest level of management within a business organized as a corporation.

Cash Currency, coins, cheques, bank credit card charge slips, and any other media that a bank will accept for deposit.

Cash equivalent Very short-term investments that are so liquid they are considered "equivalent" to cash. Examples include deposits in money market funds, treasury bills, certificates of deposit, and commercial paper.

Cash management Planning, controlling, and accounting for cash transactions and cash balances.

Deposits in transit Cash receipts that have been entered in the depositor's accounting records and mailed to the bank or left in the bank's night depository but reached the bank too late to be included in the current monthly bank statement.

Electronic funds transfer The process of transferring money in or out of a bank account electronically, without the need for the depositor to physically bring in a deposit or write a cheque.

Line of credit A prearranged loan agreement in which a bank stands ready to lend the borrower any amount up to the specified credit limit, without delay. The "unused" portion of a line of credit represents the ability to borrow cash immediately.

NSF cheque A customer's cheque that was deposited but returned because of a lack of funds (Not Sufficient Funds) in the account on which the cheque was drawn.

Outstanding cheques Cheques issued by a business to suppliers, employees, or other payees but not yet presented to the bank for payment.

Petty cash fund A small amount of cash set aside for making minor cash payments for which writing of cheques is not practicable.

Voucher A written authorization used in approving a transaction for recording and payment.

Voucher register A special journal used in a voucher system for the purpose of recording liabilities to pay approved vouchers, and the nature of the expenditures.

Voucher system An accounting system designed to provide strong internal control over cash disbursements. Requires that every transaction that will result in a cash payment be verified, approved, and recorded before a cheque is prepared.

DEMONSTRATION PROBLEM FOR YOUR REVIEW

The information listed below is available in reconciling the bank balance for the White River Company on November 30, 19__.

1 The bank statement at November 30 indicated a balance of $10,034.70. The ledger account for Cash showed a balance at November 30 of $12,761.94.

2 The November 30 cash receipts of $5,846.20 had been left in the bank's night depository on that date and did not appear among the deposits on the November bank statement.

3 Of the cheques issued in November, the following were not included among the paid cheques returned by the bank:

Cheque No.	Amount	Cheque No.	Amount
924	$136.25	944	$ 95.00
940	105.00	945	716.15
941	11.46	946	60.00
943	826.70		

4 A service charge for $40 by the bank had been made in error against the White River Company account.

5 The paid cheques returned with the November bank statement disclosed two errors in the company's cash records. Cheque no. 936 for $504.00 had been

erroneously recorded as $50.40, and cheque no. 942 for $245.50 had been recorded as $254.50. Cheque no. 936 was issued in payment of advertising expense and cheque no. 942 was for the acquisition of office equipment.

6 Included with the November bank statement was an NSF cheque for $220 signed by a customer, J. Wilson. This amount had been charged against the bank account on November 30.

7 A non-interest-bearing note receivable for $1,890 owned by the White River Company had been left with the bank for collection. On November 30 the company received a memorandum from the bank indicating that the note had been collected and credited to the company's account after deduction of a $5 collection charge. No entry has been made by the company to record collection of the note.

8 A debit memorandum for $12 was enclosed with the paid cheques at November 30. This charge covered the printing of chequebooks bearing the White River Company name and address.

INSTRUCTIONS

a Prepare a bank reconciliation at November 30.

b Prepare journal entries required at November 30 to bring the company's records up-to-date.

SOLUTION TO DEMONSTRATION PROBLEM

a

WHITE RIVER COMPANY
Bank Reconciliation
November 30, 19__

Balance per bank statement, Nov. 30			*$10,034.70*
Add: Deposit of Nov. 30 not recorded by bank		*$5,846.20*	
Service charge made by bank in error		*40.00*	*5,886.20*
Subtotal			*$15,920.90*
Deduct: Outstanding cheques:			
No. 924		*$ 136.25*	
No. 940		*105.00*	
No. 941		*11.46*	
No. 943		*826.70*	
No. 944		*95.00*	
No. 945		*716.15*	
No. 946		*60.00*	*1,950.56*
Adjusted cash balance			*$13,970.34*
Balance per depositor's records, Nov. 30			*$12,761.94*
Add: Error in recording cheque no. 942 for office equipment:			
Recorded as	*$254.50*		
Correct amount	*$245.50*	*$ 9.00*	
Note receivable collected by bank		*1,890.00*	*1,899.00*
			$14,660.94
Deduct: Error in recording cheque no. 936 for advertising expense:			
Correct amount	*$504.00*		
Recorded as	*50.40*	*$ 453.60*	
NSF cheque (J. Wilson)		*220.00*	
Collection fee	*$ 5.00*		
Printing cheques	*12.00*	*17.00*	*690.60*
Adjusted cash balance (as above)			*$13,970.34*

b Journal entries required at November 30 to bring the company's records up-to-date.

19__			
Nov. 30	*Cash*	*1,899.00*	
	Office Equipment		*9.00*
	Notes Receivable		*1,890.00*
	To record increase in Cash account as indicated by bank reconciliation.		
Nov. 30	*Advertising Expense*	*453.60*	
	Miscellaneous Expense	*17.00*	
	Accounts Receivable (J. Wilson)	*220.00*	
	Cash		*690.60*
	To record decreases in Cash account as indicated by bank reconciliation.		

ASSIGNMENT MATERIAL

DISCUSSION QUESTIONS

1 If a company has accounts in three banks, should it maintain a separate ledger account for each? Should the company's balance sheet show as three separate items the amounts on deposit in the three banks? Explain.

2 What are ***cash equivalents?*** Provide two examples. Why are these items often combined with cash for the purpose of balance sheet presentation?

3 Does the expression "efficient management of cash" mean anything more than procedures to prevent losses from fraud or theft? Explain.

4 Why are cash balances ***in excess*** of those needed to finance business operations sometimes viewed as relatively nonproductive assets?

5 Suggest several ways in which a corporation might efficiently utilize cash balances in excess of the amounts needed for current operations.

6 Among the various assets owned by a business, cash is probably the one for which strong internal control is most urgently needed. What specific attributes of cash cause this special need for internal control?

7 Mention some principles to be observed by a business in establishing strong internal control over cash receipts.

8 Explain how internal control over cash transactions is strengthened by compliance with the following rule: "Deposit each day's cash receipts intact in the bank, and make all disbursements by cheque."

9 Ringo Store sells only for cash and records all sales on cash registers before delivering merchandise to the customers. On a given day the cash count at the close of business indicated $10.25 less cash than was shown by the totals on the cash register tapes. In what account would this cash shortage be recorded? Would the account be debited or credited?

10 With respect to a ***voucher system,*** what is meant by the terms ***voucher, voucher register,*** and ***cheque register?***

11 Randall Company uses a voucher system to control its cash disbursements. With respect to a purchase of merchandise, what three documents would need to be examined to verify that the voucher should be approved?

12 Suggest an internal control procedure to prevent the documents supporting a paid voucher from being resubmitted later in support of another cash disbursement.

13 What information usually appears on a bank statement?

14 It is standard accounting practice to treat as cash all cheques received from customers. When a customer's cheque is received, recorded, and deposited, but later returned by the bank marked "NSF," what accounting entry or entries would be appropriate?

15 List two items often encountered in reconciling a bank account that may cause cash per the bank statement to be ***larger*** than the balance of cash shown in the accounts.

16 In the reconciliation of a bank account, what reconciling items necessitate a journal entry in the depositor's accounting records?

17 Briefly describe how an employer may use ***electronic funds transfers*** in meeting its payroll obligations. Describe the advantages of this system to (1) the employees and (2) the employer.

18 A basic concept of internal control is that all cash disbursements of substantial dollar amount should be made by cheque. What then is the purpose of a ***petty cash fund?*** Also, identify three types of expenditures that are likely to be made from such a fund.

19 Pico Stationery Shop has for years maintained a petty cash fund of $75, which is replenished twice a month.

- a How many debit entries would you expect to find in the Petty Cash account each year?
- b When would expenditures from the petty cash fund be entered in the ledger accounts?

20 Describe the nature and usefulness of a ***cash budget.***

MULTIPLE CHOICE QUESTIONS

1 Which of the following practices contributes to efficient cash management?

- a Never borrow money—maintain a cash balance sufficient to make all necessary payments.
- b Record all cash receipts and cash payments at the end of the month when reconciling the bank statements.
- c Prepare monthly forecasts of planned cash receipts, payments, and anticipated cash balances up to a year in advance.
- d Pay each bill as soon as the invoice arrives.

2 Each of the following measures strengthens internal control over cash receipts ***except:***

- a The use of a voucher system.
- b Preparation of a daily listing of all cheques received through the mail.
- c The deposit of cash receipts intact in the bank on a daily basis.
- d The use of cash registers.

3 When a voucher system is in use:

- a The voucher and supporting documents are perforated when the cheque is prepared for signature.

b The finance department signs the cheque and perforates the voucher and supporting documents.

c The accounting department does not have access to the perforated vouchers and support.

d The finance department signs the cheque and returns the signed cheque to the accounting department to be mailed.

Use the following data for questions 4 and 5.

Quinn Company's bank statement at January 31 shows a balance of $13,360, while the ledger account for Cash in Quinn's ledger shows a balance of $12,890 at the same date. The only reconciling items are the following:

- Deposit in transit, $890.
- Bank service charge, $24.
- NSF cheque from customer Greg Denton in the amount of $426.
- Error in recording cheque no. 389 for rent: it was written in the amount of $1,320, but was recorded in the bank statement as $1,230.
- Outstanding cheques, $?????

4 What is the total amount of outstanding cheques at January 31?
a $1,048 b $868 c $1,900 d $1,720

5 Assuming a single journal entry is made to adjust Quinn Company's accounting records at January 31, the journal entry includes:

a A debit to Rent Expense for $90.

b A credit to Accounts Receivable, G. Denton, for $426.

c A credit to Cash for $450.

d A credit to Cash for $1,720.

EXERCISES

EXERCISE 7-1
Accounting Terminology—Cash

Listed below are nine technical accounting terms introduced in this chapter.

Cash equivalents	*Cash budget*	*Cheque register*
Cash management	*Voucher system*	*Bank reconciliation*
Petty cash fund	*NSF cheques*	*Cash Over and Short*

Each of the following statements may (or may not) describe one of these technical terms. For each statement, indicate the term described, or answer "None" if the statement does not correctly describe any of the terms.

a Short-term and highly liquid investments that often are combined with cash for the purpose of balance sheet presentation.

b A sequence of procedures for assuring that every potential expenditure has been reviewed and approved before a cheque is issued.

c A control procedure that should bring to light any unrecorded cash disbursements.

d The account in which errors in making change for cash customers are recorded.

e Cheques issued by a business that have not yet been presented for payment.

f A document used in determining whether a department's cash receipts and cash expenditures are consistent with management's prior expectations.

g Includes measures to prevent the maintenance of excessively large balances in non-interest-bearing bank accounts.

h A means of conveniently making small, incidental disbursements of cash.

EXERCISE 7-2
Effects of Errors and Irregularities

DodgeTown, Inc., is an automobile dealership. The company uses a voucher system and has several bank accounts. Shown below are a series of situations that may (or may not) represent errors or irregularities that affect the reliability of the company's accounting records.

a Collection of an account receivable is recorded by debiting Sales Returns and Allowances and crediting Accounts Receivable.

b A cheque was issued in payment of voucher no. 4600, but no entry was made in the cheque register. Voucher no. 4600 was for property taxes expense.

c No entry was made to record the investment of cash in treasury bills, which are considered cash equivalents.

d No entry was made to record the investment of cash in the stock of **Canadian Pacific Limited,** which is ***not*** considered a cash equivalent.

e No entry was made to record the failure to earn any interest revenue on the large cash balances in the corporation's non-interest-bearing bank account.

f No entry is made to adjust the company's accounting records for the amount of a deposit in transit listed in the year-end bank reconciliation.

g No entry was made to adjust the company's accounting records for customers' cheques returned by the bank at year-end with the designation "NSF."

h Last month, a particular supplier was paid in full for services classified as an expense. This month, the same supporting documents were recirculated through the voucher system, and a second voucher was recorded authorizing a duplicate payment. (No cheque has yet been issued for this second payment.)

i The custodian "borrowed" $250 from the petty cash fund but replaced the money before the fund was counted or replenished.

j As the petty cash fund contained almost half of its original balance at year-end, the fund was not replenished and no entries were made in the accounting records.

INSTRUCTIONS

Indicate the effects (if any) of each of these situations upon the elements of the company's financial statements listed below. (Notice that Cash & Cash Equivalents is listed separately from other assets.) Use the code letters ***O*** to indicate overstatement, ***U*** to indicate understatement, and ***NE*** to indicate no effect. Organize your answer in tabular form, using the following column headings:

	Income Statement					Balance Sheet						
Transaction	*Net Sales*	–	*Expenses*	=	*Net Income*	*Cash & Cash Equivalents*	+	*All Other Assets*	=	*Liabilities*	+	*Owners' Equity*
a												

EXERCISE 7-3
Internal Control: Identifying Strength and Weakness

Some of the following practices are suggestive of strength in internal controls; others are suggestive of weakness. Identify each of the eight practices with the term ***Strength*** or ***Weakness.*** Give reasons for your answers.

a Vouchers and all supporting documents are stamped "PAID" before being sent to the finance department for review and signing of cheques.

b Personnel in the accounting department are not authorized to handle cash receipts. Therefore, accounts receivable records are maintained by the credit manager, who handles all collections from customers.

c Accounting department personnel are not authorized to prepare bank reconciliations. This procedure is performed in the finance department and the accounting department is notified of any required adjustments to the accounts.

d Cheques received through the mail are recorded daily by the person maintaining accounts receivable records.

e All cash receipts are deposited daily.

f Any difference between a day's over-the-counter cash receipts and the day's total shown by the cash register is added to or removed from petty cash.

g After the monthly bank reconciliation has been prepared, any difference between the adjusted balance per the depositor's records and the adjusted balance per the bank statement is entered in the Cash Over and Short account.

h Employees who handle cash receipts are not authorized to issue credit memoranda or to write off accounts receivable as uncollectible.

EXERCISE 7-4
Subdivision of Duties

Certain subdivisions of duties are highly desirable for the purpose of achieving a reasonable degree of internal control. For each of the following six responsibilities, explain whether or not assigning the duty to an employee who also handles cash receipts would represent a significant weakness in internal control. Briefly explain your reasoning.

a Responsibility for executing both cash and credit sales transactions.

b Responsibility for maintaining the general ledger.

c Responsibility for maintaining the accounts receivable subsidiary ledger.

d Responsibility for issuing credit memoranda for sales returns.

e Responsibility for preparing a control listing of all cash collections.

f Responsibility for preparing monthly bank reconciliations.

EXERCISE 7-5
Voucher System

Laser Optic, Inc., uses a voucher system. The following transactions occurred early this month:

a Voucher no. 100 prepared to purchase office equipment at cost of $4,000 from Coast Furniture Co. Ltd.

b Cheque no. 114 issued in payment of voucher no. 100.

c Voucher no. 101 prepared to establish a petty cash fund of $150.

d Cheque no. 115 issued in payment of voucher no. 101.

e Voucher no. 102 prepared to replenish the petty cash fund, which contained $40 cash, and receipts for postage $38, miscellaneous expense $54, and delivery service $18.

f Cheque no. 116 issued in payment of voucher no. 102. Cheque cashed and proceeds placed in petty cash fund.

INSTRUCTIONS

You are to record the transactions in general journal form (without explanations). Also indicate after each entry the journal (or book of original entry) in which in actual practice the transaction would be recorded. For example, your treatment of transaction **a** should be as follows:

(a) Office Equipment	*4,000*	
Vouchers Payable		*4,000*
(Voucher register)		

EXERCISE 7-6
Short Bank Reconciliation

The following information relating to the bank account is available for Music Hall at July 31:

Balance per bank statement at July 31	*$19,893.25*
Balance per depositor's records at July 31	*18,681.35*
Outstanding cheques	*2,102.50*
Deposits in transit	*872.60*
Service charge by bank	*18.00*

INSTRUCTIONS Prepare a bank reconciliation for Music Hall at July 31.

EXERCISE 7-7
Another Short Bank Reconciliation

The following information relating to the bank account is available for Wild Bill's Barbeque at May 31.

Balance per bank statement at May 31	*$9,740.15*
Outstanding cheques	*3,352.70*
Deposit in transit	*1,106.30*
Service charge by bank	*10.00*
Interest credited by the bank	*43.10*
Balance per depositor's accounting records at May 31	*7,460.65*

INSTRUCTIONS Prepare a bank reconciliation at May 31.

EXERCISE 7-8
Bank Reconciliation and Entries to Update the Accounting Records

Shown below is the information needed to prepare a bank reconciliation for Data Flow, Inc., at December 31.

1. At December 31, cash per the bank statement was $15,981; cash per the company's records was $17,445.
2. Two debit memoranda accompanied the bank statement: service charges for December of $24, and a $600 cheque drawn by Jane Jones marked "NSF."
3. Cash receipts of $4,353 on December 31 were not deposited until January 2.
4. The following cheques had been issued in December but were not included among the paid cheques returned by the bank: no. 620 for $978, no. 630 for $2,052, and no. 641 for $483.

INSTRUCTIONS

a. Prepare a bank reconciliation at December 31.
b. Prepare the necessary journal entry or entries to update the accounting records of Data Flow, Inc.

EXERCISE 7-9
Analysis of Reconciling Items

At September 30, the Cash account of Canvasback, a sole proprietorship, showed a balance of $72,900. The bank statement, however, showed a balance of $87,400 at the same date. The only reconciling items consisted of a $4,800 deposit in transit, a credit for interest earned of $200, and 30 outstanding cheques.

INSTRUCTIONS

a. Compute the amount of cash that should appear in the company's balance sheet at September 30.
b. Compute the total amount of the outstanding cheques.

EXERCISE 7-10
Adjustments to the Cash Account

In this exercise we focus on some of the basic computations required in almost all bank reconciliations. At the end of November, Glacier Lodge received a bank statement showing a balance of $105,000. The balance included interest earned during November of $450. All cheques issued by Glacier Lodge were returned with the November bank statement except for 10 cheques totalling $16,000 issued on November 30. Also, a deposit of $8,000 mailed to the bank by Glacier Lodge on November 30 did not appear on the November bank statement.

INSTRUCTIONS

a Compute the amount of cash to appear on the November 30 balance sheet of Glacier Lodge. Show all computations.

b Compute the amount of cash shown by Glacier Lodge's records ***before*** any month-end entries were made to update the company's records.

EXERCISE 7-11
Reconciling Items

In reconciling the bank account of Lane Company, the accountant had to deal with the following six items.

1 Outstanding cheques.
2 Bank service charges.
3 Cheque no. 502 was issued in the correct amount of $350 and paid by the bank in that amount, but had been incorrectly recorded in Lane Company's accounting records as $530.
4 Collection by bank of note receivable left with bank by Lane Company for collection and credit to Lane Company's account.
5 Customers' cheques deposited by Lane Company but returned by bank marked "NSF."
6 Deposit in transit.

INSTRUCTIONS

You are to classify each of the above six items under one of the following headings: (a) an addition to the balance per the bank statement; (b) a deduction from the balance per the bank statement; (c) an addition to the balance per the depositor's records; (d) a deduction from the balance per the depositor's records.

EXERCISE 7-12
Petty Cash

Prince Plaza established a petty cash fund of $200 on June 1. On June 20 the fund was replenished for the payments made to date as shown by the following petty cash vouchers: postage, $46; telephone expense, $17.50; repairs, $34.70; miscellaneous expense, $27. Prepare journal entries in ***general journal form*** to record the establishment of the fund on June 1 and its replenishment on June 20.

EXERCISE 7-13
More Petty Cash

On February 3, Executive Golf Course established a petty cash fund in the amount of $150. At February 28, the fund contained $9.20 in cash. The vouchers in the fund are summarized below:

Postage due	*$ 0.36*
Beer	*20.60*
Office supplies	*82.14*
Gas money for John	*5.00*
Mark's lunch	*8.00*
Flowers for Linda's birthday	*12.35*
Doughnuts	*6.30*

The company replenishes this fund at the end of each month. All types of expenditures that amount to less than $50 during the month are charged to Miscellaneous Expense in one debit entry. Any type of expenditure exceeding $50 is debited to an expense account that describes the nature of the expenditure. Any cash shortage or excess is debited or credited to a Cash Over and Short account, regardless of the dollar amount.

INSTRUCTIONS

Prepare all journal entries relating to the operation of this petty cash fund during the month.

PROBLEMS

Group A

PROBLEM 7A-1 Internal Control Procedures

Listed below are nine errors or problems that might occur in the processing of cash transactions. Also shown is a separate list of internal control procedures.

Possible Errors or Problems

a In serving customers who do not appear to be attentive, a salesclerk often rings up a sale at less than the actual sales amount and then removes the additional cash collected from the customer.

b John Davis, who has prepared bank reconciliations for Marlo Corporation for several years has noticed that some cheques issued by the company are never presented for payment. Davis, therefore, has formed the habit of dropping any cheques outstanding for more than six months from the outstanding cheques list and removing a corresponding amount of cash from the cash receipts. These actions taken together have left the ledger account for cash in agreement with the adjusted bank balance and have enriched Davis substantially.

c A voucher was circulated through the system twice, causing the supplier to be paid twice for the same invoice.

d Lisa Miller, an employee of Plaza Home Repairs, frequently has trouble in getting the bank reconciliation to balance. If the book balance is more than the bank balance, she writes a cheque payable to Cash and cashes it. If the book balance is less than the bank balance, she makes an accounting entry debiting Cash and crediting Cash Over and Short.

e Without fear of detection, the cashier sometimes abstracts cash forwarded to him from the mailroom or the sales department instead of depositing these receipts in the company's bank account.

f The monthly bank reconciliation continually shows a difference between the adjusted bank balance and the adjusted book balance because the cashier regularly deposits actual cash receipts, but the debits to the Cash account reflect cash register readings that differ by the amount of errors in making change in cash sales transactions.

g All cash received from Monday through Thursday was lost in a burglary on Thursday night.

h A salesclerk occasionally makes an error in the amount of change given to a customer.

i The official designated to sign cheques is able to steal blank cheques and issue them for unauthorized purposes without fear of detection.

Internal Control Procedures

1 Periodic reconciliation of bank statements to accounting records.

2 Use of a Cash Over and Short account.

3 Adequate subdivision of duties.

4 Use of prenumbered sales tickets.

5 Depositing each day's cash receipts intact in the bank.

6 Use of electronic cash registers equipped with optical scanners to read magnetically coded labels on merchandise.

7 Immediate preparation of a control listing when cash is received, and the comparison of this listing to bank deposits.

8 Cancellation of paid vouchers at the time of signing the cheques.

9 Requirement that a voucher be prepared as advance authorization of every cash disbursement.

0 None of the above control procedures can effectively prevent this type of error or problem from occurring.

INSTRUCTIONS

List the letters (**a** through **i**) designating each possible error or problem. Beside this letter, place the number indicating the internal control procedure that should prevent this type of error or problem from occurring. If none of the specified internal control procedures would effectively prevent the error or problem, place a **0** opposite the letter.

PROBLEM 7A-2
Preparing a Bank Reconciliation

At November 30, One Day Cleaners has available the following data concerning its bank account:

1 At November 30, cash per the bank statement was $37,758; per the accounting records, $42,500.

2 The cash receipts of $6,244 on November 30 were deposited on December 1.

3 Included on the bank statement was a credit for $167 interest earned on this account during November.

4 Two cheques were outstanding at November 30: no. 921 for $964 and no. 925 for $1,085.

5 Enclosed with the bank statement were two debit memoranda for the following items: service charge for November, $14; and a $700 cheque of customer Tanya Miller, marked "NSF."

INSTRUCTIONS

a Prepare a bank reconciliation at November 30.

b Prepare adjusting entries (in general journal form) based on the bank reconciliation.

PROBLEM 7A-3
A More Comprehensive Bank Reconciliation

The cash transactions and cash balances of Norfleet Farm for July were as follows:

1 The ledger account for Cash showed a balance at July 31 of $16,766.95.

2 The July bank statement showed a closing balance of $18,928.12.

3 The cash received on July 31 amounted to $4,017.15. It was left at the bank in the night depository chute after banking hours on July 31 and was therefore not recorded by the bank on the July statement.

4 Also included with the July bank statement was a debit memorandum from the bank for $7.65 representing service charges for July.

5 A credit memorandum enclosed with the July bank statement indicated that a non-interest-bearing note receivable for $4,545 from Rene Manes, left with the bank for collection, had been collected and the proceeds credited to the account of Norfleet Farm.

6 Comparison of the paid cheques returned by the bank with the entries in the accounting records revealed that cheque no. 821 for ***$835.02,*** issued July 15 in payment for office equipment, had been erroneously entered in Norfleet's records as ***$853.02.***

7 Examination of the paid cheques also revealed that three cheques, all issued in July, had not yet been paid by the bank: no. 811 for $861.12; no. 814 for $640.80; no. 823 for $301.05.

8 Included with the July bank statement was a $180 cheque drawn by Howard Williams, a customer of Norfleet Farm. This cheque was marked "NSF." It had been included in the deposit of July 27 but had been charged back against the company's account on July 31.

INSTRUCTIONS

a Prepare a bank reconciliation for Norfleet Farm at July 31.

b Prepare journal entries (in general journal form) to update the accounts at July 31. Assume that the accounts have not been closed.

c State the amount of cash that should be included in the balance sheet at July 31.

PROBLEM 7A-4
Another Comprehensive Bank Reconciliation

Daytona Recycling Centre reports the following information concerning cash balances and cash transactions for the month of September:

1 Cash balance per bank statement as of September 30 was $20,893.25.

2 Two debit memoranda accompanied the bank statement: one for $10 was for service charges for the month; the other for $64.60 was attached to an NSF cheque from A. Smith.

3 Included with the bank statement was $69 credit memorandum for interest earned on the bank account in September.

4 The paid cheques returned with the September bank statement disclosed an error in Daytona's cash records. Cheque no. 851 for $77.44 for telephone expense had erroneously been recorded as $44.77.

5 A collection charge for $26.00 (not applicable to Daytona) was erroneously deducted from the account by the bank. Notice that this was the ***bank's*** error.

6 Cash receipts of September 30 amounting to $585.25 were deposited in the bank too late to be included in the September bank statement.

7 Cheques outstanding as of September 30 were as follows: no. 860 for $151.93, no. 867 for $82.46, and no. 869 for $123.61.

8 The Cash account showed the following entries during September:

Cash

Sept	*1*	*Balance*	*18,341.82*	*Sept*	*30*	*Month's payments*	*11,598.63*
	30	*Month's receipts*	*14,441.58*				

INSTRUCTIONS

a Prepare a bank reconciliation at September 30.

b Prepare the necessary journal entries, in general journal form, to update the company's records.

PROBLEM 7A-5
Operating a Petty Cash Fund

In order to handle small cash disbursements in an efficient manner, Off Broadway established a petty cash fund on July 10. The following events relating to petty cash occurred in July.

July 10 A cheque for $300 drawn payable to Petty Cash was issued and cashed to establish the fund.

July 31 At month-end, a count of the fund disclosed the following:

Office supplies expense	*$50.40*
Postage expense	*69.00*
Travel expense	*49.38*
Miscellaneous expense	*50.62*
Currency and coin remaining in the fund	*78.60*

July 31 A cheque was issued to replenish the petty cash fund.

INSTRUCTIONS

a Prepare an entry in general journal form to record the establishment of the petty cash fund on July 10.

b Prepare an entry to record the replenishment of the petty cash fund on July 31.

c Net income for Off Broadway in July was $6,785.20. What amount of net income would have been reported in the July income statement if the company had *not* replenished the petty cash fund on July 31?

PROBLEM 7A-6
"Charmed . . ."

Equipment Rental Company had poor internal control over its cash transactions. Facts about the company's cash position at November 30, 1996, were as described below.

The accounting records showed a cash balance of $29,959.00, which included a deposit of $3,420.60 on November 30 not yet recorded by the bank. The balance indicated in the bank statement was $18,299.40. Included in the bank statement were the following debit and credit memoranda:

Adj Balance 18334.—

Debit Memoranda:

Cheque from customer G. Davis, deposited by Equipment Rental Co., but charged back as NSF	*$1,500.00*
Bank service charges for November	*25.00*

Credit Memorandum:

Proceeds from collection of a note receivable from Regal Farms that Equipment Rental Co. had left with the bank's collection department	*3,000.00*

Outstanding cheques as of November 30 were as follows:

Cheque No.	*Amount*
8231	*$ 340.30*
8263	*800.50*
8288	*145.20*
8294	*2,100.00*

Melanie Charm, the company's cashier, has been abstracting portions of the company's cash receipts for several months. Each month, Charm prepares the company's bank reconciliation in a manner that conceals her thefts. Her bank reconciliation for November is illustrated as follows:

Balance per bank statement, Nov. 30		*$18,299.40*
Add: Deposits of November 30 not recorded by bank	*$4,320.60* 900	
Collection of note from Regal Farms	*3,000.00*	*7,320.60*
Subtotal		*$26,620.00* 25620.— 1000.
Less: Outstanding cheques:		
No. 8231	*$ 340.30*	
8263	*800.50*	
8288	*145.20*	*1,186.00* 100
Adjusted cash balance per bank statement		*$25,434.00*

Balance per accounting records, Nov. 30		*$29,959.00*
Add: Credit memorandum from bank		*3,000.00* ← subtraction
Subtotal		*$26,959.00*
Less: Debit memoranda from bank:		
NSF cheque of G. Davis	*$1,500.00*	
Bank service charges	*25.00*	*1,525.00*
Adjusted cash balance per accounting records		*$25,434.00*

INSTRUCTIONS

a Determine the amount of the cash shortage that has been concealed by Charm in her bank reconciliation by preparing a correct bank reconciliation.

b Carefully review Charm's bank reconciliation and explain in detail how she concealed the amount of the shortage. Include a listing of the dollar amounts that were concealed in various ways. This listing should total the amount of the shortage determined in part **a**.

c Suggest some specific internal control measures that appear to be necessary for Equipment Rental Company.

PROBLEM 7A-7
Using Bank Statement and Records To Prepare Bank Reconciliation

At September 30, 1996, Sheraton Company's Cash account balance was exactly equal to the ending balance shown on the bank statement except for these items: a service charge by the bank of $12, interest income from the bank account of $28, and two outstanding cheques—No. 786 for $200, No. 860 for $300. The cash receipts and the cash payments from the data base showed the following transactions:

Cash Receipts

Date		Cash Dr
Oct. 1		72.80
3		361.00
6		280.00
8		510.00
10		205.60
13		180.14
15		345.00
18		427.50
20		90.00
22		360.00
27		625.00
28		130.25
29		280.50
31		690.50
		4,558.29

Cash Payments

Date		Ch. No.	Cash Cr
Oct. 1		865	130.00
1		866	90.00
1		867	35.48
2		868	31.15
4		869	60.00
4		870	70.00
5		871	515.00
8		872	62.50
9		873	13.30
10		874	28.00
13		875	650.00
19		876	125.06
19		877	40.00
19		878	85.00
20		879	24.10
21		880	38.60
22		881	65.00
22		882	162.40
23		883	150.00
26		884	15.00
28		885	270.00
28		886	105.20
28		887	225.00
28		888	355.00
30		889	25.00
31		890	35.00
31		891	255.00
			3,660.79

On November 2, the company received from its bank the following bank statement covering the month of October. Enclosed with the bank statement were 24 cheques paid by the bank during October and a $24.75 debit memorandum for service charge and a $20.50 credit memorandum for interest.

CANADIAN ROYAL BANK
380 Campbell Street, Windsor, Ontario N9B 3P6

Account No. 126890

Sheraton Company
169 Randolph Avenue
Windsor, Ontario N9C 689

	Date	Amount
Balance Forward	Sept. 30, 1996	$8,158.75

Cheques			Deposits	Date	Balance
31.15	35.48	130.00	72.80	Oct. 2	8,034.92
60.00	300.00		361.00	5	8,035.92
70.00	515.00		280.00	7	7,730.92
90.00				8	7,640.92
13.30	62.50		510.00	9	8,075.12
28.00			205.60	12	8,252.72
650.00			180.14	14	7,782.86
			345.00	16	8,127.86
85.00			427.50	19	8,470.36
24.10	125.06			20	8,321.20
40.00			90.00	21	8,371.20
162.40	65.00		360.00	23	8,503.80
15.00			625.00	27	9,113.80
355.00	270.00	225.00	130.25	29	8,394.05
255.00	25.00	24.75 SC	280.50		
			20.50 IN	31	8,390.30

INSTRUCTIONS

a Compute the amount of cash balance at October 31 according to the depositor's records, assuming the necessary journal entry or entries to update the company's records at September 30 have been made.

b Prepare a bank reconciliation at October 31.

c Prepare general journal entries to update the company's records at October 31, based on information contained in the bank reconciliation in part **b.**

Group B

PROBLEM 7B-1
Internal Control Procedures

Listed below are nine errors or problems that might occur in the processing of cash transactions. Also shown is a separate list of internal control procedures.

Possible Errors or Problems

a The bookkeeper of Centre Hardware frequently has trouble in getting the bank reconciliation to balance. If the book balance is more than the bank balance, the bookkeeper writes a cheque payable to Cash and cashes it. If the book balance is less than the bank balance, the bookkeeper makes an accounting entry debiting Cash and crediting Cash Over and Short.

b The cashier of Fun Toys Store abstracts cash forwarded to him from the mailroom or the sales department instead of depositing these receipts in the store's bank account.

c The monthly bank reconciliation continually shows a difference between the adjusted bank balance and the adjusted book balance because the cashier regularly deposits actual cash receipts, but the debits to the Cash account reflect cash register readings that differ by the amount of errors in making change in cash sales transactions.

d All cash receipts from Monday through Wednesday were stolen on Wednesday night.

e A cashier occasionally makes an error in the amount of change given to a customer.

f The official authorized to sign cheques is able to steal blank cheques and issue them for unauthorized purposes without fear of detection.

g When serving customers who do not appear to be attentive, a cashier often rings up a sale at less than the actual sales amount and then removes the additional cash collected from the customer.

h Teresa Hill, who has prepared bank reconciliations for Ross Stewart, Inc., for several years has noticed that some cheques issued by the company are never presented for payment. Hill, therefore, has formed the habit of dropping any cheques outstanding for more than six months from the outstanding cheques list and removing a corresponding amount of cash from the cash receipts. These actions taken together have left the ledger account for cash in agreement with the adjusted bank balance and have enriched Hill substantially.

i A voucher was circulated through the system twice, causing the supplier to be paid for the same voucher the second time.

Internal Control Procedures

1 Periodic reconciliation of bank statements to accounting records.

2 Use of a Cash Over and Short account.

3 Adequate subdivision of duties.

4 Use of prenumbered sales tickets.

5 Depositing each day's cash receipts intact in the bank.

6 Use of electronic cash registers equipped with optical scanners to read magnetically coded labels on merchandise.

7 Immediate preparation of a control listing when cash is received, and the comparison of this listing to bank deposits.

8 Cancellation of paid vouchers at the time of signing the cheques.

9 Requirement that a voucher be prepared as advance authorization of every cash disbursement.

0 None of the above control procedures can effectively prevent this type of error or problem from occurring.

INSTRUCTIONS

List the letters (**a** through **i**) designating each possible error or problem. Beside this letter, place the number indicating the internal control procedure that should prevent this type of error or problem from occurring. If none of the specified internal control procedures would effectively prevent the error or problem, place a **0** opposite the letter.

PROBLEM 7B-2
Preparing a Bank Reconciliation

Bluegrass Tonight is a nightclub in Halifax. The information necessary for preparing a bank reconciliation for the company at November 30 appears below:

1 As of November 30, cash per the bank statement is $41,631, per the accounting records, $48,609.

2 Cash receipts of $9,366 on November 30 were not deposited until December 1.

3 Among the paid cheques returned by the bank was a stolen cheque for $1,512 paid in error after Bluegrass Tonight had officially notified the bank not to make payment. Thus, payment of this cheque was a bank error and should not have been charged against Bluegrass Tonight's bank account.

4 The following memoranda accompanied the bank statement:

   a A debit memo for service charges, $21

   b A debit memo attached to an $1,167 cheque that Bluegrass had accepted from a customer and deposited in its account, but that the bank had returned with the marking "NSF"

   c A credit memo for interest earned on the account during November, $135

5 The following cheques had been issued by the nightclub but had not been paid by the bank as of November 30: no. 921 for $2,346; no. 924 for $1,446; and no. 925 for $1,161.

INSTRUCTIONS Prepare the November 30 bank reconciliation.

PROBLEM 7B-3
A More Comprehensive Bank Reconciliation

During July the cash transactions and cash balances of Rapid Harvest were as follows:

1 The cash balance per the bank statement at July 31 was $28,945.27.

2 The ledger account for Cash had a balance at July 31 of $26,686.95.

3 Cash receipts on July 31 amounted to $4,000. These cash receipts were left at the bank in the night depository chute after banking hours on July 31 and therefore were not included by the bank in the July bank statement.

4 Included with the July bank statement was a credit memorandum showing interest earned by the depositor on this account in the amount of $80.

5 Another credit memorandum enclosed with the July bank statement showed that a non-interest-bearing note for $3,663 from Ralph Warde, left with the bank for collection, had been collected and the proceeds credited to the account of Rapid Harvest.

6 Also included with the July bank statement was a debit memorandum from the bank for $19.45 representing service charges for July.

7 Comparison of the paid cheques returned by the bank with the entries in the accounting records revealed that cheque no. 922 for $4,521.50 issued July 15 in payment for salaries expense had been erroneously entered in the accounting records as $5,421.50.

8 Examination of the paid cheques also revealed that three cheques, all issued in July, had not yet been paid by the bank: no. 921 for $944.32; no. 924 for $320.50; no. 935 for $538.15.

9 Included with the July bank statement was a $168.20 cheque drawn by Edward Jones, a customer of Rapid Harvest. This cheque was marked "NSF." It had been included in the deposit of July 28 but had been charged back against the company's account on July 31.

INSTRUCTIONS

a Prepare a bank reconciliation for Rapid Harvest at July 31.

b Prepare journal entries (in general journal form) to update the accounts at July 31. Assume that the accounts have not been closed.

c State the amount of cash that should be included in the balance sheet at July 31.

Jan. 97 ✓ 81

PROBLEM 7B-4 Another Comprehensive Bank Reconciliation

The information needed to prepare a bank reconciliation for Wicked Pony at March 31 is listed below.

1 Cash balance per the accounting records of Wicked Pony, $18,106.69.

2 The bank statement showed a balance of $22,134.27 at March 31.

3 Accompanying the bank statement was a debit memorandum relating to a cheque for $186 from a customer, D. Otay. The cheque was returned by the bank and stamped "NSF."

4 Cheques outstanding as of March 31 were as follows: no. 84 for $1,841.02; no. 88 for $1,323.00; no. 89 for $16.26.

5 Also accompanying the bank statement was a debit memorandum for $44.80 for safety deposit box rent; the bank had erroneously charged this item to the account of Wicked Pony.

6 On March 29, the bank collected a non-interest-bearing note for Wicked Pony. The note was for $2,963.

7 A deposit of $2,008.50 on March 31 was made too late for the bank to record it on March 31.

8 In recording a $160 cheque received on account from a customer, Ross Company, the accountant for Wicked Pony erroneously recorded the amount collected as $16. The cheque appeared correctly among the deposits on the March bank statement.

9 The bank service charge for March amounted to $20.40; a debit memo in this amount was returned with the bank statement.

INSTRUCTIONS

a Prepare a bank reconciliation at March 31.

b Prepare the necessary journal entries to update the account at March 31.

c What amount of cash should be included in the company's March 31 balance sheet?

PROBLEM 7B-5 Operating a Petty Cash Fund

Santa Rosa Winery maintains a petty cash fund to control small cash payments. The company does not use a voucher system. Shown below are the transactions involving the establishment of the fund and its replenishment at September 30, the end of the company's fiscal year:

Sept. 12 A cheque for $500 was issued and cashed to establish a petty cash fund.

Sept. 30 A count of the fund showed currency and coin of $104.10 remaining on hand. Petty cash receipts in the fund were as follows:

Office supplies expense	*$100.43*
Postage expense	*43.92*
Travel & entertainment expense	*183.10*
Miscellaneous expense	*66.44*

Sept. 30 Although the fund had not been used fully, management wished to replenish the fund before the accounts were closed for the fiscal year. A cheque was therefore issued and cashed on this date in the amount necessary to restore the fund to its $500 balance.

INSTRUCTIONS

a Prepare journal entries in general journal form to record the establishment of the fund on September 12 and its replenishment on September 30.

b What would have been the effect, if any, on net income for the fiscal year ended September 30 if the company had forgotten to replenish the fund on September 30? Explain.

PROBLEM 7B-6
Bank Reconciliation and Internal Control

Carriage Towne, a successful small business, had never given much consideration to the need for internal control, and the internal controls over cash transactions were inadequate. Thom Chan, the cashier-bookkeeper, handled cash receipts, made small disbursements from these cash receipts, maintained the accounting records, and prepared the monthly reconciliations of the bank account. Recognizing the weaknesses in internal control over cash transactions, Chan began pocketing some of the company's cash receipts.

At the end of April, the bank statement indicated a balance on deposit of $37,350.90. The following cheques were outstanding: no. 7552 for $612.30, no. 7573 for $1,219.00, no. 7574 for $468.30, no. 7611 for $1,321.10, no. 7613 for $402.20, and no. 7622 for $3,211.00. All cash receipts for April (except those stolen by Chan) had been deposited in the bank, and the deposits all were listed correctly in the April 30 bank statement. The cash balance shown in the company's accounting records at April 30 was $38,467.00, including $200.00 in cash on hand. This information was known to Chan; however, he concealed the amount of his theft by preparing the bank "reconciliation" improperly, as shown below:

Balance per bank statement, April 30		*$37,350.90*
Less: Outstanding cheques:		
No. 7611	*$1,321.10*	
No. 7613	*402.20*	
No. 7622	*2,311.00*	*3,034.30*
		$34,316.60
Add: Deposit not recorded by bank (April 30 receipts)	*$3,650.40*	
Cash on hand	*500.00*	*4,150.40*
Balance per accounting records, April 30		*$38,467.00*

INSTRUCTIONS

a Determine the amount of the cash shortage concealed by Chan in his November bank reconciliation by preparing a correct bank reconciliation.

b Carefully review Chan's bank reconciliation and explain in detail how he concealed the amount of the shortage. Include a listing of the dollar amounts that were concealed in various ways. This listing should total the amount of the shortage as determined in part **a**.

c Suggest some specific internal control measures that appear to be necessary for Carriage Towne.

PROBLEM 7B-7
Using Bank Statement and Records To Prepare Bank Reconciliation

The balance of the Cash account in the ledger of Carnavan Limited, at May 31, was equal to the ending balance on the May bank statement except for these items: an outstanding cheque (No. 369) for $100, an outstanding deposit of $590 and a bank service charge of $23.80. The cash receipts and cash payments from the data base showed the following transactions during June.

Cash Receipts			Cash Payments			
Date		**Cash Dr**	**Date**		**Ch. No.**	**Cash Cr**
June 2		82.80	June 1		665	148.00
4		351.00	1		666	90.00
6		280.00	1		667	25.48
8		500.00	2		668	23.15
10		215.60	4		669	60.00
13		280.14	4		670	80.00
15		245.00	5		671	505.00
17		327.50	9		672	62.50
20		190.00	10		673	18.30
22		360.00	10		674	23.00
26		625.00	13		675	650.00
28		150.25	19		676	25.06
29		260.50	19		677	40.00
30		315.25	19		678	85.00
		4,183.04	20		679	124.10
			21		680	48.60
			22		681	65.00
			22		682	162.40
			23		683	100.00
			26		684	15.00
			28		685	290.00
			28		686	125.20
			28		687	225.00
			28		688	335.00
			29		689	45.00
			29		690	65.00
			30		691	135.00
						3,570.79

On July 3, Carnavan Limited received the following bank statement covering the month of June. Enclosed were 23 cheques paid by the bank during June, a $26.50 debit memorandum for service charges, a credit memorandum for $20 interest, and a debit memorandum for $50 for an NSF cheque from K. Jordan.

DOMINION BANK
176 Georgia Street, Vancouver B.C. V6E 4A2

Statement of Account — Account No. 3691278

Carnavan Limited 268 Front Street Vancouver, B.C. V8L 1S2		Date	Amount
	Balance Forward	May 31	$7,168.75

Cheques			Deposits	Date	Balance
			590.00	June 1	7,758.75
23.15	25.48	148.00	82.80	3	7,644.92
60.00			351.00	5	7,935.92
80.00	505.00		280.00	7	7,630.92
90.00				8	7,540.92
62.50			500.00	9	7,978.42
23.00	18.30		215.60	12	8,152.72
650.00			280.14	14	7,782.86
			245.00	16	8,027.86
85.00			327.50	19	8,270.36
124.10	25.06			20	8,121.20
40.00			190.00	21	8,271.20
162.40	65.00		360.00	23	8,403.80
15.00			625.00	27	9,013.80
335.00	290.00	225.00	150.25	29	8,314.05
135.00	45.00	26.50 SC	260.50		
50.00 DM			20.00 IN	30	8,338.05

INSTRUCTIONS

a Compute the amount of cash balance at June 30 according to the depositor's records, assuming the necessary journal entry or entries to update the company's records at June 30 have been made.

b Prepare a bank reconciliation at June 30.

c Prepare general journal entries to update the company's records at June 30, based on information contained in the bank reconciliation in part **b.**

ANALYTICAL AND DECISION PROBLEMS AND CASES

A&D 7-1
Money to Burn

St. Jude Medical, Inc., is a large public corporation engaged in the manufacture of heart valves and other medical products. In recent years, the company has accumulated large amounts of cash and cash equivalents as a result of profitable operations. A recent annual report shows cash and cash equivalents amounting to more than 50% of the company's total assets. As these large holdings of cash and cash equivalents have been accumulated, the company has paid no dividends.

INSTRUCTIONS Evaluate St. Jude's policies of accumulating liquid resources instead of paying dividends from the perspectives of:

a The company's creditors.

b The company's shareholders.

A&D 7-2 Embezzlement, She Wrote

D. J. Fletcher, a trusted employee of Bluestem Products, found herself in personal financial difficulties and decided to "borrow" (steal) $3,000 from the company and to conceal her theft.

As a first step, Fletcher removed $3,000 in currency from the cash register. This amount represented the bulk of the cash received in over-the-counter sales during the three business days since the last bank deposit. Fletcher then removed a $3,000 cheque from the day's incoming mail; this cheque had been mailed in by a customer, Michael Adams, in full payment of his account. Fletcher made no journal entry to record the $3,000 collection from Adams but deposited the cheque in Bluestem Products' bank account in place of the $3,000 over-the-counter cash receipts she had stolen.

In order to keep Adams from protesting when his month-end statement reached him, Fletcher made a journal entry debiting Sales Returns and Allowances and crediting Accounts Receivable—Michael Adams. Fletcher posted this entry to the two general ledger accounts affected and also to Adams's account in the subsidiary ledger for accounts receivable.

INSTRUCTIONS

a Did these actions by Fletcher cause the general ledger to be out of balance or the subsidiary ledger to disagree with the controlling account? Explain.

b Assume that Bluestem Products prepares financial statements at the end of the month without discovering the theft. Would any items in the balance sheet or the income statement be in error? Explain.

c Several weaknesses in internal control apparently exist in Bluestem Products. Indicate three specific changes needed to strengthen internal control over cash receipts.

A&D 7-3 Another Day, Another Dollar

Tom Pharro owns Pharro Concrete & Masonry, a small contracting business. On April 1, the company established a petty cash fund in the amount of $5,000, which was expected to last about three months. The cash was kept in a locked box in the desk of the company's receptionist. (The company has two part-time receptionists, who were designated the office custodians of the fund. The only other people with access to the petty cash box were Tom Pharro and his personal secretary, Chris Greer.) Vouchers were to be prepared for all disbursements from the fund, and these vouchers were to be placed in the petty cash box.

Unfortunately, the money in the petty cash fund did not last three months. On April 30, the receptionists reported that the vouchers in the fund totalled $4,390.90 but that the fund contained only $2.00 in cash. The vouchers were sent to the accounting department, reviewed, and cancelled. All of the vouchers included adequate documentation. Replenishment of the fund then was recorded by the following entry:

Office Supplies Expense	*160.20*	
Travel & Entertainment Expense	*1,501.00*	
Office Equipment	*804.70*	
Repairs Expense (Roof)	*925.00*	
Drawing, Tom Pharro	*1,000.00*	
Miscellaneous Expense	*607.10*	
Cash		*4,998.00*
To replenish the petty cash fund.		

INSTRUCTIONS Identify any control weaknesses relating to this fund. Explain your reasons for regarding any aspect of the fund's operations as a weakness, and make specific recommendations for improvement.

A&D 7-4
Internal Control—A Challenging Case Study

June Davis inherited a highly successful business, Solano, Inc., shortly after her twenty-second birthday and took over the active management of the business. A portion of the company's business consisted of over-the-counter sales for cash, but most sales were on credit and were shipped by truck. Davis had no knowledge of internal control practices and relied implicitly upon the bookkeeper-cashier, John Adams, in all matters relating to cash and accounting records. Adams, who had been with the company for many years, maintained the accounting records and prepared all financial statements with the help of two assistants, made bank deposits, signed cheques, and prepared bank reconciliations.

The monthly income statements submitted to Davis by Adams showed a very satisfactory rate of net income; however, the amount of cash in the bank declined steadily during the first 18 months after Davis took over the business. To meet the company's weakening cash position, a bank loan was obtained and a few months later when the cash position again grew critical, the loan was increased.

On April 1, two years after Davis assumed the management of the company, Adams suddenly left town, leaving no forwarding address. Davis was immediately deluged with claims of creditors who stated their accounts were several months past due and that Adams had promised all debts would be paid by April 1. The bank telephoned to notify Davis that the company's account was overdrawn and that a number of cheques had just been presented for payment.

In an effort to get together some cash to meet this emergency, Davis called on two of the largest customers of the company, to whom substantial sales on account had recently been made, and asked if they could pay their accounts at once. Both customers informed her that their accounts were paid in full. They produced paid cheques to substantiate their payments and explained that Adams had offered them reduced prices on merchandise if they would pay within 24 hours after delivery.

To keep the business from insolvency, Davis agreed to sell at a bargain price a half interest in the company. The sale was made to Helen Smith, who had had considerable experience in the industry. One condition for the sale was that Smith should become the general manager of the business. The cash investment by Smith for her half interest was sufficient for the company to meet the demands on it and continue operations.

Immediately after Smith entered the business, she launched an investigation of Adams's activities. During the course of this investigation the following fraudulent actions were disclosed:

1 During the last few months of Adams's employment with the company, bank deposits were much smaller than the cash receipts. Adams had abstracted most of the receipts and substituted for them a number of worthless cheques bearing fictitious signatures. These cheques had been accumulated in an envelope marked "Cash Receipts—For Deposit Only."

2 Numerous legitimate sales of merchandise on account had been charged to fictitious customers. When the actual customer later made payment for the goods, Adams abstracted the cheque or cash and made no entry. The account receivable with the fictitious customer remained in the records.

3 When cheques were received from customers in payment of their accounts, Adams had frequently recorded the transaction by debiting an expense account and crediting Accounts Receivable. In such cases Adams had removed from the cash receipts an equivalent amount of currency, thus substituting the cheque

for the currency and causing the bank deposit to agree with the recorded cash receipts.

4 More than $3,000 a month had been stolen from petty cash. Fraudulent petty cash vouchers, mostly charged to the Inventory account, had been created to conceal these thefts and to support the cheques cashed to replenish the petty cash fund.

5 For many sales made over the counter, Adams had recorded lesser amounts on the cash register or had not rung up any amount. He had abstracted the funds received but not recorded.

6 To produce income statements that showed profitable operations, Adams had recorded many fictitious sales. The recorded accounts receivable included many from nonexistent customers.

7 In preparing bank reconciliations, Adams had omitted many outstanding cheques, thus concealing the fact that the cash in the bank was less than the amount shown by the ledger.

8 Inventory had been recorded at inflated amounts in order to increase reported profits from the business.

INSTRUCTIONS

a For each of the numbered paragraphs, describe one or more internal control procedures you would recommend to prevent the occurrence of such fraud.

b Apart from specific internal controls over cash and other accounts, what general precaution could June Davis have taken to assure herself that the accounting records were properly maintained and the company's financial statements complete and dependable? Explain fully.

A&D 7-5
Analysis of Bank Reconciliation Items

The following items are related to cash balances between Macao Company and its bank for the month of December.

(1) Accompanying the bank statement was a debit memorandum for $62, representing bank service charges for Macor Limited for December. This amount was deducted from Macao's account.

(2) The bank statement does not show the cash receipts of $1,500 deposited by Macao in the bank's night depository on December 31.

(3) Enclosed with the bank statement was a credit memorandum stating that the bank had collected a $2,000 note receivable plus interest of $28 from G. Hogg. The bank charged a collection fee of $16.

(4) Macao has two cheques (one issued in payment of office supplies in October for $100 and the other in November for $320 for advertising) that still have not been cashed by the payees.

(5) Comparison of the paid cheques returned by the bank with the entries in the cash payments records revealed that a cheque for $160, in payment for advertising expense, had been erroneously recorded as $610.

(6) A cheque issued in December for $260 to settle an accounts payable (Totten Limited) was outstanding.

(7) Included with the paid cheques was a cheque for $180, marked NSF by the bank. The cheques were from Thai MacDonald in payment of his open account.

(8) A debit memorandum for $92, representing the cost of printing new cheques and service charges for December, was included with the bank statement.

INSTRUCTIONS

a Prepare the necessary entries, in general journal form but omit explanations, at December 31 to update the cash balance per company's (depositor's) records.

b Identify the item (or items) and indicate whether it should be added or deducted from the balance per bank statement to arrive at the adjusted cash balance (a bank reconciliation is **not** required).

A&D 7-6
Bank Reconciliation, Cash Management, and Internal Control

Millien Prince, owner of a small business, just came back from a conference on cash management where she learned that one key ingredient to business success is the efficient management of cash. Before she could settle down in her office, Millien was handed the following bank reconciliation for her business by Joe, the bookkeeper.

Balance per depositor's records, June 30		*$20,880*
Add: Outstanding cheques: No. 918	*$195*	
925	*360*	
931	*405*	*960*
		$21,840
Deduct: Cash on hand (receipts for three days)		*1,850*
Balance per bank statement, June 30		*$19,990*
Deduct: Unrecorded bank credit		*600*
True cash, June 30		*$19,390*

Millien took one look at the reconciliation, shook her head and said: "Joe, I don't understand this reconciliation at all. You used to start the reconciliation from the balance per bank statement and the balance per our records to arrive at two equal adjusted balances. Are you trying to confuse me or what?"

Joe, somewhat uncomfortable and irritated, countered: "Millien, you are the boss and you have time to go to conferences. But I have a lot to do here. Just in case you have forgotten, I handle cash receipts and make small payments from these receipts, do the books, and prepare the monthly bank reconciliation. I also prepare a lot of cheques for you to sign—the $960 of the outstanding cheques listed in the reconciliation is roughly 10% of the total amount of cheques that I do every month. What I did in this new reconciliation saved me time. Just one example, I saved time by excluding the five old outstanding cheques totalling $730 from the reconciliation. Since these cheques are more than six months old and cannot be cashed, there is no sense in putting them in the reconciliation. By the way, the only item that you may not understand is the unrecorded bank credit. This item represents a note collected for us by the bank."

Shortly after, Joe had a heated argument with Millien and left the company. Now Millien comes to you to see whether Joe had done anything wrong with the handling of the bank reconciliation and the cash on hand. Also, she wonders whether she has efficiently managed her cash.

INSTRUCTIONS

a Determine the adjusted cash balance per the depositor's records and the cash shortage, if any, for which Joe may be held responsible.

b Comment on the efficiency of Millien's cash management, especially the internal control on cash and suggest any improvement you deem necessary.

CHAPTER

8 Accounts Receivable and Notes Receivable

When a business sells goods or services on credit, it does so in the belief that the customer will make payment in accordance with the terms of sale. This confidence in the collectibility of receivables is the basis for showing accounts receivable and notes receivable as assets in the balance sheet and for including credit sales as revenue in the income statement. Along with our overall confidence in receivables, however, is a recognition that some customers will fail to pay as agreed. Making sales on credit inevitably leads to some credit losses. In this chapter, we explore methods of measuring the expense of uncollectible accounts receivable and of reflecting this expense in the financial statements. We also consider various forms of notes receivable and the calculation of interest. In the final pages of the chapter, we show how the concept of present value is applied to long-term notes receivable.

Learning Objectives

After studying this chapter you should be able to:

1. *Explain the nature, estimate, and statement presentation of uncollectible accounts receivable, write off any accounts known to be uncollectible, and record any later recoveries.*
2. *Compare the allowance method and the direct write-off method of accounting for uncollectible accounts.*
3. *Explain why accounts receivable may be viewed as "nonproductive" assets. Identify several ways of converting receivables quickly into cash.*
4. *Account for sales to customers using credit cards.*
5. *Explain promissory notes and the nature of interest.*
6. *Compute the accounts receivable turnover rate. Explain why this ratio is of interest to short-term creditors.*

*7 *Account for notes receivable with the interest charges included in the face amount.*

*8 *Discuss the concept of present value in accounting for long-term notes receivable.*

* *Supplemental Topic, "Notes Receivable with Interest Charges Included in the Face Amount"*

ACCOUNTS RECEIVABLE

OBJECTIVE 1 Explain the nature, estimate, and statement presentation of uncollectible accounts receivable, write off any accounts known to be uncollectible, and record any later recoveries.

One of the key factors underlying the growth of our economy is the trend toward selling goods and services on credit. Accounts receivable are liquid assets, usually being converted into cash within a period of 30 to 60 days. Therefore, accounts receivable from customers are classified as current assets, appearing in the balance sheet immediately after cash and short-term investments.

Sometimes companies sell merchandise on longer-term instalment plans, requiring 12, 24, or even 48 months to collect the entire amount receivable from the customer. By definition, the normal period of time required to collect accounts receivable is part of a company's ***operating cycle.*** Therefore, accounts receivable arising from "normal" sales transactions usually are classified as current assets, even if the credit terms extend beyond one year.[1]

Uncollectible Accounts

No business wants to sell on credit to a customer who will prove unable or unwilling to pay his or her account. Therefore, most businesses have a credit department that investigates the creditworthiness of each prospective customer. This investigation usually includes obtaining a credit report from a national credit-rating agency such as ***Dun & Bradstreet.*** If the prospective customer is a business concern, its financial statements will be obtained and analyzed to determine its financial strength and the trend of its operating results.

A business that sells its goods or services on credit will inevitably find that some of its accounts receivable are uncollectible. Regardless of how thoroughly the credit department investigates prospective customers, some uncollectible accounts will arise as a result of errors in judgment or because of unexpected developments. In fact, a limited amount of uncollectible accounts or credit loss is evidence of a sound credit policy. If the credit department should become too cautious and conservative in rating customers, it might avoid most credit losses but, in so doing, lose profitable business by rejecting many acceptable customers.

Reflecting Uncollectible Accounts in the Financial Statements An account receivable that has been determined to be uncollectible is no longer an asset. The loss of this asset represents an ***expense,*** termed ***uncollectible accounts expense*** (also called bad debts expense).

In measuring business income, one of the most fundamental principles of accounting is that revenue should be ***matched*** with (offset by) the expenses incurred in generating that revenue. Uncollectible accounts expense is ***caused by selling goods*** on credit to customers who fail to pay their bills. Therefore, this expense is incurred in the accounting period in which the ***related sales*** are made, even though specific accounts receiv-

---

[1] As explained in Chapter 5, the period used to define current assets and current liabilities is one year or the company's operating cycle, whichever is longer. The ***operating cycle*** is the period of time needed to convert cash into inventory, the inventory into accounts receivable, and the accounts receivable back into cash.

able may not be determined to be uncollectible until a later accounting period. Thus, an account receivable that originates from a sale on credit in January and is determined to be uncollectible in August represents an expense in ***January.*** Unless each month's uncollectible accounts expense is ***estimated*** and reflected in the month-end income statement and balance sheet, these financial statements may show overstated earnings and overvalued assets, because they will show accounts that will never be collected. Thus, the estimating and recording of the uncollectible accounts expense is required by the ***matching principle.***

To illustrate, assume that World Famous Toy Co. begins business on January 1, 1996, and makes most of its sales on account. At January 31, accounts receivable amount to $250,000. On this date, the credit manager reviews the accounts receivable and estimates that approximately $10,000 of these accounts will prove to be uncollectible. The following adjusting entry should be made at January 31:

Provision for uncollectible accounts

Uncollectible Accounts Expense	*10,000*	
Allowance for Doubtful Accounts		*10,000*
To record the portion of total accounts receivable estimated to be uncollectible.		

The ***Uncollectible Accounts Expense*** account created by the debit part of this entry is closed into the Income Summary account in the same manner as any other expense account. The ***Allowance for Doubtful Accounts*** that was credited in the above journal entry will appear in the balance sheet as a deduction from the face amount of the accounts receivable. It serves to reduce the accounts receivable to their ***net realizable value*** in the balance sheet, as shown by the following illustration:

WORLD FAMOUS TOY CO.
Partial Balance Sheet
January 31, 1996

How much is the estimated net realizable value of the accounts receivable?

Current assets:		
Cash and short-term investments		*$ 75,000*
Accounts receivable	*$250,000*	
Less: Allowance for doubtful accounts	*10,000*	*240,000*

The Allowance for Doubtful Accounts

There is no way of telling in advance ***which*** accounts receivable will prove to be uncollectible. It is therefore not possible to credit the accounts of specific customers for our estimate of probable uncollectible accounts. Neither should we credit the Accounts Receivable controlling account in the general ledger. If the Accounts Receivable controlling account were to be credited with the estimated amount of doubtful accounts, this controlling account would no longer be in balance with the total of the numerous customers' accounts in the subsidiary ledger. The only practical alternative, therefore, is to credit a separate account called ***Allowance for Doubtful Accounts*** with the amount estimated to be uncollectible.

The Allowance for Doubtful Accounts often is described as a ***contra-asset*** account or a ***valuation*** account. Both of these terms indicate that the Allowance for Doubtful Accounts has a credit balance, which is offset against the asset Accounts Receivable to produce the proper balance sheet value for this asset.

Estimating the Amount of Uncollectible Accounts Before financial statements are prepared at the end of the accounting period, an estimate of the expected amount of uncollectible accounts receivables should be made. This estimate is based upon past experience and modified in accordance with current business conditions. Losses from uncollectible receivables tend to be greater during periods of recession than in periods of growth and prosperity. Because the allowance for doubtful accounts is necessarily an estimate and not a precise calculation, the factor of personal judgment may play a considerable part in determining the size of this valuation account.

Conservatism as a Factor in Valuing Accounts Receivable The larger the allowance established for doubtful accounts, the lower the net valuation of accounts receivable will be. Some accountants and some business executives tend to favour the most conservative valuation of assets that logically can be supported. ***Conservatism*** in the preparation of a balance sheet implies a tendency to resolve uncertainties in the valuation of assets by reporting assets at the lower end of the range of reasonable values rather than by establishing values in a purely objective manner.

The valuation of assets at conservative amounts is a long-standing tradition in accounting, stemming from the days when creditors were the major users of financial statements. From the viewpoint of bankers and others who use financial statements as a basis for granting loans, conservatism in valuing assets has long been regarded as a desirable policy.

In considering the argument for balance sheet conservatism, it is important to recognize that the income statement also is affected by the estimate made of uncollectible accounts. The act of providing a relatively large allowance for doubtful accounts involves a correspondingly heavy charge to expense. Setting asset values at a minimum in the balance sheet has the related effect of minimizing the amount of net income reported in the current period.

Monthly Adjustments of the Allowance Account In the adjusting entry made by World Famous Toy Co. at January 31, the amount of the adjustment ($10,000) was equal to the estimated amount of uncollectible accounts. This is true because January was the first month of operations and this was the company's first estimate of its uncollectible accounts. In future months, the amount of the adjusting entry will depend upon two factors: (1) the ***estimate*** of uncollectible accounts and (2) the ***current balance*** in the Allowance for Doubtful Accounts. Before we illustrate the adjusting entry for a future month, let us first see why the balance in the allowance account may change during the accounting period.

Writing Off an Uncollectible Account Receivable

Whenever an account receivable from a specific customer is determined to be uncollectible, it no longer qualifies as an asset and should be written off.

To ***write off*** an account receivable is to reduce the balance of the customer's account to zero. The journal entry to accomplish this consists of a credit to the Accounts Receivable controlling account in the general ledger (and to the customer's account in the subsidiary ledger) and an offsetting debit to the ***Allowance for Doubtful Accounts.***

To illustrate, assume that on February 15, World Famous Toy Co. learns that a customer, Discount Stores, has gone out of business and that the $4,000 account receivable from this customer is now worthless. The entry to write off this uncollectible account receivable is:

Writing off a receivable "against the allowance"

Allowance for Doubtful Accounts	*4,000*	
Accounts Receivable (Discount Stores)		*4,000*
To write off the receivable from Discount Stores as uncollectible.		

The important thing to note in this entry is that the debit is made to the ***Allowance for Doubtful Accounts*** and ***not*** to the Uncollectible Accounts Expense account. The estimated expense of credit losses is charged to the Uncollectible Accounts Expense account at the end of each accounting period. When a particular account receivable is later determined to be worthless and is written off, this action does not represent an additional expense but merely confirms our previous estimate of the expense. If the Uncollectible Accounts Expense account were first charged with ***estimated*** credit losses and then later charged with ***proven*** credit losses, we would be double counting the actual uncollectible accounts expense.

After the entry writing off the receivable from Discount Stores has been posted, the Accounts Receivable controlling account and the Allowance for Doubtful Accounts appear as follows:

Both accounts reduced by write-off of worthless receivable

Accounts Receivable

1996		*1996*	
Jan. 31	*250,000*	*Feb. 15 (write-off)*	*4,000*

Allowance for Doubtful Accounts

1996		*1996*	
Feb. 15 (write-off)	*4,000*	*Jan. 31*	*10,000*

Notice also that the entry to write off an uncollectible account receivable reduces both the asset account and the contra-asset account by the same amount. Thus, writing off an uncollectible account ***does not change*** the net realizable value of accounts receivable in the balance sheet. The following illustration shows the net realizable value of World Famous Toy Co.'s accounts receivable before and after the write-off of the account receivable from Discount Stores:

Net value of receivables unchanged by write-off

Before the Write-Off		***After the Write-Off***	
Accounts receivable	*$250,000*	*Accounts receivable*	*$246,000*
Less: Allowance for doubtful accounts	*10,000*	*Less: Allowance for doubtful accounts*	*6,000*
Net value of receivables	*$240,000*	*Net value of receivables*	*$240,000*

The fact that writing off a worthless receivable against the Allowance for Doubtful Accounts does not change the net carrying value of accounts receivable shows that no expense is entered in the accounting records when an account receivable is written off. This example bears out the point stressed earlier in the chapter. ***Credit losses belong in the period in which the sale is made, not in a later period in which the account receivable is discovered to be uncollectible.*** This is another example of the use of the ***matching principle*** in determining net income.

Write-Offs Seldom Agree with Previous Estimates The total amount of accounts receivable actually written off will seldom, if ever, be exactly equal to the estimated amount previously credited to the Allowance for Doubtful Accounts.

If the amounts written off as uncollectible turn out to be less than the estimated amount, the Allowance for Doubtful Accounts will continue to show a credit balance. If the amounts written off as uncollectible are greater than the estimated amount, the Allowance for Doubtful Accounts will acquire a ***temporary debit balance,*** which will be eliminated by the adjustment at the end of the period.

Recovery of an Account Receivable Previously Written Off

Occasionally a receivable that has been written off as worthless will later be collected in full or in part. Such collections are often referred to as ***recoveries*** of uncollectible accounts or bad debts. Collection of an account receivable previously written off is evidence that the write-off was an error; the receivable should therefore be reinstated as an asset.

Let us assume, for example, that a past-due account receivable in the amount of $200 from J. B. Barker was written off on February 16 by the following entry:

Barker account considered uncollectible

Allowance for Doubtful Accounts	200	
Accounts Receivable (J. B. Barker)		200
To write off the receivable from J. B. Barker as uncollectible.		

On February 27, the customer, J. B. Barker, pays the account in full. The entry to restore Barker's account will be:

Barker account reinstated

Accounts Receivable (J. B. Barker)	200	
Allowance for Doubtful Accounts		200
To reinstate as an asset an account receivable previously written off.		

Notice that this entry is ***exactly the opposite*** of the entry made when the account was written off as uncollectible. A separate entry will be made to record the collection from Barker. This entry will debit Cash and credit Accounts Receivable (J. B. Barker).

Monthly Estimates of Credit Losses

At the end of each month, management should again estimate the probable amount of uncollectible accounts ***and adjust the Allowance for Doubtful Accounts to this new estimate.***

To illustrate, assume that at the end of February the credit manager of World Famous Toy Co. analyzes the accounts receivable and estimates that approximately ***$11,000*** of these accounts will prove uncollectible. Currently, the Allowance for Doubtful Accounts has a credit balance of only ***$6,000,*** determined as follows:

Current balance in the allowance account

Balance at January 31 (credit)		*$10,000*
Less: Write-offs of accounts considered worthless:		
Discount Stores	*$4,000*	
J. B. Barker	*200*	*4,200*
Subtotal		*$ 5,800*
Add: Recoveries of accounts previously written off: J. B. Barker		*200*
Balance at end of February (prior to adjusting entry)		*$ 6,000*

To increase the balance in the allowance account to $11,000 at February 28, the month-end adjusting entry must add $5,000 to the allowance because the $6,000 of accounts receivable that were considered uncollectible at the end of January are included again in the $11,000 at the end of February). The entry will be:

Increasing the allowance for doubtful accounts

Uncollectible Accounts Expense		*5,000*	
Allowance for Doubtful Accounts			*5,000*
To increase the Allowance for Doubtful Accounts to $11,000, computed as follows:			
Required allowance at Feb. 28	*$11,000*		
Credit balance prior to adjustment	*6,000*		
Required adjustment	*$ 5,000*		

Estimating Credit Losses—The "Balance Sheet" Approach The most widely used method in reviewing and analyzing accounts receivable to estimate the probable amount of uncollectible accounts is the ***aging*** of the accounts receivable. This method is sometimes called the ***balance sheet*** approach, because the method emphasizes the proper balance sheet valuation of accounts receivable.

"Aging" accounts receivable means classifying each receivable according to its age. An aging schedule for the accounts receivable of Valley Ranch Supply is illustrated below:

Analysis of Accounts Receivable by Age
December 31, 1996

	Total	Not Yet Due	1–30 Days Past Due	31–60 Days Past Due	61–90 Days Past Due	Over 90 Days Past Due
Animal Care Centre	*$ 9,000*	*$ 9,000*				
Butterfield, John D.	*2,400*			*$ 2,400*		
Citrus Groves, Inc.	*4,000*	*3,000*	*$ 1,000*			
Dairy Fresh Farms	*1,600*				*$ 600*	*$1,000*
Eastlake Stables	*13,000*	*7,000*	*6,000*			
(Other customers)	*70,000*	*32,000*	*22,000*	*9,600*	*2,400*	*4,000*
Totals	*$100,000*	*$51,000*	*$29,000*	*$12,000*	*$3,000*	*$5,000*

An aging schedule is useful to management in reviewing the status of individual accounts receivable and in evaluating the overall effectiveness of credit and collection policies. In addition, the schedule is used as the basis for estimating the amount of uncollectible accounts.

The longer an account is past due, the greater the likelihood that it will not be collected in full. Based upon past experience, the credit manager estimates the percentage of credit losses likely to occur in each age group of accounts receivable. This percentage, when applied to the total dollar amount in the age group, gives the estimated uncollectible portion for that group. By adding together the estimated uncollectible portions for all age groups, the ***required balance*** in the Allowance for Doubtful Accounts is determined. The following schedule lists the group totals from the aging schedule and shows how the estimated total amount of uncollectible accounts is computed:

Estimated Uncollectible Accounts Receivable
December 31, 1996

	Age Group Total	Percentage Considered Uncollectible*	Estimated Uncollectible Accounts
Not yet due	$ 51,000	1	$ 510
1–30 days past due	29,000	3	870
31–60 days past due	12,000	10	1,200
61–90 days past due	3,000	20	600
Over 90 days past due......	5,000	50	2,500
Totals	$100,000		$5,680

* These percentages are estimated each month by the credit manager, based upon recent experience and current economic conditions.

At December 31, Valley Ranch Supply has total accounts receivable of $100,000, of which $5,680 are estimated to be uncollectible. Thus, an adjusting entry is needed to increase the Allowance for Doubtful Accounts from its present level to $5,680. If the allowance account currently has a credit balance of, say, $4,000, the month-end adjusting entry should be in the amount of ***$1,680*** as follows:[2]

The "balance sheet" approach

Uncollectible Accounts Expense	*1,680*	
Allowance for Doubtful Accounts		*1,680*
To increase the Allowance for Doubtful Accounts to $5,680 from $4,000.		

An Alternative Approach to Estimating Credit Losses The procedures above describe the ***balance sheet*** approach to estimating and recording credit losses. This approach is based upon an aging schedule, and the Al-

[2] If accounts receivable written off during the period ***exceed*** the Allowance for Doubtful Accounts at the last adjustment date, the allowance account temporarily acquires a ***debit balance.*** This situation seldom occurs if the allowance is adjusted each month but often occurs if adjusting entries are made only at year-end.

If Valley Ranch Supply makes only an annual adjustment for uncollectible accounts, the allowance account might have a debit balance of, say, $10,000. In this case, the year-end adjusting entry should be for ***$15,680*** in order to bring the allowance to the required credit balance of $5,680.

Regardless of how often adjusting entries are made, the balance in the allowance account of Valley Ranch Supply should be ***$5,680 at year-end.*** Uncollectible accounts expense will be the same for the year regardless of whether adjusting entries are made annually or monthly. The only difference is in whether this expense is recognized in one annual adjusting entry or in 12 monthly adjusting entries, each for a smaller amount.

lowance for Doubtful Accounts is ***adjusted to a required balance.*** An alternative method, called the ***income statement*** approach, focuses upon estimating the uncollectible accounts ***expense*** for the period. Based upon past experience, the uncollectible accounts expense is estimated at some percentage of net credit sales. The adjusting entry is made in the ***full amount of the estimated expense,*** without regard for the current balance in the Allowance for Doubtful Accounts.

To illustrate, assume that a company's past experience indicates that about 2% of its net credit sales prove to be uncollectible. If net credit sales for September amount to $150,000, the month-end adjusting entry to record uncollectible accounts expense is:

The "income statement" approach

Uncollectible Accounts Expense	*3,000*	
Allowance for Doubtful Accounts		*3,000*
To record uncollectible accounts expense, estimated at 2% of net credit sales ($150,000 × 2% = $3,000).		

This approach is fast and simple—no aging schedule is required and no consideration is given to the existing balance in the Allowance for Doubtful Accounts. The aging of accounts receivable, however, provides a more reliable estimate of uncollectible accounts because of the consideration given to the age and collectibility of specific accounts receivable at the balance sheet date.

In past years, many small companies used the income statement approach as a shortcut in preparing monthly financial statements but used the balance sheet method in preparing annual financial statements. Today, however, most businesses have computer software that quickly and easily prepares monthly aging schedules of accounts receivable. Thus, most businesses today use the ***balance sheet approach*** in their monthly as well as annual financial statements.

Direct Write-Off Method

OBJECTIVE 2 Compare the allowance method and the direct write-off method of accounting for uncollectible accounts.

Some companies do not use the ***allowance method*** to value their accounts receivable. Instead of making end-of-period adjusting entries to record uncollectible accounts expense on the basis of estimates, these companies recognize no uncollectible accounts expense until specific receivables are determined to be worthless. This method makes no attempt to match revenue and related expenses. Uncollectible accounts expense is recorded in the period in which individual accounts receivable are determined to be worthless rather than in the period in which the sales were made.

When a particular customer's account is determined to be uncollectible, it is written off directly to Uncollectible Accounts Expense, as follows:

Uncollectible Accounts Expense	*250*	
Accounts Receivable (Bell Products)		*250*
To write off the receivable from Bell Products as uncollectible.		

When the direct write-off method is in use, the accounts receivable will be listed in the balance sheet at their gross amount, and ***no valuation allowance*** will be used. The receivables, therefore, are not stated at estimated net realizable value.

In some situations, use of the direct write-off method is acceptable. If a company makes most of its sales for cash, the amount of its accounts receivable will be small in relation to other assets. The expense from uncollectible accounts should also be small. Consequently, the direct write-off method is acceptable because its use does not have a ***material*** effect on the reported net income. Another situation in which the direct write-off method works satisfactorily is in a company that sells all or most of its output to a few large companies that are financially strong. In this setting there may be no basis for making advance estimates of any credit losses.

Internal Controls for Receivables

One of the most important principles of internal control is that employees who have custody of cash or other negotiable assets must not maintain accounting records. In a small business, unfortunately, it is not uncommon to find that one employee has responsibility for handling cash receipts from customers, maintaining the accounts receivable records, issuing credit memos for goods returned by or for allowance to customers, and writing off receivables judged to be uncollectible. Such a combination of duties is an invitation to errors and fraud. The errors made in performing these four functions can be covered up by the employee. Thus, the information so generated is misleading. Also, the employee in this situation is able to remove the cash collected from a customer without making any record of the collection. The next step is to dispose of the balance in the customer's account. This can be done by issuing a credit memo indicating that the customer has returned merchandise, or has been given an allowance on the sale, or by writing off the customer's account as uncollectible. Thus, the employee has the cash, the customer's account shows a zero balance due, and the books are in balance.

To avoid errors and fraud in the handling of receivables, some of the most important rules are that employees who maintain the accounts receivable subsidiary ledger must ***not have access*** to cash receipts, and employees who handle cash receipts must not have access to the records of receivables. Furthermore, ***neither*** the employees who maintain records of receivables ***nor*** those who handle cash receipts should have authority to issue credit memoranda or to authorize the write-off of receivables as uncollectible. These are classic examples of incompatible duties.

Management of Accounts Receivable

OBJECTIVE 3 Explain why accounts receivable may be viewed as "nonproductive" assets. Identify several ways of converting receivables quickly into cash.

Management has two conflicting objectives with respect to the accounts receivable. On the one hand, management wants to generate as much sales revenue as possible. Offering customers lengthy credit terms, with little or no interest, has proven to be an effective means of generating sales revenue.

Every business, however, would rather sell for cash than on account. Unless they earn interest, accounts receivable are a nonproductive asset that produce no revenue as they await collection. Therefore, another objective of management is to minimize the amount of money "tied up" in the form of accounts receivable.

Several tools are available to a management that must offer credit terms to its customers yet wants to minimize the company's investment in accounts receivable. We have already discussed offering credit customers cash discounts (such as 2/10, n/30) to encourage early payment. Other tools include factoring accounts receivable and selling to customers who use national credit cards.

Factoring Accounts Receivable

The term ***factoring*** describes transactions in which a business either sells its accounts receivable to a financial institution (often called a ***factor***) or borrows money by pledging its accounts receivable as collateral (security) for the loan. In either case, the business obtains cash immediately instead of having to wait until the receivables can be collected.

The factoring of accounts receivable may create a potential liability to reimburse the factor for any losses sustained if some of the factored accounts are uncollectible. This "potential" liability is an example of ***off-balance-sheet risk*** that must be disclosed in notes to the financial statements. The disclosure of off-balance-sheet risk such as contingencies is discussed in Chapter 11.

Factoring accounts receivable is a practice limited primarily to small business organizations that do not have well-established credit. Large and solvent organizations usually are able to borrow money using unsecured lines of credit, so they need not factor their accounts receivable.

Credit Card Sales

OBJECTIVE 4 Account for sales to customers using credit cards.

Many retailing businesses maximize sales opportunities while minimizing their investment in accounts receivable by making credit sales to customers who use well-known credit cards such as American Express, Visa, and MasterCard. A customer who makes a purchase using one of these cards must sign a multiple-copy form, which includes a ***credit card draft.*** A credit card draft is similar to a cheque that is drawn upon the funds of the credit card company rather than upon the personal bank account of the customer. The credit card company promptly pays cash to the merchant to redeem these drafts. At the end of each month, the credit card company bills the credit card holder for all the drafts it has redeemed during the month. If the credit card holder fails to pay the amount owed, it is the credit card company that sustains the loss.

By making sales through credit card companies, merchants receive cash more quickly from credit sales and avoid uncollectible accounts expense. Also, the merchant avoids the expenses of investigating customers' credit, maintaining an accounts receivable subsidiary ledger, and making collections from customers.

Bank Credit Cards Some widely used credit cards (such as Visa and MasterCard) are issued by banks. When the credit card company is a bank, the retailing business may deposit the signed credit card drafts directly in its bank account, along with the currency and personal cheques received from customers. Since banks accept these credit card drafts for immediate deposit, sales to customers using bank credit cards are recorded as ***cash sales.***

In exchange for handling the credit card drafts, the bank makes a monthly service charge that usually runs between $1\frac{1}{2}$ and 5% of the amount of the drafts deposited by the merchant during the month. This monthly service charge is deducted from the merchant's bank account and appears with other bank service charges in the merchant's monthly bank statement.

Other Credit Cards When customers use nonbank credit cards (such as EnRoute, Diners Club, and Discover), the retailing business cannot deposit the credit card drafts directly in its bank account. Instead of debiting Cash, the merchant records an account receivable from the credit card company. Periodically, the credit card drafts are mailed (or transmitted electronically) to the credit card company, which then sends a cheque to the merchant. Credit card companies, however, do not redeem the drafts at the full sales price. The agreement between the credit card company and the merchant usually allows the credit card company to take a discount of between $3\frac{1}{2}$% and 5% when redeeming the drafts.

To illustrate the procedures in accounting for these credit card sales, assume that Bradshaw Camera Shop sells a camera for $200 to a customer who uses a Quick Charge credit card. The entry would be:

This receivable is from the credit card company

Accounts Receivable (Quick Charge Company)	*200*	
Sales		*200*
To record sale to customer using Quick Charge credit card.		

At the end of the week, Bradshaw Camera Shop mails credit card drafts totalling $1,200 to Quick Charge Company, which redeems the drafts after deducting a 5% discount. When payment is received by Bradshaw, the entry is

Cash	*1,140*	
Credit Card Discount Expense	*60*	
Accounts Receivable (Quick Charge Company)		*1,200*
To record collection of account receivable from Quick Charge, less 5% discount.		

The expense account, Credit Card Discount Expense, should be included among the selling expenses in the income statement of Bradshaw Camera Shop.

NOTES RECEIVABLE

OBJECTIVE 5 Explain promissory notes and the nature of interest.

A promissory note is an unconditional promise in writing to pay on demand or at a future date a definite sum of money.

The person who signs the note and thereby promises to pay is called the ***maker*** of the note. The person to whom payment is to be made is called the ***payee*** of the note. In the following illustration, G. L. Smith is the maker of the note and A. B. Davis is the payee.

From the viewpoint of the maker, G. L. Smith, the illustrated note is a liability and is recorded by crediting the Notes Payable account. However, from the viewpoint of the payee, A. B. Davis, this same note is an asset and

Simplified form of promissory note

$100,000 Vancouver, British Columbia July 10, 19__

One year after date I promise to pay

to the order of A. B. Davis

---One hundred thousand and no/100--- dollars

payable to Canadian National Bank

for value received, with interest at 12% per annum

G.L. Smith

is recorded by debiting the Notes Receivable account. The maker of a note expects to pay cash at the ***maturity date*** (or due date); the payee expects to receive cash at that date.

Nature of Interest

Interest is a charge made for the use of money. A borrower incurs interest expense. A lender earns interest revenue. When you encounter notes payable in a company's financial statements, you know that the company is borrowing and you should expect to find interest expense. When you encounter notes receivable, you should expect interest revenue.

Computing Interest A formula used in computing interest is as follows:

Principal × Rate of Interest × Time = Interest

(Often expressed as $\mathbf{P} \times \mathbf{R} \times \mathbf{T} = \mathbf{I}$)

Of the three elements in the above formula, the rate and time elements need a brief explanation. The rate is usually stated on an annual basis, unless otherwise indicated. The time can be expressed in days, months, or on an annual basis. All notes, other than those payable on demand, are ***legally due*** and payable ***three days*** after the due date indicated on the notes. These extra three days are called the ***three days of grace.*** Thus, in counting the exact number of days for interest computation, the day on which a note is dated is not included; the date on which a note falls due is included, that is, the last day of the added three days of grace.

Suppose, for example, that a 60-day, 12% note for $100,000 is drawn on June 10. The interest charge, with the three days of grace added, is computed as follows:

$$\$100{,}000 \times 0.12 \times \tfrac{63}{365} = \$2{,}071.23$$

The principal of the note ($100,000) plus the interest ($2,071.23) equals $102,071.23 and this amount (the ***maturity value***) will be payable on ***August 12.*** The computation of days to maturity is as follows:

Note the three days of grace added

Days remaining in June (30–10; date of note is not included)	20
Days in July	31
Days in August to maturity date (date of payment is included, 9 days plus 3 days of grace)	12
Total days called for by note	63

Accounting for Notes Receivable

In some fields of business, notes receivable are seldom encountered; in other fields they occur frequently and may constitute an important part of total assets. Business concerns that sell high-priced durable goods such as automobiles and farm machinery often accept notes receivable from their customers. Many companies obtain notes receivable in settlement of past-due accounts receivable.

All notes receivable are usually posted to a single account in the general ledger. A subsidiary ledger is not essential because the notes themselves, when filed by due dates, are the equivalent of a subsidiary ledger and provide any necessary information as to maturity, interest rates, collateral pledged, and other details. The amount debited to Notes Receivable is always the ***face amount*** of the note, regardless of whether or not the note bears interest. When an interest-bearing note is collected, the amount of cash received may be larger than the face amount of the note, depending on whether the interest charge is included in the face amount of the note. (Notes receivable with interest included in the face amount will be covered in the "Supplemental Topic" at the end of this chapter.) The interest collected is credited to an Interest Revenue account, and only the face amount of the note is credited to the Notes Receivable account.

Illustrative Entries Assume that on December 1 a 90-day, 12% note receivable is acquired from a customer, Marvin White, in settlement of an existing account receivable of $30,000. The entry for acquisition of the note is as follows:

Note received to replace account receivable

Notes Receivable	30,000	
Accounts Receivable (Marvin White)		30,000
Accepted 90-day, 12% note in settlement of account receivable.		

At December 31, the end of the company's fiscal year, the interest earned to date on notes receivable should be accrued by an adjusting entry as follows:

Adjusting entry for interest revenue earned in December

Interest Receivable	295.89	
Interest Revenue		295.89
To accrue interest for the month of December on Marvin White note ($30,000 × 12% × $\frac{30}{365}$ = $295.89).		

On March 4, 93 days after the date of the note (90 days plus 3 days of grace), the note matures. The entry to record collection of the note will be:

Collection of principal and interest

Cash	30,917.26	
Notes Receivable		30,000.00
Interest Receivable		295.89
Interest Revenue		621.37
Collected 90-day, 12% note from Marvin White ($30,000 × 12% × $\frac{93}{365}$ = $917.26 interest of which $621.37 was earned in current year).		

The preceding three entries show that interest is being earned throughout the life of the note and that the interest should be apportioned between years on a time basis. The revenue of each year will then include the interest actually earned in that year.

If the Maker of a Note Defaults A note receivable that cannot be collected at maturity is said to have been ***defaulted*** by the maker. Immediately after the default of a note, an entry should be made by the holder to transfer the amount due from the Notes Receivable account to an account receivable from the debtor.

To illustrate, assume that on March 4, our customer, Marvin White, had defaulted on the note used in the preceding example. In this case, the entry on March 4 would have been:

Accounts Receivable (Marvin White)	*30,917.26*	
Notes Receivable		*30,000.00*
Interest Receivable		*295.89*
Interest Revenue		*621.37*
To record default by Marvin White on 90-day, 12% note, plus three days of grace.		

Notice that the interest earned on the note is recorded through the maturity date and is included in the account receivable from the maker. The interest receivable on a defaulted note is just as valid a claim against the maker as is the principal amount of the note.

If the account receivable from White cannot be collected, it ultimately will be written off against the Allowance for Doubtful Accounts. Therefore, the balance in the Allowance for Doubtful Accounts should provide for estimated uncollectible ***notes*** receivable as well as uncollectible ***accounts*** receivable.

CASE IN POINT For many companies, the provision for doubtful accounts is small and does not have a material effect upon net income for the period. Notes receivable, however, are the largest and most important asset for nearly every bank. Interest on these notes is a bank's largest and most important type of revenue. Thus, the collectibility of notes owned by a bank is a key factor in determining the success or failure of that bank.

A few years ago, the six Canadian chartered banks (also the six largest) added a staggering $4 billion to their allowance for doubtful loans to less developed countries. The total allowance for these doubtful loans ranges from 61% to almost 100% of the loans to these countries. This wide margin in the estimate of the allowance for doubtful loans clearly manifests the role of personal judgment in determining the size of the allowance, as pointed out in the early part of this chapter.

Renewal of a Note Receivable Sometimes the two parties to a note agree that the note shall be renewed rather than paid at the maturity date. In this situation a new note should be prepared and the old one cancelled. If the old note does not bear interest, the entry could be made as follows:

Renewal of note should be recorded

Notes Receivable	*10,000*	
Notes Receivable		*10,000*
A 60-day, non-interest-bearing note from Bell Company renewed today with new 60-day, 14% note.		

Since the above entry causes no change in the balance of the Notes Receivable account, a question may arise as to whether the entry is necessary. The renewal of a note is an important transaction requiring managerial attention; a general journal entry is needed to record the action taken by management and to provide a permanent record of the transaction. If journal entries were not made to record the renewal of notes, confusion might arise as to whether some of the notes included in the balance of the Notes Receivable account were current or defaulted. Alternatively, a memorandum noting the renewal may be attached to the new note.

Discounting Notes Receivable In past years, some companies sold their notes receivable to banks in order to obtain cash prior to the maturity dates of these notes. As the banks purchased these notes at a "discount" from their maturity values, this practice became known as ***discounting*** notes receivable.

Discounting notes receivable is not a widespread practice today, because most banks no longer purchase notes receivable from their customers. Interestingly, the discounting of notes receivable remains a common practice among banks themselves. Many banks sell large "packages" of notes receivable (loans) to other financial institutions.

If a business organization wants to convert its receivables into cash prior to their maturity dates, it usually enters into some type of factoring arrangement. Accounting for the factoring of receivables varies with the terms and conditions of the contract between the company and the factor. Various factoring arrangements will be discussed in more advanced accounting courses.

Evaluating the Quality of Notes and Accounts Receivable

In the annual audit of a company by a public accounting firm, the independent auditors will verify receivables by communicating directly with the customers of the company and with the makers of notes receivable. This ***confirmation*** process is designed to provide evidence that the customers and other debtors actually exist, and that they acknowledge the indebtedness. The auditors may also verify the credit rating of major debtors.

Any company with large amounts of receivables needs the assurance of an annual audit to guard against the possibility that sizable but worthless notes and accounts receivable from bankrupt firms or fictitious customers may have been disguised as genuine assets. The quality of receivables may also be appraised by an internal auditing staff that will study the adequacy of the internal controls over such activities as the granting of credit, accounting for receivables, and the prompt recognition of credit losses.

Accounts Receivable Turnover Collecting accounts receivable ***on time*** is important; it spells the success or failure of a company's credit and collection policies. A past-due receivable is a candidate for write-off as a credit

OBJECTIVE 6 Compute the accounts receivable turnover rate. Explain why this ratio is of interest to short-term creditors.

loss. To help us judge how good a job a company is doing in granting credit and collecting its receivables, we compute the ratio of net sales to average receivables. This ***accounts receivable turnover rate*** tells us how many times the receivables were converted into cash during the year.[3] The ratio is computed by dividing annual net sales by average accounts receivable.

For example, recent financial statements of TransCanada Pipelines Limited show net sales of \$3.1 billion. Receivables were \$.30 billion at the beginning of the year and \$.41 billion at the end of the year. Adding these two amounts and dividing the total by 2 gives us average receivables of \$.36 billion. Now we divide the year's net sales by the average receivables (\$3.1 ÷ \$.36 = 8.6); the result indicates an accounts receivable turnover rate of 8.6 times per year for TransCanada Pipelines. The higher the turnover rate the more liquid the company's receivables.

Another step that will help us judge the liquidity of a company's accounts receivable is to convert the accounts receivable turnover rate to the number of days (on average) required for the company to collect its accounts receivable. This is a simple calculation: divide the number of days in the year by the turnover rate. Continuing our example, divide 365 days by turnover of 8.6 (365 ÷ 8.6 = 42). This calculation tells us that on average, TransCanada Pipelines waited approximately 42 days to make collection of a sale on credit.

The data described above for computing the accounts receivable turnover rate and the average number of days to collect accounts receivable can be concisely stated as shown in the following equations:

Accounts Receivable Turnover

$$\frac{\text{Net Sales}}{\text{Average Accounts Receivable}} = \frac{\$3.1}{(\$.30 + \$.41) \div 2} = \frac{\$3.1}{\$.36} = 8.6 \text{ times}$$

Average Number of Days to Collect Accounts Receivable

$$\frac{\text{Days in Year}}{\text{Accounts Receivable Turnover}} = \frac{365}{8.6} = 42 \text{ days}$$

Management closely monitors these ratios in evaluating the company's policies for extending credit to customers and the effectiveness of its collection procedures. Short-term creditors, such as factors, banks, and merchandise suppliers, also use these ratios in evaluating a company's ability to generate the cash necessary to pay it short-term liabilities.

Concentrations of Credit Risk Assume that a business operates a single retail store in a town in which the major employer is a steel mill. What would happen to the collectibility of the store's accounts receivable if the steel mill were to close, leaving most of the store's customers unemployed? This situation illustrates what accountants call a ***concentration of credit risk,*** because many of the store's credit customers can be affected ***in a similar manner*** by certain changes in economic conditions. Concentra-

---

[3] From a conceptual point of view, net ***credit*** sales should be used in computing the accounts receivable turnover rate. It is common practice, however, to use the net sales figure, as the portion of net sales made on account usually is not disclosed in financial statements.

tions of credit risk occur if a significant portion of a company's receivables are due from a few major customers or from customers operating in the same industry or geographic region.

The FASB in the United States requires companies to disclose all ***significant*** concentrations of credit risk in the notes accompanying their financial statements. The disclosure includes (1) the economic characteristics defining each "concentration," (2) the amount of receivables within each concentration, and (3) the company's policies for requiring collateral (if any).[4] The basic purpose of these disclosures is to assist users of the financial statements in evaluating the extent of the company's vulnerability to credit losses stemming from changes in economic conditions.

* Supplemental Topic

Notes Receivable with Interest Charges Included in the Face Amount

OBJECTIVE 7 Account for notes receivable with the interest charges included in the face amount.

In our discussion to this point, we have used notes receivable with the interest rate ***stated separately.*** We now want to compare this form of note with an alternative form in which the interest charge is ***included in the face amount*** of the note. For example, assume that Genetic Services has a $10,000 account receivable from a customer, Biolab. The customer is short of cash and wants to postpone payment, so Genetic Services agrees to accept a 181-day promissory note from Biolab with interest at the rate of 12% a year to replace the $10,000 account receivable. The interest for the 181-day note plus 3 days of grace (a total of 184 days) will amount to $605 ($\$10,000 \times 12\% \times \frac{184}{365} = \$605$, rounded) and the total amount to be received at maturity will be $10,000 principal plus $605 interest, or $10,605 altogether.

If the note is drawn with interest stated separately, as in the illustration below, the wording will be ". . . Biolab promises to pay to Genetic Services the sum of $10,000 with interest at the rate of 12% per year."

This note is for the principal amount with interest stated separately

Montreal, Quebec November 1, 19__

181 days after this date Biolab

promises to pay to Genetic Services the sum of $ 10,000

with interest at the rate of 12% per year

Signed George Harr

Title Treasurer, Biolab

[4] FASB, *Statement No. 105,* "Disclosure about Financial Instruments with Off-Balance-Sheet Risk and Financial Instruments with Concentrations of Credit Risk" (Norwalk, Conn.: 1990), para. 20. The CICA has not issued recommendations in this area.

If the alternative form of note is used, the $605 interest will be included in the face amount and the note will appear as shown below:

Interest is included in face amount of this note

Montreal, Quebec	November 1, 19__
181 days after this date	Biolab
promises to pay to Genetic Services the sum of $	10,605
Signed	George Harr
Title	Treasurer, Biolab

Notice that the face amount of the note ($10,605) is ***greater*** than the $10,000 account receivable that it replaces. However, the value of the note receivable at November 1 is only $10,000; the other $605 included in the face amount of the note represents ***unearned interest revenue.*** As this interest revenue is earned over the life of the note, the value of the note will rise to $10,605 at maturity.

The journal entry by Genetic Services at November 1 to record the acquisition of the note will be as follows:

Interest included in face of note

Notes Receivable	10,605	
Discount on Notes Receivable		605
Accounts Receivable		10,000
Obtained from Biolab a 181-day note with a $605 interest charge included in the face amount, plus 3 days of grace.		

The asset account, Notes Receivable, was debited with the full face amount of the note ($10,605). It is, therefore, necessary to credit a contra-asset, Discount on Notes Receivable, for the $605 of future interest revenue included in the face amount of the note. The Discount on Notes Receivable will appear in the balance sheet as a deduction from Notes Receivable. In our illustration, the amounts in the balance sheet will be Notes Receivable, $10,605 ***minus*** Discount on Notes Receivable, $605, or a ***net*** asset value of $10,000 on November 1.

Discount on Notes Receivable The $605 balance of the account Discount on Notes Receivable at November 1 represents ***unearned interest revenue.*** As this interest revenue is earned over the life of the note, the amount in the discount account will be gradually transferred into Interest Revenue. Thus, at the maturity date of the note, Discount on Notes Receivable will have a zero balance and the value of the note receivable will have increased to $10,605. The process of transferring the amount in the Discount on Notes Receivable account into the Interest Revenue account is called ***amortization*** of the discount.

Amortization of the Discount The discount on ***short-term*** notes receivable usually is amortized by the straight-line method, which allocates the ***same amount*** of discount to interest revenue for each month of the note's life.[5] Thus, the $605 discount on the Biolab note will be transferred from Discount on Notes Receivable into Interest Revenue at a uniform rate over the 184-day period.

Adjusting entries should be made to amortize the discount at the end of each accounting period and at the date the note matures. At December 31, Genetic Services will make the following adjusting entry to recognize the 60-days' interest revenue earned since November 1:

Amortization of discount

Discount on Notes Receivable	197	
Interest Revenue		197
To record interest revenue earned to end-of-year on the 181-day note (plus 3 days of grace) dated Nov. 1 ($605 discount × $\frac{60}{184}$ = $197, rounded)		

At December 31, the net valuation of the note receivable will appear in the balance sheet of Genetic Services as shown below:

Asset shown net of discount

Current assets:		
Notes receivable	$10,605	
Less: Discount on notes receivable	408	$10,197

The net asset valuation of $10,197 consists of the $10,000 principal amount receivable from Biolab plus the $197 interest that has been earned since November 1.

When the note matures on May 4 of the following year, Genetic Services will recognize the $408 interest revenue earned since December 31 and will collect $10,605 from Biolab. The entry is:

Interest applicable to second year

Cash	10,605	
Discount on Notes Receivable	408	
Interest Revenue		408
Notes Receivable		10,605
To record collection of 181-day note (plus 3 days of grace) due today and to recognize interest revenue earned since year-end ($605 discount × $\frac{124}{184}$ = $408, rounded).		

Comparison of the Two Forms of Notes Receivable

We have illustrated two alternative methods that Genetic Services could use in accounting for its $10,000 receivable, depending upon the form of the note. Journal entries for both methods, along with the resulting balance sheet presentations of the asset at November 1 and December 31, are summarized on the next page. Notice that both methods result in Genetic Services recognizing the ***same amount of interest revenue*** and the ***same overall asset valuation*** in the balance sheet. The form of the note does ***not change the economic substance*** of the transaction.

---

[5] When an interest charge is included in the face amount of a ***long-term*** note, the effective interest method of amortizing the discount is often used instead of the straight-line method. The effective interest method of amortization is explained and illustrated in Chapter 11.

Comparison of the Two Forms of Notes Receivable

	Note Written for $10,000 Plus 12% Interest			Note Written with Interest Included in Face Amount		
Entry to record acquisition of note on Nov. 1	*Notes Receivable*	10,000		*Notes Receivable*	10,605	
	Accounts Receivable		10,000	*Discount on Notes Receivable*		605
				Accounts Receivable		10,000
	Current assets:			***Current assets:***		
Partial balance sheet at Nov. 1	***Notes receivable***		***$10,000***	***Notes receivable***	***$10,605***	
				Less: Discount on notes receivable	***605***	***$10,000***
Adjusting entry at Dec. 31	*Interest Receivable*	197		*Discount on Notes Receivable*	197	
	Interest Revenue		197	*Interest Revenue*		197
	Current assets:			***Current assets:***		
Partial balance sheet at Dec. 31	***Notes receivable***	***$10,000***		***Notes receivable***	***$10,605***	
	Interest receivable	***197***	***$10,197***	***Less: Discount on notes receivable***	***408***	***$10,197***
Entry to record collection of note on May 4	*Cash*	10,605		*Cash*	10,605	
	Notes Receivable		10,000	*Discount on Notes Receivable*	408	
	Interest Receivable		197	*Interest Revenue*		408
	Interest Revenue		408	*Notes Receivable*		10,605

THE CONCEPT OF PRESENT VALUE

OBJECTIVE 8 Discuss the concept of present value in accounting for long-term notes receivable.

Consider again the note receivable from Biolab in which interest is included in the face amount. The only dollar amount that appears in this note is ***$10,605***—the maturity value. Yet this note appears in Genetic Services' November 1 balance sheet at a net valuation of only ***$10,000.*** Where did this $10,000 amount come from, and what does it represent?

At November 1, $10,000 is the ***present value*** to Genetic Services of the right to collect $10,605 184 days in the future. The term ***present value*** means the economic value ***today*** of a cash flow that will occur at some future date.

It is helpful to think of present value as the ***amount that a knowledgeable investor would pay today for the right to receive the future cash amount.*** Because an investor expects to earn a profit (or interest) on an investment, the present value is ***always less*** than the full amount of the future cash flow.

The ***difference*** between the present value and the actual future amount is viewed as an ***interest charge*** included in the future amount. Often the present value of a note receivable is apparent from the current market values of the assets or services that are ***given in exchange*** for the note. In our current illustration, for example, Genetic Services accepts the note from Biolab at November 1 in full settlement of a $10,000 account receivable. This provides evidence that the current economic value (present value) of the note receivable on this date is $10,000.

In the assignment material for this chapter, the present value of notes receivable will be apparent from the value of the assets given in exchange. In practice, however, this is not always the case. When the present value of future cash flows is not apparent from the other values in a transaction, it must be computed by mathematical techniques.[6]

An Illustration of Notes Recorded at Present Value

To illustrate the use of present value in transactions involving long-term notes receivable, let us assume that on September 1, Tru-Tool, Inc., sells equipment to Everts Company and accepts as payment a one-year note (with the 3 days of grace included) in the face amount of $218,000 with no mention of an interest rate. It is not logical to assume that Tru-Tool, Inc., would extend credit for one year without charging any interest. Therefore, some portion of the $218,000 face amount of the note ***should be regarded as a charge for interest.***

Let us assume that the regular sales price of the equipment sold in this transaction is $200,000. In this case the ***present value*** of the note is apparently ***$200,000,*** and the remaining $18,000 of the face amount represents a charge for interest. (The rate of interest that will cause the $200,000 present value of the note to increase to the $218,000 maturity value in one year is 9%. Thus, the face amount of the note actually includes an interest charge computed at the effective annual interest rate of 9%.)

The selling company, Tru-Tool, Inc., should use the ***present value*** of the note in determining the amount of revenue to be recognized from the

[6] The mathematical computation of present values is discussed in Chapter 26 and in Appendix A, which is presented at the end of Chapter 16.

sale. The $18,000 interest charge included in the face amount of the note receivable from Everts Company represents ***unearned interest revenue*** to Tru-Tool, Inc., and is ***not part of the sales price of the equipment.*** If Tru-Tool, Inc., were to treat the entire face amount of the note receivable as the sales price of the equipment, the result would be to overstate sales revenue and notes receivable by $18,000, and also to understate interest revenue by this amount over the life of the note.

At September 1, the date of sale, Tru-Tool, Inc., should record as sales revenue only an amount equal to the ***present value*** of the note receivable. The portion of the note that is regarded as unearned interest revenue ($18,000) should be credited to the contra-asset account, Discount on Notes Receivable. Thus, the entry to record the sale of equipment to Everts Company at September 1 is as follows:

Present value of the note begins at $200,000—the sales price

Notes Receivable	*218,000*	
Discount on Notes Receivable		*18,000*
Sales		*200,000*
Sold equipment to Everts Company and received a one-year note (3 days of grace included) with an $18,000 interest charge included in the face amount.		

As the $18,000 interest is earned over the life of the note, this amount gradually will be transferred into Interest Revenue. At December 31, Tru-Tool, Inc., will have earned 121 days interest revenue and will make the following entry:

Present value has increased $5,967 by Dec. 31

Discount on Notes Receivable	*5,967*	
Interest Revenue		*5,967*
To record interest earned from Sept. 1 through Dec. 31 on Everts Company note ($18,000 discount × $\frac{121}{365}$ = $5,967, rounded).		

On September 1 of the following year, when the note receivable is collected from Everts Company, the required entry will be:

Present value has risen to $218,000 by maturity date

Cash	*218,000*	
Discount on Notes Receivable	*12,033*	
Interest Revenue		*12,033*
Notes Receivable		*218,000*
To record collection of Everts Company note and to recognize interest earned since year-end.		

Instalment Receivables

Another application of present value is found in the recording of ***instalment sales.*** Many retailing businesses sell merchandise on instalment sales plans, which permit customers to pay for their credit purchases through a series of monthly payments. The importance of instalment sales is emphasized by the recent balance sheets of large companies that show receivables in millions of dollars, nearly all of which call for collection in monthly instalments.

When merchandise is sold on an instalment plan, substantial interest charges are usually added to the "cash selling price" of the product in determining the total dollar amount to be collected in the series of instalment payments. The amount of sales revenue recognized at the time of sale, however, is limited to the ***present value*** of these instalment payments. In most cases, the present value of these future payments is equal to the regular sales price of the merchandise. The portion of the instalment account receivable that represents unearned finance charges is credited to the contra-asset account, Discount on Instalment Receivables. Thus, the entry to recognize the revenue on an instalment sale consists of a debit to Instalment Contracts Receivable, offset by a credit to Discount on Instalment Receivables for the unearned finance charges and a credit to Sales for the regular sales price of the merchandise. The balance of the contra-asset account, Discount on Instalment Receivables, is then amortized into Interest Revenue over the length of the collection period.

Although the collection period for an instalment receivable often runs as long as 24 to 36 months, such receivables are regarded as current assets if they correspond to customary credit terms of the industry. In published balance sheets, the Discount on Instalment Receivables is often called ***Deferred Interest Income*** or ***Unearned Finance Charges.*** A typical balance sheet presentation of instalment accounts receivable is illustrated below:

Trade accounts receivable:	
Accounts receivable	*$ 75,040,000*
Instalment contracts receivable, including $31,000,000 due after one year.	*52,640,000*
	$127,680,000
Less: Deferred interest income ($8,070,000) and allowance for doubtful accounts ($1,872,000)	*9,942,000*
Total trade accounts and notes receivable	*$117,738,000*

CHAPTER REVIEW

KEY TERMS INTRODUCED OR EMPHASIZED IN CHAPTER 8

Accounts receivable turnover A ratio used to measure the liquidity of accounts receivable and the reasonableness of the accounts receivable balance. Computed by dividing net sales by average receivables.

Aging the accounts receivable The process of classifying accounts receivable by age groups such as current, past due 1–30 days, past due 31–60 days, etc. A step in estimating the uncollectible portion of the accounts receivable.

Allowance for Doubtful Accounts A valuation account or contra account relating to accounts receivable and showing the portion of the receivables estimated to be uncollectible.

Collateral (for a loan) Assets pledged to secure a borrower's promise to repay a loan. In the event that the borrower fails to repay the loan, the creditor may foreclose against (take title to) the collateral.

Concentration of credit risk A significant portion of receivables due from one customer or from a group of customers likely to be affected in a similar manner by changes in economic conditions.

Conservatism A traditional practice of resolving uncertainties by choosing an asset valuation at the lower point of the range of reasonableness. Also refers to the policy of postponing recognition of revenue to a later date when a range of reasonable choice exists. Designed to avoid overstatement of financial strength and earnings.

Contra-asset account A ledger account that is deducted from or offset against a related account in the financial statements—for example, Allowance for Doubtful Accounts and Discount on Notes Receivable.

Default Failure to pay interest or principal of a promissory note at the due date.

Direct write-off method A method of accounting for uncollectible receivables in which no expense is recognized until individual accounts are determined to be worthless. At that point the account receivable is written off with an offsetting debit to uncollectible accounts expense. Fails to match revenue and related expenses.

Discount on Notes Receivable A contra-asset account representing any unearned interest included in the face amount of a note receivable. Over the life of the note, the balance of the Discount on Notes Receivable account is amortized into Interest Revenue.

Discounting notes receivable Selling a note receivable prior to its maturity date.

Effective interest rate The rate of interest that will cause the present value of a note to increase to the maturity value by the maturity date.

Factoring accounts receivable Transactions in which a business either sells its accounts receivable to a financial institution (often called a ***factor***) or borrows money by pledging its accounts receivable as collateral.

Interest A charge made for the use of money. The formula for computing interest is Principal × Rate of interest × Time = Interest ($P \times R \times T = I$).

Maker (of a note) A person or an entity who issues a promissory note.

Maturity date The date on which a note becomes due and payable.

Maturity value The value of a note at its maturity date, consisting of principal plus interest.

Payee The person named in a promissory note to whom payment is to be made (the creditor).

*__Present value of a future cash receipt__ The amount of money that an informed investor would pay today for the right to receive that future cash receipt. The present value is always less than the future amount, because money available today can be invested to earn interest and thereby become equivalent to a larger amount in the future.

Three days of grace The extra three days added to the due date on all notes, other than the demand notes, to determine the legal date on which the note is due and payable.

DEMONSTRATION PROBLEM FOR YOUR REVIEW

Brian's Home Centre sells custom wood furniture to decorators and the general public. Selected transactions relating to the company's receivables for the month of March follow. The company uses the allowance method in accounting for uncollectible accounts.

March 8 A $480 account receivable from S. Wilson was determined to be worthless and was written off.

March 13 Sold merchandise to Century Interiors and received a $15,000, 60-day, 8% note dated March 13.

* *Supplemental Topic, "Notes Receivable with Interest Charges Included in the Face Amount"*

March 21 Received full payment from J. Porter of a $4,500, 60-day, 12% note dated January 17. Accrued interest receivable of $62 had been recorded in prior months.

March 23 An account receivable of $325 from G. Davis had been written off in January; full payment was unexpectedly received from Davis.

March 24* Received a 60-day note from StyleCraft Co. in settlement of $3,600 open account. Interest computed at 8% was included in the face amount of the note.

March 29 Sales to ExtraCash credit card customers during March amounted to $14,800. (Summarize all credit card sales in one entry. ExtraCash Inc. is a credit card company.)

March 30 Collected cash from ExtraCash Inc. for the March credit card sales, less a 5% discount charged by ExtraCash.

March 31 As a result of substantial write-offs, the Allowance for Doubtful Accounts has a debit balance of $320. Aging of the accounts receivable indicates that the estimated uncollectible accounts are $1,800 at the end of March.

INSTRUCTIONS

a Prepare journal entries in general journal form for the March transactions.

b Prepare the necessary adjusting entries at March 31.

SOLUTION TO DEMONSTRATION PROBLEM

a *General Journal*

March 8	Allowance for Doubtful Accounts	480	
	Accounts Receivable, S. Wilson		480
	Wrote off uncollectible account from S. Wilson		
13	Note Receivable, Century Interiors	15,000	
	Sales		15,000
	Sale of merchandise for a 60-day, 8% note.		
21	Cash	4,593	
	Notes Receivable		4,500
	Interest Receivable		62
	Interest Revenue		31
	Collected note from J. Porter, including $93 interest. ($4,500 × .12 × $\frac{21}{365}$ = $31, rounded)		
23	Account Receivable, G. Davis	325	
	Allowance for Doubtful Accounts		325
	To reinstate Davis receivable previously written off.		
23	Cash	325	
	Accounts Receivable, G. Davis		325
	To record collection of Davis account.		
24	Notes Receivable	3,650	
	Discount on Notes Receivable		50
	Accounts Receivable, StyleCraft Co.		3,600
	Received 60-day note with interest at 8% included in face amount in settlement of open account ($3,600 × .08 × $\frac{63}{365}$ = $50, rounded)		
29	Accounts Receivable, ExtraCash Inc.	14,800	
	Sales		14,800
	To record credit card sales for March.		
30	Cash	14,060	
	Credit Card Discount Expense	740	
	Accounts Receivable, ExtraCash Inc.		14,800
	Collected March credit card sales invoices, less 5%.		

* *Supplemental Topic, "Notes Receivable with Interest Charges Included in the Face Amount"*

b *Adjusting Entries*

March 31	*Uncollectible Accounts Expense*		*2,120*	
	Allowance for Doubtful Accounts			*2,120*
	To provide for estimated uncollectibles as follows:			
	Required allowance at March 31	*$1,800*		
	Present balance (debit)	*320*		
	Required increase in allowance	*$2,120*		
31	*Interest Receivable*		*59*	
	Interest Revenue			*59*
	To accrue interest on the Century Interiors' note: $15,000 × .08 × $\frac{18}{365}$ = $59.			
31	*Discount on Notes Receivable*		*6*	
	Interest Revenue			*6*
	To record interest earned through March 31 on StyleCraft note receivable ($50 discount × $\frac{7}{63}$ = $6, rounded)			

ASSIGNMENT MATERIAL

DISCUSSION QUESTIONS

1 Wolf Brothers, a retailer, makes most of its sales on credit. In the first 10 years of operation, the company incurred some uncollectible accounts (bad debts) expense each year. Does this record indicate that the company's credit policies are in need of change? Explain.

2 Company A and Company B are virtually identical in size and nature of operations, but Company A is more conservative in valuing accounts receivable. Will this greater emphasis on conservatism cause A to report higher or lower net income than Company B? Assume that you are a banker considering identical loan applications from A and B and you know of the more conservative policy followed by A. In which set of financial statements would you have more confidence? Explain.

3 Explain the relationship between the ***matching principle*** and the need to estimate uncollectible accounts receivable.

4 Mako Company determines at year-end that its Allowance for Doubtful Accounts should be increased by $5,200. Give the adjusting entry to carry out this decision.

5 Clinton, Inc., which has accounts receivable of $371,520 and an allowance for doubtful accounts of $4,320, decides to write off as worthless a past-due account receivable for $1,800 from Cass Company. What effect will the write-off have upon total current assets? Upon net income for the period? Explain.

6 In making the annual adjusting entry for uncollectible accounts, a company may utilize a ***balance sheet approach*** to make the estimate or it may use an ***income statement approach.*** Explain these two alternative approaches.

7 At the end of its first year in business, Arthur Yokotake, Inc., had accounts receivable totalling $148,500. After careful analysis of the individual accounts, the credit manager estimated that $146,100 would ultimately be collected. Give the journal entry required to reflect this estimate in the accounts.

8 In February of its second year of operations, World Travel Network learned of the failure of a customer, Dale Corporation, which owed $800. Nothing could be collected. Give the journal entry to recognize the uncollectibility of the receivable from Dale Corporation, assuming World uses an allowance method.

9 Posner Company, which uses the allowance method of accounting for uncollectible accounts, wrote off as uncollectible a $1,500 receivable from Webb Company. Several months later, Webb Company obtained new long-term financing and promptly paid all its old debts in full. Give the journal entry or entries (in general journal form) that Posner Company should make to record this recovery of $1,500.

10 What is the direct write-off method of handling credit losses as opposed to the allowance method? What is its principal shortcoming?

11 Caballeros, Inc., had decided to write off its account receivable from Leisure Now because the latter has entered bankruptcy. What general ledger accounts should be debited and credited, assuming that the allowance method is in use? What general ledger accounts should be debited and credited if the direct write-off method is in use?

12 What are the advantages to a retailer of making credit sales only to customers who use nationally recognized credit cards?

13 Jade Palace, a restaurant that had always made cash sales only, adopted a new policy of honouring several nonbank credit cards. Sales did not increase, but many of its regular customers began charging dinner bills on the credit cards. Has the new policy been beneficial to Jade Palace? Explain.

14 Determine the maturity date of each of the following:

a A three-month note dated March 10.

b A 30-day note dated August 15.

c A 90-day note dated July 2.

15 On April 10, Hilltop Growers receives a 60-day, 9% note receivable from Jane Stream, a customer, in settlement of a $6,000 account receivable due today. Give the journal entries to record (1) the receipt of this note and (2) its collection at the maturity date.

16 How are the accounts receivable turnover rate and the average number of days to collect accounts receivable computed? Why is this information significant to short-term creditors?

17 How does an annual audit by a public accounting firm provide assurance that a company's accounts receivable and notes receivable are fairly presented in the company's financial statements?

*18 Define the ***present value*** of a future amount. Is the present value larger or smaller than the face amount of the future cash flow? Why?

*19 Williams Gear sold merchandise to Dayco in exchange for a one-year (3 days of grace included) note receivable. The note was drawn with a face amount of $13,310, ***including*** a 10% interest charge. Compute the amount of sales revenue to be recognized by Williams Gear.

*20 Maxline Stores sells merchandise with a sales price of $1,260 on an instalment plan requiring 12 monthly payments of $120 each. How much revenue will this sale ultimately generate for Maxline Stores? Explain the nature of this revenue and when it should be recognized in the accounting records.

*21 With reference to Question **20** above, make the journal entries required in the accounting records of Maxline Stores to record:

a Recognition of revenue from sale of merchandise on instalment contract.

* *Supplemental Topic, "Notes Receivable with Interest Charges Included in the Face Amount"*

b Collection of the first monthly instalment payment. (Assume that an equal portion of the discount is amortized at the time that each instalment payment is received.)

MULTIPLE CHOICE QUESTIONS

1 Which of the following best describes the application of generally accepted accounting principles to the valuation of accounts receivable?

a Realization principle—Accounts receivable are shown at their net realizable value in the balance sheet.

b Matching principle—The loss due to an uncollectible account is recognized in the period in which the sale is made, not in the period in which the account receivable is determined to be worthless.

c Cost principle—Accounts receivable are shown at the initial cost of the merchandise to customers, less the cost the seller must pay to cover uncollectible accounts.

d Principle of conservatism—Accountants favour using the lowest reasonable estimate for the amount of uncollectible accounts shown in the balance sheet.

2 On January 1, Dillon Company had a $3,100 credit balance in the Allowance for Doubtful Accounts. During the year, sales totalled $780,000 and $6,900 of accounts receivable were written off as uncollectible. A December 31 aging of accounts receivable indicated the amount probably uncollectible to be $5,300. (No recoveries of accounts previously written off were made during the year.) Dillon's financial statements for the current year should include:

a Uncollectible accounts expense of $9,100.

b Uncollectible accounts expense of $5,300.

c Allowance for Doubtful Accounts with a credit balance of $1,500.

d Allowance for Doubtful Accounts with a credit balance of $8,400.

3 Under the ***direct write-off*** method of accounting for uncollectible accounts:

a The current year uncollectible accounts expense is less than the expense would be under the income statement approach.

b The relationship between the current period net sales and current period uncollectible accounts expense illustrates the matching principle.

c The Allowance for Doubtful Accounts is debited when specific accounts receivable are determined to be worthless.

d Accounts receivable are not stated in the balance sheet at net realizable value, but at the balance of the Accounts Receivable ledger account.

4 On October 1, Blaine Company sold a parcel of land in exchange for a nine-month (3 days of grace included), 12% note receivable in the amount of $300,000. Interest is not included in the face amount of this note and the proper adjusting entry was made with respect to this note at December 31. Blaine's journal entry to record collection of this note at July 1 of the following year (maturity date) includes (compute interest on a monthly rather than daily basis):

a A debit to Cash for $318,000.

b A credit to Interest Revenue of $18,000.

c A debit to Interest Receivable of $9,000.

d A credit to Notes Receivable of $327,000.

*5 On September 1, 1996, Vickers Industries sold machinery in exchange for a six-month (3 days of grace included) note receivable. An interest charge, computed at an annual rate of 12%, was included in the face amount of the note. In its December 31, 1996, balance sheet, Vickers correctly presented the note receivable as follows:

Note Receivable, due March 1, 1997	*$143,100*	
Less: Discount on note receivable	*(2,700)*	*$140,400*

What was the total amount of interest charge included in the face amount of the note on ***September 1, 1996*** (interest is computed on a monthly rather than daily basis):

a $2,700 b $5,400 c $8,100 d $8,586

EXERCISES

EXERCISE 8-1 Accounting Terminology

Listed below are nine technical accounting terms introduced in this chapter.

Uncollectible accounts expense	*Allowance for Doubtful Accounts*	*Accounts receivable turnover*
Aging schedule	*Conservatism*	*Direct write-off method*
Factoring	*Default*	*Maturity value*

Each of the following statements may (or may not) describe one of these technical terms. For each statement, indicate the term described, or answer "None" if the statement does not correctly describe any of the terms.

a The principal amount of an interest-bearing note.

b Resolving uncertainties in the valuation of assets by reporting assets at the lower end of the range of reasonable values rather than by estimating values in a purely objective manner.

c The account indicating the portion of the year-end accounts receivable that are expected to prove uncollectible.

d The account indicating the amount of accounts receivable originating during the year that are expected to prove uncollectible.

e Failure to make payment of the principal or interest per the terms of a promissory note.

f A computation useful in determining how quickly a company is able to collect its accounts receivable.

g Recognition of credit losses when specific accounts receivable are determined to be uncollectible.

EXERCISE 8-2 Accounting for Uncollectible Accounts—The "Balance Sheet" Approach

At May 31, the accounts receivable of Biway Central amounted in total to $705,600. The company uses the balance sheet approach to estimate uncollectible accounts and has prepared an aging schedule of accounts receivable at May 31 that indicates $17,568 to be uncollectible. You are to prepare as of May 31 the adjusting entry required under each of the following independent assumptions. The explanation portion of each entry should include appropriate supporting computations.

a The Allowance for Doubtful Accounts has a credit balance of $12,672.

b The Allowance for Doubtful Accounts has a debit balance of $4,262.

* *Supplemental Topic, "Notes Receivable with Interest Charges Included in the Face Amount"*

EXERCISE 8-3
Accounting for Uncollectible Accounts—The "Income Statement" Approach

The income statement approach to estimating uncollectible accounts expense is used by Burgess Wholesale. On March 31 the firm had accounts receivable in the amount of $630,000. The Allowance for Doubtful Accounts had a credit balance of $3,950. The controller estimated that uncollectible accounts expense would amount to one-half of 1% of the $5,200,000 of net credit sales made during March. This estimate was entered in the accounts by an adjusting entry on March 31.

On April 12, an account receivable from Conrad Stern of $3,110 was determined to be worthless and was written off. However, on April 24, Stern won several thousand dollars in a lottery and immediately paid the $3,110 past-due account.

INSTRUCTIONS Prepare four journal entries in general journal form to record the above events.

EXERCISE 8-4
Uncollectible Accounts Expense—Allowance Method and Direct Write-Off Method

The credit manager of Olympic Sporting Goods has gathered the following information about the company's accounts receivable and credit losses during the current year:

Net credit sales for the year		*$3,000,000*
Accounts receivable at year-end		*360,000*
Uncollectible accounts receivable:		
Actually written off during the year	*$43,650*	
Estimated portion of year-end receivables expected to prove uncollectible (per aging schedule)	*18,000*	*61,650*

INSTRUCTIONS Prepare one journal entry summarizing the recognition of uncollectible accounts expense for the entire year under each of the following independent assumptions:

a Uncollectible accounts expense is estimated at an amount equal to $1\frac{1}{2}\%$ of net credit sales.

b Uncollectible accounts expense is recognized by adjusting the balance in the Allowance for Doubtful Accounts to the amount indicated in the year-end aging schedule. The credit balance in the allowance account at the beginning of the current year was $15,000.

c The company uses the direct write-off method of accounting for uncollectible accounts.

EXERCISE 8-5
Write-Offs and Recoveries

The balance sheet of Omni, Inc., at the end of last year included the following items:

Notes receivable from customers	*$ 540,000*
Interest receivable	*10,800*
Accounts receivable	*2,268,000*
Less: Allowance for doubtful accounts	*54,000*

INSTRUCTIONS You are to record the following related events of the current year in general journal entries:

a Accounts receivable of $51,840 are written off as uncollectible.

b A customer's note for $14,850, on which interest of $810 has been accrued in the accounts, is deemed uncollectible, and both balances are written off against the Allowance for Doubtful Accounts.

c An account receivable for $7,020 previously written off is collected.

d Aging of accounts receivable at the end of the current year indicates a need for an $81,000 allowance to cover possible failure to collect accounts currently outstanding.

EXERCISE 8-6
How Fast Are Accounts Receivable Collected?

In your analysis of the financial statements of Rayscan, Inc., you note that net sales for the year were $17,000,000; accounts receivable were $1,500,000 at the beginning of the year and $1,900,000 at the end of the year.

INSTRUCTIONS

a Compute the accounts receivable turnover rate for the year.

b Compute the number of days (on average) required to collect accounts receivable.

c Assume that during the following year sales increase and the accounts receivable turnover rate also increases. Would you regard this as a favourable development? Explain.

EXERCISE 8-7
Notes and Interest

On September 1, a six-month (3 days of grace included), 15% note receivable is acquired from Shaun Young, a customer, in settlement of his $12,000 account receivable. (Interest is computed on a monthly rather than daily basis.)

INSTRUCTIONS

Prepare journal entries to record:

a The receipt of the note on September 1.

b The adjustment to record accrued interest revenue on December 31.

c Collection of the principal and interest on February 28.

***EXERCISE 8-8**
Two Forms of Notes Receivable

On October 1, Blackwood Company made a loan of $300,000 to a supplier, Niagara Mills. The loan agreement provided for repayment of the $300,000 in 12 months plus interest at an annual rate of 10%. (Compute interest on a monthly basis and assume the 3 days of grace has been included.)

INSTRUCTIONS

You are to prepare two different presentations of the note receivable from Niagara Mills on Blackwood Company's balance sheet at December 31, assuming that the note was drawn as follows:

a For $300,000 with interest stated separately and payable at maturity.

b With the total interest charge included in the face amount of the note.

***EXERCISE 8-9**
Interest Included in Face Amount of Note

West Motors, a truck dealer, sold three trucks to Day & Night Truck Lines on July 1, for a total price of $78,600. Under the terms of the sale, West Motors received $21,000 cash and a promissory note due in full in 24 months. The face amount of the note was $67,968, which included interest on the note for the 24 months.

West Motors uses a perpetual inventory system. The trucks sold to Day & Night Truck Lines were carried in West's inventory at an aggregate cost of $69,000.

INSTRUCTIONS

Prepare entries in general journal form for West Motors relating to this transaction and to the note for the year ended December 31. Include the adjusting entry needed to record interest earned to December 31. (Adjusting entries are made only at year-end. Assume the discount is amortized by the straight-line method—that is, an equal amount of interest revenue is considered earned in each month. Also, compute interest on a monthly basis and assume the 3 days of grace have been included in the 24-month note.)

* *Supplemental Topic, "Notes Receivable with Interest Charges Included in the Face Amount"*

PROBLEMS

Group A

PROBLEM 8A-1
Hey, Pal . . . When You Gonna Pay for This Pop?

Shown below are the net sales and the average amounts of accounts receivable of two beverage companies in a recent year:

	(Dollars in Millions)	
	Average Accounts Receivable	Net Credit Sales
Freshdrink	$ 95	$1,315
Coldpop	337	7,677

INSTRUCTIONS

a For each of these companies, compute:

1 The number of times that the average balance of accounts receivable turned over during this fiscal year. (Round to the nearest tenth.)

2 The number of days (on average) that each company must wait to collect its accounts receivable. (Round to the nearest day.)

b Based upon your computations in part **a,** which company's accounts receivable appear to be the more "liquid" asset? Explain briefly.

PROBLEM 8A-2
Aging Accounts Receivable; Write-Offs

Chandler Associates Inc., uses the balance sheet approach to estimate uncollectible accounts and maintains an allowance account to reduce accounts receivable to realizable value. An analysis of the accounts receivable at year-end produced the following age groups:

(1) Not yet due	*$348,000*
(2) 1–30 days past due	*180,000*
(3) 31–60 days past due	*78,000*
(4) 61–90 days past due	*18,000*
(5) Over 90 days past due	*30,000*
Total accounts receivable	*$654,000*

In reliance upon its past experience with collections, the company estimated the percentages probably uncollectible for the above five age groups to be as follows: Group 1, 1%; Group 2, 4%; Group 3, 10%; Group 4, 30%; and Group 5, 50%.

Prior to adjustment at December 31 (year-end date), the Allowance for Doubtful Accounts showed a credit balance of $12,600.

INSTRUCTIONS

a Compute the estimated amount of uncollectible accounts based on the above classification by age groups.

b Prepare the adjusting entry needed to bring the Allowance for Doubtful Accounts to the proper amount.

c Assume that on February 2 of the following year, Chandler Associates learned that an account receivable that had originated on October 6 in the amount of $7,200 was worthless because of the bankruptcy of the customer, Weaver Company. Prepare the journal entry required on February 2 to write off this account receivable.

PROBLEM 8A-3
Estimating Uncollectible Accounts

KilnKraft, Inc., owned by Abby Powers, had for the past five years been engaged in selling a line of ceramic merchandise to retail stores. Sales are made on credit and each month the company has estimated its uncollectible accounts expense as a percentage of net credit sales. The percentage used has been $\frac{1}{2}$ of 1% of net credit sales. However, it appears that this provision has been inadequate because the

Allowance for Doubtful Accounts has a debit balance of $6,200 at May 31 prior to making the monthly provision. Powers has therefore decided to change the approach of estimating uncollectible accounts expense and to rely upon an analysis of the age and character of the accounts receivable at the end of each month.

At May 31, the accounts receivable totalled $380,000. This total amount included past-due accounts in the amount of $86,000. None of these past-due accounts was considered hopeless; all accounts regarded as worthless had been written off as rapidly as they were determined to be uncollectible. After careful investigation of the past-due accounts at May 31, Abby Powers decided that the probable loss contained therein was 10%, and that in addition she should anticipate a loss of 1% of the current amounts receivable.

INSTRUCTIONS

a Compute the probable amount of uncollectible accounts included in the accounts receivable at May 31, based on the analysis by the owner.

b Prepare the journal entry necessary to carry out the change in company policy with respect to providing for uncollectible accounts expense.

PROBLEM 8A-4
Accounts Receivable: A Comprehensive Problem

Nagano International has 420 accounts receivable in its subsidiary ledger. All accounts are due in 30 days. On December 31, an aging schedule was prepared. The results are summarized below:

Customer	Total	Not Yet Due	1–30 Days Past Due	31–60 Days Past Due	61–90 Days Past Due	Over 90 Days Past Due
(418 names)						
Subtotals	*$863,125*	*$458,975*	*$236,700*	*$108,350*	*$22,500*	*$36,600*

Two accounts receivable were accidentally omitted from this schedule. The following data is available regarding these accounts:

1 J. Ardis owes $10,625 from two invoices; invoice no. 218, dated Sept. 14, in the amount of $7,450; and invoice no. 568, dated Nov. 9, in the amount of $3,175.

2 N. Selstad owes $9,400 from two invoices; invoice no. 628, dated Nov. 19, in the amount of $3,375; and invoice no. 718, dated Dec. 5, in the amount of $6,025.

INSTRUCTIONS

a Complete the aging schedule as of Dec. 31 by adding to the column subtotals an aging of the accounts of Ardis and Selstad.

b Prepare a schedule to compute the estimated portion of each age group that will prove uncollectible and the required balance in the Allowance for Doubtful Accounts. Arrange your schedule in the format illustrated in this chapter. The following percentages of each age group are estimated to be uncollectible: Not yet due, 1%; 1–30 days, 4%; 31–60 days, 10%; 61–90 days, 30%; over 90 days, 50%.

c Prepare the journal entry to bring the Allowance for Doubtful Accounts up to its required balance at Dec. 31. Prior to making this adjustment, the account has a credit balance of $34,500.

d Show how accounts receivable would appear in the company's balance sheet at Dec. 31.

e On Jan. 7 of the following year, the credit manager of Nagano International learns that the $10,625 account receivable from J. Ardis is uncollectible because Ardis has declared bankruptcy. Prepare the journal entry to write off this account.

PROBLEM 8A-5
Note Receivable: Entries for Collection and for Default

Far Corners Imports sells a variety of merchandise to retail stores on open account, but it insists that any customer who fails to pay an invoice when due must replace it with an interest-bearing note. The company adjusts and closes its accounts at December 31. Among the transactions relating to notes receivable were the following:

Dec. 1 Received from a customer (Party Plus) a 60-day, 9% note for $42,000 in settlement of an account receivable due today.

Feb. 2 Collected in full the 60-day, 9% note receivable from Party Plus, including interest.

INSTRUCTIONS

a Prepare journal entries (in general journal form) to record: (1) the receipt of the note on December 1; (2) the adjustment for interest on December 31; and (3) collection of principal and interest on February 2. Assume that the company does not use reversing entries.

b Assume that instead of paying the note on February 2, the customer (Party Plus) had defaulted. Give the journal entry by Far Corners Imports to record the default. Assume that Party Plus has sufficient resources that the note eventually will be collected.

***PROBLEM 8A-6**
Notes Receivable: A Comprehensive Problem

Following are selected receivables of Clinton Agricultural Supply Company at December 1, 1995. The company adjusts and closes its accounts only at year-end.

Notes receivable:	
Flag-Is-Up; 90-day, 10% note dated Sept. 7	*$10,000*
Trust-House Co-op; 60-day, 9% note dated Oct. 29	*20,000*
Applegate Farm; 45-day, 10% note dated Nov. 1	*28,800*
W. B. McCoy; 90-day, 12% note dated Dec. 1	*32,000*
Accounts receivable:	
Morgan-Hill Farms	*$ 8,000*
T. J. Peppercorn	*12,700*
Instalment contracts receivable:	
M. Twain (19 monthly payments of $900)	*$17,100*
Unearned finance charges on instalment contracts:	
Applicable to M. Twain contract	*$ 2,280*

During December, transactions affecting these receivables were as follows:

Dec. 7 T. J. Peppercorn paid $700 on account and gave a 30-day, 10% note to cover the $12,000 balance of his account.

Dec. 9 Collected in full the maturity value of the Flag-Is-Up 90-day note.

Dec. 11 Received a 60-day note receivable from Morgan-Hill Farms in full settlement of its account receivable. The face amount of this note was $8,120, which included an interest charge.

Dec. 19 Tom Applegate wrote that Applegate Farm would be unable to pay the note due today. However, he enclosed a cheque for the interest due, along with a new 30-day, 10% note replacing the old note. Clinton Agricultural decided to accept this renewal of the Applegate note.

Dec. 31 Received notice from Trust-House Co-op that it was unable to pay its note due today. The defaulted note was not renewed, but Clinton expects that the amount due will eventually be collected.

---

* *Supplemental Topic, "Notes Receivable with Interest Charges Included in the Face Amount"*

Supplementary Section instalment — no

Dec. 31 Received the $900 payment from M. Twain on her instalment contract. The payment included $120 interest for the month of December. The interest charges included in the face amount of the instalment contract originally had been credited to the contra-asset account, Unearned Finance Charges on Instalment Contracts.

INSTRUCTIONS

a Prepare journal entries for the six December transactions listed above.

b Prepare the adjusting entries necessary at December 31 to recognize interest accrued on notes receivable through year-end.

Use one adjusting entry to accrue interest receivable on the three notes in which interest is stated separately (the Applegate, Peppercorn, and McCoy notes). Use a separate adjusting entry to recognize interest revenue earned on the note with interest included in the face amount (the Morgan-Hill note).

c Prepare the current asset section of Clinton Agricultural Supply Company's balance sheet at Dec. 31, 1995. In addition to the receivables described above, include the following items:

Cash	$ 42,500
Accounts receivable (other than described above)	120,000
Allowance for doubtful receivables (all types)	10,000
Inventory	105,000

In listing the company's receivables, include captions indicating any unamortized discount, unearned finance charges, and accrued interest. Do ***not,*** however, identify the individual debtors. (Combine all four notes under the caption "Notes receivable.")

***PROBLEM 8A-7**
Long-Term Note Receivable with Interest Included in Face Amount

On June 1, 1995, Monitor Corporation sold merchandise to Potomac Shipping in exchange for a note receivable due in ***one year*** (3 days of grace included). The note was drawn in the face amount of $325,500, which included the principal amount and an interest charge. In its December 31, 1995, balance sheet, Monitor Corporation correctly presented the note receivable as follows:

Note receivable, due May 31, 1996	$325,500	
Less: Discount on note receivable	10,625	$314,875

INSTRUCTIONS

a Determine the monthly interest revenue earned by Monitor Corporation from this note receivable.

b Compute the amount of interest revenue recognized by Monitor Corporation from the note during 1995.

c Compute the amount of sales revenue recognized by Monitor Corporation on June 1, 1995 when this note was received.

d Compute the effective annual rate of interest (stated as a percentage) represented by the interest charge originally included in the face amount of the note.

e Prepare all journal entries relating to this note in the accounting records of Monitor Corporation for 1995 and 1996. Assume that adjusting entries are made only at December 31, and that the note was collected on the maturity date.

* *Supplemental Topic, "Notes Receivable with Interest Charges Included in the Face Amount"*

Group B

PROBLEM 8B-1
Turnover of Accounts Receivable

Shown below are the net sales and the average amounts of accounts receivable of two computer makers in a recent year:

	(Dollars in Millions) Average Accounts Receivable	Net Credit Sales
P. C. Micro	$1,297	$7,102
Advantec Computers	2,108	9,390

INSTRUCTIONS

a For each of these companies, compute:

1 The number of times that the average balance of accounts receivable turned over during this fiscal year. (Round to the nearest tenth.)

2 The number of days (on average) that each company must wait to collect its accounts receivable. (Round to the nearest day.)

b Based upon your computations in part **a,** which company's accounts receivable appear to be the more "liquid" asset? Explain briefly.

PROBLEM 8B-2
Aging Accounts Receivable; Write-Offs

Public Image, a firm specializing in marketing and publicity services, uses the balance sheet approach to estimate uncollectible accounts expense. At year-end an aging of the accounts receivable produced the following classification:

(1) Not yet due	$333,000
(2) 1–30 days past due	135,000
(3) 31–60 days past due	58,500
(4) 61–90 days past due	13,500
(5) Over 90 days past due	22,500
Total	$562,500

On the basis of past experience, the company estimated the percentages probably uncollectible for the above five age groups to be as follows: Group 1, 1%; Group 2, 3%; Group 3, 10%; Group 4, 20%; and Group 5, 50%.

The Allowance for Doubtful Accounts before adjustment at December 31 (year-end date) showed a credit balance of $8,100.

INSTRUCTIONS

a Compute the estimated amount of uncollectible accounts based on the above classification by age groups.

b Prepare the adjusting entry needed to bring the Allowance for Doubtful Accounts to the proper amount.

c Assume that on January 10 of the following year, Public Image learned that an account receivable that had originated on September 1 in the amount of $8,550 was worthless because of the bankruptcy of the customer, Cranston Manufacturing. Prepare the journal entry required on January 10 to write off this account.

PROBLEM 8B-3
Estimating Uncollectible Accounts

At December 31 last year, the balance sheet prepared by Luis Montoyo included $504,000 in accounts receivable and an allowance for doubtful accounts of $26,400. During January of the current year selected transactions are summarized as follows:

(1) Sales on account	$360,640
(2) Cash collections from customers (no cash discounts)	364,800
(3) Account receivable from Acme Company written off as worthless	9,280

After a careful aging and analysis of all customers' accounts at January 31, it was decided that the allowance for doubtful accounts should be adjusted to a balance of $29,280 in order to reflect accounts receivable at net realizable value in the January 31 balance sheet.

INSTRUCTIONS

a Prepare entries in general journal form summarizing for the entire month of January the activity described in the three numbered items. Also show the adjusting entry at January 31 to provide for uncollectible accounts.

b Show the amounts of accounts receivable and the allowance for doubtful accounts as they would appear in a partial balance sheet at January 31.

c Assume that three months after the receivable from Acme Company had been written off as worthless, Acme Company won a large award in the settlement of patent litigation and immediately paid the $9,280 debt to Luis Montoyo. Give the journal entry or entries (in general journal form) to reflect this recovery of a receivable previously written off.

PROBLEM 8B-4
Estimating Uncollectible Accounts

Rivero Graphics, owned by Maria Rivero, sells paper novelty goods to retail stores. All sales are made on credit and the company has regularly estimated its uncollectible accounts expense as a percentage of net credit sales. The percentage used has been 1% of net credit sales. However, it appears that this provision has been inadequate because the Allowance for Doubtful Accounts has a debit balance of $3,900 at May 31 prior to making the monthly provision. Rivero has therefore decided to change the approach of estimating uncollectible accounts expense and to rely upon an analysis of the age and character of the accounts receivable at the end of each month.

At May 31, the accounts receivable totalled $260,000. This total amount included past-due accounts in the amount of $46,000. None of these past-due accounts was considered worthless; all accounts regarded as worthless had been written off immediately. After a careful review of the $46,000 of past-due accounts at May 31, Rivero decided that the estimated loss contained therein was 10%. In addition she decided to provide for a loss of 1% of the current accounts receivable.

INSTRUCTIONS

a Compute the estimated amount of uncollectible accounts included in the $260,000 of accounts receivable at May 31, based on the analysis by the owner.

b Prepare the journal entry necessary to carry out the change in company policy with respect to providing for uncollectible accounts expense.

PROBLEM 8B-5
Note Receivable: Entries for Collection and for Default

Hanover Mills sells merchandise to retail stores on 30-day credit, but insists that any customer who fails to pay an invoice when due must replace it with an interest-bearing note. The company adjusts and closes its accounts at December 31. Among the transactions relating to notes receivable were the following.

Nov. 1 Received from a customer (Jones Brothers) a 90-day, 9% note for $30,000 in settlement of an account receivable due today.

Feb. 2 Collected in full the 90-day, 9% note receivable from Jones Brothers, including interest.

INSTRUCTIONS

a Prepare journal entries in general journal form to record: (1) the receipt of the note on November 1, (2) the adjustment for interest on December 31, and (3) collection of principal and interest on the following February 2. Assume that the company does not use reversing entries.

b Assume that instead of paying the note on the following February 2, the customer (Jones Brothers) had defaulted. Give the journal entry by Hanover Mills to record the default. Assume that Jones Brothers has sufficient resources that the note will eventually be collected.

***PROBLEM 8B-6**
Notes Receivable: A Comprehensive Problem

Selected receivables of Hartford Building Supply at December 1, 1996, are shown below. Hartford adjusts and closes its accounts only at December 31.

Notes receivable:	
Weiss Construction Co.; 90-day, 12% note dated Sept. 29	*$25,000*
Mr. Remodel; 60-day, 10% note dated Oct. 12	*18,000*
Tillamook Homes; 45-day, 10% note dated Nov. 1	*16,000*
J. D. Walters; 60-day, 9% note dated Dec. 1	*30,000*
Accounts receivable:	
Regal Construction	*$12,000*
Dexter Dalton	*8,200*
Instalment contracts receivable:	
Jesse Cole (14 monthly payments of $600)	*$ 8,400*
Unearned finance charges on instalment contracts:	
Applicable to Jesse Cole contract	*$ 728*

During the month of December, transactions affecting these receivables were as follows:

Dec. 1 Received an 87-day note receivable from Regal Construction in full settlement of its account receivable. The face amount of this note was $12,360, which included an interest charge.

Dec. 11 Dexter Dalton paid $2,200 on his account and gave a 30-day, 12% note to cover the $6,000 balance of his account.

Dec. 14 Collected in full the maturity value of the Mr. Remodel 60-day note.

Dec. 19 Tillamook Homes paid in cash the interest due on its $16,000 note but renewed the note for the $16,000 principal amount for another 30 days. The interest rate in the new note is 12%.

Dec. 31 Received the $600 payment from Jesse Cole on his instalment contract. The payment included $52 interest for the month of December. The interest charges included in the face amount of the instalment contract originally had been credited to the contra-asset account, Unearned Finance Charges on Instalment Contracts.

Dec. 31 Received notice from Weiss Construction Company that it was unable to pay its note due today. The defaulted note was not renewed, but Hartford expects that the amount due will eventually be collectible.

INSTRUCTIONS

a Prepare journal entries for the six December transactions listed above.

b Prepare the adjusting entries necessary at December 31 to recognize interest accrued on notes receivable through year-end.

Use one adjusting entry to accrue interest receivable on the three notes in which interest is stated separately (the Tillamook Homes, J. D. Walters, and Dexter Dalton notes). Use a separate adjusting entry to recognize interest revenue earned on the note with interest included in the face amount (the Regal Construction note).

c Prepare the current asset section of Hartford Building Supply's balance sheet at Dec. 31, 1996. In addition to the receivables described above, include the following items:

* *Supplemental Topic, "Notes Receivable with Interest Charges Included in the Face Amount"*

Cash	*$ 67,900*
Accounts receivable (other than described above)	*250,000*
Allowance for doubtful receivables (all types)	*24,000*
Inventory	*350,000*

In listing the company's receivables, include captions indicating any unamortized discount, unearned finance charges, and accrued interest. Do ***not,*** however, identify the individual debtors. (Combine all four notes under the caption "Notes receivable.")

***PROBLEM 8B-7**
Long-Term Note Receivable with Interest Included in Face Amount

On April 1, 1995, Merrimac Corporation sold merchandise to Jefferson Davis Company in exchange for a note receivable due in ***one year*** (3 days of grace included). The note was drawn in the face amount of $189,200, which included the principal amount and an interest charge. In its December 31, 1995, balance sheet, Merrimac Corporation correctly presented the note receivable as follows:

Note receivable, due Mar. 31, 1996	*$189,200*	
Less: Discount on note receivable	*3,300*	*$185,900*

INSTRUCTIONS

a Determine the monthly interest revenue earned by Merrimac Corporation from this note receivable.

b Compute the amount of interest revenue recognized by Merrimac Corporation from the note during 1995.

c Compute the amount of sales revenue recognized by Merrimac Corporation on April 1, 1995, when this note was received.

d Compute the effective annual rate of interest (stated as a percentage) represented by the interest charge originally included in the face amount of the note.

e Prepare all journal entries relating to this note in the accounting records of Merrimac Corporation for 1995 and 1996. Assume that adjusting entries are made only at December 31 and that reversing entries are not used. Assume also that the note was collected on the maturity date.

ANALYTICAL AND DECISION PROBLEMS AND CASES

A&D 8-1
Which Approach for Credit Losses Did We Use?

The controller for Naturejoy Inc. is in the process of computing the uncollectible accounts expense for 1998. Unfortunately, a computer virus attacked Naturejoy's accounting system one night and destroyed the information regarding the approach that Naturejoy has consistently used for computing the uncollectible accounts expenses for the past three years. However, the following information is provided by the credit manager.

	1995	*1996*	*1997*
Accounts receivable, December 31	*$136,000*	*$184,000*	*$166,000*
Allowance for doubtful accounts (credit balance), December 31	*37,600*	*24,000*	*36,800*
Accounts receivable, written off during the year	*1,600*	*40,000*	*11,200*
Sales: cash	*480,000*	*648,000*	*560,000*
credit	*720,000*	*880,000*	*800,000*

The credit manager explains that the large write off in 1996 was due to an unexpected bankruptcy of a major customer even though the age distribution of accounts receivable has been very consistent over the past three years.

* *Supplemental Topic, "Notes Receivable with Interest Charges Included in the Face Amount"*

INSTRUCTIONS The controller wants you to determine the approach that Naturejoy has used for computing the uncollectible accounts expense for the past three years so that he can use it for 1998 to comply with the accounting principle of consistency.

A&D 8-2
How Did He Do It?

Allan Carter was a long-time employee in the accounting department of Marston Company. Carter's responsibilities included the following:

1 Maintain the accounts receivable subsidiary ledger.
2 Prepare vouchers for cash disbursements. The voucher and supporting documents were forwarded to John Marston, owner of the company.
3 Compute depreciation on all plant assets.
4 Authorize all sales returns and allowances given to credit customers and prepare the related credit memoranda. The credit memoranda were forwarded to Howard Smith, who maintains the company's journals and general ledger.

John Marston personally performs the following procedures in an effort to achieve strong internal control:

1 Prepare monthly bank reconciliations.
2 Prepare monthly trial balances from the general ledger and reconcile the accounts receivable controlling account with the subsidiary ledger.
3 Prepare from the subsidiary ledger all monthly bills sent to customers and investigate any complaints from customers about inaccuracies in these bills.
4 Review all vouchers and supporting documents before signing cheques for cash disbursements.

Carter became terminally ill and retired. Shortly thereafter, he died. However, he left a letter confessing that over a period of years he had embezzled over $300,000 from Marston Company. As part of his scheme, he had managed to obtain both a bank account and a post office box in the name of Marston Company. He had then contacted customers whose accounts were overdue and offered them a 20% discount if they would make payment within five days. He instructed them to send their payments to the post office box. When the payments arrived, he deposited them in his "Marston Company" bank account. Carter stated in his letter that he had acted alone, and that no other company employees knew of his dishonest actions.

Marston cannot believe that Carter committed this theft without the knowledge and assistance of Howard Smith, who maintained the journals and the general ledger. Marston reasoned that Carter must have credited the customers' accounts in the accounts receivable subsidiary ledger, because no customers had complained about not receiving credit for their payments. Smith must also have recorded these credits in the general ledger, or Marston would have discovered the problem by reconciling the subsidiary ledger with the controlling account. Finally, Smith must have debited some other account in the general ledger to keep the ledger in balance. Thus, Marston is about to bring criminal charges against Smith.

INSTRUCTIONS

a Explain how Carter might have committed this theft without Smith's knowledge and without being detected by Marston's control procedures. (Assume that Carter had no personal access to the journals or general ledger.)
b Which of the duties assigned to Carter should not have been assigned to an employee responsible for maintaining accounts receivable? Would internal control be strengthened if this duty were assigned to the company's cashier? Explain.

A&D 8-3
If Things Get Any Better, We'll Be Broke

Loud Max, Inc., sells stereo equipment. Traditionally, the company's sales have fallen into the following categories: cash sales, 25%; customers using national credit cards, 35%; sales on account (due in 30 days), 40%. With these policies, the company earned a modest profit, and monthly cash receipts exceeded monthly cash payments by a comfortable margin. Uncollectible accounts expense was approximately 1% of net sales. (The company uses the direct write-off method in accounting for uncollectible accounts receivable.)

Two months ago, the company initiated a new credit policy that it calls "Double Zero." Customers may purchase merchandise on account, with no down payment and no interest charges. The accounts are collected in 12 monthly payments of equal amounts.

The plan has proven quite popular with customers, and monthly sales have increased dramatically. Despite the increase in sales, however, Loud Max is experiencing cash flow problems—it hasn't been generating enough cash to pay its suppliers, most of which require payment within 30 days.

The company's bookkeeper has prepared the following analysis of monthly operating results:

	Before Double Zero	Last Month
Sales:		
Cash	$12,500	$ 5,000
National credit card	17,500	10,000
30-day accounts	20,000	–0–
Double Zero accounts	–0–	75,000
Total monthly sales	$50,000	$ 90,000
Cost of goods sold and expenses	40,000	65,000
Net income	$10,000	$ 25,000
Cash receipts:		
Cash sales	$12,500	$ 5,000
National credit card companies	17,500	10,000
30-day accounts	19,500	–0–
Double Zero accounts	–0–	11,250
Total monthly cash receipts	$49,500	$ 26,250
Accounts written off as uncollectible	$ 500	$ –0–
Accounts receivable at month-end	$20,000	$122,000

The bookkeeper offers the following assessment: "Double Zero is killing us. Since we started that plan, our accounts receivable have increased more than six-fold, and they're still growing. We can't afford to carry such a large nonproductive asset on our books. Our cash receipts are down to nearly half of what they used to be. If we don't go back to more cash sales and receivables that can be collected more quickly, we'll become insolvent."

Maxwell "Loud Max" Swartz, founder and chief executive officer, shouts back: "Why do you say that our accounts receivable are nonproductive? They're the most productive asset we have! Since we started Double Zero, our sales have nearly doubled, our profits have more than doubled, and our uncollectible accounts expense has dropped to nothing!"

INSTRUCTIONS

a Is it logical that the Double Zero plan is causing sales and profits to increase while also causing a decline in cash receipts? Explain.

b Why has the uncollectible accounts expense dropped to zero? What would you expect to happen to the company's uncollectible accounts expense in the future—say, next year? Why?

c Do you think that the reduction in monthly cash receipts is permanent or temporary? Explain.

d In what sense are the company's accounts receivable a "nonproductive" asset?

e Suggest several ways that Loud Max (the company) may be able to generate the cash it needs to pay its bills without terminating the Double Zero plan.

f Would you recommend that the company continue offering Double Zero financing, or should it return to the use of 30-day accounts? Explain the reasons for your answer and identify any unresolved factors that might cause you to change this opinion in the future.

***A&D 8-4**
How Much Is the "True" Net Income?

Record House and Concert Sound are two companies engaged in selling stereo equipment to the public. Both companies sell equipment at a price 50% greater than cost. Customers may pay cash, purchase on 30-day accounts, or make instalment payments over a 36-month period. The instalment receivables include a three-year interest charge (which amounts to 30% of the sales price) in the face amount of the contract. Condensed income statements prepared by the companies for their first year of operations follow:

	Record House	Concert Sound
Sales	$387,000	$288,000
Cost of goods sold	210,000	192,000
Gross profit	$177,000	$ 96,000
Operating expenses	63,000	60,000
Operating income	$114,000	$ 36,000
Interest revenue	-0-	10,800
Net income	$114,000	$ 46,800

When Record House makes a sale of stereo equipment on the instalment plan it immediately credits the Sales account with the face amount of the instalment receivable, which includes interest charges. The interest charges included in Record House's instalment receivables originating in the first year amount to $72,000, of which $52,000 is unearned at the end of the first year. Record House uses the direct charge-off method to recognize uncollectible accounts expense. During the year, accounts receivable of $2,100 were written off as uncollectible, but no entry was made for $37,200 of accounts estimated to be uncollectible at year-end.

Concert Sound records sales revenue equal to the present value of its instalment receivables and recognizes the interest earned during the year as interest revenue. Concert Sound provides for uncollectible accounts by the allowance method. The company wrote off $6,180 of its uncollectible accounts during the year and estimated its uncollectible accounts to be $11,100 at year end and this amount appeared to be adequate.

INSTRUCTIONS

a Identify the accounting principles that have been violated by one of the companies and determine the dollar effect of each violation on its reported net income. Also show the net income after the corrections.

b Based on the information in **a**, what do you believe to be the key factor responsible for making one of these companies more profitable than the other? What corrective action would you recommend be taken by the less profitable company to improve future performance?

* *Supplemental Topic, "Notes Receivable with Interest Charges Included in the Face Amount"*

CHAPTER

9 Inventories and the Cost of Goods Sold

Our primary goal in this chapter is to explain and illustrate the different methods of allocating the costs of purchased merchandise between inventory and the cost of goods sold. Generally accepted accounting principles permit the use of several alternative methods—each having unique characteristics and producing different financial results.

Later in the chapter, we discuss other issues relating to the valuation of inventory, including the taking of physical inventory, periodic inventory systems, and techniques for estimating the cost of goods sold.

Learning Objectives

After studying this chapter you should be able to:

1. *Use a perpetual inventory system to determine the cost of goods sold using (a) specific identification, (b) average cost, (c) FIFO, and (d) LIFO. Discuss the advantages and shortcomings of each method.*
2. *Explain the need for taking a physical inventory.*
3. *Record shrinkage losses and other year-end adjustments to inventory.*
4. *Use a periodic inventory system to determine the ending inventory and the cost of goods sold using (a) average cost, (b) FIFO, and (c) LIFO.*
5. *Explain the effects of an inventory error on the income statement of the current year and the following year.*
6. *Estimate the cost of goods sold and ending inventory by the gross profit method and by the retail method.*
7. *Identify several factors that management should consider in determining the optimal size of the company's inventory.*
8. *Compute the inventory turnover rate. Explain why this ratio is of interest to short-term creditors.*

Inventory Defined

One of the largest current assets of a retail store or of a wholesale business is the ***inventory*** of merchandise. The sale of this merchandise is the major source of revenue. In a merchandising company, the inventory consists of all goods owned and held for sale to customers. Inventory is converted into cash within the company's ***operating cycle*** and, therefore, is regarded as a current asset.[1] In the balance sheet, inventory is listed immediately after accounts receivable, because, with the exception of cash sales, it is just one step further removed from conversion into cash than are the accounts receivable.

In a merchandising company, all of the inventory is purchased in a ready-to-sell condition. A manufacturing company, however, has three types of inventory: (1) ***finished goods,*** which are ready to sell; (2) ***work in process,*** which are goods in the process of being manufactured; and (3) ***materials,*** which are the raw materials and component parts used in the manufacture of finished products. All three classes of inventory are included in the current asset section of the balance sheet.[2]

THE FLOW OF INVENTORY COSTS

Inventory is an asset and—like most other assets—usually is shown in the balance sheet at its cost.[3] As items are sold from this inventory, their costs are removed from the balance sheet and transferred into the cost of goods sold, which is offset against sales revenue in the income statement. This "flow of costs" is illustrated in the following diagram:

"Flow" of costs through financial statements

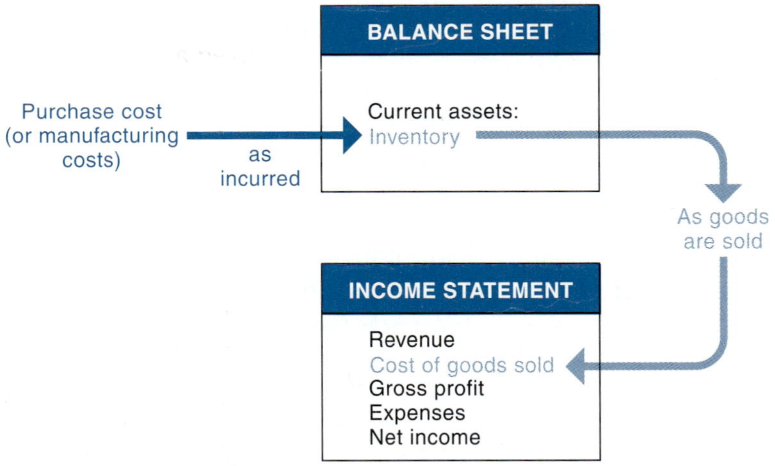

1 As explained in Chapter 5, the ***operating cycle*** of a merchandising business is the period of time required to convert cash into inventory, inventory into accounts receivable, and these accounts receivable into cash. Assets expected to be converted into cash within one year or the operating cycle, whichever is longer, are regarded as current assets.

2 In a manufacturing company, the manufacturing process is part of the operating cycle. Therefore, materials and work in process are considered current assets even if completion of the manufacturing process requires more than one year.

3 Some companies deal in inventories that can be sold in a worldwide market at quoted market prices. Examples include mutual funds, stock brokerages, and companies that deal in commodities such as agricultural crops or precious metals. Often these companies value their inventories at market price, rather than at cost. Our discussions in this chapter are directed to the far more common situation in which inventories are valued at cost.

In a perpetual inventory system, entries in the accounting records parallel this flow of costs. When merchandise is purchased, its cost (net of allowable cash discounts) is debited to the asset account Inventory. As the merchandise is sold, its cost is removed from the Inventory account and debited to the Cost of Goods Sold account.

The valuation of inventory and of the cost of goods sold are of critical importance to managers and to users of financial statements. In most cases, inventory is a company's largest current asset, and the cost of goods sold is its largest expense. These two accounts have a significant effect upon the financial statement subtotals and ratios used in evaluating the solvency and profitability of the business.

Several different methods of "pricing" inventory and of measuring the cost of goods sold are acceptable under generally accepted accounting principles. These different methods may produce significantly different results in a company's financial statements. Therefore, managers and investors alike should understand the usual effects of the different inventory valuation methods.

Which Unit Did We Sell? Does It Really Matter?

Purchases of merchandise are recorded in the same manner under all of the inventory valuation methods. The differences in these methods lie in determining ***which costs*** should be removed from the Inventory account when merchandise is sold.

We illustrated the basic entries relating to purchases and sales of merchandise in Chapter 5. In that introductory discussion, however, we made a simplifying assumption: all of the units in inventory had been acquired at the same unit costs. In practice, a company often has in its inventory units of a given product that were acquired at ***different costs.*** Acquisition costs may vary because the units were purchased at different dates, or from different suppliers.

When identical units of inventory have different unit costs, a question naturally arises as to ***which of these costs*** should be used in recording sales transactions.

Data for an Illustration

To illustrate the alternative methods of measuring the cost of goods sold, assume that Mead Electric Company sells electrical equipment and supplies. Included in the company's inventory are five Elco AC-40 generators purchased from Elco Manufacturing. These generators are identical; however, two were purchased on January 5 at a per-unit cost of ***$1,000,*** and the other three were purchased a month later, shortly after Elco had announced a price increase, at a per-unit cost of ***$1,200.*** These purchases are reflected in Mead's inventory subsidiary ledger as shown on the following page.

Notice that on February 5, the balance columns contain two "layers" of unit cost information, representing the units purchased at the two different unit costs. A new cost layer is created whenever units are acquired at a different per-unit cost. (As the units comprising a cost layer are sold, the layer is eliminated from the inventory. Therefore, a business is unlikely to have more than three or four cost layers in its inventory at any given time.)

Inventory subsidiary ledger record

Item Elco AC-40 **Primary supplier** Elco Manufacturing
Description Portable generator **Secondary supplier** Vegas Wholesale Ltd.
Location Daily St. warehouse **Inventory level: Min:** 2 **Max:** 5

	PURCHASED			SOLD			BALANCE		
Date	**Units**	**Unit Cost**	**Total**	**Units**	**Unit Cost**	**Cost of Goods Sold**	**Units**	**Unit Cost**	**Total**
Jan. 5	2	$1,000	$2,000				2	$1,000	$2,000
Feb. 5	3	1,200	3,600				2	1,000	
							3	1,200	5,600

Now assume that on March 1, Mead sells one of these Elco generators to Boulder Construction company for $1,800, cash. What cost should be removed from the Inventory account and recognized as the cost of goods sold—$1,000 or $1,200?

In answering such questions, accountants may use an approach called ***specific identification,*** or they may adopt a ***cost flow assumption.*** Either of these approaches is acceptable. Once an approach has been selected, however, it should be ***applied consistently*** in accounting for all sales of this particular type of merchandise.

Specific Identification

OBJECTIVE 1 Use a perpetual inventory system to determine the cost of goods sold using (a) specific identification, (b) average cost, (c) FIFO, and (d) LIFO. Discuss the advantages and shortcomings of each method.

The specific identification method can be used only when the actual costs of individual units of merchandise can be determined from the accounting records. For example, each of the generators in Mead's inventory may have an identification number, and these numbers may appear on the purchase invoices. With this identification number, Mead's accounting department can determine whether the generator sold to Boulder Construction had cost $1,000 or $1,200. The ***actual cost*** of this particular unit then is used in recording the cost of goods sold.

Cost Flow Assumptions

If the items in inventory are ***similar in terms of cost, function, and sales value, it is not appropriate for the seller to use the specific identification method*** in determining the cost of goods sold. Rather, the seller should follow the more convenient practice of using a ***cost flow assumption.*** (In practice, the phrase "cost flow assumption" often is shortened to "flow assumption.")

When a flow assumption is in use, the seller simply makes an ***assumption*** as to the ***sequence in which units are withdrawn from inven-***

tory. For example, the seller might assume that the oldest merchandise always is sold first, or that the most recently purchased items are the first to be sold.

Three flow assumptions are in widespread use:

1 ***Average cost.*** This assumption values all merchandise—units sold and units remaining in inventory—at the ***average*** per-unit cost. (In effect, the average-cost method assumes that units are withdrawn from the inventory in random order.)

2 ***First-in, first-out (FIFO).*** As the name implies, FIFO involves the assumption that goods sold are the ***first*** units that were purchased—that is, the ***oldest*** goods on hand. Thus, the remaining inventory is comprised of the most recent purchases.

3 ***Last-in, first-out (LIFO).*** Under LIFO, the units sold are assumed to be those ***most recently*** acquired. The remaining inventory, therefore, is assumed to consist of the earliest purchases.

The cost flow assumption selected by a company ***need not correspond to the actual physical movement of the company's merchandise.*** When the units of merchandise are identical (or nearly identical), it ***does not matter*** which units are delivered to the customer in a particular sales transaction. Therefore, in measuring the income of a business that sells units of identical merchandise, accountants consider the flow of ***costs*** to be more important than the physical flow of the merchandise.

The use of a flow assumption ***eliminates the need for separately identifying each unit sold and looking up its actual cost.*** Experience has shown that these flow assumptions provide useful and reliable measurements of the cost of goods sold, as long as they are applied consistently to all sales of the particular type of merchandise.

Average-Cost Method

When the average-cost method is in use, the ***average cost*** of all units in the inventory ***is computed after every purchase.*** This average cost is computed by dividing the total cost of goods available for sale by the number of units in inventory. As the average cost may change following each purchase, this method also is called ***moving average.***

As of January 5, Mead has only two Elco generators in its inventory, each acquired at a purchase cost of $1,000. Therefore, the average cost is $1,000 per unit. After the purchase on February 5, Mead has five Elco generators in inventory, acquired at a total cost of $5,600 (2 units @ $1,000, plus 3 units @ $1,200 = $5,600). Therefore, the ***average*** per-unit cost now is ***$1,120*** ($5,600 ÷ 5 units = 1,120).

On March 1, two entries are made to record the sale of one of these generators to Boulder Construction for $1,800. The first recognizes the revenue from this sale, and the second recognizes the cost of the goods sold. These entries follow, with the cost of goods sold measured by the average-cost method:

Cash	1,800	
Sales		1,800
To record the sale of one Elco AC-40 generator sold on account.		
Cost of Goods Sold	1,120	
Inventory		1,120
To record the cost of one Elco AC-40 generator sold to Boulder Construction. Cost determined by the average-cost method.		

(The entry to recognize the $1,800 in sales revenue remains the same, regardless of the inventory method in use. Therefore, we will not repeat this entry in our illustrations of the other cost flow assumptions.)

When the average-cost method is in use, the inventory subsidiary ledger is modified slightly from the format illustrated on page 444. Following the sale on March 1, Mead's subsidiary ledger card for Elco generators will appear as follows, modified to show the average unit cost.

Inventory subsidiary record—average cost basis

	PURCHASED			SOLD			BALANCE		
Date	Units	Unit Cost	Total	Units	Average Unit Cost	Cost of Goods Sold	Units	Average Unit Cost	Total
Jan. 5	2	$1,000	$2,000				2	$1,000	$2,000
Feb. 5	3	1,200	3,600				5	1,120*	5,600
Mar. 1				1	$1,120	$1,120	4	1,120	4,480

* $5,600 total cost ÷ 5 units = $1,120.

Notice that the unit cost column for purchases still shows actual unit costs—$1,000 and $1,200. The unit cost columns relating to sales and to the remaining inventory, however, show the ***average unit cost*** ($5,600 total ÷ 5 units = $1,120). As all units are valued at this same average cost, the inventory has only one cost layer.

Under the average-cost assumption, all items in inventory are assigned the ***same*** per-unit cost (the average cost). Hence, it does not matter which units are sold; the cost of goods sold always is based upon the current average unit cost. When one generator is sold on March 1, the cost of goods sold is $1,120; if four generators were sold on this date, the cost of goods sold would be $4,480 (4 units × $1,120 per unit).

First-In, First-Out Method

The first-in, first-out method, often called ***FIFO,*** is based upon the assumption that the ***first merchandise purchased is the first merchandise sold.*** Thus, the accountant for Mead Electric would assume that the generator sold on March 1 was one of those purchased on ***January 5.*** The entry to record the cost of goods sold would be:

Cost of Goods Sold	*1,000*	
Inventory		*1,000*
To record the cost of one Elco AC-40 generator sold to Boulder Construction. Cost determined by the FIFO flow assumption.		

Following this sale, Mead's inventory ledger would appear as follows:

Inventory subsidiary record—FIFO basis

	PURCHASED			SOLD			BALANCE		
Date	Units	Unit Cost	Total	Units	Unit Cost	Cost of Goods Sold	Units	Unit Cost	Total
Jan. 5	2	$1,000	$2,000				2	$1,000	$2,000
Feb. 5	3	1,200	3,600				2	1,000	
							3	1,200	5,600
Mar. 1				1	$1,000	$1,000	1	1,000	
							3	1,200	4,600

Notice that FIFO uses actual purchase costs, rather than an average cost. Thus, if merchandise has been purchased at several different costs, the inventory will include several different cost layers. The cost of goods sold for a given sales transaction also may involve several different cost layers. To illustrate, assume that Mead had sold ***four*** generators to Boulder Construction, instead of only one. Under the FIFO flow assumption, Mead would assume that it first sold the two generators purchased on January 5, and then two of those purchased on February 5. Thus, the total cost of goods sold ($4,400) would include items at ***two different unit costs,*** as shown below:

2 generators from January 5 purchase @ $1,000	*$2,000*
2 generators from February 5 purchase @ $1,200	*2,400*
Total cost of goods sold (4 units)	*$4,400*

As the cost of goods sold always is recorded at the oldest available purchase costs, the units remaining in inventory are valued at the more recent acquisition costs.

Last-In, First-Out Method

The last-in, first-out method, commonly known as ***LIFO,*** is one of the most interesting methods of determining the cost of goods sold and valuing inventory. As the name suggests, the ***most recently*** purchased merchandise (the "last-in") is assumed to be sold first. If Mead were using the LIFO method, it would assume that the generator sold on March 1 was one of those acquired on ***February 5,*** the most recent purchase date. Thus, the cost transferred from inventory to the cost of goods sold would be ***$1,200.***

The journal entry to record the cost of goods sold is illustrated below, along with the inventory subsidiary ledger record after this entry has been posted:

Cost of Goods Sold	*1,200*	
Inventory		*1,200*
To record the cost of one Elco AC-40 generator sold to Boulder Construction. Cost determined by the LIFO flow assumption.		

Inventory subsidiary record—LIFO basis

	PURCHASED			SOLD			BALANCE		
Date	Units	Unit Cost	Total	Units	Unit Cost	Cost of Goods Sold	Units	Unit Cost	Total
Jan. 5	2	$1,000	$2,000				2	$1,000	$2,000
Feb. 5	3	1,200	3,600				2	1,000	
							3	1,200	5,600
Mar. 1				1	$1,200	$1,200	2	1,000	
							2	1,200	4,400

The LIFO method uses actual purchase costs, rather than an average cost. Thus, the inventory may have several different cost layers. If a sale includes more units than are included in the most recent cost layer, some of the goods sold are assumed to come from the next most recent layer. For example, if Mead had sold four generators (instead of one) on March 1, the cost of goods sold determined under the LIFO assumption would be $4,600, as shown below:

3 generators from February 5 purchase @ $1,200	*$3,600*
1 generator from January 5 purchase @ $1,000	*1,000*
Total cost of goods sold (4 units)	*$4,600*

As LIFO transfers the most recent purchase costs to the cost of goods sold, the goods remaining in inventory are valued at the oldest acquisition costs.

Evaluation of the Methods

All three of the cost flow assumptions described above are acceptable for use in financial statements.[4] As we have explained, it is not necessary that the physical flow of merchandise correspond to the cost flow assumption.

[4] According to the CICA's *Financial Reporting in Canada,* Twentieth Edition (Toronto, 1993), page 92, the most common methods of valuing inventory at cost are first-in, first-out and average cost, with retail as a distant third, last-in, first-out as a distant fourth, and specific identification as a distant fifth.

Different flow assumptions may be used for different types of inventory, or for inventories in different geographical locations.

The only requirement for using a flow assumption is that the units to which the assumption is applied should be ***homogeneous*** in nature—that is, very similar in function, cost, and sales price. If each unit is unique, the specific identification method is needed in order to achieve a proper matching of sales revenue with the cost of goods sold.

As discussed below, each inventory valuation method has certain advantages and shortcomings. In the final analysis, the selection of inventory valuation methods is a managerial decision. However, the method (or methods) used in financial statements always should be disclosed in notes accompanying the statements.

Specific Identification The specific identification method is best suited to inventories of high-priced, low-volume, non-homogeneous items. This is the only method that exactly parallels the physical flow of the merchandise. If each item in the inventory is unique, as in the case of valuable paintings, custom jewellery, and most real estate, specific identification is clearly the logical choice.

The specific identification method has an intuitive appeal, because it assigns actual purchase costs to the specific units of merchandise sold or in inventory. However, when the units in inventory are identical (or nearly identical), the specific identification method may produce ***misleading results*** by implying differences in value that—under current market conditions—do not exist.

As an example, assume that a coal dealer has purchased 100 tonnes of coal at a cost of $60 per tonne. A short time later, the company purchases another 100 tonnes of the ***same grade*** of coal—but this time, the cost is $80 per tonne. The two purchases are in separate piles; thus, it would be possible for the company to use the specific identification method in accounting for sales.

Assume now that the company has an opportunity to sell 10 tonnes of coal at a retail price of $120 per tonne. Does it really matter from which pile this coal is removed? The answer is ***no;*** the coal is a homogeneous product. Under current market conditions, the coal in each pile is equally valuable. To imply that it is more profitable to sell coal from one pile rather than the other is an argument of questionable logic.

Average Cost Identical items will have the same accounting values only under the average-cost method. Assume for example that a hardware store sells a given size nail for 65 cents per kilogram. The hardware store buys the nails in 100-kilogram quantities at different times at prices ranging from 40 to 50 cents per kilogram. Several hundred kilograms of nails are always on hand, stored in a large bin. The average-cost method properly recognizes that when a customer buys a kilogram of nails it is not necessary to know exactly which nails the customer happened to select from the bin in order to measure the cost of goods sold. Therefore, the average-cost method avoids the shortcomings of the specific identification method. It is not necessary to keep track of the specific items sold and of those still in inventory. Also, it is not possible to manipulate income merely by selecting the specific items to be delivered to customers.

A shortcoming in the average-cost method is that changes in current replacement costs of inventory are concealed because these costs are averaged with older costs. Thus, neither the valuation of ending inventory nor the cost of goods sold will quickly reflect changes in the current replacement cost of merchandise.

First-In, First-Out The distinguishing characteristic of the FIFO method is that the oldest purchase costs are transferred to the cost of goods sold, while the most recent purchase costs remain in inventory.

Over the last 50 years, we have lived in an inflationary economy, which means that most prices tend to rise over time. When purchase costs are rising, the FIFO method assigns ***lower*** (older) costs to the cost of goods sold and the higher (more recent) costs to the goods remaining in inventory.

By assigning lower costs to the cost of goods sold, FIFO usually causes a business to report somewhat ***higher profits*** than would be reported under the other inventory valuation methods. Some companies favour the FIFO method for financial reporting purposes, because their goal is to report the highest net income possible.

Some accountants and decision makers believe that FIFO tends to ***overstate*** a company's profitability. Revenue is based upon current market conditions. By offsetting this revenue with a cost of goods sold based upon older (and lower) prices, gross profits may be overstated consistently.

A conceptual advantage of the FIFO method is that inventory is valued at recent purchase costs. Therefore, this asset appears in the balance sheet at an amount closely approximating its current replacement cost.

Last-In, First-Out The LIFO method is the exact opposite of FIFO. Under LIFO, the most recent purchase costs are transferred to cost of goods sold, while the oldest purchase costs remain in inventory.

Supporters of the LIFO method contend that the measurement of income should be based upon ***current market conditions.*** Therefore, current sales revenue should be offset by the ***current*** cost of the merchandise sold. Under the LIFO method, the costs assigned to the cost of goods sold are relatively current, because they stem from the most recent purchases. Under the FIFO method, on the other hand, the cost of goods sold is based upon "older" costs.

Income tax considerations, however, provide the principal reason for the popularity of the LIFO methods in the United States. Remember that the LIFO method transfers the most recent purchase costs to the cost of goods sold. In the common situation of rising prices, these "most recent" costs are also the highest costs. By reporting a higher cost of goods sold than results from the other inventory valuation methods, the LIFO method usually results in a ***lower income for tax purposes.*** In short, if purchase costs are rising, ***a company in the United States*** can reduce the amount of its income tax obligation by using the LIFO method in its income tax returns. Consequently, most companies in the United States use LIFO in their income tax returns. However, income tax regulations allow a corporation to use LIFO in its income tax return only if the company also uses LIFO in its financial statements. Thus, income tax considerations often provide an important reason for selecting the LIFO method.

However, the Canadian situation for LIFO is quite different from that for the United States. ***In Canada, LIFO is not acceptable for income tax purposes.*** This explains why only a small number of Canadian companies use LIFO.[5]

There is one significant shortcoming to the LIFO method. The valuation of the asset inventory is based upon the company's "oldest" purchase costs. After the company has been in business for many years, these "oldest" costs may greatly understate the current replacement cost of the inventory. Thus, when an inventory is valued by the LIFO method, the company also should disclose the current replacement cost of the inventory in a note to the financial statements.

During periods of rising inventory replacement costs, the LIFO method results in the lowest valuation of inventory and measurement of net income. Therefore, LIFO is regarded as the most ***"conservative"*** of the inventory pricing methods. FIFO, on the other hand, is the "least conservative" method.[6]

The Principle of Consistency

The principle of ***consistency*** is one of the basic concepts underlying reliable financial statements. This principle means that once a company has adopted a particular accounting method, it should ***follow that method consistently,*** rather than switch methods from one year to the next. Thus, once a company has adopted a particular inventory flow assumption (or the specific identification method), it should continue to apply that assumption to all sales of that type of merchandise.

The principle of consistency does ***not*** prohibit a company from ***ever*** changing its accounting methods. A company may change its method when the circumstances warrant such a change.[7] If a change is made, however, the reasons for the change must be explained, and the effects of the change upon the company's net income must be fully disclosed.

Just-in-Time (JIT) Inventory Systems

In recent years, much attention has been paid to the ***just-in-time*** inventory concept in manufacturing operations. The phrase "just-in-time" usually means that purchases of materials and component parts arrive just in time for use in the manufacturing process—often within a few hours of when the materials are scheduled for use. A second application of the just-in-time concept is completing the manufacturing process just in time to ship the finished goods to customers.

The principal advantage of a just-in-time system lies in reducing the amount of money "tied-up" in inventories of materials and finished goods. Also, the manufacturing company does not need to maintain large inventory storage facilities. The disadvantage of a just-in-time system is that a

---

[5] Op. cit., *Financial Reporting in Canada,* p. 92.

[6] During a prolonged period of ***declining*** inventory replacement costs, this situation reverses: FIFO becomes the most conservative method, and LIFO the least conservative.

[7] CICA, *CICA Handbook,* section 3030.01.

delay in the arrival of essential materials may bring manufacturing operations to a halt. Therefore, the just-in-time concept is feasible only when the suppliers of materials (and the transportation systems) are highly reliable.

CASE IN POINT One of the pioneers of just-in-time manufacturing is Toyota, a Japanese automaker. Toyota's main plant is located in an area of Japan called "Toyota City." Many of the company's suppliers of materials also are located in Toyota City and produce materials primarily for Toyota. Thus, the suppliers' economic survival depends upon their meeting their delivery schedules at the Toyota plant.

As a practical matter, a just-in-time system greatly reduces the size of the materials and finished goods inventories, but it usually does not eliminate these inventories entirely. (Just-in-time manufacturing systems are discussed further in Chapter 22.)

TAKING A PHYSICAL INVENTORY

OBJECTIVE 2 Explain the need for taking a physical inventory.

In Chapter 5, we explained the need for businesses to make a complete physical count of the merchandise on hand at least once a year. The primary reason for this procedure of "taking inventory" is to adjust the perpetual inventory records for unrecorded ***shrinkage losses,*** such as theft, spoilage, or breakage.

The physical inventory usually is taken at (or near) the end of the company's fiscal year.[8] Often a business selects a fiscal year ending in a season of low activity. For example, most large retailers use a fiscal year ending in January.

Recording Shrinkage Losses

OBJECTIVE 3 Record shrinkage losses and other year-end adjustments to inventory.

In most cases, the year-end physical count of the inventory reveals some shortages or damaged merchandise. The costs of missing or damaged units are removed from the inventory records using the same flow assumption as is used in recording the costs of goods sold.

To illustrate, assume that a company's inventory subsidiary ledger shows the following 158 units of a particular product in inventory at year-end:

8 units purchased November 2 @ $100	$ 800
150 units purchased December 10 @ $115	17,250
Total (158 units)	$18,050

[8] The reason for taking a physical inventory near year-end is to ensure that any shrinkage losses are reflected in the annual financial statements. The stronger the company's internal control over inventories, the further this procedure may be moved away from the balance sheet date. Obviously, no one wants to count inventory on New Year's Eve (as many companies have a December 31 year-end date).

A year-end physical count, however, discloses that only ***148*** of these units actually are on hand. Based upon this physical count, the company should adjust its inventory records to reflect the loss of 10 units.

If the company uses ***FIFO,*** the missing units will be valued at the oldest purchase costs shown in the inventory records. Thus, 8 of the missing units will be assumed to have cost $100 per-unit and the other 2, $115 per-unit. Under FIFO, the shrinkage loss amounts to ***$1,030*** (8 units @ $100 + 2 units @ $115). If the company uses ***LIFO,*** on the other hand, the missing units all will be assumed to have come from the most recent purchase (on December 10). Therefore, the shrinkage loss amounts to ***$1,150*** (10 units @ $115).

If shrinkage losses are small, the costs removed from inventory may be charged (debited) directly to the Cost of Goods Sold account. If these losses are ***material*** in amount, the offsetting debit should be entered in a special loss account, such as Inventory Shrinkage Losses. In the income statement, a loss account is deducted from revenue in the same manner as an expense account.

Other Write-Downs of Inventory and LCM

In addition to shrinkage losses, the value of inventory may decline because the merchandise has become obsolete or is unsalable for other reasons.

CASE IN POINT Several years ago, a deranged individual in the United States inserted a deadly poison into a few packages of Tylenol, a widely used medication. This criminal act of "product tampering" resulted in several tragic deaths. In response, Johnson & Johnson, the maker of Tylenol, promptly recalled all packages of this product and destroyed the entire inventory. The company later reintroduced Tylenol—this time in tablet form (rather than capsules) and in a tamperproof container. Other drug manufacturers quickly followed Johnson & Johnson's lead and changed the form and the packaging of their over-the-counter products.

The Tylenol tragedy often is studied by business managers and business students alike. The company's response is considered a classic example of fast, responsible, and effective action in a time of crisis.

If inventory has become obsolete or is otherwise unsalable, its carrying value in the accounting records should be ***written down*** to zero (or to its "scrap value," if any). A write-down of inventory reduces both the carrying value of the inventory and also the net income of the current period. The reduction in income is handled in the same manner as a shrinkage loss. If the write-down is relatively small, the loss is debited directly to the Cost of Goods Sold account. If the write-down is ***material in amount,*** however, it is charged to a special loss account, perhaps entitled Loss from Write-down of Inventory.

The Lower-of-Cost-and-Market (LCM) Rule An asset is an economic resource. It may be argued that no economic resource is worth more than it would cost to ***replace*** that resource in the open market. For this reason, accountants traditionally have valued inventory in the balance sheet at the lower of its (1) cost and (2) market value. In this context, "market value" means ***current replacement cost*** or ***net realizable value.*** Thus, the inventory is valued at the lower of its purchase cost or its current replacement cost or net realizable value.

For a merchandising company, current replacement cost is the amount the concern would have to pay at the present time for the goods in question, purchased in the customary quantities through the usual sources of supply and including transportation-in. Net realizable value is "the estimated selling price in the ordinary course of business less estimated costs of completion and sale" such as selling expenses in a merchandising company.[9] To avoid misunderstanding, many companies are disclosing both the cost method and the market method, such as "the lower of first-in, first-out and replacement cost," or "the lower of the average cost and net realizable value." The lower-of-cost-and-market rule is another example of the accounting concept of conservatism. A conservative valuation of inventory requires prompt recognition of losses, even though the exact amount of the loss cannot be conclusively determined.

The lower-of-cost-and-market rule may be applied in conjunction with any flow assumption and also with the specific identification method. If the current replacement cost or net realizable value of the ending inventory is substantially ***below*** the cost shown in the accounting records, the inventory is written down to the lower amount. The offsetting debit is charged to either the Cost of Goods Sold account or the Loss from Write-down of Inventory account, depending upon the materiality of the dollar amount.

In their financial statements, most companies state that inventory is valued at the lower-of-cost-and-market.[10] In our inflationary economy, however, the lower of these two amounts usually is cost, especially for companies using LIFO.[11]

The Year-End Cutoff of Transactions

Making a proper ***cutoff*** of transactions is an essential step in the preparation of reliable financial statements. A "proper cutoff" simply means that the transactions occurring near year-end are ***recorded in the right accounting period.***

One aspect of a proper cutoff is determining that all purchases of merchandise through the end of the period are recorded in the inventory records and included in the physical count of merchandise on hand at year-end. Of equal importance is determining that the cost of all merchandise sold through the end of the period has been removed from the inventory accounts and charged to the Cost of Goods Sold. This merchandise should ***not*** be included in the year-end physical count.

---

[9] CICA, *CICA Terminology for Accountants,* p. 96.

[10] Of the 268 companies surveyed by CICA, 253 used the lower-of-cost-and-market rule for inventory valuation. The most common "market methods" for inventory valuation are net realizable value and replacement cost. See CICA *Financial Reporting in Canada,* op. cit., pp. 91 and 92.

[11] A notable exception is the petroleum industry, in which the replacement cost of inventory can fluctuate very quickly and in either direction. Large oil companies occasionally report LCM adjustments of several hundred million dollars in a single year.

If some sales transactions have not been recorded as of year-end, the quantities of merchandise shown in the inventory records will exceed the quantities actually on hand. When the results of the physical count are compared with the inventory records, these unrecorded sales easily could be mistaken for inventory shortages.

Making a proper cutoff may be difficult if sales transactions are occurring while the merchandise is being counted. For this reason, most businesses count their physical inventory during nonbusiness hours, even if they must shut down their sales operations for a day.

Matching Revenue and the Cost of Goods Sold Accountants must determine that both the sales revenue and the cost of goods sold relating to sales transactions occurring near year-end are recorded in the ***same*** accounting period. Otherwise, the revenue and expense from these transactions will not be properly "matched" in the company's income statements.

Goods in Transit A sale should be recorded ***when title to the merchandise passes to the buyer.*** In making a year-end cutoff of transactions, questions may arise when goods are in transit between the seller and the buyer as to which company owns the merchandise. The answer to such questions lies in the terms of shipment. If these terms are ***F.O.B.*** (free on board) ***shipping point,*** title passes at the point of shipment and the goods are the property of the buyer while in transit. If the terms of the shipment are ***F.O.B. destination,*** title does not pass until the shipment reaches its destination and the goods belong to the seller while in transit.

Many companies ignore these distinctions, because goods in transit always arrive within a day or two. In such cases, the amount of merchandise in transit usually is ***not material*** in dollar amount, and the company may follow the ***most convenient*** accounting procedures. It usually is most convenient to record all purchases when the inbound shipments arrive and all sales when the merchandise is shipped to the customer.

In some industries, however, goods in transit may be very material. Oil companies, for example, often have millions of dollars of inventory in transit in pipelines and supertankers. In these situations, the company must consider the terms of each shipment in recording its purchases and sales.

Periodic Inventory Systems

OBJECTIVE 4 Use a periodic inventory system to determine the ending inventory and the cost of goods sold using (a) average cost, (b) FIFO, and (c) LIFO.

In our preceding discussions, we have emphasized the perpetual inventory system—that is, inventory records that are kept continuously up-to-date. Virtually all large business organizations use perpetual inventory systems.

Some small businesses, however, use ***periodic*** inventory systems. In a periodic inventory system, the cost of merchandise purchased during the year is debited to a ***Purchases*** account, rather than to the Inventory account. When merchandise is sold to a customer, an entry is made recognizing the sales revenue, but no entry is made to reduce the inventory account or to recognize the cost of goods sold.

The inventory on hand and the cost of goods sold for the year are not determined until year-end. At the end of the year, all goods on hand are counted and priced at cost. The cost assigned to this ending inventory is then used in computing the cost of goods sold, as shown below. (The dollar amounts are assumed for the purpose of completing the illustration.)

Inventory at the beginning of the year	$10,000
Add: Purchases during the year	80,000
Cost of goods available for sale during the year	$90,000
Less: Inventory at the end of the year	7,000
Cost of goods sold	$83,000

The only item in this computation that is kept continuously up-to-date in the accounting records is the Purchases account. The amounts of inventory at the beginning and end of the year are determined by annual physical counts.

Determining the cost of the year-end inventory involves two distinct steps: counting the merchandise and pricing the inventory, that is, determining the cost of the units on hand. Together, these procedures determine the proper valuation of inventory and also the cost of goods sold.

Applying Flow Assumptions in a Periodic System In our discussion of perpetual inventory systems, we have emphasized the costs that are transferred from inventory ***to the cost of goods sold.*** In a periodic system, the emphasis shifts to determining the costs that should be assigned ***to inventory*** at the end of the period.

To illustrate, assume that Cooks' Corner uses a periodic inventory system. The year-end physical inventory indicates that 12 units of a particular model food processor are on hand. Purchases of these food processors during the year are shown below:

	Number of Units	Cost Per Unit	Total Cost
Beginning inventory	10	$ 80	$ 800
First purchase (Mar. 1)	5	90	450
Second purchase (July 2)	5	100	500
Third purchase (Oct. 1)	5	120	600
Fourth purchase (Dec. 1)	5	130	650
Available for sale	30		$3,000
Units sold	18		
Units in ending inventory	12		

This schedule shows that 30 food processors were available for sale in the course of the year, of which 12 are still on hand. Thus, 18 of these food processors apparently were sold.[12] We will now use this data to determine the cost of the year-end inventory and the cost of goods sold using the specific identification method, and the average-cost, FIFO, and LIFO flow assumptions.

Specific Identification If specific identification is used, the company must identify the 12 food processors on hand at year-end and determine their

[12] The periodic inventory method does not distinguish between merchandise sold and shrinkage losses. Shrinkage losses are included automatically within the cost of goods sold.

actual costs from purchase invoices. Assume that these 12 units have an actual total cost of $1,240. The cost of goods sold then is determined by subtracting this ending inventory from the cost of goods available for sale:

Cost of goods available for sale	*$3,000*
Less: Ending inventory (specific identification)	*1,240*
Cost of goods sold	*$1,760*

Average Cost The average cost is determined by dividing the total cost of goods available for sale during the year by the total number of units available for sale. Thus, the average per-unit cost is ***$100*** ($3,000 ÷ 30 units). Under the average-cost method, the ending inventory would be priced at $1,200 (12 units × $100 per unit), and the cost of goods sold would be ***$1,800*** ($3,000 cost of goods available for sale, less $1,200 in costs assigned to the ending inventory).

FIFO Under the FIFO flow assumption, the oldest units are assumed to be the first sold. The ending inventory therefore is assumed to consist of the ***most recently*** acquired goods. (Remember, we are now talking about the goods ***in inventory,*** not the goods sold.) Thus, the inventory of 12 food processors would be valued at the following costs:

5 units from the December 1 purchase @ $130	*$ 650*
5 units from the October 1 purchase @ $120	*600*
2 units from the July 2 purchase @ $100	*200*
Ending inventory, 12 units at FIFO cost	*$1,450*

The cost of goods sold would be ***$1,550*** ($3,000 − $1,450).

Notice that the FIFO method results in an inventory valued at relatively recent purchase costs. The cost of goods sold, however, is based upon the older acquisition costs.

LIFO Under LIFO, the last units purchased are considered to be the first goods sold. Therefore, the ending inventory is assumed to contain the ***earliest*** purchases. The 12 food processors in inventory would be priced as follows:

10 units from the beginning inventory @ $80	*$800*
2 units from the March 1 purchase @ $90	*180*
Ending inventory, 12 units at LIFO cost	*$980*

The cost of goods sold under the LIFO method is ***$2,020*** ($3,000 − $980).

Notice that the cost of goods sold under LIFO is ***higher*** than that determined by the FIFO method ($2,020 under LIFO, as compared with $1,550 under FIFO). ***LIFO always results in a higher cost of goods sold when purchase costs are rising.*** Thus, LIFO tends to minimize net income during periods of rising prices for purchases.

Notice also that the LIFO method may result in an ending inventory that is priced ***well below its current replacement cost.***

Comparison between Perpetual and Periodic Inventory Systems For the FIFO and the specific identification methods, the perpetual and periodic inventory systems would both produce the same amount for cost of goods sold and for ending inventory. However, the average-cost and LIFO methods produce different amounts for cost of goods sold and for ending inventory under the perpetual and periodic inventory systems. If purchase costs are rising, the cost of goods sold under the perpetual inventory system will be smaller than that under the periodic inventory system. The reason is that the perpetual system computes the cost of goods sold on a moving average basis throughout the year while the periodic system computes cost of goods sold on the average cost for the whole year. Similarly, the LIFO method under the perpetual system produces a smaller amount of cost of goods sold than that under the periodic system when purchase costs are rising. Under the perpetual system, the amount transferred from inventory to cost of goods sold is done periodically throughout the year. Under the periodic system, the amount transferred from inventory to cost of goods sold is computed on a yearly basis. Consequently, certain "older" but lower purchase costs that would have been transferred to cost of goods sold under the perpetual system would remain in the ending inventory under the periodic system.

Pricing the Year-End Inventory by Computer If purchase records are maintained by computer, the computer can compute the value of the ending inventory automatically using any of the flow assumptions discussed above. The computer operator must only enter the number of units on hand at year-end. A computer also can apply the specific identification method, but the computer operator then must enter an identification number for each unit in the ending inventory. This is one reason why the specific identification method usually is not used for inventories consisting of a large number of low-cost items.

Importance of an Accurate Valuation of Inventory

The most important current assets in the balance sheets of most companies are cash, accounts receivable, and inventory. Of these three, the inventory of merchandise is usually by far the largest. Because of the relatively large size of the inventory, an error in the valuation of this asset may not be readily apparent. However, a large error in inventory can cause a material misstatement of financial position and of net income. An error of 20% in valuing the inventory may have as much effect on the financial statements as would the complete omission of the asset cash. Therefore, care must be taken in counting and pricing the inventory at year-end.

An error in valuing the year-end inventory will of course lead to other erroneous figures in the balance sheet, such as the total current assets, total assets, and owner's equity.

The error will also affect key figures in the ***income statement,*** such as the cost of goods sold, the gross profit on sales, and the net income for the period. Finally, it is important to recognize that ***the ending inventory of one year is also the beginning inventory of the following year.*** Consequently, the income statement of the second year will also be in error by the full amount of the original error in inventory valuation.

OBJECTIVE 5 Explain the effects of an inventory error on the income statement of the current year and the following year.

Effects of an Error in Valuing Ending Inventory To illustrate, assume that some items of merchandise in a company's inventory are overlooked during the year-end physical count. As a result of this error, the ending inventory will be ***understated.*** The costs of the uncounted merchandise erroneously will be transferred out of the Inventory account and included in the cost of goods sold. This overstatement of the cost of goods sold, in turn, results in an understatement of gross profit and net income.[13]

Inventory Errors Affect Two Years An error in the valuation of ending inventory affects not only the financial statements of the current year, but also the income statement for the ***following*** year.

Assume that the ending inventory in ***1995*** is ***understated*** by $10,000. As we have described above, the cost of goods sold in 1995 will be overstated by this amount, and both gross profit and net income will be ***understated.***

The ending inventory in 1995, however, becomes the ***beginning inventory*** in ***1996.*** An understatement of the beginning inventory results in an understatement of the cost of goods sold and, therefore, an ***overstatement*** of gross profit and net income in 1996.

Notice that the original error has exactly the ***opposite effects*** upon the net incomes of the two successive years. Net income was ***understated*** by the amount of the error of 1995, and ***overstated*** by the same amount in 1996. For this reason inventory errors are said to be "counterbalancing" or "self-correcting" over a two-year period.

The fact that offsetting errors occur in the financial statements of two successive years does not lessen the consequences of errors in inventory valuation. Rather, this ***exaggerates*** the misleading effects of the error upon ***trends*** in the company's performance from one year to the next.

CASE IN POINT Some small businesses purposely have understated ending inventory in their income tax returns as an easy—though fraudulent—means of understating taxable income. In the following year, however, the effects of this error will reverse, and taxable income will be overstated. To avoid paying income taxes on this overstated income, the business may again understate its ending inventory, this time by an even greater amount. If this type of tax fraud continues for very long, the inventory becomes so understated that the situation becomes obvious.

Effects of Errors in Inventory Valuation: A Summary The following table summarizes the effects of an error in the valuation of ending inventory over two successive years. In this table we indicate the effects of the error on various financial statement measurements using the code letters ***U*** (Understated), ***O*** (Overstated), and ***NE*** (No Effect). The effects of errors in the valuation of inventory are the same regardless of whether the company uses a perpetual or a periodic inventory system.

[13] If income tax effects are ignored, the amount of the error is exactly the same in inventory, gross profit, and net income. If tax effects are considered, the amount of the error may be lessened in the net income figure.

Original Error: Ending Inventory Understated

	Year of the Error	Following Year
Beginning inventory	NE	U
Cost of goods available for sale	NE	U
Ending inventory	U	NE
Cost of goods sold	O	U
Gross profit	U	O
Net income	U	O
Owner's equity at year-end	U	NE

Original Error: Ending Inventory Overstated

	Year of the Error	Following Year
Beginning inventory	NE	O
Cost of goods available for sale	NE	O
Ending inventory	O	NE
Cost of goods sold	U	O
Gross profit	O	U
Net income	O	U
Owner's equity at year-end	O	NE

Techniques for Estimating the Cost of Goods Sold and the Ending Inventory

OBJECTIVE 6 Estimate the cost of goods sold and ending inventory by the gross profit method and by the retail method.

Taking a physical inventory every month would be very expensive and time-consuming. Therefore, if a business using a periodic inventory system is to prepare monthly or quarterly financial statements, it usually ***estimates*** the amounts of its inventory and cost of goods sold. One approach to making these estimates is called the ***gross profit method;*** another—used primarily by retail stores—is the ***retail method.***

The Gross Profit Method

The gross profit method is a quick, simple technique for estimating the cost of goods sold and the amount of inventory on hand. In using this method, it is assumed that the rate of gross profit earned in the preceding year will remain the same for the current year. When we know the rate of gross profit, we can divide the dollar amount of net sales into two elements: (1) the gross profit and (2) the cost of goods sold. We view net sales as 100%. If the gross profit rate, for example, is 40% of net sales, the cost of goods sold must be 60%. In other words, the cost of goods sold percentage (or ***cost ratio***) is determined by deducting the gross profit rate from 100%.

When the gross profit rate is known, the ending inventory can be estimated by the following procedures:

1 Determine the ***cost of goods available for sale*** from the general ledger records of beginning inventory and net purchases.

2 Estimate the ***cost of goods sold*** by multiplying the net sales by the cost ratio.

3 Deduct the ***cost of goods sold*** from the ***cost of goods available for sale*** to find the estimated ending inventory.

To illustrate, assume that Metro Hardware has a beginning inventory of $50,000 on January 1. During the month of January, net purchases amount to $20,000 and net sales total $30,000. Assume that the company's normal gross profit rate is 40% of net sales; it follows that the cost ratio is ***60%.*** Using these facts, the inventory on January 31 may be estimated as follows:

	Goods available for sale:		
	Beginning inventory, Jan. 1		*$50,000*
	Purchases		*20,000*
Step 1 . . .	*Cost of goods available for sale*		*$70,000*
	Deduct: Estimated cost of goods sold:		
	Net sales	*$30,000*	
	Cost ratio (100% − 40%)	*60%*	
Step 2 . . .	*Estimated cost of goods sold ($30,000 × 60%)*		*18,000*
Step 3 . . .	*Estimated ending inventory, Jan. 31*		*$52,000*

The gross profit method of estimating inventory has several uses apart from the preparation of monthly financial statements. For example, if an inventory is destroyed by fire, the company must determine the amount of the inventory on hand at the date of the fire in order to file an insurance claim. The most convenient way to determine this inventory amount is often the gross profit method.

The gross profit method is also used at year-end after the taking of a physical inventory to confirm the overall reasonableness of the amount determined by the counting and pricing process.

The Retail Method

The retail method of estimating inventory and the cost of goods sold is quite similar to the gross profit method. The basic difference is that the retail method is based upon the cost ratio of the ***current period,*** rather than that of the prior year.

To determine the cost ratio of the current period, the business must keep track of both the cost of all goods purchased during the period and the ***retail sales prices*** that were assigned to these goods. To illustrate, assume that during June the cost of goods available for sale in Tennis Gallery totalled $45,000. The store had offered this merchandise for sale to its customers at retail prices totalling $100,000. The cost ratio in June was ***45%*** ($45,000 ÷ $100,000). This cost ratio is used to estimate the monthly cost of goods sold and the month-end inventory by the same procedures as are applied under the gross profit method.

Many retail stores also use their current cost ratio as a quick method of pricing the inventory counted at year-end. In a retail store, the retail sales price is clearly marked on the merchandise. Therefore, employees quickly can determine the retail price of the ending inventory. This retail price may be reduced to a close approximation of cost simply by multiplying by the cost ratio.

Assume, for example, that the annual physical inventory at Tennis Gallery indicates the merchandise on hand at year-end has a retail sales price of $120,000. If the cost ratio for the year has been 44%, the cost of this inventory is approximately \$52,800 (\$120,000 × 44%). This version of the retail method approximates valuation of the inventory at average cost.

Inventory Management

OBJECTIVE 7 Identify several factors that management should consider in determining the optimal size of the company's inventory.

How much inventory should a business keep on hand? The answer to this question is based upon many factors, including the nature of a company's business operations, the reliability and proximity of its suppliers, the physical characteristics of the inventory, marketing strategies, and management's willingness to risk the consequences of running out of merchandise or materials.

Inventory stored in a warehouse is an idle asset. Not only does this asset produce no revenue, it may require substantial storage and other costs.

Today, many manufacturing companies are implementing just-in-time inventory systems, designed to minimize their inventories of materials and finished goods. Although these systems can reduce the costs associated with carrying substantial inventories, they also involve considerable risk. As stated earlier, even a temporary delay in the arrival of key materials may bring the company's manufacturing operations to a halt.

Many retailing companies deliberately maintain large inventories to offer their customers a wide selection of merchandise. Such advertising slogans as "Largest selection in town," and "Available for immediate delivery" reflect marketing strategies that involve a large inventory.

In contrast, retailers that sell merchandise tailored to customers' specifications often maintain little or no inventory. These companies do not purchase their merchandise until ***after*** they have an order (and usually a deposit) from their customer. In essence, these businesses have just-in-time inventory systems.

Among the advantages of maintaining a ***minimum***-size inventory are:

- Less money is tied up in an asset that generates little or no revenue while it is stored in a warehouse or on a shelf. (Many companies, such as automobile dealerships, finance their purchases of inventory. Thus, a smaller inventory reduces the company's interest expense.)
- Storage costs are minimized (including the need for maintaining storage facilities).
- The risk of loss from merchandise becoming obsolete, out-of-fashion, or otherwise unsalable is held to a minimum.

On the other hand, the following considerations favour maintaining a ***larger*** inventory:

- A large selection of merchandise may attract more customers. For retailers, fewer sales opportunities are lost because items are temporarily "out of stock." In most cases, a large inventory is required to generate a high volume of sales in a retail business.
- Suppliers may offer substantial discounts if merchandise is purchased in large quantities. (Automobile manufacturers, for example, offer larger discounts to dealerships that purchase more cars.)
- For manufacturers, larger inventories of materials reduce the risk that manufacturing operations will be interrupted by shortages of key materials.

In summary, the decision as to the appropriate size of an inventory involves not only financial considerations, but also management's marketing strategy and its willingness to take risks. These issues, and the related topic of determining the optimal reorder quantity, are discussed further in later accounting courses.

Evaluating the Liquidity of Inventory

OBJECTIVE 8 Compute the inventory turnover rate. Explain why this ratio is of interest to short-term creditors.

Inventory often is the largest of a company's current assets. But how liquid is this asset? How quickly will it be converted into cash? As a step toward answering these questions, short-term creditors often compute the ***inventory turnover rate.***

Inventory Turnover Rate The inventory turnover rate is equal to the cost of goods sold divided by the average amount of inventory (beginning inventory plus ending inventory, divided by 2). This ratio indicates how many ***times*** in the course of a year the company is able to sell the amount of its average inventory. The higher this rate, the more quickly the company sells its inventory.

To illustrate, a recent annual report of Moore Corporation Limited shows a cost of goods sold of $1,631 million and average inventory of $297 million. The inventory turnover rate for Moore, therefore, is ***5.5 to 1*** ($1,631 million ÷ $297 million). We may compute the number of ***days*** required for the company to sell its inventory by dividing 365 days by the turnover rate. Thus, Moore requires ***66 days*** to turn over (sell) the amount of its average inventory (365 days ÷ 5.5).

Users of financial statements find the inventory turnover rate useful in evaluating the liquidity of the company's inventory. In addition, managers and independent auditors use this computation to help identify inventory that is not selling well and that may have become obsolete. A declining turnover rate indicates that merchandise is not selling as quickly as it used to.

Converting the Inventory into Cash Most businesses sell merchandise on account. Therefore, inventory often is not converted into cash as soon as it is sold. To determine how quickly inventory is converted into cash, we must combine the number of days required to ***sell the inventory*** with the number of days required to ***collect the accounts receivable.***

Computation of the number of days required to collect accounts receivable was illustrated and explained in the preceding chapter. To review, the ***accounts receivable turnover rate*** is computed by dividing net sales by the average accounts receivable. The number of days required to collect these receivables then is determined by dividing 365 days by this turnover rate. Data for Moore's annual report indicate that the company needed ***67 days*** (on average) to collect its accounts receivable.

Length of the Operating Cycle The ***operating cycle*** of a merchandising company is the average time period between the purchase of merchandise and the conversion of this merchandise back into cash.[14] In other words,

[14] In a ***manufacturing*** business, the operating cycle also includes the time period involved in manufacturing the inventory.

the merchandise acquired as inventory gradually is converted into accounts receivable by selling the goods on account, and these receivables are converted into cash through the process of collection.

The operating cycle of Moore was approximately ***133 days,*** computed by adding the average 66 days required to sell its inventory and the 67 days required to collect its accounts receivable from customers. From the viewpoint of short-term creditors, the shorter the operating cycle, the higher the quality of the company's current assets.

Accounting Methods Can Affect Financial Statement Subtotals and Analytical Ratios

The accounting methods selected by a company may affect the ratios and financial statement subtotals used in evaluating the company's financial position and the results of its operations. To illustrate, let us consider the effects of inventory valuation methods upon inventory turnover rates.

Assume that during a period of rising prices for purchases, Alpha Company uses LIFO, whereas Beta Company uses FIFO. In all other respects, the two companies ***are identical;*** they have the same size inventories, and they purchase and sell the same quantities of merchandise at the same prices and on the same dates. Thus, each company ***physically*** "turns over" its inventory at ***exactly the same rate.***

Because Alpha uses the LIFO method, however, its inventory is valued at older (and lower) costs than is the inventory of Beta Company. Also, Alpha's cost of goods sold includes more recent (and higher) costs than does Beta's. When these amounts are used in computing the inventory turnover rate (cost of goods sold divided by average inventory), Alpha ***appears*** to have the higher turnover rate.

We already have stated that the inventories of these two companies are turning over at exactly the same rate. Therefore, the differences in the turnover rates computed from the companies' financial statements are caused ***solely by the different accounting methods used in the valuation of the companies' inventories.***

Inventory turnover is not the only ratio that will be affected. Alpha will report lower current assets than Beta and, therefore, a lower current ratio and less working capital. In addition, using LIFO will cause Alpha to report less gross profit and lower net income than Beta.

Users of financial statements must understand the typical effects of different accounting methods. Also, a financial analyst should be able to restate on a ***comparable basis*** the financial statements of companies that use different accounting methods. Notes accompanying the financial statements usually provide the information necessary for comparing the operating results of companies using LIFO with those of companies using the FIFO method.

CHAPTER REVIEW

KEY TERMS INTRODUCED OR EMPHASIZED IN CHAPTER 9

Average-cost method A method of valuing all units in the inventory at the same average per-unit cost, which is recomputed after every purchase (for perpetual inventory system) or at the end of the year (for periodic inventory system).

Consistency in inventory valuation An accounting standard that calls for the use of the same method of inventory pricing from year to year, with full disclosure of the effects of any change in method. Intended to make financial statements comparable.

Cost flow assumptions Assumptions as to the sequence in which units are removed from inventory for the purpose of sale. Need not parallel the physical movement of merchandise if the units are homogeneous.

Cost layer Units of merchandise acquired at the same unit cost. An inventory comprised of several cost layers is characteristic of all inventory valuation methods except ***average cost.***

Cost ratio The cost of merchandise expressed as a percentage of its retail selling price. Used in inventory estimating techniques, such as the ***gross profit method*** and the ***retail method.***

First-in, first-out (FIFO) method A method of computing the cost of inventory and the cost of goods sold based on the assumption that the first merchandise acquired is the first merchandise sold, and that the ending inventory consists of the most recently acquired goods.

F.O.B. destination A term meaning the seller bears the cost of shipping goods to the buyer's location. Title to the goods remains with the seller while the goods are in transit.

F.O.B. shipping point The buyer of goods bears the cost of transportation from the seller's location to the buyer's location. Title to the goods passes at the point of shipment and the goods are the property of the buyer while in transit.

Gross profit method A method of estimating the cost of the ending inventory based upon the assumption that the rate of gross profit remains approximately the same from year to year.

Inventory turnover rate The cost of goods sold divided by the average amount of inventory. Indicates how many times the average inventory is sold during the course of the year.

Just-in-time (JIT) inventory system A technique designed to minimize a company's investment in inventory. In a manufacturing company, this means receiving purchases of materials just in time for use in the manufacturing process, and completing the manufacture of finished goods just in time to fill existing sales orders.

Last-in, first-out (LIFO) method A method of computing the cost of goods sold by use of the prices paid for the most recently acquired units. Ending inventory is valued on the basis of prices paid for the units first acquired.

Lower-of-cost-and-market (LCM) method A method of inventory pricing in which goods are valued at original cost and replacement cost or net realizable value, whichever is lower.

Operating cycle The sequence of steps (and length of time) by which a business converts cash into inventory, inventory into accounts receivable, and accounts receivable into cash. All assets expected to be converted into cash in the course of this cycle are viewed as current assets.

Physical inventory A systematic count of all goods on hand, followed by the application of unit prices to the quantities counted and development of a dollar valuation of the ending inventory.

Retail method A method of estimating the cost of goods sold and ending inventory. Similar to the gross profit method, except that the cost ratio is based upon current cost-to-retail price relationships rather than upon those of the prior year.

Shrinkage losses Losses of inventory resulting from theft, spoilage, or breakage.

Specific identification method Recording as the cost of goods sold the actual costs of the specific units sold. Required when each unit in inventory is unique, but not when the inventory consists of homogeneous products.

Write-down (of an asset) A reduction in the carrying value of an asset because it has become obsolete or its usefulness has otherwise been impaired. Involves a credit to the asset account, with an offsetting debit to a loss account.

DEMONSTRATION PROBLEM FOR YOUR REVIEW

The Audiophile sells high-performance stereo equipment. Windsor Acoustic recently introduced the Carnegie-440, a state-of-the-art speaker system. During the current year, The Audiophile purchased 9 of these speaker systems at the following dates and acquisition costs:

Date	Units Purchased	Unit Cost	Total Cost
Oct. 1	2	$3,000	$ 6,000
Nov. 17	3	3,200	9,600
Dec. 1	4	3,250	13,000
Available for sale during the year	9		$28,600

On ***November 21,*** The Audiophile sold 4 of these speaker systems to the Windsor Symphony. The other 5 Carnegie-440s remained in inventory at December 31.

INSTRUCTIONS Assume that The Audiophile uses a ***perpetual inventory system.*** Compute (1) the cost of goods sold relating to the sale of Carnegie-440 speakers to the Windsor Symphony, and (2) the ending inventory of these speakers at December 31, using each of the following flow assumptions:

a Average cost

b First-in, first-out (FIFO)

c Last-in, first-out (LIFO)

Show the number of units and the unit costs of the cost layers comprising the cost of goods sold and the ending inventory.

SOLUTION TO DEMONSTRATION PROBLEM

a (1) Cost of goods sold (at average cost):		
Average unit cost at Nov. 21 [($6,000 + $9,600) ÷ 5 units]	$ 3,120	
Cost of goods sold (4 units × $3,120 per unit)		$12,480
(2) Inventory at Dec. 31 (at average cost):		
Average unit cost at Dec. 31:		
Units remaining after sale of November 21 (1 unit @ $3,120)	$ 3,120	
Units purchased on Dec. 1 (4 units @ $3,250)	13,000	
Total cost of 5 units in inventory	$16,120	
Average unit cost at Dec. 31	$ 3,224	
Inventory at Dec. 31 (5 units × $3,224 per unit)		$16,120
b (1) Cost of goods sold (FIFO basis): (2 units @ $3,000 + 2 units @ $3,200)		$12,400
(2) Inventory at Dec. 31 (4 units @ $3,250 + 1 unit @ $3,200)		$16,200

c	*(1) Cost of goods sold (LIFO basis): (3 units @ $3,200 + 1 unit @ $3,000)*	*$12,600*
	(2) Inventory at Dec. 31 (4 units @ $3,250 + 1 unit @ $3,000)	*$16,000*

ASSIGNMENT MATERIAL

DISCUSSION QUESTIONS

1 Is the cost of merchandise acquired during the period classified as an asset or an expense? Explain.

2 Why is it necessary to use either specific identification or a flow assumption in recording the cost of goods sold?

3 Briefly describe the advantages of using a flow assumption, rather than the specific identification method.

4 Under what circumstances do generally accepted accounting principles permit the use of an inventory cost flow assumption? Must a flow assumption closely parallel the physical movement of the company's merchandise?

5 A company that uses a perpetual inventory system has in its inventory units of a particular product that were purchased at several different per-unit costs. When some of these units were sold, explain how the cost of goods sold is measured under each of the following flow assumptions:

a Average cost

b FIFO

c LIFO

6 A large art gallery has in inventory more than one hundred paintings. No two are alike. The least expensive is priced at more than $1,000 and the higher-priced items carry prices of $100,000 or more. Which of the four methods of inventory valuation discussed in this chapter would you consider to be most appropriate for this business? Give reasons for your answer.

7 During a period of steadily increasing purchase costs, which inventory flow assumption results in the highest reported profits? The valuation of inventory that is closest to current replacement cost? Briefly explain your answers.

8 Assume that during the first year of Hatton Corporation's operation, there were numerous purchases of identical items of merchandise. However, there was no change during the year in the prices paid for this merchandise. Under these special circumstances how would the financial statements be affected by the choice between the FIFO and LIFO methods of inventory valuation?

9 Apex Corporation sells two different types of products. The FIFO method is used in accounting for inventories for one type and the specific identification method is used for the other. Does this concurrent use of two inventory methods indicate that Apex is violating the accounting principles of consistency? Explain.

10 What are the characteristics of a ***just-in-time*** inventory system? Briefly explain the advantages and risks of this type of system.

11 Why do most companies that use perpetual inventory systems also take an annual ***physical inventory?*** When is this physical inventory usually taken? Why?

12 Under what circumstances might a company write down its inventory to carrying value below cost?

13 What is meant by the year-end ***cutoff*** of transactions? If merchandise in transit at year-end is material in dollar amount, what determines whether these goods should be included in the inventory of the buyer or the seller? Explain.

14 Briefly explain the operation of a ***periodic*** inventory system. Include an explanation of how the cost of goods sold is determined.

15 Assume that a ***periodic*** inventory system is in use. Explain which per-unit acquisition costs are assigned to the year-end inventory under each of the following inventory costing procedures:

a The average-cost method

b FIFO

c LIFO

16 When purchase costs are rising, do the perpetual and periodic inventory systems under LIFO produce the same amount for cost of goods sold? Explain.

17 Explain why errors in the valuation of inventory at the end of the year are sometimes called "counterbalancing" or "self-correcting."

18 Briefly explain the ***gross profit method*** of estimating inventories. In what types of situations is this technique likely to be useful?

19 Estimate the ending inventory by the gross profit method, given the following data: beginning inventory $40,000, net purchases $100,000, net sales $112,000, average gross profit rate of 25% of net sales.

20 A store using the ***retail inventory method*** takes its physical inventory by applying current retail prices as marked on the merchandise to the quantities counted. Does this procedure indicate that the inventory will appear in the financial statements at retail selling price? Explain.

21 Briefly explain the benefits to a company of minimizing the amount of inventory on hand. Also indicate the benefits that may result from maintaining a larger inventory.

22 How is the ***inventory turnover rate*** computed? Why is this measurement of interest to short-term creditors?

23 Baxter Corporation has been using FIFO during a period of rising costs. Explain whether you would expect each of the following measurements to be higher or lower if the company had been using LIFO.

a Net income

b Inventory turnover rate

c Current ratio

MULTIPLE CHOICE QUESTIONS

1 The primary purpose for using an inventory flow ***assumption*** is to:

a Parallel the physical flow of units of merchandise.

b Offset against revenue an appropriate cost of goods sold.

c Minimize income taxes.

d Maximize the reported amount of net income.

2 Ace Auto Supply uses a perpetual inventory record. On March 10, the company sells 2 Shelby four-barrel carburetors. Immediately prior to this sale, the per-

petual inventory records indicate 3 of these carburetors on hand, as shown below:

Date	Quantity Purchased	Unit Cost	Units on Hand	Total Cost
Feb. 4	1	$220	1	$220
Mar. 2	2	235	3	690

With respect to this sale on March 10: (More than one of the following answers may be correct.)

a If the average-cost method is used, the cost of goods sold is $460.

b If these carburetors have identification numbers, Ace must use the specific identification method in determining the cost of goods sold.

c If the company uses LIFO, the cost of goods sold will be $15 higher than if it were using FIFO.

d If the company uses LIFO, the carburetor ***remaining*** in inventory after the sales will be assumed to have cost $220.

3 T-Shirt City uses a ***periodic*** inventory system. During the first year of operations, the company made four purchases of a particular product. Each purchase was for 500 units and the prices paid were: $9 per unit in the first purchase, $10 per unit in the second purchase, $12 per unit in the third purchase, and $13 per unit in the fourth purchase. At year-end, 650 of these units remained unsold. Compute the cost of goods sold under the FIFO method and LIFO method, respectively.

a $13,700 (FIFO) and $16,000 (LIFO)

b $8,300 (FIFO) and $6,000 (LIFO)

c $16,000 (FIFO) and $13,700 (LIFO)

d $6,000 (FIFO) and $8,300 (LIFO)

4 Trent Department Store uses a perpetual inventory system but adjusts its inventory records at year-end to reflect the results of a complete physical inventory. In the physical inventory taken at the ends of 1995 and 1996, Trent's employees failed to count the merchandise in the store's window displays. The cost of this merchandise amounted to $13,000 at the end of 1995 and $19,000 at the end of 1996. As a result of these errors, the cost of goods sold for 1996 will be:

a Understated by $19,000.

b Overstated by $6,000.

c Understated by $6,000.

d None of the above.

5 In July, 1996, the accountant for LBJ Imports is in the process of preparing financial statements for the quarter ended June 30, 1996. The physical inventory, however, was last taken on June 5 and the accountant must establish the approximate cost at June 30 from the following data:

Physical inventory, June 5, 1996	$900,000
Transactions for the period June 5–June 30:	
Sales	700,000
Purchases	400,000

The gross profit on sales has consistently averaged 40% of sales. Using the gross profit method, compute the approximate inventory cost at June 30, 1996.

a $420,000 b $880,000 c $480,000 d $1,360,000

6 Allied Products maintains a large inventory. The company has used the LIFO inventory method for many years, during which the purchase costs of its products have risen substantially. (More than one of the following answers may be correct.)

a Allied would have reported a ***higher*** net income in past years if it had been using the average-cost method.

b Allied's financial statements imply a ***higher*** inventory turnover rate than they would if the company were using FIFO.

c If Allied were to let its inventory fall far below normal levels, the company's gross profit rate would ***rise.***

d Allied's current ratio is ***lower*** than it would be if the company were using FIFO.

EXERCISES

EXERCISE 9-1
Accounting Terminology

Listed below are nine technical accounting terms introduced in this chapter.

Retail method	*FIFO method*	*Average-cost method*
Gross profit method	*LIFO method*	*Lower-of-cost-and-market*
Flow assumption	*Shrinkage loss*	*Specific identification*

Each of the following statements may (or may not) describe one of these technical terms. For each statement, indicate the term described, or answer "None" if the statement does not correctly describe any of the terms.

a A pattern of transferring unit costs from the Inventory account to the cost of goods sold that may (or may not) parallel the physical flow of merchandise.

b The excess of the cost of the inventory determined by the perpetual records over the cost of the physical inventory of merchandise.

c The only flow assumption in which all units of merchandise are assigned the same per-unit cost.

d The method used in recording the cost of goods sold when each unit in the inventory is unique.

e The most conservative of the flow assumptions during a period of sustained inflation.

f The flow assumption that provides the most current valuation of inventory in the balance sheet.

g A technique for estimating the cost of goods sold and the ending inventory that is based upon the relationships between cost and sales price during the ***current*** accounting period.

EXERCISE 9-2
"Flow" of Inventory Costs

Micro Measurements uses a perpetual inventory system. On January 1, the Inventory account had a balance of $124,600. During the first few days of January the following transactions occurred.

Jan. 4 Purchased merchandise on credit from Laser Pen, Inc., for $23,900.

Jan. 9 Sold merchandise on account to Soho Graphics for a retail price of $36,800. This merchandise had cost Micro Measurements $27,200.

INSTRUCTIONS

a Prepare entries in general journal form to record the above transactions.

b What was the balance of the Inventory account at the close of business January 9?

c Why is the purchase of merchandise intended for resale not charged directly to an expense account, as is—say—the purchase of a tankful of gasoline in a delivery truck?

EXERCISE 9-3
Flow Assumptions

On May 10, Merlin Computers sold 70 Portex lap-top computers to College Text Publishers. At the date of this sale, Merlin's perpetual inventory records included the following cost layers for the Portex lap-tops:

Purchase Date	*Quantity*	*Unit Cost*	*Total Cost*
April 9	60	$800	$48,000
May 1	40	850	34,000
Total on Hand	100		$82,000

INSTRUCTIONS

Prepare journal entries to record the cost of the 70 Portex lap-tops sold on May 10, assuming that Merlin Computers uses the:

a Specific identification method (50 of the units sold were purchased on April 9, and the remaining 20 units were purchased on May 1).

b Average-cost method.

c FIFO method.

d LIFO method.

Exercises 9-4 and 9-5 are based upon the following data: Late in 1996, Software City began carrying WordCrafter, a new word processing software program. At December 31, Software City's perpetual inventory records included the following cost layers in its inventory of WordCrafter programs:

Purchase Date	*Quantity*	*Unit Cost*	*Total Cost*
Nov. 14	6	$400	$2,400
Dec. 12	20	310	6,200
Total available for sale at Dec. 31	26		$8,600

EXERCISE 9-4
Recording Shrinkage Losses

(This exercise is based upon the data presented above.) At December 31, Software City takes a complete physical inventory and finds only 23 WordCrafter programs on hand. Prepare the journal entry to record the shrinkage loss assuming that Software City uses (a) FIFO and (b) LIFO. Any write-down in excess of $1,000 is considered "material" in dollar amount.

EXERCISE 9-5
Lower-of-Cost-and-Market

(This exercise is based upon the data presented ***above*** Exercise ***9-4***.) Assume that at December 31, all 26 units of WordCrafter are on hand, but that the current replacement cost (wholesale price) of this product is $250 per unit.

Prepare journal entries to record (a) the write-down of the inventory of WordCrafter programs to the lower-of-cost-and-market at December 31 and (b) the cash sale of 10 WordCrafter programs on January 9 at a retail price of $350 each. Assume that Software City uses the FIFO flow assumption. (Company policy is to charge LCM adjustments of less than $2,000 to Cost of Goods Sold and larger amounts to a separate loss account.)

EXERCISE 9-6
F.O.B. Shipping Point and F.O.B. Destination

Fraser Company had two large shipments in transit at December 31. One was a $90,000 inbound shipment of merchandise (shipped December 28, F.O.B. shipping point) that arrived at the Fraser receiving dock on January 2. The other shipment was a $55,000 outbound shipment of merchandise to a customer that was shipped and billed by Fraser on December 30 (terms F.O.B. shipping point) and reached the customer on January 3.

In taking a physical inventory on December 31, Fraser counted all goods on hand and priced the inventory on the basis of average cost. The total amount was $480,000. No goods in transit were included in this figure.

What amount should appear as inventory on the company's balance sheet at December 31? Explain. If you indicate an amount other than $480,000, state which asset or liability other than inventory also would be changed in amount.

EXERCISE 9-7
Costing Inventory in a Periodic System

M. Rooney Company uses a ***periodic*** inventory system. The company's records show the beginning inventory of product no. T12 on January 1 and the purchases of this item during the current year to be as follows:

Jan. 1	*Beginning inventory*	*900 units @ $10.00*	*$ 9,000*
Feb. 23	*Purchase*	*1,200 units @ $11.00*	*13,200*
Apr. 20	*Purchase*	*3,000 units @ $11.20*	*33,600*
May 4	*Purchase*	*4,000 units @ $11.60*	*46,400*
Nov. 30	*Purchase*	*900 units @ $13.00*	*11,700*
	Totals	*10,000 units*	*$113,900*

INSTRUCTIONS

A physical count indicates 1,500 units in inventory at year-end.

Determine the cost of the ending inventory, based upon each of the following methods of inventory valuation. (Remember to use ***periodic*** inventory costing procedures.)

a Average cost
b FIFO
c LIFO

EXERCISE 9-8
Periodic Inventory Costing Methods

Pacific Plumbing uses a ***periodic*** inventory system. One of the company's products is a 2 cm brass gate valve. The company purchases these valves several times a year and makes sales of the item daily. Shown below are the inventory quantities, purchases, and sales for the year.

	Number of Units	*Cost Per Unit*	*Total Cost*
Beginning inventory (Jan. 1)	*9,100*	*$4.00*	*$ 36,400*
First purchase (Feb. 20)	*20,000*	*4.10*	*82,000*
Second purchase (May 10)	*30,000*	*4.25*	*127,500*
Third purchase (Aug. 24)	*50,000*	*4.60*	*230,000*
Fourth purchase (Nov. 30)	*10,900*	*5.00*	*54,500*
Goods available for sale	*120,000*		*$530,400*
Units sold during the year	*106,000*		
Ending inventory (Dec. 31)	*14,000*		

INSTRUCTIONS

Compute the cost of the ending inventory of gate valves, using the following ***periodic*** inventory valuation methods:

a FIFO
b LIFO
c Average cost 530,400 ÷ 120,000 = 4.42 X 14,000 = $61,880

EXERCISE 9-9
Periodic LIFO, Comparison with Perpetual LIFO, and Inventory Shrinkage

Marsden Products uses a perpetual inventory system and a LIFO flow assumption. At year-end, the perpetual inventory records indicate the following units of Product RB-21 are in inventory:

Purchase Date	Quantity	Unit Cost	Total Cost
Beginning inventory	50	$40	$ 2,000
June 18	300	45	13,500
Nov. 7	150	50	7,500
Total available for sale at Dec. 31	500		$23,000

A physical count of the merchandise indicates that only 490 units of Product RB-21 are on hand. Applying ***periodic LIFO*** costing procedures, these 490 units would be assigned the following unit costs:

Purchase Date	Quantity	Unit Cost	Total Cost
Beginning inventory	220	$40	$ 8,800
June 18	270	45	12,150
Total available for sale at Dec. 31	490		$20,950

INSTRUCTIONS

a Prepare a journal entry to record the shrinkage loss of 10 units in the LIFO-based perpetual inventory records. Charge any loss of less than $1,000 directly to Cost of Goods Sold.)

b Prepare a journal entry to record the shrinkage loss of 10 units under the periodic LIFO costing procedures.

c Explain ***why*** the perpetual LIFO inventory system produces a higher year-end inventory than the periodic LIFO costing procedures.

EXERCISE 9-10
Effects of Errors in Inventory Valuation

Norfleet Company prepared the following condensed income statements for two successive years:

	1996	1995
Sales	$1,500,000	$1,440,000
Cost of goods sold	879,600	914,400
Gross profit	$ 620,400	$ 525,600
Operating expenses	460,500	447,000
Net income	$ 159,900	$ 78,600

At the end of 1995 (right-hand column above) the inventory was understated by $50,400, but the error was not discovered until after the accounts had been closed and financial statements prepared at the end of ***1996***. The balance sheets for the two years showed owner's equity of $414,200 at the end of 1995 and $460,400 at the end of 1996. (Norfleet is organized as a sole proprietorship and does not incur income taxes expense.)

INSTRUCTIONS

a Compute the corrected net income figures for 1995 and 1996.

b Compute the gross profit amounts and the gross profit percentages for each year based upon corrected data.

c What correction, if any, should be made in the amounts of the company's owner's equity at the end of 1995 and at the end of 1996?

EXERCISE 9-11
Estimating Inventory by the Gross Profit Method

When Anne Blair arrived at her store on the morning of January 29, she found empty shelves and display racks; thieves had broken in during the night and stolen the entire inventory. Blair's accounting records showed that she had had $55,000 inventory on January 1 (cost value). From January 1 to January 29, she had made net sales of $200,000 and net purchases of $141,800. The gross profit during the last several years had consistently averaged 30% of net sales. Blair wishes to file an insurance claim for the theft loss. You are to use the ***gross profit method*** to estimate the cost of her inventory at the time of the theft. Show computations.

EXERCISE 9-12
Estimating Inventory by the Retail Method

Westlake Accessories needs to determine the approximate amount of inventory at the end of each month without taking a physical inventory of merchandise in the shop. From the following information, you are to estimate the cost of goods sold and the cost of the July 31 inventory by the ***retail method*** of inventory valuation.

	Cost Price	Retail Selling Price
Inventory of merchandise, June 30	*$264,800*	*$400,000*
Purchases during July	*170,400*	*240,000*
Goods available for sale during July	*$435,200*	*$640,000*
Net sales during July		*$275,200*

EXERCISE 9-13
Inventory Turnover Rates

In your analysis of the financial statements of Retail Outlet, you note that the cost of goods sold for the year was $13,200,000; inventory was $2,000,000 at the beginning of the year and $2,400,000 at year-end.

INSTRUCTIONS

a Compute the inventory turnover rate for the year.

b Using the assumption of 365 days in a year, compute the number of days required for the company to sell the amount of its average inventory (round to the nearest day).

c Assume that an average of 45 days is required for Retail Outlet to collect its accounts receivable. What is the length of the company's operating cycle?

PROBLEMS

Note: This chapter contains an unusually wide variety of problem assignments. In order to make these assignments readily available to all users of the text, we present them in one consecutive series, rather than splitting them into A and B groups. This series is supported in both the Group A and Group B packages of accounting work sheets.

PROBLEM 9-1
Evaluating Different Inventory Methods

A note to the recent financial statements of a large public company includes the following information:

Inventories Inventories are valued at the lower-of-cost-or-market, using various cost methods. The percentage of year-end inventories valued using each of the methods is as follows:

June 30 (fiscal year-end)	
Average cost	*54%*
Last-in, first-out (LIFO)	*29%*
First-in, first-out (FIFO)	*17%*

INSTRUCTIONS

a Does the company's use of three different inventory methods violate the accounting principle of consistency?

b Assuming that the replacement cost of inventories has been steadily rising, would the company's reported net income be higher or lower if all inventories were valued by the FIFO method?

c Assume that management's primary objective is to minimize income taxes and that the three inventory valuation methods are acceptable for income tax purposes. Which inventory valuation method would you recommend? Explain.

PROBLEM 9-2
Perpetual Inventory Records

A perpetual inventory system is used by Black Hawk, Inc., and an inventory record card is maintained for each type of product in stock. The following transactions show beginning inventory, purchases, and sales of product KR9 for the month of May:

May 1	*Balance on hand, 20 units, cost $40 each*	*$800*
May 5	*Sale, 8 units, sales price $60 each*	*480*
May 6	*Purchase, 20 units, cost $45 each*	*900*
May 21	*Sale, 10 units, sales price $60 each*	*600*
May 31	*Sale, 15 units, sales price $65 each*	*975*

INSTRUCTIONS

a Record the beginning inventory, the purchases, the cost of goods sold, and the running balance on an inventory record card like the one illustrated in this chapter. Use the ***last-in, first-out*** (LIFO) method.

b Prepare general journal entries to record the purchases and sales in May. Assume that all transactions were on account.

PROBLEM 9-3
Perpetual Inventory Records in a Small Business

Executive Suites, Inc., uses a perpetual inventory system. This system includes a perpetual inventory record card for each of the 60 types of products the company keeps in stock. The following transactions show the purchases and sales of a particular desk chair (product code DC-SB2) during September.

Sept. 1	*Balance on hand, 50 units, cost $60 each*	*$3,000*
Sept. 4	*Purchase, 20 units, cost $65 each*	*1,300*
Sept. 8	*Sale, 35 units, sales price $100 each*	*3,500*
Sept. 9	*Purchase, 40 units, cost $65 each*	*2,600*
Sept. 20	*Sale, 60 units, sales price $100 each*	*6,000*
Sept. 25	*Purchase, 40 units, cost $70 each*	*2,800*
Sept. 30	*Sale, 5 units, sales price $110 each*	*550*

INSTRUCTIONS

a Record the beginning inventory, the purchases, the cost of goods sold, and the running balance on an inventory record card like the one illustrated in this chapter. Use the ***first-in, first-out*** (FIFO) method.

b Prepare general journal entries to record the purchases and sales in September. Assume that all transactions were on account.

PROBLEM 9-4
Four Methods of Inventory Valuation

On January 15, 1996, California Irrigation sold 2,000 RainMaster-30 oscillating sprinkler heads to Rancho Landscaping. Immediately prior to this sale, California's perpetual inventory records for this sprinkler head included the following cost layers:

Purchase Date	*Quantity*	*Unit Cost*	*Total Cost*
December 12, 1995	*1,200*	*$18.50*	*$22,200*
January 9, 1996	*1,800*	*19.00*	*34,200*
Total on hand	*3,000*		*$56,400*

INSTRUCTIONS (***Note:*** We present this problem in the normal sequence of the accounting cycle—that is, journal entries before ledger entries. However, you may find it helpful to work part **b** first.)

a Prepare a separate journal entry to record the cost of goods sold relating to the January 15 sale of 2,000 RainMaster-30 sprinkler heads, assuming that California Irrigation uses:

1 Specific identification (1,000 of the units sold were purchased on December 12, and the remaining 1,000 were purchased on January 9).

2 Average cost.

3 FIFO.

4 LIFO.

b Complete a subsidiary ledger record for RainMaster-30 sprinkler heads using each of the four inventory valuation methods listed above. Your inventory records should show both purchases of this product, the sale on January 15, and the balance on hand at December 12, January 9, and January 15. Use the formats for inventory subsidiary records illustrated in this chapter.

Problems 9-5 and 9-6 are based upon the following data: SK Marine sells high-performance marine equipment to power boat owners. Apollo Outboard recently introduced the world's first 400 horsepower outboard motor—the Apollo 400. During the current year, SK purchased 8 of these motors—all intended for resale to customers—at the following dates and acquisition costs:

Purchase Date	*Units Purchased*	*Unit Cost*	*Total Cost*
July 2	*2*	*$4,450*	*$ 8,900*
July 22	*3*	*4,600*	*13,800*
Aug. 3	*3*	*4,700*	*14,100*
Available for sale during the year	*8*		*$36,800*

On ***July 28,*** SK sold 4 of these motors to Mr. G Racing Associates. The other 4 motors remained in inventory at September 30, the end of SK's fiscal year.

PROBLEM 9-5
Alternative Flow Assumptions

Assume that SK Marine uses a ***perpetual inventory system.***

INSTRUCTIONS

a Compute (a) the cost of goods sold relating to the sale on July 28 and (b) the ending inventory of Apollo outboard motors at September 30, using each of the following flow assumptions:

1 Average cost

2 FIFO

3 LIFO

Show the number of units and the unit costs of each cost layer comprising the cost of goods sold and the ending inventory.

b In part **a,** you have determined SK's cost of Apollo motors sold using three different inventory flow assumptions.

1 Which of these methods will result in SK Marine reporting the ***highest net income*** for the current year? Would this always be the case? Explain.

2 Assume that these methods are acceptable for income tax purposes, which method will ***minimize the income taxes owed*** by SK for the year? Would you expect this usually to be the case? Explain.

PROBLEM 9-6
Periodic Costing Procedures

Assume that SK Marine uses a ***periodic inventory system.***

INSTRUCTIONS

a Compute the ending inventory of Apollo motors at September 30 and the cost of goods sold through this date under each of the following periodic costing procedures:

1 Average cost

2 FIFO

3 LIFO

Show the number of units and the unit costs in each cost layer of the ***ending inventory.*** (You may determine the cost of goods sold by deducting ending inventory from the cost of goods available for sale.)

b Would the amount for ending inventory for each of the methods in (a) be different if the perpetual inventory system were used? Explain.

PROBLEM 9-7
Year-End Adjustments; Shrinkage Losses and LCM

Bunyon's Trees & Shrubs uses a perpetual inventory system. At December 31, 1996, the perpetual inventory records indicate the following quantities of a particular 5-gallon tree:

	Quantity	Unit Cost	Total Cost
First purchase (oldest)	230	$18	$ 4,140
Second purchase	200	19	3,800
Third purchase	170	20	3,400
Total	600		$11,340

A year-end physical inventory, however, shows only 570 of these trees on hand and alive.

In its financial statements, Bunyon's values its inventories at the lower-of-cost-and-market. At year-end, the per-unit net realizable value of this tree is $21. (Use $2,000 as the "level of materiality" in deciding whether to debit losses to Cost of Goods Sold or to a separate loss account.)

INSTRUCTIONS

Prepare the journal entries required to adjust the inventory records at year-end, assuming that:

a Bunyon's uses:

1 Average cost.

2 Last-in, first-out.

b Bunyon's uses the first-in, first-out method. However, the net realizable value of the trees at year-end is ***$15*** apiece, rather than the $21 stated originally. [Make separate journal entries to record (1) the shrinkage losses, and (2) the restatement of the inventory at a "market" value lower than cost. Record the shrinkage losses first.]

PROBLEM 9-8
Periodic Inventory Costing Procedures

Audio Shop uses a periodic inventory system. One of the most popular items carried in stock by Audio Shop is a 16 cm speaker unit. The inventory quantities, purchases, and sales of this unit for the most recent year follow.

	Number of Units	Cost Per Unit	Total Cost
Inventory, Jan. 1	2,700	$30.00	$ 81,000
First purchase (May 12)	3,540	30.60	108,324
Second purchase (July 9)	2,400	31.05	74,520
Third purchase (Oct. 4)	1,860	32.10	59,706
Fourth purchase (Dec. 18)	3,000	32.55	97,650
Goods available for sale	13,500		$421,200
Units sold during the year	9,600		
Inventory, Dec. 31	3,900		

INSTRUCTIONS

a Using ***periodic*** costing procedures, compute the cost of the December 31 inventory and the cost of goods sold for the 16 cm speaker units during the year under each of the following:

1 First-in, first-out

2 Last-in, first-out

3 Average-cost

b Which of the three inventory pricing methods provides the most realistic balance sheet valuation of inventory in light of the current replacement cost of the speaker units? Does this same method also produce the most realistic measure of income in light of the costs being incurred by Audio Shop to replace the speakers when they are sold? Explain.

PROBLEM 9-9
Comparisons of Perpetual and Periodic Inventory Systems

During 1996, Playground Specialists purchased 6 BigGym redwood playground sets at the following dates and acquisition costs:

Date	Units Purchased	Unit Cost	Total Cost
Aug. 4	2	$2,100	$ 4,200
Sep. 23	2	2,300	4,600
Oct. 2	2	2,560	5,120
Available for sale during the year	6		$13,920

On ***September 25,*** the company sold 3 of these BigGym sets to the Department of Parks and Recreation. The other 3 sets remained in inventory at December 31.

INSTRUCTIONS

a Assume that Playground Specialists uses a ***perpetual inventory system.*** Using each of the flow assumptions listed below, compute (a) the cost of goods sold relating to the sale of BigGym playground sets on September 25 and (b) the cost of the BigGym sets in inventory at December 31.

1 Average cost

2 FIFO

3 LIFO

Show the number of units and the unit costs of each cost layer comprising the cost of goods sold and the ending inventory.

b Assume that Playground Specialists uses a ***periodic inventory system.*** Compute the ending inventory of BigGym playground sets at December 31 and the related cost of goods sold under each of the following year-end costing procedures:

1 Average cost

2 FIFO

3 LIFO

Show the number of units and the unit costs in each cost layer of the ending inventory. (You may determine the cost of goods sold by deducting ending inventory from the cost of goods available for sale.)

c Would the amount for ending inventory for each of the three methods be different between the perpetual and periodic inventory systems? Explain.

PROBLEM 9-10
Inventory Errors: Effects on Earnings

The owners of Night & Day Window Coverings are offering the business for sale as a going concern. The income statements of the business for the three years of its existence are summarized below:

	1997	1996	1995
Net sales	$860,000	$850,000	$800,000
Cost of goods sold	481,600	486,000	480,000
Gross profit	$378,400	$364,000	$320,000
Gross profit percentage	44%	43%*	40%

* Rounded to nearest full percentage point.

In negotiations with prospective buyers of the business, the owners of Night & Day are calling attention to the rising trends of the gross profit and of the gross profit percentage as very favourable elements.

Assume that you are retained by a prospective purchaser of the business to make an investigation of the fairness and reliability of Night & Day's accounting records and financial statements. You find everything in order except for the following: (1) An arithmetical error in the computation of inventory at the end of 1995 had caused a $24,000 understatement in that inventory, (2) a counting error in the physical inventory at the end of 1996 had caused an overstatement of $10,000 in that inventory, and (3) a duplication of figures in the computation of inventory at the end of 1997 had caused an overstatement of $70,000 in that inventory. The company uses the periodic inventory system and these errors had not been brought to light prior to your investigation.

INSTRUCTIONS

a Prepare a revised three-year schedule similar to the one illustrated above.

b Comment on the trend of gross profit and gross profit percentage before and after the revision.

PROBLEM 9-11
Retail Method

Cherry Vanilla is called a "record" store, but its sales consist almost entirely of tapes and CDs. The company uses a periodic inventory system but also uses the retail method to estimate its monthly, quarterly, and annual cost of goods sold and ending inventory.

During the current year, Cherry Vanilla offered for sale merchandise that had cost a total of ***$392,000.*** As required by the retail method, the company also kept track of the retail sales values of this merchandise, which amounted to ***$700,000.*** The store's net sales for the year were ***$610,000.***

INSTRUCTIONS

a Using the retail method, estimate (1) the cost of goods sold during the year and (2) the inventory at the end of the year.

b At year-end, Cherry Vanilla takes a physical inventory. The manager walks through the store counting each type of product and reading its retail price into a tape recorder. From this tape recording, an employee prepares a schedule listing the entire ending inventory at retail sales prices. The inventory on hand at year-end had a retail sales value of ***$82,400.***

1 Use the cost ratio determined in part **a** to reduce the inventory counted by the manager from its retail value to an estimate of its cost.

2 Determine the estimated shrinkage losses (measured at cost) incurred by Cherry Vanilla during the year.

3 Compute the store's gross profit for the year. (Include shrinkage losses in the cost of goods sold.)

PROBLEM 9-12
What If They'd Used FIFO?

O & B Corporation uses LIFO. Recent financial statements included the following data (dollars in thousands):

Average inventory (throughout the year)	*$ 81,554*
Ending inventory	*89,334*
Current assets (at year-end)	*115,852*
Current liabilities (at year-end)	*27,175*
Net sales	*315,076*
Cost of goods sold	*209,006*
Gross profit	*106,070*

A note accompanying these statements indicated that had the company used the ***FIFO*** inventory method (dollars in thousands):

1 Average inventory would have been $88,474 ($6,920 ***higher*** than the LIFO amount).

2 Ending inventory would have been valued at a cost of $96,115 ($6,781 ***higher*** than the LIFO cost).

3 The cost of goods sold would have been $209,284 ($278 ***higher*** than that reported in the company's income statement).*

* ***Note to student:*** Notice that the cost of goods sold is ***higher*** under FIFO than LIFO. This is a somewhat unusual situation, indicating that the company has encountered ***declining*** replacement costs for its merchandise during the year.

INSTRUCTIONS

a Using the data contained in the company's financial statements (based upon the LIFO method), compute the following analytical measurements. (Round to the nearest tenth.)

1 Inventory turnover rate

2 Current ratio

3 Gross profit rate

b ***Recompute*** the three ratios required in part **a** in a manner that will be ***directly comparable*** to those of a company using the FIFO method in its financial statements. (Round to the nearest tenth.)

ANALYTICAL AND DECISION PROBLEMS AND CASES

A&D 9-1
Have I Got a Deal for You!

You are the sales manager of Continental Motors, an automobile dealership specializing in European imports. Among the automobiles in Continental Motors' showroom are two Italian sports cars, which are identical in every respect except for colour: one is red and the other white. The red car had been ordered last February, at a cost of $48,300. The white car had been ordered early last March, but because of a revaluation of the Italian lira relative to the dollar, the white car had cost only $47,000. Both cars arrived on the same boat and had just been delivered to your showroom. Since the cars were identical except for colour and both colours were equally popular, you had listed both cars at the same suggested retail price,

$58,000. This price is about $2,000 less than competing dealerships are asking for this particular model.

Smiley Miles, one of your best sales agents, comes into your office with a proposal. He has a customer in the showroom who wants to buy the red car for $58,000. However, when Miles pulled the inventory card on the red car to see what options were included, he happened to notice the inventory card of the white car. Continental Motors, like most automobile dealerships, uses the specific identification method to value inventory. Consequently, Miles noticed that the red car had cost $48,300, while the white one had cost Continental Motors only $47,000. This gave Miles the idea for the following proposal.

"Have I got a deal for you! If I sell the red car for $58,000, Continental Motors makes a gross profit of $9,700. But if you'll let me discount that white car $500, I think I can get my customer to buy that one instead. If I sell the white car for $57,500, the gross profit will be $10,500, so Continental Motors is $800 better off than if I sell the red car for $58,000. Since I came up with this plan, I feel I should get part of the benefit, so Continental Motors should split the extra $800 with me. That way, I'll get an extra $400 commission, and the company still makes $400 more than if I sell the red car."

INSTRUCTIONS Would you accept Miles's proposal? Explain your reasoning.

A&D 9-2
Just-in-Time or NQIT (Not-Quite-in-Time)

Fargo Manufacturing is located in Windsor, Ontario. In the past, the company has rented several warehouses to store its inventories of materials and finished goods. Recently, management has been working to implement the principles of a just-in-time inventory system. At present, almost 70% of the company's materials arrive on a just-in-time basis, and all finished goods are shipped to customers immediately upon completion of the production process.

INSTRUCTIONS

a Explain what is meant by "just-in-time," with respect to both materials and finished goods.

b What are the advantages to Fargo of just-in-time manufacturing? What is the biggest risk?

A&D 9-3
Are these Inventory Transactions Okay?

The bookkeeper of FunBuy Souvenir Shop is not sure whether the following transactions have been handled properly. FunBuy uses a perpetual inventory system.

(1) Merchandise costing $1,000 was shipped to FunBuy by a supplier on December 30, 1995. Since the merchandise was not received until January 3, 1996, it was not included in the physical ending inventory of 1995. The supplier's invoice, with terms n/30, F.O.B. shipping point, was received on December 31, 1995 and was recorded immediately.

(2) Merchandise costing $2,900 was shipped to a regular customer in the late afternoon of December 31, 1995, after it was counted and included in the physical inventory. Since this customer had done a lot of business with the company, FunBuy did not want to bill the customer until January 8, 1996. On that day, the invoice for $3,600, with terms 2/10, n/30, F.O.B. shipping point, was prepared and the transaction was recorded.

INSTRUCTIONS Indicate, in a tabulation format, the items in the 1995 and 1996 income statements and in the 1995 balance sheet that are affected by the manner in which the two transactions were handled and how these items are affected (that is, whether they are understated or overstated and by what amount). FunBuy charges inventory shrinkage loss to cost of goods sold.

A&D 9-4
Inventory Management

In this chapter, we discussed several factors that management should consider in deciding upon the size of inventory to be kept on hand. In each of the following cases, you are to indicate what you consider to be the most important factor (or factors) favouring (1) increasing the size of the company's inventory and (2) ***not*** increasing the size of the inventory.

a Morgan Chevrolet is an automobile dealership in a large metropolitan area. It currently has an opportunity to buy several hectares of land adjacent to the dealership that it could use to store additional inventory. The cost of this land would be approximately $200,000. General Motors—Morgan Chevrolet's supplier—allows substantial discounts to dealers that purchase a large volume of cars. Like most auto dealers, Morgan Chevrolet finances purchases of inventory through a bank and repays the bank as individual automobiles are sold.

b Marc's Furniture sells name-brand furniture to homeowners at discount prices. The company is located in a small rented office. At present, the company's inventory consists of five or six different pieces of furniture that are kept on hand primarily for purposes of display. Customers place their orders from catalogues and wait six to eight weeks for delivery. The manager has noticed that customers most frequently order those items that the company has on display.

c Captain's Choice is a fish market located near the waterfront. All of the fish is purchased fresh each day from the local fishing fleet. Captain's Choice sells the fish at a retail price of approximately five times its cost.

A&D 9-5
Comparison of LIFO and FIFO

You are making a detailed analysis of the financial statements of two companies in the same industry: APM and BFC. Both businesses are organized as corporations and, therefore, must pay income taxes on their earnings. Both companies maintain large inventories, and the replacement costs of their products have been rising steadily for several years. A note to APM's financial statements discloses that the company's inventory is shown at a cost that is ***far below*** current replacement cost. BFC's inventory, in contrast, is presented at a cost that is ***very close*** to its current replacement cost.

INSTRUCTIONS

Answer the following questions. Explain the reasoning behind your answers.

a What method of inventory valuation is probably used by APM? By BFC?

b If we assume that the two companies are identical except for the method used in valuing inventory:

  1 Which company probably has been reporting the higher net income in recent years?

  2 Which company's financial statements probably imply the higher inventory turnover rate?

  3 Which company's financial statements probably imply the higher current ratio?

  4 Comment upon your answers to parts **2** and **3** above. If the only difference between these companies is their method of inventory valuation, is one company actually more solvent than the other? Assume that the inventory valuation methods are all acceptable for income tax purposes.

c If both companies sold their entire inventory at the same sales prices, which company would you expect to report the larger amount of gross profit?

A&D 9-6
Inventory: Attracting Attention?

Carla Fontana is an auditor with Revenue Canada. She has been assigned to audit the income tax return of Square Deal Lumber Company (a corporation). Selected figures from the company's income tax return are shown on the next page.

Sales	$12,000,000
Beginning inventory	360,000
Purchases of merchandise	9,600,000
Ending inventory	260,000
Cost of goods sold	9,700,000
Gross profit	2,300,000

As Fontana examined these figures, she became suspicious that Square Deal had understated its taxable income by a significant amount and may have been engaging in this practice for several years.

Fontana looked up several ratios for the retail lumber industry in a recent publication of industry averages. She found that retail lumberyards, on average, had annual sales of $10 million, an inventory turnover rate of 10, and a gross profit rate of 20%. Fontana also noticed a newspaper advertisement by Square Deal, which read, "Many unique products in our huge yard. We carry what the other yards don't. This week's special: roofing materials—15% discount on shake, shingle, and composition. Large selection in stock." Fontana then sent a letter to Square Deal to arrange a date for visiting the company and performing an audit of its latest income tax return.

When Fontana arrived at Square Deal Lumber, she was met in the parking lot by Sam "Square Deal" Delano, president and owner of the business. Fontana noticed that Square Deal looked like most other retail lumberyards. There was one main building, containing offices and displays of such merchandise as power tools and electrical supplies. Behind this building was a large fenced yard, with many stacks of lumber, and several storage sheds. These sheds contained plywood, fiberglass insulation, and other products that required protection from the weather.

Fontana asked to see the company's perpetual inventory records. Delano told her that Square Deal uses a periodic inventory system, as it is not a publicly owned company and does not have to issue quarterly financial statements to shareholders or other outsiders. He pointed out that he and the general manager were on hand every day, and they both knew exactly what was in stock—down to the very last board.

By examining various accounting records, Fontana concluded that the amounts of sales revenues and merchandise purchases were correctly stated in Square Deal's income tax return. She noticed, however, that most types of merchandise were reordered at intervals of about five weeks.

INSTRUCTIONS

a What was it about the figures in Square Deal Lumber Company's income tax return that originally made Fontana suspect that the company might be understating its taxable income?

b What happened to confirm Fontana's suspicions? Identify all of the factors that have come to her attention and yours.

c Does it appear that Square Deal is engaging in a deliberate scheme to evade income taxes, or that the company has simply made an "honest mistake"? Explain.

d Assume that the industry averages correctly approximate the financial position and operating results of the Square Deal. Estimate for the current year the correct amounts of the company's (1) cost of goods sold, (2) gross profit, (3) average amount of inventory. (Show supporting computations.)

e Estimate the amount by which Square Deal appears to have understated its taxable income over a period of years. Explain the basis for your conclusion.

CHAPTER

10 Capital Assets: Plant and Equipment, Intangible Assets, and Natural Resources

Our primary goal in this chapter is to illustrate and explain the accounting concepts relating to the acquisition, use, and disposal of capital assets. An important element of this discussion is our coverage of alternative depreciation methods used for plant and equipment, including the straight-line, units-of-output, declining-balance, and sum-of-the-years'-digits methods. In the final portions of the chapter, we address the special topics of accounting for intangible assets and for natural resources.

Learning Objectives

After studying this chapter you should be able to:

1 *Determine the cost of plant assets.*

2 *Distinguish between capital expenditures and revenue expenditures.*

3 *Explain the relationship between depreciation and the matching principle.*

4 *Compute depreciation by the straight-line, units-of-output, declining-balance, and sum-of-the-years'-digits methods.*

5 *Record the disposal of a plant asset.*

6 *Explain the nature of goodwill and indicate when this asset should appear in the accounting records.*

7 *Account for the depletion of natural resources.*

8 *Identify some problems that may arise in accounting for the impairment of long-lived assets.*

PLANT AND EQUIPMENT

The *CICA Handbook*[1] uses the general term ***capital assets*** to encompass three groups of long-term assets: property, plant, and equipment; intangible assets; and natural resources. Each of these three groups of assets is usually presented separately in the financial statements, and they will be discussed individually in this chapter.

The term ***plant and equipment*** is used to describe long-lived capital assets acquired for use in the operation of the business and not intended for resale to customers. Among the more common examples are land, buildings, machinery, furniture and fixtures, office equipment, and automobiles. A cargo van in the showroom of an automobile dealer is inventory; when this same vehicle is sold to a furniture store for use in making deliveries to customers, it becomes a unit of plant and equipment.

The term ***fixed assets*** has long been used in accounting literature to describe all types of plant and equipment and is still used in the published financial statements of large corporations. ***Plant and equipment,*** however, appears to be a more descriptive term. Another alternative title used on many corporation balance sheets is ***property, plant, and equipment.***

Plant and Equipment—A Stream of Services

It is convenient to think of a plant asset as a stream of services to be received by the owner over a period of years. Ownership of a delivery truck, for example, may provide about 100,000 kilometres of transportation. The cost of the delivery truck is customarily entered in a plant and equipment account entitled Delivery Truck, which in essence represents the advance purchase of many years of transportation service. Similarly, a building may be regarded as advance purchase of many years' supply of housing services. As the years go by, these services are utilized by the business and the cost of the plant asset gradually is transferred into depreciation expense.

An awareness of the similarity between plant assets and prepaid expenses is essential to an understanding of the accounting process by which the cost of plant assets is allocated to the accounting periods in which the benefits of ownership are received.

Major Categories of Plant and Equipment

Plant and equipment items are often classified into the following groups:

1 **Tangible plant assets.** The term "tangible" denotes physical substance, as exemplified by land, a building, or a machine. This category may be subdivided into two distinct classifications:

---

[1] Section 3060. Also, the terms "property, plant and equipment," and "intangible assets" are most widely used in published financial statements. In fact, these terms are used in the most recent CICA's *Financial Reporting in Canada* (Twentieth Edition, 1993).

   a Plant property subject to depreciation; included are plant assets of limited useful life such as buildings and office equipment.
   b Land. The only plant asset not subject to depreciation is land, which has an unlimited term of existence.
2 **Intangible assets.** The term "intangible assets" is used to describe capital assets that are used in the operation of the business but have no physical substance and are noncurrent. Examples include patents, copyrights, trademarks, franchises, and goodwill. Current assets such as accounts receivable or prepaid rent are not included in the intangible classification, even though they are lacking in physical substance.
3 **Natural resources.** A site acquired for the purpose of extracting or removing some valuable resource such as oil, minerals, or timber is classified as a ***natural resource,*** not as land. This type of capital (plant) asset is gradually converted into inventory as the natural resource is extracted from the site.

Determining the Cost of Plant and Equipment

OBJECTIVE 1 Determine the cost of plant assets.

The cost of plant and equipment includes all expenditures reasonable and necessary in acquiring the asset and placing it in a position and condition for use in the operations of the business. Only ***reasonable*** and ***necessary*** expenditures should be included. For example, if the company's truck driver receives a traffic ticket while hauling a new machine to the plant, the traffic fine is ***not*** part of the cost of the new machine. If the machine is dropped and damaged while being unloaded, the cost of repairing the damage should be recognized as expense in the current period and should ***not*** be added to the cost of the machine.

Cost is most easily determined when an asset is purchased for cash. The cost of the asset is then equal to the cash outlay necessary to acquire the asset plus any expenditures for freight, legal services, duties, insurance while in transit, installation, trial runs, and any other costs necessary to make ***the asset ready for use.*** If plant assets are ***purchased*** on the instalment plan or by issuance of notes payable, the interest element or carrying charge should be recorded as interest expense and ***not*** as part of the cost of the plant assets. However, if a company ***constructs*** a plant asset for its own use, interest costs incurred ***during the construction period*** are viewed as part of the cost of the asset when it is the company's accounting policy to capitalize such costs.[2]

This principle of including in the cost of a plant asset all the incidental charges necessary to put the asset in use is illustrated by the following example. A factory in Windsor orders a machine from a tool manufacturer at a list price of $10,000, with a $200 cash discount. Sales and goods and services taxes of $1,500 must be paid, as well as freight charges of $1,250. Transportation from the railroad station to the factory costs $150, and installation labour amounts to $400. The cost of the machine to be entered in the Machinery account is computed as follows:

---
[2] CICA, *CICA Handbook* (Toronto), section 3060.26.

Items included in cost of machine

List price of machine	*$10,000*
Less: Cash discount	*200*
Net cash price	*$ 9,800*
Sales and goods and services taxes	*1,500*
Freight	*1,250*
Transportation from railroad station to factory	*150*
Installation labour	*400*
Cost of machine	*$13,100*

Why should all the incidental charges relating to the acquisition of a machine be included in its cost? Why not treat these incidental charges as expenses of the period in which the machine is acquired?

The answer is to be found in the basic accounting principle of ***matching costs and revenue.*** The benefits of owning the machine will be received over a span of years, for example, 10 years. During those 10 years the operation of the machine will contribute to revenue. Consequently, the total costs of the machine should be recorded in the accounts as an asset and allocated against the revenue of the 10 years. All costs incurred in acquiring the machine are costs of the services to be received from using the machine.

Land When land is purchased, various incidental costs are generally incurred, in addition to the purchase price. These additional costs may include commissions to real estate brokers, land transfer tax, legal fees for examining the title, delinquent taxes paid by the purchaser, and fees for surveying, draining, clearing, and grading the property. All these expenditures become part of the cost of the land.

Apportionment of a Lump-Sum Purchase Separate ledger accounts are necessary for land and buildings, because buildings are subject to depreciation and land is not. The treatment of land as a nondepreciable asset is based on the premise that land used as a building site has an unlimited life. When land and building are purchased for a lump sum, the purchase price must be apportioned between the land and the building. An appraisal may be necessary for this purpose. Assume, for example, that land and a building are purchased for a bargain price of $400,000. The apportionment of this cost on the basis of an appraisal may be made as follows:

Apportioning cost between land and building

	Value per Appraisal	*Percentage of Total*	*Apportionment of Cost*
Land	*$200,000*	*40%*	*$160,000*
Building	*300,000*	*60%*	*240,000*
Total	*$500,000*	*100%*	*$400,000*

Sometimes a tract of land purchased as a building site has on it an old building that is not suitable for the buyer's use. The Land account should be charged with the entire purchase price ***plus any costs incurred in tearing down or removing the building.*** Proceeds received from sale of the materials salvaged from the old building are recorded as a credit in the Land account.

Land Improvements Improvements to real estate such as driveways, fences, parking lots, landscaping, and sprinkler systems have a limited life and are therefore subject to depreciation. For this reason they should be recorded in a separate account entitled Land Improvements.

Buildings Old buildings are sometimes purchased with the intention of repairing them prior to placing them in use. Repairs made under these circumstances are charged to the Buildings account. After the building has been placed in use, ordinary repairs are considered as maintenance expense when incurred.

Capital Expenditures and Revenue Expenditures

OBJECTIVE 2 Distinguish between capital expenditures and revenue expenditures.

Expenditures for the purchase or expansion of plant assets are called ***capital expenditures*** and are recorded in asset accounts. Expenditures for ordinary repairs, maintenance, fuel, and other items necessary to the ownership and use of plant and equipment are called ***revenue expenditures*** and are recorded by debiting expense accounts. The charge to an expense account is based on the assumption that the benefits from the expenditure will be used up in the current period, and the cost should therefore be deducted from the revenue of the period in determining the net income.

A business may purchase many small items that will benefit several accounting periods but that have a relatively low cost. Examples of such items include auto batteries, wastebaskets, and pencil sharpeners. Such items are theoretically capital expenditures, but if they are recorded as assets in the accounting records it will be necessary to compute and record the related depreciation expense in future periods. We have previously mentioned the idea that the extra work involved in developing more precise accounting information should be weighed against the benefits that result. Thus, for reasons of convenience and economy, expenditures that are ***not material*** in dollar amount are treated in the accounting records as expenses of the current period. In brief, ***any material expenditure that will benefit several accounting periods is considered a capital expenditure. Any expenditure that will benefit only the current period or that is not material in amount is treated as a revenue expenditure.***

Many companies develop formal policy statements defining capital and revenue expenditures as a guide toward consistent accounting practice from year to year. These policy statements often set a minimum dollar limit for a capital expenditure (such as $500).

Effect of Errors in Distinguishing between Capital and Revenue Expenditures Because a capital expenditure is recorded by debiting an asset account, the transaction has no immediate effect upon net income. However, the depreciation of the amount entered in the asset account will be reflected as an expense in future periods. A revenue expenditure, on the other hand, is recorded by debiting an expense account and therefore represents an immediate deduction from earnings in the current period.

Assume that the cost of a new delivery truck is erroneously debited to the Repairs Expense account. The result will be to overstate repairs expense, thereby understating the current year's net income. If the error is not corrected, the net income of subsequent years will be overstated because no depreciation expense will be recognized during the years in which the truck is used.

On the other hand, assume that ordinary truck repairs are erroneously debited to the asset account, Delivery Truck. The result will be to understate repairs expense, thereby overstating the current year's net income. If the error is not corrected, the net income of future years will be understated because of excessive depreciation charges based upon the inflated balance of the Delivery Truck account.

These examples indicate that a careful distinction between capital and revenue expenditures is essential to attainment of one of the most fundamental objectives of accounting—the determination of net income for each year of operation of a business.

Capital Budgeting

The process of planning and evaluating proposals for capital expenditures is called ***capital budgeting.*** Capital budgeting includes such decisions as whether to build new factories or automate old ones, buy competing businesses, and develop new products.

Decisions regarding the acquisition of plant assets may be among management's most significant responsibilities. These acquisitions often involve large dollar amounts, perhaps hundreds of millions—even billions—of dollars. If the company has the plant assets designed and constructed, the cash outlays to acquire these assets may continue over a period of years. In addition, acquisitions of plant assets may affect the nature and profitability of the company's operations for many years to come.

A major factor in most capital budgeting decisions is management's estimates of the ***future cash flows*** relating to the project—that is, the cash outlays needed to acquire the new assets, and the annual net cash receipts that these assets are expected to generate.

One approach widely used in the evaluation of capital budgeting proposals is ***discounting*** the expected future cash flows to their ***present value.*** Another approach is to compute the return on investment (ROI) expected from each proposed expenditure. These and other capital budgeting techniques are discussed in depth in Chapter 26. Our objective at this time is simply to emphasize the following points:

1 Decisions concerning the acquisition of plant assets are of considerable importance, as they may affect business operations for many years.

2 Accounting information—especially estimates of future cash flows and earnings—plays a vital role in these decisions.

Capital Expenditures Budget In Chapter 7, we explained that most well-managed companies prepare ***cash budgets***—forecasts of expected cash receipts and cash payments for the coming year. In addition, these companies often prepare ***capital expenditures budgets,*** which forecast the company's capital expenditures over a period of several years.

The long-term capital expenditures budget and the annual cash budgets are interrelated. Both budgets should agree as to the amount of cash to be spent on capital expenditures during the current year.

DEPRECIATION

Allocating the Cost of Plant and Equipment over the Years of Use

Tangible plant assets, with the exception of land, are of use to a company for only a limited number of years. ***Depreciation,*** as the term is used in accounting, is the ***allocation of the cost of a tangible plant asset to expense in the periods in which services are received from the asset.***[3] In short, the basic purpose of depreciation is to achieve the ***matching principle***—that is, to offset the revenue of an accounting period with the costs of the goods and services being consumed in the effort to generate that revenue.

OBJECTIVE 3 Explain the relationship between depreciation and the matching principle.

Earlier in this chapter, we described a delivery truck as a "stream of transportation services" to be received over the years that the truck is owned and used. The cost of the truck initially is debited to an asset account, because this purchase of these "transportation services" will benefit many future accounting periods. As these services are received, however, the cost of the truck gradually is removed from the balance sheet and allocated to expense in the income statement, through the process called "depreciation."

Depreciation: a process of allocating the cost of an asset to expense

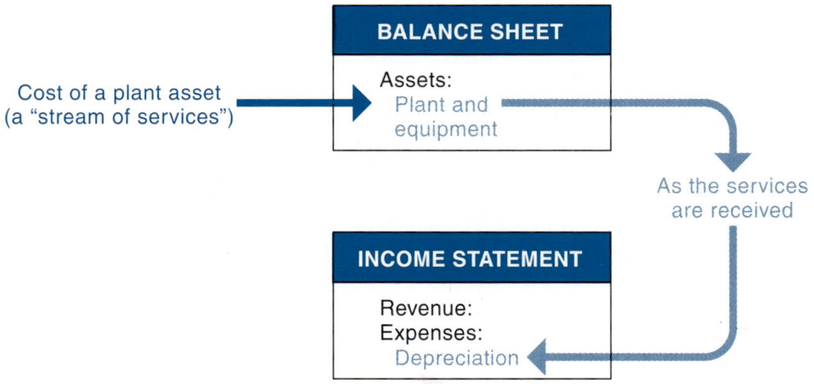

The journal entry to record depreciation expense consists of a debit to Depreciation Expense and a credit to Accumulated Depreciation. The credit portion of the entry removes from the balance sheet that portion of the asset's cost estimated to have been used up during the current period. The debit portion of the entry allocates this expired cost to expense.

---

[3] While section 3060 of the *CICA Handbook* uses the term "amortization" to encompass the commonly used terms "depreciation" and "depletion," it indicates that the latter two terms may also be used. In practice, the terms "depreciation" and "depletion" are still most widely used. Also, these two terms are used in the most recent CICA's *Financial Reporting In Canada* (Twentieth Edition, 1993). Accordingly, the terms "depreciation" and "depletion" are used in this text.

Separate Depreciation Expense and Accumulated Depreciation accounts are maintained for different types of depreciable assets, such as factory buildings, delivery equipment, and office equipment. These separate accounts help accountants to measure separately the costs of different business activities, such as manufacturing, sales, and administration.

Depreciation Is Not a Process of Valuation Depreciation is a process of ***cost allocation,*** not a process of valuation. Accounting records do not attempt to show the current market values of plant assets. The market value of a building, for example, may increase during some accounting periods within the building's useful life. The recognition of depreciation expense continues, however, without regard to such temporary increases in market value. Accountants recognize that the building will render useful services only for a limited number of years, and that the full cost of the building should be ***systematically allocated to expense*** during these years.

Book Value Plant assets are shown in the balance sheet at their book values (or ***carrying values***). The ***book value*** of a plant asset is its ***cost minus the related accumulated depreciation.*** Accumulated depreciation is a contra-asset account, representing that portion of the asset's cost that has ***already*** been allocated to expense. Thus, book value represents the portion of the asset's cost that remains to be allocated to expense in future periods.

Depreciation and Cash Flows Depreciation differs from most expenses in that it does not depend upon a cash payment at or near the time the expense is recorded. For this reason, depreciation sometimes is called a "noncash" expense. Bear in mind, however, that "payment" of many years' depreciation expense may be made in advance, when the plant asset is purchased. Also, when the asset eventually wears out, an even larger cash payment may be required immediately or over a period of time to replace it.

Some people mistakenly believe that accumulated depreciation represents a fund of cash being accumulated for the purpose of replacing the plant assets when they wear out. This is a misconception. Accumulated depreciation is ***not*** an asset—it is the portion of the asset's cost that ***already has been allocated to expense.*** The amount of cash owned by a company is shown in the asset account, Cash.

Causes of Depreciation

The two major causes of depreciation are physical deterioration and obsolescence.

Physical Deterioration Physical deterioration of a plant asset results from use, as well as from exposure to sun, wind, and other climatic factors. When a plant asset has been carefully maintained, it is not uncommon for the owner to claim that the asset is as "good as new." Such statements are not literally true. Although a good repair policy may greatly lengthen the useful life of a machine, every machine eventually reaches the point at which it must be discarded. In brief, the making of repairs does not lessen the need for recognition of depreciation.

Obsolescence The term ***obsolescence*** means the process of becoming out of date or obsolete. A computer, for example, may become obsolete even though it is in excellent physical condition; it becomes obsolete because better computers of superior design and performance have become available.

The usefulness of plant assets may also be reduced because the rapid growth of a company renders such assets inadequate. ***Inadequacy*** of a plant asset may necessitate replacement with a larger unit even though the asset is in good physical condition. Obsolescence and inadequacy are often closely associated; both relate to the opportunity for economical and efficient use of an asset rather than to its physical condition.

Methods of Computing Depreciation

OBJECTIVE 4 Compute depreciation by the straight-line, units-of-output, declining-balance, and sum-of-the-years'-digits methods.

There are several alternative methods of computing depreciation. A business need not use the same method of depreciation for all its various assets. For example, a company may use straight-line depreciation on some assets and a declining-balance method for other assets. Furthermore, the methods used for computing depreciation expense in financial statements ***may differ*** from the methods used in the preparation of the company's income tax return.

Data for Our Illustrations Our illustrations of four depreciation methods will be based upon the following data: On January 2, S&G Wholesale Grocery acquires a new delivery truck. S&G has December 31 year-end date. The data and estimates needed for the computation of the annual depreciation expense are:

Cost	*$17,000*
Estimated residual value	*$ 2,000*
Estimated useful life	*5 years (or 100,000 kilometres)**

* The estimated life stated in kilometres will be used only in the **units-of-output** depreciation method.

Straight-Line Method The simplest and most widely used method of computing depreciation is the straight-line method. Under this method an ***equal portion*** of the asset's cost is recognized as depreciation expense in each period of the asset's useful life. (The straight-line method was described in Chapter 3 and has been used in all of our illustrations and problems involving depreciation up to this point.)

Annual depreciation expense is computed by deducting the estimated ***residual value*** (or salvage value) from the cost of the asset and dividing the remaining ***depreciable cost*** by the years of estimated useful life. Using the data in our example, the annual straight-line depreciation is computed as follows:

Computing depreciation by straight-line method

$$\frac{\text{Cost} - \text{Residual Value}}{\text{Years of Useful Life}} = \frac{\$17{,}000 - \$2{,}000}{5} = \$3{,}000$$

This same depreciation computation is shown below in tabular form.

Cost of the depreciable asset	*$17,000*
Less: Estimated residual value (amount to be realized by sale of asset when it is retired from use)	*2,000*
Total amount to be depreciated (depreciable cost)	*$15,000*
Estimated useful life	*5 years*
Depreciation expense each year ($15,000 ÷ 5)	*$ 3,000*

The following schedule summarizes the effects of straight-line depreciation over the entire life of the asset:

Depreciation Schedule: Straight-Line Method

Constant annual depreciation expense

Year	Computation	Depreciation Expense	Accumulated Depreciation	Book Value
				$17,000
First	*($15,000 × $\frac{1}{5}$)*	*$ 3,000*	*$ 3,000*	*14,000*
Second	*($15,000 × $\frac{1}{5}$)*	*3,000*	*6,000*	*11,000*
Third	*($15,000 × $\frac{1}{5}$)*	*3,000*	*9,000*	*8,000*
Fourth	*($15,000 × $\frac{1}{5}$)*	*3,000*	*12,000*	*5,000*
Fifth	*($15,000 × $\frac{1}{5}$)*	*3,000*	*15,000*	*2,000*
Total		*$15,000*		

Notice that the depreciation expense over the life of the truck totals ***$15,000***—the cost of the truck ***minus the estimated residual value.*** The residual value is ***not*** part of the cost "used up" in business operations. Instead, the residual value is expected to be recovered in cash upon disposal of the asset.

In practice, residual values are ignored if they are not expected to be ***material*** in amount. Traditionally, buildings, office equipment, furniture, fixtures, and special-purpose equipment seldom are considered to have significant residual values. Assets such as vehicles, aircraft, and computer systems, in contrast, often do have residual values that are material in amount.

In our example, S&G acquired the delivery truck on January 2. Therefore, we computed a "full year's" depreciation for the year of acquisition. Assume, however, that the truck had been acquired later in the year, say, on ***October 1.*** Thus, the truck would have been in use for only 3 months (or $\frac{3}{12}$) of the first year. In this case, depreciation expense for the first year would be limited to only ***$750,*** or $\frac{3}{12}$ of a "full year's" depreciation ($3,000 × $\frac{3}{12}$ = $750). (An alternative method of computing depreciation for fractional periods is explained later in this chapter.)

It often is convenient to state the portion of an asset's depreciable cost that will be written off during the year as a percentage, called the ***depreciation rate.*** When straight-line depreciation is in use, the depreciation rate is simply ***1*** divided by the ***life*** (in years) of the asset. The delivery truck in our example has an estimated life of 5 years, so the depreciation expense each year is $\frac{1}{5}$, or ***20%,*** of the depreciable amount. Similarly, an asset with a 10-year life has a depreciation rate of $\frac{1}{10}$, or ***10%;*** and an asset with an 8-year life, a depreciation rate of $\frac{1}{8}$, or ***12$\frac{1}{2}$%.***

Units-of-Output (Production) Method For certain kinds of assets, more equitable allocation of the cost can be obtained by dividing the cost (minus residual or salvage value, if significant) by the estimated units of output or production rather than by the estimated years of useful life. A car rental company, for example, might compute depreciation on its vehicles on the kilometres used.

If we assume that the delivery truck in our example has an estimated useful life of 100,000 kilometres, the depreciation rate ***per kilometre of operation*** is ***15 cents*** ($15,000 ÷ 100,000 kilometres). This calculation of the depreciation rate may be stated as follows:

$$\frac{\text{Cost} - \text{Residual Value}}{\text{Estimated Units of Output (Kilometres)}} = \text{Depreciation per Unit of Output (Kilometre)}$$

$$\frac{\$17{,}000 - \$2{,}000}{100{,}000 \text{ kilometres}} = \$.15 \text{ depreciation per kilometre}$$

At the end of each year, the amount of depreciation to be recorded would be determined by multiplying the 15-cent rate by the number of kilometres the truck had been driven during the year. After the truck has gone 100,000 kilometres, it is fully depreciated, and the depreciation program is stopped. This method is suitable only when the total units of output of the asset over its entire useful life can be estimated with reasonable accuracy.

Accelerated Depreciation Methods The term ***accelerated depreciation*** means recognition of relatively large amounts of depreciation in the early years of use and reduced amounts in the later years. Many types of plant and equipment are most efficient when new and therefore provide more and better services in the early years of useful life. If we assume that the benefits derived from owning an asset are greatest in the early years when the asset is relatively new, then the amount of the asset's cost that we allocate as depreciation expense should be greatest in these same early years. This is consistent with the basic accounting concept of matching costs with related revenue. Accelerated depreciation methods have been widely used in income tax returns because they reduce the current year's tax burden by recognizing a relatively large amount of depreciation expense.

Fixed-Percentage-of-Declining-Balance (Diminishing-Balance) Method The most widely used form of accelerated depreciation is the fixed-percentage-of-declining-balance method. This method involves computing an ***accelerated depreciation rate*** that is a ***specified percentage of the straight-line depreciation rate.*** Depreciation expense is computed each year by applying this accelerated depreciation rate ***to the remaining book value*** (undepreciated cost) of the asset. This computation may be summarized as follows:

$$\text{Depreciation Expense} = \text{Remaining Book Value} \times \text{Accelerated Depreciation Rate}$$

The accelerated depreciation rate ***remains constant*** throughout the life of the asset. Hence, this rate represents the "fixed-percentage" described in the name of this depreciation method. The book value (cost minus accumulated depreciation) ***decreases every year,*** and represents the "declining-balance" or "diminishing balance."

Thus far, we have described the accelerated depreciation rate as a "specified percentage" of the straight-line rate. Most often, this specified percentage is ***200%,*** meaning that the accelerated rate is exactly twice the straight-line rate. As a result, the declining-balance method of depreciation often is called ***double-declining-balance*** (or 200%-declining-balance). Tax rules, however, often specify a ***lower*** percentage, such as 150% of the straight-line rate. This version of the declining-balance method may be described as "150%-declining-balance."[4] In this text, we will limit our illustrations and problems to the widely used version of the declining-balance method, in which the accelerated depreciation rate is ***double*** the straight-line rate.

To illustrate double-declining-balance, consider our example of the $17,000 delivery truck. The estimated useful life is 5 years; therefore, the straight-line depreciation rate is ***20%*** (1 ÷ 5 years). Doubling this straight-line rate indicates an accelerated depreciation rate of ***40%.***[5] Each year, we will recognize as depreciation expense 40% of the truck's current book value, as shown below:

Accelerated depreciation: declining-balance

Depreciation Schedule: Double Declining-Balance Method

Year	Computation	Depreciation Expense	Accumulated Depreciation	Book Value
				$17,000
First	($17,000 × 40%)	$6,800	$ 6,800	10,200
Second	($10,200 × 40%)	4,080	10,880	6,120
Third	($6,120 × 40%)	2,448	13,328	3,672
Fourth	($3,672 × 40%)	1,469	14,797	2,203
Fifth	($2,203 × 40%) = ~~881~~	203	15,000	2,000
Total		$15,000		

Notice that the estimated residual value of the delivery truck ***does not*** enter into the computation of depreciation expense until the very end. This is because the declining-balance method provides an ***"automatic"*** residual value. As long as each year's depreciation expense is equal to only a portion of the undepreciated cost of the asset, the asset ***will never be entirely written off.*** However, if the asset has a significant residual value, depreciation should ***stop at this point.*** Since our delivery truck has an estimated residual value of ***$2,000,*** the depreciation expense for the fifth year should be ***limited to $203,*** rather than the $881 indicated by taking 40% of the remaining book value. By limiting the last year's depreci-

---

[4] The higher the specified percentage of the straight-line rate, the "more accelerated" this depreciation method becomes. Experience and tradition have established 200% of the straight-line rate as the maximum level. Tax rules often specify lower percentages in order to "slow down" the rates at which taxpayers may depreciate specific types of assets in their income tax returns.

[5] Under the 150%-declining-balance method, the accelerated depreciation rate would be ***30%*** (20% straight-line rate × 150% = 30%).

ation expense in this manner, the book value of the truck at the end of the fifth year will be equal to its $2,000 estimated residual value.

If the asset in the above illustration had been acquired on October 1 rather than on January 2, depreciation for only 3 months would be recorded in the first year. The computation would be $17,000 × 40% × $\frac{3}{12}$, or $1,700. For the next calendar year the calculation would be ($17,000 − $1,700) × 40%, or $6,120.

Sum-of-the-Years'-Digits Method Another form of accelerated depreciation is the sum-of-the-years'-digits method, sometimes called SYD. In this method, the depreciation rate is stated as a ***fraction,*** which gets smaller each year. These "shrinking fractions" determine the percentage of the asset's ***depreciable amount*** (cost minus residual value) charged to depreciation expense each year.

The key to the sum-of-the-years'-digits method is computing the series of fractions used as depreciation rates. The method draws its name from the ***denominator*** of these fractions, which is the ***sum*** of the numbers that designate the years of the asset's useful life. To illustrate, consider our example of the delivery truck with a 5-year life. The sum of the numbers 1 through 5 is ***15,*** as shown below:

$$1 + 2 + 3 + 4 + 5 = 15$$

Thus, the ***denominator*** of the depreciation rates for an asset with a 5-year useful life is 15. Notice that the denominator ***varies substantially*** with the estimated useful life of the asset. An asset with a 4-year life will have a denominator of 10 (1 + 2 + 3 + 4 = 10), whereas the denominator for assets with a 6-year life is 21 (1 + 2 + 3 + 4 + 5 + 6 = 21).[6]

The ***numerator*** of each depreciation rate fraction is the number of years ***remaining*** in the asset's useful life as of the ***beginning*** of the current year. Thus, the numerator becomes smaller each year.

In the example involving S&G's delivery truck, the amount to be depreciated is ***$15,000*** ($17,000 cost − $2,000 residual value). At the beginning of the first year, all 5 years of useful life remain; therefore, the depreciation rate is ***$\frac{5}{15}$,*** and depreciation expense for the year amounts to ***$5,000*** ($15,000 depreciable amount × $\frac{5}{15}$). In the second year, only 4 years of useful life remain; the depreciation rate is lowered to ***$\frac{4}{15}$,*** and depreciation expense is ***$4,000*** ($15,000 × $\frac{4}{15}$). This pattern continues over the asset's entire useful life; the depreciation rates are $\frac{3}{15}$ in the third year, $\frac{2}{15}$ in the fourth year, and $\frac{1}{15}$ in the fifth and final year. The depreciation program is summarized on the next page.

---

[6] Alternatively, the denominator may be computed by using the formula $n\left(\frac{n+1}{2}\right)$, where n is the useful life of the asset. According to this formula, the sum of the years' digits for an asset with a 5-year life is computed as follows: $5\left(\frac{5+1}{2}\right) = 5(3) = 15$. Similarly, the sum of the years' digits for an asset with a 10-year life would be computed as follows: $10\left(\frac{10+1}{2}\right) = 10(5.5) = 55$.

Accelerated depreciation: sum-of-the-years'-digits

Depreciation Schedule: Sum-of-the-Years'-Digits Method

Year	Computation	Depreciation Expense	Accumulated Depreciation	Book Value
				$17,000
First	($15,000 × $\frac{5}{15}$)	$ 5,000	$ 5,000	12,000
Second	($15,000 × $\frac{4}{15}$)	4,000	9,000	8,000
Third	($15,000 × $\frac{3}{15}$)	3,000	12,000	5,000
Fourth	($15,000 × $\frac{2}{15}$)	2,000	14,000	3,000
Fifth	($15,000 × $\frac{1}{15}$)	1,000	15,000	2,000
Total		$15,000		

Assume that the asset being depreciated by the sum-of-the-years'-digits method was acquired on October 1 rather than on January 2. Since the asset was in use for only 3 months during the first accounting period, the depreciation to be recorded in this first period will be for only $\frac{3}{12}$ of a full year, that is, $\frac{3}{12}$ × $5,000, or $1,250. For the second accounting period the depreciation computation will be:

$\frac{9}{12}$ × ($\frac{5}{15}$ × $15,000)	$3,750
$\frac{3}{12}$ × ($\frac{4}{15}$ × $15,000)	1,000
Depreciation expense, second period	$4,750

A similar pattern of allocation will be followed for each accounting period of the asset's life.

Depreciation for Fractional Periods When an asset is acquired in the middle of an accounting period, it is not necessary to compute depreciation expense to the nearest day or week. In fact, such a computation would give a misleading impression of great precision. Since depreciation is based upon an estimated useful life of many years, the depreciation applicable to any one year is ***only an approximation.***

One widely used method of computing depreciation for part of a year is to round the calculation to the nearest whole month. Thus, if an asset is acquired on July 12, depreciation is computed for the six months beginning July 1. If an asset is acquired on July 16 (or any date in the latter half of July), depreciation is recorded for only five months (August through December) in the current calendar year.

Another acceptable approach, called the ***half-year convention,*** is to record six months' depreciation on all assets acquired during the year. This approach is based upon the assumption that the actual purchase dates will "average out" to approximately midyear. The half-year convention is widely used for assets such as office equipment, automobiles, and machinery.

The half-year convention enables us to treat similar assets acquired at different dates during the year as a single group. For example, assume that an insurance company purchases hundreds of desk-top computers throughout the current year at a total cost of $600,000. The company depreciates these computers by the straight-line method, assuming a 5-year life and no residual value. Using the half-year convention, the depreciation expense on all of the computers purchased during the year may be computed as follows: $600,000 ÷ 5 years × $\frac{6}{12}$ = $60,000. If we did not use the half-year convention, depreciation would have to be computed separately for computers purchased in different months. This would not be cost effective.

Management's Responsibility for Depreciation Methods and Related Estimates

Management is responsible for selecting the methods to be used in depreciating company assets. For purposes of financial reporting, management usually elects to use the straight-line method, because this method allows the company to report higher earnings. In fact, a recent survey of large corporations shows that more than 87% of these companies used straight-line depreciation in their financial statements for at least some of their plant assets.[7]

The Principle of Consistency The ***consistent*** application of accounting methods is a generally accepted accounting principle. With respect to depreciation methods, this principle means that a company should ***not change*** from year to year the method used in computing the depreciation expense for a given plant asset. However, management ***may*** use different methods in computing depreciation for different assets. Also, management may use different depreciation methods in the company's financial statements and in its income tax returns.

Financial Statement Disclosures A company should ***disclose*** in notes to its financial statements the methods used to depreciate plant assets. Readers of these statements should recognize that accelerated depreciation methods transfer the costs of plant assets to expense more quickly than does the straight-line method. Thus, accelerated methods result in more ***conservative*** (lower) balance sheet valuations of plant assets and measurements of net income in the early years in the life of the plant assets. Moreover, when a change in depreciation method is made, both the reason for the change and the effect of the change on reported net income should be fully disclosed in a note to the financial statements.

Estimates of Useful Life and Residual Value Estimating the useful lives and residual values of plant assets also is a responsibility of management. These estimates usually are based upon the company's past experience with similar assets, but they also reflect the company's current circumstances and management's future plans. Thus, the estimated lives and residual values of similar assets may vary from one company to another.

The estimated lives and residual values of plant assets affect the amount of net income reported each period. The longer the estimated useful life and the larger the residual value, the smaller the amount of cost

---

[7] CICA, *Financial Reporting in Canada,* Twentieth Edition (Toronto, 1993), p. 154. The straight-line method was used by 262 of the 300 companies surveyed; 108 of these 262 companies also used either the diminishing (declining) balance or unit-of-production (output) method. In addition, 16 and 14 of the 300 companies used the diminishing-balance and units of production methods respectively.

transferred each period to depreciation expense, and the larger the amount of reported net income. Bear in mind, however, that all large public corporations are ***audited*** annually by a firm of independent public accountants. One of the responsibilities of these auditors is to determine that management's estimates of the useful lives and residual values of plant assets are reasonable under the circumstances.

Automobiles typically are depreciated over relatively short estimated lives—say, from 3 to 5 years. Most other types of equipment are depreciated over a period of from 5 to 15 years. Buildings are depreciated over much longer lives—perhaps 20 to 40 years for a new building, and 15 years or more for a building acquired used.

Revision of Estimated Useful Lives What should be done if, after a few years of using a plant asset, management decides that the asset actually is going to last for a considerably longer or shorter period than was originally estimated? When this situation arises, a ***revised estimate*** of useful life should be made and the periodic depreciation expense decreased or increased accordingly.

The acceptable procedure for correcting the depreciation program is to spread the remaining undepreciated cost of the asset ***over the years of remaining useful life.***[8] This correction affects only the amount of depreciation expense that will be recorded in the current and future periods. The financial statements of past periods are ***not*** revised to reflect changes in the estimated useful lives of depreciable assets. It is desirable to disclose the nature and effect of such a change.

To illustrate, assume that a company acquires a $10,000 asset that is estimated to have a 10-year useful life and no residual value. Under the straight-line method, the annual depreciation expense is $1,000. At the end of the sixth year, accumulated depreciation amounts to $6,000, and the asset has an undepreciated cost (or book value) of $4,000.

At the beginning of the seventh year, it is decided that the asset will last for 8 more years. The revised estimate of useful life is, therefore, a total of 14 years. The depreciation expense to be recognized for the seventh year and for each of the remaining years is $500, computed as follows:

Revision of depreciation program

Undepreciated cost at end of sixth year ($10,000 – $6,000)	*$4,000*
Revised estimate of remaining years of useful life	*8 years*
Revised amount of annual depreciation expense ($4,000 ÷ 8)	*$ 500*

Inflation and Depreciation

We have illustrated that depreciation expense is based upon ***historical costs,*** that is, the costs actually incurred when the asset was acquired. For long-lived assets such as buildings, these costs may have been incurred 20, 30, perhaps even 50 years ago.

We live in an inflationary economy, which is characterized by rising prices. Sometimes inflation is severe, while at other times it is quite moderate. Still, prices have risen significantly over the long term. Prices today are about four times their levels of 40 years ago.

---

8 CICA, *CICA Handbook* (Toronto), section 1506.25.

Many accountants, business executives, and economists believe that the "old" historical costs used in financial reporting should be ***adjusted*** to reflect the changes in prices over time. Without such an adjustment, they argue, expenses such as depreciation substantially ***understate*** the "current economic values" of the resources being consumed in business operations, thereby causing an overstatement of net income.

A Past Effort at "Inflation Accounting" In the early 1980s, the CICA conducted an experiment in which it required large corporations to ***disclose*** in their financial statements the ***current replacement costs*** of their plant assets, and also depreciation expense based upon these current costs. In early 1992, the CICA's Accounting Standards Board ***discontinued*** these disclosure requirements. The main reason was that these disclosures were not ***cost-effective***—that is, the cost to businesses of developing this information each year ***exceeded*** the value of the information to decision makers. A basic concept of financial reporting is that all accounting information should be ***cost-effective*** when viewed from the perspective of our society as a whole.

Today, there appears to be a renewed interest in the use of current market values in the valuation of various types of assets. The fact that the CICA has discontinued one experiment in the use of current costs does not mean that financial statements will remain based upon historical costs forever. It does suggest, however, that a shift away from historical cost is not likely to occur quickly, or without considerable public discussion and debate.

DISPOSAL OF PLANT AND EQUIPMENT

OBJECTIVE 5 Record the disposal of a plant asset.

When depreciable assets are disposed of at any date other than the end of the year, an entry should be made to record depreciation for the ***fraction of the year*** ending with the date of disposal. If the half-year convention is in use, six months' depreciation should be recorded on all assets disposed of during the year. In the following illustrations of the disposal of items of plant and equipment, it is assumed that any necessary entries for fractional-period depreciation already have been recorded.

As units of plant and equipment wear out or become obsolete, they must be scrapped, sold, or traded in on new equipment. Upon the disposal or retirement of a depreciable asset, the cost of the property is removed from the asset account, and the accumulated depreciation is removed from the related contra-asset account. Assume, for example, that office equipment purchased 10 years ago at a cost of $20,000 has been fully depreciated and is no longer useful. The entry to record the scrapping of the worthless equipment is as follows:

Scrapping fully depreciated asset

Accumulated Depreciation: Office Equipment	*20,000*	
Office Equipment		*20,000*
To remove from the accounts the cost and the accumulated depreciation on fully depreciated office equipment now being scrapped. No salvage value.		

Once an asset has been fully depreciated, no more depreciation should be recorded on it, even though the property is in good condition and is still in use. The objective of depreciation is to spread the ***cost*** of an asset over the estimated period of its usefulness; in no case can depreciation expense be greater than the amount paid for the asset. When a fully depreciated asset remains in use beyond the original estimate of useful life, the asset account and the Accumulated Depreciation account should remain in the accounting records without further entries until the asset is retired.

Gains and Losses on Disposals of Plant and Equipment

Since the residual value and useful life of plant assets are only estimates, it is not uncommon for plant assets to be sold at a price that differs from their book value at the date of disposal. When plant assets are sold, any gain or loss on the disposal is computed by comparing the ***book value with the amount received from the sale.*** A sales price in excess of the book value produces a gain; a sales price below the book value produces a loss. These gains or losses, if material in amount, should be shown separately in the income statement in computing the income from operations.

Disposal at a Price Above Book Value Assume that a machine that cost $10,000 and has a book value of $2,000 is sold for $3,000 cash. The journal entry to record this disposal is as follows:

Gain on disposal of plant asset

Cash	*3,000*	
Accumulated Depreciation: Machinery	*8,000*	
Machinery		*10,000*
Gain on Disposal of Plant Assets		*1,000*
To record sale of machinery at a price above book value.		

Disposal at a Price Below Book Value Now assume that the same machine is sold for $500 cash. The journal entry in this case would be as follows:

Loss on disposal of plant asset

Cash	*500*	
Accumulated Depreciation: Machinery	*8,000*	
Loss on Disposal of Plant Assets	*1,500*	
Machinery		*10,000*
To record sale of machinery at a price below book value.		

The disposal of a depreciable asset at a price equal to book value would result in neither a gain nor a loss. The entry for such a transaction would consist of a debit to Cash for the amount received, a debit to Accumulated Depreciation for the balance accumulated, and a credit to the asset account for the original cost.

Trading in Used Assets on New

Certain types of depreciable assets, such as automobiles and trucks, sometimes are traded in on new assets of the same kind. In most instances, a trade-in is viewed as both a ***sale*** of the old asset and a purchase of a new one as the cash payment involved is significant.[9]

---

[9] The CICA's Accounting Standards Board takes the position that, in general, when 10% or more of the transaction value is comprised of monetary consideration (cash or monetary obligations), the transaction should be viewed as ***monetary,*** rather than nonmonetary. Thus, gains and losses on most routine trade-ins should be ***recognized in full.*** See *CICA Handbook,* section 3830.04.

To illustrate, assume that Rancho Landscape has an old pickup truck that originally cost $15,000 but that now has a book value of $2,000. Rancho trades in this old truck on a new one with a fair market value of $23,000. The truck dealership grants Rancho a "trade-in allowance" of $3,500 for the old truck, and Rancho pays the remaining $19,500 cost of the new truck in cash. Rancho Landscape should record this transaction as follows:

Entry to record a typical trade-in

Vehicles (new truck)	*23,000*	
Accumulated Depreciation: Trucks (old truck)	*13,000*	
Vehicles (old truck)		*15,000*
Gain on Disposal of Plant Assets		*1,500*
Cash		*19,500*
Traded-in old truck on a new one costing $23,000. Received $3,500 trade-in allowance on the old truck, which had a book value of $2,000.		

Notice that Rancho views the $3,500 trade-in allowance granted by the truck dealership as the ***sales price*** of the old truck. Thus, Rancho recognizes a ***$1,500 gain*** on the disposal (trade-in) of this asset ($3,500 trade-in allowance − $2,000 book value = $1,500 gain).

However, if the trade-in allowance is $1,200 rather than $3,500 a ***loss of $800*** ($2,000 book value − $1,200 trade-in allowance) is incurred by Rancho in this transaction. Also, the amount of cash to be paid is $21,800 rather than $19,500.

Accordingly, gains and losses on routine trade-ins are recorded in the accounting records whenever the transaction involves the payment of a significant amount of cash (or the creation of debt).

INTANGIBLE ASSETS

Characteristics

As the word ***intangible*** suggests, assets in this classification have no physical substance. Leading examples are goodwill, patents, and trademarks. Intangible assets are classified in the balance sheet as a separate section called intangible assets (or other assets), following plant assets. However, not all assets that lack physical substance are regarded as intangible assets. An account receivable, for example, or a short-term prepayment is of nonphysical nature but is classified as a current asset and is not regarded as an intangible. In brief, ***intangible assets are assets that are used in the operation of the business but that have no physical substance and are noncurrent.***

The basis of valuation for intangible assets is cost. In some companies, certain intangible assets such as trademarks may be of great importance but may have been acquired without the incurring of any cost. An intangible asset should appear in the balance sheet ***only*** if a cost of acquisition or development has been incurred.

Operating Expenses versus Intangible Assets

For an expenditure to qualify as an intangible asset, there must be reasonable evidence of future benefits. Many expenditures offer some prospects of yielding benefits in subsequent years, but the existence and life-span of these benefits is so uncertain that most companies treat these expenditures as operating expenses. Examples are the expenditures for intensive advertising campaigns to introduce new products and the expense of training employees to work with new types of machinery or office equipment. There is little doubt that some benefits from these outlays continue beyond the current period, but because of the uncertain duration of the benefits, it is almost universal practice to treat expenditures of this nature as expense of the current period.

Amortization

The term ***amortization*** is used to describe the systematic write-off to expense of the cost of an intangible asset over its useful life.[10] The usual accounting entry for amortization consists of a debit to Amortization Expense and a credit to the intangible asset account. There is no theoretical objection to crediting an accumulated amortization account rather than the intangible asset account, but this method is seldom encountered in practice.

Although it is difficult to estimate the useful life of an intangible such as a trademark, it is highly probable that such an asset will not contribute to future earnings on a permanent basis. The cost of the intangible asset should, therefore, be deducted from revenue during the years in which it may be expected to aid in producing revenue. Under the current accounting practices the maximum period for amortization of an intangible asset cannot exceed ***40 years,*** unless a longer life can be estimated and clearly demonstrated.[11] The straight-line method normally is used for amortizing intangible assets.

Goodwill

OBJECTIVE 6 Explain the nature of goodwill and indicate when this asset should appear in the accounting records.

Business executives used the term ***goodwill*** in a variety of meanings before it became part of accounting terminology. One of the most common meanings of goodwill in a nonaccounting sense concerns the benefits derived from a favourable reputation among customers. To accountants, however, goodwill has a very specific meaning not necessarily limited to customer relations. It means the ***present value of future earnings in excess of the normal return on net identifiable assets.*** Above-average earnings may arise not only from favourable customer relations but also from such factors as superior management and manufacturing efficiency.

The present value of future cash flows is the amount that a knowledgeable investor would pay today for the right to receive those future cash flows. (The present value concept is discussed further in later chapters and in Appendix A at the end of Chapter 16.)

The phrase ***normal return on net identifiable assets*** also requires explanation. ***Net assets*** means the owner's equity in a business, or assets minus liabilities. Goodwill, however, is not an ***identifiable*** asset. The existence of goodwill is implied by the ability of a business to earn an above-

---

[10] As mentioned in footnote 3 earlier, section 3060 of the *CICA Handbook* uses the term "amortization" to describe the allocation of the cost of tangible and intangible capital assets.

[11] CICA, *CICA Handbook* (Toronto), section 3060.32.

average return; however, the cause and precise dollar value of goodwill are largely matters of personal opinion. Therefore, ***net identifiable assets*** mean all assets ***except goodwill,*** minus liabilities. A ***normal return*** on net identifiable assets is the rate of return that investors demand in a particular industry to justify their buying a business at the ***fair market value*** of its net identifiable assets. A business has goodwill when investors will pay a higher price because the business earns more than the normal rate of return.

Assume that two similar restaurants are offered for sale and that the normal return on the fair market value of the net identifiable assets of restaurants of this type is 15% a year. The relative earning power of the two restaurants during the past five years is shown below:

	Mandarin Coast	Silver Dragon
Fair market value of net identifiable assets	$1,000,000	$1,000,000
Normal rate of return on net assets	15%	15%
Normal earnings, computed as 15% of net identifiable assets	150,000	150,000
Average net income for past five years	$ 150,000	$ 190,000
Earnings in excess of normal	$ —0—	$ 40,000

An investor presumably would be willing to pay $1,000,000 to buy Mandarin Coast, because this restaurant earns the normal 15% return that justifies the fair market value of its net identifiable assets. Although Silver Dragon has the same amount of net identifiable assets, an investor would be willing to pay ***more*** for Silver Dragon than for Mandarin Coast, because Silver Dragon has a record of superior earnings that will presumably continue for some time in the future. The ***extra amount*** that a buyer would pay to purchase Silver Dragon represents the value of this business's ***goodwill.***

Estimating Goodwill How much will an investor pay for goodwill? Above-average earnings in past years are of significance to prospective purchasers only if they believe that these earnings ***will continue*** after they acquire the business. Investors' appraisals of goodwill, therefore, will vary with their estimates of the future earning power of the business. Very few businesses, however, are able to maintain above-average earnings for more than a few years. Consequently, the purchaser of a business will usually limit any amount paid for goodwill to not more than four or five times the amount by which annual earnings exceed normal earnings.

Arriving at a fair value for the goodwill of an ongoing business is a difficult and subjective process. Any estimate of goodwill is in large part a matter of personal opinion. The following are several methods that a prospective purchaser might use in estimating a value for goodwill:

1 Agreement on the amount of goodwill may be reached through negotiation between buyer and seller. For example, it might be agreed that the fair market value of net identifiable assets is $1,000,000 and that the total purchase price for the business will be $1,180,000. This negotiated price implies a $180,000 payment for goodwill.
2 Goodwill may be determined as a multiple of the amount by which average annual earnings exceed normal earnings. Referring to our example

involving Silver Dragon, a prospective buyer might be willing to pay four times the amount by which average earnings exceed normal earnings, indicating a value of $160,000 (4 × $40,000) for goodwill. The purchase price of the business, therefore, would be $1,160,000.

The multiple applied to the excess annual earnings will vary widely from perhaps 1 to 10. An investor who pays four times the excess earnings for goodwill must, of course, expect these earnings to continue for ***at least*** four years so as to recover the amount paid for the goodwill.

3 Goodwill may be estimated by ***capitalizing*** the amount by which average earnings exceed normal earnings. Capitalizing an earnings stream means dividing those earnings by the investor's required rate of return. The result is the maximum amount that the investor could pay for the excess earnings in order to achieve the required rate of return on the investment. To illustrate, assume that the prospective buyer decides to capitalize the $40,000 annual excess earnings of Silver Dragon at a rate of 20%. This approach results in a $200,000 estimate ($40,000 ÷ .20 = $200,000) for the value of goodwill. (Note that $40,000 per year represents a 20% return on a $200,000 investment.)

A weakness in the capitalization method is that ***no provision is made for the recovery*** of the investment. If the prospective buyer is to earn a 20% return on the $200,000 investment in goodwill, either the excess earnings must continue ***forever*** (an unlikely assumption) or the buyer must be able to recover the $200,000 investment at a later date by selling the business at a price above the fair market value of net identifiable assets.

Recording Goodwill in the Accounting Records Goodwill is recorded in the accounting records ***only when it is purchased;*** this situation usually occurs only when a going business is purchased in its entirety. After the fair market values of all identifiable assets have been recorded in the accounting records of the new owners, any additional amount paid for the business may properly be debited to an asset account entitled Goodwill. Generally accepted accounting principles require goodwill to be amortized to expense over a period not to exceed 40 years (unless a longer life can be estimated and clearly demonstrated), although a much shorter amortization period often is appropriate.[12]

Many businesses have never purchased goodwill but have generated it internally through developing good customer relations, superior management, or other factors that result in above-average earnings. Because there is no objective means of determining the dollar value of goodwill unless the business is sold, internally developed goodwill is ***not recorded*** in the accounting records. Thus, goodwill may be a very important asset of a successful business but may not even appear in the company's balance sheet.

Patents

A patent is an exclusive right granted by the federal government for manufacture, use, and sale of a particular product. The purpose of this exclusive

[12] Ibid.

grant is to encourage the invention of new machines and processes. When a company acquires a patent by purchase from the inventor or other holder, the purchase price should be recorded by debiting the intangible asset account Patents.

For patents filed before October 1, 1989, their duration is 17 years from the date of issue. For patents filed on or after October 1, 1989, their duration is 20 years from the date of application. Thus, the period of amortization for patents must not exceed their legal life of either 17 or 20 years. However, if the patent is likely to lose its usefulness in less than the legal life, amortization should be based on the shorter period of estimated useful life. Assume that a patent is purchased from the inventor at a cost of $100,000, after five years of its 17-year legal life have expired. The remaining ***legal*** life is, therefore, 12 years, but if the estimated ***useful*** life is only four years, amortization should be based on this shorter period. The entry to be made to record the annual amortization expense would be:

Entry for amortization of patent

Amortization Expense: Patents	*25,000*	
Patents		*25,000*
To amortize cost of patent on a straight-line basis over an estimated life of 4 years.		

Trademarks and Trade Names

Coca-Cola's distinctive bottle is an example of a trademark known around the world. A trademark is a word, symbol, or design that identifies a product or group of products and affords a measure of protection to the owner whether or not registration has occurred. However, registration of a trademark in Canada serves as evidence of ownership and facilitates a higher degree of protection. Registration has a term of 15 years but may be renewed indefinitely for further terms of 15 years.

A trade name is the name under which a business is carried on whether or not it is the legally incorporated name of the business. If a trade name is used as a trademark it may be registered as a trademark.

The costs of developing a trademark or trade name often consist of advertising campaigns, which should be treated as expense when incurred. If a trademark or trade name is purchased, however, the cost may be substantial. Such cost should be capitalized and amortized to expense over a reasonable period of time, which generally would not be more than 40 years. If the use of the trademark is discontinued or its contribution to earnings becomes doubtful, any unamortized cost should be written off immediately.

Franchises

A franchise is a right granted by a company or a governmental unit to conduct a certain type of business in a specific geographical area. An example of a franchise is the right to operate a McDonald's restaurant in a specific neighbourhood. The cost of franchises varies greatly and often may be quite substantial. When the cost of a franchise is small, it may be charged immediately to expense or amortized over a short period such as 5 years. When the cost is material, amortization should be based upon the life of the franchise (if limited); the amortization period, however, may not exceed 40 years.

Copyrights

A copyright is an exclusive right granted by the federal government to protect the production and sale of literary or artistic materials for the life of the creator plus 50 years. The cost of obtaining a copyright in some cases is minor and therefore is chargeable to expense when paid. Only when a copyright is ***purchased*** will the expenditure be ***material enough*** to warrant its being capitalized and spread over the useful life. The revenue from copyrights is usually limited to only a few years, and the purchase cost should, of course, be amortized over the years in which the revenue is expected.

Other Intangibles and Deferred Charges

Among the other intangibles found in the published balance sheets of large corporations are moving costs, plant rearrangement costs, organization costs, formulas, processes, name lists, and film rights. Some companies group items of this type under the title of Deferred Charges, meaning expenditures that will provide benefits beyond the current year and will be written off to expense over their useful economic lives. It is also common practice to combine these items under the heading of Other Assets, which is listed at the bottom of the balance sheet.

Research and Development (R&D) Costs

The spending of millions of dollars a year on research and development leading to all kinds of new products is a striking characteristic of modern industry. In the past, some companies treated all research and development costs as an expense in the year incurred; other companies in the same industry recorded these costs as intangible assets to be amortized over future years. This diversity of practice prevented the financial statements of different companies from being comparable.

The lack of uniformity in accounting for R&D was ended when the *CICA Handbook* recommended that all research and development costs be charged to expense when incurred except when the ***development costs*** have met the following specific criteria; (1) the product is clearly defined and the attributable costs can be identified, (2) the product is technically and commercially feasible and adequate resources are available to complete the project, and (3) the future benefits of the product could be considered as reasonably certain and the enterprise intends to sell or use the product.[13] Those development costs that have met ***all*** these criteria should be ***deferred*** to future periods. The amortization of these deferred development costs should be on a systematic and rational basis so as to result in a fair matching of such costs with related benefits.[14] In the United States,

---

13 CICA, *CICA Handbook,* (Toronto), section 3450.20 and 3450.21.

14 Ibid., section 3450.26, 3450.27, and 3450.28.

however, the FASB requires that all research and development costs be charged to expense when incurred.[15]

NATURAL RESOURCES

Accounting for Natural Resources

OBJECTIVE 7 Account for the depletion of natural resources.

Mining properties, oil and gas reserves, and tracts of standing timber are leading examples of natural resources. The distinguishing characteristics of these assets are that they are physically removed from their natural environment and are converted into inventory. Theoretically, a coal mine might be regarded as an underground "inventory" of coal; however, such an "inventory" is certainly not a current asset. In the balance sheet, mining property and other natural resources are classified as property, plant, and equipment. Once the coal is removed from the ground, however, this coal ***does*** represent inventory.

We have explained that plant assets such as buildings and equipment depreciate because of physical deterioration or obsolescence. A mine or an oil reserve does not "depreciate" for these reasons, but it is gradually ***depleted*** as the natural resource is removed from the ground. Once all of the coal has been removed from a coal mine, for example, the mine is "fully depleted" and will be abandoned or sold for its residual value.

To illustrate the depletion of a natural resource, assume that Rainbow Minerals pays $45 million to acquire the Red Valley Mine, which is believed to contain 10 million tonnes of coal. The residual value of the mine after all of the coal is removed is estimated to be $5 million. The depletion that will occur over the life of the mine is the original cost minus the residual value, or $40 million. This depletion will occur at the rate of ***$4 per tonne*** ($40 million ÷ 10 million tonnes) as the coal is removed from the mine. If we assume that 2 million tonnes are mined during the first year of operations, the entry to record the depletion of the mine would be as follows:

Recording depletion

Inventory	*8,000,000*	
Accumulated Depletion: Red Valley Mine		*8,000,000*
To record depletion of the Red Valley Mine for the year; 2,000,000 tonnes mined @ $4 per tonne.		

Once removed from the mine, coal becomes merchandise available for sale. Therefore, the estimated costs to this coal are debited to the Inventory account. As the coal is sold, these costs are transferred from the Inventory account to the Cost of Goods Sold account.

Accumulated Depletion is a ***contra-asset account*** similar to the Accumulated Depreciation account; it represents the portion of the mine that has been used up (depleted) to date. In Rainbow Mineral's balance sheet, the Red Valley Mine now appears as follows:

Property, Plant & Equipment:		
Mining properties: Red Valley Mine	*$45,000,000*	
Less: Accumulated depletion	*8,000,000*	*$37,000,000*

[15] *FASB, Statement No. 2,* "Accounting for Research and Development Costs" (Norwalk, Conn.: 1974), par. 12.

Depreciation of Buildings and Equipment Closely Related to Natural Resources Buildings and equipment installed at a mine or drilling site may be useful only at that particular location. Consequently, such assets should be depreciated over their normal useful lives, or over the life of the natural resource, ***whichever is shorter.*** Often depreciation on such assets is computed using the units-of-output method, thus relating the depreciation expense to the rate at which units of natural resource are removed.

Depreciation, Amortization, and Depletion—A Common Goal

The processes of depreciation, amortization, and depletion discussed in this chapter all have a common goal. That goal is to ***allocate the acquisition cost of a long-lived asset to expense over the years in which the asset contributes to revenue.*** By allocating the acquisition cost of long-lived assets over the years that benefit from the use of these assets, we stress again the importance of the ***matching principle.*** The determination of income requires the matching of revenue with the expenses incurred to produce that revenue.

Impairment of Long-Lived Assets

OBJECTIVE 8 Identify some problems that may arise in accounting for the impairment of long-lived assets.

On occasion, it may become apparent that a company cannot reasonably expect to recover the cost of certain plant assets, either through use or through sale. For example, an oil company may pay a high price for land that it hopes contains large deposits of oil. If the company finds no oil, however, it may become apparent that the land is worth far less than its cost.

If the cost of an asset cannot be recovered through future use or sale, the asset should be ***written down*** to its net recoverable value.[16] The offsetting debit is to a loss account. Such a write-down is not reversable if the net recoverable amount increases in subsequent periods.

This idea is a simple one—an asset should not be carried in the accounting records at an amount that clearly exceeds its economic worth. In practice, however, this concept may be very difficult to apply. What criteria should be used in determining when an asset has become "impaired"? Is the impairment likely to be permanent, or only temporary? How should the "net recoverable value" of such an asset be estimated? There are no definitive answers to these questions. Therefore, accounting for the possible impairment of long-lived assets is an area in which management, professional accountants, and auditors must exercise professional judgment on a case-by-case basis.

In summary, the possible impairment of long-lived assets may involve such uncertainty that the amount of the company's loss cannot be determined with any objectivity. Regardless of whether or not potentially impaired assets are written down, the circumstances should be fully disclosed in notes accompanying the financial statements.

The possible impairment of long-lived assets is one type of ***contingent loss.*** Contingent losses are discussed in the following chapter.

---

16 CICA, *CICA Handbook* (Toronto), section 3060.42.

CHAPTER REVIEW

KEY TERMS INTRODUCED OR EMPHASIZED IN CHAPTER 10

Accelerated depreciation Methods of depreciation that call for recognition of relatively large amounts of depreciation in the early years of an asset's useful life and relatively small amounts in the later years.

Amortization The systematic write-off to expense of the cost of an intangible asset over the periods of its economic usefulness.

Book value The cost of a plant asset minus the total recorded depreciation, as shown by the Accumulated Depreciation account. The remaining undepreciated cost is also known as ***carrying value.***

Capital assets Capital assets consist of property, plant, and equipment, intangible properties, and natural resources that are held for use in the operation of the business and not intended for sale to customers.

Capital budgeting The process of planning and evaluating proposals for making capital expenditures.

Capital expenditure A cost incurred to acquire a long-lived asset. An expenditure that will benefit several accounting periods.

Deferred charge An expenditure expected to yield benefits for several accounting periods and therefore capitalized and written off during the periods benefited.

Depletion Allocating the cost of a natural resource to the units removed as the resource is mined, pumped, cut, or otherwise consumed.

Depreciation The systematic allocation of the cost of an asset to expense over the years of its estimated useful life.

Fixed-percentage-of-declining-balance depreciation An accelerated method of depreciation in which the rate may be a multiple of the straight-line rate, which is applied each year to the ***undepreciated cost*** of the asset. Most commonly used is double the straight-line rate.

Goodwill The present value of expected future earnings of a business in excess of the earnings normally realized in the industry. Recorded when a business entity is purchased at a price in excess of the fair value of its net identifiable assets (excluding goodwill) less liabilities.

Half-year convention The practice of taking six months' depreciation in the year of acquisition and the year of disposition, rather than computing depreciation for partial periods to the nearest month. The half-year convention generally is ***not*** used for assets that are purchased very infrequently during the year, e.g., buildings.

Impairment (of an asset) A change in economic conditions that reduces the economic usefulness of an asset. May necessitate writing down the carrying value of the asset.

Intangible assets Those assets that are used in the operation of a business but have no physical substance and are noncurrent.

Natural resources Mines, oil fields, standing timber, and similar assets that are physically consumed and converted into inventory.

Net identifiable assets Total of all assets ***except goodwill*** minus liabilities.

Present value The amount that a knowledgeable investor would pay today for the right to receive future cash flows. The present value is always less than the sum of the future cash flows because the investor requires a return on the investment.

Replacement cost The estimated cost of replacing an asset at the current balance sheet date.

Residual (salvage) value The portion of an asset's cost expected to be recovered through sale or trade-in of the asset at the end of its useful life.

Revenue expenditure Any expenditure that will benefit only the current accounting period.

Straight-line depreciation A method of depreciation that allocates the cost of an asset (minus any residual value) equally to each year of its useful life.

Sum-of-the-years'-digits depreciation An accelerated method of depreciation. The depreciable cost is multiplied each year by a fraction of which the numerator is the remaining years of useful life (as of the beginning of the current year) and the denominator is the sum of the years of useful life.

Units-of-output depreciation A depreciation method in which cost (minus residual value) is divided by the estimated units of lifetime output. The unit depreciation cost is multiplied by the actual units of output each year to compute the annual depreciation expense.

DEMONSTRATION PROBLEM FOR YOUR REVIEW

On April 1, 1995, Argo Industries purchased new equipment at a cost of $325,000. Useful life of this equipment was estimated at 5 years, with a residual value of $25,000.

INSTRUCTIONS Compute the annual depreciation expense for each year until this equipment becomes fully depreciated under each depreciation method listed below. (Because you will record depreciation for only a fraction of a year in 1995, depreciation will extend through 2000 in all methods.) Show supporting computations.

- **a** Straight-line, with depreciation for fractional years rounded to the nearest whole month.
- **b** Double-declining-balance, with the half-year convention.
- **c** Sum-of-the-years'-digits, with the half-year convention.

SOLUTION TO DEMONSTRATION PROBLEM

	Method of Depreciation		
Year	a Straight-Line	b Double-Declining-Balance	c Sum-of-the-Years'-Digits
1995	$ 45,000	$ 65,000	$ 50,000
1996	60,000	104,000	90,000
1997	60,000	62,400	70,000
1998	60,000	37,440	50,000
1999	60,000	22,464	30,000
2000	15,000	8,696	10,000
Totals	$300,000	$300,000	$300,000

Supporting computations:

a

1995: ($325,000 − $25,000) × $\frac{1}{5}$ × $\frac{9}{12}$ = $45,000
1996–1999: $300,000 × $\frac{1}{5}$ = $60,000
2000: $300,000 × $\frac{1}{5}$ × $\frac{3}{12}$ = $15,000

b

	Undepreciated Cost		Rate		Depreciation Expense
1995:	$325,000	×	40% × $\frac{1}{2}$	=	$ 65,000
1996:	260,000	×	40%	=	104,000
1997:	156,000	×	40%	=	62,400
1998:	93,600	×	40%	=	37,440
1999:	56,160	×	40%	=	22,464
2000:	33,696	−	$25,000	=	8,696

c

1995:	$300,000 × $\frac{5}{15}$ × $\frac{1}{2}$ =		$50,000
1996:	$300,000 × $\frac{5}{15}$ × $\frac{1}{2}$ =	$50,000	
	+300,000 × $\frac{4}{15}$ × $\frac{1}{2}$ =	40,000	$90,000
1997:	$300,000 × $\frac{4}{15}$ × $\frac{1}{2}$ =	$40,000	
	+300,000 × $\frac{3}{15}$ × $\frac{1}{2}$ =	30,000	$70,000
1998:	$300,000 × $\frac{3}{15}$ × $\frac{1}{2}$ =	$30,000	
	+300,000 × $\frac{2}{15}$ × $\frac{1}{2}$ =	20,000	$50,000
1999:	$300,000 × $\frac{2}{15}$ × $\frac{1}{2}$ =	$20,000	
	+300,000 × $\frac{1}{15}$ × $\frac{1}{2}$ =	10,000	$30,000
2000:	$300,000 × $\frac{1}{15}$ × $\frac{1}{2}$ =		$10,000

ASSIGNMENT MATERIAL

DISCUSSION QUESTIONS

1 Which of the following characteristics would prevent an item from being included in the classification of plant and equipment? (a) Tangible asset used in the operation, (b) limited life, (c) unlimited life, (d) held for sale in the regular course of business, (e) not capable of rendering benefits to the business in the future.

2 The following expenditures were incurred in connection with a large new machine acquired by a metals manufacturing company. Identify those that should be included in the cost of the asset. (a) Freight charges, (b) sales tax on the machine, (c) payment to a passing motorist whose car was damaged by the equipment used in unloading the machine, (d) wages of employees for time spent in installing and testing the machine before it was placed in service, (e) wages of employees assigned to lubrication and minor adjustments of machine one year after it was placed in service.

3 What is the distinction between a ***capital expenditure*** and a ***revenue expenditure?***

4 If a capital expenditure is erroneously treated as a revenue expenditure, will the net income of the current year be overstated or understated? Will this error have any effect upon the net income reported in future years? Explain.

5 Which of the following statements best describes the nature of depreciation?

a Regular reduction of asset value to correspond to the decline in market value as the asset ages.

b A process of correlating the book value of an asset with its gradual decline in physical efficiency.

c Allocation of cost in a manner that will ensure that plant and equipment items are not carried on the balance sheet at amounts in excess of net recoverable value.

d Allocation of the cost of a plant asset to the periods in which services are received from the asset.

6 Should depreciation continue to be recorded on a building when ample evidence exists that the current market value is greater than original cost and that the rising trend of market values is continuing? Explain.

7 Criticize the following quotation:
"We shall have no difficulty in paying for new plant assets needed during the coming year because our estimated outlays for new equipment amount to only $80,000, and we have more than twice that amount in our accumulated depreciation account at present."

8 A factory machine acquired at a cost of $94,200 was to be depreciated by the sum-of-the-years'-digits method over an estimated life of 8 years. Residual salvage value was estimated to be $15,000. State the amount of depreciation during the ***first*** year and during the ***eighth*** year.

9 Explain two approaches to computing depreciation for a fractional period in the year in which an asset is purchased. (Neither of your approaches should require the computation of depreciation to the nearest day or week.)

10 a Does the accounting principle of consistency require a company to use the same method of depreciation for all of its plant assets?

b Is it acceptable for a corporation to use different depreciation methods in its financial statements and its income tax returns?

11 After 4 years of using a machine acquired at a cost of $15,000, Office Construction Company determined that the original estimated life of 10 years had been too short and that a total useful life of 12 years was a more reasonable estimate. Explain briefly the method that should be used to revise the depreciation program, assuming that straight-line depreciation has been used. Assume that the revision is made after recording depreciation and closing the accounts at the end of four years of use of the machine.

12 Explain what is meant by the following quotation: "In periods of rising prices companies do not recognize adequate depreciation expense, and reported corporate net income is overstated in terms of current market values."

13 Newton Products purchased for $2 million a franchise making it the exclusive distributor of Gold Creek Beer in three Atlantic provinces. This franchise has an unlimited legal life and may be sold by Newton Products to any buyer who meets with Gold Creek Beer's approval. The accountant at Newton Products believes that this franchise is a permanent asset, which should appear in the company's balance sheet indefinitely at $2 million, unless it is sold. Is this treatment in conformity with generally accepted accounting principles, as prescribed by the CICA?

14 Define ***intangible assets.*** Would an account receivable arising from a sale of merchandise qualify as an intangible asset under your definition?

15 Over what period of time should the cost of various types of intangible assets be amortized by regular charges against revenue? (Your answer should be in the form of a principle or guideline rather than a specific number of years.) What method of amortization is generally used?

16 Several years ago March Metals purchased for $120,000 a well-known trademark for padlocks and other security products. After using the trademark for three years, March Metals discontinued it altogether when the company withdrew from the lock business and concentrated on the manufacture of aircraft parts. Amortization of the trademark at the rate of $3,000 a year is being continued on the basis of a 40-year life, which the owner of March Metals says is required by accounting standards. Do you agree? Explain.

17 Under what circumstances should ***goodwill*** be recorded in the accounts?

18 In reviewing the financial statements of Digital Products Company with a view to investing in the company's stock, you notice that net tangible assets total $1 million, that goodwill is listed at $400,000, and that average earnings for the past five years have been $50,000 a year. How would these relationships influence your thinking about the company?

19 Mineral King recognizes $20 depletion for each tonne of ore mined. During the current year the company mined 600,000 tonnes but sold only 500,000 tonnes, as it was attempting to build up inventories in anticipation of a possible strike by employees. How much depletion should be deducted from revenue of the current year?

20 Identify two problems that may arise in attempting to account for the possible impairment of long-lived assets.

MULTIPLE CHOICE QUESTIONS

1 In which of the following situations should the named company ***not*** record any depreciation expense on the asset described?

- a Commuter Airline is required by law to maintain its aircraft in "as good as new" condition.
- b Metro Advertising owns an office building that has been increasing in value each year since it was purchased.
- c Computer Sales Company has in inventory a new type of computer designed "never to become obsolete."
- d None of the above answers is correct—in each case, the named company should record depreciation on the asset described.

2 Which of the following statements is (are) correct?

- a Accumulated depreciation represents a fund being accumulated for the replacement of plant assets.
- b The cost of a machine includes the cost of repairing damage to the machine during the installation process.
- c A company may use different depreciation methods in its financial statements.
- d The use of an accelerated depreciation method causes an asset to wear out more quickly than does use of the straight-line method.

3 On April 1, 1995, Sanders Construction paid $10,000 for equipment with an estimated useful life of 10 years and a residual value of $2,000. The company uses the double-declining-balance method of depreciation and applies the half-

year convention to fractional periods. In ***1996,*** the amount of depreciation expense to be recognized on this equipment is:

a $1,600 b $1,440 c $1,280 d Some other amount

4 Delta Company sold a plant asset that originally had cost $50,000 for $22,000 cash. If Delta correctly reports a $5,000 gain on this sale, the ***accumulated depreciation*** on the asset at the date of sale must have been:

a $33,000 b $28,000 c $23,000 d Some other amount

5 In which of the following situations would Burton Industries include goodwill in its balance sheet?

a The fair market value of Burton's net identifiable assets amounts to $2,000,000. Normal earnings for this industry is 15% of net identifiable assets. Burton's net income for the past five years has averaged $390,000.

b Burton spent $800,000 during the current year for research and development for a new product that promises to generate substantial revenue for at least 10 years.

c Burton acquired Baxter Electronics at a price in excess of the fair market value of Baxter's net identifiable assets.

d A buyer wishing to purchase Burton's entire operation has offered a price in excess of the fair market value of Burton's net identifiable assets.

EXERCISES

EXERCISE 10-1
Accounting Terminology

Listed below are nine technical accounting terms introduced or emphasized in this chapter:

Intangible asset	*Revenue expenditure*	*Amortization*
Book value	*Depletion*	*Double declining-balance*
Goodwill	*Impairment*	*Accelerated depreciation methods*

Each of the following statements may (or may not) describe one of these technical terms. For each statement, indicate the accounting term described, or answer "None" if the statement does not correctly describe any of the terms.

a A type of asset usually found only in the financial statements of a company that has purchased another going business in its entirety.

b Noncurrent assets lacking in physical substance.

c A depreciation method that often consists of doubling the straight-line rate and applying this doubled rate to the undepreciated cost of the asset.

d A depreciation method designed to allocate more depreciation in the later years than in the early years.

e The cost of a plant asset minus the total recorded depreciation on the asset.

f A material expenditure that will benefit several accounting periods.

g The systematic allocation to expense of the cost of an intangible asset.

h A sudden reduction in the usefulness of an asset that may necessitate writing down the carrying value in the accounting records.

EXERCISE 10-2
Identifying Costs to Be Capitalized

New machinery was purchased by HydroTech at a list price of $40,000, with a cash discount of $800. Payment of the invoice was made within the discount period. Sales tax was $2,352. HydroTech also paid transportation charges of $610 on the new machinery as well as $760 for installing the machinery in the appropriate locations. During the unloading and installation work, some of the machines fell from a forklift and were damaged. Repair of the damaged parts cost $2,170. After the machinery had been in use for 3 months, it was thoroughly cleaned and lubricated at a cost of $260. Prepare a list of the items that should be capitalized by a debit to the Machinery account and state the total cost of the new machinery.

EXERCISE 10-3
Distinguishing Capital Expenditures from Revenue Expenditures

Identify the following expenditures as capital expenditures or revenue expenditures:

a Immediately after acquiring a new delivery truck at a cost of $25,500, paid $890 to have the name of the store and other advertising material painted on the truck.

b Painted delivery truck at a cost of $250 after 2 years of use.

c Purchased new battery at a cost of $99 for 2-year-old delivery truck.

d Installed an escalator at a cost of $18,500 in a three-story building that had previously been used for some years without elevators or escalators.

e Purchased a pencil sharpener at a cost of $8.50.

f Original life of the delivery truck had been estimated at 4 years and straight-line depreciation of 25% yearly had been recognized. After 3 years' use, however, it was decided to recondition the truck thoroughly, including a new engine and transmission, at a cost of $4,000. By making this expenditure it was believed that the useful life of the truck would be extended from the original estimate of 4 years to a total of 6 years.

EXERCISE 10-4
Units-of-Output Method

During the current year, Airport Auto Rentals purchased 60 new automobiles at a cost of $13,000 per car. The cars will be sold to a wholesaler at an estimated $4,000 each as soon as they have been driven 50,000 kilometres. Airport Auto Rentals computes depreciation expense on its automobiles by the units-of-output method, based upon kilometres used.

INSTRUCTIONS

a Compute the amount of depreciation to be recognized for each kilometre that a rental automobile is driven.

b Assuming that the 60 rental cars are driven a total of 1,650,000 kilometres during the current year, compute the total amount of depreciation expense that Airport Auto Rentals should recognize on this fleet of cars for the year.

EXERCISE 10-5
Double-Declining-Balance Method

Machinery with an estimated useful life of 5 years was acquired by VPI Industries at a cost of $55,000 at the beginning of the year. The estimated residual value of the machinery is $6,000. Compute the annual depreciation on this machinery for each of the 5 years using the double-declining-balance method.

EXERCISE 10-6
Sum-of-the-Years'-Digits Method

On January 2, Bartel Company acquired a machine at a cost of $14,000. The machine is expected to have a useful life of 5 years with a residual value of $2,000. You are to compute the annual depreciation on the machine in each of the 5 years of its useful life using the sum-of-the-years'-digits method. (One full year's depreciation will be taken each year.)

EXERCISE 10-7
Three Depreciation Methods

Delta Company acquired new equipment with an estimated useful life of 5 years. Cost of the equipment was $50,000 and the residual value was estimated to be $5,000. Compute the annual depreciation expense for each of the first 2 years under each of the following methods of depreciation. (Compute on full year's depreciation in each year.)

a Straight-line

b Sum-of-the-years'-digits

c Double-declining-balance

EXERCISE 10-8
Depreciation for Fractional Years

On November 2, Glass Recycling Company purchased special-purpose equipment at a cost of $600,000. Useful life of the equipment was estimated to be 5 years and the residual value $90,000. Compute the depreciation expense to be recognized in each calendar year during the life of the equipment under each of the following methods:

a Straight-line (round computations for a partial year to the nearest full month).

b Straight-line (use the half-year convention).

EXERCISE 10-9
Revision of Depreciation Rates

Grain Products uses straight-line depreciation on all its depreciable assets. The accounts are adjusted and closed at the end of each calendar year. On January 4, 1994, the corporation purchased machinery for cash at a cost of $80,000. Useful life was estimated to be 10 years and residual value $12,000. Depreciation for partial years is recorded to the nearest full month.

In 1996, after almost 3 years of experience with the equipment, management decided that the estimated life of the equipment should be revised from 10 years to 6 years. No change was made in the estimate of residual value. The revised estimate of useful life was decided upon ***prior*** to recording depreciation for the period ended December 31, 1996.

INSTRUCTIONS

Prepare journal entries in chronological order for the above events, beginning with the purchase of the machinery on January 4, 1994. Show separately the depreciation for 1994, 1995, and 1996.

EXERCISE 10-10
Trade-in and Cost Basis

Ogilvie Construction traded in a used crane on a similar new one. The original cost of the old crane was $60,000 and the accumulated depreciation was $48,000. The new crane carried a list price of $75,000 and the trade-in allowance was $18,000. What amount of cash must Ogilvie pay? Compute the indicated gain or loss on disposal of the old crane.

EXERCISE 10-11
Disposal of Equipment by Sale, Trade-in, or as Scrap

A tractor that cost $30,000 had an estimated useful life of 5 years and an estimated residual value of $10,000. Straight-line depreciation was used. Give the entry (in general journal form) required by each of the following alternative assumptions:

a The tractor was sold for cash of $19,500 after 2 years' use.

b The tractor was traded in after 3 years on another tractor with a fair market value of $37,000. Trade-in allowance was $21,000.

c The tractor was scrapped after 5 years' use. Since scrap dealers were unwilling to pay anything for the tractor, it was given to a scrap dealer for his services in removing it.

EXERCISE 10-12
Estimating Goodwill

During the past several years the annual net income of Goldtone Appliance Company has averaged $540,000. At the present time the company is being offered for sale. Its accounting records show the book value of net assets (total assets minus all liabilities) to be $2,800,000. The fair market value of Goldtone's net identifiable assets, however, is $3,000,000.

An investor negotiating to buy the company offers to pay an amount equal to the fair market value for the net identifiable assets and to assume all liabilities. In addition, the investor is willing to pay for goodwill an amount equal to net earnings in excess of 15% on the fair market value of net identifiable assets, capitalized at a rate of 25%.

On the basis of this agreement, what price should the investor offer for Goldtone Appliance?

EXERCISE 10-13
Depletion: Recording and Reporting

King Mining Corporation purchased the Lost Creek Mine for $15,000,000 cash. The mine was estimated to contain 2 million tonnes of ore and to have a residual value of $3,000,000.

During the first year of mining operations at the Lost Creek Mine, 400,000 tonnes of ore were mined, of which 300,000 tonnes were sold.

INSTRUCTIONS

a Prepare a journal entry to record depletion of the Lost Creek Mine during the year.

b Show how the mine and the accumulated depletion would appear in King Mining company's balance sheet after the first year of operations.

c Will the entire amount of depletion computed in part **a** be deducted from revenue in determining the income for the year? Explain.

EXERCISE 10-14
Evaluation of Disclosures in Annual Reports

A recent annual report of a large public company includes the following note:

> ***Depreciation:*** For financial reporting purposes, depreciation is provided on the straight-line method over the estimated useful lives of the assets. Accelerated depreciation methods are used for income tax purposes.

INSTRUCTIONS

a Is the company violating the accounting principle of consistency by using different depreciation methods in its financial statements and in its income tax returns? Explain.

b Why do you think that the company uses accelerated depreciation methods in its income tax returns?

c Would the use of accelerated depreciation methods in the financial statements be more "conservative," or less "conservative," than the practice of using the straight-line method? Explain.

PROBLEMS

Group A

PROBLEM 10A-1
Determining the Cost of Plant Assets

Early this summer, Crystal Car Wash purchased new "brushless" car washing equipment for all 10 of its car washes. The following information refers to the purchase and installation of this equipment.

1 The list price of the brushless equipment was $7,200 for the equipment needed at each car wash. Because Crystal Car Wash purchased 10 sets of equipment at one time, it was given a special "package price" of $63,000 for all of the equipment. Crystal paid $23,000 of this amount in cash (no cash discount was allowed) and issued a 90-day, 8% note payable for the remaining $40,000. Crystal paid this note promptly at its maturity date, along with $800 in accrued interest charges.

2 In addition to the amounts described above, Crystal paid sales taxes of $3,780 at the date of purchase.

3 Freight charges for delivery of the equipment totalled $3,320.

4 Crystal paid a contractor $2,250 per location to install the equipment at six of Crystal's car washes. Management was able to find a less expensive contractor who installed the equipment in the remaining four car washes at a cost of $1,900 per location.

5 During installation, one of the new machines was accidentally damaged by an employee of Crystal Car Wash. The cost to repair this damage, $914, was paid by Crystal.

6 As soon as the machines were installed, Crystal Car Wash paid $5,700 for a series of radio commercials advertising the fact that it now uses brushless equipment in all of its car washes.

INSTRUCTIONS

a In one sentence, make a general statement summarizing the nature of the expenditures properly included in the cost of plant and equipment.

b For each of the six numbered paragraphs, indicate which items should be included by Crystal Car Wash in the cost debited to the Equipment account. Also briefly indicate the accounting treatment that should be accorded to any items that you ***do not*** regard as part of the cost of the equipment.

c Prepare a list of the expenditures that should be included in the cost of the equipment. (Determine the total cost of the equipment at all 10 locations; do not attempt to separate costs by location.)

d Prepare a journal entry at the end of the current year to record depreciation on this equipment. Crystal depreciates this equipment by the straight-line method over an estimated useful life of 10 years, assumes zero salvage value, and applies the half-year convention.

PROBLEM 10A-2
Basic Depreciation Methods —No Fractional Years

Integrated Waste Management purchased new equipment on January 3, 1995, at a cost of $240,000. The equipment had an estimated useful life of 8 years, with an estimated residual value of $24,000.

INSTRUCTIONS

Compute the annual depreciation expense throughout the 8-year life of this equipment under the three depreciation methods listed below. Company policy is to round depreciation for fractional periods to the nearest month.

a Straight-line.

b Sum-of-the-years'-digits.

c Double-declining-balance.

PROBLEM 10A-3
Alternative Depreciation Methods— Including Fractional Periods

On March 29, 1995, Global Manufacturing purchased new equipment with a cost of $100,000, an estimated useful life of 5 years, and an estimated residual value of $10,000.

INSTRUCTIONS

a Compute the annual depreciation expense for each year until this equipment becomes fully depreciated under each of the depreciation methods listed below. Show supporting computations.

  1 Straight-line, with depreciation for fractional years rounded to the nearest whole month.

  2 Double-declining-balance, with the half-year convention.

  3 Sum-of-the-years'-digits, with the half-year convention.

b Global has two conflicting objectives. Management wants to report the highest possible earnings to shareholders in the near future, yet also wants to minimize the taxable income. Indicate the depreciation method that the company will probably use in (1) its financial statements and (2) its income tax return. Explain the reasons for your answers.

PROBLEM 10A-4
Depreciation: A Comprehensive Problem

In the first few years of business, Midwest Agricultural Cooperative acquired several expensive pieces of machinery. Because there was no set policy on depreciation methods, the various machines are being depreciated according to a variety of methods. Information concerning four of the machines follows:

Machine	Date Acquired	Cost	Estimated Useful Life, Years	Estimated Residual Value	Method of Depreciation
A	Aug. 25, 1994	$308,000	6	10%	Straight-line
B	Apr. 3, 1994	160,000	8	None	Double-declining-balance
C	Jan. 8, 1995	250,000	6	$40,000	Sum-of-the-years'-digits
D	Sept. 5, 1996	204,000	10	$25,000	Double-declining-balance

INSTRUCTIONS

a Compute the amount of accumulated depreciation, if any, on each machine at December 31, 1995. In the year of acquisition, assume that depreciation was computed to the nearest month.

b Prepare a depreciation schedule for use in the computation of the depreciation expense. Use the following column headings:

Machine	Method of Depre-ciation	Date of Acquisi-tion	Cost	Estimated Residual Value	Amount to Be Depre-ciated	Useful Life, Years	Accu-mulated Depre-ciation, Dec. 31, 1995	Depre-ciation Expense, 1996

c Prepare a journal entry to record depreciation expense for 1996 in the general ledger accounts.

PROBLEM 10A-5
Disposal of Plant Assets

During 19__, Cabrillo Moving and Storage disposed of plant assets in the following transactions:

Mar. 12 Cabrillo traded in an old moving van for a new one. The old moving van had cost $27,000 and accumulated depreciation amounted to $19,000. The price of the new moving van was $38,000. Cabrillo received a $12,000 trade-in allowance for the old moving van and paid the $26,000 balance in cash. (Moving vans are included in the Vehicles account.)

May 23 Cabrillo sold land and an unused storage facility to Self-Store, Inc., for $850,000, receiving $300,000 in cash and a 5-year, 10% note receivable for $550,000. Cabrillo's accounting records showed the following amounts: Land, $120,000; Building, $570,000; Accumulated Depreciation: Building (as of May 23), $230,000.

Sept. 20 Cabrillo traded in its old computer system as part of the purchase of a new system. The old computer had cost $126,000 and, as of September 20, accumulated depreciation amounted to $98,000. The new computer had a list price of $95,000. Cabrillo was granted a $10,000 trade-in allowance for the old computer system, paid $35,000 in cash, and issued a $50,000, 2-year, 12% note payable to Business Systems for the balance. (Computers are included in the Office Equipment account.)

Nov. 8 Office equipment costing $11,000 was given to a scrap dealer. No proceeds were received from the scrap dealer. At the date of disposal, accumulated depreciation on the office equipment amounted to $8,900.

INSTRUCTIONS

Prepare journal entries to record each of these transactions. Assume that depreciation expense on each asset already has been recorded up to the date of disposal. Thus, you need not update the accumulated depreciation figures stated in the problem.

PROBLEM 10A-6
Acquisition, Disposal, and Trade-in of Plant Asset; Depreciation and Revision of Depreciation

Malden Tool & Die purchased a precision machine on March 16, 1994 for $225,000 cash. The machine was installed in the factory for $5,000 cash. At this date, management considered it appropriate to depreciate this machine at an annual rate of 20%, based on the declining-balance method. This machine was to be used to make automobile parts and estimated to have a residual value of $30,000.

To accommodate added office staff, Malden purchased office equipment for $15,000 cash on June 7, 1995. The office equipment was estimated to have a useful life of 7 years and a residual value of $1,000. The straight-line method of depreciation was to be used for the equipment.

Late in 1996, Malden's management decided that the machine's annual depreciation rate should be changed from 20% to 40% because of heavy usage. Also, the estimated residual value should be revised from $30,000 to $10,000.

On June 15, 1997, the office equipment was traded-in for the more sophisticated office equipment. Malden received a trade-in allowance of $9,500 for the old office equipment and paid $10,000.

On December 8, 1997, the pipes in the factory froze and broke, flooding the area where the precision machine was located. Because of the heavy damage, the machine was beyond repair. As a result, a cash payment of $70,000 was received from the insurance company that took possession of the machine.

Malden adjusts and closes its books at the end of each calendar year and uses the half-year convention for depreciation in the year of acquisition and disposal of its machines and equipment.

INSTRUCTIONS

Based on the above information, prepare the necessary journal entries from March 16, 1994 to December 8, 1997.

PROBLEM 10A-7
Intangible Assets or Operating Expense: GAAP

During the current year Magnum Industries incurred the following expenditures that should be recorded either as operating expenses of the current year or as intangible assets.

a Expenditure to acquire a franchise as one of four Canadian distributors of an Italian automobile. The franchise expires in 49 years.

b Incurred research and development costs in an effort to produce a 200,000-kilometre tire. At year-end, the project looks promising. If successful, the product will be patented for 20 years, but it should contribute to revenue for at least 25 years.

c Purchased a patent on a fuel-saving device. The patent has a remaining legal life of 13 years, but Magnum Industries expects to produce and sell the device for a period of 5 years.

d Expenditures to advertise a new product. The product is patented and is expected to contribute to company revenue for the entire 20-year life of the patent.

e Expenditures for management training programs. The average manager stays with the company for a period of 9½ years but attends a management training program every 2 years.

INSTRUCTIONS

Explain whether each of the above expenditures should be recorded as an operating expense of the current year or as an intangible asset. If you view the expenditure as creating an intangible asset, indicate the number of years over which the asset should be amortized. Explain your reasoning.

PROBLEM 10A-8
Depreciation and Disposal

On October 12, 1994, Speedy Print purchased a colour photocopy machine at a cost of $20,000. Management estimated that the machine would have a useful life of 8 years and a residual value of $4,000. Speedy Print uses straight-line depreciation in its financial statements, rounding depreciation for partial periods to the nearest full month.

Speedy Print found that not many of its customers used the colour copier. Therefore, on March 19, 1996, Speedy Print sold this machine to Commercial Graphics Company for $10,000 cash.

INSTRUCTIONS

a Prepare a schedule showing the annual amounts of depreciation expense that management originally expects to recognize over the 8-year life of this asset.

b Compute (1) the book value of the copier at the date of disposal and (2) the gain or loss on the sale.

c Prepare journal entries to record in Speedy Print's accounting records (1) depreciation on the copier for 1996 and (2) the sale of the colour copier. (Prepare both entries in general journal form.)

Group B

PROBLEM 10B-1
Determining Cost of Plant Assets

Brenner Graphics, a newly organized corporation, purchased typesetting equipment having a list price of $204,000 from a manufacturer, plus sales tax of $13,994. Brenner Graphics paid the invoice within the discount period and received a $4,080 discount. Other payments relating to the acquisition of the equipment were a freight bill of $2,596 and a labour cost for installing the equipment of $4,210. During the installation process, an accident caused damage to the equipment, which was repaired at a cost of $5,900. As soon as the equipment was in place, the company obtained insurance on it for a premium of $1,800. All the items described above were charged to the Typesetting Equipment account. No entry for depreciation has yet been made and the accounts have not yet been closed.

INSTRUCTIONS

a Prepare a list of the expenditures that should have been capitalized by debiting the Typesetting Equipment. Show the correct total cost for this asset.

b Prepare one compound journal entry to ***correct*** the error or errors by the company in recording these transactions.

c Prepare a journal entry at the end of the current year to record depreciation on this equipment. Brenner Graphics depreciates typesetting equipment by the straight-line method over an estimated useful life of 10 years, assumes no residual value, and applies the half-year convention.

d In one sentence state the accounting principle or concept that indicates the nature of expenditures properly included in the cost of equipment. (Do not list individual types of expenditure.)

PROBLEM 10B-2
Basic Depreciation Methods—No Fractional Years

On January 2, 1996, Atlantic Iron Works acquired new machinery at a cost of $270,000. The useful life of the machinery was estimated at 5 years, with a residual value of $24,000.

INSTRUCTIONS

Compute the annual depreciation expense throughout the 5-year life of this equipment under each of the following depreciation methods. As the equipment was acquired early in January, one full year's depreciation will be taken in each year.

a Straight-line.

b Sum-of-the-years'-digits.

c Double-declining-balance.

PROBLEM 10B-3
Alternative Depreciation Methods—Including Fractional Periods

Micro Circuit Company purchased new equipment on September 4, 1995, at a cost of $80,000. Useful life of this equipment was estimated at 4 years, with an estimated residual value of $5,000.

INSTRUCTIONS

Compute the annual depreciation expense for each year until this equipment becomes fully depreciated under each of the depreciation methods listed below. Show supporting computations.

a Straight-line, with depreciation for fractional years rounded to the nearest whole month.

b Sum-of-the-years'-digits, with the half-year convention.

c Double-declining-balance, with the half-year convention.

PROBLEM 10B-4
Depreciation: A Comprehensive Problem

During the last few years, Sunhill Corporation has acquired four machines but has given little consideration to depreciation policies. At the time of acquisition of each machine, a different accountant was employed; consequently, various methods of depreciation have been adopted for the several machines. For machines A and D, assume that the depreciation rate was double the rate under the straight-line method. Information concerning the four machines appears below.

Machine	*Date Acquired*	*Cost*	*Estimated Useful Life, Years*	*Estimated Residual Value*	*Method of Depreciation*
A	Jan. 1, 1995	$150,000	5	None	Declining-balance
B	June 30, 1995	360,000	8	10%	Straight-line
C	Jan. 1, 1996	221,600	10	$23,600	Sum-of-the-years'-digits
D	May 27, 1997	237,000	10	None	Declining-balance

INSTRUCTIONS

a Compute the amount of accumulated depreciation, if any, on each machine at December 31, 1996. In the year of acquisition, assume that depreciation was computed to the nearest month.

b Prepare a depreciation schedule for use in the computation of the depreciation expense. Use the following column headings:

Machine	*Method of Depreciation*	*Date of Acquisition*	*Cost*	*Estimated Residual Value*	*Amount to Be Depreciated*	*Useful Life, Years*	*Accumulated Depreciation, Dec. 31, 1996*	*Depreciation Expense, 1997*

c Prepare a journal entry to record the total depreciation expense relating to these machines for 1997 in Sunhill's general ledger accounts.

PROBLEM 10B-5
Disposal of Plant Assets

During 19__, Crown Developers disposed of plant assets in the following transactions:

Feb. 10 Office equipment costing $14,000 was given to a scrap dealer. No proceeds were received from the scrap dealer. At the date of disposal, accumulated depreciation on the office equipment amounted to $11,900.

Apr. 1 Crown sold land and a building to Villa Associates for $630,000, receiving $200,000 in cash and a 5-year, 10% note receivable for $430,000. Crown's accounting records showed the following amounts: Land, $120,000; Building, $350,000; Accumulated Depreciation: Building (as of April 1), $115,000.

Aug. 15 Crown traded in an old truck for a new one. The old truck had cost $11,000, and accumulated depreciation amounted to $7,000. The price of the new truck was $17,000; Crown received a $5,000 trade-in allowance for the old truck and paid the $12,000 balance in cash. (Trucks are included in the Vehicles account.)

Oct. 1 Crown traded in its old computer system as part of the purchase of a new system. The old computer had cost $150,000 and, as of October 1, accumulated depreciation amounted to $110,000. The new computer had a list price of $90,000. Crown was granted a $10,000 trade-in allowance for the old computer system, paid $30,000 in cash, and issued a $50,000, 2-year, 9% note payable to Action Computers for the balance. (Computers are included in the Office Equipment account.)

INSTRUCTIONS Prepare journal entries to record each of these transactions. Assume that depreciation expense on each asset already has been recorded up to the date of disposal. Thus, you need not update the accumulated depreciation figures stated in the problem.

PROBLEM 10B-6 Acquisition and Disposal of Plant Asset; Depreciation and Revision of Depreciation

Granville Company makes "Wonder Toys" for young adults. It has a December 31 year-end. On January 3, 1995, it purchased high-tech toy making equipment for cash at a cost of $120,000. It was estimated that the equipment would produce 100,000 units during its 5-year useful life, after which it would be sold for $20,000.

In order to get operating information on a more timely basis, an advanced data processing system was purchased on March 8, 1996 for $38,000 cash. This system was estimated to have a useful life of 6 years and a residual value of $2,000.

Granville decided that the equipment should be depreciated by the units-of-output method and the data processing system by the straight-line method.

On December 31, 1997, Granville was disappointed that, based on the production of the equipment (20,000 units for 1995, 18,000 units for 1996, and 15,000 units for 1997), the total production for the toy making equipment during its five-year useful life would be 12,000 units less than the original estimate. The residual value also would be reduced by $10,000.

The early part of 1998 was also disappointing for Granville. Since the production for the equipment up to March 30 was only 2,000 units, the equipment was sold for $30,000 cash on that day. In addition, Granville finally decided to get a more sophisticated system even though the existing data processing system was working well and still was very popular. So, on April 18, the system was sold for $26,900 on account, payable in 30 days.

INSTRUCTIONS Based on the above information, prepare the necessary journal entries for the period of January 3, 1995 to April 18, 1998. Depreciation in the year of acquisition and in the year of disposal should be rounded to the nearest full month.

PROBLEM 10B-7 Intangible Assets or Operating Expenses: GAAP

During the current year, Home Sales Corporation incurred the following expenditures that should be recorded either as operating expenses of the current year or as intangible assets:

- **a** Expenditures for the training of new employees. The average employee remains with the company for 7 years, but is retrained for a new position every 3 years.
- **b** Purchased from another company the trademark to a household product. The trademark has an unlimited legal life, and the product is expected to contribute to revenue indefinitely.
- **c** Incurred significant research and development costs to develop a dirt-resistant fiber. The company expects that the fiber will be patented and that sales of the resulting products will contribute to revenue for at least 50 years. The legal life of the patent, however, will be 20 years.
- **d** An expenditure to acquire the patent on a popular video game. The patent has a remaining life of 14 years, but Home Sales expects to produce and sell the game for only 3 years.
- **e** Spent a large amount to sponsor a television mini-series about the French Revolution. The purpose in sponsoring the program was to make television viewers more aware of the company's name and its product lines.

INSTRUCTIONS Explain whether each of the above expenditures should be recorded as an operating expense or an intangible asset. If you view the expenditure as an intangible asset, indicate the number of years over which the asset should be amortized. Explain your reasoning.

PROBLEM 10B-8
Depreciation and Disposal

On March 2, 1994, Gourmet Market purchased a used delivery truck for $10,000. This asset was depreciated by the straight-line method, using an estimated useful life of 5 years, a residual value of $2,000, and the half-year convention. On September 4, 1996, Gourmet Market sells the truck for $5,200 cash.

INSTRUCTIONS

a Prepare a schedule showing the annual amounts of depreciation expense until the asset is fully depreciated.

b Compute (1) the book value of the truck at the date of disposal and (2) the amount of gain or loss on the sale.

c Prepare journal entries (in general journal form) to record in Gourmet Market's accounting records (1) depreciation on the truck for the year of disposal and (2) the sale of the truck.

ANALYTICAL AND DECISION PROBLEMS AND CASES

A&D 10-1
Depreciation Policies in Annual Reports

Shown below is a note accompanying a recent financial statement of a large public company.

Plant, Properties, and Equipment

Plant, properties, and equipment are stated at cost less accumulated depreciation.

For financial reporting purposes, the company uses the units-of-production method of depreciating its major pulp and paper mills and certain wood products facilities, and the straight-line method for other plants and equipment.

Annual straight-line depreciation rates for financial reporting purposes are as follows: buildings $2\frac{1}{2}$% to 8%; machinery and equipment 5% to 33%; woods equipment 10% to 16%. For tax purposes, depreciation is computed utilizing accelerated methods.

INSTRUCTIONS

a Are the depreciation methods used in the company's financial statements determined by current income tax laws? If not, who is responsible for selecting these methods? Explain.

b Does the company violate the consistency principle by using different depreciation methods for its paper mills and wood products facilities than it uses for its other plant and equipment? If not, what does the principle of consistency mean? Explain.

c What is the estimated useful life of the machinery and equipment being depreciated with a straight-line depreciation rate of:

1 5%.

2 33% (round to the nearest year).

Who determines the useful lives over which specific assets are to be depreciated?

d Why do you think the company uses accelerated depreciation methods for income tax purposes, rather than using the straight-line method (assuming both are acceptable for income tax purposes)? Explain.

A&D 10-2
Effects of Depreciation Policies upon Earnings

Two independent cases are described below. You are to comment separately on each case.

Case A Assume that Adams Limited and Barnes Corporation are in the same line of business, have similar plant assets that were acquired a few years ago, and report the same amount of net income. In their financial statements, Adams uses straight-line depreciation and Barnes uses an accelerated method.

INSTRUCTIONS Do you have any reason for considering one of these companies to be more profitable than the other? Explain.

Case B The income statement of Morris Foods includes depreciation expense of $200,000 and net income of $100,000. A note accompanying the financial statements discloses the following information about the company's depreciation policies:

Depreciation. For financial statement purposes, depreciation is computed by the straight-line method using the following estimated useful lives:

Automobiles	*12 years*
Furniture and equipment	*25 to 30 years*
Buildings	*60 to 90 years*

For tax purposes, depreciation is computed using accelerated methods.

INSTRUCTIONS In general terms, evaluate the effects of these depreciation policies upon the net income reported by the company in its income statement.

A&D 10-3 Depreciation Method and Journal Entries on Disposal

Holeless Donuts began operations on January 1, 1993. On that date, it purchased donut making equipment that was estimated to have a five-year useful life and a residual value of $15,000. The first year's business was a huge success and a computer system was needed to cope with the increased business volume. So, on January 1, 1994, a new computer with a four-year useful life and a $6,000 residual value was purchased.

The equipment and computer were depreciated over their respective useful lives as follows:

	Equipment	Computer
Depreciation expense for: 1993	$72,000	
1994	43,200	$12,800
1995	25,920	9,600
1996	15,552	6,400
1997	8,328	3,200

On January 1, 1998, the equipment was sold for $16,200 cash and the computer was traded-in for a new one with a list price of $28,000. Since the trade-in allowance was $5,200, Holeless Donuts only paid $22,800 for the new computer.

INSTRUCTIONS

a Determine the depreciation method used for the equipment and for the computer.

b Prepare the entries, in general journal form, to record the sale of the equipment and the trade-in of the computer.

A&D 10-4 Depreciation Method and Disposals

Evergreen Company, a clothing manufacturer, purchased a delivery truck on January 1, 1994. This truck was estimated to have a useful life of 5 years and a residual value of $3,000. Its depreciation expenses for 1994, 1995, 1996, and 1997 were: $12,000, $7,200, $4,320, and $2,592.

On January 1, 1996, the company purchased sewing equipment with a useful life of four years and a residual value of $3,000.

As Evergreen's business was booming, it needed a bigger truck. Accordingly, on January 1, 1998 the old delivery truck was traded in for a new truck with a retail price of $46,000. Since the trade-in allowance was $5,000, a cash payment of $41,000 was made. The gain on the trade-in was $1,112. On the same day, the sewing equipment was sold for $8,000 cash, resulting in a loss of $1,600. The depreciation expenses of the sewing equipment for 1996 and 1997 were: $8,800 and $6,600.

INSTRUCTIONS

a Prepare the entries, in general journal form, to record the trade-in of the delivery truck and the sale of the sewing equipment.

b Determine the depreciation method used for the delivery truck and for the sewing equipment.

A&D 10-5
Did I Do This Right?

Protein Plus is a processor and distributor of frozen foods. The company's management is anxious to report the maximum amount of net income allowable under generally accepted accounting principles and, therefore, uses the longest acceptable lives in depreciating or amortizing the company's plant assets. Depreciation and amortization computations are rounded to the nearest full month.

Near year-end the company's regular accountant was in an automobile accident, so a clerk with limited accounting experience prepared the company's financial statements. The income statement prepared by the clerk indicated a net loss of $45,000. However, the clerk was unsure that he had properly accounted for the following items:

1 On April 4, the company purchased a small food processing business at a cost $80,000 above the value of that business's net identifiable assets. The clerk classified this $80,000 as goodwill on Protein Plus's balance sheet and recorded no amortization expense because the food processor's superior earnings are expected to continue indefinitely.

2 During the year the company spent $32,000 on a research project to develop a method of freezing avocados. The clerk classified these expenditures as an intangible asset on the company's balance sheet and recorded no amortization expense because it was not yet known whether the project would be successful.

3 Two gains from the disposal of plant assets were included in the income statement. One gain, in the amount of $4,300, resulted from the sale of a plant asset at a price above its book value. The other gain, in the amount of $2,700 on December 31, was based on receiving an offer for equipment that has not yet been sold.

4 A public accounting firm had determined that the company's depreciation expense for income tax purposes was $51,400. The clerk used this figure as depreciation expense in the income statement, although in prior years the company had used the straight-line method of depreciation in its financial statements. Depreciation for the current year amounts to $35,600 when computed by the straight-line method over realistic estimates of useful lives.

5 On January 4, the company paid $90,000 to purchase a 10-year franchise to become the exclusive distributor in three eastern provinces for a brand of Mexican frozen dinners. The clerk charged this $90,000 to expense in the current year because the entire amount had been paid in cash.

6 During the year, the company incurred advertising costs of $22,000 to promote the newly acquired line of frozen dinners. The clerk did not know how many periods would be benefited from these expenditures, so he included the entire amount in the selling expenses of the current year.

INSTRUCTIONS

a For each of the numbered paragraphs, explain whether the clerk's treatment of the item is in conformity with generally accepted accounting principles.

b Prepare a schedule determining the correct net income (or net loss) for the year. Begin with "Net loss originally reported . . . $45,000," and indicate any adjustments that you consider appropriate. If you indicate adjustments for the amortization of intangible assets acquired during the year, round the amortization to the nearest month.

A&D 10-6
Any Word from Kuwait?

It is early 1991 and you are a public accountant auditing the 1990 financial statements of Norco, a multinational corporation. One of Norco's assets is a large plant located in the country of Kuwait; this facility currently is carried in Norco's accounting records at a book value of $140 million. In August of 1990, Kuwait was invaded by neighbouring Iraq, and currently is under Iraqi control.

Early in 1991 (but before the issuance of Norco's 1990 financial statements), a U.S.-led coalition initiated military action to "liberate Kuwait." Most military experts expect the coalition forces ultimately to prevail, although the extent of physical damage that may be caused within Kuwait cannot be predicted. (Losses caused by acts of war are not covered by insurance.)

Norco has received no communication from its Kuwait facility since last August. The company has no way of knowing the current physical condition of this facility, nor what may happen to it in the coming months.

INSTRUCTIONS

Summarize briefly the arguments for and against Norco immediately writing down the carrying value of its Kuwait plant. What actions would you require Norco to take before you would consider that the company's 1990 financial statements provide a "fair presentation" of this situation?

COMPREHENSIVE PROBLEM 3

ALPINE VILLAGE AND NORDIC SPORTS

CONCEPTS OF ASSET VALUATION AND EFFECTS UPON NET INCOME

Chris Scott, a former Olympic skier, wants to purchase an established ski equipment and clothing shop in Banff, Alberta. Two such businesses currently are available for sale: Alpine Village and Nordic Sports. Both businesses are organized as sole proprietorships and have been in business for three years. Summaries of the current balance sheet data of both shops are shown below:

Assets	*Alpine Village*	*Nordic Sports*
Cash	$ 31,200	$ 37,800
Accounts receivable	169,300	188,500
Inventory	141,700	150,400
Plant and equipment:		
Land	33,000	42,000
Building (net of accumulated depreciation)	87,480	99,900
Equipment (net of accumulated depreciation)	8,200	7,600
Goodwill		22,200
Total assets	$470,880	$548,400
Liabilities & Owner's Equity		
Total liabilities	$194,400	$176,200
Owner's equity	276,480	372,200
Total liabilities & owner's equity	$470,880	$548,400

Income statements for the last three years show that Alpine Village has reported total net income of $201,480 since the business was started. The income statements of Nordic Sports show total net income of $256,200 for the same three-year period.

With the permission of the owners of the two businesses, Scott arranges for a public accountant to review the accounting records of both companies. This investigation discloses the following information:

Accounts Receivable Nordic Sports uses the direct write-off method of recording uncollectible accounts expense. The accountant believes that the $188,500 of accounts receivable appearing in the company's balance sheet includes about $18,000 in uncollectible accounts. Alpine Village makes monthly estimates of its uncollectible accounts and shows accounts receivable in its balance sheet at estimated net realizable value.

Inventories Nordic Sports uses the first-in, first-out ***(FIFO)*** method of pricing its inventory. Had the company used the last-in, first-out ***(LIFO)*** method, the balance sheet valuation of inventory would be about $12,000 lower. Alpine Village uses the LIFO method to value inventory; if it had used FIFO, the balance sheet valuation of inventory would be about $10,000 greater.

Buildings Nordic Sports depreciates its building over an estimated life of 40 years using the straight-line method. Alpine Village depreciates its building over 20 years using the double-declining-balance method. Alpine has owned its building for 3 years, and the accumulated depreciation on the building now amounts to $32,520.

Goodwill Three years ago, each business provided $24,000 in prize money for ski races held in the area. Nordic Sports charged this expenditure to goodwill, which it is amortizing over a period of 40 years. Alpine Village charged its $24,000 prize money expenditure directly to advertising expense.

INSTRUCTIONS

a Prepare a revised summary of the balance sheet data in a manner that makes the information about the two companies more comparable. You will adjust the asset values of one company or the other so that the balance sheet data for both companies meet the following standards:

1 Accounts receivable are valued at estimated net realizable value.

2 Inventories are valued by the method that will minimize income during a period of rising prices.

3 Depreciation on the buildings is based upon the straight-line method and an estimated useful life of 40 years.

4 The cost of the $24,000 payment of prize money is treated in the manner required by generally accepted accounting principles.

After making the indicated adjustments to the valuation of certain assets, show "owner's equity" at the residual amount needed to bring total liabilities & owner's equity into agreement with total assets.

When you revalue an asset of either company, show supporting computations.

b Revise the cumulative amount of net income reported by each company during the last three years, taking into consideration the changes in accounting methods and policies called for in part **a.**

c Assume that after revision of asset values as described in part **a,** the revised book value of net identifiable assets is not materially different from aggregate fair market value of net identifiable assets. Therefore, Scott is willing to buy either company at a price equal to the revised amount of owner's equity as determined in part **a,** plus an amount for goodwill. For goodwill, Scott is willing to pay four times the amount by which average annual net income exceeds a 20% return on this revised owner's equity.

Determine the price that Scott is willing to pay for each of the two companies. Base your computations on the revised data about owner's equity and net income that you developed in parts **a** and **b.**

PART

4 Liabilities and Accounting Principles

Part 4 consists of two chapters. In Chapter 11 we discuss the types of liabilities commonly found in most business organizations. Chapter 12 is intended as a "capstone" chapter for the first semester course. It includes a review of many accounting principles introduced in earlier chapters, and also a discussion of the professional ethics relating to the practice of accounting.

CHAPTER

11 Liabilities Common to Most Business Organizations

Our primary coverage of liabilities is split between this chapter and Chapter 16. In this chapter, we address the types of liabilities likely to arise in almost any type or size of business organization, and also the accounting and disclosure requirements relating to contingent losses and commitments. Accounting for payrolls is discussed in a Supplemental Topic section at the end of the chapter.

In Chapter 16, we will address the special types of liabilities that appear primarily in the balance sheets of large, publicly owned corporations.

Learning Objectives

After studying this chapter you should be able to:

1 *Define* liabilities; *distinguish between liabilities and owner's equity.*

2 *Distinguish between current and long-term liabilities.*

3 *Account for notes payable and the accrual of interest.*

4 *Account for notes payable with the interest included in the face amount.*

5 *Prepare an amortization table allocating payments on an instalment loan between interest and repayment of principal.*

6 *Compute the quick ratio, debt ratio, and interest coverage ratio, and explain their usefulness.*

7 *Define* contingent losses and commitments. *Explain the criteria for determining their presentation in financial statements.*

*8 *Describe the basic separation of duties in a payroll system, and explain how this plan contributes to strong internal control.*

*9 *Account for a payroll, including computation of amounts withheld and payroll taxes on the employer.*

* *Supplemental Topic, "Accounting for Payrolls"*

Companies that cannot pay their liabilities eventually will be forced out of business—and, perhaps, into bankruptcy. In evaluating the solvency of a business, or its ability to finance future growth, users of financial statements should consider carefully the nature and amount of the company's liabilities.

The Nature of Liabilities

OBJECTIVE 1 Define liabilities; distinguish between liabilities and owner's equity.

Liabilities may be defined as ***debts or obligations arising from past transactions or events and requiring settlement at a future date.*** Thus, liabilities represent ***existing obligations*** for the business to part with its resources in the future. All liabilities have certain characteristics in common; however, the terms of different liabilities vary greatly, as do the rights of the specific creditors.

Distinctions between Debt and Equity Businesses have two basic sources of financing: debt (liabilities) and equity. Liabilities differ from owner's equity in several respects. The feature that most clearly distinguishes the claims of creditors from owner's equity is that all liabilities eventually ***mature***—that is, they come due. Owner's equity ***does not*** mature. The date upon which a liability comes due is called the ***maturity date.***[1]

Although all liabilities mature, their maturity dates vary. Some liabilities are so short in term that they are paid right after the year-end date. Long-term liabilities, in contrast, may not mature for many years. The maturity dates of key liabilities may be a critical factor in the solvency of a business.

The providers of borrowed capital are ***creditors*** of the business, not owners. As creditors, they have financial claims against the business, but they usually do ***not*** have the right to control business operations. The traditional roles of owners, managers, and creditors may be modified, however, in an ***indenture contract.*** Creditors sometimes insist upon being granted some control over business operations as a condition of making a loan, particularly if the business is in poor financial condition. Indenture contracts may impose such restrictions as limits upon management salaries and upon dividends, and may require the creditor's approval for additional borrowing or for large capital expenditures.

The claims of creditors have ***legal priority*** over the claims of owners. If a business ceases operations and liquidates, creditors must be ***paid in full*** before any distributions are made to the owners. The relative security of creditors' claims, however, can vary among the creditors. Sometimes the borrower pledges title to specific assets as ***collateral*** for a loan. If the borrower defaults on a secured loan, the creditor may foreclose upon the pledged assets. Assets that have been pledged as security for loans should be identified in notes accompanying the borrower's financial statements.

---

[1] Some liabilities are ***due on demand,*** which means that the liability is payable upon the creditor's request. From a bank's point of view, customers' chequing accounts are "demand liabilities." Liabilities due on demand may come due at any time and in a classified balance sheet are shown as current liabilities.

Liabilities that are not secured by specific assets are termed ***general credit obligations.*** The priorities of general credit obligations vary with the nature of the liability, and the terms of indenture contracts.

Most long-term liabilities, and some short-term ones, require the borrower to pay interest. In some companies, the requirements to pay future interest charges are so large that they threaten the very survival of the business. Obligations to pay interest ***stem only from liabilities;*** a company does ***not*** pay interest upon its owner's equity.

Estimated Liabilities Most liabilities are for a definite dollar amount, clearly stated by contract. Examples include notes payable, accounts payable, and accrued expenses, such as interest payable and salaries payable. In some cases, however, the dollar amount of a liability must be ***estimated*** at the balance sheet date.

Estimated liabilities have two basic characteristics: The liability is ***known to exist,*** but the precise dollar amount cannot be determined until a later date. For instance, the automobiles sold by most auto makers are accompanied by a warranty obligating the auto maker to replace defective parts for a period of several years. As each car is sold, the auto maker ***incurs a liability*** to perform any work that can be required under the warranty. The dollar amount of this liability, however, can only be estimated.

CURRENT LIABILITIES

OBJECTIVE 2 ***Distinguish between current and long-term liabilities.***

Current liabilities are obligations that must be paid within one year or within the operating cycle, whichever is longer. Another requirement for classification as a current liability is the expectation that the debt will be paid from current assets (or through the rendering of services). Liabilities that do not meet these conditions are classified as long-term liabilities.

The time period used in defining current liabilities parallels that used in defining current assets. As explained in Chapter 5, the amount of ***working capital*** (current assets less current liabilities) and the ***current ratio*** (current assets divided by current liabilities) are valuable indicators of a company's ability to pay its debts in the near future.

Among the most common examples of current liabilities are accounts payable, short-term notes payable, the current portion of long-term debt, accrued liabilities (such as interest payable, income taxes payable, and payroll liabilities), and unearned revenue.

Accounts Payable

Accounts payable often are subdivided into the categories of trade accounts payable and other accounts payable. Trade accounts payable are short-term obligations to suppliers for purchases of merchandise. Other accounts payable include liabilities for any goods and services other than merchandise.

Accounts payable may be recorded at an amount ***net*** of any available cash discounts. If payment is not made until after the discount period has lapsed, the additional amount paid is charged to an expense account entitled Purchase Discounts Lost.

Technically, the date at which a trade account payable comes into existence depends upon whether goods are purchased F.O.B. shipping point or F.O.B. destination. However, unless ***material*** amounts of merchandise are purchased on terms of F.O.B. shipping point, most companies follow the convenient practice of recording the transaction when the merchandise is received.

Notes Payable

OBJECTIVE 3 Account for notes payable and the accrual of interest.

Notes payable are issued whenever bank loans are obtained. Other transactions that may give rise to notes payable include the purchase of real estate or costly equipment, the purchase of merchandise, and the substitution of a note for a past-due account payable.

Notes payable generally require the borrower to pay an interest charge. Accounting for interest charges is easiest if the interest rate is stated separately from the ***principal*** amount of the note. To illustrate, assume that on November 1 Porter Company borrows $10,000 from its bank for a period of six months (with the three days of grace included) at an annual interest rate of 12%. Six months later, on May 1, Porter Company will have to pay the bank the ***principal*** amount of $10,000, plus $600 interest ($\$10,000 \times \frac{6}{12} \times .12$).[2]

The journal entry in Porter Company's accounting records for this November 1 borrowing is:

Face amount of note

Cash	10,000	
Notes Payable		10,000
Borrowed $10,000 for six months at 12% interest per year.		

Notice that no liability is recorded for the interest charges when the note is issued. At the date that money is borrowed, the borrower has a liability ***only for the principal amount of the loan;*** the liability for interest accrues day by day over the life of the loan. At December 31, two months' interest expense has been incurred, and the following year-end adjusting entry is made:

A liability for interest accrues day by day

Interest Expense	200	
Interest Payable		200
To record interest expense incurred through year-end on a six-month, 12% note dated Nov. 1 ($\$10,000 \times \frac{2}{12} \times 12\% = \$200$).		

If we assume that the company does not use reversing entries, the entry on May 1 when the note is paid will be:

Payment of principal and interest

Notes Payable	10,000	
Interest Payable	200	
Interest Expense	400	
Cash		10,600
To record payment of six-month, 12% note on maturity date and to recognize interest expense incurred since year-end ($\$10,000 \times \frac{4}{12} \times .12 = \$400$).		

[2] For notes stated in months, interest will be computed on the basis of months rather than days, so as to stress concept rather than unnecessary precision.

Notes Payable with Interest Charges Included in the Face Amount

OBJECTIVE 4 Account for notes payable with the interest included in the face amount.

Instead of stating the interest rate separately as in the preceding illustration, the note payable issued by Porter Company could have been drawn to ***include the interest charge in the face amount of the note.*** Thus, the face amount of this note is $10,600 ($10,000 + $600), $600 greater than the $10,000 amount borrowed. Porter Company's liability at November 1 is only $10,000—the ***present value*** of the note.[3] The other $600 included in the face amount of the note represents ***future interest charges.*** As interest expense is incurred over the life of the note, Porter Company's liability will grow to $10,600, just as in the preceding illustration.

The entry to record Porter Company's $10,000 borrowing from the bank at November 1 will be as follows for this type of note payable:

Interest included in face of note

Cash	10,000	
Discount on Notes Payable	600	
Notes Payable		10,600
Issued to bank a six-month, 12% note payable with interest charge included in the face amount of note.		

The liability account, Notes Payable, was credited with the full face amount of the note ($10,600). It is therefore necessary to debit a ***contra-liability*** account, ***Discount on Notes Payable,*** for the future interest charges included in the face amount of the note. Discount on Notes Payable is shown in the balance sheet as a deduction from Notes Payable. In our illustration, the amounts in the balance sheet would be Notes Payable, $10,600, minus Discount on Notes Payable, $600, or a net liability of $10,000 at November 1.

Discount on Notes Payable The balance of the account Discount on Notes Payable represents ***interest charges applicable to future periods.*** As this interest expense is incurred, the balance of the discount account gradually is transferred into the Interest Expense account. Thus, at the maturity date of the note, Discount on Notes Payable will have a zero balance, and the net liability will have increased to $10,600. The process of transferring the amount in the Discount on Notes Payable account into the Interest Expense account is called ***amortization*** of the discount.

Amortization of the Discount The discount on ***short-term*** notes payable usually is amortized by the straight-line method, which allocates the same amount of discount to interest expense for each month the note is outstanding. Thus, the $600 discount on the Porter Company note payable will be transferred from Discount on Notes Payable into Interest Expense at the rate of $100 per month ($600 ÷ 6 months).

Adjusting entries should be made to amortize the discount at the end of each accounting period and at the date the note matures. At December 31, Porter Company will make the following adjusting entry to recognize the two months' interest expense incurred since November 1:

[3] The concept of present value was introduced in Chapter 8. The mechanics of computing present values is explained in Appendix A at the end of Chapter 16.

Amortization of discount

Interest Expense	*200*	
Discount on Notes Payable		*200*
To record interest expense incurred to end of year on a six-month, 12% note dated Nov. 1 ($600 discount × $\frac{2}{6}$).		

Notice that the liability for accrued interest is recorded by crediting Discount on Notes Payable rather than Interest Payable. The credit to Discount on Notes Payable reduces the debit balance in this contra-liability account from $600 to $400, thereby increasing the ***net liability*** for notes payable by $200.

At December 31, Porter Company's net liability for the bank loan will appear in the balance sheet as shown below:

Liability shown net of discount

Current liabilities:		
Note payable	*$10,600*	
Less: Discount on notes payable	*400*	*$10,200*

The net liability of $10,200 consists of the $10,000 principal amount of the debt plus the $200 interest that has accrued since November 1.

When the note matures on May 1, Porter Company will recognize the four months' interest expense incurred since year-end and will pay the bank $10,600. The entry is:

Two-thirds of interest applicable to second year

Notes Payable	*10,600*	
Interest Expense	*400*	
Discount on Notes Payable		*400*
Cash		*10,600*
To record payment of a six-month, 12% note due today and recognize interest expense incurred since year-end ($10,000 × $\frac{4}{12}$ × 12% = $400).		

Comparison of the Two Forms of Notes Payable

We have illustrated two alternative methods that Porter Company could use in accounting for its $10,000 bank loan, depending upon the form of the note payable. The journal entries for both methods, along with the resulting balance sheet presentations of the liability at November 1 and December 31, are summarized on the next page. Notice that both methods result in Porter Company recognizing the ***same amount of interest expense*** and the ***same total liability*** in its balance sheet. The form of the note does not change the economic substance of the transaction.

The Current Portion of Long-Term Debt

Notes payable usually are classified as current liabilities or as long-term liabilities based upon the maturity date. Thus, notes payable maturing in one year or less normally are classified as current liabilities, whereas notes maturing after one year are classified as long-term liabilities.

As the maturity date of a long-term liability approaches, the obligation eventually becomes due within the current period. Long-term liabilities

Comparison of the Two Forms of Notes Payable

	Note Written for $10,000 Plus 12% Interest			Note Written with Interest Included in Face Amount		
Entry to record borrowing on Nov. 1	*Cash*	*10,000*		*Cash*	*10,000*	
	Notes Payable		*10,000*	*Discount on Notes Payable*	*600*	
				Notes Payable		*10,600*
Partial balance sheet at Nov. 1	***Current liabilities:***			***Current liabilities:***		
	Notes payable		***$10,000***	***Notes payable***	***$10,600***	
				Less: Discount on notes payable	***600***	***$10,000***
Adjusting entry at Dec. 31	*Interest Expense*	*200*		*Interest Expense*	*200*	
	Interest Payable		*200*	*Discount on Notes Payable*		*200*
Partial balance sheet at Dec. 31	***Current liabilities:***			***Current liabilities:***		
	Notes payable	***$10,000***		***Notes payable***	***$10,600***	
	Interest payable	***200***	***$10,200***	***Less: Discount on notes payable***	***400***	***$10,200***
Entry to record payment of note on May 1	*Notes Payable*	*10,000*		*Notes Payable*	*10,600*	
	Interest Payable	*200*		*Interest Expense*	*400*	
	Interest Expense	*400*		*Discount on Notes Payable*		*400*
	Cash		*10,600*	*Cash*		*10,600*

that become payable within the current year generally are ***reclassified*** in the balance sheet as current liabilities.[4]

Some long-term notes payable, such as mortgage loans, are payable in a series of monthly or quarterly ***instalments.*** In these cases, the principal amount to be repaid within the coming year is classified as a current liability, and the remainder of the principal amount is classified as a long-term liability. (Notice that the current portion of an instalment note payable includes only the ***principal amount*** to be repaid within one year, ***not the interest payments*** scheduled for the year.)

Accrued Liabilities

Accrued liabilities arise from the recognition of expenses for which payment will be made in future periods. Thus, accrued liabilities also may be called ***accrued expenses.*** Examples of accrued liabilities include interest payable, income taxes payable, and payroll liabilities. As accrued liabilities stem from the recording of expenses, the timing and amounts of these liabilities are governed by the ***matching principle.***

All companies incur accrued liabilities. In most cases, however, these liabilities are paid at frequent intervals—usually within a month or less. Therefore, accrued liabilities ***usually do not accumulate to large dollar amounts.*** In the balance sheet, accrued liabilities often are combined with accounts payable, rather than being listed separately.

Interest Payable Interest—the cost of borrowing—accrues with the passage of time. When companies enter into long-term borrowing agreements, they may become committed to paying large amounts of interest for many years to come. At any balance sheet date, however, only a ***small portion*** of this total interest obligation represents a "liability."

Remember, liabilities stem from ***past transactions.*** Therefore, the only interest obligation that represents a "liability" is the unpaid interest that has ***already*** accrued. (At the end of each period, any accrued interest payable is recorded by debiting Interest Expense and crediting Interest Payable.)

To illustrate this point, assume that HighTech Stores borrows $500,000 from its bank for a period of five years at an interest rate of 12%. Although the principal amount of this loan will not be due for five years, interest is to be paid monthly—on the first day of each month.

The interest expense on this loan amounts to ***$60,000*** per year ($500,000 × 12%). Over the life of the loan, HighTech will pay ***$300,000*** in interest charges. At the end of each month, however, HighTech will have a liability for only ***one month's interest***—the interest that has accrued since the last interest payment date. Thus, HighTech's balance sheets normally will show accrued interest payable of only ***$5,000*** ($500,000 × $\frac{1}{12}$ × 12%).

If this loan had called for the accrued interest to be paid on the ***last*** day of each month, HighTech's balance sheets would include ***no*** liability for accrued interest payable.

---

[4] Exceptions are made to this rule if the maturing liability will be ***refinanced*** (that is, extended or renewed) on a long-term basis or if a special ***sinking fund*** has been accumulated for the purpose of repaying the liability. In these cases, the debt continues to be classified as a long-term liability, as it is not expected to be paid from current assets.

A borrower's contractual obligation to pay interest in future periods is ***not yet a liability*** and ***does not appear*** in the borrower's balance sheet. However, this information may be of vital importance to investors and creditors in evaluating the company's solvency and its ability to finance future growth. For this reason, accounting principles require businesses to ***disclose*** the terms of major borrowing arrangements in the notes that accompany their financial statements.

To determine the amount of a company's interest ***expense*** for the year, the reader of financial statements should look in the ***income statement,*** not the balance sheet. For information about the company's interest obligations in ***future*** years, this reader must study the ***notes*** that accompany the financial statements.

Income Taxes Payable Profitable corporations are required to pay income taxes equal to a portion of their taxable income. Income taxes expense accrues ***as profits are earned.*** At the end of each accounting period, income taxes expense is estimated and recorded in an adjusting entry, as shown below:[5]

Adjusting entry to accrue estimated income taxes

Income Taxes Expense	*72,750*	
Income Taxes Payable		*72,750*
To accrue estimated income taxes expense for the first quarter of the year (Jan. 1 through Mar. 31).		

The account debited in this entry, Income Taxes Expense, is an expense account and usually appears as the very last deduction in the income statement. For example, the income taxes expense recorded above would appear as follows in an income statement for the quarter ended March 31:

Income before income taxes	*$200,000*
Less: Income taxes expense	*72,750*
Net income	*127,250*

Only businesses organized as ***corporations*** incur income taxes expense. Unincorporated businesses—sole proprietorships and partnerships—do not pay income taxes. The incomes earned by unincorporated businesses are taxable directly to the ***owners*** of these businesses, not to the business entities themselves.

The liability account, Income Taxes Payable, ordinarily will be paid within a few months and, therefore, appears in the current liability section of the balance sheet.

Payroll Liabilities Every business incurs a number of accrued liabilities relating to its payroll. The largest of these liabilities is the obligation to pay employees for services rendered during the period. Payroll ***expense*** often is among the largest expenses of a business organization. Accrued payroll liabilities, however, seldom accumulate to large amounts because they are paid in full at frequent intervals.

---

[5] Actual income tax expense for the year cannot be determined until after year-end, when the company prepares its income tax return. Therefore, monthly or quarterly adjusting entries recognizing income taxes expense are based upon ***estimated*** amounts.

Accounting for payrolls involves much more than merely recording the liability for accrued wages and salaries payable. Employers must compute numerous taxes that the government levies either upon employees or upon the employer. The employer then is responsible for withholding the taxes upon employees from the employees' paycheques and forwarding these amounts directly to the government. The employer also is responsible for maintaining records indicating for ***each employee*** the amounts earned during the year and the amounts of taxes withheld. All of this information must be computed separately for every pay period—usually every one or two weeks. Thus, payroll accounting is a specialized function within most accounting departments.

Every business student should have some familiarity with payrolls, including the purpose and relative size of the various payroll taxes, and whether these taxes are paid by the employees or by the employer. An introduction to accounting for payrolls is presented in the Supplemental Topic section at the end of this chapter.

Unearned Revenue

A liability for unearned revenue arises when a customer pays in advance. Upon receipt of an advance payment from a customer, the company debits Cash and credits a liability account such as Unearned Revenue, or Customers' Deposits. As the services are rendered to the customer, an entry is made debiting the liability account and crediting a revenue account. Notice that the liability for unearned revenue normally is "paid" by rendering services to the creditor, rather than by making cash payments.

Unearned revenue ordinarily is classified as a current liability, as the activities involved in earning revenue are part of the business's normal operating cycle.

LONG-TERM LIABILITIES

Long-term obligations usually arise from major expenditures, such as acquisitions of plant assets, the purchase of another company, or refinancing an existing long-term obligation that is about to mature. Thus, transactions involving long-term liabilities are relatively few in number but often involve large dollar amounts. In contrast, current liabilities usually arise from routine operating transactions.

Many businesses regard long-term liabilities as an alternative to owners' equity as a source of "permanent" financing. Although long-term liabilities eventually mature, they often are ***refinanced***—that is, the maturing obligation simply is replaced with a new long-term liability.

Maturing Obligations Intended to Be Refinanced

One special type of long-term liability is an obligation that will mature in the current period but is expected to be refinanced on a long-term basis. For example, a company may have a bank loan that "comes due" each year but is routinely extended for the following year. Both the company and the bank may intend for this arrangement to continue on a long-term basis.

If management has both the ***intent*** and the ***ability*** to refinance soon-to-mature obligations on a long-term basis, these obligations are classified as long-term liabilities. In this situation, the accountant looks to the ***economic substance*** of the situation, rather than to its legal form.

When the economic substance of a transaction differs from its legal form or its outward appearance, financial statements should reflect the ***economic substance.*** Accountants summarize this concept with the phrase, ***"Substance takes precedence over form."*** Today's business world is characterized by transactions of ever-increasing complexity. Recognizing those situations in which the substance of a transaction differs from its form is one of the greatest challenges confronting the professional accountant.

Instalment Notes Payable

Purchases of real estate and certain types of equipment often are financed by the issuance of long-term notes that call for a series of instalment payments. These payments (often called ***debt service***) may be due monthly, quarterly, semiannually, or at any other interval. If these instalments continue until the debt is completely repaid, the loan is said to be "fully amortizing." Often, however, instalment notes contain a "due date" at which the remaining unpaid balance is to be repaid in a single "balloon" payment.

Some instalment notes call for instalment payments equal to the periodic interest charges (an "interest only" note). Under these terms, the principal amount of the loan is payable at a specified maturity date. More often, however, the fixed-amount instalment payments are ***greater*** than the amount of interest accruing during the period. Thus, only a portion of each instalment payment represents interest expense, and the remainder of the payment reduces the principal amount of the liability. As the amount owed is reduced by each payment, the portion of each successive payment representing interest expense will ***decrease,*** and the portion going toward repayment of principal will ***increase.***

OBJECTIVE 5 Prepare an amortization table allocating payments on an instalment loan between interest and repayment of principal.

Allocating Instalment Payments between Interest and Principal In accounting for an instalment note, the accountant must determine the portion of each payment that represents interest expense, and the portion that reduces the principal amount of the liability. This distinction is made in advance by preparing an ***amortization table.***

To illustrate, assume that on October 15, 1995, King's Inn purchases furnishings at a total cost of $16,398. In payment, the company issues an instalment note payable for this amount, plus interest at 12% per annum (or 1% per month). This note will be paid in 18 monthly instalments of $1,000 each, beginning on November 15. An amortization table for this instalment note payable appears at the top of the following page. (Amounts of interest expense are ***rounded to the nearest dollar.***)

Preparing an Amortization Table Let us explore the content of this table. First, notice that the payments are made on a ***monthly*** basis. Therefore,

Amortization Table
(12% Note Payable for $16,398; Payable in 18 Monthly Instalments of $1,000)

Interest Period	Payment Date	(A) Monthly Payment	(B) Interest Expense (1% of the Last Unpaid Balance)	(C) Reduction in Unpaid Balance (A) − (B)	(D) Unpaid Balance
Issue date	Oct. 15, 1995	—	—	—	$16,398
1	Nov. 15	$1,000	$164	$836	15,562
2	Dec. 15	1,000	156	844	14,718
3	Jan. 15, 1996	1,000	147	853	13,865
4	Feb. 15	1,000	139	861	13,004
5	Mar. 15	1,000	130	870	12,134
6	Apr. 15	1,000	121	879	11,255
7	May 15	1,000	113	887	10,368
8	June 15	1,000	104	896	9,472
9	July 15	1,000	95	905	8,567
10	Aug. 15	1,000	86	914	7,653
11	Sept. 15	1,000	77	923	6,730
12	Oct. 15	1,000	67	933	5,797
13	Nov. 15	1,000	58	942	4,855
14	Dec. 15	1,000	49	951	3,904
15	Jan. 15, 1997	1,000	39	961	2,943
16	Feb. 15	1,000	29	971	1,972
17	Mar. 15	1,000	20	980	992
18	Apr. 15	1,000	8*	992	-0-

* In the last period, interest expense is equal to the amount of the final payment minus the remaining unpaid balance. This compensates for the cumulative effect of rounding interest amounts to the nearest dollar.

the amounts of the payments (column A), interest expense (column B), and reduction in the unpaid balance (column C) are all ***monthly amounts.***

The interest rate used in the table is of special importance; this rate must coincide with the period of time ***between payment dates***—in this case, one month. Thus, if payments are made monthly, column B must be based upon the ***monthly*** rate of interest. If payments were made quarterly, this column would use the quarterly rate of interest.

An amortization table begins with the original amount of the liability ($16,398) listed at the top of the unpaid balance column. The amounts of the monthly payments, shown in column A, are specified by the instalment contract. The monthly interest expense, shown in column B, is computed for each month by applying the monthly interest rate to the unpaid balance at the ***beginning of that month.*** The portion of each payment that reduces the amount of the liability (column C) is simply the remainder of the payment (column A minus column B). Finally, the unpaid balance of the liability (column D) is reduced each month by the amount indicated in column C.

Rather than continuing to make monthly payments, King's Inn could settle this liability at any time by paying the amount currently shown as the unpaid balance.

Notice that the amount of interest expense listed in column B ***changes every month.*** In our illustration, the interest expense is ***decreasing*** each month, because the unpaid balance is continually decreasing.[6]

Preparing each horizontal line in an amortization table involves making the same computations, based upon a new unpaid balance. Thus, an amortization table of any length can be easily and quickly prepared by computer. (Most "money management" software includes a program for preparing amortization tables.) The data that must be entered into the computer consist of only three items: (1) the original amount of the liability, (2) the amount of periodic payments, and (3) the interest rate (per payment period).

Using an Amortization Table Once an amortization table has been prepared, the entries to record each payment are taken directly from the amounts shown in the table. For example, the entry to record the first monthly payment (November 15, 1995) is:

Payment is allocated between interest and principal

Interest Expense	*164*	
Instalment Note Payable	*836*	
Cash		*1,000*
Made November payment on instalment note payable.		

Similarly, the entry to record the ***second*** payment, made on ***December 15, 1995,*** is:

Notice that interest expense is less in December

Interest Expense	*156*	
Instalment Note Payable	*844*	
Cash		*1,000*
Made December payment on instalment note payable.		

At December 31, 1995, King's Inn should make an adjusting entry to record one-half month's accrued interest on this liability. The amount of this adjusting entry is based upon the unpaid balance shown in the amortization table as of the last payment (December 15). This entry is:

Year-end adjusting entry

Interest Expense	*74*	
Interest Payable		*74*
Adjusting entry to record interest expense on instalment note for the last half of December: \$14,718 × 1% × $\frac{1}{2}$ = \$74.		

The Current Portion of Long-Term Debt Notice that as of December 31, ***1995,*** the unpaid balance of this note is \$14,718. As of December 31, ***1996,*** however, the unpaid balance will be only \$3,904. Thus, the principal amount of this note will be reduced by ***\$10,814*** during 1996 (\$14,718 − \$3,904 = \$10,814). In the balance sheet prepared at December 31, 1995, the \$10,814 portion of this debt that is scheduled for repayment within the ***next 12 months*** should be classified as a ***current liability.*** The remaining \$3,904 should be classified as a long-term liability.

[6] If the monthly payments were ***less*** than the amount of the monthly interest expense, the unpaid balance of the note would ***increase*** each month. This, in turn, would cause the interest expense to increase each month. This pattern, termed ***negative amortization,*** occurs temporarily in some "adjustable-rate" home mortgages.

Disclosure Requirements for Long-Term Debt

A company should disclose in notes to its financial statements the interest rates, the assets pledged as security, and the maturity dates of all long-term notes payable.[7] In addition, the company should disclose the total amounts of long-term debt maturing in each of the next five years. These disclosures are intended to assist users of the financial statements in evaluating the company's solvency—not just today, but over a period of several years.

EVALUATING THE SAFETY OF CREDITORS' CLAIMS

OBJECTIVE 6 ***Compute the quick ratio, debt ratio, and interest coverage ratio, and explain their usefulness.***

In recent years, some companies with profitable business operations have incurred so much debt that they have been unable to make the required interest payments. If a company cannot pay its debts and is forced into bankruptcy, creditors and investors alike may sustain large losses. Management, too, is concerned with the company's debt-paying ability. Not only does management want the business to remain solvent, but it wants the company to maintain a high ***credit rating*** with agencies such as Dun & Bradstreet and Standard & Poor's. A high credit rating helps the company borrow money more easily and at lower interest rates.

Analysis by Short-Term Creditors

In evaluating debt-paying ability, short-term creditors and long-term creditors look at different financial relationships. Short-term creditors are interested in the company's immediate solvency and look toward such measures of liquidity as working capital and the current ratio. As explained in earlier chapters, they also may compute the turnover rates for receivables and for inventory, in order to evaluate the liquidity of these assets.

Quick Ratio Although inventories and prepaid expenses are classified as current assets, they are further removed from conversion into cash than are other current assets. Therefore, short-term creditors often use a statistic called the ***quick ratio*** or ***acid test ratio,*** rather than the current ratio, to provide a quick evaluation of a company's short-term solvency.

The quick ratio is computed by dividing ***quick assets*** by current liabilities. Quick assets include only cash, investments in marketable securities,[8] and short-term receivables. Thus, the quick ratio provides a more rigid test of short-term solvency than does the current ratio.

A quick ratio of 1.0 to 1 or better usually is considered satisfactory, and a quick ratio of over 1.5 to 1 indicates a high degree of liquidity. Of course, all ratios vary substantially among companies of different sizes or in different industries. However, an analyst familiar with the nature of a compa-

---

[7] If a company has many different notes payable, it is not practicable to disclose separately the terms of each note. In such cases, the notes are grouped into categories of similar liabilities, and the ***range*** of interest rates and maturity dates of each category is disclosed. Drafting disclosures that are informative, yet not excessively detailed, requires professional judgment.

[8] Investments in marketable securities are investments that can be sold readily at quoted market prices. They include, for example, investments in government bonds and in the stocks and bonds issued by major corporations. Marketable securities are discussed in Chapter 17.

ny's operations generally can determine from the quick ratio whether the company represents a good credit risk in the short run.

Analysis by Long-Term Creditors

Long-term creditors are less concerned than short-term creditors with the amount of liquid assets a business has on hand today. Rather, they are interested in the borrower's ability to meet its interest obligations ***over a period of years,*** and also its ability to repay or refinance large obligations years in the future.

Debt Ratio One measurement often used in evaluating the overall safety of long-term creditors' investments is the debt ratio. This ratio is computed by dividing total liabilities by total assets. Basically, the debt ratio indicates the ***percentage*** of total assets that are financed with borrowed money (liabilities), in comparison with the percentage financed with equity capital.

Creditors prefer a ***low*** debt ratio, as this means that their claims amount to only a small percentage of total assets. This relationship increases the prospects that the creditors will be paid in full, even if the company ceases operations and liquidates its assets.

Of course, individual creditors should look beyond the overall debt ratio to determine the safety of their claims. Holders of subordinated debt, for example, should consider the priority of their claims relative to those of other creditors. The holders of secured debt should consider the value and salability of the specific assets that secure their claims.

Interest Coverage Ratio Creditors, investors, and managers all feel more comfortable when a company has enough income to cover its interest payment obligations by a wide margin. One widely used measure of the relationship between earnings and interest expense is called the ***interest coverage ratio.***

The interest coverage ratio is computed by dividing annual ***operating income*** by the annual interest expense. From the creditors' point of view, the higher this ratio, the better. In past years, most companies with high credit ratings had interest coverage ratios of, perhaps, 4 to 1 or more. With the spree of corporate borrowing that characterized the 1980s, many large corporations have let their interest coverage ratios decline below 2 to 1. In most cases, their credit ratings have dropped accordingly.

ESTIMATED LIABILITIES, CONTINGENT LOSSES, AND COMMITMENTS

Estimated Liabilities

The term ***estimated liabilities*** refers to ***liabilities that appear in financial statements at estimated dollar amounts.*** Let us again consider the example of the auto maker's liability to honour its "new car warranties." A manufacturer's liability for warranty work is recorded by an entry debiting Warranty Expense and crediting Liability for Warranty

Claims. The ***matching principle*** requires that the expense of performing warranty work be recognized in the period in which the products are ***sold,*** in order to offset this expense against the related sales revenue. As the warranty may extend several years into the future, the dollar amount of this liability (and expense) must be estimated. Rather than estimate when warranty work will be performed, accountants traditionally have classified the liability for warranty claims as a current liability.

By definition, estimated liabilities involve some degree of uncertainty. However, the liabilities are (1) known to exist, and (2) the uncertainty is ***not so great*** as to prevent the company from making a reasonable estimate and recording the liability.

Contingent Losses

OBJECTIVE 7 Define contingent losses and commitments. Explain the criteria for determining their presentation in financial statements.

Contingent losses are similar to estimated liabilities, but may involve much more uncertainty. A ***contingent loss*** is a ***possible loss*** (or expense), stemming from ***past events,*** that will be resolved as to existence and amount by some future event confirming or rejecting the loss.

Central to the definition of a contingent loss is the element of ***uncertainty***—uncertainty to the amount of loss and, in some cases, uncertainty as to ***whether or not any loss actually has been incurred.*** A common example of a contingent loss is a lawsuit pending against a company. The lawsuit is based upon past events, but until the suit is resolved, uncertainty exists as to the amount (if any) of the company's liability.

Contingent losses differ from estimated liabilities in two ways. First, a contingent loss involves a ***greater degree of uncertainty.*** Often the uncertainty extends to whether or not any loss or expense actually has been incurred. In contrast, the loss or expense relating to an estimated liability is ***known to exist.***

Second, the concept of a contingent loss extends not only to possible liabilities but also to possible ***impairments of assets.*** Assume, for example, that a bank has made large loans to a foreign country that is now experiencing political instability. Uncertainty exists as to the amount of loss, if any, associated with this loan. From the bank's point of view, this loan is an ***asset that may be impaired,*** not a liability.

Contingent Losses in Financial Statements The manner in which contingent losses are presented in financial statements depends upon the ***degree of uncertainty involved.***

Contingent losses are ***recorded*** in the accounting records only when both of the following criteria are met: (1) it is ***likely*** that a loss has been incurred, and (2) the amount of loss can be ***reasonably estimated.***[9] When these criteria are ***not*** met, contingent losses still are ***disclosed*** in financial statements if the occurrence of the confirming future event (1) is likely but the amount of loss cannot reasonably be estimated, or (2) is likely and there exists an exposure to loss in excess of the amount accrued in the records, or (3) is not determinable. Pending lawsuits, for example, usually are disclosed in notes accompanying the financial statements, but the loss, if any, is not recorded in the accounting records until the lawsuit is settled.

---

[9] CICA, *CICA Handbook* (Toronto), section 3290.12.

Companies generally need not disclose contingent losses if the risk of a material loss is considered ***remote.***

Notice the ***judgmental nature*** of the criteria used in accounting for contingent losses. These criteria involved assessments as to whether the material loss is "likely," or "reasonably estimated," or "remote." Thus, the ***professional judgment*** of the company's management, accountants, legal counsel, and auditors is the deciding factor in accounting for contingent losses.

When contingent losses are disclosed in footnotes to the financial statements, the footnote should describe the nature of the contingency and, if possible, provide an estimate of the amount of possible loss. If a reasonable estimate of the amount of possible loss cannot be made, the footnote should include the range of possible loss or a statement that an estimate cannot be made. The following footnote is typical of the disclosure of the contingent loss arising from pending litigation:

Footnote disclosure of a contingent loss

Note 8: Contingencies

In October of the current year, the Company was named as defendant in a lawsuit alleging patent infringement and claiming damages of $408 million. The Company denies all charges in this case and is preparing its defenses against them. The Company is advised by legal counsel that it is not possible at this time to determine the ultimate legal or financial responsibility with respect to this litigation.

As mentioned earlier, in certain cases, a ***portion*** of a contingent loss qualifies for immediate recognition, whereas the remainder only meets the criteria for disclosure. Assume, for example, that a company has been sued for $10 million. Legal counsel cannot predict the outcome of this litigation, but considers it "likely" that the company will lose at least $1 million. The company should recognize this $1 million expected loss and record it as a liability. In addition, the company should disclose the nature and amount of the litigation, stating that the loss ultimately may exceed the recorded amount.

Potential Significance of Contingent Losses Users of financial statements should pay close attention to the notes disclosing contingent losses. Even if no loss has yet been recorded in the accounting records, contingent losses may be so material as to threaten the continued existence of the company.

The risk that losses may result from ***future*** events is ***not*** a contingent loss. The risk of future losses generally is ***not*** disclosed in financial statements for several reasons. For one, any disclosure of future losses would be sheer speculation. For another, no one can foresee all of the events that might give rise to future losses.

Commitments

Contracts for future transactions are called ***commitments.*** They are not liabilities. However, commitments (contractual obligations) that are significant or material should be disclosed in footnotes to the financial statements. For example, a professional baseball club may issue a three-year contract to a player at an annual salary of, say, $2 million. This is a commitment to pay for services to be rendered in the future. There is no obligation to make payment until the services are received. As liabilities stem only from ***past transactions,*** this commitment has not yet created a liability.

Other examples of commitments include a corporation's long-term employment contract with a key officer, a contract for construction of a new plant, and a contract to buy or sell inventory at future dates. The common quality of all these commitments is an intent to enter into transactions ***in the future.***

Losses on Commitments A basic concept of accounting is that losses should be recorded as soon as evidence exists that a loss has been incurred. Therefore, if a commitment existing at the balance sheet date appears to "lock the company into a loss," that loss should be recorded. The offsetting credit entry is to a liability account, which will be paid when the company honours its commitment.

To illustrate, assume that in December of 1995 an independent oil refinery entered into a firm contractual commitment to purchase 1 million barrels of oil in January 1996 at a price of ***$30*** per barrel. By December 31, 1995, however, the price of oil unexpectedly had declined to only ***$20*** per barrel.

The refinery's purchase commitment obligated it to buy 1 million barrels of oil at a per-barrel price ***$10 above*** current replacement cost. Thus, under the terms of this agreement, the refinery contractually was obligated to sustain a $10 million economic loss. At December 31, 1995, the refinery recognized this loss by making the following adjusting entry:

Recognition of a "locked-in" loss

Loss on Purchase Commitment	*10,000,000*	
Liability for Loss on Purchase Commitment		*10,000,000*
To record loss from commitment to purchase 1 million barrels of oil at a price $10 per barrel in excess of market.		

When the oil was received in January, the refinery recorded the purchase as shown below:

Purchases recorded at market value below cost

Inventory	*20,000,000*	
Liability for Loss on Purchase Commitment	*10,000,000*	
Cash		*30,000,000*
To record purchase of 1 million barrels of oil at $30 per barrel under terms of an unfavourable purchase commitment.		

Notice that when the inventory is received, it is recorded at its current replacement cost, not at the $30 per barrel price specified in the purchase commitment. This practice is consistent with the idea that inventories should be valued at the ***lower-of-cost-and-market*** value.

"Gains" on Commitments Are Not Recognized Assume for a moment that at the end of 1995, the price of oil has been ***$35*** per barrel—a price well in excess of the cost specified in the refinery's purchase commitment. The facts underlying a favourable purchase commitment may be disclosed in notes to the financial statements, but no "gain" is recorded in the accounting records. A gain is not ***realized*** merely because inventory is purchased on favourable terms; gains are realized only when that inventory is ***sold*** at a price above cost.

Topics Deferred to Chapter 16

In this chapter, we have discussed the types of liabilities that are common to almost every business organization. Our discussion, however, does not address some of the largest liabilities of many large, publicly owned corporations.

In a large corporation, such liabilities as bonds payable, pensions and other post-retirement benefits, and deferred income taxes often dwarf such obligations as accounts payable and instalment debt. Liabilities that relate primarily to large corporations will be discussed in Chapter 16, after we have explored more fully the nature and characteristics of the corporate form of business entity.

* *Supplemental Topic*
Accounting for Payrolls

In most business organizations, the largest expense accruing on a daily basis is payroll. In the airlines industry, for example, labour costs usually represent 40% to 50% of total operating expenses.

The task of accounting for payroll costs would be an important one simply because of the large amounts involved; however, it is further complicated by the many federal and provincial laws that require employers to maintain certain specific information in their payroll records not only for the business as a whole but also for each individual employee. Frequent reports of wages paid and amounts withheld must be filed with government authorities. These reports are prepared by every employer and must be accompanied by ***payment*** to the government of the amounts withheld from employees and of the payroll taxes levied on the employer.

A basic rule in most business organizations is that every employee must be paid on time, and the payment must be accompanied by a detailed explanation of the computations used in determining the net amount received by the employee. The payroll system must therefore be capable of processing the input data (such as employee names, social insurance numbers, hours worked, pay rates, overtime, and taxes) and producing a prompt and accurate output of paycheques, payroll records, withholding statements, and reports to governmental authorities. In addition, the payroll system must have built-in safeguards against overpayments to employees, the issuance of duplicate paycheques, payments to fictitious employees, and the continuance on the payroll of persons who have been terminated as employees.

INTERNAL CONTROL OVER PAYROLLS

Every business needs to establish adequate internal control over payrolls. With such controls, a business has assurance that employees will be paid the correct amounts and that payroll-related taxes will be computed correctly and paid on time. Failure to pay employees promptly and in the proper amounts is certain to damage employee morale. Failures to remit

OBJECTIVE 8 ***Describe the basic separation of duties in a payroll system, and explain how this plan contributes to strong internal control.***

payroll taxes to tax authorities on schedule may result in severe fines and penalties. Finally, payroll historically has been an area in which poor internal control has sometimes led to employee fraud.

Payroll fraud can take many forms. Small-scale payroll fraud may consist of employees overstating the number of hours (or days) that they have actually worked. "Padding" the payroll—adding fictitious employees to the payroll in order to generate extra paycheques—is a larger-scale payroll fraud.

A basic means of achieving adequate internal control over payrolls is an appropriate separation of duties. In most organizations, payroll activities include (1) employing workers, (2) timekeeping, (3) payroll preparation and record keeping, and (4) the distribution of pay to employees. Internal control is strengthened if each of these functions is handled by a separate department.

Human Resources Department The work of the human resources department begins with interviewing and hiring job applicants. When a new employee is hired, the department prepares records showing the date of employment, the authorized rate of pay, and payroll deductions. It then sends a written notice to the payroll department to place the new employee on the payroll. The human resources department also is responsible for notifying the payroll department of changes in employees' rates of pay and of persons whose employment has been terminated.

Timekeeping For employees paid by the hour, the time of arrival and departure should be punched on time cards. A new time card should be placed in the rack by the time clock at the beginning of each week or other pay period. Control procedures should exist to ensure that each employee punches his or her own time card and no other. The timekeeping function should be lodged in a separate department that will control the time cards and transmit these source documents to the payroll department.

In a computer-based payroll system, record keeping is simplified if the time clocks are on-line devices—that is, if they are connected directly with the computer system. In this way, the hours worked by each employee are entered automatically into the payroll accounting system.

The Payroll Department The input of information to the payroll department consists of hours reported by the timekeeping department and authorized names, pay rates, and payroll deductions received from the human resources department. The output of the payroll department includes (1) payroll cheques, (2) individual employee records of earnings and deductions, and (3) regular reports to the government showing employee earnings and taxes withheld.

Distribution of Paycheques The paycheques prepared in the payroll department are transmitted to the ***paymaster,*** who distributes them to the employees. The paymaster should ***not*** have responsibility for hiring or firing employees, timekeeping, or preparation of the payroll.

Paycheques for absent employees should never be turned over to other employees or to supervisors for delivery. Instead, the absent employee should later pick up the paycheque from the paymaster after presenting proper identification and signing a receipt. The distribution of paycheques by the paymaster provides assurance that paycheques will not continue to be issued to fictitious employees or employees who have been terminated.

The Operation of a Payroll System: A Summary

The operation of a typical payroll system is illustrated in the following flowchart. Notes have been made indicating the major internal control points within the system.

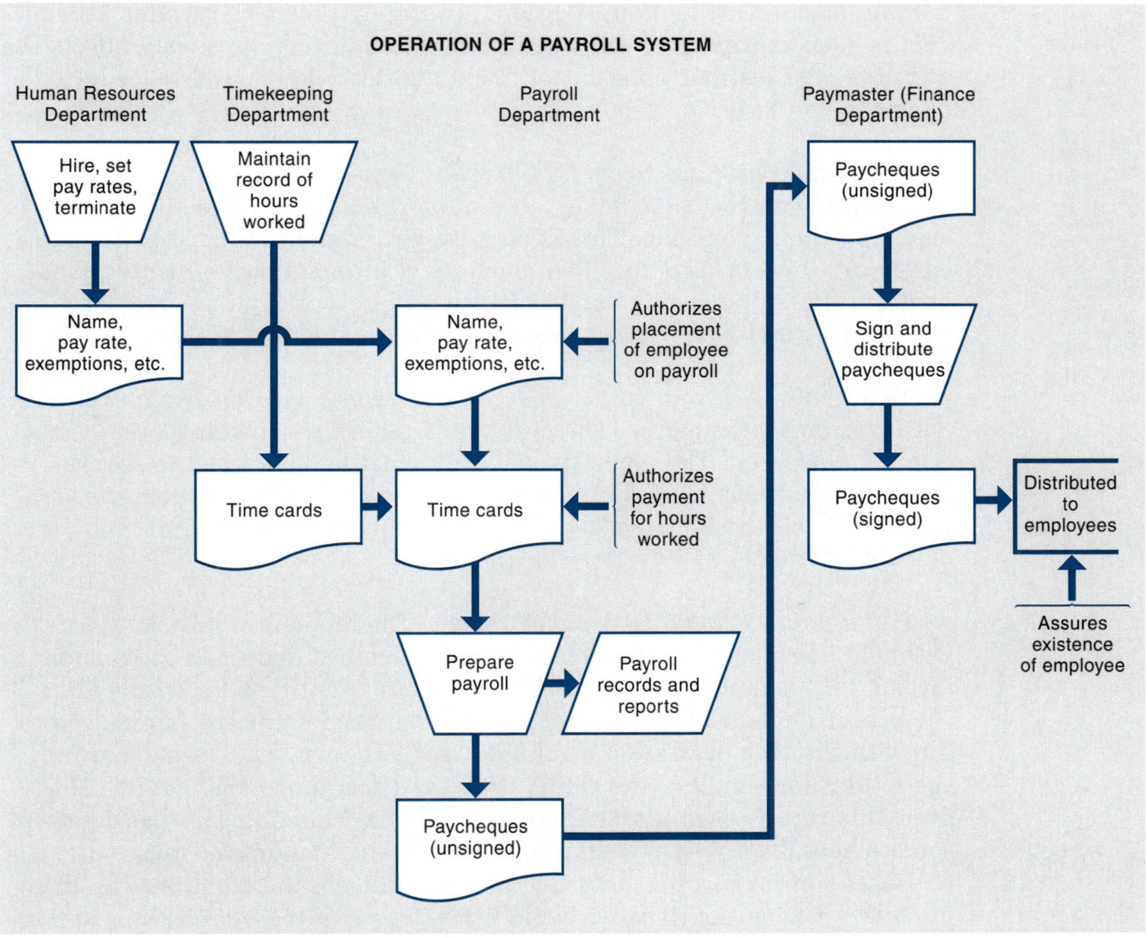

THE COMPUTATION OF PAYROLL AMOUNTS

OBJECTIVE 9 Account for a payroll, including computation of amounts withheld and payroll taxes on the employer.

The actual preparation of a payroll, including the computation of dollar amounts, maintenance of payroll records, and printing of paycheques, is the responsibility of the payroll department. The dollar amounts associated with payrolls fall into three categories: (1) employees' gross pay, (2) amounts withheld from employees' gross pay, and (3) payroll taxes levied on the employer.

Gross Pay

Gross pay (earnings) is the amount earned by the employees during the pay period. Except to the extent that employers ***withhold*** amounts for taxes or other purposes, all gross pay is payable directly to the employees.

Gross pay also includes compensation during sick days, holidays, and vacations. However, it does not include ***fringe benefits,*** such as group life insurance paid by the employer or the use of a "company car." The distinction is that fringe benefits are not payable directly to the employees.

Gross pay must be computed separately for each employee. For employees paid an hourly wage, the payroll system must keep track of the ***number of hours*** that each employee works each day. In many cases, current laws require that employees be paid at an overtime rate for hours worked in excess of 8 per day or 40 per week. For employees who receive sales commissions, the system must record separately the sales revenue attributable to each salesperson. The amount of an employee's gross pay affects the amounts of taxes that must be withheld and also the payroll taxes levied upon the employer.

Amounts Withheld from Employees' Pay

The ***net pay*** (or "take-home pay") of most employees is substantially less than their gross pay. This is because government authorities require employers to ***withhold*** specified amounts of income taxes, unemployment insurance premiums, and Canada Pension Plan contributions from each employee's gross pay. (Employees often refer to amounts withheld as ***deductions.***)

Taxes withheld from employees' pay are taxes levied ***on the employees,*** not taxes on the employer. The employer's role in withholding taxes is that of a tax ***collector.*** The amounts withheld must be forwarded to governmental tax authorities weekly, twice-monthly, or monthly, depending on the size of the amount involved. Therefore, the employer records the amounts withheld as ***current liabilities.***

Federal and Provincial Income Taxes The amount of income taxes withheld depends upon the amount of the earnings and upon the amount of income tax exemptions to which the employee is entitled. To ensure that the proper amount of income tax is withheld, each employee is required to file with the employer a Personal Tax Credit Return, TD1 form, showing the total claim amount, the Claim Code, and the supporting details. However, this return need not be filed by employees claiming the "basic personal amount" only—i.e., claiming the minimum amount for tax credit.

Based on the earnings and the amount claimed, the employer can determine the income tax to be withheld from the employee by referring to the income tax deduction tables provided by Revenue Canada, Taxation. The amount withheld from employees is remitted to Revenue Canada, Taxation. This amount includes both the federal and provincial income taxes for all provinces except the province of Quebec, which collects its own income tax. Employers in Quebec must withhold separate deductions for federal and Quebec income taxes.

Unemployment Insurance Since its inception in 1940, the federal Unemployment Insurance Act has undergone significant changes. The current act requires, with a few exceptions, both employers and employees to contribute to unemployment insurance. The purpose of the act is to provide relief from financial hardships for those who are unemployed even though they are willing and able to work. The eligibility for, and the amount of, unemployment benefits depend on a number of factors, including past insurable earnings, length of insurable employment, and regional unemployment rate.

The employers are responsible for withholding an appropriate amount of unemployment insurance premium from their employees. The amount of premium withheld together with the premium contributed by the employer is remitted to Revenue Canada, Taxation. Employees are subject to unemployment insurance premium when they have cash earnings of 20% of the maximum weekly insurable earnings (this maximum amount changes annually; in 1993 it was $745) or when they have worked 15 hours a week. For the year 1993, the employees' premium is 3% of their insurable earnings; the employers' premium is 1.4 times that of the employees'. For example, if an employee's monthly insurable earnings are $1,000, the premiums for the employee and the employer are $30 (1,000 × 3%) and $42 ($30 × 1.4) respectively. In 1993, the rate of premium of 3% is applicable to annual insurable earnings of up to a maximum of $38,740, or up to a maximum of $3,228.33 on a monthly basis. In other words, employees with annual earnings of $38,740 (or monthly earnings of $3,228.33) or more are required to pay premium on the annual maximum amount of $38,740 (or $3,228.33 monthly). Accordingly, the maximum annual premium for an employee is $1,162.20 ($38,740 × 3%), or on a monthly basis the maximum is $96.85 ($3,228.33 × 3%). The premium rate as well as the maximum amounts subject to unemployment insurance premium may change from year to year.

On occasion, employees may have contributed more than the maximum amount of premium. In such cases, the employees should claim a refund by reporting the overpayment in their income tax returns.

While the individual contribution is small, the total contribution for unemployment insurance is huge. For example, the total contribution of unemployment insurance in a recent year was more than $12 billion.

Canada Pension Plan The Canada Pension Plan Act requires, with a few exceptions, both employers and employees, including those who are self-employed, to make contributions to the Canada Pension Plan. Its purpose is to provide retirement, disability, and similar benefits. The eligibility for, and the amount of, benefits depend on a number of factors, including the amount of pensionable earnings, the length of the contribution period, and the age of the individual.

The employers are responsible for withholding an appropriate amount of Canada Pension Plan contribution from the pensionable earnings of each of their employees and are required to contribute an amount equal to that of the employees'. The amount withheld together with the amount contributed by the employers is remitted to Revenue Canada, Taxation. For the year 1993, the employees' contribution is 2.5% of the annual pensionable earnings, with the first $3,300 exempted, and the employers' contribution is the same as that of the employees'. For example, if an employee's annual pensionable earnings are $18,500, both the employee and the employer are required to contribute $380 each [($18,500 less $3,300 basic annual exemption) times 2.5%]. In 1993, the rate of contribution of 2.5% is applicable to annual pensionable earnings of over $3,300, up to a maximum of $30,100 (i.e., earnings of $33,400 less the $3,300 basic annual exemption). In other words, employees with annual pensionable earnings of $3,300 or less are not required to contribute, and employees with pensionable earnings of $33,400 or more are required to contribute on the maximum amount of $30,100. Accordingly, the maximum annual contribution for an employee is $752.50 ($30,100 × 2.5%).

Since contributions are made periodically, employees with annual earnings exceeding the maximum pensionable earnings may pay up the $752.50 maximum contribution in the early part of the year. If an employee, for example, earns $60,000 a year, the monthly contribution is $118.12 ($5,000 less the monthly exemption of $275 at 2.5%), and the employee will have contributed $708.72 in the first six months and will only be required to contribute the balance of $43.78 in the seventh month.[10] The rate, and the amount subject to, Canada Pension Plan, may change from year to year. On occasion, an employee may have contributed more than the maximum amount. In such cases, the employee should claim a refund by reporting the overpayment in his or her income tax return.

The Canada Pension Plan applies to all provinces except the province of Quebec, which has its own similar pension plan. The two plans are closely coordinated so that contributing employees are protected wherever they may work in Canada.

The total contribution to Canada Pension Plan is very large; a recent year's contribution amounted to more than $6 billion.

Other Deductions from Employees' Earnings In addition to the compulsory deductions for unemployment insurance, Canada (or Quebec) Pension Plan, and income taxes, many other deductions are voluntarily authorized by employees. Union dues, insurance premiums, savings bond purchases, charitable contributions, retirement programs, and pension plans are examples of voluntary payroll deductions.

Employer's Responsibility for Amounts Withheld In withholding amounts from an employee's earnings for either voluntary or involuntary deductions, the employer acts merely as a collection agent. The amounts withheld are paid to the designated organization, such as a government department or labour union. The employer is also responsible for maintaining accounting records that will enable it to file required reports and make timely payments of the amounts withheld. From the employer's viewpoint, the amounts withheld from employee's earnings represent current liabilities.

Basic Payroll Records

The formats of payroll records vary greatly among different businesses, depending upon the number of employees and the extent of automation. However, there are two basic records common to the payroll system of

[10] The monthly exemption is arrived at by dividing the annual exemption of $3,300 by 12. The proper amounts of contributions can be obtained from the deduction tables provided by Revenue Canada, Taxation. Since the exemption has already been taken into account in these tables, there is no need to deduct the monthly or weekly exemption from the earnings. For example, if the monthly earnings plus taxable benefits, if any, are $5,000, look up the earnings' bracket between $4,993.60 and $5,003.59 to obtain the proper amount of contribution, which is $118.09.

every organization: the ***payroll register*** and the ***employees' individual earnings records.***

Payroll Register The payroll register is a special journal used for developing all of the information needed for processing and recording the payroll of a specific pay period. This journal includes a separate line of data about each employee. On this line, the employee's gross pay, various amounts withheld, and net pay are entered in separate columns. Thus, each line of the payroll register provides the data necessary for preparing one employee's paycheque, and also for updating the employee's individual earnings record. Totalling each column, on the other hand, provides information about the ***entire*** payroll, which is posted to the general ledger accounts.

To illustrate, assume that Data Management Limited has 35 salaried employees, who are paid monthly. A payroll register containing data relating to the March payroll is illustrated on the following page (along with the individual earnings record for one employee).

The illustrated payroll register includes separate columns for gross pay, four different types of withholding, and net pay.[11] The ***totals*** of these columns represent the expenses and liabilities associated with the issuance of paycheques to employees. (These totals do ***not*** reflect the payroll taxes on the employer for March.)

One common practice is to summarize the column totals of the payroll register in the form of a general journal entry, as follows:[12]

Journal entry summarizing the March payroll—except for taxes on the employer

Salaries Expense	80,000	
Liability for Income Tax Withheld		14,572
Liability for Unemployment Insurance Withheld		2,400
Liability for Canada Pension Plan Withheld		1,768
Liability for Group Insurance Withheld		1,860
Accrued Payroll		59,400
To record the monthly payroll for March.		

All of the accounts credited in this entry are current liabilities of the employer. Accrued payroll represents the net pay owed to employees; this liability will be discharged almost immediately through the issuance of paycheques. The liabilities for amounts withheld will be discharged within a short period of time by remitting these amounts to the appropriate recipients.

Employees' Individual Earnings Records An employer also must maintain an ***individual earnings record*** for each employee. These records contain basically the same information as does the payroll register: each employee's gross pay, amounts withheld, and net pay. The differences

---

[11] The illustrated payroll register is highly simplified. An actual payroll register includes many more columns for such items as employees' social insurance numbers and several other types of withholding. For employees paid an hourly wage, additional columns would indicate pay rates and regular hours and overtime hours worked during the pay period. Actual payroll registers generally are a computer printout with, perhaps, 15 or more data columns.

[12] A general journal entry is not actually necessary; the column totals could be posted directly from the payroll register to the general ledger accounts.

PAYROLL REGISTER

Payroll period ended: March 31, 19__

Employee	Gross Pay	Amounts Withheld: Income Taxes	Amounts Withheld: Unemployment Insurance	Amounts Withheld: Canada Pension Plan	Amounts Withheld: Group Insurance	Net Pay	Cheque No.
Abrams, H	$ 1,600	$ 262	$ 48	$ 33	$ 35	$ 1,222	841
Boice, C	2,000	347	60	43	42	1,508	842
Cato, Y	3,000	637	90	68	66	2,139	843
Zucco, R	2,400	450	72	53	51	1,774	875
Totals	$80,000	$14,572	$2,400	$1,768	$1,860	$59,400	— —

EMPLOYEE EARNINGS RECORD

Name: Carol Boice
Address: 900 Lake View Lane, Apt. D
Windsor, Ontario, N9B 8P9
Position: Commercial artist-grade 1
Marital status: M
Claim Code: 2

Soc. Ins. # 483-724-690
Date of Birth: July 17, 1970
Date employed: July 24, 1994
Date of termination:
Reason for termination:
Monthly salary: $2,000

Pay Period	Gross Pay	Year-to-Date	Amounts Withheld: Income Taxes	Amounts Withheld: Unemployment Insurance	Amounts Withheld: Canada Pension Plan	Amounts Withheld: Group Insurance	Net Pay	Cheque No.
Jan.	$2,000	$2,000	$347	$60	$43	$42	$1,508	772
Feb.	2,000	4,000	347	60	43	42	1,508	807
Mar.	2,000	6,000	347	60	43	42	1,508	842
Total for quarter	$6,000	$6,000	$1,041	$180	$129	$126	$4,524	— —
Apr.								
May								

between a payroll register and the employees' individual earnings records are primarily in the manner in which the data are ***organized.***

A payroll register shows in one place all of the payroll data for ***one payroll period,*** including data for all employees. An earnings record shows in one place all of the payroll data ***for one employee,*** including data for every payroll period. The individual earnings record for one of Data Management's salaried employees is illustrated above.

An employee's earnings record always includes a column showing the employee's ***cumulative*** gross pay earned thus far during the year. This year-to-date earnings figure determines when (and if) the employee's earnings exceed the bases subject to Canada Pension Plan contribution. In addition, employers must report each employee's gross earnings for the year to the employee and to Revenue Canada.

By the end of February of each year, employers must furnish each employee and Revenue Canada with a copy of the Statement of Remuneration Paid (T4), showing the employee's gross earnings for the preceding calendar year and the amounts of all taxes withheld. When the employee files an income tax return, he or she must attach a copy of this statement.

Payroll Taxes Levied upon the Employer

As discussed earlier in this chapter, employers are required to contribute to unemployment insurance and Canada Pension Plan. These contributions are expenses to the business and are commonly called "payroll taxes expense."

Entry Recording an Employer's Payroll Taxes The entry to record the employer's payroll taxes is made at the end of each pay period, along with the entry recording the payroll. To illustrate, let us again consider the $80,000 March payroll of Data Management Limited. The entry to record this payroll, including the taxes withheld from employees, appeared on page 557. Now, however, we are addressing the payroll taxes levied directly upon the ***employer.***

The employer's liability for unemployment insurance premium is 1.4 times the amounts withheld from the employees—$3,360 (1.4 × $2,400). The employer's liability for Canada Pension Plan is equal to the amount withheld from the employees—$1,768. A general journal entry recording the payroll taxes levied upon Data Management in March appears below:

Journal entry to record payroll taxes on the employer

Payroll Taxes Expense	*5,128*	
Unemployment Insurance Taxes Payable		*3,360*
Canada Pension Plan Taxes Payable		*1,768*
To record employer's payroll taxes relating to the March payroll.		

All of the accounts credited represent current liabilities that must be paid within a short period of time.

Payroll by Computer

Because of the repetitious nature of payroll computations, payrolls are ideally suited to computer processing. In fact, accounting for payrolls was among the first applications of the computer in the business world. As an alternative to accounting for payrolls "in-house," small businesses often delegate this function to an outside agency.

Given the complexities of payroll accounting, computer-based payroll systems are amazingly efficient. Often, the only input required for processing the entire payroll is the ***number of hours*** worked by each employee receiving an hourly wage. If time clocks are on-line devices, payrolls sometimes can be prepared without any manual input of data or manual computations. (Of course, the computer-based files must be updated for changes in pay rates, tax rates, or the personnel comprising the work force.)

In conclusion, it simply is ***not cost-efficient*** to account for payrolls manually in a business that has more than just a few employees.

Fringe Benefits

Many companies provide employees with various fringe benefits, such as group life insurance and a pension plan. The cost of fringe benefits usually is determined for the work force as a whole, rather than computed separately for each employee. Separate expense accounts and liability accounts are used in recording each type of fringe benefit.

To illustrate, assume that Data Management pays life insurance for its employees and also contributes an amount equal to 5% of their gross pay to an employees' registered pension plan. A general journal entry recording the cost of fringe benefits relating to the March 31 payroll is shown below:

Journal entry to record the cost of fringe benefits

Life Insurance Expense	4,600	
Pension Expense	4,000	
Insurance Premiums Payable		4,600
Liability to Employees' Pension Plan		4,000
To record the cost of fringe benefits provided to employees in March.		

The Total Cost of Employee Compensation

Our discussion of payrolls has been based upon the $80,000 March payroll of Data Management Limited. Notice, however, that the company's ***total*** payroll cost in March actually amounts to ***$93,728***—a figure substantially higher than the employees' gross pay. The "total payroll cost" includes the following elements:

Employees cost more than they're paid

Gross pay earned by employees	$80,000
Payroll taxes levied upon employer	5,128
Fringe benefits paid by employer	8,600
Total employee compensation costs for the pay period	$93,728

These results are not at all unusual. An employer's total payroll cost generally exceeds employees' gross pay by 15% to 25%.

Distinction between Employees and Independent Contractors

Every business obtains personal services from ***employees*** and also from ***independent contractors.*** The employer-employee relationship exists when the company paying for the services has a right to direct and supervise the person rendering the services. Independent contractors, on the other hand, are retained to perform a specific task and exercise their own judgment as to the best methods for performing the work. Examples of independent contractors include public accountants engaged to perform an audit, lawyers retained to represent a company in a law suit, and a plumber called in to repair a broken pipe.

The ***fees*** paid to independent contractors are not included in payroll records and are ***not subject to withholding or payroll taxes.*** Also, independent contractors do not participate in the fringe benefits provided to employees.

CHAPTER REVIEW

KEY TERMS INTRODUCED OR EMPHASIZED IN CHAPTER 11

Accrued liabilities The liability to pay an expense that has accrued during the period. Also called ***accrued expenses.***

Amortization of discount The process of systematically writing off to interest expense each period a portion of the discount on a note payable. Causes the carrying value of the liability to rise to the face value of the note by the maturity date.

Amortization table A schedule that indicates how instalment payments are allocated between interest expense and repayments of principal.

***Canada Pension Plan** A national plan established by a federal act that requires both the employer and the employee to make contributions to the plan. Its purpose is to provide retirement, disability, and similar benefits.

Commitments Agreements to carry out future transactions. Not a liability because the transaction has not yet been performed, but should be disclosed in footnotes to the financial statements if the commitment is significant.

Contingent loss A possible loss that either will develop into a full-fledged loss or will be eliminated entirely by a future event.

Contra-liability account A ledger account that is deducted from or offset against a related liability account in the balance sheet; for example, Discount on Notes Payable.

Debt ratio Total liabilities divided by total assets. Indicates the percentage of total assets financed by borrowing.

Discount on Notes Payable A contra-liability account representing any interest charges applicable to future periods included in the face amount of a note payable. Over the life of the note, the balance of the Discount on Notes Payable account is amortized into Interest Expense.

Estimated liabilities Liabilities known to exist but that must be recorded in the accounting records at estimated dollar amounts.

***Fringe benefits** Portions of the compensation package offered to employees that are not paid directly to the employees. Paid life insurance is an example.

***Gross pay** The total amount earned by an employee that is payable, at least in part, to that employee. Does not include fringe benefits.

***Independent contractor** A person or firm providing services to a company for a fee or commission. Not controlled or supervised by the client company. Not subject to payroll taxes.

Interest coverage ratio Operating income divided by interest expense. Indicates the number of times that the company was able to earn the amount of its interest charges.

Maturity value The value of a note at its maturity date, consisting of principal plus any interest payable at that date.

Operating income A subtotal in the income statement representing the revenue earned from customers less only operating expenses. Widely used in evaluating the relationship between earnings and interest expense, as operating income represents the earnings ***before*** deductions for interest expense and other "nonoperating" items.

***Payroll register** A form of payroll record showing for each pay period all payroll information for employees individually and in total.

* *Supplemental Topic, "Accounting for Payrolls"*

***Personal Tax Credit Return (TD1)** A form prepared and signed by the employee that shows the total amount of claims and the supporting details. It is used to determine the proper amount of income tax to be withheld from the employee's remuneration.

Principal amount That portion of the maturity value of a note that is attributable to the amount borrowed or to the cost of the asset acquired when the note was issued, rather than being attributable to interest charges.

Quick ratio Quick assets divided by current liabilities. A more stringent measure of immediate solvency than the current ratio.

***Statement of Remuneration Paid (T4)** A form furnished by the employer to every employee that shows the gross earnings for the calendar year and the amounts withheld for unemployment insurance, Canada Pension Plan, income tax, and other items such as registered pension plan.

***Unemployment insurance** An insurance plan established by a federal act that imposes a premium contribution on both the employer and the employee. Its purpose is to provide relief from financial hardships for the unemployed.

DEMONSTRATION PROBLEM FOR YOUR REVIEW

Listed below are selected items from the financial statements of G & H Pump Mfg. Corporation for the year ended December 31, 1995:

Note payable to Royal Bank	$100,000
Discount on note payable (to Royal Bank)	1,000
Income taxes payable	63,000
Contingent liability relating to lawsuit	200,000
Accounts payable	163,230
Mortgage note payable	240,864
Interest payable (mortgage note)	1,606
Accrued payroll	18,700
Amounts withheld from employees' pay	2,940
Payroll taxes payable	1,260
Unearned revenue	25,300

OTHER INFORMATION

1 The note payable owed to Royal Bank is due in 30 days. G & H has arranged with this bank to renew the note for an additional 2 years.

2 G & H has been sued for $200,000 by someone claiming the company's pumps are excessively noisy. It is reasonably possible, but not probable, that a loss has been sustained.

3 The mortgage note is payable at $8,000 per month over the next 3 years. During the next 12 months, the principal amount of this note will be reduced to $169,994.

INSTRUCTIONS

a Using this information, prepare the current liabilities and long-term liabilities sections of a classified balance sheet at December 31, 1995.

b Explain briefly how the information in each of the three numbered paragraphs affected your presentation of the company's liabilities.

* *Supplemental Topic, "Accounting for Payrolls"*

SOLUTION TO DEMONSTRATION PROBLEM

a

G & H PUMP MFG. CORPORATION
Partial Balance Sheet
December 31, 1995

Liabilities:		
Current liabilities:		
Accounts payable		*$163,230*
Income taxes payable		*63,000*
Interest payable (mortgage note)		*1,606*
Accrued payroll		*18,700*
Amounts withheld from employees' pay		*2,940*
Payroll taxes payable		*1,260*
Unearned revenue		*25,300*
Current portion of long-term debt (mortgage note)		*70,870*
Total current liabilities		*$346,906*
Long-term liabilities:		
Note payable	*100,000*	
Less: Discount on note payable	*1,000*	*$ 99,000*
Mortgage note payable		*169,994*
Total long-term liabilities		*$268,994*
Total liabilities		*$615,900*

b **1** Although the note payable to Royal Bank is due in 30 days, it is classified as a long-term liability as it will be refinanced on a long-term basis.

2 The pending lawsuit is a contingent liability requiring disclosure, but it is not listed in the liability section of the balance sheet.

3 The $70,870 of the mortgage note that will be repaid within the next 12 months ($240,864 − $169,994) is a current liability; the remaining balance, due after December 31, 1995, is long-term debt.

ASSIGNMENT MATERIAL

DISCUSSION QUESTIONS

1 Define ***liabilities.*** Identify several characteristics that distinguish liabilities from owner's equity.

2 Explain the relative priority of the claims of owners and of creditors to the assets of a business. Do all creditors have equal priority? Explain.

3 Define ***estimated liabilities*** and provide three examples. Are estimated liabilities recorded in accounting records?

4 Jonas Company issues a 3-month (3 days of grace included), 12% note payable to replace an account payable to Smith Supply Company in the amount of $8,000. Draft the journal entries (in general journal form) to record the issuance of the note payable and the payment of the note at the maturity date.

5 Howard Benson applied to the City Bank for a loan of $20,000 for a period of 3 months (with the 3 days of grace included). The loan was granted at an annual interest rate of 12%. Write a sentence illustrating the wording of the note signed by Benson if

a Interest is stated separately in the note.

b Interest is included in the face amount of the note.

6 With reference to Question **5** above, give the journal entry required on the books of Howard Benson for issuance of each of the two types of notes.

7 What kind of account is Discount on Notes Payable? Where and how should it appear in the financial statements? What is the eventual disposition of amounts in Discount on Notes Payable?

8 Define ***current liabilities*** and ***long-term liabilities.*** Under what circumstances might a 5-year note payable be classified as a current liability? Under what circumstances might a note payable maturing 30 days after the balance sheet date be classified as a long-term liability?

9 Is the failure to record an accrued liability likely to affect the income statement as well as the balance sheet? Explain.

10 Trong Corporation had a $300,000 note payable outstanding throughout the entire year. The note calls for interest to be computed at the annual rate of 9% and to be paid monthly on the last day of each month. How much accrued interest payable will appear in Trong's December 31 balance sheet? Explain.

11 Ace Garage has an unpaid mortgage loan of $63,210, payable at $1,200 per month. An amortization table indicates that $527 of the current monthly payment represents interest expense. What will be the amount of this mortgage obligation immediately ***after*** Ace makes this current payment?

12 A friend of yours has just purchased a house and has incurred a $50,000, 11% mortgage, payable at $476.17 per month. After making the first monthly payment, he received a receipt from the bank stating that only $17.84 of the $476.17 had been applied to reducing the principal amount of the loan. Your friend computes that at the rate of $17.84 per month, it will take over 233 years to pay off the $50,000 mortgage. Do you agree with your friend's analysis? Explain.

13 Among the long-term liabilities listed on Reese Corporation's balance sheet is "Long-term instalment debt . . . $2,300,000." What ***disclosures*** should be made concerning this debt to assist users of the financial statements in evaluating the company's financial position?

14 Why is the ***quick ratio*** often considered a more useful measure of short-term solvency than the current ratio?

15 Would long-term creditors prefer that a corporation's ***debt ratio*** be high or low? How about its ***interest coverage ratio?*** Explain your answers.

16 What is the meaning of the term ***contingent loss?*** Give two examples. How are contingent losses presented in financial statements? Explain.

17 What is the meaning of the term ***commitment?*** Give several examples. How are commitments usually presented in financial statements? Explain.

*18 MetroScape has 210 employees, but no liability for accrued payroll appears in the company's balance sheet. Assuming no error has been made, how can this be? Explain.

* *Supplemental Topic, "Accounting for Payrolls"*

*19 The personnel department of Meadow Company failed to notify the payroll department that five hourly factory workers had been terminated at the end of the last pay period. Assuming a normal subdivision of duties regarding personnel, timekeeping, preparation of payroll, and distribution of paycheques, what control procedure will prevent the payroll department from preparing paycheques for these five employees in the current period?

*20 The type of payroll fraud known as "padding" a payroll is a more difficult maneuver under today's payroll accounting practices than it was a generation or more ago. What present-day factors make the padding of payrolls a complex and more difficult type of fraud?

*21 Explain which of the following taxes relating to an employee's wages are borne by the employee and which by the employer:

- a Unemployment insurance
- b Canada Pension Plan
- c Income taxes

*22 Is the Salaries Expense account equal to take-home pay or to gross pay? Why?

*23 Why is the cost to an employer of having an employee on the payroll greater than that person's gross pay?

*24 Distinguish between an employee and an independent contractor. Why is this distinction important with respect to payroll accounting?

MULTIPLE CHOICE QUESTIONS

1 Which of the following is characteristic of liabilities, rather than of equity? (More than one answer may be correct.)

- a The obligation matures.
- b The capital providers frequently are entitled to receive interest payments.
- c The capital providers' claims are ***residual*** in the event of liquidation of the business.
- d The capital providers normally have the right to exercise control over business operations.

2 Which of the following situations require recording a liability in 1995? (More than one answer may be correct.)

- a In 1995, a company manufactures and sells stereo equipment that carries a three-year warranty.
- b In 1995, a theatre group receives payments in advance from season ticket holders for productions to be performed in 1996.
- c A company is a defendant in a legal action. At the end of 1995, the company's lawyer feels it is possible the company will lose, and that the amount of the loss might be material.
- d During 1995, a western agricultural co-operative is concerned about the risk of loss if inclement weather destroys the crops.

Use the following data for questions 3 and 4.

On May 1, 1995, Thompkins Company borrowed $350,000 from the bank and agreed to repay that amount plus 12% interest at the end of one year (including the three days of grace).

---

* *Supplemental Topic, "Accounting for Payrolls"*

2,3,4

3 Assume the note payable is drawn in the amount of $350,000 with interest stated separately. With respect to this note, Thompkins's financial statements for the year ended December 31, 1995 include:

a Interest expense of $42,000.

b An overall current liability for this loan of $392,000.

c An overall current liability for this loan of $378,000.

d Unamortized Discount on Notes Payable of $14,000.

4 Assume the note payable is drawn with interest included in the face of the note. Thompkins's adjusting entry on December 31, 1995 with regard to this note includes:

a A credit to Notes Payable of $14,000.

b A debit to Interest Expense of $14,000.

c A credit to Interest Payable of $28,000.

d A credit to Discount on Notes Payable of $28,000.

*5 Each of the following indicates a significant weakness in internal control over payrolls ***except:***

a The paymaster is responsible for timekeeping and for distributing paycheques to employees.

b The human resources department is responsible for hiring and firing employees and for the distribution of paycheques.

c The payroll department is responsible for preparing the payroll cheques for signature by the paymaster, maintaining individual employees' earnings records of earnings and deductions, and filing required payroll reports with the government.

d The payroll department prepares the payroll, the paymaster prepares and signs paycheques, and the paycheques are distributed by the timekeeping department.

*6 Hennesey receives a salary of $60,000 per year from Carling Limited. Income taxes withheld amounted to $18,260. Unemployment insurance premium and Canada Pension Plan contribution withheld were $1,162.20 and $752.50 respectively. Registered pension plan of $3,500 and union dues of $360 were also withheld. Hennesey's take-home pay and the total cost to Carling of having Hennesey on the payroll are, respectively:

a $35,965.30 and $62,379.58

b $41,740 and $61,914.70

c $37,492 and $61,914.70

d $37,880 and $63,829.40

EXERCISES

EXERCISE 11-1 Accounting Terminology

Listed below are nine technical terms introduced or emphasized in this chapter:

Contingent losses	**Unemployment insurance*	*Quick ratio*
Amortization table	**Canada Pension Plan*	*Debt ratio*
Maturity value of a note payable	*Discount on notes payable*	*Interest coverage ratio*

Each of the following statements may (or may not) describe one of these technical terms. For each statement, indicate the term described, or answer "None" if the statement does not correctly describe any of the terms.

* *Supplemental Topic, "Accounting for Payrolls"*

a Future interest charges included in the face amount of a note payable.

b A tax levied upon employees but not upon employers.

c A more stringent measure of short-term solvency than the current ratio.

d A schedule allocating payments on an instalment note payable between the portion representing interest expense of the current period and the portion reducing the principal amount of the debt.

e Total liabilities divided by annual interest expense.

f The risk that a loss may occur in a future period as a result of risks inherent in the nature of a company's business operations.

g The amount owed on a note payable ***excluding*** any interest charges.

EXERCISE 11-2
Effects of Transactions on the Accounting Equation

Listed below are eight events or transactions of GemStar Corporation.

a Made an adjusting entry to record interest on a short-term note payable that has the interest charge included in the face amount.

b Made a monthly instalment payment of a fully amortizing, 6-month, interest-bearing instalment note payable.

c Entered into a contractual commitment with a television network to purchase sixty 30-second commercials in each of the next 18 months. The cost is $75,000 per month, payable on the last day of the month in which the commercial is aired.

d Came within 12 months of the maturity date of a note payable originally issued for a period of 3 years.

e Made an adjusting entry recognizing the accrued interest on a 30-year mortgage that is payable in 360 monthly instalments.

f Estimated the income taxes expense relating to this month's business income.

*g Recorded a regular bi-weekly payroll, including the amounts withheld from employees, the issuance of paycheques, and payroll taxes upon the employer.

*h Remitted the amounts withheld from employees' paycheques to the designated recipients.

INSTRUCTIONS

Indicate the effects of each of these transactions upon the financial statement categories shown below. Organize your answer in tabular form, using the illustrated column headings. Use the following code letters to indicate the effects of each transaction upon the accounting element listed in the column heading:

I = Increase *D* = Decrease *NE* = No Effect

	Income Statement			Balance Sheet			
Transaction	*Revenue* –	*Expenses* =	*Net Income*	*Assets* =	*Current Liab.* +	*Long-Term Liab.* +	*Owner's Equity*
a							

EXERCISE 11-3
Financial Statement Presentation of Liabilities

Using the following information, prepare a listing and descriptions of the amounts that you would classify as (a) current liabilities and (b) long-term liabilities. If you do not list part or all of an item in either classification, briefly explain your reasoning.

* *Supplemental Topic, "Accounting for Payrolls"*

Interest expense that will arise on interest bearing notes over the next 12 months	*$134,000*
Long-term mortgage note payable (of which $3,200 will be paid within the next 12 months)	*800,000*
Interest payable on the mortgage note payable	*2,600*
Lawsuit pending against the company, claiming $500,000 in damages. Legal counsel can make no reasonable estimate of company's potential liability at this time	*500,000*
Note payable due in 60 days, but which will be extended for an additional 18 months	*75,000*
Three-year commitment to Charlene Doyle as chief financial officer at a salary of $140,000 per year	*420,000*
**Amounts withheld from employees' pay*	*6,100*

EXERCISE 11-4
Two Forms for Notes Payable

On November 1, Metals Exchange, Inc., borrowed $250,000 from a bank, and promised to repay that amount plus 12% interest (per year) at the end of 6 months (three days of grace included). You are to prepare two different presentations of the liability to the bank on Metals Exchange's December 31 balance sheet, assuming that the note payable to the bank was drawn as follows:

a For $250,000, with interest stated separately and payable at maturity.

b With the total interest charge included in the face amount of the note.

EXERCISE 11-5
Interest Included in Face Amount of Note Payable

On April 1, Tiger Truck Lines bought four trucks from Freeway Motors for a total price of $272,000. The transactions required Tiger Truck Lines to pay $80,000 cash and to issue a promissory note due in full 18 months later (three days of grace included). The face amount of the note was $215,040, which included interest on the note for the 18 months.

Prepare all entries (in general journal form) for Tiger Truck Lines relating to the purchase of the trucks and the note for the current fiscal year ended December 31. Include the adjusting entries to record interest expense and depreciation expense to December 31. (The trucks are to be depreciated over an 8-year service life by the straight-line method. There is no estimated salvage value.)

EXERCISE 11-6
The Nature of an Accrued Liability

Late in 1994, Marco Construction borrowed $1 million, signing a 5-year (three days of grace included), 7.2% note payable. The note calls for payment of interest charges monthly, on the sixteenth day of each month. Compute the following amounts relating to this note payable:

a Total interest that will be paid over the life of the note.

b Interest expense that will appear in Marco's income statement for ***1996.***

c Accrued interest payable that will appear in Marco's balance sheet at ***December 31, 1996.*** (Compute interest payable based on a 365-day year.)

EXERCISE 11-7
Use of an Amortization Table

Blue Cays Marina has a $200,000 mortgage liability. This mortgage is payable in monthly instalments of $2,057, which include interest computed at the rate of 12% per year (1% per month).

INSTRUCTIONS

a Prepare a partial amortization table showing the original balance of this loan and the allocation of the ***first two*** monthly payments between interest expense and reduction in the unpaid balance. (Round amounts to the nearest dollar.)

b Prepare the journal entry to record the ***second*** monthly payment.

---

* *Supplemental Topic, "Accounting for Payrolls"*

EXERCISE 11-8
Safety of Creditors' Investments

wed. 10.904
Thu. day

Shown below are data from the recent annual reports of two large toy makers. Amounts are stated in thousands.

	Mattel Inc.	Hasbro Inc.
Total assets	*$830,273*	*$1,246,485*
Total liabilities	*554,103*	*444,161*
Interest expense	*50,029*	*24,288*
Operating income	*163,116*	*170,079*

INSTRUCTIONS

a Compute for each company (1) the debt ratio and (2) the interest coverage ratio. (Round the debt ratio to one-tenth of 1%, and interest coverage to one decimal place.)

b In your opinion, which of these companies would a long-term creditor probably view as the safer investment? Explain.

EXERCISE 11-9
"He's Outta There!"

The Iron Dukes, a major league baseball team, signed a 2-year employment contract with Antonio Ramirez, a promising young catcher. The contract calls for Ramirez to receive an annual salary of $1.5 million, even if he is unable to play because of a "baseball-related" injury. Prepare the journal entry (if any is required) to record in the Dukes' accounting records each of the following events.

a Signing the contract with Ramirez.

b After one season, Ramirez sustains a "baseball-related" injury that terminates his major league baseball career.

If you do not consider a journal entry necessary for recording either of these events, explain.

***EXERCISE 11-10**
Internal Control over Payroll

A supervisor in the factory of Barton Products, a large manufacturing company, discharged an employee but did not notify the human resources department of this action. The supervisor then began forging the employee's signature on time cards. When giving out paycheques, the supervisor diverted to his own use the paycheques drawn payable to the discharged worker. What internal control measure would be most effective in preventing this fraudulent activity?

***EXERCISE 11-11**
Journal Entries for Payroll and Payroll Taxes

The payroll record of ALG Company for the month of January showed the following amounts for total earnings: sales employees, $16,000; office employees, $10,000. Amounts withheld consisted of unemployment insurance premiums, $795, Canada Pension Plan, $582, and income tax, $4,860.

a Prepare a general journal entry to record the payroll. Do not include taxes on the employer.

b Prepare a general journal entry to record the payroll taxes expense to ALG Company relating to this payroll. Assume that the employer's rate for unemployment insurance is 1.4 times the employees' premium and that the employer's contribution to Canada Pension Plan is the same as the employees'.

***EXERCISE 11-12**
Employer's Payroll Taxes

The payroll of Fields Company may be summarized as follows:

Gross earnings of employees	*$250,000*
Employee earnings subject to unemployment insurance	*238,000*
Employee earnings subject to Canada Pension Plan	*221,000*

* *Supplemental Topic, "Accounting for Payrolls"*

Assuming that the employer is required to contribute unemployment insurance at 1.4 times the employee's rate of 3.5% and to contribute 3% to Canada Pension Plan, compute the amount of Fields Company's payroll taxes expense for the year, showing separately the amount of each of the two taxes and prepare a general journal entry to record the company's payroll taxes expense.

PROBLEMS

Note: In this chapter, we provide an unusually wide variety of problem assignments. In order to make the full range of these assignments available to all users of the text, we present them in one consecutive series, rather than splitting them into A and B groups. This entire series is supported in both the Group A and Group B accounting work sheets.

PROBLEM 11-1
The Nature of Liabilities

Listed below are seven publicly owned corporations and a liability that regularly appears in each corporation's balance sheet:

- a **Bank of Montreal:** Deposits
- b **Maclean Hunter Limited:** Unearned revenue
- c **The Windsor Raceway Inc.** (horse racing): Outstanding mutuel tickets
- d **American Greetings** (greeting cards and gift wrap products manufacturer): Sales returns
- e **Dofasco Inc.:** Current requirements on long-term debt
- f **Club Med., Inc.** (resorts): Amounts received for future vacations
- g **Apple Computer, Inc.:** Accrued marketing and distribution

INSTRUCTIONS

Briefly explain what you believe to be the nature of each of these liabilities, including how the liability arose and the manner in which it is likely to be discharged.

PROBLEM 11-2
Effects of Transactions on Financial Statements

Twelve transactions or events affecting Laptop Computer, Inc., are listed below:

- a Made a year-end adjusting entry to accrue interest on a note payable that has the interest rate stated separately from the principal amount.
- b Made a year-end adjusting entry to amortize the discount on a 120-day note payable with interest included in the face amount.
- c A liability classified for several years as long-term becomes due within the next 12 months.
- d Earned an amount previously recorded as unearned revenue.
- e Made arrangements to extend for 18 months a bank loan due in 60 days.
- f Made a monthly payment on a fully amortizing instalment note payable. (Assume this note is classified as a current liability.)
- g Recorded income taxes expense for the fourth quarter in the year (October 1 through December 31). Payment will be made within 3 months.
- h Recorded an estimated liability for future warranty claims on products sold during the current year.
- i Entered into a 2-year commitment to buy all hard drives from a particular supplier at a price 10% below market.
- j The company has a noncancellable commitment to purchase a specified number of semiconductors during each of the next 3 months at a fixed price. As of the balance sheet date, the current replacement cost of these semiconductors was well ***below*** this contractual purchase price.

k Received notice that a lawsuit has been filed against the company for $7 million. The amount of the company's liability, if any, cannot be reasonably estimated at this time.

***l** Recorded the regular bi-weekly payroll, including amounts withheld from employees, the issuance of paycheques, and payroll taxes levied upon the employer.

INSTRUCTIONS Indicate the effects of each of these transactions upon the following elements of the company's financial statements. Organize your answer in tabular form, using the column headings shown below. Use the following code letters to indicate the effects of each transaction upon the accounting element listed in the column heading:

I = Increase ***D*** = Decrease ***NE*** = No Effect

	Income Statement			Balance Sheet			
Transaction	*Revenue* –	*Expenses* =	*Net Income*	*Assets* =	*Current Liab.* +	*Long-Term Liab.* +	*Owner's Equity*
a							

PROBLEM 11-3
Balance Sheet Presentation of Liabilities

Listed below are selected items from the accounting records of GOOD 'N' LITE Candy Co. for the year ended December 31, 1995:

Note payable	*$200,000*
Discount on note payable	*2,000*
Income taxes payable	*43,000*
Accrued expenses and payroll taxes	*59,800*
Mortgage note payable	*301,080*
Accrued interest on mortgage note payable	*2,508*
Trade accounts payable	*129,345*
Unearned revenue	*52,100*
Potential liability in pending lawsuit	*750,000*

OTHER INFORMATION

1 The note payable to Northwest Bank is due in 60 days. Arrangements have been made to renew this note for an additional 12 months.

2 The mortgage note payable requires payments of $10,000 per month for the next 36 months. An amortization table shows that as of December 31, ***1996,*** this note will be paid down to $212,430.

3 Accrued interest on the mortgage note payable is paid monthly.

4 GOOD 'N' LITE has been sued for $750,000 in a contract dispute. It is not possible at this time to make a reasonable estimate of the possible loss, if any, which the company may have sustained.

INSTRUCTIONS

a Using this information, prepare the current liabilities section and long-term liabilities section of a classified balance sheet at December 31, 1995. (Within each classification, items may be listed in any order.)

b Explain briefly how the information in each of the four numbered paragraphs affected your presentation of the company's liabilities.

* *Supplemental Topic, "Accounting for Payrolls"*

PROBLEM 11-4
Notes Payable; Adjusting Entries for Interest

In the fiscal year ended October 31, Harbour Corporation carried out several transactions involving notes payable. Listed below are the transactions relating to notes payable.

June 1 Borrowed $20,000 from Holden Investments, by issuing a 2-month (3 days of grace included), 12% note payable to Holden as evidence of the indebtedness.

July 15 Bought office equipment from Western Office Supply. The invoice amount was $18,000 and Western Office Supply accepted as full payment a 3-month (3 days of grace included), 10% note for this amount.

Aug. 1 Paid the Holden note for $20,000 plus interest.

Sept. 1 Borrowed $240,000 from Western Bank at an annual interest rate of 8%; signed a 3-month note (3 days of grace included) with interest included in the face amount of the note.

Oct. 1 Purchased merchandise for $16,200 from Earthware Imports. Gave in settlement a 3-month note (3 days of grace included) bearing interest at 10%. (Harbour Corporation uses a perpetual inventory system.)

Oct. 15 The $18,000 note payable to Western Office Supply matured today. Paid the interest accrued and issued a new 1-month (3 days of grace included), 12% note to replace the matured note.

INSTRUCTIONS

a Prepare journal entries (in general journal form) to record the above transactions.

b Prepare the adjusting entries needed at October 31, prior to closing the accounts. Use one adjusting entry to accrue interest on the two notes in which interest is stated separately (the Earthware Imports note and the Western Office Supply note). Use a separate adjusting entry to record interest expense accrued on the note with interest included in the face amount (the Western Bank note).

PROBLEM 11-5
Notes Payable Accruing Interest—An Alternate Problem

During the fiscal year ended December 31, Dunleer Corporation carried out the following transactions involving notes payable.

Aug. 6 Borrowed $11,200 from Tom Hutchins, issuing to him a 2-month (3 days of grace included), 12% note payable.

Sept. 15 Purchased office equipment from Harper Company. The invoice amount was $16,800 and Harper Company agreed to accept as full payment a 3-month (3 days of grace included), 12% note for the invoice amount.

Oct. 6 Paid the Hutchins note plus accrued interest.

Oct. 31 Borrowed $235,200 from National Bank at an interest rate of 12% per annum; signed a 3-month (3 days of grace included) note payable for $242,256, which included a $7,056 interest charge in the face amount.

Dec. 1 Purchased merchandise in the amount of $3,000 from Kramer Company. Gave in settlement a 3-month note (3 days of grace included) bearing interest at 14%. (A perpetual inventory system is in use.)

Dec. 15 The $16,800 note payable to Harper Company matured today. Paid the interest accrued and issued a new 1-month (3 days of grace included), 12% note to replace the maturing note.

INSTRUCTIONS

a Prepare journal entries (in general journal form) to record the above transactions.

b Prepare the adjusting entries needed at December 31, prior to closing the accounts. Use one entry for the two notes on which interest is stated separately and a separate entry for the National Bank note in which interest is included in the face amount of the note.

maybe

PROBLEM 11-6
Notes Payable: A Comprehensive Problem

The following transactions relating to notes payable were completed by Desktop Graphics during the three months ended June 30.

Apr. 1	Bought office equipment for use in the business from Stylecraft, Inc., for $39,000, making a $5,400 cash down payment and issuing a 1-year (3 days of grace included) note payable for the balance. The face amount of the note was $38,976, which included a 16% interest charge.
Apr. 15	Paid $15,000 cash and issued a 3-month (3 days of grace included), 8%, $27,000 note to Hall Company in settlement of open account payable in the amount of $42,000.
Apr. 25	Purchased office equipment from ADM Company for $52,200, issuing a 2-month (3 days of grace included), 9% note payable in settlement.
May 15	Borrowed $216,000 from Manufacturers Bank, issuing a 3-month (3 days of grace included) note payable as evidence of indebtedness. An interest charge computed at 17% per year was included in the face amount of the note.
June 10	Purchased merchandise on account from Courtway Company, $54,000. (The company uses a perpetual inventory system.)
June 15	Issued a 2-month (3 days of grace included) note bearing interest at 9% in settlement of the account payable to Courtway Company.
June 25	Paid the 2-month (3 days of grace included), 9% note due to ADM Company, which matured today.

INSTRUCTIONS

a Prepare journal entries (in general journal form) to record the listed transactions for the 3 months ended June 30.

b Prepare adjusting entries to record the interest expense on notes payable through June 30. Prepare one adjusting entry to record the accrued interest payable on the two notes for which interest is stated separately (the Hall Company note and the Courtway Company note). The other adjusting entry should record the amortization of discount on the two notes in which interest is included in the face amount (the Stylecraft, Inc., note and the Manufacturers Bank note).

c Prepare a partial balance sheet at June 30 reflecting the above transactions. Show "Notes Payable to Bank" as one item and "Notes Payable: Other" as a separate liability. Also include the interest payable in the current liability section of the balance sheet.

PROBLEM 11-7
Amortization Table and Instalment Debt

On December 31, 1995, Kay Architectural Services purchased equipment at a cost of $20,215, paying $5,000 cash and issuing a 2-year instalment note payable for $15,215. This note calls for four semiannual instalments of $4,800, which include interest computed at the annual rate of 20% per year (10% per semiannual period). Payments are due on June 30 and December 31. The first payment is due June 30, 1996, and the note will be fully amortized at December 31, 1997.

Kay can retire this note at any interest payment date by paying the unpaid balance plus any accrued interest.

INSTRUCTIONS

a Prepare an amortization table showing the allocation of each of the four semiannual payments between interest expense and reductions in the principal amount of the note.

b Prepare journal entries to record the issuance of this note and each of the four semiannual payments in 1996 and 1997.

c Assume that on December 31, ***1996,*** Kay decided to pay the entire unpaid balance of this note. Prepare a journal entry to record the early retirement of this note. (Assume that the semiannual payment due on this date already has been paid.)

d Illustrate the presentation of this note in the company's balance sheet at December 31, ***1995.***

This part is confusing — eliminate it

PROBLEM 11-8
Preparation and Use of an Amortization Table

On September 1, 1996, H-K Steak House signed a 30-year, $540,000 mortgage note payable to Union Bank in conjunction with the purchase of a restaurant. This mortgage note calls for interest at the rate of 12% per year (1% per month), and monthly payments of $5,555. The note is fully amortizing over a period of 360 months (30 years).

Union Bank sent H-K Steak House an amortization table showing the allocation of the monthly payments between interest and principal over the life of the loan. A small part of this amortization table is illustrated below. (For convenience, amounts have been rounded to the nearest dollar.)

Amortization Table
(12%, 30-Year Mortgage Note Payable for $540,000;
Payable in 360 Monthly Instalments of $5,555)

Interest Period	*Payment Date*	*Monthly Payment*	*Interest Expense*	*Reduction in Unpaid Balance*	*Unpaid Balance*
Issue date	*Sept. 1, 1996*	—	—	—	*$540,000*
1	*Oct. 1*	*$5,555*	*$5,400*	*$155*	*539,845*
2	*Nov. 1*	*$5,555*	*5,398*	*157*	*539,688*

INSTRUCTIONS

a Explain whether the amounts of interest expense and the reductions in the unpaid balance are likely to change in any predictable pattern from month to month.

b Prepare journal entries to record the first two monthly payments on this mortgage.

c Complete this amortization table for two more monthly instalments—those due on December 1, 1996, and January 1, 1997. (Round amounts to the nearest dollar.)

d Will any amounts relating to this 30-year mortgage be classified as ***current*** liabilities in the December 31, 1996, balance sheet of H-K Steak House? Explain, but you need not compute any additional dollar amounts.

***PROBLEM 11-9**
Payroll—A Short Problem

The payroll records of Copper Kettle for the first week in January showed total salaries earned by employees of $25,000.

The amounts withheld from employees' pay consisted of unemployment insurance of $720, Canada Pension Plan of $530, income taxes of $4,372, and union dues of $380.

* *Supplemental Topic, "Accounting for Payrolls"*

As a fringe benefit, Copper Kettle contributes an amount equal to 3% of employees' gross pay to an employee registered pension plan and 1% to an employee group life insurance plan.

The weekly payroll is recorded on Friday, January 6, and paycheques will be issued to employees on Monday, January 9.

INSTRUCTIONS

a Prepare separate general journal entries to record the (1) salaries earned by employees, amounts withheld, and liability for net pay; (2) payroll taxes levied upon the employer; (3) cost of fringe benefits; and (4) issuance of paycheques.

b Compute the ***total cost*** to Copper Kettle of employee compensation for the first week of January.

c Assuming no change in pay rates, tax rates, or number of employees, would you expect the total cost of Copper Kettle's weekly payroll to increase or decrease as the year progresses? Explain.

***PROBLEM 11-10**
Payroll—A Comprehensive Problem

The individual employees' earnings records of Surveillance Systems show the following cumulative gross pay (earnings) as of year-end.

Employee	Cumulative Gross Pay	Employee	Cumulative Gross Pay
Arthur, D. S.	$28,500	Hamilton, A. J.	$35,000
Barnett, S. T.	42,000	Maison, G. R.	49,600
Donahue, E. G.	60,000		

Assume that the rate of unemployment insurance for employees is 3.5% and the rate for the employer is 1.4 times that of the employees. The maximum annual insurable earnings for each employee is $40,620. The rate for Canada Pension Plan is assumed to be 3% for both the employees and the employer and the rate is applied to the employees' first $31,800 annual pensionable earnings (i.e., gross pay of $35,400 less $3,600 exemption).

During the year, the employer has withheld income taxes of $54,920 from employees' pay and has incurred costs of $23,120 relating to fringe benefits.

INSTRUCTIONS

a Prepare a schedule with four data columns for each employee. In the first column, enter the employee's cumulative gross pay, as indicated above. In the remaining three columns, indicate the amounts of this gross pay that were subject to (1) unemployment insurance and (2) Canada Pension Plan. Show totals for each column.

b Compute the following total amounts for the current year (round amounts to the nearest dollar):

1 Total amount withheld from employees' pay (combine all types of withholdings).

2 Employees' net pay.

3 Payroll taxes levied upon the employer.

4 The employer's total payroll costs.

c Reconcile the total amount of employees' net pay [**b(2)**] with the total payroll costs incurred by the employer [**b(4)**].

* *Supplemental Topic, "Accounting for Payrolls"*

***PROBLEM 11-11 Payroll—A More Comprehensive Problem**

The Daily Chronicle is a large business organization, with perhaps 1,500 employees. For illustrative purposes, however, we will demonstrate certain payroll procedures using the earnings of ***only three*** of these employees in the month of July.

The monthly salaries of these three employees, and their cumulative gross pay for the year as of June 30, appear below:

Employee	Monthly Salary	Year-to-Date, June 30
Adams	$5,500	$33,000
Colbert	2,000	6,500**
Henderson	6,300	37,800

** Colbert started work in late March.

This information is obtained from the employees' individual earnings records.

Assume that the rate of unemployment insurance for employees is 3.5% and the rate for the employer is 1.4 times that of the employees. The maximum monthly insurable earnings for each employee is $3,385. The rate for Canada Pension Plan is assumed to be 3% for both the employees and the employer and the rate is applied to the employees' first $31,800 pensionable earnings (i.e., gross earnings of $35,400 less $3,600 exemption).

The Daily Chronicle provides the following fringe benefits to all employees:

- Paid group life insurance (cost: $100 per month for the three employees)
- Contributions to an employees' registered pension plan (at the rate of 5% of each employee's monthly salary)

Liabilities relating to fringe benefits are paid at the end of each calendar quarter.

INSTRUCTIONS

a Prepare a four-column schedule showing payroll data for each employee. In the first column, enter each employee's gross pay for July. In the remaining columns, show the amount of this July's gross pay that is subject to (1) unemployment insurance and (2) Canada Pension Plan. (If none of an employee's July salary is subject to a particular tax, explain why not. If only part of the employee's July salary is subject to a particular type of tax, show a supporting computation.)

Show totals in each of the four columns.

b Prepare three separate general journal entries, each dated ***July 31,*** summarizing for the month:

1 The gross pay, amounts withheld, and net pay of these employees. In addition, the amount withheld for income taxes is $4,260. Paycheques will be issued on the next business day (August 3).

2 The payroll taxes ***levied upon the employer.***

3 The cost of fringe benefits.

c Compute the ***total cost*** to The Daily Chronicle of having these three employees on the payroll during the month of July.

d List all of the current liabilities at July 31 resulting from this monthly payroll. Sequence this listing by dollar amount, from the largest liability to the smallest.

ANALYTICAL AND DECISION PROBLEMS AND CASES

A&D 11-1 Liabilities: Recognition and Measurement

The eight events listed below occurred at National Products on or near the end of the fiscal year, December 31, 1995:

a On October 12, the company was named as a defendant in a lawsuit alleging $20 million in damages caused by lead paint used on products manufactured by

* *Supplemental Topic, "Accounting for Payrolls"*

the company in the late 1980s. National's legal counsel believes it is likely that National has liability of at least $2 million. The suit is not expected to be settled for several years.

b On November 1, borrowed $900,000 from a bank, signing a 3-month (3 days of grace included) note payable for $918,000 with interest included in the face amount.

c On December 15, signed a contract for the purchase of 50,000 barrels of oil per month in 1996 at a price of $18 per barrel, a price slightly below current market price.

d On December 31, purchased machinery at a price of $200,000 and signed a note payable due in 6 months with interest stated at the annual rate of 9%.

e On December 31, signed a 2-year contract with a labour union providing for a 6% increase in wage rates each year. The increase in wages for the first year is estimated at $540,000.

***f** On December 31, processed the bi-weekly payroll. Paycheques totalling $289,000 were issued to employees. As these cheques were issued after banking hours on December 31, no cash will be disbursed from National's payroll bank account until early in January 1996. The amount withheld from employees' pay and payroll taxes on the employer of $67,600 was remitted to tax authorities on January 3, 1996.

g On December 31, estimated that warranty work costing $200,000 probably will need to be performed in future months on products that were sold in 1995 with a 12-month warranty.

h On January 5, 1996, a preliminary estimate was made of the company's income taxes expense for 1995. This expense was estimated at $2,800,000, of which $2,100,000 had already been paid in quarterly tax payments made during 1995. In March 1996 the company completed the preparation of its 1995 income tax return, and income taxes expense for 1995 was determined to be $2,779,806.

INSTRUCTIONS For each of these eight events, indicate the dollar amounts (if any) that should appear in either the current or long-term liability sections of National's 1995 year-end balance sheet. Also indicate any information that should be disclosed in the notes accompanying the 1995 financial statements. Briefly explain the reasons underlying your answers. (***Note:*** As a practical matter, much of the task of preparing the 1995 financial statements must be performed in January 1996. Assume the financial statements are completed and issued on January 31.)

A&D 11-2
Contingent Losses?

Discuss each of the following situations, indicating whether the situation is a contingent loss that should be recorded or disclosed in the financial statements of Aztec Airlines. If the situation is not a contingent loss, explain how (if at all) it should be reported in the company's financial statements. (Assume that all dollar amounts are material.)

a The company's president is in poor health and has previously suffered two heart attacks.

b As with any airline, Aztec faces the risk that a future airplane crash could cause considerable loss.

c Aztec is being sued for $2 million for failing to adequately provide for passengers whose reservations were cancelled as a result of the airline overbooking certain flights. This suit will not be resolved for a year or more.

* *Supplemental Topic, "Accounting for Payrolls"*

A&D 11-3
Liabilities, Contingencies, or ???

Marian Rogers, a CA on the audit staff of a national public accounting firm, is in charge of the annual audit of Crystal Corporation, a successful medium-size client. On December 31, Rogers receives a telephone call from John Arnold, the controller of Crystal. Arnold explains that the company's board of directors has just signed two contractual arrangements with its former president, who has retired. The first agreement provides that Crystal will pay its ex-president $10,000 a month for five years if during that time he does not compete with the company in a rival business. The second agreement states that Crystal will pay the ex-president $8,000 per month for five years, for which he is to provide such advisory services as the company may request.

The controller asks Rogers if the year-end balance sheet would include $216,000 as a current liability to the ex-president and $864,000 as a long-term liability, or whether the total amount of $1,080,000 should be disclosed as a contingency in a note to the financial statements. The controller emphasized that these amounts were material in terms of the company's earnings and resources.

INSTRUCTIONS Explain fully how you think Marian Rogers should respond to the question raised by the controller.

***A&D 11-4**
"Hey—Can't We Do This by Computer?"

A W Clausen's is a large department store with a highly automated accounting system. The computer program used in processing payrolls includes all tax rates and withholding tables, employees' individual earnings records, and every employee's rate of compensation. Employees' gross pay is determined as follows:

Warehouse workers	*Hourly wages*
Office workers and management	*Monthly salaries*
Salespeople	*Monthly salary plus commissions*

Sales commissions are based upon the gross profit generated by the individual salesperson during the pay period.

Employees are paid twice each month. Every payroll period, the computer program compiles a payroll register, updates the employees' earnings records, prints paycheques, and records in the general ledger both the payroll and the payroll taxes upon the employer.

INSTRUCTIONS

a Indicate the ***additional information*** that must be entered into this computerized system ***each pay period*** to enable the computer to perform the processing tasks described above. Suggest means by which each type of additional information might be entered into the computerized payroll system ***automatically,*** instead of manually.

b Describe a plan for distributing paycheques to the company's employees that is both efficient and contributes to strong internal control.

* *Supplemental Topic, "Accounting for Payrolls"*

CHAPTER 12

Accounting Concepts, Professional Judgment, and Ethical Conduct

Throughout this text, we have tried to explain the theoretical rationale for each new accounting concept, principle, and practice as it has first come under discussion. In this chapter, we look back and review some of the major concepts, principles, and assumptions that comprise the theoretical framework of financial reporting. In addition, we discuss independent auditors' reports, the indispensible role of professional judgment in the financial reporting process, and some of the ethical considerations associated with careers in accounting.

Learning Objectives

After studying this chapter you should be able to:

1. *Explain the need for recognized accounting standards.*
2. *Discuss the nature and sources of generally accepted accounting principles.*
3. *Discuss the accounting principles and concepts presented on pages 582–592.*
4. *Explain the instalment method and the percentage-of-completion method of income recognition.*
5. *Define an independent audit and discuss the assurances provided by the auditors' report.*
6. *Describe the role of professional judgment in the financial reporting process.*
7. *Discuss international accounting standards.*
8. *Describe the nature of ethics and explain the basic purpose of a code of ethics within a profession.*
9. *Identify and explain the basic principles underlying a professional code of ethics.*
10. *Apply the basic principles of ethical conduct to various situations likely to arise in an accountant's work.*

The Need for Recognized Accounting Standards

OBJECTIVE 1 Explain the need for recognized accounting standards.

The basic purpose of financial statements is to provide information about a business entity—information that will be ***useful in making economic decisions.*** Investors, managers, creditors, financial analysts, economists, and government policy makers all rely upon financial statements and other accounting reports in making the decisions that shape our economy. Therefore, it is of vital importance that the information contained in financial statements possess certain characteristics. The information should be:[1]

1 **Relevant** to the information needs of the decision makers.
2 As **reliable** as possible.
3 **Comparable** to the financial statements of prior accounting periods and also to the statements of other companies.
4 **Understandable** to the users of the financial statements.

We need a well-defined body of accounting principles or standards to guide accountants in preparing financial statements that possess these characteristics. The users of financial statements also must be familiar with these principles in order to interpret properly the information contained in these statements.

GENERALLY ACCEPTED ACCOUNTING PRINCIPLES (GAAP)

The principles that constitute the ground rules for financial reporting are called ***generally accepted accounting principles.*** Accounting principles may also be termed ***standards, assumptions, conventions,*** or ***concepts.*** The various terms used to describe accounting principles stem from the many efforts that have been made to develop a satisfactory framework of accounting theory.[2] For example, the word ***standards*** was chosen rather than ***principles*** by the CICA for its Accounting Standards Board as the top standard-making body. The effort to construct a satisfactory body of accounting theory is an ongoing process, because accounting theory must continually change with changes in the business environment and changes in the needs of financial statement users.

When a new accounting principle is promulgated, it must be adopted by the companies in their financial reporting. The application of the new principle can have a very significant impact on the financial statements.

CASE IN POINT Recently, the Financial Accounting Standards Board in the United States issued a new accounting principle that requires companies to recognize the costs of future retiree health care benefits in the year

---

1 Adapted from *CICA Handbook* (Toronto) section 1000.18-.23.

2 See, in Canada, *Corporate Reporting: Its Future Evolution,* CICA (Toronto: 1980). In the United States, see for example, *Accounting Research Study No. 3,* "A Tentative Set of Broad Accounting Principles for Business Enterprises," AICPA (New York: 1962), *APB Statement No. 4,* "Basic Concepts and Accounting Principles Underlying Financial Statements of Business Enterprises," AICPA (New York: 1970); and *Statements of Financial Accounting Concepts Nos. 1–6,* FASB (Norwalk, Conn.: 1978–1985).

they are incurred rather than when they are actually paid. The adoption of this new principle in financial reporting resulted in huge charges to income in one single year: American Telephone and Telegraph, $7 billion; Ford Motor, $7.5 billion; and General Motors, $21 billion. One estimate put the total charges created by this new principle on the Standard & Poor's 500 index at $148 billion.

Nature of Accounting Principles

OBJECTIVE 2 Discuss the nature and sources of generally accepted accounting principles.

Accounting principles do not exist in nature; rather, they are developed by humans in light of what we view as the most important objectives of financial reporting. In Chapter 1, we drew a parallel between generally accepted accounting principles and the rules established for an organized sport, such as basketball or football. For example, both accounting principles and sports rules originate from a combination of experience, tradition, and official decree. Also, both may change over time as gaps or shortcomings in the existing rules come to light.

An important aspect of accounting principles is the ***need for consensus*** within the economic community. If these principles are to provide a useful framework for financial reporting, they must be understood and observed by the participants in the financial reporting process. Thus, the words ***generally accepted*** are an important part of the phrase "generally accepted accounting principles."

As accounting principles are closely related to the needs, objectives, and traditions of a society, they vary somewhat from one country to another. Our discussion is limited to accounting principles "generally accepted" within Canada. An effort is underway to create greater uniformity in accounting principles among nations (as discussed in the last section of this chapter), but this effort will be a difficult and slow process.

Authoritative Support for Accounting Principles

To qualify as generally accepted, an accounting principle must have substantial authoritative support. This support may come from official sources, such as the CICA, or from unofficial sources, such as common sense, tradition, and widespread use.

Official Sources of GAAP The most influential authoritative group in Canada is the ***Accounting Standards Board (AcSB)*** of the Canadian Institute of Chartered Accountants (CICA).[3] The AcSB is responsible for the development and promulgation of accounting principles, and its recommendations are contained in the "Accounting Recommendations" section of the *CICA Handbook.* These recommendations are considered as generally

---

[3] The CICA's Accounting Standards Board is composed of a cross section of individuals with various backgrounds and occupations: eight members are appointed by the CICA, and one member is appointed by each of these five organizations—the Canadian Academic Accounting Association, Canadian Council of Financial Analysts, Certified General Accountants' Association of Canada, Financial Executives Institute Canada, and Society of Management Accountants of Canada. However, the Certified General Accountants' Association of Canada has declined to appoint its representative to serve on the Board.

accepted accounting principles (GAAP) by the accounting profession, the administrators of provincial securities commissions, and a number of corporations acts, including the Canada Business Corporations Act.

In the United States, the official sources of accounting principles include (1) the American Institute of Certified Public Accountants, (2) the Financial Accounting Standards Board, and (3) the Securities and Exchange Commission.

Unofficial Sources of GAAP Not all of what we call generally accepted accounting principles can be found in the "official pronouncements" of the standard-setting organizations. The business community is too complex and changes too quickly for every possible type of transaction to be covered by an official pronouncement. Thus, practicing accountants often must account for situations that have never been addressed by the official sources.

When the method of accounting for a particular situation is not explained in any official literature, generally accepted accounting principles are based upon such considerations as:

- Accounting practices that are in widespread use.
- Accounting guidelines and consensus issued by the CICA's Accounting Standards Board and the Emerging Issues Committee respectively.
- Broad theoretical concepts that underlie most accounting practices.

Thus, an understanding of generally accepted accounting principles requires a familiarity with (1) authoritative accounting literature, (2) accounting practices in widespread use, and (3) the broad theoretical concepts that underlie accounting practices. We will discuss these "broad theoretical concepts" in the following sections of this chapter.

The Accounting Entity Concept

OBJECTIVE 3 Discuss the accounting principles and concepts presented on pages 582–592.

One of the basic principles of accounting is that information is compiled for a clearly defined accounting entity. An ***accounting entity*** is any economic unit that controls resources and engages in economic activities. An individual is an accounting entity. So is a business enterprise, whether organized as a proprietorship, partnership, or corporation. Governmental agencies are accounting entities, as are nonprofit clubs and organizations. An accounting entity may also be defined as an identifiable economic unit ***within a larger accounting entity.*** For example, the Chevrolet Division of General Motors may be viewed as an accounting entity separate from GM's other activities.

The basic accounting equation, Assets = Liabilities + Owner's Equity, reflects the accounting entity concept because the elements of the equation relate ***to the particular entity whose economic activity is being reported in the financial statements.*** Although we have considerable flexibility in defining our accounting entity, we must be careful to use the ***same definition*** in the measurement of assets, liabilities, owners' equity, revenue, and expense. An income statement would not make sense, for example, if it included all the revenue of General Motors but listed the expenses of only the Chevrolet Division.

Although the entity concept appears straightforward, it can pose some judgmental allocation problems for accountants. Assume, for example, that we want to prepare an income statement for only the Chevrolet Division of General Motors. Also assume that a given plant facility is used in the production of Chevrolets, Pontiacs, and school buses. How much of the depreciation on this factory building should be regarded as an expense of the Chevrolet Division? Such situations illustrate the importance of the entity concept in developing meaningful financial information.

The Going-Concern Assumption

An underlying assumption in accounting is that an accounting entity will continue in operation for a period of time sufficient to carry out its existing commitments. The assumption of continuity, especially in the case of corporations, is in accord with experience in our economic system. This assumption leads to the concept of the ***going concern.*** In general, the going-concern assumption justifies ignoring immediate liquidating values in presenting assets and liabilities in the balance sheet.

For example, suppose that a company has just purchased a three-year insurance policy for $5,000. If we assume that the business will continue in operation for three years or more, we will consider the $5,000 cost of the insurance as an asset that provides services (freedom from certain risks) to the business over a three-year period. On the other hand, if we assume that the business is likely to terminate in the near future, the insurance policy should be recorded at its cancellation value—the amount of cash that can be obtained from the insurance company as a refund on immediate cancellation of the policy, which may be, say $3,500.

Although the assumption of a going concern is justified in most normal situations, it should be dropped when it is not in accord with the facts. For example, accountants are sometimes asked to prepare a statement of financial position for an enterprise that is about to liquidate. In this case the assumption of continuity is no longer valid and the accountant drops the going-concern assumption and reports assets at their current liquidating value and liabilities at the amount required to settle the debts immediately.

The Time Period Principle

The users of financial statements need information that is reasonably current and that is comparable to the information relating to prior accounting periods. Therefore, for financial reporting purposes, the life of a business must be divided into a series of relatively short accounting periods of equal length. This concept is called the time period principle.

The need for periodic reporting creates many of the accountant's most challenging problems. Dividing the life of an enterprise into relatively short time segments, such as a year or a quarter of a year, requires numerous estimates and assumptions. For example, estimates must be made of the useful lives of depreciable assets and judgments must be made as to appropriate depreciation methods. Thus periodic measurements of net income and financial position are at best only informed estimates. The tentative nature of periodic measurements should be understood by those who rely on periodic accounting information.

The Stable-Dollar Assumption

The stable-dollar assumption means that money is used as the basic measuring unit for financial reporting. The dollar, or any other monetary unit, is a measure of value—that is, it indicates the relative price (or value) of different goods and services.

When accountants add or subtract dollar values originating in different years, they imply that the dollar is a ***stable unit of measure,*** just as the litre, the hectare, and the kilometre are stable units of measure. Unfortunately, the dollar is ***not*** a stable measure of value.

To illustrate, assume that in 1980, you purchased land for $20,000. In 1995, you sell this land for $30,000. Under generally accepted accounting principles, which include the stable-dollar assumption, you have made a $10,000 "gain" on the sale. Economists would point out, however, that $30,000 in 1995 represents less "buying power" than did $20,000 in 1980. When the relative buying power of the dollar in 1980 and 1995 is taken into consideration, you came out behind on the purchase and the sale of this land.

Let us stress, however, that despite its shortcomings, the stable-dollar assumption remains a generally accepted accounting principle. In periods of low inflation, this assumption does not cause serious problems. During periods of severe inflation, however, the assumption of a stable dollar may cause serious distortions in accounting information.

The Objectivity Principle

The term ***objective*** refers to measurements that are ***unbiased*** and subject to verification by independent experts. For example, the price established in an arm's-length transaction is an objective measure of exchange value at the time of the transaction. Exchange prices established in business transactions constitute much of the raw material from which accounting information is generated. Accountants rely on various kinds of evidence to support their financial measurements, but they seek always the most objective evidence available. Invoices, contracts, paid cheques, and physical counts of inventory are examples of objective evidence.

If a measurement is objective, 10 competent investigators who make the same measurement will come up with substantially identical results. However, 10 competent accountants who set out independently to measure the net income of a given business would ***not*** arrive at an identical result. Despite the goal of objectivity, ***it is not possible to insulate accounting information from opinion and personal judgment.*** For example, the cost of a depreciable asset can be determined objectively but not the periodic depreciation expense. Depreciation expense is merely an estimate, based upon estimates of the useful life and the residual value of the asset, and a judgment as to which depreciation method is most appropriate. Such estimates and judgments can produce significant variations in the measurement of net income.

Objectivity in accounting has its roots in the quest for reliability. Accountants want to make their economic measurements reliable and, at the same time, as relevant to decision makers as possible. However, the most relevant information may not be the most reliable. Thus, where to draw the line in the trade-off between ***reliability*** and ***relevance*** is one of the crucial issues in accounting theory. Accountants are constantly faced with the necessity of compromising between what users of financial information would like to know and what it is possible to measure with a reasonable degree of reliability.

Asset Valuation: The Cost Principle

Both the balance sheet and the income statement are affected by the cost principle. Assets are initially recorded in the accounts at cost, and no adjustment is made to this valuation in later periods, except to allocate a portion of the original cost to expense as the assets expire. At the time an asset is originally acquired, cost represents the "fair market value" of the goods or services exchanged, as evidenced by an arm's-length transaction. With the passage of time, however, the fair market value of such assets as land and buildings may change greatly from their historical cost. These later changes in fair market value generally have been ignored in the accounts, and the assets have continued to be valued in the balance sheet at historical cost (less the portion of that cost which has been allocated to expense.)

Many accountants and users of financial statements believe that current market value is more relevant than historical cost, and thus should be used as the basis for asset valuation. This group argues that the use of current values would result in a more meaningful balance sheet. Also, they claim that expenses shown in the income statement should reflect the current market values of the goods and services consumed in the effort to generate revenue.

The cost principle is derived, in large part, from the principle of objectivity. Those who support the cost principle argue that it is important that users have confidence in financial statements, and that this confidence can best be maintained if accountants recognize changes in assets and liabilities only on a basis of completed transactions. Objective evidence generally exists to support cost; current market values, however, may be largely a matter of personal opinion.

The question of whether to value assets at cost or estimated market value is a classic illustration of the "trade-off" between the relevance and the reliability of accounting information.

Revenue Recognition: The Realization (Recognition) Principle

When is revenue realized and when should it be recognized in the accounting records? Under the assumptions of accrual accounting, revenue should be recognized "when it is earned." However, the "earning" of revenue usually is an extended ***economic process*** and does not actually take place at a single point in time.

Some revenue, such as interest earned, is directly related to time periods. For this type of revenue, it is easy to determine how much revenue has been earned by computing how much of the earning process is complete. However, the earning process for sales revenue is related to ***economic activity*** rather than to a specific period of time. In a manufacturing business, for example, the earning process involves (1) acquisition of direct or raw materials, (2) production of finished goods, (3) sale of the finished goods, and (4) collection of cash from credit customers.

In the manufacturing example, there is little objective evidence to indicate how much revenue has been earned during the first two stages of the earning process. Accountants therefore usually do not recognize revenue until the revenue has been ***realized.*** Section 3400 of the *CICA Handbook* stipulates these criteria for revenue realization or recognition: (1) the significant risks and rewards of ownership of goods have been transferred from the seller to the buyer or the services have been performed, (2) reasonable assurance exists regarding the measurement of the consideration from the sale of goods or service rendered, and the extent to which goods may be returned, and (3) ultimate collection of the consideration from the sale of goods or services rendered is reasonably assured.[4] Accordingly, revenue is realized when both of the following conditions are met: (1) the earning process is ***essentially complete*** and (2) ***objective evidence*** exists as to the amount of revenue earned.

In most cases, the realization principle indicates that revenue should be recognized ***at the time goods are sold or services are rendered.***[5] At this point the business has essentially completed the earning process and the sales value of the goods or services can be measured objectively. At any time prior to sale, the ultimate sales value of the goods or services sold can only be estimated. After the sale, the only step that remains is to collect from the customer, and this is usually a relatively certain event.

In Chapter 3, we described a ***cash basis*** of income measurement whereby revenue is recognized only when cash is collected from customers and expenses are recorded only when cash is actually paid out. Cash basis accounting ***does not conform*** to generally accepted accounting principles, but it may be used by individuals in determining their ***taxable*** income. (Remember that the accounting methods used in income tax returns often differ from those used in financial statements.)

OBJECTIVE 4 Explain the instalment method and the percentage-of-completion method of income recognition.

The Instalment Method Under the instalment method, the seller recognizes the gross profit on sales gradually over an extended time span as the cash is actually collected from customers. If the gross profit rate on instalment sales is 30%, then out of every dollar collected on instalment receivables, the sum of 30 cents represents gross profit.

To illustrate, assume that on December 15, 1994, a retailer sells for $400 a television set that cost $280, or 70% of the sales price. The terms of the sale call for a $100 cash down payment with the balance payable in 15 monthly instalments of $20 each, beginning on January 1, 1995. (Interest charges are ignored in this illustration.) The collections of cash and recognition of profit under the instalment method are summarized as follows:

Instalment method illustrated

Year	Cash Collected –	Cost Recovery (70%) =	Profit Earned (30%)
1994	$100	$ 70	$ 30
1995	240	168	72
1996	60	42	18
Totals	$400	$280	$120

[4] CICA, *CICA Handbook* (Toronto), section 3400.06, .07 and .08.

[5] Ibid., section 3400.06, .07, .08 and .11.

Since the instalment method delays the recognition of profit beyond the point of sale, there is little theoretical justification for its use. Under generally accepted accounting principles, use of the instalment method is permissible only when the amounts likely to be collected on instalment sales are so uncertain that no reasonable basis exists for estimating an allowance for doubtful accounts. However, this is usually a rare occurrence. Consequently, the instalment method is seldom used for financial reporting.

Percentage-of-Completion Under certain circumstances, accountants recognize income during the production process.[6] An example arises in the case of long-term construction contracts, such as the building of a dam over a period of several years. Clearly the income statements of a company engaged in such a project would be of little use to managers or investors if no profit or loss were reported until the dam was finally completed. The accountant therefore estimates the portion of the project completed during each accounting period, and recognizes the gross profit on the project ***in proportion*** to the work completed. This is known as the percentage-of-completion method of accounting for long-term contracts.

The percentage-of-completion method works as follows:

1 An estimate is made of the total costs to be incurred and the total profit to be earned over the life of the project.

2 Each period, an estimate is made of the portion of the total project completed during the period. This estimate is usually made by expressing the costs incurred during the period as a percentage of the estimated total cost of the project.

3 The percentage figure determined in step **2** is applied to the estimated total profit on the contract to compute the amount of profit applicable to the current accounting period.

4 No estimate is made of the percentage of work during the final period. In the period in which the project is completed, any remaining profit is recognized.

To illustrate, assume that Reed Construction Limited enters into a contract with the government to build an irrigation canal at a price of $50,000,000. The canal will be built over a three-year period at an estimated total cost of $40,000,000. Therefore, the estimated total profit on the project is $10,000,000. The following schedule shows the actual costs incurred and the amount of profit to be recognized in each of the three years using the percentage-of-completion method:

Profit recognized as work progresses

Year	(A) Actual Costs Incurred	(B) Percentage of Work Done in Year (Column A ÷ $40,000,000)	(C) Profit Considered Earned ($10,000,000 × Column B)
1	$ 6,000,000	15	$1,500,000
2	20,000,000	50	5,000,000
3	14,520,000	*	2,980,000 balance
Totals	$40,520,000		$9,480,000

* Balance required to complete the contract.

[6] Op. cit., *CICA Handbook,* section 3400.08 and .14.

The percentage of the work completed during Year 1 was estimated by dividing the actual cost incurred in the year by the estimated total cost of the project ($6,000,000 ÷ $40,000,000 = 15%). Because 15% of the work was done in Year 1, 15% of the estimated total profit of $10,000,000 was considered earned in that year ($10,000,000 × 15% = $1,500,000). Costs incurred in Year 2 amounted to 50% of the estimated total costs ($20,000,000 ÷ $40,000,000 = 50%); thus, 50% of the estimated total profit was recognized in Year 2 ($10,000,000 × 50% = $5,000,000). Note that no percentage-of-work-completed figure was computed for Year 3. In Year 3, the total actual cost (including the cost overrun of $520,000) is known ($40,520,000), and the actual total profit on the contract is determined to be $9,480,000 ($50,000,000 − $40,520,000). Since profits of $6,500,000 were previously recognized in Years 1 and 2, the ***remaining*** profit ($9,480,000 − $6,500,000 = $2,980,000) is recognized in Year 3.

Although an expected ***profit*** on a long-term construction contract is recognized in proportion to the work completed, a different treatment is accorded to an expected ***loss.*** If at the end of any accounting period it appears that a loss will be incurred on a contract in progress, the ***entire loss should be recognized at once.***

The percentage-of-completion method should be used only when the total profit expected to be earned can be ***reasonably estimated in advance*** and the ***ultimate collection*** of the contract price is ***reasonably assured.*** If there are substantial uncertainties in the amount of profit that will ultimately be earned or in the amount of the contract price to be collected, no profit should be recognized until ***production is completed.*** This approach is often referred to as the ***completed-contract method.*** If the completed-contract method had been used in the preceding example, no profit would have been recognized in Years 1 and 2; the entire profit of $9,480,000 would have been recorded in Year 3 when the contract was completed and actual costs known.

Expense Recognition: The Matching Principle

The relationship between expenses and revenue is one of ***cause and effect.*** Expenses are ***causal factors*** in the earning of revenue. To measure the profitability of an economic activity, we must consider not only the revenue earned, but also all the expenses incurred in the effort to produce this revenue. Thus, accountants attempt to ***match*** (or ***offset***) the revenue appearing in an income statement with all the expenses incurred in generating that revenue. This concept, called the ***matching principle,*** governs the timing of expense recognition in financial statements.

To illustrate, assume that in June a painting contractor purchases paint on account. The contractor uses the paint on jobs completed in July but does not pay for the paint until August. In which month should the contractor recognize the cost of the paint as expense? The answer is ***July,*** because this is the month in which the paint was ***used in the process of earning revenue.***

Because of the matching principle, costs that are expected to benefit future accounting periods are debited to asset accounts. These costs are then allocated to expense in the periods that the costs contribute to the production of revenue. The matching principle underlies such accounting practices as depreciating plant assets, computing the cost of goods sold each period, and amortizing the cost of unexpired insurance policies. All end-of-the-period adjusting entries involving recognition of expense are applications of the matching principle.

Costs are matched with revenue in one of two ways:

1. **Direct association of costs with specific revenue transactions.** The ideal method of matching revenue with expenses is to determine the amount of expense associated with the specific revenue transactions occurring during the period. However, this approach works only for those costs and expenses that can be directly associated with specific revenue transactions. The cost of goods sold and commissions paid to salespeople are examples of costs and expenses that can be ***directly associated*** with the revenue of a specific accounting period.
2. **Systematic allocation of costs over the "useful life" of the expenditure.** Many expenditures contribute to the earning of revenue for a number of accounting periods but cannot be directly associated with specific revenue transactions. Examples include the costs of insurance policies, depreciable assets, and intangible assets such as goodwill. In these cases, accountants attempt to match revenue and expenses by ***systematically allocating the cost to expense*** over its useful life. Straight-line amortization and the various methods of depreciation are examples of the "systematic allocation" techniques used to match revenue with the related costs and expenses.

Unfortunately, it is not possible to apply the matching principle objectively to every type of expenditure. Many expenditures offer at least some hope of producing revenue in future periods; however, there may be little or no objective evidence to support these hopes. Accountants defer recognition of an expense to the future only when there is ***reasonable evidence*** that the expenditure will, in fact, benefit future operations. If this evidence is not available, or is not convincing, accountants do not attempt to apply the matching principle; rather, they charge the expenditure ***immediately to expense.*** Expenditures generally considered "too subjective" for accountants to apply the matching principle include advertising, research, and the cost of employee training programs.[7]

The Consistency Principle

The principle of ***consistency*** implies that a particular accounting method, once adopted, will not be changed from period to period. This assumption is important because it assists users of financial statements in interpreting changes in financial position and changes in net income between two periods.

Consider the confusion that would result if a company ignored the principle of consistency and changed its method of depreciation every year. The company could cause its net income for any given year to increase or decrease merely by changing its depreciation method.

---

[7] Section 3450.16 of the *CICA Handbook* recommends that research costs be charged to expense immediately.

The principle of consistency does not mean that a company should ***never*** make a change in its accounting methods. In fact, a company ***should*** make a change if a proposed new accounting method will provide more useful information than does the method presently in use. But when a significant change in accounting methods does occur, the fact that a change has been made and the dollar effects of the change should be ***fully disclosed*** in the financial statements.

Consistency applies to a single accounting entity and increases the comparability of financial statements from period to period. Different companies, even those in the same industry, may follow different accounting methods. For this reason, it is important to determine the accounting methods used by companies whose financial statements are being compared.

The Disclosure Principle

Adequate disclosure means that all ***material*** and ***relevant facts*** concerning financial position and the results of operations ***are communicated to users.*** This can be accomplished either in the financial statements or in the notes accompanying the statements. Such disclosure should make the financial statements more useful and less subject to misinterpretation.

Adequate disclosure does not require that information be presented in great detail; it does require, however, that no important facts be withheld. For example, if a company has been named as a defendant in a large lawsuit, this information must be disclosed. Other examples of information that should be disclosed in financial statements include:

1 A summary of the ***accounting policies*** (for example, principles and methods) used in the preparation of the statements.

2 Dollar effects of any ***changes*** in these accounting policies during the current period.

3 Any ***contingent losses*** that may have a material effect upon the financial position of the business.

4 Contractual provisions that will affect future cash flows, including the terms and conditions of borrowing agreements, employee pension plans, and commitments to buy or sell material amounts of assets.

Even significant events that occur ***after*** the end of the accounting period but before the financial statements are issued may need to be disclosed.

Naturally, there are practical limits to the amount of disclosure that can be made in financial statements and the accompanying notes. The key point to bear in mind is that the supplementary information should be ***relevant to the interpretation*** of the financial statements.

Materiality

The term ***materiality*** refers to the ***relative importance*** of an item or an event. An item is “material” if knowledge of the item might reasonably ***influence the decisions*** of users of financial statements. Accountants must be sure that all material items are properly reported in the financial statements.

However, the financial reporting process should be ***cost-effective***—that is, the value of the information should exceed the cost of its preparation. By definition, the accounting treatment accorded to ***immaterial*** items is of little or no value to decision makers. Therefore, accountants should not waste time accounting for immaterial items; these items may be treated in the ***easiest and most convenient manner.*** In short, the concept of materiality allows accountants to ***ignore other accounting principles*** with respect to items that are not material.

An example of the materiality concept is found in the manner in which most companies account for low-cost plant assets, such as pencil sharpeners or wastebaskets. Although the matching principle calls for depreciating plant assets over their useful lives, these low-cost items usually are charged immediately to an expense account. The resulting "distortion" in the financial statement is too small to be of any importance.

If a large number of immaterial items occur in the same accounting period, accountants should consider the ***cumulative effect*** of these items. Numerous "immaterial" items may, in aggregate, ***have a material effect upon the financial statements.*** In these situations, the numerous immaterial events must be properly recorded to avoid a material distortion of the financial statements.

We must recognize that the materiality of an item is a relative matter; what is material in a small business organization may not be material in a larger one. The materiality of an item depends not only upon its dollar amount but also upon its nature. In a large corporation, for example, it may be immaterial whether a given $50,000 expenditure is classified as an asset or as an expense. However, if the $50,000 item is a misuse of corporate funds, such as an unauthorized payment of the personal living expense of the chief executive, the ***nature*** of the item may make it quite material to users of the financial statements.

Conservatism as a Guide in Resolving Uncertainties[8]

We have previously referred to the use of ***conservatism*** in connection with the measurement of net income and the reporting of accounts receivable and inventories in the balance sheet. Although the concept of conservatism may not qualify as an accounting principle, it has long been a powerful influence upon asset valuation and income determination. Conservatism is most useful when matters of judgment or estimates are involved. Ideally, accountants should base their estimates on sound logic and select those accounting methods that neither overstate nor understate the facts. When some doubt exists about the valuation of an asset or the realization of a gain, however, accountants traditionally select the accounting option that produces a lower net income for the current period and a less favourable financial position.

An example of conservatism is the traditional practice of pricing inventory at the lower-of-cost-and-market. Decreases in the market value of the inventory are recognized as a part of the cost of goods sold in the current period, but increases in market value of inventory are ignored. Failure to

---

[8] CICA, *CICA Handbook* (Toronto), section 1000.21.

apply conservatism when valuations are especially uncertain may produce misleading information and result in losses to creditors and shareholders.

Audited Financial Statements

OBJECTIVE 5 Define an independent audit and discuss the assurances provided by the auditors' report.

The annual financial statements of large corporations are used by great numbers of shareholders, creditors, government regulators, and members of the general public. What assurance do these people have that the information in these statements is reliable and is presented in conformity with generally accepted accounting principles? The answer is that the annual financial statements of large corporations are ***audited*** by independent public accountants.

An audit is a thorough investigation of every material item, dollar amount, and disclosure that appears in the financial statements. (Keep in mind that many ledger balances and other types of information are combined and condensed in preparing financial statements. Consequently, each caption appearing in financial statements usually is considered material.)

After completing the audit, the auditors express their opinion as to the ***fairness*** of the financial statements. This opinion is contained in the ***auditors' report,*** which is published with the financial statements in the company's annual report to its shareholders. A report by a firm might read as follows:

> To the Shareholders of CD Technologies Limited
>
> We have audited the balance sheet of CD Technologies Limited as at December 31, 19__, and the statements of income, retained earnings, and changes in financial position for the year then ended. These financial statements are the responsibility of the company's management. Our responsibility is to express an opinion on these financial statements based on our audit.
>
> We conducted our audit in accordance with generally accepted auditing standards. Those standards require that we plan and perform the audit to obtain reasonable assurance as to whether the financial statements are free of material misstatement. An audit includes examining, on a test basis, evidence supporting the amounts and disclosures in the financial statements. An audit also includes assessing the accounting principles used and significant estimates made by management, as well as evaluating the overall financial statement presentation.
>
> In our opinion, these financial statements present fairly, in all material respects, the financial position of the company as at December 31, 19__ and the results of its operations and the changes in its financial position for the year then ended in accordance with generally accepted accounting principles.
>
> Calgary, Alberta — *Blue, White & Company*
> February 18, 19__ — Chartered Accountants

Over many decades, audited financial statements have developed an excellent track record of reliability. Note, however, that the auditors ***do not guarantee*** the accuracy of financial statements; rather, they render their ***professional opinion*** as to the overall ***fairness*** of the statements. "Fairness," in this context, means that the financial statements are ***not misleading.*** However, just as a physician may make an error in the diagnosis of a particular patient, there is always a possibility that an auditor's opinion may be in error. The primary responsibility for the reliability of financial statements rests with the management of the issuing company, not with the independent auditors.

PROFESSIONAL JUDGMENT: AN ESSENTIAL ELEMENT IN FINANCIAL REPORTING

OBJECTIVE 6 Describe the role of professional judgment in the financial reporting process.

Judgment plays a major role in financial reporting. For those situations not specifically covered by an official pronouncement, accountants must exercise professional judgment in determining the treatment that is most consistent with generally accepted accounting principles. Judgment also is exercised in selecting appropriate accounting methods (as for example, deciding whether to use the FIFO or LIFO method of inventory valuation), in estimating the useful lives of depreciable assets, and in deciding what events are "material" to a given business entity.

Judgment is a personal matter; different accountants often will make different judgments, even for similar situations. This explains why the financial statements of different companies are not likely to be directly comparable in all respects.

International Accounting Standards

OBJECTIVE 7 Discuss international accounting standards.

As mentioned in Chapter 1, the increasing growth in international trade and capital financing as well as the rapid expansion of multinational enterprises have made international accounting standards (that is, international GAAP) an indispensable element in financial reporting. The fundamental rationale for internationalization of accounting standards is to enhance the comparability of external financial reporting by multinational and other large enterprises whose economic and financial influences and effects transcend national boundaries.

While the root for the development of international accounting standards can be traced back to the first conference of the International Congress of Accountants in 1904, the establishment of The Accountants International Study Group (AISG) in 1966 by the accounting profession of Canada, the United Kingdom, and the United States provided an impetus to the creation of the International Accounting Standards Committee (IASC).

In 1973, the International Accounting Standards Committee was established by the professional accounting bodies in Australia, Canada, France, Germany, Japan, Mexico, the Netherlands, the United Kingdom and Ireland, and the United States as an independent, private sector standard setting organization. The primary objective of the IASC is to formulate and publish basic international accounting standards and to promote their worldwide acceptance and observance. Since its inception, the IASC has devoted its effort to expand its membership and to harmonize the divergence of accounting standards among nations. At present, it has about 100 accounting bodies from some 80 nations as members. (Canada has three members: The Canadian Institute of Chartered Accountants, the Certified General Accountants' Association of Canada, and the Society of Management Accountants of Canada.) It has issued more than thirty pronouncements on international accounting standards. These pronouncements provide sufficient flexibility by allowing the use of a fair number of accounting alternatives. However, the IASC has attempted to eliminate a number of free choices among alternative accounting treatments.

While the establishment of international accounting standards is a difficult and slow process, the IASC has accomplished a certain degree of harmonizing the standards by refining the boundaries for acceptable accounting standards. It has been able to narrow the choice of the number of accounting alternatives in some cases. Also, it has provided a source of accounting standards for some countries. For example, Malaysia, Singapore, and Yugoslavia, which do not have their own standards, have recognized the IASC's standards as the accepted standards. Moreover, in countries such as Nigeria and India where standard setting is emerging, the IASC's standards are the basis for the development of their accounting standards. Another significant manifestation of the IASC's accomplishment is that some stock exchanges, such as London and the Netherlands, consider the IASC's standards as generally accepted accounting principles in granting listing of foreign-based companies.

It is important to note two limitations of the IASC's accounting standards. First, compliance with these standards is voluntary; their acceptance is dependent on the persuasion of the IASC and the goodwill of its members. Second, these standards do not override those of the member countries.

ETHICAL CONDUCT IN THE ACCOUNTING PROFESSION

What Are "Ethics"?

OBJECTIVE 8 Describe the nature of ethics and explain the basic purpose of a code of ethics within a profession.

Ethics are the moral principles that an individual uses in governing his or her behaviour. In short, ethics are the personal criteria by which an individual distinguishes "right" from "wrong."

Every society has a strong interest in the ethical standards of its citizens. If people had no ethics, for example, they would see nothing "wrong" in cheating, stealing, or even committing murder as a means of achieving their goals. Obviously a society without ethics would be a chaotic and dangerous place in which to live. For this reason, governments, organized religions, and educators have long attempted to create or promote certain ethical standards among all members of society. Governments pass laws requiring or prohibiting certain types of behaviour; organized religions attempt to define "right" and "wrong" through sermons and religious teachings. Throughout the educational process, educators attempt to teach students to distinguish between "right" and "wrong" using criteria (ethics) acceptable to the greater society.

Ethics Relating to Certain Types of Activities Some ethical concepts, such as a belief that it is wrong to steal, apply to almost all situations. Other ethical concepts, however, apply specifically to some particular type of activity. For example, many of us have ethical principles relating directly to sports. Assume that you are playing a competitive sport and the umpire or referee makes a "bad call" ***in your favour.*** Do you challenge the call? Your answer to this question will depend upon your ***personal*** ethical principles concerning participation in competitive sports.

Some ethical concepts relate specifically to doing business. For example, if a member of the royal family or a government official in a foreign country demands a secret cash payment before allowing you to do business in that country, is it "ethical" for you to make this payment? If you manufacture a product that is useful, legal, and profitable, but evidence shows that its use is harmful to the environment, should you continue to produce this product? These are ethical decisions unique to the field of business. There also are many ethical decisions that relate specifically to the practice of ***professions,*** such as medicine, law, and accounting.

To understand and appreciate the ethics applicable to a specialized type of activity, one must first understand the ***nature of that activity.*** Consider, for example, a painter who encounters a building badly in need of new paint. The painter has no "ethical obligation" to stop and paint this building. Now consider a physician encountering an accident victim who is unconscious and badly in need of immediate medical attention. The physician ***does*** have an ethical obligation to stop and render emergency medical care. The obligation to render immediate service simply because it is needed is an ethical concept somewhat unique to the medical profession, because that profession is devoted to the public's health and safety.[9]

Ethics Relating to the Practice of Accounting Accountants, too, have unique ethical responsibilities. For example, public accountants auditing financial statements have an ethical obligation to be ***independent*** of the company issuing the statements. An accountant preparing an income tax return has an ethical obligation to prepare the return ***honestly,*** even though the taxpayer paying the accountant's fee may want the return prepared in a manner that understates taxable income. An accountant employed by a private company has the conflicting ethical obligations of respecting the ***confidentiality*** of information gained on the job and also making ***appropriate disclosures*** to people outside the organization.

The Concept of a "Profession" Accountants are proud to consider themselves members of a recognized ***profession.*** Just what is a "profession"? Actually, there exists no single definition or criterion that distinguishes a profession from other fields of endeavour. Over time, however, some occupations have come to be regarded as professions, while others have not. Among the occupations most commonly regarded as professions are the practices of medicine, law, engineering, architecture, and theology. Accounting, too, is widely viewed as having achieved the status of a profession.

Although a profession is not easily defined, all professions do have certain characteristics in common. Perhaps the most important of these characteristics is the special responsibility of persons practicing a profession to ***serve the public interest,*** even at the sacrifice of personal gain.

---

[9] Similar ethical responsibilities also exist for people working in a variety of "public safety" occupations.

Professional Codes of Ethics

All recognized professions have developed ***codes of professional ethics.*** The basic purpose of these codes is to provide members of the profession with guidelines for conducting themselves ***in a manner consistent with the responsibilities of the profession.*** Codes of ethics have been developed by several professional organizations of accountants. In addition to these codes, there are laws and professional pronouncements that govern the conduct of professional accountants.

Codes of ethics developed by professional organizations generally hold their members to ***higher*** standards of conduct than do the laws regulating that profession. In part, this tendency evolves from the fact that professional organizations have a vested interest in enhancing the public image of the profession. Also, these organizations have a better understanding than do lawmakers of the special problems confronting the professional. For these reasons, all professions are, to some extent, ***self-regulating.*** (The term ***self-regulating*** means that society expects the profession to establish its own rules of "professional conduct" for its members, and also to develop methods of enforcing these rules.)

OBJECTIVE 9 Identify and explain the basic principles underlying a professional code of ethics.

In this introductory discussion of ethical principles applicable to the accounting profession, we will explore briefly the following fundamental principles underlying the rules of professional conduct of the Institute of Chartered Accountants of Ontario[10]:

1 A member or student shall conduct himself or herself at all times in a manner which will maintain the good reputation of the profession and its ability to serve the public interest.

2 A member or student shall perform his or her professional services with integrity and care and accept an obligation to sustain his or her professional competence by keeping himself or herself informed of, and complying with, developments in professional standards.

3 A member who is engaged in an attest function such as an audit or review of financial statements shall hold himself or herself free of any influence, interest, or relationship, in respect of his or her client's affairs, which impairs his or her professional judgment or objectivity or which, in the view of a reasonable observer, would impair the member's professional judgment or objectivity.

4 A member or student has a duty of confidence in respect of the affairs of any client and shall not disclose, without proper cause, any information obtained in the course of his or her duties, nor shall he or she in any way exploit such information to his or her advantage.

5 The development of a member's practice shall be founded upon a reputation for professional excellence, and the use of methods of advertising which do not uphold professional good taste, which could be characterized as self-promotion, and which solicit, rather than inform, is not in keeping with this principle.

---

[10] Since these principles express the general spirit underlying the rules of professional conduct, they are essential in governing the conduct of professional accountants, regardless of the organization of affiliation. However, these principles are selected for purposes of illustration only.

6 A member shall act in relation to any other member with the courtesy and consideration due between professional colleagues and which, in turn, he or she would wish to be accorded by the other member.

While these principles focus mainly on public accountants (those who practise public accounting), they also apply to management accountants (those who are employed by private companies, not-for-profit organizations, and governmental agencies). For example, the principles of integrity and confidentiality, to a large extent, are applicable to public accountants as well as management accountants. Also, the principle of independence applies primarily to attestation engagements such as an audit or a review (attesting to the plausibility of financial information or financial statements), not to income tax work or the rendering of other professional services.

These principles call for an unswerving commitment to honourable behaviour, even at the sacrifice of personal advantage. A member or student who is found guilty of violating any provisions of the rules of professional conduct derived from these principles will be admonished, reprimanded, suspended, or expelled. A member who is expelled will lose his or her professional accounting certificate.

A Closer Look at Some Key Principles

OBJECTIVE 10 ***Apply the basic principles of ethical conduct to various situations likely to arise in an accountant's work.***

Three ethical principles of special importance to public accountants and management accountants are independence (or objectivity), integrity, and confidentiality.

Independence, or Objectivity When public accountants ***audit*** a company's financial statements, they express their ***professional opinion*** as to whether the financial statements represent a fair presentation of the company's financial position and the results of its operations. Shareholders, creditors, and potential investors all rely on these audited financial statements in deciding how to allocate their investment resources. The auditors' report will lend ***credibility*** to audited financial statements only if users of the statements view the auditors as impartial.

For auditors to be viewed as impartial, the profession feels that they must be ***independent*** of the company issuing the financial statements. By ***"independent,"*** we mean in fact and in appearance. Independence ***in fact*** refers to the ability of public accountants to maintain an objective mental attitude in all aspects of their work. Since it is not subject to objective measurement, mental attitude can usually be judged only by the public accountants themselves. On the other hand, independence ***in appearance*** means that the auditor must not be perceived as being under the company's influence or control or as having any ***vested interest*** in the results reported in the financial statements. Assume, for example, that an auditor owned shares in the common stock of an audit client. Many users of the financial statements might assume that the auditor would be reluctant to insist upon the disclosure of facts that might lower the price of the company's shares. Thus, the auditor would not be regarded as impartial by these users of the statements.

Public accountants take extensive measures ***to appear*** independent of their audit clients. This aspect of independence places a number of constraints upon the auditor's relationship with the audit client. Auditors must not have any financial interest in a client firm, must not accept expensive gifts from the client, and must not be employees of the client organization. Other restrictions require that close relatives of the auditors not have major investments or hold key management positions with a client company. In terms of inspiring public confidence, the ***appearance*** of independence is just as important as being independent in fact.

Public accountants need be independent only when they are expressing an opinion on the representations made by another party. Thus, the concept of independence applies ***primarily*** to the public accountant's role as an ***auditor.*** In rendering income tax services, consulting services, and many types of accounting services, public accountants are ***not*** required to be independent of their clients.

An important distinction between a management accountant and a public accountant is that the management accountant is an ***employee*** of the company for which he or she performs accounting services. The public accountant, on the other hand, is an independent contractor who provides services for a variety of different clients. Employees are not regarded as independent of their employers, so management accountants cannot perform independent audits of their employers' financial statements.

Although management accountants are not independent of their employers, they still are expected to develop accounting information that is fair, honest, and free from bias.

Integrity One of the most important principles underlying professional conduct is that both public and management accountants shall ***not knowingly misrepresent facts.*** This concept of integrity goes to the very heart of the professional accountant's responsibility to the public interest.

Facts may be misrepresented even if the facts themselves are stated correctly. For example, facts are considered to be misrepresented if the financial statements or accounting documents do not contain ***adequate disclosure*** of relevant information that may reasonably influence the intended user's ***interpretation*** of the facts.

Accordingly, public and management accountants ***must not be associated*** with misleading financial statements, income tax returns, or other accounting reports. If a client or employer insists upon preparing financial statements or documents in a misleading manner, the public or management accountant must ***resign from the engagement or employment.***

Confidentiality If individuals are to discuss sensitive and private matters openly with professionals, they must trust those professionals not to misuse the information provided. Thus, most professions have ethical requirements that information provided to the professionals must be held in strict confidence. Physicians, lawyers, and clergy, for example, are ethically and legally prohibited from disclosing to others personal information obtained from persons who have sought their professional services.

By the nature of their work, public and management accountants must have access to much financial information about their clients or their employers, information that is regarded as "confidential." If public and management accountants are to earn the trust and respect of their clients, their employers, and the public, they must respect the confidential nature of this information. They should not divulge sensitive information about a client or employer company to the company's competitors or to other outsiders, or use that information for their personal gain.

CASE IN POINT Both public and management accountants often have advance knowledge that a company's earnings for the year will be higher or lower than most investors are expecting. It would be unethical for the accountants to use this confidential information to profit from changes in the company's stock price, either personally or by passing such information to third parties.

The principle that information obtained by public and management accountants is to be held in confidence differs somewhat between the accounting profession and other professions. In all aspects of their work, these accountants have an ethical obligation ***not to misrepresent facts.*** They may face a conflict between their professional obligation to correctly and fully disclose facts, and a company's desire that certain information be held in confidence. In such a situation, they should insist that company make the necessary disclosure. If such disclosure is not made, they should resign.

It should be noted that the confidentiality requirement is not valid when there is a legal obligation for the accountants to make such disclosure.

The Challenge of Adhering to a Code of Ethics

In principle, a professional code of ethics is a good thing. Society benefits when professionals conduct themselves in an honourable and ethical manner. (Surely, no one would argue against professionals striving toward such goals as increased competence and integrity.) A professional code of ethics provides professionals with some general guidelines in conducting themselves in an ethical manner.

However, even an "honest" person may find it difficult to act in an ethical manner in some situations. Let us briefly consider a few of the "barriers" to ethical conduct.

The "Price" of Ethical Behaviour We would like to think that professionals will do the "right" (ethical) thing, regardless of the amount of personal sacrifice involved. This is an easier course of action to advocate than to follow. Management accountants, interestingly, may have to pay a far greater "price" for ethical conduct than the public accountants. Let us first consider the case of a public accountant.

Assume that a public accountant has a client that intends to issue misleading financial statements or to understate taxable income in an income tax return. The public accountant should not be associated with such misrepresentation and should resign from the engagement. This, of course, may mean that the public accountant is unable to collect his or her fee from this engagement, but this is a relatively small price to pay.

First, this "unethical" client is but one of many clients for the typical public accountant. Thus, the fee from this engagement probably represents only a small percentage of the public accountant's total revenue. More importantly, public accountants simply ***cannot afford*** to be associated with misleading financial statements or fraudulent income tax returns. Such associations could leave the public accountant personally liable to persons deceived by the misleading accounting documents, create adverse publicity that could destroy the public accountant's practice, cause the public accountant to lose his or her licence to practise public accounting, and result in the public accountant going to prison for committing fraud. Thus, the public accountant's choice is relatively clear: it is far better to give up an unethical client than to continue the association.

Now consider the situation of the management accountant. If the management accountant's employer rejects the accountant's concerns over an ethical problem, the management accountant may have no further recourse other than to resign. This may mean giving up a high and steady income, losing future pension rights, and joining the ranks of the unemployed. Clearly, this management accountant is asked to pay a much higher price for choosing the "ethical path" than is the public accountant in the preceding example.

Incomplete Information A professional accountant may "suspect" that activities in which he or she is asked to participate are unethical, but not be sure.

CASE IN POINT Wilson, a management accountant for International Equipment Company, is asked to process the paper work to reimburse the Vice-President of International Operations for a $50,000 "advertising expenditure" claimed in the executive's expense account. Wilson considers it improbable that the Vice-President actually spent $50,000 in personal funds for company advertising. More likely, Wilson thinks, the funds were paid as a bribe to some foreign official. However, Wilson has no facts concerning the expenditure, other than that top management wants the vice-president reimbursed.

In most situations, accountants have neither the responsibility nor the right to investigate their employers or clients. If a further investigation of the facts is not directly related to the accountant's professional responsibilities, the accountant simply may never have enough information to reach an informed decision as to whether or not specific activities are "ethical."

Just What Is the "Ethical" Thing to Do? Codes of ethics consist of broad, general guidelines, intended to be useful to practitioners in identifying and resolving ethical problems. However, no code of ethics can address every situation that might arise. Every "ethical dilemma" is somewhat unique, having its own facts and circumstances.

CASE IN POINT Assume that Barnes, a public accountant, is performing income tax services for Regis Limited: Regis insists that Barnes prepare the company's income tax return in a manner that understates the amount of taxes owed. What should Barnes do?

Answer: Barnes cannot ethically comply with the client's instructions. Therefore, Barnes should resign from the engagement.

In many situations, however, the ethical course of action ***is not readily apparent.***

CASE IN POINT Assume that Riley, a public accountant, is auditing the 1996 financial statements of Quest Corporation. During this audit, Quest Corporation is acquired by Gordon Communications. Riley's step-brother is the Controller of Gordon Communications. Has Riley's independence been impaired with respect to the Quest audit? Must Riley resign from this engagement?

Answer: ???[11]

Codes of ethics, including the "official interpretations," typically do not address such specific questions. Therefore, it often is not possible to simply "look up" the solution to an ethical problem. In deciding when an ethical problem exists, and in determining what constitutes ethical behaviour, the practitioner must often rely primarily upon his or her own ***professional judgment.***

In addition to studying a code of ethics, professionals attempting to resolve an ethical dilemma might ask themselves the following questions: "Would the action that I am considering be fair to everyone involved?" and "If my friends and family knew all the facts, would they be proud of my actions?" "Ethical conduct" means more than abiding by a list of rules; it means an ***unswerving commitment to honourable behaviour;*** even at the sacrifice of personal advantage.

CHAPTER REVIEW

KEY TERMS INTRODUCED OR EMPHASIZED IN CHAPTER 12

Accounting Standards Board (ASB) The unit authorized by the CICA to issue recommendations with respect to matters of accounting practices. The board's recommendations are recognized as an authoritative source of generally accepted accounting principles.

---

[11] Our Case in Point involving Riley and his step-brother is intended to show that ethical dilemmas ***do not always have clear-cut answers.*** This case hinges upon personal judgments, including the closeness of the relationship between Riley and his step-brother, and what impairs the "appearance" of independence. Thus, even with all the facts in hand, experts are likely to disagree on the answer to this case.

Auditors' report The report issued by a firm of public accountants after auditing the financial statements of a business. The auditors' report expresses an opinion on the fairness of the financial statements and indicates the nature and limits of the responsibility being assumed by the independent auditors.

Conservatism A traditional practice of resolving uncertainties by choosing an asset valuation at the lower point of the range of reasonableness. This term refers to the policy of postponing recognition of revenue to a later date when a range of reasonable choice exists. Conservatism is designed to avoid overstatement of financial strength and earnings.

Consistency An assumption that once a particular accounting method is adopted, it will not be changed from period to period. Consistency is intended to make financial statements of a given company comparable from year to year.

Cost principle The traditional, widely used policy of accounting for assets at their historical cost determined through arm's-length bargaining. Justified by the need for objective evidence to support the valuation of assets.

Disclosure principle Financial statements should include all material and relevant information about the financial position and operating results of the business. The notes accompanying financial statements are an important means of making the necessary disclosures.

Emerging Issues Committee The committee established by CICA's Accounting Standards Board to review emerging accounting issues and to provide guidance so as to minimize divergent or unsatisfactory treatments in practice.

Entity concept Any economic unit that controls economic resources and is accountable for these resources may be considered an accounting entity.

Ethical conduct Doing "what is right," even at the sacrifice of personal advantage.

Financial Accounting Standards Board (FASB) The organization in the United States with primary responsibility for formulating new accounting standards. The FASB is part of the private sector and is not a governmental agency.

Generally accepted accounting principles (GAAP) The "ground rules" for financial reporting. This concept includes principles, concepts, and methods that have received authoritative support, such as the accounting recommendations in the *CICA Handbook,* or that have become "generally accepted" through widespread use.

Going-concern assumption An assumption that a business entity will continue in operation indefinitely and thus will carry out its existing commitments.

Instalment method An accounting method that provides for recognition of realized profit on instalment contracts in proportion to cash collected.

Management accountant An accountant employed within a specific organization. Management accountants develop accounting information to meet the various needs of the organization and also assist management in the interpretation of this information.

Matching principle The accounting principle that governs the timing of expense recognition. This principle indicates that expenses should be offset against revenue on a basis of cause and effect. That is, the revenue of an accounting period should be offset by those costs and expenses that were causal factors in producing that revenue.

Materiality The relative importance of an amount or item. An item that is not significant enough to influence the decisions of users of financial statements is considered to be ***not*** material. The accounting treatment of immaterial items may be guided by convenience rather than by theoretical principles.

Objectivity (objective evidence) The valuation of assets and the measurement of income are to be based as much as possible on objective evidence, such as exchange prices in arm's-length transactions.

Percentage-of-completion method A method of accounting for long-term construction projects that recognizes revenue and profits in proportion to the work completed, based on an estimate of the portion of the project completed each accounting period.

Professional judgment Using one's professional knowledge, experience, and ethics to make decisions that have no prescribed or obvious answer.

Public Accountant A person who is licensed or otherwise permitted by provincial laws to engage in the practice of public accounting, the primary functions of which are to attest to the fairness of financial statements or financial information and to provide accounting services.

Realization principle The principle of recognizing revenue in the accounts only when the earning process is virtually complete, which is usually at the time of sale of goods or rendering service to customers.

Review An engagement designed to lend only a limited degree of assurance relating to financial statements or financial information.

Stable-dollar assumption In using money as a measuring unit and preparing financial statements expressed in dollars, accountants make the assumption that the dollar is a stable unit of measurement. This assumption is faulty in an environment of continued inflation.

Time period principle The idea that to be useful, financial statements should be prepared for relatively short accounting periods of equal length. While this principle contributes to the timeliness of financial statements, it conflicts with the objectivity principle by forcing accountants to make many estimates, such as the useful lives of depreciable assets.

ASSIGNMENT MATERIAL

DISCUSSION QUESTIONS

1 Briefly explain the meaning of the term ***generally accepted accounting principles.***

2 Why is it important that the accounting principles be "generally accepted"?

3 Name the organization in Canada that has been the most influential in developing generally accepted accounting principles.

4 To be "generally accepted," must an accounting method be set forth in the official pronouncements of an accounting standard-making organization? Explain.

5 Are generally accepted accounting principles in worldwide use? Explain.

6 What is the ***time period principle?*** Does this principle tend to increase or decrease the objectivity of accounting information? Explain.

7 What is meant by the term ***stable-dollar assumption?*** Is this assumption completely valid? Explain.

8 What is the meaning of the term ***objectivity*** as it is used by accountants? Is accounting information completely objective? Explain.

9 An argument has long existed as to whether assets should be valued in financial statements at cost or at estimated market value. Explain the implications of the ***objectivity principle*** in this controversy.

10 Explain what is meant by the expression "trade-off between ***reliability*** and ***relevance***" in connection with the preparation of financial statements.

11 What two conditions should be met before accountants consider revenue to be ***realized?***

12 Long-term construction projects often are accounted for by the percentage-of-completion method.

a Is this method consistent with the realization principle? Explain.

b What is the justification for the use of this method?

13 Briefly explain the ***matching principle.*** Indicate two approaches that accountants follow in attempting to "match" revenue with expense.

14 Does the concept of ***consistency*** mean that all companies should use the same accounting methods? Explain.

15 Briefly define the principle of ***disclosure.*** List four examples of information that should be disclosed in financial statements or in notes accompanying the statements.

16 Briefly explain the concept of ***materiality.*** If an item is not material, how is the item treated for financial reporting purposes?

17 Does ***conservatism*** mean that assets should be deliberately understated in accounting records? Explain fully.

18 Indicate how the concept of ***conservatism*** would apply to:

a Estimating the allowance for doubtful accounts receivable.

b Estimating the useful lives of depreciable assets.

19 What are ***audited*** financial statements? Is the auditing of financial statements made easier or more difficult by the principle of objectivity? Explain.

20 Professional judgment plays an important role in financial reporting. Explain at least three areas in which the accountant preparing financial statements must make professional judgments that will affect the content of the statements.

21 Briefly explain why society benefits from "ethical conduct" by all citizens. Next, explain why a society expects professionals to observe additional ethical standards, beyond those which pertain to all citizens.

22 Explain why all recognized professions have developed their own codes of professional ethics.

23 Identify an ethical concept that is unique to the auditing of financial statements. Explain why this ethical concept is important in the auditing function.

24 Briefly describe the ethical concept of ***confidentiality.*** Does this concept apply to public accountants, to management accountants, or to both? Does this concept prevent public accountants from insisting that their clients make "adequate disclosure" in financial statements intended for use by outsiders?

25 Why may a management accountant have to "pay a higher price" in resolving an ethical conflict than the "price paid" by a public accountant?

26 Briefly explain several reasons why even an honest person may have difficulty in always following the "ethical" course of action.

MULTIPLE CHOICE QUESTIONS

1 Generally accepted accounting principles (GAAP):

a Include only the official pronouncements of the standard-setting organizations, such as the CICA and FASB.

b May include customary accounting practices in widespread use even if not mentioned specifically in official pronouncements.

c Eliminate the need for professional judgment in the area in which an official pronouncement exists.

d Are laws of the provincial and federal governments.

2 Which of the following situations best illustrates the application of the ***realization*** principle?

a A company sells merchandise on the instalment method and recognizes gross profit as the cash is collected from customers.

b A construction company engaged in a three-year project determines the portion of profit to be recognized each year using the percentage-of-completion method.

c A construction company engaged in a three-month project during the year recognizes no profit until the project is completed.

d A manufacturer that sells washing machines with a three-year warranty recognizes warranty expense related to current year sales, based upon the estimated future liability.

3 Which of the following concepts has the ***least*** influence in determining the depreciation expense reported in the income statement under current GAAP?

a Reliability—The price of a depreciable asset established in an exchange transaction can be supported by verifiable, objective evidence.

b Cost principle—Assets are initially recorded in the account at cost and no adjustment is made to this valuation in subsequent periods, except to allocate a portion of the original cost to expense as assets expire.

c Relevance—Amounts shown in the financial statements should reflect current market values, as these are the most relevant to decision makers.

d Matching principle—Accountants attempt to match revenue with the expenses incurred in generating that revenue by systematically allocating an asset's cost to expense over its useful life.

4 The existence of generally accepted accounting principles has eliminated the need for professional judgment in:

a Estimating the useful lives and residual values of depreciable plant assets.

b Selecting an appropriate inventory valuation method, such as LIFO, FIFO, average cost, or specific identification.

c Determining which events are "material" to a given entity.

d None of the above is correct; each of the above situations requires the use of professional judgment.

5 The fact that a corporation's financial statements have been audited means that:

a An independent firm of public accountants has expressed an opinion upon the fairness of the statements.

b Revenue Canada has examined the financial statements to investigate compliance with tax laws.

- **c** The financial statements are guaranteed to be accurate by the public accountants who prepared them.
- **d** The financial statements were prepared by a public accounting firm, rather than by the company itself.

6 The concept of ethical conduct would ***prohibit*** a professional accountant from which of the following?

- **a** Resolving issues based upon professional judgment.
- **b** After resigning because of an ethical dispute with an employer, accepting employment elsewhere in the same industry.
- **c** Using for personal gain information that has not yet been released to the public about the financial position of a publicly owned employer or client.
- **d** Investing in the common stocks of any publicly owned companies.

EXERCISES

EXERCISE 12-1
Accounting Terminology

Listed below are nine technical accounting terms introduced or emphasized in this chapter.

GAAP	*Professional judgment*	*Realization*
CICA	*Materiality*	*Matching*
Objectivity	*Conservatism*	*Consistency*

Each of the following statements may (or may not) describe one of these technical terms. For each statement, indicate the accounting term described, or answer "None" if the statement does not correctly describe any of the terms.

- **a** The concept of associating expenses with revenue on a basis of cause and effect.
- **b** An essential element for an accountant making estimates, selecting appropriate accounting methods, and resolving trade-offs between the goals of conflicting accounting principles.
- **c** The organization that is primarily responsible for developing new accounting standards in Canada.
- **d** The goal of having all companies use the same accounting methods.
- **e** The accounting principles developed by the CICA.
- **f** The accounting principle used in determining when revenue should be recognized in financial statements.
- **g** An accounting concept that may justify departure from other accounting principles for purposes of convenience and economy.

EXERCISE 12-2
Asset Valuation

Milestone Manufacturing Company has just purchased expensive machinery that was custom-made to suit the firm's manufacturing operations. Because of the custom nature of this machinery, it would be of little value to any other company. Therefore, the controller of Milestone is considering writing these machines down to their estimated resale value in order to provide a conservative valuation of assets in the company's balance sheet. In the income statement, the write-down would appear as a "loss on revaluation of machinery."

Separately discuss the idea of writing down the carrying value of the machinery in light of each of the four following accounting concepts:

- **a** The going-concern assumption
- **b** The matching principle
- **c** Objectivity
- **d** Conservatism

EXERCISE 12-3
Revenue Recognition

In deciding when to recognize revenue in financial statements, accountants normally apply the realization principle.

a Revenue is considered realized when two conditions are met. What are these conditions?

b Indicate when the conditions for recognition of revenue have been met in each of the following situations. (Assume that financial statements are prepared monthly.)

1 An airline sells tickets several months in advance of its flights.

2 An appliance dealer sells merchandise on 24-month payment plans.

3 A professional sports team sells season tickets in July for eight home games to be played in the months of August through December.

4 Interest revenue relating to a 2-year note receivable is all due at the maturity of the note.

EXERCISE 12-4
Expense Recognition

Mystery Playhouse prepares monthly financial statements. At the beginning of its 3 month summer season, the company has programs printed for each of its 48 upcoming performances. Under certain circumstances, either of the following accounting treatments of the costs of printing these programs would be acceptable. Justify both of the accounting treatments using accounting principles discussed in this chapter.

a The cost of printing the programs is recorded as an asset and is allocated to expense in the month in which the programs are distributed to patrons attending performances.

b The entire cost of printing the programs is charged to expense when the invoice is received from the printer.

EXERCISE 12-5
Violations of Accounting Principles

For each situation described indicate the principle of accounting that is being violated. You may choose from the following:

Accounting entity	*Materiality*
Consistency	*Objectivity*
Disclosure	*Realization*
Matching	*Stable-dollar assumption*

a The bookkeeper for a large metropolitan auto dealership depreciates metal wastebaskets over a period of 5 years.

b Upon completion of the construction of a condominium project that will soon be offered for sale, Townhome Developers increased the balance sheet valuation of the condominiums to their sales value and recognized the expected profit on the project.

c Plans to dispose of a major segment of the business are not communicated to readers of the financial statements.

d The cost of expensive, custom-made machinery installed in an assembly line is charged to expense because it is doubtful that the machinery would have any resale value if the assembly line were shut down.

e A small commuter airline recognizes no depreciation on its aircraft because the planes are maintained in "as good as new" condition.

EXERCISE 12-6
Profit Recognition: Installment Method

On September 15, 1995, Susan Moore sold a piece of property that cost her $56,000 for $80,000, net of commissions and other selling expenses. The terms of sale were as follows: down payment, $8,000; balance, $3,000 on the fifteenth day of each month for 24 months, starting October 15, 1995. Compute the gross profit to be recognized by Moore in 1995, 1996, and 1997 using the ***accrual basis*** of accounting and (b) the ***instalment basis*** of accounting. Moore uses a fiscal year ending December 31.

EXERCISE 12-7
Profit Recognition: Percentage-of-Completion Method

The Clinton Corporation recognizes the profit on a long-term construction project as work progresses. From the information given below, compute the profit that should be recognized each year, assuming that the original cost estimate on the contract was $6,000,000 and that the contract price is $7,500,000.

Year	Costs Incurred	Profit Considered Realized
1994	$1,800,000	$?
1995	3,000,000	?
1996	1,171,000	?
Total	$5,971,000	$1,529,000

EXERCISE 12-8
Audits of Financial Statements

The annual financial statements of all large, publicly owned corporations are audited.

a What is an audit of financial statements?

b Who performs these audits?

c What is the basic purpose of an audit?

EXERCISE 12-9
Ethical Responsibilities of a Public Accountant

Teresa Ortiz, a public accountant, was engaged to audit the financial statements of Meglo Corporation and also to prepare the company's income tax return. During the course of her work, Ortiz discovered that in its income tax return, Meglo had claimed $75,000 of the amortization of goodwill even though this amount is not deductible in determining taxable income. Ortiz discussed this problem with her client, but the client insisted on deducting the amortization. A representative of management stated: If 100% amortization of goodwill isn't deductible, it should be. After all, it's the same as any other expenses that the company incurred."

Also during this engagement, Ortiz learned that Meglo has owed $36,000 to Martin Advertising Agency for a period of 17 months. Apparently, Martin had underbilled Meglo for services rendered 2 years ago and has made no request for the $36,000 additional payments due.

In the financial statements, Meglo included appropriate amounts of income taxes expense and income taxes payable. The company also properly included the $36,000 among its liabilities. However, management has told Ortiz that it has no intention of making payment of this amount unless it receives a bill from Martin.

Discuss Ortiz's ethical responsibilities with respect to (a) completing her professional engagements for Meglo, and (b) personally disclosing the facts directly to the affected third parties (Revenue Canada and/or Martin).

EXERCISE 12-10
The Honourable Mr. Chan

Hong-Ching Chan, CMA, was hired this year as a management accountant for Drexel, Inc. While working for Drexel, Chan learns that in the preceding year the company understated its tax liability in its income tax return by more than $400,000.

a Can Chan ethically report Drexel to Revenue Canada?

b Would your answer be different if Chan had been fired by Drexel?

c Would your answer be different if Chan were a public accountant engaged by Drexel to conduct an audit of the company's financial statements?

PROBLEMS

Note: Due to the nature of the problem material in this chapter, two sets of problems would result in substantial repetition. For this reason, we present the problems in one series, rather than in our usual A and B groups. Both the A and B sets of accounting work sheets support this series of problems. However, most of the problems also can be answered either on ordinary notebook paper or by using a word processor.

PROBLEM 12-1
Rationale Behind Acceptable Practices

Paragraphs **a** through **e** describe accounting practices that ***are in accord*** with generally accepted accounting principles. From the following list of accounting principles, identify those principles that you believe justify or explain each described accounting practice. (Most of the described practices are explained by a single principle; however, more than one principle may relate to a given practice.) Briefly explain the relationship between the described accounting practice and the underlying accounting principle.

Accounting Principles

Consistency	*Accounting entity concept*
Materiality	*Matching revenue with expense*
Objectivity	*Going-concern assumption*
Realization	*Disclosure*
Conservatism	*Stable-dollar assumption*

Accounting Practices

a If land costing $60,000 were sold for $65,000, a $5,000 gain would be reported regardless of inflation during the years that the land has been owned.

b When equipment is purchased an estimate is made of its useful life and its residual value, and the equipment is then depreciated over this period.

c The personal assets of the owner of a sole proprietorship are not disclosed in the financial statements of the business, even when these personal assets are sufficient to assure payment of all the business's liabilities.

d In estimating the appropriate size of the allowance for doubtful accounts, most accountants would, under conditions of uncertainty, rather see this allowance be a little too large rather than a little too small.

e The methods used in the valuation of inventory and for the depreciation of plant assets are described in a footnote to the financial statements.

PROBLEM 12-2
Accounting Principles

Paragraphs **a** through **e,** below, describe accounting practices that ***are in accord*** with generally accepted accounting principles. From the following list of accounting principles, identify those principles that you believe justify or explain each described accounting practice. (Most of the practices are explained by a single principle; however, more than one principle may relate to a particular practice.) Briefly explain the relationship between the described accounting practice and the underlying accounting principle.

Accounting Principles

Consistency	*Accounting entity concept*
Materiality	*Matching revenue with expense*
Objectivity	*Going-concern assumption*
Realization	*Disclosure*
Conservatism	*Stable-dollar assumption*

Accounting Practices

a The purchase of a 2-year fire insurance policy is recorded by debiting an asset account even though no refund will be received if the policy is cancelled.

b Hand tools with a small unit cost are charged to expense when purchased even though the individual tools have a useful life of several years.

c An airline records depreciation on its aircraft even though an excellent maintenance program keeps the planes in "as good as new" condition.

d A lawsuit filed against a company is described in footnotes to the company's financial statements even though the lawsuit was filed with the court shortly after the company's balance sheet date.

e A real estate developer carries an unsold inventory of condominiums in its accounting records at cost rather than at a much higher estimated sales value.

PROBLEM 12-3
Violations of GAAP

Six independent situations are described below.

a Morris Construction, Inc., does not have sufficient current assets to qualify for a much needed loan. Therefore, the corporation included among its current assets the personal savings accounts of several major shareholders, as these shareholders have promised to invest more money in the corporation if necessary.

b First Bank incurred large losses on uncollectible agricultural loans. On average, these loans call for payments to be received over a period of 10 years. Therefore, First Bank is amortizing its losses from the uncollectible loans against the revenue that will be earned over this 10-year period.

c The Ghost of Bay Street, a popular play, has sold out in advance for the next 2 years. These ticket sales were recognized as revenue at the time cash was received from the customers.

d Bay Street Advisory Service has been sued by clients for engaging in illegal securities transactions. No mention is made of this lawsuit in the company's financial statements, as the suit has not been settled and the company cannot objectively estimate the extent of its liability.

e Carver Company sold for $200,000 land that had been purchased 10 years ago for $150,000. As the general price level had doubled during this period, Carver Company restated the cost of the land at $300,000 and recognized a $100,000 loss.

f In a recent downturn in the economy, many small businesses have become bankrupt. Although Red River Stores was in no danger of bankruptcy, it reduced the carrying value of its assets to liquidation value to make its financial statements more in tune with the economy.

INSTRUCTIONS For each situation, identify the accounting principle that has been violated and explain the nature of the violation.

PROBLEM 12-4
Applying Accounting Principles

Five independent situations are described below.

a Pearl Cove Hotel recognizes room rental revenue on the date that a reservation is received. For the summer season, many guests make reservations as much as a year in advance of their intended visit.

b In prior years Regal Corporation had used the declining-balance method of depreciation for both financial reporting purposes and for income tax purposes. In the current year, Regal began to use straight-line depreciation on all assets for financial reporting purposes but continued to depreciate assets by the declining-balance method for income tax purposes.

c The liabilities of Ellis Construction are substantially in excess of the company's assets. In order to present a more impressive balance sheet for the business, Roy Ellis, the owner of the company, included in the company's balance sheet such personal assets as his saving account, automobile, and real estate investments.

d On January 9, 1996, Gable Company's only plant was badly damaged by a tornado and will be closed for much of the coming year. No mention was made of this event in the financial statements for the year ended December 31, 1995, as the tornado occurred after year-end.

e Friday Production follows a policy of valuing its plant assets at liquidation values in the company's balance sheet. No depreciation is recorded on these assets. Instead, a loss is recognized if the liquidation values decline from one year to the next. If the liquidation values increase during the year, a gain is recognized.

INSTRUCTIONS For each situation, indicate the accounting principle or concept, if any, that has been violated and explain briefly the nature of the violation. If you believe the treatment ***is in accord with generally accepted principles,*** state this as your position and briefly defend it.

PROBLEM 12-5
Evaluating Applications of Accounting Principles

Assume that you are an independent public accountant performing audits of financial statements. In the course of your work, you encounter the following situations:

a Reliable Appliance Company sells appliances on long-term payment plans. The company uses the instalment method of recognizing revenue in its financial statements. Uncollectible accounts consistently range between 1.5% and 2.0% of net sales.

b Akron Labs has spent $700,000 during the year in a very imaginative advertising campaign. The controller is sure that the advertising will generate revenue in future periods, but he has no idea how much revenue will be produced or over what period of time it will be earned. Therefore, he has decided to follow the "conservative" policy of charging the advertising expenditures to expense in the current period.

c Taylor Corporation has purchased special-purpose equipment, designed to work with other equipment already in place in Taylor's assembly line. Due to the special nature of this equipment, it has virtually no resale value to any other company. Therefore, Taylor's accountant has charged the entire cost of this special-purpose machinery to expense in the current period.

d Architectural Associates charges all purchases of drafting supplies directly to expense. At year-end, the company makes no entry to record the fact that $100 to $200 of these supplies remain on hand.

e Newton Company prepares financial statements four times each year. For convenience, these statements are prepared when business is slow and the accounting staff is not busy with other matters. Last year, financial statements were prepared for the two-month period ended February 28, the five-month period ended July 31, the three-month period ended October 31, and the one-month period ended November 30.

INSTRUCTIONS Discuss each of the above situations. If you consider the treatment to be in conformity with generally accepted accounting principles, explain why. If you do not, explain which principle or principles have been violated, and also explain how the situation should have been reported.

PROBLEM 12-6
Alternative Methods of Revenue Recognition

Early in 1995 Roadbuilders, Inc., was notified that it was the successful bidder on the construction of a section of a highway. The bid price for the project was $24 million. Construction began in 1995 and will take about 27 months to complete; the deadline for completion is in April of 1997.

The contract calls for payments of $6 million per year to Roadbuilders, Inc., for 4 years, beginning in 1995. (After the project is complete, the government will also pay a reasonable interest charge on the unpaid balance of the contract.) The company estimates that construction costs will total $16 million, of which $6 million will be incurred in 1995, $8 million in 1996, and $2 million in 1997.

The controller of the company, Joe Morgan, recognizes that there are a number of ways he might account for this contract. He might recognize income at the time the contract is completed (completed-contract method), in April of 1997. Alternatively, he might recognize income during construction (percentage-of-completion method), in proportion to the percentage of the total cost incurred in each of the 3 years. Finally, he might recognize income in proportion to the percentage of the total contract price collected in instalment receipts during the 4-year period (instalment method).

INSTRUCTIONS

a Prepare a schedule (in millions of dollars) showing the profit that would be recognized on this project in each of the 4 years (1995 through 1998) under each of the three accounting methods being considered by the controller. Assume that the timing and construction costs go according to plan. (Ignore the interest revenue relating to the unpaid balance of the contract.)

b Explain which accounting method you consider to be ***most*** appropriate in this situation. Also explain why you consider the other two methods less appropriate.

PROBLEM 12-7
Alternative Methods of Revenue Recognition

Halifax Boat Works builds custom sailboats. During the first year of operations, the company built four boats for Island Charter, a well-established and profitable company. The four boats had a total cost of $216,000 and were sold for a total price of $360,000, due on an instalment basis. Island Charter paid $120,000 of this sales price during the first year, plus an additional amount for interest charges.

At year-end, work is in progress on two other boats that are 40% complete. The contract price for these two boats totals $250,000 and costs incurred on these boats during the year total $60,000 (40% of estimated total costs of $150,000).

INSTRUCTIONS

a Compute the gross profit for Halifax Boat Works during its first year of operations under each of the following methods. (Interest earned from Island Charter Company does not enter into the computation of gross profit.)

(1) Gross profit is recognized by a percentage-of-completion method.

(2) Gross profit is recognized by the instalment method.

b Which method is more appropriate from the revenue recognition viewpoint? Explain.

PROBLEM 12-8
Ethical Dilemmas

Below are five independent cases that may confront professional accountants. In each case, identify the specific fundamental principle(s) that should guide the accountant's conduct, and indicate the ethical course of action. If the situation does not create any ethical problem, briefly explain why not.

a Brewster, a management accountant, works for the Defence Ministry. Part of her job is to evaluate bids of various defence contractors for Defence Ministry business. In the course of her work, she has come to know many people in the defence industry quite well. Today John Helms, a vice-president with General Systems Corporation, a defence contractor, offered Brewster the use of a condominium at a nearby ski resort any time she wanted to use it. He explained, "I know you like to ski. Our company owns this condominium, but no one ever seems to use it. Here's the key; just consider the place yours."

b Bello, a public accountant, has been requested to audit the financial statements of Bello Corporation, a family business. The business is owned and operated entirely by Bello's parents, brothers, and sisters. Bello has no direct financial interest in the business and does not personally participate in its management.

c Ross, a management accountant, works for One Million Auto Parts. The vice-president of marketing has asked Ross to prepare a summary of the market value of the company's inventory, arranged by geographic sales territories. Ross does not know the intended use of this summary. He does know, of course, that generally accepted accounting principles do not permit the valuation of inventories at market value in financial statements.

d Jacobs, a public accountant, is a member of a public accounting firm that audits four banks in the area. Jacobs is the firm's specialist in the banking industry. Yesterday, she received a request that her firm audit the financial statements of First National, the largest bank in the country.

e Two months ago, Arnold Chiou, a management accountant, worked as a cost accountant for Ewing Oil, but he is now employed by WestStar Oil. A manager at WestStar tells Chiou that WestStar is thinking of cutting its prices to win market share from Ewing. However, the manager needs to know Ewing Oil's per-litre production cost in order to know which company is likely to win a price war.

PROBLEM 12-9
More Ethical Dilemmas

Below are five independent cases that may confront professional accountants. In each case, identify the specific fundamental principles that should guide the accountant's conduct, and indicate the ethical course of action. If the situation does not create any ethical problem, briefly explain why not.

a Brown, a public accountant, has been engaged by Marshal Corporation to help the company design a more efficient accounting system. In the course of this engagement, Brown learns that in the preceding year, Marshal prepared its income tax return in a manner that understated the amount of income taxes due. Brown was not involved in the preparation of this tax return. However, assume that she will receive a 10% "finder's fee" by providing information that assists the government in collecting additional taxes owed by Marshal.

Brown is considering alerting the government to the additional taxes owed by Marshal.

b Huang, a management accountant, is asked by his employer to prepare financial statements in which depreciation expense is computed by the straight-line method. Huang knows that the company uses declining-balance depreciation methods in its income tax return.

c Porter, a public accountant, considers Commuter Airlines to be a well-managed company with a good future. For years, Porter has been purchasing stock in Commuter Airlines as a means of saving for her children's university education. Recently, Porter has received a request from Commuter Airlines to assist them in the preparation of its income tax return.

d DMX Corporation does custom manufacturing and bills each of its customers on a "cost plus" basis. In advertising, DMX uses the slogan, "We'll treat you like our only customer."

DMX has just purchased for $300,000 special machinery that will be used on seven separate contracts. Swartz, a management accountant at DMX, is told by his supervisor to charge each of these contracts with the entire $300,000 cost. The supervisor explains, "We would have had to buy this machinery if we were working on just one contract, and in that case, the customer would be charged the entire $300,000. So we'll just treat each customer as if it were our only customer."

e Mandella, a public accountant, is engaged in the audit of Wells Medical Products. Wells is in financial difficulties and will be using the audited financial statements in its effort to raise much needed capital. The company hopes to issue 10-year bonds payable in the near future.

Mandella learns that Wells is a defendant in numerous lawsuits alleging that Microtain, a product produced by Wells in the early 1960s, caused birth defects. The lawsuits probably will not be resolved for perhaps 5, 10, or 15 years. If Wells should lose the suit, the damages awarded to the plaintiffs could bankrupt the company.

The chief financial officer for Wells tells Mandella, "Look, we aren't about to disclose this stuff in our financial statements. First, we're innocent; Microtain never hurt anyone. When it's all said and done, we won't owe a dime. Also, if we lose, we'll appeal. These suits won't even be settled until long after our 10-year bond issue has been repaid. If you insist on disclosing this mess in the financial statements, we'll never get our financing. We'll have to close up, and thousands of our employees will lose their jobs. In short, I can't allow disclosure of this information; you'll just have to regard it as 'confidential'."

ANALYTICAL AND DECISION PROBLEMS AND CASES

A&D 12-1
Gotta Match?

In determining when to recognize an expenditure as expense, accountants attempt to apply the matching principle. Listed below are 10 types of costs frequently encountered by business organizations.

Types of Costs

1 The cost of merchandise purchased for resale.
2 The cost to an auto dealer of a training program for mechanics. On average, mechanics stay with the dealership for 4 years.
3 Sales commissions owed to employees for sales in the current period but payable in the next period.
4 The cost of a 2-year insurance policy.
5 The amount of accounts receivable estimated to be uncollectible.
6 The cost of expensive factory equipment with an estimated life of 10 years.
7 Research costs that may benefit the company for a decade or more if successful products are discovered and brought to market.
8 The cost of four wastebaskets with an estimated useful life of 10 years.
9 Interest on notes payable that has accrued during one period but is not payable until a future period.
10 The cost of an advertising campaign promoting the opening of a new store that is expected to remain in operation for 20 years.

INSTRUCTIONS Indicate in which period or periods these costs should be recognized as expense.

A&D 12-2
"Trade-Offs" among Accounting Principles

It is not possible to be consistent with all accounting principles all the time. Sometimes trade-offs are necessary; accountants may need to compromise one accounting principle or goal in order to achieve another more fully.

INSTRUCTIONS Describe a situation that requires a trade-off between the following sets of principles or goals:

a The relevance of accounting information to decision makers and the need for this information to be reliable.
b The comparability of information reported by different companies and the idea that a company should consistently apply the same accounting methods from year-to-year.

c The realization principle and the need for relatively timely information.

d The desire to match revenue with expenses and the quest for objectivity.

A&D 12-3
GAAP from an Auditor's Perspective

Assume that you are an independent public accountant performing audits of financial statements. In the course of your work, you encounter the following situations:

a Gala Magazine receives most of its revenue in the form of 12-month subscriptions. Even though this subscription revenue has already been received in cash, the company's controller defers recognition in the income statement; the revenue is recognized on a monthly basis as the monthly issues of the magazine are mailed to subscribers.

b Due to the bankruptcy of a competitor, Regis Trucking was able to buy plant assets worth at least $400,000 for the "bargain price" of $300,000. In order to reflect the benefits of this bargain purchase in the financial statements, the company recorded the assets at a cost of $400,000 and reported a $100,000 "gain on purchase of plant assets."

c Metro Development Company built a 400-unit furnished apartment complex. All materials and furnishings used in this project that had a unit cost of less than $200 were charged immediately to expense. The total cost of these items amounted to $6 million.

d In January 1996, the main plant of Hillside Manufacturing Company was destroyed in a fire. As this event happened in 1996, no loss was shown in the income statement for 1995. However, the event was thoroughly disclosed in notes to the 1995 financial statements.

e In an effort to match revenue with all related expenses in an objective manner, Brentwood Company has established "useful life" standards for all types of expenditures. For example, expenditures for advertising are amortized over 12 months; the costs of employee training programs, 24 months; and research costs, 10 years.

INSTRUCTIONS

Discuss each of the above situations. If you consider the treatment to be in conformity with generally accepted accounting principles, explain why. If you do not, explain which principle or principles have been violated, and also explain how the situation should have been reported.

A&D 12-4
How Much Is the Restaurant?

Rich & Famous, a luxury ski resort hotel located in Whistler, has been expanding its operation in the past few years to meet the increasing influx of affluent skiers from all over the globe. Last summer, Rich & Famous decided to add a gourmet restaurant for its wealthy guests. A contract was signed with a contractor to build the restaurant for $800,000. Since the skiing season usually begins in mid-December and the new restaurant was expected to attract more skiers to the hotel, Rich & Famous extracted a guarantee from the contractor to complete the construction of the restaurant by December 15; otherwise, a penalty of $8,000 a day will be deducted from the contract price until the restaurant is completed.

Unfortunately, the restaurant was not completed until December 31. Consequently, Rich & Famous deducted $128,000 (16 days × $8,000) from the contract price and paid only $672,000. In spite of the rather heavy penalty, Rich & Famous felt that it had lost not only some goodwill but also revenue as a few of the guests left earlier than expected because the restaurant was not in place as promised.

At the end of the year, the president of Rich & Famous wanted to show the restaurant at its contract price of $800,000 and the penalty of $128,000 as revenue in the financial statements. However, the controller argued that the restaurant should be shown at its actual cost of $672,000. This upset the president and he shot back at the controller: "I don't know on what accounting principles you based your argument. But it simply doesn't make sense to me. Are you telling me that if the construction delay were 102 days rather than 16, you wouldn't even show the restaurant in the balance sheet because the contract price would be reduced to zero? Are you then saying that this new gourmet restaurant is not an asset? What do I do with the $16,000 penalty in excess of the contract price? I certainly think that it should be reported as revenue. Now, let me tell you one more thing: you and I know that the delay cost us more than $8,000 a day in revenue."

INSTRUCTIONS Discuss the accounting principles and concepts underlying the position of the controller and of the president and defend their respective positions.

A&D 12-5 "What? Me? Fired?"

Christine Davis is a management accountant for CalTex Industries. Davis believes that she is being asked to accumulate inappropriate costs on a "cost plus" contract. All costs accumulated on the contract (along with a markup representing CalTex's profit margin) ultimately are billed to the customer, an agency of the government.

a Does this situation represent an ethical problem for Davis? Explain.

b If you believe that an ethical problem exists, briefly explain how Davis should resolve it.

c Assume that as a result of taking the steps that you suggested in part **b,** Davis is fired. Does Davis have an ethical obligation to inform the governmental agency of her suspicions that it is being overcharged? Explain.

A&D 12-6 Ethics in the "Real World"

Bring into class a copy of a newspaper or magazine article describing a situation in which professional accountants probably faced an ethical dilemma. (Your article need not specifically mention the accountants' roles in the situation. Also, your article need not be current; you may select any article from any business publication.)

Describe the ethical problems that you believe confronted the accountants in this situation and the course of action they should have considered. Also, express your ***personal opinion*** as to whether or not the accountants acted in an ethical manner, including the reasons behind your opinion. Finally, discuss what ***you*** would have done in the accountants' place, identifying any factors that may have made your decision difficult.

PART

5 Partnerships and Corporations

The next five chapters focus on accounting issues that affect partnerships and corporations. In Chapter 13, the specialized field of accounting for partnership is explored. In the other chapters, issues unique to corporations are discussed. Corporations play the dominant role in our economy. Corporations own more assets, earn more revenue, provide more jobs, and attract more capital than all other forms of business organizations combined.

Part 5 also contains Comprehensive Problem 4. This problem provides a review of much of the material of the first twelve chapters, as well as some corporate accounting issues.

CHAPTER

13 Partnerships

In prior chapters we have used the sole proprietorship as a model in our study of basic accounting concepts. In this chapter we focus on the partnership and the accounting issues related to this form of business organization. Among these topics are the accounting for the formation of a partnership, the equitable division of partnership net income or net loss among the partners, the admission and the withdrawal of individual partners, and finally the liquidation of a partnership business.

Learning Objectives

After studying this chapter you should be able to:

1. *Describe the basic characteristics of a partnership.*
2. *Discuss the advantages and disadvantages of the partnership as a form of business organization.*
3. *Distinguish between a regular partnership and a limited partnership.*
4. *Account for the formation of a partnership.*
5. *Divide the net income of a partnership among the partners.*
6. *Account for the admission of a new partner and the withdrawal of a partner.*
7. *Account for the liquidation of a partnership.*

Three types of business organization are common to Canadian business: the sole proprietorship, the partnership, and the corporation. Partnerships are a popular form of organization because they provide a convenient, inexpensive means of combining the capital and the special abilities of two or more persons. The partnership form of organization is widely used in all types of small business and also in the professions. A partnership is often referred to as a ***firm;*** the name of the firm often includes the word ***company,*** as, for example, "Adams, Barnes, and Company."

In Canada, each province has its own partnership legislation. The provincial partnership legislation may consist of one or more acts. All provincial partnership legislation covers essentially the same ground and provides essentially the same fundamental rules on the nature, organization, and operation of partnerships.

What constitutes a partnership? The answer can be found in the partnerships act. The legal definition of a partnership is essentially the same in all provincial legislation, except for minor differences in wording. The Ontario Partnerships Act, for example, has the following definition:

> Partnership is the relation that subsists between persons carrying on a business in common with a view to profit, but the relation between the members of a company or association that is incorporated by or under the authority of any special or general Act in force in Ontario or elsewhere, or registered as a corporation under any such Act, is not a partnership within the meaning of this Act.

In this chapter, we shall concentrate on the significant features of and the accounting problems peculiar to a partnership.

Significant Features of a Partnership

OBJECTIVE 1 Describe the basic characteristics of a partnership.

Before taking up the accounting problems peculiar to partnerships, it will be helpful to consider briefly some of the distinctive characteristics of the partnership form of organization. These characteristics (such as limited life and unlimited liability) all stem from the concept that a partnership is not a separate legal entity in itself but merely a voluntary association of individuals.

Ease of Formation Generally, a partnership can be created with a minimum of formality. When two or more persons agree, orally or in writing, to carry on a business with a view to profit, such agreement constitutes a contract and a partnership is automatically created. The contract should be in writing in order to lessen the chances for misunderstanding and future disagreement. The voluntary aspect of a partnership agreement means that no one can be forced into a partnership or forced to continue as a partner.

CASE IN POINT Richard and Mike were friends and employees of the same large corporation. They became interested in forming a partnership to acquire a nearby small business being offered for sale for a down payment of $50,000. They felt that they could manage the business (which had two employees) in their spare time. Richard and Mike agreed that each would deposit $25,000 in a partnership bank account. There was no written agreement of partnership. Richard made his deposit from his personal savings; Mike had only $10,000 of his own but was able to obtain the other $15,000 from his brother-in-law, Joe, to whom he described the business with great enthusiasm. Mike then deposited $25,000 in the partnership bank account and the business was purchased. Richard had never met Joe and was not aware of his $15,000 investment.

A few months later, Joe became annoyed because he had received no return on his investment. He appeared suddenly at the business while Richard was there, stating that he was a partner and demanding to see the accounting records and the bank statements. Richard refused, and after an angry argument, Joe was forcibly ejected. The question of whether Joe was a "silent partner" caused bitter disagreement among all three of the principals. During this dispute, the business was forced to shut down because of lack of working capital. Richard, Mike, and Joe each retained a lawyer to seek damages from the others.

Although a partnership may be at times a somewhat unstable form of organization, a written agreement of partnership might have avoided the problems encountered by Richard and Mike—and by Joe.

Limited Life A partnership may be ended at any time by the death or withdrawal of any member of the firm. Other factors that may bring an end to a partnership include the bankruptcy or incapacity of a partner, the expiration of the period specified in the partnership contract, or the completion of the project for which the partnership was formed. The admission of a new partner or the retirement of an existing member means an end to the old partnership, although the business may be and usually is continued by the formation of a new partnership.

Mutual Agency Each partner acts as an agent of the partnership, with authority to enter into contracts for the purchase and sale of goods and services. The partnership is bound by the acts of any partner as long as these acts are within the scope of normal operations. The factor of mutual agency suggests the need for exercising great caution in the selection of a partner. To be in partnership with an irresponsible person or one lacking in integrity is an intolerable situation.

Unlimited Liability Each partner is ***personally*** responsible for all the debts of the firm. The lack of any ceiling on the liability of a partner may deter a wealthy person from entering a partnership.

A new member joining an existing partnership may or may not assume liability for debts incurred by the firm prior to his or her admission. A partner withdrawing from membership must give adequate public notice of withdrawal; otherwise the former partner may be held liable for partnership debts incurred subsequent to his or her withdrawal. The retiring partner remains liable for partnership debts existing at the time of withdrawal unless the creditors agree to a release of this obligation.

Co-ownership of Partnership Property and Income When a partner invests a building, inventory, or other property in a partnership, he or she does not retain any personal right to the assets contributed. The property becomes jointly owned by all partners. Each member of a partnership also has an ownership right in the income of the partnership.

Advantages and Disadvantages of a Partnership

OBJECTIVE 2 Discuss the advantages and disadvantages of the partnership as a form of business organization.

Perhaps the most important advantage of most partnerships is the opportunity to bring together sufficient capital to carry on a business. The opportunity to combine special skills, as, for example, the specialized talents of an engineer and an accountant, may also induce individuals to join forces in a partnership. To form a partnership is much easier and less expensive than to organize a corporation. Members of a partnership enjoy more freedom from government regulation and more flexibility of action than do the owners of a corporation. The partners may withdraw funds and make business decisions of all types without the necessity of formal meetings or legalistic procedures.

Operating as a partnership ***may*** in some cases produce income tax advantages as compared with doing business as a corporation. The partnership itself is neither a legal entity nor a taxable entity. A partnership does not pay income taxes. However, the individual partners must pay income taxes on their respective shares of the partnership's net income.

Offsetting these advantages of a partnership are such serious disadvantages as limited life, unlimited liability (except for a limited partner in a limited partnership, as discussed in the following section), and mutual agency. Furthermore, if a business is to require a large amount of capital, the partnership is a less effective device for raising funds than is a corporation. Many persons who invest freely in common stocks of corporations are unwilling to enter a partnership because of the unlimited liability imposed on partners.

Limited Partnerships

OBJECTIVE 3 Distinguish between a regular partnership and a limited partnership.

In past years a number of businesses have been organized as "limited partnerships." This form of organization is widely used for businesses that provide tax-sheltered income to investors, such as real estate syndications and mining ventures. However, limited partnerships are ***not*** appropriate for businesses in which the owners intend to be active managers. Recent tax legislation has also reduced greatly the income tax advantages formerly available to investors in limited partnerships.

A limited partnership must have at least one ***general partner*** as well as one or more ***limited partners.*** The general partners are partners in the traditional sense, with unlimited liability for the debts of the business and the right to make managerial decisions. The limited partners, however, are basically ***investors*** rather than traditional partners. They have the right to participate in the income of the business, but their liability for losses is limited to the amount of their investment. Also, limited partners do not actively participate in management of the business. Thus, the concepts of unlimited liability and mutual agency apply only to the general partners in a limited partnership.

In this chapter, we emphasize the characteristics and accounting practices of conventional partnerships rather than limited partnerships. Limited partnerships are discussed in depth in courses on business law and income taxes.

The Partnership Contract

Although a partnership can be formed by an oral agreement, it is highly desirable that a written partnership agreement be prepared, summarizing the partners' mutual understanding on such points as:

1 Names of the partners
2 The duties and rights of each partner, effective the specified date of formation of the partnership
3 Amount to be invested by each partner, including the procedure for valuing any noncash assets invested or withdrawn by partners
4 Methods of sharing net income and net losses
5 Withdrawals to be allowed each partner
6 Provision for liquidation, including the method for sharing a deficiency in a partner's capital account by other partners

Partnership Accounting

As mentioned earlier in this chapter, a partnership ***does not*** constitute a ***legal*** entity with an identity separate from its owners. However, from a record-keeping and reporting point of view, a partnership does constitute a ***separate and distinct accounting entity.***

An adequate accounting system and an accurate measurement of income are needed by every business, but they are especially important in a partnership because the net income is divided among two or more owners. Each partner needs current, accurate information on operations so that he or she can make intelligent decisions on such questions as additional investments, expansion of the business, or sale of an interest in the partnership.

CASE IN POINT Rowe and Davis were partners in an automobile dealership and auto repair shop. Rowe was the active manager of the business, but Davis had supplied nearly all the capital. Aware that the firm was quite profitable, Rowe devised a scheme to become the sole owner by buying out his partner. In order to persuade Davis to sell his interest at a bargain price, Rowe deliberately began falsifying the accounting records and financial statements in a manner to understate the earnings of the business. Much of the revenue from auto repair work was not recorded at all, depreciation expense was overstated, ending inventories were understated, and the cost of new items of plant and equipment were charged to expense. The result was a series of monthly income statements that showed the business operating at a larger loss each month. Faced with these discouraging financial statements, Davis became pessimistic over the prospects for the business and was on the verge of selling his interest to Rowe at a price far below the balance in his capital account.

However, a friend suggested that before selling out, Davis should insist upon an audit of the business by a public accounting firm. An audit was performed and revealed that the business was in fact highly profitable. When confronted by Davis with the auditors' findings, Rowe withdrew from the partnership and Davis became the sole owner.

Opening the Accounts of a New Partnership

OBJECTIVE 4 Account for the formation of a partnership.

When a partner contributes assets other than cash, a question always arises as to the value of such assets. The valuations assigned to noncash assets should be their ***current market values*** at the date of transfer to the partnership. The valuations assigned must be agreed to by all partners.

To illustrate the opening entries for a newly formed partnership, assume that on January 1, Joan Blair and Richard Cross, who operate competing retail stores, decide to form a partnership by consolidating their two businesses. A capital account will be opened for each partner and credited with the agreed valuation of the ***net assets*** (total assets less total liabilities) that the partner contributes. The journal entries to open the accounts of the partnership of Blair and Cross are as follows:

Entries for formation of partnership.

Cash	40,000	
Accounts Receivable	60,000	
Inventory	90,000	
Accounts Payable		30,000
Joan Blair, Capital		160,000
To record the investment by Joan Blair in the partnership of Blair and Cross.		
Cash	10,000	
Inventory	60,000	
Land	60,000	
Building	100,000	
Accounts Payable		70,000
Richard Cross, Capital		160,000
To record the investment by Richard Cross in the partnership of Blair and Cross.		

Partnership accounting is similar to that in a sole proprietorship, except that separate capital and drawing accounts are maintained for each partner. These capital and drawing accounts show for each partner the amounts invested, the amounts withdrawn, and the appropriate share of partnership net income. In brief, each partner is provided with a history of his or her equity in the firm.

The values assigned to assets in the accounts of the new partnership may be quite different from the amounts at which these assets were carried in the accounts of their previous owners. For example, the land contributed by Cross and valued at $60,000 might have appeared in his accounting records at a cost of $20,000. The building that he contributed was valued at $100,000 by the partnership, but it might have cost Cross only $80,000 some years ago and might have been depreciated on his records to a net value of $60,000. Assuming that market values of land and buildings had risen sharply while Cross owned this property, it is only fair to recognize the ***current market value*** of these assets at the time he transfers them to the partnership and to credit his capital account accordingly. Depreciation of the building in the partnership accounts will be based on the assigned value of $100,000 at the date of acquisition by the partnership.

Additional Investments

Assume that after six months of operation the firm is in need of more cash, and the partners make an additional investment of $10,000 each on July 2. These additional investments are credited to the capital accounts as shown below:

Entry for additional investment

Cash	*20,000*	
Joan Blair, Capital		*10,000*
Richard Cross, Capital		*10,000*
To record additional investments.		

Drawing Accounts

The drawing account maintained for each partner serves the same purpose as the drawing account of the owner of a sole proprietorship. The transactions calling for debits to the drawing accounts of partners may be summarized as follows:

1 Cash or other assets withdrawn by a partner
2 Payments from partnership funds of the personal debts of a partner
3 Partnership cash collected on behalf of the firm by a partner but retained by the partner personally

Loans from Partners

Ordinarily any funds furnished to the firm by a partner are recorded by crediting that partner's capital account. Occasionally, however, a partnership may be in need of funds but the partners do not wish to increase their capital investment in the business, or perhaps one partner is willing to advance funds when the others are not. Under these circumstances, the advance of funds may be designated as a loan from the partner and credited to a liability account. However, partnership liabilities to outsiders always take precedence over liabilities to partners.

Closing the Accounts of a Partnership at Year-End

At the end of the accounting period, the balance in the Income Summary account is closed into the partners' capital accounts. The net income or losses of a partnership may be divided among the partners in ***any manner agreed upon*** by the partners. However, this agreement should be carefully stipulated in the partnership contract. In the event that the partners ***do not*** have a formal income-and-loss sharing agreement, the law requires all net income or losses to be ***divided equally*** among the partners.

In our illustration, let us assume that Blair and Cross have agreed to share net income equally. (We will discuss other income-and-loss sharing arrangements later in this chapter.) Assuming that the partnership earns net income of $60,000 in the first year of operations, the entry to close the Income Summary account is as follows:

Closing income summary: net income shared equally

Income Summary	*60,000*	
Joan Blair, Capital		*30,000*
Richard Cross, Capital		*30,000*
To divide net income for the year in accordance with partnership agreement to share it equally.		

The next step in closing the accounts is to transfer the balance of each partner's drawing account to his capital account. Assuming that withdrawals during the year amounted to $24,000 for Blair and $16,000 for Cross, the entry at December 31 to close the drawing accounts is as follows:

Closing the drawing accounts to capital accounts

Joan Blair, Capital	*24,000*	
Richard Cross, Capital	*16,000*	
Joan Blair, Drawing		*24,000*
Richard Cross, Drawing		*16,000*
To transfer debit balances in partners' drawing accounts to their respective capital accounts.		

Income Statement for a Partnership The income statement for a partnership differs from that of a sole proprietorship in only one respect: a final section may be added to show the division of the net income between the partners, as illustrated below for the firm of Blair and Cross. The income statement of a partnership is consistent with that of a sole proprietorship in showing no income taxes expense and no salaries expense relating to services rendered by partners.

Note division of net income

BLAIR AND CROSS
Income Statement
For the Year Ended December 31, 19__

Sales		*$600,000*
Cost of goods sold		*400,000*
Gross profit		*$200,000*
Operating expenses:		
Selling expenses	*$100,000*	
General & administrative expenses	*40,000*	*140,000*
Net income		*$ 60,000*
Division of net income:		
To Joan Blair (50%)	*$ 30,000*	
To Richard Cross (50%)	*30,000*	*$ 60,000*

Statement of Partners' Equity The partners will usually want an explanation of the change in their capital accounts from one year-end to the next. A supplementary schedule called a ***statement of partners' equity*** is prepared to show this information. A statement of partners' equity for Blair and Cross follows:

Changes in capital accounts during the year

BLAIR AND CROSS
Statement of Partners' Equity
For the Year Ended December 31, 19__

	Blair	Cross	Total
Balances, Jan. 1, 19__	$160,000	$160,000	$320,000
Add: Additional investments	10,000	10,000	20,000
Net income for the year	30,000	30,000	60,000
Subtotals	$200,000	$200,000	$400,000
Less: Drawings	24,000	16,000	40,000
Balances, Dec. 31, 19__	$176,000	$184,000	$360,000

The balance sheet of Blair and Cross would show the capital balance for each partner, as well as the total capital of $360,000.

Partnership Income and Income Taxes

Partnerships Are Not Required to Pay Income Taxes Partners must include their shares of the partnership net income (after certain technical adjustments) on their individual income tax returns. Partnership net income is thus taxable to the partners individually in the year in which it is earned. The income tax rules applicable to investment in a partnership are covered in advanced accounting courses.

Note that partners report and pay tax on their respective shares of the net income earned by the partnership during the year and ***not*** on the amounts that they have drawn out of the business during the year. ***The net income of the partnership is taxable to the partners each year,*** even though there may have been no withdrawals. This treatment is consistent with that accorded a sole proprietorship.

The Nature of Partnership Net Income

The net income earned by partnerships, like those earned by sole proprietorships, compensate the owners for (1) personal services rendered to the business, (2) capital invested in the business, and (3) "entrepreneurial risk"—that is, taking the risk that the investments of personal services and of capital may be lost if the business is unsuccessful. Recognition of these three factors is helpful in developing an equitable plan for the division of partnership net income.

If one partner devotes full time to the business while another devotes little or no time, the difference in the partners' contributions of time and effort should be reflected in the income-sharing agreement. If one partner possesses special skills, the income-sharing agreement should reward this partner's talent. Also, partners may each provide different amounts of capital to the business entity. Again, the differences in the value of the partners' contributions to the business should be reflected in the income-and-loss sharing agreement.

To recognize the particular contributions of each partner to the business, partnership income-and-loss sharing agreements often include "salary allowances" to partners and "interest" on the balances of partners' capital accounts. These "salaries" and "interest" are ***not expenses*** of the business; rather, they are ***steps in the computation made to divide partnership net income among the partners.***

In the preceding illustrations of the partnership of Blair and Cross, we assumed that the partners invested equal amounts of capital, rendered equal services, and divided net income equally. We are now ready to consider cases in which the partners invest ***unequal*** amounts of capital and services.

Dividing Partnership Net Income among the Partners

Partners can share net income or loss in any manner they decide upon; however, most income-sharing agreements fall under one of the following types:

OBJECTIVE 5 Divide the net income of a partnership among the partners.

1 A fixed ratio. The fixed ratio method has already been illustrated in the example of the Blair and Cross partnership in which net income was shared equally, that is, 50% and 50%. Partners may agree upon any fixed ratio such as 60% and 40%, or 70% and 30%.
2 Salary allowances to the partners, with remaining net income or loss divided in a fixed ratio.
3 Interest allowances on partners' capital balances, with remaining net income or loss divided in a fixed ratio.
4 Salary allowances to the partners, interest allowances on partners' capital balances, and remaining net income or loss divided in a fixed ratio.

All these methods of sharing partnership net income are intended to recognize differences in the personal services rendered by partners and in the amounts of capital invested in the firm.

In the illustrations that follow, it is assumed that beginning balances in the partners' capital accounts were Brooke Adams, $160,000, and Ben Barnes, $40,000. At year-end, the Income Summary account showed a credit balance of $96,000, representing the net income for the year before any allowances for partners' salaries or interest on capital account balances.

Salaries to Partners, with Remainder in a Fixed Ratio Because partners often contribute different amounts of personal services, partnership agreements often provide for partners' salaries as a factor in the division of net income.

For example, assume that Adams and Barnes agree to annual salary allowances of $24,000 for Adams and $48,000 for Barnes. These salaries, that total $72,000 per year, are agreed upon by the partners in advance. Of course, the net income of the business is not likely to be exactly $72,000 in a given year. Therefore, the income-and-loss sharing agreement should also specify a fixed ratio for dividing any income or loss remaining after giving consideration to the agreed-upon salary allowances. We will assume that Adams and Barnes agree to divide any remaining income or loss equally.

The division of the $96,000 in partnership net income between Adams and Barnes is illustrated in the following schedule. The first step is to allocate to each partner his or her agreed-upon salary allowance. This step allocates $72,000 of the partnership net income. The remaining $24,000 is then divided in the agreed-upon fixed ratio (50-50 in this example).

Income sharing; salary allowances and remainder in a fixed ratio

Division of Partnership Net Income

	Adams	Barnes	Net income
Net income to be divided			*$96,000*
Salary allowances to partners	*$24,000*	*$48,000*	*(72,000)*
Remaining income after salary allowances			*$24,000*
Allocated in a fixed ratio:			
Adams (50%)	*12,000*		
Barnes (50%)		*12,000*	*(24,000)*
Total share to each partner	*$36,000*	*$60,000*	*$ –0–*

Under this agreement, Adams's share of the $96,000 net income amounts to $36,000 and Barnes's share amounts to $60,000. The entry to close the Income Summary account would be:

Income Summary	*96,000*	
Brooke Adams, Capital		*36,000*
Ben Barnes, Capital		*60,000*
To close the Income Summary account by crediting each partner with agreed-upon salary allowance and dividing the remaining income equally.		

The "salary allowances" used in dividing partnership net income are sometimes misinterpreted, even by the partners. These salary allowances are merely an agreed-upon device for dividing net income; they are ***not expenses*** of the business and are ***not recorded in any ledger account.*** A partner is considered an owner of the business, not an employee. Therefore, the services that a partner renders to the firm are assumed to be rendered in anticipation of earning a share of the net income, not a salary.

The amount of cash or other assets that a partner withdraws from the partnership may be greater than or less than the partner's salary allowance. Even if a partner decides to withdraw an amount of cash equal to his or her "salary allowance," the withdrawal should be recorded by debiting the partner's drawing account, ***not by debiting an expense account.*** Let us repeat the main point: ***"salary allowances" to partners should not be recorded as expenses of the business.***[1]

Because of this treatment of salary allowances, the net income reported by a partnership will differ from the net income that would be reported if the business were organized as a corporation. Corporations do record as expenses any salaries paid to owners.[2]

[1] Some exceptions to this general rule will be discussed in advanced accounting courses.

[2] The net income reported by a corporation also differs from that reported by an unincorporated business because the corporation is subject to income taxes on its earnings. Accounting practices of corporations are discussed in later chapters.

Interest Allowances on Partners' Capital, with Remainder in a Fixed Ratio Next we shall assume a business situation in which the partners spend very little time in the business and net income depends primarily on the amount of money invested. The income-sharing plan then might emphasize invested capital as a basis for the first step in allocating income.

For example, assume that Adams and Barnes agree that both partners are to be allowed interest at ***15%*** on their beginning capital balances, with any remaining income or loss to be divided equally. Net income to be divided is $96,000, and the beginning capital balances are Adams, ***$160,000,*** and Barnes, ***$40,000.***

Income sharing; interest on capital and remainder in a fixed ratio

Division of Partnership Net Income

	Adams	Barnes	Net Income
Net income to be divided			$96,000
Interest allowances on beginning capital:			
Adams ($160,000 × 15%)	$24,000		
Barnes ($40,000 × 15%)		$ 6,000	
Total allocated as interest allowances			(30,000)
Remaining income after interest allowances			$66,000
Allocated in a fixed ratio:			
Adams (50%)	33,000		
Barnes (50%)		33,000	(66,000)
Total share to each partner	$57,000	$39,000	$ -0-

The entry to close the Income Summary account in this example would be:

Income Summary	96,000	
Brooke Adams, Capital		57,000
Ben Barnes, Capital		39,000
To close the Income Summary account by crediting each partner with interest at 15% on beginning capital and dividing the remaining income equally.		

Interest allowances on partners' capital, like partners' salary allowances, are computational devices used in dividing partnership net income. This "interest" is not recorded as an expense of the business.

Salary Allowances, Interest Allowances on Capital, and Remainder in a Fixed Ratio The preceding example took into consideration the difference in amounts of capital provided by Adams and Barnes but ignored any difference in personal services performed. In the next example, we shall assume that the partners agree to an income-sharing plan providing for salaries and for interest on beginning capitals. Salary allowances, as before, are authorized at $24,000 for Adams, $48,000 for Barnes. Beginning capital balances are $160,000 for Adams, $40,000 for Barnes. Partners are to be allowed interest at 10% on their beginning capital balances, and any income or loss remaining after authorized salary and interest allowances is to be divided equally.

Income sharing; salaries, interest, and remainder in a fixed ratio

Division of Partnership Net Income

	Adams	Barnes	Net Income
Net income to be divided			*$96,000*
Salary allowances to partners	*$24,000*	*$48,000*	*(72,000)*
Income after salary allowances			*$24,000*
Interest allowances on beginning capital:			
Adams ($160,000 × 10%)	*16,000*		
Barnes ($40,000 × 10%)		*4,000*	
Total allocated as interest allowances			*(20,000)*
Remaining income after salary and interest allowances			*$ 4,000*
Allocated in a fixed ratio:			
Adams (50%)	*2,000*		
Barnes (50%)		*2,000*	*(4,000)*
Total share to each partner	*$42,000*	*$54,000*	*$ -0-*

The journal entry to close the Income Summary account in this case will be:

Income Summary	*96,000*	
Brooke Adams, Capital		*42,000*
Ben Barnes, Capital		*54,000*
To close the Income Summary account by crediting each partner with authorized salary, interest at 10% on beginning capital, and dividing the remaining income equally.		

Authorized Salary and Interest Allowance in Excess of Net Income In the preceding example the total of the authorized salaries and interest was $92,000 and the net income to be divided was $96,000. Suppose that the net income had been only ***$80,000;*** how should the division have been made?

If the partnership contract provides for salaries and interest on invested capital, these provisions are to be followed even though the net income for the year is ***less*** than the total of the authorized salaries and interest. If the net income of the firm of Adams and Barnes amounted to only $80,000, this amount would be allocated as follows:

Authorized salary and interest allowances in excess of net income

Division of Partnership Net Income

	Adams	Barnes	Net Income
Net income to be divided			*$ 80,000*
Salary allowances to partners	*$24,000*	*$48,000*	*(72,000)*
Income after salary allowances			*$ 8,000*
Interest allowances on beginning capital:			
Adams ($160,000 × 10%)	*16,000*		
Barnes ($40,000 × 10%)		*4,000*	
Total allocated as interest allowances			*(20,000)*
Residual loss after salary and interest allowances			*$(12,000)*
Allocated in a fixed ratio:			
Adams (50%)	*(6,000)*		
Barnes (50%)		*(6,000)*	*12,000*
Total share to each partner	*$34,000*	*$46,000*	*$ -0-*

Notice that after deducting for the specified salary and interest allowances, there is a residual loss of $12,000 to be divided equally between Adams and Barnes. ***This does not mean that the partnership has generated a loss for the period.*** The partnership earned net income of $80,000. The residual loss allocation is simply a computational step in the process of dividing net income according to the partnership contract. The entry to close the Income Summary account will be as follows:

Income Summary	80,000	
Brooke Adams, Capital		34,000
Ben Barnes, Capital		46,000
To close the Income Summary account by crediting each partner with authorized salary and with interest on invested capital and by dividing the residual loss equally.		

Admission of a New Partner

OBJECTIVE 6 Account for the admission of a new partner and the withdrawal of a partner.

An individual may gain admission to an existing partnership in either of two ways: (1) by buying an equity interest from one or more of the present partners or (2) by making an investment in the partnership. When an incoming partner purchases an equity interest from a present member of the firm, the payment goes personally to the old partner, and there is no change in the assets or liabilities of the partnership. On the other hand, if the incoming partner acquires an equity interest by making an investment in the partnership, the assets of the firm are increased by the amount paid in by the new partner.

By Purchase of an Interest When a new partner buys an equity interest from a present member of a partnership, the only change in the accounts will be a transfer from the capital account of the selling partner to the capital account of the incoming partner.

Assume, for example, that Pam Lee has an $80,000 equity interest in the partnership of Lee, Martin, and Nash. Lee arranges to sell her entire interest to Paul Trent for $100,000 cash. Partners Martin and Nash agree to the admission of Trent, and the transaction is recorded in the partnership accounts by the following entry:

Incoming partner buys interest from present partner

Pam Lee, Capital	80,000	
Paul Trent, Capital		80,000
To record the transfer of Pam Lee's equity interest to the incoming partner, Paul Trent.		

Note that the entry in the partnership accounts is for ***$80,000,*** the balance of Lee's capital account. The entry does ***not*** indicate the price paid by Trent to the retiring partner. The payment of $100,000 by Trent to Lee was a ***personal transaction*** between these two individuals; it does not affect the assets or liabilities of the partnership and, therefore, is ***not*** entered in the partnership accounting records.

As a separate but related example, assume that Trent is to gain admission to the firm of Lee, Martin, and Nash by purchasing one-fourth of the equity interest of each partner. The present capital accounts are as follows: Lee $80,000; Martin, $60,000; Nash, $100,000. Assume also that Trent makes payment directly to the old partners, ***not to the partnership.*** The amount paid to each existing partner for one-fourth of his or her equity interest is a privately negotiated matter, and the amounts of these payments are ***not*** recorded in the partnership records. The only entry required in the partnership accounting records is the following:

Pam Lee, Capital	*20,000*	
Pat Martin, Capital	*15,000*	
Tom Nash, Capital	*25,000*	
Paul Trent, Capital		*60,000*
To record purchase of 25% of each partner's equity by Paul Trent.		

This entry transfers to Paul Trent one-fourth of the balance formerly appearing in the capital accounts of each of the existing partners. The amounts actually paid to these partners by Trent are ***not recorded*** in the partnership accounts, because these payments did not flow into the partnership business entity. Thus, the transfer of ownership equity among the partners does not affect the assets, liabilities, or ***total*** partners' equity in the business.

By Investing in the Firm Now let us assume that an incoming partner acquires his or her equity interest by making an investment directly into the firm. In this case the payment by the new partner goes to the partnership and not to the partners as individuals; the investment therefore increases the partnership assets and also the total owners' equity of the firm. The portion of total equity granted to a new partner is based upon the terms negotiated by both existing and incoming partners. This equity interest (credited to the new partner's capital account) may be equal to, less than, or greater than the amount invested in the partnership by the incoming partner.

Assume that Ann Phillips and Judy Ryan are partners, each having a capital account of $100,000. They agree to admit Bart Smith and negotiate to grant him a one-half equity interest in the business upon his investment of $200,000 in cash. The recording of Smith's admission to the partnership is based on the following calculations:

Net assets (owners' equity) of old partnership	*$200,000*
Cash investment by Bart Smith	*200,000*
Net assets (owners' equity) of new partnership	*$400,000*
Smith's one-half interest	*$200,000*

To acquire an interest of $200,000 in the net assets of $400,000, Smith invested $200,000. In this situation, the amount of equity interest acquired is equal to the amount of Smith's investment. The entry to record the admission of Smith would be as follows:

Investment in business by new partner

Cash	*200,000*	
Bart Smith, Capital		*200,000*
To record the admission of Bart Smith to a one-half interest in the firm.		

Although Smith has a one-half equity interest in the net assets of the new firm of Phillips, Ryan, and Smith, he is not necessarily entitled to receive one-half of the net income. Income sharing is a matter for agreement among the partners; if the new partnership contract contains no mention of income sharing, the assumption is that the three partners intended to share net income and losses equally.

Allowing a Bonus to Former Partners If an existing partnership has exceptionally high earnings year after year, the present partners may demand a ***bonus*** as a condition of admission of a new partner. In other words, to acquire an equity interest of, say, $80,000, the incoming partner may be required to invest $120,000 in the partnership. The excess investment of $40,000 may be regarded as a bonus to the old partners and credited to their capital accounts in the established ratio for income sharing.

To illustrate the recording of a bonus to the old partners, let us assume that Jane Rogers and Richard Steel are members of a highly successful partnership. Their partnership agreement calls for net income and losses to be divided 60% to Rogers and 40% to Steel. As a result of profitable operations, the partners' capital accounts have doubled within a few years and presently stand at $100,000 each. David Taylor desires to join the firm and offers to invest $100,000 for a one-third equity interest. Rogers and Steel refuse this offer but extend a counteroffer to Taylor of $120,000 for a one-fourth equity interest in the capital of the firm and a one-fourth interest in net income. Taylor accepts these terms because of his desire to share in the unusually large net income of the business. The recording of Taylor's admission to the partnership is based on the following calculations:

Calculation of bonus to old partners

Net assets (owners' equity) of old partnership	*$200,000*
Cash investment by David Taylor	*120,000*
Net assets (owners' equity) of new partnership	*$320,000*
Taylor's one-fourth equity interest	*$ 80,000*

To acquire an interest of $80,000 in the net assets of $320,000, Taylor has invested $120,000. His ***excess investment,*** or ***bonus,*** of $40,000 will be allocated 60% to Rogers ($24,000) and 40% to Steel ($16,000), in accordance with the income-sharing arrangement in effect prior to Taylor's admission.

The entry to record Taylor's admission to the partnership follows:

Recording bonus to old partners

Cash	*120,000*	
David Taylor, Capital		*80,000*
Jane Rogers, Capital		*24,000*
Richard Steel, Capital		*16,000*
To record admission of David Taylor as a partner with a one-fourth interest in capital and net income.		

The total capital of the new partnership is now $320,000, in which Taylor has a one-fourth equity interest ($80,000). Rogers' capital account is $124,000 and Steel's capital account is $116,000 after admission of Taylor. Although in this case Taylor was also granted a one-fourth share of future partnership net income, ***the equity interest and the income-sharing ratio of a partner are not necessarily the same.*** Old partners Rogers and Steel will set a new income-sharing arrangement for the remaining 75% of net income to be divided between themselves.

The term ***relative income-sharing ratio*** describes the relationship between the income- and loss-sharing ratios of the continuing partners, excluding the share formerly received by the retiring partner. The relative income- and loss-sharing ratio of each continuing partner is computed by the following formula:

$$\frac{\text{Percentage Formerly Received by This Partner}}{\text{Total Percentage Formerly Received by All Continuing Partners}}$$

Based upon this formula, the relative income- and loss-sharing ratios of Acres and Bundy are as follows:

Acres (20% ÷ 50%)	*40%*
Bundy (30% ÷ 50%)	*60%*

Assume now that Coe receives ***$140,000*** in cash from the partnership in full settlement of his equity in the firm. As Coe's capital account has a balance of only $100,000, he is receiving a ***$40,000 bonus*** from Acres and Bundy. This bonus is charged against the capital accounts of Acres and Bundy in relation to their relative income- and loss-sharing ratios (Acres, 40%; Bundy, 60%). Thus, Coe's withdrawal from the firm is recorded as follows:

Bonus paid to withdrawing partner

John Coe, Capital (retiring partner)	*100,000*	
Chris Acres, Capital	*16,000*	
Brit Bundy, Capital	*24,000*	
Cash		*140,000*
To record the withdrawal of partner Coe, and payment of his capital account plus a bonus of $40,000. Bonus charged 40% to Acres, 60% to Bundy.		

Partnership Pays Coe Less Than the Balance in His Capital Account Now assume that Coe is willing to accept a cash payment of ***only $80,000*** in full settlement of his $100,000 capital account. This situation might arise if, for example, Coe has a pressing need for cash or the future of the firm is jeopardized by contingent losses not yet recorded in its balance sheet accounts. In our example, the continuing partners' equity in the firm will ***increase*** by a total of $20,000 as a result of Coe's withdrawal. Acres and Bundy should divide this ***"bonus to the continuing partners"*** in their relative income- and loss-sharing ratios. The entry is:

Payment to withdrawing partner of less than book equity

John Coe, Capital	*100,000*	
Cash		*80,000*
Chris Acres		*8,000*
Brit Bundy		*12,000*
To record the withdrawal of Coe, and settlement in full for $20,000 less than the balance of his capital account. Bonus to continuing partners allocated 40% to Acres, 60% to Bundy.		

Death of a Partner

A partnership is dissolved by the death of any member. To determine the amount owing to the estate of the deceased partner, it is usually necessary to close the accounts and prepare financial statements. This serves to credit all partners with their individual shares of the net income earned during the fractional accounting period ending with the date of ***dissolution.***

The partnership agreement may prescribe procedures for making settlement with the estate of a deceased partner. Such procedures often include an audit by public accountants, appraisal of assets, and computation of goodwill. If payment to the estate must be delayed, the amount owed should be carried in a liability account replacing the deceased partner's capital account.

Insurance on Lives of Partners Members of a partnership often obtain life insurance policies that name the partnership as the beneficiary. Upon the death of a partner, the cash collected from the insurance company is used to pay the estate of the deceased partner. In the absence of insurance on the lives of partners, there might be insufficient cash available to pay the deceased partner's estate without disrupting the operation of the business.

Liquidation of a Partnership

OBJECTIVE 7 Account for the liquidation of a partnership.

A partnership is terminated or dissolved whenever a new partner is added or an old partner withdraws. The termination or dissolution of a partnership, however, does not necessarily indicate that the business is to be discontinued. Often the business continues with scarcely any outward evidence of the change in membership of the firm. Termination of a partnership indicates a change in the membership of the firm, which may or may not be followed by liquidation.

The process of breaking up and discontinuing a partnership business is called ***liquidation.*** Liquidation of a partnership spells an end to the business. If the business is to be discontinued, the assets will be sold, the liabilities paid, and the remaining cash distributed to the partners.

Sale of the Business The partnership of Royal, Simms, and Tate sells its business to the North Corporation. The balance sheet appears as follows:

Partnership at time of sale

ROYAL, SIMMS, AND TATE
Balance Sheet
December 31, 19__

Assets		*Liabilities & Partners' Equity*	
Cash	$ 50,000	Accounts payable	$100,000
Inventory	200,000	Ann Royal, capital	140,000
Other assets	150,000	Ed Simms, capital	120,000
		Jon Tate, capital	40,000
Total	$400,000	Total	$400,000

The terms of sale provide that the inventory and other assets will be sold to the North Corporation for a consideration of $230,000, a price resulting in a loss of $120,000. The liabilities will not be transferred to North Corporation, but will be paid by the partnership out of existing cash plus the proceeds of the sale, prior to any distribution of cash to the partners.

The entry to record the sale of the inventory and other assets to North Corporation is:

Entry to record the sale of the business

Cash	*230,000*	
Loss on Sale of Business	*120,000*	
Inventory		*200,000*
Other Assets		*150,000*
To record the sale of all assets other than cash to North Corporation.		

Division of the Gain or Loss from Sale of the Business The gain or loss from the sale of the business must be divided among the partners in the agreed income- and loss-sharing ratio ***before*** any cash is distributed to them. The amount of cash to which each partner is entitled in liquidation cannot be determined until each capital account has been increased or decreased by the proper share of the gain or loss on disposal of the assets. Assuming that Royal, Simms, and Tate share net income and losses equally, the entry to allocate the $120,000 loss on the sale of the business will be as follows:

Entry to divide loss on sale

Ann Royal, Capital	*40,000*	
Ed Simms, Capital	*40,000*	
Jon Tate, Capital	*40,000*	
Loss on Sale of Business		*120,000*
To divide the loss on the sale of the business among the partners in the established ratio for sharing net income and losses.		

Distribution of Cash The balance sheet of Royal, Simms, and Tate appears as follows after the loss on the sale of the assets has been entered in the partners' capital accounts:

Balance sheet after sale of assets

ROYAL, SIMMS, AND TATE
Balance Sheet
(After the Sale of All Assets Except Cash)

Assets		*Liabilities & Partners' Equity*	
Cash	*$280,000*	*Accounts payable*	*$100,000*
		Ann Royal, capital	*100,000*
		Ed Simms, capital	*80,000*
		Jon Tate, capital	*-0-*
Total	*$280,000*	*Total*	*$280,000*

The creditors must be paid in full before cash is distributed to the partners. The sequence of entries will be as follows:

(1) Pay creditors

Accounts Payable	*100,000*	
Cash		*100,000*
To pay the creditors in full.		

(2) Pay partners

Ann Royal, Capital	*100,000*	
Ed Simms, Capital	*80,000*	
Cash		*180,000*
To complete liquidation of the business by distributing the remaining cash to the partners according to the balances in their capital accounts.		

Note that the equal division of the $120,000 loss on the sale of the business reduced the capital account of Jon Tate to zero; therefore, Tate received nothing when the cash was distributed to the partners. This action is consistent with the original agreement of the partners to share net income and losses equally. In working partnership liquidation problems, accounting students sometimes make the error of dividing the cash among the partners in the income- and loss-sharing ratio. An income- and loss-sharing ratio means just what the name indicates; it is a ratio for sharing net income and losses, ***not a ratio for sharing cash or any other asset.*** The amount of cash that a partner should receive in liquidation will be indicated by the balance in his or her capital account ***after*** the gain or loss from the disposal of assets has been divided among the partners in the agreed ratio for sharing net income and losses.

Treatment of Debit Balance in a Capital Account To illustrate this situation, let us change our assumptions concerning the sale of the assets by the firm of Royal, Simms, and Tate, and say that the partnership assets (except cash) are sold to North Corporation for $206,000. The amount of cash received by the partnership is $24,000 less than in the prior example, and the loss incurred on the sale of assets is ***$144,000*** rather than the ***$120,000*** previously illustrated. Tate's one-third share of a $144,000 loss would be $48,000, which would wipe out the $40,000 credit balance in his capital account and create an ***$8,000 debit balance.*** After the liabilities are paid, a balance sheet for the partnership would appear as follows:

Tate now owes $8,000 to the partnership

ROYAL, SIMMS, AND TATE
Balance Sheet
(After the Sale of All Assets Except Cash)

Assets		*Partners' Equity*	
Cash	$156,000	Ann Royal, capital	$ 92,000
		Ed Simms, capital	72,000
		Jon Tate, capital (deficiency)	(8,000)
Total	$156,000	Total	$156,000

To eliminate the debit balance in his capital account, Tate should pay $8,000 to the partnership. If Tate makes this payment, the balance in his capital account will become zero, and the cash on hand will be increased to $164,000, which is just enough to pay Royal and Simms the balances shown in their capital accounts.

If Tate is unable to pay the $8,000 due to the firm, how should the $156,000 of cash on hand be divided between Royal and Simms, whose capital accounts stand at $92,000 and $72,000, respectively? Failure of Tate to pay in the debit balance means an additional loss to Royal and Simms. According to the original partnership agreement, Royal and Simms have equal income- and loss-sharing ratios. Since partnership agreements generally specify that such a debit balance or deficiency be shared in the net income and loss ratio, let us assume that this was included in the liquidation provisions of the partnership agreement. Therefore, each must absorb $4,000 additional loss caused by Tate's inability to pay the $8,000 due to the partnership. The $156,000 of cash on hand should be divided between Royal and Simms in such a manner that the capital account of each will be paid down to $4,000, their respective shares of the additional loss. The journal entry to record this distribution of cash to Royal and Simms is as follows:

Entry to record distribution of cash on hand

Ann Royal, Capital	*88,000*	
Ed Simms, Capital	*68,000*	
Cash		*156,000*
To divide the remaining cash by paying down the capital accounts of Royal and Simms to a balance of $4,000 each, representing the division of Tate's loss between them.		

After this entry has been posted, the only accounts still open in the partnership records will be the capital accounts of the three partners. A trial balance of the ledger will appear as follows:

Trial balance after cash distribution

ROYAL, SIMMS, AND TATE
Trial Balance
(After Distribution of Cash)

Ann Royal, capital		*$4,000*
Ed Simms, capital		*4,000*
Jon Tate, capital (deficiency)	*$8,000*	
	$8,000	*$8,000*

If Tate is able later to pay in the $8,000 debit balance, Royal and Simms will then receive the additional $4,000 each indicated by the credit balances in their accounts. However, if Tate is definitely unable to pay the $8,000, these accounts should be closed.

The sharing of a debit balance may become a rather difficult issue if the partnership agreement is silent or the partners fail to agree on how such a debit balance is to be shared. Even though there are provisions on this issue in the partnership legislation, they are potentially subject to different interpretations. One interpretation was provided in the English case *Garner v. Murray* (1904), where it was ruled that the debit balance was to be shared among the other partners in the ratio of their capital account balances as at the date of liquidation. The reason was that the debit balance was considered a personal debt of one partner to the other partners rather than a business or operating loss. As a practical matter, however, the issue of how the debit balance should be shared rarely arises, apparently because partnership agreements generally specify a method for such a situation.

In solving the problems on partnership liquidation in this text, it is assumed that the partnership agreement specifies the sharing of a debit balance of a partner's capital account by other partners in the net income and loss ratio.

CHAPTER REVIEW

KEY TERMS INTRODUCED OR EMPHASIZED IN CHAPTER 13

Dissolution (of a partnership) Termination of an existing partnership by any change in the personnel of the partners or by liquidating the business.

General partner A partner in a limited partnership who has the traditional rights and responsibilities of a partner, including mutual agency and unlimited personal liability for the debts of the business.

Limited partner A partner in a limited partnership who has the right to participate in income, but whose liability for losses is limited to the amount he or she has invested and who does not have the right to participate in management of the business. A limited partner's role is that of an investor rather than that of a traditional partner.

Limited partnership A partnership that has one or more ***limited partners*** as well as one or more ***general partners.*** Limited partnerships are used primarily to attract investment capital from the limited partners for such ventures as mining and real estate development.

Liquidation of a partnership The process of breaking up and discontinuing a partnership, including the sale of assets, payment of creditors, and distribution of remaining assets to the partners.

Mutual agency Authority of each partner to act as agent for the partnership within its normal scope of operations and to enter into contracts that bind the partnership.

Partnership contract An agreement among partners on the formation and operation of the partnership. Usually includes such points as a plan for sharing net income, amounts to be invested, and provision for dissolution and liquidation.

Statement of partners' equity A financial statement that shows for each partner and for the firm the amounts of beginning capitals, additional investments, net income, drawings, and ending capitals.

ASSIGNMENT MATERIAL

DISCUSSION QUESTIONS

1 Jane Miller is the proprietor of a small manufacturing business. She is considering the possibility of joining in partnership with Mary Bracken, whom she considers to be thoroughly competent and congenial. Prepare a brief statement outlining the advantages and disadvantages of the potential partnership to Miller.

2 Allen and Baker are considering forming a partnership. What do you think are the two most important factors for them to include in their partnership agreement?

3 What is meant by the term ***mutual agency?***

4 A real estate development business is managed by two experienced developers and is financed by 50 investors from throughout the country. To allow maximum income tax benefits to the investors, the business is organized as a partnership. Explain why this type of business would probably be a limited partnership rather than a regular partnership.

5 What factors should be considered in drawing up an agreement as to the way in which net income shall be shared by two or more partners?

6 Scott has land having a book value of $50,000 and a current market value of $80,000 and a building having a book value of $70,000 and a current market value of $60,000. The land and building become Scott's sole capital contribution to a partnership. Assuming no bonus to any partner, what is Scott's capital balance in the new partnership? Why?

7 Is it possible that a partnership agreement containing interest and salary allowances as a step toward dividing net income could cause a partnership net loss to be distributed so that one partner's capital account would be decreased by ***more*** than the amount of the entire partnership net loss?

8 Partner John Young has a choice to make. He has been offered by his partners a choice between no salary allowance and a one-third share in the partnership net income or a salary of $16,000 per year and a one-quarter share of residual income. Write a brief memorandum explaining the factors he should consider in reaching a decision.

9 Helen Lee withdraws $25,000 from a partnership during the year. When the financial statements are prepared at the end of the year, Lee's share of the partnership net income is $45,000. Which amount must Lee report on her income tax return?

10 What factors should be considered when comparing the net income figure of a partnership to that of a corporation of similar size?

11 Explain the difference between being admitted to a partnership by buying an equity interest from an existing partner and by making an investment in the partnership.

12 If C is going to be admitted to the partnership of A and B, why is it first necessary to determine the current market value of the assets of the partnership of A and B?

13 Shirley Bray and Carl Carter are partners who share net income and losses equally. The current balances in their capital accounts are: Bray, $50,000; Carter, $35,000. If Carter sells his equity interest in the firm to Deacon for $70,000 and Bray consents to the sale, what entry should be made in the partnership accounting records?

14 Farley invests $80,000 cash in the partnership of Dale and Erskin, but is granted an equity interest of only $60,000 upon his admission to the partnership. What is the nature of the $20,000 difference between the amount invested by Farley and the equity interest he received? How is this $20,000 difference handled in the partnership accounting records?

15 Majors, who has a capital account balance of $90,000, received cash of $120,000 from the partnership of Linden, Majors, & Napp upon his retirement. Discuss the nature of the $30,000 paid to Majors in excess of his capital account balance and how this excess payment is handled in the partnership books upon Majors' withdrawal.

16 Describe how a ***liquidation*** of a partnership may differ from a ***dissolution*** of a partnership.

17 What measure can you suggest to prevent a partnership from having insufficient cash available to pay the estate of a deceased partner without disrupting the operation of the business?

18 Upon the death of Robert Bell, a partner in the firm of Bell, Cross, and Davis, Charles Bell, the son of Robert Bell, demanded that he replace his father as a member of the partnership. Can Charles Bell enforce this demand? Explain.

MULTIPLE CHOICE QUESTIONS

1 When a partnership is formed,

a A written partnership agreement, signed by all partners, must be filed in the jurisdiction in which the partnership is formed.

b Each partner may bind the business to contracts and may withdraw an unlimited amount of assets from the partnership, unless these rights are limited in the partnership contract.

c Each member of the partnership is entitled to participate equally in the net income of and management of the partnership, unless the partnership is a limited partnership.

d The partnership must file an income tax return and pay income taxes on its net income.

2 Carter and Dixie have capital account balances of $80,000 and $100,000, respectively, at the beginning of 1996. Their partnership agreement provides for interest on beginning capital account balances, 10%; salaries to Carter, $30,000, and to Dixie, $24,000; residual income or loss divided 60% to Carter and 40% to Dixie. Partnership net income for 1996 is $62,000. Neither partner made any additional investment in the partnership during 1996, but Carter withdrew $1,500 monthly and Dixie withdrew $1,000 monthly throughout 1996. The partnership balance sheet at December 31, 1996, should include:

a Capital, Carter, $94,000

b Capital, Carter, $100,000

c Capital, Dixie, $30,000

d Total partners' equity, $242,000

3 Quinn and Ryan are partners who divide net income and losses 30% to Quinn and 70% to Ryan. At the present time, Quinn's capital account balance is $80,000 and Ryan's capital account balance is $160,000. Stone is admitted to a one-third equity interest in the partnership for an investment of $60,000. Each of the following statements relating to the admission of Stone is true with the exception of:

a Quinn has a capital account balance of $68,000 after recording Stone's admission.

b Stone has a capital account balance of $60,000 upon his admission to the partnership.

c Stone received a "bonus" of $40,000 from Quinn and Ryan.

d Total capital (equity) of the new partnership is $300,000 after Stone's admission is recorded.

4 Link, Martin, and Nolan are partners dividing net income and losses 30% to Link, 40% to Martin, and 30% to Nolan. Their capital accounts are as follows: Link, $500,000; Martin, $100,000; Nolan, $400,000. Nolan decides to retire and receives $393,000 from the partnership in exchange for his equity interest. Recording Nolan's withdrawal involves:

a A debit to Nolan's capital account for $393,000.

b Debits to Link's and to Martin's capital accounts for $3,500 each.

c A credit to Link's capital account for $3,000 and a credit to Martin's capital account for $4,000.

d Credits to Link's and to Martin's capital accounts for $200,000 each.

5 When a partnership is liquidated:

a Any cash distribution to partners is allocated according to the income- and loss-sharing ratios.

b Cash is distributed to each partner in an amount equal to his or her capital account balance prior to the sale of partnership assets.

c Any gain or loss on disposal of partnership assets is divided among the partners according to their relative capital account balances.

d A partner who maintained a credit balance in his or her capital account prior to liquidation may end up owing cash to the partnership if partnership assets are sold at a loss.

EXERCISES

EXERCISE 13-1
Accounting Terminology

Listed below are nine technical terms introduced in this chapter:

Unlimited liability	*Partnership contract*	*Dissolution of partnership*
Liquidation	*Current market value*	*Interest on partners' capital*
General partner	*Limited partner*	*Partnership net income*

Each of the following statements may (or may not) describe one of these technical terms. For each statement, indicate the accounting term described, or answer "None" if the statement does not correctly describe any of the terms.

a Serves to identify partners, specify capital contributions, and establish income-sharing formula.

b The process of breaking up and discontinuing a partnership business.

c Amounts to be entered in asset accounts of a partnership to record the investment of noncash assets by partners.

d A method of dividing partnership net income to ensure that no partner's share of net income will be less than the prime rate of interest applied to his or her capital account.

e A characteristic of the partnership type of organization that causes many wealthy investors to choose investments in limited partnerships or corporations rather than in regular partnerships.

f Results from the retirement of a partner from the firm or the admission of a new partner.

g A partner whose financial responsibility does not exceed the amount of his or her investment and who does not actively participate in management.

h An income-sharing provision designed to compensate for differences in dollar amounts invested by different partners.

EXERCISE 13-2
Formation of a Partnership

A business owned by Fern Douglas was short of cash and Douglas therefore decided to form a partnership with Andy McKuen, who was able to contribute cash to the new partnership. The assets contributed by Douglas appeared as follows in the balance sheet of her business: cash, $600; accounts receivable, $34,900, with an allowance for doubtful accounts of $960; inventory, $45,600; and store equipment, $21,600. Douglas had recorded depreciation of $1,800 during her use of the store equipment in her sole proprietorship.

Douglas and McKuen agreed that the allowance for doubtful accounts was inadequate and should be $1,800. They also agreed that a current market value for the inventory was $54,000 and that the current market value of the store equipment was $19,000. You are to open the partnership accounts by making a general journal entry to record the investment by Douglas.

EXERCISE 13-3
Partners' Capital and Drawing Accounts

Explain briefly the effect of each of the transactions given below on a partner's capital and drawing accounts:

a Partner borrows funds from the business.

b Partner collects a partnership account receivable while on vacation and uses the funds for personal purposes.

c Partner receives in cash the salary allowance provided in the partnership agreement.

d Partner takes home merchandise (cost $80, selling price $120) for personal use.

e Partner has loaned money to the partnership. The principal together with interest at 15% is now repaid to the partner in cash.

EXERCISE 13-4
Dividing Partnership Income

Guenther and Firmin, both of whom are CAs, form a partnership, with Guenther investing $100,000 and Firmin, $80,000. They agree to share net income as follows:

1 Salary allowances of $80,000 to Guenther and $60,000 to Firmin.

2 Interest allowances at 15% of beginning capital account balances.

3 Any partnership net income in excess of the amount required to cover the interest and salary allowances to be divided 60% to Guenther and 40% to Firmin.

INSTRUCTIONS

The partnership net income for the first year of operations amounted to $247,000 before interest and salary allowances. Show how this $247,000 should be divided between the two partners. Use a three-column schedule of the type illustrated in this chapter. List on separate lines the amounts of interest, salaries, and the residual amount divided.

EXERCISE 13-5
Admission of a New Partner; Bonus to Old Partners

Abrams and Boling are partners with capital account balances of $102,000 and $63,000. They divide net income and losses one-third to Abrams and two-thirds to Boling. The partnership has been quite profitable and has an excellent reputation. Abrams and Boling agree to admit Cato to a one-third equity interest in the partnership for an investment of $105,000. The assets of the business are ***not*** to be revalued. Explain how the bonus to the old partners is computed and prepare a general journal entry to record the admission of Cato.

EXERCISE 13-6
Admission of a New Partner; Bonus Computation

Randall and Dirks are partners who divide net income and losses 60% to Randall and 40% to Dirks. At the present time, each partner's capital account balance is $140,000. Randall and Dirks agree to admit Foster to a one-fourth equity interest in the partnership for an investment of $80,000. Prepare a general journal entry to record the admission of Foster. Explain how any bonus (to existing partners ***or*** to the incoming partner) is computed.

EXERCISE 13-7
Withdrawal of a Partner

The capital accounts of the Triple D partnership are as follows: Drake, $90,000; Dunlap, $210,000; Dyson, $180,000. Net income and losses are allocated 25% to Drake, 50% to Dunlap, and 25% to Dyson. Dyson is withdrawing from the partnership and it is agreed that he shall be paid $240,000 for his interest because the earnings of the business are high in relation to the assets of the firm. Assuming that the excess of the settlement over the amount of Dyson's capital account is to be recorded as a bonus to Dyson, prepare a general journal entry to record Dyson's retirement from the firm.

EXERCISE 13-8
Liquidation of a Partnership

The CDE partnership is being liquidated. After all liabilities have been paid and all assets sold, the balances of the partners' capital accounts are as follows: Cooley, $42,000 credit balance; Dean, $16,000 ***debit*** balance; Emmett, $53,000 credit balance. The partners share net income and losses: Cooley, 10%; Dean, 60%; Emmet, 30%.

a How should the available cash (the only remaining asset) be distributed if it is impossible to determine at this date whether Dean will be able to pay the $16,000 he owes the firm? Draft the journal entry to record payment of all available cash at this time.

b Draft the journal entries to record a subsequent partial payment of $13,000 to the firm by Dean, and the distribution of this cash. Prepare a schedule (similar to the one prepared in part **a**) showing computation of amount to be distributed to each partner.

PROBLEMS

Group A

PROBLEM 13A-1
Formation of a Partnership; Closing the Income Summary Account

The partnership of Barton and Liu was formed on July 2, when Tina Barton and Sam Liu agreed to invest equal amounts and to share net income and losses equally. The investment by Barton consists of $40,000 cash and an inventory of merchandise valued at $56,000.

Liu also is to contribute a total of $96,000. However, it is agreed that his contribution will consist of the following assets of his business along with the transfer to the partnership of his business liabilities. The agreed values of the various items as well as their carrying values on Liu's records are listed below. Liu also contributes enough cash to bring his capital account to $96,000.

	Investment by Liu	
	Balances on Liu's Records	*Agreed Value*
Accounts receivable	*$89,600*	*$89,600*
Allowance for doubtful accounts	*3,840*	*8,000*
Inventory	*9,600*	*12,800*
Office equipment (net)	*12,800*	*9,000*
Accounts payable	*28,800*	*28,800*

INSTRUCTIONS

a Draft entries (in general journal form) to record the investments of Barton and Liu in the new partnership.

b Prepare the beginning balance sheet of the partnership (in report form) at the close of business July 2, reflecting the above transfers to the firm.

c On the following June 30 after one year of operation, the Income Summary account showed a credit balance of $78,000 and the Drawing account for each partner showed a debit balance of $32,000. Prepare journal entries to close the Income Summary account and the drawing accounts at June 30.

PROBLEM 13A-2 Dividing Partnership Income; Financial Statements

The adjusted trial balance of B & G Distributors indicates the following account balances at the end of the current year:

	Debit	Credit
Cash	$ 32,620	
Accounts receivable (net)	81,000	
Inventory	28,200	
Prepaid expenses	3,900	
Equipment	90,000	
Accumulated depreciation		$ 18,000
Notes payable		9,600
Accounts payable		38,520
Accrued expenses		2,880
Bolton, capital (beginning of year)		70,000
Bolton, drawing	10,080	
Gorman, capital (beginning of year)		60,000
Gorman, drawing	7,200	
Sales		648,960
Cost of goods sold	390,960	
Selling expenses	112,380	
Administrative expenses	91,620	
Totals	$847,960	$847,960

A perpetual inventory system is used by the company. The partnership agreement provided that partners are to be allowed 10% interest on invested capital as of the beginning of the year and that the residual net income is to be divided equally.

INSTRUCTIONS

a Prepare an income statement for the current year, using the appropriate accounts from the above list. At the bottom of the income statement, prepare a schedule showing the division of net income.

b Prepare a statement of partners' equity for the current year.

c Prepare a balance sheet at the end of the current year.

PROBLEM 13A-3 Various Methods for Dividing Partnership Net Income

Alicia Dunn and Roberto Pascal, both real estate appraisers, formed a partnership, with Dunn investing $40,000 and Pascal investing $60,000. During the first year, the net income of the partnership amounted to $45,000.

INSTRUCTIONS

a Determine how the $45,000 net income would be divided under each of the following four independent assumptions as to the agreement for sharing net income and losses. Using schedules of the types illustrated in this chapter, show all steps in the division of net income between the partners.

1 The partnership agreement does not mention income sharing.

2 Interest at 15% to be allowed on beginning capital investments and balance to be divided equally.

3 Salaries of $24,000 to Dunn and $20,000 to Pascal; balance to be divided equally.

4 Salaries of $18,000 to Dunn and $26,000 to Pascal; interest at 15% to be allowed on beginning capital investments; balance to be divided equally.

b Prepare the journal entry to close the Income Summary account, using the division of net income developed in part 4 above.

PROBLEM 13A-4
Dividing Partnership Net Income and Loss

Financial Planners has three partners—Reed, Stein, and Trump. At the beginning their capital balances were: Reed, \$140,000; Stein, \$100,000; and Trump, \$60,000. The partnership agreement provides that partners shall receive salary allowances as follows: Reed, none; Stein, \$60,000; and Trump, \$38,000. The partners shall also be allowed 12% interest annually on their beginning capital balances. Residual income or loss is to be divided: Reed, 50%; Stein, 30%; Trump, 20%.

INSTRUCTIONS Prepare separate schedules showing how net income or loss will be divided among the three partners in each of the following cases. The figure given in each case is the annual partnership net income or loss to be allocated among the partners.

a Net income of \$554,000

b Net income of \$83,000

c Net loss of \$19,000

PROBLEM 13A-5
Admission of a New Partner

Aspen Lodge is a partnership with a record of profitable operations. At the end of the current year the capital accounts of the three partners and the ratio for sharing net income and losses are as shown in the following schedule. At this date, it is agreed that a new partner, Wolfgang Ritter, is to be admitted to the firm.

	Capital	Income-Sharing Ratio
Olga Svenson	\$300,000	60%
Jill Kidd	240,000	30%
Miles Kohl	180,000	10%

INSTRUCTIONS For each of the following situations involving the admission of Ritter to the partnership, give the necessary journal entry to record his admission.

a Ritter purchases one-half of Kidd's equity interest in the firm, paying Kidd personally \$150,000.

b Ritter buys a one-quarter equity interest in the firm for \$200,000 by purchasing one-fourth of the present equity interest of each of the three partners. Ritter pays the three individuals directly.

c Ritter invests \$200,000 in the firm and receives a one-fourth interest in the equity and net income of the business. In addition to the journal entry to record Ritter's admission, show computation of the equity interest received and bonus (if any) to either the old partners or to Ritter.

d Ritter invests \$360,000 in the firm and receives a one-fourth interest in the equity and net income of the business. In addition to the journal entry to record Ritter's admission, show computation of the equity interest received and bonus (if any) to either the old partners or to Ritter.

PROBLEM 13A-6
Retirement of a Partner

In the partnership of World Travel Agency, the partners' capital accounts at the end of the current year were as follows: Roy Kim, \$220,000; Susan John, \$148,000; and Mark Ray, \$60,000. The partnership agreement provides that net income will be shared 40% to Kim, 50% to John, and 10% to Ray. At this time Kim decides to retire from the firm.

INSTRUCTIONS Described below are a number of independent situations involving the retirement of Kim. In each case prepare the journal entries necessary to reflect the withdrawal of Kim from the firm.

a Kim sells three-fourths of his equity interest to Ray for $208,000 and the other one-fourth to John for $64,000. The payments to Kim are made from the personal funds of Ray and John, not from the partnership.

b Kim accepts $90,000 in cash and a patent having a book value of $100,000 in full payment for his equity interest in the firm. This payment consists of a transfer of partnership assets to the retiring partner. As the fair value of the patent is approximately $100,000, the continuing partners agree that a revaluation of assets is not needed. The excess of Kim's capital account over the payment to him for withdrawal should be credited to the continuing partners.

c Kim receives $100,000 in cash and a 10-year, 12% note for $180,000 in full payment for his equity interest. Assets are not to be revalued.

PROBLEM 13A-7 Liquidation of a Partnership

The partnership of Talent Scouts has ended its operations and is in the process of liquidation. All assets except for cash and accounts receivable have already been sold. The task of collecting the accounts receivable is now to be carried out as rapidly as possible. The general ledger balances are as follows:

	Debit	Credit
Cash	$ 27,200	
Accounts receivable	116,800	
Allowance for doubtful accounts		$ 6,400
Liabilities		36,800
May, capital (income-loss share 30%)		43,200
Nix, capital (income-loss share 50%)		33,600
Peat, capital (income-loss share 20%)		24,000

INSTRUCTIONS For each of the two independent situations shown below, prepare journal entries to record the collection or sale of the receivables, the payment of liabilities, and the distribution of all remaining cash to the partners. Support all entries with adequate explanation; the entries for distribution of cash to the partners should have explanations showing how the amounts were determined.

a Collections of $66,400 are made on receivables, and the remainder are deemed uncollectible.

b Receivables are sold to a collection agency; the partnership receives in cash as a final settlement 30% of the gross amount of its receivables. The personal financial status of the partners is uncertain, but all available cash is to be distributed at this time.

Group B

PROBLEM 13B-1 Formation of a Partnership

The partnership of Silver and Hawk was formed on January 1, when Anna Silver and John Hawk agreed to invest equal amounts and to share net income equally. The investment by Silver consists of $44,000 cash and an inventory of merchandise valued at $76,000. Hawk is also to contribute a total of $120,000. However, it is agreed that his contribution will consist of the following assets of his business along with the transfer to the partnership of his business liabilities. The agreed value of the various items as well as their carrying values on Hawk's records are listed as follows:

	Investment by Hawk	
	Balances on Hawk's Records	Agreed Value
Accounts receivable	$117,600	$117,600
Allowance for doubtful accounts	5,040	8,500
Inventory	16,600	20,800
Office equipment (net)	16,800	19,500
Accounts payable	37,800	37,800

Hawk also contributed enough cash to bring his capital account to $120,000.

INSTRUCTIONS

a Draft general journal entries to record the investments of Silver and Hawk in the new partnership.

b Prepare the beginning balance sheet of the partnership (in report form) at the close of business January 1, reflecting the above transfers to the firm.

c On the following December 31 after one year of operations, the Income Summary account had a credit balance of $92,000 and the Drawing account for each partner showed a debit balance of $36,000. Prepare journal entries to close the Income Summary and the drawing accounts at December 31.

PROBLEM 13B-2 Dividing Income; Financial Statement

The adjusted trial balance of Design for Living indicates the following account balances at the end of the current year:

	Debit	Credit
Cash	$ 17,800	
Accounts receivable	105,200	
Allowance for doubtful accounts		$ 2,000
Inventory	28,500	
Showroom fixtures	32,400	
Accumulated depreciation		6,400
Notes payable		9,000
Accounts payable		38,000
Lloyd, capital		70,000
Lloyd, drawing	32,000	
Johnson, capital		60,000
Johnson, drawing	24,000	
Sales		648,000
Cost of goods sold	391,000	
Selling expenses	110,000	
Administrative expenses	92,500	
Totals	$833,400	$833,400

There were no changes in partners' capital accounts during the year. Design for Living uses a perpetual inventory system. The partnership agreement provided that partners are to be allowed 15% interest on invested capital as of the beginning of the year and that the residual net income is to be divided equally.

INSTRUCTIONS

a Prepare an income statement for the current year, using the appropriate accounts from the above list. At the bottom of the income statement, prepare a schedule showing the distribution of net income.

b Prepare a statement of partners' equity for the current year.

c Prepare a balance sheet at the end of the current year.

PROBLEM 13B-3 Sharing Partnership Net Income: Various Methods

A small nightclub called Comedy Tonight was organized as a partnership with Lewis investing $80,000 and Martin investing $120,000. During the first year, net income amounted to $110,000.

INSTRUCTIONS

a Determine how the $110,000 net income would be divided under each of the following three independent assumptions as to the agreement for sharing net income and losses. Use schedules of the type illustrated in this chapter to show all steps in the division of net income between the partners.

1. Net income is to be divided in a fixed ratio: 40% to Lewis and 60% to Martin.
2. Interest at 15% to be allowed on beginning capital investments and balance to be divided equally.
3. Salaries of $36,000 to Lewis and $56,000 to Martin; interest at 15% to be allowed on beginning capital investments; balance to be divided equally.

b Prepare the journal entry to close the Income Summary account, using the division of net income developed in part **3** above.

PROBLEM 13B-4 Dividing Partnership Net Income and Loss

Research Consultants has three partners—Axle, Brandt, and Conrad. During the current year their capital balances were: Axle, $180,000; Brandt, $140,000; and Conrad, $80,000. The partnership agreement provides that partners shall receive salary allowances as follows: Axle, $10,000; Brandt, $50,000; Conrad, $28,000. The partners shall also be allowed 12% interest annually on their capital balances. Residual net income or loss is to be divided: Axle, one-half; Brandt, one-third; Conrad, one-sixth.

INSTRUCTIONS

Prepare separate schedules showing how net income will be divided among the three partners in each of the following cases.

a Net income of $526,000

b Net income of $67,000

c Net loss of $32,000

PROBLEM 13B-5 Admission of a New Partner

Art of Asia is a partnership organized by Howell and So. On this date the two partners agreed to admit a new partner, Lee. Howell and So have been dividing net income in a ratio of 3:2 (that is, 60% and 40%). The new partnership will have an income- and loss-sharing ratio of Lee, 50%; Howell, 25%; and So, 25%. The following is the condensed balance sheet at September 30.

ART OF ASIA
Balance Sheet
September 30

Assets		Liabilities & Partners' Equity		
Current assets	$180,000	Liabilities		$160,000
Plant & equipment (net)	420,000	Partners' equity:		
		Howell, capital	$280,000	
		So, capital	160,000	440,000
Total	$600,000	Total		$600,000

INSTRUCTIONS Described below are four different situations under which Lee might be admitted to partnership. Considering each independently, prepare the journal entries necessary to record the admission of Lee to the firm.

a Lee purchases a one-half equity interest in the partnership from Howell for $260,000. Payment is made to Howell as an individual.

b Lee purchases one-half of Howell's equity interest and one-half of So's equity interest, paying Howell $168,000 and So $96,000.

c Lee invests $300,000 in the firm and receives a one-half interest in capital and net income. In addition to the journal entry to record Lee's admission, show computation of the equity interest received and bonus (if any) to either the old partners or to Lee.

d Lee invests $560,000 in the firm and receives a one-half interest in the capital and net income of the business. In addition to the journal entry to record Lee's admission, show computation of the equity interest received and bonus (if any) to either the old partners or to Lee.

PROBLEM 13B-6
Withdrawal of a Partner

Terra Management is a partnership of three individuals that specializes in the management of professional office buildings. The partnership owns and maintains offices in one such professional centre and provides management services for several other buildings owned by clients. At the end of the current year, the firm had the following balance sheet:

TERRA MANAGEMENT
Balance Sheet
December 31, 19__

Assets		*Liabilities & Partners' Equity*		
Cash	*$175,000*	*Liabilities*		*$198,000*
Receivables	*67,000*	*Partners' equity:*		
Land	*210,000*	*Spence, capital*	*$264,000*	
Building (net of accumulated		*Carver, capital*	*180,000*	
depreciation)	*260,000*	*Drake, capital*	*168,000*	*612,000*
Furniture & fixtures (net of				
accumulated depreciation)	*98,000*			
Total	*$810,000*	*Total*		*$810,000*

The partners share net income and losses in the ratio of 50% to Spence, 30% to Carver, and 20% to Drake. It is agreed that Drake is to withdraw from the partnership on this date.

INSTRUCTIONS Following are a number of different assumptions involving the withdrawal of Drake from the firm. Considering each case independently, prepare the general journal entry or entries needed to record Drake's withdrawal.

a Drake, with the permission of the other partners, gives his equity to his brother-in-law, Holmes, who is accepted as a partner in the firm.

b Drake sells one-fourth of his equity interest to Carver for $48,000 cash and sells the other three-fourths to Spence for $104,000 cash. The payments are made by Carver and Spence personally and not by the partnership.

c Drake retries and agrees to accept as full settlement of his partnership interest $120,000 cash and accounts receivable having a book value of $36,000. These assets come from the firm. The partners agree that no revaluation of assets will be made.

d The partners agree that land is worth $390,000 at present market prices. They do not wish to write up this asset in the accounts but believe that Drake is entitled to a settlement that includes his 20% interest in the increase in value. Drake is paid $96,000 in cash and given a 2-year, 12% note for $108,000.

PROBLEM 13B-7
Liquidation; Insolvent Partners

The December 31 balance sheet of MRC Group, a partnership specializing in market research and consulting, appears below. In order to focus attention on the principles involved in liquidating a partnership, the balance sheet has been shortened by combining all assets other than cash under the caption of "Other assets."

Merit, Rush, and Carroll share net income in a ratio of 3:2:1, respectively. At the date of the balance sheet the partners decided to liquidate the business.

MRC GROUP
Balance Sheet
December 31, 19__

Assets		Liabilities & Partners' Equity		
Cash	$ 90,000	Liabilities		$180,000
Other assets	450,000	Partners' equity:		
		Merit, capital	$135,000	
		Rush, capital	120,000	
		Carroll, capital	105,000	360,000
Total	$540,000	Total		$540,000

INSTRUCTIONS

For each of the three independent situations shown below, prepare journal entries to record the sale of the "other assets," payment of liabilities, division of the loss on the sale of "other assets" among the partners, and distribution of the available cash to the partners. Support all entries with adequate explanation; the entries for distribution of cash to the partners should have explanations showing how the amounts were determined.

a Other assets are sold for $378,000.

b Other assets are sold for $144,000. Each partner has personal assets and will contribute the amount necessary to cover any debit balance in his or her capital account that may arise in the liquidation process.

c Other assets are sold for $117,000. Rush has personal assets and will contribute any necessary amount. Merit and Carroll are both personally bankrupt; any deficiency in either capital account must be absorbed by remaining partners.

ANALYTICAL AND DECISION PROBLEMS AND CASES

A&D 13-1
Developing an Equitable Plan for Dividing Partnership Income

Juan Ramirez and Robert Cole are considering forming a partnership to engage in the business of aerial photography. Ramirez is a licensed pilot, is currently earning $48,000 a year, and has $50,000 to invest in the partnership. Cole is a professional photographer who is currently earning $30,000 a year. He has recently inherited $70,000 that he plans to invest in the partnership.

Both partners will work full-time in the business. After careful study, they have estimated that expenses are likely to exceed revenue by $10,000 during the first year of operations. In the second year, however, they expect the business to become profitable, with revenue exceeding expenses by an estimated $90,000. (Bear in mind that these estimates of expenses do not include any salaries or interest to the partners.) Under present market conditions, a fair rate of return on capital invested in this type of business is 20%.

INSTRUCTIONS

a On the basis of this information, prepare a brief description of the income-sharing agreement that you would recommend for Ramirez and Cole. Explain the basis for your proposal.

b Prepare a separate schedule for each of the next two years showing how the estimated amounts of net income would be divided between the two partners under your plan. (Assume that the original capital balances for both partners remain unchanged during the 2-year period. This simplifying assumption allows you to ignore the changes that would normally occur in capital accounts as a result of divisions of net income, or from drawings or additional investments.)

c Write a brief statement explaining the differences in allocation of income to the two partners and defending the results indicated by your income-sharing proposal.

A&D 13-2
An Offer of Partnership

Upon graduation from university, Ray Bradshaw began work as a staff assistant for a national CA firm. During the next few years, Bradshaw received his CA certificate and was promoted to the level of senior on the firm's audit staff.

At this time, Bradshaw received an offer from a small local CA firm, Ames and Bolt, to join that firm as a third partner. Both Ames and Bolt have been working much overtime and they would expect a similar workload from Bradshaw. Ames and Bolt draw salaries of $60,000 each and share residual income equally. They offer Bradshaw a $60,000 salary plus one-third of residual income. The offer provides for Bradshaw to receive a one-third equity interest in the firm and requires him to make a cash investment of $120,000. Balance sheet data for the firm of Ames and Bolt are as follows:

Current assets	*$ 72,000*	*Current liabilities*	*$ 36,000*
Property & equipment	*288,000*	*Long-term liabilities*	*174,000*
		Ames, capital	*75,000*
		Bolt, capital	*75,000*
Total	*$360,000*	*Total*	*$360,000*

Projected net income of the local CA firm for the next four years is estimated below. These estimated earnings are before partners' salaries and are based on the assumption that Bradshaw joins the firm and makes possible an increased volume of business.

1st year	*$192,000*	*3rd year*	*$228,000*
2nd year	*$204,000*	*4th year*	*$240,000*

If Bradshaw decides to continue in his present position with the national CA firm rather than join the local firm, he estimates that his salary over the next four years will be as follows:

1st year	*$62,000*	*3rd year*	*$73,000*
2nd year	*$66,000*	*4th year*	*$80,000*

INSTRUCTIONS

a Assuming that Bradshaw accepts the offer from Ames and Bolt, determine the amount of his beginning capital and prepare the entry in the partnership accounts to record Bradshaw's admission to the firm.

b Compute the yearly amounts of Bradshaw's income from the partnership for the next four years. Compare these amounts with the salary that he will receive if he continues in his present employment and write a memo explaining the factors Bradshaw should consider in deciding whether to accept or decline the offer from Ames and Bolt.

c Assuming that Bradshaw declines the offer, suggest some alternatives that he might propose if he decides to present a counteroffer to Ames and Bolt.

CHAPTER 14

Corporations: Organization and Shareholders' Equity

This chapter begins our study of businesses organized as corporations. First, we describe the nature of a corporation, explain the concept of a "separate legal entity," and discuss the advantages and disadvantages of the corporate form of organization. Next, we focus attention upon the shareholders' equity section of a corporate balance sheet. Contributed capital is distinguished from retained earnings, and preferred stock is contrasted with common stock. Distinctions are drawn among the concepts of no par value, par value, book value, and market value. Various shareholders' equity transactions are illustrated and explained, including the issuance of capital stock and the declaration and payment of cash dividends. Also covered are such topics as subscriptions to capital stock, accounting for donated capital, and the computation of book value per share.

Learning Objectives

After studying this chapter you should be able to:

1. *Discuss the advantages and disadvantages of organizing a business as a corporation.*
2. *Explain the rights of shareholders and the roles of corporate directors and officers.*
3. *Contrast the balance sheet presentation of the ownership equity in a corporation and in a sole proprietorship.*
4. *Account for the issuance of capital stock.*
5. *Discuss the features of preferred stock and common stock.*
6. *Discuss the factors affecting the market price of preferred stock and of common stock.*
7. *Explain the meaning and significance of book value and market value of capital stock.*

Who owns a corporation? The owners of a corporation are called ***shareholders.*** Shareholders in a large corporation such as Canadian Pacific or BCE, Inc. (Bell Canada Enterprises) include thousands of men and women, as well as many pension funds, mutual investment funds, labour unions, banks, universities, and other organizations. Because a corporation can be used to pool the savings of any number of investors, it is an ideal means of obtaining the capital necessary for large-scale business activities.

Nearly all large businesses and many small ones are organized as corporations. There are many more sole proprietorships and partnerships than corporations, but in dollar volume of business activity, corporations hold an impressive lead. Because of the dominant role of the corporation in our economy, it is important for everyone interested in business, economics, or politics to have an understanding of corporations and their accounting practices.

What Is a Corporation?

A corporation is a ***legal entity*** having an existence separate and distinct from that of its owners. In the eyes of the law a corporation is an "artificial person," having many of the rights and responsibilities of a real person.

A corporation, as a separate legal entity, may own property in its own name. Thus, the assets of a corporation belong to the corporation itself, ***not to the shareholders.*** A corporation has legal status in court—that is, it may sue and be sued as if it were a person. As a legal entity, a corporation may enter into contracts, is responsible for its own debts, and pays income taxes on its earnings.

Advantages of the Corporate Form of Organization

The corporation offers a number of advantages not available in other forms of organization. Among these advantages are the following:

OBJECTIVE 1 Discuss the advantages and disadvantages of organizing a business as a corporation.

1 **No personal liability for shareholders.** Creditors of a corporation have a claim against the assets of the corporation, not against the personal property of the shareholders. Thus, the amount of money that shareholders risk by investing in a corporation is ***limited to the amount of their investment.*** To many investors, this is the most important advantage of the corporate form.

2 **Ease of accumulating capital.** Ownership of a corporation is evidenced by transferable ***shares of capital stock.*** The sale of corporate ownership in units of one or more shares permits both large and small investors to participate in ownership of the business. Some corporations have half a million or more individual shareholders. A corporation whose ownership shares are offered for sale to the general public is said to be ***publicly owned.*** Of course not all corporations are large. Many small businesses are organized as corporations and restrict ownership to a limited group of shareholders. Such corporations are said to be ***closely held or privately owned.***

3 **Readily transferable ownership shares.** Shares of capital stock may be sold by one investor to another without dissolving or disrupting the business organization. The shares of most large corporations may be

bought or sold by investors in organized markets, such as the ***Toronto Stock Exchange.*** Investments in these shares have the advantage of ***liquidity,*** because investors may easily convert their corporate ownership into cash by selling their capital stock.

4 **Continuous existence.** A corporation is a separate legal entity with a perpetual existence. The continuous life of the corporation, despite changes in ownership, is made possible by the issuance of transferable shares of capital stock. By way of contrast, a partnership is a relatively unstable form of organization that is dissolved by the death or retirement of any of its members. The continuity of the corporate entity is essential to most large-scale business activities.

5 **Professional management.** The shareholders own the corporation, but they do not manage it on a daily basis. To administer the affairs of the corporation, the shareholders elect a ***board of directors.*** The directors, in turn, hire a president and other corporate officers to manage the business. There is no mutual agency in a corporation; thus, an individual shareholder has no right to participate in the management of the business unless he or she has been hired as a corporate officer.

Disadvantages of the Corporate Form of Organization

Among the disadvantages of the corporation are:

1 **Greater regulation.** A corporation comes into existence under the terms of federal or provincial laws and these same laws may provide for considerable regulation of the corporation's activities and disclosures. For example, the withdrawal of funds from a corporation is subject to certain limits set by law. Moreover, various securities acts administered by the provincial securities commissions require publicly owned corporations to make extensive disclosure of their affairs.

2 **Separation of ownership and control.** The separation of the functions of ownership and management may be an advantage in some cases but a disadvantage in others. On the whole, the excellent record of growth and earnings in most large corporations indicates that the separation of ownership and control has benefited rather than injured shareholders. In a few instances, however, a management group has chosen to operate a corporation for the benefit of insiders. The shareholders may find it difficult in such cases to take the concerted action necessary to oust the officers.

3 **Taxation.** The income of a partnership or a sole proprietorship is taxable only as personal income to the owners of the business. The income of a corporation, on the other hand, is subject to income taxes that must be paid by the corporation. Federal and provincial corporate income taxes take a share of a corporation's before-tax income. If a corporation distributes its earnings to shareholders, the shareholders must pay personal income taxes on the amounts they receive. This practice of first taxing corporate income to the corporation and then taxing distributions of that income to the shareholders is sometimes called ***double taxation.*** However, this double taxation is minimized by the federal dividend tax credit claimed by the shareholders.

Income Taxes in Corporate Financial Statements

As mentioned previously, a corporation is subject to income taxes on its earnings. Income taxes are levied as a percentage of ***taxable income.*** Taxable income is an amount developed in an income tax return, consisting of those revenues subject to income taxes, minus the expenses (deductions) allowed by income tax laws.

At the end of every accounting period, the estimated amount of a corporation's income taxes expense for the period is recorded in an adjusting entry. As illustrated in Chapter 11, this entry consists of a debit to ***Income Taxes Expense*** and a credit to the current liability ***Income Taxes Payable.***[1]

Corporate income taxes expense cannot be determined with precision until several months after year-end, when the corporation completes the preparation of its annual income tax return. Thus, the end-of-period adjusting entries are based upon estimates.

The topic of corporate income taxes is discussed further in Chapter 18.

Formation of a Corporation

A corporation is created by obtaining ***a certificate of incorporation*** or ***a corporate charter*** from the federal or provincial government where the company is to be incorporated. To obtain a certificate of incorporation or a corporate charter, an application called the ***articles of incorporation*** is submitted to the federal or provincial government. Once the certificate or charter is obtained, the shareholders in the new corporation hold a meeting to elect ***directors*** and to pass ***bylaws*** as a guide to the company's affairs. The directors in turn hold a meeting at which officers of the corporation are appointed.

Organization Costs The formation of a corporation is a much more costly step than the organization of a partnership. The necessary costs include the payment of an incorporation fee to the federal or provincial government, the payment of fees to lawyers for their services in drawing up the articles of incorporation, payments to promoters, and a variety of other outlays necessary to bring the corporation into existence. These costs are charged to an asset account called Organization Costs. In the balance sheet, organization costs appear under the "Other assets" caption, as illustrated on page 679.

The incurring of these organization costs leads to the existence of the corporate entity; consequently, the benefits derived from these costs may be regarded as extending over the entire life of the corporation. Since the life of a corporation may continue indefinitely, one might argue that organization costs are an asset with an unlimited life. However, such intangible assets as organization costs should be amortized over a maximum period of 40 years.[2] Income tax rules, on the other hand, permit three-quarters of the organization costs to be written off at an annual rate of 7% based on the

[1] The recognition of income taxes expense may also involve "deferred" income taxes. This topic is addressed in Chapter 16.

[2] CICA, *CICA Handbook* (Toronto), section 3060.32.

declining balance method. Consequently, most companies have elected to write off organization costs in this manner. Accountants have been willing to accept this practice, because organization costs are not material in dollar amount. The accounting principle of ***materiality*** permits departures from theoretical concepts on the grounds of convenience if the practice in question will not cause any material distortion of net income or financial position.

Rights of Shareholders The ownership of capital stock in a corporation usually carries the following basic rights:

OBJECTIVE 2 ***Explain the rights of shareholders and the roles of corporate directors and officers.***

1 To vote for directors, and thereby to be represented in the management of the business. The approval of a majority of shareholders may also be required for such important corporate actions as mergers and acquisitions, the selection of independent auditors, the incurring of long-term debts, the establishment of stock option plans, or the splitting of capital stock into a larger number of shares.
   When a corporation issues two classes of capital stock such as common stock and preferred stock, voting rights generally are granted only to the holders of common stock. These two different types of capital stock will be discussed in detail later in this chapter.
2 To share in income by receiving ***dividends*** declared by the board of directors. Shareholders in a corporation may not make withdrawals of company assets, as may an owner of an unincorporated business. However, the income of a profitable corporation may be distributed to shareholders in the form of cash dividends. The payment of a dividend always requires formal authorization by the board of directors.
3 To share in the distribution of assets if the corporation is liquidated. When a corporation ends its existence, the creditors of the corporation must first be paid in full; any remaining assets are divided among shareholders in proportion to the number of shares owned.
4 To subscribe for additional shares in the event that the corporation decides to increase the amount of capital stock outstanding. This ***preemptive right*** entitles shareholders to maintain their percentages of ownership in the company by subscribing, in proportion to their present shareholdings, to any additional shares issued. Under the Canada Business Corporations Act, a corporation may provide such a pre-emptive right in its articles of incorporation if it so wishes.

Shareholders' meetings usually are held once a year. Each share of capital stock generally is entitled to one vote. (Some corporations have shares with more than one vote, such as Norcen's "multiple voting ordinary shares" with five votes each and its "subordinate voting ordinary shares" with one vote each.) In large corporations, these annual meetings are usually attended by relatively few persons, often by less than 1% of the shareholders. Prior to the meeting, the management group will request shareholders who do not plan to attend in person to send in ***proxy statements*** assigning their votes to the existing management. Through this use of the proxy system, management may secure the right to vote as much as, perhaps, 80% or more of the total outstanding shares.

Functions of the Board of Directors The primary functions of the board of directors are to manage the corporation and to protect the interests of the shareholders. At this level, management may consist principally of formulating policies and reviewing acts of the officers. Specific duties of the directors include declaring dividends, setting the salaries of officers, reviewing the system of internal control with the internal auditors and with the company's independent auditors, and authorizing important contracts of various kinds.

In recent years increasing importance has been attached to the inclusion of outside directors on the boards of large corporations. The term ***outside directors*** refers to individuals who are not officers of the company and who thus have a view independent of that of the corporate officers. The influence of these outside directors on the corporation can be very significant. Also, the board of directors of large publicly owned corporations have recently become more aggressive and more responsive to the shareholders' interests.

CASE IN POINT In recent years, a number of chief executive officers of giant corporations have resigned or changed position or "retired" under the pressures of the corporations' boards of directors. These corporations include General Motors and IBM in the United States, and Petro-Canada in Canada.

Functions of Corporate Officers Corporate officers are the top level of the professional managers appointed by the board of directors to run the business. These officers usually include a president or chief executive officer (CEO), one or more vice presidents, a controller, a treasurer, and a secretary. A vice president is often made responsible for the sales function; other vice presidents may be given responsibility for such important functions as human resources, finance, and production.

The responsibilities of the controller, treasurer, and secretary are most directly related to the accounting phase of business operation. The ***controller,*** or chief accounting officer, is responsible for the maintenance of adequate internal control and for the preparation of accounting records and financial statements. Such specialized activities as budgeting, tax planning, and preparation of tax returns are usually placed under the controller's jurisdiction. The ***treasurer*** has custody of the company's funds and is generally responsible for planning and controlling the company's cash position. The ***secretary*** represents the corporation in many contractual and legal matters and maintains minutes of the meetings of directors and shareholders. Another responsibility of the secretary is to coordinate the preparation of the annual report, which includes the financial statements and other information relating to corporate activities. In small corporations, one officer frequently acts as both secretary and treasurer. The following organization chart indicates lines of authority extending from shareholders to the directors to the president and other officers.

Typical corporate organization

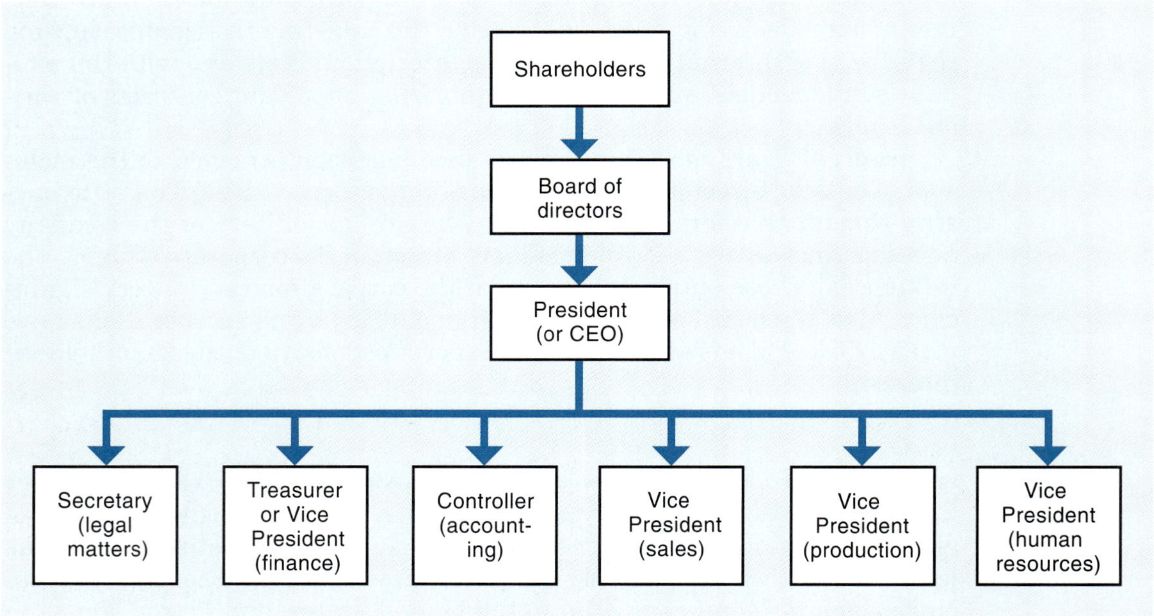

Shareholders' Equity[3]

OBJECTIVE 3 Contrast the balance sheet presentation of the ownership equity in a corporation and in a sole proprietorship.

The sections of the balance sheet showing assets and liabilities are much the same for a corporation as for a sole proprietorship. The owner's equity section is the principal point of contrast. In the balance sheet of a corporation, the term ***shareholders' equity*** is used instead of owners' equity.

The owners' equity in a corporation, as in other types of business organizations, is equal to the assets of the business minus the liabilities. However, corporation laws require that the shareholders' equity section of a corporate balance sheet clearly indicate the ***source*** of the owners' equity. The two basic sources of owners' equity are (1) investment by the shareholders ***(contributed capital),*** and (2) earnings from profitable operation of the business ***(retained earnings).***

When shareholders invest cash or other assets in the business, the corporation issues to them in exchange shares of capital stock as evidence of their ownership. In the simplest case, capital invested by the shareholders is recorded in the corporation's accounting records by a credit to an account entitled ***Capital Stock.*** The capital paid in by shareholders is regarded as permanent capital not ordinarily subject to withdrawal.

The increase in shareholders' equity arising from profitable operations is called ***retained earnings.*** At the end of the year the balance of the Income Summary account is closed into the Retained Earnings account.

---

[3] According to the CICA's *Financial Reporting in Canada,* Twentieth Edition, 1993, pp. 135–136, the terms "shareholders' equity" and "capital stock" are most commonly used; thus, the first two terms are used in this book.

For example, if net income for the year is $70,000, the closing entry will be as follows:

Income Summary	*70,000*	
Retained Earnings		*70,000*
To close the Income Summary account by transferring the year's net income into the Retained Earnings account.		

If the company operates at a loss of, say, $25,000, the Income Summary account will have a debit balance. The account must then be credited to close it. The closing entry will be:

Retained Earnings	*25,000*	
Income Summary		*25,000*
To close the Income Summary account by transferring the year's net loss into the Retained Earnings account.		

If a corporation has sufficient cash, a distribution of income or earnings may be made to shareholders. Distributions of this nature are termed ***dividends*** and decrease both total assets and total shareholders' equity. Because dividends are regarded as distributions of earnings, the decrease in shareholders' equity is recorded in the Retained Earnings account. Thus, the amount of retained earnings at any balance sheet date represents the ***accumulated earnings of the company since the date of incorporation, minus any losses, and minus all dividends.***

Some people mistakenly believe that retained earnings represents a fund of cash available to a corporation. ***Retained earnings is not an asset; it is an element of shareholders' equity.*** Although the amount of retained earnings indicates the portion of total assets that are ***financed*** by the earnings retained by the corporation, it does ***not*** indicate the ***form*** in which these resources are currently held. The resources generated by retaining earnings may have been invested in land, buildings, equipment, or any other kind of asset. The total amount of cash owned by a corporation is shown by the balance of the Cash account, which appears in the asset section of the balance sheet.

Shareholders' Equity in the Balance Sheet For a corporation with $1,000,000 of capital stock and $600,000 of retained earnings, the shareholders' equity section of the balance sheet (omitting certain details) will appear as follows:

Contributed capital and retained earnings

Shareholders' equity:		
Capital stock	*$1,000,000*	
Retained earnings	*600,000*	*$1,600,000*

If this same company had been unprofitable and had incurred losses totalling $300,000 since its incorporation, the shareholders' equity section of the balance sheet would be as follows:

Contributed capital less losses incurred

Shareholders' equity:		
Capital stock	*$1,000,000*	
Less: Deficit	*300,000*	*$700,000*

This second illustration tells us that $300,000 of the original $1,000,000 invested by shareholders has been lost. Note that the capital stock in both illustrations remains at the fixed amount of $1,000,000, the shareholders' original investment. The accumulated income or losses since the organization of the corporation are shown as ***retained earnings*** or as a ***deficit*** and are not intermingled with the contributed capital. The term ***deficit*** indicates a negative amount of retained earnings.

Cash Dividends

The term ***dividend,*** when used by itself, is generally understood to mean a distribution of cash by a corporation to its shareholders. Dividends are stated as a specific amount per share of capital stock, as, for example, a dividend of $1 per share. The amount received by each shareholder is in proportion to the number of shares owned. Thus, a shareholder who owns 100 shares will receive $100.

Dividends are paid only through action by the board of directors. The board has full discretion to declare a dividend or to refrain from doing so. Once the declaration of a dividend has been announced, the obligation to pay the dividend is a current liability of the corporation and cannot be rescinded.

Because a dividend is declared on one date by the board of directors and paid at a later date, two separate journal entries are necessary. To illustrate the entries for declaration and payment of a cash dividend, assume that a corporation declares a dividend of $1 per share on 100,000 shares of outstanding capital stock. The dividend is declared on December 15 and is payable on January 25. The two entries would be as follows:

Dividends are first declared . . .

Dec. 15	Retained Earnings	100,000	
	Dividends Payable		100,000
	To record declaration by the board of directors of a cash dividend of $1 per share on the 100,000 shares of capital stock outstanding.		

. . . and then paid

Jan. 25	Dividends Payable	100,000	
	Cash		100,000
	To record payment of the $1 per share dividend declared Dec. 15 on the 100,000 shares of capital stock outstanding.		

The account ***Dividends Payable,*** which was credited at the date of declaring the dividend, is a current liability. If a company has more than one issue of capital stock (such as both common stock and preferred stock or class A and class B), it may use a separate Dividends Payable account for each issue.

Some companies in recording the declaration of a dividend will debit an account entitled Dividends instead of debiting the Retained Earnings account. Whenever a Dividends account is used, a closing entry will be required at the end of the year to transfer the debit balance in the Dividends account into the Retained Earnings account. Under either method the end result is a reduction in retained earnings for the amount of the dividends ***declared.*** (In our end-of-chapter material we will debit the Retained Earnings account, as illustrated above.)

What Is Capital Stock?

As previously mentioned, the caption ***capital stock*** in the balance sheet of a corporation represents the amount invested by the owners of the business. When the owners of a corporation invest cash or other assets in the business, the corporation issues capital stock as evidence of the investors' ownership equity.

The basic unit of capital stock is called a ***share,*** but a corporation may issue capital stock certificates in denominations of 1 share, 100 shares, or any other number. The total number of shares of capital stock outstanding at any given time represents 100% ownership of the corporation. ***Outstanding*** shares are those in the hands of shareholders. The number of shares owned by an individual investor determines the extent of his or her ownership of the corporation.

Assume, for example, that Star Corporation issues a total of 50,000 shares of capital stock to investors in exchange for cash. If you were to acquire 5,000 shares of the 50,000 shares, you would own a 10% interest in the corporation.

Authorization and Issuance of Capital Stock

OBJECTIVE 4 Account for the issuance of capital stock.

While the articles of incorporation ***may*** specify any maximum number of shares of capital stock that a corporation is authorized to issue, a corporation is ***not required*** to do so under the Canada Business Corporations Act. Thus, a corporation governed by the federal act does not have a limit on the maximum number of shares of capital stock it can issue unless it chooses to have one by stating such a limit in its articles of incorporation. The federal act does require, however, that the shares of capital stock of corporations be ***without par or nominal value.*** Provincial corporation legislation, such as the Ontario Business Corporations Act, parallels that of the federal act in these respects. On the other hand, certain provincial legislation (as well as legislation in the United States) still requires corporations to specify the maximum number of shares of capital stock they are authorized to issue and permits corporations to issue capital stock with a par value. Thus, some of the large corporations still have a maximum number of authorized capital stock and par value capital stock.

CASE IN POINT Maritime Telegraph and Telephone has maximum authorized preferred and common stock, some with par value, and the premium on common stock (the excess of issue price over par value) is in excess of $38 million; Bow Valley Industries has 200 million shares of no-par common stock authorized, with only slightly over 54 million shares issued and outstanding.[4] In the United States, the common stock of Ford, AT&T, and Coca-Cola all have a par value of $1.

It should be noted that mere authorization of a capital stock issue (with or without a maximum limit) does not bring an asset into existence, nor

[4] These corporations ranked among the 500 largest in Canada. See the annual Summer issue of *The Financial Post 500.*

does it give the corporation any capital. The obtaining of authorization from the federal or provincial government for a capital stock issue merely affords a legal opportunity to obtain assets through the sale of capital stock.

No-par Value Capital Stock

Federal and provincial corporation legislation clearly indicates that no-par value capital stock will become increasingly common in Canada. The following are some of the important reasons for the emergence of the concept of no-par value capital stock:

1. It avoids the assignment of an arbitrary amount as par value that is subject to misunderstanding by investors. For example, issued capital stock traded on stock exchanges at below its par value may sometimes be interpreted as a bargain even though the stock is at its fair market value. Thus, no-par stock eliminates such an opportunity for misunderstanding. Of course, the market value of any stock fluctuates according to the changes in the investors' perception about the value of the business, not according to the par value.
2. It provides a corporation with greater flexibility in the arrangement of its capital structure. For example, a corporation can split the existing no-par shares into a greater number of shares (as will be discussed in Chapter 15) without having to consider the effect on the par value. Also, no-par stock eliminates the problem of issuing stock at a discount, which generally is not allowed by law. Of course, since the par value is usually set at a very low amount, in reality the question of issuing stock at a discount seldom arises.
3. It eliminates the confusion and misunderstanding associated with the nature and meaning of such accounts as premium on capital stock, since no-par stock does not result in the establishment of these premium accounts.

Issuance of No-par Value Capital Stock When no-par value capital stock is issued, the entire proceeds on the issue are credited to the Capital Stock account. Assuming that 60,000 shares of no-par value capital stock are issued at a price of $10 each, the entry to record the issue is as follows:

Entry for no-par capital stock

Cash	*600,000*	
Capital Stock		*600,000*
Issued 60,000 shares of no-par capital stock at a price of $10 a share.		

The amount credited to the Capital Stock account represents the ***legal capital*** or the ***stated capital***[5]—the amount that cannot be reduced except by (1) losses from business operations or (2) legal action taken by a majority vote of shareholders or permitted by the legislation governing the corporation.

[5] "Stated capital" is the term used in the Canada Business Corporations Act and certain provincial corporations acts.

The shareholders' equity section of the balance sheet is illustrated as follows (assuming an unlimited number of authorized shares and the existence of $280,000 in retained earnings in order to have a complete illustration).

Shareholders' equity:	
Capital stock, no-par value, authorized, an unlimited number of shares, issued and outstanding, 60,000 shares	*$600,000*
Retained earnings	*280,000*
Total shareholders' equity	*$880,000*

Par Value Capital Stock

The par value of capital stock represents the arbitrary amount assigned by a corporation as its legal capital per share. It merely indicates the amount per share to be entered in the Capital Stock account; it is ***not*** an indication of its market value. Par value may be $1, $2, $5, per share, or any amount decided upon by the corporation. Generally, the par values of most corporations are very small.

Issuance of Par Value Capital Stock When par value capital stock is issued, the Capital Stock account is credited with the par value of the shares sold. Assuming that 80,000 shares of $2 par value capital stock are issued at a price of $2 each, the entry would be:

Entry for par value capital stock issued at par

Cash	*160,000*	
Capital Stock		*160,000*
Issued 80,000 shares of $2 par value capital stock at their par value.		

When capital stock is sold for more than its par value, the Capital Stock account is credited with the par value of the shares issued, and a separate account, Premium on Capital Stock, is credited for the excess of selling price over par. If, for example, the issuance price is $3 rather than $2, as in the previous illustration, the entry for the 80,000 shares would be:

Capital stock issued in excess of par value

Cash	*240,000*	
Capital Stock		*160,000*
Premium on Capital Stock		*80,000*
Issued 80,000 shares of $2 par value capital stock at a price of $3 a share.		

The premium (the amount in excess of par value) does not represent an income to the corporation. It is part of the invested capital, and it will be added to the capital stock on the balance sheet to show the total contributed capital.[6] The shareholders' equity section of the balance sheet is illustrated as follows. (An authorization for 1,800,000 shares and the existence of $70,000 in retained earnings are assumed in order to have a complete illustration.)

[6] It is more appropriate to treat the premium on capital stock as part of the contributed capital than as part of contributed surplus, even though the latter is preferred by the *CICA Handbook*.

Corporation's capital classified by source

Shareholders' equity:	
Capital stock, $2 par value, authorized, 1,800,000 shares, issued and outstanding, 80,000 shares	*$160,000*
Premium on capital stock	*80,000*
Total contributed capital	*$240,000*
Retained earnings	*70,000*
Total shareholders' equity	*$310,000*

If capital stock is issued by a corporation for less than par, the account Discount on Capital Stock should be debited for the difference between the issuance price and the par value. The issuance of capital stock at a discount is not permitted under the federal and most provincial business corporations acts.

Preferred Stock and Common Stock

OBJECTIVE 5 Discuss the features of preferred stock and common stock.

The account title ***capital stock*** is widely used when a corporation has issued ***one class*** of capital stock. In order to appeal to as many investors as possible, a corporation may issue more than one class of capital stock. Under the Canada Business Corporations Act, a corporation may have more than one class of capital stock, provided that the rights, privileges, restrictions, and conditions of each class are set forth in the articles of incorporation and that at least one class of capital stock has the rights typically associated with what is traditionally known as "common stock." These rights are identical with the first three rights mentioned earlier, namely, (1) to vote at any meeting of shareholders of the corporation, (2) to receive any dividend declared by the corporation, and (3) to receive the remaining property of the corporation on dissolution. The federal act does not use the terms "common" and "preferred" to distinguish the different classes of capital stock. However, since the terms "preferred stock" and "common stock" are still widely used in practice and have been proven useful in distinguishing classes of capital stock, they will be used throughout this book.

The basic type of capital stock issued by every corporation is generally called common stock. Common stock has the three basic rights previously mentioned. Whenever these rights are modified, the term preferred stock (or sometimes Class B Common) is used to describe this second type of capital stock. Some corporations issue two or more classes of preferred stock, each class having certain distinctive features designed to interest a particular type of investor. In summary, every business corporation has common stock; a good many corporations also issue preferred stock; and some companies have two or more types of preferred stock.

CASE IN POINT The amount of preferred stock issued has been impressive. In recent years, the annual dollar amount of preferred stock issued ranged from around $400 million to over $3 billion. Many of these issues were cumulative preferred stock and the amount ranged from $50 million (Consumers' Gas) to $300 million (Canutilities Holdings) per issue.

Common stock may be regarded as the basic, residual element of ownership. It carries voting rights and, therefore, is the means of exercising control over the business. Common stock has unlimited possibilities of increase in value; during periods of business expansion, the market prices of common stocks of some leading corporations may rise to many times their former values. On the other hand, common stocks lose value more rapidly than other types of securities when corporations encounter periods of unprofitable business.

The following shareholders' equity section illustrates the balance sheet presentation for a corporation having both preferred and common stock; note that the item of retained earnings is not apportioned between the two groups of shareholders.

Balance sheet presentation of shareholders' equity

Shareholders' equity:	
$12 cumulative preferred stock, no-par value, authorized, an unlimited number of shares, issued and outstanding, 200,000 shares	*$ 5,000,000*
Common stock, no-par value, authorized, an umlimited number of shares, issued and outstanding, 2,000,000 shares	*10,000,000*
Retained earnings	*3,500,000*
Total shareholders' equity	*$18,500,000*

Characteristics of Preferred Stock

The characteristics of preferred stocks vary from one issue to the next. The term ***preferred*** stems from the fact that these stocks almost always have "preference"—or priority—over the common stock in receiving dividends and in the event of liquidation. However, preferred shares usually ***lack*** significant advantages found in common stock. For example, the dividends paid to preferred shareholders normally ***do not increase*** if the company prospers. Also, preferred shareholders usually do ***not*** have voting rights and, therefore, have little say in management.

Among the features usually associated with preferred stock are the following:

1 Preferred as to dividends
2 Cumulative dividend rights
3 Preferred as to assets in event of the liquidation of the company
4 Callable or redeemable at the option of the corporation
5 No voting power

Another very important feature is a clause permitting the ***conversion*** of preferred stock into common at the option of the holder. Preferred stocks vary widely with respect to the special rights and privileges granted. Careful study of the terms of the individual preferred stock contract is a necessary step in the evaluation of any preferred stock.

Stock Preferred as to Dividends Stock preferred as to dividends is entitled to receive each year a dividend of specified amount before any dividend is paid on the common stock. The dividend is usually stated as a dollar amount per share. Some preferred stocks state the dividend preference as a ***percentage of par value.*** For example, a ***9%*** preferred stock with a par value of $100 per share would mean that $9 must be paid yearly on each share of preferred stock before any dividends are paid on the common. This dividend rate remains unchanged or fixed during the life of the preferred stock.

CASE IN POINT Bell Canada has a series of preferred stock at various dividend rates. For example, series 9 and 10 have dividend rates of $1.875 and $1.86 per share respectively; series 11, on the other hand, has a dividend rate of 7.64% per share.

In recent years, corporations also issued preferred stock with a ***floating rate*** of dividend rather than a fixed rate as discussed above. The floating rate is tied to the bank prime rate (an interest rate given to the most credit worthy customers). Thus, the amount of dividends the preferred shareholders receive changes as the bank prime rate changes. This means that these shareholders will receive and the corporations will pay a dividend rate that reflects the rate in the current market.

CASE IN POINT George Weston Limited has a number of "floating rate" preferred stock, among them: senior preferred stock-series A at 71% of average bank prime rate, junior preferred stock-series E at two-thirds average bank prime rate plus $\frac{3}{4}$%. Similarly, the "floating rate" preferred shares of Loblaw Companies Limited include: second preferred shares-first series at one-half of bank prime rate plus $\frac{7}{8}$%, second preferred shares-second series at one-half of bank prime rate plus $1\frac{1}{4}$%, and junior preferred shares-third series at two-thirds of average bank prime rate plus $\frac{3}{4}$%.

The holders of preferred stock have no assurance that they will always receive the indicated dividend. A corporation is obligated to pay dividends to shareholders only when the board of directors declares a dividend. Dividends must be paid on preferred stock before anything is paid to the common shareholders, but if the corporation is not prospering, it may decide not to pay dividends on either preferred or common stock. For a corporation to pay dividends, income must be earned and cash must be available. However, preferred stocks in general offer ***more assurance*** of regular dividend payments than do common stocks.

Cumulative Preferred Stock The dividend preference carried by most preferred stocks is a ***cumulative*** one. If all or any part of the regular dividend on the preferred stock is omitted in a given year, the amount omitted is said to be ***in arrears*** and must be paid in a subsequent year before any dividend can be paid on the common stock. Assume that a corporation was organized January 1, 1994, with 10,000 shares of $8 cumulative preferred stock and 50,000 shares of common stock. Dividends paid in 1994 were at the rate of $8 per share of preferred stock and $2 per share of common. In

1995, earnings declined sharply and the only dividend paid was $2 per share on the preferred stock. No dividends were paid in 1996. What is the status of the preferred stock at December 31, 1996? Dividends are in arrears in the amount of $14 per share ($6 omitted during 1995 and $8 omitted in 1996). On the entire issue of 10,000 shares of preferred stock, the dividends in arrears amount to $140,000.

Dividends in arrears ***are not listed among the liabilities of a corporation, because no liability exists until a dividend is declared by the board of directors.*** Nevertheless, the amount of any dividends in arrears on preferred stock is an important factor to investors and should always be ***disclosed.*** This disclosure is usually made by a note accompanying the balance sheet such as the following:

Footnote disclosure of dividends in arrears

Note 6: Dividends in arrears

As of December 31, 1996, dividends on the $8 cumulative preferred stock were in arrears to the extent of $14 per share and amounted in total to $140,000.

In 1997, we shall assume that the company earned a large income and wished to pay dividends on both the preferred and common stocks. Before paying a dividend on the common, the corporation must pay the $140,000 in arrears on the cumulative preferred stock ***plus*** the regular $8 per share applicable to the current year. The preferred shareholders would, therefore, receive a total of $220,000 in dividends in 1997; the board of directors would then be free to declare dividends on the common stock.

For a ***noncumulative*** preferred stock, any omitted dividend is lost forever. Because of this factor, investors view the noncumulative feature as an unfavourable element, even though noncumulative preferred stocks are still issued.

CASE IN POINT The investors' confidence that default on dividend obligations by large national financial institutions would be highly unlikely has enabled banks and trust companies to issue ***noncumulative*** preferred stocks. In a recent year, a number of banks and trust companies such as the Royal Bank, Toronto Dominion Bank, Bank of Montreal, Bank of Nova Scotia, and Royal Trustco issued over $1 billion of noncumulative preferred stock.

Stock Preferred as to Assets Most preferred stocks carry a preference as to assets in the event of liquidation of the corporation. If the business is terminated, the preferred stock is entitled to payment in full of its par value or a higher stated liquidation value before any payment is made on the common stock. This priority also includes any dividends in arrears.

Callable or Redeemable Preferred Stock Most preferred stocks include a ***call*** or ***redemption provision.*** This provision grants the issuing corporation the right to repurchase the stock from the shareholders at a stipulated ***call (redemption) price.*** The call price is usually slightly higher than the issued price or par value of the stock. For example, $100 par value preferred stock may be callable at $105 or $110 per share. In addition to paying the call price, a corporation that redeems its preferred stock must pay any dividends in arrears. A call provision gives a corporation flexibility in adjusting its financial structure, for example, by eliminating a preferred stock and replacing it with other securities if future growth of the company makes such change advantageous.

Convertible Preferred Stock In order to add to the attractiveness of preferred stock as an investment, corporations sometimes offer a ***conversion privilege*** that entitles the preferred shareholders to exchange their shares for common stock in a stipulated ratio. If the corporation prospers, its common stock will probably rise in market value, and dividends on the common stock will probably increase. The investor who buys a convertible preferred stock rather than common stock has greater assurance of regular dividends. In addition, through the conversion privilege, the investor is assured of sharing in any substantial increase in value of the company's common stock.

As an example, assume that Remington Corporation issued a $9, no-par, convertible preferred stock on January 2, at a price of $100 per share. Each share was convertible into four shares of the company's no-par value common stock at any time. The common stock had a market price of $20 per share on January 2, and an annual dividend of $1 per share was being paid. During the next few years, Remington Corporation's earnings increased, the dividend on the common stock was raised to an annual rate of $3, and the market price of the common stock rose to $40 per share. At this point the preferred stock would have a market value of ***at least $160,*** since it could be converted at any time into four shares of common stock with a market value of $40 each. In other words, the market value of a convertible preferred stock will tend to move in accordance with the price of the common.

When the dividend rate is increased on the common stock, some holders of the preferred stock may convert their holdings into common stock in order to obtain a higher cash return on their investments. If the holder of 100 shares of the preferred stock presented these shares for conversion, Remington Corporation would make the following journal entry:

Conversion of preferred stock into common

$9 Convertible Preferred Stock	*10,000*	
Common Stock		*10,000*
To record the conversion of 100 shares of no-par preferred stock into 400 shares of no-par value common stock.		

Note that the issue price recorded for the 400 shares of common stock is based upon the ***carrying value*** of the preferred stock in the accounting records, not upon market prices at the date of conversion.

Participating Preferred Stock On rare occasions, a corporation may issue a participating preferred stock. A ***participating*** preferred stock is one that, in addition to the regular specified dividend, is entitled to participate (or share) in some manner in additional dividends declared by the board of directors.

For example, assume a corporation has outstanding both common stock and $8 ***fully participating,*** no-par value preferred stock issued at $100 each. Any dividends declared are first allocated (at $8 per share or 8%) to the preferred shareholders. After the common shareholders are allocated an equivalent dividend (8% of the amount of the common stock issued and outstanding), the preferred and common shareholder groups share proportionally the residual amount, if any. ***Partially participating*** preferred stock is subject to limits on amounts received in excess of the stated preferred dividend.

Market Price of Preferred Stock

Investors buy preferred stocks primarily to receive the dividends that these shares pay. Thus, the dividend rate is one important factor in determining the market price of a preferred stock.

OBJECTIVE 6 Discuss the factors affecting the market price of preferred stock and of common stock.

But what happens to the market price of an \$8 preferred stock, originally issued at \$100, if government policies and other factors cause long-term interest rates to rise to, say, 15% or 16%? If investments offering a return of 16% are readily available, investors will no longer pay \$100 for a share of preferred stock that provides a dividend of only \$8 per year. Thus, the market price of the preferred stock will fall to about half of its original issue price, or about \$50 per share. At this market price, the stock offers a 16% return (called the ***dividend yield***) to an investor purchasing the stock (\$8 per year ÷ \$50 = 16%). However, if the prevailing long-term interest rates decline to the 8% range, the market price of this \$8 preferred stock should rise quickly to approximately the original issued price of \$100.[7]

In conclusion, the market price of preferred stock ***varies inversely with interest rates.*** As interest rates rise, preferred stock prices decline; as interest rates fall, preferred stock prices rise.

Market Price of Common Stock

Interest rates also have a significant effect upon the market prices of common stocks. However, common stock dividends are not fixed in amount. If the company prospers, these dividends are likely to increase—perhaps every year. Therefore, ***investors' expectations*** as to the profitability of ***future operations*** greatly affect the market value of common shares.

In addition, many large corporations grow by acquiring smaller companies with excellent future prospects. This generally is accomplished by offering to buy all (or most) of the smaller company's common stock at a price that will induce the existing shareholders to sell. As preferred shareholders usually have no voting rights, an investor seeking control of a business entity need not acquire these shares.

Bear in mind that after shares have been issued they belong to the ***shareholders,*** not to the issuing corporation. Therefore, changes in the market price of the shares ***do not affect the financial statements of the corporation,*** and these changes are not recorded in the corporation's accounting records. The contributed capital shown in a corporate balance sheet represents the amount ***received when the stock was issued,*** not the current market value of shares.

Issuing Capital Stock: The Role of an Underwriter

When a large amount of capital stock is to be issued, most corporations use the services of an investment dealer, frequently referred to as an ***under-***

[7] To simplify the discussion, the effect of dividend tax credit is ignored.

writer. The underwriter guarantees the issuing corporation a specific price for the stock and makes a profit by selling the shares to the investing public at a slightly higher price. The corporation records the issuance of the stock at the net amount received from the underwriter. The use of an underwriter assures the corporation that the entire capital stock issue will be sold without delay and that the entire amount of funds to be raised will be available on a specific date.

The price that a corporation will ask for a new issue of capital stock is based upon such factors as (1) expected future earnings and dividends, (2) the financial strength of the company, and (3) the current state of the investment markets. However, if the corporation asks too much, it simply will not find an underwriter or other buyers willing to purchase the shares.

Stock Issued for Assets Other Than Cash

Corporations generally sell their capital stock for cash and use the cash to buy the various types of assets needed in the business. Sometimes, however, a corporation may issue shares of its capital stock in a direct exchange for land, buildings, or other assets. Capital stock may also be issued in payment for services rendered by lawyers and promoters in the formation of the corporation.

When a corporation issues capital stock in exchange for services or for assets other than cash, the transaction should be recorded at the current ***market value*** of the goods or services received. For some types of assets such as land or buildings, the services of a firm of professional appraisers may be useful in establishing current market value. Often, the best evidence as to the market value of these goods or services is the market value of the shares issued in exchange. For example, assume that a company issues 10,000 shares of its no-par value common stock in exchange for land. Competent appraisers may have differing opinions as to the market value of the land. But let us assume that the company's stock is currently selling on a stock exchange for $90 per share. It is logical to say that the cost of the land to the company is $900,000, the market value of the shares issued in exchange.

Once the valuation has been decided, the entry to record the issuance of the stock in exchange for the land is as follows:

Notice the use of current market values

Land	*900,000*	
Common Stock		*900,000*
To record the issuance of 10,000 shares of no-par value common stock in exchange for land. Current market value of stock ($90 per share) used as basis for valuing the land.		

Similarly, if 100 shares of the no-par value common stock with a market value of $90 per share are issued to lawyers and promoters for their services of $9,000 in the formation of the corporation, the entry to record the exchange is:

Organization costs	*9,000*	
Common Stock		*9,000*
To record the issuance of 100 shares of no-par value common stock in exchange for organization costs of $9,000.		

As mentioned earlier, the fair market value of the assets such as land and building may also be used as a basis of valuation if it is proven to be more objective and reliable than the market value of the shares used in the exchange. The responsibility for the determination of market value rests with the board of directors of the corporation. Thus, the board must assess all available evidence to ensure that the most objective and reliable basis of valuation is used.

Subscriptions to Capital Stock

Small, newly formed corporations sometimes offer investors an opportunity to **subscribe** to shares of the company's capital stock. Under a subscription plan, the investors agree to purchase specified numbers of shares at a stated price ***at a future date,*** often by making a series of instalment payments. The stock is issued after the entire subscription price has been collected.

In summary, selling stock through subscriptions is similar to selling merchandise on a "layaway" plan. One reason for this procedure is to attract small investors. Another reason is to appeal to investors who prefer not to invest cash until the corporation is ready to start business operations.

When stock is subscribed, the company debits Stock Subscriptions Receivable for the subscription price and credits Capital Stock Subscribed for the subscription price of the shares. Later, as instalments are collected, the entry is a debit to Cash and a credit to Stock Subscriptions Receivable. When the entire subscription price has been collected, the stock certificates are issued. The issuance of the stock is recorded by debiting Capital Stock Subscribed and crediting Capital Stock. The following illustration demonstrates the accounting procedures for stock subscriptions.

In this example, 10,000 shares of no-par value common stock are subscribed at a price of $15. Subscriptions for 6,000 of these shares are then collected in full from one subscriber. A partial payment is received from another subscriber on the other 4,000 shares.

Entry for subscription of common stock

Stock Subscriptions Receivable	*150,000*	
Common Stock Subscribed		*150,000*
Received subscriptions for 10,000 shares of no-par value common stock at price of $15 a share.		

When the subscriptions for 6,000 shares are collected in full, certificates for 6,000 shares will be issued. The following entries are made:

Entries for subscriptions collected in full

Cash	*90,000*	
Stock Subscriptions Receivable		*90,000*
Collected subscriptions in full for 6,000 shares at $15 each.		
Capital Stock Subscribed	*90,000*	
Common Stock		*90,000*
Issued certificates for 6,000 fully paid shares of no-par common stock at $15 a share.		

The subscriber to the remaining 4,000 shares paid only half of the amount of the subscription but promised to pay the remainder within a month. Stock certificates will not be issued until the subscription is collected in full, but the partial collection is recorded by the following entry:

Entry for partial collection of subscription

Cash	*30,000*	
Stock Subscriptions Receivable		*30,000*
Collected partial payment on subscription for 4,000 shares.		

From the corporation's point of view, Stock Subscriptions Receivable is a current asset, which ordinarily will be collected within a short time. If financial statements are prepared between the date of obtaining subscriptions and the date of issuing the stock, the Capital Stock Subscribed account is regarded as legal capital and will appear in the shareholders' equity section of the balance sheet.

Donated Capital

On occasion, a corporation may receive assets as a gift. To increase local employment, for example, some cities have given corporations the land upon which to build factories. When a corporation receives such a gift, both total assets and total shareholders' equity increase by the market value of the assets received. ***No income is recognized when a gift is received;*** the increase in shareholders' equity is regarded as contributed capital. The receipt of a gift is recorded by debiting the appropriate asset accounts and crediting an account entitled ***Donated Capital.***

For example, the entry to record the donation of land with a market value of $390,000 is as follows:

Land	*390,000*	
Donated Capital		*390,000*
To record the donation of land with a market value of $390,000.		

Donated capital appears in the shareholders' equity section of the balance sheet, as illustrated on page 680.

Shareholder Records in a Corporation

A large corporation with shares listed on the Toronto Stock Exchange or other exchanges usually has millions of shares outstanding and hundreds of thousands of shareholders. Each day many shareholders sell their shares; the buyers of these shares become new members of the company's family of shareholders. An investor purchasing capital stock in a corporation receives a ***stock certificate*** from the company indicating the number of shares acquired. If the investor later sells these shares, this stock certificate must be surrendered to the corporation for cancellation before a new certificate is issued to the new owner of the shares.

A corporation must have an up-to-date record of the names and addresses of this constantly changing army of shareholders so that it can send dividend cheques, financial statements, and voting forms to the right people. Also, the corporation must make sure that old stock certificates are cancelled as new ones are issued so that no excess certificates become outstanding.

Shareholders Subsidiary Ledger When there are numerous shareholders, it is not practical to include a separate account for each shareholder in the general ledger. Instead, a single controlling account entitled Capital Stock appears in the general ledger, and a ***shareholders subsidiary ledger*** is maintained. This ledger contains an account for each individual shareholder. Entries in the shareholders subsidiary ledger are made in number of shares rather than in dollars. Thus, each shareholder's account shows the number of shares owned and the dates of acquisitions and sales. This record enables the corporation to send each shareholder a single dividend cheque, even though the shareholder may have acquired several stock certificates at different dates.

A corporation that has one or more issues of preferred stock outstanding, as well as common stock, will maintain a separate set of shareholders subsidiary records for each issue.

Stock Transfer Agent and Stock Registrar Large, publicly owned corporations use an independent stock transfer agent and a stock registrar to maintain their shareholder records and to establish strong internal control over the issuance of stock certificates. These transfer agents and registrars usually are large banks or trust companies. When stock certificates are to be transferred from one owner to another, the old certificates are sent to the transfer agent, who cancels them, makes the necessary entries in the shareholders subsidiary ledger, and prepares a new certificate for the new owner of the shares. This new certificate then must be registered with the stock registrar before it represents valid and transferable ownership of stock in the corporation.

Small, closely held corporations generally do not use the services of independent registrars and transfer agents. In these companies, the shareholder records usually are maintained by a corporate officer. To prevent the accidental or fraudulent issuance of an excessive number of stock certificates, even a small corporation should require that each certificate be signed by at least two designated corporate officers.

Book Value per Share of Common Stock

Jan-'99

OBJECTIVE 7 Explain the meaning and significance of book value and market value of capital stock.

Because the equity of each shareholder in a corporation is determined by the number of shares he or she owns, an accounting measurement of interest to many shareholders is book value per share of common stock. Book value per share is equal to the ***net assets*** represented by one share of common stock. The term ***net assets*** means total assets minus total liabilities; in other words, net assets are equal to total shareholders' equity. Thus in a corporation that has issued common stock only, the book value per share is computed by dividing total shareholders' equity by the number of shares outstanding (or subscribed).

For example, assume that a corporation has 4,000 shares of common stock outstanding and the shareholders' equity section of the balance sheet is as follows:

How much is book value per share?

Common stock, no-par value (4,000 shares outstanding)	$ 44,000
Retained earnings	76,000
Total shareholders' equity	$120,000

The book value per share is $30; it is computed by dividing the shareholders' equity of $120,000 by the 4,000 shares of outstanding stock. In computing book value, we are not concerned with the number of authorized shares but merely with the ***outstanding*** shares, because the total of the outstanding shares represents 100% of the shareholders' equity.

CASE IN POINT Book value per share is regularly reported in such financial news media as *The Financial Post* and in the annual reports of such large corporations as Dofasco Inc., George Weston Limited, Bombardier, Ivaco, and United Dominion. For example, Dofasco's book value in a recent year was $12.98.

Book Value When a Company Has Both Preferred and Common Stock Book value is usually computed only for common stock. If a company has both preferred and common stock outstanding, the computation of book value per share of common stock requires two steps. First, the ***redemption value*** or ***call price*** of the entire preferred stock issue and any dividends in arrears are deducted from total shareholders' equity. Second, the remaining amount of shareholders' equity is divided by the number of common shares outstanding to determine book value per common share. This procedure reflects the fact that the common shareholders are the residual owners of the corporate entity.

To illustrate, assume that the shareholders' equity of Video Corporation at December 31 is as follows:

Two classes of stock

$8 preferred stock, no-par, callable at $110, issued and outstanding, 10,000 shares	*$1,000,000*
Common stock, no-par, issued and outstanding, 50,000 shares	*1,250,000*
Retained earnings	*130,000*
Total shareholders' equity	*$2,380,000*

Because of a weak cash position, Video Corporation has paid no dividends during the current year. As of December 31, dividends in arrears on the cumulative preferred stock total ***$80,000.***

All the equity belongs to the common shareholders, except the $1.1 million call price ($110 × 10,000 shares) applicable to the preferred stock and the $80,000 of dividends in arrears on preferred stock. The calculation of book value per share of common stock is shown below:

Total shareholders' equity		*$2,380,000*
Less: Equity of preferred shareholders:		
Call price of preferred stock	*$1,100,000*	
Dividends in arrears	*80,000*	*1,180,000*
Equity of common shareholders		*$1,200,000*
Number of common shares outstanding		*50,000*
Book value per share of common stock ($1,200,000 ÷ 50,000 shares)		*$24*

Book Value and Market Price To some extent, book value may be used in evaluating the reasonableness of the market price of a stock. However, it must be used with great caution; the fact that a stock is selling at less than book value does not necessarily indicate a bargain.

Book value is a historical concept, representing the amounts invested by shareholders plus the amounts earned and retained by the corporation. If a stock is selling at a price well ***above*** book value, investors believe that management has created a business worth substantially more than the historical cost of the resources entrusted to its care. This, in essence, is the sign of a successful corporation. If the excess of market price over book value becomes very great, however, investors should consider whether the company's prospects really justify a market price so much above the underlying book value of the company's resources.

On the other hand, if the market price of a stock is ***less than*** book value, investors believe that the company's resources are worth less than their cost while under the control of current management. Thus, the relationship between book value and market price is one measure of investors' confidence in a company's management.

Balance Sheet for a Corporation Illustrated

A fairly complete balance sheet for a corporation is illustrated below and on the following page. Note the inclusion in this balance sheet of liabilities for income taxes payable and dividends payable. These liabilities do not appear in the balance sheet of an unincorporated business. Note also that the caption for each capital stock account indicates the type of capital stock and the number of shares authorized and issued. The caption for preferred stock also indicates the dividend rate, call price, and other important features.

Bear in mind that current practice includes many alternatives in the choice of terminology and the arrangement of items in financial statements.

DEL MAR CORPORATION
Balance Sheet
December 31, 1996

Assets

Current assets:		
Cash and cash equivalents		*$ 305,600*
Accounts receivable (net)		*1,215,200*
Inventories (lower of FIFO and net realizable value)		*1,300,800*
Short-term prepayments		*125,900*
Total current assets		*$2,947,500*
Plant and equipment:		
Land—at cost		*900,000*
Buildings and equipment—at cost	*$5,283,000*	
Less: Accumulated depreciation	*1,250,000*	*4,033,000*
Other assets: *Organization costs*		*14,000*
Total assets		*$7,894,500*

Liabilities & Shareholders' Equity

Current liabilities:		
Accounts payable		$ 998,100
Income taxes payable		324,300
Dividends payable		109,700
Interest payable		20,000
Total current liabilities		$1,452,100
Long-term liabilities: Bonds payable, 12%, due Oct. 1, 2006		1,000,000
Total liabilities		$2,452,100
Shareholders' equity:		
Cumulative $8 preferred stock, no-par, callable at $104, authorized, an unlimited number of shares, issued and outstanding, 10,000 shares	$1,000,000	
Common stock, no-par, authorized, an unlimited number of shares, issued and outstanding, 600,000 shares	2,670,000	
Common stock subscribed, 2,500 shares	20,000	
Donated capital	210,000	
Total contributed capital	$3,900,000	
Retained earnings	1,542,400	
Total shareholders' equity		$5,442,400
Total liabilities & shareholders' equity		$7,894,500

CHAPTER REVIEW

KEY TERMS INTRODUCED OR EMPHASIZED IN CHAPTER 14

Board of directors Persons elected by common shareholders to direct the affairs of a corporation.

Book value per share The shareholders' equity represented by each share of common stock, computed by dividing common shareholders' equity by the number of common shares outstanding.

Call (redemption) price The price to be paid by a corporation for each share of callable (redeemable) preferred stock if the corporation decides to call (redeem) the preferred stock.

Capital stock Transferable units of ownership in a corporation. A broad term that may refer to common stock, preferred stock, or both.

Closely held corporation A corporation owned by a limited group of shareholders, usually a small corporation.

Common stock A type of capital stock that possesses the basic rights of ownership including the right to vote. Represents the residual element of ownership in a corporation.

Contributed capital The amounts invested in a corporation by its shareholders (also includes donated capital).

Cumulative preferred stock A class of preferred stock with a provision that if dividends are reduced or omitted in any year, this amount of dividends accumulates and must be paid prior to payment of dividends on common stock.

Deficit Accumulated losses incurred by a corporation. A negative amount of retained earnings.

Dividend A distribution of cash by a corporation to its shareholders.

Floating rate A dividend rate for preferred stock that is tied to the bank prime interest rate.

Legal capital Equal to the ***proceeds of no-par value*** or the ***par value*** of capital stock issued. This amount represents a "permanent commitment" of capital by the owners of a corporation and cannot be removed without special legal action. Of course, it may be eroded by losses.

Non-cumulative preferred stock A class of preferred stock with a provision that any dividends omitted in any year are lost forever.

No-par value Capital stock without nominal or par value.

Organization costs Costs incurred to form a corporation.

Par value The ***legal capital*** of a corporation. Represents the minimum amount per share to be invested in the corporation by its owners and cannot be withdrawn except by special legal action.

Preferred stock A class of capital stock usually having preferences as to dividends and in the distribution of assets in event of liquidation.

Premium on capital stock The amount paid in by shareholders for the capital stock in excess of its par value.

Publicly owned corporation A corporation whose ownership shares are offered for sale to the general public.

Retained earnings That portion of shareholders' equity resulting from income earned and retained in the business. Retained earnings is increased by the earning of net income and is decreased by the incurring of net losses and by the declaration of dividends.

Shareholder Someone with an ownership interest in a corporation. The percentage of this ownership interest is determined by the percentage of the outstanding shares owned.

Shareholders' equity The excess of assets over liabilities. The two main sources are investments by the shareholders and earnings from profitable operations.

Shareholders subsidiary ledger A record showing the number of shares owned by each shareholder.

Stock certificate A document issued by a corporation (or its transfer agent) as evidence of the ownership of the number of shares stated on the certificate.

Stock registrar An independent agent retained by a corporation to provide assurance against overissuance of stock certificates.

Stock transfer agent A bank or trust company retained by a corporation to maintain its records of capital stock ownership and to make transfers from one investor to another.

Underwriter An investment dealer who handles the sale of a corporation's capital stock to the public.

DEMONSTRATION PROBLEM FOR YOUR REVIEW

At the close of the current year, the shareholders' equity section of Rockhurst Corporation's balance sheet was as follows:

Shareholders' equity:		
$8 preferred stock, no-par value, authorized, an unlimited number of shares, callable at $102 per share, issued and outstanding, 120,000 shares		*$12,360,000*
Common stock, no-par value, authorized, an unlimited number of shares:		
Issued and outstanding 2,000,000	*$32,000,000*	
Subscribed, 800,000 shares	*12,800,000*	*44,800,000*
Retained earnings		*2,680,000*
Total shareholders' equity		*$59,840,000*

Assets of the corporation include ***subscriptions receivable, $7,200,000.***

INSTRUCTIONS On the basis of this information, answer the following questions and show any necessary supporting computations.

a What is the total annual dividend requirement on the outstanding preferred stock?

b What was the average price per share received by the corporation for its common stock, including shares subscribed?

c What is the average amount per share that subscribers to common stock have yet to pay on their subscriptions?

d What is the total amount of legal capital, including shares subscribed?

e What is the book value per share of common stock? (Assume no dividends in arrears.)

SOLUTION TO DEMONSTRATION PROBLEM

a $960,000 (120,000 shares × $8 per share)

b	*Total issue price of common shares (including subscribed)*	*$44,800,000*
	Shares issued and subscribed (2,000,000 + 800,000)	*2,800,000*
	Average issue price per share ($44,800,000 ÷ 2,800,000 shares)	*$16*
c	*Subscriptions receivable*	*$ 7,200,000*
	Shares subscribed	*800,000*
	Average amount due per share ($7,200,000 ÷ 800,000 shares)	*$9*
d	*$57,160,000 ($12,360,000 preferred, $44,800,000 common)*	
e	*Total shareholders' equity*	*$59,840,000*
	Less: Claims of preferred shareholders (120,000 shares × $102 call price)	*12,240,000*
	Equity of common shareholders	*$47,600,000*
	Common shares outstanding or subscribed (2,000,000 + 800,000)	*2,800,000*
	Book value per share ($47,600,000 ÷ 2,800,000 shares)	*$17*

ASSIGNMENT MATERIAL

DISCUSSION QUESTIONS

1 Why are large corporations often said to be ***publicly owned?***

2 Distinguish between corporations and partnerships in terms of the following characteristics:

a Owners' liability for debts of the business
b Transferability of ownership interest
c Continuity of existence
d Taxation on income

3 What are the basic rights of the owner of a share of corporate stock? In what way are these basic rights commonly modified with respect to the owner of a share of preferred stock?

4 Distinguish between ***contributed capital*** and ***retained earnings*** of a corporation. Why is such a distinction useful?

5 If the Retained Earnings account has a debit balance, how is it presented in the balance sheet and what is it called?

6 Explain the reasons for the emergence of the concept of no-par value capital stock in federal and provincial corporation legislation.

7 Explain the significance of ***par value.*** Does par value indicate the reasonable market price for a share of capital stock? Explain.

8 Describe the usual nature of the following features as they apply to a share of preferred stock: (a) cumulative, (b) convertible, and (c) callable (redeemable).

9 Why is noncumulative preferred stock considered a very unattractive form of investment?

10 When capital stock is issued by a corporation in exchange for assets other than cash, accountants face the problem of determining the dollar amount at which to record the transaction. Discuss the factors to be considered and explain their significance.

11 State the classification (asset, liability, shareholders' equity, revenue, or expense) of each of the following accounts:
a Subscriptions receivable
b Organization costs
c Preferred stock
d Retained earnings
e Capital stock subscribed
f Premium on common stock
g Income taxes payable

12 A professional baseball team received as a gift from the city the land upon which to build a stadium. What effect, if any, will the receipt of this gift have upon the baseball team's balance sheet and income statement? Explain.

13 Explain the following terms:
a Stock transfer agent
b Shareholders subsidiary ledger
c Underwriter
d Stock registrar

14 What does ***book value per share*** of common stock represent? Does it represent the amount common shareholders would receive in the event of liquidation of the corporation? Explain briefly.

15 How is book value per share of common stock computed when a company has both preferred and common stock outstanding?

16 What would be the effect, if any, on book value per share of common stock as a result of each of the following independent events: (a) a corporation obtains a bank loan; (b) a dividend is declared (to be paid in the next accounting period).

17 In the great stock market crash of October 19, 1987, the market price of **IBM's** capital stock fell by over $31 per share. Explain the effects, if any, of this decline in share price on IBM's balance sheet.

MULTIPLE CHOICE QUESTIONS

1 When a business is organized as a corporation:

a Shareholders are liable for the debts of the business only in proportion to their percentage ownership of capital stock.

b Shareholders do ***not*** have to pay personal income taxes on dividends received, because the corporation is subject to income taxes on its earnings.

c Fluctuations in the market value of outstanding shares of capital stock do ***not*** affect the amount of shareholders' equity shown in the balance sheet.

d Each shareholder has the right to bind the corporation to contracts and to make other managerial decisions.

2 Great Plains Corporation was organized with authorization to issue 100,000 shares of no-par value common stock. Forty thousand shares were issued to Tom Morgan, the company's founder, at a price of $5 per share. No other shares have yet been issued.

a Morgan owns ***40%*** of the shareholders' equity of the corporation.

b The corporation should recognize a $200,000 gain on the issuance of these shares.

c If the balance sheet includes retained earnings of $50,000, total ***contributed*** capital amounts to $250,000.

d In the balance sheet, the Common Stock account will have a $200,000 balance, regardless of the income earned or losses incurred since the corporation was organized.

3 Which of the following is ***not*** a characteristic of the ***common stock*** of a large, publicly owned corporation?

a The shares may be transferred from one investor to another without disrupting the continuity of business operations.

b Voting rights in the election of the board of directors.

c A cumulative right to receive dividends.

d After issuance, the market value of the stock is unrelated to its issued price or par value.

4 Tri-County Electric is a profitable utility company that has increased its dividend to ***common*** shareholders every year for 62 consecutive years. Which of the following is ***least*** likely to affect the market price of the company's ***preferred*** stock?

a The company's earnings are expected to increase significantly over the next several years.

b An increase in long-term interest rates.

c The annual dividend paid to preferred shareholders.

d Whether or not the preferred stock carries a conversion privilege.

5 The following information is taken from the balance sheet and related disclosures of Blue Oyster Corporation:

Total contributed capital	*$5,400,000*
Outstanding shares:	
Common stock, no-par value	*100,000 shares*
$6 preferred stock, no-par value, callable at $108 per share, issued at $100 per share	*10,000 shares*
Preferred dividends in arrears	*2 years*
Total shareholders' equity	*$4,700,000*

Which of the following statements is true? (More than one answer may be correct.)

a The preferred dividends in arrears amount to $120,000 and should appear as a liability in the corporate balance sheet.

b The book value per share of common stock is $35.

c The shareholders' equity section of the balance sheet should include a deficit of $700,000.

d The company has paid no dividend on its ***common*** stock during the past two years.

EXERCISES

EXERCISE 14-1
Accounting Terminology

Listed below are nine technical accounting terms introduced or emphasized in this chapter:

Retained earnings	*Preferred stock*	*No-par value*
Deficit	*Common stock*	*Book value*
Dividend in arrears	*Contributed capital*	*Market value*

Each of the following statements may (or may not) describe one of these technical terms. For each statement, indicate the term described, or answer "None" if the statement does not correctly describe any of the terms.

a That portion of shareholders' equity arising from the issuance of capital stock.

b The type of capital stock most likely to increase in value as a corporation becomes increasingly profitable.

c The net assets represented by one share of common stock.

d A distribution of cash by a corporation to its owners.

e The type of capital stock for which the dividend usually is fixed in amount.

f Cash provided by profitable operations that is available for distribution to shareholders as dividends.

g The per-share value of common stock that reflects investors' expectations of future profitability.

h A dividend paid to common shareholders that is smaller than the dividend paid in the prior year.

EXERCISE 14-2
Computing Retained Earnings

Johnson Pump, Inc., began operations in 1995. In that year, the corporation earned net income of $195,000 and paid dividends of $2.25 per share on its 40,000 outstanding shares of capital stock. In 1996, the corporation incurred a net loss of $127,000 and paid no dividends.

INSTRUCTIONS

a Prepare the journal entry to close the Income Summary account at December 31, 1996 (the year of the $127,000 net loss).

b Compute the amount of retained earnings or deficit that will appear in the company's balance sheet at December 31, 1996.

EXERCISE 14-3
Recording Dividends

Westfall Corporation has outstanding 60,000 shares of no-par value common stock, which were issued for $22 per share. The net income in the first year of operations was $235,000. On December 31, the board of directors declared a dividend of $1.50 per share, payable on January 31 of the following year.

INSTRUCTIONS

a Prepare the journal entries at December 31 of the first year (1) to close the Income Summary account and (2) to record declaration of the dividend.

b Prepare the journal entry to record payment of the dividend on January 31 of the second year.

c Compute the amount of retained earnings reported in Westfall's balance sheet at ***December 31,*** the end of the first year of operations.

d Assume that the board of directors of Westfall did not meet on December 31 as above but waited until January 15 of the second year because the chairperson was on vacation. On January 15, they declared the dividend of $1.50 per share payable on February 15. Compute the amount of retained earnings that would have been reported in Westfall's balance sheet at ***December 31,*** the end of the first year of operations in this situation.

EXERCISE 14-4
Shareholders' Equity Section of a Balance Sheet

When Enviro Systems, Inc., was formed, the company was authorized to issue an unlimited number of shares of no-par value, $8 cumulative preferred stock, and an unlimited number of no-par value common stock. The preferred stock is callable at $106.

Then 2,500 shares of the preferred stock were issued at a price of $103 per share, and 70,000 shares of the common stock were sold for $13 per share. At the end of the current year, Enviro Systems, Inc., has retained earnings of $297,000. Prepare the shareholders' equity section of the company's balance sheet at the end of the current year.

EXERCISE 14-5
Dividends: Preferred and Common

The shareholders' equity at December 31, 1996, of Palermo Corporation appears below:

Shareholders' equity:	
Preferred stock, $4.50 cumulative, no-par, 40,000 shares issued and outstanding	*$2,000,000*
Preferred stock, $12, noncumulative, no-par, 8,000 shares issued	*800,000*
Common stock, no-par, 400,000 shares issued and outstanding	*4,800,000*
Retained earnings	*890,000*
Total shareholders' equity	*$8,490,000*

INSTRUCTIONS

Assume that all the stock was issued on January 1, 1994, and that no dividends were paid during the first two years of operations. During 1996 Palermo Corporation declared and paid total cash dividends of $736,000.

a Compute the amount of cash dividends paid during 1996 to each of the three classes of stock.

b Compute the dividends paid ***per share*** during 1996 for each of the three classes of stock.

c Palermo Corporation generated a net loss of $190,000 in 1994 and earned net income of $627,000 in 1995. Compute the amount of net income (or net loss) generated by Palermo during 1996.

EXERCISE 14-6
Computing Retained Earnings

Wolfe Company has outstanding two classes of no-par value stock: 5,000 shares of $8 cumulative preferred and 25,000 shares of common. The company had a $50,000 deficit at the beginning of the current year, and preferred dividends had not been paid for two years. During the current year, the company earned $300,000. What will be the balance in retained earnings at the end of the current year, if the company pays a dividend of $2 per share on the common stock?

EXERCISE 14-7
Analyzing Shareholders' Equity

The year-end balance sheet of Maui Corporation includes the following shareholders' equity section (with certain details omitted):

Shareholders' equity:	
$8.25 cumulative preferred stock, $100 par value, callable at $105	*$ 12,000,000*
Common stock, $5 par value, 5,000,000 shares authorized	*20,000,000*
Premium on preferred	*240,000*
Premium on common	*31,200,000*
Retained earnings	*57,160,000*
Total shareholders' equity	*$120,600,000*

INSTRUCTIONS

From this information, compute answers to the following questions:

a How many shares of preferred stock have been issued?

b What is the total amount of the annual dividends paid to preferred shareholders?

c What was the average issuance price per share of common stock?

d What is the amount of total contributed capital?

e What is the book value per share of common stock?

EXERCISE 14-8
Issuing Stock for Assets Other Than Cash

Kato Manufacturing issued 45,000 shares of common stock in exchange for land with a fair market value of $790,000. Prepare the journal entry to record this transaction under each of the following independent assumptions:

a The stock has a $2 par value.

b The stock has a $10 par value.

c The stock has no par value.

EXERCISE 14-9
Stock Subscriptions

To raise capital for a new polo field, Santa Fe Polo Club offered shares of its common stock to club members on a subscription plan. Prepare journal entries in the club's accounting records to record the following transactions:

Sept. 15 Members subscribed to 30,000 shares of no-par value common stock at a subscription price of $25 per share.

Dec. 20 Collected $300,000 cash in full payment of 12,000 of the subscribed shares. Issued stock certificates for these shares.

EXERCISE 14-10
Computing Book Value

Presented below is the information necessary to compute the net assets (shareholders' equity) and book value per share of common stock for Ahora Advertising, Inc.:

$8 cumulative preferred stock, no-par (callable at $110), issued and outstanding, 3,000 shares	*$ 300,000*
Common stock, no-par, issued and outstanding, 90,000 shares	*1,129,200*
Deficit	*130,200*
Dividends in arrears on preferred stock, 1 full year	*24,000*

INSTRUCTIONS

a Compute the amount of net assets (shareholders' equity).

b Compute the book value per share of common stock.

EXERCISE 14-11
Nature of Market, Par, and Book Values

International Business Micro-comp (IBM), the world's largest manufacturer of microcomputers, has had a long track record of growing sales and earnings. In December 1994, however, IBM announced projected revenue growth of only 6% for 1995, below the computer industry average. In addition, heavy competition would enable IBM to hold gross profit margins at just 51% to 53%, several points below what analysts had expected. According to company management, this lower-than-expected growth projection will not affect the company's ability or commitment to continue paying dividends at the current rate.

What would you expect the immediate effect of this announcement to be upon the following values of IBM's common stock? Explain.

a Par value

b Market value

c Book value

PROBLEMS

Group A

PROBLEM 14A-1
Journal Entries for Corporate Transactions

Shown below are five selected transactions of Reclamation Systems, Inc., for the year ended December 31, 1996:

Jan. 15 Paid a cash dividend totalling $45,000. This dividend was declared on December 15, 1995, payable on January 15, 1996.

June 19 Issued an additional 20,000 shares of no-par value capital stock to Baldwin Development Corporation in exchange for an adjoining parcel of land needed for expansion. The stock of Reclamation Systems is not widely traded. Although Baldwin paid $385,000 for the land 5 years ago, two independent appraisals have estimated the value of the real estate to be $310,000 on this date.

Dec. 15 The board of directors declared a dividend of 30 cents per share, payable on January 15, 1997, to the owners of the corporation's 170,000 outstanding shares of capital stock.

Dec. 31 Recorded income tax expense for the three-month period ended December 31, 1996, $54,200. These taxes will be paid in early 1997. (Income taxes for the first nine months of 1996, amounting to $184,600, have already been recorded and paid.)

Dec. 31 Closed the Income Summary account at the end of a profitable year. Net income, $472,000.

INSTRUCTIONS

a Prepare journal entries to record the above transactions.

b Assume the balance sheet of Reclamation Systems at December 31, 1995, reported retained earnings of $1,516,000. Compute the amount of retained earnings to be reported in the corporation's balance sheet at December 31, ***1996.*** Show computation.

PROBLEM 14A-2
Shareholders' Equity in the Balance Sheet

Bauman Pharmaceutics was organized early in 1990 with authorization to issue an unlimited number of no-par value preferred stock and of no-par value common stock. Fifty thousand preferred stock were issued at $100 each, and 600,000 shares of common stock were sold for $16 per share. The preferred stock pays a $9 cumulative dividend and is callable at $110.

During the first five years of operations (1990 through 1994), the corporation earned a total of $6,920,000 and paid dividends of 50 cents per share each year on the common stock. In 1995, however, the corporation reported a net loss of $2,400,000 and paid no dividends.

INSTRUCTIONS

a Prepare the shareholders' equity section of the balance sheet at December 31, 1995. Prepare a separate supporting schedule showing your computation of the amount of retained earnings or deficit.

b Draft a footnote to accompany the financial statements disclosing any dividends in arrears at the end of 1995.

PROBLEM 14A-3 Shareholders' Equity Section—A More Challenging Problem

Tomahawk Tools, Inc., was organized in January 1992. The corporation issued at $8 per share 100,000 of its unlimited authorized shares of no-par common stock. On January 2, ***1993,*** the company sold at $60 per share the entire 10,000 authorized shares of $50 par value, 8% cumulative preferred stock. On January 2, ***1994,*** the company again needed money and issued 5,000 shares of its unlimited authorized shares of $11, no-par, cumulative preferred stock for a total of $518,000.

The company suffered losses and paid no dividends during 1992 and 1993, reporting a deficit of $200,000 at the end of 1993. During 1994 and 1995 combined, the company earned a total of $800,000. Dividends of $0.75 per share were paid on common stock in 1994 and $1.50 per share in 1995.

INSTRUCTIONS

Prepare the shareholders' equity section of the balance sheet at December 31, 1995. Include a separate supporting schedule showing your computation of retained earnings or deficit at this balance sheet date.

PROBLEM 14A-4 Journal Entries and Shareholders' Equity: A Short, Comprehensive Problem

Pat Breeden has been working in the child care field for many years as both a child care provider and as a consultant. She and several associates recently formed a corporation, Wee Care, Inc., to provide organization and administration of on-site child care programs for large employers. The corporation is authorized to issue 100,000 shares of $100 par value, $8 cumulative preferred stock and an unlimited number of shares of no-par value common stock. The following transactions (among others) occurred during the first year of operations:

Jan. 5 Issued for cash 20,000 shares of common stock at $14 per share. The shares were issued to Breeden and 10 other investors.

Jan. 8 Issued 4,500 shares of preferred stock for cash of $518,400.

Feb. 10 Issued an additional 500 shares of common stock to Breeden in exchange for her services in organizing the corporation. The shareholders agreed that these services were worth $7,000.

Nov. 15 The board of directors declares the first annual dividend on the preferred stock, to be paid on December 15.

Nov. 27 Acquired land as a future building site in exchange for 15,000 shares of common stock. Wee Care's stock is not widely traded on any organized exchange, but the parcel of land has been appraised at approximately $225,000 by two different independent appraisers.

Dec. 15 Paid the cash dividend declared on November 15.

Dec. 31 After the revenue and expenses (except income taxes) were closed into the Income Summary account, that account showed a before-tax income of $216,000. Income taxes were determined to be $59,440.

INSTRUCTIONS

a Prepare journal entries in general journal form to record the above transactions. Include entries at December 31 to (1) record the income tax liability, (2) close the Income Taxes Expense account into the Income Summary account, and (3) close the Income Summary account.

b Prepare the shareholders' equity section of the Wee Care, Inc., balance sheet at December 31.

PROBLEM 14A-5
Starting a New Corporation; Includes Stock Subscriptions

Pancho's Cantina is the best Mexican restaurant in town—maybe the best anywhere. For years, the restaurant was a sole proprietorship owned by Wayne Label. Many of Label's friends and customers had offered to invest in the business if he ever decided to open new locations. So, early this year, Label decided to expand the business. He formed a new corporation, called Pancho's Cantinas, Inc., which planned to issue capital stock and use the money received to open new restaurants in various locations.

The new corporation is authorized to issue an unlimited number of shares of no-par value capital stock. In May the corporation entered into the following transactions:

May 1 Received subscriptions from various investors for 30,000 shares of capital stock to be issued at a price of $25 per share.

May 24 Received an invoice from a lawyer for $7,100 for services relating to the formation of the new corporation. This invoice is due in 30 days.

May 28 Received $75,000 cash as full payment from Alan Richmond, an investor who had subscribed to 3,000 shares of capital stock. A stock certificate was immediately issued to Richmond for 3,000 shares. (No payments have been received from the subscribers to the other 27,000 shares.)

May 31 Issued 30,000 shares of capital stock to Label in exchange for the assets of the original Pancho's Cantina. These assets and their current market values on this date are listed below.

Inventory	*$ 23,000*
Land	*325,000*
Building	*260,000*
Equipment and fixtures	*142,000*

May 31 Issued 200 shares of capital stock to Label in exchange for $5,000 cash, thus assuring Label voting control of the corporation even after the other investors pay for their subscribed shares.

The new corporation will begin operation of the original Pancho's Cantina on June 1. Therefore, the corporation had no revenue or expenses relating to restaurant operations during May. No depreciation of plant assets or amortization of organization costs will be recognized until June, when operations get under way.

INSTRUCTIONS

a Prepare journal entries to record the May transactions in the accounting records of the new corporation.

b Prepare a classified balance sheet for the corporation as of May 31, 19__.

PROBLEM 14A-6
Analysis of an Equity Section of a Balance Sheet

The year-end balance sheet of DeskTop Products includes the following shareholders' equity section (with certain details omitted):

Shareholders' equity:	
$9.60 cumulative preferred stock, no-par value, redeemable at $110, authorized unlimited shares, issued and outstanding 28,000 shares	*$ 2,800,000*
Common stock, no-par value, authorized unlimited shares, issued and outstanding 420,000 shares	*8,400,000*
Donated capital	*600,000*
Retained earnings	*6,400,000*
Total shareholders' equity	*$18,200,000*

INSTRUCTIONS From this information, compute answers to the following questions:

a What was the average issuance price of a share of preferred stock?

b What is the total dollar amount of the annual dividend requirement on preferred stock?

c What was the average issuance price of a share of common stock?

d What is the current book value per share of common stock?

e What is the total contributed capital?

f Total dividends of $1,012,000 were declared on the preferred and common stock during the year, and the balance of retained earnings at the beginning of the year was $5,184,000. What was the amount of net income for the year?

Group B

PROBLEM 14B-1
Journal Entries for Corporate Transactions

Shown below are selected transactions of St. Claire Vineyards for the year ended December 31, 1996:

Jan. 19 Issued capital stock to Martin DiBello in exchange for land. Two firms hired to appraise the land have differing opinions as to the fair market value of the real estate. DiBello, however, agrees to accept 10,000 shares of no-par value capital stock as a fair exchange. St. Claire's stock is widely traded and is quoted at $19 per share on a stock exchange on this date.

June 10 At their June meeting, the board of directors declared a dividend of 20 cents per share, payable on July 15, to owners of the corporation's 200,000 outstanding shares of capital stock.

July 15 Paid the dividend declared on June 10.

Dec. 10 At their December meeting, the board of directors declared a dividend of 25 cents per share, payable on January 15 of the following year. No capital stock has been issued since the January 19 transaction.

Dec. 31 Recorded income tax expense for the three months ended December 31, 1996, $34,900. These taxes will be paid in early 1997. (Income taxes for the first nine months of 1996 have already been recorded and paid.)

Dec. 31 Closed the Income Summary account at the end of a profitable period. Net income, $365,000.

INSTRUCTIONS

a Prepare journal entries to record the above transactions.

b Assume the balance sheet of St. Claire Vineyards at December 31, 1995, reported retained earnings of $1,215,000. Compute the amount of retained earnings to be reported in the corporation's balance sheet at December 31, ***1996.*** Show computation.

PROBLEM 14B-2
Shareholders' Equity in a Balance Sheet

Early in 1992, Sinclair Press was organized with authorization to issue an unlimited number of shares of no-par value preferred stock and of no-par value common stock. Ten thousand shares of the preferred stock were issued at $100 each, and 170,000 shares of common stock were sold for $15 per share. The preferred stock pays an $8 cumulative dividend and is callable at $105.

During the first four years of operations (1992 through 1995), the corporation earned a total of $1,025,000 and paid dividends of 75 cents per share each year on the common stock. In 1996, however, the corporation reported a net loss of $340,000 and paid no dividends.

INSTRUCTIONS

a Prepare the shareholders' equity section of the balance sheet at December 31, 1996. Include a supporting schedule showing your computation of the amount of retained earnings or deficit.

b Draft a footnote to accompany the financial statements disclosing any dividends in arrears at the end of 1996.

PROBLEM 14B-3 Shareholders' Equity Section—A More Challenging Problem

Maria Martinez organized Manhattan Transport Limited in January 1993. The corporation immediately issued at $7.50 per share 100,000 of its unlimited authorized shares of no-par common stock. On January 2, ***1994,*** the corporation sold at $110 per share the entire 5,000 authorized shares of 8%, $100 par value, cumulative preferred stock. On January 2, ***1995,*** the company again needed money and issued 5,000 shares of its unlimited authorized shares of $9, no-par, cumulative preferred stock for a total of $512,000.

The company suffered losses in its first two years reporting a deficit of $170,000 at the end of 1994. During 1995 and 1996 combined, the company earned a total of $890,000. Dividends of 50 cents per share were paid on common stock in 1995 and $1.60 per share in 1996.

INSTRUCTIONS

Prepare the shareholders' equity section of the balance sheet at December 31, 1996. Include a supporting schedule showing your computation of retained earnings or deficit at the balance sheet date.

PROBLEM 14B-4 Dividends, Closing Entries, and Shareholders' Equity

Hua Lai organized Pacific Rim Corporation early in 1995. On January 9, the corporation issued to Hua Lai and other investors 100,000 of its unlimited authorized shares of no-par value common stock at a price of $9 per share.

After the revenue and expense accounts (except income taxes expense) were closed into the Income Summary account at the end of the year, that account showed a before-tax income of $288,000. Income taxes were determined to be $64,000. No dividends were paid during 1995.

On January 15, 1996, the board of directors declared a cash dividend of 75 cents per share, payable February 15.

INSTRUCTIONS

a Prepare the journal entries for 1995 to (1) record the issuance of the common stock, (2) record the income tax liability at December 31, (3) close the Income Taxes Expense account into the Income Summary account, and (4) close the Income Summary account.

b Prepare the journal entries in 1996 for the declaration of the dividend on January 15 and payment of the dividend on February 15.

c Operations in 1996 resulted in a $158,800 net loss. Prepare the journal entry to close the Income Summary account at December 31, 1996.

d Prepare the shareholders' equity section of the balance sheet at December 31, 1996. Include a separate supporting schedule showing your determination of retained earnings or deficit at that date. Disregard the possibility of an income tax refund.

PROBLEM 14B-5 Issuance of Capital Stock and Stock Subscriptions

For several years, Kathryn Mead has operated a successful business organized as a sole proprietorship. In order to raise the capital to operate on a larger scale, she decided to organize a new corporation to continue in the same line of business. In January, Mead organized Down Home, Inc., which was authorized to issue unlimited shares of no-par value common stock. During January, Down Home, Inc., completed the following transactions:

Jan. 9 Issued 8,000 shares of common stock to various investors for cash at $32 per share.

Jan. 12 Issued 27,000 shares of common stock to Mead in exchange for assets with a current market value as follows:

Inventory	*$198,000*
Land	*235,000*
Building	*124,000*
Equipment	*307,000*

Jan. 14 Received an invoice from a lawyer for $8,950 for services relating to the formation of Down Home, Inc. The invoice will be paid in 30 days.

Jan. 15 Received subscriptions for 7,000 shares of common stock at $32 per share; 2,000 of the shares were subscribed by Mead and 5,000 were subscribed by other investors.

Jan. 31 Collected from Mead the full amount of her subscription to 2,000 shares of common stock and issued a stock certificate for these shares. (No collection has yet been made from the subscribers to the other 5,000 shares.)

The corporation will begin operations in February; no revenue was earned and no expenses were incurred during January. No depreciation of plant assets and no amortization of organization cost will be recognized until February, when operations get under way.

INSTRUCTIONS

a Prepare journal entries to record the transactions for January in the accounting records for Down Home, Inc.

b Prepare a classified balance sheet for the corporation at January 31.

PROBLEM 14B-6
Analysis of Shareholders' Equity

The year-end balance sheet of LaserTech, Inc., includes the following shareholders' equity section (with certain details omitted):

Shareholders' equity:	
$8.80 cumulative preferred stock, $100 par value, callable at $110, authorized 30,000 shares	*$ 1,200,000*
Common stock, no-par value, authorized unlimited shares, issued and outstanding, 310,000 shares	*7,440,000*
Premium on preferred stock	*60,000*
Donated capital	*960,000*
Retained earnings	*4,680,000*
Total shareholders' equity	*$14,340,000*

INSTRUCTIONS

On the basis of this information, answer the following questions and show any necessary supporting computations:

a How many shares of preferred stock are outstanding?

b What is the amount of the annual dividend requirement on preferred stock?

c What was the average issuance price of a share of common stock?

d What was the average issuance price of a share of preferred stock?

e What is the current book value per share of common stock?

f What is the total contributed capital?

g Assume that net income for the year was $2,100,000 and the balance of retained earnings at the beginning of the year was $3,302,000. What was the amount of dividend declared during the year for the preferred and common stock?

ANALYTICAL AND DECISION PROBLEMS AND CASES

A&D 14-1
Par, Book, and Market Values. An Open-Ended Discussion

Microsoft Corp. is the producer of such software products as ***Windows, Excel,*** and ***Word.*** In mid-1990, an investment service published the following per-share amounts relating to Microsoft's only class of capital stock:

Par value	*$ 0.001*
Book value (estimated)	*6.50*
Market value	*73.00*

INSTRUCTIONS

a Without reference to dollar amounts, explain the nature and significance of ***par value, book value,*** and ***market value.***

b Comment upon the ***interrelationships,*** if any, among the per-share amounts shown for Microsoft Corp. What do these amounts imply about the company and its operations? Also comment upon what these amounts imply about the security of ***creditors'*** claims against the company.

A&D 14-2
Issuing Stock for Assets Other Than Cash

The following independent cases involve the issuance of capital stock in exchange for assets other than cash.

1 DuPar Corporation, a successful, family-owned company, is in the process of acquiring a tract of land suitable for the construction of a factory. The DuPar Corporation has agreed to offer 26,000 shares of common stock in exchange for the land, which has an agreed fair market value of $650,000, based on two independent appraisals. DuPar Corporation stock is not traded on any stock exchange.

INSTRUCTIONS

Give the journal entry that should be made to record this transaction under each of the following assumptions:

a The stock has a $2 par value.

b The stock has ***no*** par value.

2 Irwin Products, a well-established company, issued 3,800 shares of its $5 par value common stock in exchange for certain patents. The patents were entered in the accounts at $19,000. At this time, Irwin Products common stock was quoted on the over-the-counter market at "25 bid and 27 asked"; that is, sellers were offering stock at $27 per share, and buyers were offering to buy at $25 per share.

INSTRUCTIONS

a Comment on the company's treatment of this transaction. Write a brief statement explaining whether you agree or disagree, and why.

b What is the essential difference between the evidence available to the accountant as a basis for the record of DuPar Corporation and the evidence available for Irwin Products?

A&D 14-3
Factors Affecting the Market Prices of Preferred and Common Stocks

ADM Labs is a publicly owned company with several issues of capital stock outstanding. Over the past decade, the company has consistently earned modest income and has increased its common stock dividend annually by 5 or 10 cents per share. Recently the company introduced several new products that you believe will cause future sales and income to increase dramatically. You also expect a gradual increase in long-term interest rates from their present level of about 9% to, perhaps, 10% or $10\frac{1}{2}$%. Based upon these forecasts, explain whether you would expect to see the market prices of the following issues of ADM capital stock increase or decrease. Explain your reasoning in each answer.

a 8%, $100 par value, preferred stock (currently selling at $90 per share)

b No-par value common stock (currently paying an annual dividend of $1.20 and selling at $40 per share)

c $5, no-par value, convertible preferred stock (currently selling at $119 per share)

A&D 14-4
Whether or Not To Incorporate

Mario Valenti owns Valenti Ford, a successful automobile dealership. For 25 years, Valenti has operated the business as a sole proprietorship and has acted as both owner and manager. Now, he is 70 years old and is planning on retiring from active management. However, he wants the dealership to stay in the family; his long-term goal is to leave the business to his two children and five grandchildren.

Valenti is wondering whether or not he should incorporate his business. If he were to reorganize Valenti Ford as a corporation, he could then leave an appropriate number of shares of capital stock to each of his heirs. Otherwise, he could leave the entire business to his heirs to be operated as a partnership. In selecting the appropriate form of business entity, Valenti has formulated the following objectives:

1 **Ownership:** Valenti wants each of his two children to own 25% of the business and each of his five grandchildren to own 10%.

2 **Continuity of existence:** Valenti wants the business to continue indefinitely, even if one or more of the heirs should die or should no longer want to participate in ownership.

3 **Management:** When Valenti retires, he plans to give Joe Heinz, a long-time employee, responsibility for managing the business. Although Valenti wants to keep the ownership of the business in the family, he does not believe that any of his family members have the time or experience to manage the business on a daily basis. In fact, Valenti believes that two of his grandchildren simply have no "business sense," and he does not want them to participate in management.

4 **Income taxes:** Valenti wants to organize the business in a manner that will minimize the income taxes to be paid by his heirs. He expects that all the earnings of the business normally will be distributed to its owners on an annual basis.

5 **Owners' liability:** Valenti recognizes that an automobile dealership might become liable for vast amounts of money, if, for example, improper repairs caused a customer's car to be involved in an accident. Although the business carries insurance, he wants to be sure that his heirs' equity in the business does not place their personal assets at risk in the event of business losses.

INSTRUCTIONS

a For each of the five numbered paragraphs above, explain how the choice of business organization (partnership or corporation) relates to Valenti's stated objective.

b In light of your analysis in part **a**, above, would you recommend that Valenti reorganize Valenti Ford as a corporation, or leave the business unincorporated so that his heirs may operate it as a partnership?

A&D 14-5
Dividend Distribution and Policy

Sarkis Corporation has been in business for a number of years. Even though it has been profitable, Sarkis Corporation's performance has been erratic: 1995, net loss of $182,000; 1996, net income of $212,000; and 1997, net income of $298,000. The shareholders' equity of Sarkis at December 31, 1994 showed, among other items, the following:

Capital stock issued and outstanding:	
$8 noncumulative preferred, 5,000 shares	*$ 500,000*
$6 cumulative preferred, 6,000 shares	*600,000*
$5 cumulative fully-participating preferred, 10,000 shares	*1,000,000*
Common, 100,000 shares	*2,000,000*
Retained earnings	*810,000*

There were no capital stock transactions for the years 1995 to 1997.

INSTRUCTIONS

a Compute the amount of dividends for each of the four classes of capital stock for the years 1995, 1996 and 1997, based on the following dividend policies:
  1 Distribute an amount that is the greater of the regular dividends or the net income for the year.
  2 Distribute an amount that is equal to the net income for the year.

b Based on the answers in **a** above, which dividend policy is more beneficial to the common shareholders? Explain.

CHAPTER

15 Corporations: Operations and Additional Shareholders' Equity Transactions

In this chapter we explore special topics relating primarily to the financial statements of large corporations. The chapter is divided into two major parts. In the first part, we show how an income statement is organized to present certain "unusual" items separately from the income or loss from normal business activities. Also, we illustrate and explain the presentation of earnings per share, with emphasis upon the interpretation of the different per-share amounts. In the second part, we look at various shareholders' equity transactions, including cash dividends, stock dividends, stock splits, prior period adjustments, and treasury stock transactions. Also, we explain the presentation of the statement of retained earnings.

Learning Objectives

After studying this chapter you should be able to:

1. *Explain predictive information and its relation to the presentation of discontinued operations, extraordinary items, and accounting changes in the income and other financial statements.*
2. *Compute earnings per share.*
3. *Distinguish between basic and fully diluted earnings per share.*
4. *Account for stock dividends and stock splits, and explain the probable effect of these transactions upon market price.*
5. *Describe and prepare a statement of retained earnings.*
6. *Define prior period adjustments and explain how they are presented in financial statements.*
7. *Account for treasury stock transactions.*

REPORTING THE RESULTS OF OPERATIONS

The most important aspect of corporate financial reporting, in the view of most shareholders, is the determination of periodic net income. Both the market price of common stock and the amount of cash dividends per share depend to a considerable extent on the current level of earnings (net income). Even more important than the absolute amount of net income is the ***trend*** of earnings over time.

Developing Predictive Information in the Income Statement

OBJECTIVE 1 ***Explain predictive information and its relation to the presentation of discontinued operations, extraordinary items, and accounting changes in the income and other financial statements.***

An income statement tells us a great deal about the performance of a company over the past year. For example, study of the income statement makes clear the types and amounts of revenue earned and expenses incurred as well as the amounts of gross profit and net income. But can we expect this year's income statement to predict ***next year's*** performance? If the transactions summarized in the income statement for the year just completed were of a normal recurring nature, such as selling merchandise, paying employees, and incurring other normal expenses, we can reasonably assume that the operating results were typical and that somewhat similar results can be expected in the following year. However, in any business, unusual and nonrecurring events may occur that cause the current year's net income to be quite different from the net income we should expect the company to earn in the future. For example, the company may have sustained large losses in the current year from an earthquake or some other event that is not likely to recur in the near future.

Ideally, the results of unusual and nonrecurring events should be shown in a separate section of the income statement ***after*** the income or loss from normal business activities has been determined. Income from ***normal and recurring*** activities presumably should be a more useful figure for ***predicting future earnings*** than is a net income figure that includes the results of nonrecurring events. The problem in creating such an income statement, however, is in determining which events are so unlikely to recur that they should be excluded from the results of "normal" operations. The categories of events that require special treatment in the income statement are (1) the results of discontinued operations and (2) extraordinary items. An income statement with such separate disclosure can serve as a basis for evaluating past performance and for predicting future performance.

Reporting Unusual Events—An Illustration

To illustrate the presentation of these events, assume that Ross Corporation operates both a small chain of retail stores and two motels. Near the end of the current year, the company sells both motels to a national hotel chain. In addition, Ross Corporation reports two "extraordinary items." An income statement illustrating the correct format for reporting these events appears as follows:

ROSS CORPORATION
Income Statement
For the Year Ended December 31, 1996

Net sales		*$8,000,000*
Cost and expenses:		
Cost of goods sold	*$4,580,000*	
Selling expenses	*1,500,000*	
General and administrative expenses	*920,000*	
Income taxes (on continuing operations)	*300,000*	*7,300,000*
Income from continuing operations		*$ 700,000*
Discontinued operations:		
Operating loss on motels (net of $90,000 income tax benefit)	*$ (210,000)*	
Gain on sale of motels (net of $195,000 income taxes)	*455,000*	*245,000*
Income before extraordinary items		*$ 945,000*
Extraordinary items:		
Gain on expropriation of land for a highway (net of $45,000 income taxes)	*$ 105,000*	
Loss from earthquake damage to a retail store (net of $75,000 income tax benefit)	*(175,000)*	*(70,000)*
Net income		*$ 875,000*

Notice the order in which the "special items" are reported

This income statement is designed to illustrate the presentation of various "unusual events." Rarely, if ever, will all these types of events appear in the income statement of one company within a single year.

Continuing Operations

The first section of the income statement contains only the results of ***continuing business activities***—that is, the retail stores. Notice that the income taxes expense shown in this section relates ***only to continuing operations.*** The income taxes relating to the "unusual events" are shown separately in the income statement as adjustments to the amounts of these items.

Income from Continuing Operations The subtotal ***income from continuing operations*** measures the profitability of the ongoing operations. This subtotal should be helpful in making predictions of the company's future earnings. For example, if we predict no significant change in the profitability of its retail stores, we would expect Ross Corporation to earn a net income of approximately $700,000 next year.

Discontinued Operations

If management has sold or discontinued a ***segment*** of the business, or enters into a formal plan to sell or discontinue a ***segment*** of the business, the results of that segment's operations are shown separately in the income statement. This enables users of the financial statements to better evaluate the performance of the company's ongoing (continuing) operations and to better predict the company's future performance.

Two items are included in the "discontinued operations" section of the income statement: (1) the income or loss from ***operating*** the segment prior to its disposal, net of applicable income taxes and (2) the gain or loss on ***disposal*** of the segment, net of applicable income taxes. Notice also that the income taxes relating to the discontinued operations are ***shown separately*** from the income taxes expense relating to continuing business operations.

Discontinued Operations Must Be a "Segment" of the Business To qualify for separate presentation in the income statement, the discontinued operations must represent an ***entire segment*** of the business. A "segment" of a business is a separate line of business activity or an operation that services a particular class of customers. For example, the sale of an oil and gas operation by a real estate company or the sale of the wholesale division selling food to retail stores by a company whose other operations consist of selling food through its restaurants would constitute a disposal of a segment of business.[1]

CASE IN POINT Large corporations usually have many segments of business. Imasco has four segments, one of which is the Shoppers Drug Mart. If Imasco closes an individual Shoppers Drug Mart store, such a closure does not qualify as "discontinued operations" because Imasco remains in the drug store business. However, if Imasco were to sell the entire Shoppers Drug Mart operation, the drug store activities would be shown in Imasco's income statement as "discontinued operations."

Discontinued Operations Are Not Really "Unusual" In recent years, a characteristic of the Canadian economy has been the "restructuring" of many large corporations. As part of this restructuring, corporations often sell one or more segments of the business. Thus, the presence of "discontinued operations" is not uncommon in the income statements of large corporations.

CASE IN POINT Some time ago, George Weston Limited (the fourth largest company in Canada) disposed of its Canadian InterBake biscuit business, its Peter J. Schmitt wholesale operation in the U.S., and its White Swan consumer and industrial tissue product business for a total price tag of more than $389 million. Similarly, Placer Dome, a giant mining company, agreed to sell its U.S. oil and gas operation at about $336 million U.S. so that it could concentrate on mining activities.

[1] CICA, *CICA Handbook* (Toronto), section 3475.05.

Extraordinary Items

The second category of events requiring disclosure in a separate section of the income statement is extraordinary items. Extraordinary items are those items resulting from events or transactions that have met all of the following three characteristics or criteria:

1 not expected to occur frequently over several years
2 not typical of the normal business activities of the entity
3 not dependent primarily on decisions or determinations by management or owners[2]

To clarify the application of these characteristics, the Accounting Standards Board of the CICA has provided some explanations and examples. First, the determination of whether an event is expected to occur frequently over several years requires the determination of the frequency of the occurrence of such events in the recent past and in the foreseeable future. Accordingly, a farmer's crop loss from drought does not meet this first criterion if drought conditions in the area are normally experienced every three or four years.[3]

Second, the factors that determine whether a transaction or event typifies the normal business activities of the entity should include: "type and scope of operations, characteristics of the industry, operating policies, nature of products and services, and the environment in which the entity operates."[4] Thus, the following, regardless of size, do not qualify because they are from normal business activities: (1) losses and provisions for losses with respect to bad debts and inventories, (2) gains and losses from fluctuations in foreign exchange rates, (3) adjustments with respect to contract prices, (4) gains and losses from write-down or sale of property, plant, equipment or other investments, (5) income tax reductions on utilization of prior period losses or reversal of previously recorded tax benefits.[5]

Third, a transaction or event would not depend primarily on decisions or determinations by management or owners "if their decisions or determinations would not normally influence the transactions or events."[6] Therefore, sale of land originally intended for plant expansion, but later held for appreciation, would not meet this criterion.

Because the criteria for extraordinary items are very restrictive, extraordinary items are quite rare. The following are examples that are likely to meet the three criteria recommended in the *CICA Handbook:*

1 The expropriation of a corporation's land and buildings for a highway.
2 The destruction of a large portion of a wheat crop by a tornado.

---

[2] CICA, *CICA Handbook* (Toronto), section 3480.02.

[3] Ibid., section 3480.03.

[4] Ibid., section 3480.04.

[5] Ibid.

[6] Ibid., section 3480.05.

3 An explosion in a nuclear reactor resulting in high-level radioactive emission.

4 The destruction of an airplane of a major airline by a terrorist attack.[7]

When a gain or loss resulting from a transaction or an event qualifies as an extraordinary item, it appears under a ***separate heading*** called ***extraordinary items,*** following the sub-heading "income before extraordinary items," net of applicable income taxes. The nature of the gain or loss should be adequately and clearly described. Such a separate and distinct presentation, as illustrated in the income statement of Ross Corporation, enables users of the financial statements to better evaluate and predict the performance of the company's on-going (continuing) operations.

Accounting Changes

Other matters having an effect on the evaluation and prediction of the trend of earnings include: (1) a change in an accounting policy, (2) a change in an accounting estimate, and (3) a correction of an error in prior period financial statements. These matters are covered by Section 1506, *"Accounting Changes,"* of the *CICA Handbook.* The recommendations of the *CICA Handbook* are highlighted in the following paragraphs.

Changes in Accounting Policy encompass changes in accounting principles as well as accounting methods used in the preparation of financial statements. As stated in Chapter 12 and other chapters, the consistent application of accounting principles and methods from one accounting period to another enhances the usefulness of financial statements on a comparative basis. Also, management may justify a change to another acceptable accounting principle on the grounds that it is more appropriate. For example, a change in determining inventory cost from a weighted-average to a first-in first-out method or a change in recognizing depreciation expense from a straight-line to a declining-balance method constitutes a change in accounting policy, when such a change is ***not*** the result of changed circumstances, experience, or new information.[8]

Since a change in accounting policy affects two or more accounting periods, Section 1506 of the *CICA Handbook* recommends that the effect of an accounting policy change be reflected on a ***retroactive*** basis with a ***restatement*** of those prior period financial statements affected by the change. Thus, each of those prior period financial statements presented on a comparative basis is to be restated to reflect the new accounting policy. In addition, the cumulative effect of the change on the periods preceding the earliest period included in the comparative financial statements is treated as an adjustment to the beginning balance of retained earnings of the earliest period. If comparative statements are not prepared, an adjustment

[7] Ibid., section 3480.05 and .06.

[8] Ibid., section 1506.03.

should be made to the current period's beginning retained earnings for the cumulative effect of the change on prior periods.

Changes in Accounting Estimates include such items as a revision of the estimate of the amount of allowance for doubtful accounts or a revision of the estimate of a nine-year useful life of a depreciable asset to a six-year life. A change in an estimate is a result of ***new*** information. For example, a change in the method of depreciation of a plant asset that results from changed circumstances, experience, or new information would be treated as a change in accounting estimate. Section 1506 of the *CICA Handbook* recommends that the effect of such a change be accounted for in the period of change or in the period of change and the applicable future periods, depending on whether the change affects one or more periods. Thus, this differs from the treatment of a change in accounting policy in that a restatement of prior periods or a cumulative adjustment is ***not*** required.

Corrections of Errors are required when errors are discovered in prior period financial statements. Errors may result from a mistake in computation, a misinterpretation or misrepresentation of information, an oversight of available information, or a misappropriation of assets.[9] Examples of corrections of errors include the discovery that inventories were materially overstated and depreciation expenses were substantially understated in prior period financial statements. Section 1506 of the *CICA Handbook* recommends that a correction of an error be accounted for ***retroactively*** and that the prior period financial statements presented for comparative purposes be ***restated.*** In addition, it requires disclosure in the current period regarding: (1) a description of the error, (2) the effect of the correction of the error on the financial statements of the current and prior periods, and (3) the fact that the prior period financial statements presented for comparative purposes have been restated. The disclosure of the effect of the correction on such significant items as net income, earnings per share, and working capital also may be appropriate. These requirements for a correction of an error are logical because they make comparisons of performance of a business enterprise over a number of periods more meaningful and not misleading.

The chart at the top of page 704 summarizes the accounting and reporting requirements of Section 1506 of the *CICA Handbook.* It is interesting to note that both a change in an accounting policy and a correction of an error in prior period financial statements receive the same treatment—retroactive application and restatement. Such a treatment is also accorded to prior period adjustments as discussed later in this chapter. Thus, although these two types of accounting changes do not have the four characteristics of a prior period adjustment, both of them are required to have the same retroactive application and restatement of prior period financial statements.

[9] Ibid., section 1506.26.

Type of Accounting Change	Financial Statements Affected: Income	Financial Statements Affected: Retained Earnings	Accounting and Reporting Requirements
1. Change in accounting policy	Prior period	Current and prior periods	Retroactive application and restatement
2. Change in accounting estimate	Current or current and future periods	Not applicable	Current or current and prospective application
3. Correction of error in prior period	Prior period	Current and prior periods	Retroactive application and restatement

The in-depth coverage of the topic of accounting changes is more appropriately covered in the intermediate accounting course.

Earnings per Share (EPS)

OBJECTIVE 2 Compute earnings per share.

Perhaps the most widely used of all accounting statistics is ***earnings per share*** of common stock. Everyone who buys or sells stock in a corporation needs to know the annual earnings per share. Stock market prices are quoted on a per-share basis. If you are considering investing in Canadian Pacific stock at a price of, say, $20 per share, you need to know the earnings per share and the annual dividend per share in order to decide whether this price is reasonable. In other words, how much earning power and how much dividend income would you be getting for each share you buy?

To compute earnings per share, the annual net income applicable to the common shareholders is divided by the average number of common shares outstanding. The concept of earnings per share applies ***only to common stock;*** preferred stock has no claim to earnings beyond the stipulated preferred stock dividends.

Many financial analysts express the relationship between earnings per share and market price per share as a ***price-earnings ratio*** (p/e ratio). This ratio is computed by dividing the market price per share of common stock by the annual earnings per share.

Weighted-Average Number of Shares Outstanding The simplest example of computing earnings per share is found when a company has issued only common stock and the number of shares outstanding has not changed during the year. In this situation, the net income for the year divided by the number of shares outstanding at year-end equals earnings per share.

In many companies, however, the number of shares of stock outstanding changes one or more times during the year. When additional shares are issued in exchange for assets during the year, the computation of earnings per share is based upon the ***weighted-average*** number of shares outstanding.[10]

The weighted-average number of shares for the year is determined by multiplying the number of shares outstanding by the fraction of the year that said number of shares outstanding remained unchanged. For example, assume that 100,000 shares of common stock were outstanding during the first nine months of 1996 and 140,000 shares during the last three months. Assume also that the increase in shares outstanding resulted from the sale of 40,000 shares for cash. The weighted-average number of shares outstanding during 1996 would be ***110,000*** determined as follows:

100,000 shares × $\frac{9}{12}$ of a year	75,000
140,000 shares × $\frac{3}{12}$ of a year	35,000
Weighted-average number of common shares outstanding	110,000

This procedure gives more meaningful earnings per share data than if the total number of shares outstanding at the end of the year were used in the calculations. By using the weighted-average number of shares, we recognize that the proceeds from the sale of the 40,000 shares were available to generate earnings only during the last three months of the year. Although the weighted-average number of shares outstanding must be used in earnings-per-share computations, this figure does not appear in the shareholders' equity section of the balance sheet. A balance sheet prepared at year-end reports the ***actual*** number of shares outstanding at that date, regardless of when the shares were issued during the year.

Preferred Dividends and Earnings per Share When a company has preferred stock outstanding, the preferred shareholders participate in net income to the extent of the preferred stock dividends. To determine the earnings ***applicable to the common stock,*** we first deduct from net income the amount of current year preferred stock dividends. The annual dividend on ***cumulative*** preferred stock is ***always*** deducted, even if not declared by the board of directors for the current year. Noncumulative preferred stock dividends are deducted only if declared.

To illustrate, let us assume that Tanner Corporation has 200,000 shares of common stock and 10,000 shares of $6 cumulative preferred stock outstanding throughout the year. Net income for the year 1996 totals $560,000. Earnings per share of common stock would be computed as follows:

Net income	$560,000
Less: Dividends on preferred stock (10,000 shares × $6)	60,000
Earnings applicable to common stock	$500,000
Weighted-average number of common shares outstanding	200,000
Earnings per share of common stock ($500,000 ÷ 200,000 shares)	$2.50

---

[10] When the number of shares outstanding changes as a result of a stock split or a stock dividend (discussed later in this chapter), the computation of the weighted-average number of shares outstanding should be adjusted ***retroactively*** to the beginning of the period, as if the shares had been outstanding for the whole period. Earnings per share data for prior years thus will be consistently stated in terms of the current capital structure.

Even when there are dividends in arrears, only the ***current year's*** cumulative preferred stock dividend is deducted in the earnings per share computation. Dividends in arrears from previous years have already been deducted in the prior years' earnings per share computations.

Presentation of Earnings per Share in the Income Statement All publicly owned corporations are ***required*** to present earnings per share data in their ***income statements.***[11] If an income statement includes subtotals for income from continuing operations, or for income before extraordinary items, per-share figures are shown for income before discontinued operations and extraordinary items as well as for net income. Also, it is desirable to show the earnings per share for discontinued operations and extraordinary items to stress their effect on the final earnings per share.[12] This additional per-share amount is computed by substituting the amount of the appropriate subtotal for the net income figure in the preceding calculation.

To illustrate all of the potential per-share computations, we will expand our Tanner Corporation example to include income from continuing operations and income before extraordinary items. We should point out, however, that all of these figures seldom appear in the same income statement. Very few companies have both discontinued operations and an extraordinary item to report in the same year. The following condensed income statement is intended to illustrate the proper format for presenting earnings per share figures and to provide a review of the calculations.

Earnings per share figures are required in the income statement

TANNER CORPORATION
Condensed Income Statement
For the Year Ended December 31, 1996

Net sales	*$9,000,000*
Costs and expenses (including income taxes on continuing operations)	*8,310,000*
Income from continuing operations	*$ 690,000*
Loss from discontinued operations (net of income tax benefits)	*(90,000)*
Income before extraordinary items	*$ 600,000*
Extraordinary loss (net of income tax benefit)	*(40,000)*
Net income	*$ 560,000*
Earnings per share of common stock:	
Earnings from continuing operations	*$3.15*[a]
Loss from discontinued operations	*(.45)*
Earnings before extraordinary items	*$2.70*[b]
Extraordinary loss	*(.20)*
Net earnings	*$2.50*[c]

[a] ($690,000 − $60,000 preferred dividends) ÷ 200,000 shares
[b] ($600,000 − $60,000) ÷ 200,000 shares
[c] ($560,000 − $60,000) ÷ 200,000 shares

[11] CICA, *CICA Handbook* (Toronto), section 3500.06.

[12] Ibid., section 3500.12.

Interpreting the Different Per-Share Amounts To knowledgeable users of financial statements, each of these figures has a different significance. Earnings per share from continuing operations represents the results of continuing and ordinary business activity. This figure is the most useful one for evaluating current operating results and for predicting future operating results. ***Net earnings*** per share, on the other hand, shows the overall operating results of the current year, including any discontinued operations and extraordinary items.

Unfortunately the term ***earnings per share*** often is used without qualification in referring to various types of per-share data. When using per-share information, it is important to know exactly which per-share statistic is being presented. For example, the price-earnings ratios (market price divided by earnings per share) for common stocks listed on major stock exchanges are reported daily in ***The Financial Post*** and many other newspapers. Which earnings per share figures are used in computing these ratios? If a company reports an extraordinary gain or loss, the price-earnings ratio is computed using the per-share ***earnings before the extraordinary item.*** Otherwise, the ratio is based upon ***net earnings*** (net income) per share.

Basic and Fully Diluted Earnings per Share

OBJECTIVE 3 Distinguish between basic and fully diluted earnings per share.

Let us assume that a company has an outstanding issue of preferred stock that is convertible into shares of common stock at a rate of, say, two shares of common for each share of preferred. The conversion of this preferred stock would increase the number of common shares outstanding and might ***dilute*** (reduce) earnings per share. Any common shareholder interested in the trend of earnings per share will want to know what effect the conversion of the preferred stock would have upon this statistic.

To inform investors of the potential dilution that might occur, two figures are presented for each earnings per share statistic. The first figure, called ***basic*** earnings per share, is based upon the weighted-average number of common shares actually outstanding during the year. Thus, this figure ignores the potential dilution represented by the convertible preferred stock.[13] The second figure, called ***fully diluted*** earnings per share, shows the impact that conversion of the preferred stock would have upon basic earnings per share.

Basic earnings per share are computed in the same manner illustrated in our preceding example of Tanner Corporation. Fully diluted earnings per share, on the other hand, are computed on the assumption that all the preferred stock ***had been converted into common stock at the beginning of the current year.***[14] (The mechanics of computing fully diluted earnings per share are covered in the intermediate accounting course.)

---

[13] If certain criteria are met, preferred shares are treated, for example, as **"common stock"** and are entered into the computation of basic earnings per share. This and other complex issues relating to earnings per share are discussed in section 3500 of the *CICA Handbook* and in intermediate accounting texts.

[14] If the preferred stock had been issued during the current year, we would assume that it was converted into common stock on the date it was issued.

It is important to remember that fully diluted earnings per share represent a ***hypothetical case.*** This statistic is computed even though the preferred stock actually was ***not*** converted during the year. The purpose of showing fully diluted earnings per share is to warn common shareholders what ***could*** have happened. When the difference between basic and fully diluted earnings per share becomes significant, investors should recognize the ***risk*** that future earnings per share may be reduced by conversions of other securities into common stock.

When a company reports both basic and fully diluted earnings per share, the price-earnings ratio shown in newspapers is based upon the ***basic*** figure (and before discontinued operations and extraordinary items).

OTHER SHAREHOLDERS' EQUITY TRANSACTIONS

Cash Dividends

The prospect of receiving cash dividends is a principal reason for investing in the capital stocks of corporations. An increase or a decrease in the established rate of dividends will usually cause an immediate rise or fall in the market price of the company's capital stock. Shareholders are keenly interested in prospects for future dividends and as a group are strongly in favour of more generous dividend payments. The board of directors, on the other hand, is primarily concerned with the long-run growth and financial strength of the corporation; it may prefer to restrict dividends to a minimum in order to conserve cash for the purchase of plant and equipment or for other needs of the company. Many of the so-called "growth companies" plow back into the business most of their earnings and pay only very small cash dividends.

The preceding discussion suggests three requirements for the payment of a cash dividend. These are:

1 **Retained earnings.** Since dividends represent a distribution of earnings to shareholders, the theoretical maximum for dividends is the total undistributed net income of the company, represented by the credit balance of the Retained Earnings account. As a practical matter, many corporations limit dividends to somewhere near 40% of annual net income, in the belief that a major portion of the net income must be retained in the business if the company is to grow and to keep pace with its competitors.

2 **An adequate cash position.** The fact that the company reports large earnings does not mean that it has a large amount of cash on hand. Cash generated from earnings may have been invested in such assets as inventory, new plant and equipment, or used in paying off debts. There is no necessary relationship between the balance in the Retained Earnings account and the balance in the Cash account. The traditional expression of "paying dividends out of retained earnings" is misleading. Cash dividends can be paid only "out of" cash.

3 **Dividend action by the board of directors.** Even though a company's net income is substantial and its cash position seemingly satisfactory, dividends are not paid automatically. A formal action by the board of directors is necessary to declare a dividend.

Dividend Dates

Four significant dates are involved in the distribution of a dividend. These dates are:

1 **Date of declaration.** On the day on which the dividend is declared by the board of directors, a liability to make the payment comes into existence.

2 **Date of record.** The date of record always follows the date of declaration, usually by a period of two to four weeks, and is always stated in the dividend declaration. In order to be eligible to receive the dividend, a person must be listed as the owner of the stock on the date of record.

3 **Ex-dividend date.** The ex-dividend date is significant for investors in companies with stocks traded on the stock exchanges. To permit the compilation of the list of shareholders as of the record date, it is customary for the stock to go ***ex-dividend*** four business days before the date of record. A stock is said to be selling ex-dividend on the day that it loses the right to receive the latest declared dividend. A person who buys the stock before the ex-dividend date is entitled to receive the dividend; conversely, a shareholder who sells shares before the ex-dividend date does not receive the dividend.

4 **Date of payment.** The declaration of a dividend always includes announcement of the date of payment as well as the date of record. Usually the date of payment comes from two to four weeks after the date of record.

The journal entries to record the declaration and payment of a cash dividend were illustrated in Chapter 14 but are repeated here with emphasis on the date of declaration and date of payment.

Entries made on declaration date and . . .

June 1	*Retained Earnings*	*100,000*	
	Dividends Payable		*100,000*
	To record declaration of a cash dividend of $1 per share on the 100,000 shares of common stock outstanding. Payable July 10 to shareholders of record on June 20.		

. . . on payment date

July 10	*Dividends Payable*	*100,000*	
	Cash		*100,000*
	To record payment of $1 per share dividend declared June 1 to shareholders of record on June 20.		

As mentioned in Chapter 14, some companies record the declaration of a dividend by debiting a Dividends account instead of debiting Retained Earnings. In this case, a closing entry is required at the end of the year to transfer the debit balance of the Dividends account into the Retained Earnings account. Under either method, the balance of the Retained Earnings account ultimately is reduced by the amount of all dividends ***declared*** during the period.

Most dividends are paid in cash, but occasionally a dividend declaration calls for payment in assets other than cash. A large distillery once paid a dividend consisting of a bottle of whiskey for each share of stock. When a corporation goes out of existence (particularly a small corporation with only a few shareholders), it may choose to distribute noncash assets to its owners rather than to convert all its assets into cash.

In some cases, a cash dividend may be "paid" in common stock through an "automatic dividend reinvestment plan" whereby the cash dividends may be ***automatically*** reinvested. Thus, those shareholders who have chosen this plan will receive the cash dividends in common stock and the entry would debit retained earnings and credit common stock. To make such a plan attractive to the shareholders, the price for these new shares is usually below the current market price. Such a plan is beneficial to the company as it can conserve the cash needed for operations and expansion.

CASE IN POINT MacLean Hunter has an automatic dividend reinvestment plan, which offers its shareholders the opportunity to reinvest their cash dividends for new common stock at 95% of the current market price. In a recent year, $6 million of the $45 million of cash dividends were reinvested.

Liquidating Dividends

A ***liquidating dividend*** occurs when a corporation pays a dividend that ***exceeds the balance in the Retained Earnings account.*** Thus, the dividend returns to shareholders all or part of their paid-in capital investment. Liquidating dividends usually are paid only when a corporation is going out of existence or is making a permanent reduction in the size of its operations. Normally dividends are paid as a result of profitable operations; shareholders may assume that a dividend represents a distribution of earnings unless they are notified by the corporation that the dividend is a return of invested capital.

Stock Dividends

OBJECTIVE 4 ***Account for stock dividends and stock splits, and explain the probable effect of these transactions upon market price.***

Stock dividend is a term used to describe a distribution of ***additional shares of stock*** to a company's shareholders in proportion to their present holdings. In brief, the dividend is payable in ***additional shares of stock*** rather than in cash. Most stock dividends consist of additional shares of common stock distributed to holders of common stock, and our discussion will be limited to this type of stock dividend.

An important distinction must be drawn between a cash dividend and a stock dividend. In a ***cash dividend,*** assets are distributed by the corporation to the shareholders. Thus, a cash dividend reduces both assets and shareholders' equity. In a ***stock dividend,*** however, ***no assets are distributed.*** Thus, a stock dividend causes ***no change*** in assets or in total shareholders' equity. Each shareholder receives additional shares, but his or her total ownership in the corporation is ***no larger than before.***

To illustrate this point, assume that a corporation with 2,000 shares of stock is owned equally by James Davis and Susan Miller, each owning 1,000 shares of stock. The corporation declares a stock dividend of 10% and distributes 200 additional shares (10% of 2,000 shares), with 100 shares going to each of the two shareholders. Davis and Miller now hold 1,100 shares apiece, but each ***still owns one-half of the business.*** Furthermore, the corporation has not changed in size; its assets and liabilities and its total shareholders' equity are exactly the same as before the stock dividend.

Now let us consider the logical effect of this stock dividend upon the ***market price*** of the company's stock. Assume that before the stock dividend, the outstanding 2,000 shares in our example had a market price of $110 per share. This price indicates a total market value for the corporation of $220,000 (2,000 shares × $110 per share). As the stock dividend does not change total assets or total shareholders' equity, the total market value of the corporation ***should remain $220,000*** after the stock dividend. As 2,200 shares are now outstanding, the market price of each share ***should fall*** to $100 ($220,000 ÷ 2,200 shares). In short, the market value of the stock ***should fall in proportion*** to the number of new shares issued. Whether the market price per share ***will*** fall in proportion to a small increase in number of outstanding shares is another matter. The market prices of common stocks are influenced by many different factors.

Reasons for Issuing Stock Dividends Although stock dividends cause no change in total assets or total shareholders' equity, they are popular both with management and with shareholders. Management likes stock dividends because they do not cost anything (other than administrative costs)—the corporation does not have to surrender any assets. Shareholders enjoy stock dividends because often the market price of the stock ***does not fall enough*** to reflect fully the increased number of shares. While this failure of the stock price to fall proportionately is not logical, it is nonetheless a common phenomenon. In such cases, the stock dividend actually does increase the total market value of the corporation and of each shareholder's investment.

Entries to Record a Stock Dividend In accounting for ***small*** stock dividends (say, less than 20%), the ***market value*** of the new shares is transferred from the Retained Earnings accounts to the contributed capital accounts. This process sometimes is called ***capitalizing*** retained earnings. The overall effect is the same as if the dividend had been paid in cash, and the shareholders had immediately reinvested the cash in the business in exchange for additional shares of stock. Of course, no cash actually changes hands—the new shares of stock are sent directly to the shareholders.

To illustrate, Aspen Corporation, on June 1, has outstanding 100,000 shares of no-par value common stock with a market value of $22 per share. On this date, the company declares a 10% stock dividend, distributable on July 15 to shareholders of record on June 20. The entry at June 1 to record the ***declaration*** of this dividend is:

Stock dividend declared; note use of market price of stock

Retained Earnings	*220,000*	
Stock Dividend to Be Distributed		*220,000*
Declared a 10% stock dividend consisting of 10,000 shares (100,000 shares × 10%) of no-par value common stock, market price $22 per share. Distributable July 15 to shareholders' of record on June 20.		

The Stock Dividend to Be Distributed account is ***not a liability,*** because there is no obligation to distribute cash or any other asset. If a balance sheet is prepared between the date of declaration of a stock dividend and the date of distribution of the shares, this account should be presented in the shareholders' equity section of the balance sheet.

Notice that the Retained Earnings account was debited for the ***market value*** of the shares to be issued (10,000 shares × $22 per share = $220,000). Notice also that ***no change*** occurs in the total amount of shareholders' equity. The amount removed from the Retained Earnings account was simply transferred into another shareholders' equity account.

On July 15, the entry to record the ***distribution*** of the dividend shares is:

Stock dividend distributed

Stock Dividend to Be Distributed	*220,000*	
Common Stock		*220,000*
Distributed 10,000 share stock dividend declared June 1.		

Large stock dividends (for example, those in excess of 20 to 25%), on the other hand, generally have the effect of proportionately reducing the market price of the stock. For example, a 100% stock dividend would reduce the market price by about 50%, because twice as many shares would be outstanding. A 100% stock dividend is very similar to the 2-for-1 ***stock split*** discussed in the following section of this chapter.

Stock Splits

A corporation may split its stock by increasing the number of outstanding shares of common stock. The purpose of the split is to reduce substantially the market price of the common stock, with the intent of making the stock more attractive to investors.

For example, assume that Pelican Corporation has outstanding 1 million shares of no-par value stock. The market price is $90 per share. The corporation now increases the number of shares from 1 million to 2 million. This action would be called a 2-for-1 stock split. A shareholder who owned 100 shares of the stock before the split would own 200 shares after the split. Since the number of outstanding shares has been doubled without any change in total assets or total shareholders' equity, the market price of the stock should drop from $90 to approximately $45 a share.

A stock split does not change the balance of any ledger account; consequently, the transaction may be recorded merely by ***a memorandum entry*** in the general journal and in the Common Stock account. For Pelican Corporation, this memorandum entry might read:

Memorandum entry to record a stock split

Sept. 30 Memorandum: Issued additional 1 million shares of common stock in a 2-for-1 stock split.

The description of common stock also is changed in the balance sheet to reflect the greater number of shares outstanding.

Stock may be split in any desired ratio. Among the more common ratios are 2 for 1, 3 for 2, and 3 for 1. The determining factor is the number of shares needed to bring the price of the stock into the desired trading range.

For example, assume that a stock is selling at a price of $150 per share and that management wants to reduce the price to approximately $30 per share. This objective may be accomplished with a ***5-for-1*** stock split ($150 ÷ 5 = $30).

Distinction between Stock Splits and Large Stock Dividends What is the difference between a 2-for-1 stock split and a 100% stock dividend? There is very little difference; both will double the number of outstanding shares without changing total shareholders' equity, and both should serve to cut the market price of the stock approximately in half. The stock dividend, however, will cause a transfer from the Retained Earnings account to the Common Stock account equal to the declared dollar amount for no-par value or to the par value of the dividend shares. A 2-for-1 stock split will reduce the par value per share by one-half, but it will not change the dollar balance of any account.

After an increase in the number of shares as a result of a stock split or stock dividend, earnings per share are computed in terms of the increased number of shares. In presenting 5- or 10-year summaries, the earnings per share for earlier years are ***retroactively restated*** to reflect the increased number of shares currently outstanding and thus make the trend of earnings per share from year to year a valid comparison.

Statement of Retained Earnings

OBJECTIVE 5 Describe and prepare a statement of retained earnings.

The term ***retained earnings*** refers to the portion of shareholders' equity derived from profitable operations. Retained earnings is increased by earning net income and is reduced by incurring net losses and by the declaration of dividends.

In addition to a balance sheet and an income statement, a complete set of financial statements includes a statement of retained earnings and a statement of changes in financial position. The statement of changes in financial position will be discussed in Chapter 19; a statement of retained earnings is illustrated below:

SHORE LINE CORPORATION
Statement of Retained Earnings
For the Year Ended December 31, 1996

Retained earnings, December 31, 1995		$600,000
Net income for 1996		180,000
Subtotal		$780,000
Less: Cash dividends:		
Preferred stock ($5 per share)	$ 17,500	
Common stock ($2 per share)	55,300	
10% stock dividend	140,000	212,800
Retained earnings, December 31, 1996		$567,200

Appropriations and Restrictions of Retained Earnings A few corporations transfer a portion of their retained earnings into separate accounts called ***appropriations*** or ***reserves.*** The purpose of such appropriations or reserves is to indicate to users of financial statements that a portion of retained earnings is not available for the declaration of cash dividends. The limitation on cash dividends may be established voluntarily by the board of directors or it may be required by law or contract.

Most corporations disclose restrictions on the declaration of cash dividends in notes accompanying the financial statements. For example, a company with total retained earnings of $10,000,000 might include the following note in its financial statements:

Footnote disclosure of restrictions placed on retained earnings

Note 7: Restriction of retained earnings

As of December 31, 1996, certain long-term debt agreements prohibited the declaration of cash dividends that would reduce the amount of retained earnings below $5,200,000. Retained earnings not so restricted amounted to $4,800,000.

Prior Period Adjustments

OBJECTIVE 6 Define prior period adjustments and explain how they are presented in financial statements.

Prior period adjustments are those gains or losses that have ***all four*** of the following characteristics:

1 are specifically identified with and directly related to the business activities of particular prior periods
2 are not attributable to economic events occurring subsequent to the date of the financial statements for such prior periods
3 depend primarily on decisions or determinations by persons other than management or owners
4 could not be reasonably estimated prior to such decisions or determinations[15]

Because of the restrictiveness of these characteristics, prior period adjustments are rare. The *CICA Handbook* provides only two examples:

1 nonrecurring adjustments or settlements of income taxes
2 settlements of claims resulting from litigation[16]

In contrast to extraordinary items described earlier in the chapter, ***prior period adjustments*** are excluded from the determination of net income for the current accounting period and are applied retroactively to the income of the related prior periods.[17] The financial statements affected by such an adjustment, when presented for comparative purposes, are to be ***restated,*** together with any related income tax effect. In the period where a prior period adjustment occurs, the following disclosures are required:

1 a description of the adjustment
2 its effects on the financial statements of the current and prior periods

[15] CICA, *CICA Handbook,* section 3600.03.

[16] Ibid., section 3600.02.

[17] Ibid., section 3600.06.

3 the fact regarding the restatement of the financial statements of prior periods that are presented.[18]

Also, the beginning balance of retained earnings for the periods subsequent to the period to which the adjustment relates should be ***restated.***

To illustrate, assume that in 1996 Jilin Corporation settled with the tax authority the assessment of additional income taxes of $60,000 for 1992. This prior period adjustment is presented in the comparative statements of earnings for 1996 and 1995 as follows:

Statement of retained earnings shows prior period adjustments, net income, and dividends

JILIN CORPORATION
Statement of Retained Earnings
For Years Ended December 31

	1996	1995
Retained earnings at beginning of year:		
As originally reported	$860,000	$820,000
Prior period adjustment—additional income taxes for 1992	(60,000)	(60,000)
As restated	$800,000	$760,000
Net income	160,000	110,000
Subtotal	$960,000	$870,000
Less: Cash dividends on common stock	80,000	70,000
Retained earnings at end of year	$880,000	$800,000

The additional income taxes for 1992 are shown as an adjustment to the beginning balance of retained earnings for both 1996 and 1995 because these beginning amounts were overstated by $60,000. Also, this presentation serves to explain all changes in retained earnings during the accounting period.

Treasury Stock

Corporations sometimes acquire shares of their own capital stock by purchase in the open market. Paying out cash to acquire shares will reduce the assets of the corporation and reduce the shareholders' equity by the same amount. One reason for such purchases is to have stock available to reissue to officers and employees under bonus plans. Other reasons may include a desire to increase the reported earnings per share or to support the current market price of the stock.

Treasury stock may be defined as shares of a corporation's own capital stock that have been issued and later ***acquired by the issuing company,*** but that have not been cancelled or permanently retired. Treasury shares may be held indefinitely or may be issued again at any time. Shares of capital stock held in the treasury are not entitled to receive dividends, to vote, or to share in assets upon dissolution of the company. In the computation of earnings per share, shares held in the treasury are not regarded as outstanding shares.

A corporation may, under certain provincial legislation, acquire its own capital stock for the purpose of reissuing or cancelling it in the future.

[18] Ibid., section 3600.08.

However, other legislation such as the Canada Business Corporations Act and the Ontario Business Corporations Act require that such acquired capital stock be cancelled or restored to the authorized but unissued status. Thus, corporations under such legislation are prohibited from having treasury stock. Also, corporation legislation does not permit a corporation to acquire its own capital stock when it is insolvent or if such an acquisition would render it insolvent.

Recording Purchases of Treasury Stock

OBJECTIVE 7 Account for treasury stock transactions.

Purchases of treasury stock should be recorded by debiting the Treasury Stock account with the cost of the stock. For example, if Torrey Corporation acquires 1,500 shares of its own no-par stock at a price of $100 per share, the entry is as follows:

Treasury Stock	150,000	
Cash		150,000
Purchased 1,500 shares of no-par treasury stock at $100 per share.		

Treasury Stock Is Not an Asset When treasury stock is purchased, the corporation is eliminating part of its shareholders' equity by a payment to one or more shareholders. The purchase of treasury stock should be regarded as a ***reduction of shareholders' equity,*** not as the acquisition of an asset. For this reason, the Treasury Stock account should appear in the balance sheet ***as a deduction in the shareholders' equity section.*** The presentation of treasury stock in a corporate balance sheet is illustrated on page 718.

Reissuance of Treasury Stock

When treasury shares are reissued, the Treasury Stock account is credited for the cost of the shares reissued and Contributed Capital from Treasury Stock Transactions account is debited or credited for any difference between ***cost*** and the reissue price. To illustrate, assume that 1,000 of the treasury shares acquired by Torrey Corporation at a cost of $100 per share are now reissued at a price of $115 per share. The entry to record the reissuance of these shares at a price above cost would be:

Treasury stock reissued at a price above cost

Cash	115,000	
Treasury Stock		100,000
Contributed Capital from Treasury Stock Transactions		15,000
Sold 1,000 shares of treasury stock, which cost $100,000, at a price of $115 per share.		

If treasury stock is reissued at a price below cost, contributed capital from previous treasury stock transactions of the same class is reduced (debited) by the excess of cost over the reissue price.[19] To illustrate, assume that Torrey Corporation reissues its remaining 500 shares of treasury stock (cost $100 per share) at a price of $90 per share. The entry would be:

[19] CICA, *CICA Handbook* (Toronto), section 3240.20.

Reissued at a price below cost

Cash	*45,000*	
Contributed Capital from Treasury Stock Transactions	*5,000*	
Treasury Stock		*50,000*
Sold 500 shares of treasury stock, which cost $50,000, at a price of $90 each.		

If there is insufficient or no contributed capital from previous treasury stock transactions to cover the excess, the balance or the entire excess of the cost of the treasury shares over the reissue price may be recorded as a debit to Retained Earnings.[20]

No Income or Loss on Treasury Stock Transactions Notice that ***no income or loss is recognized on treasury stock transactions,*** even when the shares are reissued at a price above or below cost. A corporation earns income by selling goods and services to outsiders, not by issuing or reissuing shares of its own capital stock. When treasury shares are reissued at a price above cost the corporation receives from the new shareholder an amount of contributed capital larger than the reduction in shareholders' equity when the corporation acquired the treasury shares. Conversely, if treasury shares are reissued at a price below cost, the corporation ends up with less contributed capital as a result of the purchase and reissuance of the shares. Thus, any changes in shareholders' equity resulting from treasury stock transactions are regarded as changes in ***contributed capital*** and are ***not*** included in the measurement of net income.

Restriction of Retained Earnings for Treasury Stock Owned Purchases of treasury stock, like cash dividends, are distributions of assets to the shareholders in the corporation. Corporate laws generally require that distributions to shareholders (including purchases of treasury stock) cannot exceed the balance in the Retained Earnings account. Therefore, retained earnings usually are restricted by an amount equal to the ***cost*** of any shares held in the treasury.

Stock "Buyback" Programs

In past years, most treasury stock transactions involved relatively small dollar amounts. Hence, the topic was not of much importance to investors or other users of financial statements. Late in 1987, however, many corporations in the United States initiated large "buyback" programs, in which they repurchased huge amounts of their own common stock.[21] As a result of these programs, treasury stock has become a very material item in the balance sheets of many corporations.

---

[20] Ibid.

[21] On October 19, 1987, a date known as ***Black Monday,*** stock prices around the world suffered the largest one-day decline in history. Many economists and investors believed that this stock market "crash" would trigger a worldwide economic depression. Within hours of the market's close on Black Monday, many large corporations announced their intention to enter the market and spend hundreds of millions of dollars repurchasing their own shares. In the opinions of the authors, the announcement of these buyback programs did much to stabilize the world's financial markets, restore investors' confidence, and possibly avoid a depression.

CASE IN POINT Shown below is the cost of the treasury stock listed in the balance sheets of several publicly owned corporations in the United States at the end of a recent year.

	Treasury Stock	
Company	At Cost (in Thousands)	As a % of Other Elements of Shareholders' Equity*
Coca-Cola	$ 3,235,963	48
Exxon	16,224,000	35
Lotus	194,937	41
King World	159,587	72

* To place these holdings in perspective, we have shown the cost of the treasury stock as a percentage of total shareholders' equity **before** deducting the cost of the repurchased shares.

These large buyback programs serve several purposes. First, by creating demand for the company's stock in the marketplace, these programs tend to increase the market value of the shares. Also, reducing the number of shares outstanding usually increases earnings per share. When stock prices are low, some companies find that they can increase earnings per share by a greater amount through repurchasing shares than through expanding business operations.

Illustration of a Shareholders' Equity Section

The following shareholders' equity section of a balance sheet illustrates the various items discussed in this chapter. You should be able to explain the nature and origin of each account and disclosure.

The published financial statements of leading corporations indicate that there is no one standard arrangement for the various items making up the shareholders' equity section. Variations occur in the selection of titles, in the sequence of items, and in the extent of detailed classification.

Shareholders' equity:	
Capital stock:	
$9 preferred stock, no-par value, unlimited authorized shares, 1,000 shares issued and outstanding	$260,000
Common stock, no-par value, unlimited authorized shares, issued 60,000 shares, of which 1,000 are held in treasury	543,000
Common stock subscribed, 6,000 shares	30,000
Contributed capital from treasury stock transactions	5,000
Total contributed capital	$838,000
Retained earnings (of which $12,000, an amount equal to the cost of treasury stock purchased, is unavailable for dividends)	162,000
	$1,000,000
Less: Treasury stock, common, 1,000 shares at cost	12,000
Total shareholders' equity	$988,000

CHAPTER REVIEW

KEY TERMS INTRODUCED OR EMPHASIZED IN CHAPTER 15

Basic earnings per share Net income applicable to the common stock divided by weighted-average number of common shares outstanding during the year (or some other accounting period).

Book value The shareholders' equity represented by each share of common stock. Book value is computed by dividing the common shareholders' equity by the number of common shares outstanding during the year.

Changes in accounting estimates Include such items as a revision of the estimate of the amount of allowance for doubtful accounts or a revision of the estimate of a nine-year useful life of a depreciable asset to a six-year life.

Changes in accounting policy Encompass changes in accounting principles as well as accounting methods used in the preparation of financial statements.

Comparative financial statements Financial statements of the current year and the preceding year that are presented together to facilitate comparison.

Corrections of errors Required when errors are discovered in prior period financial statements. Such errors may result from a mistake in computation, a misinterpretation or misrepresentation of information, an oversight of available information, and a misappropriation of assets.

Date of record The date on which a person must be listed as a shareholder in order to be eligible to receive a dividend. Follows the date of declaration of a dividend by two to four weeks.

Discontinued operations The net operating results (revenue and expenses) of a segment of a company that has been or is being sold.

Earnings per share Net income applicable to the common stock divided by the weighted-average number of common shares outstanding during the year.

Ex-dividend date A date generally four days prior to the date of record specified in a dividend declaration. A person buying a stock prior to the ex-dividend date also acquires the right to receive the dividend. The four-day interval permits the compilation of a list of shareholders as of the date of record.

Extraordinary items Transactions and events that are not dependent on decisions by management or owners, unusual in nature, and occur infrequently—for example, a large earthquake loss. Such items are shown separately in the income statement after the determination of Income before Extraordinary Items.

Fully diluted earnings per share Earnings per share computed under the assumption that all convertible securities had been converted into additional common shares at the beginning of the current year. The purpose of this hypothetical computation is to warn common shareholders of the risk that future earnings per share might be diluted by the conversion of other securities into common stock.

Price-earnings (p/e) ratio Market price of a share of common stock divided by annual earnings per share.

Prior period adjustment An adjustment to the earnings reported in the financial statements of a prior year. Prior period adjustments are recorded directly in the Retained Earnings account and are not included in the income statement of the current period; examples, settlement of income taxes and litigations.

Segment of a business Those elements of a business that represent a separate and distinct line of business activity or that service a particular class of customers.

Statement of retained earnings A basic financial statement explaining the change during the year in the amount of retained earnings.

Stock dividend A distribution of additional shares to common shareholders in proportion to their holdings.

Stock split An increase in the number of shares outstanding. The additional shares are distributed proportionately to all common shareholders. Purpose is to reduce market price per share and encourage wider public ownership of the company's stock. A 2-for-1 stock split will give each shareholder twice as many shares as previously owned.

Treasury stock Shares of a corporation's stock that have been issued and then acquired, but not cancelled by the corporation.

DEMONSTRATION PROBLEM FOR YOUR REVIEW

The shareholders' equity of Sutton Corporation at December 31, 1995, is shown below:

Shareholders' equity:	
Common stock, no-par, unlimited shares authorized, 40,000 shares issued and outstanding	*$ 600,000*
Retained earnings	*1,500,000*
Total shareholders' equity	*$2,100,000*

Transactions affecting shareholders' equity during 1996 are as follows:

Mar. 31 A 5-for-4 stock split proposed by the board of directors was approved by vote of the shareholders. The 10,000 new shares were distributed to shareholders.

Apr. 1 The company purchased 2,000 shares of its common stock on the open market at $37 per share.

July 1 The company reissued 1,000 shares of treasury stock at $45 per share.

July 1 Issued for cash 20,000 shares of previously unissued no-par value common stock at a price of $45 per share.

Dec. 1 A cash dividend of $1 per share was declared, payable on December 30, to shareholders of record at December 14.

Dec. 22 A 10% stock dividend was declared; the dividend shares are to be distributed on January 15 of the following year. The market price of the stock on December 22 was $48 per share.

The net income for the year ended December 31, 1996, amounted to $177,000, after an extraordinary loss of $35,400 (net of $17,600 income tax benefits).

INSTRUCTIONS

a Prepare journal entries (in general journal form) to record the transactions relating to shareholders' equity that took place during the year.

b Prepare the lower section of the income statement for 1996, beginning with the ***income before extraordinary items*** and showing the extraordinary loss and the net income. Also illustrate the presentation of earnings per share in the income statement, assuming that earnings per share is determined on the basis of the ***weighted-average*** number of shares outstanding during the year.

c Prepare a statement of retained earnings for the year ending December 31, 1996.

SOLUTION TO DEMONSTRATION PROBLEM

a

General Journal

Mar. 31	Memorandum: Shareholders approved a 5-for-4 stock split. This action increased the number of shares of common stock outstanding from 40,000 to 50,000. The 10,000 new shares were distributed.		
Apr. 1	Treasury Stock	74,000	
	Cash		74,000
	Acquired 2,000 shares of treasury stock at $37 per share.		
July 1	Cash	45,000	
	Treasury Stock		37,000
	Contributed Capital from Treasury Stock Transactions		8,000
	Sold 1,000 shares of treasury stock at $45 per share.		
1	Cash	900,000	
	Common Stock		900,000
	Issued 20,000 shares of previously unissued no-par value common stock for cash of $45 per share.		
Dec. 1	Retained Earnings	69,000	
	Dividends Payable		69,000
	To record declaration of cash dividend of $1 per share on 69,000 shares of common stock outstanding (1,000 shares in treasury are not entitled to receive dividends).		

Note: Entry to record the payment of the cash dividend is not shown here since the action does not affect the shareholders' equity.

22	Retained Earnings	331,200	
	Stock Dividends to Be Distributed		331,200
	To record declaration of 10% stock dividend consisting of 6,900 shares of no-par value common stock to be distributed on Jan. 15 of next year.		
31	Income Summary	177,000	
	Retained Earnings		177,000
	To close Income Summary account.		

b

SUTTON CORPORATION
Partial Income Statement
For Year Ended December 31, 1996

Income before extraordinary items	$212,400
Extraordinary loss (net of $17,600 income tax benefits)	(35,400)
Net income	$177,000
Earnings per share:*	
Income before extraordinary items	$3.60
Extraordinary loss	(0.60)
Net income	$3.00

* On 59,000 weighted-average number of shares of common stock outstanding during 19__, determined as follows:

Jan. 1–Mar. 31: (40,000 + 10,000 shares issued pursuant to a 5 for 4 split) × $\frac{1}{4}$ of year	12,500
Apr. 1–June 30: (50,000 − 2,000 shares of treasury stock) × $\frac{1}{4}$ of year	12,000
July 1–Dec. 31: (50,000 + 20,000 shares of new stock − 1,000 shares of treasury stock) × $\frac{1}{2}$ of year	34,500
Weighted-average number of shares outstanding	59,000

c

SUTTON CORPORATION
Statement of Retained Earnings
For Year Ended December 31, 1996

Retained earnings, December 31, 1995		*$1,500,000*
Add: Net income for 1996		*177,000*
Subtotal		*$1,677,000*
Less: Cash dividends ($1 per share)	*$ 69,000*	
10% stock dividend	*331,200*	*400,200*
Retained earnings, December 31, 1996		*$1,276,800*

ASSIGNMENT MATERIAL

DISCUSSION QUESTIONS

1 What is the purpose of arranging an income statement to show subtotals for ***Income from Continuing Operations*** and for ***Income before Extraordinary Items?***

2 Pappa Joe's owns 30 pizza parlors and a minor league baseball team. During the current year, the company sold three of its pizza parlors and closed another when the lease on the building expired. Should any of these events be classified as "discontinued operations" in the company's income statement? Explain.

3 Define ***extraordinary items.*** Give three examples of losses that qualify as extraordinary items and three examples of losses that would ***not*** be classified as extraordinary.

4 Briefly describe the nature and accounting treatment of each of the following:

a A change in an accounting policy

b A change in an accounting estimate

c A correction of an error in prior period financial statements

5 In past years, the management of St. Thomas Medical Supply had consistently estimated the allowance for doubtful accounts at 2% of total accounts receivable. At the end of the current year, management estimated that uncollectible accounts would equal 4% of accounts receivable. Should the uncollectible accounts expense of prior years be recomputed in order to show in the comparative income statements of previous years the effect of this change in accounting estimate?

6 Even though ***a change in accounting principle*** and ***prior period adjustment*** affect the income of past accounting periods, their natures are different. Explain how they are reported in the financial statements.

7 In the current year, Garden Products decided to switch from use of an accelerated method of depreciation to the straight-line method. Will the cumulative effect of this change in accounting principle increase or decrease the amount of retained earnings reported at the beginning of the preceding year (assume a two-year comparative statement is presented)? Explain.

8 ***Earnings per share*** and ***book value per share*** are statistics that relate to common stock. When both preferred and common stock are outstanding, explain the computation involved in determining the following:

a Earnings allocable to the common shareholders

b Aggregate book value allocable to the common shareholders

9 Assume a corporation has only common stock outstanding. Is the number of common shares used in the computation of earnings per share ***always*** the same as the number of common shares used in computing book value per share for this corporation? Is the number of common shares used in computing these two statistics ***ever*** the same? Explain.

10 Explain how each of the following is computed:

a Price-earnings ratio

b Basic earnings per share

c Fully diluted earnings per share

11 Throughout the year, Gold Seal Nineteen Limited had 4 million shares of common stock and 120,000 shares of convertible preferred stock outstanding. Each share of preferred is convertible into four shares of common. What number of shares should be used in the computation of (a) basic earnings per share and (b) fully diluted earnings per share?

12 A financial analyst notes that Baxter Corporation's earnings per share have been rising steadily for the last five years. The analyst expects the company's net income to continue to increase at the same rate as in the past. In forecasting future basic earnings per share, what special risk should the analyst consider if Baxter's basic earnings are significantly larger than its fully diluted earnings?

13 Explain the significance of the following dates relating to dividends: date of declaration, date of record, date of payment, ex-dividend date.

14 What is the purpose of a ***stock split?***

15 Distinguish between a ***stock split*** and a ***stock dividend.*** Is there any reason for the difference in accounting treatment of these two events?

16 What are ***prior period adjustments?*** How are they presented in financial statements?

17 Identify three items that may appear in a statement of retained earnings as changes in the amount of retained earnings.

18 What is ***treasury stock?*** Why do corporations purchase their own shares? Is treasury stock an asset? How should it be reported in the balance sheet?

19 Corporation laws generally require that retained earnings be restricted for dividend purposes to the extent of the cost of treasury shares. What is the reason for this legal rule?

MULTIPLE CHOICE QUESTIONS

1 The primary purpose of showing unusual types of events separately in the income statement is to:

a Increase earnings per share.

b Assist users of the income statement in evaluating and predicting the profitability of normal, ongoing operations.

c Minimize the income taxes paid on the results of ongoing operations.

d Prevent unusual losses from recurring.

2 Which of the following situations would be presented in a separate section of the current year's income statement of Marlow Corporation? During the current year:

a Marlow's Vancouver headquarters are destroyed by a tornado.

b Marlow sells its entire juvenile furniture operations and concentrates upon its remaining children's clothing segment.

c Marlow changes from the straight-line method of depreciation to the declining-balance method.

d Marlow's accountant discovers that the entire price paid several years ago to purchase company offices in Winnipeg had been charged to a Land account; consequently, no depreciation has ever been taken on these buildings.

3 When a corporation has outstanding both common and preferred stock:

a Basic and fully diluted earnings per share are reported only if the preferred stock is cumulative.

b Earnings per share are reported for each type of stock outstanding.

c Earnings per share may be computed without regard to the amount of dividends declared on common stock.

d Earnings per share may be computed without regard to the amount of the annual preferred dividends.

4 The statement of retained earnings:

a Is a basic financial statement that shows such items as prior period adjustments, net income, and dividends declared.

b Indicates the amount of cash available for the payment of dividends.

c Includes prior period adjustments and cash dividends, but not stock dividends.

d Shows revenue, expenses, and dividends for the accounting period.

5 On December 10, 1995, Totem Corporation acquired 2,000 of its own no-par stock at a price of $60 per share. In 1996, 500 of the treasury shares are reissued at a price of $70 per share. Which of the following statements is correct?

a The treasury stock purchased is recorded at cost and is shown in Totem's December 31, 1995, balance sheet as an asset.

b The two treasury stock transactions result in an overall reduction in Totem's shareholders' equity of $85,000.

c Totem recognizes a gain of $10 per share on the reissuance of the 500 treasury shares in 1996.

d Totem's shareholders' equity was increased by $110,000 when the treasury stock was acquired.

EXERCISES

EXERCISE 15-1
Accounting Terminology

Listed below are nine technical accounting terms introduced or emphasized in this chapter:

p/e ratio	*Treasury stock*	*Discontinued operations*
Stock dividend	*Extraordinary item*	*Prior period adjustment*
Basic earnings per share	*Change in accounting policy*	*Fully diluted earnings per share*

Each of the following statements may (or may not) describe one of these technical terms. For each statement, indicate the term described, or answer "None" if the statement does not correctly describe any of the terms.

a A gain or loss that is beyond management's control, unusual in nature, and not expected to recur in the foreseeable future.

b The asset represented by shares of capital stock that have not yet been issued.

c A distribution of additional shares of stock that reduces retained earnings but causes no change in total shareholders' equity.

d The inventory costing method has been changed from weighted average to first-in, first-out.

e An adjustment to the beginning balance of retained earnings to correct an error previously made in the measurement of net income.

f A statistic expressing a relationship between the current market value of a share of common stock and the underlying earnings per share.

g A separate section sometimes included in an income statement as a step in helping investors to evaluate and predict the profitability of ongoing business activities.

h A hypothetical figure indicating what earnings per share would have been if all securities convertible into common stock had been converted at the beginning of the current year.

EXERCISE 15-2
Discontinued Operations

During the current year, SunSports, Inc., operated two business segments: a chain of surf and dive shops and a small chain of tennis shops. The tennis shops were not profitable and were sold near year-end to another corporation. SunSports' operations for the current year are summarized below. The first two captions, "Net sales" and "Costs and expenses," relate only to the company's continuing operations.

Net sales	*$9,800,000*
Costs and expenses (including applicable income taxes)	*8,600,000*
Operating loss from tennis shops (net of $76,800 income tax benefit)	*192,000*
Loss on sale of tennis shops (net of $129,200 income tax benefit)	*348,000*

The company had 150,000 shares of a single class of capital stock outstanding throughout the year.

INSTRUCTIONS Prepare a condensed income statement for the year. At the bottom of the statement, show any appropriate earnings-per-share figures.

EXERCISE 15-3
Extraordinary Items, Accounting Changes, and Prior Period Adjustments

Select the ***best*** answer for each of the following multiple-choice questions:

1 Accounting changes include
  a A change in accounting policy and in accounting estimate
  b A correction of error in a prior period
  c A prior period adjustment
  d **a** and **b**
  e **a**, **b**, and **c**

2 An extraordinary item reflects an event that is
  a Unusual, material, and beyond management's control
  b Not reasonably estimated, not related to economic events, but within management's control
  c Not typical, infrequent, and beyond management's control
  d Not typical, irregular, but a recurring factor for ordinary operation evaluation
  e An element of an accounting change

3 Changes in accounting policy encompass
  a Changes in the statement of changes in financial position

b Changes in accounting principles and methods
c Changes in accounting estimates
d Corrections of errors in prior period financial statements
e Extraordinary items and prior period adjustments

4 Changes in accounting estimates include
a Revision of the amount of allowance for doubtful accounts
b Revision of the useful life of a depreciable asset
c Revision of the residual value of a depreciable asset
d A change of depreciation method
e **a**, **b**, and **c**

5 Retroactive application and restatement are required by
a A change in accounting policy
b A change in accounting estimate
c A correction of an error in a prior period
d **a** and **c**
e **a** and **c** and a prior period adjustment.

6 An accounting change requiring a current or current and prospective application is
a A change in accounting estimate
b A change in accounting policy and accounting estimate
c A change in accounting policy and accounting estimate as well as a correction of a prior period error
d An extraordinary item
e A prior period adjustment

EXERCISE 15-4 Reporting an Extraordinary Item

For the year ended December 31, Union Chemical had net sales of $8,000,000, costs and other expenses (including income taxes) of $7,060,000, and an extraordinary gain (net of $200,000 income taxes) of $400,000. Prepare a condensed income statement (including earnings per share), assuming that 500,000 shares of common stock were outstanding throughout the year.

EXERCISE 15-5 Computing Earnings Per Share: Changes in Number of Shares Outstanding

In the year just ended, Sunshine Citrus earned net income of $6,300,000. The company has issued only one class of no-par value capital stock, of which 1 million shares were outstanding at January 1. Compute the company's earnings per share under each of the following ***independent*** assumptions:

a No change occurred during the year in the number of shares outstanding.
b On October 1, the company issued an additional 200,000 shares of capital stock in exchange for cash of $1,500,000.
c On July 1, the company distributed an additional 200,000 shares of capital stock as a 20% stock dividend. On July 1, Sunshine's stock had a market value of $7.25 per share.

EXERCISE 15-6 Computing Earnings Per Share: Effect of Preferred Stock

The net income of Carriage Trade Clothiers amounted to $2,550,000 for the current year. Compute the amount of earnings per share assuming that the shares of capital stock outstanding throughout the year consisted of:

a 300,000 shares of no-par value common stock and no preferred stock.
b 200,000 shares of $9, no-par value preferred stock and 300,000 shares of no-par value common stock.

EXERCISE 15-7
Restating Earnings per Share After a Stock Dividend

The 1994 annual report of **R&W Ko Corporation** included the following comparative summary of earnings per share over the last three years:

	1994	1993	1992
Earnings per share	$3.03	$2.22	$1.30

Early in 1995, the company declared and distributed a 100% stock dividend. Following this stock dividend, the company reported earnings per share of $2.35 for 1995.

INSTRUCTIONS

a Prepare a three-year schedule similar to the one above, but compare earnings per share during the years 1995, 1994, and 1993.

b In preparing your schedule, which figure (or figures) did you have to restate? Why? Explain the logic behind your computation.

EXERCISE 15-8
Restating Earnings per Share After a Stock Split

The 1994 annual report of **Nathan Corporation** included the following comparative summary of earnings per share over the last three years:

	1994	1993	1992
Earnings per share	$6.69	$4.86	$3.78

During 1995, the company split its common stock 3 for 1. Following this stock split, the company reported earnings per share of $3.05 in 1995 and $3.78 in 1996.

INSTRUCTIONS

a Prepare a three-year schedule similar to the one above, but compare earnings per share during the years 1996, 1995, and 1994.

b In preparing your schedule, which figure (or figures) did you have to restate? Why? Explain the logic behind your computation.

EXERCISE 15-9
Cash Dividends, Stock Dividends and Stock Splits

Global Technology Corporation has 500,000 shares of no-par value capital stock outstanding on January 1. The following equity transactions occurred during the current year:

Apr. 30 Distributed additional shares of capital stock in a 2-for-1 stock split. Market price of stock was $35 per share.

June 1 Declared a cash dividend of 60 cents per share.

July 2 Paid the 60-cent cash dividend to shareholders.

Aug. 1 Declared a 5% stock dividend. Market price of stock was $19 per share.

Sept. 10 Issued shares pursuant to the 5% stock dividend declared on August 1.

INSTRUCTIONS

a Prepare journal entries to record the above transactions.

b Compute the number of shares of capital stock outstanding at year-end.

EXERCISE 15-10
Effect of Stock Dividends on Stock Price

Tarreytown Corporation has a total of 80,000 shares of common stock outstanding and no preferred stock. Total shareholders' equity at the end of the current year amounts to $5 million and the market value of the stock is $66 per share. At year-end, the company declares a 10% stock dividend—one share for each ten shares held. If all parties concerned clearly recognize the nature of the stock dividend, what should you expect the market price per share of the common stock to be on the ex-dividend date?

EXERCISE 15-11
Recording Treasury Stock Transactions

Cachet, Inc., engaged in the following transactions involving treasury stock:

Feb. 10 Purchased for cash 14,500 shares of treasury stock at a price of $30 per share.

June 4 Reissued 6,000 shares of treasury stock at a price of $33 per share.

Dec. 22 Reissued 4,000 shares of treasury stock at a price of $28 per share.

INSTRUCTIONS

a Prepare general journal entries to record these transactions.

b Compute the amount of retained earnings that should be restricted because of the treasury stock still owned at December 31.

EXERCISE 15-12
Effects of Various Transactions upon Earnings per Share

Explain the immediate effects, if any, of each of the following transactions upon a company's net earnings per share:

a Split the common stock 3 for 1.

b Realized a gain from the sale of a discontinued operation.

c Declared and paid a cash dividend on common stock.

d Declared and distributed a stock dividend on common stock.

e Acquired several thousand shares of treasury stock.

EXERCISE 15-13
Where to Find Financial Information

You have now been exposed to the following financial statements issued by corporations: balance sheet, income statement and statement of retained earnings. Listed below are various items frequently of interest to a corporation's owners, potential investors, and creditors, among others. You are to specify which of the above corporate financial statements, if any, reports the desired information. If the listed item is not reported in any formal financial statement issued by a corporation, indicate an appropriate source for the desired information.

a Number of shares of stock outstanding as of year-end

b Total dollar amount of cash dividends declared during the current year

c Market value per share at balance sheet date

d Cumulative dollar effect of an accounting error made in a previous year

e The disposal of a segment of the business.

f Loss from an earthquake

g Earnings per share of common stock

h Book value per share

i Price/earnings (p/e) ratio

j The total amount the corporation paid to buy back shares of its own stock that it now holds

PROBLEMS

Group A

PROBLEM 15A-1
Reporting Unusual Events; Using Predictive Subtotals

Gulf Coast Airlines operated both an airline and several motels located near airports. During the year just ended, all motel operations were discontinued and the following operating results were reported:

Continuing operations (airlines):	
Net sales	*$51,120,000*
Costs and expenses (including income taxes on continuing operations)	*43,320,000*
Other data:	
Operating income from motels (net of $388,000 income taxes)	*864,000*
Gain on sale of motels (net of $2,230,000 income taxes)	*4,956,000*
Extraordinary loss (net of $1,512,000 income tax benefit)	*3,360,000*

The extraordinary loss resulted from the destruction of an airliner by terrorists.

Gulf Coast Airlines had 1,200,000 shares of capital stock outstanding throughout the year.

INSTRUCTIONS

a Prepare a condensed income statement including proper presentation of the discontinued motel operations and the extraordinary loss. Include all appropriate earnings per share figures.

b Assume that you expect the profitability of Gulf Coast's airlines operations to ***decline by*** 6% next year, and the profitability of the motels to decline by 10%. What is your estimate of the company's net earnings per share next year?

PROBLEM 15A-2
Accounting Changes

The following comparative statement of retained earnings relates to Waterloo Corporation, which began operations in 1993.

	December 31	
	1995	*1994*
Retained earnings at beginning of year	*$ 900,000*	*$680,000*
Net income	*260,000*	*220,000*
Retained earnings at end of year	*$1,160,000*	*$900,000*

Waterloo decided on January 1, 1996, to change its depreciation method from declining-balance to straight-line. The information for the depreciation expense is as follows:

Year	*Declining-Balance*	*Straight-Line*
1993	*$100,000*	*$42,000*
1994	*75,000*	*42,000*
1995	*56,250*	*42,000*

INSTRUCTIONS

a Compute the amount of cumulative effect on the beginning balance of retained earnings for 1995, as a result of the change in depreciation method and indicate whether the effect is an increase or a decrease. (Disregard income tax considerations.)

b How would the income statements for 1994 and 1995 be affected by the change in depreciation method? (Disregard income tax considerations.)

c Assuming that after the 1996 net income of $188,000 was recorded, the company discovered that it should have changed the useful life of the assets in 1996. This change would have increased the depreciation expense by $12,000 for each of 1995, 1996, and 1997. Explain how this change would affect the net income and retained earnings for these three years. (Disregard income tax considerations.)

PROBLEM 15A-3
Format of an Income Statement and a Statement of Retained Earnings

The following data are relating to the operations of Academic Testing Services, Inc., during 1996:

Continuing operations:	
Net sales	*$15,750,000*
Costs and expenses (including applicable income taxes)	*12,800,000*
Other data:	
Operating income during 1996 on segment of the business discontinued near year-end (net of $112,500 income taxes)	*225,000*
Loss on disposal of discontinued segment (net of $337,500 income tax benefit)	*675,000*
Extraordinary loss (net of $390,000 income tax benefit)	*780,000*
Cumulative effect of change in accounting principle for a three-year period to December 31, 1995, resulted in an increase in total net income	*135,000*
Settlement of income tax assessment for 1992	*150,000*
Cash dividends declared	*925,000*

INSTRUCTIONS

a Prepare a condensed income statement for 1996, including earnings per share statistics. Academic Testing Services, Inc., had 300,000 shares of no-par value common stock and 40,000 shares of $6.25, no-par value preferred stock outstanding throughout the year.

b Prepare a statement of retained earnings for the year ended December 31, 1996. As originally reported, retained earnings at December 31, 1995 amounted to $6,450,000.

c Compute the amount of cash dividend ***per share*** of ***common stock*** declared by the board of directors for 1996. Assume no dividends in arrears on the preferred stock.

PROBLEM 15A-4
Reporting Unusual Events: A Comprehensive Problem

The following income statement was prepared by a new and inexperienced employee in the accounting department of Keller Interiors, a business organized as a corporation.

KELLER INTERIORS
Income Statement
For the Year Ended December 31, 1996

Net sales		*$10,800,000*
Gain on sale of treasury stock		*54,000*
Premium on capital stock		*510,000*
Prior period adjustment (net of $30,000 income taxes)		*60,000*
Extraordinary gain (net of $18,000 income taxes)		*36,000*
Total revenue		*$11,460,000*
Less:		
Cost of goods sold	*$6,000,000*	
Selling expenses	*1,128,000*	
General and administrative expenses	*1,896,000*	
Income taxes (on continuing operations)	*720,000*	
Operating loss on discontinued operations (net of $126,000 income tax benefit)	*252,000*	
Loss on disposal of discontinued operations (net of $210,000 income tax benefit)	*420,000*	
Cumulative effect of change in accounting principle	*84,000*	
Dividends declared on capital stock	*350,000*	
Total costs and expenses		*10,850,000*
Net income		*$ 610,000*

INSTRUCTIONS

a Prepare a corrected income statement for the year ended December 31, 1996. Include at the bottom of your income statement all appropriate earnings per share figures. Assume that throughout the year, the company had outstanding a weighted average of 200,000 shares of a single class of capital stock.

b Prepare a statement of retained earnings for 1996. (As originally reported, retained earnings at December 31, 1995 amounted to $1,400,000.)

PROBLEM 15A-5
Effects of Stock Dividends, Stock Splits, and Treasury Stock Transactions

At the beginning of the year, Recovery Sciences, Inc., has total shareholders' equity of $660,000 and 20,000 outstanding shares of a single class of capital stock. During the year, the corporation completes the following transactions affecting its shareholders' equity accounts:

Jan. 10 A 10% stock dividend is declared and distributed. (Market price, $40 per share.)

Mar. 15 The corporation acquires 1,000 shares of its own capital stock at a cost of $40.50 per share.

May 30 All 1,000 shares of the treasury stock are reissued at a price of $44.90 per share.

July 31 The capital stock is split 2 for 1.

Dec. 15 The board of directors declares a cash dividend of $1.10 per share, payable on January 15.

Dec. 31 Net income of $127,600 (equal to $2.90 per share) is reported for the year ended December 31.

INSTRUCTIONS

Compute the amount of total shareholders' equity, the number of shares of capital stock outstanding, and the book value per share following each successive transaction. Organize your solution as a three-column schedule with these separate column headings: (1) Total Shareholders' Equity, (2) Number of Shares Outstanding, and (3) Book Value per Share.

PROBLEM 15A-6
Recording Stock Dividends and Treasury Stock Transactions

At the beginning of 1996, OverNight Letter showed the following amounts in the shareholders' equity section of its balance sheet:

Shareholders' equity:	
Capital stock, no-par value, unlimited shares authorized, issued and outstanding, 382,000 shares	*$4,584,000*
Retained earnings	*2,704,600*
Total shareholders' equity	*$7,288,600*

The transactions relating to shareholders' equity accounts during the year are as follows:

Jan. 3 Declared a dividend of $1 per share to shareholders of record on January 31, payable on February 15.

Feb. 15 Paid the cash dividend declared on January 3.

Apr. 12 The corporation purchased 6,000 shares of its own capital stock at a price of $40 per share.

May 9 Reissued 4,000 shares of the treasury stock at a price of $44 per share.

June 1 Declared a 5% stock dividend to shareholders of record at June 15, to be distributed on June 30. The market price of the stock at June 1 was $42 per share.

June 30 Distributed the stock dividend declared on June 1.

Aug. 4 Reissued 600 of the 2,000 remaining shares of treasury stock at a price of $37 per share.

Dec. 31 The Income Summary account, showing net income for the year of $1,928,000 was closed into the Retained Earnings account.

INSTRUCTIONS

a Prepare in general journal form the entries to record the above transactions.

b Prepare the shareholders' equity section of the balance sheet at December 31, 1996. Use the format illustrated in this chapter. Include a supporting schedule showing your computation of retained earnings at that date.

c Compute the maximum cash dividend per share that legally could be declared at December 31, 1996 without impairing the contributed capital of OverNight Letter.

PROBLEM 15A-7
Preparing the Shareholders' Equity Section: A Challenging Case

The Mandella family decided early in 1995 to incorporate their family-owned vineyards under the name Mandella Corporation. The corporation was authorized to issue unlimited shares of a single class of no-par value capital stock. Presented below is the information necessary to prepare the shareholders' equity section of the company's balance sheet at the end of 1995 and at the end of 1996.

1995. In January the corporation issued to members of the Mandella family 150,000 shares of capital stock in exchange for cash and other assets used in the operation of the vineyards. The fair market value of these assets indicated an issue price of $30 per share. In December, Joe Mandella died, and the corporation purchased 10,000 shares of its own capital stock from his estate at $34 per share. Because of the large cash outlay to acquire this treasury stock, the directors decided not to declare cash dividends in 1995 and instead declared a 10% stock dividend to be distributed in January of 1996. The stock price at the declaration date was $35 per share. Net income for 1995 was $940,000.

1996. In January the corporation distributed the stock dividend declared in 1995, and in February, the 10,000 treasury shares were sold to Maria Mandella at $39 per share. In June, the capital stock was split 2 for 1. On December 15, the directors declared a cash dividend of $2 per share, payable in January of 1997. Net income for 1996 was $1,080,000.

INSTRUCTIONS

Using the format illustrated in this chapter, prepare the shareholders' equity section of the balance sheet at:

a December 31, 1995

b December 31, 1996

Show any necessary computations in supporting schedules.

Group B

PROBLEM 15B-1
Reporting Unusual Events; Using Predictive Subtotals

Sea Quest Corporation operated both a fleet of commercial fishing vessels and a chain of six seafood restaurants. The restaurants continuously lost money and were sold to a large restaurant chain near year-end. The operating results of Sea Quest Corporation for the year ended December 31, 1996, are shown below:

Continuing operations (fishing fleet):	
Net sales	*$23,000,000*
Costs and expenses (including applicable income taxes)	*20,100,000*
Other data:	
Operating loss from restaurants (net of $770,000 income tax benefit)	*1,540,000*
Gain on sale of restaurant properties (net of $230,000 income taxes)	*460,000*
Extraordinary loss (net of $360,000 income tax benefit)	*720,000*

The extraordinary loss resulted from the expropriation of a fishing vessel by a foreign government.

Sea Quest Corporation had 500,000 shares of capital stock outstanding throughout the year.

INSTRUCTIONS

a Prepare a condensed income statement including proper presentation of the discontinued restaurant operations and the extraordinary loss. Include all appropriate earnings per share figures.

b Assume that you expect the profitability of Sea Quest's fishing operations to ***increase by 5%*** in the next year and the profitability of the restaurants to remain unchanged. What is your estimate of the company's net earnings per share for 1997?

PROBLEM 15B-2
Accounting Changes

The following is a comparative statement of retained earnings for Fudan Limited for the last two years.

	December 31	
	1996	1995
Retained earnings at beginning of year	$480,000	$300,000
Net income	200,000	180,000
Retained earnings at end of year	$680,000	$480,000

Fudan Limited was incorporated on January 2, 1994, and used a straight-line method of depreciation for its depreciable assets until January 1, 1997. At that time, Fudan changed its depreciation method from straight-line to double-declining. The net income for 1997, based on the new depreciation method, is $286,000. The information for depreciation expense is as follows:

Year	Straight-Line	Declining-Balance
1994	$54,000	$120,000
1995	54,000	72,000
1996	54,000	43,200

INSTRUCTIONS

a Prepare a comparative statement of retained earnings for 1996 and 1997. (Disregard income tax considerations.)

b How would the income statement for 1995 be affected by the change in depreciation method? Explain. (Disregard income tax considerations.)

c Assuming that after the net income of $286,000 for 1997 was recorded, an engineering report showed that the company should have changed the useful life of its depreciable assets in 1997. Such a change would have decreased the depreciation expense by $14,600 for 1996 and by $8,620 for 1997. Explain how this change would affect the net income and retained earnings for 1996, 1997, and 1998. (Disregard income tax considerations.)

PROBLEM 15B-3
Format of an Income Statement and a Statement of Retained Earnings

Shown on the next page are data relating to the operations of Synthetic Genetics, Inc., during 1996:

Continuing operations:	
Net sales	*$21,000,000*
Costs and expenses (including applicable income taxes)	*18,300,000*
Other data:	
Operating loss during 1996 on segment of the business discontinued near year-end (net of $150,000 income tax benefit)	*300,000*
Loss on disposal of discontinued segment (net of $450,000 income tax benefit)	*900,000*
Extraordinary gain (net of $310,000 income taxes)	*620,000*
Cumulative effect of change in accounting principle from 1992 to 1995 resulted in an increase in total net income	*140,000*
Settlement of lawsuit against the company related to 1990, net of $120,000 income tax benefit	*240,000*
Cash dividends declared	*1,200,000*

INSTRUCTIONS

a Prepare a condensed income statement for 1996, including earnings per share statistics. Synthetic Genetics had 400,000 shares of no-par value common stock as well as 50,000 shares of $8, no-par value preferred stock outstanding throughout 1996.

b Prepare a statement of retained earnings for the year ended December 31, 1996. As originally reported, retained earnings at December 31, 1995, amounted to $7,400,000.

c What was the cash dividend ***per share*** of ***common stock*** declared by Synthetic Genetics' board of directors for 1996? Assume there were no dividends in arrears on the preferred stock.

PROBLEM 15B-4
Reporting the Results of Operations—A Comprehensive Problem

Katherine McCall, the accountant for Alternative Energy Systems, was injured in a skiing accident, and the following income statement was prepared by a temporary employee with little knowledge of accounting:

ALTERNATIVE ENERGY SYSTEMS
Income Statement
For the Year Ended December 31, 1996

Net sales		*$5,400,000*
Gain on sale of treasury stock		*30,000*
Premium on capital stock		*120,000*
Operating income from segment of business discontinued during the year (net of $100,000 income taxes)		*200,000*
Cumulative effect of change in accounting principle		*75,000*
Total revenue		*$5,825,000*
Less:		
Prior period adjustment (net of $125,000 income tax benefit)	*$ 250,000*	
Cost of goods sold	*2,480,000*	
Selling expenses	*1,160,000*	
General and administrative expenses	*820,000*	
Income taxes on continuing operations	*270,000*	
Extraordinary loss (net of $115,000 income tax benefit)	*230,000*	
Loss on sale of discontinued segment (net of $225,000 income tax benefit)	*450,000*	
Dividends declared on capital stock	*300,000*	*5,960,000*
Net loss		*$ 135,000*

INSTRUCTIONS

a Prepare a corrected income statement for the year ended December 31, 1996. Include at the bottom of your income statement all appropriate earnings per share figures. Assume that throughout the year the company had outstanding a weighted average of 50,000 shares of a single class of capital stock.

b Prepare a statement of retained earnings for 1996. Assume that retained earnings at December 31, 1995, were originally reported at $2,300,000.

PROBLEM 15B-5
Effects of Stock Dividends, Stock Splits, and Treasury Stock Transactions

On January 1, Alton Pump & Compressor Corporation has total shareholders' equity of $4,400,000 and 50,000 outstanding shares of a single class of capital stock. During the year, the corporation completes the following transactions affecting its shareholders' equity accounts:

Jan. 10 The board of directors declares a cash dividend of $4.20 per share, payable on February 15.

Apr. 30 The capital stock is split 2 for 1.

June 11 The corporation acquires 2,000 shares of its own capital stock at a cost of $56.60 per share.

July 21 All 2,000 shares of the treasury stock are reissued at a price of $61.60 per share.

Nov. 10 A 5% stock dividend is declared and distributed (market value $60 per share).

Dec. 31 Net income of $378,000 (equal to $3.60 per share) is reported for the year.

INSTRUCTIONS

Compute the amount of total shareholders' equity, the number of shares of capital stock outstanding, and the book value per share following each successive transaction. Organize your solution as a three-column schedule with these separate column headings: (1) Total Shareholders' Equity, (2) Number of Shares Outstanding, and (3) Book Value per Share.

PROBLEM 15B-6
Recording Stock Dividends and Treasury Stock Transactions

The shareholders' equity of Cornish Productions, Inc., at January 1, 1996, is as follows:

Shareholders' equity:	
Common stock, no-par value, authorized, unlimited shares, issued and outstanding, 260,000 shares	$5,365,000
Retained earnings	2,810,000
Total shareholders' equity	$8,175,000

During the year the following transactions relating to shareholders' equity occurred:

Jan. 15 Paid a $1.50 per share cash dividend declared in December of the preceding year. This dividend was properly recorded at the declaration date and was the only dividend declared during the preceding year.

June 10 Declared a 10% stock dividend to shareholders of record on June 30, to be distributed on July 15. At June 10, the market price of the stock was $35 per share.

July 15 Distributed the stock dividend declared on June 10.

Aug. 4 Purchased 10,000 shares of treasury stock at a price of $30 per share.

Oct. 15 Reissued 6,000 shares of treasury stock at a price of $32 per share.

Dec. 10 Reissued 2,000 shares of treasury stock at a price of $28.50 per share.

Dec. 15 Declared a cash dividend of $1.50 per share to be paid on January 15 to shareholders of record on December 31.

Dec. 31 The Income Summary account, showing net income of $1,620,000, was closed into the Retained Earnings account.

INSTRUCTIONS

a Prepare in general journal form the entries necessary to record these transactions.

b Prepare the shareholders' equity section of the balance sheet at December 31, 1996, following the format illustrated in this chapter. Include a note following your shareholders' equity section indicating any portion of retained earnings that is not available for dividends. Also include a supporting schedule showing your computation of the balance of retained earnings at year-end.

c Comment on whether Cornish Productions, Inc., increased or decreased the total amount of cash dividends declared during the year in comparison with dividends declared in the preceding year.

PROBLEM 15B-7
Preparing the Shareholders' Equity Section of a Balance Sheet

David Klein was a free-lance engineer who developed and patented a highly efficient turbocharger for automotive engines. In 1995, Klein and Scott Harris organized Performance, Inc., to manufacture the turbocharger. The corporation was authorized to issue unlimited shares of no-par value capital stock. Presented below is the information necessary to prepare the shareholders' equity section of the company's balance sheet at the end of 1995 and at the end of 1996.

1995. On January 20, the corporation issued 80,000 shares of common stock to Harris and other investors for cash at $34 per share. In addition, 10,000 shares of common stock were issued on that date to Klein in exchange for his patents. In November, Klein was killed while auto racing in Europe. At the request of Klein's heirs, Performance, Inc., purchased the 10,000 shares of its stock from Klein's estate at $45 per share. Because of the unexpected cash outlay to acquire treasury stock, the directors decided against declaring any cash dividends in 1995. Instead, they declared a 5% stock dividend that was distributed on December 31. The stock price at the declaration date was $42 per share. Net income for the year was $415,000.

1996. In March, the 10,000 treasury shares were reissued at a price of $52 per share. In August, the stock was split 4 for 1. On December 20, the directors declared a cash dividend of 70 cents per share, payable in January of 1997. Net income for the year was $486,000.

INSTRUCTIONS

Prepare the shareholders' equity section of the balance sheet at:

a December 31, 1995

b December 31, 1996

Use the format illustrated in this chapter and show any necessary supporting computations.

ANALYTICAL AND DECISION PROBLEMS AND CASES

A&D 15-1
What's This?

The following events have been reported in the financial statements of large corporations.

a **TransCanada PipeLines** sold all of its United States oil and gas properties held by its wholly owned subsidiary for approximately $150 million. In the year of disposal, the U.S. operation had an operating income of $2.4 million. Also, the loss on disposal of the U.S. operation amounted to $52.7 million.

b **Banister Continental Ltd.** reduced the remaining useful lives of certain older pieces of construction equipment. This change increased depreciation expense and decreased net income for the year by $1,030,000.

c **Union Carbide Corp.** sustained a large loss as a result of the explosion of a chemical plant.

d **Algoma Central Railway** received $951,000 in settlement of a claim relating to a fire aboard one of its vessels a few years ago. Income taxes applicable to the settlement amounted to $422,000.

e **Derlan Industries Limited** changed its policy of accounting for capital stock issue costs by charging these costs to retained earnings rather than capitalizing them as an asset. The cumulative effect of this change affecting the beginning balance of retained earnings for the preceding year was $2,370,000. Also, the effect of this change for the preceding year was $2,734,000.

INSTRUCTIONS Indicate how each of these items should be accounted for or presented in the financial statements. Briefly explain the reasons for your answers.

A&D 15-2
The Case of the Extraordinarily Ordinary Loss

In 1994, a large corporation recognized a $68 million loss from the write-off of certain foreign-based assets due to "escalating war, social upheaval, the weakening economies of oil-producing nations, and growing political instability." (The operations in these foreign countries were not discontinued.) The company originally classified this loss as an extraordinary item. Upon reviewing the company's financial statements, however, the securities commission requested that the company reclassify this item as a normal operating loss. In 1995, the company revised its 1994 income statement to comply with the commission's request.

INSTRUCTIONS Indicate the effect of the reclassification of this loss upon the company's:

a Net income for 1994.

b Income before extraordinary items for 1994.

c Income from continuing operations in 1994.

d Price-earnings ratio as shown in financial newspapers such as *The Financial Post.*

e 1995 financial statements.

f Ability to pay cash dividends.

Explain the reasoning behind your answers.

A&D 15-3
Is There Life without Baseball?

Midwestern Publishing, Inc., publishes two newspapers and until recently owned a professional baseball team. The baseball team had been losing money for several years and was sold at the end of 1995 to a group of investors who plan to move it to a larger city. Also in 1995, Midwestern suffered an extraordinary loss when its Raytown printing plant was damaged by a tornado. The damage has since been repaired. A condensed income statement follows:

MIDWESTERN PUBLISHING, INC.
Income Statement
For the Year Ended December 31, 1995

Net revenue		$41,000,000
Costs and expenses		36,500,000
Income from continuing operations		$ 4,500,000
Discontinued operations:		
Operating loss on baseball team	$(1,300,000)	
Gain on sale of baseball team	4,700,000	3,400,000
Income before extraordinary items		$ 7,900,000
Extraordinary loss:		
Tornado damage to Raytown printing plant		(600,000)
Net income		$ 7,300,000

INSTRUCTIONS On the basis of this information, answer the following questions. Show any necessary computations and explain your reasoning.

a What would Midwestern's net income have been for 1995 if it ***had not*** sold the baseball team?

b Assume that for 1996, you expect a 7% increase in the profitability of Midwestern's newspaper business but had projected a $2,000,000 operating loss for the baseball team if Midwestern had continued to operate the team in 1996. What amount would you forecast as Midwestern's 1996 net income ***if the company had continued to own and operate the baseball team?***

c Given your assumptions in part **b,** but given that Midwestern ***did*** sell the baseball team in 1995, what would you forecast as the company's estimated net income for 1996?

d Assume that the expenses of operating the baseball team in 1995 amounted to $32,200,000, net of any applicable income tax effects. What was the team's ***net revenue*** for the year?

A&D 15-4
Using Earnings per Share Statistics

For many years Canadian Studios has produced television shows and operated several FM radio stations. Late in the current year, the radio stations were sold to Times Publishing, Inc. Also during the current year, Canadian Studios sustained an extraordinary loss when one of its camera trucks caused an accident in a grand prix auto race. Throughout the current year, the company had 3 million shares of common stock and a large quantity of convertible preferred stock outstanding. Earnings per share reported for the current year were as follows:

	Basic	Fully Diluted
Earnings from continuing operations	$8.20	$6.80
Earnings before extraordinary items	$6.90	$5.50
Net earnings	$3.80	$2.40

INSTRUCTIONS

a Briefly explain why Canadian Studios reports fully diluted earnings per share amounts as well as earnings per share computed on a basic basis. What is the purpose of showing investors the fully diluted figures?

b What was the total dollar amount of the extraordinary loss sustained by Canadian Studios during the current year?

c Assume that the price-earnings ratio shown in the morning newspaper for Canadian Studios' common stock indicates that the stock is selling at a price equal to 10 times the reported earnings per share. What is the approximate market price of the stock?

d Assume that you expect both the revenue and expenses involved in producing television shows to increase by 10% during the coming year. What would you forecast as the company's net earnings per share (basic basis) for the coming year under each of the following independent assumptions? (Show your computations and explain your reasoning.)

1. ***None*** of the convertible preferred stock is converted into common stock during the coming year.
2. ***All*** of the convertible preferred stock is converted into common stock at the beginning of the coming year.

CHAPTER

16 Special Types of Liabilities

"Routine" types of business liabilities were discussed in Chapter 11. In this second chapter about liabilities we explore many special types of liabilities. We will consider such questions as: How can a corporation borrow a huge amount of money on a long-term basis from many small, short-term investors? Why are some long-term lease agreements viewed as liabilities, whereas others are not? How can the balance sheet of a large corporation that has promised millions of dollars of retirement benefits to its employees include no liability for this obligation? And just what are deferred taxes, anyway?

The liabilities discussed in this chapter appear primarily in the financial statements of large, publicly owned corporations. Some, however, also affect the financial statements of smaller organizations.

Learning Objectives:

After studying this chapter you should be able to:

1 *Describe the typical characteristics of corporate bonds.*

2 *Explain the tax advantage of raising capital by issuing bonds instead of stock.*

3 *Account for the issuance of bonds, accrual and payment of interest, and retirement of bonds.*

4 *Describe the relationship between interest rates and bond prices.*

5 *Explain the effects of amortizing bond discount and premium upon bond interest expense.*

6 *Amortize bond discount and premium by the straight-line and the effective interest methods.*

7 *Explain the accounting treatment of operating leases and of capital leases.*

8 *Account for the costs of pensions and other postretirement benefits.*

9 *Explain the nature of deferred income taxes.*

*10 *Explain the accounting treatment of convertible bonds payable.*

---

* *Supplemental Topic, "Convertible Bonds Payable"*

BONDS PAYABLE

Financially sound corporations may arrange limited amounts of long-term financing by issuing notes payable to banks or to insurance companies. But to finance a large project, such as developing an oil field or purchasing a controlling interest in the capital stock of another company, a corporation may need more capital than any single lender can supply. When a corporation needs to raise large amounts of long-term capital—perhaps 50, 100, or 500 million dollars (or more)—it generally sells additional shares of capital stock or issues ***bonds payable.***

What Are Bonds?

OBJECTIVE 1 Describe the typical characteristics of corporate bonds.

The issuance of bonds payable is a technique for splitting a very large loan into a great many transferable units, called bonds. Each bond represents a ***long-term, interest-bearing note payable,*** usually in the face amount (or par value) of $1,000, or some multiple of $1,000. The bonds are sold to the investing public, enabling many different investors (bondholders) to participate in the loan.

Bonds usually are very long-term notes, maturing in perhaps 15 or 20 years. The bonds are transferable, however, so individual bondholders may sell their bonds to other investors at any time. Most bonds call for semiannual interest payments to the bondholders, with interest computed at a specified ***contract rate*** (the interest rate printed on the bonds) throughout the life of the bond. Thus, investors often describe bonds as "fixed income" investments. An example of a corporate bond issue is the 10.25% bonds payable of Maritime Telegraph & Telephone, which were issued some years ago and are due August 1, 2006. With this bond issue, Maritime Telegraph & Telephone borrowed $50 million by issuing 50,000 bonds of $1,000 each, at an annual contract interest rate of 10.25%. Each bondholder is issued a single ***bond certificate*** indicating the number of bonds purchased. Investors such as mutual funds, banks, and insurance companies often buy thousands of bonds at one time.

Bonds payable differ from capital stock in several ways. First, bonds payable are a liability; thus, bondholders are ***creditors*** of the corporation, not owners. Bondholders generally do not have voting rights and do not participate in the earnings of the corporation beyond receiving contractual interest payments. Next, bond interest payments are ***contractual obligations*** of the corporation. Dividends, on the other hand, do not become legal obligations of the corporation until they have been formally declared by the board of directors. Finally, bonds have a specified ***maturity date,*** upon which the corporation must redeem the bonds at their face amount. Capital stock, on the other hand, does not have a maturity date and may remain outstanding indefinitely.

Authorization of a Bond Issue Formal approval of the board of directors and the shareholders may be required before bonds can be issued. If the bonds are to be sold to the general public, certain requirements of the provincial securities commissions must be met, just as for an issue of capital stock that is offered to the public.

When bonds are issued, the corporation usually utilizes the services of an investment dealer, called an ***underwriter.*** The underwriter guarantees the issuing corporation a specific price for the entire bond issue and makes a profit by selling the bonds to the investing public at a higher price. The corporation records the issuance of the bonds at the net amount received from the underwriter. The use of an underwriter assures the corporation that the entire bond issue will be sold without delay, and the entire amount of the proceeds will be available at a specific date.

Transferability of Bonds Corporate bonds, like capital stocks, are traded daily on organized securities exchanges, such as the ***Toronto Stock Exchange.*** The holders of a 20-year bond issue need not wait 20 years to convert their investments into cash. By placing a telephone call to a broker, an investor may sell bonds within a matter of minutes at the going market price. This quality of ***liquidity*** is one of the most attractive features of an investment in corporate bonds.

Quoted Market Prices Bond prices are quoted as a ***percentage*** of their face value or ***maturity*** value, which is usually $1,000. The maturity value is the amount the issuing company must pay to redeem the bond at the date it matures (becomes due). A $1,000 bond quoted at ***102*** would therefore have a market price of $1,020 (102% of $1,000). The following line from *The Financial Post* summarizes certain information on one of Bell Canada's bonds:

What is the market value of this bond?

Bonds	*Interest Rate*	*Maturity date*	*Bid*	*Yield*
Bell Can.	12.650%	Nov. 15, 03	$122.50	7.38%

This line of condensed information indicates that Bell Canada's 12.650% (contract interest rate) bonds will be matured on November 15, 2003, the buyers were willing to pay $122.50 or $1,225 for a bond of $1,000 face value, and the yield rate (the effective interest rate) on the bid price is 7.38%.

The primary factors that determine the market value of a bond are (1) the relationship of the bond's interest rate to other investment opportunities, (2) the length of time until the bond matures, and (3) investors' confidence that the issuing company has the financial strength to make all future interest and principal payments promptly. Thus, a bond with a 10% interest rate will command a higher market price than an 8% bond with the same maturity date if the two companies issuing the bonds are of equal financial strength.

A bond selling at a market price greater than its maturity value is said to be selling at a ***premium;*** a bond selling at a price below its maturity value is selling at a ***discount.*** As a bond nears its maturity date, the market price of the bond moves toward the maturity value. At the maturity date the market value of the bond will be exactly equal to its maturity value, because the issuing corporation will redeem the bond for that amount.

Types of Bonds Bonds secured by the pledge of specific assets are called ***mortgage bonds.*** An unsecured bond is called a ***debenture bond;*** its value rests upon the general credit of the corporation. A debenture bond issued by a very large and strong corporation may have a higher investment rating than a secured bond issued by a corporation in less satisfactory financial condition.

Bond interest is usually paid semiannually by mailing to each bondholder a cheque for six months' interest on the bonds he or she owns.[1] Almost all bonds are ***callable (redeemable),*** which means that the corporation has the right to redeem the bonds ***in advance*** of the maturity date by paying a specified ***call (redemption) price.*** To compensate bondholders for being forced to give up their investments, the call price usually is somewhat higher than the face value of the bonds.

Corporations must maintain a ***bondholders subsidiary ledger,*** showing each bondholder's name and address and the face value of bonds owned. This record provides the information necessary for determining the amount of interest payable to each bondholder and for notifying bondholders if their bonds are called.

Traditionally, bonds have appealed to conservative investors, interested primarily in a reliable income stream and in the safety of the principal that they have invested. To make a bond issue more attractive to these investors, some corporations create a bond ***sinking fund,*** designated for repaying the bonds at maturity. At regular intervals, the corporation deposits cash into this sinking fund. A bond sinking fund is not classified as a current asset, because it is not available for the payment of current liabilities. Such funds are shown in the balance sheet under the caption "Long-term Investments," which appears just below the current asset section.

As an additional attraction to investors, corporations sometimes include a conversion privilege in the bond indenture. A ***convertible bond*** is one that may be exchanged at the option of the bondholder for a specified number of shares of common stock. Thus, the market value of a convertible bond tends to fluctuate with the market value of an equivalent number of shares of common stock.

"Junk Bonds" In recent years, some corporations have issued securities that have come to be known as ***junk bonds.*** This term describes a bond issue that involves a substantially greater risk of default than normal. A company issuing junk bonds usually has so much long-term debt that its ability to meet interest and principal repayment obligations has become questionable. To compensate bondholders for this unusual level of risk, junk bonds promise a substantially higher rate of interest than do more "highly rated" bonds.

---

[1] In recent years, corporations have issued only ***registered*** bonds, for which interest is paid by mailing a cheque to the registered owners of the bonds. In past decades, some companies issued ***coupon bonds*** or ***bearer bonds,*** which had a series of redeemable coupons attached. At each interest date, the bondholder was to "clip" the coupon and present it to a bank to collect the interest. These bonds posed a considerable hazard to investors—if the investor lost the coupon, or forgot about an interest date, he or she received no interest.

Tax Advantage of Bond Financing

OBJECTIVE 2 Explain the tax advantage of raising capital by issuing bonds instead of stock.

A principal advantage of raising money by issuing bonds instead of stock is that interest payments are ***deductible*** in determining income subject to corporate income taxes. Dividends paid to shareholders, however, are ***not deductible*** in computing taxable income.

To illustrate, assume that a corporation pays income taxes at a rate of ***30%*** on its taxable income. If this corporation issues \$10 million of 10% bonds payable, it will incur interest expense of \$1 million per year. This interest expense, however, will reduce taxable income by \$1 million, thus reducing the corporation's annual income taxes by \$300,000. As a result, the ***after-tax*** cost of borrowing the \$10 million is only ***\$700,000,*** as shown below:

Interest expense (\$10,000,000 × 10%)	\$1,000,000
Less: Income tax savings (\$1,000,000 deduction × 30%)	300,000
After-tax cost of borrowing	\$700,000

A short-cut approach to computing the after-tax cost of borrowing is simply multiplying the interest expense by ***1 minus the company's tax rate,*** as follows: $\$1,000,000 \times (1 - .30) = \$700,000$.

Accounting for Bonds Payable

OBJECTIVE 3 Account for the issuance of bonds, accrual and payment of interest, and retirement of bonds.

Accounting for bonds payable closely parallels accounting for notes payable. The "accountable events" in the life of a bond issue usually are (1) issuance of the bonds, (2) semiannual interest payments, (3) accrual of interest payable at the end of each accounting period,[2] and (4) retirement of the bonds at maturity.

To illustrate these events, assume that on March 1, 1995, Wells Corporation issues \$1 million of 12%, 20-year bonds payable.[3] These bonds are dated March 1, 1995, and interest is computed from this date. Interest on the bonds is payable semiannually, each September 1 and March 1. If all of the bonds are sold at par value (face amount), the issuance of the bonds on March 1 will be recorded by the following entry:

Cash	1,000,000	
Bonds Payable		1,000,000
Issued 12%, 20-year bonds payable at a price of 100.		

Every September 1 during the life of the bond issue, Wells Corporation must pay \$60,000 to the bondholders ($\$1,000,000 \times .12 \times \frac{1}{2} = \$60,000$). This semiannual interest payment will be recorded as shown below:

Bond Interest Expense	60,000	
Cash		60,000
Semiannual payment of bond interest.		

---

2 To simplify our illustrations, we assume in all of our examples and assignment material that adjusting entries for accrued bond interest payable are made ***only at year-end.*** In practice, these adjustments usually are made on a monthly basis.

3 The amount of \$1 million is used only for purposes of illustration. As explained earlier, actual bond issues are for many millions of dollars.

Every December 31 (the year-end date), Wells Corporation must make an adjusting entry to record the four months' interest that has accrued since September 1:

Bond Interest Expense	*40,000*	
Bond Interest Payable		*40,000*
To accrue bond interest payable for four months ended Dec. 31 ($1,000,000 × .12 × $\frac{4}{12}$ = $40,000).		

The accrued liability for bond interest payable will be paid within a few months and, therefore, is classified as a current liability.

Two months later, on March 1, a semiannual interest payment is made to bondholders. This transaction represents payment of the four months' interest accrued at December 31, and of two months' interest that has accrued since year-end. If we assume that the company does not use reversing entries, the entry to record the semiannual payments every March 1 will be:

Bond Interest Expense	*20,000*	
Bond Interest Payable	*40,000*	
Cash		*60,000*
To record semiannual interest payment to bondholders, and to recognize two months' interest expense accrued since year-end ($1,000,000 × .12 × $\frac{2}{12}$ = $20,000).		

When the bonds mature 20 years later on March 1, 2015, two entries are required: one entry to record the regular semiannual interest payment (which is the same as the above entry on March 1) and a second entry to record the retirement of the bonds. The entry to record retirement of the bond issue is:

Bonds Payable	*1,000,000*	
Cash		*1,000,000*
Paid face amount of bonds at maturity.		

Bonds Issued between Interest Dates The semiannual interest dates (such as January 1 and July 1, or April 1 and October 1) are printed on the bond certificates. However, bonds are often issued between the specified interest dates. The ***investor*** is then required to pay the interest accrued to the date of issuance ***in addition*** to the stated price of the bond. This practice enables the corporation to pay a full six months' interest on all bonds outstanding at the semiannual interest payment date. The accrued interest collected from investors purchasing bonds between interest payment dates is thus returned to them on the next interest payment date.

To illustrate, let us modify our illustration to assume that Wells Corporation issues $1 million of 12% bonds at a price of 100 on ***May 1***—two months ***after*** the date printed on the bonds. The amount received from the bond purchasers now will include two months' accrued interest, as follows:

Bonds issued between interest dates

Cash	*1,020,000*	
Bonds Payable		*1,000,000*
Bond Interest Payable		*20,000*
Issued $1,000,000 face value of 12%, 20-year bonds at 100 plus accrued interest for two months ($1,000,000 × 12% × $\frac{2}{12}$ = $20,000).		

Four months later on the regular semiannual interest payment date, a full six months' interest ($60 per each $1,000 bond) will be paid to all bondholders, ***regardless of when they purchased their bonds.*** The entry for the semiannual interest payment is illustrated below:

Notice only part of the interest payment is charged to expense

Bond Interest Payable	20,000	
Bond Interest Expense	40,000	
Cash		60,000
Paid semiannual interest on $1,000,000 face value of 12% bonds.		

Now consider these interest transactions from the standpoint of the ***investors.*** They paid for two months' accrued interest at the time of purchasing the bonds, and then received cheques for six months' interest after holding the bonds for only four months. They have, therefore, been compensated properly for the use of their money for four months.

When bonds are subsequently sold by one investor to another, they sell at the quoted market price ***plus accrued interest*** since the last interest payment date. This practice enables the issuing corporation to pay all the interest for an interest period to the investor owning the bond at the interest date. Otherwise, the corporation would have to make partial payments to every investor who bought or sold the bond during the interest period. This would be costly and impractical.

The amount that investors will pay for bonds is the ***present value*** of the principal and interest payments they will receive. Before going further in our discussion of bonds payable, it will be helpful to review the concepts of present value and effective interest rate.

The Concept of Present Value

The concept of present value is based upon the "time value" of money—the idea that receiving money today is preferable to receiving money at some later date. Assume, for example, that a bond will have a maturity value of $1,000 five years from today but will pay no interest in the meantime. Investors would not pay $1,000 for this bond today, because they would receive no return on their investment over the next five years. There are prices less than $1,000, however, at which investors would buy the bond. For example, if the bond could be purchased for $600, the investor could expect a return (interest) of $400 from the investment over the five-year period.

The ***present value*** of a future cash receipt is the amount that a knowledgeable investor will pay ***today*** for the right to receive that future payment. The exact amount of the present value depends upon (1) the amount of the future payment, (2) the length of time until the payment will be received, and (3) the rate of return required by the investor. However, the present value will always be ***less*** than the future amount. This is because money received today can be invested to earn interest and thereby becomes equivalent to a larger amount in the future.

The rate of interest that will cause a given present value to grow to a given future amount is called the ***discount rate*** or ***effective interest rate.*** The effective interest rate required by investors at any given time is regarded as the going ***market rate*** of interest. (The procedures for computing the present value of a future amount are illustrated in Appendix A at the end of this chapter.)

OBJECTIVE 4 Describe the relationship between interest rates and bond prices.

The Present Value Concept and Bond Prices The price at which bonds will sell is the present value to investors of the future principal and interest payments. If the bonds sell at par, the market interest rate is equal to the ***contract interest rate*** (or nominal rate) printed on the bonds. The ***higher*** the effective interest rate that investors require, the ***less*** they will pay for bonds with a given contract rate of interest. For example, if investors insist upon a 10% return, they will pay less than $1,000 for a 9%, $1,000 bond. Thus, if investors require an effective interest rate ***greater*** than the contract rate of interest for the bonds, the bonds will sell at a ***discount*** (price less than face value). On the other hand, if investors require an effective interest rate of ***less*** than the contract interest rate, the bonds will sell at a ***premium*** (price above face value).

A corporation wishing to borrow money by issuing bonds must pay the going market rate of interest. Since market rates of interest are fluctuating constantly, it must be expected that the contract rate of interest may vary somewhat from the market interest rate at the date the bonds are issued. Thus, bonds may be issued at either a discount or a premium.

Bonds Issued at a Discount

To illustrate the sale of bonds at a discount, assume that SCUBA TECH plans to issue $1 million face value of 9%, 10-year bonds, interest payable semiannually. At the issuance date of January 1, the going market rate of interest is slightly above 9% and the bonds sell at a price of only ***98*** ($980 for each $1,000 bond). The issuance of the bonds will be recorded by the following entry:

Issuance of bonds at a discount

Cash	980,000	
Discount on Bonds Payable	20,000	
Bonds Payable		1,000,000
Issued $1,000,000 face value of 9%, 10-year bonds at 98.		

If a balance sheet is prepared immediately after the issuance of the bonds, the liability for bonds payable will be shown as follows:

Reporting the net liability

Long-term liabilities:		
9% bonds payable, due in 10 years	$1,000,000	
Less: Discount on bonds payable	20,000	$980,000

The amount of the discount is deducted from the face value of the bonds payable to show the ***carrying value*** or book value of the liability. At the date of issuance, the carrying value of bonds payable is equal to the amount for which the bonds were sold. In other words, the amount of the company's liability at the date of issuing the bonds is equal to the ***amount of money borrowed.*** Over the life of the bonds, however, we shall see that this carrying value gradually increases until it reaches the face value of the bonds at the maturity date.

Bond Discount as Part of the Cost of Borrowing In Chapter 11, we illustrated two ways in which interest charges can be specified in a note payable: the interest may be stated as an annual percentage rate of the face amount of the note, or it may be included in the face amount. Bonds issued at a discount include ***both*** types of interest charge. The $1 million bond issue in our SCUBA TECH example calls for cash interest payments of $90,000 per year ($1,000,000 × 9% contract interest rate), payable semiannually. In addition to making the semiannual interest payments, the corporation must redeem the bond issue for $1 million on the maturity date. This maturity value is ***$20,000 more*** than the $980,000 received when the bonds were issued. Thus, the $20,000 discount in the issue price may be regarded as an ***interest charge included in the maturity value of the bonds.***

Although the interest charge represented by the discount will not be paid to bondholders until the bonds mature, SCUBA TECH benefits from this cost during the entire period that it has the use of the bondholders' money (that is, from the date of issue, which is not necessarily the date of the bonds, to the maturity date of the bonds). Therefore, the cost represented by the discount should be allocated over the life of the bond issue. The process of allocating bond discount to interest expense is termed ***amortization*** of the discount.

OBJECTIVE 5 Explain the effects of amortizing bond discount and premium upon bond interest expense.

Bonds are sometimes issued between interest dates. In this situation the bonds are outstanding for a shorter time; therefore, the amortization period is shorter. For example, if a 10-year bond issue dated January 1, 1996, is issued on March 1, 1996, the bonds will be outstanding for 9 years and 10 months, or a total of ***118 months.*** Under the straight-line method of amortization, the discount amortized per month will be $\frac{1}{118}$ of the total discount.

Whenever bonds are issued at a discount, the total interest cost over the life of the bonds is equal to the total of the regular cash interest payments ***plus the amount of the discount.*** For the $1 million bond issue in our example, the total interest cost over the 10-year life of the bonds is ***$920,000*** of which $900,000 represents the 20 semiannual cash interest payments and $20,000 represents the discount. The average annual interest expense, therefore, is ***$92,000*** ($920,000 ÷ 10 years), consisting of $90,000 paid in cash and $2,000 amortization of the bond discount (which will be paid in one lump sum of $20,000 when the bonds mature). This analysis is illustrated below:

Total cash interest payments to bondholders		
($1,000,000 × 9% × 10 years)		*$900,000*
Add: Interest charge included in face amount of bonds:		
Maturity value of bonds	*$1,000,000*	
Amount borrowed	*980,000*	*20,000*
Total cost of borrowing over life of bond issue		*$920,000*
Average annual interest expense ($920,000 ÷ 10 years)		*$ 92,000*

Similarly, bond premium reduces the interest cost, as explained later.

OBJECTIVE 6 Amortize bond discount and premium by the straight-line and the effective interest methods.

Amortization of Bond Discount The simplest method of amortizing bond discount is the ***straight-line method,*** which allocates an equal portion of the discount to Bond Interest Expense in each period.[4] In our example, the Discount on Bonds Payable account has a beginning debit balance of

[4] An alternative method of amortization, called the ***effective interest method,*** is illustrated later in this chapter. Although the effective interest method is theoretically preferable to the straight-line method, the resulting differences generally are not material in dollar amount.

$20,000; each year $\frac{1}{10}$ of this amount, or $2,000, will be amortized into Bond Interest Expense. Assuming that the interest payment dates are June 30 and December 31, the entries to be made each six months to record bond interest expense are as follows:

Payment of bond interest and straight-line amortization of bond discount

Bond Interest Expense	*45,000*	
Cash		*45,000*
Paid semiannual interest on $1,000,000 of 9%, 10-year bonds.		
Bond Interest Expense	*1,000*	
Discount on Bonds Payable		*1,000*
Amortized discount for six months on 10-year bond issue ($20,000 discount × $\frac{1}{20}$).		

The two entries shown above to record the cash payment of bond interest and to record the amortization of bond discount can conveniently be combined into one compound entry, as follows:

Bond Interest Expense	*46,000*	
Cash		*45,000*
Discount on Bonds Payable		*1,000*
To record payment of semiannual interest on $1,000,000 of 9%, 10-year bonds ($1,000,000 × 9% × $\frac{1}{2}$) and to amortize $\frac{1}{20}$ of the $20,000 discount on the 10-year bond issue.		

Regardless of whether the cash payment of interest and the amortization of bond discount are recorded in separate entries or combined in one entry, the amount recognized as Bond Interest Expense is the same—$46,000 each six months, or a total of $92,000 a year. An alternative accounting procedure that will produce the same results is to amortize the bond discount only at year-end rather than at each interest-payment date.

Note that the additional interest expense resulting from amortization of the discount does not require any additional cash payment. The credit portion of the entry is to the contra-liability account, Discount on Bonds Payable, rather than to the Cash account. Crediting this contra-liability account increases the carrying value of bonds, which is a long-term liability. The original $20,000 discount will be completely amortized by the end of the tenth year, and the net liability (carrying value) will be the full face value of the bonds.

In this example, the bonds were outstanding for the full term of 10 years or 120 months. If the bonds had been issued between interest dates, say, March 1, rather than January 1, the amortization period would have been the shortened life of 118 months.

Zero Coupon Bonds Some companies have issued bonds that pay ***no interest*** over the life of the bond. Thus, the entire interest charge is included in the face amount of the bonds and is represented by a ***very large discount*** at the issuance date. Such bonds, called ***zero coupon*** (or ***zeros***), usually are issued at a price of less than 20% of their maturity value.

The discount on zero coupon bonds is so material that the straight-line method of amortization produces misleading results. Therefore, generally accepted accounting principles require that the discount on such bonds be amortized by the ***effective interest method,*** which is discussed later in this chapter.

Further discussion of zero coupon bonds is deferred to the intermediate accounting course and to courses in corporate finance.

Bonds Issued at a Premium

Bonds will sell ***above*** par if the contract rate of interest specified on the bonds is ***higher*** than the current market rate for bonds of this grade. Let us now change our basic illustration by assuming that the $1 million issue of 9%, 10-year bonds is sold at a price of 102 ($1,020 for each $1,000 bond). The entry is as follows:

Issuance of bonds at a premium

Cash	1,020,000	
Bonds Payable		1,000,000
Premium on Bonds Payable		20,000
Issued $1,000,000 face value of 9%, 10-year bonds at price of 102.		

If a balance sheet is prepared immediately following the sale of the bonds, the liability will be shown as follows:

Reporting the carrying value of the liability

Long-term liabilities:		
9% bonds payable, due in 10 years	$1,000,000	
Add: Premium on bonds payable	20,000	$1,020,000

The amount of any unamortized premium is ***added*** to the maturity value of the bonds payable to show the current carrying value of the liability. Over the life of the bond issue, this carrying value will be ***reduced*** toward the maturity value of $1 million.

Bond Premium as Reduction in the Cost of Borrowing We have illustrated how issuing bonds at a discount increases the cost of borrowing above the amount of the regular cash interest payments. Issuing bonds at a premium, on the other hand, ***reduces the cost of borrowing below the amount of the regular cash interest payments.***

The amount received from issuance of the bonds is $20,000 greater than the amount that must be repaid at maturity. This $20,000 premium is not a gain but is to be offset against the periodic interest payments in determining the net cost of borrowing.

Whenever bonds are issued at a premium, the total interest cost over the life of the bonds is equal to the regular cash interest payments ***minus the amount of the premium.*** In our example, the total interest cost over the life of the bonds is computed as $900,000 of cash interest payments, minus $20,000 of premium amortized (which is not paid back to the bondholders), or a net borrowing cost of ***$880,000.*** The average annual interest expense will be ***$88,000,*** consisting of $90,000 paid in cash each year, less an offsetting $2,000 reduction in the net liability for bonds payable that results from amortization of the premium.

The semiannual entries on June 30 and December 31 to record the payment of bond interest and amortization of bond premium (by the straight-line method) are as follows:

Payment of bond interest and straight-line amortization of bond premium

Bond Interest Expense	45,000	
Cash		45,000
Paid semiannual interest on $1,000,000 of 9%, 10-year bonds.		
Premium on Bonds Payable	1,000	
Bond Interest Expense		1,000
Amortized premium for six months on 10-year bond issue ($20,000 premium × $\frac{1}{20}$).		

In our prior discussion of bond discount, we stated that if bonds are issued between interest dates, the amortization period will be shortened. This concept also applies to bonds issued at a premium. In brief, the period for amortization of either bond discount or premium is determined by the number of years and months the bonds are actually outstanding (that is, from the date the bonds are sold to the maturity date).

Year-End Adjustments for Bond Interest Expense

In the preceding illustration, it was assumed that one of the semiannual dates for payment of bond interest coincided with the end of the company's accounting year. In many cases, however, the semiannual interest payment dates will fall during an accounting period rather than on the last day of the year.

For purposes of illustration, assume that $1 million of 12%, 10-year bonds are issued at a price of 97 on ***October 1,*** 1996. Interest payment dates are April 1, and October 1. The total discount to be amortized amounts to $30,000, or $1,500 in each six-month interest period. (Notice that the discount is amortized at a rate of $250 per month, using a straight-line method of amortization.) Now also assume that the corporation closes its accounts at the end of each calendar year. At December 31, an ***adjusting entry*** will be needed to (1) record accrued interest at the 12% contract rate for the three months since October 1 and (2) amortize the bond discount for the three months since October 1. This adjusting entry will be:

Bond Interest Expense	30,750	
Bond Interest Payable		30,000
Discount on Bonds Payable		750

To adjust for accrued interest on bonds and to amortize discount for period from Oct. 1 to Dec. 31. Accrued interest: $\$1,000,000 \times .12 \times \frac{3}{12} = \$30,000$. Amortization: $\$30,000 \times \frac{3}{120} = \$750$.

A similar adjusting entry will be required every December 31 throughout the life of the bond issue.

In the December 31, 1996 balance sheet, the bond interest payable of $30,000 will appear as a current liability. The long-term liability for bonds payable will appear as follows:

Long-term liabilities:		
12% Bonds payable, due Oct. 1, 2006	$1,000,000	
Less: Discount on bonds payable	29,250	$970,750

When the bonds were issued on October 1, the net liability for bonds payable was $970,000. Notice that the carrying value of the bonds has ***increased*** over the three months by the amount of discount amortized. When the entire discount has been amortized, the carrying value of the bonds will be $1 million, which is equal to their maturity value.

On April 1, we must record interest expense and discount amortization only for the ***three-month period since year-end.*** Of the semiannual $60,000 cash payment to bondholders, one-half, or $30,000, represents payment of the liability for bond interest payable recorded on December 31. The entry on April 1 is:

Bond Interest Expense	30,750	
Bond Interest Payable	30,000	
Discount on Bonds Payable		750
Cash		60,000
To record bond interest expense and amortization of discount for three-month period since year-end and to record semiannual payment to bondholders.		

Straight-Line Amortization: A Theoretical Shortcoming

Although the straight-line method of amortizing bond discount or premium recognizes the full cost of borrowing over the life of a bond issue, the method has one conceptual weakness: The same dollar amount of interest expense is recognized each year. Amortizing a discount, however, causes a gradual increase in the liability for bonds payable; amortizing a premium causes a gradual decrease in the liability. If the uniform annual interest expense is expressed as a ***percentage*** of either an increasing or a decreasing liability, it appears that the borrower's cost of capital is changing over the life of the bonds.

This problem can be avoided by using the ***effective interest method*** of amortizing bond discount or premium. The effective interest method recognizes annual interest expense equal to a ***constant percentage of the carrying value of the related liability.*** This percentage is the effective rate of interest incurred by the borrower. For this reason, the effective interest method of amortization is considered theoretically preferable to the straight-line method. Whenever the two methods would produce ***materially different*** annual results, the use of the effective interest method is preferable. In fact, the Financial Accounting Standards Board in the United States has taken such a position.

Over the life of the bonds, both amortization methods recognize the ***same total amount*** of interest expense. Even on an annual basis, the results produced by the two methods are quite similar (unless the bonds were issued at an enormous discount, as are zero coupon bonds).

Effective Interest Method of Amortization

When bonds are sold at a discount, the effective interest rate incurred by the issuing corporation is ***higher*** than the contract rate printed on the bonds. Conversely, when bonds are sold at a premium, the effective rate of interest is ***lower*** than the contract rate.

When the effective interest method is used, bond interest expense is determined by multiplying the ***carrying value of the bonds*** at the beginning of the period by the ***effective rate of interest*** for the bond issue. The amount of discount or premium to be amortized is the ***difference*** between the interest expense computed in this manner and the amount of interest paid (or payable) to bondholders for the period. The computation of effective interest expense and the amount of discount or premium amortization for the life of the bond issue is made in advance in a specially designed ***amortization table.***

Sale of Bonds at a Discount To illustrate the effective interest method, assume that on May 1 a corporation issues $1 million face value, 9%, 10-year bonds with interest dates of November 1 and May 1. The bonds sell for ***$937,689,*** a price resulting in an effective interest rate of 10%.[5] An amortization table for this bond issue is shown below. (Amounts of interest expense have been ***rounded to the nearest dollar.***)

Amortization Table for Bonds Sold at a Discount
($1,000,000, 10-year bonds, 9% interest payable semiannually, sold at $937,689 to yield 10% compounded semiannually)

Six-Month Interest Period	(A) Interest Paid Semiannually ($4\frac{1}{2}$% of Face Value)	(B) Effective Semiannual Interest Expense (5% of Bond Carrying Value)	(C) Discount Amortization (B − A)	(D) Bond Discount Balance	(E) Carrying Value of Bonds, End of Period ($1,000,000 − D)
Issue date	—	—	—	$62,311	$937,689
1	$45,000	$46,884	$1,884	60,427	939,573
2	45,000	46,979	1,979	58,448	941,552
3	45,000	47,078	2,078	56,370	943,630
4	45,000	47,182	2,182	54,188	945,812
5	45,000	47,291	2,291	51,897	948,103
6	45,000	47,405	2,405	49,492	950,508
7	45,000	47,525	2,525	46,967	953,033
8	45,000	47,652	2,652	44,315	955,685
9	45,000	47,784	2,784	41,531	958,469
10	45,000	47,923	2,923	38,608	961,392
11	45,000	48,070	3,070	35,538	964,462
12	45,000	48,223	3,223	32,315	967,685
13	45,000	48,384	3,384	28,931	971,069
14	45,000	48,553	3,553	25,378	974,622
15	45,000	48,731	3,731	21,647	978,353
16	45,000	48,918	3,918	17,729	982,271
17	45,000	49,114	4,114	13,615	986,385
18	45,000	49,319	4,319	9,296	990,704
19	45,000	49,535	4,535	4,761	995,239
20	45,000	49,761*	4,761	-0-	1,000,000

* In the last period, interest expense is equal to interest paid to bondholders plus the remaining balance on the bond discount. This compensates for the accumulated effects of rounding amounts.

This amortization table can be used to illustrate the concepts underlying the effective interest method of determining interest expense and discount amortization. Note that the "interest periods" in the table are the ***semiannual*** (six-month) interest periods. Thus, the interest payments (column A), interest expense (column B), and discount amortization (column C) are for six-month periods. Similarly, the balance of the Discount on

[5] Computation of the exact effective interest rate involves mathematical techniques beyond the scope of this discussion. A close approximation of the effective interest rate can be obtained by dividing the ***average*** annual interest expense by the ***average*** carrying value of the bonds.

Bonds Payable account (column D) and the carrying value of the liability (column E) are shown as of each semiannual interest payment date.

The original issuance price of the bonds ($937,689) is entered at the top of column E. This represents the carrying value of the liability throughout the first six-month interest period. The semiannual interest payment, shown in column A, is $4\frac{1}{2}\%$ (one-half of the original contract rate) of the $1 million face value of the bond issue. The semiannual cash interest payment does not change over the life of the bonds. The interest expense shown in column B, however, ***changes every period.*** This expense is always a ***constant percentage*** of the carrying value of the liability as of the end of the preceding period. The "constant percentage" is the effective interest rate of the bond issue. The bonds have an effective annual interest rate of 10%, indicating a semiannual rate of 5%. Thus, the effective interest expense for the first six-month period is $46,884 (5% of $937,689). The discount amortization for Period 1 is the difference between this effective interest expense and the contract interest paid to bondholders.

After the discount is reduced by $1,884 at the end of Period 1, the carrying value of the bonds in column E ***increases*** by $1,884 (from $937,689 to $939,573). In Period 2, the effective interest expense is determined by multiplying the effective semiannual interest rate of 5% by this new carrying value of $939,573 (5% × $939,573 = $46,979).

Semiannual interest expense may be recorded every period directly from the data in the amortization table. For example, the entry to record bond interest expense at the end of the first six-month period is:

Amortization of discount increases interest expense

Bond Interest Expense	46,884	
Discount on Bonds Payable		1,884
Cash		45,000
To record semiannual interest payment and amortize discount for six months.		

Similarly, interest expense at the end of the ***fifteenth*** six-month period would be recorded by the following journal entry:

Bond Interest Expense	48,731	
Discount on Bonds Payable		3,731
Cash		45,000
To record semiannual interest payment and amortize discount for six months.		

When bond discount is amortized, the carrying value of the liability for bonds payable ***increases*** every period toward the maturity value. Since the effective interest expense in each period is a constant percentage of this increasing carrying value, the interest expense also increases from one period to the next. This is the basic difference between the effective interest method and straight-line amortization.

Sale of Bonds at a Premium Let us now change our illustration by assuming that the $1 million issue of 9%, 10-year bonds is sold on May 1 at a price of ***$1,067,952***, resulting in an effective interest rate of 8% annually (4% per six-month interest period). An amortization table for this bond issue follows:

Amortization Table for Bonds Sold at a Premium
($1,000,000, 10-year bonds, 9% interest payable semiannually, sold at $1,067,952 to yield 8% compounded semiannually)

Six-Month Interest Period	(A) Interest Paid Semiannually ($4\frac{1}{2}$% of Face Value)	(B) Effective Semiannual Interest Expense (4% of Bond Carrying Value)	(C) Premium Amortization (A − B)	(D) Bond Premium Balance	(E) Carrying Value of Bonds, End of Period ($1,000,000 + D)
Issue date	—	—	—	$67,952	$1,067,952
1	$45,000	$42,718	$2,282	65,670	1,065,670
2	45,000	42,627	2,373	63,297	1,063,297
3	45,000	42,532	2,468	60,829	1,060,829
4	45,000	42,433	2,567	58,262	1,058,262
5	45,000	42,330	2,670	55,592	1,055,592
6	45,000	42,224	2,776	52,816	1,052,816
7	45,000	42,113	2,887	49,929	1,049,929
8	45,000	41,997	3,003	46,926	1,046,926
9	45,000	41,877	3,123	43,803	1,043,803
10	45,000	41,752	3,248	40,555	1,040,555
11	45,000	41,622	3,378	37,177	1,037,177
12	45,000	41,487	3,513	33,664	1,033,664
13	45,000	41,347	3,653	30,011	1,030,011
14	45,000	41,200	3,800	26,211	1,026,211
15	45,000	41,048	3,952	22,259	1,022,259
16	45,000	40,890	4,110	18,149	1,018,149
17	45,000	40,726	4,274	13,875	1,013,875
18	45,000	40,555	4,445	9,430	1,009,430
19	45,000	40,377	4,623	4,807	1,004,807
20	45,000	40,193*	4,807	-0-	1,000,000

* In the last period, interest expense is equal to interest paid to bondholders minus the remaining balance of the bond premium. This compensates for the accumulated effects of rounding amounts.

In this amortization table, the interest expense for each six-month period is equal to ***4%*** of the carrying value of the liability at the beginning of that period. This amount of interest expense is ***less*** than the amount of cash being paid to bondholders, illustrating that the effective interest rate is less than the contract rate.

Based upon this amortization table, the entry to record the interest payment and amortization of the premium for the first six months of the bond issue is:

Amortization of premium decreases interest expense

Bond Interest Expense	*42,718*	
Premium on Bonds Payable	*2,282*	
Cash		*45,000*
To record semiannual interest payment and amortization of premium.		

As the carrying value of the liability declines, so does the amount recognized as bond interest expense.

Year-End Adjusting Entries Since the amounts recognized as interest expense change from one period to the next, we must refer to the appropriate interest period in the amortization table to obtain the dollar amounts for use in year-end adjusting entries. To illustrate, consider our example of the bonds sold at a premium on May 1. The entry shown on the previous page records interest and amortization of the premium through November 1. If the company keeps its accounts on a calendar-year basis, two months' interest has accrued as of December 31, and the following adjusting entry is made at year-end:

Year-end adjusting entry

Bond Interest Expense	*14,209*	
Premium on Bonds Payable	*791*	
Bond Interest Payable		*15,000*
To record two months' accrued interest and amortize one-third of the premium for the interest period.		

This adjusting entry covers one-third (two months) of the second interest period. Consequently, the amounts shown as bond interest expense and amortization of premium are ***one-third*** of the amounts shown in the amortization table for the second interest period. Similar adjusting entries must be made at the end of every accounting period while the bonds are outstanding. The dollar amounts of these adjusting entries will vary, however, because the amounts of interest expense and premium amortization change in every interest period. The amounts applicable to any given adjusting entry will be the appropriate fraction of the amounts for the interest period then in progress.

Following the year-end adjusting entry illustrated above, the interest expense and premium amortization on May 1 of the second year, are recorded as follows:

Interest payment in the following year

Bond Interest Expense	*28,418*	
Bond Interest Payable	*15,000*	
Premium on Bonds Payable	*1,582*	
Cash		*45,000*
To record semiannual interest payment, a portion of which had been accrued, and amortize remainder of premium applicable to interest period.		

Bond Prices after Issuance

As stated earlier, many corporate bonds are traded daily on organized securities exchanges at quoted market prices. After bonds are issued, their market prices vary ***inversely*** with changes in market interest rates. As interest rates rise, investors will be willing to pay less money to own a bond that pays a given contract rate of interest. Conversely, as interest rates decline, the market prices of bonds rise.

CASE IN POINT A large corporation sold to underwriters $500 million of $9\frac{3}{8}$%, 25-year debenture bonds. The underwriters planned to sell the bonds to the public at a price of $99\frac{5}{8}$. Just as the bonds were offered for sale, however, a change in general business conditions and government policy started an upward surge in interest rates. The underwriters encountered great difficulty selling the bonds. Within one week, the market price of the bonds had fallen to $94\frac{1}{2}$. The underwriters dumped their unsold inventory at this price and sustained one of the largest underwriting losses in the history of the underwriting business.

During the months subsequent to the issuance, interest rates soared to record levels. Within five months, the price of the bonds had fallen to $76\frac{3}{8}$. Thus, nearly one-fourth of the market value of these bonds evaporated in less than half a year. The financial strength of the corporation was never in question; this dramatic loss in market value was caused entirely by rising interest rates.

Changes in the current level of interest rates are not the only factor influencing the market prices of bonds. The length of time remaining until the bonds mature is another major force. As a bond nears its maturity date, its market price normally moves closer and closer to the maturity value. This trend is dependable because the bonds are redeemed at par value on the maturity date.

CASE IN POINT Ontario Hydro has outstanding two issues of 10% bonds, one issue maturing in 5 years and the other in 12 years. When the going market rate of interest was much greater than 10%, both bonds were selling at a discount. The bonds maturing in 5 years, however, were selling at a market price of $91.10, whereas the bonds maturing in 12 years were selling at a price of only $86.20. Both bonds pay the same amount of interest, were issued by the same company, and have the same credit ratings. Thus, the difference in the market prices is caused mainly by the difference in the bonds' maturity dates.[6]

Volatility of Short-Term and Long-Term Bond Prices When interest rates fluctuate, the market prices of long-term bonds are affected to a far greater extent than are the market prices of bonds due to mature in the near future. To illustrate, assume that market interest rates suddenly soar from 9% to 12%. A 9% bond scheduled to mature in but a few days will still have a market value of approximately $1,000—the amount to be collected in a few days from the issuing corporation. However, the market price of a 9% bond maturing in 10 years will drop significantly. Investors who must accept these "below market" interest payments for many years will buy the bonds only at a discounted price.

In summary, fluctuations in interest rates have a far greater effect upon the market prices of long-term bonds than upon the prices of short-term bonds.

Remember that after bonds have been issued, they belong to the bondholder, ***not to the issuing corporation.*** Therefore, changes in the market price of bonds subsequent to their issuance ***do not*** affect the amounts shown in the financial statements of the issuing corporation, and these changes are not recorded in the company's accounting records.

6 The expected future interest rate is also a factor. The yield rates for these two bonds are 12.60% and 12.32% respectively, suggesting an expected decline in future long-term interest rates.

Early Retirement of Bonds Payable

Bonds are sometimes retired before the maturity date. The principal reason for retiring bonds early is to relieve the issuing corporation of the obligation to make future interest payments. If interest rates decline to the point that a corporation can borrow at an interest rate below that being paid on a particular bond issue, the corporation may benefit from retiring those bonds and issuing new bonds at a lower interest rate.

Bond issues generally contain a call (redemption) provision, permitting the corporation to redeem the bonds by paying a specified price, usually a few points above par. Even without a call provision, the corporation may retire its bonds before maturity by purchasing them in the open market. If the bonds can be purchased by the issuing corporation at less than their carrying value, a ***gain*** is realized on the retirement of the debt. If the bonds are acquired by the issuing corporation at a price in excess of their carrying value, a ***loss*** must be recognized. If material in dollar amount, any gain or loss from the early retirement of debt should be presented separately in the income statement.

For example, assume that Briggs Corporation has outstanding a 13%, $10 million bond issue, callable on any interest date at a price of 104. Assume also that the bonds were issued at par and will not mature for nine years. Recently, however, market interest rates have declined to less than 13%, and the market price of Briggs' bonds has increased to 104.[7]

Regardless of the market price, Briggs can call these bonds at 104. If the company exercises this call provision for 10% of the bonds ($1 million face value), the entry will be:

Bonds called at a price above carrying value

Bonds Payable	*1,000,000*	
Loss on Early Retirement of Bonds	*40,000*	
Cash		*1,040,000*
To record the call of $1,000,000 in 13% bonds payable at a call price of 104.		

Notice that Briggs ***called*** these bonds, rather than purchasing them at market prices, which may be higher than the call price. Therefore, Briggs is able to retire these bonds at their call price of 104.

Classification of Bonds Payable in a Balance Sheet

Bonds payable generally are classified as ***long-term*** liabilities, even when the bonds are within one year of maturity. This is because the obligation for maturing bonds usually is paid either (1) by issuing new bonds and using the proceeds to retire the maturing bond issue or (2) from a bond ***sinking fund.***

If new bonds are issued, the maturing bond liability has been ***refinanced.*** As explained in Chapter 11, maturing obligations that will be

[7] Falling interest rates cause bond prices to rise. On the other hand, falling interest rates also provide the issuing company with an incentive to call the bonds and, perhaps, replace them with bonds bearing a lower rate of interest. For this reason, call prices often serve as an approximate "ceiling" on market prices.

refinanced on a long-term basis are classified as long-term liabilities rather than current liabilities. Now consider maturing bonds that will be repaid from a sinking fund accumulated over the years specifically for this purpose. A sinking fund is not regarded as a current asset, because its contents ***cannot be used*** for paying operating expenses or the claims of most short-term creditors. The bonds payable, therefore, do not become a current liability, as they will be paid from the sinking fund ***rather than from current assets.***

Accrued interest payable on long-term bonds ***is*** regarded as a current liability, because accrued interest normally is paid in cash within six months or less.

Commercial Paper

The term ***commercial paper*** describes ***very short-term*** notes payable issued by financially strong corporations. These notes mature generally in 30 days to 270 days and are issued in denominations of $25,000 or more. Commercial paper is similar to bonds payable in that it splits a large loan into small units, enabling many different investors to act as the lender. Also, an organized marketplace exists in which the holders of commercial paper may sell their investment immediately at a quoted market price.

Because commercial paper matures so quickly, it is regarded as a safer and more liquid investment than are stocks or bonds. The market price of commercial paper does not fluctuate significantly as a result of changes in interest rates. Rather, the market price tends to progress day by day toward maturity value.

Many investors purchase commercial paper as a means of earning interest revenue on idle cash balances for very short periods of time—perhaps over a weekend. For this reason, investors usually regard commercial paper as a cash equivalent. The issuing corporation, of course, views these notes as a current liability.

Commercial paper is issued at a discount; that is, with the interest charges included in the face amount. (Accounting for short-term notes payable with interest charges included in the face amount was discussed in Chapter 11.)

OTHER "CORPORATE" LIABILITIES

Bonds payable and commercial paper are issued only by large corporations. These debt instruments are attractive to investors only if the continued existence and solvency of the business enterprise can be taken for granted.

We now will discuss the liabilities arising from lease agreements, pension plans, and the deferral of income taxes. These liabilities appear primarily in the financial statements of large corporations, but they may also affect smaller business organizations. Many small businesses, however, do not have financial reporting obligations to investors and creditors. Therefore, these businesses sometimes use income tax rules, rather than accounting principles, in recording the liabilities and expenses. Our discussion of these topics emphasizes generally accepted accounting principles—the accounting standards used in the financial statements of publicly owned companies.

Lease Payment Obligations

OBJECTIVE 7 Explain the accounting treatment of operating leases and of capital leases.

A company may purchase the assets needed in its business operations or, as an alternative, it may lease them. A ***lease*** is a contract in which the lessor gives the lessee the right to use an asset for a specified period of time in exchange for periodic rental payments. The ***lessor*** is the owner of the property; the ***lessee*** is a tenant or renter. Examples of assets frequently acquired by lease include automobiles, building space, computers, and equipment. Two types of leases—operating and capital—are presented below.

Operating Leases

When the lessor gives the lessee the right to use leased property for a limited period of time but retains the usual risks and rewards of ownership, the contract is known as an ***operating lease.*** An example of an operating lease is a contract leasing office space in an office building. If the building increases in value, the ***lessor*** can receive the benefits of this increase by either selling the building or increasing the rental rate once the lease term has expired. On the other hand, if the building declines in value, it is the lessor who bears the loss.

In accounting for an operating lease, the lessor views the monthly lease payments received as rental revenue, and the lessee regards these payments as rental expense. No asset or liability (other than a short-term liability for rent payable) relating to the lease appears in the lessee's balance sheet. Thus, operating leases are sometimes termed off-balance-sheet financing.

Capital Leases

Some lease contracts are intended to provide financing to the lessee for the eventual purchase of the property or to provide the lessee with use of the property over most of its useful life. These lease contracts are called ***capital leases*** (or sales-type or direct financing leases). In contrast to an operating lease, a capital lease transfers most of the risks and rewards of ownership from the lessor to the ***lessee.*** Assume, for example, that City Realty leases a new automobile for a period of three years. Also assume that at the end of the lease, title to the automobile transfers to City Realty at no additional cost. Clearly, City Realty is not merely "renting" the use of the automobile; rather, it is using the lease agreement as a means of ***financing the purchase*** of the car.

From an accounting viewpoint, capital leases are regarded as ***essentially equivalent to a sale*** of the property by the lessor to the lessee, even though title to the leased property has not been transferred. Thus, a capital lease should be recorded by the ***lessor as a sale*** of property and by the ***lessee as a purchase.*** In such lease agreements, an appropriate interest charge usually is added to the regular sales price of the property in determining the amount of the lease payments.

Some companies use capital lease agreements as a means of financing the sale of their products to customers. In accounting for merchandise "sold" through a capital lease, the lessor debits ***Lease Payments Receivable*** and credits ***Sales*** for an amount equal to the ***present value*** of the future lease payments.[8] In most cases, the present value of these future payments is equal to the regular sales price of the merchandise. In addition, the lessor transfers the cost of the leased merchandise from the Inventory account to the Cost of Goods Sold account. When lease payments are received, the lessor should recognize an appropriate portion of the payment as representing interest revenue and the remainder as a reduction in Lease Payments Receivable.

When equipment is acquired through a capital lease, the lessee should ***debit an asset account,*** Leased Equipment, and ***credit a liability account,*** Lease Payment Obligation, for the present value of the future lease payments. Lease payments made by the lessee are allocated between Interest Expense and a reduction in the liability, Lease Payment Obligation. The portion of the lease payment obligation that will be repaid within the next year is classified as a current liability, and the remainder is classified as long-term.

No rent expense is involved in a capital lease. The asset account, Leased Equipment, is depreciated over the life of the equipment rather than the life of the lease. (The journal entries used in accounting for a capital lease are illustrated in Appendix A at the end of this chapter.)

Distinguishing between Capital Leases and Operating Leases The *CICA Handbook* recommended the following distinction.[9]

1 A lease that transfers substantially all of the benefits and risks of ownership related to the leased property from the lessor to the lessee should be accounted for as a capital lease by the lessee and as a sales-type or direct financing lease by the lessor.

2 A lease where the benefits and risks of ownership related to the leased property are substantially retained by the lessor should be accounted for as an operating lease by the lessee and lessor.

Liabilities for Pensions and Other Postretirement Benefits

OBJECTIVE 8 Account for the costs of pensions and other postretirement benefits.

Pensions Many employers agree to pay their employees a pension; that is, monthly cash payments for life, beginning upon retirement. Pensions are not an expense of the years in which cash payments are made to retired workers. Employees earn the right to receive the pension ***while they are working for their employer.*** Therefore, the employer's cost of future pension payments ***accrues*** over the years that each employee is "on the payroll."

Of course, the amounts of the retirement benefits that will be paid to today's workers after they retire is not known with certainty. Among other things, these amounts depend upon how long retired employees live.

[8] We have elected to record the present value of the future lease payments by a single debit entry to Lease Payments Receivable. An alternative is to debit Lease Payments Receivable for the total amount of the future payments and to credit Discount on Lease Payments Receivable, a contra-asset account, for the unearned finance charges included in the contractual amount. Either approach results in the lessor recording a net receivable equal to the present value of the future lease payments.

[9] CICA, *CICA Handbook* (Toronto), section 3065.09 and .10.

Therefore, the employer's obligation for future pension payments arising during the current year ***can only be estimated.***

Employers do not usually pay retirement pensions directly to retired employees. Most employers meet their pension obligations by making periodic deposits in a ***pension fund*** (or pension plan) throughout the years of each worker's employment.

A pension fund is ***not an asset*** of the employer. Rather, it is an ***independent entity*** managed by a trustee (usually a bank or an insurance company). As the employer makes deposits in the pension fund, the trustee invests the money in securities such as stocks and bonds. Over time, the pension fund earns investment income and normally accumulates to a balance far in excess of the employer's deposits. It is the ***pension fund***—not the employer—that disburses monthly pension benefits to retired workers.

If the employer meets ***all*** of its estimated pension obligations by promptly depositing cash in a pension fund, the pension fund is said to be ***fully funded.*** The operation of a fully funded pension plan is summarized in the following illustration:

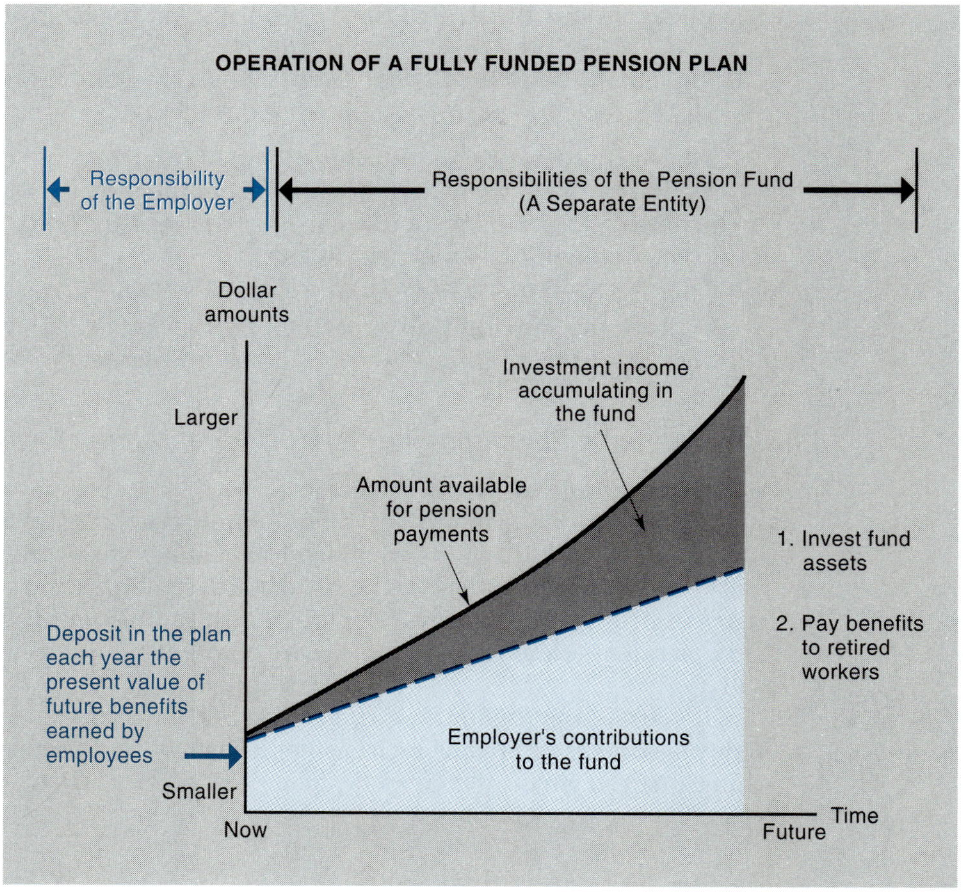

If a pension plan is fully funded, ***no liability*** for pension payments appears in the employer's balance sheet. The employer's obligation is discharged in the ***current period*** through the payments made to the pension fund. The employer records each payment to this fund by debiting Pension Expense and crediting Cash.

Most pension plans are fully funded; therefore, most corporations do ***not*** report any pension liability. However, an employer must credit a liability account, Unfunded Pension Liability, for any portion of its periodic pension expense that ***is not*** paid immediately to the pension fund.

Determining Pension Expense From a conceptual point of view, the pension expense of a given period is the ***present value*** of the future pension rights granted to employees as a result of their services during the period. The computation of annual pension expense is complex and involves many assumptions. The amount of this expense is not computed by accountants, but rather by a professional ***actuary.*** Among the factors considered by the actuary are:

- Average age, retirement age, and life expectancy of employees.
- Employee turnover rates.
- Compensation levels and estimated rate of pay increases.
- Expected rate of return to be earned on pension fund assets.

As a step in determining the pension expense for the year, the actuary estimates the employer's total pension liability as of year-end. Thus, the estimates are updated annually, and estimating errors in prior years are "corrected" in the current year.

Postretirement Benefits Other Than Pensions In addition to pension plans, many companies have promised their employees other types of postretirement benefits, such as dental or other health insurance. In most respects, these "nonpension" postretirement benefits are accounted for in the same manner as are pension benefits. Most companies, however, have not fully funded their obligations for nonpension postretirement benefits. Thus, recognition of the annual expense often involves a credit to an unfunded liability.

To illustrate, assume that at the end of 1996 Cable Corporation receives the following report from its actuaries:

CABLE CORPORATION
Summary of Postretirement Benefits Expenses
For the Year Ended December 31, 1996
Prepared by Gibson & Holt, Professional Actuaries

Pension Plan:	
Estimated liability at Dec. 31, 1996	*$4,500,000*
Estimated liability at Dec. 31, 1995	*4,100,000*
Pension expense for 1996	*$ 400,000*
Payments during the year to National Trust (trustee for the pension plan)	*400,000*
Increase (decrease) in unfunded pension liability	*$ -0-*
Nonpension Postretirement Benefits:	
Estimated liability at Dec. 31, 1996	*$1,600,000*
Estimated liability at Dec. 31, 1995	*1,350,000*
Nonpension postretirement benefits expense for 1996	*$ 250,000*
Payments during the year to National Trust (trustee for the nonpension postretirement benefits plan)	*140,000*
Increase (decrease) in unfunded liability	*$ 110,000*

As the pension plan is fully funded, an entry summarizing Cable Corporation's pension expense for 1996 is shown as follows:[10]

Pension Expense	*400,000*	
Cash		*400,000*
Pension expense for the year as determined by actuarial firm of Gibson & Holt. Fully funded by payments to National Trust.		

The company's "nonpension" postretirement benefits expense was only partially paid in cash. The entry to summarize this expense for the year is:

Nonpension Postretirement Benefits Expense	*250,000*	
Cash		*140,000*
Unfunded Liability for Nonpension Postretirement Benefits		*110,000*
To record nonpension postretirement benefits expense per report of Gibson & Holt, actuaries. Expense funded to the extent of $140,000.		

Any portion of the unfunded liability that the company intends to fund during the next year is classified as a current liability; the remainder is classified as a long-term liability.

There are many complex issues involved in computing and reporting unfunded liabilities for postretirement benefits. These issues will be discussed in more advanced accounting courses.

Deferred Income Taxes

OBJECTIVE 9 Explain the nature of deferred income taxes.

Differences sometimes exist between the dates certain types of revenue or expense are recognized in financial statements and the dates these items are reported in income tax returns. For example, the amount of depreciation reported for financial purposes may be different for income tax purposes. Because of such ***timing differences*** between accounting principles and tax rules, income or expense may be reported in the income statement of one year but in the income tax return of a different year. Most timing differences result in ***postponing*** (deferring) the recognition of income or in early recognition of expenses for tax purposes.[11] The recognition of income in income tax returns is postponed by those tax rules that enable taxpayers either to (1) delay the recognition of revenue or (2) accelerate the recognition of expense.

In summary, income appearing in the income statement today may not be subject to income taxes until future years. However, the ***matching principle*** requires that the income shown in an income statement be offset by all related income taxes expense, regardless of when these taxes will be paid. Thus, the entry to record a corporation's income taxes expense often appears as follows:

---

[10] This entry summarizes the pension expense and payments to the trustee for the ***entire year.*** In practice, payments to the trustee often are made on a monthly or quarterly basis.

[11] In some situations, income may be subject to income taxes ***prior*** to recognition of the income for financial reporting purposes. In these instances, the taxpayer ***prepays*** its income taxes expense. Prepaid income taxes is an asset, similar to prepaid rent. In this chapter, we limit our discussion to the more common situation in which the payment of income taxes is ***deferred*** to later periods.

Payment of some taxes expense often can be deferred

Income Taxes Expense	*1,000,000*	
Income Taxes Payable		*800,000*
Deferred Income Taxes		*200,000*
To record corporate income taxes applicable to the income of the current year.		

Income Taxes Payable is a current liability representing the portion of the income taxes expense that must be paid when the company files its income tax return for the current year. That portion of the income taxes expense that is deferred to future tax returns is credited to a liability account entitled Deferred Income Taxes. Notice that deferred income taxes are tax obligations that have been ***postponed*** to future periods; the company has ***not eliminated*** its obligation to pay these taxes.

Growing businesses often are able to defer part of their income taxes expense every year. Of course, some of the income taxes deferred in prior years constantly are coming due. Nonetheless, the liability for deferred taxes usually continues to grow as the company grows.

Accounting for deferred taxes involves a number of complex issues that will be addressed in the intermediate accounting course.

Disclosures about Financial Instruments

Except for deferred income taxes, all the liabilities discussed in this chapter are among the contracts often regarded as financial instruments. The term ***financial instruments*** describes cash, equity investments in another business, and any contracts calling for the receipt or payment of cash. Notice that this term applies to certain assets, as well as to most liabilities.

Many financial instruments, such as bonds payable, investments in stocks and bonds, and long-term loans receivable or payable, have market values that can ***differ substantially*** from their carrying values in financial statements. In such cases, current practices require companies to ***disclose*** the ***fair value*** of these instruments, usually in notes accompanying the financial statements.

Fair value generally means ***current market value.*** As the disclosures of fair value generally appear in ***notes*** to the financial statements, these disclosures do ***not*** affect the carrying values of the financial instruments in the company's balance sheet.

There are two basic reasons for requiring disclosures of fair values. First, the fair value represents the current "economic" value of the financial instruments. Thus, it is the best indication of the ***value today*** of the resources owned or owed. Second, financial instruments often can be settled (sold or discharged) at their fair value. If these settlement prices differ from the book values of the financial instruments, the settlement transactions will result in the recognition of gains or losses. Disclosures of the fair values of these instruments may alert investors to the possibility—or probability—of such future gains or losses.

Measuring Fair Value Bonds payable usually have quoted market prices. Thus, the fair value of an issue of bonds payable is determined by multiplying the quoted price by the number of bonds outstanding. Investments in stocks and bonds also are financial instruments that usually have readily determinable market values. For financial instruments that ***do not*** have quoted market prices, fair value often is considered to be the ***present value*** of the future cash flows, computed under current market conditions. (Computation of the present value of future cash flows is explained and illustrated in Appendix A, at the end of this chapter.)

The fair market value of financial instruments must be disclosed only if this value (1) is reasonably determinable and (2) is ***significantly different*** from the carrying value in the financial statements. These conditions greatly limit the types of financial instruments for which this disclosure is required. Cash, accounts receivables, accounts payable, and commercial paper, for example, normally have carrying values that ***closely approximate*** their fair values.

Bonds payable, long-term notes payable or receivable, and investments in stocks and bonds, however, often ***do*** have fair values differing substantially from their carrying values. Thus, the requirement for disclosure of fair value applies primarily to these types of financial instruments.

Disclosure of Off-Balance-Sheet Risk Some financial instruments do not create assets or liabilities that appear in financial statements but still create a risk of ***future losses.*** When a financial instrument does not appear in the balance sheet, the risk of loss created by the instrument is called an ***off-balance-sheet risk.***

The possibility of ***future losses*** ordinarily is ***not*** disclosed in financial statements, because all of the situations that may cause future losses cannot be identified. However, if the risk of a future loss ***is created by an existing contract*** (financial instrument), current practices require disclosure of the potential for loss.

As an example, large and financially strong corporations sometimes guarantee bank loans or other specific liabilities of less financially sound corporations. In these situations, the guarantor promises to repay the loan if the original borrower is unable to do so. The basic purpose of a loan guarantee is to enable the weaker company to borrow money at more favourable terms than its own credit rating would justify.

Why would one company guarantee the debts of another? Often the borrower pays the guarantor a fee for this service. In other cases, the borrower may be an important customer or supplier of the guarantor.

A loan guarantee (also called an ***accommodation endorsement***) creates a contingent loss for the guarantor.[12] Unless a loss is considered ***likely*** and ***reasonably determinable,*** however, no liability appears in the guarantor's financial statements. Therefore, the guarantor's risk of loss—that is, the possibility of having to assume responsibility for the guaranteed loan—is an ***off-balance-sheet risk.***

Current practices require companies to disclose any material off-balance-sheet risk created by financial instruments. The required disclosure is to include a written explanation of the nature and terms of the financial instrument, and the maximum amount of loss that might be sustained.

---

[12] Accounting for contingent losses is discussed in Chapter 11.

Some Old Ratios Take on New Importance

In Chapter 11, we discussed two ratios widely used by long-term creditors in evaluating the safety of their investments: the ***debt ratio*** and the ***interest coverage ratio.***

The debt ratio, which is total liabilities divided by total assets, indicates the percentage of total assets financed with borrowed money. Creditors prefer a ***low*** debt ratio, as this indicates that their claims amount to only a small percentage of the company's total assets. The interest coverage ratio, which equals operating income divided by interest expense, indicates how many times the company's earnings for the period "covered" its interest obligations. Creditors prefer a high interest coverage ratio.

The ability of large corporations to meet their interest obligations has taken on new importance in recent years. During the 1980s, a number of well-known corporations borrowed startling amounts of money by issuing "junk bonds" bearing interest rates of 12, 14, and 16 percent—and sometimes even higher. As a result, the very existence of some of these corporations now is threatened by the size of the companies' annual interest obligations. Such a long-established company as Federated Department Stores in the United States (owned by Campeau Corporation, a Canadian company) already has declared bankruptcy, and others are sure to follow.

Bankruptcy affects much more than the claims of long-term creditors. Shareholders have only a residual claim to assets; therefore, capital stocks are the first securities to lose value. Top management often is replaced, and many employees usually lose their jobs. Perhaps most devastating in human terms, bankrupt companies may be unable to meet unfunded post-retirement obligations.

In conclusion, debt ratios and interest coverage ratios have become measurements of importance to ***everyone*** concerned with the long-run survival and health of a business organization.

* Supplemental Topic
Convertible Bonds Payable

OBJECTIVE 10 Explain the accounting treatment of convertible bonds payable.

Convertible bonds represent a popular form of financing, particularly during periods when common stock prices are rising. The conversion feature gives bondholders an opportunity to profit from a rise in the market price of the issuing company's common stock while still maintaining their status as creditors rather than shareholders. Because of this potential gain, convertible bonds generally carry lower interest rates than nonconvertible bonds.

The number of shares of common stock into which each bond may be converted is termed the ***conversion ratio.*** The market value of this number of shares represents the ***stock value*** of the bond. When the bond is originally issued, a conversion ratio is selected that sets the stock value well below the face value of the bond. In future periods, however, both the price of the stock and the stock value of the bond may increase without limit.

For example, assume that the current market rate of interest on long-term bonds with a face value of $1,000 each is 9%, and that the common stock of Ling Corporation has a current market price of ***$27*** per share. Instead of issuing 9% bonds payable, the company might issue ***7% convertible bonds,*** with a conversion ratio of 20 to 1 or a ***conversion price*** of $50 ($1,000 face value ÷ by 20 shares). At the issuance date, the stock value of each convertible bond would be only $540 (20 shares × $27). If the value of the common stock rises above ***$50*** per share, however, the stock value will rise above the $1,000 face value of the bond.

When the price of the common stock rises above the conversion price, the stock value of the bond becomes far more important than the current level of interest rates in establishing the market price of a convertible bond. (See, for example, the Case in Point below.)

Ling Corporation benefits from issuing these convertible bonds because it is able to pay less than the going market rate of interest. The bondholders also may benefit from the conversion feature, ***but only if the price of the common stock rises above the conversion price*** ($50 per share) during the life of the bonds.

Let us assume that Ling Corporation issues $5 million of these convertible bonds at par. Some years later, when the price of the common stock has risen to $90 per share, holders of 100 bonds decide to convert their bonds into common stock. Ling Corporation will record this conversion as follows:

Conversion of bonds into common stock

Convertible Bonds Payable	*100,000*	
Common Stock		*100,000*
To record the conversion of 100 bonds payable into 2,000 shares of common stock.		

Notice that the current market price of the stock ($90 per share) ***does not*** affect this entry. The carrying value of the bonds is simply assigned to the common stock issued in exchange. Thus, the effect of the entry is to transfer the carrying value of the bonds from the liability section to the shareholders' equity section of the balance sheet. (If the bonds had been issued at a price above or below the face amount, any unamortized premium or discount relating to the converted bonds would be written off at the time of conversion in order to assign the carrying value of the bonds to the common stock.)

CONVERSION OF BONDS FROM THE INVESTOR'S VIEWPOINT

Investors do not always convert their investment in convertible bonds into capital stock as soon as the market value of the capital stock they would receive rises above the $1,000 maturity value of their bonds. As the bonds easily can be converted into capital stock, their market value ***rises right along*** with that of the capital stock.

CASE IN POINT Norcen had an outstanding issue of more than $149 million of 6% bonds payable (maturing December 15, 2006) in which each bond was convertible into 64.52 shares of the company's capital stock. The company's capital stock was selling at $24 per share, indicating a market value for 64.52 shares of $1,548. The market value of the convertible bonds was quoted at 154 (that is, $1540 for a $1,000 bond), even though the bonds would mature at a price of only 100 (that is, at $1,000 for a $1,000 bond) in the near future. Also, the going market interest rate of about 13% was more than twice the 6% for the bonds, indicating that the stock value of the bonds was more important than the market interest rate in establishing the market price of a convertible bond.

When are the owners of convertible bonds likely to exchange their bonds for shares of capital stock? The exchange point is reached when the dividends that would be received from the capital stock ***exceed the interest payments*** currently being received from the investment in bonds. When the capital stock dividends increase to this level, the bondholders can ***increase their cash receipts*** by converting their bonds into shares of capital stock. Regardless of the relationship between interest and dividends, convertible bonds should be converted prior to their maturity date if the market price of the common stock exceeds the conversion price.

CHAPTER REVIEW

KEY TERMS INTRODUCED OR EMPHASIZED IN CHAPTER 16

Amortization of discount or premium on bonds payable The process of systematically writing off a portion of bond discount to increase interest expense or writing off a portion of bond premium to decrease interest expense each period the bonds are outstanding.

Capital lease A lease contract that, in essence, finances the eventual purchase by the lessee of leased property. The lessor accounts for a capital lease as a sale of property; the lessee records an asset and a liability equal to the present value of the future lease payments. Also called a ***sales-type*** or ***direct financing lease.***

Commercial paper Very short-term notes payable issued by financially strong corporations. Highly liquid from the investors' point of view.

Contract interest rate The contractual rate of interest printed on bonds. The contract interest rate, applied to the face value of the bonds, determines the amount of the annual cash interest payments to bondholders. Also called the ***nominal interest rate.***

*__Convertible bond__ A bond that may be exchanged (at the bondholders' option) for a specified number of shares of the company's capital stock.

Deferred income taxes Income taxes upon income that already has been reported for financial reporting purposes but that will not be reported in income tax returns until future periods.

Discount on bonds payable Amount by which the face amount of the bond exceeds the price received by the corporation of the date of issuance. Indicates that the contractual rate of interest is lower than the market rate of interest.

Effective interest method of amortization A method of amortizing bond discount or premium that causes bond interest expense to be a constant percentage of the carrying value of the liability.

* *Supplemental Topic, "Convertible Bonds Payable"*

Effective interest rate The actual rate of interest expense to the borrowing corporation, taking into account the contractual cash interest payments and the discount or premium to be amortized.

Fair value A measure of current economic value. Usually means current market value, if determinable.

Financial instrument Cash, equity investments in another business, and contracts involving the receipt or payment of cash.

Junk bonds Bonds payable that, when issued, were abnormally risky but also offered an abnormally high contract rate of interest.

Lessee The tenant, user, or renter of leased property.

Lessor The owner of property leased to a lessee.

Off-balance-sheet financing An arrangement in which the use of resources is financed without the obligation for future payments appearing as a liability in the balance sheet. An operating lease is a common example of off-balance-sheet financing.

Off-balance-sheet risk The risk of future losses resulting from an existing financial instrument that does not currently appear on the balance sheet. An example is the risk of loss from a loan guarantee.

Operating lease A lease contract that is in essence a rental agreement. The lessee has the use of the leased property, but the lessor retains the usual risks and rewards of ownership. The periodic lease payments are accounted for as rent expense by the lessee and as rental revenue by the lessor.

Pension fund A fund managed by an independent trustee into which an employer company makes periodic payments. The fund is used for the purpose of paying retirement benefits to company employees.

Premium on bonds payable Amount by which the issuance price of a bond exceeds the face value. Indicates that the contractual rate of interest is higher than the market rate.

Present value of a future amount The amount of money that an informed investor would pay today for the right to receive the future amount, based upon a specific rate of return required by the investor.

Zero coupon bonds Bonds payable that do not provide for periodic interest payments. Instead, the bonds are issued at a large discount, and all interest charges are included in the face amount.

ASSIGNMENT MATERIAL

DISCUSSION QUESTIONS

1 Distinguish between the two terms in each of the following pairs:

- a Bonds payable; commercial paper
- b Mortgage bond; debenture
- c Callable bond; convertible bond
- d Junk bond; zero coupon bond

2 A financial newspaper recently quoted a market price of ***102*** for an issue of 8% bonds of a large corporation. What would be the market price for $25,000 face value of these bonds (ignoring accrued interest)? Is the market rate of interest for bonds of this quality higher or lower than 8%? Explain.

3 Briefly explain the income tax advantage of raising capital by issuing bonds rather than by capital stock.

4 Tampa Boat Limited pays income taxes at a rate of 30% on taxable income. Compute the company's annual ***after-tax*** cost of borrowing on a 10%, $5 million bond issue. Express this after-tax cost as a percentage of the borrowed $5 million.

5 Why is the ***present value*** of a future amount always less than the future amount?

6 Does issuing bonds at a discount increase or decrease the issuing company's cost of borrowing? Explain.

7 Explain why the effective rate of interest differs from the contract rate when bonds are issued (a) at a discount and (b) at a premium.

8 Why do bond prices ***vary inversely*** with interest rates?

9 When the effective interest method is used to amortize bond discount or premium, the amount of bond interest expense will differ in each period from that of the preceding period. Explain how the amount of bond interest expense changes from one period to another when the bonds are issued (a) at a discount and (b) at a premium.

10 Explain why the effective interest method of amortizing bond discount or premium is considered to be theoretically preferable to the straight-line method.

11 Some bonds now being bought and sold by investors on organized securities exchanges were issued when interest rates were much higher than they are today. Would you expect these bonds to be trading at prices above or below their face values? Explain.

12 The 6% bonds of Central Gas & Electric Limited are selling at a market price of 72, whereas the 6% bonds of Power Corporation are selling at a price of 97. Does this mean that Power has a better credit rating than Central Gas & Electric? Explain. (Assume current long-term interest rates are in the 11% to 13% range.)

13 Discuss the advantages and disadvantages of a ***call (redemption) provision*** in a bond contract from the viewpoint of (a) the bondholder and (b) the issuing corporation.

14 Explain how the lessee accounts for an operating lease and a capital lease. Why is an operating lease sometimes called ***off-balance-sheet financing?***

15 Ortega Industries has a fully funded pension plan. Each year, pension expense runs in excess of $10 million. At the present time, employees are entitled to receive pension benefits with a present value of $125 million. Explain what liability, if any, Ortega Industries should include in its balance sheet as a result of this pension plan.

16 What is meant by the term ***deferred income taxes?*** Explain.

17 Define ***financial instruments.*** What are the basic reasons for disclosing the fair value of these instruments when this value differs significantly from the carrying values shown in the balance sheet?

18 Why does the requirement for disclosure of fair value often apply to financial instruments such as bonds payable, long-term notes payable and receivable, and investments in stocks and bonds, but usually ***not*** to cash, accounts payable or receivable, or commercial paper?

19 What is meant by a financial instrument creating ***off-balance-sheet risk?*** Provide an example.

20 As a result of issuing 20-year bonds payable, Low-Cal Foods now has an interest coverage ratio of ***.75 to 1.*** Should this ratio be of greater concern to short-term creditors or to shareholders? Explain.

21 A $200 million bond issue of Waterloo Corporation (a solvent company) recently matured. The entire maturity value was paid from a bond sinking fund. What effect did this transaction have upon the company's current ratio? Upon its debt ratio? Explain.

*22 What is a ***convertible bond?*** Discuss the advantages and disadvantages of convertible bonds from the standpoint of (a) the investor and (b) the issuing corporation.

*23 What situation or condition is most likely to cause the holders of convertible bonds to convert their bonds into shares of common stock? (Do not assume that the bonds have been called or that they are about to mature.)

MULTIPLE CHOICE QUESTIONS

1 Which of the following statements are correct? (More than one statement may be correct.)

- a A bond issue is a technique for subdividing a very large loan into a great many small, transferable units.
- b Bond interest payments are contractual obligations, whereas the board of directors determines whether or not dividends will be paid.
- c As interest rates rise, the market prices of bonds fall; as interest rates fall, bond prices tend to rise.
- d Bond interest payments are deductible in determining income subject to income taxes, whereas dividends paid to shareholders are not deductible.

2 A few years ago, Glasco issued 30-year, 9% bonds payable, callable at 105. At the issuance date, the market interest rate for such bonds was about $8\frac{1}{2}$%; today, it is about 11%. Indicate statement(s) with which you agree. (More than one answer may be correct.)

- a The bonds probably were issued at a discount.
- b Glasco's disclosure of current fair value probably shows these bonds trading at a discount.
- c The market price of these bonds probably has increased since the issuance date.
- d Glasco is unlikely to call these bonds in the near future even if it has the resources to do so.

3 Lawton International leases its manufacturing equipment from Atlas under an arrangement that qualifies as a capital lease. Lawton's financial statements should include which of the following? (More than one answer may be correct.)

- a Depreciation expense on the leased equipment.
- b Rent expense each period for the amount of the lease payment made.
- c A liability for the present value of all future lease payments.
- d A liability for the total amount of all future lease payments.

---

* *Supplemental Topic, "Convertible Bonds Payable"*

4 Silverado maintains a fully funded pension plan. During 1996, $1 million was paid to retired workers, and workers currently employed by the company earned the right to receive pension payments expected to total $3 million ***over their lifetimes.*** Silverado's pension ***expense*** for 1996 amounts to:

a $1

b $3 million

c $4 million

d Some other amount

5 Deferred income taxes result from:

a The fact that bond interest is deductible in the computation of taxable income.

b Depositing income taxes due in future years in a special fund managed by an independent trustee.

c Timing differences between when income or expense is recognized in financial statements and in income tax returns.

d The inability of a bankrupt company to pay its income tax liability on schedule.

6 Waste Disposal Corporation issued 30-year bonds at a price very close to par value. The company uses the effective interest method of amortizing bond discount and premium. Indicate any of the following statements with which you ***agree.*** (More than one statement may be correct.).

a If these bonds were issued at a discount, bond interest expense will ***increase*** from year to year.

b If these bonds were issued at a premium, bond interest expense will ***decrease*** from year to year.

c Total interest expense over the life of the bond issue will be the ***same*** as would result from use of the straight-line method of amortization.

d The annual differences between interest expense computed by the effective interest method and the straight-line method will not be material in dollar amount.

EXERCISES

EXERCISE 16-1
Accounting Terminology

Listed below are nine technical accounting terms introduced or emphasized in this chapter.

Unfunded pension liability	*Deferred income taxes*	*Effective interest method (of amortization)*
Off-balance-sheet risk	*Present value of future amounts*	*Straight-line method (of amortization)*
Operating lease	*Bond premium*	*Commercial paper*

Each of the following statements may (or may not) describe one of these technical terms. For each statement, indicate the term described, or answer "None" if the statement does not correctly describe any of the terms.

a The measurement concept applied to the liabilities for capital lease obligations and to unfunded pension liabilities.

b Income taxes applicable to earnings that have already been included in the income statement but that appear in the income tax returns of a future year.

- **c** Cash, equity investments in another business organization, or contracts calling for receipts or payments of cash.
- **d** Amortizing bond discount or premium in a manner that results in the same amount of interest expense every period.
- **e** Future interest charges included in the maturity value of bonds payable.
- **f** A long-term liability appearing in the balance sheet of any company that offers a pension to retired workers.
- **g** A lease agreement that results in the lessee recording ownership of an asset and a long-term liability to the lessor.
- **h** Potential future losses that could result from existing financial instruments that are not listed either as assets or as liabilities.

EXERCISE 16-2
Effects of Bond Transactions upon the Accounting Equation

Listed below are seven events relating to debt instruments issued by Wizard Computer, Inc.:

- **a** Issued 30-year bonds payable at a discount.
- **b** Issued 90-day commercial paper at a discount.
- **c** Made a semiannual interest payment and amortized discount on the bond issue described in part **a,** above.
- **d** Made a semiannual interest payment and amortized premium on a 20-year bond issue that has been outstanding for nine years.
- **e** Due to a decline in interest rates, the market value of the bond issues described in both parts **a** and **d** have increased in market value.
- **f** Called bonds payable described in part **d,** above, at a price above carrying value but below current market value. (Assume all interest expense already has been properly recorded.)
- **g** Redeemed at face value the commercial paper described in part **b,** above.

INSTRUCTIONS

Indicate the effects of each of these transactions upon the financial statement categories shown below. Organize your answer in tabular form, using the illustrated column headings. Use the following code letters to indicate the effects of each transaction upon the accounting element listed in the column heading:

I = Increase ***D*** = Decrease ***NE*** = No Effect

	Income Statement					Balance Sheet						
Transaction	*Revenue*	−	*Expenses and Losses*	=	*Net Income*	*Assets*	=	*Current Liab.*	+	*Long-Term Liab.*	+	*Owners' Equity*
a												

EXERCISE 16-3
Effects upon the Accounting Equation—Transactions Other Than Bonds

The following seven items are among the transactions of Commuter Train Corporation during the current year:

- **a** Leased equipment, signing a five-year capital lease payable in monthly instalments.
- **b** Leased land to be used as a storage yard, signing a one-year lease payable in monthly instalments.
- **c** Paid a monthly instalment on a capital lease (assume all remaining payments on this particular lease are due within one year).
- **d** Made a monthly payment on an operating lease (assume all remaining payments on this particular lease are due within one year).

e Recorded pension expense on a fully funded pension plan and remitted in cash the amount owed to the trustee.

f Recorded expense relating to postretirement benefits other than pensions earned by employees during the current period. This liability is ***partially*** funded; no payments are made now, but 50% of the obligation arising this period will be funded within the next 12 months.

g Made an adjusting entry recording income taxes expense for the period, including a considerable amount of deferred taxes.

INSTRUCTIONS

Indicate the effects of each of these transactions upon the financial statement categories shown below. Organize your answer in tabular form, using the illustrated column headings. Use the following code letters to indicate the effects of each transaction upon the accounting element listed in the column heading:

I = Increase ***D*** = Decrease ***NE*** = No Effect

	Income Statement			Balance Sheet			
Trans-action	*Revenue* −	*Expenses* =	*Net Income*	*Assets* =	*Current Liab.* +	*Long-Term Liab.* +	*Owners' Equity*
a							

EXERCISE 16-4
After-Tax Cost of Borrowing

NY Central, Inc., issued $20 million of 12% bonds payable at face value. The company pays income taxes at an average rate of 35% of its taxable income.

Compute the company's annual ***after-tax*** cost of borrowing on this bond issue, stated as (a) a total dollar amount and (b) a percentage of the amount borrowed.

EXERCISE 16-5
Bond Interest (Bonds Issued at Par)

On March 31, Bancor Corporation received authorization to issue $30 million of 12%, 20-year debenture bonds. Interest payment dates were March 31 and September 30. The bonds were all issued at par on April 30, one month after the interest date printed on the bonds.

INSTRUCTIONS

a Prepare the journal entry at April 30, to record the sale of the bonds.

b Prepare the journal entry at September 30, to record the semiannual bond interest payment.

c Prepare the adjusting entry at December 31, to record bond interest accrued since September 30.

EXERCISE 16-6
Basic Entries for a Bond Issue: Issuance, Interest Payment, and Retirement

La Paloma Corporation issued $10 million of 15-year, $10\frac{1}{2}$% bonds on July 1, 1995, at $98\frac{1}{2}$. Interest is due on June 30 and December 31 of each year, and the bonds mature on June 30, 2010. The fiscal year ends on December 31; bond discount is amortized by the straight-line method. Prepare the following journal entries:

a July 1, 1995, to record the issuance of the bonds

b December 31, 1995, to pay interest and amortize the bond discount (make two entries)

c June 30, 2010, to pay interest, amortize the bond discount, and retire the bonds at maturity (make three entries)

EXERCISE 16-7
Amortizing Bond Discount and Premium: Straight-line Method

North Corporation issued $80 million of 12%, 10-year bonds on January 1. Interest is payable semiannually on June 30 and December 31. The bonds were sold to an underwriting group at 105.

South Limited issued $80 million of 11%, 10-year bonds on January 1. Interest is payable semiannually on June 30 and December 31. The bonds were sold to an underwriting group at 95.

Prepare journal entries to record all transactions during the year for (a) the North bond issue; and (b) the South bond issue; assume that both companies amortize bond discount or premium by the straight-line method at each interest payment date. (c) Comment on the effect of the bond premium and discount on the interest expense for the two companies.

EXERCISE 16-8
Bond Prices and Accrued Interest

On August 1, 1996, Cellular Industries issued $10 million face value, 9%, 20-year bonds payable to an underwriter for total cash proceeds of $10,064,000. The bonds were dated April 1, 1996, and pay interest semiannually at October 1 and April 1.

a State the issue price of these bonds as a ***percentage*** of the face amount. (Round to the nearest $\frac{1}{10}$ of 1%.)

b Compute the amount of cash paid to bondholders at each semiannual interest date.

c Compute the company's semiannual bond interest expense (for a full six-month period), assuming that any discount or premium is amortized by the straight-line method.

EXERCISE 16-9
Effective Interest Method—Bond Discount

Three Flags Corporation issued on the authorization date $1 million of 10-year, 9% bonds payable and received proceeds of $937,689, resulting in an effective interest rate of 10%. The discount is amortized by the effective interest method; the amortization table for this bond issue is illustrated in this chapter. Interest is payable semiannually.

INSTRUCTIONS

a Show how the liability for the bonds would appear on a balance sheet prepared immediately after issuance of the bonds.

b Show how the liability for the bonds would appear on a balance sheet prepared after ***14*** semiannual interest periods (three years prior to maturity).

c Show the necessary calculations to determine interest expense by the effective interest method for the ***second*** six-month period; the discount amortized at the end of that second period; and the cash payment of interest. Round all amounts to the nearest dollar.

EXERCISE 16-10
Effective Interest Method—Premium

On April 1, Financial Publications issued $1 million of 10-year, 9% bonds payable and received proceeds of $1,067,952 resulting in an effective interest rate of 8%. Interest is payable on September 30 and March 31. The effective interest method is used to amortize bond premium; an amortization table for this bond issue is illustrated in this chapter.

INSTRUCTIONS

Prepare the necessary journal entries (rounding all amounts to the nearest dollar) on:

a April 1, to record the issuance of the bonds

b September 30, to record the payment of interest and amortization of premium at the first semiannual interest payment date

c December 31, to accrue bond interest expense through year-end

d March 31, to record payment of interest and amortization of bond premium at the second semiannual interest payment date.

EXERCISE 16-11
Partial Retirement of a Bond Issue

The following liability appears on the balance sheet of Pearl Limited on December 31, 1995:

Long-term liabilities:		
Bonds payable, 11%, due Dec. 31, 2009	*$10,000,000*	
Premium on bonds payable	*210,000*	*$10,210,000*

On January 1, 1996, 25% of the bonds are retired at 98. Interest had been paid on December 31, 1995.

a Record the retirement of $2,500,000 of bonds on January 1, 1996.

b Record the interest payment for the six months ending December 31, 1996, and the amortization of the premium on December 31, 1996 (using the straight-line method).

EXERCISE 16-12
Accounting for Leases

On July 1, City Hospital leased equipment from MedTech Instruments for a period of five years. The lease calls for monthly payments of $2,000, payable in advance on the first day of each month, beginning July 1.

INSTRUCTIONS

Prepare the journal entry needed to record this lease in the accounting records of City Hospital on July 1 under each of the following independent assumptions:

a The lease represents a simple rental arrangement.

b At the end of five years, title to this equipment will be transferred to City Hospital at no additional cost. The present value of the 60 monthly lease payments is $90,809, of which $2,000 is paid in cash on July 1.

EXERCISE 16-13
Pension Plans

During the current year, Deltron Corporation paid $3 million into a fully funded pension plan for the company's employees. At year-end, the plan has total assets of $42 million, and the present value of all future pension payments earned to date is estimated at $40 million. During the current year, the plan paid $5 million in pension benefits to retired Deltron employees.

INSTRUCTIONS

a What is Deltron's pension expense for the year?

b Identify any assets or liabilities relating to this pension plan that will appear in Deltron's balance sheet, and indicate the appropriate dollar amount.

c If Deltron becomes insolvent in future years, what prospects, if any, do today's employees have of receiving the pension benefits that they have earned to date?

EXERCISE 16-14
Accounting for Retirement Benefits

At the end of the current year, Krepshaw Power Tools, Inc., received the following information from its actuary:

Pension expense	*$1,790,000*
Nonpension postretirement benefits	*316,000*

The pension plan is fully funded. Krepshaw has funded only $23,000 of the nonpension postretirement benefits this year.

Prepare a separate journal entry to summarize for the entire year (a) the pension expense and (b) the nonpension postretirement benefits expense.

EXERCISE 16-15
Deferred Income Taxes

The following journal entry summarizes for the current year the income taxes expense of Kowloon Coachworks:

Income Taxes Expense	*14,000,000*	
Cash		*9,000,000*
Income Taxes Payable		*2,900,000*
Deferred Income Taxes Payable		*2,100,000*
To record income taxes expense for the current year.		

Of the deferred income taxes, only $240,000 is classified as a current liability.

INSTRUCTIONS

a Define ***deferred income taxes payable.***

b What is the amount of income taxes that the company has paid or expects to pay in conjunction with its income tax return for the current year?

c Illustrate the allocation of the liabilities shown in the above journal entry between the classifications of ***current liabilities*** and ***long-term liabilities.***

***EXERCISE 16-16**
Convertible Bonds

A recent annual report of a large corporation shows that 406 of the company's $3\frac{7}{8}\%$, \$1,000 face amount, convertible bonds are still outstanding. These bonds mature in less than 3 years and have a conversion ratio of 32 to 1. The company's common stock has a current market price of \$60 per share, and currently pays dividends of \$1.68 per share.

INSTRUCTIONS

a Prepare the journal entry that would be made by the corporation to record the conversion of these outstanding convertible bonds into shares of common stock. (Assume the bonds originally were issued at par.)

b Under the circumstances described above, would it be advantageous for the bondholders to exchange the bonds for common stock? Explain.

PROBLEMS

Note: In this chapter, we provide an unusually wide variety of problem assignments. In order to make the full range of these assignments available to all users of the text, we present them in one consecutive series, rather than in the usual A and B groups. This entire series is supported in both the Group A and Group B accounting work sheets.

PROBLEM 16-1
Bond Interest (Bonds Issued at Par)

Bar Harbor Gas & Electric obtained authorization to issue \$90 million face value of 10%, 20-year bonds, dated May 1, 1995. Interest payment dates were November 1 and May 1. Issuance of the bonds did not take place until August 1, 1995. On this date all the bonds were sold at a price of 100 plus accrued interest.

INSTRUCTIONS

Prepare the necessary entries in general journal form on:

a August 1, 1995, to record the issuance of the bonds

b November 1, 1995, to record the first semiannual interest payment on the bond issue

c December 31, 1995, to accrue bond interest expense through year-end

d May 1, 1996, to record the second semiannual interest payment

PROBLEM 16-2
Amortization of Bond Discount: Straight-line Method

On May 1, 1996, Festival Cruise Ships, Inc., sold a \$60 million face value, 11%, 10-year bond issue to an underwriter at a price of 98. Interest is payable semiannually on May 1 and November 1. Company policy is to amortize bond discount by the straight-line method at each interest payment date and at year-end. The company's fiscal year ends at December 31.

INSTRUCTIONS

a Prepare journal entries to record the issuance of these bonds, the payment of interest at November 1, 1996, and the bond interest expense through year-end.

b Show the proper balance sheet presentation of all liabilities relating to this bond issue at December 31, 1996. Include captions indicating whether the liabilities are classified as current or long-term.

c Why do you think that Festival was able to receive a price of only 98 for these bonds, rather than being able to issue them at par? What will issuing these bonds at a discount mean about the relationship between Festival's annual

---

* *Supplemental Topic, "Convertible Bonds Payable"*

bond interest expense and the amount of cash paid annually to bondholders? Explain.

PROBLEM 16-3
Amortizing Bond Discount and Premium: Straight-line Method

On September 1, 1995, North American Farm Equipment issued $60 million in 10% debenture bonds. Interest is payable semiannually on March 1 and September 1, and the bonds mature in 20 years. Company policy is to amortize bond discount or premium by the straight-line method at each interest payment date and at year-end. The company's fiscal year ends at December 31.

INSTRUCTIONS

a Make the necessary adjusting entries at December 31, 1995, and the journal entry to record the payment of bond interest on March 1, 1996, under each of the following assumptions:

1 The bonds were issued at 98.

2 The bonds were issued at 101.

b Compute the carrying value of bond liability at December 31, 1996, under assumptions **1** and **2** above.

PROBLEM 16-4
Comprehensive Problem: Straight-line Amortization

Country Recording Studios obtained the necessary approvals to issue $30 million of 12%, 10-year bonds, dated March 1, 1995. Interest payment dates were September 1 and March 1. Issuance of the bonds did not occur until June 1, 1995. On this date, the entire bond issue was sold to an underwriter at a price that included three months' accrued interest. Country Recording Studios follows the policy of amortizing bond discount or premium by the straight-line method at each interest date as well as for year-end adjusting entries at December 31.

INSTRUCTIONS

a Prepare all journal entries necessary to record the issuance of the bonds and bond interest expense during 1995, assuming that the total proceeds from issuance of the bonds on June 1 amounted to ***$30,315,000*** including accrued interest.

b Assume that the proceeds received from the underwriter on June 1 had amounted to ***$31,180,800*** including accrued interest. Prepare journal entries for 1995 parallel to those in part **a** above.

c Show the proper balance sheet presentation of the liability for bonds payable (including accrued interest) in the balance sheet prepared at December 31, ***2000,*** assuming that the total proceeds from issuance of the bonds (including accrued interest) had been:

1 $30,315,000, as described in part **a**

2 $31,180,800, as described in part **b**

PROBLEM 16-5
An Alternate to Problem 16-4

Liberty Broadcasting Corporation obtained authorization to issue $80 million of 12%, 10-year bonds, dated May 1, 1995. Interest payment dates were May 1 and November 1. Issuance of the bonds did not take place until July 1, 1995. On this date, the entire bond issue was sold to an underwriter at a price that included the two months' accrued interest. Liberty Broadcasting follows the policy of amortizing bond discount or premium by the straight-line method at each interest date as well as for year-end adjusting entries at December 31.

INSTRUCTIONS

a Prepare all journal entries necessary to record the issuance of the bonds and bond interest expense during 1995, assuming that the sales price of the bonds on July 1 was $83,960,000 ***including accrued interest.***

b Assume that the total proceeds from issuance of the bonds on July 1 had been $79,830,000 including accrued interest. Prepare journal entries for 1995 parallel to those in part **a** above.

c Show the proper balance sheet presentation of the liability for bonds payable in the balance sheet prepared at December 31, ***2001,*** assuming that the total proceeds from issuance of the bonds (including accrued interest) had been:

1 $83,960,000, as described in part **a**

2 $79,830,000, as described in part **b**

PROBLEM 16-6 Accrual and Payment of Interest, Amortization of Bond Premium, and Bond Redemption

The items shown below appear in the balance sheet of Majestic Corporation at December 31, 1995:

Current liabilities:		
Bond interest payable (for three months from Sept. 30 to Dec. 31)		*$ 200,000*
Long-term debt:		
Bonds payable, 10%, due Sept. 30, 2000	*$8,000,000*	
Add: Premium on bonds payable	*136,800*	*8,136,800*

The bonds are redeemable on any interest date. On September 30, 1996, Majestic redeemed $2 million of the bonds at 101.

INSTRUCTIONS

a Prepare journal entries to record the semiannual interest payment on March 31, 1996. Premium is amortized by the straight-line method at each interest payment date and was amortized to December 31, 1995.

b Prepare journal entries to record the amortization of bond premium and payment of bond interest at September 30, 1996, and also to record the redemption of $2,000,000 of the bonds at this date.

c Prepare a journal entry to record the accrual of interest at December 31, 1996. Include the amortization of bond premium to the year-end.

PROBLEM 16-7 Accrual and Payment of Interest, Amortization of Bond Discount, and Bond Redemption

The following items appear in the balance sheet of International Limited at December 31, 1995:

Current liabilities:		
Bond interest payable (for three months from Sept. 30 to Dec. 31)		*$ 300,000*
Long-term debt:		
Bonds payable, 12%, due Mar. 31, 2006	*$10,000,000*	
Less: Discount on bonds payable	*196,800*	*9,803,200*

The bonds are redeemable on any interest date. On September 30, 1996, International redeemed $2,000,000 of the bonds at 102.

INSTRUCTIONS

a Prepare journal entries to record the semiannual payment on March 31, 1996. Discount is amortized by the straight-line method at each interest payment date and was amortized to December 31, 1995.

b Prepare journal entries to record the amortization of bond discount and payment of bond interest at September 30, 1996, and also to record the redemption of $2,000,000 of the bonds at this date.

c Prepare a journal entry to record the accrual of interest at December 31, 1996. Include the amortization of bond discount to the year-end.

PROBLEM 16-8 Effective Interest Method: Bonds Issued at Discount

Arcades R Fun maintains its accounts on a calendar-year basis. On June 30, 1996, the company issued $6 million face value of 7.6% bonds at a price of $97\frac{1}{4}$, resulting in an effective rate of interest of 8%. Semiannual interest payment dates are June 30 and December 31. Bond discount is amortized by the effective interest method. The bonds mature on June 30, 2006.

INSTRUCTIONS

a Prepare the required journal entries on:

1 June 30, 1996, to record the sale of the bonds.

2 December 31, 1996, to pay interest and amortize the discount using the effective interest method.

3 June 30, ***2006,*** to pay interest, amortize the discount, and retire the bonds. Assume that at the beginning of this last interest period, the carrying value of the bonds is ***$5,988,462.*** (Use a separate journal entry to show the retirement of the bonds.)

b Show how the accounts Bonds Payable and Discount on Bonds Payable should appear on the balance sheet at December 31, ***1996.***

PROBLEM 16-9
Effective Interest Method of Amortizing Bond Discount

On December 31, 1994, city of Glenview issued $10 million face value, 10%, 10-year bonds to an underwriter at a price of 94. This price results in an effective annual interest rate of 11%. Interest is payable semiannually on June 30 and December 31. City of Glenview amortizes bond discount by the effective interest method.

INSTRUCTIONS

a Prepare an amortization table for the first two years (four interest periods) of this bond issue. Round all amounts to the nearest dollar and use the following column headings for your table:

Six Month Interest Period	(A) Interest Paid Semi-annually ($10,000,000 × 5%)	(B) Effective Semi-annual Interest Expense (Carrying Value × $5\frac{1}{2}$%)	(C) Discount Amorti-zation (B − A)	(D) Bond Discount Balance	(E) Carrying Value of Bonds, End of Period ($10,000,000 − D)
Issue date	—	—	—	$600,000	$9,400,000

b Using the information from your amortization table, prepare all journal entries necessary to record issuance of the bonds in ***1994,*** and bond interest for ***1995.*** (Use a compound entry for interest payment and amortization of bond discount at each semiannual interest payment date.)

c Show the proper balance sheet presentation of Bonds Payable and Discount on Bonds Payable at December 31, ***1996.***

PROBLEM 16-10
Effective Interest Method: Bonds Issued at Premium

On December 31, 1995, Rocky Mountain Railroad sold a $10 million, $10\frac{1}{4}$%, 20-year bond issue to an underwriter at a price of 102. This price results in an effective annual interest rate of 10%. The bonds were dated December 31, and the interest payment dates were June 30 and December 31. Rocky Mountain Railroad follows a policy of amortizing the bond premium by the effective interest method at each semiannual payment date.

INSTRUCTIONS

a Prepare an amortization table for the first two years (four interest periods) of the life of this bond issue. Round all amounts to the nearest dollar and use the following column headings:

Six-Month Interest Period	(A) Interest Paid Semi-annually ($10,000,000 × $5\frac{1}{8}$%)	(B) Effective Semi-annual Interest-Expense (Carrying Value × 5%)	(C) Premium Amortization (A − B)	(D) Bond Premium Balance	(E) Carrying Value of Bonds, End of Period ($10,000,000 + D)

b Using the information in your amortization table, prepare all journal entries necessary to record the issuance of the bonds in ***1995,*** and the bond interest expense during ***1996.***

c Show the proper balance sheet presentation of the liability for bonds payable at December 31, ***1997.***

PROBLEM 16-11
Effective Interest Method: Discount and Premium

On September 1, 1995, Camelot Hotel & Casino issued $9 million face (par) value, $8\frac{1}{2}$%, 10-year bonds payable with interest dates of March 1 and September 1. The company maintains its accounts on a calendar-year basis and follows the policy of amortizing bond discount and bond premium by the effective interest method at the semiannual interest payment dates as well as at the year-end adjusting of the accounts.

INSTRUCTIONS

a Prepare the necessary journal entries to record the following transactions, assuming that the bonds were sold for ***$8,700,000,*** a price resulting in an effective annual interest rate of ***9%.***
  1 Sale of the bonds on September 1, 1995
  2 Adjustment of the accounts at December 31, 1995, for accrued interest and amortization of a discount
  3 Payment of bond interest and amortization of discount on March 1, 1996

b Assume that the sales price of the bonds on September 1, 1995, had been ***$9,300,000,*** resulting in an effective annual interest rate of ***8%.*** Prepare journal entries parallel to those called for in **a** above at the dates of September 1, 1995; December 31, 1995; and March 1, 1996.

c State the amounts of bond interest expense for 1995 and the amount of the liability for the bonds payable at December 31, 1995, under the independent assumptions set forth in both **a** and **b** above. Show your computations.

PROBLEM 16-12
Factors Affecting Bond Prices

Shown below are three independent cases, each involving two bond issues of a large corporation. In each case, both bond issues have identical credit ratings.

a **Ontario Hydro** has two bond issues maturing in the year 2010; one has a contract interest rate of 10.5%, and the other, a contract rate of 13.375%.

b **Bell Canada** has outstanding two issues of $10\frac{1}{2}$% bonds—one issue maturing in 1998 and the other in 2009.

*c **John Labatt Limited** has issued the following convertible bonds: (1) 6% bonds maturing in 2006, with a conversion price of $17.875 per share of common stock, and (2) 5% bonds maturing in 2007, with a conversion price of $27 per share of common stock. In February, 1994, the market price of Labatt's common stock was 22\frac{1}{2}$ per share.

INSTRUCTIONS

For each case, explain which of the two bonds you would expect to have been selling at the higher market price in February, ***1994.*** Also indicate whether each bond should have been selling at a premium or a discount at that time. Explain the reasoning behind your answers. Assume that in February, 1994, market interest rates for bonds of this quality were as follows:

Maturity	*Market Interest Rate*
Years 1994–1996	*13%*
Years 1997–1999	*12%*
Year 2000 and beyond	*11%*

* *Supplemental Topic, "Convertible Bonds Payable"*

PROBLEM 16-13
Capital Leases: A Comprehensive Problem

Beach Equipment frequently uses long-term contracts as a means of financing the sale of its products. On November 1, 1996, Beach Equipment leased to Star Industries a machine carried in the perpetual inventory records at a cost of $18,120. The terms of the lease called for 48 monthly payments of $650 each, beginning November 30, 1996. The present value of these payments, after considering a built-in interest charge of 1% per month, is equal to $24,680, the regular sales price of the machine. At the end of the 48-month lease, title to the machine will transfer to Star Industries.

INSTRUCTIONS

a Prepare journal entries for 1996 in the accounts of Beach Equipment on:
   1 November 1 to record the sale financed by the lease and the related cost of goods sold.
   2 November 30, to record receipt of the first $650 monthly payment.
   3 December 31, to record receipt of the second monthly payment.

b Prepare journal entries for 1996 in the accounts of Star Industries on:
   1 November 1, to record acquisition of the leased machine.
   2 November 30, to record the first monthly lease payment.
   3 December 31, to record the second monthly lease payment.
   4 December 31, to recognize depreciation on the leased machine through year-end. Compute the depreciation expense by the straight-line method, using a 10-year service life and an estimated salvage value of $6,680.

c Compute the net carrying value of the leased machine in the balance sheet of Star Industries at December 31, 1996.

d Compute the amount of Star Industries' lease payment obligation at December 31, 1996.

PROBLEM 16-14
Reporting Liabilities in a Balance Sheet

Listed below are selected items from the accounting records of Gulf Coast Telephone Limited (GulfTel) for the year ended December 31, ***1996*** (dollar amounts in thousands):

Accounts payable	*$ 65,600*
Accrued expenses payable (other than interest)	*11,347*
$6\frac{3}{4}$% Bonds payable, due Feb. 1, 1997	*100,000*
$8\frac{1}{2}$% Bonds payable, due June 1, 1997	*250,000*
Unamortized bond discount ($8\frac{1}{2}$% bonds of 1997)	*260*
11% Bonds payable, due June 1, 2006	*300,000*
Unamortized bond premium (11% bonds of '06)	*1,700*
Accrued interest payable	*7,333*
Bond interest expense	*61,000*
Other interest expense	*17,000*
Commercial paper (net of unamortized discount)	*110,000*
Lease payment obligations—capital leases	*23,600*
Pensions obligation	*410,000*
Unfunded obligation for postretirement benefits other than pensions	*72,000*
Deferred income taxes	*130,000*
Income taxes expense	*66,900*
Income taxes payable	*17,300*
Accommodation endorsements (loan guarantees)	*28,600*
Operating income	*280,800*
Net income	*134,700*
Total assets	*2,093,500*

OTHER INFORMATION (dollar amounts in thousands)

1 The $6\frac{3}{4}\%$ bonds due in February 1997 will be refinanced in January 1997 through the issuance of \$150,000 in 9%, 20-year general debentures.

2 The $8\frac{1}{2}\%$ bonds due June 1, 1997, will be repaid entirely from a bond sinking fund.

3 GulfTel is committed to total lease payments of \$14,400 in 1997. Of this amount, \$7,479 is applicable to operating leases, and \$6,921 to capital leases. Payments on capital leases will be applied as follows: \$2,300 to interest expense and \$4,621 to reduction in the capitalized lease payment obligation.

4 GulfTel's pension plan is fully funded with an independent trustee.

5 The obligation for postretirement benefits other than pensions consists of a commitment to maintain dental and other health insurance for retired workers. During 1997, GulfTel will fund \$18,000 of this obligation.

6 The \$17,300 in income taxes payable relates to income taxes levied in 1996 and must be paid on or before March 15, 1997. No portion of the deferred tax liability is regarded as a current liability.

7 The accommodation endorsements are guarantees of bank loans and other indebtedness of various suppliers of specialized telecommunications equipment. In the opinion of management, the risk of material losses arising from these loan guarantees is not likely.

INSTRUCTIONS

a Using this information, prepare the current liabilities and long-term liabilities sections of a classified balance sheet as of December 31, 1996. (Within each classification, items may be listed in any order.)

b Explain briefly how the information in each of the seven numbered paragraphs affected your presentation of the company's liabilities.

c Compute as of December 31, 1996, the company's (1) debt ratio and (2) interest coverage ratio.

d Based solely upon information stated in this problem, indicate whether this company appears to be an outstanding, medium, or poor long-term credit risk. State specific reasons for your conclusion.

ANALYTICAL AND DECISION PROBLEMS AND CASES

A&D 16-1 Don't Call Us . . . We'll Call You

On December 31 of the current year, Synex Corporation has outstanding \$200 million of $14\frac{1}{2}\%$ bonds payable that mature in 20 years. These bonds were issued at par and are callable at a price of 106. Because of a recent decline in market interest rates, the company today can issue, at par, \$200 million of 20-year bonds with an interest rate of only 11% and use the proceeds to call the $14\frac{1}{2}\%$ bonds; the issuing cost is \$3,000,000.

INSTRUCTIONS

a Would you recommend that Synex replace the $14\frac{1}{2}\%$ bond issue, or leave it outstanding? Justify your recommendation.

b Assume that you are an investor willing to earn the current market rate of return of 11%. If you were to purchase the Synex $14\frac{1}{2}\%$ bonds at a price of 113 and hold these bonds until their maturity date, you would earn a return slightly greater than 11%. Does this investment sound attractive? Explain.

A&D 16-2 Accounting for Leases

At the beginning of the current year, Cable TV entered into the two long-term lease agreements described below:

Building Lease. Leased from Lamden Properties the use of an office building for a period of 5 years. The monthly lease payments are based upon the square metres of the building and increase by 5% each year. The estimated useful life of the building is 40 years.

Satellite Lease. Leased from SpaceNet, Inc., the use of a communications satellite for a period of 5 years. The monthly payments are intended to pay SpaceNet the current sales price of the satellite, plus a reasonable charge for interest. At the end of the lease, ownership of the satellite will transfer to Cable TV at no additional cost. The estimated useful life of the satellite is 15 years.

INSTRUCTIONS Answer each of the following questions as they relate to the building lease. After answering all four questions, answer them again as they relate to the satellite lease.

a Is this agreement an operating lease or a capital lease? Why?

b Will this lease result in any assets or liabilities being included in Cable TV's future balance sheets? If so, identify these assets and liabilities.

c Indicate the nature of any expenses that will appear in Cable TV's future income statements as a result of the lease, and indicate the number of years for which the expense will be incurred.

d Briefly explain how the ***lessor*** should account for this lease agreement, including the receipt of future lease payments. Indicate whether the lessor should recognize depreciation on the leased asset.

***A&D 16-3 Convertible Bonds**

Dreyer's Grand Ice Cream, Inc., has outstanding $50 million face value of $6\frac{1}{2}\%$ convertible bonds payable, callable at $106\frac{1}{2}$, maturing in 2011. Each $1,000 bond is convertible into 31.25 shares of the company's common stock. Today's newspaper indicates a market price for the company's common stock, which pays a dividend of 20 cents per share, of $36. On this date, the market rate of interest for bonds of similar quality and maturity date but ***without*** a conversion feature is approximately 10%.

INSTRUCTIONS

a Compute the conversion price and the stock value for one of these bonds.

b Prepare journal entries in the company's accounting records to record the following alternative possibilities:

1 Dreyer's calls the bonds (assume the bonds were originally issued at par).

2 Bondholders convert the entire bond issue into common stock.

c Given the circumstances described above, would you expect:

1 The bonds to be selling at a discount or a premium?

2 Dreyer's to call the bonds in the immediate future?

3 Bondholders to convert the bonds into common stock in the immediate future?

Explain the reasons for your answers to each question in part **c.**

COMPREHENSIVE PROBLEM 4

SHADOW MOUNTAIN HOTEL

A CORPORATE "PRACTICE SET"

Note to Students and Instructors: This problem ***requires*** use of the partially completed working papers that accompany this textbook.

* *Supplemental Topic, "Convertible Bonds Payable"*

Shadow Mountain Hotel is a profitable resort hotel and convention centre that has been in operation for several years. Max Griffith, a motion picture producer, organized a new corporation called Shadow Mountain Corporation to purchase and operate the Shadow Mountain Hotel. The new corporation raised capital by issuing both capital stock and bonds payable, and on July 1, 1996, purchased the Shadow Mountain Hotel from the previous owners.

You have been hired as the corporation's controller. The hotel's accounting staff records and posts all the routine transactions, but you have instructed them ***not*** to record any transaction that they do not understand. Rather, they are to prepare a written description of these items for your review, and you will handle the recording of these transactions. You also perform the end-of-period procedures, including the preparation of a work sheet, adjusting and closing entries, and financial statements. The corporation adjusts and closes its accounting records at the end of each ***calendar quarter*** (three-month period).

It is now September 30, 1996, the end of the first calendar quarter after Shadow Mountain Corporation acquired the Shadow Mountain Hotel. Management has asked you to provide an income statement and statement of retained earnings for this three-month period, and also a balance sheet as of September 30. Almost all of the routine transactions have ***already been recorded*** in the accounting records and posted to ledger accounts by your staff. Per your instructions, they have prepared the following written description of each transaction or event ***not yet recorded,*** as well as information necessary for end-of-period adjustments.

Transactions or Events Not Recorded by Staff

Date 1996	Transaction or Event
June 2	Max Griffith organized Shadow Mountain Corporation, with an unlimited number of authorized no-par common stock, and $100 par value, 6% convertible preferred stock (each convertible into six shares of common stock).
June 3	Griffith and other investors subscribed to 480,000 shares of the corporation's common stock at a price of $16 per share. Griffith states that he expects to have another 70,000 shares subscribed by the end of the month.
June 4	Issued to Dianna Trump all 25,000 shares of the convertible preferred stock at par, receiving $2,500,000 cash.
June 6	Underwriters Milken & Burnham agreed to purchase $10 million of 15%, 20-year bonds payable to be issued by the corporation on July 1, 1996. The bonds will pay interest every December 31 and June 30. The exact issue price will be determined at the date of issuance, based upon an index of interest rates and bond prices.
June 25	Collected in cash all $7,680,000 receivable from subscribers to the common stock. Issued stock certificates for 480,000 shares.
June 29	Issued an additional 2,000 shares of common stock to Griffith for his services in organizing the corporation. The board of directors agrees that these services were worth the $32,000 market value of these shares.

July 1 Issued the $10 million of 15%, 20-year bonds payable, dated today, to underwriters Milken & Burnham. The issue price was 98, and the corporation received $9,800,000 in cash from the underwriters.

July 1 Purchased Shadow Mountain Hotel by assuming the liabilities of the hotel and paying an additional $19 million cash to National Resorts, Inc. Exhibit 1 indicates the current values of the specific assets purchased, and also the amounts of the liabilities assumed. The excess of our $19 million purchase price over the current value of the net ***identifiable*** assets is regarded as a purchase of unrecorded goodwill.

Exhibit 1
Shadow Mountain Hotel
Valuation of Assets Purchased and Liabilities Assumed
July 1, 1996

Assets acquired:		
Accounts receivable	*$ 50,800*	
Allowance for doubtful accounts	*(1,000)*	*(credit)*
Inventory	*36,200*	
Supplies	*44,000*	
Land	*10,570,000*	
Buildings	*14,000,000*	
Furnishings & equipment	*1,200,000*	
Total identifiable assets	*$25,900,000*	
Liabilities assumed:		
Accounts payable	*$ 99,000*	
Interest payable	*41,000*	
Unearned deposits	*615,000*	
Income taxes payable	*305,000*	
Mortgage note payable (10%)	*9,840,000*	
Total liabilities	*$10,900,000*	
Current value of net identifiable assets purchased	*$15,000,000*	
Purchase price	*$19,000,000*	

July 4 Isadora Duncan, a shareholder who owned 12,000 shares of common stock in Shadow Mountain Corporation, was killed in an automobile accident. Duncan was a personal friend of Max Griffith.

July 10 Shadow Mountain Corporation purchased 12,000 shares of its common stock from the estate of Isadora Duncan at a price of $18 per share. These shares will be held temporarily as treasury stock and will be reissued in the near future.

July 11 Milken & Burnham, the underwriters of the bond issue, reported that they had resold all the bonds to investors at an average price of 101.

July 12 As part of the normal refurbishing of hotel rooms, older furniture was sold to Freight Liquidators for $119,900 cash. In the acquisition transaction on July 1, these furnishings had been assigned a cost of $200,000. (As these assets were sold less than one-half month after acquisition, there is no related accumulated depreciation, and no depreciation need be computed through the date of sale.)

July 14 Purchased new furnishings for $500,000 cash to replace those sold on July 12.

Aug. 10 Dianna Trump converted 10,000 shares of her $100 par value convertible preferred stock into 60,000 shares of no-par value common stock.

In light of her increased voting rights, Trump was given a seat on the corporation's board of directors.

Aug. 18 The City of Shadow Mountain gave to Shadow Mountain Corporation several hectares of land including the riverbed along the western boundary of the hotel parking lot. The land was given to the corporation at no cost, but with the understanding that the corporation would build a flood control channel in this riverbed to prevent land erosion. The corporation intends to build this flood control channel underground, and then to expand the parking lot on top of the riverbed and the donated land.

The donated land currently is estimated to be worth $320,000 in its present condition.

Sept. 2 Received a $48,000 advance deposit from the Canadian Academic Accounting Association to reserve a block of 300 rooms for its national convention next June.

Sept. 10 The board of directors declared the regular quarterly dividend of $1.50 per share on the shares of 6% convertible preferred stock still outstanding. The dividend is payable on October 10 to shareholders of record on September 20.

Sept. 10 The board of directors declared a 2% stock dividend on currently outstanding shares of common stock. The current market price of the common stock is $20 per share. The dividend will be distributed on September 30 to shareholders of record on September 20.

Sept. 20 Date of record for the stock dividend declared on September 10. The market value of the stock today is $21 per share.

Sept. 24 Reissued 10,400 shares of the common stock held in the treasury at a price of $21, receiving $218,400 in cash.

Sept. 26 The provincial government paid Shadow Mountain Corporation cash of $310,000 in compensation for land that was expropriated by the province to permit widening of a highway. The cost of this land to the corporation, based upon the July 1 purchase transaction, was $200,000. In this case, the transaction also is ***material in dollar amount.***

Sept. 27 Max Griffith sold 100,000 shares of his common stock in Shadow Mountain Corporation to Dianna Trump at a price of $20 per share. On this date, Griffith resigned as the corporation's chief executive officer, and the board named Trump as his replacement.

You remain the company's controller.

Sept. 30 Distributed the 10,600 share stock dividend declared on September 10. The market price of the common stock today is $22 per share.

Sept. 30 Although paycheques have been prepared and distributed, no entries have yet been made in the accounting records to record the biweekly payroll occurring on this date. Your accounting staff has provided you with the following information:

The wages and salaries earned by employees in the two weeks ended September 30 amounted to $108,000. Amounts withheld from employees' cheques consisted of $14,320 in income taxes, unemployment insurance of $4,300, and Canada Pension Plan of $3,500. Shadow Mountain contributes an equal amount for unemployment insurance and 1.4 times for Canada Pension Plan.

Company policy is to make two entries to record biweekly payrolls: one recording the payroll and amounts withheld and the other recording the payroll taxes upon the employer.

Sept. 30 Paid in cash all the liabilities at month-end for unemployment insurance and Canada Pension Plan, as well as for income taxes withheld from employees. This payment included the liabilities arising from the September 30 payroll. (Make one compound journal entry to record payment of these liabilities.)

Information for End-of-Period Adjustments

a Hotel guests normally are billed for their room rental when they check out. As of September 30, guests currently registered at the hotel owe $44,100 in room rental charges that have not yet been recorded or billed.

b The hotel's accounts receivable consist primarily of amounts owed by current guests who have not yet checked out. Based upon experience, the company's policy is to provide an allowance for uncollectible accounts equal to 2% of these receivables. The amount of the allowance determined in this manner is rounded to the nearest $100.

c The Unearned Deposits account represents advance deposits made by conventions and other groups to reserve large blocks of rooms for future dates. As of September 30, $402,300 of the amounts credited to this account have been earned, and $642,000 remains unearned.

d Supplies on hand at September 30 amount to $40,000.

e The insurance policies were purchased on July 1 for $300,000 and cover a period of 12 months.

f Depreciation on the hotel building and other structures is computed by the ***straight-line*** method, assuming a 25-year life and no salvage value.

g Depreciation on furniture and equipment is computed by the ***double-declining-balance*** method, assuming a 5-year life. (Depreciation for fractional periods is rounded to the nearest full month. In this case, you are to take 3 full months' depreciation on all assets included in the Furniture & Equipment account at September 30.)

h Goodwill is amortized by the straight-line method over a 40-year amortization period.

i Organization costs are amortized by the straight-line method over a five-year period.

j Property taxes payable accrue at the rate of $30,000 per month, beginning on July 1. These taxes are payable within a year.

k Interest accrues on the mortgage note payable at the annual rate of 10%, and accrued interest is payable on the 15th of each month. Thus, at September 30, one-half month's interest expense has accrued. (The principal amount of this note is not due until April 30, 1997.)

l In recognizing interest expense on the 15% bonds payable, bond discount is amortized by the straight-line method.

m A public accountant has determined that the company's income taxes applicable to the quarter ended September 30 amount to $256,000, including $212,000 in taxes applicable to normal operations, and $44,000 in taxes resulting from the gain from the condemnation of land by the state government. The $44,000 in taxes relating to this gain should be debited to ***account no. 600,*** Gains on Disposals of Plant Assets, rather than to the Income Taxes Expense account.
All income tax obligations will be paid within 90 days.

INSTRUCTIONS

a Prepare general journal entries to record any of the transactions and events listed above that should be recorded in the accounting records of Shadow Mountain Corporation.

Next, post your journal entries to the general ledger accounts in the partially completed accounting work sheets (a supplement to the text). You will find the company's chart of accounts in the work sheets.

Remember, your accounting staff ***already*** has recorded and posted the routine transactions occurring during the quarter ended September 30. Entries summarizing the transactions recorded by your staff ***already appear*** in the general ledger accounts and are identified by the caption "Summary of entries posted by staff." After ***you*** post an entry to the ledger, enter the new balance of the ledger account.

b Prepare a 10-column work sheet for the ***three months*** ended September 30, 1996 using the information for end-of-period adjustments provided. (We have included in this work sheet a ***correct and complete unadjusted trial balance*** as of September 30, 1996. By comparing your September 30 account balances to the amounts shown, you may determine whether or not you have correctly completed the earlier portions of this problem.)

c Prepare the following financial statements:

1 An income statement for the three months ended September 30, 1996 using single-step format.

Your income statement is to include the ***earnings per share figures*** normally found in the income statement of a publicly owned corporation. (Round per-share amounts to the nearest cent. Fully diluted amounts are not required.)

2 A statement of retained earnings for the three months ended September 30, 1996.

3 A classified balance sheet as of September 30, 1996. Include a separate classification in your balance sheet for Intangible Assets, immediately following the Plant and Equipment section. For retained earnings, show only the ending balance as of September 30.

d Journalize and post the adjusting and closing entries.

e Prepare an after-closing trial balance as of September 30, 1996.

APPENDIX A

Applications of Present Value

Several chapters have included brief references to the concept of present value in discussions of the valuation of certain assets and liabilities. The purpose of this appendix is to discuss this concept more fully and also to demonstrate the use of present value tables as an aid to making present value computations. In addition, the appendix summarizes in one location the various applications of the present value concept that have been discussed throughout the book.

Learning Objectives

After studying this appendix you should be able to:

1. *Explain the concept of present value.*
2. *Identify the three factors that affect the present value of a future amount.*
3. *Compute the present value of a future amount and of an annuity using present value tables.*
4. *Discuss accounting applications of the present value concept.*

The Concept of Present Value

OBJECTIVE 1 Explain the concept of present value.

The concept of present value has many applications in accounting, but it is most easily explained in the context of evaluating investment opportunities. In this context, the present value of an expected future cash receipt is the amount that a knowledgeable investor would pay ***today*** for the right to receive that future amount. The present value is always ***less*** than the future amount, because the investor will expect to earn a return on the investment. The amount by which the future cash receipt exceeds its present value represents the investor's profit; in short, this difference may be regarded as ***interest revenue*** included in the future amount.

OBJECTIVE 2 Identify the three factors that affect the present value of a future amount.

The present value of a particular investment opportunity depends upon three factors: (1) the expected dollar amount to be received in the future, (2) the length of time until the future amount will be received, and (3) the rate of return (called the ***discount rate***) required by the investor. The process of determining the present value of a future cash receipt or payment is called ***discounting*** the future amount.

To illustrate the present value concept, assume that a specific investment is expected to result in a $1,000 cash receipt at the end of one year. An investor requiring a 10% annual rate of return would be willing to pay $909 today (computed as $1,000 ÷ 1.10) for the right to receive this future amount. This computation may be verified as follows (amounts rounded to the nearest dollar):

Amount to be invested (present value)	$ 909
Required return on investment ($909 × 10%)	91
Amount to be received in one year (future value)	$1,000

If the $1,000 is to be received ***two years*** in the future, the investor would pay only $826 for the investment today [($1,000 ÷ 1.10) ÷ 1.10]. This computation may be verified as follows (amounts rounded to the nearest dollar):

Amount to be invested (present value)	$ 826
Required return on investment in first year ($826 × 10%)	83
Amount invested after one year	$ 909
Required return on investment in second year ($909 × 10%)	91
Amount to be received in two years (future value)	$1,000

The amount that our investor would pay today, $826, is the ***present value*** of $1,000 to be received two years later, discounted at an annual rate of 10%. The $174 difference between the $826 present value and the $1,000 future amount may be regarded as the return (interest revenue) to be earned by the investor over the two-year period.

Present Value Tables

Although we can compute the present value of future amounts by a series of divisions as illustrated above, a more convenient method is available. We can use a ***table of present values*** to find the present value of $1 at a specified discount rate and then multiply that value by the future amount. For example, in ***Table 1*** below, the present value of $1 to be received in two years, discounted at an annual rate of 10%, is ***$0.826.*** If we multiply .826 by the expected future cash receipt of $1,000, we get an answer of $826, the same amount produced by the series of divisions in our previous illustration.

TABLE 1
Present Values of $1 Due in *n* Periods*

Number of Periods (*n*)	Discount Rate 1%	$1\frac{1}{2}$%	5%	6%	8%	10%	12%	15%	20%
1	.990	.985	.952	.943	.926	.909	.893	.870	.833
2	.980	.971	.907	.890	.857	.826	.797	.756	.694
3	.971	.956	.864	.840	.794	.751	.712	.658	.579
4	.961	.942	.823	.792	.735	.683	.636	.572	.482
5	.951	.928	.784	.747	.681	.621	.567	.497	.402
6	.942	.915	.746	.705	.630	.564	.507	.432	.335
7	.933	.901	.711	.665	.583	.513	.452	.376	.279
8	.923	.888	.677	.627	.540	.467	.404	.327	.233
9	.914	.875	.645	.592	.510	.424	.361	.284	.194
10	.905	.862	.614	.558	.463	.386	.322	.247	.162
20	.820	.742	.377	.312	.215	.149	.104	.061	.026
24	.788	.700	.310	.247	.158	.102	.066	.035	.013
36	.699	.585	.173	.123	.063	.032	.017	.007	.001

* The present value of $1 is computed by the formula $p = 1/(1 + i)^n$, where **p** is the present value of $1, *i* is the discount rate, and ***n*** is the number of periods until the future cash flow will occur. Amounts in this table have been rounded to three decimal places and are shown for a limited number of periods and discount rates. Many calculators are programmed to use this formula and can compute present values when the future amount is entered along with values for *i* and ***n***.

Selecting an Appropriate Discount Rate

The ***discount rate*** may be viewed as the investor's required rate of return. All investments involve some degree of risk that actual future cash flows may turn out to be less than expected. Investors usually will expect a rate of return that justifies taking this risk. Under today's market conditions, investors require annual returns of between 7% and 9% on low-risk investments, such as government bonds and term deposits. For relatively high-risk investments, such as the introduction of a new product line, investors may expect to earn an annual return of perhaps 15% or more.

In addition to the amount of risk involved, the "appropriate" discount rate for determining the present value of a specific investment depends upon the investor's cost of capital and the returns available from other investment opportunities. When a higher discount rate is used, the resulting present value will be lower and the investor, therefore, will be interested in the investment only at a lower price.

Discounting Annual Cash Flows

Let us now assume that an investment is expected to produce an ***annual net cash flow*** of $10,000 in ***each of the next three years.***[1] If Camino Company expects a 12% return on this type of investment, it may compute the present value of these cash flows as follows:

OBJECTIVE 3 Compute the present value of a future amount and of an annuity using present value tables.

Year	Expected Net Cash Flow	×	Present Value of $1 Discounted at 12%	=	Present Value of Net Cash Flows
1	$10,000		.893		$ 8,930
2	10,000		.797		7,970
3	10,000		.712		7,120
Total present value of the investment					$24,020

This analysis indicates that the present value of the expected net cash flows from the investment, discounted at an annual rate of 12%, amounts to $24,020. This is the maximum amount that Camino Company could afford to pay for this investment and still expect to earn the 12% required rate of return.

In the preceding schedule, we multiplied each of the expected annual cash flows by the present value of $1 in the appropriate future period, discounted at 12% per year. The present values of the annual cash flows were then added to determine the total present value of the investment. Separately discounting each annual cash flow to its present value is necessary only when the cash flows vary in amount from one year to the next. Since the annual cash flows in our example are ***uniform in amount,*** there are two easier ways to compute the total present value.

One way is to add the three decimal figures representing the present value of $1 in the successive years (.893 + .797 + .712) and then to multiply this total (2.402) by the $10,000 annual cash flow. This approach produces the same result ($10,000 × 2.402 = $24,020) we obtained by determining the present value of each year's cash flow separately and adding the results.

An even easier approach to determining the present value of uniform annual cash flows is to refer to an ***annuity table,*** which shows the present value of ***$1 to be received periodically*** for a given number of periods. An annuity table appears on the following page and is labelled as ***Table 2.***[2]

Note that the present value of $1 to be received periodically (annually) for three years, discounted at 12% per year, is ***$2.402.*** Thus, $10,000 received annually for three years, discounted at 12%, is ***$24,020*** ($10,000 × 2.402).

---

[1] An "annual net cash flow" normally is the net result of a series of cash receipts and cash payments occurring throughout the year. For convenience, we follow the common practice of assuming that the entire net cash flow for each year occurs at ***year-end.*** This assumption causes relatively little distortion and greatly simplifies computations.

[2] This table assumes that the periodic cash flows occur at the ***end*** of each period.

TABLE 2
Present Values of $1 to Be Received Periodically for *n* Periods

Number of Periods (*n*)					Discount Rate				
	1%	$1\frac{1}{2}$%	5%	6%	8%	10%	12%	15%	20%
1	0.990	0.985	0.952	0.943	0.926	0.909	0.893	0.870	0.833
2	1.970	1.956	1.859	1.833	1.783	1.736	1.690	1.626	1.528
3	2.941	2.912	2.723	2.673	2.577	2.487	2.402	2.283	2.106
4	3.902	3.854	3.546	3.465	3.312	3.170	3.037	2.855	2.589
5	4.853	4.783	4.329	4.212	3.993	3.791	3.605	3.352	2.991
6	5.795	5.697	5.076	4.917	4.623	4.355	4.111	3.784	3.326
7	6.728	6.598	5.786	5.582	5.206	4.868	4.564	4.160	3.605
8	7.652	7.486	6.463	6.210	5.747	5.335	4.968	4.487	3.837
9	8.566	8.361	7.108	6.802	6.247	5.759	5.328	4.772	4.031
10	9.471	9.222	7.722	7.360	6.710	6.145	5.650	5.019	4.192
20	18.046	17.169	12.462	11.470	9.818	8.514	7.469	6.259	4.870
24	21.243	20.030	13.799	12.550	10.529	8.985	7.784	6.434	4.937
36	30.108	27.661	16.547	14.621	11.717	9.677	8.192	6.623	4.993

Discount Periods of Less Than One Year

The interval between regular periodic cash flows is termed the ***discount period.*** In our preceding examples we have assumed cash flows and, therefore, discount periods of one year. Often a note or a contract may call for cash payments on a more frequent basis, such as monthly, quarterly, or semiannually. The illustrated present value tables can be used with discount periods of any length, ***but the discount rate must relate to the time interval of the discount period.*** Thus, if we use the annuity table to find the present value of a series of equal monthly cash payments, the discount rate must be expressed as a monthly interest rate.

To illustrate, assume that StyleMart purchases merchandise from Western Fashions, issuing in exchange a $96,000 note payable to be paid in 24 monthly instalments of $4,000 each. Both companies should record this transaction at the present value of the note. If a reasonable ***annual*** interest rate for this type of note is 12%, we should discount the monthly cash payments at the ***monthly*** rate of ***1%.*** The annuity table shows the present value of $1 to be received (or paid) for 24 monthly periods, discounted at 1% per month, is 21.243. Thus, the present value of the instalment note issued by StyleMart is ***$84,972*** ($4,000 × 21.243).

ACCOUNTING APPLICATIONS OF THE PRESENT VALUE CONCEPT

Accounting applications of the concept of present value have been discussed at appropriate points throughout this textbook. We will now demon-

OBJECTIVE 4 Discuss accounting applications of the present value concept.

strate these applications with examples that make use of our present value tables.

Valuation of Long-Term Notes Receivable and Payable (Chapters 8 and 11)

When a long-term note receivable or payable does not bear a realistic stated rate of interest, a portion of the face amount of the note should be regarded as representing an interest charge. The amount of this interest charge can be determined by discounting the note to its present value using as a discount rate a realistic rate of interest.

To illustrate, consider our preceding example in which StyleMart purchases merchandise from Western Fashions by issuing an instalment note payable with a face amount of $96,000 and no stated rate of interest. The present value of this note, discounted at the realistic market interest rate of 1% per month, was $84,972. The difference between the $96,000 face amount of the note and its present value of $84,972 is $11,028, which represents the interest charge included in the face amount.

StyleMart should use the ***present value*** of the note in determining the cost of the merchandise and the amount of the related net liability, as shown by the following entry:

The net liability is recorded at its present value

Inventory	*84,972*	
Discount on Notes Payable	*11,028*	
Notes Payable		*96,000*
Purchased merchandise by issuing a 24-month instalment note payable with a 1% monthly interest charge included in the face amount.		

The $11,028 discount represents the interest charges included in the face amount of the note. To determine how much of this discount will be recognized as interest expense each month, StyleMart should prepare an ***amortization table*** similar to the one illustrated in Chapter 11. This table will be based upon 24 monthly payments of $4,000, a monthly interest rate of 1%, and an original unpaid balance (principal amount) of $84,972. Therefore, the interest expense for the first month (rounded to the nearest dollar) will be $850 ($84,972 × 1%), and the remaining $3,150 ($4,000 payment, less $850 interest expense) will reduce the unpaid principal amount. Interest expense will decline in each successive month, as a result of the decline in the unpaid principal amount.

The entries to record the first $4,000 payment on the face amount of this note and the related monthly interest expense are illustrated below:

Notes Payable	*4,000*	
Cash		*4,000*
To record $4,000 payment on a note payable.		

Interest Expense	*850*	
Discount on Notes Payable		*850*
To record interest expense and amortize discount on an instalment note payable with interest included in the face amount (interest expense equal to unpaid principal amount, $84,972, times 1% monthly interest rate).		

Capital Budgeting (Chapter 10)[3]

Capital budgeting is the process of planning and evaluating proposals for capital expenditures, such as the acquisition of plant assets or the introduction of a new product line. Perhaps the most widely used approach in the evaluation of proposed capital expenditures is ***discounting*** the expected future cash flows to their ***present value.***

Assume that Globe Mfg. Ltd. is considering a proposal to purchase new equipment in order to produce a new product. The equipment costs $400,000, has an estimated 10-year service life, and has an estimated salvage value of $50,000. Globe estimates that production and sale of the new product will increase the company's annual net cash flow by $100,000 per year for the next 10 years. If Globe requires a 15% annual rate of return on investments of this nature, the present value of these cash flows may be computed as shown below:

Present value of expected annual net cash inflows of $100,000 for 10 years, discounted at 15% per year: $100,000 × 5.019 (from Table 2, page 795)	$501,900
Present value of estimated salvage value to be received at the end of the tenth year: $50,000 × .247 (from Table 1, page 793)	12,350
Present value of estimated future cash inflows	$514,250
Less: Amount to be invested (already a present value)	400,000
Net present value of proposal	$114,250

This analysis indicates that the present value of the expected net cash flows from this investment, discounted at an annual rate of 15%, amounts to $514,250. This is the maximum amount that Globe could afford to invest in this project and still expect to earn the required 15% annual rate of return. As the cost of this investment is only $400,000, Globe can expect to earn more than its required 15% return.

The ***net present value*** of a proposal is the ***difference*** between the total present value of the future net cash flows and the cost of the investment. When the net present value is equal to zero, the investment provides a rate of return exactly equal to the rate used in discounting the cash flows. A ***positive*** net present value means that the investment provides a rate of return ***greater*** than the discount rate; a ***negative*** net present value means that the investment yields a return of ***less*** than the discount rate.

Since the discount rate usually is the minimum rate of return required by the investor, proposals with a positive net present value are considered acceptable, and those with a negative net present value are viewed as unacceptable.

Capital budgeting techniques are discussed further in courses in management accounting, cost accounting, and finance.

Estimating the Value of Goodwill (Chapter 10)

The asset goodwill may be defined as the present value of expected future earnings in excess of the normal return on net identifiable assets. One

[3] Capital budgeting also is discussed in Chapter 26.

method of estimating goodwill is to estimate the annual amounts by which earnings are expected to exceed a normal return and then to discount these amounts to their present value.

To illustrate, assume that LiteHouse, a chain of restaurants, is negotiating to purchase Little Nell's, a highly profitable restaurant in Toronto. In addition to paying for the fair market value of Little Nell's net identifiable assets, LiteHouse is willing to pay an appropriate amount for goodwill. The management of LiteHouse estimates that Little Nell's will earn at least $80,000 in excess of "normal earnings" for this size restaurant in each of the next five years. If LiteHouse requires a 20% annual return on purchased goodwill, it can pay as much as $239,280 for this expected 5-year $80,000 annuity. [$80,000 × 2.991 (from Table 2) = $239,280.]

Market Prices of Bonds (Chapter 16)

The market price of bonds may be regarded as the ***present value*** to bondholders of the future principal and interest payments. To illustrate, assume that a corporation issues $1,000,000 face value of 10-year, 9% bonds when the going market rate of interest is 10%. Since bond interest generally is paid semiannually, we must use 20 ***semiannual*** periods as the life of the bond issue and a 5% ***semiannual*** market rate of interest in our present value calculations. The expected issuance price of this bond issue may be computed as follows:

Present value of future principal payments:	
$1,000,000 due after 20 semiannual periods, discounted at 5% per period:	
$1,000,000 × .377 (from Table 1, page 793)	*$377,000*
Present value of future interest payments:	
$45,000 per period ($1,000,000 × 9% × ½) for 20 semiannual periods,	
discounted at 5%: $45,000 × 12.462 (from Table 2, page 795)	*560,790*
Expected issuance price of bond issue	*$937,790*

Capital Lease (Chapter 16)

A capital lease is regarded as a sale of the leased asset by the lessor to the lessee. At the date of this sale, the lessor recognizes sales revenue equal to the ***present value*** of the future lease payments receivable, discounted at a realistic rate of interest. The lessee also uses the present value of the future payments to determine the cost of the leased asset and the valuation of the related liability.

To illustrate, assume that on December 1, Pace Tractor uses a ***capital lease*** to finance the sale of a tractor to Kelly Grading Co. The tractor was carried in Pace Tractor's perpetual inventory records at a cost of $15,000. Terms of the lease call for Kelly Grading Co. to make ***24*** monthly payments of ***$1,000*** each, beginning on December 31. These lease payments include an interest charge of ***1%*** per month. At the end of the 24-month lease, title to the tractor will pass to Kelly Grading Co. at no additional cost.

Accounting by the Lessor (Pace Tractor) ***Table 2*** shows that the present value of $1 to be received monthly for 24 months, discounted at 1% per month, is ***21.243.*** Therefore, the present value of the 24 future lease payments is $1,000 × 21.243, or ***$21,243.*** Pace Tractor should record this capital lease as a sale of the tractor at a price equal to the present value of the lease payments, as follows:

Lease Payment Receivable (net)	*21,243*	
Sales		*21,243*
Financed sale of a tractor to Kelly Grading Co. using a capital lease requiring 24 monthly payments of $1,000. Payments include a 1% monthly interest charge.		

Cost of Goods Sold	*15,000*	
Inventory		*15,000*
To record cost of tractor sold under capital lease.		

Notice that the sales price of the tractor is only $21,243, even though the gross amount to be collected from Kelly Grading Co. amounts to $24,000 ($1,000 × 24 payments). The difference between these two amounts, $2,757, will be recognized by Pace Tractor as interest revenue over the life of the lease.[4]

To illustrate the recognition of interest revenue, the entry on December 31 to record collection of the first monthly lease payment (rounded to the nearest dollar) is:

Cash		*1,000*	
Interest Revenue			*212*
Lease Payments Receivable (net)			*788*
Received first lease payment from Kelly Grading Co.:			
Lease payment received	*$1,000*		
Interest revenue ($21,243 × 1%)	*(212)*		
Reduction in lease payments receivable	*$ 788*		

After this first monthly payment is collected, the present value of the lease payments receivable is reduced to $20,455 ($21,243 original balance, less $788). Therefore, the interest revenue earned during the ***second*** month of the lease (rounded to the nearest dollar) will be ***$205*** ($20,455 × 1%).[5]

Accounting by the Lessee (Kelly Grading Co.) Kelly Grading Co. also should use the present value of the lease payments to determine the cost of the tractor and the amount of the related liability, as shown below:

Leased Equipment	*21,243*	
Lease Payment Obligation		*21,243*
To record acquisition of a tractor through a capital lease from Pace Tractor. Terms call for 24 monthly payments of $1,000, which include a 1% monthly interest charge.		

4 We have elected to record the present value of the future lease payments by a single debit entry to Lease Payments Receivable. An alternative is to debit Lease Payments Receivable for the total amount of the future payments and to credit Discount on Lease Payments Receivable, a contra-asset account, for the unearned finance charges included in the contractual amount. Either approach results in the lessor recording a net receivable equal to the present value of the future lease payments.

5 Both Pace Tractor and Kelly Grading Co. would prepare ***amortization tables*** showing the allocation of each lease payment between interest and the amount due.

The entry on December 31 to record the first monthly lease payment (rounded to the nearest dollar) is:

Interest Expense		*212*	
Lease Payment Obligation		*788*	
Cash			*1,000*
To record first monthly lease payment to Pace Tractor:			
Amount of payment	*$1,000*		
Interest expense ($21,243 × 1%)	*(212)*		
Reduction in lease payment obligation	*$ 788*		

ASSIGNMENT MATERIAL

PROBLEMS

PROBLEM 1
Using Present Value Tables

Use Tables 1 and 2 to determine the present value of the following cash flows.

a $10,000 to be paid annually for seven years, discounted at an annual rate of 10%. Payments are to occur at the end of each year.

b $7,500 to be received today, assuming that money can be invested to earn 15% annually.

c $350 to be paid monthly for 24 months, with an additional "balloon payment" of $15,000 due at the end of the twenty-fourth month, discounted at a monthly interest rate of $1\frac{1}{2}$%. The first payment is to be one month from today.

d $30,000 to be received annually for the first three years, followed by $20,000 to be received annually for the next two years (total of five years in which collections are received), discounted at an annual rate of 12%. Assume collections occur at year-end.

PROBLEM 2
Present Value and Bond Prices

On June 30 of the current year, Rural Gas & Electric Ltd. issued $10,000,000 face value, 11%, 10-year bonds payable, with interest dates of December 31 and June 30. The bonds were issued at a discount, resulting in an effective ***semiannual*** interest rate of 6%. The company maintains its accounts on a calendar-year basis and amortizes the bond discount by the effective interest method.

INSTRUCTIONS

a Compute the issuance price for the bond issue that results in an effective semiannual interest rate of 6%.

b Prepare a journal entry to record the issuance of the bonds at the sales price you computed in part **a.**

PROBLEM 3
Valuation of a Note Payable

On December 1, Showcase Interiors purchased a shipment of furniture from Colonial House by paying $10,500 cash and issuing an instalment note payable in the face amount of $28,800. The note is to be paid in 24 monthly instalments of $1,200 each. Although the note makes no mention of an interest charge, the rate of interest usually charged to Showcase Interiors in such transactions is $1\frac{1}{2}$% per month.

INSTRUCTIONS

a Compute the present value of the note payable, using a discount rate of $1\frac{1}{2}$% per month.

b Prepare the journal entries in the accounts of Showcase Interiors on:

1 December 1, to record the purchase of the furniture (debit Inventory).

2 December 31, to record the first $1,200 monthly payment on the note and to recognize interest expense for one month by the effective interest method. (Round interest expense to the nearest dollar.)

c Show how the liability for this note would appear in the balance sheet at December 31. (Assume that the note is classified as a current liability.)

PROBLEM 4
Discounting Lease Agreements to Present Value

Metropolitan Transit District (MTD) plans to acquire a large computer system by entering into a long-term lease agreement with the computer manufacturer. The manufacturer will provide the computer system under either of the following lease agreements:

Five-year lease. MTD is to pay $2,500,000 at the beginning of the lease (delivery date) and $1,000,000 annually at the end of each of the next 5 years. At the end of the fifth year, MTD may take title to the system for an additional payment of $3,000,000.

Ten-year lease. MTD is to pay $2,000,000 at the beginning of the lease and $900,000 annually at the end of each of the next 10 years. At the end of the tenth year, MTD may take title for an additional payment of $1,300,000.

Under either proposal, MTD will buy the computer at the end of the lease. MTD is a governmental agency that does not seek to earn a profit and is not evaluating alternative investment opportunities. However, MTD does attempt to minimize its costs and it must borrow the money to finance either lease agreement at an annual interest rate of 10%.

INSTRUCTIONS

a Determine which lease proposal results in the lower cost for the computer system when the future cash outlays are discounted at an annual interest rate of 10%.

b Prepare a journal entry to record the acquisition of the computer system under the lowest cost lease agreement as determined in part **a.** (This journal entry will include the initial cash payment to the computer manufacturer required at the beginning of the lease.)

PROBLEM 5
Capital Leases: A Comprehensive Problem

Custom Truck Builders frequently uses long-term lease contracts to finance the sale of its trucks. On November 1, 1995, Custom Truck Builders leased to Central Van Lines a truck carried in the perpetual inventory records at $33,520. The terms of the lease call for Central Van Lines to make 36 monthly payments of $1,400 each, beginning on November 30, 1995. The present value of these payments, after considering a built-in interest charge of 1% per month, is equal to the regular $42,150 sales price of the truck. At the end of the 36-month lease, title to the truck will transfer to Central Van Lines.

INSTRUCTIONS

a Prepare journal entries for 1995 in the accounts of Custom Truck Builders on:
  1 November 1 to record the sale financed by the lease and the related cost of goods sold. (Debit Lease Payments Receivable for the $42,150 present value of the future lease payments.)
  2 November 30, to record receipt of the first $1,400 monthly payment. (Prepare a compound journal entry that allocates the cash receipt between interest revenue and reduction of Lease Payments Receivable. Round all interest computations to the nearest dollar.)
  3 December 31, to record receipt of the second monthly payment.

b Prepare journal entries for 1995 in the accounts of Central Van Lines on:
  1 November 1, to record acquisition of the leased truck.
  2 November 30, to record the first monthly lease payment. (Determine the portion of the payment representing interest expense in a manner parallel to that described in part **a.**)

3 December 31, to record the second monthly lease payment.

4 December 31, to recognize depreciation on the leased truck through year-end. Compute depreciation expense by the straight-line method, using a 10-year service life and an estimated salvage value of $6,150.

c Compute the net carrying value of the leased truck in the balance sheet of Central Van Lines at December 31, 1995.

d Compute the amount of Central Van Lines' lease payment obligation at December 31, 1995.

PROBLEM 6
Valuation of a Note Receivable with an Unrealistic Interest Rate

On December 31, Richland Farms sold a tract of land, which had cost $930,000, to Skyline Developers in exchange for $150,000 cash and a five-year, 4%, note receivable for $900,000. Interest on the note is payable annually, and the principal amount is due in five years. The accountant for Richland Farms did not notice the unrealistically low interest rate on the note and made the following entry on December 31 to record this sale:

Cash	*150,000*	
Notes Receivable	*900,000*	
Land		*930,000*
Gain on Sale of Land		*120,000*
Sold land to Skyline Developers in exchange for cash and a five-year note with interest due annually.		

INSTRUCTIONS

a Compute the present value of the note receivable from Skyline Developers at the date of sale, assuming that a realistic rate of interest for this transaction is 12%.

b Prepare the journal entry on December 31 to record the sale of the land correctly. Show supporting computations for (1) the gain or loss on the sale and (2) the discount on the note receivable.

c Explain what effects the error made by Richland Farms' accountant will have upon (1) the net income in the year of the sale and (2) the combined net income of the next five years. Ignore income taxes.

CHAPTER

17 Investments in Corporate Securities

In this chapter, we discuss investments in corporate securities (stocks and bonds) from the viewpoint of the investor. We first focus upon short-term investments in marketable securities—that is, highly liquid investments made primarily for the purpose of earning dividend or interest revenue. Next, we discuss long-term investments in common stock made for the purpose of exercising significant influence or control over the issuing corporation. We illustrate the equity method of accounting for these investments and explain how a parent company and its subsidiaries function as one economic entity. The chapter concludes with a discussion of consolidated financial statements.

Learning Objectives

After studying this chapter you should be able to:

1. *Account for short-term investments in stocks and bonds.*
2. *Account for an investment in common stock by the equity method.*
3. *Explain how a parent company "controls" its subsidiaries.*
4. *Describe the distinctive feature of consolidated financial statements.*
5. *Explain why intercompany transactions must be eliminated as a step in preparing consolidated financial statements.*
6. *Prepare a consolidated balance sheet.*

The term ***corporate securities*** refers to the stocks and bonds issued by corporations. The securities issued by large, publicly owned corporations such as BCE, Inc., Canadian Pacific, and Alcan Aluminum are owned by literally millions of different investors. On the other hand, all of the common stock issued by a small, closely held corporation may be owned by one individual or by a small group of investors, such as the members of a family. From the investor's point of view, most investments in corporate securities fall into one of two broad categories: (1) investments in ***marketable securities*** and (2) investments for purposes of ***significant influence or control.***

INVESTMENTS IN MARKETABLE SECURITIES

Marketable securities consist primarily of government bonds and the bonds and stocks of large corporations. These securities are traded on organized securities exchanges, such as the Toronto Stock Exchange. Thus, they are easily purchased or sold at quoted market prices. Investments in marketable securities earn a return for the investor, yet are almost as liquid as cash itself. For this reason, marketable securities usually are listed in the balance sheet second among current assets, immediately after cash.

To qualify as a current asset, an investment in marketable securities must be readily marketable. ***Readily marketable*** means immediately salable at a quoted market price. In addition, management must be ***willing*** to use the invested funds to pay current liabilities or to use in current operations. Investments that are not readily marketable, or that management intends to hold on a long-term basis, are ***not*** current assets. Such investments should be shown in the balance sheet just below the current asset section under the caption Long-Term Investments.

Quoted Market Prices The current market prices of most marketable securities are quoted daily by securities exchanges, by brokerage houses, and in the financial pages of major newspapers. The market prices of stocks are quoted in terms of dollars per share. As illustrated in Chapter 16, bond prices are stated as a percentage of the bond's maturity value, which usually is $1,000. Thus, a bond with a quoted price of ***87*** has a market value of ***$870*** ($1,000 × 87%).

Accounting for Marketable Securities

OBJECTIVE 1 Account for short-term investments in stocks and bonds.

Accounting differs somewhat between investments in marketable equity securities (stocks) and in marketable debt securities (bonds). The principal distinction in accounting for investments in stocks and in bonds is that ***interest on bonds accrues*** from day to day. An investor in bonds must account for this accrued interest when the bonds are purchased, at the end of each accounting period, and when the bonds are sold. Dividends on stock, however, ***do not accrue.*** For this reason, separate controlling accounts are used in the general ledger for each type of investment. For each controlling account, a subsidiary ledger is maintained, which shows for each security owned the acquisition date, total cost, number of shares (or bonds) owned, and the cost per share (or bond). This subsidiary ledger provides the information necessary to determine the amount of gain or loss when an investment in a particular stock or bond is sold.

Marketable Debt Securities (Bonds)

The amount of interest paid annually to bondholders is equal to a stated percentage of the bond's maturity value. Thus, the owner of a 10% bond receives $100 interest ($1,000 × 10%) every year. Since bond interest usually is paid semiannually, the bondholder receives two semiannual interest payments of $50 each.

When bonds are purchased between interest dates, the purchaser pays the quoted market price for the bond ***plus*** the interest accrued since the last interest payment date. By this arrangement the new owner becomes entitled to receive in full the next semiannual interest payment. An account called Bond Interest Receivable should be debited for the amount of accrued interest purchased.

To illustrate the accounting entries for an investment in bonds, assume that on August 1 an investor purchases ten 9%, $1,000 bonds of Rider Corporation that pay interest on June 1 and December 1. The investor buys the bonds on August 1 at a price of 99 (or $9,900), plus a brokerage commission of $50 and two months' accrued interest of $150 ($10,000 × 9% × $\frac{2}{12}$ = $150). The brokerage commission is viewed as part of the cost of the bonds. However, the accrued interest receivable at the time of purchase must be accounted for separately. Therefore, the journal entry made by the investor on August 1 is:

Separate account for accrued bond interest purchased

Marketable Debt Securities	*9,950*	
Bond Interest Receivable	*150*	
Cash		*10,100*
Purchased ten 9% bonds of Rider Corporation for $9,900 plus a brokerage commission of $50 and two months' accrued interest.		

On December 1, the semiannual interest payment date, the investor will receive an interest cheque for $450, which will be recorded as follows:

Note portion of interest cheque earned

Cash	*450*	
Bond Interest Receivable		*150*
Bond Interest Revenue		*300*
Received semiannual interest on Rider Corporation bonds.		

The $300 credit to Bond Interest Revenue represents the amount actually earned during the four months the bonds were owned by the investor (9% × $10,000 × $\frac{4}{12}$ = $300).

If the investor's accounting records are maintained on a calendar-year basis, the following adjusting entry is required at December 31 to record bond interest earned since December 1:

Bond Interest Receivable	*75*	
Bond Interest Revenue		*75*
To accrue one month's interest earned (Dec. 1–Dec. 31) on Rider Corporation bonds ($10,000 × 9% × $\frac{1}{12}$ = $75).		

Amortization of Bond Discount or Premium from the Investor's Viewpoint

We have discussed the need for the corporation issuing bonds payable to amortize any bond discount or premium to measure correctly the bond interest expense. But what about the ***purchaser*** of the bonds? Should an investor in bonds amortize any difference between the cost of the investment and its future maturity value in order to measure investment income correctly? The answer to this question depends upon whether the investor considers the bonds to be a current asset (short-term investment) or a long-term investment.

When an investment in bonds is classified as a current asset, the investor usually ***does not*** amortize discount or premium. The justification for this practice is the accounting principle of ***materiality.*** Given that the investment may be held for but a short period of time, amortization of bond discount or premium probably will not have a material effect upon reported net income. When an investment in bonds will be held for the long term, however, the investor should amortize discount or premium. Amortization of a discount will increase the amount of interest revenue recognized by the investor; amortization of a premium will reduce the amount of interest revenue recognized.

Marketable Equity Securities (Stocks)

Since dividends on stock do not accrue, the ***entire cost*** of purchasing stock (including brokerage commissions) is debited to the Marketable Equity Securities account. Dividend revenue usually is recognized when the dividend cheque arrives; the entry consists of a debit to Cash and a credit to Dividend Revenue. No adjusting entries are needed to recognize dividend revenue at the end of an accounting period.

Additional shares of stock received in stock splits or stock dividends ***are not income*** to the shareholder, and only a ***memorandum entry*** is used to record the increase in the number of shares owned. The ***cost basis per share*** is decreased, however, because of the larger number of shares comprising the investment after receiving additional "free" shares from a stock split or a stock dividend.

As an example, assume that an investor purchases 100 shares of Delta Limited common stock at a total cost of $7,200, including commission. The investor's original cost basis is $72 per share ($7,200 ÷ 100 shares). Later the investor receives an additional 20 shares as the result of a 20% stock dividend. The investor's cost basis per share is thereby reduced to ***$60*** per share, computed by dividing the total cost of $7,200 by the ***120*** shares owned after the stock dividend. The memorandum entry to be made in the investor's general journal would be:

July 10	*Memorandum: Received 20 additional shares of Delta Limited common stock as a result of 20% stock dividend. Now own 120 shares with a cost basis of $7,200, or $60 per share.*

Gains and Losses from Sales of Investments

The sale of an investment in ***stocks*** is recorded by debiting Cash for the amount received and crediting the Marketable Equity Securities account for the cost of the securities sold. Any difference between the proceeds of the sale and the cost of the investment is recorded by a debit to Loss on Sale of Marketable Securities or by a credit to Gain on Sale of Marketable Securities.

At the day of sale of an investment in ***bonds,*** any interest that has accrued since the last interest payment date (or year-end) should be recognized as interest revenue. For example, assume that 10 bonds of the Elk Corporation carried in the accounts of an investor at $9,600 are sold at a price of ***94,*** plus accrued interest of ***$90,*** and less a brokerage commission of ***$50.*** The gain or loss may be computed as follows:

Proceeds from sale ($9,400 + $90 − $50)	*$9,440*
Less: Proceeds representing interest revenue	*90*
Sales price of investment in bonds	*$9,350*
Cost of investment in bonds	*9,600*
Loss on sale	*$ 250*

This sale should be recorded by the following journal entry:

Investment in bonds sold at a loss

Cash	*9,440*	
Loss on Sale of Marketable Securities	*250*	
Marketable Debt Securities		*9,600*
Bond Interest Revenue		*90*
Sold 10 bonds of Elk Corporation at 94 and accrued interest of $90, less broker's commission of $50.		

Balance Sheet Valuation of Marketable Securities

The market values of securities such as bonds and stocks fluctuate from day to day. An investor who sells an investment in marketable securities at a price above or below cost will recognize a gain or loss on the sale. But what if the investor continues to hold securities after a significant change in their market value? In this case, should any gain or loss be recognized in the financial statements? The answer depends on whether the securities are short-term or long-term investments and whether the change in market value is temporary in nature.

Short-term marketable securities should be shown as a current asset in the balance sheet at the ***lower*** of their aggregate cost and market value. The effect of the ***lower-of-cost-and-market*** (LCM) rule is to recognize losses from drops in market value without recognizing gains from rising prices.

Marketable securities classified as long-term investments are accounted for in the balance sheet by either the cost method or the equity method. The ***cost method*** is used for long-term ***portfolio investments*** where the investor is not able to exercise significant influence over the investee. The account title for this type of investment is commonly called Marketable Securities—Long-Term. The ***equity method*** is used for those long-term investments where ***the investor is able to exercise significant influence over the investee.*** The common account title for this type of investment is Investment in X Corporation. When there is a decline in the market value of these long-term investments that is other than a temporary decline, these investments should be shown in the balance sheet at their lower market value. Consequently, a lower market value is also used for long-term investments if the decline in market value is not temporary in nature.

The lower-of-cost-and-market rule produces ***conservative results*** in both the balance sheet and the income statement. In the balance sheet, the investment in marketable securities is shown at the lowest justifiable amount—that is, the lower of its cost and market value. In the income statement, declines in market value below cost immediately are recognized as losses. Increases in market value above cost or the carrying value (if lower), however, are not recognized until the securities are sold.

Accountants traditionally have applied different criteria in recognizing gains and losses. One of the basic principles in accounting is that gains shall not be recognized until they are ***realized,*** and the usual test of realization is the sale of the asset in question. Losses, on the other hand, are recognized as soon as ***objective evidence*** indicates that a loss has been incurred.

Applying the Lower-of-Cost-and-Market Rule: An Illustration

In applying the lower-of-cost-and-market rule, the total cost of the marketable securities is compared with their current market value, and the ***lower*** of these two amounts is used as the balance sheet valuation. If the market value is below cost, an entry is made to reduce the carrying value of the marketable securities to current market value and to recognize a ***loss*** for the amount of the market decline. The write-down of an investment in marketable securities to a market value below cost is an end-of-period adjusting entry and should be based upon market prices at the balance sheet date.

To illustrate the lower-of-cost-and-market adjustment, assume the following facts for the investment of Eagle Corporation at December 31, 1996:

	Cost	Market Value
Common stock of Adams Corporation	$100,000	$106,000
Common stock of Barnes Limited	60,000	52,000
Preferred stock of Parker Industries	200,000	182,000
Other marketable securities	25,000	25,000
Totals	$385,000	$365,000

Since the total market value of the securities in our example is less than their cost to Eagle Corporation, the balance sheet valuation would be the lower amount of $365,000. This downward adjustment of $20,000 means that a loss of $20,000 will be included in the determination of the year's net income. Also the $365,000 market value becomes the ***carrying value*** for these securities and is used as the "new cost" for future applications of the lower-of-cost-and-market rule. The balance sheet presentation would be:

Current assets:	
Marketable securities (at the lower of cost and market, cost—$385,000)	$365,000

The significance of the carrying value deserves an explanation. Since the carrying value is considered to be the "new cost" for the marketable securities, if there is a further decline in market value, this carrying value will be adjusted to the lower market value.[1] However, if there is a recovery in market value, the recovery is not recognized because the market value is higher than the carrying value even though it is still lower than the original cost. For example, if the marketable securities of Eagle Corporation were held until December 31, 1997, and the market value were $380,000 (still $5,000 below the original cost of $385,000), these securities would be stated in the balance sheet at the carrying value of $365,000 because it is lower than the current market value of $380,000. Consequently, the recovery in market value of $15,000 was not recognized. This practice of not recognizing the recovery in the decline of market value below cost lacks logical support.

In the United States, the FASB recommended that for marketable equity securities such as common stock the recovery in the decline of market value below cost should be recognized. The decline and recovery in market value are considered as ***unrealized loss*** and ***unrealized gain,*** so as to distinguish them from a loss or a gain by an actual sale of securities. Based on the Eagle Corporation example, the $20,000 decline in market value would be recorded as follows:

1996			
Dec. 31	*Unrealized Loss on Marketable Securities ....*	*20,000*	
	Valuation Allowance for Marketable Securities ...		*20,000*
	To reduce the cost of the investment in marketable equity securities to the lower of cost and market.		

The Valuation Allowance for Marketable Securities is a ***contra-asset*** account or ***valuation*** account. In the balance sheet, this valuation account is offset against the asset Marketable Securities in the same manner as the Allowance for Doubtful Accounts is offset against Accounts Receivable. The following partial balance sheet illustrates the use of the Valuation Allowance for Marketable Securities:

Current assets:		
Marketable securities	*$385,000*	
Less: Valuation allowance for marketable securities	*20,000*	*365,000*

At the end of every period, the balance of the valuation account is adjusted so that marketable equity securities will be shown in the balance sheet at the lower of cost and current market value. If the valuation allowance must be increased because of further declines in market value, the adjusting entry will recognize an additional unrealized loss. On the other hand, if market prices have gone up since the last balance sheet date, the adjusting entry will reduce or eliminate the valuation allowance and recognize an ***unrealized gain.***

To illustrate the adjustment of the valuation account, let us assume that by the end of 1997 the market value of Eagle Corporation's investment has ***increased*** to an amount greater than cost. Since market value is no longer below cost, the valuation allowance, which has a credit balance of $20,000, is no longer needed. Thus, the following entry would be made to eliminate the balance of the valuation allowance:

---

[1] CICA, *CICA Handbook* (Toronto), paragraph 3010.06.

Unrealized gain cannot exceed the former balance of the valuation account

1997			
Dec. 31	*Valuation Allowance for Marketable Securities ....*	*20,000*	
	Unrealized Gain on Marketable Securities		*20,000*
	To increase the carrying value of marketable equity securities to original cost following recovery of market value.		

Note that the amount of unrealized gain recognized is limited to the amount in the valuation account. ***Increases in market value above cost are not recognized in the accounting records.*** In brief, when marketable equity securities have been written down to the lower of cost and market, they can be written back up only ***to original cost*** if the market prices recover.

Because the valuation allowance is based upon a comparison of ***total*** cost and market value, the allowance cannot be directly associated with individual investments. The valuation allowance reduces the carrying value of the total investment but does not affect the individual carrying values of the investments. Lower-of-cost-and-market adjustments, therefore, have ***no effect*** upon the gain or loss recognized when an investment is sold. When specific securities are sold, the gain or loss realized from the sale is determined by comparing the ***cost*** of the securities (without regard to lower-of-cost-and-market adjustments) to their selling price.[2]

Presentation of Marketable Securities in Financial Statements

Gains and losses from the decline in market value of marketable securities or on the sale of marketable securities, as well as interest and dividend revenue, are types of nonoperating income. These items should be specifically identified in the income statement and shown after the determination of operating income.

Those marketable securities classified as current assets should be presented in the balance sheet at the lower of cost and market; those classified as long-term investments should be presented in the balance sheet at cost, unless the decline in market value is permanent, in which case the lower of cost and market should be used.

We mentioned earlier that separate controlling accounts are usually used in the general ledger for marketable equity securities and marketable debt securities. In the balance sheet, however, these two types of investments are combined and shown under a single caption, such as ***Marketable Securities.***

Presentation of Investments That Are Not Readily Marketable Securities issued by small businesses may not be traded on securities exchanges and, therefore, may not have quoted market prices. These securities are not

[2] The reader may notice that a decline in the market value of securities owned could be reported in the income statement on two separate occasions: first, as an unrealized loss in the period in which the price decline occurs; and second, as a realized loss in the period in which the securities are sold. However, after securities with market values below cost have been sold, the valuation allowance may be reduced or eliminated. The entry to reduce the valuation allowance involves the recognition of an unrealized gain, which offsets the unrealized losses reported in earlier periods.

"readily marketable"; an investor owning such securities should classify the investment as long-term, rather than as a current asset. Also, such investments should be identified as "Other Long-Term Investments," rather than as marketable securities. As these securities do not have quoted market prices, the lower-of-cost-and-market rule is not applied. These investments normally are shown in the investor's balance sheet at ***cost.***[3]

INVESTMENTS FOR PURPOSES OF SIGNIFICANT INFLUENCE OR CONTROL

An investor may acquire enough of a company's common stock to ***significantly influence or control*** that company's strategic operating, investing, and financing policies through the voting rights of the shares owned. Such large holdings of common stock create an important business relationship between the investor and the issuing company (called the ***investee***). Since investments of this type cannot be sold without disrupting this relationship, they are not included in the portfolio of marketable securities. Such investments are shown in the investor's balance sheet under the caption Long-Term Investments and are accounted for quite differently from an investment in marketable securities.

If an investor is able to exercise ***significant influence*** over the investee's management, dividends paid by the investee may no longer be a good measure of the investor's income from the investment. This is because the investor may influence the investee's dividend policy. In such cases, dividends paid by the investee are likely to reflect the ***investor's*** cash needs and income tax considerations, rather than the profitability of the investment.

For example, assume that Sigma Corporation owns 49% of the common stock of Davis Limited. For three years Davis is very profitable but pays no dividends, because Sigma has no need for additional cash. In the fourth year, Davis pays a large cash dividend to Sigma despite operating at a loss for that year. Clearly, it would be misleading for Sigma to report no investment income while the company it owns is operating profitably, and then to show large investment income in a year when Davis incurred a net loss.

The investor does not have to own 49% of the common stock of the investee to exercise a significant degree of influence. An investor with much less than 49% of the voting stock may have significant influence, since the remaining shares are not likely to vote as an organized block. In the absence of other evidence (such as another large shareholder), ownership of ***20% or more*** (but below 50%) of the investee's common stock is viewed as giving the investor significant influence over the investee's policies and operations. In such cases, the investor should account for the investment by using the ***equity method.***[4]

---

[3] As with any asset valued at cost, the asset should be written down to an estimated recoverable amount if it becomes apparent that the original cost cannot be recovered.

[4] CICA, *CICA Handbook* (Toronto), section 3050.06.

The Equity Method

OBJECTIVE 2 Account for an investment in common stock by the equity method.

When the equity method is used, an investment in common stock is first recorded at cost but later is adjusted each year for changes in the shareholders' equity in the investee. As the investee earns net income, the shareholders' equity in the company increases. An investor using the equity method recognizes its ***proportionate share of the investee's net income*** as an increase in the carrying value of its investment. A proportionate share of a net loss reported by the investee is recognized as a decrease in the investment.

When the investee pays dividends, the shareholders' equity in the company is reduced. The investor, therefore, treats dividends received from the investee as a conversion of part of the investment into cash, thus reducing the carrying value of the investment. In effect, the equity method causes the carrying value of the investment (the amount reported in the balance sheet) to rise and fall with changes in the book value of the shares. As mentioned earlier, if the market value is lower than cost (or carrying value) and the decline is not temporary, the lower market value should be used.[5]

Illustration of the Equity Method Assume that Cove Corporation purchases 10,000 shares (25%) of the common stock of Bay Limited for $200,000, which corresponds to 25% of the underlying book value of Bay. During the following year, Bay earns net income of $120,000 and pays dividends of $80,000. Cove Corporation would account for its investment as follows:

Investment in Bay Limited	*200,000*	
Cash		*200,000*
To record acquisition of 25% of the common stock of Bay Limited.		
Investment in Bay Limited	*30,000*	
Investment Income		*30,000*
To increase the investment for 25% share of net income earned by Bay Limited (25% × $120,000).		
Cash	*20,000*	
Investment in Bay Limited		*20,000*
To reduce investment for dividends received from Bay Limited (25% × $80,000).		

The net result of these entries by Cove Corporation is to increase the carrying value of the Investment in Bay Limited account by $10,000, to $210,000. This corresponds to 25% of the increase reported in Bay Limited's retained earnings during the period [25% × ($120,000 − $80,000) = $10,000]. Cove Corporation ***reports in its balance sheet*** the investment in Bay Limited at $210,000 under the caption Long-Term Investments.

In this illustration of the equity method, we have made several simplifying assumptions: (1) Cove Corporation purchased the stock of Bay Limited at a price equal to the underlying book value; (2) Bay Limited had issued common stock only and the number of shares outstanding did not

---

[5] Ibid., section 3050.25.

change during the year; and (3) there were no intercompany transactions between Cove Corporation and Bay Limited. If we were to change any of these assumptions, the computations in applying the equity method would become more complicated. Application of the equity method in more complex situations is discussed in advanced accounting courses.

Parent and Subsidiary Companies

OBJECTIVE 3 Explain how a parent company "controls" its subsidiaries.

A corporation that owns ***all or a majority*** of another corporation's outstanding voting stock is called a ***parent*** company, and the corporation that is wholly owned or majority-held is called a ***subsidiary.***[6] Through the voting rights of the owned shares, the parent company can elect the board of directors of the subsidiary company and thereby control the subsidiary's resources and policies. In effect, the ***affiliated companies*** (the parent and its subsidiaries) function as a ***single economic unit*** controlled by the directors of the parent company. This relationship is illustrated in the following diagram.

PARENT COMPANY AND TWO SUBSIDIARIES

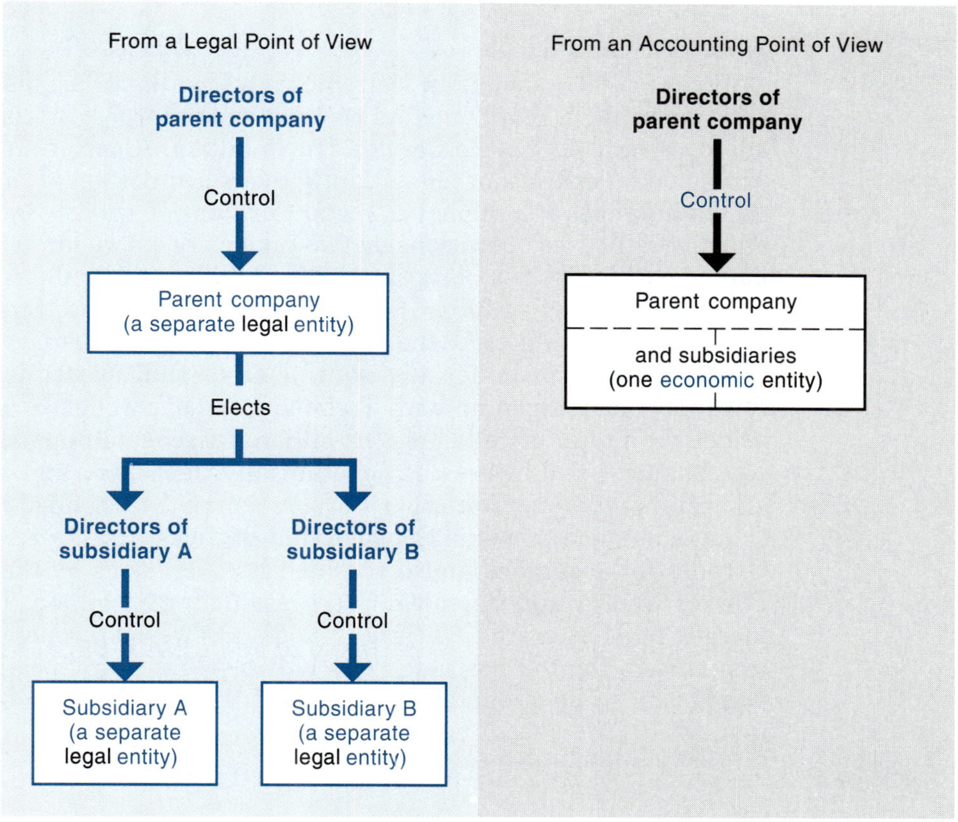

For simplicity, our illustration shows a parent company with only two subsidiaries. It is not unusual, however, for a parent company to own and control a dozen or more subsidiaries.

---

[6] Ownership of a majority of a company's voting stock means holding at least 50% plus one share.

There are a number of economic, legal, and income tax advantages that encourage large business organizations to operate through subsidiaries rather than through a single legal entity. Although we think of BCE, Inc., Canadian Pacific, or George Weston Ltd. as single companies, each of these organizations is really a parent company with many subsidiaries. Since the parent company in each case controls the resources and policies of its subsidiaries, it is logical for us to consider an organization such as BCE (which owns 100% of Bell Canada) as one ***economic*** entity.

Growth through the Acquisition of Subsidiaries

A parent company may acquire another corporation as a subsidiary by purchasing more than 50% of the other corporation's voting stock. The purchase of one corporation by another may be termed a ***merger,*** a ***business combination,*** an ***acquisition,*** or a ***takeover.*** The acquisition of new subsidiaries is a fast and effective way for a company to grow, to diversify into new product lines, and to acquire new technology. In recent years, the price tag for these acquisitions and mergers has run into billions of dollars.

CASE IN POINT Just a few well-known billion-dollar acquisitions or mergers: Imperial Oil reaffirmed its position as the largest oil company in Canada by acquiring Texaco Canada for $5 billion. Amoco Canada Petroleum expanded its operations significantly by its acquisition of Dome Petroleum for slightly over $5 billion. Campeau Corporation greatly increased its size and diversified its operations by two takeovers of two large American companies—Allied Stores Corporation for $5 billion ($3.6 billion U.S.) and Federated Department Stores Incorporated at $8.2 billion ($6.6 billion U.S.). Imasco Limited entered the financial institution business by acquiring Genstar Corporation for the control of Canada Trust for $2.6 billion. Noranda Inc. teamed up with Trelleborg AB of Sweden to acquire Falconbridge for a total price tag of $2.2 billion, thereby adding nickel as another core business and increasing substantially the copper and zinc production and reserves. Stone Container Corporation (U.S) extended its operation to Canada by its takeover of Consolidated Bathurst Inc. for $2.6 billion. Nova Corporation expanded and diversified its operations by the acquisition of Polysar Energy and Chemical Corporation for $1.4 billion. The $1.6 billion merger of Molson and Carling O'Keefe Breweries propelled the merged company to the top position in its industry. Interprovincial Pipe Line expanded its scope of operation by acquiring Home Oil Limited for $1.1 billion.

The acquisition of one corporation by another is, perhaps, the largest and most interesting of all business transactions. Such transactions may involve billions of dollars, bidding wars among prospective buyers, and dramatic increases in the value of a sought-after company's capital stock. Sometimes a company borrows vast amounts of money and acquires a corporation much larger than itself, thus doubling or tripling the size of the parent company overnight.

Financial Statements for a Consolidated Economic Entity

OBJECTIVE 4 Describe the distinctive feature of consolidated financial statements.

Because the parent company and its subsidiaries are separate legal entities, separate financial statements are prepared for each company. In the ***separate*** financial statements of the parent company, the subsidiaries appear only as assets classified as long-term investments. Since the affiliated companies function as a single economic unit, the parent company also prepares ***consolidated financial statements*** that show the financial position and operating results of the ***entire group of companies.***[7] It is these consolidated financial statements that are of greatest interest to the investing public and that are included in the parent company's annual report to its shareholders.

In consolidated financial statements, the parent company and its subsidiaries are viewed as ***one economic*** or ***business entity.*** The distinctive feature of these statements is that the assets, liabilities, revenue, and expenses of ***two or more separate legal entities*** are combined in a single set of financial statements. For example, the amount shown as cash in a consolidated balance sheet is the total of the cash owned by all of the affiliated companies. Liabilities of the parent and subsidiary companies also are combined. Similarly, in a consolidated income statement, the revenue and expenses of the affiliated companies are combined to show the operating results of the consolidated economic entity.

Shareholders and creditors of the parent company have a vital interest in the financial results of all operations under the parent company's control, including those conducted by subsidiaries. Therefore, it is the consolidated financial statements that are included in the parent company's annual and quarterly reports to shareholders.

There are many interesting accounting issues involved in the preparation of consolidated financial statements. A brief introduction to some of these issues is provided in the following section of this chapter. However, ***no special problems are posed in reading a set of consolidated financial statements.*** The number of separate legal entities within the consolidated organization is an unimportant detail. For most purposes, consolidated financial statements may be interpreted as if the parent company and its subsidiaries ***were just one organization.***

CONSOLIDATED FINANCIAL STATEMENTS: CONCEPTS AND MECHANICS

Methods of Consolidation

The purchase of an entire corporation usually is a very big investment. To accumulate the money necessary to buy another corporation, the parent company often needs to issue capital stock or bonds payable. If the parent

[7] In the past, some subsidiaries were omitted from the consolidated financial statements for such reasons as the subsidiaries being engaged in business activities substantially different from those of the parent company. New rules, however, require every subsidiary controlled by the parent company to be included in the consolidated statements unless this control will be temporary. In this case, the investment in the subsidiary is shown in the balance sheet at cost and is classified as a long-term investment; dividends received are recorded as revenue.

company pays cash or issues debt securities to purchase the other corporation's capital stock, the business combination is accounted for by the ***purchase method.***

A second method of accounting for a business combination is called a ***pooling of interests.*** The pooling method may be appropriate if the stock of a subsidiary is obtained in direct exchange for shares of the parent company's capital stock and neither company can be identified as the acquirer.[8] A key aspect of such a transaction is that the former shareholders of the subsidiary ***become shareholders in the parent corporation.*** The vast majority of business combinations are viewed as purchases, rather than poolings. In this textbook, we shall illustrate only the purchase method of accounting for business combinations. The special case of a pooling of interests will be covered in more advanced accounting courses.

Consolidated financial statements are prepared by combining the amounts that appear in the separate financial statements of the parent and subsidiary companies. In the combining process, however, certain adjustments are made to ***eliminate the effects of intercompany transactions*** and thus to reflect the assets, liabilities, and shareholders' equity as those of a single economic entity.

Intercompany Transactions The term ***intercompany transactions*** refers to transactions between affiliated companies. These transactions may include, for example, the sale of merchandise, the leasing of property, and the making of loans. When the affiliated companies are viewed separately, these transactions may create assets and liabilities for the individual companies. However, when the affiliated companies are viewed as a single business entity, these assets and liabilities are merely the result of internal transfers within the business organization and should ***not appear*** in the consolidated financial statements.

OBJECTIVE 5 Explain why intercompany transactions must be eliminated as a step in preparing consolidated financial statements.

For example, if a subsidiary borrows money from the parent company, a note payable will appear as a liability in the balance sheet of the subsidiary company and a note receivable will appear as an asset in the separate balance sheet of the parent. When the two companies are viewed as a single consolidated entity, however, this "loan" is nothing more than a transfer of cash from one part of the business to another. Transferring assets between two parts of a single business entity does not create either a receivable or a payable for that entity. Therefore, the parent company's note receivable and the subsidiary's note payable should not appear in the consolidated financial statements.

Preparing Consolidated Financial Statements Separate accounting records are maintained for each company in an affiliated group, but no accounting records are maintained for the consolidated entity. The amounts shown in consolidated financial statements ***do not come from a ledger;*** they are determined on a ***working paper*** by combining the amounts of like items on the financial statements of the affiliated companies. For example, the inventories of all the affiliated companies are combined into one amount for inventories. Entries to eliminate the effects of intercompany

8 CICA, *CICA Handbook* (Toronto), section 1580.08.

transactions are made ***only*** on this working paper. These elimination entries are ***not recorded in the accounting records*** of either the parent company or its subsidiaries.

Consolidation at the Date of Acquisition

OBJECTIVE 6 Prepare a consolidated balance sheet.

To illustrate the basic principles of consolidation, we will now prepare a consolidated balance sheet. Assume that on January 1 Post Corporation purchases for cash 100% of the capital stock of Sun Limited at its book value of $3,000,000. (The shares are purchased from Sun's former shareholders.) Also on this date, Post Corporation lends $200,000 cash to Sun, receiving a note as evidence of the loan. Immediately after these two transactions, the separate balance sheet accounts of Post Corporation and Sun Limited are as shown in the first two columns of the following working paper:

POST CORPORATION AND SUBSIDIARY
Working Paper—Consolidated Balance Sheet
January 1, 19__ (Date of Acquisition)

	Post Corporation	Sun Limited	Intercompany Eliminations		Consolidated Balance Sheet
			Debit	Credit	
Cash & cash equivalents	500,000	350,000			850,000
Notes receivable	200,000			(b) 200,000	—
Accounts receivable (net)	300,000	400,000			700,000
Inventories	1,100,000	950,000			2,050,000
Investment in Sun Limited	3,000,000			(a) 3,000,000	—
Plant & equipment (net)	2,800,000	1,800,000			4,600,000
Totals	7,900,000	3,500,000			8,200,000
Notes payable		200,000	(b) 200,000		—
Accounts payable	425,000	300,000			725,000
Capital stock—					
Post Corporation	4,000,000				4,000,000
Sun Limited		2,000,000	(a) 2,000,000		—
Retained earnings—					
Post Corporation	3,475,000				3,475,000
Sun Limited		1,000,000	(a) 1,000,000		—
Totals	7,900,000	3,500,000	3,200,000	3,200,000	8,200,000

Explanation of elimination:
(a) To eliminate the Investment in Sun Limited against Sun Limited's shareholders' equity.
(b) To eliminate intercompany note receivable against related note payable.

Intercompany Eliminations

Before the balance sheet amounts of Post Corporation and Sun Limited are combined, entries are made in the working paper to eliminate the effects of intercompany transactions. Intercompany eliminations may be classified into three basic types:

1 Elimination of intercompany stock ownership
2 Elimination of intercompany debt
3 Elimination of intercompany revenue and expenses

The first two types of eliminations are illustrated in our example of Post Corporation and Sun Limited. The elimination of intercompany revenue and expenses will be discussed later in this chapter.

To understand the need for elimination entries, we must adopt the viewpoint of the consolidated entity, in which Post Corporation and Sun Limited are regarded as two business operations within a single company.

Entry (a): Elimination of Intercompany Stock Ownership The purpose of entry (*a*) in the working paper on page 817 is to eliminate from the consolidated balance sheet both the asset account and the shareholders' equity accounts representing the parent company's ownership of the subsidiary.

Post Corporation's ownership interest in Sun Limited appears in the ***separate*** balance sheets of both corporations. In the parent's balance sheet, this ownership interest is shown as the asset Investment in Sun Limited. In the separate balance sheet of the subsidiary, the parent company's ownership interest is represented by the shareholders' equity accounts Capital Stock and Retained Earnings. In the ***consolidated*** balance sheet, however, this "ownership interest" is neither an asset nor a part of shareholders' equity.

From the viewpoint of the single consolidated entity, ***there are no shareholders in Sun Limited.*** "Shareholders" are outside investors who have an ownership interest in the business. All of Sun's capital stock is "internally owned" by another part of the consolidated entity. A company's "ownership" of its own stock does not create either an asset or shareholders' equity. Therefore the asset account Investment in Sun Limited and Sun Limited's related shareholders' equity accounts must be eliminated from the consolidated balance sheet.

Entry (b): Elimination of Intercompany Debt When Post Corporation loaned $200,000 to Sun Limited, the parent company recorded a note receivable and the subsidiary recorded a note payable. This "receivable" and "payable" exist only when Post Corporation and Sun Limited are viewed as two separate entities. When both corporations are viewed as a single company, this "loan" is merely a transfer of cash from one part of the business to another. Such internal transfers of assets do not create either a receivable or a payable for the consolidated entity. Therefore, entry (*b*) is made to eliminate Post Corporation's note receivable and Sun Limited's note payable from the consolidated balance sheet.

After the necessary eliminations have been entered in the working paper, the remaining balance sheet amounts of Post Corporation and Sun Limited are combined to determine the assets, liabilities, and shareholders' equity of the consolidated entity. The following consolidated balance sheet is then prepared from the last column of the working paper.

POST CORPORATION AND SUBSIDIARY
Consolidated Balance Sheet
January 1, 19__

Assets		
Current assets:		
Cash & cash equivalents		*$ 850,000*
Accounts receivable (net)		*700,000*
Inventories		*2,050,000*
Total current assets		*$3,600,000*
Plant & equipment (net)		*4,600,000*
Total assets		*$8,200,000*
Liabilities & Shareholders' Equity		
Current liabilities:		
Accounts payable		*725,000*
Shareholders' equity:		
Capital stock	*$4,000,000*	
Retained earnings	*3,475,000*	
Total shareholders' equity		*7,475,000*
Total liabilities & shareholders' equity		*$8,200,000*

Notice the shareholders' equity is that of the parent company

Acquisition of Subsidiary's Stock at a Price above Book Value

When a parent company purchases a controlling interest in a subsidiary, it usually pays a price for the shares ***in excess of*** their book value.[9] We cannot ignore a difference between the cost of the parent company's investment and the underlying book value of these shares. In consolidation, the parent's investment is offset against the shareholders' equity accounts of the subsidiary, and if the two amounts are not equal, we must determine what the difference between them represents.

To illustrate, let's use the preceding example with one significant change. Assume that on January 1 Post Corporation purchases all of the outstanding shares of Sun Limited for $3,400,000 instead of $3,000,000. On this date, Sun Limited's balance sheet shows total shareholders' equity of $3,000,000, consisting of capital stock of $2,000,000 and retained earnings of $1,000,000. In preparing the elimination entry on the working papers for a consolidated balance sheet, we must determine what to do with the $400,000 difference between the price paid, $3,400,000, and the shareholders' equity (book value) of Sun Limited, $3,000,000.

Why would Post Corporation pay a price in excess of book value for Sun Limited's stock? Post's management must believe that either (1) the fair market value of certain specific assets of Sun (such as land or buildings) is in excess of book value or (2) Sun's future earnings prospects are so favourable as to justify paying $400,000 for Sun's unrecorded ***goodwill.***

If we assume that the $400,000 represents unrecorded goodwill, entry

[9] The parent company also might acquire the shares of the subsidiary at a price below book value. This situation will be discussed in an advanced accounting course.

(*a*) in the working papers to eliminate Post Corporation's investment account against the shareholders' equity accounts of Sun Limited would be:

Note: This entry is made only in the working papers, not in the accounting records of either company

Capital Stock—Sun Limited	*2,000,000*	
Retained Earnings—Sun Limited	*1,000,000*	
Goodwill	*400,000*	
Investment in Sun Limited (Post Corporation's asset account)		*3,400,000*
To eliminate the cost of Post Corporation's 100% interest in Sun Limited against Sun's shareholders' equity accounts and to recognize Sun Limited's unrecorded goodwill.		

Although we have shown this entry in general journal form, it actually would be made ***only*** in the Intercompany Eliminations columns of the working paper for a consolidated balance sheet, as illustrated below:

POST CORPORATION AND SUBSIDIARY
Working Paper—Consolidated Balance Sheet
January 1, 19__ (Date of Acquisition)

	Post Corporation	Sun Limited	Intercompany Eliminations: Debit	Intercompany Eliminations: Credit	Consolidated Balance Sheet
Cash & cash equivalents	100,000	350,000			450,000
Notes receivable	200,000			(b) 200,000	—
Accounts receivable (net)	300,000	400,000			700,000
Inventories	1,100,000	950,000			2,050,000
Investment in Sun Limited	3,400,000			(a) 3,400,000	
Plant & equipment (net)	2,800,000	1,800,000			4,600,000
Goodwill			(a) 400,000		400,000
Totals	7,900,000	3,500,000			8,200,000
Notes payable		200,000	(b) 200,000		—
Accounts payable	425,000	300,000			725,000
Capital stock—					
Post Corporation	4,000,000				4,000,000
Sun Limited		2,000,000	(a) 2,000,000		
Retained earnings—					
Post Corporation	3,475,000				3,475,000
Sun Limited		1,000,000	(a) 1,000,000		
Totals	7,900,000	3,500,000	3,600,000	3,600,000	8,200,000

Explanation of elimination:
(a) To eliminate the Investment in Sun Limited against Sun Limited's shareholders' equity, and to recognize goodwill.
(b) To eliminate intercompany note receivable against related note payable.

The following consolidated balance sheet is then prepared from the last column of the working paper. It is important to note that the $400,000 of goodwill will appear as an asset only in the ***consolidated*** balance sheet,

not in the accounting records of Sun Limited or Post Corporation.[10] This asset will be amortized to expense over its useful life.

Notice that goodwill appears only in the consolidated balance sheet

POST CORPORATION AND SUBSIDIARY
Consolidated Balance Sheet
January 1, 19__

Assets		
Current assets:		
Cash & cash equivalents		*$ 450,000*
Accounts receivable (net)		*700,000*
Inventories		*2,050,000*
Total current assets		*$3,200,000*
Plant & equipment (net)		*4,600,000*
Goodwill		*400,000*
Total assets		*$8,200,000*
Liabilities & Shareholders' Equity		
Current liabilities:		
Accounts payable		*725,000*
Shareholders' equity:		
Capital stock	*$4,000,000*	
Retained earnings	*3,475,000*	
Total shareholders' equity		*7,475,000*
Total liabilities & shareholders' equity		*$8,200,000*

Less Than 100% Ownership in Subsidiary

If a parent company owns a majority interest in a subsidiary but less than 100% of the outstanding shares, a new kind of ownership equity known as the ***non-controlling (minority) interest*** will appear in the consolidated balance sheet. This non-controlling interest represents the ownership interest in the subsidiary held by shareholders other than the parent company.

When there are non-controlling (minority) shareholders, only the portion of the subsidiary's shareholders' equity owned by the parent company is eliminated. The remainder of the shareholders' equity of the subsidiary is included in the consolidated balance sheet under the caption Non-controlling Interest.

To illustrate, assume that on January 1 Park Limited purchases 75% of the outstanding capital stock of Sims Corporation for $150,000 cash, an amount equal to 75% of the book value (shareholders' equity) of Sims. The working paper to prepare a consolidated balance sheet on the date that control of Sims Corporation is acquired appears as follows:

---

[10] If specific assets of Sun Limited had been undervalued, the $400,000 would be allocated to increase the valuation of those assets in the consolidated working papers. The revaluation of specific assets is beyond the scope of our introductory discussion.

PARK LIMITED AND SUBSIDIARY
Working Paper—Consolidated Balance Sheet
January 1, 19__ (Date of Acquisition)

	Park Limited	Sims Corporation	Intercompany Eliminations Debit	Intercompany Eliminations Credit	Consolidated Balance Sheet
Cash	200,000	50,000			250,000
Other assets	500,000	210,000			710,000
Investment in Sims Corporation	150,000			(a) 150,000	
Totals	850,000	260,000			960,000
Liabilities	250,000	60,000			310,000
Capital stock—					
Park Limited	500,000				500,000
Sims Corporation		120,000	(a) 90,000 (b) 30,000		
Retained earnings—					
Park Limited	100,000				100,000
Sims Corporation		80,000	(a) 60,000 (b) 20,000		
Non-controlling interest (25% of $200,000)				(b) 50,000	50,000
Totals	850,000	260,000	200,000	200,000	960,000

Explanation of elimination:
(a) To eliminate Park Limited's investment in 75% of Sims Corporation's shareholders' equity.
(b) To classify the remaining 25% of Sims Corporation's shareholders' equity as a non-controlling interest.

Entry (*a*) in this working paper offsets Park's asset, Investment in Sims Corporation, against 75% of Sims Corporation's capital stock and retained earnings. The purpose of this entry is to eliminate intercompany stock ownership from the assets and shareholders' equity shown in the consolidated balance sheet. Entry (*b*) reclassifies the remaining 25% of Sims Corporation's capital stock and retained earnings into a special account entitled Non-controlling Interest. The CICA recommends that the non-controlling interest appear separately from the shareholders' equity section of the consolidated balance sheet usually between total liabilities and shareholders' equity.[11]

Non-Controlling Interest Why is the non-controlling interest shown separately in the consolidated balance sheet instead of being included in the amounts shown for capital stock and retained earnings? The reason for this separate presentation is to distinguish between the ownership equity of the controlling shareholders and the equity of the non-controlling shareholders.

The shareholders in the parent company own the controlling interest in the consolidated entity. Because these shareholders elect the directors of the parent company, they control the entire group of affiliated companies.

[11] CICA, *CICA Handbook* (Toronto), section 1600.69.

The non-controlling interest, however, has ***no control*** over any of the affiliated companies. Because they own shares only in a subsidiary, they cannot vote for the directors of the parent company. Also, they can never outvote the parent shareholder (the parent company) in electing the directors or establishing the policies of the subsidiary.

The non-controlling shareholders receive 25% of the dividends declared by Sims but do not participate in dividends declared by the parent company. The controlling shareholders, on the other hand, receive all the dividends declared by Park but do not receive directly dividends declared by the subsidiary.

Consolidated Income Statement

At date of acquisition of a controlling interest, the consolidated balance sheet is the only appropriate financial statement, as no revenue or expenses have yet occurred. Once operations begin, however, a complete set of four corporate financial statements is required: consolidated income statement, consolidated statement of retained earnings, consolidated balance sheet, and consolidated statement of changes in financial position. We shall discuss briefly some of the basic concepts involved in the preparation of a consolidated income statement.

A ***consolidated income statement*** is prepared simply by combining the revenue and expense accounts of the parent and subsidiary. Revenue or expenses that are the result of ***intercompany transactions*** are eliminated because they do not change the net assets from a consolidated viewpoint—they merely reflect transfers of assets from one affiliated company to another. Assume a subsidiary pays $12,000 to its parent company for rent of warehouse facilities during the year. The subsidiary's $12,000 rent expense as well as the parent's $12,000 rental income should be disregarded (eliminated) in reporting the results of operations for the consolidated entity. This rental transaction neither increased nor decreased the net assets ***of the consolidated entity.***

Elimination of Intercompany Revenue and Expenses Some of the more common examples of intercompany items that should be eliminated in preparing a consolidated income statement are:

- Sales to affiliated companies
- Cost of goods sold resulting from sales to affiliated companies
- Interest expense on loans from affiliated companies
- Interest revenue on loans made to affiliated companies
- Rent or other revenue received for services rendered to affiliated companies
- Rent or other expenses paid for services received from affiliated companies

Because of the complexity of the intercompany eliminations, the preparation of a consolidated income statement, a consolidated statement of retained earnings, and a consolidated statement of changes in financial position are topics appropriately deferred to an advanced accounting course.

Accounting for Investments in Corporate Securities: A Summary

In this chapter, we have discussed the accounting principles applied to investments in corporate securities under various circumstances. The accounting treatment accorded to investments in ***bonds*** depends upon whether the investment is viewed as a current asset or a long-term investment. The accounting treatment of an investment in ***stock*** depends primarily upon the ***degree of influence*** or ***control*** that the investor is able to exercise over the issuing corporation. These relationships are summarized as follows:

Situation	Accounting Practice
Investments in bonds:	
Classified as current asset	*Combined with current asset portfolio of stocks and shown as marketable securities. Interest revenue accrues each period. Difference between cost and maturity value (discount or premium) generally not amortized.*
Classified as a long-term investment	*Combined with long-term portfolio of stocks and shown as marketable securities, under the classification Long-Term Investments. Interest revenue accrues each period. Difference between cost and maturity value is amortized.*
Investment in stocks:	
Noninfluential interest (ownership of less than 20% of the voting stock)	*(Readily marketable) Shown as a marketable security (may be classified as a current asset or a long-term investment). For those classified as current assets, each portfolio is valued at lower-of-cost-and-market. For those classified as long-term investments, each portfolio is valued at cost; when the decline in the lower market value is* not *temporary in nature, the lower market value is used. Dividends recorded as revenue when received.*
	(Not readily marketable) Shown as a long-term investment and carried at cost. Dividends recorded as revenue when received.
Influential but noncontrolling interest (ownership from 20% to 49% of the voting stock)	*Shown as a long-term investment, accounted for by the equity method. A lower market value is used if the decline in market value is* not *temporary in nature.*
Controlling interest (ownership of more than 50% of voting stock)	*The assets, liabilities, revenue, and expenses of controlled subsidiary are combined with those of the parent corporation in consolidated financial statements.*

CHAPTER REVIEW

KEY TERMS INTRODUCED OR EMPHASIZED IN CHAPTER 17

Business combination The combining of two or more companies into a single economic or business entity. Also called a ***merger,*** an ***acquisition,*** or a ***takeover.***

Consolidated financial statements A set of statements presenting the combined financial position and operating results of a consolidated entity consisting of a parent company and one or more subsidiaries.

Equity method The method of accounting used when the investment by one corporation in another is large enough to significantly influence the policies of the ***investee.*** The investor recognizes as investment income its proportionate share of the investee's net income, rather than considering dividends received as income.

Intercompany transactions Transactions between two affiliated companies. The effects of intercompany transactions, such as intercompany loans, are eliminated as a step in preparing consolidated financial statements.

Lower-of-cost-and-market (LCM) The conservative practice of valuing marketable securities in the balance sheet at the lower of total cost and current market value.

Marketable securities Investments in stocks (equity securities) and bonds (debt securities). These are highly liquid investments that may be sold at any time. Classified as a current asset second only to cash in liquidity.

Non-controlling (minority) interest Shares of a subsidiary owned by investors other than the parent.

Parent company A corporation that owns a controlling interest in another company.

Purchase method The method used in preparing consolidated financial statements when the parent company has purchased the shares of its subsidiary by paying cash or issuing debt securities. The purchase method is not used for those special transactions that qualify as a ***pooling of interests.***

Subsidiary A corporation in which a controlling stock interest is held by another corporation (the parent).

ASSIGNMENT MATERIAL

DISCUSSION QUESTIONS

1 Why are investments in marketable securities usually regarded as current assets?

2 Why must an investor who owns numerous marketable securities maintain a marketable securities subsidiary ledger?

3 If an investor buys a bond between interest dates, he or she pays as a part of the purchase price the accrued interest since the last interest date. On the other hand, if the investor buys a share of common or preferred stock, no "accrued dividend" is added to the quoted price. Explain why this difference exists.

4 Should stock dividends received be considered revenue to an investor? Explain.

5 In the current asset section of its balance sheet at December 31, 1995, Delta Industries shows marketable securities at a market value of $3,000,000, which

is $190,000 below cost. If the market value of these securities rises by $250,000 during 1996, how should Delta Industries account for such an increase in its 1996 income statement under the recommendations of the CICA and the FASB?

6 Ancaster Corporation has a large investment in stocks and bonds. The market value of this investment is significantly below cost at December 31, 1995, but is slightly above cost at April 30, 1996. Explain how Ancaster should value this investment in the balance sheet if it is (a) a short-term investment (b) a long-term portfolio investment.

7 When should investors use the equity method to account for an investment in common stock?

8 Dividends on stock owned are usually recognized as income when they are received. Does an investor using the ***equity method*** to account for an investment in common stock follow this policy? Explain fully.

9 When the equity method is used to account for an investment in common stock that is traded on organized exchanges, is the investment adjusted to the lower-of-cost-and-market at the end of each accounting period? Explain your answer.

10 Alexander Corporation owns 80% of the outstanding stock of Benton Limited. Explain the basis for the assumption that these two companies constitute a single economic entity operating under unified control.

11 What are consolidated financial statements? Explain briefly how these statements are prepared.

12 List the three basic types of intercompany eliminations that should be made as a step in the preparation of consolidated financial statements.

13 Explain why the price paid to acquire a controlling interest in a subsidiary company may be different from the book value of the equity acquired.

14 The following items appear on a consolidated balance sheet: "Non-controlling interest in subsidiary . . . $620,000." Explain the nature of this item, and where you would expect to find it on the consolidated balance sheet.

15 Briefly explain when a business combination is viewed as a ***purchase*** and when it might be viewed as a ***pooling of interests.***

16 As a general rule, when are consolidated financial statements appropriate?

17 What groups of investors are likely to be primarily interested in consolidated financial statements? Why?

MULTIPLE CHOICE QUESTIONS

1 During 1995, Bonner Company bought and sold a short-term investment in $200,000 face value, 9% bonds that pay interest each April 1 and October 1. Bonner purchased the bonds at 98 plus accrued interest on February 1, 1995, and held the bonds until December 1, 1995, when the entire investment was sold for $200,000, including accrued interest. Each of the following is true, ***except:***

a Bonner recognizes bond interest revenue of $15,000 for 1995.

b Bonner paid a total of $202,000 to acquire the investment on February 1, 1995.

c Bonner recognizes a gain of $1,000 on the sale of these marketable securities on December 1, 1995.

d Bonner received semiannual interest cheques in the amounts of $3,000 on April 1 and $9,000 on October 1.

2 Early in 1993, Rodgers Corp. purchased for $1,000,000 several marketable equity securities as a short-term investment. The market value of this investment was $900,000 at the end of 1993, $990,000 at the end of 1994, and $1,180,000 at the end of 1995. Based on these facts:

a Rodgers will recognize in its income statement a loss of $100,000 in 1993, and a gain of $90,000 in both 1994 and 1995.

b At the end of 1994, Rodgers will recognize a gain of $90,000.

c In 1995, Rodgers will report the investment in the balance sheet at $1,000,000.

d Rogers will recognize in its 1993 income statement a loss of $100,000.

3 Which of the following is ***true*** with regard to investments in corporate securities?

a When an investor acquires more than 20% of the common stock of a company, the investment is no longer classified as a marketable security even if it is traded on the stock exchanges.

b An investor who owns more than 20% of the outstanding bonds of a company should account for this investment by using the equity method.

c Whenever an investor owns less than 50% of the common stock of a corporation, the investment is valued at the lower-of-cost-and-market value.

d Regardless of percentage ownership, an investor in the common stock of another corporation records dividends as revenue when they are received.

4 On January 1, 1996, Stockdale Limited purchased 30% (30,000 shares) of the common stock of Equus, Inc., for $600,000. At December 31, 1996, Equus reported net income of $200,000 and paid cash dividends of $80,000. At December 31, 1996, Equus' stock is trading at $19 per share. With regard to this investment, Stockdale's financial statements for 1996 should report:

a Dividend revenue of $24,000.

b Investment in Equus, Inc., of $636,000.

c Investment income of $36,000.

d A loss on marketable securities of $30,000.

5 When consolidated financial statements are issued by a parent and a subsidiary:

a The consolidated balance sheet includes the shareholders' equity accounts of both the parent and the subsidiary.

b Intercompany transactions are reported in separate sections of the income statement and the balance sheet.

c There is no need for the parent and the subsidiary to maintain separate accounting records or prepare separate financial statements.

d Non-controlling interest appears in the consolidated balance sheet whenever the parent does not own 100% of the outstanding shares of the subsidiary.

EXERCISES

EXERCISE 17-1
Accounting Terminology

Listed below are nine technical accounting terms emphasized in this chapter:

Consolidated financial statements	*Lower-of-cost-and-market*	*Elimination of intercompany transactions*
Parent company	*Non-controlling interest*	*Equity method*
Goodwill	*Subsidiary*	*Marketable securities*

Each of the following statements may (or may not) describe one of these technical terms. For each statement, indicate the accounting term described, or answer "None" if the statement does not correctly describe any of the terms.

a A separate legal entity owned and controlled by another corporation.

b An accounting procedure that is a necessary step in preparing consolidated financial statements, but that does not involve making entries in the ledger accounts.

c A single set of financial statements showing the assets, liabilities, revenue, and expenses of all companies in a given industry.

d An investment in voting stock of a large corporation that is too small to give the investor significant influence within the issuing company and that is almost as liquid an asset as cash.

e Procedures used to account for an investment in which a corporate investor has significant influence over the policies of another corporation.

f An unrecorded asset that often explains why a parent company pays far more than book value to acquire the capital stock of a subsidiary.

g The equity in a subsidiary held by shareholders other than the parent company.

h Method used in the balance sheet valuation of an investment in marketable securities.

EXERCISE 17-2
Investment in Bonds

Yamato Limited purchased as a short-term investment $300,000 face value of the 7% bonds of Lorenzo, Inc., on May 31 of the current year, at a total cost of $305,750, including interest accrued since January 1. Interest is paid by Lorenzo, Inc., on June 30 and December 31. On October 31, five months after the purchase, Yamato sold the bonds and interest accrued since July 1 for a total price of $304,900.

INSTRUCTIONS Prepare in general journal form all entries required in the accounting records of Yamato relating to the investment in Lorenzo, Inc., bonds. (Commissions are to be ignored.)

EXERCISE 17-3
Investment in Stocks

During the current year, the following events occurred with respect to the Deutz Corporation's investments in stocks:

Jan. 17 Purchased as a short-term investment 5,000 shares of Cooper Industries common stock at a price of $83.50 per share, plus a brokerage commission of $2,500.

Mar. 10 Received a cash dividend of $1.25 per share on the investment in Cooper Industries stock.

July 9 Received an additional 250 shares of Cooper Industries common stock as a result of a 5% stock dividend.

Sept. 11 Sold 2,500 shares of Cooper Industries common stock at a price of $85 per share, less a brokerage commission of $1,450.

INSTRUCTIONS

a Prepare the journal entries in the accounting records of the Deutz Corporation to record the above transactions. Include a memorandum entry on July 9 to show the change in the cost basis per share.

b Assume the stock of Cooper Industries is widely traded and has a quoted market price of $87 per share at the end of the current year. What is the amount reported in Deutz company's year-end ***balance sheet*** for this investment?

EXERCISE 17-4
Valuation at Lower-of-Cost-and-Market

The cost and market value of Escobar Corporation's marketable securities (in common stock) at the end of 1995 and 1996 are shown below. The marketable securities are viewed as a current asset.

	Cost	*Market Value*
1995	*$395,000*	*$334,000*
1996 (carrying value $334,000)	*395,000*	*415,000*

INSTRUCTIONS

Show how the investment would appear ***in the balance sheet*** at the end of 1995 and at the end of 1996, based on the recommendations of the CICA and FASB. If appropriate, use a valuation account in your presentation.

EXERCISE 17-5
The Equity Method

On January 1, 1995, Southern Transport purchases 40% of the common stock of Delta Shipping, Inc., for $900,000, which corresponds to the underlying book value. Delta Shipping, Inc., has issued common stock only. At December 31, 1995, Delta Shipping reported net income for the year of $400,000 and paid cash dividends of $180,000. Southern Transport uses the equity method to account for this investment.

INSTRUCTIONS

a Prepare all journal entries in the accounting records of Southern Transport relating to the investment during 1995.

b During 1996, Delta Shipping, Inc., reports a net loss of $300,000 and pays no dividends. Compute the carrying value of Southern Transport's investment in Delta Shipping, Inc., at the end of 1995 (refer to your answer to part **a**) and at the end of 1996.

c Based upon quoted market prices, the fair market value of Southern Transport's investment in Delta Shipping, Inc. was $995,000 at the end of 1995 but has temporarily fallen to $850,000 at the end of 1996. Do these market values affect amounts reported ***in the balance sheet*** for this investment? Are these market values reflected ***in any way*** in the financial statements?

EXERCISE 17-6
Eliminating Intercompany Stock Ownership; Recording Goodwill

Merit Brands, Inc., has purchased all the outstanding shares of Eduardo Foods for $670,000. At the date of acquisition, Eduardo Foods' balance sheet showed total shareholders' equity of $600,000, consisting of $250,000 capital stock and $350,000 retained earnings. The excess of this purchase price over the book value of Eduardo Foods' shares is regarded as payment for Eduardo Foods' unrecorded goodwill.

In general journal entry form, prepare the eliminating entry necessary on the working paper to consolidate the balance sheets of these two companies.

EXERCISE 17-7
Computing Consolidated Amounts

Selected account balances from the separate balance sheets of Primis Corporation and its wholly owned subsidiary, Syntech, Inc., immediately after acquisition, are as follows:

	Primis Corporation	Syntech, Inc.	Consolidated
Accounts receivable	$ 300,000	$ 140,000	$
Rent receivable—Primis Corporation		7,000	
Investment in Syntech, Inc.	1,475,000		
Accounts payable	390,000	120,000	
Accrued expenses payable	29,000		
Bonds payable	1,400,000	900,000	
Capital stock	4,000,000	1,000,000	
Retained earnings	2,934,000	475,000	

Primis Corporation owes Syntech, Inc., $7,000 in accrued rent payable and Syntech, Inc., owes Primis Corporation $24,000 on account for services rendered prior to acquisition.

INSTRUCTIONS Indicate the amount that should appear in the consolidated balance sheet for each of these selected accounts. If the account would not appear in the consolidated balance sheet, enter –0– as the consolidated account balance. Show supporting computations.

EXERCISE 17-8
Preparing a Consolidated Balance Sheet; Non-controlling Interest

On June 30 Peabody, Inc., ***purchased*** 80% of the stock of Stern Ltd. for $1,200,000 in cash. The separate condensed balance sheets immediately after the purchase are as follows:

	Peabody, Inc.	Stern Ltd.
Cash	$ 350,000	$ 225,000
Investments in Stern Ltd.	1,200,000	
Other assets	5,450,000	1,775,000
	$7,000,000	$2,000,000
Liabilities	$1,500,000	$ 500,000
Capital stock	3,000,000	1,000,000
Retained earnings	2,500,000	500,000
	$7,000,000	$2,000,000

INSTRUCTIONS Prepare a consolidated balance sheet immediately after Peabody, Inc., acquired control of Stern Ltd.

PROBLEMS

Group A

PROBLEM 17A-1
Investments in Marketable Debt Securities

On April 1, 1995, Imperial Motors purchased $450,000 face value of the 8% bonds of Crest Theatres, Inc., at a price of 98 plus accrued interest. The bonds pay interest semiannually on March 1 and September 1. Imperial regards these bonds as a short-term investment.

INSTRUCTIONS

a In general journal form, prepare the entries required in 1995 to record:
   1 Purchase of the bonds on April 1.
   2 Receipt of the semiannual interest payment on September 1.

3 Adjustment of the accounts at December 31 for bond interest earned since September 1. (Imperial Motors adjusts and closes its accounts annually, using the calendar year.)

b Assume that on January 31, 1996, Imperial Motors sells the entire investment in Crest Theatres bonds for $444,700 plus accrued interest. Prepare the entries to:

1 Accrue bond interest earned from December 31, 1995 through the date of sale.

2 Record the sale of the bonds on January 31, 1996.

PROBLEM 17A-2
Investments in Marketable Equity Securities

During the current year, the following transactions occurred relating to Talley Manufacturing Limited's investments in marketable equity securities:

Jan. 31 Purchased as a short-term investment 4,000 shares of Raleigh Corporation common stock at $64.75 per share, plus broker's commission of $1,400.

Mar. 31 Received a cash dividend of $1.25 per share from Raleigh Corporation. Raleigh declared the dividend on February 15, payable on March 31 to shareholders of record on March 15.

June 30 Raleigh Corporation distributed a 5% stock dividend.

July 31 Raleigh Corporation shares were split 2 for 1; Talley Manufacturing received additional shares pursuant to this stock split.

Sept. 30 Raleigh Corporation paid a cash dividend of 70 cents per share. Dividend was declared on August 25 payable on September 30 to shareholders of record on September 15.

Dec. 21 Talley Manufacturing sold 3,000 shares of Raleigh Corporation stock at $29 per share. Commission charges on the sale amounted to $600.

As of December 31, Raleigh Corporation common stock had a market value of $28.50 per share. Talley Manufacturing classifies its Raleigh Corporation stock as a current asset and owns no other marketable equity securities.

INSTRUCTIONS

Prepare journal entries to account for this investment in Talley Manufacturing's accounting records. Include memorandum entries when appropriate. For journal entries involving computations, the explanation portion of the entry should include the computation. Also show how the investment should appear in the balance sheet at December 31.

PROBLEM 17A-3
Accounting for Marketable Securities: A Comprehensive Problem

The marketable securities owned by Freitag Development at the beginning of the current year are listed below. Management considers all investments in marketable securities to be current assets.

$300,000 maturity value of Micro Computer 12% bonds due Apr. 30, 1999. Interest payable on Apr. 30 and Oct. 31 of each year. Cost basis $990 per bond	*$297,000*
4,000 shares of Ryan Corporation common stock. Cost basis $52.50 per share	*210,000*

Transactions relating to marketable securities during the current year were as follows:

Jan. 21 Received semiannual cash dividend of 90 cents per share on the 4,000 shares of Ryan Corporation common stock.

Feb. 8 Purchased 1,500 shares of Gramm Ltd. common stock at $39\frac{3}{4}$ per share. Brokerage commissions amounted to $375.

Mar. 15 Received an additional 1,500 shares of Gramm Ltd. common stock as a result of a 2-for-1 split.

Apr. 30 Received semiannual interest on Micro Computer 12% bonds. Accrued interest of $6,000 had been recorded on December 31 of last year in the Bond Interest Receivable account.

May 31 Sold $200,000 face value of Micro Computer 12% bonds at a price of 103, plus one month's accrued interest, less a brokerage commission of $575.

July 21 Received cash dividend on 4,000 shares of Ryan Corporation common stock. Amount of dividend has increased to $1.05 per share.

Oct. 18 Received an additional 200 shares of Ryan Corporation common stock as a result of a 5% stock dividend.

Oct. 19 Sold 1,200 shares of Ryan Corporation common stock at $47 per share, less a brokerage commission of $250.

Oct. 31 Received semiannual interest payment on remaining $100,000 face value of Micro Computer 12% bonds.

At December 31 of the current year, the quoted market prices of the marketable securities owned by Freitag Development were as follows: Ryan Corporation, $46 per share; Gramm Ltd. $21.50 per share; Micro Computer 12% bonds, $1,025 per bond.

INSTRUCTIONS

a Prepare journal entries to record the transactions listed above. Include an adjusting entry to record the accrued interest on the remaining Micro Computer bonds through December 31.

b Prepare a schedule showing the cost and market value of the marketable securities owned by Freitag Development at December 31.

c Show how the marketable securities should appear in the balance sheet at December 31.

PROBLEM 17A-4
Equity Method—Financial Statement Effects

On January 1, 1995, Minelli Foods purchased 30% (300,000 shares) of the widely traded common stock of Kansas Grain Products, Inc., for $5,100,000. (This price was equal to 30% of Kansas Products' book value at that date.) The following data is available regarding Kansas Grain Products, Inc., for 1995 and 1996:

	1995	*1996*
Net income (loss)	*$2,500,000*	*$(900,000)*
Dividends declared & paid	*$1,300,000*	*$ 650,000*
Quoted market price per share at December 31	*$ 19*	*$ 14*

INSTRUCTIONS

a Briefly describe how Minelli Foods should account for this investment. Identify the principal factors that determine the accounting treatment.

b Compute each of the following amounts relating only to Minelli's investment in Kansas Grain Products, Inc.

1 Cash dividends received by Minelli in 1995 and in 1996.

2 Amounts (if any) reported in Minelli's ***income statement*** in 1995 and in 1996 for each of the following: Dividend Revenue; Investment Income (or Loss).

3 Carrying value of this investment reported in Minelli's ***balance sheet*** at December 31, 1995, and at December 31, 1996.

c Compute the ***market value*** of Minelli Foods' investment in Kansas Grain Products, Inc., at the end of 1995 and 1996. How are these market values reflected in Minelli Foods' financial statements, if at all? Assume that the market value of Kansas' stock went up to $17.50 per share in early 1997.

PROBLEM 17A-5
Basic Elements of a Consolidated Balance Sheet

On December 31, 1995, the Home Club, Inc., purchased for cash 70% of the capital stock of Winston Paint Ltd. The separate year-end balance sheets of the two companies include the following items:

	Home Club, Inc.	Winston Paint Ltd.
Accounts receivable—Home Club, Inc.	–0–	315,000
Investments in Winston Paint Ltd.	1,050,000	–0–
Total assets	6,500,000	2,180,000
Accounts payable—Winston Paint Ltd.	315,000	–0–
Total liabilities	3,900,000	980,000
Total shareholders' equity	2,600,000	1,200,000

The excess of the $1,050,000 purchase price over the book value of the acquired shares in Winston Paint Ltd. is regarded as a purchase of Winston Paint's unrecorded goodwill.

INSTRUCTIONS

Compute the amounts to appear in the year-end consolidated balance sheet for each of the following (show supporting computations):

a Goodwill

b Non-controlling interest

c Total assets

d Total liabilities

e Total shareholders' equity.

PROBLEM 17A-6
Preparing a Consolidated Balance Sheet

On January 1, 1996, Maxwell Entertainment purchased all the outstanding common stock of Video Scene, Inc., for $800,000. Immediately ***before*** the acquisition, the condensed separate balance sheets of the two companies were as shown below. (As these balance sheets were prepared just ***before*** the purchase, the current assets of Maxwell Entertainment still include the $800,000 in cash that was paid to acquire Video Scene, Inc.)

Assets	Maxwell Entertainment	Video Scene, Inc.
Current assets	$1,630,000	$240,000
Other assets	1,970,000	660,000
Total assets	$3,600,000	$900,000
Liabilities & Shareholders' Equity		
Current liabilities	$ 580,000	$120,000
Long-term debt	900,000	208,000
Capital stock	1,000,000	200,000
Retained earnings	1,120,000	372,000
Total liabilities & shareholders' equity	$3,600,000	$900,000

The excess, if any, of the purchase price over the book value of Video Scene's acquired shares is regarded as payment for Video Scene's unrecorded goodwill.

INSTRUCTIONS Prepare a consolidated balance sheet for Maxwell Entertainment and its newly acquired subsidiary (Video Scene, Inc.) on January 1, 1996, the date of acquisition.

PROBLEM 17A-7 Working Paper for a Consolidated Balance Sheet

On March 31, 1996, Connor Yacht Design purchased for $375,000 cash 90% of the capital stock of Wing Sails, Inc. The separate balance sheets of the two corporations immediately ***after*** this purchase are as follows:

Assets	Connor Yacht Design	Wing Sails, Inc.
Cash	$ 69,000	$ 40,000
Accounts receivable	150,000	60,000
Inventories	120,000	80,000
Investment in Wing Sails, Inc.	375,000	
Plant and equipment	500,000	360,000
Accumulated depreciation	(100,000)	(80,000)
Total assets	$1,114,000	$460,000
Liabilities & Shareholders' Equity		
Accounts payable	$ 80,000	$ 80,000
Accrued liabilities	50,000	20,000
Common stock	600,000	200,000
Retained earnings	384,000	160,000
Total liabilities & shareholders' equity	$1,114,000	$460,000

ADDITIONAL INFORMATION

1 Connor Yacht's asset account, Investment in Wing Sails, Inc., represents ownership of 90% of Wing Sails' shareholders' equity, which has a book value of $324,000 [90% × ($200,000 + $160,000) = $324,000]. The remainder of the Investment account balance represents the purchase of Wing Sails, Inc.'s unrecorded goodwill.

2 Wing Sails owes Connor Yacht Design $14,000 in accrued rent payable. This amount is included in the accrued liabilities of the subsidiary and the accounts receivable of the parent company.

3 Connor Yacht Design owes Wing Sales $32,000 for services rendered. This amount is included in the parent company's accounts payable and the subsidiary's accounts receivable.

INSTRUCTIONS Prepare a working paper for a consolidated balance sheet at March 31, 1996—the date of this business acquisition. Include at the bottom of the working paper explanations of the elimination entries.

Group B

PROBLEM 17B-1 Investments in Marketable Debt Securities

On June 1, 1995, Allied Chemical purchased $600,000 face value of the 9% bonds of Tiger Trucking at a price of 102 plus accrued interest. The bonds pay interest semiannually on April 1 and October 1. Allied Chemical regards these bonds as a short-term investment.

INSTRUCTIONS

a In general journal form, prepare the entries required in 1995 to record:

1 Purchase of the bonds on June 1.

2 Receipt of the semiannual interest payment on October 1.

3 Adjustment of the accounts at December 31 for bond interest earned since October 1. (Allied Chemical adjusts and closes its accounts annually, using the calendar year.)

b Assume that on February 28, 1996, Allied Chemical sells the entire investment in Tiger Trucking bonds for total proceeds of $628,900, which includes accrued interest. Prepare the entries to:

1 Accrue bond interest earned from December 31, 1995, through the date of sale.

2 Record the sale of the bonds on February 28, 1996.

PROBLEM 17B-2
Investments in Marketable Securities

During the current year, Overnight Air Freight (OAF) engaged in the following transactions relating to marketable securities in stock:

Feb. 28 Purchased 5,000 shares of National Products common stock for $88.50 per share plus a broker's commission of $1,500.

Mar. 15 National Products paid a cash dividend of 75 cents per share that had been declared on February 20, payable on March 15 to shareholders of record on March 6.

May 31 National Products distributed a 20% stock dividend.

Nov. 15 National Products distributed additional shares as the result of a 2-for-1 stock split.

Dec. 5 OAF sold 3,500 shares of its National Products stock at $39 per share, less a broker's commission of $450.

Dec. 10 National Products paid a cash dividend of 30 cents per share. Dividend was declared November 20, payable December 10 to shareholders of record on November 30.

As of December 31, National Products common stock had a market value of $35 per share. OAF classifies its National Products stock as a current asset and owns no other marketable securities.

INSTRUCTIONS Prepare journal entries to account for this investment in OAF's accounting records. Include memorandum entries when appropriate. For journal entries involving computations, the explanation portion of the entry should include the computation. Also show how the investment should appear in the balance sheet at December 31.

PROBLEM 17B-3
Accounting for Marketable Securities: A Comprehensive Problem

The marketable securities owned by Bar Harbour Corporation at January 1 consisted of the three securities listed below. All marketable securities are classified as current assets.

$200,000 maturity value Copper Products Ltd. 9% bonds due Apr. 30, 2002. Interest is payable on Apr. 30 and Oct. 31 of each year. Cost basis $990 per bond	*$198,000*
3,000 shares of Aztec Corporation common stock. Cost basis $38.50 per share	*115,500*
1,500 shares of Donner-Pass, Inc., $7.00 cumulative preferred stock. Cost basis $55 per share	*82,500*

Jan. 10 Acquired 1,000 shares of Rhodes Ltd. common stock at $65.50 per share. Brokerage commissions paid amounted to $500.

Jan. 21 Received quarterly dividend on $1.75 per share on 1,500 shares of Donner-Pass, Inc., preferred stock.

Mar. 5 Sold all 1,500 shares of Donner-Pass, Inc., preferred stock at $58 per share less a brokerage commission of $375.

Apr. 1 Received additional 2,000 shares of Rhodes Ltd. common stock as a result of a 3-for-1 split.

Apr. 30 Received semiannual interest on Copper Products Ltd. 9% bonds. Accrued interest of $3,000 had been recorded on December 31 of last year in the Bond Interest Receivable account.

June 30 Sold $100,000 face value of Copper Products Ltd. 9% bonds at 93, plus two months' accrued interest, less a commission of $125.

July 10 Received additional 300 shares of Aztec Corporation common stock as a result of 10% stock dividend.

Sept. 24 Sold 1,300 shares of Aztec Corporation common stock at $40 per share, less a brokerage commission of $250.

Oct. 31 Received semiannual interest payment on remaining $100,000 face value of Copper Products Ltd. 9% bonds.

At December 31, 19__, the quoted market prices of the marketable securities owned by Bar Harbour Corporation were as follows: Aztec Corporation common stock, $37; and Rhodes common stock, $18. Copper Products 9% bonds, $960 per bond.

INSTRUCTIONS

a Prepare journal entries to record the transactions listed above. Include an adjusting entry to record accrued interest on the remaining Copper Products bonds through December 31.

b Prepare a schedule showing the cost and market value of the marketable securities owned by Bar Harbour Corporation at December 31.

c Show how the marketable securities should be presented in the balance sheet at December 31.

PROBLEM 17B-4
Equity Method—Financial Statement Effects

On January 1, 1996, Bishop Industries purchased 60,000 shares of the widely traded common stock of Franklin-Parker Corporation for $1,500,000. On this date, Franklin-Parker had 150,000 shares of a single class of stock outstanding and total shareholders' equity of $3,750,000. The following data is available regarding Franklin-Parker Corporation for 1996 and 1997:

	1996	*1997*
Net income (loss)	*$(300,000)*	*$1,500,000*
Dividends declared & paid	*$ 75,000*	*$ 600,000*
Quoted market price per share at December 31	*$ 22*	*$ 30*

INSTRUCTIONS

a Briefly describe how Bishop Industries should account for this investment. Identify the principal factors that determine the accounting treatment.

b Compute each of the following amounts relating only to Bishop's investment in Franklin-Parker Corporation.

1 Cash dividends received by Bishop in 1996 and in 1997.

2 Amounts (if any) reported in Bishop's ***income statement*** in 1996 and in 1997 for each of the following: Dividend Revenue; Investment Income (or Loss).

3 Carrying value of this investment reported on Bishop's ***balance sheet*** at December 31, 1996, and at December 31, 1997.

c Compute the ***market value*** of Bishop Industries' investment in Franklin-Parker at December 31, 1996, and December 31, 1997. How are these market values reflected in Bishop's financial statements, if at all?

PROBLEM 17B-5
Basic Elements of a Consolidated Balance Sheet

On December 31, 1996, Northwest Building Materials purchased for cash 80% of the capital stock of Corning Electrical Supply. The separate year-end balance sheets of the two companies include the following items:

	Northwest Building Materials	Corning Electrical Supply
Accounts receivable—Corning Electrical Supply	130,000	-0-
Investment in Corning Electrical Supply	1,600,000	-0-
Total assets	9,800,000	2,200,000
Accounts payable—Northwest Building Materials	-0-	130,000
Total liabilities	3,600,000	700,000
Total shareholders' equity	6,200,000	1,500,000

The excess of the $1,600,000 purchase price over the book value of the acquired shares in Corning is regarded as a purchase of Corning's unrecorded goodwill.

INSTRUCTIONS Compute the amounts to appear in the year-end consolidated balance sheet for each of the following (show supporting computations):

a Goodwill

b Non-controlling interest

c Total assets

d Total liabilities

e Total shareholders' equity.

PROBLEM 17B-6 Preparing a Consolidated Balance Sheet

On June 30, 19__, Pokfulam Sportswear paid $1,800,000 cash to acquire all the outstanding capital stock of Jeans by Jorge. Immediately ***before*** this acquisition, the condensed separate balance sheets of the two companies were as shown below. (As these balance sheets were prepared immediately ***before*** the acquisition, the current assets of Pokfulam Sportswear still include the $1,800,000 in cash that will be paid to acquire Jeans by Jorge.)

Assets	Pokfulam Sportswear	Jeans by Jorge
Current assets	$3,760,000	$ 640,000
Plant and equipment	3,040,000	1,800,000
Total assets	$6,800,000	$2,440,000
Liabilities & Shareholders' Equity		
Current liabilities	$1,080,000	$ 560,000
Long-term debt	2,400,000	400,000
Capital stock	1,200,000	600,000
Retained earnings	2,120,000	880,000
Total liabilities & shareholders' equity	$6,800,000	$2,440,000

The excess, if any, of the purchase price over the book value of Jeans by Jorge shares acquired is regarded as payment for unrecorded goodwill.

INSTRUCTIONS Prepare a consolidated balance sheet for Pokfulam Sportswear and its newly acquired subsidiary (Jeans by Jorge) on June 30, 19__, the date of acquisition.

PROBLEM 17B-7 Working Paper for a Consolidated Balance Sheet

On September 30, 1996, Morse Communications purchased 80% of the stock of Graham Cable for cash. The separate balance sheets of the two companies immediately after this purchase are as follows:

Assets	Morse Communications	Graham Cable
Cash	$ 52,000	$ 45,000
Note receivable from Graham Cable	50,000	
Accounts receivable	108,000	60,000
Inventories	120,000	174,000
Investment in Graham Cable	570,000	
Plant and equipment	420,000	540,000
Accumulated depreciation	(168,000)	(100,000)
Total assets	$1,152,000	$719,000
Liabilities & Shareholders' Equity		
Notes payable	$ 120,000	$ 50,000
Accounts payable	144,000	45,000
Accrued liabilities	36,000	24,000
Common stock	500,000	350,000
Retained earnings	352,000	250,000
Total liabilities & shareholders' equity	$1,152,000	$719,000

ADDITIONAL INFORMATION

1 Morse Communications' asset account Investment in Graham Cable represents ownership of 80% of Graham Cable's shareholders' equity, which has a book value of $480,000 [80% × ($350,000 + $250,000) = $480,000]. The remainder of the investment account balance represents the purchase of Graham Cable's unrecorded goodwill.

2 Graham Cable's $50,000 note payable is owed to Morse Communications. (All interest has been paid through September 30.)

3 The accounts payable of Morse Communications include $15,000 owed to Graham Cable. This amount also is included in the accounts receivable of Graham Cable.

INSTRUCTIONS Prepare a working paper for a consolidated balance sheet at September 30, 1996—immediately after the purchase of Graham Cable. Include at the bottom of the working paper explanations of the elimination entries.

ANALYTICAL AND DECISION PROBLEMS AND CASES

A&D 17-1 Apples and Oranges

Dane Electronics has the following investments in the securities of other corporations:

a 2,000 shares of the common stock of Apple Computer. Apple is a large publicly owned corporation and sells at a quoted market price in excess of Dane's cost. Dane's management stands ready to sell these shares at any time.

b $100,000 face amount of Central Telephone's $3\frac{5}{8}$% bonds maturing in 10 years. The bonds were acquired at a substantial discount. These bonds are readily marketable, and Dane's management stands ready to sell them to meet any current cash requirements.

c 5 million of the 15 million voting shares in Micro-Desk, Inc. Micro-Desk is a publicly owned corporation, and its quoted stock price recently has declined to a level below Dane's cost.

d $300,000 face value of Carver Stores $12\frac{1}{4}$% bonds maturing in 10 years. These bonds are readily marketable at a quoted price. However, Dane intends to hold these bonds until their maturity date. The bonds were acquired at a premium.

e 51% of the voting stock in Consumer Corp. Consumer is a profitable company, but it is not publicly owned. There is no quoted market price for Consumer's capital stock.

f 50,000 of the 1 million outstanding shares of SIMCO Products, a publicly owned corporation. The market price of SIMCO's shares has declined steadily since Dane purchased its shares. Dane's management, however, believes in the long-run prospects of SIMCO and intends to hold this investment for at least 10 years.

g 5,000 shares of voting stock of Orange Express. Orange Express operates profitably, but it is not publicly owned and has no quoted market value. This investment does not give Dane an influential interest in Orange Express. Dane's management stands ready to sell these shares at any time that an attractive offer is received.

INSTRUCTIONS Explain how Dane Electronics should account for each of these investments. Your explanations should include discussion of the three topics listed below.

1 Whether the investment qualifies for consolidation and, if not, the appropriate balance sheet classification of the investment account.

2 The basis for balance sheet valuation (e.g., consolidation, equity method, cost, cost adjusted for amortization of bond discount or premium, or lower-of-cost-and-market).

3 The factors involved in the recognition of income (or loss) from the investment (e.g., Does the lower-of-cost-and-market rule enter into the determination of net income? Is bond discount or premium amortized? Are dividends recorded as income when received? Is the equity method in use?).

A&D 17-2
Success or Failure and Why?

There have been many well-known, well-publicized business acquisitions and mergers in recent years. The results of these acquisitions and mergers have been mixed—some successes, some failures, and a few disasters. In addition, the fate of the more recent acquisitions and mergers is still pending.

INSTRUCTIONS Select one of the acquisitions or mergers cited in the "CASE IN POINT" in this chapter and determine why it has been a success or a failure.

PART

6

Special Purpose Reports and Financial Statement Analysis

In the next three chapters we discuss several specialized uses of accounting information, including the determination of taxable income, the measurement of cash flows, and the analysis of financial statements by investors.

Part 6 also includes Comprehensive Problem 5, which provides an opportunity to analyze and evaluate the financial statements of a well-known corporation.

CHAPTER

18 Income Taxes and Business Decisions

For many college and university students, this chapter may be their only academic exposure to the truly remarkable system known as income taxes. The early part of the chapter presents a brief history, rationale, and basic structure of the federal tax structure, including the tax reform measures introduced in 1988. This introduction also stresses the pervasive influence of income taxes upon economic activity. The next section portrays the basic process of determining taxable income and the tax liability for individual taxpayers. The income tax computations for a corporation are also explained and illustrated. The final section of the chapter gives students an understanding of the important role that tax planning can play in the affairs of individuals and also in the decision-making of a business entity.

Learning Objectives

After studying this chapter you should be able to:

1. *Describe the history of the federal income tax, the highlights of the tax reform measures introduced in 1988, and the basic structure of the tax system.*
2. *Explain the formula for determining the taxable income and tax liability of an individual taxpayer.*
3. *Explain the income tax treatment of dividends received by individuals.*
4. *Determine the tax liability of an individual.*
5. *Determine the taxable income and income tax of a corporation.*
6. *Determine the amount of capital cost allowance.*
7. *Describe the circumstances that create a liability for deferred income taxes.*
8. *Explain how tax planning is used in choosing the form of business organization, timing and nature of transactions, and the capital structure.*

The Federal Income Tax: History and Objectives

OBJECTIVE 1 Describe the history of the federal income tax, the highlights of the tax reform measures introduced in 1988, and the basic structure of the tax system.

The federal income tax legislation, the ***Income Tax Act,*** has undergone many changes since its inception as the ***Income War Tax Act*** in 1917. The more significant changes occurred in the years 1948, 1952, and 1972. In 1988, major tax reform measures were introduced, as highlighted in the following section and discussed in this chapter. Similarly, the objectives of income tax legislation also have been changed and expanded over the years. The administration and enforcement of the Income Tax Act rest with the Department of National Revenue for Taxation, commonly known as Revenue Canada, Taxation.

Originally, the objective of the federal income tax was simply to obtain revenue to help meet Canada's growing war expenditures. It was intended as a temporary measure and the tax rates were quite low. Today, the objectives are many and the tax rates are significantly higher.

The objectives of federal income tax today include a number of broad ones in addition to raising revenue. Among these broad objectives are to combat inflation, to influence the rate of economic growth, to encourage full employment, to provide incentive for small businesses, and to redistribute national income on a more equal basis.

Tax Reform Measures of 1988

In 1988, the federal government enacted new income tax legislation that brought sweeping changes in income tax rules and rates. Although annual changes in the income tax law have become normal practice, the changes in this new legislation represented some of the most drastic in the history of the federal income tax. Annual changes, however, will continue. The five most striking characteristics of this major tax legislation are the broadening of the tax base, the lowering of tax rates, the reduction of the number of tax brackets, the replacement of various exemptions and deductions with tax credits, and a shifting of the tax burden from individuals to corporations and to sales tax.

Provincial Income Tax

All ten provinces as well as the Northwest Territories and Yukon levy income tax. The federal government collects the income tax of individuals and corporations except for the Provinces of Ontario, Alberta, and Quebec; Ontario and Alberta collect their corporate income tax and Quebec collects its income tax on both individuals and corporations. The rate of income tax varies among the jurisdictions. The tax rate for individuals is expressed as a percentage of the individual's basic federal tax. The tax rate for corporations, on the other hand, applies to the corporation's taxable income. The computations of provincial income tax will be illustrated later.

Tax Planning versus Tax Evasion

Tax Planning Taxpayers who manage their affairs in ways that ***legally*** minimize their income tax obligations are engaging in a practice called ***tax planning.*** Tax planning is both legal and ethical.

The goals of tax planning usually are either to minimize the total amount of taxes owed or to postpone into future years the dates at which the taxes become due. Tax planning may take many forms; for example: Should business automobiles be leased or purchased? Should needed capital be financed by issuing bonds or preferred stock? Should a business be incorporated? Some of these choices may significantly affect the amount and timing of the taxpayer's income tax obligations.

If tax planning is to be efficient, it should be undertaken ***before*** the taxpayer engages in the related transactions. Once a transaction is complete, it usually is ***too late*** to change its tax consequences. Every taxpayer, whether an individual or a corporation, can benefit from thoughtful tax planning. Tax planning is one of the major services that public accounting firms offer their clients.

Tax Evasion In contrast to tax planning, ***tax evasion*** refers to ***illegal*** efforts by taxpayers to avoid their tax obligations. Examples include failure to file an income tax return or fraudulently understating the amount of taxable income reported in the return. By definition, tax evasion is a crime, punishable by fines, imprisonment, or both.

CASE IN POINT Al Capone, one of the most infamous gangsters in American history, was believed to have committed many crimes, including bootlegging, extortion, and murder. Capone was the subject of an intense criminal investigation conducted by the American federal law enforcement agents—including the legendary Elliot Ness and "The Untouchables."

The only crime for which the American government was able to convict Capone was income tax evasion. The result, however, was the same as if he had been convicted of murder and given a life sentence. He died in prison while serving his term.

The Critical Importance of Income Taxes

Taxes levied by federal and provincial governments are a significant part of the cost of operating a typical household, as well as a business enterprise. Every manager who makes business decisions, and every individual who makes personal investments, urgently needs some knowledge of income taxes. A general knowledge of income taxes will help any business manager or owner to benefit more fully from the advice of the professional tax accountant.

Some understanding of income taxes will also aid the individual citizen in voting intelligently, because a great many of the issues decided in every election have tax implications. Such issues as pollution, inflation, foreign policy, and employment are quite closely linked with income taxes. For example, the offering of special tax incentives to encourage businesses to launch massive programs to reduce pollution is one approach to protection of the environment.

In terms of revenue generated, income taxes constitute one of the most important sources of revenue in Canada. Income taxes also exert a pervasive influence on all types of business decisions and affect millions of individuals. For example, tax returns filed annually in recent years were about 19 million for individuals and 900,000 for corporations. The annual income tax revenue from individuals and corporations in recent years was about

$96 billion. For this reason we shall limit our discussion to the basic federal and provincial income tax rules applicable to individuals and corporations.

Income tax returns are based on accounting information. In many respects this information is consistent with the accounting concepts we have discussed in earlier chapters. However, the measurement of ***taxable income*** includes some unique principles and computations that differ from those used for published financial statements. An understanding of the unique aspects of taxable income can assist an individual or a business in minimizing the amount of income taxes owed.

Classes of Taxpayers and Liability of Tax

In the eyes of the income tax law, the classes of taxpayers are: individuals, corporations, and trusts. Since trusts are taxed as individuals, there are in essence two classes of taxpayers.

Proprietorships and partnerships are not taxed as business units; their income is taxed directly to the individual proprietor or partners, ***whether or not actually withdrawn from the business.*** A proprietor reports his or her business income on an individual tax return; the members of a partnership include on their individual tax returns their respective shares of the partnership net income. An individual taxpayer's income tax return must include not only any business income from a proprietorship or partnership, but also any salary or income from other sources and any deductions affecting the tax liability.

A corporation is a separate taxable entity; it must file an income tax return and pay a tax on its annual taxable income. In addition, individual shareholders must report dividends received as part of their personal taxable income. This is sometimes called "double taxation" of corporate income—once to the corporation and again when it is distributed as dividends to shareholders. However, this double taxation is minimized by the "dividend tax credit" claimed by the shareholders.

The income tax law stipulates that income tax is payable on the taxable income for each taxation year of every person resident in Canada. Moreover, income tax is payable on the taxable income earned in Canada by a nonresident person. The word "person" may include an individual or a corporation.

Enforcement of Income Tax Laws

Our system of income taxes relies upon taxpayers measuring their own taxable income, computing the taxes that they owe, and filing an income tax return in which these amounts are reported to governmental income tax authorities. For this reason, our system of collecting income taxes often is described as a system of ***self-assessment.***

However, income tax authorities have several means of enforcing this "self-assessment" system. To begin with, much of the taxable income earned by taxpayers is reported to the tax authorities by a third party. For example, employers must send ***T4*** forms to the government indicating the total salary or wages paid to each employee during the year. Corporations and banks are required to send ***T5*** forms reporting to the government the dividends and interest earned by each investor and creditor. Through the use of its computers, Revenue Canada traces many of these reported amounts directly into the recipient's income tax return.

Next, each year income tax authorities ***audit*** selected tax returns filed by taxpayers. Only a small percentage of the returns filed each year are audited; however, Revenue Canada has considerable experience in identifying those returns in which taxable income may be understated. Many of the returns selected for audit are those that appear "suspicious" in some way, or in which taxpayers have claimed deductions to which they might not be entitled. Thus, by claiming certain deductions (such as expenses relating to a "home office" or a large business loss), a taxpayer may increase the chances that his or her return will be audited.

An interesting quirk in the tax law is that when a tax return is audited, ***the burden of proof rests with the taxpayer.*** Thus, taxpayers who do not maintain adequate records may lose deductions to which they otherwise would be entitled.

Finally, tax authorities may impose financial penalties upon taxpayers who have understated their taxable incomes. First, the taxpayer must pay interest on any additional taxes owed. In addition, substantial fines and penalties may be levied if the taxpayer has been careless or fraudulent. As previously stated, fraudulent tax evasion is a criminal offense and may be punishable by imprisonment, as well as by financial penalties.

INCOME TAXES: INDIVIDUALS

Cash Basis of Accounting for Individual Tax Returns

Most of the individual tax returns are prepared on the cash basis of measuring income. The cash basis is advantageous for the individual taxpayer for several reasons. It is simple and requires a minimum of record keeping. Moreover, the income of most individuals comes in the form of salaries, interest, and dividends. At the end of each year, employers are required to inform each employee (and Revenue Canada, Taxation) of the salary earned and the income tax withheld during the year. The report (a T4 form) must be prepared on the cash basis without any accrual of unpaid wages. Generally, companies paying interest and dividends also use the cash basis in reporting the amounts paid during the year. Thus, most individuals are provided with reports prepared on a cash basis for use in preparing their individual tax returns. However, businesses and professional practices, with rare exceptions such as a farming business, are not allowed to use the cash basis for tax purposes.

Tax Rates for Individuals

All taxes may be characterized as progressive, proportional, or regressive with respect to any given base. A ***progressive*** tax becomes a larger portion of the base as that base increases. A ***proportional*** tax remains a constant percentage of the base no matter how that base changes. For example, an 8% sales tax remains a constant percentage of sales regardless of changes in the dollar amount of sales. A ***regressive*** tax becomes a smaller percentage of the base as the base increases. Regressive taxes, however, are extremely rare.

Federal income tax is ***progressive*** with respect to income, since a higher tax ***rate*** applies as the amount of taxable income increases. Since provincial income tax is expressed as a percentage of "basic federal tax," it is also progressive with respect to income. The 1993 federal and provincial tax rates for individuals are as follows:

Federal Tax Rates for Individuals—1993

Taxable Income	*Marginal Tax Rate*
$0–29,590	17%
$29,591–59,180	26%
over $59,180	29%

Provincial Tax Rates for Individuals*—1993

Alberta	45.5%
British Columbia	52.5%
Manitoba	52%
New Brunswick	62%
Newfoundland	69%
Nova Scotia	59.5%
Ontario	58%
Prince Edward Island	59.5%
Saskatchewan	50%

* There was a surtax or flat tax or both for all provinces except Newfoundland.

(The province of Quebec collects its own individual income tax. The 1993 rate ranges from 16% to 24%, and the rate applies to taxable income as computed under the Quebec Taxation Act.)

As mentioned earlier, two of the most striking characteristics of the 1988 tax reform legislation are the reduction of the number of tax brackets and the lowering of tax rates. In contrast to the 10 tax brackets and marginal tax rates ranging from 6% to 34% prior to the tax reform, the current tax legislation provides for only 3 tax brackets and 3 marginal tax rates ranging from 17% to 29%.

To minimize the impact of severe inflation, the tax legislation provides for the indexing of the three tax brackets and tax credits relating to "personal amount" by any annual increase in the Consumers Price Index in excess of 3%.

Income Tax Formula for Individuals

OBJECTIVE 2 Explain the formula for determining the taxable income and tax liability of an individual taxpayer.

The federal government supplies a standard income tax form (T1 General) on which individual taxpayers are guided to a proper computation of their taxable income and the amount of the tax. It is helpful to visualize the computation in terms of an income tax formula. Moreover, it is easier to understand the structure and logic of income tax and to analyze tax rules and their effect by referring to a tax formula. The general income tax formula, based on the standard income tax form for individuals, is outlined on the next page. The items in the formula are explained in more detail in the following paragraphs.

Total Income

The total income of an individual taxpayer is his or her world income from all sources except those explicitly excluded by the income tax law. If an amount received by an individual is income and not a return of capital and it is not explicitly excluded by the tax law, then it should be included as income. To identify whether an amount is excluded as income for tax purposes, it is necessary to refer to the income tax law, regulations, and court decisions.

The major categories of income for tax purposes are on page 850.

General Income Tax Formula for Individuals

Total Income → This is world income from all sources: including income from office, employment, business, property, pension, and capital gains.

minus

Deductions → These are deductions from total income and include registered pension plan contributions, registered retirement savings plan contributions (for the taxpayer or the spouse), union and professional dues, and child care expenses.

equals

Net Income → This net income amount is used as the basis for the computation of the amounts eligible for medical expense and charitable donation tax credits.

minus

Other Deductions → These other deductions include non-capital and allowable capital losses of previous years, and capital gains deduction.[1]

equals

Taxable Income → This is the amount to which appropriate federal income tax rates are applied.

basis for

Federal Income Tax Calculation → This amount is the gross federal tax. It is a preliminary basis for determining the federal tax payable.

minus

Tax Credits → These include tax credits relating to Canada Pension Plan contributions, unemployment insurance premiums, personal amounts, tuition fees, and charitable donations.

equals

Basic Federal Tax → This is the amount used to compute provincial income tax. Then, it may be reduced by any foreign tax credit.

basis for

Provincial Income Tax → This is computed by applying the appropriate provincial income tax rate to the "basic federal tax."[2]

---

1 Only those capital gains accrued as of February 22, 1994 are eligible for the $100,000 lifetime capital gains exemption. This capital gains exemption is no longer available after February 22, 1994.

2 As mentioned earlier, the province of Quebec applies its tax rate to taxable income under the Quebec Taxation Act.

1 **Income from an office or employment** This category includes salaries, wages, directors' fees, and other remuneration and taxable fringe benefits[3] such as bonuses, tips, honoraria, and certain allowances for personal or living expenses.

2 **Income from a business or property** This category includes net income from a proprietorship, partnership, or a professional business, as well as rental, royalty, interest, and dividend income. Also, income from a business of an illegal nature is to be included in income for tax purposes.

3 **Capital gains** This category includes gains from selling capital assets such as stocks, bonds, and depreciable properties used in the business at prices higher than their costs or adjusted costs. For 1993, ***three-quarters*** of capital gains (known as "taxable capital gains") were to be included as income for tax purposes. These gains may be offset by the same proportion of capital losses (known as "allowable capital losses") for a given year. Any remaining allowable capital losses may be carried back against taxable capital gains of the three preceding years and may be carried forward indefinitely against taxable capital gains in future years. However, there is a cumulative lifetime capital gains exemption of $100,000. In other words, up to $100,000 of the capital gain is not subject to tax.[4]

4 **Other sources of income** This category includes all income items not covered by the preceding three categories. The more common items are: benefits from Old Age Security Pension, Canada or Quebec Pension Plan, other pensions or superannuation, and unemployment insurance benefits.

As mentioned earlier, certain items are explicitly excluded as income for tax purposes; the more common items include lottery winnings, war disability pensions, inheritance, and income from personal injury awards.[5]

Deductions

There are a number of deductions from total income. The more common ones include: registered pension plan contributions, registered retirement savings plan contributions, annual union and professional dues, child care expenses, moving expenses, alimony or separation allowance paid, carrying charges such as interest expense on money borrowed to earn investment income, safety deposit box charges for storing investment documents, and social benefits repayment for unemployment insurance and old age security when the amount of net income before the repayment, called "net income before adjustments," is over a certain limit. The amount of repayment is first deducted from "net income before adjustments" and then added back to the federal and provincial taxes to arrive at the total amount of taxes payable to the government.

[3] Effective July 1, 1994, the premium on group term life insurance paid by the employer is considered to be a taxable fringe benefit. Previously, only the premium on coverage exceeding $25,000 was taxable.

[4] As indicated in footnote 1, the lifetime capital gains exemption is no longer available after February 22, 1994.

[5] Workers' compensation payments are first included in total income and then deducted, as "other deductions," from net income.

Net Income

The net income of an individual taxpayer is his or her total income minus the deductions. This amount is important because it is the basis for computing the amounts eligible for medical expense and charitable donation tax credits.

Other Deductions

There are very few items in this category. The deductions for 1993 include: workers' compensation payments, social assistance payments, non-capital and net capital losses of previous years, and capital gain deductions (i.e., taxable capital gain). For many taxpayers, their net income would be the same as taxable income unless they had business and allowable capital losses in prior years to be carried forward to the current year, or they have capital gains eligible for exemption from tax this year (the cumulative lifetime capital gains exemption of $100,000 was mentioned earlier).[6]

Taxable Income

This is the amount subject to federal income tax. It is computed by deducting from total income the allowable deductions to arrive at net income and then deducting from net income the allowable other deductions. The concept of taxable income is most important because it is the amount to which the appropriate tax rate is applied to determine the amount of "gross" federal income tax.

Federal Income Tax Calculation

This is the amount of "gross" federal income tax. It is not the amount of tax payable because there are a number of tax credits to be deducted from it to determine the basic federal tax and the federal tax payable.

Tax Credits

As mentioned earlier, one of the most striking characteristics of the tax reform legislation was the replacement of various deductions and exemptions with tax credits. Deductions such as Canada Pension Plan contributions, unemployment insurance premiums, tuition fees, education deductions, medical expenses in excess of 3% of net income, and charitable donations were substituted by tax credits. Similarly, all the personal exemptions—basic, married, infirm dependant aged 18 and over, and age—were replaced by tax credits. While some of the tax credits may be transferred to a spouse or a parent, any unused tax credits are not refundable. Since the tax credits are set at the lowest rate of 17%, this is an example of the broadening of the tax base as taxpayers with taxable income above the 17% bracket will be paying more income tax. The more common tax credits and the amounts for 1993 are:

---

6 As indicated in footnote 1, the lifetime capital gains exemption is no longer available after February 22, 1994.

1 Personal tax credits[7]

(a) basic, for the taxpayer ($6,456 × 17%)	$1,098
(b) married, for the taxpayer's spouse ($5,380 × 17%)*	915
(c) infirm dependants aged 18 and over ($1,583 × 17%)*	269
(d) age, 65 and over ($3,482[8] × 17%)	592

* A spouse and an infirm dependant aged 18 and over can earn a net income of $538 and $2,690 respectively without reduction in the amount of tax credits. The tax credit will be reduced by 17% of net income in excess of these limits.

2 Deduction tax credits based on 17% of the amount of the allowable deductions.

(a) Canada Pension Plan contributions

EIC **(b)** Unemployment insurance premiums

(c) Tuition fees

(d) Education amount of $80 for each month in full-time attendance at a designated educational institution and enrolled in a qualifying educational program.

(e) Medical expenses in excess of $1,614 or 3% of net income (this excess is commonly called "allowable medical expenses"), ***whichever is less***

(f) Charitable donations (the 17% is for the first $250 in donations and 29% for the amount in excess of $250, up to a maximum of 20% of net income)[9]

It should be mentioned that the tax reform legislation eliminated two common deductions—the employment expense deduction and the interest and dividend income deduction. Such an elimination is an example of the broadening of the tax base, one of the most striking characteristics of this tax reform legislation that was mentioned earlier.

Basic Federal Tax

The amount of basic federal tax is "gross" federal income tax (federal income tax calculation) minus tax credits. It is the basis for computing the provincial income tax. This amount plus the federal surtax of 3% on basic federal tax and 5% of basic federal tax over $12,500 and minus any foreign tax credit becomes the amount of federal tax payable.

Provincial Income Tax

The amount of provincial income tax is determined by applying the appropriate provincial tax rate to the amount of basic federal tax. Since the tax

7 On January 1, 1993, the tax credit for dependants under age 18 (as well as the family allowance payments) was replaced by the "child tax benefits." However, these benefits do not affect the computation of taxable income or income taxes.

8 This amount is reduced by the amount of net income exceeding $25,921 times 7.5% in 1994 and 15% in 1995. For example, if net income is $49,134 in both 1994 and 1995, the reduction for 1994 is $1,741 [($49,134 − $25,921) × 7.5%] and the reduction for 1995 is $3,482 [($49,134 − $25,921) × 15%]. In other words, for 1995 and subsequent years, if a senior's net income is $49,134 or more, he or she is not entitled to the age tax credit.

9 Commencing in 1994, the threshold amount is decreased from $250 to $200; that is, the 17% is applied to the first $200 of donations and the 29% to donations exceeding $200.

rate varies among provinces, an average rate of 58% (surtax or flat tax included) will be used as a provincial tax rate for illustration purposes and for the assignment materials.

Federal Dividend Tax Credit for Individuals

OBJECTIVE 3 Explain the income tax treatment of dividends received by individuals.

To minimize the impact of double taxation on corporate income upon its subsequent distribution as dividends to individual shareholders, income tax law allows a special deduction from tax called "federal dividend tax credit." However, an individual taxpayer must first include in his or her income the dividends from taxable Canadian corporations at 125% for 1993 (known as the "gross-up" or "taxable" amount of dividends). This "gross-up" amount is taxed at the normal rate of the taxpayer. The federal income tax is then reduced by the dividend tax credit at 13⅓% of the "gross-up" amount of dividends. Since income tax is progressive, the dividend tax credit provides more tax benefit to taxpayers with lower income. To illustrate, let us assume that the federal tax rates for three individuals are 17%, 26%, and 29% and each has $8,000 of dividends from taxable Canadian corporations.

Tax Rate		17%	26%	29%
Dividends	(a)	$ 8,000	$ 8,000	$ 8,000
Add: "gross-up" of 25%		2,000	2,000	2,000
Taxable (gross-up) amount of dividends (125% of dividends received)		$10,000	$10,000	$10,000
Federal income tax on taxable amount of dividends		$ 1,700	$ 2,600	$ 2,900
Less: dividend tax credit of 13⅓% on taxable (gross-up) amount of dividends (13⅓% × $10,000)		1,333	1,333	1,333
Federal tax on dividends	(b)	$ 367	$ 1,267	$ 1,567
Effective rate of federal tax on dividends (b) ÷ (a)		4.6%	15.8%	19.6%

It is clear from the preceding illustration that the difference in the effective tax rate on the dividend income between the lowest and the highest tax brackets is very substantial—a 15% difference. The 15% difference is greater than the 12% (29% − 17%) difference between the tax rates for these two tax brackets. This is, of course, in keeping with the progressive nature or the "ability to pay" philosophy of our current income tax system.

Instalment Payment of Estimate Tax for Individuals

For self-employed persons such as public accountants, doctors, dentists, and owners of unincorporated businesses, there is, of course, no salary and no tax withholding. Other examples of income on which no withholding occurs are rental income, dividends, and interest income. In these cases, instalment tax is required if tax is not withheld from at least three-quarters of a taxpayer's net income and if the taxpayer's tax in the year or in the preceding year is $1,000 or more.[10] The amount of instalment payments, due on or before March 15, June 15, September 15, and December 15, is based either on a reasonable estimate or on the tax applicable to the taxable income of the preceding year, whichever is lower. Any additional tax is due on or before April 30 of the following year.

Tax Returns, Tax Refunds, and Payment of the Tax

All individuals with tax owing must file an income tax return on or before April 30 for the preceding calendar year; otherwise, late filing penalties and interest will be charged. The payment of income taxes is on a "pay as you go" basis. The procedure by which employers withhold income taxes from the salaries of employees has been discussed previously in Chapter 11. The amounts withheld from an employee's salary for income taxes can be considered as payment on account. If the amount of income taxes as computed by preparing a tax return is less than the amount withheld during the year, the taxpayer is entitled to a refund. On the other hand, if the tax computed is more than the amount withheld, the balance should be paid with the filing of the tax return. Individuals who are entitled to a refund will have to file a tax return (within three years from the end of the year for which a refund is due) to obtain a refund.

Computation of Individual Income Tax Illustrated

OBJECTIVE 4 Determine the tax liability of an individual

The computation of the 1993 federal and provincial income tax for Sam Lee is illustrated on the next page. The illustration highlights some of the main features of the income tax law and is based on the following assumed data:

1 Mr. Sam Lee is married and has a sixteen-year-old son who has $860 net income from various part-time jobs. Also, Mrs. Lee has a net income of $500.

2 Mr. Lee's income, withholdings, and disbursements include:

Income:	
Salary from employment (before tax withholding)	*$60,000*
Dividends from taxable Canadian corporations	*8,000*
Interest from Canada Savings Bonds	*1,800*
Gain on sale of shares of Canadian Ltd.	*1,200*
Withholdings:	
Income taxes	*16,000*
Canada Pension Plan contributions	*753*
Unemployment insurance premiums	*1,162*
*Contribution to a registered pension plan**	*4,869*
Union membership dues	*530*
Disbursements:	
Medical expenses	*900*
Charitable donations	*1,600*
Professional membership dues	*690*

** Assumed amount for the year. The determination of the maximum amount can be very complex, depending on the types of pension plan and such elements as pensionable earnings, years of services, etc.*

[10] Effective September 15, 1994, instalment tax is required if the difference between tax payable (federal and provincial) and tax withheld at source is greater than $2,000 in both the current year and either of the two preceding years.

3 Provincial tax rate is 58%.

SAM LEE
Illustrative Federal and Provincial Income Tax Computation
For the Year 1993

Total income:		
Salary		$60,000
Dividends ($8,000 plus 25% gross-up)		10,000
Interest		1,800
Taxable capital gain (¾ of the $1,200 gain)		900
		$72,700
Deductions		
Registered pension plan contributions	$4,869	
Union and professional dues	1,220	6,089
Net income		$66,611
Other deductions		
Capital gains deduction (¾ of the $1,200 gain)*		900
Taxable income		$65,711
Federal income tax calculation:		
$29,590 at 17%		$ 5,030
$29,590 at 26%		7,693
$ 6,531 at 29%		1,894
$65,711		$14,617
Tax credits:		
Canada Pension Plan contributions credit	$ 128	
Unemployment insurance premiums credit	198	
Basic personal credit	1,098	
Spousal (married) credit	915	
Charitable donations credits		
($250 at 17% and $1,350 at 29%)**	434	
Dividend credit (13⅓% of the gross-up amount of $10,000)	1,333	4,106
Basic federal tax		$10,511
3% federal surtax		315
Federal tax payable		$10,826
Add:		
Provincial tax—58% of "basic federal tax"		6,096
Total tax payable		$16,922
Less: income taxes withheld		16,000
Amount to be paid		$ 922

** Assuming the $100,000 lifetime capital gains exemption has not been reached. Also note, this exemption is no longer available after February 22, 1994.*
*** As mentioned in footnote 9, the threshold amount of $250 is decreased to $200 for 1994 and subsequent years.*
Note: Since the amount of medical expenses of $900 is less than 3% of net income, there is no tax credit for medical expenses.

INCOME TAXES: CORPORATIONS

Taxation and Tax Rates

A corporation is a separate taxable entity. Every corporation, unless specifically exempt from taxation, must file an income tax return (Form T2) within six months from the end of its taxation year, whether or not it has taxable income or owes any tax. Also, corporations are required to pay their income taxes on a monthly instalment basis. Our discussion is focussed on the ordinary business public corporations, with only brief references to certain other types of corporations for which special tax treatment applies.

As with individuals, the federal income tax rate applies to the corporation's taxable income. The tax rates for 1993 are as shown below:

Type of Business	Tax Rate
General business	28%
Manufacturing business	22%[11]
Small business	12%[12]

Also, there is a 3% surtax on federal corporate income tax that increases all the above rates by 0.8%.

In addition to federal tax, all provinces levy income tax on corporations. The provincial tax rate for 1993 for general business public corporations ranges from 9% to 17%. Also, provincial rates are lower for certain businesses, such as manufacturing and processing and small businesses.

Computation of Taxable Income of Corporations

While the taxable income of corporations is computed in much the same way as for individuals there are a number of differences. The major ones include:

1 **Tax credits of a personal nature** Corporations are not allowed tax credits of a personal nature, such as basic personal, married, dependant (for infirm dependant aged 18 and over) tax credits and medical expenses tax credits, which are allowed for individuals.

2 **Dividends received** The dividends received by a corporation from other taxable Canadian corporations are ***not*** included in the corporation's taxable income. Since these dividends are not taxable, the dividend tax credit for individuals does not apply to corporations. However, certain private corporations pay a special refundable tax on certain dividends received, which will be refunded when the corporation subsequently pays a taxable dividend to its shareholders.

---

[11] The 1994 tax rate for a manufacturing business is 21%.

[12] This low tax rate is no longer available to those corporations with taxable capital employed in Canada of $15 million or more for taxation years ending after June 30, 1994. Also, for corporations with taxable capital between $10 and $15 million, the amount subject to this low rate is reduced on a straight-line basis.

Capital gains and losses Corporations, like individuals, may deduct the ***allowable*** capital losses ***only*** to the extent of ***taxable*** capital gains. Also, corporations may carry back and forward the remaining allowable capital losses against taxable capital gains in the same manner as for individuals, as discussed earlier. However, the lifetime cumulative capital gains exemption of $100,000 for individuals is ***not*** available for corporations.[13]

Computation of Taxable Income and Federal Income Tax for Corporation Illustrated

OBJECTIVE 5 Determine the taxable income and income tax of a corporation.

To highlight some of the main features of income tax law as it applies to corporations, the computation of federal tax for Stone Corporation, a general business operation, for the 1993 taxation year follows. Remember this illustration is not an income statement and does not show items in the sequence of an income statement.

Notice the difference between accounting income ($184,000) and taxable income ($176,000)

STONE CORPORATION
Illustrative Federal Tax Computation
(In thousands of dollars)

Revenue:		
Sales		$780,000
Dividends received from taxable Canadian corporations		10,000
Total revenue		$790,000
Expenses:		
Cost of goods sold	$510,000	
Other expenses (includes capital loss of $2,000)	96,000	606,000
Income for accounting purposes		$184,000
Add back:		
Capital loss deducted as part of operating expenses		2,000
Subtotal		$186,000
Deduct (item not subject to tax)		
Dividends received from taxable Canadian corporations		10,000
Taxable income		$176,000
Federal tax computation:		
28% on $176,000	$49,280	
3% surtax (3% × $49,280)	1,478	$ 50,758
Deduct: Monthly instalment payments		50,600
Balance of federal tax payable		$ 158

Accounting Income versus Taxable Income

In the determination of ***accounting income,*** the objective is to measure business operating results as accurately as possible in accordance with generally accepted accounting principles. ***Taxable income,*** on the other hand, is a legal concept governed by statute and subject to frequent change

[13] As indicated in footnote 1, the lifetime capital gains exemption is no longer available after February 22, 1994.

by Parliament. In setting the rules for determining taxable income, Parliament is interested not only in meeting the revenue needs of government but also in achieving certain public policy objectives. Since accounting income and taxable income are determined with different purposes in mind, it is not surprising that they often differ by material amounts.

The following are some of the major areas of difference between accounting income and taxable income:

1 Certain income and expense items included in computing accounting income are either excluded or partly excluded from computing taxable income. For example, dividends received by a taxable Canadian corporation from other taxable Canadian corporations are included in accounting income but are excluded from taxable income; goodwill and organization costs incurred after 1971 may be amortized for accounting purposes, but only three-quarters of them can be amortized for tax purposes.
2 Capital gains and losses are fully included in computing accounting income, but only a portion (¾) of these gains and losses is included in computing taxable income.
3 Methods used for computing accounting income may differ from those used for computing taxable income. For example, lifo method of inventory may be used for accounting purposes, but is not allowed for tax purposes; straight-line or sum-of-the-years'-digits method of depreciation may be used for computing accounting income, but a declining balance method based on tax regulations is used to compute depreciation, called "capital cost allowance," for tax purposes.

Capital Cost Allowance

OBJECTIVE 6 Determine the amount of capital cost allowance.

There are special tax regulations for recognizing a portion of a depreciable asset as an expense each year. This expense is called ***capital cost allowance*** rather than depreciation. The recognition of capital cost allowance for tax purposes differs significantly from depreciation for accounting purposes. The main features of capital cost allowance are:

1 Depreciable assets of a similar nature are grouped into a particular class or pool.
2 Costs of additions are added to, and proceeds of disposals (up to the original cost of the asset) and capital cost allowances are deducted from, the balance of the class or pool.
3 When a class or pool has a credit balance at the end of a taxation year, the credit balance, known as "recaptured capital cost allowance," is to be included in income for tax purposes.
4 A stipulated rate is applied to the balance of each class or pool to obtain the amount of capital cost allowance for the year. However, in the year where there is net addition of assets (i.e., total addition exceeds total disposal), only one-half of such net addition is eligible for capital cost allowance for that year.

Some of the more common classes of depreciable assets and their stipulated rates are:

Class		Maximum Rate
1	Brick, stone, cement buildings, and most buildings (other than those in Classes 6, 31, or 32)	4%*
8	Machinery, equipment, and furniture**	20%
10	Automobiles, trucks, and tractors	30%

* For buildings acquired in 1988 and subsequent years. Buildings acquired prior to 1988 are in class 3, with a 5% rate.
** If the machinery and equipment are for manufacturing, they are included in class 43.

Taxpayers may claim an amount of capital cost allowance in each taxation year up to the maximum amount allowed for each class. The following example illustrates the application of the main features of capital cost allowance.

X Ltd. has a number of trucks (Class 10) used in its business operations. The beginning balance is $100,000. During the year, two trucks costing $48,000 were purchased and one old truck, with an original cost of $12,000, was sold for $8,000.

The capital cost allowance for the year is computed as follows:

Beginning balance	$100,000
Add: purchase of two trucks	48,000
	$148,000
Deduct: proceeds of disposal of one truck	8,000
Ending balance	$140,000
Capital cost allowance: 30% on beginning balance of $100,000	$ 30,000
30% on ½ of net asset addition of $40,000 [($48,000 − $8,000) × ½ × 30%)]	6,000
	$ 36,000

X Ltd. may claim a capital cost allowance for class 10 of up to a maximum of $36,000 for the year.

Deferred Income Taxes

OBJECTIVE 7 Describe the circumstances that create a liability for deferred income taxes.

We have seen that differences between generally accepted accounting principles and income tax rules can be material. Some businesses might consider it more convenient to maintain their accounting records in conformity with the tax rules, but the result would be to distort financial statements. It is clearly preferable to maintain accounting records by the principles that produce relevant information about business operations. The data in the records can then be adjusted by use of work sheets to arrive at taxable income.

When a corporation follows one method in its accounting records and financial statements but uses a different method for its income tax return, a financial reporting problem arises. The difference in method will usually have the effect of postponing the recognition of income on the tax return. The items causing this difference fall into two broad categories: permanent differences and timing (temporary) differences.

Permanent differences are revenue or expenses that enter into the computation of one type of income, but never are considered in determining the other. Most permanent differences are the result of special tax law provisions unrelated to accounting principles. For example, dividends received by a corporation from other taxable Canadian corporations are included in the determination of accounting income but are excluded from the computation of taxable income. Also, certain expenses such as political contributions are deducted from accounting income but are not deducted from the computation of taxable income.

Timing differences arise when the ***same dollar amount*** of revenue or expense is recognized for tax purposes and for accounting purposes, but the ***timing*** of the recognition under tax rules differs from that under accounting principles. For example, a company may use an accelerated method of depreciation in its income tax return but use the straight-line method in its income statement. Over the life of the depreciable asset, however, the total amount of depreciation claimed in the tax returns will be the same as that reported in the company's income statements.

Most businesses have a policy of using in their income tax returns those accounting methods that will ***accelerate as much as possible the recognition of expenses, and delay as long as possible the recognition of revenue.*** As a result of using these methods, many businesses are able to defer the recognition of significant portions of their pretax accounting income into the tax returns of future years. Hence, they are able to defer payment of the related income taxes.

Accounting for Deferred Taxes: An Illustration

When differences between pretax accounting income and taxable income are caused by timing differences, a business bases its income tax expense for the period upon its pretax accounting income. This practice achieves a proper ***matching*** of income taxes expense with the related earnings. However, some of this income taxes expense will not be paid until later years, when the income is included in future tax returns. Through timing differences, payment of part of a company's income taxes expense may be deferred on a long-term basis.

To illustrate, let us consider a very simple case involving only one timing difference. Assume that Pryor Corporation has before-tax accounting income of $600,000 in both 1995 and 1996. However, the company takes as a tax deduction in 1995 an expense of $200,000, which is not deducted as expense in the income statement until 1996. The company's accounting income, taxable income, and the actual income taxes due (assuming an average federal and provincial tax rate of 46%) are shown below.

	1996	1995
Accounting income (before income taxes)	$600,000	$600,000
Taxable income	800,000	400,000
Actual income taxes due each year at 46% rate:		
1995: $600,000 – $200,000 = $400,000 taxable income × 46%		$184,000
1996: $600,000 + $200,000 = $800,000 taxable income × 46%	$368,000	

Let us assume the Pryor Corporation reports as an expense in its income statement each year the amount of income taxes due for that year. The effect on reported net income as shown in the company's financial statements would be as follows:

Company reports actual taxes

	1996	1995
Accounting income (before income taxes)	$600,000	$600,000
Income taxes expense (amount actually due)	368,000	184,000
Net income	$232,000	$416,000
Income taxes expense as a percentage of pretax accounting income	61%	31%

The readers of Pryor Corporation's income statement might well wonder why the same $600,000 accounting income before income taxes in the two years produced such widely varying amounts of tax expense and net income.

To deal with this distortion between pretax income and after-tax income, an accounting policy known as ***interperiod income tax allocation*** is required for financial reporting purposes.[14] Briefly, the objective of income tax allocation is to ***accrue income taxes expense*** in ***relation to accounting income,*** even if the items comprising accounting income will be taxable or deductible in a different period.

In the Pryor Corporation example, this means we would report in the 1995 income statement a tax expense based on $600,000 of accounting income even though a portion of this income ($200,000) will not be subject to income tax until the second year. The effect of this accounting procedure is demonstrated by the following journal entries to record the income tax expense in each of the two years:

Entries to record income tax allocations

1995	*Income Taxes Expense*	276,000	
	Income Taxes Payable		184,000
	Deferred Income Taxes		92,000
	To record current and deferred income taxes at 46% of accounting income of $600,000.		

Deferred income taxes are a liability. As explained in Chapter 16, classification of deferred income taxes as current or long-term depends upon the nature of the items causing the tax deferral.[15]

In 1996, the timing difference will "reverse," and Pryor will report taxable income of $200,000 in excess of its pretax accounting income. Thus, the income taxes deferred in 1995 are coming due. The entry to record income taxes expense in 1996 is:

[14] For a more complete discussion of tax allocation procedures, see *CICA Handbook,* section 3470, on "Corporate income taxes."

[15] Timing differences also may require a company to pay some income taxes ***before*** the related income appears in accounting income. This situation creates an asset, which might be called Prepaid Income Taxes. In this chapter, we illustrate only the more common situation in which the payment of taxes is deferred, thereby creating a liability.

1996	*Income Taxes Expense*	276,000	
	Deferred Income Taxes	92,000	
	Income Taxes Payable		368,000
	To record income taxes at 46% of accounting income of $600,000 and to record actual income taxes due.		

Notice that as in 1995, income tax expense is based upon the pretax accounting income shown in the company's income statement.

Using these interperiod tax allocation procedures, Pryor Corporation's financial statements would report net income during the two-year period as follows:

	1996	1995
Accounting income (before income taxes)	$600,000	$600,000
Income taxes expense (tax allocation basis)	276,000	276,000
Net income	$324,000	$324,000
Income taxes expense as a percentage of pretax accounting income	46%	46%

Deferred Taxes: An Evaluation In 1996, Pryor Corporation faces the unpleasant prospect of paying an amount of income taxes that is ***greater*** than its income taxes expense for the current year. Although this situation can arise, it does not usually happen as long as a company continues to grow.

A growing company usually defers more taxes each year than the previous deferrals that are coming due. Thus, a growing company may pay less in taxes each year than the amount of its current tax expense, and its liability for deferred income taxes continues to grow. The liability for deferred taxes is, in essence, an ***interest-free loan***—capital made available to the business by selecting advantageous accounting methods for use in the company's income tax returns. Hence, deferring income taxes generally is viewed as a desirable business strategy.

CASE IN POINT The balance sheets of many companies showed large amounts of deferred income taxes. As of a recent year, the deferred income taxes for Petro-Canada were $460 million; Canadian Pacific, $420 million; Dofasco, $394 million; and Bow Valley Industries, $133 million.

TAX PLANNING OPPORTUNITIES

Income tax laws have become so complex that careful tax planning has become a way of life for most business firms. Almost all companies today engage professional tax specialists to review the tax aspects of major business decisions and to develop plans for legally minimizing income taxes. We will now consider some areas in which tax planning may offer substantial benefits.

Form of Business Organization

OBJECTIVE 8 Explain how tax planning is used in choosing the form of business organization, timing and nature of transactions, and the capital structure.

Tax factors should be carefully considered at the time a business is organized. As a sole proprietor or partner, a business owner will pay taxes at individual rates on the business income earned in any year ***whether or not it is withdrawn from the business.*** On the other hand, corporations deduct salaries paid to owners for services but cannot deduct dividends paid to shareholders. Both ***salaries and dividends*** are taxable income to the persons receiving them. However, the tax on dividends is reduced by a dividend tax credit.

These and other factors must be weighed in deciding in any given situation whether the corporate or noncorporate form of business organization is preferable. There is no simple answer, even considering only these basic differences. To illustrate, suppose that Able, a married man, starts a small business that he expects will produce, before any compensation to himself and before income taxes, an average annual income of $80,000. Able plans to recognize a salary of $20,000 and to withdraw all income from the business. The combined corporate and individual taxes (based on 1993 tax rates) under the corporate and sole proprietorship form of business organization are summarized below (surtax is excluded to simplify the computations).

Which form of business organization produces a lower tax?

		Corporation	Sole Proprietorship
Business income		$80,000	$80,000
Salary to Able		20,000	
		$60,000	$80,000
Corporate taxes (on the $60,000 taxable income of a small business)			
Federal 12%	$7,200		
Provincial 10%*	6,000	13,200	
Amount to Able (the $46,800 as dividends)		$46,800	$80,000
Combined corporate and individual tax:			
Corporate tax on $60,000 taxable income		$13,200	
Individual tax (assume a total deduction of $8,500, tax credits of $2,123, and dividend tax credit of $7,800)			
On Able's $20,000 salary and $46,800 dividends		9,382	
On Able's $80,000 share of business income			$22,393
Total income taxes on business income		$22,582	$22,393

* The more common rate for 1993.

Under these assumptions, the formation of a corporation is not favourable from an income tax viewpoint. However, the tax difference between the corporation and sole proprietorship of $189 is very small. Another factor to be considered is that, with the corporation, Able can postpone the amount of tax payable by retaining the income in the corporation rather than paying it out as dividends. Of course, factors other than income tax (such as limited liability) must be considered in deciding whether to incorporate the business.

Planning Business Transactions to Minimize or Postpone Income Taxes

Business transactions may often be arranged in such a way as to produce favourable tax treatment. For example, timing of disposal of investments (usually at or near the year-end date) in securities can postpone income taxes because capital losses from securities can be offset against capital gains. However, the sale of an investment in securities to generate a capital loss must not be accompanied by the purchase of the same securities within 30 days or the capital loss would be disallowed as it would be considered as a "wash transaction."

Sometimes sellers try to arrange a transaction one way to their tax benefit and buyers try to shape it another way to produce tax savings for them. Income tax effects thus become a part of price negotiation. For example, in buying business property, the purchasers will try to allocate as much of the cost of the property to the building and as little to the land as possible, since building costs can be depreciated for tax purposes. Similarly, in buying a business, the buyers will want as much as possible of the total purchase price to be attributed to inventories or to depreciable assets rather than goodwill. The cost of goods sold and depreciation are deductible against income, whereas only three-quarters of goodwill can be amortized for tax purposes. Thus, the main point is: ***any failure to consider tax effects on major business transactions can be costly.***

Tax Planning in the Choice of Financial Structure

In deciding upon the best means of raising capital to start or expand a business, consideration should be given to income taxes. Different forms of business financing produce different amounts of tax expense. Interest on debt, for example, is ***fully deductible,*** but dividends on preferred or common stock are not. This factor operates as a strong incentive to finance expansion by borrowing.

Let us suppose that a company subject to a 45% marginal tax rate needs $100,000 to invest in productive assets on which it can earn a 16% annual return. If the company obtains the needed money by issuing $100,000 in 9% preferred stock, it will earn ***after taxes*** only $8,800, which is not even enough to cover the $9,000 preferred dividend. (This after-tax amount is computed as $16,000 income less taxes at 45% of $16,000.)

Now let us assume, on the other hand, that the company borrowed $100,000 at 12% interest. (Interest rate is usually higher than dividend rate because interest is tax deductible and dividend provides a dividend tax credit.) The additional gross income would be $16,000 but interest expense of $12,000 would be deducted, leaving taxable income of $4,000. The tax on the $4,000 at 45% would be $1,800, leaving after-tax income of $2,200. Analysis along these lines is also needed in choosing between debt financing and financing by issuing common stock.

CHAPTER REVIEW

KEY TERMS INTRODUCED OR EMPHASIZED IN CHAPTER 18

Basic federal tax The gross amount of federal tax minus tax credits. The basic federal tax is the basis for computing provincial tax.

Capital cost allowance The amount of expense for depreciable assets for tax purposes.

Capital gain or loss The difference between the cost or adjusted-cost base of a capital asset and the amount received from its sale.

Dividend tax credit This credit is intended to minimize the impact of "double taxation" on corporate income. It is computed by applying 13⅓% to the taxable (gross-up) amount of dividends and is deducted from federal income tax.

Gross federal tax Taxable income times federal tax rate equals gross federal tax.

Interperiod tax allocation Allocation of income tax expense among accounting periods because of timing differences between accounting income and taxable income. Causes income tax expense reported in financial statements to be in logical relation to accounting income.

Marginal tax rate The tax rate to which a taxpayer is subject on the additional dollar of income received.

Tax credit An amount to be subtracted from gross federal income tax to arrive at basic federal tax, including credits for Canada Pension Plan contributions, unemployment insurance premiums, basic personal, married, dependant (infirm and aged 18 and over), tuition fees, and charitable donations.

Tax planning A systematic process of legally minimizing income taxes by considering in advance the tax consequences of alternative business or investment actions.

Taxable income The computed amount to which the appropriate tax rate is to be applied to arrive at the gross amount of federal tax.

Total income An individual's world income from all sources, including income from office, employment, business, property and pension, and capital gain.

ASSIGNMENT MATERIAL

DISCUSSION QUESTIONS

1 What are some broad objectives of the federal income tax legislation other than providing revenue for the government?

2 List the five most striking characteristics of the 1988 tax reform legislation.

3 List three examples of tax credits other than dividend tax credit.

Jan./99 → 4 Explain the differences between ***tax planning*** and ***tax evasion,*** and give an example of each.

5 What are the major classes of taxpayers under the federal income tax law?

6 It has been claimed that corporate income is subject to "double taxation." Explain the meaning of this expression, and indicate whether there is provision in the tax law to minimize it.

7 Why is the income tax system described as one of ***self-assessment?*** What means do tax authorities have of enforcing this system?

8 Taxes are characterized as either ***progressive, proportional,*** or ***regressive*** with respect to any given base. Describe an income tax rate structure that would fit each of these characterizations.

9 State whether you agree with the following statement and explain your reasoning: A person in a very high tax bracket who makes a cash contribution to a charitable organization will reduce his or her federal income tax liability by more than the amount of the donation.

10 State the federal income tax formula for individuals, beginning with total income and ending with basic federal tax.

11 From an individual taxpayer's viewpoint, it is better to have a $10,000 capital gain than $10,000 of ordinary income. Explain.

12 Cite two examples to illustrate the broadening of the tax base originated from the tax reform legislation.

13 Even when a corporation uses the accrual method of accounting, taxable income may differ from accounting income. Give four ***examples*** of differences between the tax treatment and accounting treatment of items that are included in the determination of income.

14 Under what circumstances is the accounting procedure known as ***interperiod income tax allocation*** appropriate? Explain the objective of this procedure.

15 The depreciation expense computed by Zane Corporation as the capital cost allowance (permitted by the income tax law) appeared in the tax return as $150,000. In the accounting records and financial statements, Zane's depreciation was computed on the straight-line basis and amounted to $100,000. Under interperiod tax allocation procedures, would Zane's balance sheet show deferred income taxes as a debit or credit? Explain.

16 List some tax factors to be considered in deciding whether to organize a new business as a corporation or as a partnership.

17 Explain the principal factors that should be considered by a taxpayer in determining ***when*** it would be most advantageous to sell an investment that will result in the recognition of a capital loss.

18 Explain how the corporate income tax makes debt financing in general more attractive than financing through the issuance of preferred stock.

19 Some of the decisions that business owners must make in the organization and operation of a business will affect the amount of income taxes to be paid. List some of these decisions that affect the amount of income taxes legally payable.

MULTIPLE CHOICE QUESTIONS

1 Which of the following is applicable to the income tax system?

a The only objective of income tax laws is to raise as much revenue as possible to finance government spending.

b A taxpayer is required to pay instalment tax if tax withheld at source is greater than $2,000.

c One of the most striking characteristics of the 1988 tax reform legislation is the lowering of tax rates and the broadening of the tax base.

d The three classes of taxpayers are: individuals, partnerships, and corporations.

2 In preparing the income tax return for an individual taxpayer:

a Income taxes withheld from an individual's salary are deducted from total income.

b Income from sources outside Canada must be included in the determination of total income.

c Income from illegal sources is excluded from the computation of total income.

d Receipt of a large refund each year indicates better tax planning than receipt of a small refund.

3 Which of the following are eligible for tax credits? (More than one answer may be correct.)

a Registered pension plan contributions and unemployment insurance premiums.

b Tuition fees, charitable donations, and education amount.

c Basic personal amount for the taxpayer, Canada Pension Plan contributions, and unemployment insurance premium.

d Medical expenses, union dues, and allowable capital losses.

4 When a business is organized as a corporation:

a Income taxes expense recorded in the accounting records is based upon accounting income and may differ from the income taxes liability shown in the corporate income tax return.

b The treatment of capital gains and losses is the same as for individuals, including the cumulative capital gain exemption of $100,000.

c Taxable income is the same as net income before income taxes in the income statement.

d Dividends received from other taxable Canadian corporations must be included in the corporation's taxable income.

5 Which of the following are valid statements regarding tax planning and the choice of business organization? (More than one answer may be correct.)

a When a business is organized as a corporation, no income tax is paid on earnings that remain invested in the business.

b In computing a corporation's taxable income, the corporation may deduct salaries paid to owners, but may not deduct dividends.

c When a business is organized as a sole proprietorship, the owner must pay taxes at individual rates on the entire amount of business income, regardless of amounts withdrawn by the owner.

d An individual who organizes a business as a corporation must pay individual income taxes on any salary and dividends received from the corporation after deducting the appropriate amount of dividend tax credit.

EXERCISES

EXERCISE 18-1
Accounting and Tax Terminology

Listed below are nine technical accounting and tax terms introduced in this chapter:

Capital gain	*Taxable income*	*Interperiod tax allocation*
Tax credit	*Gross federal tax*	*Cash basis of accounting*
Basic federal tax	*Tax planning*	*Capital cost allowance*

Each of the following statements may (or may not) describe one of these technical terms. For each statement, indicate the term described, or answer "None" if the statement does not correctly describe any of the terms.

- **a** Net income minus other deductions, which serves as a basis to compute gross federal tax.
- **b** Taxable income multiplied by an appropriate federal tax rate.
- **c** Gross federal tax minus tax credits.
- **d** Income tax recognized each period as a constant percentage of net sales.
- **e** Causes income tax expense reported in financial statements to be in logical relationship to accounting income.
- **f** Profit from disposal of such assets as stock and bonds acquired as long-term investments.
- **g** Revenue recorded when received in cash and expenses recorded in period payment is made.
- **h** An amount to be subtracted from gross federal tax.
- **i** Depreciation calculated according to tax law and regulations.

EXERCISE 18-2
Inclusion or Exclusion?

Some of the following items should be included in income; others on the list should be excluded. For each item listed, write the identifying letter and the word ***included*** or ***excluded*** to show whether the item belongs in income on the income tax return of an individual.

- **a** Kickbacks received by automobile salespeople from insurance brokers to whom they referred customers.
- **b** Dividends from investment in a taxable Canadian corporation.
- **c** Compensation received for damages suffered in automobile accident.
- **d** Gain on sale of shares of Canadian Ltd. common stock.
- **e** Gift from an uncle.
- **f** Money received from lottery winnings.
- **g** Tips received by waiter.
- **h** Interest received on investment bonds.

EXERCISE 18-3
Deductible or Nondeductible?

Susan Rooney has a total income of $68,000 and a net income of $54,000. For each item listed, write the identifying letter and the word ***deductible*** or ***nondeductible.***

a Interest paid on instalment contract on automobile	$ 180
b Gift to an unemployed relative	300
c Professional dues	660
d Contribution to Red Cross	575
e Cost of commuting between home and work	800
f Canada Pension Plan contributions	753
g Unemployment insurance premiums	1,162
h Registered pension plan contributions	4,800
i Medical expenses (not covered by insurance)	500
j Cash stolen while on business trip	80
k Interest paid on a bank loan for investment purposes	450
l Safety deposit box fee (to keep investment certificates)	35

EXERCISE 18-4
Determine Total, Net, and Taxable Income, and Federal Tax for an Individual

Angela Lambert has the following information for her first tax return, one year after graduation from a top university.

Salary	*$88,000*
Interest from a bank account	*388*
Canada Pension Plan contributions	*753*
Unemployment insurance premiums	*1,162*
Professional dues	*800*
Registered pension plan contributions	*3,500*
Basic personal tax credits	*1,098*
Dental expenses	*2,980*
Charitable donations	*2,600*

Compute (a) total income, (b) net income, (c) taxable income, (d) gross federal tax, and (e) basic federal tax for Angela Lambert. The federal tax rates are assumed to be: 17% the first $29,590, 26% on the second $29,590, and 29% on the remaining taxable income.

EXERCISE 18-5
Determine Taxable Income for an Individual

Pier Fiorino has the following sources of income for 1993:

Interest from Canada Savings Bonds	*$ 1,000*
Dividends from taxable Canadian corporations	*12,000*
Gains on sales of shares in Canadian National Ltd.	*3,000*

Compute the ***net*** amount that should be included as taxable income, assuming no capital gain was reported in prior years.

EXERCISE 18-6
Determine Taxable Income and Federal Tax Liability for a Corporation

Sunset Limited reports the following income during Year 1:

Operating income (after deducting depreciation of $100,000)	*$600,000*
Capital gains	*180,000*
Dividends received from taxable Canadian corporations	*60,000*
Capital cost allowances	*116,000*

Compute the taxable income and ***federal*** income tax liability for Sunset Limited for Year 1. Assume a 28% federal tax rate and ignore any surtax.

EXERCISE 18-7
Interperiod Tax Allocation

Sea King Corporation deducted on its tax return for Year 1 an expense of $50,000 that was not recognized as an expense for accounting purposes until Year 2. The corporation's accounting income before income taxes in each of the two years was $485,000. The company uses tax allocation procedures.

a Prepare the journal entries required at the end of Year 1 and Year 2 to record income tax expense, assuming a combined federal and provincial tax rate of 46%.

b Prepare a two-column schedule showing the net income to appear on the financial statements for Year 1 and Year 2, assuming tax allocation procedures are used. Also prepare a similar schedule on the assumption that tax allocation procedures are not used.

PROBLEMS

Group A

PROBLEM 18A-1
Inclusion in or Exclusion from Income?

State whether each item listed below should be included in or excluded from an individual's income for federal income tax purposes. Add explanatory comments if needed.

1 Lottery winnings.
2 Cash dividends received on stock of Canadian Ltd.
3 Proceeds of life insurance policy received on death of a taxpayer.
4 Tips received by a door attendant at a luxury hotel.
5 Income from a business of an illegal nature.
6 Unemployment insurance benefits.
7 Drawing received from a proprietorship in excess of its income.
8 Income from personal injury awards.
9 Interest received on a savings account in Scotia Bank.
10 Gain on sale of Loris Ltd. shares of common stock.
11 Painted a building owned by the creditor in return for the cancellation of a note payable of $1,000.
12 Las Vegas vacation paid by employer as reward for outstanding service.

PROBLEM 18A-2
Deductible or Not Deductible?

State whether each item listed below is deductible or not deductible by an individual for federal income tax purposes, and if deductible, whether it is from total income or net income, or as a tax credit.

1 Fees for preparation of personal income tax return.
2 Lawyer's fee for appealing an assessment by Revenue Canada, Taxation.
3 Registered pension plan contributions.
4 Professional membership fee.
5 Interest on a loan that was used to invest in a taxable Canadian corporation.
6 Interest paid on mortgage covering personal residence.
7 Capital loss on the sale of securities.
8 Life insurance premium paid by a taxpayer.
9 Lottery losses.
10 Expenses incurred in moving from Calgary to Vancouver to accept a new position with a different company, not reimbursed by employer.
11 Alimony paid.
12 Education amount.

PROBLEM 18A-3
Determine Income Tax for an Individual

The following information is related to Gloria Hoysum, a resident of a province with a tax rate of 58%.

Income:	
Salary from employment	*$70,000*
Director's fee (on the board of directors of Toysun Ltd.)	*8,000*
Dividends from taxable Canadian corporations	*6,000*
Interest from savings account with Bank of Nova Scotia	*600*
Gain on sale of shares of Halifax Ltd.	*1,800*

Withholdings:	
Income taxes	22,000
Canada Pension Plan contributions	753
Unemployment insurance premiums	1,162
Contribution to a registered pension plan	4,980
Disbursements:	
Charitable donations	3,200
Professional membership fees	1,200
Others:	
Loss on sale of shares of Sydney Mines Ltd.	600
Lottery losses	890
Tax credits relating to the taxpayer	1,098

INSTRUCTIONS Compute Hoysum's federal and provincial income tax for the year by using the following federal tax rates: 17% on the first $29,590, 26% on the second $29,590, and 29% on the remaining amount. Assume that Hoysum had not reported any capital gains or losses in prior years and that there is a 3% federal surtax on basic federal tax and a 5% surtax on basic federal tax in excess of $12,500. The provincial rate is 58%.

PROBLEM 18A-4 Determine Capital Cost Allowance, Federal Tax, and Deferred Tax

The following information is related to Macri Corporation for the current year:

Operating income (before depreciation, dividends, capital gains, and capital losses)	$980,000
Depreciation (automobiles and trucks, straight-line basis)	150,000
Dividends received from taxable Canadian corporations	80,000
Capital gains from sale of securities	30,000
Capital losses from sale of securities	50,000
Automobiles and trucks (class 10, maximum rate 30%):	
Beginning balance	700,000
Additions during the last month of the year	350,000
Proceeds from disposal of trucks (original cost $460,000) during the year	250,000

INSTRUCTIONS

a Compute the amount of capital cost allowance for the current year.

b Compute the federal income tax for the current year, based on a 28% tax rate.

c Compute the amount of federal income tax deferred by claiming the maximum capital cost allowance rather than the amount of depreciation for accounting purposes.

PROBLEM 18A-5 Determine Accounting and Taxable Income, Income Tax and Deferred Tax, and Tax Advantage of Financing Method

The accounting records of Garden Corporation included the following information for the current year:

Net sales	$8,600,000
Cost of goods sold	6,000,000
Dividends received from a taxable Canadian corporation	53,000
Operating expenses (including depreciation of $250,000)	1,700,000
Capital gains from sales of securities	28,000
Capital losses from sales of securities	12,000
Capital cost allowance	360,000

Garden is considering expanding its facilities as a result of increased sales, financed either by issuing $500,000, 12% bonds or 9% cumulative preferred stock.

INSTRUCTIONS

a Compute the accounting income for the current year.

b Compute the taxable income for the current year.

c Compute the federal and provincial income taxes for the current year. Assume that the federal rate is 28% and provincial rate is 14%.

d Prepare the journal entry to record the current and deferred income taxes for the year.

e Explain which method of financing the $500,000 expansion is more beneficial to the company from an income tax viewpoint.

Group B

PROBLEM 18B-1 Inclusion in or Exclusion from Income?

State whether each item listed below should be included in or excluded from an individual's income for federal income tax purposes. Add explanatory comments if they are necessary.

1 Share of income from partnership in excess of drawings.
2 An honorarium of $100 for a speech to charitable organizations.
3 Interest received on Canada Savings Bonds.
4 Salary received from a corporation by a shareholder who owns directly or indirectly all the shares of the corporation's outstanding stock.
5 Amount received as damages in a libel lawsuit.
6 Trip to Hawaii given by employer as reward for outstanding service.
7 Taxpayer owed $1,500 on a note payable. During the current year the taxpayer painted a building owned by the creditor, and in turn the creditor cancelled the note.
8 Gain on sale of taxable Canadian Ltd. capital stock.
9 Value of a colour TV set won as a prize in a quiz contest.
10 Inheritance received on death of a rich uncle.
11 Cash dividends received from Canadian Oil Ltd.
12 Unemployment insurance benefits.

PROBLEM 18B-2 Deductible or Not Deductible?

State whether each of the following items is deductible or not deductible by an individual for federal income tax purposes, and if deductible, whether it is from total income or net income, or as a tax credit.

1 Tuition fees.
2 Fee paid to chartered accountant for services in contesting assessment of additional income taxes by Revenue Canada, Taxation.
3 Expenses incurred in moving across country to accept a position with different employer. Not reimbursed.
4 Charitable donations.
5 Loss on sale of investment in securities.
6 Cost of commuting between home and place of employment.
7 Registered retirement savings plan contributions for spouse.
8 Unemployment insurance premiums.
9 Registered pension plan contributions.

10 Interest paid on mortgage on personal residence.
11 Union dues.
12 Interest expense for a loan to finance investment in securities.

PROBLEM 18B-3
Determine Income Tax for an Individual

Christine Levy, a resident of a province with a 58% tax rate, asks you to prepare her tax return for the current year. She provides you with the following information:

Income:	
Salary from employment	*$68,000*
Dividends from taxable Canadian corporations	*3,000*
Interest from Canada Savings Bonds	*1,200*
Gains on sale of shares of B.C. Ltd.'s common stock	*2,000*
Rental income (net)	*8,000*
Withholdings:	
Income taxes	*20,000*
Canada Pension Plan contributions	*753*
Unemployment insurance premiums	*1,162*
Registered pension plan contributions	*4,680*
Disbursements:	
Dental expenses	*2,200*
Charitable donations	*2,500*
Professional membership fees	*800*
Others:	
Loss on sale of shares in Victoria Mines Ltd.	*5,000*
Lottery winnings	*9,600*
Basic personal tax credit	*1,098*

INSTRUCTIONS

Compute Levy's federal and provincial income taxes for the year by using the following federal tax rates: 17% on the first $29,590, 26% on the second $29,590 and 29% on the balance. There is also a 3% federal surtax on basic federal tax and a 5% surtax on basic federal tax in excess of $12,500.

PROBLEM 18B-4
Determine Capital Cost Allowance, Federal Tax, and Deferred Tax

Colitti Limited has the following operation results for the current year:

Operating income (after depreciation of $138,000 and before capital gains and losses and dividends)	*$800,000*
Net capital gains from sale of securities (capital gains of $30,000 less capital losses of $18,000)	*12,000*
Dividends received from taxable Canadian corporations	*45,000*

The company's only depreciation assets are machinery, equipment, and furniture. The ending balance from last year's tax return was $600,000. During the current year, the company added equipment and furniture at a cost of $450,000 and sold a machine (original cost $66,000) for $50,000. The capital cost allowance rate for tax purposes is 20%.

INSTRUCTIONS

a Compute the amount of capital cost allowance for the current year.

b Compute the federal income tax for the current year, based on 28% tax rate.

c Compute the amount of federal income tax deferred by claiming the maximum capital cost allowance rather than the amount of depreciation for accounting purposes.

PROBLEM 18B-5
Determine Accounting and Taxable Income, Income Tax and Deferred Tax, and Tax Advantage of Financing Method

The following information appears in the records of Macor Corporation for the current year:

Net sales	*$988,000*
Cost of goods sold	*707,000*
Operating expenses (including depreciation of $90,000)	*151,000*
Dividends received from taxable Canadian corporations	*38,000*
Net capital losses from sale of securities (capital losses of $37,000 less capital gains of $19,000)	*18,000*
Capital cost allowance	*190,000*

The company is considering whether it should issue bonds or cumulative preferred stock to finance its expanded operations. The amount needed would be $600,000. The interest rate would be 11% and the dividend rate would be at 8%.

INSTRUCTIONS

a Compute the accounting income for the current year.

b Compute the taxable income for the current year.

c Compute the federal and provincial income taxes for the current year, based on the respective rates of 28% and 14%.

d Prepare the journal entry to record the current and deferred income taxes for the year.

e Explain which method of financing the $600,000 expansion is more beneficial to the company from an income tax viewpoint.

ANALYTICAL AND DECISION PROBLEMS AND CASES

A&D 18-1
What's Wrong with My Tax Return?

After one look at his tax return, Tim Pearl is stunned by the income tax he has to pay. "After I inherited $500,000 from Uncle Tom and won a $30,000 lottery this year, I thought I was O.K. for life. Now, this year's tax is more than double last year's and I have to pay thousands of dollars on April 30. I just don't have this much cash every April 30 to pay the taxes," Tim complains to his wife. The tax return that Tim is complaining about shows the following information:

Total income:	
Salary	*$ 46,000*
Dividends received	*22,000*
Interest	*25,500*
Capital gains	*6,000*
Lottery winnings	*30,000*
	$129,500
Deduct: union dues	*500*
Net income and taxable income	*$129,000*

Federal income tax calculation:		
$ 29,590 at 17%		*$ 5,030*
29,590 at 26%		*7,693*
69,820 at 29%		*20,248*
$129,000		*$ 32,971*
Tax credits		
Registered pension plan contributions (17% × $3,820)	*$ 649*	
Canada Pension Plan contributions (17% × $753)	*128*	
Unemployment insurance premium (17% × $1,162)	*198*	
Basic personal amount (17% × $6,456)	*1,098*	
Married amount (17% × $5,380)	*915*	
Medical (17% × $2,188)	*372*	*3,360*
Basic federal tax		*$ 29,611*
Provincial tax: 57% of basic federal tax		*16,878*
Total tax payable		*$ 46,489*
Deduct: amount withheld (on salary)		*10,966*
Tax payable		*$ 35,523*

INSTRUCTIONS

Explain how each of the errors in Tim's return should be corrected. (Do ***not*** prepare a corrected return.) Assume that Tim has not claimed any capital gains before and is subject to a 57% provincial tax and federal tax of: 17% on the first $29,590, 26% on the second $29,590, and 29% on the remaining taxable income. (Ignore surtax.) Also, comment on Tim's concern regarding the cash need on April 30 in future years.

A&D 18-2 Investors Choose between Debt and Equity

Bill and Hannah Bailey own a successful small company, Bailey Corporation. The outstanding capital stock consists of 1,000 shares, of which 400 shares are owned by Bill and 600 by Hannah. In order to finance a new branch operation, the corporation needs an additional $100,000 in cash. Bill and Hannah have this amount on deposit with a bank and intend to put these personal funds into the corporation in order to establish the new branch. They will either arrange for the corporation to issue to them an additional 1,000 shares of stock, or they will make a loan to the corporation at an interest rate of 12%.

Income before taxes of the corporation has been consistently averaging $150,000 a year, and annual dividends of $64,000 have been paid regularly on the $100,000 of capital stock. It is expected that the new branch will cause income before taxes to increase by $30,000. If new common stock is issued to finance the expansion, the total annual dividend of $64,000 will be continued unchanged. If a loan of $100,000 is arranged, the dividend will be reduced by $12,000, the amount of annual interest on the loan.

INSTRUCTIONS

a From the income tax standpoint of Bill and Hannah Bailey (with a federal marginal tax rate of 29%), would there be any savings as between the stock issuance and the loan? Explain.

b From the standpoint of getting their money out of the corporation (assuming that the new branch is profitable), should Bill and Hannah choose capital stock or a loan for the infusion of new funds to the corporation?

c Prepare a two-column schedule, with one column headed If New Stock Is Used and the other headed If Loan Is Used. For each of these proposed methods of financing, show (1) the present corporate income ***before taxes;*** (2) the corporate income ***before taxes*** after the expansion; (3) the corporate income taxes (12% federal tax rate) after the expansion; and (4) the corporate net income after the expansion.

A&D 18-3
Tax Advantage: Sole Proprietorship versus Corporation

Stephen Glenn is in the process of organizing a business that is expected to produce, before any compensation to him and before income taxes, an income of $98,000 per year. In deciding whether to operate as a sole proprietorship or as a corporation, he is willing to make the choice on the basis of the relative income tax advantage under either form of organization.

If the business is organized as a sole proprietorship, Glenn plans to withdraw the entire income of $98,000 each year.

If the business is organized as a corporation, Glenn will own all the shares and will pay himself a salary of $32,000. He will distribute the remaining after-tax income as dividends.

It may be assumed that the accounting income and the taxable income for the corporation would be the same and that the corporation would be qualified as a small business for income tax purposes.

Glenn is a resident of a province where the tax rate for individuals is 58% and has a total deduction of $8,000, and a total tax credit (not including any dividend tax credit) of $1,800.

INSTRUCTIONS

Determine the relative income tax advantage to Stephen Glenn of operating the business as a sole proprietorship or as a corporation, and make a recommendation as to the form of organization he should adopt. Would it be beneficial to Glenn, from an income tax viewpoint, to keep the remaining after-tax income in the corporation rather than distribute it as dividend? Assume a combined federal and provincial tax rate of 20% for a corporation qualified as a small business and that the federal income tax rates for individuals are: 17% for the first $29,590, 26% for the second $29,590, and 29% on the balance. (Ignore surtax.)

CHAPTER

19 Statement of Changes in Financial Position

In this chapter we introduce a new major financial statement—a statement of changes in financial position. First, we differentiate this statement from the balance sheet and the income statement. Second, we explain the nature and objective of, as well as the disclosure and presentation requirements for, a statement of changes in financial position. Third, we explain how cash flows are determined and the underlying rationale. Fourth, we show step-by-step how a statement of changes in financial position can be developed, using both a simple and a comprehensive case. Finally, we demonstrate how a statement of changes in a financial position may be analyzed and interpreted. Also, the T account method for the preparation of the statement of changes in financial position is presented in Appendix B.

Learning Objectives

After studying this chapter you should be able to:

1. *Differentiate a statement of changes in financial position from an income statement and a balance sheet.*
2. *Explain the nature and objective of the statement of changes in financial position.*
3. *Explain the disclosure and presentation requirements for a statement of changes in financial position.*
4. *Explain how cash flows are determined and why.*
5. *Develop a statement of changes in financial position—a simple and a comprehensive illustration.*
6. *Analyze and interpret a statement of changes in financial position.*

OBJECTIVE 1 Differentiate a statement of changes in financial position from an income statement and a balance sheet.

In Chapter 1, we introduced two key financial objectives of every business organization: ***operating profitably*** and ***staying solvent.*** Operating profitably means increasing the amount of the owners' equity through the activities of the business; in short, providing the owners with a satisfactory return on their investment. Staying solvent means being able to pay the debts and obligations of the business as they come due.

An income statement is designed to measure the success or failure of the business in achieving its objective of profitable operations. To some extent, a balance sheet shows whether or not the business is solvent. It shows, for example, the nature and amounts of current assets and current liabilities. From this information, users of the financial statements may compute such measures of solvency as the current ratio and the amount of working capital.

However, assessing the ability of a business to remain solvent involves more than just evaluating the liquid resources on hand at the balance sheet date. In this chapter we introduce a major financial statement, the ***statement of changes in financial position,*** which provides ***additional*** information on the solvency and liquidity of a business. Liquidity means the ability to generate and maintain an adequate amount of the most liquid financial resources—cash and cash equivalents. Thus, this statement complements the balance sheet and the income statement.

STATEMENT OF CHANGES IN FINANCIAL POSITION

Nature and Objective

OBJECTIVE 2 Explain the nature and objective of the statement of changes in financial position.

A statement of changes in financial position summarizes the operating, financing, and investing activities of a business for a period on a ***cash basis*** (i.e., cash and cash equivalents).[1] Thus, it explains how and why the cash position of a business has changed during a period. The objective of this statement is to provide information to financial statement users to assess the liquidity and solvency of a business, that is, its ability to generate cash from internal and external sources to finance its operations and investments.[2] With this information on how cash has flowed into the business and how cash has been used, we can begin to answer such important questions as: Do the normal operations of the business generate sufficient cash to enable the company to continue paying dividends? Did the company have to borrow to finance the acquisition of new plant assets, or was it able to generate the cash from current operations? Is the business becoming more or less solvent? And perhaps the most puzzling question: How can a ***profitable*** business be running low on cash? Even though a business operates profitably, its cash may decline and the business may even become insolvent.

The statement of changes in financial position gives us answers to these questions, because it shows in detail the amount of cash inflows (or sources) and outflows (or uses) relating to the operating, financing, and investing activities throughout the year. In fact, this statement is also called a "cash flow statement," a "statement of changes in cash resources,"

[1] CICA, *CICA Handbook* (Toronto), section 1540.01, 1540.02, and 1540.03.

[2] The terms "operations" and "operating activities" are used interchangeably.

and a "statement of changes in cash position." However, the most commonly used title for this statement is the ***statement of changes in financial position.***[3]

Prior to 1985, the statement of changes in financial position was prepared on a working capital (current assets less current liabilities) basis, that is, it focussed on the sources and uses of working capital. In September, 1985, the Accounting Standards Board, through Section 1540 of the *CICA Handbook,* recommended that the statement of changes in financial position should be prepared on a basis of cash rather than of working capital. The reason for this change is to accommodate the financial statement users' increasing interest and preference for information on cash flows.

Cash Defined

Section 1540 of the *CICA Handbook* recommends that the statement of changes in financial position "should report the changes in ***cash and cash equivalents*** resulting from the activities of the enterprise during the period." (Emphasis added.) Thus, this statement shows the changes not only for cash but also for cash equivalents. Cash and cash equivalents are described in Section 1540 as follows: "Cash and cash equivalents would normally include cash, net of short-term borrowings, and temporary investments and may, in some cases, include ***certain other elements of working capital when they are equivalent to cash.***" (Emphasis added.) It should be noted that it is the short-term ***borrowings*** (such as bank loans), not short-term debts (such as accounts payable), that are included in the calculation of cash and cash equivalents.

Unfortunately, Section 1540 neither identifies these "other elements" nor explains the conditions under which these elements are considered as equivalent to cash. It has been suggested that these elements would include such working capital items as "receivables, inventories, and payables when they are equivalent to cash."[4]

Disclosure and Presentation

OBJECTIVE 3 ***Explain the disclosure and presentation requirements for a statement of changes in financial position.***

While the exact format of the statement of changes in financial position may vary from company to company, Section 1540 stipulates the items that should be disclosed and the manner in which these items should be presented. To ensure that the statement of changes in financial position is as informative as possible, Section 1540 recommends that it disclose the components of cash and cash equivalents and that it contain separate disclosures of at least the following items:

1 Cash from operations: the amount of cash from operations should be reconciled to the income statement, or the components of cash from operations should be disclosed.[5]

---

3 According to the CICA's *Financial Reporting in Canada,* 20th ed. (Toronto), 1993, p. 212, of the 300 companies surveyed, 205 used this title.

4 Sam Marinucci, "Changes to Statement of Changes," *CA Magazine,* October, 1985, p. 68.

5 *Financial Reporting in Canada,* p. 213. Of the 300 companies surveyed, 294 reconcile the amount of cash from operations to net income in the income statement. This approach is used here in Chapter 19.

2 Cash flows resulting from discontinued operations.
3 Cash flows resulting from extraordinary items.
4 Outlays for acquisition and proceeds on disposal of assets, by major category, not included in **1, 2** or **3** above.
5 The issue, assumption, redemption, and repayment of debt not included in **1, 2** or **3** above.
6 The issue, redemption, and acquisition of share capital (capital stock).
7 The payment of dividends, identifying separately dividends paid by subsidiaries to non-controlling interests.

Furthermore, it recommends that the above items be classified into three categories: ***operating, financing,*** and ***investing.*** Cash flows from ***operating activities*** relate to cash from operations and would include net income (or income from continuing operations if there are discontinued operations and extraordinary items) and changes in noncash current accounts. Cash flows from ***financing activities*** refer to those items affecting the size and composition of a company's long-term debt and equity capital structure and would include items **5** and **6** above. Also, cash dividends (item **7** above) are usually treated as a financing activity even though Section 1540 of the *CICA Handbook* allows a choice of presenting them as a financing activity, as an operating activity, or as an activity apart from both financing and operating.[6] It is more logical to treat cash dividends as a financing activity because they are an important factor in attracting equity capital. The amount of cash dividends affects the market price of a company's stock and the ability of the company to raise equity capital. Cash flows from ***investing activities*** pertain to those items affecting the non-current assets such as long-term investments, plant, and equipment implied in item **4** above.

Certain financing and investing activities such as the acquisition of plant assets or long-term investments by issuing long-term debt or capital stock, the conversion of long-term debt to equity or of preferred stock to common stock, and stock dividends where the shareholder has an option of receiving cash or shares (optional stock dividend), even though they do not involve cash, are to be disclosed, since the effect of these activities is "similar to a cash inflow followed immediately by a cash outflow, or vice versa."[7] These activities are often referred to as ***exchange transactions.***

While most transactions affecting ***only long-term (noncurrent) accounts*** are exchange transactions, there are four exceptions: (1) stock dividends where shareholders can only receive shares of capital stock (non-optional stock dividends); (2) stock splits; (3) transfers to and from reserve accounts; and (4) appraisal adjustments.[8] These exceptions do not involve an exchange and ***are not*** regarded as financing and investing activities. For this reason, they are not shown in a statement of changes in financial position.

6 *Financial Reporting in Canada,* p. 214. Of the 212 companies surveyed, 134 presented dividends as a financing activity and 55 classified dividends as a separate category.

7 CICA, *CICA Handbook,* Section 1540.20.

8 Ibid., Section 1540.21.

The rationale for the recommended disclosure and presentation is to provide information to financial statement users to assess a company's ability to generate cash from internal and external sources to finance its operating and investing activities, as well as to show the changes in the structure of a company's long-term assets, long-term debts, and equity capital. Consequently, these users are better able to evaluate the company's liquidity and solvency position, and its cash policies on operating, financing, and investing activities.

The cash flow from operations is of critical importance because, in the long run, a business must generate a positive net cash flow from operations if the business is to survive. A business with a negative net cash flow from operations will not be able to raise cash from other sources indefinitely. In fact, the ability of a business to raise cash through financing activities is highly dependent upon its ability to generate cash from operations. Creditors and shareholders are reluctant to invest in a company that does not generate enough cash from operations to assure prompt payment of maturing liabilities, interest, and dividends.

DETERMINATION OF CASH FLOWS

OBJECTIVE 4 Explain how cash flows are determined and why.

Transactions involving a debit to cash represent an inflow (source) of cash. The sales of merchandise for cash, the collection of accounts receivable and the issuance of long-term debt or equity instruments for cash are the common examples of sources of cash inflows. On the other hand, transactions involving a credit to cash represent an outflow (use) of cash. The purchase of merchandise for cash, the payment of accounts payable or expenses, and the payment for redemption or retirement of long-term debt or preferred stock are common examples of cash outflows (uses of cash).

However, since the statement of changes in financial position is on a cash and cash equivalent basis, transactions affecting only the cash and cash equivalent accounts ***equally*** do not produce an inflow or outflow of cash. The reason is that there is no change in the amount of cash and cash equivalents. For example, the purchase of temporary investments such as marketable securities with cash (debiting marketable securities and crediting cash for an equal amount) changes the components but does not change the total amount of cash and cash equivalents. Similarly, short-term borrowings such as bank loans (debiting cash and crediting bank loans for an equal amount) change the components but do not change the total amount of cash and cash equivalents. Of course, if a transaction affects more than the cash and cash equivalent accounts, there will be either an inflow or outflow of cash. For example, selling temporary investments at a gain will increase the amount of cash and cash equivalents (that is, increased by the amount of the gain) and the increase is included in the net income. Also, obtaining a short-term bank loan at a discount (that is, with prepaid interest deducted from the loan) or selling temporary investments at a loss will decrease the amount of cash and cash equivalents and the decrease is included in net income.

Since the accounting records and the other financial statements are on an accrual basis, how do we determine the cash inflows and outflows for the statement of changes in financial position? We will answer this question by presenting explanations under the three categories of the statement of changes in financial position—operating, financing, and investing activities.

Operating Activities

The determination of cash flow for operating activities requires the reconciliation or conversion from net income (the accrual basis of accounting) to net cash flow (cash basis of accounting).[9] Thus, ***changes*** in the ***noncash current asset*** and ***current liability*** accounts such as accounts receivable, inventory, unexpired insurance, accounts payable, and accrued liabilities, which have a ***different effect on net income than on cash flows,*** must be taken into account in the reconciliation. However, certain current liability accounts, such as dividends payable, and the current portion of the long-term debts are ***not*** related to the income statement and therefore have no effect on cash flow for operation. Now, let's explain how the changes in the noncash current assets and current liability accounts are handled in the reconciliation from net income to net cash flow resulting from operating activities.

Changes in Accounts Receivable Accounts receivable increases as credit sales are made, and decreases as cash is collected from customers. A net increase in accounts receivable over an accounting period indicates that revenue from credit sales exceeds collections from customers. In other words, the increase represents the portion of credit sales (which have been recognized as revenue and reflected in net income) that have not been collected. Thus, net income measured on the accrual basis is greater than net cash flow. Consequently, a net increase in accounts receivable is deducted from net income in the reconciliation from net income to net cash flow.

On the other hand, a net decrease in accounts receivable indicates that revenue from credit sales is less than collections from customers. Thus, net income on the accrual basis is smaller than net cash flow. Consequently, a net decrease in accounts receivable is added to net income in the reconciliation from net income to net cash flow.

Changes in Inventory The balance in the Inventory account increases as merchandise is purchased, and decreases as goods are sold. A net increase during the accounting period in the Inventory account indicates that purchases during the period exceed the cost of goods sold. Thus, to reconcile net income with net cash flow, we deduct from net income the amount of these additional purchases (the net increase in the balance of the Inventory account).

A net decrease over the period in the balance of the Inventory account indicates that the cost of goods sold exceeds purchases made during the

---

[9] The cash basis of accounting was explained in Chapter 3. Under the cash basis, revenue is not recorded until cash is collected from the customer; purchases of merchandise and expenses incurred are recorded in the period in which payment is made. Under the accrual basis, on the other hand, revenue is recognized at the date of sale and expenses are recorded when the related goods or services are used.

period. Thus, to reconcile net income with net cash flow, we add to net income the net decrease in inventory.

It should be noted that the adjustment of the increase or decrease of inventory to net income is really to convert the amount of cost of goods sold to the amount of credit purchases. The amount of credit purchases will be converted to cash payments for purchases (as required by the cash basis of accounting) by incorporating the change in accounts payable, as discussed later.

Changes in Prepaid Expenses Prepaid expenses are current assets. Increases in these assets result from cash payments, and decreases result from recognizing the expired portion as expenses. Thus, a net increase of prepaid expenses over the period indicates that cash payments made for these items exceed the amount recognized as expenses. Consequently, we deduct from net income the net increase in prepaid expenses in determining net cash flows for operating activities.

A net decrease in prepaid expenses indicates that cash outlays during the period are less than the amounts deducted as expenses in the determination of net income. Consequently, a net decrease in prepaid expenses is added back to net income in determining net cash flows for operating activities.

Changes in Accounts Payable Accounts payable are increased by purchases on account and are reduced by cash payments to suppliers. A net increase in accounts payable indicates that the credit purchases are greater than the cash payments made to suppliers. Thus, in converting net income to net cash flow, we add back to net income the amount of purchases financed by a net increase in accounts payable. (In the earlier discussion on changes in inventory, we ***deduct*** a net increase in inventory to net income to convert the amount of cost of goods sold to credit purchases. An increase in accounts payable means that the portion of the credit purchases has not been paid. Therefore, such an increase must be added back to net income to arrive at the amount of cash payments for purchases.)[10]

A net decrease in accounts payable indicates that cash payments to suppliers exceed the purchases during the period. Thus, a net decrease in accounts payable is deducted from net income to arrive at the cash flows for operating activities.

Changes in Accrued Expenses (Accrued Liabilities) The liability for accrued expenses rises with the recognition of expenses that will be paid in the future, and decreases as cash payments are made. A net increase in accrued expenses indicates that expenses in the period exceed the related cash payments. Thus, net income is less than net cash flow, and the increase in accrued expenses should be added to net income in determining the net cash flow for operating activities.

A net decrease in accrued expenses indicates that cash payments exceed the related amounts of expense. This decrease, therefore, is deducted from net income in determining the net cash flow from operating activities.

---

[10] This situation is illustrated in the Claire Company example in a later section.

Income Statement Items Not Affecting Cash Items such as depreciation, amortization of intangible assets, and amortization of discount on bonds payable reduce net income, but do not reduce cash flow. Thus, the amount of depreciation and amortization must be added back to net income to convert it to net cash flow.

Let us use depreciation as an example to illustrate this point. Assume that on December 31, 1995, City Delivery Service buys two trucks for cash at a cost of $30,000. As of January 1, 1996, the company does business on a cash basis, collecting revenue of $40,000 and paying expenses of $22,000, thus showing an $18,000 increase in cash. The company then records depreciation expense of $6,000 on its trucks, resulting in a $12,000 net income for 1996. What is the amount of cash provided by operations in 1996? The recording of depreciation expense reduces net income, ***but it does not reduce cash flow;*** cash flow for operating activities remains at $18,000. The $12,000 net income figure therefore ***understates*** the amount of cash flow for operating activities by the amount of depreciation expense recorded during the period. Thus, to convert the $12,000 net income of City Delivery Service to the amount of cash flow for operating activities of $18,000, we must ***add back*** the depreciation expense of $6,000.

On the other hand, certain items in the income statement increase net income without increasing cash flow; such items must be deducted from net income in the conversion of net income to net cash flow for operating activities. An example is the amortization of premium on bonds payable, which causes interest expense to be less than the cash payments of interest to bondholders.

"Nonoperating" Gains and Losses These gains and losses usually result from the disposal of long-term assets or the retirement of long-term debts. While these gains and losses do not affect operating activities, they do enter into the determination of net income. Therefore, in converting net income to net cash flow for operating activities, we ***add back any nonoperating losses*** and ***deduct any nonoperating gains*** included in net income.

Discontinued Operations and Extraordinary Items The income or loss from discontinued operations as well as gains or losses for discontinued operations and extraordinary items are included in the determination of net income (as presented in Chapter 15). To determine the net cash flow for "normal" operating activities, we must exclude such income or loss as well as gains or losses. Consequently, we add back to net income the losses and deduct from net income the income or gains in the conversion of net income to net cash flow. (The resulting figure represents income from continuing operations.) The income or loss from discontinued operations is converted to net cash flow and presented as a separate item called "cash from discontinued operations" under the operating activities. The gains or losses are combined with the related proceeds for discontinued operations and extraordinary items, and presented separately under the investing activities.

A Summary for Cash Flows of Operating Activities The foregoing discussion on the determination of cash flows of operating activities can be summarized by the following formula:

Cash provided or used by operating activities = Net income +

{
- Decrease in accounts receivable
- Decrease in inventory
- Decrease in prepaid expenses
- Increase in accounts payable
- Increase in accrued expenses
- Depreciation
- Amortization of intangibles
- Amortization of discount on bonds payable
- Nonoperating losses
- Loss from discontinued operations
- Extraordinary losses

} −

{
- Increase in accounts receivable
- Increase in inventory
- Increase in prepaid expenses
- Decrease in accounts payable
- Decrease in accrued expenses
- Amortization of premium on bonds payable
- Nonoperating gains
- Income and gain from discontinued operations
- Extraordinary gains

}

A few observations may be noted from the formula. First, decreases in noncash current asset accounts are added to net income because they cause a lower net income to be reported than net cash flow. Second, increases in noncash current asset accounts are deducted from net income because they cause a higher net income to be reported than net cash flow. Third, increases in current liability accounts (other than short-term borrowings, such as bank loans, which are included in the computation of cash and cash equivalents) are added because they cause a lower net income to be reported than net cash flow. Fourth, decreases in current liability accounts are deducted because they cause a higher net income to be reported than net cash flow. As mentioned earlier, the changes in the dividends payable or the current instalment of long-term debt have no effect on cash flow for operations as these two liabilities are not related to the income statement.

Financing Activities

Cash flows for financing activities are determined by analyzing the debit and credit changes recorded during the period in the long-term liability and shareholders' equity accounts. Credit changes in such accounts as bonds payable and preferred or common stock indicate cash receipts (inflow of cash), while debit changes of these accounts indicate cash payments (outflow of cash), unless these changes are the result of exchange transactions (which are discussed later).

The amount of cash dividends can be determined by analyzing the debit changes recorded during the period in the Retained Earnings account and the changes in the Dividends Payable account.

As mentioned earlier, exchange transactions such as issuing long-term debt or capital stock for plant assets, conversion of long-term debt or preferred stock into common stock, and optional stock dividends where shareholders have a choice of receiving cash or shares of common stock are considered financial activities even though no cash is involved. Thus, the debits and credits recorded during the period in the plant asset, long-term debt, preferred stock, common stock, and retained earnings account must be analyzed to determine exchange transactions.

Investing Activities

Cash flows for investing activities can be determined by analyzing the changes in such noncurrent accounts as long-term investments, intangible assets, plant, and equipment. Debit entries in these accounts represent purchases of the assets or cash outlay (unless an exchange transaction is involved as discussed in the paragraph below). Credit entries in these accounts, however, represent only the ***cost*** or ***book value*** of the assets sold. Therefore, to determine the cash proceeds from these sales transactions, we must adjust the amount of the credit entries for any gains or losses recognized on the sales (unless an exchange transaction is involved as discussed in the paragraph below). Also, the gains will be deducted from, and the losses added to, net income in the determination of cash flow for operating activities.

Similar to the discussion in the section on financing activities, exchange transactions—such as the acquisition of long-term investments or plant assets by issuing long-term debt or capital stock and the exchange of long-term investments or plant assets for other noncurrent assets—are considered investing activities even though no cash is involved. Thus, the debits and credits recorded during the period in these noncurrent asset accounts must be analyzed to determine exchange transactions.

DEVELOP A STATEMENT OF CHANGES IN FINANCIAL POSITION

Cash Flow: A Simple Illustration

OBJECTIVE 5 Develop a statement of changes in financial position—a simple and a comprehensive illustration.

Assume that John Claire started a business, Claire Company, as a sole proprietorship on April 30 by investing $40,000 cash; the company rented a building on May 1 and completed the following transactions during the month of May:

(1) Claire invested an additional $27,000 cash in the business.

(2) Purchased merchandise costing $40,000 on credit and sold three-fourths of this, also on credit, for $58,000.

(3) Collected $45,000 on receivables; paid $31,000 on accounts payable.

(4) Incurred $20,500 of operating expenses, of which $18,500 was paid, $2,000 was accrued.

(5) Purchased land for the construction of a store by issuing a six-year mortgage note for $17,000.

(6) Paid $30,000 for equipment purchased on May 31.

(7) Paid $1,000 for a one-year insurance policy that begins on June 1.

(8) Withdrew $2,000 cash from the business for personal use.

The company's income statement and balance sheet at May 31 follow:

CLAIRE COMPANY
Income Statement
For the Month Ended May 31

Sales	$58,000
Cost of goods sold (three-fourths of purchases)	30,000
Gross profit	$28,000
Operating expenses	20,500
Net income	$7,500

CLAIRE COMPANY
Comparative Balance Sheet

Assets	*May 31*	*Apr. 30*
Cash	$ 29,500	$40,000
Accounts receivable	13,000	
Inventory	10,000	
Unexpired insurance	1,000	
Land	17,000	
Equipment	30,000	
Total assets	$100,500	$40,000
Liabilities & Owner's Equity		
Accounts payable	$ 9,000	
Accrued liabilities (Accrued expenses)	2,000	
Mortgage payable (due in six years)	17,000	
John Claire, capital	72,500	$40,000
Total liabilities & owner's equity	$100,500	$40,000

The cash account amounted to $40,000 on April 30 but was only $29,500 on May 31, a decrease of $10,500. In analyzing the transactions completed during the month of May, we see that cash was increased and decreased as follows:

Transactions increasing cash:		
Additional investment by owner		$27,000
Collection of accounts receivable		45,000
Total increases in cash		$72,000
Transactions decreasing cash:		
Payment of accounts payable	$31,000	
Payment of operating expenses	18,500	
Payment for purchase of equipment	30,000	
Payment for unexpired insurance	1,000	
Withdrawal of cash by owner	2,000	
Total decrease in cash		82,500
Decrease in cash during May		$10,500

A complete list of transactions for a fiscal period may not be readily available, and even if it were, analysis of such a list would be a laborious process. In practice, a statement of changes in financial position is prepared by analyzing the changes that occurred ***in the noncash accounts*** (that is, all accounts other than the accounts for cash, temporary investment, and short-term borrowing such as bank loans) during the fiscal period. An analysis of the comparative balance sheet for Claire Company indicates the following changes in the noncash accounts:

(1) Increase in accounts receivable, $13,000.

(2) Increase in inventory, $10,000.

(3) Increase in unexpired insurance, $1,000.

(4) Increase in land, $17,000.

(5) Increase in equipment, $30,000.

(6) Increase in accounts payable, $9,000.

(7) Increase in accrued liabilities, $2,000.

(8) Increase in mortgage payable, $17,000.

(9) Increase in Claire's capital, $32,500, resulting from additional cash investment of $27,000, net income of $7,500, and a withdrawal of cash of $2,000.

Based on this analysis and the discussion on the determination of cash flows in the preceding section, we can prepare the following statement of changes in financial position for the month of May to account for the $10,500 decrease in cash.

A simple statement of changes in financial position

CLAIRE COMPANY
Statement of Changes in Financial Position
For Month of May

Operating activities:		
Net income		$ 7,500
Deduct: Increase in accounts receivable	$(13,000)	
Increase in inventory	(10,000)	
Increase in unexpired insurance	(1,000)	(24,000)
Add: Increase in accounts payable	$9,000	
Increase in accrued liabilities	2,000	11,000
Cash used by operating activities		$ (5,500)
Financing activities:		
Additional investment by owner	$27,000	
Withdrawal by owner	(2,000)	
Issuance of mortgage note for land	17,000	
Cash provided by financing activities		42,000
Investing activities:		
Purchase of land in exchange for a mortgage note	$(17,000)	
Purchase of equipment	(30,000)	
Cash used in investing activities		(47,000)
Decrease in cash		$(10,500)

The difference between net income and net cash flow should be carefully noted in this example. Although Claire Company's net income for May was $7,500, it experienced a ***cash deficiency*** of $5,500 from operating activities and its cash account ***decreased*** by $10,500. This is not unusual for a company just beginning its business. However, a company will experience financial difficulty if there is a continuing cash deficiency from its operations and a continuing decline in its most liquid asset—cash.

The Claire Company illustrates clearly the application of many of the concepts on the determination of cash flows presented in the preceding section.

Operating Activities

To determine the net cash flows for operating activities, we have to reconcile the net income to net cash flow. This reconciliation is a conversion of net income on an accrual basis to a cash basis. Thus, changes in such noncash current accounts as accounts receivable, inventory, unexpired insurance, accounts payable, and accrued liabilities must be accounted for as follows:

Increase in Accounts Receivable The $13,000 increase in accounts receivable is deducted from net income because it represents the portion of credit sales that has not been collected but that has been reflected in net income.

Increase in Inventory The $10,000 increase in inventory is deducted from net income to convert the amount of cost of goods sold to the amount of credit purchases. (Deducting the increase in inventory from net income has the same effect as adding the increase to the cost of goods sold.) This amount of credit purchases will be converted to cash payments for purchases with the adjustment of the change in accounts payable, as explained later.

Increase in Unexpired Insurance The $1,000 increase in unexpired insurance is deducted from net income because this prepayment has not been recognized as an expense in the determination of net income.

Increase in Accounts Payable The $9,000 increase in accounts payable is added to net income to convert the amount of credit purchases (which was determined by deducting the $10,000 increase in inventory from net income as presented earlier) to cash payments for purchases. The following will further clarify this point.

Cost of goods sold	*$30,000*
*Add: Increase in inventory**	*10,000*
Credit purchases	*$40,000*
*Deduct: Increase in accounts payable for purchases**	*9,000*
Cash payments for purchases	*$31,000*

* In converting the accrual basis to the cash basis of accounting, adding the increase in inventory to cost of goods sold has the same effect as deducting the increase from net income, and deducting the increase in accounts payable from credit purchases has the same effect as adding the increase to net income.

It should also be observed from the above example that if the increase in inventory is equal to the increase in accounts payable, then cost of goods sold is equal to cash payments for purchases. Consequently, the equal but opposite adjustments have no net effect on net income.

Increase in Accrued Liabilities The $2,000 increase in accrued liabilities is added back to net income because the expenses recognized ($20,500) are more than the cash payments for expenses ($18,500) by $2,000.

Financing Activities

The additional investment and the withdrawal by the owner represent financial activities. The investment increases cash and the withdrawal decreases cash. The issuance of a mortgage note for land is an exchange transaction. Thus, this transaction should be shown as both a financing activity and an investing activity. The issuance of a mortgage note is treated in the same manner as if it is for cash.

Investing Activities

The purchase of equipment is an investing activity involving a cash outflow. The purchase of land in exchange for a mortgage note, an exchange transaction (as pointed out in the preceding section), constitutes an investing activity, as if it is purchased with cash from the issuance of the mortgage note.

Cash Flow: A Comprehensive Illustration

To illustrate more fully the concepts discussed in the section on determination of cash flows, we shall prepare a statement of changes in financial position for the Allison Corporation from the comparative balance sheet and the condensed income statement that appear on page 891. A summary of the transactions completed by Allison Corporation that resulted in a change in ***noncash accounts*** during 1996 follows:

1 **Changes in noncash current accounts:**
- a Increase in accounts receivable, $20,000
- b Increase in inventory, $80,000
- c Increase in prepaid expenses, $13,000
- d Increase in accounts payable, $55,000
- e Decrease in accrued expenses, $19,500

2 **Changes in noncurrent assets:**
- a A plant asset costing $50,000 was sold for $53,000 cash. This asset was acquired in 1995 and was not used in operation. Thus, no depreciation was recorded.
- b A segment of business with a book value of $215,000 was sold for $180,000 cash (ignore the income tax effect and assume no operating income or loss, as these matters are more appropriate for a higher level accounting course).
- c A parcel of land was acquired for $150,000 by issuing a long-term note payable for the entire purchase price.

d Equipment was purchased for $140,000; the invoice was paid within 10 days.

e Depreciation of $67,500 was recorded.

Analysis of these financial statements will explain the sources and uses of cash

ALLISON CORPORATION
Comparative Balance Sheet
At December 31

Assets	*1996*	*1995*
Current assets:		
Cash	$ 12,000	$ 35,000
Marketable securities	23,000	-0-
Accounts receivable (net)	105,000	85,000
Inventory	150,000	70,000
Prepaid expenses	25,000	12,000
Total current assets	$315,000	$202,000
Land	300,000	150,000
Plant and equipment	470,000	380,000
Less: accumulated depreciation	(192,500)	(125,000)
Other: assets of a business segment	-0-	215,000
Total assets	$892,500	$822,000
Liabilities & Shareholders' Equity		
Current liabilities:		
Bank loan	$ 20,000	$ -0-
Accounts payable (for purchases)	145,000	90,000
Accrued expenses	22,500	42,000
Total current liabilities	$187,500	$132,000
Notes payable, long-term	170,000	20,000
Bonds payable, due June 30, 2008	60,000	300,000
Capital stock, no-par	310,000	160,000
Retained earnings	165,000	210,000
Total liabilities & shareholders' equity	$892,500	$822,000

ALLISON CORPORATION
Condensed Income Statement
For Year Ended December 31, 1996

Sales (net)	$900,000
Cost of goods sold	500,000
Gross profit	$400,000
Operating expenses and income taxes (less $3,000 gain on sale of plant asset)	340,000
Income from continuing operations	$ 60,000
Loss on sale of a business segment	35,000
Net income	$ 25,000

3 Changes in noncurrent liabilities:

a As stated in transaction **2c,** a $150,000 long-term note payable was issued in exchange for land.

b Bonds payable of $240,000 were retired at a price equal to face value.

4 Changes in shareholders' equity accounts:

a A stock dividend (non-optional) was declared in January, requiring a transfer of $30,000 from the Retained Earnings account to the Capital Stock account.

b In February, 8,000 shares of no-par value stock were issued for $120,000 cash.

c Cash dividends of $40,000 were declared and paid, causing a reduction in retained earnings.

d The net income for the year, $25,000 (including the $3,000 nonoperating gain on sale of a plant asset and the $35,000 loss on sale of a business segment), was transferred to the Retained Earnings account.

From the comparative balance sheets, the income statement, and the summary of transactions affecting noncash accounts, we can prepare a statement of changes in financial position by completing the following three steps:

1 Compute the change in cash (i.e., cash and cash equivalents) during the period.
2 Prepare a working paper for analysis of changes in noncash accounts.
3 Prepare the statement of changes in financial position.

Computation of Increase in Cash during the Period The first step in preparing a statement of changes in financial position is to determine the net increase or decrease in cash during the period covered by the statement.

Cash of the Allison Corporation decreased by $20,000 during 1996, determined as follows:

Uses of cash exceed sources by $20,000

ALLISON CORPORATION
Computation of Decrease in Cash during 1996

	Dec. 31 1996	Dec. 31 1995
Cash and cash equivalents (cash and marketable securities)	$35,000	$35,000
Less: Short-term borrowing (bank loan)	20,000	–0–
Cash and cash equivalents	$15,000	$35,000
Decrease in cash during 1996 ($15,000 – $35,000)	$20,000	

The purpose of the statement of changes in financial position is to explain the ***reasons*** for the change in cash. This is accomplished by listing the specific sources (inflows) and uses (outflows) of cash during the period. Since cash for the Allison Corporation decreases by $20,000, the uses of cash during 1996 exceeded the sources by this amount. But before a statement of changes in financial position can be prepared, we must analyze the changes that took place during the year in the noncash accounts.

Preparation of Working Paper for Analysis of Changes in Noncash Accounts

A working paper showing the analysis of changes in noncash accounts for Allison Corporation is illustrated below and on page 894. The amount of cash and the balances in noncash accounts at the beginning of the period are listed in the first column of the working paper; balances at the end of the year are listed in the last (right-hand) column. The two middle columns are used to ***explain the changes*** in each ***noncash*** account during the year and to indicate whether each change represents a source or a use of cash. Transactions for the year (in summary form) are recorded in these middle columns, and an offsetting entry is made in the lower section of the working paper indicating the effect of each transaction upon cash.

ALLISON CORPORATION
Working Paper for Statement of Changes in Financial Position
For Year Ended December 31, 1996

Debits	Account Balances, End of 1995	Analysis of Transactions for 1996: Debit	Analysis of Transactions for 1996: Credit	Account Balances, End of 1996
Cash and marketable securities, net of bank loan	35,000		(x) 20,000	15,000
Accounts receivable (net)	85,000	(7) 20,000		105,000
Inventory	70,000	(8) 80,000		150,000
Prepaid expenses	12,000	(9) 13,000		25,000
Land	150,000	(12) 150,000		300,000
Plant and equipment	380,000	(13) 140,000	(4) 50,000	470,000
Assets of a business segment	215,000		(5) 215,000	-0-
Total	947,000			1,065,000
Credits				
Accumulated depreciation	125,000		(6) 67,500	192,500
Accounts payable	90,000		(10) 55,000	145,000
Accrued expenses	42,000	(11) 19,500		22,500
Notes payable, long-term	20,000		(12) 150,000	170,000
Bonds payable, due June 30, 2008	300,000	(14) 240,000		60,000
Capital stock, no-par	160,000		(3) 30,000 (15) 120,000	310,000
Retained earnings	210,000	(2) 40,000 (3) 30,000	(1) 25,000	165,000
Total	947,000	732,500	732,500	1,065,000

	Sources	Uses	
Operating activities:			
Net income	*(1) 25,000*		*Income from continuing operations, $60,000; cash provided by operating activities, $47,000*
Deduct: Gain on sale of plant		*(4) 3,000*	
Increase in accounts receivable		*(7) 20,000*	
Increase in inventory		*(8) 80,000*	
Increase in prepaid expenses		*(9) 13,000*	
Decrease in accrued expenses		*(11) 19,500*	
Add: Loss on sale of a business segment	*(5) 35,000*		
Depreciation	*(6) 67,500*		
Increase in accounts payable	*(10) 55,000*		
Financing activities:			
Cash dividends		*(2) 40,000*	*Cash used in financing activities, $10,000*
Issuance of long-term note payable for land	*(12) 150,000*		
Retirement of bonds payable		*(14) 240,000*	
Issuance of capital stock	*(15) 120,000*		
Investing activities:			
Sale of plant, including a gain of $3,000	*(4) 53,000*		*Cash used in investing activities, $57,000*
Sale of a business segment	*(5) 180,000*		
Purchase of land in exchange for long-term note payable		*(12) 150,000*	
Purchase of equipment		*(13) 140,000*	
Total sources and uses of cash	*685,500*	*705,500*	
Decrease in cash during the year	*(x) 20,000*		
	705,500	*705,500*	

Explanation of transactions for 1996:

(1) Net income, $25,000 (including a gain of $3,000 on sale of plant asset and $35,000 loss on sale of a business segment), is transferred to Retained Earnings and is classified as a tentative source of cash [to be adjusted by entries (4) through (11) below].
(2) Cash dividends paid, $40,000, reduce retained earnings and cash, and this is a use of cash.
(3) A stock dividend has no effect on cash.
(4) Sale of plant asset for $53,000. Explains a $50,000 credit change in the Plant and equipment account. The $3,000 nonoperating gain on the sale is reclassified within the sources of cash from the "operating activities" section to the "investing activities" section.
(5) Sale of a business segment for $180,000. Explains the $215,000 credit in the assets of business segment account. The $35,000 loss is added back to net income to show income from continuing operations.
(6) Depreciation, $67,500, is added to net income in arriving at cash provided by operating activities.
(7) Increase in accounts receivable of $20,000 is deducted from net income in arriving at cash provided by operating activities.
(8) Increase in inventory of $80,000 is deducted from net income in arriving at cash provided by operating activities.
(9) Increase in prepaid expenses of $13,000 is deducted from net income in arriving at cash provided by operating activities.
(10) Increase in accounts payable of $55,000 is added to net income in arriving at cash provided by operating activities.
(11) Decrease in accrued expenses of $19,500 is deducted from net income in arriving at cash provided by operating activities.
(12) A $150,000 long-term note payable was issued (a source of cash) to acquire land (a use of cash).
(13) Cash of $140,000 was used to purchase equipment, an investing activity.
(14) Cash of $240,000 was used to retire bonds payable, a financing activity.
(15) Issued capital stock, increasing cash by $120,000, a financing activity.
(x) Balancing figure—decreases in cash during the year.

Explanation of Entries in the Middle Columns By studying the changes in the noncash accounts during 1996, we are able to find the specific reasons for the $20,000 decrease in cash. The noncash accounts may be analyzed in any sequence; however, we recommend the following approach.

1 Explain all transactions affecting the Retained Earnings account.
2 Explain the adjustment and reclassification of nonoperating gain and loss on sale of a business segment.

3 Explain the expense items that have no effect on cash.
4 Explain the changes in the ***noncash current*** accounts.
5 Explain any remaining changes in ***noncurrent*** accounts.
6 Make an entry explaining the net change in cash. This entry should bring both the upper and lower sets of middle columns into balance.

Using this approach, the entries in our illustrated working paper are explained as follows:

Entry

Step 1: Explain the changes in retained earnings

(1) Allison Corporation's net income explains a $25,000 credit change in the Retained Earnings account. In the bottom portion of the working papers, an offsetting entry is made identifying net income as a source of cash, which is shown in the "operating activities" section.

(2) Cash dividends of $40,000 declared and paid during 1996 caused a debit change in the Retained Earnings account and were a use of cash, which is shown in the "financing activities" section.

(3) The stock dividend (non-optional) caused a $30,000 debit change in the Retained Earnings account and a $30,000 credit change in the Capital Stock account. Notice that both the debit and credit portions of this entry appear in the ***top portion*** of the working papers. As previously stated, non-optional stock dividends (and stock splits) are an exception to the general rule that changes in noncurrent accounts represent either sources or uses of cash. Non-optional stock dividends have ***no effect*** upon cash.

With these first three entries, we have explained how the Retained Earnings account increased during 1996 from $210,000 to its ending balance of $165,000.

Step 2: Explain the adjustment and reclassification of nonoperating gain and loss on sale of a business segment.

(4) To compute the cash provided by operating activities, we must remove from net income the $3,000 nonoperating gain from the sale of a plant asset from the "operating activities" section and show the entire $53,000 proceeds from the sale as a source of cash in the "investing activities" section in the bottom portion of the working paper. In the top portion of the working paper, entry (4) shows that the sale of this plant asset caused a $50,000 credit change in the Plant and Equipment account.

(5) The $35,000 loss on sale of a business segment is added back to net income to show the amount of income from continuing operations of $60,000. The $180,000 proceeds are treated as a source of cash under the "investing activities" section in the bottom portion of the working paper. In the top portion of the working paper, entry (5) shows that the sale of the business segment reduced the assets of a business segment account to zero.

Step 3: Explain the expense items having no effect on cash.

(6) The $25,000 net income figure appearing in the bottom portion of the working paper is only a tentative measure of the cash provided by operating activities. Depreciation expense, for example, must be added back to this figure, because the recording of depreciation expense reduced net income but did not reduce cash. Entry (6) shows that depreciation expense explains the $67,500 credit change in the Accumulated Depreciation account and adds this amount to net income as a step in determining cash provided by operating activities.

Step 4: Explain the changes in the noncash current accounts.

(7) To complete the computation of cash provided by operating activities, we must convert the net income of $25,000 from an accrual to a cash basis by also taking into consideration the changes in these noncash current accounts that are related to the income statement. The rationale for involving the changes of these accounts in the conversion has been explained in the section on the determination of cash flows and in the Claire Company example. The changes in the noncash current accounts of Allison Corporation are considered in entries (7) through (11) in the working paper.

Entry (7) shows the increase in accounts receivable of $20,000 as a deduction from net income in the "operating activities" section in arriving at cash provided by operating activities, and as a debit change in accounts receivable in the top portion of the working paper.

(8) This entry shows the $80,000 increase in inventory as a deduction from net income in the "operating activities" section and as a debit change in inventory in the top portion of the working paper.

(9) This entry shows the $13,000 increase in prepaid expenses as a deduction from net income in the "operating activities" section and as a debit change in the prepaid expenses in the top portion of the working paper.

(10) This entry shows the $55,000 increase in accounts payable as an addition to net income in the "operating activities" section and as a credit change in accounts payable in the top portion of the working paper.

(11) This entry shows the $19,500 decrease in accrued expenses as a deduction from net income in the "operating activities" section and as a debit change in accrued expenses in the top portion of the working paper.

We have now determined that cash of $47,000 was provided by operating activities, and income from continuing operations was $60,000.

Step 5: Explain any remaining changes in non-current accounts.

(12) The issuance of a $150,000 long-term note payable in exchange for land is an exchange transaction, representing both a source and a use of cash. First, an entry is made in the top portion of the working paper explaining the $150,000 increase in the Notes Payable account and an offsetting entry is made in the "financing activities" section below showing a $150,000 source of cash. Next, a debit entry is made in the upper portion of the working paper explaining the $150,000 increase in the Land account, and an offsetting entry is made in the following "investing activities" section showing this $150,000 use of cash.

(13) The purchase of equipment explains the $140,000 debit change in the Equipment account and is a use of cash for investing activities.

(14) During the year, Allison Corporation retired $240,000 of bonds payable at par. A reduction in long-term debt is a use of cash. This transaction is recorded in the working paper by a debit to the Bonds Payable account and an offsetting entry describing the use of cash for financing activities.

(15) The issuance of capital stock in February for $120,000 is recorded in the upper section of the working paper by credits to Capital Stock. The issuance of capital stock is a source of cash; therefore, the offsetting entry in the lower section of the working papers is entered in the "financing activities" section as a source of cash.

At this point we should check carefully to determine that our entries in the Debit and Credit columns correctly explain the difference between the beginning and ending balances of each noncash account. If the top section of the working paper explains the change in every noncash account, the bottom section should include all of the sources and uses of cash for the year.

Step 6: Record the net change in cash.

(x) We now total the Sources column ($685,500) and the Uses column ($705,500) in the bottom section of the working paper. The $20,000 difference between these column totals represents the net change in cash during the year. Since cash decreased, this $20,000 is entered as a credit to cash on the top line of the working paper and as the balancing figure in the Sources column at the bottom of the working paper.

Totals can now be determined for the Debit and Credit columns in the top section of the working paper. If these totals agree, we know that our analysis is correct, at least so far as the mechanics are concerned.

Preparation of Statement of Changes in Financial Position The preceding working paper analysis explained all changes in noncash accounts that took place during 1996. In making this analysis, we listed the sources and uses of cash in the lower section of the working paper on pages 893–894. The decrease of $20,000 in cash has been confirmed and a statement of changes in financial position, including a schedule showing the change in cash, can now be prepared as follows:

Statement of changes in financial position shows sources and uses of cash relating to operating, financing, and investing activities

ALLISON CORPORATION
Statement of Changes in Financial Position
For Year Ended December 31, 1996

Operating activities:		
*Income from continuing operations**		*$ 60,000*
Deduct: Gain on sale of plant asset	*$ (3,000)*	
Increase in accounts receivable	*(20,000)*	
Increase in inventory	*(80,000)*	
Increase in prepaid expenses	*(13,000)*	
Decrease in accrued expenses	*(19,500)*	*(135,500)*
Add: Expenses not requiring the use of cash—depreciation	*$ 67,500*	
Increase in accounts payable	*55,000*	*122,500*
Cash provided by operating activities		*$ 47,000*
Financing activities:		
Cash dividends	*$ (40,000)*	
Issuance of long-term note payable for land	*150,000*	
Retirement of bonds payable	*(240,000)*	
Issuance of capital stock	*120,000*	
Cash used by financing activities		*(10,000)*
Investing activities:		
Sale of a plant asset including a gain of $3,000	*$ 53,000*	
Sale of a business segment at a $35,000 loss	*180,000*	
Purchase of land in exchange for long-term note payable	*(150,000)*	
Purchase of equipment	*(140,000)*	
Cash used in investing activities		*(57,000)*
Decrease in cash and cash equivalents		*$ (20,000)*

* If there are no discontinued operations or extraordinary items, this will be "net income."

This supporting schedule shows the change in cash

Schedule of Changes in Cash and Cash Equivalents

	December 31	
	1996	*1995*
Cash	*$ 12,000*	*$35,000*
Marketable securities	*23,000*	*–0–*
	$ 35,000	*$35,000*
Deduct: Bank loan (short-term)	*20,000*	*–0–*
Cash and cash equivalents	*$ 15,000*	*$35,000*
	(35,000)	
Decrease in cash and cash equivalents	*$(20,000)*	

The preceding statement of changes in financial position illustrates the disclosure and presentation requirements of Section 1540 of the *CICA Handbook* in a clear and understandable manner. The schedule of changes in cash and cash equivalents is included here to enhance understanding of the "cash and cash equivalents" definition for cash. In published financial statements, such a schedule is seldom presented because the change can be easily determined from the few items involved. Instead, the items included as "cash and cash equivalents" are simply described in a note below the statement or in the last heading in the statement.

In published financial statements, the changes in noncash current accounts are usually presented in the statement of changes in financial position as one lump sum amount entitled "Changes in noncash working capital components" or "Changes in noncash working capital." This amount is sometimes supported by a schedule or a footnote showing the changes in the individual noncash current or working capital accounts.

ANALYSIS AND INTERPRETATION OF A STATEMENT OF CHANGES IN FINANCIAL POSITION

OBJECTIVE 6 Analyze and interpret a statement of changes in financial position.

As discussed in the early part of this chapter, the statement of changes in financial position provides information on the liquidity and solvency position of a business, as well as the cash policies on its operating, financing, and investing activities. The amount of cash and cash equivalents together with the changes in noncash current account in the statement will provide insights into the liquidity position and the cash policy on operating activities. The changes in the noncurrent accounts shown in the financing and investing activities sections of the statement will provide information on the cash policies regarding the extent of financing and investing activities. Thus, a careful analysis and interpretation of this statement will enable management and other users to logically assess the soundness of the business's liquidity position and its cash policies on operating, financing, and investing activities.

The following analysis and interpretation of a statement of changes in financial position is based on the Allison Corporation example.

The Allison Corporation's liquidity position is deteriorating; its cash and cash equivalents at the end of 1996 are less than half that in 1995, as shown in the Schedule of Changes in Cash and Cash Equivalents on page 898. Moreover, the amount of cash and cash equivalents of $15,000 seems to be inadequate to meet the need for paying the $167,500 of account payable and accrued expenses, especially if the company continues its existing policy on collection from customers, which is explained later.

The company does not appear to have a well-coordinated and satisfactory cash policy on operating activities. The increase in accounts receivable means that credit sales are greater than the cash collected from customers. Since there is an increase in both inventory and accounts payable and the increase in inventory exceeds the increase in accounts payable, more goods are being purchased on credit than are being sold and payments are less than the credit purchases. The increase in prepaid expenses indicates that more expenses are being prepaid than are being incurred. Similarly, the decrease in accrued liabilities means that payments are being made faster than the expenses are being incurred. These analyses show that the company seems to be slow in collecting its accounts receivable and in paying its suppliers but too quick in paying its other expenses. Consequently, the company should evaluate its credit, collection, and payment policies for their soundness and coordination. The fact that the cash provided from operating activities is much less than the amount of depreciation indicates that the company will have to borrow more, or issue additional capital stock, in order to maintain its present operating capacity, unless this is a temporary situation. However, this had already occurred in 1996 as the company had to issue long-term notes payable and capital stock to finance its purchase of land and equipment (in addition to the proceeds from the sale of a business segment).

The company's cash policy on financing activities seems unsound. The retirement of $240,000 bonds payable, in spite of an unsatisfactory cash position, was ill-advised. The cash dividends of about two-thirds of income from continuing operations and 80% of the amount of cash from operations were unusually large and caused a further strain on the cash resources. Consequently, the company should amend its policy in each of these areas. It should also be noted that, by presenting the information on financing activities in one place, it is easier for users to analyze and interpret the extent and reasonableness of these activities.

The company's cash policy on investing activities reflects the desire to finance its investments through long-term debt and capital stock. The heavier emphasis on debt than equity financing appeared to be logical in view of the relationship between the amount of long-term debts and the amount of long-term assets on the one hand, and the amount of long-term debts and the amount of shareholders' equity on the other. However, since the total amount of debts is about 50% of the total assets, the company may find borrowing increasingly difficult and risky in the future, unless there is a substantial increase in shareholders' equity. The sale of a business segment at a loss may have reflected the need to get rid of an unprofitable segment and to generate more cash. Since the investing activities are presented in one place, it is easier for users to analyze and interpret the extent and reasonableness of these activities.

CHAPTER REVIEW

KEY TERMS INTRODUCED OR EMPHASIZED IN CHAPTER 19

Accrual basis A method of summarizing operating results in terms of revenue earned and expenses incurred, rather than cash receipts or cash payments.

Cash basis A method of summarizing operating results in terms of cash receipts and cash payments rather than revenue earned and expenses incurred.

Cash and cash equivalents Cash and cash equivalents encompass cash, net of short-term borrowings, and temporary investments. In some cases, cash and cash equivalents may include certain other elements of working capital when they are equivalent to cash.

Cash flows from financing activities Cash flows that affect the size and composition of a company's long-term debt and equity capital structure.

Cash flows from investing activities Cash flows that affect the noncurrent assets such as long-term investments, plant, and equipment.

Cash flows from operating activities Cash flows from operations, including net income or income from continuing operation and changes in noncash current accounts.

Exchange transaction In the context of a statement of changes in financial position, exchange transactions are financing or investing activities that do not directly affect cash. An example of such a transaction is the purchase of plant assets by issuing common stock. Such transactions should be shown in a statement of changes in financial position as both a source and a use of cash.

Noncash current accounts All current asset and current liability accounts other than cash or cash equivalents. Also referred to as noncash working capital accounts.

Noncurrent account Any balance sheet account ***other than*** a current asset or a current liability. Noncurrent accounts include long-term investments, plant assets, intangible assets, long-term liabilities, and shareholders' equity accounts.

Noncurrent assets All long-term assets such as long-term investments, plant, and equipment; they are part of the noncurrent accounts.

Non-optional stock dividends Stock dividends where shareholders can only receive shares of capital stock.

Optional stock dividends Stock dividends where shareholders have an option of receiving cash or shares of capital stock.

Statement of changes in financial position A financial statement showing the sources and uses of cash from operating, financing, and investing activities during the accounting period. In addition, this statement shows financing and investing activities, such as exchange transactions, that do not directly affect cash.

Working capital Current assets minus current liabilities. Working capital represents the net amount of liquid resources available to a business.

DEMONSTRATION PROBLEM FOR YOUR REVIEW

Comparative financial data for Liquid Gas Limited for the last two years are shown on page 902.

OTHER DATA

(1) During 1996, the board of directors of the company authorized a transfer of $15,000 from retained earnings to reflect a stock dividend on the common stock. (This is a non-optional stock dividend.)

(2) Cash dividends of $6,000 were declared and paid on the preferred stock, and cash dividends of $50,000 were declared and paid on the common stock.

(3) Three hundred shares of preferred stock were retired for $30,000 cash.

(4) The only entries recorded in the Retained Earnings account were for dividends and to close the Income Summary account, which had a credit balance of $66,000 after the loss on the sale of the land.

(5) There were no sales or retirements of building and equipment during the year; land was sold for $8,000, resulting in a loss of $2,000.

Debits	December 31 1996	December 31 1995
Cash	$ 29,220	$ 15,800
Marketable securities	20,000	28,000
Accounts receivable (net of allowance for doubtful accounts)	41,400	24,000
Inventories, lower of cost and market	27,600	36,800
Prepaid expenses	4,180	4,400
Land	9,000	19,000
Buildings	280,000	250,000
Equipment	478,600	450,000
Total	$890,000	$828,000
Credits		
Accumulated depreciation: buildings	$ 95,000	$ 77,000
Accumulated depreciation: equipment	153,000	120,000
Bank loan	12,000	23,000
Accounts payable	67,200	35,000
Accrued expenses	20,000	10,000
Bonds payable	90,000	90,000
Premium on bonds payable	2,800	3,000
Preferred stock (no-par)	70,000	100,000
Common stock (no-par)	305,000	290,000
Retained earnings	75,000	80,000
Total	$890,000	$828,000

INSTRUCTIONS

a Compute the change in cash and cash equivalents during 1996.

b Prepare a working paper for a statement of changes in financial position for 1996.

c Prepare a statement of changes in financial position for 1996, without showing the schedule of change in cash.

SOLUTION TO DEMONSTRATION PROBLEM

a Computation of change in cash and cash equivalents:

	December 31 1996	December 31 1995
Cash	$29,220	$15,800
Marketable securities	20,000	28,000
	$49,220	$43,800
Less: Bank loan	12,000	23,000
Cash and cash equivalents	$37,220	$20,800
Increase in cash during 1996 ($37,220 – $20,800)	$16,420	

b

LIQUID GAS LIMITED
Working Paper for Statement of Changes in Financial Position
For Year Ended December 31, 1996

Debits	Account Balances, End of 1995	Analysis of Transactions for 1996 Debit	Analysis of Transactions for 1996 Credit	Account Balances, End of 1996
Cash and marketable securities,				
net of bank loan	20,800	(x) 16,420		37,220
Accounts receivable (net)	24,000	(6) 17,400		41,400
Inventories	36,800		(7) 9,200	27,600
Prepaid expenses	4,400		(8) 220	4,180
Land	19,000		(4) 10,000	9,000
Buildings	250,000	(11) 30,000		280,000
Equipment	450,000	(12) 28,600		478,600
Total	805,000			878,000
Credits				
Accumulated depreciation: buildings	77,000		(5) 18,000	95,000
Accumulated depreciation: equipment	120,000		(5) 33,000	153,000
Accounts payable	35,000		(9) 32,200	67,200
Accrued expenses	10,000		(10) 10,000	20,000
Bonds payable	90,000			90,000
Premium on bonds payable	3,000	(13) 200		2,800
Preferred stock, no-par	100,000	(14) 30,000		70,000
Common stock, no-par	290,000		(2) 15,000	305,000
Retained earnings	80,000	(2) 15,000	(1) 66,000 }	75,000
		(3) 56,000		
Total	805,000	193,620	193,620	878,000

	Sources	Uses	
Operating activities:			
Net income	*(1) 66,000*		*Cash provided by operating activities, $153,020.*
Add: Loss on sale of land	*(4) 2,000*		
Depreciation	*(5) 51,000*		
Decrease in inventories	*(7) 9,200*		
Decrease in prepaid expenses	*(8) 220*		
Increase in accounts payable	*(9) 32,200*		
Increase in accrued expenses	*(10) 10,000*		
Deduct: Increase in accounts receivable		*(6) 17,400*	
Amortization of premium on bonds payable		*(13) 200*	
Financing Activities:			
Cash dividends		*(3) 56,000*	*Cash used in financing activities, $86,000.*
Retirement of preferred stock		*(14) 30,000*	
Investing activities:			*Cash used in investing activities, $50,600.*
Sale of land, at a loss of $2,000	*(4) 8,000*		
Purchase of building		*(11) 30,000*	
Purchase of equipment		*(12) 28,600*	
Total sources and uses of cash	*178,620*	*162,200*	
Increase in cash during the year		*(x) 16,420*	
	178,620	*178,620*	

Explanation of transactions for 1996:

(1) Net income, $66,000, including a loss of $2,000 on sale of land, transferred to Retained Earnings account.
(2) Entry to record stock dividend; no effect on cash.
(3) Cash dividends declared, $56,000 (preferred stock, $6,000, and common, $50,000).
(4) To record sale of land for $8,000; the $2,000 nonoperating loss is reclassified from the "operating activities" section to "investing activities" section.
(5) Depreciation, $51,000, is added to net income because it is an expense that did not reduce cash.
(6) Increase in accounts receivable of $17,400 is deducted from net income in arriving at cash provided by operating activities.
(7) Decrease in inventory of $9,200 is added to net income in arriving at cash provided by operating activities.
(8) Decrease in prepaid expenses of $220 is added to net income in arriving at cash provided by operating activities.
(9) Increase in accounts payable of $32,200 is added to net income in arriving at cash provided by operating activities.
(10) Increase in accrued expenses of $10,000 is added to net income in arriving at cash provided by operating activities.
(11) To record cash used for purchase of building.
(12) To record cash used for purchase of equipment.
(13) Amortization of premium on bonds payable decreased expense and thus increased net income but had no effect on cash.
(14) To record cash used for retirement of preferred stock.
(x) Balancing figure—increase in cash during the year.

c

LIQUID GAS LIMITED
Statement of Changes in Financial Position
For Year Ended December 31, 1996

Operating activities:		
Net income		*$ 66,000*
Add: Loss on sale of land	*$ 2,000*	
Expenses not requiring the use of cash—depreciation	*51,000*	
Decrease in inventory	*9,200*	
Decrease in prepaid expenses	*220*	
Increase in accounts payable	*32,200*	
Increase in accrued expenses	*10,000*	*104,620*
Deduct: Increase in accounts receivable	*$(17,400)*	
Expense reduction that increased income but with no effect on cash—amortization of premium on bonds payable	*(200)*	*(17,600)*
Cash provided by operating activities		*$153,020*
Financing activities:		
Cash dividends	*$(56,000)*	
Retirement of preferred stock	*(30,000)*	
Cash used in financing activities		*(86,000)*
Investing activities:		
Sale of land at a loss of $2,000	*$ 8,000*	
Purchase of building	*(30,000)*	
Purchase of equipment	*(28,600)*	
Cash used in investing activities		*(50,600)*
Increase in cash and cash equivalents		*$ 16,420*

* *Appendix B*

T Account Method for the Preparation of Statement of Changes in Financial Position

The "T account method," as the name suggests, utilizes T accounts to summarize the same information as the working paper method illustrated in the chapter. First, all the accounts required for the preparation of the statement of changes in financial position are set up in the T account format rather than in the working paper format. Second, the changes between the beginning and ending balances for these accounts are noted in the T accounts. (With the working paper method, the beginning and ending balances of a period rather than their changes are noted.) Third, these changes are accounted for by reconstructing the entries posted to these accounts during the period. (With the working paper method, the beginning and ending balances of a period are reconciled by reconstructing the entries posted to these accounts.) The following examples, selected from the demonstration problem—Liquid Gas Limited—delineate these three basic differences.

Working Paper Method

	Account Balances, End of 1995	Analysis of Transactions for 1996		Account Balances, End of 1996
Debits		Debit	Credit	
Buildings	*250,000*	*(11) 30,000*		*280,000*
Credits				
Preferred stock, no-par	*100,000*	*(14) 30,000*		*70,000*
		Sources	**Uses**	
Financing activities:				
Retirement of preferred stocks			*(14) 30,000*	
Investing activities:				
Purchase of building			*(11) 30,000*	

T Account Method

Buildings

Change	*30,000*	
(11) Purchase of building	*30,000*	

Preferred Stock, No-Par

Change	*30,000*	
(14) Retirement of Preferred Stock	*30,000*	

Financing Activities

	(14) Retirement of Preferred Stock	*30,000*

Investing Activities

	(11) Purchase of building	*30,000*

A careful study of these examples shows that both the working paper and the T accounts contain the same information needed for the preparation of the statement of changes in financial position. The T account method may be more efficient, particularly for solving relatively simple problems, but the essential difference is really the format in which the information is presented. In the above example, the two items in the credit column in the use of cash section of the working paper—purchase of building, $30,000, and retirement of preferred stock, $30,000—are the same as the two items in the credit column of the financing and investing activities accounts. Similar parallels can be made for all the other accounts in the Liquid Gas Limited demonstration problem.

The T account method generally involves the following steps:

1 Open a T account for "Cash" (that is, cash and cash equivalents) and debit or credit the account with the increase or decrease (change) in cash. Double underline this amount.

2 Open a T account for each noncash account with the change between the beginning and ending balances and debit or credit the change to these accounts. Double underline the amount in each of these accounts.

3 Add the debits and credits of the T account for cash and for the noncash accounts. The equality of the debit and credit totals proves that the amounts have been correctly noted on these accounts (unless there are exact offsetting errors, which are usually unlikely).

4 Open a T account for "Operating Activities" for the reconstruction of the posting of entries related to cash from operations such as net income, nonoperating gains or losses, items included in the income statement but not providing cash or requiring the use of cash (e.g., amortization of premium on bonds payable or depreciation), and changes in noncash current accounts. This account shows the details of cash provided or used by operating activities.

5 Open a T account for "Financing Activities" for the reconstruction of the postings of entries related to cash flows on such activities as the issuance, redemption, and retirement of long-term debt and capital stock. This account shows the details of cash provided by or used in financing activities.

6 Open a T account for "Investing Activities" for the reconstruction of the postings of entries related to cash flows on such activities as the acquisition and disposal of long-term assets such as plant and equipment. This account shows the details of cash provided by or used in investing activities.

7 Analyze all available information, and reconstruct the postings to account for the changes in the T accounts set up thus far.

8 Check that the changes in each noncash T account have been accounted for.

9 Add the Operating Activities, Financing Activities, and Investing Activities T accounts and transfer the balances (these are the amounts of cash provided by or used in operating, financing and investing activities) to the Cash T account.

10 Check that the total amount of the balances transferred from step 9 is the same amount and on the same side of the T account as that already noted in the cash T account.

11 Review all the noncurrent T accounts to ensure that exchange transactions have been accounted for.

12 Prepare the statement of changes in financial position from

   i The Operating Activities T account, which provides all the details on cash provided by or used in operations.

   ii The Financing Activities T account, which provides all the details on cash provided by or used in financing activities.

iii The Investing Activities T account, which provides all the details on cash provided by or used in investing activities.

These twelve steps are used to illustrate the T account method using the information of the Liquid Gas Limited demonstration problem.

a The information contained in the T accounts after steps 1 to 6 is as follows [the total of debits ($127,620) equals the total of credits ($127,620)]:

Account	Debit	Credit
Cash*	16,420	
Accounts Receivable	17,400	
Inventories		9,200
Prepaid Expenses		220
Land		10,000
Buildings	30,000	
Equipment	28,600	
Acc. Depr.—Buildings		18,000
Acc. Depr.—Equipment		33,000
Accounts Payable		32,200
Accrued Expenses		10,000
Premium on Bonds Payable	200	
Preferred Stock	30,000	
Common Stock		15,000
Retained Earnings	5,000	
Operating Activities		
Financing Activities		
Investing Activities		

* Cash and cash equivalents

b After analyzing all available information and reconstructing the postings to account for the differences in the T accounts as required by step 7, the T accounts are as follows. (Comparing the numbered items in these T accounts with the numbered items in the middle columns of the working paper on pages 903–904 will show that the information is identical in both places.)

Cash

	16,420		

Accounts Receivable

	17,400		
(6)	17,400		

Inventories

			9,200
		(7)	9,200

Prepaid Expenses

			220
		(8)	220

Land

			10,000
		(4)	10,000

Buildings

	30,000		
(11)	30,000		

Equipment

	28,600		
(12)	28,600		

Acc. Depr.—Buildings

			18,000
		(5)	18,000

Acc. Depr.—Equipment

			33,000
		(5)	33,000

Accounts Payable

			32,200
		(9)	32,200

Accrued Expenses

			10,000
		(10)	10,000

Premium on Bonds Payable

	200		
(13)	200		

Preferred Stock

	30,000		
(14)	30,000		

Common Stock

			15,000
		(2)	15,000

Retained Earnings

	5,000		
(2)	15,000	(1)	66,000
(3)	56,000		
	71,000		
	5,000		

(Check that the difference in each noncash T account has been accounted for.)

Operating Activities

(1) Net income	66,000	(6) Increase in accounts receivable	17,400
(4) Loss on sale of land	2,000	(13) Amortization of premium on bonds payable	200
(5) Depreciation	51,000		
(7) Decrease in inventories	9,200		
(8) Decrease in prepaid expenses	220		
(9) Increase in accounts payable	32,200		
(10) Increase in accrued expenses	10,000		

Financing Activities

		(3) Cash dividends	56,000
		(14) Retirement of preferred stock	30,000

Investing Activities

(4) Sale of land, at a loss of $2,000	8,000	(11) Purchase of building	30,000
		(12) Purchase of equipment	28,600

c Add the Operating Activities, Financing Activities, and Investing Activities T accounts and transfer the balances to the Cash T account. Check that the total amount of the balances transferred to and the amount already noted in the Cash T account are in agreement. These are required by steps 9 and 10. These four accounts, after the two steps have been performed, are as follows:

Operating Activities

(1) Net income	66,000	(6) Increase in accounts receivable	17,400
(4) Loss on sale of land	2,000	(13) Amortization of premium on bonds payable	200
(5) Depreciation	51,000		
(7) Decrease in inventories	9,200		
(8) Decrease in prepaid expenses	220		
(9) Increase in accounts payable	32,200		
(10) Increase in accrued expenses	10,000		
	170,620		17,600
		(x) Transfer to cash T acct	153,020
	170,620		170,620

Financing Activities

		(3) Cash dividends	56,000
		(14) Retirement of preferred stock	30,000
(x) Transfer to cash T account	86,000		86,000

Investing Activities

(4) Sale of land, at a loss of $2,000	8,000	(11) Purchase of building	30,000
		(12) Purchase of equipment	28,600
	8,000		58,600
(x) Transfer to cash T account	50,600		
	58,600		58,600

Cash

	16,420		
(x) Transfer from operating activities	153,020	(x) Transfer from:	
		Financing activities	86,000
		Investing activities	50,600
	136,600		136,600
	16,420		

d Review all the noncurrent T accounts to ensure that exchange transactions have been accounted for.

e Use the information in the Operating Activities, Financing Activities, and Investing Activities T accounts to prepare the statement of changes in financial position. This statement is the same as that on page 905.

ASSIGNMENT MATERIAL

DISCUSSION QUESTIONS

1 Does a statement of changes in financial position or an income statement best measure the profitability of a financially sound business? Explain.

2 What is the nature and objective of the statement of changes in financial position?

3 What information can a reader gain from a statement of changes in financial position that is not apparent from reading a balance sheet?

4 How is "cash and cash equivalents" defined by Section 1540 of the *CICA Handbook*?

5 List the items required to be separately disclosed in a statement of changes in financial position by Section 1540 of the *CICA Handbook*.

6 How should the items in **5** be classified?

7 Briefly describe the meaning of: cash flows from operating activities; cash flows from financing activities; cash flows from investing activities.

8 Explain the rationale of Section 1540 of the *CICA Handbook* for the recommended disclosure and presentation for the statement of changes in financial position.

9 List six items that are added to or deducted from net income in computing cash provided or used by operating activities.

10 List four items that are included in computing cash provided by or used in financing activities.

11 List four items that are included in computing cash provided by or used in investing activities.

12 How should an increase and a decrease in accounts receivable be handled in converting net income to cash provided or used by operating activities? Why?

13 How should an increase and a decrease in inventory and in accounts payable be handled in converting net income to cash provided or used by operating activities? Why?

14 How should an increase and a decrease in prepaid expenses be handled in converting net income to cash provided or used by operating activities? Why?

15 How should an increase and a decrease in accrued expenses be handled in converting net income to cash provided or used by operating activities? Why?

16 In converting net income to cash provided or used by operating activities, are all

(a) increases in noncash current asset accounts handled in the same manner? Explain.

(b) decreases in noncash current asset accounts handled in the same manner? Explain.

17 In converting net income to cash provided or used by operating activities, are all

(a) increases in current liability accounts other than bank loans handled in the same manner? Explain.

(b) decreases in current liability accounts other than bank loans handled in the same manner? Explain.

18 What is an "exchange transaction"? List two examples and explain how they are handled in a statement of changes in financial position.

19 List four exceptions to "exchange transactions" that are not disclosed in a statement of changes in financial position.

20 Sources of cash include long-term borrowing, sale of noncurrent assets, operations, and sale of capital stock. Which of these possible sources of cash do you consider to be most important to the long-run survival of a business?

21 Give examples of expenses, other than depreciation expense, that reduce net income but do not result in the use of cash during the period.

22 Give an example of an increase in net income that does not result in an increase in cash during the period.

23 Miller Corporation acquired a building for $300,000, paying $60,000 cash and issuing a long-term note payable for the balance. What is the effect of this transaction upon the cash of Miller Corporation? How should the transaction be shown in a statement of changes in financial position?

24 During the year, holders of $4 million of Sommersby Limited convertible bonds converted their bonds into shares of Sommersby common stock. The president of Sommersby Limited made the following statement: "By issuing common stock to retire these bonds, the company has saved $4 million in cash. Our statement of changes in financial position will not have to show the retirement of bonds among the uses of cash." Do you agree with this statement? Explain.

25 An outside member of the board of directors of a small corporation made the following comment after studying the comparative financial statements for the past two years: "I have trouble understanding why our cash has increased steadily during the past two years, yet our profits have been negligible; we have paid no dividends; and inventories, receivables, payables, cost of plant and equipment, long-term debt, and capital stock have remained essentially unchanged." Write a brief statement explaining how this situation might occur.

MULTIPLE CHOICE QUESTIONS

1 The statement of changes in financial position is designed to assist users in assessing each of the following, ***except:***

a The ability of a company to remain solvent.

✓ b The company's profitability.

c The major sources of cash receipts during the period.

d The reasons why net cash flow from operating activities differ from net income.

2 Which of the following is ***not*** included in the statement of changes in financial position?

✓ a Disclosure of the amount of cash invested in temporary investments during the accounting period.

b A reconciliation of net income to net cash flow from operating activities.

c Disclosure of investing or financing activities that did not involve cash.

d The amount of cash and cash equivalents owned by the business at the end of the accounting period.

3 The cash flows shown in the statement of changes in financial position are grouped into the following major categories:

a Operating activities, investing activities, and financing activities.

b Cash receipts, cash disbursements, and noncash activities.

c Direct cash flows and indirect cash flows.

d Operating activities, investing activities, and collecting activities.

4 The following information is obtained from Owen Limited.

Increase in accounts receivable	*$12,000*
Decrease in inventory	*19,000*
Increase in accounts payable	*16,000*
Decrease in accrued expenses	*8,000*
Depreciation expense	*67,000*
Gain on sale of plant assets	*3,000*

Based only upon the above items, net cash flow from operating activities is:

a $85,000 b $15,000 c $79,000 d $125,000

5 During the current year, two transactions were recorded in the Land account of Cliffhanger Industries. One involved a debit of $320,000 to the Land account; the second was a $210,000 credit to the Land account. Cliffhanger Industries' income statement for the year reported a loss on sale of land in the amount of $25,000. All transactions involving the Land account were cash transactions. These transactions would be shown in the statement of cash flows as:

a $320,000 cash provided by investing activities, and $210,000 cash disbursed for investing activities.

b $210,000 cash provided by investing activities, and $320,000 cash disbursed for investing activities.

c $235,000 cash provided by financing activities, and $320,000 cash disbursed for investing activities.

d $185,000 cash provided by investing activities, and $320,000 cash disbursed for investing activities.

EXERCISES

EXERCISE 19-1 Accounting Terminology

Listed below are nine technical accounting terms introduced in this chapter:

Operating activities	*Statement of changes in financial position*	*Working capital*
Investing activities	*Income statement*	*Accrual basis*
Financing activities	*Cash equivalents*	*Cash basis*

Each of the following statements may (or may not) describe one of these technical terms. For each statement, indicate the accounting term described, or answer "None" if the statement does not correctly describe any of the terms.

a A method of accounting that summarizes operating results in terms of cash receipts and cash payments.

b The financial statement that shows the financial position of the business at a particular date.

c An asset consisting of temporary investments in marketable securities.

d The financial statement that best describes the profitability of a business that receives most of its revenue in cash.

e Transactions involving the issuance and repayment of debt, investments by owners, and distributions to owners.

f The section of a statement of changes in financial position summarizing the cash effects of most transactions that enter into the determination of net income.

g The section of a statement of changes in financial position summarizing the acquisition and disposal of plant and equipment.

EXERCISE 19-2
Computing Cash Equivalents

Compute the amount of the increase or decrease in cash and cash equivalents during 1996 from the following information:

	December 31 1996	December 31 1995
Cash	$ 26,000	$ 20,000
Marketable securities	32,000	28,000
Accounts receivable (net)	87,000	79,000
Unexpired insurance	6,000	1,500
Bank loans	30,000	38,000
Accounts payable	80,000	78,000
Mortgage payable	200,000	200,000

EXERCISE 19-3
Effect of Transactions on Cash and Cash Equivalents

Indicate the amount of the increase or decrease (if any) in cash and cash equivalents as a result of each of the following situations:

a In the first year of operations, cash sales were $240,000, credit sales were $600,000, and accounts receivable at the end of the year were $120,000.

b Issued $600,000 of bonds payable for an office building.

c Land costing $18,000 was sold for $26,000; the purchaser paid $12,000 and issued a mortgage note for $14,000.

d Issued capital stock to investors for $860,000 cash.

e Purchased temporary investments for $90,000 cash.

f Purchased equipment costing $300,000 for $100,000 cash and $200,000 mortgage payable.

g Declared cash dividends of $80,000.

h Obtained a short-term bank loan of $180,000.

EXERCISE 19-4
Items To Be Reported in the Statement of Changes in Financial Position

Briefly explain how each of the following situations should be reported in the statement of changes in financial position for 1997.

a Cash of $80,000 was paid and capital stock with a market value of $450,000 was issued to acquire land worth $530,000.

b Depreciation of $200,000 was recorded for the year.

c In June, the 20,000 shares of no-par value capital stock of $500,000 were split 3 for 6, and in November, a 10% stock dividend in common stock was distributed to shareholders.

d Classified a portion of long-term debt as current liabilities, $190,000.

e Sold a plant asset for $2,160,000 cash, resulting in a gain of $160,000 that was reported in the income statement.

EXERCISE 19-5
Conversion of Accrual to Cash Basis

Indicate whether each of the following changes during the year should be added or deducted in converting net income to cash provided or used by operating activities:

a Increase in accounts receivable.
b Increase in accounts payable.
c Decrease in inventory.
d Decrease in prepaid expenses.
e Decrease in accrued expenses.

EXERCISE 19-6
Classification of Items in the Statement of Changes in Financial Position

Indicate in which of the three categories of activities in the statement of changes in financial position each of the following items should be presented:

a Redeemed preferred stock.
b Purchased equipment for cash.
c Sold land for cash.
d Paid cash dividends of $800,000.
e Depreciation expense.
f Increase in inventory.
g Decrease in accrued liabilities.
h Purchased a building costing $60,000 by issuing capital stock.
i Issued bonds payable for cash.

EXERCISE 19-7
Determine Cash from Operations

The London Corporation reported a net loss of $54,000 on its income statement. In arriving at this figure, the following items, among others, were included:

Gain on sale of a plant asset	$28,000
Depreciation expense	88,400
Amortization of patents	28,000
Amortization of premium on bonds payable	10,000

In addition, the changes in noncash current accounts were:

Increase in accounts receivable	$ 8,000
Decrease in inventory	12,000
Increase in prepaid expenses	2,200
Increase in accounts payable	13,000
Decrease in accrued expenses	2,000

From the information above, compute the amount of cash provided or used by operating activities.

EXERCISE 19-8
Converting Net Income to Cash from Operations

The following data are taken from the records of the Eaton Company:

	End of Year	Beginning of Year
Accounts receivable	$ 19,700	$ 7,700
Inventories	32,000	40,000
Prepaid expenses	2,800	2,000
Accounts payable (merchandise creditors)	28,000	25,000
Accrued expenses	1,000	1,200
Net credit sales	398,000	
Cost of goods sold	260,000	
Operating expenses (includes depreciation of $10,000)	100,000	

From the foregoing information prepare the operating activities section of the statement of changes in financial position.

EXERCISE 19-9
Converting Income Statement Items to a Cash Basis

From the information provided in Exercise 19-8, compute the following:

a Cash collected from customers during the year.

b Cash paid to merchandise creditors during the year.

c Cash paid for operating expenses during the year.

d Cash provided or used by operating activities during the year.

EXERCISE 19-10
Preparing a Statement of Changes in Financial Position

A summary of the comparative financial position for Landscape Consultants, Inc., for the current year appears as follows:

	End of Current Year	Beginning of Current Year
Cash (cash and cash equivalents)	$ 18,000	$ 14,000
Accounts receivable (net)	98,000	88,000
Inventory	64,000	73,000
Land	90,000	50,000
Buildings	160,000	100,000
Less: Accumulated depreciation	(40,000)	(35,000)
Totals	$390,000	$290,000
Accounts payable (for purchases)	$ 42,000	$ 31,000
Accrued expenses	8,000	9,000
Notes payable, due in five years	70,000	-0-
Capital stock, no-par value	220,000	210,000
Retained earnings	50,000	40,000
Totals	$390,000	$290,000

The net income was $17,000. Depreciation expense for the current year was $5,000. A cash dividend of $7,000 was paid at the end of the current year.

Prepare a statement of changes in financial position for the current year without using a working paper.

PROBLEMS

Group A

PROBLEM 19A-1
Effect of Transactions on Cash and Cash Equivalents and on Net Income Conversion, and Identifying Exchange Transactions

For each of the following business transactions and adjustments, you are to indicate the effect, first, on cash and cash equivalents, and second, on net income in its conversion to cash provided or used by operating activities. In each case, the possible effects are an increase, decrease, or no change.

1 One-year fire insurance policy paid in advance at year-end date.

2 Inventory destroyed in an accident; one-half of its carrying value covered by insurance and paid by the insurance company.

3 Charging the portion of unexpired insurance expense that expired during the current year.

4 A plant asset sold for cash at a price below its carrying value.

5 Declaration of a cash dividend.

6 Payment of a previously declared cash dividend.

7 Purchase of patent, which gives 200 shares of the company's common stock in exchange.

8 Marketable securities (temporary investments) sold for cash at a price above cost.

9 Amortization of premium on bonds payable.

10 Temporary investments in marketable securities sold for cash at cost, i.e., its carrying value.

INSTRUCTIONS

a List the numbers 1 to 10 on your answer sheet, and set up two columns headed "Effect on cash and cash equivalents" and "Effect on net income conversion." For each item, write the words ***increase, decrease,*** or ***no change*** in the appropriate column to indicate the effect of the item on cash and cash equivalents, and on net income conversion.

b Are any of the items listed above considered "exchange transactions," which would be listed as both a source and use of cash in a statement of changes in financial position? Explain.

PROBLEM 19A-2 Computation of Net Cash Flow from Operating Activities

The data below are taken from the income statement and balance sheets of Discount Pharmacies, Inc.:

	1996	1995
Income statement:		
Net income	$300,000	
Depreciation expense	140,000	
Amortization of intangible assets	20,000	
Gain on sale of plant assets	70,000	
Loss on sale of long-term investments	25,000	
Balance sheets:		
Accounts receivable	$365,000	$410,000
Inventory	513,000	585,000
Prepaid expenses	22,000	10,000
Accounts payable (to merchandise suppliers)	369,000	410,000
Accrued expenses	190,000	155,000

INSTRUCTIONS

Using this information, prepare a partial statement of changes in financial position for the year ended December 31, 1996, showing the determination of net cash flow from operating activities.

PROBLEM 19A-3 Prepare and Comment on a Statement of Changes in Financial Position

The information that is illustrated below is taken from the financial statements of Toro Corporation:

	1996	1995
Cash	$ 65,000	$ 85,000
Temporary investments	35,000	20,000
Accounts receivable (net)	180,000	125,000
Inventories	220,000	250,000
Prepaid expenses	20,000	15,000
Long-term investments	110,000	130,000
Equipment	600,000	420,000
Less: Accumulated depreciation	(190,000)	(110,000)
Bank loan	75,000	55,000
Accounts payable	140,000	165,000
Accrued expenses	25,000	20,000
Capital stock	300,000	255,000
Retained earnings	500,000	440,000

Depreciation for 1996 amounted to $80,000; no equipment items were sold; long-term investments were sold at a gain of $10,000; capital stock was issued for $45,000; and net income was $135,000. Cash dividends of $75,000 were declared and paid.

INSTRUCTIONS

a Compute the amount of increase or decrease in cash and cash equivalents for 1996.

b Prepare a statement of changes in financial position for 1996, without using working papers.

c Briefly comment on the company's liquidity position and cash policies on operating, financing, and investing activities for 1996.

PROBLEM 19A-4
Working Paper

Using the information provided in Problem 19A-3, prepare a working paper for a statement of changes in financial position. (If you have already worked Problem 19A-3, determine that your solutions to both problems are in agreement.)

PROBLEM 19A-5
Show How the Increase in Cash and Cash Equivalents Is Determined and Prepare a Statement of Changes in Financial Position

During the year, Montiris Limited showed the following changes in amount for the following groups of accounts. For example, cash and cash equivalents increased by $16,000 during the year, and this amount therefore appears in the Debit change column.

14,000

	Changes during the Year	
	Debit	*Credit*
Cash and cash equivalents	*$ 16,000*	
Accounts receivable	*54,000*	
Inventories		*$ 10,000*
Building	*200,000*	
Equipment	*120,000*	
Accumulated depreciation		*80,000*
Accounts payable	*120,000*	
Accrued expenses		*4,000*
Capital stock, no-par		*320,000*
Retained earnings		*96,000*
Totals	*$510,000*	*$510,000*

During the year the company sold 12,800 shares of capital stock and applied the proceeds to the purchase of building and equipment. There were no retirements of building and equipment during the year. Net income was $284,000 and cash dividends declared and paid during the year amounted to $188,000.

INSTRUCTIONS

a Show how the $16,000 increase in cash and cash equivalents may be determined by using some necessary ***assumed*** amounts.

b Prepare a statement of changes in financial position without using working papers.

PROBLEM 19A-6
Prepare a Schedule of Cash and Cash Equivalents, and Working Paper and Statement of Changes in Financial Position

Comparative after-closing trial balances for Vancouver Limited follow:

	December 31 1996	1995
Debits		
Cash	$ 82,000	$ 88,000
Marketable securities		96,000
Accounts receivable	192,000	190,000
Inventories	152,000	200,000
Prepaid expenses	46,000	34,000
Land	130,000	
Buildings	510,000	
Patents (net of amortization)	68,000	78,000
Totals	$1,180,000	$686,000
Credits		
Allowance for doubtful accounts	$ 6,000	$ 12,000
Bank loans	30,000	10,000
Accounts payable	138,000	92,000
Accrued expenses	72,000	78,000
Long-term notes payable	300,000	60,000
Capital stock	396,000	226,000
Retained earnings	238,000	208,000
Totals	$1,180,000	$686,000

During 1995, the company operated in rented space. Early in 1996, it acquired suitable land and made arrangements to borrow funds on long-term notes to finance the construction of new buildings. The company also sold additional stock for $170,000 and all its marketable securities at a gain of $2,000. Construction of the buildings was not completed until the end of 1996; therefore, no depreciation expense was recorded in 1996. Net income was $88,000; cash dividends declared and paid amounted to $58,000.

INSTRUCTIONS

a Prepare a schedule of change in cash and cash equivalents.

b Prepare a working paper for a statement of changes in financial position.

c Prepare a statement of changes in financial position for 1996.

PROBLEM 19A-7
Prepare Schedule of Cash and Cash Equivalents, and Working Paper and Statement of Changes in Financial Position

Comparative account balances for Caron Corporation at the end of 1996 and 1997 follow:

Debit	*1997*	*1996*
Cash	*$ 100,000*	*$ 180,000*
Marketable securities		*30,000*
Accounts receivable (net)	*250,000*	*275,000*
Inventory	*450,000*	*350,000*
Land for future expansion	*200,000*	
Plant and equipment	*1,850,000*	*1,725,000*
Patents (net of amortization)	*190,000*	*200,000*
Other: assets of a business segment		*500,000*
Totals	*$3,040,000*	*$3,260,000*

Credit	*1997*	*1996*
Accumulated depreciation	*$ 262,500*	*$ 300,000*
Bank loan	*10,000*	
Accounts payable	*232,500*	*200,000*
Dividends payable	*10,000*	
Notes payable (long-term)	*225,000*	*100,000*
Bonds payable	*1,000,000*	*1,500,000*
Premium on bonds payable	*50,000*	*60,000*
Capital stock	*1,100,000*	*850,000*
Retained earnings	*150,000*	*250,000*
Totals	*$3,040,000*	*$3,260,000*

ADDITIONAL DATA

1 The net loss for 1997 amounted to $40,000.

2 Cash dividends of $10,000 were declared.

3 The company incurred the following expenses, among others: depreciation, amortization of patents, and amortization of premium on bonds payable.

4 The company issued 10,000 shares of its common stock in exchange for land to be held for future expansion. The land was appraised at $200,000.

5 The abandonment of an obsolete and fully depreciated plant with an original cost of $100,000 resulted in a $25,000 cash penalty (a nonoperating loss).

6 Sold a business segment with a carrying value of $500,000 for $530,000 cash (ignore income tax effect and assume no operating income or loss).

7 Equipment was purchased for $225,000. The company paid $100,000 of this amount in cash and issued a 12%, long-term note payable for the balance.

8 Capital stock of $50,000 was issued for stock dividends.

INSTRUCTIONS

a Prepare a schedule of change in cash and cash equivalents during 1997.

b Prepare working papers for a statement of changes in financial position for 1997.

c Prepare a statement of changes in financial position for 1997.

Group B

PROBLEM 19B-1
Effect of Transactions on Cash and Cash Equivalents and on Net Income Conversion, and Identifying Exchange Transactions

A list of business transactions and adjustments follows. For each item you are to indicate the effect, first, on cash and cash equivalents, and second, on net income in its conversion to cash provided or used by operating activities. In each case, the possible effects are an increase, a decrease, or no change.

1 Empty warehouse destroyed by fire; one-half of its carrying value covered by insurance and paid by the insurance company.
2 Amortization of discount on bonds payable.
3 Premium paid for a one-year insurance policy (debit to Unexpired Insurance) at year-end date.
4 Short-term loan from bank.
5 Temporary investments sold for cash at a price below cost.
6 Payment of an account payable.
7 Depreciation recorded for the period.
8 Sale of long-term investment at a price above its carrying value, resulting in a gain.
9 Payment of last year's income tax liability, which was previously recorded in the accounting records.
10 Shares of common stock issued in exchange for convertible bonds converted by bondholders.

INSTRUCTIONS

a List the numbers 1 to 10 on your answer sheet, and set up two columns headed "Effect on cash and cash equivalents" and "Effect on net income conversion." For each item write the words ***increase, decrease,*** or ***no change*** in the appropriate column to indicate the effect of the item on cash and cash equivalents, and on net income conversion.
b Are any of the items listed above considered "exchange transactions," which would be listed as both a source and a use of cash in a statement of changes in financial position? Explain.

PROBLEM 19B-2
An Analysis of Possible Reconciling Items

An analysis of the annual financial statements of K-G Train Corporation reveals the following:

a Prepaid expenses decreased by $500,000 over the year.
b The company had a $2 million nonoperating loss from the early retirement of bonds payable.
c Depreciation for the year amounted to $8 million.
d During the year, $3 million in cash was transferred from the company's bank account into temporary investments.
e Accounts receivable from customers increased by $6 million over the year.
f Accounts payable (to suppliers of merchandise) increased by $3 million during the year.
g Dividends declared during the year, $8 million; dividends paid during the year, $6 million.
h The liability for income taxes payable amounted to $6 million at the beginning of the year and $4 million at year-end.

INSTRUCTIONS

In the reconciliation of net income to net cash flow from operating activities, explain whether each of the above items should be ***added to net income, deducted from net income,*** or ***omitted from the reconciliation.*** Briefly explain your reasons for each answer.

PROBLEM 19B-3
Prepare and Comment on a Statement of Changes in Financial Position

The following information is taken from the 1997 annual report of Just-Arrived Fashion, Inc.:

	End of 1997	End of 1996
Cash	$ 42,000	$ 20,000
Temporary investments	29,000	12,000
Accounts receivable	63,000	54,000
Inventories	95,000	109,000
Prepaid expenses	3,000	4,000
Long-term investments	50,000	62,000
Equipment	435,000	275,000
Less: Accumulated depreciation	(120,000)	(70,000)
Bank loan	27,000	10,000
Accounts payable	70,000	68,000
Accrued expenses	–0–	8,000
Bonds payable	60,000	–0–
Capital stock	150,000	150,000
Retained earnings	290,000	230,000

Depreciation for 1997 amounted to $50,000; no equipment items were sold; long-term investments were sold at a gain of $6,000; bonds were issued for $60,000 cash; and net income was $100,000. Cash dividends of $40,000 were declared and paid.

INSTRUCTIONS

a Compute the amount of increase or decrease in cash and cash equivalents for 1997.

b Prepare a statement of changes in financial position for 1997, without using working papers.

c Briefly comment on the company's liquidity position and cash policies on operating, financing, and investing activities.

PROBLEM 19B-4
Working Paper

Using the information provided in Problem 19B-3, prepare a working paper for a statement of changes in financial position. (If you have already worked Problem 19B-3, determine that your solutions to both problems are in agreement.)

PROBLEM 19B-5
Show How the Increase in Cash and Cash Equivalents Is Determined and Prepare a Statement of Changes in Financial Position

During the year Sun Publishers showed the following ***changes*** in amount for the following groups of accounts. For example, cash and cash equivalents increased by $24,000 during the year, and this amount therefore appears in the Debit change column.

	Changes during the Year	
	Debit	Credit
Cash and cash equivalents	$ 24,000	
Accounts receivable		$ 16,000
Inventories	140,000	
Prepaid equipment rental	12,000	
Land	200,000	
Buildings	880,000	
Accumulated depreciation		460,000
Accounts payable		212,000
Accrued salaries	20,000	
Capital stock, no-par		324,000
Retained earnings		264,000
Totals	$1,276,000	$1,276,000

During the year the company issued 18,000 shares of capital stock at a price of $18 per share. There were no retirements of land and buildings during the year. Net income was $504,000, and cash dividends declared and paid during the year amounted to $240,000.

INSTRUCTIONS

a Show how the $24,000 increase in cash and cash equivalents may be determined by using some ***assumed*** amounts.

b Prepare a statement of changes in financial position for the year without using working papers.

PROBLEM 19B-6 Prepare Schedule of Cash and Cash Equivalents, and Working Paper, and Statement of Changes in Financial Position

Comparative balance sheets for Sierra Hot Tub Ltd. at the end of 1996 and 1997 are shown below:

	1997	1996
Cash	$ 55,000	$ 70,000
Marketable securities	20,000	28,000
Accounts receivable (net)	190,000	205,000
Inventory	245,000	200,000
Prepaid rent	20,000	18,000
Land for future expansion	85,000	
Plant and equipment (see accumulated depreciation below)	520,000	395,000
Patents (net of amortization)	65,000	70,000
Totals	$1,200,000	$986,000
Accumulated depreciation	$157,500	$120,000
Bank loan	36,000	30,000
Accounts payable (suppliers)	161,500	145,000
Accrued salaries	24,000	26,000
Dividends payable	16,000	
Notes payable due in 2000	55,000	
Capital stock, no-par	700,000	575,000
Retained earnings	50,000	90,000
Totals	$1,200,000	$986,000

ADDITIONAL DATA

1 The net loss for 1997 amounted to $24,000.

2 Cash dividends of $16,000 were declared.

3 The company incurred the following expenses, which did not require the use of cash: depreciation, $37,500; and amortization of patents, $5,000.

4 Land for future expansion was acquired at a cost of $85,000. This acquisition was financed by paying $30,000 cash and issuing a 10% note payable due in three years for the balance of the purchase price.

5 The company issued 12,500 shares of its capital stock for cash. The market value of the stock was $10 per share. The proceeds were used to purchase equipment.

INSTRUCTIONS

a Prepare a schedule of cash and cash equivalents for 1997.

b Prepare a working paper for a statement of changes in financial position for 1997.

c Prepare a statement of changes in financial position for 1997.

PROBLEM 19B-7
Prepare Schedule of Cash and Cash Equivalents, and Working Paper and Statement of Changes in Financial Position

Comparative after-closing trial balances for Emerging Technologies, Inc., at the ends of 1996 and 1997 follow:

Debits	1997	1996
Cash	$ 180,000	$ 100,000
Marketable securities	190,000	160,000
Accounts receivable (net)	390,000	320,000
Inventories	710,000	875,000
Prepaid expenses	30,000	45,000
Land	700,000	850,000
Buildings & equipment	1,700,000	1,135,000
Goodwill	288,000	300,000
Other: assets of a business segment		620,000
Discount on bonds payable	23,000	25,000
Totals	$4,211,000	$4,430,000
Credits		
Bank loan (short-term)	$ 30,000	$ 175,000
Accounts payable	545,000	525,000
Accrued expenses	28,000	40,000
Accumulated depreciation	688,000	580,000
Long-term notes payable	250,000	
Bonds payable	1,100,000	1,100,000
11% preferred stock, $100 par		800,000
Common stock, no-par	905,000	630,000
Retained earnings	665,000	580,000
Totals	$4,211,000	$4,430,000

ADDITIONAL DATA

1 Net income for 1997 was $260,000.

2 Land with a cost of $150,000 was sold for $170,000 cash.

3 A segment of business with a book value of $620,000 was sold for $520,000 cash (ignore the income tax effect and assume no operating income or loss).

4 The company incurred, among others, the following expenses: depreciation, amortization of goodwill, and amortization of discount on bonds payable.

5 Equipment was purchased for $565,000 by paying $315,000 in cash and issuing a 12% long-term note payable for the remaining $250,000.

6 The company issued 5,000 shares of common stock at a price of $20 per share. The proceeds, along with some additional cash, were used to retire the entire issue of 11% preferred stock at its par value.

7 Stock dividends of $175,000 in common stock were issued where shareholders were given a choice of receiving cash or common stock.

INSTRUCTIONS

a Prepare a schedule of change in cash and cash equivalents during 1997.

b Prepare a working paper for a statement of changes in financial position for 1997.

c Prepare a statement of changes in financial position for 1997.

ANALYTICAL AND DECISION PROBLEMS AND CASES

A&D 19-1
Convert Income Statement from Accrual to Cash Basis, Prepare and Comment on the Statement of Changes in Financial Position

When the controller of Southern King Corporation presented the following condensed comparative financial statements to the board of directors, the reaction of the board members was very favourable.

SOUTHERN KING CORPORATION
Comparative Financial Position
As of December 31
(in thousands of dollars)

	1997	1996
Current assets	$ 410	$395
Less: Current liabilities	200	225
Working capital	$ 210	$170
Plant and equipment (net)	962	660
Patents (net of amortization)	8	10
Other—assets of a business segment	-0-	150
Total assets minus current liabilities	$1,180	$990
Long-term liabilities	$ 250	$-0-
Preferred stock (non-cumulative)	-0-	170
Common stock	500	500
Retained earnings	430	320
Total long-term debt and capital	$1,180	$990

SOUTHERN KING CORPORATION
Comparative Income Statements
(in thousands of dollars)

	1997	1996
Net sales	$1,000	$680
Cost of goods sold	590	480
Gross profit	$ 410	$200
Operating expenses, including depreciation of $80 in 1997 and $60 in 1996	(180)	(140)
Loss on sale of a business segment	(30)	-0-
Income taxes	(90)	(25)
Net income	$ 110	$ 35

Noting that net income rose from $3.50 per share of capital stock to $11 per share, one member of the board proposed that a substantial cash dividend be paid. "Our working capital is up by $40,000; we should be able to make a distribution to shareholders," he commented. The controller replied that the company's cash position was precarious and pointed out that at the end of 1997 a cash balance of only $15,000 was on hand, a decline from $145,000 at the end of 1996. The controller also reminded the board that the company bought some new equipment during 1997. When a board member asked for an explanation of the increase of $40,000 in working capital, the controller presented the following schedule (in thousands of dollars):

		EFFECT ON WORKING CAPITAL
Increase in working capital:		
Accounts receivable increased by		*$ 83*
Inventories increased by		*72*
Accounts payable reduced by		*62*
Accrued expenses reduced by		*28*
Total increases in working capital		*$245*
Decreases in working capital:		
Cash decreased by	*$130*	
Prepaid expenses reduced by	*10*	
Income tax liability increased by	*65*	*205*
Increase in working capital during 1997		*$ 40*

After examining this schedule, the board member shook his head and said, "I still don't understand how our cash position can be so tight in the face of a tripling of net income and a substantial increase in working capital! Also, I am not sure what our cash policies in the operating, financing, and investing areas are. The information provided by the controller really does not help me at all."

INSTRUCTIONS

a Prepare a statement converting Southern King Corporation's income statement to a cash basis, determining the cash generated by operations during 1997.

b From the information and the comparative statement of financial position provided above, prepare a statement of changes in financial position for 1997, explaining the $130,000 decrease in the cash balance. (Check that the cash from operating activities is the same in both **a** and **b.**)

c Comment on the issues raised by the board member.

A&D 19-2
Can We Make It?

Olympic Sportswear Limited has a cash balance of $6,450,000 at the beginning of 1996. Restrictions contained in the bank loan agreement require that the cash balance not fall below $6,000,000. The following projected information is available for 1996.

1 Budgeted net income (including the gain on sale of plant assets) is $7,200,000. The following items are included in estimating net income: depreciation, $2,100,000; amortization of premium on bonds payable, $150,000. Also, accounts receivable and inventory are expected to increase by $3,200,000 and $3,600,000 respectively. Accounts payable are expected to increase by $6,800,000. The company's sales are expected to be similar to 1995.

2 Sale of plant assets with a carrying value of $1,200,000 is expected to bring in $1,500,000 cash.

3 Additional plant assets costing $15,000,000 will be acquired. Payment will be as follows: 40% cash, and 60% through issuance of capital stock.

4 Long-term investment will be sold at cost, $300,000 cash.

5 Bonds payable in the amount of $1,500,000, bearing interest at 11%, will be redeemed at 105, approximately 10 years prior to maturity in order to eliminate the high interest expense of $165,000 per year. The elimination of this interest and the gain or loss on the retirement of bonds payable were taken into account in estimating net income for 1996. These bonds had been issued at par.

6 Tentative planned cash dividend, $4,500,000.

INSTRUCTIONS

a Consider all the information that has been given and prepare a projected statement of changes in financial position in order to determine the estimated increase or decrease in cash for 1996.

b The planned cash dividend of $4,500,000 represents the same dividend per share as paid last year. The company would like to maintain dividends at this level. Does it appear likely that the past dividend policy can be maintained in 1996? What factors other than cash position should be considered in determining the level of cash dividends declared by the board of directors?

c Comment on the company's cash policy on operating activities.

A&D 19-3
On Target or Not?

Lancaster Corporation is assessing its three-year plan on plant modernization and expansion. The company is in a capital-intensive industry where plant and equipment can become obsolete in a few years. This plan is as follows:

1995 Modernization by replacing obsolete equipment.

1996 Commencing the expansion by constructing a new plant and by purchasing equipment, financed partly by selling the remaining long-term investments of $32 million.

1997 Completing the expansion and starting the operating of the new plant at the beginning of 1998. Of the total cost of $190 million incurred in 1997 ($52 million for plant and $138 million for equipment), $170 million will be financed equally by issuing bonds payable and capital stock.

To enhance the attractiveness of its capital stock issue, the company wants to continue its long-established dividend policy of about 8% on capital, which will require a cash dividend of $38 million in 1997. Also, the company will have more than half of its assets financed by debts after issuing the bonds payable in 1997. The new and old bond indentures (bonds were also issued prior to 1995) will require the company to maintain a minimum cash balance of $30 million for 1997 and subsequent years. It is expected that the net income for 1997 will be similar to that for 1996.

The comparative statements of changes in financial position for 1995 and 1996 are presented below and on page 929.

LANCASTER CORPORATION
Comparative Statements of Changes in Financial Position
For 1996 and 1995
(in millions of dollars)

	1996	1995
Operating activities:		
Net income	$ 12	$ 16
Add: Expenses not requiring the use of cash—Depreciation	8	6
Decrease in accounts receivable	5	2
Decrease in inventories	2	2
Increase in accounts payable	10	3
Increase in accrued liabilities	2	1
Cash provided by operating activities	$ 39	$ 30

	1996	1995
Financing activities:		
Sale of long-term investments	$ 32	$ 62
Issuance of bonds payable	116	
Cash dividends	(30)	(30)
Cash provided by financing activities	$ 118	$ 32
Investing activities:		
Construction of plant	$ (90)	
Purchase of equipment	(36)	$(60)
Cash used in investing activities	$(126)	$(60)
Increase in cash	$ 31	$ 2
Cash Balance	$ 41	$ 10

INSTRUCTIONS

a Assess the company's liquidity position for 1996.

b Comment on the company's cash policies on operating, financing, and investing activities in 1996.

c Will the company be able to finance its activities in 1997 as planned? If yes, explain. If not, explain and suggest alternatives.

CHAPTER

20 Analysis and Interpretation of Financial Statements

In preceding chapters we have explained how decision makers analyze, interpret, and use various types of accounting information, including the statement of changes in financial position presented in Chapter 19. Now we are ready to examine the balance sheet, the income statement, and the statement of retained earnings, and to see how investors and creditors may use these statements in evaluating the profitability, solvency, and future prospects of a business. Also, the importance of the information in corporate annual reports is highlighted. A major goal of this chapter is to demonstrate how different types of investors select the accounting information that is most relevant to their decisions.

Learning Objectives

After studying this chapter you should be able to:

1. *Put a company's net income into perspective by relating it to sales, assets, and shareholders' equity.*
2. *Describe several sources of financial information about a business.*
3. *Explain the uses of dollar and percentage changes, trend percentages, component percentages, and ratios.*
4. *Discuss the "quality" of a company's earnings, assets, and working capital.*
5. *Analyze financial statements from the viewpoints of common shareholders, creditors, and others.*
6. *Compute the ratios widely used in financial statement analysis and explain the significance of each.*

Financial statements are the instrument panel of a business enterprise. They constitute a report on managerial performance, attesting to managerial success or failure and flashing warning signals of impending difficulties. To read a complex instrument panel, one must understand the gauges and their calibration to make sense out of the array of data they convey. Similarly, one must understand the inner workings of the accounting system and the significance of various financial relationships to interpret the data appearing in financial statements. To a reader with a knowledge of accounting, a set of financial statements tells a great deal about a business enterprise.

The financial affairs of a business may be of interest to a number of different groups: management, creditors, investors, politicians, union officials, and government agencies. Each of the groups has somewhat different needs, and accordingly each tends to concentrate on particular aspects of a company's financial picture.

What Is Your Opinion of the Level of Corporate Earnings?

OBJECTIVE 1 Put a company's net income into perspective by relating it to sales, assets, and shareholders' equity.

As a college or university student who has completed (or almost completed) a course in accounting, you have a much better understanding of corporate earnings than do people who have never studied accounting. The level of earnings of large corporations is often a controversial topic, a favourite topic in many political speeches and at cocktail parties. Some of the statements one reads or hears from these sources are emotional rather than rational, fiction rather than fact. Public opinion polls show that the public believes the average manufacturing company has an after-tax net income of about 30% of sales, when in fact such net income has been ***about 5% of sales*** in recent years. A widespread public belief that net income is six times the actual rate may lead to some unwise decisions.

An in-depth knowledge of accounting does not enable you to say at what level corporate earnings ***should be;*** however, a knowledge of accounting does enable you to read audited financial statements that show what the level of corporate earnings ***actually is.*** Moreover, you are aware the information in published financial statements of corporations has been audited by public accounting firms. Consequently, you know that the earnings reported in these published financial statements are reasonably reliable; they have been determined in accordance with generally accepted accounting principles and verified by independent experts.

There are many ways of appraising the adequacy of corporate earnings. Certainly, earnings should be compared with total assets and with invested capital as well as with sales. In this chapter we shall look at a number of ways of evaluating corporate earnings and solvency.

Sources of Financial Information

For the most part, our discussion will be limited to the kind of analysis that can be made by "outsiders" who do not have access to internal accounting records. Investors must rely to a considerable extent on financial statements in published annual and quarterly reports. In the case of largely publicly owned corporations, additional information is presented in their

OBJECTIVE 2 Describe several sources of financial information about a business.

annual report. For example, large corporations include in their annual reports a ***discussion and analysis*** by top management of the results of the company's operations and of its current financial position. (Comprehensive Problem 5 at the end of this chapter contains an example of such information.)

Many financial analysts also study the financial position and future prospects of publicly owned corporations and sell their analyses, conclusions, and investment recommendations for a fee. For example, detailed financial analyses of most large corporations are published by *The Financial Post,* Dun & Bradstreet of Canada, Canadian Business Service *(The Investment Reporter),* Moody's Investors Service, Standard & Poor's, and The Value Line Investment Survey. Anyone may subscribe to these investment advisory services.

Bankers and major creditors usually are able to obtain detailed financial information from borrowers simply by requesting it as a condition for granting a loan. Suppliers and other trade creditors may obtain some financial information about almost any business from credit-rating agencies, such as Dun & Bradstreet of Canada.

Comparative Financial Statement

Significant changes in financial data are easy to see when financial statement amounts for two or more years are placed side by side in adjacent columns. Such a statement is called a ***comparative financial statement.*** The amounts for the most recent year are usually placed in the left-hand money column. All financial statements are usually prepared in the form of comparative statements. A highly condensed comparative income statement covering three years is shown below.

Condensed three-year income statement

BENSON CORPORATION
Comparative Income Statement
For the Years Ended December 31, 1997, 1996, and 1995
(in thousands of dollars)

	1997	1996	1995
Net sales	$600	$500	$400
Cost of goods sold	370	300	235
Gross profit	$230	$200	$165
Expenses	194	160	115
Net income	$ 36	$ 40	$ 50

Tools of Analysis

Few figures in a financial statement are highly significant in and of themselves. It is their relationship to other quantities or the amount and direction of change that is important. Analysis is largely a matter of establishing significant relationships and identifying changes and trends. Four widely used analytical techniques are (1) dollar and percentage changes, (2) trend percentages, (3) component percentages, and (4) ratios.

OBJECTIVE 3
Explain the uses of dollar and percentage changes, trend percentages, component percentages, and ratios.

Dollar and Percentage Changes

The dollar amount of change from year to year is significant, but expressing the change in percentage terms adds perspective. For example, if sales this year have increased by $100,000, the fact that this is an increase of 10% over last year's sales of $1 million puts it in a different perspective than if it represented a 1% increase over sales of $10 million for the prior year.

The dollar amount of any change is the difference between the amount for a ***comparison*** year and for a ***base*** year. The percentage change is computed by dividing the amount of the change between years by the amount for the base year. This is illustrated in the tabulation below, using data from the comparative income statement on page 932.

Dollar and percentage changes

	In Thousands			Increase or (Decrease)			
				1997 over 1996		1996 over 1995	
	Year 1997	Year 1996	Year 1995	Amount	%	Amount	%
Net sales	$600	$500	$400	$100	20%	$100	25%
Net income	36	40	50	(4)	(10%)	(10)	(20%)

Although net sales increased $100,000 in both 1996 and 1997, the percentage of change differs because of the shift in the base from 1995 to 1996. These calculations present no problems when the figures for the base year are positive amounts. If a negative amount or a zero amount appears in the base year, however, a percentage change cannot be computed. Thus if Benson Corporation had incurred a net loss in 1996, the percentage change in net income from 1996 to 1997 could not have been calculated.

Evaluating Percentage Changes in Sales and Earnings Computing the percentage changes in sales, gross profit, and net income from one year to the next gives insight into a company's rate of growth. If a company is experiencing growth in its economic activities, sales and earnings should increase at ***more than the rate of inflation.*** Assume, for example, that a company's sales increase by 6% while the general price level rises by 10%. It is probable that the entire increase in the dollar amount of sales may be explained by inflation, rather than by an increase in sales volume (the number of units sold). In fact, the company may well have sold ***fewer*** goods than in the preceding year.

In measuring the dollar or percentage change in ***quarterly*** sales or earnings, it is customary to compare the results of the current quarter with those of the ***same quarter in the preceding year.*** Use of the same quarter of the preceding year as the base period prevents our analysis from being distorted by seasonal fluctuations in business activity.

Percentages Become Misleading When the Base Is Small Percentage changes may create a misleading impression when the dollar amount used as a base is unusually small. Occasionally we hear a television newscaster say that a company's net income has increased by a very large percentage, such as 900%. The initial impression created by such a statement is that the company's net income must now be excessively large. But assume, for example, that a company had net income of $100,000 in its first year; that in the second year net income drops to $10,000; and that in the third year net income returns to the $100,000 level. In this third year, net income has increased by $90,000, representing a 900% increase over the net income of the second year. What needs to be added is that this 900% increase in net income in the third year ***exactly offsets*** the 90% decline in net income in the second year. Few people realize that a 90% decline in earnings must be followed by a 900% increase just to get back to the starting point.

CASE IN POINT In 1990, Maclean Hunter Limited had a net income of $15.3 million, as compared to 1989's net income of $89 million. This represented an 83% decline in net income ($89 million minus $15.3 million divided by $89 million). How much of an increase in net income would be required in 1991 in order for the net income to return to the 1989 level? The answer is 482%, as computed as follows:

Required increase to reach the 1989 net income level (from $15.3 million to $89 million)	*$73.7 million*
Base period earnings (1990)	*$15.3 million*
Required percentage increase ($73.7 million ÷ $15.3 million)	*482%*

Thus, even when Maclean Hunter's net income increased by 231% in 1991 over the net income in 1990, the 1991 net income was only $50.6 million. In fact, a 431% increase in net income in 1992 over the net income in 1990 resulted only in an $81.2 million net income for 1992, still short of the 1989 net income level.

Trend Percentages

The changes in financial statement items from a base year to following years are often expressed as ***trend percentages*** to show the extent and direction of change. Two steps are necessary to compute trend percentages. First, a base year is selected and each item in the financial statements for the base year is given a weight of 100%. The second step is to express each item in the financial statements for following years as a percentage of its base-year amount. This computation consists of dividing an item such as Sales in the years after the base year by the amount of Sales in the base year.

For example, assume that 1991 is selected as the base year and that Sales in the base year amounted to $300,000 as shown below. The trend percentages for Sales are computed by dividing the Sales amount of each following year by $300,000. Also shown in the illustration are the yearly amounts of net income. The trend percentages for net income are computed by dividing the Net Income amount for each following year by the base-year amount of $15,000.

	1996	1995	1994	1993	1992	1991
Sales	*$450,000*	*$360,000*	*$330,000*	*$320,000*	*$312,000*	*$300,000*
Net income	*22,950*	*14,550*	*21,450*	*19,200*	*15,600*	*15,000*

When the computations described above have been made, the trend percentages will appear as shown below.

	1996	1995	1994	1993	1992	1991
Sales	150%	120%	110%	107%	104%	100%
Net income	153%	97%	143%	128%	104%	100%

The above trend percentages indicate a very modest growth in sales in the early years and accelerated growth in 1995 and 1996. Net income also shows an increasing growth trend with the exception of the year 1995, when net income declined despite a solid increase in sales. This variation could have resulted from an unfavourable change in the gross profit margin or from unusual expenses. However, the problem was overcome in 1996 with a sharp rise in net income. Overall the trend percentages give a picture of a profitable growing enterprise.

As another example, assume that sales are increasing each year but that the cost of goods sold is increasing at a faster rate. This means that the gross profit margin is shrinking. Perhaps the increases in sales are being achieved through excessive price cutting. The company's net income may be declining even though sales are rising.

Component Percentages

Component percentages indicate the ***relative size*** of each item included in a total. For example, each item on a balance sheet could be expressed as a percentage of total assets. This shows quickly the relative importance of current and noncurrent assets as well as the relative amount of financing obtained from current creditors, long-term creditors, and shareholders. By computing component percentages for several successive balance sheets, we can see which items are increasing in importance and which are becoming less significant.

Common Size Income Statement Another application of component percentages is to express all items in an income statement as a percentage of net sales. Such a statement is called a common size income statement. A condensed income statement in dollars and in common size form is illustrated below.

Are the year-to-year changes favourable?

Income Statement

	Dollars		Component Percentages	
	1996	1995	1996	1995
Net sales	$1,000,000	$600,000	100.0%	100.0%
Cost of goods sold	700,000	360,000	70.0	60.0
Gross profit	$ 300,000	$240,000	30.0%	40.0%
Expenses (including income taxes)	250,000	180,000	25.0	30.0
Net income	$ 50,000	$ 60,000	5.0%	10.0%

Looking only at the component percentages, we see that the decline in the gross profit rate from 40% to 30% was only partially offset by the decrease in expenses as a percentage of net sales, causing net income to decrease from 10% to 5% of net sales.

Ratios

A ratio is a simple mathematical expression of the relationship of one item to another. Every percentage may be viewed as a ratio—that is, one number expressed as a percentage of another.

Ratios may be stated in several ways. To illustrate, let us consider the current ratio, which expresses the relationship between current assets and current liabilities. If current assets are \$100,000 and current liabilities are \$50,000, we may say either that the current ratio is 2 to 1 (which is written as 2:1) or that current assets are 200% of current liabilities. Either statement correctly summarizes the relationship—that is, that current assets are twice as large as current liabilities.

If a ratio is to be useful, the two amounts being compared must be logically related. Our interpretation of a ratio often requires investigation of the underlying data.

Comparative Data in Annual Reports of Major Corporations

The annual reports of major corporations usually contain comparative balance sheets covering two years and comparative income statements for two or three years. Supplementary schedules showing sales, net income, and other key amounts are often presented for periods of five to 10 years. Shown below are selected items from an annual report of Bombardier, Inc. showing some interesting trends for a five-year period.

BOMBARDIER, INC.
(Dollars in millions, except per share data)

	1993	1992	1991	1990	1989
Revenue	\$4,448	\$3,059	\$2,892	\$2,143	\$1,426
Net income	132	108	100	92	68
Net earnings per common share	0.85	0.73	0.71	0.68	0.52
Dividends per share (class A)	0.20	0.16	0.16	0.13	0.11
Market price per share (year-end), class A	11.88	17.13	8.44	7.81	6.69
Book value per common share	6.16	5.67	4.64	3.54	2.92

Standards of Comparison

In using dollar and percentage changes, trend percentages, component percentages, and ratios, financial analysts constantly search for some standard of comparison against which to judge whether the relationships that they have found are favourable or unfavourable. Two such standards are (1) the past performance of the company and (2) the performance of other companies in the same industry.

Past Performance of the Company Comparing analytical data for a current period with similar computations for prior years affords some basis for judging whether the condition of the business is improving or worsening. This comparison of data over time is sometimes called ***horizontal*** or ***trend*** analysis, to express the idea of reviewing data for a number of consecutive periods. It is distinguished from ***vertical*** or ***static*** analysis, which refers to the review of the financial information for only one accounting period.

In addition to determining whether the situation is improving or becoming worse, horizontal analysis may aid in making estimates of future prospects.

Because changes may reverse their direction at any time, however, projecting past trends into the future is always a somewhat risky statistical endeavour.

A weakness of horizontal analysis is that comparison with the past does not afford any basis for evaluation in absolute terms. The fact that net income was 2% of sales last year and is 3% of sales this year indicates improvement, but if there is evidence that net income ***should be*** 7% of sales, the record for both years is unfavourable.

Industry Standard The limitations of horizontal analysis may be overcome to some extent by finding an appropriate "yardstick" against which to measure a particular company's performance. The yardsticks most widely used by most analysts are the performance of comparable companies and the average performance of several companies in the same industry.[1]

CASE IN POINT Dun & Bradstreet Canada Limited publishes *Key Business Ratios Canada-Corporations* for many industries. The following are "industry ratios" selected from a recent issue of this publication:

	Average Ratios			
Industry Group	***Gross Margin***	***Current Ratio***	***Net Income to Sales***	***Rate of Return on Equity***
Retail trade	*25.7%*	*1.4*	*2.5%*	*20.9%*
Wholesale trade	*18.2%*	*1.3*	*1.9%*	*14.0%*
Manufacturers	*22.7%*	*1.5*	*4.5%*	*12.4%*
Construction	*24.5%*	*1.3*	*3.2%*	*23.3%*
Services	*79.6%*	*1.0*	*7.0%*	*23.5%*
Transportation, Storage & Utilities (including radio and T.V.)	*78.0%*	*0.8*	*6.6%*	*9.9%*

Assume, for example, that the revenue of Alpha Airlines drops by 5% during the current year. If the revenue for the airlines industry had dropped an average of 15% during this year, Alpha's 5% decline might be viewed as a ***favourable*** performance. As another example, assume that Omega Limited earns a net income equal to 2% of net sales. This would be substandard if Omega were a manufacturer of commercial aircraft, but it would be satisfactory performance if it were a grocery chain.

When we compare a given company with its competitors or with industry averages, our conclusions will be valid only if the companies in question

[1] Industry data are available from a number of sources. For example, Robert Morris Associates publishes *Annual Statement Studies* that include data from many thousands of annual reports, grouped into several hundred industry classifications. Industry classifications are subdivided further by company size. Dun & Bradstreet annually publishes *Key Business Ratios* for several hundred lines of business.

are reasonably comparable. Because of the large number of diversified companies formed in recent years, the term ***industry*** is difficult to define, and companies that fall roughly within the same industry may not be comparable in many respects. For example, one company may engage only in the marketing of oil products; another may be a fully integrated producer from the well to the gas pump, yet both are said to be in the "oil industry."

Quality of Earnings

OBJECTIVE 4 Discuss the "quality" of a company's earnings, assets, and working capital.

Earnings are the lifeblood of a business entity. No entity can survive for long and accomplish its other goals unless it is profitable. On the other hand, continuous losses will drain assets from the business, consume owners' equity, and leave the company at the mercy of creditors. In assessing the prospects of a company, we are interested not only in the total ***amount*** of earnings but also in the ***rate*** of earnings on sales, on total assets, and on owner's equity. In addition, we must look at the ***stability*** and ***source*** of earnings. An erratic earnings performance over a period of years, for example, is less desirable than a steady level of earnings. A history of increasing earnings is preferable to a "flat" earnings record.

A breakdown of sales and earnings by ***major product lines*** is useful in evaluating the future performance of a company. Publicly owned companies include with their financial statements supplementary schedules showing sales and earnings by product line and by geographical area. These schedules assist financial analysts in forecasting the effect upon the company of changes in consumer demand for particular types of products.

Financial analysts often express the opinion that the earnings of one company are of higher quality than earnings of other similar companies. This concept of ***quality of earnings*** arises because each company management can choose from a variety of accounting principles and methods, all of which are considered generally acceptable. A company's management often is under heavy pressure to report rising earnings, and accounting policies may be tailored toward this objective. We have already pointed out the impact on current reported earnings of the choice between the LIFO and FIFO methods of inventory valuation and the choice of depreciation policies. In judging the quality of earnings, the financial analyst should consider whether the accounting principles and methods selected by management lead to a conservative measurement of earnings or tend to inflate reported earnings.

Quality of Assets and the Relative Amount of Debt

Although a satisfactory level of earnings may be a good indication of the company's long-run ability to pay its debts and dividends, we must also look at the composition of assets, their condition and liquidity, the relationship between current assets and current liabilities, the cash flows, and the total amount of debt outstanding. A company may be profitable and yet be unable to pay its liabilities on time; sales and earnings may appear satisfactory, but plant and equipment may be deteriorating because of poor maintenance policies; valuable patents may be expiring; substantial losses may be imminent due to slow-moving inventories and past-due receivables. Companies with large amounts of debt often are vulnerable to increases in interest rates and to even temporary reductions in cash inflows.

Impact of Inflation

During a period of significant inflation, financial statements prepared in terms of historical costs do not reflect fully the economic resources or the real income (in terms of purchasing power) of a business enterprise. It is desirable that companies include in their annual reports supplementary schedules showing the effects of inflation upon their financial statements. Most companies, however, do ***not*** include these supplementary schedules because of the high cost of developing this information.

Illustrative Analysis for Seacliff Corporation

Keep in mind the preceding discussion of analytical principles as you study the illustrative financial analysis that follows. The basic information for our analysis is contained in a set of condensed two-year comparative financial statements for Seacliff Corporation shown below and on the following page.[2] Summarized statement data, together with computations of dollar increases and decreases, and component percentages where applicable, have been compiled. For convenience in this illustration, relatively small dollar amounts have been used in the Seacliff financial statements.

Using the information in these statements, let us consider the kind of analysis that might be of particular interest to (1) common shareholders, (2) long-term creditors, (3) preferred shareholders, and (4) short-term creditors.

SEACLIFF CORPORATION
Comparative Income Statement
For the Years Ended December 31, 1996 and December 31, 1995

			Increase or (Decrease)		Percentage of Net Sales	
	1996	1995	Dollars	%	1996	1995
Net sales	$900,000	$750,000	$150,000	20.0	100.0	100.0
Cost of goods sold	530,000	420,000	110,000	26.2	58.9	56.0
Gross profit	$370,000	$330,000	$ 40,000	12.1	41.1	44.0
Operating expenses:						
Selling expenses:	$117,000	$ 75,000	$ 42,000	56.0	13.0	10.0
General and administrative expenses	126,000	95,000	31,000	32.6	14.0	12.7
Total operating expenses	$243,000	$170,000	$ 73,000	42.9	27.0	22.7
Operating income	$127,000	$160,000	$(33,000)	(20.6)	14.1	21.3
Interest expense	24,000	30,000	(6,000)	(20.0)	2.7	4.0
Income before income taxes	$103,000	$130,000	$(27,000)	(20.8)	11.4	17.3
Income taxes	28,000	40,000	(12,000)	(30.0)	3.1	5.3
Net income	$ 75,000	$ 90,000	$(15,000)	(16.7)	8.3	12.0
Earnings per share of common stock	$13.20	$20.25	$(7.05)	(34.8)		

[2] Since the statement of changes in financial position was presented and analyzed in Chapter 19, it is not included here again.

SEACLIFF CORPORATION
Statement of Retained Earnings
For the Years Ended December 31, 1996 and December 31, 1995

			Increase or (Decrease)	
	1996	1995	Dollars	%
Retained earnings, beginning of year	$176,000	$115,000	$61,000	53.0
Net income	75,000	90,000	(15,000)	(16.7)
	$251,000	$205,000	$46,000	22.4
Less: Dividends on common stock ($5.00 per share in 1995, $4.80 per share in 1996)	$ 24,000	$ 20,000	$ 4,000	20.0
Dividends on preferred stock ($9 per share)	9,000	9,000		
	$ 33,000	$ 29,000	$ 4,000	13.8
Retained earnings, end of year	$218,000	$176,000	$42,000	23.9

SEACLIFF CORPORATION
Condensed Comparative Balance Sheet*
December 31, 1996 and December 31, 1995

			Increase or (Decrease)		Percentage of Total Assets	
Assets	1996	1995	Dollars	%	1996	1995
Current assets	$390,000	$288,000	$102,000	35.4	41.1	33.5
Plant and equipment (net)	500,000	467,000	33,000	7.1	52.6	54.3
Other assets (loans to officers)	60,000	105,000	(45,000)	(42.9)	6.3	12.2
Total assets	$950,000	$860,000	$ 90,000	10.5	100.0	100.0
Liabilities & Shareholders' Equity						
Liabilities:						
Current liabilities	$112,000	$ 94,000	$ 18,000	19.1	11.8	10.9
12% bonds payable	200,000	250,000	(50,000)	(20.0)	21.1	29.1
Total liabilities	$312,000	$344,000	$(32,000)	(9.3)	32.9	40.0
Shareholders' equity:						
$9 preferred stock, no-par, callable at 105, 1,000 shares	$100,000	$100,000			10.5	11.6
Common stock (1996, 5,000 shares; 1995, 4,000 shares)	320,000	240,000	$ 80,000	33.3	33.7	27.9
Retained earnings	218,000	176,000	42,000	23.9	22.9	20.5
Total shareholders' equity	$638,000	$516,000	$122,000	23.6	67.1	60.0
Total liabilities & shareholders' equity	$950,000	$860,000	$ 90,000	10.5	100.0	100.0

* In order to focus attention on important subtotals, this statement is highly condensed and does not show individual asset and liability items. These details will be introduced as needed in the next discussion. For example, a list of Seacliff Corporation's current assets and current liabilities appears on page 949.

Analysis by Common Shareholders

OBJECTIVE 5 Analyze financial statements from the viewpoints of common shareholders, creditors, and others.

Common shareholders and potential investors in common stock look first at a company's earnings record. Their investment is in shares of stock, so ***earnings per share and dividends per share*** are of particular interest.

Earnings per Share of Common Stock As indicated in Chapter 15, earnings per share of common stock are computed by dividing the income applicable to the common stock by the weighted-average number of shares of common stock outstanding during the year. Any preferred dividend requirements must be subtracted from net income to determine income applicable to common stock, as shown in the following computations for Seacliff Corporation:

Earnings per Share of Common Stock

Earnings related to number of common shares outstanding

		1996	1995
Net income		$75,000	$90,000
Less: Preferred dividend requirements		9,000	9,000
Income applicable to common stock	(a)	$66,000	$81,000
Shares of common stock outstanding, during the year	(b)	5,000	4,000
Earnings per share of common stock (a ÷ b)		$13.20	$20.25

Notice that earnings per share have decreased by ***$7.05*** in 1996, representing a decline of nearly ***35%*** from their level in 1995 ($7.05 ÷ $20.25 = 34.8%). Common shareholders consider a decline in earnings per share to be an extremely unfavourable development. A decline in earnings per share generally represents a decline in the profitability of the company, and creates doubt as to the company's prospects for future growth.

With such a significant decline in earnings per share, we should expect to see a ***substantial*** decline in the market value of Seacliff's common stock during 1996. [For purposes of our illustration, we will assume the common stock had a market value of ***$160*** at December 31, 1995 and of ***$132*** at the end of 1996. This drop of $28 per share represents a ***17½%*** decline in the market value of every common shareholder's investment ($28 decline ÷ $160 = 17.5%).]

Price-Earnings Ratio The relationship between the market price of common stock and earnings per share is so widely recognized that it is expressed as a ratio, called the price-earnings ratio (or ***p/e*** ratio). The p/e ratio is determined by dividing the market price per share by the annual earnings per share.

The p/e ratio of the 300 stocks included in the TSE 300 Composite (Toronto Stock Exchange) has varied widely in recent years. The outlook for future earnings is the major factor influencing a company's p/e ratio. Companies with track records of rapid growth may sell at p/e ratios of perhaps 20 to 1, or even higher. Companies with "flat" earnings or earnings expected to decline in future years often sell at price-earnings ratios below, say, 10 to 1.

At the end of 1995, Seacliff's p/e ratio was approximately ***8 to 1*** ($160 ÷ $20.25 = 7.9), suggesting that investors ***were expecting*** earnings to decline in 1996. At December 31, 1996, the price earnings ratio was ***10 to 1***

($132 ÷ $13.20 = 10.0). A p/e ratio in this range suggests that investors expect future earnings to stabilize around the current level.

Dividend Yield Dividends are of prime importance to some shareholders but a secondary factor to others. In other words, some shareholders invest primarily to receive regular cash income, while others invest in stocks principally with the hope of securing capital gains through rising market prices. If a corporation is profitable and retains its earnings for expansion of the business, the expanded operations should produce an increase in the net income of the company and thus tend to make each share of stock more valuable.

In comparing the merits of alternative investment opportunities, we should relate earnings and dividends per share to the ***market value*** of the stock. Dividends per share divided by market price per share determine the ***yield*** rate of a company's stock. Dividend yield is especially important to those investors whose objective is to maximize the dividend revenue from their investments.

Summary of Earnings and Dividend Data for Seacliff The relationships of Seacliff's per-share earnings and dividends to its year-end stock prices are summarized below:

Earnings and dividends related to market price of common stock

Earnings and Dividends per Share of Common Stock

Date	Assumed Market Value per Share	Earnings per Share	Price-Earnings Ratio	Dividends per Share	Dividend Yield, %
Dec. 31, 1995	$160	$20.25	8	$5.00	3.1
Dec. 31, 1996	132	13.20	10	4.80	3.6

The decline in market value during 1996 presumably reflects the decreases in both earnings and dividends per share. Investors appraising this stock at December 31, 1996, should consider whether a price-earning ratio of ***10*** and a dividend yield of ***3.6%*** represent a satisfactory situation in the light of alternative investment opportunities. These investors will also place considerable weight on estimates of the company's prospective future earnings and the probable effect of such estimated earnings on the market price of the stock and on dividend payments.

Book Value per Share of Common Stock The procedures for computing book value per share were fully described in Chapter 14 and will not be repeated here. We will, however, determine the book value per share of common stock for Seacliff:

Why did book value per share increase?

Book Value per Share of Common Stock

		1996	1995
Total shareholders' equity		$638,000	$516,000
Less: Equity of preferred shareholders (1,000 shares at call price of $105)		105,000	105,000
Equity of common shareholders	(a)	$533,000	$411,000
Shares of common stock outstanding	(b)	5,000	4,000
Book value per share of common stock (a ÷ b)		$106.60	$102.75

Book value indicates the net assets represented by each share of stock. This statistic is often helpful in estimating a reasonable price for a company's stock, especially for small corporations whose shares are not publicly traded.[3] However, if a company's future earnings prospects are unusually good or unusually poor, or the market value of the company's assets is different from their carrying (book) value, the market price of its shares may differ significantly from their book value.

CASE IN POINT A study on Canada's top 100 public corporations (in terms of the market value of their listed shares) compared the market values with book values of the common stock of these corporations and computed a "premium market/book value" statistic. For example, a premium market/book value of plus 100% means that the market value of common stock is twice the book value. The percentages of the premium market/book value of these top 100 public corporations range from a negative 18% for a bank and a resource company to a plus 887% for a real estate developer. A recent annual report of Bombardier, Inc. showed a premium market/book value of 192.8.

Revenue and Expense Analysis The trend of earnings of Seacliff is unfavourable, and shareholders will want to know the reasons for the decline in net income. The comparative income statement shows that despite a 20% increase in net sales, net income fell from $90,000 in 1995 to $75,000 in 1996, a decline of 16.7%. As a percentage of net sales, net income fell from 12% to only 8.3%. The primary causes of this decline were the increases in selling expenses (56.0%), in general and administrative expenses (32.6%), and in the cost of goods sold (26.2%), all of which exceeded the 20% increase in net sales.

Let us assume that further investigation reveals Seacliff decided in 1996 to reduce its sales prices in an effort to generate greater sales volume. This would explain the decrease in gross profit rate from 44% to 41.1% of net sales. Since the dollar amount of gross profit increased $40,000 in 1996, the strategy of reducing sales prices to increase volume would have been successful if there had been little or no increase in operating expenses. However, operating expenses rose by $73,000, resulting in a $33,000 decrease in operating income.

The next step is to find which expenses increased and why. An investor may be handicapped here, because detailed operating expenses are not usually shown in published financial statements. Some conclusions, however, can be reached on the basis of even the condensed information available in the comparative income statement for Seacliff.

The substantial increase in selling expenses presumably reflects greater selling effort during 1996 in an attempt to improve sales volume. However, the fact that selling expenses increased $42,000 while gross profit increased only $40,000 indicates that the cost of this increased sales

---

[3] As pointed out in Chapter 14, book value per share is regularly reported in such financial news media as *The Financial Post* and *The Financial Times,* and also in the annual reports of large corporations such as Dofasco Inc., Royal Bank of Canada, and Moore Corporation Limited.

effort was not justified in terms of results. Even more disturbing is the increase in general and administrative expenses. Some growth in administrative expenses might be expected to accompany increased sales volume, but because some of the expenses are fixed, the growth generally should be ***less than proportional*** to any increase in sales. The increase in general and administrative expenses from 12.7 to 14% of sales would be of serious concern to informed investors.

Management generally has greater control over operating expenses than over revenue. The ***operating expense ratio*** is often used as a measure of management's ability to control its operating expenses. The unfavourable trend in this ratio for Seacliff is shown below:

Does a higher operating expense ratio indicate higher net income?

Operating Expense Ratio

	1996	1995
Operating expenses	(a) $243,000	$170,000
Net sales	(b) $900,000	$750,000
Operating expense ratio (a ÷ b)	27.0%	22.7%

If management were able to increase the sales volume while at the same time increasing the gross profit rate and decreasing the operating expense ratio, the effect on net income could be quite dramatic. For example, if in 1997 Seacliff can increase its sales by 11% to $1,000,000, increase its gross profit rate from 41.1 to 44%, and reduce the operating expense ratio from 27 to 24%, its operating income will increase from $127,000 to $200,000 ($1,000,000 − $560,000 − $240,000), an increase of over 57%.

Return on Investment (ROI)

The rate of return on investment (often called ROI) is a measure of management's efficiency in using available resources. Regardless of the size of the organization, capital is a scarce resource and must be used efficiently. In judging the performance of branch managers or of companywide management, it is reasonable to raise the question: What rate of return have you earned on the resources under your control? The concept of return on investment can be applied to a number of situations: for example, evaluating a branch, a total business, a product line, or an individual investment. A number of different ratios have been developed for the ROI concept, each well suited to a particular situation. We shall consider the ***return on assets*** and the ***return on common shareholders' equity*** as examples of the return on investment concept.

Return on Assets An important test of management's ability to earn a return on funds supplied from all sources is the rate of return on total assets.

The income figure used in computing this ratio should be ***operating income,*** since interest expense and income taxes are determined by factors other than the efficient use of resources. Operating income is earned throughout the year and therefore should be related to the ***average*** investment in assets during the year. The computation of this ratio of Seacliff is as follows (assuming the 1995 beginning balance of total assets is $820,000):

Percentage Return on Assets

Earnings related to investment in assets

	1996	1995
Operating income	(a) $127,000	$160,000
Total assets, beginning of year	(b) $860,000	$820,000
Total assets, end of year	(c) $950,000	$860,000
Average investment in assets [(b + c) ÷ 2]	(d) $905,000	$840,000
Return on assets (a ÷ d)	14%	19%

This ratio shows that the rate of return earned on the company's assets has fallen off in 1996. Before drawing conclusions as to the effectiveness of Seacliff's management, however, we should consider the trend in the return on assets earned by other companies of similar kind and size.

Return on Common Shareholders' Equity Because interest and dividends paid to creditors and preferred shareholders are fixed in amount, a company may earn a greater or smaller return on the common shareholders' equity than on its total assets. The computation of return on shareholders' equity for Seacliff is shown below:

Return on Common Shareholders' Equity

Does the use of leverage benefit common shareholders?

	1996	1995
Net income	$ 75,000	$ 90,000
Less: Preferred dividend requirements	9,000	9,000
Net income applicable to common stock	(a) $ 66,000	$ 81,000
Common shareholders' equity, beginning of year	(b) $416,000	$355,000*
Common shareholders' equity, end of year	(c) $538,000	$416,000
Average common shareholders' equity [(b + c) ÷ 2]	(d) $477,000	$385,500
Return on common shareholders' equity (a ÷ d)	13.8%	21.0%

*Assumed

In both years, the rate of return on common shareholders' equity was higher than the 12% rate of interest paid to long-term creditors or the 9% dividend rate paid to preferred shareholders. This result was achieved through the favourable use of leverage.

Leverage

The term ***leverage*** means operating a business with borrowed money. If the borrowed capital can be used in the business to earn a return ***greater*** than the cost of borrowing, then the net income and the return on common shareholders' equity will ***increase.*** In other words, if you can borrow money at 12% and use it to earn 20%, you will benefit by doing so. However, leverage can act as a "double-edged sword"; the effects may be favourable or unfavourable to the holders of common stock.

If the rate of return on total assets should fall ***below*** the average rate of interest on borrowed capital, leverage will ***reduce*** net income and the return on common shareholders' equity. In this situation, paying off the loans that carry high interest rates would appear to be a logical move. However, most companies do not have enough cash to retire long-term debt on short notice. Therefore, the common shareholders may become "locked in" to the unfavourable effects of leverage.

In deciding how much leverage is appropriate, the common shareholders should consider the ***stability*** of the company's return on assets as well as the relationship of this return to the average cost of borrowed capital. If a business incurs so much debt that it becomes unable to meet the required interest and principal payments, the creditors may force liquidation or reorganization of the business.

CASE IN POINT After two mega acquisitions in the United States for a total price tag of over $13 billion, most of which was financed by debt, Campeau Corporation was highly leveraged. With more than $11 billion in debt and only slightly over $110 million in equity, Campeau's equity ratio was exceedingly low. The rising interest rate, coupled with poor operating results, led to serious financial trouble for Campeau. In a span of six months, Campeau's stock plummeted from a high of $22 per share to less than $2. Consequently, the company had to be restructured, reorganized, and drastically "downsized."

Equity Ratio One indicator of the amount of leverage used by a business is the equity ratio. This ratio measures the proportion of the total assets financed by shareholders, as distinguished from creditors. It is computed by dividing total shareholders' equity by total assets. A ***low*** equity ratio indicates an extensive use of leverage, that is, a large proportion of financing provided by creditors. A high equity ratio, on the other hand, indicates that the business is making little use of leverage.

The equity ratio at year-end for Seacliff is determined as follows:

Proportion of assets financed by shareholders

Equity Ratio

		1996	1995
Total shareholders' equity	(a)	$638,000	$516,000
Total assets (or total liabilities & shareholders' equity)	(b)	$950,000	$860,000
Equity ratio (a ÷ b)		67.2%	60.0%

Seacliff has a higher equity ratio in 1996 than in 1995. Is this favourable or unfavourable?

From the viewpoint of the common shareholder, a low equity ratio will produce maximum benefits if management is able to earn a rate of return on assets greater than the rate of interest paid to creditors. However, a low equity ratio can be very ***unfavourable*** if the return on assets falls ***below*** the rate of interest paid to creditors. Since the return on total assets earned by Seacliff has declined from 19% in 1995 to a relatively low 14% in 1996, the common shareholders probably would ***not*** want to risk a low equity ratio. The action by management in 1996 of retiring $50,000 in long-term liabilities will help to protect the common shareholders from the unfavourable effects of leverage if the rate of return on assets continues to decline.

Analysis by Long-Term Creditors

Bondholders and other long-term creditors are primarily interested in three factors: (1) the rate of return on their investment, (2) the firm's ability to meet its interest requirements, and (3) the firm's ability to repay the principal of the debt when it falls due.

Yield Rate on Bonds The yield rate on bonds or other long-term indebtedness cannot be computed in the same manner as the yield rate on shares of stock, because bonds, unlike stocks, have a definite maturity date and amount. The ownership of a 12%, 10-year, $1,000 bond represents the right to receive $120 each year for 10 years plus the right to receive $1,000 at the end of 10 years. If the market price of this bond is $950, the yield rate on an investment in the bond is the rate of interest that will make the present value of these two contractual rights equal to $950. When bonds sell at maturity value, the yield rate is equal to the bond interest rate. ***The yield rate varies inversely with changes in the market price of the bond.*** If interest rates rise, the market price of existing bonds will fall; if interest rates decline, the price of bonds will rise. If the price of a bond is above maturity value, the yield rate is less than the bond interest rate; if the price of a bond is below maturity value, the yield rate is higher than the bond interest rate.

Interest Coverage Ratio Bondholders feel that their investments are relatively safe if the issuing company earns enough income to cover its annual interest obligations by a wide margin.

A common measure of creditors' safety is the ratio of operating income available to cover the annual interest expense, called the ***interest coverage ratio.*** This computation for Seacliff would be:

Long-term creditors watch this ratio

Interest Coverage Ratio

	1996	1995
Operating income (before interest and income taxes)	(a) $127,000	$160,000
Annual interest expense	(b) $ 24,000	$ 30,000
Interest coverage (a ÷ b)	5.3 times	5.3 times

The ratio remained unchanged at a satisfactory level during 1996. A ratio of 5.3 times interest earned would be considered strong in many industries. In the electric utilities industry, for example, the interest coverage ratio for the leading companies generally averages about 3, with the ratios of individual companies varying from 2 to 6.

Debt Ratio Long-term creditors are interested in the percentage of total assets financed by debt, as distinguished from the percentage financed by shareholders. The percentage of total assets financed by debt is measured by the debt ratio. This ratio is computed by dividing total liabilities by total assets, shown below for Seacliff.

What portion of total assets is financed by creditors?

Debt Ratio

	1996	1995
Total liabilities	(a) $312,000	$344,000
Total assets (or total liabilities & shareholders' equity)	(b) $950,000	$860,000
Debt ratio (a ÷ b)	32.8%	40.0%

From a creditor's viewpoint, the lower the debt ratio (or the higher the equity ratio) the better, since this means that shareholders have contributed the bulk of the funds to the business, and therefore the margin of protection to creditors against a shrinkage of the assets is high.

Analysis by Preferred Shareholders

Some preferred stocks are convertible into common stock at the option of the holder. However, many preferred stocks do not have the conversion privilege. If a preferred stock is convertible, the interests of the preferred shareholders are similar to those of common shareholders. If a preferred stock is not convertible, the interests of the preferred shareholders are more like those of long-term creditors.

Preferred shareholders are interested in the yield on their investment. The yield is computed by dividing the dividend per share by the market value per share. The dividend per share of Seacliff preferred stock is $9. If we assume that the market value at December 31, 1996, is $75 per share, the yield rate at that time would be 12% ($9 ÷ $75).

The primary measurement of the safety of an investment in preferred stock is the ability of the firm to meet its preferred dividend requirements. The best test of this ability is the ratio of the net income to the amount of the annual preferred dividends, as follows:

Is the preferred dividend safe?

Preferred Dividends Coverage Ratio

	1996	1995
Net income	*(a) $75,000*	*$90,000*
Annual preferred dividend requirements	*(b) $ 9,000*	*$ 9,000*
Preferred dividend coverage (a ÷ b)	*8.3 times*	*10 times*

Although the margin of protection declined in 1996, the annual preferred dividend requirement still appears well protected.

As previously discussed in Chapter 14 the market price of a preferred stock tends to ***vary inversely*** with interest rates. When interest rates are moving up, preferred stock prices tend to decline, when interest rates are dropping, preferred stock prices rise.

Analysis by Short-Term Creditors

Bankers and other short-term creditors share the interest of shareholders and bondholders in the profitability and long-run stability of a business. Their primary interest, however, is in the current position of the firm—its ability to generate sufficient funds (working capital) to meet current operating needs and to pay current debts promptly. Thus the analysis of financial statements by a banker considering a short-term loan, or by a trade creditor investigating the credit status of a customer, is likely to centre on the working capital position of the prospective debtor.

Amount of Working Capital The details of the working capital of Seacliff are as follows:

SEACLIFF CORPORATION
Comparative Schedule of Working Capital
As of December 31, 1996 and December 31, 1995

			Increase or (Decrease)		Percentage of Total Current Items	
	1996	1995	Dollars	%	1996	1995
Current assets:						
Cash	$ 38,000	$ 40,000	$ (2,000)	(5.0)	9.7	13.9
Receivables (net)	117,000	86,000	31,000	36.0	30.0	29.9
Inventories	180,000	120,000	60,000	50.0	46.2	41.6
Prepaid expenses	55,000	42,000	13,000	31.0	14.1	14.6
Total current assets	$390,000	$288,000	$102,000	35.4	100.0	100.0
Current liabilities:						
Notes payable to creditors	$ 14,600	$ 10,000	$ 4,600	46.0	13.1	10.7
Accounts payable	66,000	30,000	36,000	120.0	58.9	31.9
Accrued liabilities	31,400	54,000	(22,600)	(41.9)	28.0	57.4
Total current liabilities	$112,000	$ 94,000	$ 18,000	19.1	100.0	100.0
Working capital	$278,000	$194,000	$84,000	43.3		

The amount of working capital is measured by the ***excess of current assets over current liabilities.*** Thus, working capital represents the amount of cash, near-cash items, and cash substitutes (prepayments) on hand after providing for payment of all current liabilities.

This schedule shows that current assets increased $102,000, while current liabilities rose by only $18,000, with the result that working capital increased $84,000.

Quality of Working Capital In evaluating the debt-paying ability of a business, short-term creditors should consider the quality of working capital as well as the total dollar amount. The principal factors affecting the quality of working capital are (1) the nature of the current assets and (2) the length of time required to convert these assets into cash.

The preceding schedule shows an unfavourable shift in the composition of Seacliff's working capital during 1996; cash decreased from 13.9% to 9.7% of current assets, while inventory rose from 41.6% to 46.2%. Inventory is a less liquid resource than cash. Therefore, the quality of working capital is not as liquid as in 1995. ***Turnover rates*** (or ***ratios***) may be used to assist short-term creditors in estimating the time required to turn assets such as receivables and inventory into cash.

Accounts Receivable Turnover Rate As explained in Chapter 8, the accounts receivable turnover rate indicates how quickly a company converts its accounts receivable into cash. The accounts receivable turnover ***rate*** is determined by dividing net sales by the average balance of accounts receivable.[4] The number of ***days*** required (on average) to collect accounts receivable then may be determined by dividing the number of days in a year (365) by the turnover rate. These computations are shown below using the data in our Seacliff example:

Accounts Receivable Turnover

Are customers paying promptly?

	1996	1995
Net sales	(a) $900,000	$750,000
Receivables, beginning of year	$ 86,000	$ 80,000*
Receivables, end of year	$117,000	$ 86,000
Average receivables	(b) $101,500	$ 83,000
Receivable turnover per year (a ÷ b)	8.9 times	9.0 times
Average number of days to collect receivables (divide 365 days by receivable turnover)	41 days	41 days

*Assumed

There has been no significant change in the average time required to collect receivables. The interpretation of the average age of receivables depends upon the company's credit terms and the seasonal activity immediately before year-end. For example, if the company grants 30-day credit terms to its customers, the above analysis indicates that accounts receivable collections are lagging. If the terms are for 60 days, however, collections are being made ahead of schedule.

Inventory Turnover Rate The inventory turnover rate indicates how many times during the year the company is able to sell a quantity of goods equal to its average inventory. Mechanically, this rate is determined by dividing the cost of goods sold for the year by the average amount of inventory on hand during the year. The number of days required to sell this amount of inventory may be determined by dividing 365 days by the turnover rate. These computations were explained in Chapter 9, and are demonstrated below using the data of Seacliff:

Inventory Turnover

	1996	1995
Cost of goods sold	(a) $530,000	$420,000
Inventory, beginning of year	$120,000	$100,000*
Inventory, end of year	$180,000	$120,000
Average inventory	(b) $150,000	$110,000
Average inventory turnover per year (a ÷ b)	3.5 times	3.8 times
Average number of days to sell inventory (divide 365 days by inventory turnover)	104 days	96 days

*Assumed

The trend indicated by this analysis is unfavourable, since the length of time required for Seacliff to turn over (sell) its inventory is increasing.

4 Ideally, the accounts receivable turnover is computed by dividing net ***credit*** sales by the ***monthly*** average of receivables. Such detailed information, however, generally is not provided in annual financial statements.

Companies that have low gross profit rates often need high inventory turnover rates in order to operate profitably. This is merely another way of saying that if the gross profit rate is low, a high volume of transactions is necessary to produce a satisfactory amount of profits. Companies that sell "high markup" items, such as jewellery stores and art galleries, can operate successfully with much lower inventory turnover rates.

Operating Cycle In Chapter 5 we defined the term ***operating cycle*** as the average time period between the purchase of merchandise and the conversion of this merchandise back into cash. In other words, the merchandise acquired for inventory is gradually converted into accounts receivable by selling goods to customers on credit, and these receivables are converted into cash through the process of collection. The word ***cycle*** refers to the circular flow of assets from cash to inventory to receivables and back into cash.

Seacliff's operating cycle in 1996 was approximately 145 days, computed by adding the 104 days required to turn over inventory and the average 41 days required to collect receivables. This compares to an operating cycle of only 137 days in 1995, computed as 96 days to dispose of the inventory plus 41 days to collect the resulting receivables. From the viewpoint of short-term creditors, the shorter the operating cycle, the better the quality of the borrower's working capital. Therefore, these creditors would regard the lengthening of Seacliff's operating cycle as an unfavourable trend.

Current Ratio The current ratio (current assets divided by current liabilities) expresses the relationship between current assets and current liabilities. As debts come due, they must be paid out of current assets. Therefore, short-term creditors frequently compare the amount of current assets with the amount of current liabilities. The current ratio indicates a company's short-run, debt-paying ability. It is a measure of liquidity and of solvency. A strong current ratio provides considerable assurance that a company will be able to meet its obligations coming due in the near future. The current ratio for Seacliff is computed as follows:

Does this indicate satisfactory debt-paying ability?

Current Ratio

	1996	1995
Total current assets	(a) $390,000	$288,000
Total current liabilities	(b) $112,000	$ 94,000
Current ratio (a ÷ b)	3.5	3.1

A general rule is that a current ratio of 2 to 1 or better is satisfactory. By this standard, Seacliff's current ratio appears quite strong. Creditors tend to feel that the higher the current ratio the better. From a managerial point of view, however, there is an upper limit. Too high a current ratio may indicate that capital is not being used productively in the business as the amount of cash, accounts receivable, and inventories may be excessive.

Use of both the current ratio and the amount of working capital helps to place debt-paying ability in its proper perspective. For example, if Company X has current assets of $200,000 and current liabilities of $100,000 and Company Y has current assets of $2,000,000 and current liabilities of $1,900,000, each company has $100,000 of working capital, but the current position of Company X is clearly superior to that of Company Y. The current ratio for Company X is quite satisfactory at 2 to 1, but Company Y's current ratio is very low—only slightly above 1 to 1.

As another example, assume that Company A and Company B both have current ratios of 3 to 1. However, Company A has working capital of $50,000 and Company B has working capital of $500,000. Although both companies appear to be good credit risks, Company B would no doubt be able to qualify for a much ***larger*** bank loan than would Company A.

Quick Ratio Because inventories and prepaid expenses are further removed from conversion into cash than other current assets, a statistic known as the ***quick ratio*** is sometimes computed as a supplement to the current ratio. The quick ratio compares the highly liquid current assets (cash, marketable securities, and receivables) with current liabilities. Seacliff has no marketable securities; its quick ratio is computed as follows:

A measure of liquidity

Quick Ratio

	1996	1995
Quick assets (cash and receivables)	(a) $155,000	$126,000
Current liabilities	(b) $112,000	$ 94,000
Quick ratio (a ÷ b)	1.4	1.3

Here again the analysis reveals a favourable trend and a strong position. If the credit periods extended to customers and granted by creditors are roughly equal, a quick ratio of 1.0 or better is considered satisfactory.

Unused Lines of Credit From the viewpoint of a short-term creditor, a company's unused lines of credit represent a "resource" almost as liquid as cash. An unused line of credit means that a bank has agreed in advance to lend the company any amount, up to the specified limit. As long as this line of credit remains available, creditors know that the business can borrow cash quickly and easily for any purpose, including payments of creditors' claims.

Existing unused lines of credit are ***disclosed*** in notes accompanying the financial statements and in the management's discussion and analysis section of the annual report.

CASE IN POINT The unused lines of credit can be substantial in amount. The recent annual reports of the following corporations provide a glimpse of such a picture: NOVA Corporation of Alberta, unutilized lines of credit of $1.2 billion; Canadian Pacific Limited, unused commitments for long-term financing in excess of $1.1 billion and unused lines of credit for short-term financing of $738.9 million; Maclean Hunter Limited, unused credit lines of approximately $340 million; Univa Inc., unused lines of credit of $307 million; Bow Valley Industries Ltd., unused long- and short-term lines of credit of approximately $265 million and $18 million, respectively; and Hayes-Dana Inc., unused lines of credit of approximately $100 million. Of course, there is a cost for such unused lines of credit. For one of the corporations, the annual commitment fees on the unused long-term credit lines were $\frac{1}{10}$ to $\frac{1}{8}$ of one percent of the unused amount.

Usefulness of the Notes to Financial Statements

A set of financial statements normally is accompanied by several pages of ***notes,*** disclosing information useful in interpretation of the statements. Users should view these notes as an ***integral part*** of the financial statements.

In our preceding chapters, we have identified many items that are disclosed in notes to the financial statements. Among the most useful disclosures are (a) a summary of the accounting methods in use, (b) material contingent losses, (c) current market value of financial instruments, (d) identification of the assets pledged to secure specific liabilities, (e) maturity dates of significant liabilities, (f) unused lines of credit, and (g) preferred stock dividends in arrears. The notes also supplement the financial statements by providing further explanation of such items as extraordinary gains and losses, changes in accounting principle, and significant financial events occurring after the balance sheet date.

In summary, the notes often contain information ***essential*** to a proper interpretation of the company's financial position, operating results, and future prospects.

OBJECTIVE 6 Compute the ratios widely used in financial statement analysis and explain the significance of each.

Summary of Analytical Measurements

The basic ratios and other measurements discussed in this chapter and their significance are summarized below.

The student should keep in mind the fact that the full significance of any of these ratios or other measurements depends on the ***direction of its trend*** and its ***relationship to some predetermined standard*** or industry average.

Ratio or Other Measurement	Method of Computation	Significance
1 Earnings per share of common stock	$\frac{\text{Net income} - \text{preferred dividends}}{\text{Shares of common outstanding}}$	Indicates the amount of earnings applicable to a share of common stock.
2 Price-earnings ratio	$\frac{\text{Market price per share}}{\text{Earnings per share}}$	Indicates if price of stock is in line with earnings.
3 Dividend yield	$\frac{\text{Dividend per share}}{\text{Market price per share}}$	Shows the rate of return earned by shareholders based on current price for a share of stock.
4 Book value per share of common stock	$\frac{\text{Common shareholders' equity}}{\text{Shares of common outstanding}}$	Measures the recorded value of net assets behind each share of common stock.
5 Operating expense ratio	$\frac{\text{Operating expenses}}{\text{Net sales}}$	Indicates management's ability to control expenses.

6 Return on assets	$\dfrac{\text{Operating income}}{\text{Average total assets}}$	*Measures the productivity of assets regardless of capital structure.*
7 Return on common shareholders' equity	$\dfrac{\text{Net income} - \text{preferred dividends}}{\text{Average common shareholders' equity}}$	*Indicates the earning power of common stock equity.*
8 Equity ratio	$\dfrac{\text{Total shareholders' equity}}{\text{Total assets}}$	*Shows the protection to creditors and the extent of leverage being used.*
9 Debt ratio	$\dfrac{\text{Total liabilities}}{\text{Total assets}}$	*Indicates the percentage of assets financed through borrowing; it shows the extent of leverage being used.*
10 Interest coverage ratio	$\dfrac{\text{Operating income}}{\text{Annual interest expense}}$	*Measures the coverage of interest requirements, particularly on long-term debt.*
11 Preferred dividends coverage ratio	$\dfrac{\text{Net income}}{\text{Annual preferred dividends}}$	*Shows the adequacy of current earnings to cover dividends on preferred stocks.*
12 Working capital	*Current assets – current liabilities*	*Measures short-run debt-paying ability.*
13 Accounts receivable turnover rate	$\dfrac{\text{Net sales}}{\text{Average receivables}}$	*Indicates reasonableness of accounts receivable balance and effectiveness of collections.*
14 Inventory turnover rate	$\dfrac{\text{Cost of goods sold}}{\text{Average inventory}}$	*Indicates marketability of inventory and reasonableness of quantity on hand.*
15 Current ratio	$\dfrac{\text{Current assets}}{\text{Current liabilities}}$	*Measures short-run debt-paying ability.*
16 Quick ratio	$\dfrac{\text{Quick assets}}{\text{Current liabilities}}$	*Measures the short-term liquidity of a firm.*

Annual Reports

Annual reports of corporations contain a plethora of information. In addition to the audited financial statements and the auditors' reports, these corporate annual reports include such information as: financial or operating highlights; message to shareholders from the chief executive and chief operating officers on the current operations and future outlook of the company; profile of the company, focusing on the nature of operations, products, and personnel; management's discussion and analysis on the financial statements regarding liquidity, capital resources, and results of operations; statistical reports such as five- or ten-year summary; stock market prices, book value per share, and dividends; list of directors and officers; shareholder information; and a host of other items. This information takes up between twenty and fifty pages in an annual report.

Much of this material complements the information in the financial statements and is useful in assessing the present and future prospects of a company. Consequently, investors, creditors, and other interested parties should review and analyze this information in the corporate annual report in order to get a more complete picture of the company.

The following excerpts, selected from the 1992 annual report of Maclean Hunter Limited, provide a glimpse of such information. (Additional information in the annual report is presented in Comprehensive Problem 5 at the end of this chapter.)

Corporate Highlights

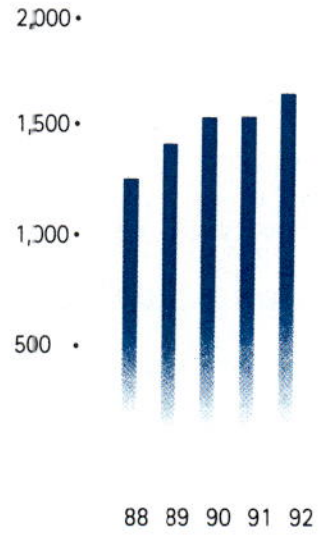

Revenue
(in millions)

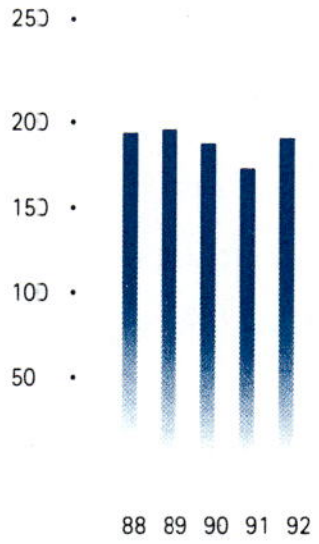

Operating income before amortization
(in millions)

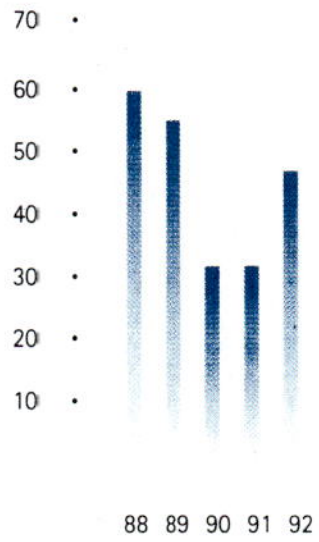

Earnings per share before unusual items
(in cents)

(millions of dollars except per share data)	**1992**	1991	1990
Operating Summary			
Revenue	**$ 1,635**	$ 1,535	$ 1,536
Operating income before amortization	**194**	171	189
Income before unusual items	**81**	51	49
Unusual items	**–**	–	(34)
Consolidated net income	**81**	51	15
Cash Flow			
Earnings before interest, taxes, depreciation and amortization	**302**	276	287
Cash flow from operations	**200**	170	161
Dividends	**45**	42	40
Purchase of property, plant and equipment	**99**	105	128
Per Share Data			
Income before unusual items	**47¢**	32¢	32¢
Unusual items	**–**	–	(21)
Consolidated earnings per share	**47¢**	32¢	11¢
Earnings before interest, taxes, depreciation and amortization	**$ 1.71**	$ 1.70	$ 1.79
Cash flow from operations	**$ 1.14**	$ 1.05	$ 1.01
Dividends	**25¢**	25¢	25¢
Financial Position at Year-End			
Working capital (excluding current indebtedness)	**183**	77	141
Total assets	**1,872**	1,754	1,831
Total debt	**468**	616	725
Shareholders' equity plus convertible debentures	**887**	667	655
Ratios			
Operating return on revenue	**12%**	11%	12%
Operating return on assets employed	**13%**	11%	13%
Return on average shareholders' equity plus convertible debentures	**10%**	8%	8%*
Total debt to capital employed	**29%**	40%	45%
Employees			
Number of employees	**12,432**	11,850	12,425
Share Prices			
Year-end closing	**$ 12.13**	$ 11.50	$ 9.63
Current (March 12, 1993)	**$ 11.75**		

*Before unusual items.

LETTER TO SHAREHOLDERS

An interview with Ron Osborne

Q *How would you characterize the year 1992 for Maclean Hunter?*

It's been a very good year for us in many respects. We're by no means back where we should be in terms of operating results and profitability, but clearly we are heading in the right direction. It's been first-rate for cable, but disappointing from an advertising recovery point of view. Given that the economy is not yet "firing on eight cylinders", we are pleased to report a 7% increase in revenue to $1.6 billion, a 14% increase in operating income before amortization to $194 million for 1992, and a 47% increase in earnings per share.

Q *What factors had the greatest bearing on results?*

Four major factors. First, we have the stability of our cable television operations, which, even in relatively tough economic times, have found ways to be creative in providing relevant services to customers and generating additional revenue.

Second, the significant drop in interest rates has had a beneficial effect on financing costs and our Treasury Department has taken full advantage of that decline with an aggressive but appropriate policy on our rate and debt structure, maximizing the use of short-term money market instruments.

Third, our cyclical operations, which are more dependent on economic conditions, have yet to benefit from major fixed cost reductions implemented over the past two to three years.

Fourth, partly as a reflection of the cyclical nature of our publishing business, we have benefited from significant paper price discounts.

Q *What were the areas of strength and weakness, beginning with the strengths?*

Clearly cable had another excellent year in both the United States and Canada. Our commercial printing division has recovered nicely from 1991, and the Aurora web operation and Yorkville group continued to outperform their markets. Davis + Henderson, our specialty printing group, also had another fine year.

In television, our Calgary CTV-affiliate, CFCN, performed extremely well, and the CTV network also saw significantly improved results. CHCH-TV in Hamilton turned in excellent results after a successful turnaround, and has now been sold to WIC Western International Communications.

I would say the improvement in The Financial Post should be characterized as an area of strength, although in absolute terms it continues to incur significant operating losses over a period that's extended beyond what anybody anticipated as a result of the recession. These losses have declined substantially in 1992 and should continue to do so in 1993. That has to be counted as a major plus.

Q *And the weaknesses?*

On the negative side of the ledger, our business forms operations, both in Canada and in the U.S., have softened due to weak demand and excess capacity in that industry. Our radio operations have had a rougher time, reflecting the weakness in the retail sector in the Maritimes and in Ontario.

Business publishing in Canada has been a mixed bag with a few notable exceptions such as medical publishing. Our U.S. publishing operations have done very well, not only in the medical field, but also in a number of industrial fields and in training and development. Britain had a very difficult year due to the economic climate, and despite the strength of our construction industry publications in Germany, we're starting to see signs of a slowdown in Europe. However, overall, our European operations are performing quite respectably.

The Toronto Sun's financial results were down compared to its peak of two or three years ago – essentially a function of the soft retail and employment market. This was somewhat offset by reductions in newsprint costs, which are a major factor in the performance of our newspapers. The Ottawa Sun continues to gain ground and it's only a matter of time before it's a significant contributor to the Sun group. The Calgary Sun had an excellent year with Edmonton somewhat weaker.

Q *What plans are in place to minimize weaknesses and build on strengths?*

I would refer the reader to the Review of Operations for details, as I will only list the main points here.

- Radio – Our format switch in Kitchener will enable us to repatriate significant listenership. The new broadcast centre we're building in Toronto will bring operating synergies and we're completely revamping the sound and operating style of CFNY.
- Television – The restructuring of CTV has been finalized and will enable the network to complete its financial turnaround. Maclean

Hunter will continue to play a role and have an increased share in future profits.

• Cable – We've successfully introduced the Full Cable Service tier in Ontario and are developing additional revenue streams in the area of "alternate access" in Canada and the U.S., allowing customers to choose how they wish to interconnect with telephone services.

• Consumer Magazines – In conjunction with the Sun newspapers, we've launched Modern Woman to extend the audience for our women's magazines and to offer customers a broader advertising base.

• Business Publishing – Having rationalized some of our non-performing assets, we will concentrate on developing our existing areas of strength and extending our expertise in these areas into new markets in the form of international, even global, publishing networks. We continue to invest in electronic publishing, which is still something of a "Holy Grail", but we have a number of initiatives in this area in our international directory operations.

• Business Forms – We doubled our volumes at a very favourable cost with the acquisition of Southam Business Forms. ...

Q *What is your number one priority for 1993?*

If I had to choose one, it would be to maintain our earnings growth without sacrificing product quality. We will continue looking for new revenue streams, controlling our costs, capitalizing on existing products, and turning those around that need to be turned around without turning a blind eye to potential acquisitions that offer a fair return for our shareholders over the short to medium term. We've made some major longer-term investments in recent years and launched some major new products, so our focus, as in 1992, will be on maximizing those.

Q *What is the outlook for 1993?*

We expect to show growth in earnings per share throughout 1993. The worst of the recession appears to be over in the U.S. and that can only be good for Canada. The first quarter is not necessarily much of an indication, because the first and third quarters are always softer in our advertising-based products, which tend to lag behind economic recovery. Any significant improvement in earnings would require a strong and sustained upturn in these more cyclical products.

Community Involvement

Maclean Hunter has been designated "a caring company" by the Canadian Centre for Philanthropy for its practice of contributing a portion of its pre-tax earnings and providing in-house services to worthy organizations in the various communities we serve. Our cash and non-cash contribution to hospitals and cultural and community organizations was approximately $15 million in 1992. Much of this consisted of contributed advertising space and broadcast airtime.

We make additional cultural contributions through The Maclean Hunter Television Fund, established as part of the Selkirk acquisition in 1989. In 1992, the Fund invested over $3 million in the production of Canadian dramatic television series. In education, we fund six chairs in journalism and business at academic institutions across Canada. This $3 million endowment made in 1987 was our way of investing in the future of Canada and giving something back to the communities we serve. ...

On behalf of the Board

Donald G. Campbell
Chairman

Ronald W. Osborne
President and Chief Executive Officer

CHAPTER REVIEW

KEY TERMS INTRODUCED OR EMPHASIZED IN CHAPTER 20

Comparative financial statements Financial statement data for two or more successive years placed side by side in adjacent columns to facilitate study of changes.

Component percentage The percentage relationship of any financial statement item to a total including that item. For example, each type of asset as a percentage of total assets.

Horizontal analysis Comparison of the change in a financial statement item such as inventories during two or more accounting periods.

Leverage Refers to the practice of financing assets with borrowed capital. Extensive leverage creates the possibility for the rate of return on common shareholders' equity to be substantially above or below the rate of return on total assets. When the rate of return on total assets exceeds the average cost of borrowed capital, leverage increases net income and the return on common shareholders' equity. However, when the return on total assets is less than the average cost of borrowed capital, leverage reduces net income and the return on common shareholders' equity.

Quality of assets The concept that some companies have assets of better quality than others, such as well-balanced composition of assets, well-maintained plant and equipment, and receivables that are all current. A lower quality of assets might be indicated by poor maintenance of plant and equipment, slow-moving inventories with high danger of obsolescence, past-due receivables, and patents approaching an expiration date.

Quality of earnings Earnings are said to be of high quality if they are stable, the source seems assured, and the methods used in measuring income are conservative. The existence of this concept suggests that the range of alternative but acceptable accounting principles may still be too wide to produce financial statements that are comparable.

Rate of return on investment (ROI) A measure of management's ability to earn a satisfactory return on the assets under its control. Numerous variations of the ROI concept are used, such as return on total assets, return on total shareholders' equity, and return on common shareholders' equity.

Ratios See pages 953–954 for list of ratios, methods of computation, and significance.

Trend percentages The purpose of computing trend percentages is to measure the increase or decrease in financial items (such as sales, net income, cash, etc.) from a selected base year to a series of following years. For example, the dollar amount of net income each year is divided by the base year net income to determine the trend percentage.

Vertical analysis Comparison of a particular financial statement item to a total including that item, such as inventories as a percentage of current assets, or operating expenses in relation to net sales.

DEMONSTRATION PROBLEM FOR YOUR REVIEW

The accounting records of King Corporation showed the following balances at the end of 1995 and 1996:

	1996	1995
Cash	$ 35,000	$ 25,000
Accounts receivable (net)	91,000	90,000
Inventory	160,000	140,000
Short-term prepayments	4,000	5,000
Investment in land	90,000	100,000
Equipment	880,000	640,000
Less: Accumulated depreciation	(260,000)	(200,000)
Total assets	$1,000,000	$ 800,000
Accounts payable	$ 105,000	$ 46,000
Income taxes payable and other accrued liabilities	40,000	25,000
Bonds payable—8%	280,000	280,000
Premium on bonds payable	3,600	4,000
Capital stock (33,000 shares in 1996; 22,000 shares in 1995)	165,000	110,000
Retained earnings	406,400	335,000
Total liabilities and shareholders' equity	$1,000,000	$ 800,000
Sales (net of discounts and allowances)	$2,200,000	$1,600,000
Cost of goods sold	1,606,000	1,120,000
Gross profit	$ 594,000	$ 480,000
Expenses (including $22,400 interest expense)	(336,600)	(352,000)
Income taxes	(91,000)	(48,000)
Net income	$ 166,400	$ 80,000

Cash dividends of $40,000 were paid and a 50% stock dividend was distributed early in 1996. All sales were made on credit at a relatively uniform rate during the year. Inventory and receivables did not fluctuate materially. The market price of the company's stock on December 31, 1996, was $86 per share; on December 31, 1995, it was $43.50 (before the 50% stock dividend distributed in 1996).

INSTRUCTIONS Compute the following for 1996 and 1995:

1 Quick ratio.
2 Current ratio.
3 Equity ratio.
4 Debt ratio.
5 Book value per share of capital stock (based on shares outstanding after 50% stock dividend in 1996).
6 Earnings per share of capital stock.
7 Price-earnings ratio.
8 Gross profit percentage.
9 Operating expense ratio.
10 Net income as a percentage of net sales.
11 Inventory turnover. (Assume an average inventory of $150,000 for both years.)

12 Accounts receivable turnover. (Assume average accounts receivable for $90,000 for 1995.)

13 Interest coverage ratio.

SOLUTION TO DEMONSTRATION PROBLEM

	1996	1995
(1) Quick ratio:		
$126,000 ÷ $145,000	.9 to 1	
$115,000 ÷ $71,000		1.6 to 1
(2) Current ratio:		
$290,000 ÷ $145,000	2 to 1	
$260,000 ÷ $71,000		3.7 to 1
(3) Equity ratio:		
$571,400 ÷ $1,000,000	57%	
$445,000 ÷ $800,000		56%
(4) Debt ratio:		
$428,600 ÷ $1,000,000	43%	
$355,000 ÷ $800,000		44%
(5) Book value per share of capital stock:		
$571,400 ÷ 33,000 shares	$17.32	
$445,000 ÷ 33,000* shares		$13.48
(6) Earnings per share of capital stock:		
$166,400 ÷ 33,000 shares	$5.04	
$80,000 ÷ 33,000* shares		$2.42
(7) Price-earnings ratio:		
$86 ÷ $5.04	17 times	
$43.50 ÷ 1.5* = $29, adjusted market price; $29 ÷ $2.42		12 times
(8) Gross profit percentage:		
$594,000 ÷ $2,200,000	27%	
$480,000 ÷ $1,600,000		30%
(9) Operating expense ratio:		
($336,600 − $22,400) ÷ $2,200,000	14%	
($352,000 − $22,400) ÷ $1,600,000		20.6%
(10) Net income as a percentage of net sales:		
$166,400 ÷ $2,200,000	7.6%	
$80,000 ÷ $1,600,000		5%
(11) Inventory turnover:		
$1,606,000 ÷ $150,000	10.7 times	
$1,120,000 ÷ $150,000		7.5 times
(12) Accounts receivable turnover:		
$2,200,000 ÷ $90,500	24.3 times	
$1,600,000 ÷ $90,000		17.8 times
(13) Interest coverage ratio:		
($166,400 + $22,400 + $91,000) ÷ $22,400	12.5 times	
($80,000 + $22,400 + $48,000) ÷ $22,400		6.7 times

*Adjusted retroactively for 50% stock dividend.

ASSIGNMENT MATERIAL

DISCUSSION QUESTIONS

1 a What groups are interested in the financial affairs of publicly owned corporations?

b List some of the more important sources of financial information for investors.

2 In financial statement analysis, what is the basic objective of observing trends in data and ratios? Suggest some other standards of comparison.

3 Distinguish between ***trend percentages*** and ***component percentages.*** Which would be better suited to analyzing the change in sales over a term of several years?

4 In financial statement analysis, what information is produced by computing a ratio that is not available in a simple observation of the underlying data?

5 "Although net income declined this year as compared with last year, it increased from 3% to 5% of net sales." Are sales increasing or decreasing?

6 Differentiate between ***horizontal*** and ***vertical*** analysis.

7 Assume that Chemco Corporation is engaged in the manufacture and distribution of a variety of chemicals. In analyzing the financial statements of this corporation, why would you want to refer to the ratios and other measurements of companies in the chemical industry? In comparing the financial results of Chemco Corporation with another chemical company, why would you be interested in the accounting practices used by the two companies?

8 Explain how the following accounting practices will tend to raise or lower the quality of a company's earnings. (Assume the continuance of inflation.)

a Adoption of an accelerated depreciation method rather than straight-line depreciation.

b Adoption of FIFO rather than LIFO for the valuation of inventories.

c Adoption of a 7-year life rather than a 10-year life for the depreciation of equipment.

9 What single ratio do you think should be of greatest interest to:

a A banker considering a short-term loan?

b A common shareholder?

c An insurance company considering a long-term mortgage loan?

10 Modern Corporation earned a 16% return on its total assets. Current liabilities are 10% of total assets. Long-term bonds carrying a 13% interest rate are equal to 30% of total assets. There is no preferred stock. Is this application of leverage favourable or unfavourable from the viewpoint of Modern's shareholders?

11 In deciding whether a company's equity ratio is favourable or unfavourable, creditors and shareholders may have different views. Why?

12 Ahi Ltd. has a current ratio of 3 to 1. Ono Corp. has a current ratio of 2 to 1. Does this mean that Ahi's operating cycle is longer than Ono's? Why?

13 An investor states, "I bought this stock for $50 several years ago and it now sells for $100. It paid $5 per share in dividends last year so I'm earning 10% on my investment." Criticize this statement.

14 Alpine Products experiences a considerable seasonal variation in its business. The high point in the year's activity comes in November, the low point in July. During which month would you expect the company's current ratio to be higher? If the company were choosing a fiscal year for accounting purposes, how would you advise them?

15 Auto Parts' inventory turnover and accounts receivable turnover both increased from 1995 to 1996, but net income decreased. Can you offer some possible reasons for this?

16 Is the rate of return on investment (ROI) intended primarily to measure liquidity, solvency, or some other aspect of business operations? Explain.

17 Mention three financial amounts to which corporate earnings can logically be compared in judging their adequacy or reasonableness.

18 Under what circumstances would you consider a corporate net income of $1 million for the year as being unreasonably low? Under what circumstances would you consider a corporate net income of $1 million as being unreasonably high?

MULTIPLE CHOICE QUESTIONS

1 Which of the following is ***not*** an accurate statement?

- a Expressing the various items in the income statement as a percentage of net sales illustrates the use of component percentages.
- b An increase in the market price of bonds causes the yield rate to decline.
- c A high debt ratio is viewed favourably by long-term creditors as long as the number of times interest earned is at least 1.
- d In measuring the dollar or percentage change in quarterly sales or earnings, it is appropriate to compare the results of the current quarter with those of the same quarter in the preceding year.

2 Which of the following actions will improve the "quality" of earnings, even though the total dollar amount of earnings may not increase?

- a Increasing the uncollectible accounts expense from 1% to 2% of net credit sales to reflect current conditions.
- b Switching from an accelerated method to the straight-line method for depreciating assets.
- c Changing from LIFO to the FIFO method of inventory valuation during a period of rising prices.
- d Lengthening the estimated useful lives of depreciable assets.

3 Hunter Corporation's net income was $400,000 in 1995 and $160,000 in 1996. What percentage increase in net income must Hunter achieve in 1997 to offset the decline in profits in 1996?

a 60% b 150% c 600% d 67%

4 Of the following situations, which would be considered the most favourable for the common shareholders?

- a The company stops paying dividends on its cumulative preferred stock; the price-earnings ratio of common stock is low.
- b Equity ratio is high; return on assets exceeds the cost of borrowing.
- c Book value per share of common stock is substantially higher than market value per share; return on common shareholders' equity is less than the rate of interest paid to creditors.
- d Equity ratio is low; return on assets exceeds the cost of borrowing.

5 During 1996, Ganey Corporation had sales of $4,000,000, all on credit. Accounts receivable averaged $400,000 and inventory levels averaged $250,000 throughout the year. If Ganey's gross profit rate during 1996 was 25% of net sales, which of the following statements are correct? (More than one statement may be correct. Assume 360 days in a year.)

- a Ganey "turns over" its accounts receivable more times per year than it turns over its average inventory.
- b Ganey collects the amount of its average accounts receivable in about 36 to 37 days.
- c Ganey's operating cycle is 66 days.
- d The quality of Ganey's working capital would improve if the company could reduce its inventory and receivables turnover rates.

EXERCISES

EXERCISE 20-1 Accounting Terminology

Listed below are nine technical accounting terms introduced or emphasized in this chapter.

Inventory turnover	*Trend percentages*	*Leverage*
Operating cycle	*Vertical analysis*	*Yield*
Price-earning ratio	*Return on assets*	*Quick ratio*

Each of the following statements may (or may not) describe one of these technical terms. For each statement, indicate the accounting term described, or answer "None" if the statement does not correctly describe any of the terms.

- a The proportion of total assets financed by shareholders, as distinguished from creditors.
- b Market price per common share divided by earnings per common share.
- c Changes in financial statement items from a base year to following years expressed as a percentage of the base year amount and designed to show the extent and direction of change.
- d Dividends per share divided by market price per share.
- e Average time period between the purchase of merchandise and the conversion of this merchandise back into cash.
- f Study of relationships among the data of a single accounting period.
- g Net sales divided by average inventory.
- h Comparison of highly liquid current assets (cash, marketable securities, and receivables) with current liabilities.
- i Buying assets with money raised by borrowing.

EXERCISE 20-2 Percentage Changes

Selected information taken from financial statements of Kowloon Corporation for two successive years follows. You are to compute the percentage change from 1995 to 1996 whenever possible.

	1996	1995
a Accounts receivable	$126,000	$150,000
b Marketable securities	–0–	250,000
c Retained earnings	80,000	(80,000)
d Notes receivable	120,000	–0–
e Notes payable	860,000	800,000
f Cash	82,400	80,000
g Sales	990,000	900,000

EXERCISE 20-3
Intuition versus Calculation

Tait Corporation had net income of $4 million in its first year. In the second year, net income decreased by 75%. In the third year, due to an improved business environment, net income increased by 250%.

INSTRUCTIONS

a Prior to making any computations, do you think Tait's net income was higher or lower in the third year than in the first year?

b Compute Tait's net income for the second year and for the third year. Do your computations support your initial response in part **a**?

EXERCISE 20-4
Trend Percentages

Compute ***trend percentages*** for the following items taken from the financial statements of Water-Wise Plumbing Fixtures over a five-year period. Treat 1992 as the base year. State whether the trends are favourable or unfavourable. (Dollar amounts are stated in thousands.)

	1996	1995	1994	1993	1992
Sales	$85,000	$74,000	$61,500	$59,000	$50,000
Cost of goods sold	$58,500	$48,000	$40,500	$36,000	$30,000

EXERCISE 20-5
Common Size Income Statements

Prepare ***common size*** income statements for Toyoda Company, a sole proprietorship, for the two years shown below by converting the dollar amounts into percentages. For each year, sales will appear as 100% and other items will be expressed as a percentage of sales. (Income taxes are not involved as the business is not incorporated.) Comment on whether the changes from 1995 to 1996 are favourable or unfavourable.

	1996	1995
Sales	$500,000	$400,000
Cost of goods sold	330,000	268,000
Gross profit	$170,000	$132,000
Operating expenses	140,000	116,000
Net income	$ 30,000	$ 16,000

EXERCISE 20-6
Ratios for a Retail Store

Selected financial data for Vashon's, a retail store, appear below. Since monthly figures are not available, the average amounts for inventories and for accounts receivable should be based on the amounts shown for the beginning and end of 1996.

	1996	1995
Sales (terms 2/10, n/30)	$750,000	$600,000
Cost of goods sold	495,000	408,000
Inventory at end of year	85,500	94,500
Accounts receivable at end of year	87,500	100,000

INSTRUCTIONS

Compute the following for 1996:

a Gross profit percentage

b Inventory turnover

c Accounts receivable turnover

EXERCISE 20-7
Computing Ratios

A condensed balance sheet for Durham Corporation prepared at the end of the year appears below.

Assets		Liabilities & Shareholders' Equity	
Cash	$ 55,000	Notes payable (due in 6 months)	$ 40,000
Accounts receivable	155,000	Accounts payable	110,000
Inventory	270,000	Long-term liabilities	330,000
Prepaid expenses	60,000	Capital stock (60,000 shares)	300,000
Plant & equipment (net)	570,000	Retained earnings	420,000
Other assets	90,000		
Total	$1,200,000	Total	$1,200,000

During the year the company earned a gross profit of $1,116,000 on sales of $2,790,000. Accounts receivable, inventory, and plant assets remained almost constant in amount throughout the year.

INSTRUCTIONS Compute the following:

a Current ratio
b Quick ratio
c Working capital
d Equity ratio
e Accounts receivable turnover (all sales were on credit)
f Inventory turnover
g Book value per share of capital stock

EXERCISE 20-8
Current Ratio, Debt Ratio, and Earnings per Share

Selected items from successive annual reports of Hastings, Inc., appear below.

	1996	1995
Total assets (40% of which are current)	$400,000	$325,000
Current liabilities	$ 80,000	$100,000
Bonds payable, 12%	100,000	50,000
Capital stock (20,000 shares)	100,000	100,000
Retained earnings	120,000	75,000
Total liabilities & shareholders' equity	$400,000	$325,000

Dividends of $26,000 were declared and paid in 1996.

INSTRUCTIONS Compute the following:

a Current ratio for 1996 and 1995
b Debt ratio for 1996 and 1995
c Earnings per share for 1996

EXERCISE 20-9
Ratio Analysis for Two Similar Companies

Selected data from the financial statements of Italian Marble Ltd. and Toro Stone Products for the year just ended follow. Assume that for both companies dividends declared were equal in amount to net earnings during the year and therefore shareholders' equity did not change. The two companies are in the same line of business.

	Italian Marble Ltd.	Toro Stone Products
Total liabilities	$ 200,000	$ 100,000
Total assets	800,000	400,000
Sales (all on credit)	1,800,000	1,200,000
Average inventory	240,000	140,000
Average receivables	200,000	100,000
Gross profit as a percentage of sales	40%	30%
Operating expenses as a percentage of sales	36%	25%
Net income as a percentage of sales	4%	5%

INSTRUCTIONS Compute the following for each company:

a Net income

b Net income as a percentage of shareholders' equity

c Accounts receivable turnover

d Inventory turnover

PROBLEMS

Note: In this chapter, we provide an unusually wide variety of problem assignments. In order to make the full range of these assignments available to all users of the text, we present them in one consecutive series, rather than splitting them into A and B groups. This entire series is supported in both the Group A and Group B accounting work sheets.

PROBLEM 20-1
Analysis to Identify Favourable and Unfavourable Trends

The following information was developed from the December 31, year-end financial statements of Custom Logos, Inc. At the beginning of 1996, the company's former supplier went bankrupt, and the company began buying merchandise from another supplier.

	1996	1995
Gross profit	$1,008,000	$1,134,000
Income before income taxes	230,400	252,000
Net income	172,800	189,000
Net income as a percentage of net sales	6.0%	7.5%

INSTRUCTIONS

a Compute the net sales for each year.

b Compute the cost of goods sold in dollars and as a percentage of net sales for each year.

c Compute operating expenses in dollars and as a percentage of net sales for each year. (Income taxes expense is not an operating expense.)

d Prepare a condensed comparative income statement for 1995 and 1996. Include the following items: net sales, cost of goods sold, gross profit, operating expenses, income before income taxes, income taxes expense, and net income. Omit earnings per share statistics.

e Identify the significant favourable trends and unfavourable trends in the performance of Custom Logos, Inc. Comment on any unusual changes.

PROBLEM 20-2
Comparing Operating Results with Average Performance in the Industry

Sub Zero, Inc., manufactures camping equipment. Shown below for the current year are the income statement for the company and a common size summary for the industry in which the company operates. (Notice that the percentages in the right-hand column are ***not*** for Sub Zero, Inc., but are average percentages for the industry.)

	Sub Zero, Inc.	Industry Average
Sales (net)	$20,000,000	100%
Cost of goods sold	9,800,000	57
Gross profit	$10,200,000	43%
Operating expenses:		
Selling	$ 4,200,000	16%
General and administrative	3,400,000	20
Total operating expenses	$ 7,600,000	36%
Operating income	$ 2,600,000	7%
Income taxes	1,200,000	3
Net income	$ 1,400,000	4%
Return on assets	18%	9%

INSTRUCTIONS

a Prepare a two-column common size income statement. The first column should show for Sub Zero, Inc., all items expressed as a percentage of net sales. The second column should show as an industry average the percentage data given in the problem. The purpose of this common size statement is to compare the operating results of Sub Zero, Inc., with the average for the industry.

b Comment specifically on differences between Sub Zero, Inc., and the industry average with respect to gross profit, selling expenses, general and administrative expenses, operating income, net income, and return on assets. Suggest possible reasons for the more important disparities.

PROBLEM 20-3
Ratios Based on Balance Sheet and Income Statement Data

Barnum Corporation has issued common stock only. The company has been successful and has a gross profit rate of 25%. The information shown below was derived from the company's financial statements.

Beginning inventory	$ 700,000
Ending inventory	800,000
Average accounts receivable	250,000
Average common shareholders' equity	1,800,000
Sales (80% on credit)	4,000,000
Net income	225,000

INSTRUCTIONS

On the basis of the above information, compute the following:

a Accounts receivable turnover and the average number of days required to collect the accounts receivable

b The inventory turnover and the average number of days required to turn over the inventory

c Length of Barnum Corporation's operating cycle

d Return on common shareholders' equity

PROBLEM 20-4
Ratios; Consider Advisability of Incurring Long-Term Debt

At the end of the year, the following information was obtained from the accounting records of Carleton Office Products:

Sales (all on credit)	*$2,700,000*
Cost of goods sold	*1,755,000*
Average inventory	*351,000*
Average accounts receivable	*300,000*
Interest expense	*45,000*
Income taxes	*84,000*
Net income	*159,000*
Average investment in assets	*1,800,000*
Average shareholders' equity	*795,000*

INSTRUCTIONS

a From the information given, compute the following:
1 Inventory turnover
2 Accounts receivable turnover
3 Total operating expenses
4 Gross profit percentage
5 Return on average shareholders' equity
6 Return on average assets

b Carleton has an opportunity to obtain a long-term loan at an annual interest rate of 12% and could use this additional capital at the same rate of profitability as indicated above. Would obtaining the loan be desirable from the viewpoint of the shareholders? Explain.

PROBLEM 20-5
Ratios; Consider Advisability of Incurring Long-Term Debt— A Second Problem

At the end of the year, the following information was obtained from the accounting records of Santa Fe Boot Limited.

Sales (all on credit)	*$800,000*
Cost of goods sold	*480,000*
Average inventory	*120,000*
Average accounts receivable	*80,000*
Interest expense	*6,000*
Income taxes	*8,000*
Net income for the year	*36,000*
Average investment in assets	*500,000*
Average shareholders' equity	*400,000*

The company declared no dividends of any kind during the year and did not issue or retire any capital stock.

INSTRUCTIONS

a From the information given, compute the following for the year:
1 Inventory turnover
2 Accounts receivable turnover
3 Total operating expenses
4 Gross profit percentage
5 Return on average shareholders' equity
6 Return on average assets

b Santa Fe Boot Limited has an opportunity to obtain a long-term loan at an annual interest rate of 12% and could use this additional capital at the same rate of profitability as indicated in **a.** Would obtaining the loan be desirable from the viewpoint of the shareholders? Explain.

PROBLEM 20-6
Analysis and Interpretation from Viewpoint of Short-Term Creditor

Shown below are selected financial data for Mondo Corporation and Global, Inc., at the end of the current year.

	Mondo Corporation	Global, Inc.
Net sales (all on credit)	$1,440,000	$1,190,000
Cost of goods sold	1,260,000	825,000
Cash	36,000	70,000
Accounts receivable (net)	180,000	140,000
Inventory	504,000	165,000
Current liabilities	240,000	150,000

Assume that the year-end balances shown for accounts receivable and for inventory also represent the average balances of these accounts throughout the year.

INSTRUCTIONS

a For each company, compute the following:
1 Working capital.
2 Current ratio.
3 Quick ratio.
4 Number of times inventory turned over during the year and the average number of days required to turn over inventory.
5 Number of times accounts receivable turned over during the year and the average number of days required to collect accounts receivable. (Round to the nearest day.)
6 Operating cycle.

b From the viewpoint of a short-term creditor, comment upon the ***quality*** of each company's working capital. To which company would you prefer to sell $50,000 in merchandise on a 30-day open account?

PROBLEM 20-7
Ratios: Evaluation of Two Companies

Shown below are selected financial data for Another World and Imports, Inc., at the end of the current year:

	Another World	Imports, Inc.
Net credit sales	$675,000	$560,000
Cost of goods sold	504,000	480,000
Cash	51,000	20,000
Accounts receivable (net)	75,000	70,000
Inventory	84,000	160,000
Current liabilities	105,000	100,000

Assume that the year-end balances shown for accounts receivable and for inventory also represent the average balances of these items throughout the year.

INSTRUCTIONS

a For each of the two companies, compute the following:
1 Working capital.
2 Current ratio.

3 Quick ratio.

4 Number of times inventory turned over during the year and the average number of days required to turn over inventory. (Round computation to the nearest day.)

5 Number of times accounts receivable turned over during the year and the average number of days required to collect accounts receivable. (Round computation to the nearest day.)

6 Operating cycle.

b From the viewpoint of a short-term creditor, comment upon the ***quality*** of each company's working capital. To which company would you prefer to sell $30,000 in merchandise on a 30-day open account?

PROBLEM 20-8
Evaluating Short-Term Debt-Paying Ability

Listed below is the working capital information for Imperial Products, Inc., at the beginning of the year.

Cash	*$405,000*
Temporary investments in marketable securities	*216,000*
Notes receivable—current	*324,000*
Accounts receivable	*540,000*
Allowance for doubtful accounts	*27,000*
Inventory	*432,000*
Prepaid expenses	*54,000*
Notes payable within one year	*162,000*
Accounts payable	*445,500*
Accrued liabilities	*40,500*

The following transactions are completed during the year:

0 Sold on account inventory costing $72,000 for $65,000.
1 Issued additional shares of capital stock for cash, $800,000.
2 Sold temporary investments costing $60,000 for $54,000 cash.
3 Acquired temporary investments, $105,000. Paid cash.
4 Wrote off uncollectible accounts, $18,000.
5 Sold on account inventory costing $75,000 for $90,000.
6 Acquired plant and equipment for cash, $480,000.
7 Declared a cash dividend, $240,000.
8 Declared a 10% stock dividend.
9 Paid accounts payable, $120,000.
10 Purchased goods on account, $90,000.
11 Collected cash on accounts receivable, $180,000.
12 Borrowed cash from a bank by issuing a short-term note, $250,000.

INSTRUCTIONS

a Compute the amount of quick assets, current assets, and current liabilities at the beginning of the year as shown by the above account balances.

b Use the data compiled in part **a** to compute: (1) current ratio; (2) quick ratio; and (3) working capital.

c Indicate the effect (Increase, Decrease, and No Effect) of each independent transaction listed above on the current ratio, quick ratio, and working capital. Use the following four-column format (item **0** is given as an example):

	Effect on		
Item	*Current Ratio*	*Quick Ratio*	*Working Capital*
0	*Decrease*	*Increase*	*Decrease*

PROBLEM 20-9
Effects of Transactions on Various Ratios

Listed in the left-hand column below is a series of 12 business transactions and events relating to the activities of Wabash Industries. Opposite each transaction is listed a particular ratio used in financial analysis.

Transaction	*Ratio*
(1) Purchased inventory on open account.	*Quick ratio*
(2) A larger physical volume of goods was sold at smaller unit prices.	*Gross profit percentage*
(3) Corporation declared a cash dividend.	*Current ratio*
(4) An uncollectible account receivable was written off against the allowance account.	*Current ratio*
(5) Issued additional shares of common stock and used proceeds to retire long-term debt.	*Debt ratio*
(6) Paid stock dividend on common stock, in common stock.	*Earnings per share*
(7) Conversion of a portion of bonds payable into common stock. (Ignore income taxes.)	*Interest coverage ratio*
(8) Appropriated retained earnings.	*Rate of return on shareholders' equity*
(9) During period of rising prices, company changed from FIFO to LIFO method of inventory pricing.	*Inventory turnover*
(10) Paid a previously declared cash dividend.	*Debt ratio*
(11) Purchased factory supplies on open account.	*Current ratio (assume that ratio is greater than 1:1)*
(12) Issued shares of capital stock in exchange for patents.	*Equity ratio*

INSTRUCTIONS What effect would each transaction or event have on the ratio listed opposite to it; that is, as a result of this event would the ratio increase, decrease, or remain unchanged? Your answer for each of the 12 transactions should include a brief explanation.

PROBLEM 20-10
Building Financial Statements from Limited Information, Including Ratios

Pete Mitchell, the accountant for Hercules Construction, prepared the year-end financial statements, including all ratios, and was invited to bring them along on a wilderness retreat with the executives of the corporation. To his embarrassment, he found that only certain fragmentary information had been placed in his briefcase and the completed statements had been left in his office. One hour before Mitchell was to present the financial statements to the executives, he was able to come up with the following information:

HERCULES CONSTRUCTION
Balance Sheet
December 31, 19__
(in thousands of dollars)

Assets			*Liabilities & Shareholders' Equity*		
Current assets:			*Current liabilities*		$?
Cash		?	*Long-term debt, 8% interest*		?
Accounts receivable (net)		?	*Total liabilities*		$?
Inventory		?	*Shareholders' equity:*		
Total current assets		$?	*Capital stock*	$300	
Plant assets:			*Retained earnings*	100	
Machinery and equipment	$580		*Total shareholders' equity*		400
Less: Accumulated depreciation	80	500			
Total assets		$?	*Total liabilities & shareholders' equity*		$?

HERCULES CONSTRUCTION
Income Statement
For the Year Ended December 31, 19__
(in thousands of dollars)

Net sales	$?
Cost of goods sold	?
Gross profit (25% of net sales)	$?
Operating expenses	?
Operating income (10% of net sales)	$?
Interest expense	28
Income before income taxes	$?
Income taxes—40% of income before income taxes	?
Net income	$60

ADDITIONAL INFORMATION

1 The equity ratio was 40%; the debt ratio was 60%.
2 The only interest expense was on the long-term debt.
3 The beginning inventory was $150,000; the inventory turnover was 4.8 times.
4 The current ratio was 2 to 1; the quick ratio was 1 to 1.
5 The beginning balance in accounts receivable was $80,000; the accounts receivable turnover for the year was 12.8 times. All sales were made on account.

INSTRUCTIONS The accountant asks you to help complete the financial statements for Hercules Construction, using only the information available. Present supporting computations and explanations for all amounts appearing in the balance sheet and the income statement.

PROBLEM 20-11
Analysis and Interpretation from Viewpoint of Common Shareholders and of Bondholders

The following financial information for Continental Transfer and Canadian Van Lines (except market price per share of stock) is stated in ***thousands of dollars.*** The figures are as of the end of the current year. The two companies are in the same industry and are quite similar as to operations, facilities, and accounting methods. Assume that both companies pay income taxes equal to 50% of income before income taxes.

Assets	*Continental Transfer*	*Canadian Van Lines*
Current assets	*$ 97,500*	*$132,320*
Plant and equipment	*397,500*	*495,680*
Less: Accumulated depreciation	*(55,000)*	*(78,000)*
Total assets	*$440,000*	*$550,000*
Liabilities & Shareholders' Equity		
Current liabilities	*$ 34,000*	*$ 65,000*
Bonds payable, 12%, due in 15 years	*120,000*	*100,000*
Capital stock, no par	*150,000*	*200,000*
Retained earnings	*136,000*	*185,000*
Total liabilities & shareholders' equity	*$440,000*	*$550,000*
Analysis of retained earnings:		
Balance, beginning of year	*$125,200*	*$167,200*
Net income for the year	*19,800*	*37,400*
Dividends	*(9,000)*	*(19,600)*
Balance, end of year	*$136,000*	*$185,000*
Market price of capital stock, per share	*$30*	*$61*
Number of shares of capital stock outstanding	*6 million*	*8 million*

INSTRUCTIONS

a Compute for each company:
  1 The interest coverage ratio (number of times bond interest was earned during the current year).
  2 The debt ratio.

b In light of the information developed in **a** above, write a paragraph indicating which company's bonds you think would trade in the market at the higher price. Which would probably provide the higher yield? Explain how the ratios developed influence your answer. (It may be assumed that the bonds were issued several years ago and are traded on an organized securities exchange.)

c For each company compute the dividend yield, earnings per share, the price-earnings ratio, and the book value per share. (Show supporting computations. Remember that dollar amounts in the problem are in thousands of dollars, that is, three zeros omitted.)

d Assume that you expect both companies to grow at the same rate. Express an opinion, based solely on the data developed in **c** above, as to which company's stock is a better investment at the present market price.

PROBLEM 20-12
A Financial Taste Test

Selected data from recent annual reports of ***The Coca-Cola Company*** and ***PepsiCo, Inc.*** (and subsidiaries) are shown below. (Dollar amounts are stated in millions.)

	Coca-Cola	PepsiCo*
Balance sheet statistics:		
At year-end:		
Quick assets	$2,002	$ 2,774
Current assets	3,604	3,551
Total assets	8,283	15,127
Current liabilities	3,658	3,692
Total liabilities	4,798	11,236
Total shareholders' equity	3,485	3,891
Average throughout the year:		
Accounts receivable	802	1,110
Inventory	784	494
Total assets	7,867	13,131
Total shareholders' equity	3,415	3,526
Income statement statistics:		
Net sales	8,966	15,242
Cost of goods sold	3,892	7,468
Interest expense	308	610
Operating income	1,726	1,783
Net income	1,724	901

* More than one-half of PepsiCo's revenue and profits stem from its snack food and restaurant operations, rather than from soft drink sales.

INSTRUCTIONS

a Compute the following for each company:

1 Net income as a percentage of sales
2 Return on assets
3 Return on equity
4 Working capital
5 Accounts receivable turnover rate
6 Inventory turnover rate
7 Quick ratio
8 Debt ratio
9 Interest coverage ratio

b Both Coca-Cola and PepsiCo are highly successful companies with excellent credit ratings. Based on your analysis in part **a**, however, indicate which of these companies you believe:

1 Provides the greatest degree of safety for its ***short-term*** creditors.
2 Provides the greatest degree of safety for its ***long-term*** creditors.
3 Would have the higher p/e ratio (that is, the stock would sell at the greater market value relative to the current earnings per share).

In each case, ***explain your reasoning.***

ANALYTICAL AND DECISION PROBLEMS AND CASES

A&D 20-1
Season's Greetings

Holiday Greeting Cards is a local company organized late in July of 1995. The company's net income for each of its first six calendar quarters of operations is summarized below. The amounts are stated in thousands of dollars.

	1996	1995
First quarter (January through March)	$ 253	—
Second quarter (April through June)	308	—
Third quarter (July through September)	100	$ 50
Fourth quarter (October through December)	450	500
Total for the calendar year	$1,111	$550

Glen Wallace reports the business and economic news for a local radio station. On the day that Holiday Greeting Cards released the above financial information, you heard Wallace make the following statement during his broadcast: "Holiday Greeting Cards enjoyed a 350% increase in its net income for the fourth quarter, and net income for the entire year was up by over 100%."

INSTRUCTIONS

a Show the computations that Wallace probably made in arriving at his statistics.

b Do you believe that Wallace's percentage changes present a realistic impression of Holiday Greeting Cards' rate of growth in 1996? Explain.

c What figure would you use to express the percentage change in Holiday's fourth quarter net income in 1996? Explain why you would compute the change in this manner.

A&D 20-2
Limit on Dividends

During each of the last 10 years, Reese Corporation has increased the common stock dividend per share by about 10%. Total dividends now amount to $9 million per year, consisting of $2 million paid to preferred shareholders and $7 million paid to common shareholders. The preferred stock is cumulative but not convertible. Annual net income had been rising steadily until two years ago, when it peaked at $44 million. Last year, increased competition caused net income to decline to $37 million. Management expects net income to stabilize around this level for several years. This year, Reese Corporation issued bonds payable. The contract with bondholders requires Reese Corporation to limit total dividends to not more than 25% of net income.

INSTRUCTIONS Evaluate this situation from the perspective of:

a Common shareholders

b Preferred shareholders

A&D 20-3
Improving Cash Flow

Reynolds Labs develops and manufactures pharmaceutical products. The company has been growing rapidly during the past 10 years, due primarily to having discovered, patented, and successfully marketed dozens of new products. Net income has increased annually by 30% or more. The company pays no dividend but has a very high price-earnings ratio. Due to its rapid growth and large expenditures for research and development, the company has experienced occasional cash shortages. To solve this problem, Reynolds has decided to improve its cash position by (1) requiring customers to pay for products purchased on account from the company in 30 days instead of 60 days and (2) reducing expenditures for research and development by 20%.

INSTRUCTIONS Evaluate this situation from the perspective of:

a Short-term creditors.

b Common shareholders.

A&D 20-4
Declining Interest Rate

Metro Utilities has outstanding 16 issues of bonds payable, with interest rates ranging from $5\frac{1}{2}\%$ to 14%. The company's rate of return on assets consistently averages 12%. Almost every year, the company issues additional bonds to finance growth, to pay maturing bonds, or to call outstanding bonds when advantageous. During the current year, long-term interest rates have fallen dramatically. At the beginning of the year, these rates were between 12% and 13%; now, however, they are down to between 8% and 9%. Management currently is planning a large 8% bond issue.

INSTRUCTIONS Evaluate this situation from the perspective of:

a Holders of $5\frac{1}{2}\%$ bonds, maturing in 11 years but redeemable now at 103.

b Holders of 14% bonds, maturing in 23 years but redeemable now at 103.

c Common shareholders.

A&D 20-5
Which One Is Better?

The following presents certain financial information relating to two companies, London Toyland and Nathan Toymart as of the end of the current year. All figures (except market price per share of stock) are in ***thousands of dollars.***

Assets	*London Toyland*	*Nathan Toymart*
Cash	$ 252	$ 360
Marketable securities, at lower of cost and market	258	906
Accounts receivable, net	290	334
Inventories, at lower of cost and market	1,510	770
Prepaid expenses	50	30
Plant and equipment, net	3,360	3,140
Intangibles and other assets	280	60
Total assets	$6,000	$5,600
Liabilities & Shareholders' Equity		
Accounts payable	$ 690	$ 608
Accrued liabilities, including income taxes	310	192
Bonds payable, 8%, due in 10 years	400	1,000
Capital stock (London, 150,000 shares; Nathan, 120,000 shares)	2,780	2,700
Retained earnings	1,820	1,100
Total liabilities & shareholders' equity	$6,000	$5,600
Analysis of retained earnings:		
Balance, beginning of year	$1,424	$ 860
Add: Net income	690	480
Less: Dividends	(294)	(240)
Balance, end of year	$1,820	$1,100
Market price per share of stock, end of year	46	40
Net sales	$6,900	$6,000

INSTRUCTIONS London Toyland and Nathan Toymart are generally comparable in the nature of their operations, products, and accounting procedures used. Use whatever analytical computations you feel will best support each of the following evaluations.

a Evaluate these two companies from the perspective of short-term creditors and explain which company you feel is more credit worthy.

b Evaluate these two companies from the perspective of common shareholders and explain which company you feel is a better investment.

COMPREHENSIVE PROBLEM 5

MACLEAN HUNTER LIMITED

ANALYSIS OF THE FINANCIAL STATEMENTS OF A PUBLICLY OWNED CORPORATION

The purpose of this Comprehensive Problem is to acquaint you with the financial statements of a publicly owned company. The financial statements included in the 1992 annual report of **Maclean Hunter Limited** (the company) were selected because they illustrate many of the financial reporting issues discussed in this textbook. Notice that several pages of explanatory notes are included with the basic statements. These explanatory notes supplement the condensed information in the financial statements and are intended to carry out the generally accepted accounting principle of adequate disclosure. Also, selected information in the annual report is included.

This Comprehensive Problem is subdivided into three parts. **Part 1** is designed to familiarize you with the content of these financial statements and other information in the annual report. **Part 2** requires analysis from the viewpoint of a short-term creditor, and **Part 3,** from the perspective of a shareholder.

PART 1
An Overview of the Statements and the Related Notes, Reports, and Other Information

A corporate annual report includes not only the financial statements, but also notes, auditors' reports, corporate profile, corporate plan, management's discussion and analysis, management's responsibility for financial reporting, consolidated financial statement—summary of accounting policies, an 11-year financial summary. Our purpose in Part 1 of this comprehensive problem is to acquaint you with the form and content of these materials.

INSTRUCTIONS Answer each of the following questions and briefly explain where in the statements, notes, reports by the auditors, other information in the annual report (presented in this problem) you located the information used in your answer.

a What is the nature and scope of Maclean Hunter's operations?

b What is Maclean Hunter's corporate plan?

c The comparative financial statements include the statements of income, retained earnings, changes in cash position, and financial position. Were all of these statements audited by a firm of public accountants? Name the firm that audited these statements. What were the auditors' conclusions?

d Who is responsible for the content of these statements—management, the company's board of directors, or the auditors? In general terms, what measures have been undertaken by ***management*** to ensure the reliability of these statements?

(Continued on page 994.)

CORPORATE PROFILE

Maclean Hunter is a diversified communications company operating across Canada and in the United States and Europe, with 12,000 employees and 1992 revenue of $1.6 billion. Almost half of our 1992 operating income was earned in the United States.

With more than 1.2 million subscribers, our cable television operations in Canada and the United States have been a sustaining force in our growth accounting for 72% of our operating income before amortization of $194 million in 1992.

We began in periodical publishing in 1887, and are best known in Canada for Maclean's, L'actualité, Chatelaine and Flare. In total, we publish more than 200 consumer and business periodicals in 10 countries.

We produce business forms and specialty printing items in both Canada and the United States and are major commercial printers in Canada.

We have a 62% interest in The Toronto Sun Publishing Corporation, which publishes Sun newspapers in four Canadian cities, The Financial Post, and 62 community newspapers in Canada and the U.S.

Our broadcasting interests include a CTV-affiliated television station in Calgary and 21 radio stations in Ontario and the Maritimes.

Related communication services include radio paging, trade and consumer shows, co-op advertising and media monitoring, and post-production services.

Corporate Plan

We will stay exclusively within the communications business, primarily in North America and Europe.

All investments that fall into the normal-risk category will achieve a minimum after-tax return on net assets employed of 15%. In lower-risk investments (e.g. in most cable TV operations), a minimum after-tax return of 12% may be more appropriate.

All properties that do not measure up to the corporate plan's objectives will require approval for continuance.

We will own, if not a majority interest, at least effective control of all activities.

The Company has a target of paying 40% of the previous year's after-tax earnings in dividends.

We will manage our growth so that any new venture or acquisition will not jeopardize the future stability of the Company.

Management's Discussion and Analysis

This analysis is supplemental to the Consolidated Financial Statements . . . and is intended to provide investors with additional information on the recent performance of the Company, its current financial situation, and its future prospects. For a more complete understanding of the Company's operations, readers should refer to the Letter to Shareholders and the Review of Operations sections of this annual report, which include other detailed information which has not been duplicated in this analysis.

OPERATING RESULTS

Overview

Revenue

Revenue for the year increased by $100 million or 7% compared to 1991. Approximately $29 million or 2% of this growth was due to acquisitions completed during the last two years, the largest being the acquisition in the fourth quarter of 1992 of the Southam business forms operations. Offsetting this, revenue declined by approximately $11 million due to dispositions. An additional $22 million of the increase was due to the weakening of the Canadian dollar compared to the U.S. dollar during 1992.

(millions)	1992		1991	
Cable television	**$ 398**	**24%**	$ 358	23%
Periodicals	**366**	**22**	354	23
Business forms and commercial printing	**409**	**25**	354	23
Newspapers	**329**	**20**	322	21
Broadcasting	**74**	**5**	77	5
Communication services	**59**	**4**	70	5
	1,635	**100**	1,535	100
Canada	**1,094**	**67**	1,046	68
United States and Europe	**541**	**33**	489	32
Total revenue	**$1,635**	**100%**	$1,535	100%

The above breakdown of revenue by industry and geographic segments shows that the growth occurred mainly in cable television and business forms and commercial printing, and there were slight declines in revenue from the broadcasting and communication services segments. These developments did not, however, significantly change the proportion of revenue generated by each segment, and the proportion of revenue generated outside Canada has also remained stable relative to 1991.

The Company's objective over the long term is to maintain a balance between advertising and non-advertising revenue. As a result of growth and investment in cable television, together with depressed advertising markets during the last three years, revenue from non-advertising sources was a greater percentage of the total in 1992 than it has been for many years. A sustained economic recovery should result in faster growth of advertising revenues compared to non-advertising revenues, and may therefore slow or reverse this trend.

LIQUIDITY AND CAPITAL RESOURCES

Cash Flow

(millions)	1992	1991
Cash flow from operations	**$200**	$170
Dividends	**(45)**	(42)
Purchase of property, plant and equipment	**(99)**	(105)
Business acquisitions	**(56)**	(13)
Business divestitures	**9**	22
Receipt of mortgage	**–**	43
Other	**59**	25
Surplus cash	**68**	100
Issue of common shares	**173**	–
Net repayment of debt	**(190)**	(105)
Increase (decrease) in cash	**$ 51**	$ (5)

Cash flow from operations (defined as operating income plus depreciation and amortization and other items, less net interest expense and current income taxes) increased from $170 million in 1991 to $200 million in 1992. Cash flow from operations per share increased from $1.05 per share in 1991 to $1.14 per share in 1992. The increase in operating cash flow is due to higher operating income and lower interest expense.

In the publishing and cable television industries, subscribers prepay for services to be rendered. As a result of this deferred revenue, together with the minimal current assets of cable television operations, the Company does not have a large investment in non-cash working capital.

1992 dividends amounted to $45 million and dividends declared per common share were 25¢ per share in 1992 and 1991. It is the Company's target to pay 40% of the previous year's after-tax earnings in dividends with the dividend rate being reviewed beginning with the second quarter dividend payable in August. The Company has an Automatic Dividend Reinvestment Plan whereby cash dividends may be automatically reinvested in new shares at 95% of the current stock price. Cash dividends reinvested amounted to $6 million in 1992 and $3 million in 1991.

1992 additions to property, plant and equipment totalled $99 million including $60 million in cable television and $13 million at The Toronto Sun. Business acquisitions amounted to $56 million in 1992, including $24 million for working capital and $21 million for property, plant and equipment.

The remaining surplus cash, together with the proceeds of the common share issue, enabled $190 million of debt to be repaid and cash balances were $51 million higher at the end of the year.

Capital Expenditures

An analysis of capital expenditures and depreciation by business segment is provided in note 1 to the Consolidated Financial Statements. Major individual projects were to complete construction and refurbishment of new premises for our New Jersey cable operations ($5 million), and to rebuild and upgrade channel capacity of the Florida cable system ($12 million).

The Company has planned capital expenditures for 1993 amounting to approximately $100 million, $49 million of which is for cable television in Ontario and the United States.

Debt

Details of the Company's debt position are included in note 9 to the Consolidated Financial Statements.

One important source of debt financing for the Company continues to be short-term notes in its commercial paper program. At December 31, 1992, notes outstanding totalled $285 million, comprised of 19 separate issues with terms mostly from 30-90 days and representing an average maturing amount to be "rolled over" on any one day of approximately $15 million. Notes are generally issued at interest rates related to LIBOR in U.S. dollars or Banker's Acceptances in Canadian dollars; at December 31, 1992, all commercial paper was either denominated in U.S. dollars, or converted thereto using currency exchanges, at interest rates ranging from 3.3% to 4.1%.

While these notes are classified as current liabilities in the Consolidated Statement of Financial Position since the terms of the individual notes are for periods under one year, it is the Company's intention that the commercial paper program will represent an ongoing source of financing. Although the Company to date always has been able to roll over maturing notes, there are approximately $340 million of unused bank credit lines available for general corporate purposes, $150 million of which is dedicated as back-up for the commercial paper program.

The proceeds received on the sale of CHCH-TV in January 1993 were used to repay commercial paper by approximately $53 million.

Management's Responsibility for Financial Reporting

The preparation of the Consolidated Financial Statements accompanying this annual report and the presentation of all other information in the report are the responsibilities of management. The Consolidated Financial Statements have been prepared in accordance with appropriate and generally accepted accounting principles, and reflect management's estimates and judgements in situations where a precise determination of the value of certain assets and liabilities is dependent on future events. Management has also ensured that the financial information presented elsewhere in this annual report is consistent with the Consolidated Financial Statements.

Management is also responsible for a system of internal control which is designed to provide reasonable assurance that assets are safeguarded and accounting systems provide timely, accurate financial reports.

The Board of Directors is responsible for ensuring that management fulfils its responsibilities for financial reporting and internal control and is ultimately responsible for reviewing and approving the Consolidated Financial Statements. The Board is assisted in exercising its responsibilities through its Audit Committee, which is composed of outside Directors. The Committee meets periodically with management, as well as the internal and external auditors, to discuss internal controls, auditing matters and financial reporting issues, to satisfy itself that each party is properly discharging its responsibilities, and to review the interim and annual Consolidated Financial Statements. The Committee also considers, for review by the Board and approval by the shareholders, the engagement or re-appointment of the external auditors.

Ernst & Young, the external auditors appointed by the shareholders of the Company, have audited the Consolidated Financial Statements and their report follows. The external auditors have full and unrestricted access to the Audit Committee to discuss their audit and their related findings as to the Company's financial reporting and the system of internal controls.

February 12, 1993

R.W. Osborne

Ronald W. Osborne
President and Chief Executive Officer

J. Furse

J. Robert Furse
Vice President, Finance and Chief Financial Officer

Auditors' Report

To the Shareholders of Maclean Hunter Limited:

We have audited the consolidated statements of financial position of Maclean Hunter Limited as at December 31, 1992 and 1991 and the consolidated statements of income, retained earnings and changes in cash position for the years then ended. The preparation of these financial statements is the responsibility of the Company's management. Our responsibility is to express an opinion on these financial statements based on our audits.

We conducted our audits in accordance with generally accepted auditing standards. Those standards require that we plan and perform an audit to obtain reasonable assurance whether the financial statements are free of material misstatement. An audit includes examining, on a test basis, evidence supporting the amounts and disclosures in the financial statements. An audit also includes assessing the accounting principles used and estimates made by management, as well as evaluating the overall financial statement presentation.

In our opinion, these consolidated financial statements present fairly, in all material respects, the financial position of the Company as at December 31, 1992 and 1991 and the results of its operations and the changes in its financial position for the years then ended in accordance with generally accepted accounting principles.

Ernst + Young

Chartered Accountants
Toronto, Canada
February 12, 1993

Consolidated Financial Statements
Summary of Accounting Policies

Consolidation and Investments

The accounts of subsidiaries are consolidated with those of the Company. Certain subsidiary companies hold a non-controlling interest in Maclean Hunter Holdings Limited which owns shares of the Company. The Company's proportionate interest in the cost of such shares is deducted from shareholders' equity. Earnings and cash flow per share are calculated after eliminating the Company's indirect interest in its own shares. Similarly, the dividends deducted from retained earnings exclude that portion which relates to the Company's indirect interest in its own shares.

Investments in entities where the Company exercises significant influence but does not have voting control are accounted for using the equity method whereby the Company includes its proportionate share of their net income or loss in consolidated net income. Investments held for resale are valued at the lower of cost and estimated net realizable value.

Translation of Foreign Currencies

Foreign currency amounts and the financial statements of foreign subsidiaries are translated into Canadian dollars on the following basis:

- assets and liabilities at the year-end rate of exchange (1992 – $1 U.S. = $1.271 Cdn.; 1991 – $1 U.S. = $1.156 Cdn.)
- revenue and expenses at the average rate calculated monthly (1992 – $1 U.S. = $1.210 Cdn.; 1991 – $1 U.S. = $1.149 Cdn.)

Exchange gains or losses arising from the translation of the Company's net investment in self-sustaining foreign operations, net of the Company's U.S. dollar denominated debt, are accumulated in the foreign currency translation adjustment account in shareholders' equity and included in income if realized through sale of the investment or distribution of foreign assets.

Unearned Revenue

Prepaid subscriptions for business magazines that are substantially dependent on subscription revenue, for cable television and for newspapers are deferred and taken into income as the services are provided to the subscribers. These deferred amounts are included in accounts payable.

Net revenue pertaining to prepaid subscriptions from consumer magazines is also deferred and taken into income over the terms of the various subscriptions. These magazines derive a substantial majority of their net revenue from advertising and, since current assets will not be used to discharge any obligations to subscribers, no portion of such unearned revenue is included in current liabilities.

Income Taxes

The deferral method is used in accounting for income taxes whereby timing differences between income reported in the financial statements and taxable income result in deferred income taxes. Such timing differences occur when revenue or expenses are recognized in the accounts in one year and are included in taxable income in another year.

Inventories

Inventories, principally materials for printing and business forms, are valued at the lower of cost, calculated using the first-in, first-out method, and replacement cost.

Capital Assets

Property, plant and equipment are recorded at cost less related investment tax credits. Interest on borrowings is capitalized during the construction of new plant and equipment.

For newly licensed areas within a cable television system, all costs are capitalized prior to the prematurity period. During the prematurity period, a portion of the fixed system costs attributable to future operations is capitalized. Prematurity begins with the first subscriber hook-up and ends when construction is planned to be substantially complete.

Capital leases, which transfer substantially all the benefits and risks of ownership, are recorded as the acquisition of an asset and the incurrence of an obligation based on the present value of future rental payments.

Property, plant and equipment, including capital leases, is depreciated in a rational and systematic manner appropriate to the nature of the assets using straight-line or diminishing balance methods over the estimated life of the assets as follows:

	Amortization Period
Buildings	20 to 40 years
Leasehold improvements	Lease term
Cable television equipment	5 to 15 years
Presses and printing equipment	5 to 15 years
Broadcasting equipment	5 to 20 years
Office furniture and fixtures	5 to 10 years
Vehicles	3 to 5 years
Pagers and paging equipment	5 to 10 years
Computer hardware and software	2 to 7 years
Other equipment	3 to 15 years

The excess of the cost of acquiring businesses over the value assigned to identifiable net tangible assets acquired is allocated first to intangible assets and the residual is allocated to goodwill.

Intangible assets which include broadcast licences, circulation bases, subscriber lists, radio paging frequencies, favourable contracts and non-compete agreements are amortized on a straight-line basis over their estimated economic life up to a maximum of forty years. Cable television franchises are amortized using the sinking fund method with an interest rate of 4% over periods not exceeding forty years.

Goodwill is amortized on a straight-line basis over ten years for trade and consumer shows and over periods not exceeding forty years for other operations.

Periodically, management re-evaluates the remaining useful life of all capital assets, and extends or shortens the amortization periods accordingly. Management also periodically reviews the carrying amount of all capital assets, and writes them down when the long-term expectation is that the net carrying amount will not be recovered.

Pension Costs and Obligations

For defined benefit plans, pension costs are actuarially determined on the basis of management's estimates using the projected benefit method prorated over the service lives of the employees. Actuarial surpluses or deficiencies are amortized to income over the expected average remaining service life of pension plan members. Pension fund assets are valued using market prices averaged over a five year period.

Consolidated Statement of Income

(millions)	Notes	December 31 1992	1991
Revenue			
Cable television		$ 398.3	$ 357.6
Periodicals		365.4	353.5
Business forms and commercial printing		408.9	353.7
Newspapers		329.4	322.5
Broadcasting		73.6	76.9
Communication services		59.0	70.4
Total revenue		1,634.6	1,534.6
Operating income			
Cable television		139.0	120.3
Periodicals		16.1	10.1
Business forms and commercial printing		31.2	31.6
Newspapers		4.3	3.5
Broadcasting		6.3	6.0
Communication services		(2.8)	(0.8)
Operating income before amortization		194.1	170.7
Amortization of intangible assets and goodwill	*1(b)*	(17.0)	(16.2)
Total operating income		177.1	154.5
Other income, net	*5(b)*	10.8	3.8
Interest expense	*9 and 10*	(31.0)	(59.2)
Minority interest		–	2.2
Income taxes	*3*	(75.7)	(50.7)
Consolidated net income		$ 81.2	$ 50.6
Earnings per share	*2*	47¢	32¢

Consolidated Statement of Retained Earnings

(millions)	Notes	December 31 1992	1991
Retained earnings, beginning of year		$ 438.4	$ 429.3
Consolidated net income		81.2	50.6
Dividends declared	*11(b)*	(45.4)	(41.5)
Cost of common share issue (net of tax)	*11(e)*	(4.5)	–
Retained earnings, end of year		$ 469.7	$ 438.4

Consolidated Statement of Changes in Cash Position

(millions)	Notes	December 31 1992	1991
Operating activities			
Operating income before amortization		**$ 194.1**	$ 170.7
Depreciation	*1(b)*	**100.6**	96.1
Other items, net		**7.1**	9.1
Earnings before interest, taxes, depreciation and amortization		**301.8**	275.9
Interest expense		**(31.0)**	(59.2)
Current income taxes	*3*	**(70.9)**	(46.4)
Cash flow from operations		**199.9**	170.3
Decrease in non-cash working capital		**33.9**	12.4
Total cash provided by operating activities		**233.8**	182.7
Investment activities			
Purchase of property, plant and equipment	*1(d)*	**(99.4)**	(105.4)
Business acquisitions	*1(d) and 5(a)*	**(56.1)**	(13.2)
Business divestitures	*5(b)*	**8.6**	22.2
Other		**2.4**	(1.3)
Total cash used in investment activities		**(144.5)**	(97.7)
Financing activities			
Issue of common shares	*11*	**179.3**	3.1
Repayment of notes and other indebtedness	*9*	**(189.6)**	(105.2)
Dividends declared	*11(b)*	**(45.4)**	(41.5)
Received from minority shareholders		**6.2**	10.4
Distribution from Barden Cablevision, Partnership	*8*	**11.2**	–
Receipt of mortgage		**–**	43.0
Total cash used in financing activities		**(38.3)**	(90.2)
Increase (decrease) in cash		**51.0**	(5.2)
Cash and short-term investments, beginning of year		**36.7**	41.9
Cash and short-term investments, end of year		**$ 87.7**	$ 36.7
Cash flow per share	*2*		
Earnings before interest, taxes, depreciation and amortization		**$ 1.71**	$ 1.70
Cash flow from operations		**$ 1.14**	$ 1.05

Consolidated Statement of Financial Position

Maclean Hunter Limited
(Incorporated under the laws of Ontario)

(millions)	Notes	December 31 1992	1991
Assets			
Current assets			
Cash and short-term investments		**$ 87.7**	$ 36.7
Accounts receivable		**195.4**	179.2
Inventories		**66.2**	50.6
Prepaids and other receivables	*5(b)*	**89.0**	35.7
Total current assets		**438.3**	302.2
Property, plant and equipment	*6*	**658.8**	632.4
Intangible assets	*7*	**383.5**	377.2
Goodwill		**293.8**	295.2
Investments and other assets	*8*	**97.5**	146.6
Total Assets		**$1,871.9**	$1,753.6
Liabilities and Shareholders' Equity			
Current liabilities			
Accounts payable		**$ 222.2**	$ 201.5
Income and other taxes payable		**32.8**	24.1
		255.0	225.6
Indebtedness due within one year	*9*	**301.2**	449.7
Total current liabilities		**556.2**	675.3
Long-term debt	*9*	**166.7**	166.5
Unearned revenue		**36.6**	37.7
Deferred income taxes		**119.4**	102.0
Minority interest		**106.3**	105.5
Convertible debentures	*10*	**21.4**	23.0
Shareholders' equity			
Share capital	*11*	**490.1**	292.2
Retained earnings		**469.7**	438.4
Foreign currency translation adjustment	*12*	**(17.3)**	(18.6)
		942.5	712.0
Less the Company's indirect interest in its own shares	*13*	**(77.2)**	(68.4)
Total shareholders' equity		**865.3**	643.6
Total Liabilities and Shareholders' Equity		**$1,871.9**	$1,753.6

On behalf of the Board:

Radcliffe R. Latimer
Director

Ronald W. Osborne
Director

Notes to Consolidated Financial Statements

1. Industry and Geographic Segment Information

(a) Revenue and operating income before amortization

(millions)	1992	1991
Revenue		
Canada	**$1,093.9**	$1,045.5
United States and Europe	**540.7**	489.1
	1,634.6	1,534.6
Operating income before amortization		
Canada	**99.6**	86.4
United States and Europe	**94.5**	84.3
	$ 194.1	$ 170.7

(b) Depreciation and amortization

	Depreciation		Amortization of intangible assets and goodwill	
(millions)	1992	1991	1992	1991
Industry				
Cable television	**$ 46.4**	$44.0	**$ 6.0**	$ 5.5
Periodicals	**7.4**	7.4	**3.5**	3.3
Business forms and commercial printing	**20.1**	17.6	**2.2**	2.1
Newspapers	**16.3**	15.8	**2.7**	2.4
Broadcasting	**3.1**	3.2	**1.1**	1.1
Communication services	**7.3**	8.1	**1.5**	1.8
	100.6	96.1	**17.0**	16.2
Geographic				
Canada	**64.4**	63.0	**10.2**	10.2
United States and Europe	**36.2**	33.1	**6.8**	6.0
	$100.6	$96.1	**$17.0**	$16.2

6. Property, Plant and Equipment

(millions)	1992			1991
	Cost	Accumulated depreciation	Net	Net
Land	$ 36.4	$ –	$ 36.4	$ 34.6
Buildings	165.8	40.0	125.8	120.2
Leasehold improvements	28.3	17.3	11.0	13.8
Cable television systems				
– equipment	464.0	219.2	244.8	230.1
– deferred prematurity costs	24.1	15.4	8.7	10.5
Presses and printing equipment	280.1	152.1	128.0	119.6
Broadcasting equipment	53.6	37.8	15.8	20.2
Office furniture and fixtures	53.3	33.8	19.5	11.3
Vehicles	16.6	10.1	6.5	5.6
Pagers and paging equipment	28.8	14.0	14.8	17.1
Computer hardware and software	64.9	39.8	25.1	20.8
Other equipment	84.9	63.6	21.3	27.7
Construction in progress	1.1	–	1.1	0.9
Total 1992	**$1,301.9**	**$643.1**	**$658.8**	$632.4
Total 1991	$ 1,185.4	$ 553.0	$ 632.4	

The above amounts include net property, plant and equipment of $2.9 million (1991 – $8.1 million) under capital leases.

The Company has planned capital expenditures for 1993 amounting to approximately $100 million, $49 million of which is for cable television in Ontario and the United States.

9. Debt

(millions)	1992	1991
Short-term notes	**$285.4**	$374.2
Medium-term notes	**2.0**	50.9
Debentures, due July 1995	**164.2**	150.8
Bank loans, revolving credit lines, capital leases and other	**16.3**	40.3
Total	**467.9**	616.2
Classified as:		
Indebtedness due within one year	**301.2**	449.7
Long-term debt	**166.7**	166.5
Total	**467.9**	616.2
Total debt is denominated in, or converted using forward currency and interest rate swap agreements into, currencies as follows:		
Canadian dollars	**3.1**	207.6
United States dollars	**458.4**	403.3
European currencies	**6.4**	5.3
	$467.9	$616.2

(a) Short-term notes

The Company issues short-term notes in the form of commercial paper in both Canadian and U.S. dollars. At December 31, 1992, the notes bear interest at rates ranging from 3.3% to 4.1% (1991 – 4.5% to 8.5%), with a weighted average interest rate at December 31, 1992 of 3.8% (1991 – 6.0%). From time to time, the Company purchases future rate agreements to fix the future interest cost with respect to these short-term notes. While the notes are classified as a current liability on the Consolidated Statement of Financial Position as the terms of the individual notes are less than one year, it is the Company's intention that the commercial paper program will represent an ongoing source of financing.

Interest expense on commercial paper amounted to $11.7 million in 1992 ($31.2 million in 1991).

(b) Medium-term notes

The medium-term notes outstanding are due in 1993 and bear interest at 11.8%.

Interest expense on the medium-term notes amounted to $4.4 million in 1992 ($5.3 million in 1991).

(c) Debentures, due July 1995

The debentures bear interest at 12.2%, are unsecured and are due on July 19, 1995. Interest is payable in equal semi-annual instalments on January 19 and July 19 in each year. At December 31, 1992, the original debentures had all been swapped into three month U.S. floating rates for which the effective interest rate was 6.2%. The interest rate has been fixed until July 19, 1993 using future rate agreements at 6.4%.

Interest expense on the debentures amounted to $11.0 million in 1992 ($16.2 million in 1991).

(d) Bank loans, revolving credit lines, capital leases and other

Interest rates on bank revolving credits lines are based on various options including bank prime, banker's acceptances for Canadian funds and London Interbank Offered Rate (LIBOR) for U.S. funds.

Interest expense on these other financial instruments amounted to $2.0 million in 1992 ($4.5 million in 1991).

The Company has approximately $340 million of unused bank credit lines available for general corporate purposes, $150 million of which is dedicated as back-up for the commercial paper program.

(e) Principal repayments of indebtedness other than short-term notes are as follows:

	(millions)
1993	$ 15.8
1994	1.1
1995	165.3
1996	0.3
Total	$182.5

Eleven-Year Financial Summary

Maclean Hunter Limited

(dollar amounts in millions)	1992	1991	1990
Operating Results			
Revenue			
Cable television	**$ 398.3**	$ 357.6	$ 326.1
Periodicals	**365.4**	353.5	372.0
Business forms and commercial printing	**408.9**	353.7	351.7
Newspapers	**329.4**	322.5	323.3
Broadcasting	**73.6**	76.9	82.8
Communication services	**59.0**	70.4	80.1
Total revenue	**1,634.6**	1,534.6	1,536.0
Operating Income			
Cable television	**139.0**	120.3	106.0
Periodicals	**16.1**	10.1	23.3
Business forms and commercial printing	**31.2**	31.6	38.3
Newspapers	**4.3**	3.5	5.1
Broadcasting	**6.3**	6.0	12.4
Communication services	**(2.8)**	(0.8)	3.7
Operating income before amortization	**194.1**	170.7	188.8
Net Income			
Income before unusual items	**81.2**	50.6	49.5
Unusual items	**–**	–	(34.2)
Consolidated net income	**$ 81.2**	$ 50.6	$ 15.3
Per Share Data			
Income before unusual items	**47¢**	32¢	32¢
Unusual items	**–**	–	(21)
Consolidated earnings per share	**47¢**	32¢	11¢
Cash flow from operations	**$ 1.14**	$ 1.05	$ 1.01
Dividends	**25.0¢**	25.0¢	25.0¢
Number of shares less indirect interest (thousands)			
Year end	**171,616**	155,713	154,803
Weighted average (fully diluted)	**176,219**	162,579	160,514
Cash Flow			
Cash flow from operations	**$ 199.9**	$ 170.3	$ 160.9
Capital expenditures			
Business acquisitions	**56.1**	13.2	44.7
Purchase of property, plant and equipment	**99.4**	105.4	128.1
Dividends declared	**45.4**	41.5	39.5
Year-End Financial Position			
Working capital (excluding current indebtedness)	**$ 183.3**	$ 76.6	$ 140.8
Property, plant and equipment	**658.8**	632.4	628.7
Intangible assets and goodwill	**677.3**	672.4	682.3
Assets and capital employed	**1,616.9**	1,528.0	1,619.5
Total debt	**467.9**	616.2	724.9
Minority interest	**106.3**	105.5	102.5
Convertible debentures	**21.4**	23.0	24.9
Shareholders' equity	**865.3**	643.6	630.5
Ratios			
Operating return on revenue	**12%**	11%	12%
Return on average shareholders' equity plus convertible debentures	**10%**	8%	8%
Annual Stock Prices			
High	**$ 13.00**	$ 11.75	$ 12.38
Low	**11.00**	9.13	7.88
Close	**12.13**	11.50	9.63

1989	1988	1987	1986	1985	1984	1983	1982
$ 255.9	$ 219.7	$ 199.5	$ 177.8	$ 162.1	$ 137.1	$ 115.1	$ 92.6
355.7	336.0	316.8	292.4	238.8	212.4	184.0	168.4
353.6	337.6	293.6	237.7	134.9	125.9	100.2	95.6
312.2	278.2	213.3	183.8	166.0	153.7	140.5	94.1
77.8	72.2	69.0	53.3	51.1	52.1	51.5	51.4
71.0	58.4	32.8	28.9	32.1	28.0	26.5	22.8
1,426.2	1,302.1	1,125.0	973.9	785.0	709.2	617.8	524.9
87.4	75.6	70.2	60.3	53.0	39.2	31.4	24.1
29.2	32.7	34.1	32.9	27.5	24.4	14.4	10.3
41.2	38.7	33.5	31.5	18.7	18.0	11.7	10.0
15.7	26.3	35.0	26.7	23.4	20.8	19.9	8.2
14.6	13.3	14.7	9.0	11.3	12.3	13.2	15.3
9.0	9.4	7.2	6.1	6.8	5.6	4.8	3.7
197.1	196.0	194.7	166.5	140.7	120.3	95.4	71.6
87.1	93.6	82.8	69.5	59.7	49.5	31.0	21.8
1.9	1.3	50.5	—	5.2	—	16.9	2.9
$ 89.0	$ 94.9	$ 133.3	$ 69.5	$ 64.9	$ 49.5	$ 47.9	$ 24.7
56¢	60¢	53¢	45¢	40¢	34¢	22¢	17¢
1	1	32	—	3	—	12	2
57¢	61¢	85¢	45¢	43¢	34¢	34¢	19¢
$ 1.28	$ 1.10	$ 1.10	98¢	86¢	81¢	59¢	48¢
24.3¢	21.0¢	17.5¢	15.4¢	12.6¢	9.6¢	8.5¢	8.3¢
153,937	151,512	147,514	148,716	146,697	143,972	142,777	118,585
159,492	159,016	160,073	158,229	155,331	150,797	142,412	141,244
$ 202.0	$ 173.3	$ 174.2	$ 151.9	$ 131.6	$ 120.7	$ 82.3	$ 65.7
62.0	723.7	58.8	96.2	35.2	7.5	122.5	71.7
167.2	124.5	97.4	72.2	48.0	51.1	58.9	71.5
37.8	32.5	26.9	23.0	18.6	14.2	11.6	10.1
$ 78.0	$ 99.7	$ 140.9	$ 97.0	$ 127.4	$ 80.7	$ 27.1	$ 36.7
589.7	446.0	370.4	338.7	303.0	298.6	288.4	268.7
601.8	282.3	213.6	197.5	140.4	110.6	104.5	93.5
1,545.4	1,604.1	884.2	821.0	733.2	657.9	548.5	415.6
655.4	771.7	105.9	175.8	187.3	216.8	269.6	168.0
110.5	107.5	106.8	82.2	71.3	61.3	36.4	31.7
27.7	33.1	52.3	54.3	55.0	55.0	—	45.0
607.1	551.5	479.6	392.6	318.3	247.9	203.9	119.5
14%	15%	17%	17%	18%	17%	15%	14%
15%	17%	17%	18%	18%	20%	18%	15%
$ 14.25	$ 14.88	$ 12.88	$ 10.75	$ 7.82	$ 5.91	$ 4.66	$ 3.06
11.50	9.88	8.25	7.32	5.50	4.10	2.63	2.00
12.13	13.25	9.81	9.50	7.44	5.69	4.25	2.69

e Are these financial statements prepared for a single legal entity or for a parent corporation and its subsidiaries?

f What are the company's four major sources of revenue and which of these sources provides the largest operating income?

g What are the company's accounting policies on unearned revenue?

h What valuation method was used for inventories in 1992?

i How much cash did the company spend during 1992 on additions to property, plant, and equipment and on business acquisitions?

j How much are the expected capital expenditures for 1993?

k What are the rates of return on average shareholders' equity plus convertible debentures for 1990, 1991, 1992? Are these rates increasing or decreasing?

l Has the company maintained a stable dividend policy over the years 1990 to 1992? What is its dividend policy?

m Indicate for the years 1992 and 1988 the following per share amount: (1) earnings, (2) cash dividends, and (3) stock price range (high and low).

PART 2
Evaluation of Credit Worthiness

Assume that in early 1993 you are the credit manager of a potential supplier of Maclean Hunter Limited. Maclean Hunter wants to make credit purchases from your company of between $5 million and $10 million per month, with payment due in 60 days.

INSTRUCTIONS

a As part of your credit investigation, compute the following for the years ended December 31, 1992 and 1991. (Follow the company's policy of stating dollar amounts in millions.)

1 Current ratio.

2 Quick ratio.

3 Working capital.

4 Percentage of current assets comprised of cash and cash equivalents.

5 The increase (or decrease) in cash and cash equivalents in 1991 and 1992.

6 Accounts receivable turnover rate and the average number of days required to collect accounts receivable. (Assume that the 1990 accounts receivable amounted to $179.4 million.)

b Does the company have lines of credit that could assist it in meeting its short-term obligations for cash payments?

c Based upon your above analyses, has this company's liquidity ***increased*** or ***decreased*** during 1992? Explain. If you indicated that liquidity has decreased, explain whether you consider this a serious problem.

d Your company assigns each customer one of the four credit ratings listed below. Assign a credit rating to Maclean Hunter and write a memorandum explaining your decision. (In your memorandum, you may use any of your computations in parts **a** or **b**, and may refer to other information in the financial statements and in the annual report.)

POSSIBLE CREDIT RATINGS

A **Outstanding.** Little or no risk of inability to pay. For customers in this category, we fill any reasonable order, without imposing a credit limit. The customer's credit is reevaluated annually.

B **Good.** Customer has good debt-paying ability, but is assigned a credit limit that is reviewed every six months. Orders above the established credit limit are accepted only on a cash basis.

C **Marginal.** Customer appears sound, but credit should be extended only on a 30-day basis with a relatively low credit limit. Credit status and credit limit are reevaluated every 90 days.

D **Unacceptable.** Customer does not qualify for credit.

PART 3
Analysis of Common Stock

Assume that you are an investment advisor who publishes a monthly newsletter with recommendations to your clients as to whether to buy, hold, or sell specific stocks. One of the common stocks that you will evaluate this month is Maclean Hunter. It is now almost mid 1993, and the price of the company's common stock is ***$12*** per share.

INSTRUCTIONS

a As a starting point, compute the following for the years ended December 31, 1992 and 1991. (Follow the company's policy of stating dollar amounts in millions, except for per share amounts. Round percentage computations to $\frac{1}{10}$ of 1%.)

1 Price-earnings ratio. (For 1992, use the current stock price of $12 per share; for 1991, use the high stock price for the year.)

2 Dividend yield. (Use the stock prices indicated in item **1**.)

3 Return on average total assets. Assume that the total assets for 1990 amounted to $1,844.2 (in millions).

4 Return on average shareholders' equity. Assume that the shareholders' equity for 1990 amounted to $630.5 (in millions).

5 Equity ratio.

b Prepare trend analyses of (1) total revenue, (2) net income, (3) dividends per share, and (4) highest market price per share for the three years from 1990 through 1992. (Use 1990 as the base year, which will be stated at 100% in each trend analysis. Round to the nearest percent.)

c Maclean Hunter has a target of paying 40% of the previous year's after-tax earnings as dividends. Write a memorandum indicating whether this target has been met in the past 3 years and evaluating the company's ability to meet this target in the near future without reducing its dividend of 25 cents per share.

d Write a brief memorandum on the topic of leverage as it relates to Maclean Hunter. Does the company make extensive use of long-term debt financing? Assuming that long-term interest rates are about 9%, would the use of long-term debt as a means of financing future growth be desirable from the viewpoint of common shareholders?

e Write a brief memorandum on the "quality" of the company's earnings. As a basis for this memorandum, review trends in the comparative income statements and in the 11-year summary. Also consider management's discussion and analysis of the company's operations results.

f Write a statement for your newsletter in which you recommend that your clients take one of the following actions with respect to Maclean Hunter's common stock:

Buy (Your positive recommendation; you think the market price of the stock will go up.)

Sell (Your negative recommendation; you feel that the stock is overpriced and will fall in value.)

Hold (A relatively neutral position: you feel that the stock is priced at a fair value with good but not exceptional prospects.)

Explain the reasoning behind your recommendation.

In addition to the information developed in other parts of this problem, your recommendation should consider the following facts about the economic environment in early and mid 1993.

The country had recently entered a recession. Corporate earnings were declining in many industries. Interest rates remained low. Many economists were forecasting a period of slow recovery and modest economic growth.

Dividend yields for growth-oriented companies ranged from zero to about 3%; for slow-growth companies, yields were from 5% to 7%.

g Look up the current market price of Maclean Hunter's common stock in the financial pages of a newspaper. (The stock trades on the Toronto Stock Exchange.) How did your recommendation work out in the long run?

Index